D1641211

The Leading Economic Indicators and Business Cycles in the United States

John B. Guerard

The Leading Economic Indicators and Business Cycles in the United States

100 Years of Empirical Evidence and the Opportunities for the Future

John B. Guerard
McKinley Capital Management, LLC
Anchorage, AK, USA

ISBN 978-3-030-99417-4   ISBN 978-3-030-99418-1   (eBook)
https://doi.org/10.1007/978-3-030-99418-1

This Palgrave Macmillan imprint is published by the registered company Springer Nature Switzerland AG
The registered company address is: Gewerbestrasse 11, 6330 Cham, Switzerland

Preface

The purpose of this monograph is to introduce the reader to economic history and its impact on U.S. economists who developed theories from much of the data they observed. These theories addressed why and how the economy can grow, the impact of this growth on corporate profits and stock prices, and how investors can profit. The reader will be surprised, perhaps stunned, that Wesley Clair Mitchell pointed out the small-stock effect in 1910, noting that stocks had outperformed bonds, that smaller priced firms outperformed larger priced firms for the 1890–1909 period, and that stock prices could rise over a very long period which included the very severe depression of 1893.

As the reader becomes familiar with several major Wesley C. Mitchell texts, the first two texts of the National Bureau of Economic Research (NBER) studies in business cycles, the reader becomes aware of the phases of the business cycle. The phases of prosperity, crises, and depression of Mr. Mitchell's *Business Cycles*, (University of California Press, 1913). Mr. Mitchell based his observations of the phases of the business cycles on the U.S. economic data of 1890–1920. There were several periods of prosperity, crises, and depression. In Mr. Mitchell's 1922 monograph, *Business Cycles and Unemployment* (NBER, 1923), resulted from a presidential commission to study how the steep, but short, recession of 1921 unemployed so many Americans. Mr. Mitchell worked with the presidents of major U.S. corporations and the U.S. Secretary of Commerce, Herbert Hoover, to present recommendations that were surprising for their "progressive" tone in 1923. Mr. Mitchell's thoughts on business fluctuations and cycles evolved, leading to his

1927 NBER monograph *Business Cycles: The Problem and Its Setting* (NBER, 1927). Finally, very near his death, Mr. Mitchell and Mr. Arthur Burns published their *Measuring Business Cycles* (NBER, 1946). Mr. Burns became Mr. Mitchell's successor as Director of Research at the NBER and continued their work. Mr. Burns and Mr. Mitchell modeled over 800 time series of U.S. data during the 1857–1933 period.

One of the great research volumes of business cycles is the Geoffrey Moore *Business Cycle Indicators* (NBER, 1961), a two-volume set. The first volume contained much of NBER research papers, written during the 1938–1958 period. The second volume contained the data used in these NBER papers, several series covering the 1919–1958 period. The period of Mr. Moore's Director of Research at the NBER was an extremely productive period for research publications, including his *Business Cycles, Inflation, and Forecasting* (NBER, 1983). In 1991, Mr. Moore, then Director for International Business Cycle Research at Columbia University, continued his publishing works on business cycles. Mr. Moore and Mr. Zarnowitz were concerned with real world of business forecasting. Their works consistently addressed whether the then-current business recession was "new" or resembled previous recessions. Mr. Moore and his colleague, Victor Zarnowitz, produced many outstanding papers on business cycles, and the rise of Mr. Zarnowitz to lead the NBER business cycle research team was seamless. Mr. Zarnowitz, Professor-Emeritus of Economics and Finance at the University of Chicago Graduate School of Business published his magnum opus, the *Business Cycles: Theory, History, Indicators, and Forecasting,* (NBER, 1992). Mr. Zarnowitz thanked his NBER program colleagues for their joint work on business cycles 1952–1991. The reader should not think for a moment that Mr. Zarnowitz retired from the University of Chicago in 1992 and was not productive. Mr. Zarnowitz joined The Conference Board (TCB) in 1997 when TCB took over the U.S. and global Leading Economic Indicators, LEI. From 1997 until his death in 2006, Mr. Zarnowitz was most productive in producing outstanding business cycle research. Mr. Zarnowitz and his team at TCB built and maintained the LEI data and research. The author is indebted to the TCB research department for making an updated November 5, 2021, TCB LEI database available. This data is used in Chapter 10 of this monograph.

The history of U.S. business cycles and research has not been entirely written by NBER authors, although the Mr. Mitchell, Mr. Burns, Mr. Moore, and Mr. Zarnowitz tradition of research is the basis of this monograph. The author included a chapter of business cycle research developed within the Harvard University Department of Economics, where Mr. Persons, Mr. Schumpeter, Mr. Haberler, Mr. Hansen, and Mr. Eckstein wrote great texts on business cycles, economic growth, and econometric modeling and business cycles.

I wrote this monograph as I transitioned from serving as Director of Quantitative Research to serving on its Scientific Advisory Board (SAB), along with Harry Markowitz, Ganlin Xu, Ian Domowitz, Rochester Cahan, and Jose Menchero. The SAB, created by Robert A. Gillam, the McKinley Capital Management then Chief Investment Officer (CIO), now Chief Executive Officer (CEO), leverages its Quantitative Research department. The Quants at McKinley Capital generally are 23–32-year-old men and women with MS degrees in Quantitative and Computational Finance, most from the Georgia Institute of Technology, more commonly known as Georgia Tech, a top-10 Financial Engineering school. The Quants at McKinley and I crunched trade-off curves to develop effective and statistically significant portfolio selection models. Certainly, working with Harry Markowitz, Ganlin Xu, "Rocky" Cahan, and Jose Menchero, with whom I published during my time as Director of Quantitative Research, greatly leveraged our talents. I enjoyed my years at McKinley Capital in Anchorage, Alaska, and this monograph was a great learning experience for my transition. I want to thank Harry Markowitz, the Nobel Prize laurate, for reading several chapters of this monograph, and for the 25 years of co-authorship that we shared with Ganlin Xu. The three of us worked very well together, publishing 4–5 peer-reviewed articles and 4–5 practitioner-oriented, articles, and we thoroughly enjoyed our times together. I want to thank Rob Gillam, the McKinley Capital Management (MCM) CEO, for creating an atmosphere where we could work long hours to develop statistically significant stock selection models, but also for me to write, and publish, on weekends as research director. I must thank Martin Gruber, Professor-Emeritus, at New York University, for reading several chapters and his friendship and support for over 40 years. Victor Zarnowitz and I served as Associate Editors of the *International Journal of Forecasting, IJF*, a peer-reviewed Elsevier journal of forecasting. Special thanks to Professors Edward Tower and James Vander Weide, at Duke, my alma mater, for their friendship of forty-plus years, their encouragement, and support of my research. I wish to thank Bernell Stone, Professor-Emeritus, at BYU, Richard Ashley, of Virginia Tech, and Dimitrios Thomakos, at The University of Athens, yes, Greece, long-time co-authors, for our work and friendships. I would like to thank several IJF Editors and Associate Editors, Robert Fildes, Keith Ord, Jan De Goiijer, Kahal Lahiri, David Hendry, Spyros Makridakis, and Fred Joutz, who taught me a great deal about forecasting and its applications. Special thanks to Jennifer Castle, of Oxford, and David Hendry, who have made the use of OxMetrics so pleasant.

I thank Julie, my wife of 40 years, our children, Richard (and Hannah, my favorite daughter-in-law), Katherine, and Stephanie for their love and support. Finally, I would like to thank several gentlemen with whom I have enjoyed cocktails over the past several decades, H.T. Vaught, Dave Tomasko, Peter Dupak, Peter Hunter, Tom Seay, and Kent Hiser. Their friendships have raised our spirits!

Anchorage, USA   John B. Guerard
                                            Scientific Advisory Board

Contents

1 Economic Growth and Business Cycles in the U.S   1
   1.1   Depression in the Late Nineteenth-Century U.S.
          Economy   4
          1.1.1   The Panic of 1873   6
          1.1.2   The Cycle of 1879–1885   7
          1.1.3   The Cycle of 1885–1888   8
          1.1.4   The Panic of 1893 and the Cycle
                  of 1894–1897   9
          1.1.5   Monetary Policy and Prices, 1890–1909   10
   1.2   Mr. Fisher and the Purchasing Power of Money
          and Depressions   12
   1.3   Post-War Economic History and Measuring U.S.
          Economic Growth   15
   1.4   Our Path Ahead   19

**2 Wesley Clair Mitchell: The Advent of U.S. And NBER
Business Cycle Research**   23
   2.1   Mitchell's Early Business Cycles Analysis: What
          Investors Needs to Know About the Cumulation
          of Prosperity   24
          2.1.1   Mitchell's Early Business Cycles Analysis:
                  Prosperity Breeding Crisis   26

2.1.2 Mitchell's Early Business Cycles Analysis:
       Crisis   28
2.1.3 Mitchell's Early Business Cycles Analysis:
       Business Depression   31
2.1.4 Mitchell's Early Business Cycles Analysis:
       Wider Aspects of Business Cycles   34
2.2   Mr. Mitchell and His Business Cycles
       and Unemployment   36
2.3   Mitchell's Business Cycles Analysis at the NBER:
       Volume 1   39
2.4   Summary and Conclusions of Mr. Mitchell and His
       Business Cycles and His Business Cycles   48

3 **Measuring Business Activity: An Introductions
   to the Contributions of Mr. Persons, Mr. Schumpeter,
   Mr. Haberler, and Mr. Eckstein**   49
3.1   Mr. Persons and the General Business Conditions
       Index   50
3.2   Mr. Schumpeter and His Business Cycles   58
3.3   Mr. Haberler and Prosperity and Depression   63
3.3.1 Mr. Haberler and the Prosperity
       and Depression Phases   65
3.3.2 Mr. Haberler and His the Expansion
       and Contraction Phases   67
3.3.3 Mr. Haberler on Crisis and Revival   69
3.4   Econometric Modelling and Mr. Eckstein and His
       DRI Model   71
3.4.1 Mr. Eckstein: The DRI Model
       and the Business Cycle   74
3.5   Summary and Conclusions to the Contributions
       of Mr. Persons, Schumpeter, Haberler, and Eckstein   77

4 **Mr. Burns and Mr. Mitchell on *Measuring Business Cycles***   79
4.1   Comments on Measuring Business Cycles   88
4.2   Mr. Burns on Mr. Mitchell and the Progress
       on Business Cycle Research   92
4.3   Summary and Conclusions of the Mr. Burns and Mr.
       Mitchell Business Cycle Research   99
References   99

5   Mr. Geoffrey Moore and NBER Business Cycle Research   101
  5.1   Mr. Moore and his *Business Cycles Indicators* (1961)   102
  5.2   Mr. Moore and his *Business Cycles, Inflation, and Forecasting* (1983)   109
  5.3   What is a Recession?   109
    5.3.1   Mr. Moore and His Leading Group Indicators   111
    5.3.2   Unemployment   113
    5.3.3   The Money Supply and Stock Prices   113
  5.4   Mr. Moore and the Mildness and Shortness of Postwar Recessions   116
  5.5   Mr. Moore and his *Leading Indicators for the 1990s*   118
  5.6   Mr. Moore and Mr. Lahiri and Their *Leading Economic Indicators* (1991)   120
  5.7   Mr. Zarnowitz and his Tribute to Mr. Moore: The Ms. Dua Volume   121
  5.8   Summary and Conclusions   124

6   Mr. Victor Zarnowitz and Economic Forecasting, and NBER Business Cycle Research   125
  6.1   Forecast Rationality   127
  6.2   Absolute and Relative Forecast Accuracy   132
  6.3   Extending the Mincer-Zarnowitz Forecasting Benchmark   134
  6.4   Mr. Zarnowitz, the NBER, and Business Cycle Research in 1992   138
    6.4.1   Mr. Zarnowitz and the Lists of Leading Indicators, 1950–1989   142
    6.4.2   Econometric Model Simulations and Business Cycles   143
  6.5   Mr. Zarnowitz and The Major Market Economies during the Post-World War II Period   146
    6.5.1   Estimated Dimensions of Business Cycles in Eight Countries   147
    6.5.2   Growth Cycles   150
    6.5.3   Mr. Zarnowitz and Exogenous Business Cycle Variables: Money   152
    6.5.4   Mr. Zarnowitz, Business Cycles and Expectational Shocks   153

	6.5.5 What is a Business Cycle: Some General Conclusions	155
6.6	Summary and Conclusions	156
	Appendix 6.1: Exponential Smoothing	157
	References	160
7	**Regression and Time Series Modeling of Real GDP, the Unemployment Rate, and the Impact of Leading Economic Indicators on Forecasting Accuracy**	**163**
7.1	Estimating an Ordinary Least Square Regression Line	165
7.2	Estimating Multiple Regression Lines	169
7.3	Influential Observations and Possible Outliers and the Application of Robust Regression	171
7.4	Estimating Simple and Multiple Regression Models in SAS	173
	7.4.1 Estimating OLS and Robust Regression Real GDP Models in SAS	175
	7.4.2 Estimating OLS and Robust Regression Models of the Unemployment Rate in SAS	191
7.5	Estimating Robust Regression Simple and Multiple Regression Model in SAS	230
7.6	Estimating Automatic Time Series Models and Forecasting	241
	7.6.1 Automatic Time Series Model Selection Using OxMetrics	242
	7.6.2 Automatic Time Series Modeling of Real GDP Using Leading Economic Indicators (LEI), 1959–2020	245
7.7	Automatic Time Series Modeling of the Unemployment Rate Using Leading Economic Indicators (LEI)	250
7.8	Forecasting the Unemployment Series with Leading Indicators and Adaptive Learning	265
7.9	Concluding Remarks and Extensions	268
	Appendix: OxMetrics Modeling in the COVID Period	268
	BOLD Notes the Statistically Significant AR1 and LEI Coefficients and the WkUNCL Component Variables	274
	BOLD Denotes Statistically Significant Coefficients on the AR1 and LEI and Its WkUNCL Components	280
	References	286

**8   Granger Causality Testing and LEI Forecasting
of Quarterly Mergers and the Unemployment Rate**   291
8.1   Causal Analysis for Economic Policy   292
8.2   Regression Modeling of Quarterly Mergers, Stock
Prices, and the LEI   293
8.3   Time Series Model Selection and Granger Causality
Modeling   298
8.4   Granger Causality Testing in the SCA System   300
8.5   Rolling Forecast Windows Modeling Efficiency   309
8.5.1   Rolling Windows and Real GDP with the LEI
and Money Supply   316
8.6   Summary and Conclusions   324
References   326

**9   Active Management in Portfolio Selection
and Management Within Business Cycles
and Present-Day COVID**   331
9.1   The Risk-Return Trade-Off Work of Markowitz,
Sharpe, and Elton and Gruber   332
9.1.1   Markowitz Optimization Analysis   337
9.1.2   Multi-Beta Risk Control Models   344
9.1.3   The BARRA Model: The Primary
Institutional Risk Model   349
9.2   Implementing Optimal Portfolio Selection   355
9.2.1   What We Knew in 1991 Tests of Fundamental
Data   355
9.2.2   What We Learned After 1993   363
9.2.3   Markowitz Risk Modeling with Barra
and Axioma Risk Models: Constructing
Mean-Variance Efficient Frontiers   368
9.2.4   The Stone Mathematical Assignment Program
Trade-off Curve   371
9.3   The Existence and Continued Persistence of Financial
Anomalies, 2003–2108   372
9.3.1   Portfolio Selection Through Much of COVID   386
9.4   Summary and Conclusions   406
References   406

**10 Testing and Forecasting the Unemployment Rate
with the Most Current Data, TCB LEI, Data
as of 11/05/2021**   415
   10.1   OLS Modeling of the PJD Unemployment Rate,
       TCB LEI 11052021 in 1959–11/2021   416
   10.2   Robust Regression of the Modeling the PJD
       Unemployment Rate, TCB LEI 11052021   478
   10.3   Robust Regression Estimations of the DUE,
       DLLEIL1, and DkWkUNCLL1 Relationships Using
       M, S, and MM-Estimations   503
   10.4   OLS Modeling of the PJD Unemployment Rate,
       TCB LEI 11052021 in 1999–11/2021   518
   10.5   Robust Regression of the Modeling the PJD
       Unemployment Rate, TCB LEI 11052021,
       1999–11/2021   532
   10.6   Automatic Time Series Modeling and Forecasting
       the PJD Unemployment Rate, the Application
       of OxMetrics to TCB LEI 11052021   543
   10.7   Automatic Time Series Modeling and Forecasting
       the PJD Unemployment Rate, the Application
       of OxMetrics to TCB LEI 11052021 to the MZTT
       Post-publication Period, 1999–11/2021   569
   10.8   Concluding Remarks and Extensions   578
   References   579

11 Conclusions and Summary   581
   11.1   Where Do We Go from Here?   590

**Appendix: The Theory and Estimation of Regression,
        Time Series Analysis, and Causality Modeling
        of the Unemployment Rate and the Leading
        Economic Indicators (LEI)**   591

Selected References   639

Index   643

About the Author

John B. Guerard, Jr., Ph.D. is a member of the McKinley Capital Management Scientific Advisory Board. He served almost 15 years as Director of Quantitative Research at McKinley Capital Management, in Anchorage, Alaska. John is an Affiliate Instructor in the Department of Applied Mathematics, the Computational Finance and Risk Management Program, The University of Washington, Seattle, WA. He earned his B.A. in Economics from Duke University, M.A. in Economics from the University of Virginia, MSIM from the Georgia Institute of Technology, and Ph.D. in Finance from the University of Texas, Austin. Mr. Guerard took three of his doctoral seminars at Texas from Jan Mossin, a co-developer of the Capital Asset Pricing model. John taught at the McIntire School of Commerce, the University of Virginia, Lehigh University, and Rutgers University. John taught as an adjunct faculty member at New York University, and the University of Pennsylvania. He worked with the DAIS Group at Drexel, Burnham, Lambert, Daiwa Securities Trust Company, where he co-managed the Japanese Equity Fund portfolio with Harry Markowitz. While serving as Director of Quantitative Research at Vantage Global Advisors, Mr. Guerard was awarded the first Moskowitz Prize for research in socially responsible investing. John has published several monographs, including *Corporate Financial Policy and R&D Management* (Wiley, 2006), *Quantitative Corporate Finance* (Kluwer, now Springer, 2007, with Eli Schwartz, the third edition is at press, 2021), *The Handbook of Portfolio Construction: Contemporary Applications of Markowitz*

Techniques (Springer, 2010), *Introduction to Financial Forecasting in Invest-ment Analysis* (Springer, 2013), and *The Handbook of Applied Investment Research* (World Scientific Publishing, 2020, with William T. Ziemba). John serves as Associate Editor of the *Journal of Investing* and *The International Journal of Forecasting* and has published research in *The International Journal of Forecasting*, *Management Science*, the *IBM Journal of Research and Devel-opment*, *Annals of Operations Research*, *Journal of Forecasting*, *Journal of Investing*, *Journal of Portfolio Management*, *The Financial Analysts Journal*, *Research in Finance*, *Research Policy*, and the *Journal of the Operational Research Society*.

List of Figures

Chart 6.1   The relationship between Predicted Change and Actual
            Change should be represented by a line with a Positive
            Slope when the Turning Point is Correctly Forecast   128
Chart 6.2   The relationship between Predicted and Actual Values
            should be represented by a line with a Positive Slope
            when the Value Correctly Forecast   129
Chart 6.3   A Negative slope relationship between Predicted and Actual
            Values reports an Incorrect Forecast   129
Chart 7.1   Residuals indicate that the model is not adequately
            estimated   270
Chart 7.2   Residuals indicate that the model is adequately estimated   280

Fig. 8.1   Cross-correlation of pre-whitened unemployment and LEI,
            1959–1965   314
Fig. 8.2   Cross-correlation of pre-whitened unemployment
            and weekly unemployment claims, 1959–1965   314
Fig. 8.3   Cross-correlation of pre-whitened unemployment and LEI,
            1959-1/2020   315
Fig. 8.4   Cross-correlation of pre-whitened unemployment
            and weekly unemployment claims, 1959-1/2020   315
Fig. 8.5   Cross-correlation of pre-whitened unemployment and LEI,
            1959-12/2020   316
Fig. 8.6   Cross-correlation of pre-whitened unemployment
            and weekly unemployment claims, 1959-12/2020   316
Fig. 9.1   Cash or bonds   333

Fig. 9.2	Mr. Tobin and the risk-return trade-off	334
Fig. 9.3	Mr. Tobin and landing and borrowing	335
Fig. 9.4	Mr. Markowitz and optimal portfolio selection	335
Fig. 9.5	The critical line	338
Fig. 9.6	Observed risk-return trade-off, Japan (WLRR,4Q,4), TCR = 2%	338
Fig. 9.7	Observed risk-return trade-off, TSE Section 1, standard composite model	339
Fig. 9.8	The Barra-estimated trade-off curve of the USER Model, 1998–2007	371
Fig. 9.9	Large Cap U.S. Stock Portfolios	383
Fig. 9.10	MSCI Japan Stock Portfolios	384
Fig. 9.11	MSCI Non-U.S. Stock Portfolios	384
Fig. 9.12	MSCI All World (Global) Stock Portfolios	385
Fig. 9.13	Russell 3000 U.S. Stock Portfolios	385
Fig. 9.14	MSCI Emerging Markets Stock Portfolios	386
Fig. 9.15	ACW Donuts	388
Fig. 10.1	Model UER AR1 LS	545
Fig. 10.2	Model UER AR1 large residuals	545
Fig. 10.3	Model UER AR1 with IIS, DIIS, and TIS saturation variables	547
Fig. 10.4	Model UER AR1 LS with LEI L1	550
Fig. 10.5	Model UER AR1 with IIS, DIIS, and TIS saturation and LEI L1 variables	551
Fig. 10.6	Model UER AR1 LS with WkUNCL L1	554
Fig. 10.7	Model UER AR1 with IIS, DIIS, and TIS saturation and WkUNCL L1 variables	555
Fig. 10.8	Model UER AR1 LS with LEI, WkUNCL L1	558
Fig. 10.9	Model UER AR1 with IIS, DIIS, and TIS saturation and WkUNCL LEI L1 variables	560
Fig. 10.10	Model UER AR1 with IIS, DIIS, and TIS saturation and WkUNCL L12 variables	562
Fig. 10.11	Model UER AR1 with Tiny IIS, DIIS, and TIS saturation and WkUNCL L12 variables	566
Fig. 10.12	Model DLGDP AR1 IIS DIIS TIS saturation variables	571
Fig. 10.13	Model PS UER AR1 IIS, DIIS, TIS saturation variables	573
Fig. 10.14	Model PS UER AR1 IIS, DIIS, TIS saturation and LEI L1 variables	575
Fig. 10.15	Model PS DUE AR1 IIS DIIS TIS saturation and DLWkUNCL DLLEI L12 variables	578
Fig. 11.1	The DLGDP AR1 LS, 1959–2020 is plagued by outliers, particularly in 2020	583
Fig. 11.2	DLGDP AR1 with IIS DIIS TIS Saturation Variables, 1959–2020	585

Fig. 11.3   DLGDP with DLLEI L4 Lags with IIS DIIS And TIS
Saturation Variables, 1959–2029   586

List of Tables

Table 1.1	NBER chronology of expansions and contractions	2
Table 3.1	The persons correlation coefficients of wholesale prices, 1879–1913	51
Table 3.2	The persons correlation coefficients on first differences of wholesale prices and time series, 1879–1913	51
Table 3.3	The persons correlation coefficients with business barometer, 1879–1913	52
Table 5.1	Estimated *Autometrics* Time Series Model of Stock Prices, 1991–September 2020	115
Table 5.2	Performance Summary for Models for levels of the S&P 500 Index and the Money Supply, M1, 1991–2020	116
Table 7.1	Forecasting performance comparison, US unemployment rate, 1959–2018	267
Table 8.1	OLS and Robust regression analysis of mergers, stock prices, and the LEI quarterly data, 1975 Q1 to 2018 Q4	294
Table 8.2	FactSet Mergerstat 1975–2018	295
Table 8.3	Mergers explained by Stock Prices with 4-period Lags	296
Table 8.4	Causal paths between mergers and LEI, SP500 and Unemployment at lag value specified in the "lag" column	297
Table 8.5	Summary for univariate time series model for the U.S. Unemployment rate	301
Table 8.6	Summary for univariate time series model with outliers—TFM1	302

Table 8.7   SCA transfer function modelling of the U.S.
             unemployment rate   304
Table 8.8   Stepwise autoregression summary   310
Table 8.9   Summary of final parameter estimates and their standard
             errors   312
Table 8.10   TCB LEI as an input to forecasting the unemployment
             rate in the U.S., 1959–2020 and 1995–2020   317
Table 8.11   TCB unemployment claims as an input to forecasting
             the unemployment rate in the U.S., 1959–2020
             and 1995–2020   319
Table 8.12   MZTT data, 1964.03–2020.11 unemployment is
             a function of LEI   321
Table 8.13   The LEI and real GDP, 1995–11/2020 the 10-year rolling
             windows approach   323
Table 8.14   The money supply and real GDP, 1995–11/2020
             the 10-year rolling windows approach   325
Table 9.1   Mr. Markowitz and DPOS Japanese and U.S. simulations   359
Table 9.2   BARRA-estimated USER, EQ efficient frontiers,
             1998.01–2007.12   370
Table 9.3   The Stone MAP trade-off curve   373
Table 9.4   An anomalies-based risk-return trade-off curve, 2001–2018   378
Table 9.5   Donuts and portfolio selection (Donut portfolio analysis
             time period: 12/2002–11/2018)   387
Table 9.6   Monthly ICs of US Factors within the Rissell 3000 Index
             Consitiunents   389
Table 9.7   Monthly ICs of Non–US Factors within the MSCI ex
             USA Index Consitiunents   392
Table 9.8   Monthly ICs of Global Factors within the Russell 3000
             and MSCI ex USA Index Consitiunents   395
Table 9.9   Top Six Factors within Stock Universes   398
Table 9.10   Portfolio Dashboard of Non-US Portfokios   400
Table 9.11   Global Portfolio Dashboard, 2001–2021   403

1

Economic Growth and Business Cycles in the U.S

The reader should rightfully ask why business cycles are important. Why has the National Bureau of Economic Research, the NBER, published so many volumes on the topic? Has the business cycle has abolished, as was the topic of a Social Science Research Council Committee conference?[1] The answer to that question is clearly no, as the American public has experienced in the March 2020—November 22, 2021 period. But more recent studies ask "has the business cycle changed? More recently, distinguished authors have addressed this question by asking if postwar (World War II, denoted WWII) business cycles are similar to pre-WWII cycles. The answers appear to be no, business cycles have not been abolished, nor have they been tamed, if one looks at GDP in the COVID period. It appears to the author that we need to review Mr. Mitchell to see what economists believed and taught in 1913 regarding business cycles. One must remember that the Federal Reserve Banking System had been created in 1913, partially to prevent the repeat of the Panics of 1873, 1893, and 1907. The economic history of the U.S. has been characterized by many booms and busts, depressions. This is particularly true during the time periods of booms and depressions analyzed by the NBER. The U.S. has enjoyed its longest peak-to-peak expansion, by far, in 2020.

What should the reader remember from Table 1.1, in Chapter 1? There were numerous and the longest, 1873–1879, contraction prior to the creation

---

[1] Is the Business Cycle Obsolete? *Martin Bronfenbrenner*, Editor (New York: John Wiley & Sons, 1969).

© The Author(s), under exclusive license to Springer Nature
Switzerland AG 2022
J. B. Guerard, *The Leading Economic Indicators and Business Cycles
in the United States*, https://doi.org/10.1007/978-3-030-99418-1_1

Table 1.1 NBER chronology of expansions and contractions

Peak month (Peak Quarter)	Trough month (Trough Quarter)	Contraction Duration, peak to trough	Expansion Duration, peak to trough	Cycle Duration, peak to trough	Cycle Duration, peak to peak
June 1857 (1857Q2)	December 1854 (1854Q4)		30		
October 1860 (1860Q3)	December 1858 (1858Q4)	18	22	48	40
April 1865 (1865Q1)	June 1861 (1861Q3)	8	46	30	54
June 1869 (1869Q2)	December 1867 (1868Q1)	32	18	78	50
October 1873 (1873Q3)	December 1870 (1870Q4)	18	34	36	52
March 1882 (1882Q1)	March 1879 (1879Q1)	65	36	99	101
March 1887 (1887Q2)	May 1885 (1885Q2)	38	22	74	60
July 1890 (1890Q3)	April 1888 (1888Q1)	13	27	35	40
January 1893 (1893Q1)	May 1891 (1891Q2)	10	20	37	30
December 1895 (1895Q4)	June 1894 (1894Q2)	17	18	37	35
June 1899 (1899Q3)	June 1897 (1897Q2)	18	24	36	42
September 1902 (1902Q4)	December 1900 (1900Q4)	18	21	42	39
May 1907 (1907Q2)	August 1904 (1904Q3)	23	33	44	56
January 1910 (1910Q1)	June 1908 (1908Q2)	13	19	46	32
January 1913 (1913Q1)	January 1912 (1911Q4)	24	12	43	36
August 1918 (1918Q3)	December 1914 (1914Q4)	23	44	35	67
January 1920 (1920Q1)	March 1919 (1919Q1)	7	10	51	17
May 1923 (1923Q2)	July 1921 (1921Q3)	18	22	28	40
October 1926 (1926Q3)	July 1924 (1924Q3)	14	27	36	41
August 1929 (1929Q3)	November 1927 (1927Q4)	13	21	40	34
May 1937 (1937Q2)	March 1933 (1933Q1)	43	50	64	93
February 1945 (1945Q1)	June 1938 (1938Q2)	13	80	63	93
November 1948 (1948Q4)	October 1945 (1945Q4)	8	37	88	45
July 1953 (1953Q2)	October 1949 (1949Q4)	11	45	48	56
August 1957 (1957Q3)	May 1954 (1954Q2)	10	39	55	49
April 1960 (1960Q2)	April 1958 (1958Q2)	8	24	47	32
December 1969 (1969Q4)	February 1961 (1961Q1)	10	106	34	116
November 1973 (1973Q4)	November 1970 (1970Q4)	11	36	117	47
January 1980 (1980Q1)	March 1975 (1975Q1)	16	58	52	74
July 1981 (1981Q3)	July 1980 (1980Q3)	6	12	64	18
	November 1982 (1982Q4)	16		28	

Peak month	Trough month	Contraction	Expansion	Cycle	Cycle
July 1990 (1990Q3)	March 1991 (1991Q1)	8	92	100	108
March 2001 (2001Q1)	November 2001 (2001Q4)	8	120	128	128
December 2007 (2007Q4)	June 2009 (2009Q2)	18	73	91	81
February 2020 (2019Q4)	April 2020 (2020Q2)	2	128	130	146
1854–2020		17	41.4	58.4	59.2
1854–1919		21.6	26.6	48.2	48.9
1919–1945		18.2	35.0	53.2	53.0
1945–2020		10.3	64.2	74.5	75.0

Source US Business cycle expansions and contractions, https://www.nber.org/research/data/us-business-cycle-expansions-and-contractions. Business cycle data last updated: 07/19/2021

of the Fedral Reserve, "The Fed." Second, the time surrounding the creation of the Fed, 1907–1913, saw three rather severe (contractions) recessions. Third, the Great Depression of 1929–1933 and the subsequent recession of 1937–1938 created a decade of severe economic downturn, that affected the economic mentality of many U.S. citizens. The author asks the reader to consider if your grandmother and grandfather did not seem cheap? Fourth, the duration of expansions has increased relative to the duration of contractions over time, particularly in the post-WWII time period, 1945–2020. The fourth fact may be of less interest to the political parties currently debating the COVID relief efforts. Fifth, the post-1973 recessions have been few, and the contractions a very short period of the entire business cycle, with the exception of 1973–1975 and 1981–1982. In the author's business career, 1979–2020, the U.S. economy has been characterized by prosperity, or certainly the lack of depressions and severe recessions, rising Gross Domestic Product, GDP, and rising stocks prices, as measured by the Dow Jones Industrial Index, the S&P 500 Index, and /or the Center for Research in Security Prices (CRSP) value-weighted indexes.

It is necessary in this chapter to review much of the U.S. economic and political history of the 1865–1897 and 1874–1914 periods, and its relevance to business cycles, to understand why so many economists wanted to create the Fed and use its monetary policy to booster the economy and prevent or at least dampen contractions and depressions. The reader notes the emphasis on recessions and depressions. Most people understand volatility. They just prefer markets to be "active" or volatile, when economic activity and market prices are rising. Few people enjoy volatility when markets fall.

1.1   Depression in the Late Nineteenth-Century U.S. Economy

The U.S. suffered several major depressions in the second half of the nineteenth century. From the end of the Civil War, 1865 to 1897, the U.S. economy experienced falling prices, deflation. Borrowers, many of them farmers, were repaying bank loans with depreciating currency and agriculture, where debt was widely used, was particularly hard hit. The depression of 1873–1879, 1882–1885, and 1893–1897, were very long and pronounced depressions. Falling prices were accompanied by falling interest rates. Commercial paper rates fell dramatically from over 10% in 19,873 to less than 5% in 1878; rising thereafter.[2] Mr. Fels suggested that speculation in the U.S. would resume the gold standard at an appreciated value abnormally lowered interest rates during the depressions and silver problems dominated the 1890s money market. Much of the U.S. monetary theory was developed and reported in 1911 at the American Economic Association meeting regarding price movements during the 1896–1909 period.

What was happening in the post-Civil War U.S. economy? First, the U.S. war economy produced great output in the 1874–1913 period. In the Fels presentation of the GNP tables of Professor Simon Kuznets, GNP rose by 44% (in 1929 prices).[3] The U.S. economy continued its growth during the 1879–1888, 1884–1893, 1889–1898, 1894–1903, 1889–1903, and 1904–1913 periods of 31, 19, 16, 21, 25, and 21%, respectively. The corresponding implicit price deflators (measuring inflation) of GNP rose by −12, −8, −7, −8, −6, 0, 8, and 12%, respectively. Wholesale prices, reported by the Bureau of Labor Statistics, rose by − 4, −11, −7, −8, 1, 14, and 10%, respectively. Thus, the reader sees that GNP, the market value of goods and services, rose during the 1874–1913 period, whereas prices from 1874 to 1898 and rose from 1899 to 1909 and 1899–1913.[4] Railroad bond yields followed the same pattern. Crop production and manufacturing output rose dramatically from 9 to 34% during the intervals.[5] Crop production fell during the 1879–1888 and 1884–1893 period. This was not true in manufacturing, transportation and communications, and railroad capital formation. Unemployment data was virtually non-existent.[6]

Prices and profit margin fell in the U.K. as well. Mr. Fels, commented on the money supply issue, stating that the depression had two explanations, monetary and real.[7] The money supply might not have been growing fast enough and thus prices fell. As the money supply eventually increased, due to gold production, prices rose. Real explanations stress over-production and the lack of investment opportunities.[8] Mr. Fels stated that the relative strength of the monetary and real factors is of great importance.

Following the Civil War, the U.S. economy was posed for a burst of investment activity. Railroad building was one of the most important investment opportunities. The population was growing and railroad construction in the

---

[2] Rendings Fels, *American Business Cycles, 1865–1897* (Chapel Hill: University of North Carolina Press, 1959), pp. 63–65.

[3] Fels, *American Business Cycles, 1865–1897*, p. 66.

[4] Ibid.

[5] Ibid.

[6] Fels, *American Business Cycles, 1865–1897*, p. 67.

[7] Fels, *American Business Cycles, 1865–1897*, p. 68.

[8] Ibid.

West was financed by domestic and foreign sales of bonds with high interest rates.[9] There was a housing shortage in 1865. Despite the investment boom in housing and railroads, 1865–1872, wholesale prices fell in all but one year from 1865 to 1879. Agricultural output doubled in the period from 1866 to 1878 and agricultural prices fell.[10]Agricultural prices dominated the wholesale price index, not just because they were included in.

the index computation and they served as raw materials for other industries, depressing the gold premium, and making imports cheaper. Between 1865 and 1869, the currency supply fell, as did transportation costs and great technological advances in the steel industry, such as the Bessemer process led to production cost reductions. The currency fell 30% while railroad mileage construction doubled.

In September 1869, Mr. Jay Gould and Mr. Jim Fisk attempted to corner the gold market. They ran the price of gold from $131 to $162. The housing index peaked in 1871, although the national economic growth was stagnant (not declining).[11] Wholesale prices rose during 1871–1873 and railroad earnings jumped substantially. The NBER cyclical peak occurred in October 1873, following a bank panic in September 1873, with the failure of Jay Cooke & Company. Mr. Cooke had financed the Civil War and the Northern Pacific Railroad. Tight money caused higher interest rates and 25 railroads defaulted on bonds.[12] Stock prices and New York bank clearings fell sharply in the first half of 1873. NY bank problems spread throughout the country because the National Banking System did not have the later power of The Federal Reserve Banks.[13] On Thursday, September 18th, Jay Cooke failed in its advances to the Northern Pacific Railroad.

1.1.1   The Panic of 1873

A monetary contraction and a shortage of capital caused the downturn. At the beginning of the upswing, interest rates were low and induced businessmen to build railroads and take advantage of technical progress, opening up new countries, and launch new investment projects. The production of fixed capital grew at the expense of consumer's goods. Profits were initially higher but fell off as wages and interest rates rose. The rising interest rates forced abandonment of capital projects.

---

[9] Fels, *American Business Cycles, 1865–1897*, pp. 84–85.

[10] Fels, *American Business Cycles, 1865–1897*, pp. 89–90.

[11] Fels, *American Business Cycles, 1865–1897*, pp. 96–97.

[12] Fels, *American Business Cycles, 1865–1897*, p. 99.

[13] Fels, *American Business Cycles, 1865–1897*, pp. 100–101.

The long cyclical contraction following the Panic of 1873 was the longest in the history of American business cycles, 5.5 years, at that point in time.[14] The decline of bank clearings of 1875–1878 was greater than all other periods except 1893–1897 and 1929–1933. In the U.K., prices and interest rates fell, but industrial production rose. Had the U.S. been on the gold standard, the depression and corresponding falling net income would have reduced its imports, and created a favorable balance of payments, if exports are maintained, if not increased, as expected. The greenbacks appreciated in 1877.[15]

1.1.2 The Cycle of 1879–1885

The lower turning point of the cycle of 1879–1885 was 1877–1879 when wholesale prices were still declining. The U.S. economy returned to the gold standard in 1879, reviving confidence, and good crop harvests and railroad construction led to the 1879–1891 upswing.[16] Large gold imports created an easy money market in 1880–1881. American railroads floated their bonds in the U.S., rather than Europe. Interest rates fell with prices between 1873 and 1876. Prosperity appeared in September 1879 and investment increased on the basis that the rate of increase in demand would be maintained in the future.[17] Railroad expansion created opportunities favoring agriculture, mining, mills, and foundries. Unemployment reached a seven-year low.[18] The upper turning point of 1881–1883 was reached in the summer of 1881. By 1883, business grew worse and in 1884, the contraction became pronounced. The reduction of railroad construction started the downturn of 1883. A bank panic developed in 1884, when on May 8, 1883, Grant and Ward, a brokerage firm, failed. The Marine Bank was a banker for Grant and Ward

---

[14] Fels, *American Business Cycles, 1865–1897*, p. 107. Milton Friedman and Anna J. Schwartz, "Money and Business Cycles," *The Review of Economics and Statistics* (Feb. 1963) Vol. 45, No. 1, Part 2, Supplement, pp. 32–64, noted that the depression of 1873–1879 was accompanied by a 4.9% reduction in the money supply, M1. The "Panic of 1873" had the third largest reduction in the money supply of depressions of the 1867–1960 time period, trailing only the 5.8% decline of the 1892–1894 period and the 35.2% decline of the 1929–1933 period, see p. 34. The Friedman and Schwartz association of the role of the money supply and real GDP is tested in our Chapter 8 for the 1995–2020 period and confirmed. That is, the money supply is statistically associated with real GDP. Initial results of research with Professor Dimitrios Thomakos and the author report statistically significant Granger-causality findings.

[15] Fels, *American Business Cycles, 1865–1897*, p. 109.

[16] Fels, *American Business Cycles, 1865–1897*, p. 114.

[17] Fels, *American Business Cycles, 1865–1897*, p. 122.

[18] Fels, *American Business Cycles, 1865–1897*, p. 123.

and it initially failed, as did the Second National Bank. Actions by The Treasury created a rescue that allowed both banks to reopen. The panic of 1883 was short-lived. In 1885, interest rates were low and new building construction eventually brought forth a weak revival. Immigration increased the labor force and new buildings were established in new territories opened by railroad expansion.[19]

1.1.3   The Cycle of 1885–1888

The trough of the business cycle was in May 1885. Railroad construction would again spur the economic recovery. In 1885, railroad managers agreed to raise railroad rates and railroad traffic was expanding throughout the U.S., and the railroads previously n default were being re-organized.[20] Railroad prices rose during the second half of 1885. The upswing was generated by better crop harvests in 1886 and the number of railroad miles built doubled to 6000 miles in 1886 from the 3000 miles built in 1885. Total merchandise exports were only 6–7% of Gross National Product in 1886.[21] Improved business conditions in railroads helped drive the U.S. economy in the 1880s. Improved business in railroads allowed the railroads to maintain rates, generating better earnings prospects and higher stock prices. Interest rates were low as capital was abundant in the upswing of 1886.[22] The business peak occurred in March 1887. The downturn that followed the peak was one of the mildest recessions during the 1869–1933 period. Railroad construction peaked in 1887 and supply-chain issues developed in the steel and iron industries. Interest rates peaked during the business cycle peak. Business failures increased as interest rates rose.

---

[19] Fels, *American Business Cycles, 1865–1897*, p. 133. See also Rendigs Fels, "The Long-Wave Depression, 1873–1897", *The Review of Economics and Statistics* 31 (1949), pp. 69–73.

Mr. James Laurence Laughlin, later of the University of Chicago, wrote in 1887 that when one reviews the history of gold and prices during the 1870–1874 to 1885 period, the gold supply increased in the money supply United States (and Italy), while the U.K. money supply slightly fell. See James Laurence Laughlin, "Gold and Prices Since 1873" *The Quarterly Journal of Economics* 1 (1887), pp. 319–355. The Table referenced is on p. 349. Mr. Laughlin commented the effective growth of checks and the clearinghouses that created an effective system and an elastic currency that met the needs of trade, pp. 350–351.

To Mr. Laughlin, the fall of prices during the 1870 -1885 period was independent of the quantity of gold and silver. Despite the coincidental demonetization of silver in 1873, a new of technology and enhancements in the production of many commodities drove down prices since 1873.

[20] Fels, *American Business Cycles, 1865–1897*, pp. 137–138.

[21] Fels, *American Business Cycles, 1865–1897*, p. 138.

[22] Fels, *American Business Cycles, 1865–1897*, p. 139.

1.1.4   The Panic of 1893 and the Cycle of 1894–1897

The Panic of 1893 was the trough of the cycle of 1891–1893.[23] The upswing of 1891–1893 was spurred by railroad construction and its accompanying pig-iron production, and bank clearings. In fact, pig-iron production reached a new high in 1892, although output started to fall in September. Indeed, the Kondratieff cycle of steam and steel was coming to its end in 1892–1893. A large cotton crop in 1891 forced cotton prices low and brought depression to (only) The South, and the agricultural boom continued in 1892. Agricultural output drove the boom of 1892. New issues rose on the New York Stock Exchange in 1892.[24] The NBER turning point of January 1893 is the upper turning point of the cycle. GNP growth had been 4%, annually, but this would not continue. Weak firms, a weak banking structure, a weak gold standard, and weak banking opportunities would cause a major depression.[25] The depression onset occurred on February 29, 1893, with the Reading Railroad bankruptcy. The Reading floated $3 million of debt in 1893 to pay interest on its $18.5 million debt obligations and held cash of less than $100,000 at the time of its filing. Additional failures drove down the stock market in 1893. Net gold exports were $29 million in the first quarter of 1893 and the U.S. gold reserve fell below $100 million. In 1893, gold exports ceased with the repeal of The Sherman Purchase Act of 1890. The bank and railroad failures of 1893 created a severe depression. The U.S. government would no longer purchase silver of 4.5 million ounces of silver per month. The McKinley Tariff of 1890, passed together with The Sherman Silver Act, was not repealed.[26] Low U.S. interest rates and a poor crop harvest led to the export of gold.

Only pig-iron production spurred a minor swing in 1895, and the recovery, or revival, was unsatisfactory. Another cyclical downturn occurred in December 1895. The May –June 1896 period marked the peak for wholesale prices and building permits. The reader will remember from American history that the Presidential election featured William Jennings Bryan and his famous cross-of-gold speech on July 7, 1896, calling for the free coinage of

---

[23] Fels, *American Business Cycles, 1865–1897*, p. 179.

[24] Fels, *American Business Cycles, 1865–1897*, pp. 180–182.

[25] Fels, *American Business Cycles, 1865–1897*, p. 184. We noted previously that the 5.8% decline of the 1892–1894 period was the second largest money supply decline in the 1867–1960 period, trailing only the 35.2% decline of the 1929–1933 period, see Friedman and Schwartz, "Money and Business Cycles, *The Review of Economics and Statistics* 45 (1963), p. 34.

[26] Fels, *American Business Cycles, 1865–1897*, pp. 185–187. A central bank, Mr. Fels stated, could have raised short-term interest rates and attracted foreign capital and ended the gold exports, *American Business Cycles, 1865–1897*, p. 194.

silver at a ratio of 16:1.[27] The overvalued ratio would have driven out gold and raised prices. Gold hoarding began in June 1896 and interest rates rose substantially.

The Depression of the 1890s was very severe. It had both internal and external factors. Mr. Schumpeter characterized the depression of 1893 in terms of the exhaustion of innovative opportunities and the U.S. currency factor. Mr. Friedman and Ms. Schwartz characterized the depression of 1893 as the second largest contraction of the money supply of 90 years. Monetary constraints, crop failures, railroad failures created a lack of confidence in the U.S. economy. The sixth and last Juglar cycle prosperity phase, of the Kondratieff railroad, stem, and steel cycle extended from 1889–1891. The Panic of 1893 resulted from the end of the preceding Juglar prosperity phase and the entire Kondratieff cycle.[28]

1.1.5 Monetary Policy and Prices, 1890–1909

Why did we stress the 1873 and 1893 depressions in this Chapter? The depressions of 1873 and 1893 were two of the three worst depressions involving contracting money supplies in the monetary history of the U.S. 1867–1960, as we noted from Mr. Milton Friedman and Ms. Anna Schwartz, in their *A Monetary History of the U.S., 1867–1960*. The relationship among the money supply, Gross National Product, and the price level raged among economists from the late nineteenth century to the creation of the Federal Reserve System in 1913.[29]

At the American Economic Association meeting of 1911, Mr. James Laurence Laughlin and Mr. Irving Fisher hotly debated the cause of raising prices from 1896 to 1909. Mr. Laughlin stated there was a proposition on which can all agree. An increase in the quantity of the monetary standard,

---

[27] Fels, *American Business Cycles, 1865–1897*, pp. 202–203. The read might think of Senator Bryan was an earlier version of Senator Bernie Sanders.

[28] Fels, *American Business Cycles, 1865–1897*, pp. 221–223. See also Alvin H. Hansen, *Fiscal Policy and Business Cycles* (New York: W.W. Norton & Company, Inc., 1941, pp. 29–30.

[29] H. Parker Willis, of Columbia University, earned his Ph.D. at Chicago under Professor James Laurence Laughlin. Mr. Willis taught at Washington & Lee University, George Washington University, and Columbia University. Mr. Willis served as an economic advisor to Carter Glass, of the Ways and Means and Banking and Currency House of Representatives committees. Mr. Glass, as a member of the U.S. House of Representatives, Carter Glass co-sponsored the Federal Reserve Act. As secretary of the Treasury from 1918 to 1920, Mr. Glass also served as ex officio chairman of the Federal Reserve Board. Later, as U.S. senator from the Commonwealth of Virginia, and chairman of the Senate Banking Committee during the Great Depression, Mr. Glass co-sponsored major legislation that changed the structure and responsibilities of the Federal Reserve System. The reader will immediately recognize the Glass-Owen of 1913 and the Glass-Steagall Act of February 1932 Act among these legislations. Source: https://www.federalreservehistory.org/people/carter-glass.

such as gold, would, holding other things being equal, lower its value and raise prices. In trying to find the causes in the price level at any given time (as in 1896–1909) it is necessary, therefore, after stating the facts as to the increase of gold, to examine into the influence of "the other things".[30] There is abundant evidence to show that the demand for gold, in this recent period of rising prices (1896–1909) has been as strong as, or even stronger than, the demand for gold in the previous period (1873–1896) of falling prices. Mr. Laughlin attributed price increases of the 1896 to 1909 period to the high tariff of President McKinley, the Dingley Act of 1897, and the high price of food, due to changing conditions in agricultural production.[31] Tariffs and agriculture are external factors that can influence prices and business cycles and are independent of monetary policy.

Mr. Fisher, presenting materials of his forthcoming *The Purchasing Power of Money* (1911) attributed the rising price level to increasing money supply of currency and demand deposits, and their respective velocities.[32] Mr. Fisher presented the Equation of Exchange as the factors affecting the price level.

$$MV + M'V' = PT$$

The five factors affecting prices are.

1. The quantity of money in circulation (M').
2. The volume of bank deposits subject to check considered relatively to money (M,)
3. The velocity of the former (V).

---

[30] James Laurence Laughlin, "Causes of the Changes in Prices Since 1896", *The American Economic Review* 1 (1911) pp. 26–36. The reader is referred to page 30.

[31] Laughlin, "Causes of the Changes in Prices Since 1896", *The American Economic Review*, p. 35. Mr. Laughlin answered Mr. Fisher's equation of M V + MV'= PT is to my mind not a solution, but only a statement, of the problem of price levels. His equation does not show causes; it states a static situation, into which various causes may be read. Mr. Laughlin noted that bank deposits increased 500–600% between 1876 and 1896 and yet that period was distinguished as one of falling prices. Therefore M' cannot be regarded as having been proved to be a cause of higher prices. Further, as Mr. Laughlin continued "In my paper, I purposely included the general movement from 1850 to 1896 to serve as a corrective to hasty inference in the period of 1896–1909, when prices were rising; for the same group of forces were at work in both periods.", p. 68. See also D. F. Houston, E. W. Kemmerer, Joseph French Johnson, Murray S. Wildman, T. N. Carver, F. W. Taussig, Ralph H. Hess, J. Laurence Laughlin and Irving Fisher, "Money and Prices: Discussion", *The American Economic Review* 1 (1911), pp. 46–70, particularly pp. 67–70.

[32] Irving Fisher, "Recent Changes in Price Levels and Their Causes", *The American Economic Review* 1 (1911), pp. 37–45. Mr. Fisher began with the statement that the supply and demand are terms which help in the discussion of individual prices but not in the consideration of the general price level.

4. The velocity of the latter (V').
5. The volume of trade (T).

This equation restates the old quantity theory of money. Mr. Fisher attributed the Equation of Exchange to Mr. Simon Newcomb.[33]

Mr. Fisher compared the relative importance of these five magnitudes by answering the question: What would the result have been had any one of these magnitudes remained unchanged during these years, assuming that the other four changed in the same manner that they actually did change. We find (1) that if the money in circulation, M, had not changed, the price level of 1909 would have been 45% lower than it actually was; (2) that if, the relative deposits, had not changed, the price level in 1909 would have been 23% lower than it actually was; (3) if the velocity of circulation of money, V, had not changed, the price level for 1909 would have been 1% lower; (4) if the velocity of circulation of deposits, V', had not changed, the price level in 1909 would have been 28% lower. Thus, the increase in the quantity of money has an importance nearly double that of any other one price-raising factor.[34] Mr. Fisher concluded that the chief cause of the rise in prices during the last fifteen years has been due to the increase in the money in circulation.[35]

1.2   Mr. Fisher and the Purchasing Power of Money and Depressions

In equilibrium, the Quantity Theory of Money held that increases in the money supply created proportional changes in the price level. As long as the economy is "normal," then an increase in the money in circulation, M, merely raises prices, P, proportionally. Furthermore, the equation of exchange says that $MV = PT$, where V is the velocity of money and T is real output. In periods of transition, the economy can experience real effects from increases in the money supply, such as increases in V and PT. Fisher created a dramatic

---

[33] See Mr. Simon Newcomb, *Principles of Political Economy* (New York: Harper & Brothers, 1885), pp. 329–349 for one of the first equation of exchange presentations.

[34] Fisher, "Recent Changes in Price Levels and Their Causes", *AER* (1911), pp. 43–44. Furthermore, if T had not changed, the price level in 1909 would have been 106% higher.

[35] Robert W. Dimond, "J. Laurence Laughlin versus Irving Fisher on the Quantity Theory of Money, 1894 to 1913" *Oxford Economic Papers*, 72 (2020), pp. 1032–1049. The Dimond paper is a very good review of Laughlin, his Ph.D. students and the University of Chicago, including H. Parker Willis, their views on bimetallism; the Bryan Campaign of 1896 and "sound money"; and the Laughlin debate with Mr. Fisher in 1911. https://doi.org/10.1093/oep/gpaa014.

example in his Chapter 4, of *The Purchasing Power of Money,* he discusses a sudden doubling of the money supply, creating a period of transition, the doubling of the money supply will double the price level in the long run.[36] However, the price level may not initially double, and the increased money supply can initially cause interest rates to fall, which can change prices and profits, and generate booms and depressions. Fisher distinguished between the period of transition and the period of permanent effect; i. e., the period of the new equilibrium. In Chapter 4, Mr. Fisher distinguished between rising prices and high prices, and falling prices from low prices.[37] It is rising and falling prices that lead to changes in the rate of interest. It is the change in the interest rate during transitionary periods that is responsible for crises and depressions.[38] If the interest rate is initially 5% and rising pricing (inflation) is 3%, then the lender must receive slightly more than 8% to maintain his/her purchasing power. Rising prices require a higher interest rate than stable prices. Lenders require a higher rate and borrowers can afford to pay higher interest rates. Businessmen's' profits initially increase faster than prices because the interest rate is a cost of doing rate, because the interest rate will not immediately adjust. Businessman can afford to pay higher interest rates because the interest rate does not immediately adjust, and profits initially rise. The businessman, finding that his profits will rise faster than prices. These increasing profits encourage further borrowing to expand his business. These borrowings are short-term bank loans. As load demand rises and the nominal interest rate is forced upward.[39] Mr. Fisher stated that the lenders (the banks) extend the loans because of the higher nominal interest rates. As prices rise, the value of the collateral rises, and it is easier for bowers to get larger credits.

The Fisher transitionary sequence is that prices rise, interest rates rise, but not sufficiently. Enterprises are encouraged by larger profits to expand their loans. Deposit currency rises relative to money, further driving up prices. The increase in prices leads to further increases in prices as long as the nominal interest rate lags behind the normal figure. Deposits based on loans increase relative to the money driving prices upward further. Trade is stimulated by the easy terms for loans and business is "good or booming." The entrepreneur is excited by rising prices, but not so the creditor, the salaried man, or the laborer because they are not receiving proportionally higher incomes. The

---

[36] Fisher, *The Purchasing Power of Money,* p. 55.

[37] Fisher, *The Purchasing Power of Money,* p. 56.

[38] Ibid..

[39] Fisher, *The Purchasing Power of Money,* p. 60. See David Laidler, *The Golden Age of The Quantity Theory of Money.* Princeton, NJ: Princeton University Press, 1991, pp. 76–81, for an analysis of the Fisherian transition period and the inflation of 1896–1909.

volume of trade purchases is higher than the case had prices and costs risen promptly or proportionally. The amount of trade is dependent on factors other than currency, and an increase in money cannot greatly increase trade. In periods of transition, there is some increase in trade. The increase in prices and the fall in purchasing power accelerates the circulation of money. Money is depreciating and holders want to get rid of it.[40] Prices are pushed still higher. Prices rise, velocity rises, and the rate of interest rises, but not sufficiently, and profits increase. Mr. Fisher notes that all the variables in the equation of exchange change within the transition period.

The check in the expansion is caused by the interest rate. The late rise in the interest rate is responsible for the abnormal condition.[41] the boom continues until the interest rate rises to the rate of price increases. As interest rates rise, bond prices fall, and the value of collateral falls. The securities cannot be used for collateral for loans as before. The rising interest rates mean that businessmen cannot renew their loans at their former rates. Some firms will fail. The failure of firms that borrow heavily induces fears for the bank's depositors. The depositors may demand cash and can create a "run on the bank."[42] Banks will curtail loans and the interest rate may rise to a panic figure. The culmination of an upward price movement is called a crisis, a condition characterized by bankruptcies. The essential fault of every crisis is a collapse of bank credit brought by a loss of confidence. Monetary causes are most important in crises when taken into connection with the maladjustments in the rate of interest. "Overconsumption" and "overinvestment" are caused by people spending more than they could afford on the basis of the consumer relying on a stable dollar that is falling rapidly in its purchs. asing power.[43] Borrowers blame the high interest rates for their inability would get "easy loans" and the borrowers would not have overborrowed had the interest rate risen proportionally in the first place. The contraction of loans and deposits leads to a decrease in velocity and leads to falling prices. Liquidation begins even when interest rates fall because the rate of interest falls slowly. Entrepreneurs are discouraged by smaller profits and contract their borrowers with falling prices.[44] Deposit currency (M') falls relative to money, M, and prices continue to fall. Business is "bad" and there is a depression of trade. During depressions, velocities are abnormally low and the quantity in trade declines. Why? Initiators of trade, the entrepreneurs, are discouraged

---

[40] Fisher, *The Purchasing Power of Money*, p. 63.
[41] Fisher, *The Purchasing Power of Money*, p. 64.
[42] Fisher, *The Purchasing Power of Money*, p. 65.
[43] Fisher, *The Purchasing Power of Money*, p. 66.
[44] Fisher, *The Purchasing Power of Money*, p. 68.

and higher prices lead to a falling off of expenditure and trade in money may give way to barter.[45] Profits decline until the change in the rate of interest equals the rate of falling prices.

We introduced the reader to the economic history of 1865–1909 for two reasons. The nineteenth-century depressions were severe, and Mr. Mitchell refers to them in his *Business Cycles* (1913), the subject of Chapter 2. Second, Mr. Mitchell's research philosophy was developed from his dissertation under Mr. Laughlin. The Mitchell approach to empiricism, and criticisms of it, are discussed in Chapters 2–4.

1.3   Post-War Economic History and Measuring U.S. Economic Growth

In 1961, Mr. Robert A. Gordon presented a very compelling graphical presentation of the U.S. manufacturing production index, 1866–1956, and real GNP, Gross National Product, in 1947 dollars, for the 1900–1956 period. The graph was one of reporting tremendous growth. Despite the Great Depression of the 1930s and two world wars, the U.S. economy has produced great growth. There is volatility associated with that growth. In 1961, economic income was measured by Gross National Product, national income, the market value of goods and services produced in the economic, GNP rose from 1929 to 1961, from $105.32 billion to $565.73 billion, a 5.37 multiple, a 6.43% average annual growth rate. The U.S. GNP rose to $21,116.09 billion in 2020, a 200.49 multiplier, a 6.00% average annual growth rate. Economic activities include all activities of corporations and the government. [46]Mr. Gordon commented that calculations used on GNP are nominally calculated, including inflation, and not just real national income. Had one used real GNP based on 2012 dollars, the real GNP of $18,582.30 billion in 2020 divided by the real GNP of $1,120.718 billion in 1929 gives a 16.581 multiple which is a 3.13% average annual growth for 91 years. The corresponding average annual growth rate for real GNP for the 1929–1961 period was 3.50%. Thus, when the reader hears on "the news" that the growth in the U.S. economy is 3% annually, one should not be excited. An average annual growth rate of 3% is merely a long-term average for the U.S. economy.

Mr. Gordon offers an explanation as to how the economy generates business cycles. In major cycles, there are periods of rising (or high level)

---

[45] Fisher, *The Purchasing Power of Money,* p. 69.
[46] Robert A. Gordon, *Business Fluctuations* (New York: Harper & Brothers Publishers, 1962, Second edition), p. 158.

activity where long-term investment opportunities are favorable and even short-term set bucks, or short recessions. are not sufficient to offset new revivals or recoveries.[47] Mild recessions in 1947 and pre-World War II recessions, such as 1924 and 1927, are examples of short-term recessions. In major downturns, long-term investment opportunities appear bleak, and a long and severe downturn can result from the depressed view of business. There is no backlog of continuing investment opportunities, and there is no self-correcting economic factors sufficient enough to alter the downward movement. Short-term recoveries fail to restore income and employment to the levels before the major downturn began. Major cycles result from long-term investment planning of businessmen and consumers.[48] The study of major cycles centers on analyzing investment opportunities, changes in the growth rate of the economy, and possible speculative promotion of capital projects. Monetary and fiscal policies effect the profitable long-term investment opportunities. Let us consider a major business contraction that has gone on for several years. Production has declined, prices have fallen, unemployment is rising, stock prices have fallen, and long-term investment is at a very low level. The marginal efficiency of capital, the discounted investment output on investment inputs, is shifted down during the business contraction, and income and consumption are falling. As the economy spirals downward, production falls faster than consumption and retail sales. Inventory cannot decline forever. As inventories are reduced there is eventually a low level, where further inventory decreases diminish, businessmen pay off their bank loans and convert investments to cash. Businessmen tend to hold off on replacing older equipment and cash positions increase; liquidity increases. Businessmen eventually replace depleted inventories and obsolete equipment. Banks increase their liquidity as consumers pay off bank loans and banks accumulate excess reserves. As prices fall, goods become cheaper internationally and exports may rise, and gold flows into the country. Bank reserves increase and bankers purchase securities and invest in more mortgages with their "excess cash." Bond prices rise while bond yields and interest rates fall. Low interest rates induce corporations to refund outstanding bond issues, issued when interest rates were higher, and lower interest rates are beneficial to home builders and buyers.[49] Stock prices generally lead business activity, and start to rise before businesses turn up. The greater liquidity tempts investors

[47] Robert A. Gordon, Business Fluctuations, p. 299.
[48] Robert A. Gordon, *Business Fluctuations* , p. 300.
[49] Robert A. Gordon, *Business Fluctuations*, pp. 303–304.

to buy stocks. Business confidence improves, stock prices rise, and confidence spreads throughout the economy.[50]

Prices decline through the contraction and wholesale prices of raw materials fall faster than finished goods prices, resulting in the reduction of fixed costs per unit. Prices fall at a slower rate and businessmen seek to replenish inventory. Labor costs decline during the downturn and labor productivity rises. Profit margins begin to increase. Often the reader may hear about an "over-production" period of business activity. The bottom of the contraction before profit margins increase, production increases, and inventories are replenished are such periods. Consumption falls in downturns, but not as much as production and income, and government payments and transfers in unemployment benefits and farm subsidies. Higher real consumption and lower interest rates create a more favorable outlook for long-term investment. There must be demand for loanable funds and for investment to increase. The demand for loanable funds must respond to a lower interest rate. A strong demand for housing with a growing population can lead to an increased demand for residential building with lower interest rates.[51] Chronic home over-building can create longer periods for the economy to recover. Consumers replace obsolete consumer goods in downturns.

New industries can begin and spend on new equipment mid plant-expansion with lower interest rates. Mr. Gordon reminds the reader that the reduction in costs and interest rates, inventories, and higher real spending are self-correcting endogenous factors. Outside, or exogenous factors, such as government spending (defense or public works), or foreign country demands for U.S. products can affect the push to an economic revival. As the expansion increases, speculation can occur and drive up commodity prices, raw material prices, and output may increase and create bottlenecks in the supply chain. Businessmen increase new order spending, and the number of unfilled orders can rise. Stock price speculation continues to increase, and higher corporation profits lead to higher earnings per share and increases in the price-to-earnings ratios.[52] Enhanced optimism expands stock prices, real estate prices, and there is an increase in the volume of new mortgages, creating a real estate boom. Capacity to fill orders may expand too quickly because of speculation. Full employment is reached, and wages rise. Increases in aggregate demand push up prices. Expansions and prosperity end as profit margins start to

---

[50] Robert A. Gordon, *Business Fluctuations*, p. 304.
[51] Robert A. Gordon, *Business Fluctuations*, p. 308.
[52] Robert A. Gordon, *Business Fluctuations*, p. 314.

decline because of higher labor costs and interest rates.[53] Expectations eventually are reduced and there may be an over investment in new industries, perhaps because businessmen are often mistaken in forecasting new product demand. Investment eventually declines, reducing incomes and consumption. The upper turning point can occur when output and employment reach their maximum levels, and profit margins start to fall, and bankruptcies may start to rise because of faulty expectations and excessive inventories. Prosperity ends and the recession begins, further driving down stock and commodity prices. Long-term investment declines. A short-term decline may only lead to a moderate decline in business confidence and investment and consumption are relatively maintained. In a major downturn, confidence and business activity deteriorate quickly and investment opportunities are impaired. There is a scramble for liquidity and a lack of confidence in the future of stock prices, leading to security sells that accelerate stock price declines.[54]

In summary, economic forces generate business cycles, and several points should be made.

1. Prosperity and contraction levels are created by almost mirror-image processes which are different from the turning points of the business cycles.
2. It is important to distinguish between major and minor cycles in the business cycle. In major cycles, long-term investment is a driver of expansion and contraction. In minor cycles, short-term plans and businessmen's expectations drive the processes.
3. Major and minor cycles occur in combination and no two cycles are alike
4. Self-correcting mechanisms are present in minor cycles, such as liquidation of excessive inventories, and liquidity positions of firms. Lower interest rate cost, greater mortgage availability, and the replacement of obsolete equipment drives major cycles.
5. Minor recessions are caused by declines in new orders and inventory investment.
6. Depressions can be caused by private investment decreases, and further aggregate demand declines.
7. Major downturns can be made worse by capital asset value decline and impaired debtor solvency can create credit contraction, liquidity issues, and bank failures.
8. External, or exogenous factors, can occur and cut short expansions or contractions.

[53] Robert A. Gordon, *Business Fluctuations*, pp. 315–316.
[54] Robert A. Gordon, *Business Fluctuations*, p. 333.

9. Structural changes in the U.S. economy since the 1930s have modified the self-correcting factors and yet, despite these changes, minor cycles self-correcting mechanism have continued to operate to minimize, or moderate, minor cycles.

1.4   Our Path Ahead

The reader what makes this monograph different from a traditional business cycles textbook. We introduce the reader to the NBER Studies in Business Cycles primary authors. In Chapter 2, we introduce the reader to several major Wesley C. Mitchell texts, the first two texts of the National Bureau of Economic Research (NBER) studies in business cycles. The reader becomes aware of the phases of the business cycle. The phases of prosperity, crises, and depression of Mr. Mitchell's *Business Cycles*, (University of California Press, 1913). Mr. Mitchell based his observations of the phases of the business cycles on the U.S. economic data of 1890–1912. There were several periods of prosperity, crises, and depression. The reader will be surprised, perhaps stunned, that Wesley Clair Mitchell pointed out the small-stock effect in 1910, noting that stocks had outperformed bonds, that smaller-priced firms outperformed larger-priced firms for the 1890–1909 period, and that stock prices could rise over a very long period which included the very severe depression of 1893.

In Mr. Mitchell's 1922 monograph, *Business Cycles and Unemployment* (NBER, 1923), resulted from a presidential commission to study how the steep, but short, recession of 1921 unemployed so many Americans. Mr. Mitchell worked with the presidents of major U.S. corporations and the U.S. Secretary of Commerce, Herbert Hoover, to present to recommendations that were surprising for their "progressive" tone in 1923. Mr. Mitchell's thoughts on business fluctuations and cycles evolved, leading to his 1927 NBER monograph *Business Cycles: The Problem and its Setting* (NBER, 1927). Finally, very near his death, Mr. Mitchell and Mr. Arthur Burns, published their *Measuring Business Cycles* (NBER, 1946). Mr. Burns became Mr. Mitchell's successor as Director of Research at the NBER and continued their work. Mr. Burns and Mr. Mitchell modeled over 800-time series of U.S. data during the 1857–1933 period. In Chapter 4, we review the Burns and Mitchell NBER monograph.

One of the great research volume of business cycles is the Geoffrey Moore *Business Cycle Indicators* (NBER, 1961), a two-volume set. The first volume contained much of NBER research papers, written during the 1938–1958 period. The second volume contained the data used in these

NBER papers, several series covering the 1919–1958 period. The period of Mr. Moore's Director of Research at the NBER was an extremely productive period for research publications, including his *Business Cycles, Inflation, and Forecasting* (NBER, 1983). We introduce the reader to Mr. Moore in Chapter 5. Mr. Moore and his colleague, Victor Zarnowitz, produced many outstanding papers on business cycles. Mr. Moore and Mr. Zarnowitz were concerned with real world of business forecasting. Their works consistently addressed whether the then-current business recession was "new" or resembled previous recessions. Mr. Moore and Mr. Zarnowitz wrote so many research papers together that the rise of Mr. Zarnowitz to lead the NBER business cycle research team was seamless. Mr. Zarnowitz, a Professor Emeritus of Economics and Finance at the University of Chicago Graduate School of Business, and Director for International Business Cycle Research at Columbia University, published his magnum opus, the *Business Cycles: Theory, History, Indicators, and Forecasting,* (NBER, 1992). Mr. Zarnowitz thanked his NBER program colleagues for their joint work on business cycles 1952–1991. The reader should not think for a moment that Victor retired from the University of Chicago in 1992 and was not productive. Mr. Zarnowitz joined The Conference Board (TCB) in 1997 when TCB took over the U.S. and global Leading Economic Indicators, LEI. From 1997 until his death in 2006, Mr. Zarnowitz was most productive in producing outstanding business cycle research. Mr. Zarnowitz and his team at TCB built and maintained the LEI data and research. We model the LEI, real GDP, unemployment rate relations in Chapter 7, for regression modeling and forecasting, and Chapter 8, for Granger causality modelling and testing. The author is indebted to the TCB research department for making an updated November 5, 2021 TCB LEI database available. This data is used in Chapter 10 of this monograph.

The history of U.S. business cycles and research has not been entirely written by NBER authors, although the Mr. Mitchell, Mr. Burns, Mr. Moore, and Mr. Zarnowitz tradition of research is the basis of this monograph. The author included a chapter of business cycle research developed within the Harvard University Department of Economics, where Mr. Persons, Mr. Schumpeter, Mr. Haberler, Mr. Hansen, and Mr. Eckstein wrote great texts on business cycles, economic growth, and econometric modelling and business cycles.

Mr. Harry Markowitz, the famed Nobel Prize winner in economic sciences, the author of the seminal monograph *Portfolio Selection* (Wiley, 1959), and the author published a paper in 2018 that reported the stock performance of the S&P 500 index for the 1985–2018 time period, rising by a multiple of almost 7.0. The U.S. economy has generated economic growth, produced business fluctuations, and generated great stockholder returns for long-run investors. We analyze Markowitz models and extensions of portfolio selection in Chapter 9.

The purpose of this monograph is to introduce the reader to economic history and its impact on U.S. economists who developed theories from much of the data they observed. These theories addressed why and how the economy can grow, the impact of this growth on corporate profits and stock prices, and how investors can profit in business cycles.

2

Wesley Clair Mitchell: The Advent of U.S. And NBER Business Cycle Research

Business cycles often begin with the work of Mr. Wesley Clair Mitchell, the first Director of Research at the National Bureau of Economic Research, NBER. Mr. Mitchell was elected the NBER Director of Research on February 2, 1920, shortly after its chartering.[1] He held that position for over 25 years. In that capacity, Mr. Mitchell produced the first two NBER volumes of research on Business Cycles. In fact, prior to his NBER appointment, Mr. Mitchell had conducted extensive research on the history of the greenbacks, currency issued during the U.S. Civil War, and business cycles, producing several large monographs on these topics.[2]

---

[1] The NBER was chartered on December 29, 1919. The National Bureau was formed "to encourage, in the broadest and most liberal manner, investigation, research and discovery, and the application of knowledge to the well-being of mankind; and in particular to conduct, or assist in the making of, exact and impartial investigations in the field of economic. Social, and industrial science". National Bureau Charter and By-Laws. The quote is taken from *Wesley Clair Mitchell: The Economic Scientist*, Arthur F. Burns, Editor (New York: National Bureau of Economic Research, 1952), pp. 30–31. Mr. Burns edited a volume shortly after Mr. Mitchell passed on October 29, 1948. Contributors to the volume included Joseph Dorfman, John Maurice Clark, Milton Friedman, Joseph Schumpeter, and Alvin Hansen. A personal sketch was included by his wife, Lucy Spague Mitchell.

[2] Wesley Clair Mitchell, *A History of the Greenbacks, with Special References to the Economic Consequences of Their Issue, 1862–1865* (The Decennial Publications of the University of Chicago, 2d. Series, V.9, the University of Chicago Press, 1903). Before we plunge into Mr. Mitchell's *Business Cycles* (1913), we should give the reader a slight biographical sketch of Mr. Mitchell. He was born in 1874, in Rushville, Illinois, and entered the University of Chicago, under President Harper at its creation in 1982. Wesley studied with John Dewey and James Laurence Laughlin, the noted "sound money" economist, and by his graduation in 1896, had published two articles on the Quantity Theory of Money in Mr. Laughlin's *Journal of Political Economy, JPE*, edited at The University of Chicago. His next several articles were on the history of the Greenbacks during the Civil War and

---

J. B. Guerard, *The Leading Economic Indicators and Business Cycles in the United States*, https://doi.org/10.1007/978-3-030-99418-1_2

Let us begin with Part III of Mr. Mitchell's *Business Cycles* (1913) and review prosperity, crises, and depressions, his stages of economic activity. Mr. Mitchell wrote his book with an intended audience of businessmen. In this monograph, we stress money profits by business enterprises, as did Mr, Mitchell when he stated, "Since the quest of money profits is the controlling factor among the economic activities of men who live in a money economy, the whole discussion must center about the prospects of profits."[3]

2.1   Mitchell's Early Business Cycles Analysis: What Investors Needs to Know About the Cumulation of Prosperity

Mr. Mitchell began his discussion of business cycles with the revival of business activities between 1890 and 1910.[4] U.S. revivals began with highly profitable grain harvests in 1891 and 1897 and a successful defense of the gold reserve standard in 1895. Depressions eventually create conditions for recovery, such as falling prime and supplemental costs of manufacturing commodities (inputs) and in inventory of wholesale and retail merchants, low rates of interest, and a liquidation of business debts. Falling costs and lower interest rates tend to widen profit margins and facilitate bank borrowing. Once started, a revival of economic activity spreads across most, if not all, of the business world. The industries producing the raw materials and supplemental supplies are the first industries stimulated. Transportation, railroads,

---

the suspension and resumption of specie payments. His dissertation on the Greenbacks, *History of the Legal-Tender Acts*, was accepted in 1899 and he graduated *summa cum laude* from the University of Chicago. He joined the faculty at Chicago, leaving in 1903 to follow Adolph Miller, one of his teachers at Chicago, to the University of California. It was at California, that he published his *A History of the Greenbacks, with Special References to the Economic Consequences of Their Issue, 1862–1865* (1903) and took up his business cycle research. See Arthur F. Burns, "Introductory Sketch", in *Wesley Clair Mitchell: The Economic Scientist*, Arthur Burns, Editor, New York: National Bureau of Economic Research, Inc. 1952), pp. 7–10, and Frederick C. Mills, "A Professional Sketch", in *Wesley Clair Mitchell: The Economic Scientist*, Arthur Burns, Editor, New York: National Bureau of Economic Research, Inc. 1952), pp. 107–124. Upon completion of *Business Cycles*, Mr. Mitchell joined the faculty at Columbia University, in 1913.

[3] Wesley Clair Mitchell, *Business Cycles and Their Causes* (Berkeley and Los Angeles: University of California Press, 1963, Fifth printing), p. xi. Mitchell, 1963, is the fifth printing of Wesley Clair Mitchell , *Business Cycles and Their Causes*, 1941, reprinting of Part III of the original *Business Cycles: University of California Press*, 1913. The reader seeks to read the original 1913 on the National Bureau of Economic Research website. See Mr. Clark's discussion of Mr. Mitchell and his "money economy" in John Maurice Clark, "Theory of Business Cycles", in *Wesley Clair Mitchell: The Economic Scientist*, Arthur F. Burns, Editor (New York: National Bureau of Economic Research, 1952), pp. 198–199.

[4] Mr. Mitchell frequently uses business fluctuations in lieu of business cycles. Joseph A. Schumpeter, "The General Economist", in *Wesley Clair Mitchell: The Economic Scientist*, Arthur F. Burns, Editor (New York: National Bureau of Economic Research, 1952), pp. 302–333.

and banking industries start to boom. Employees earn higher salaries and proprietors earn higher profits, enabling workers and owners to pay off debts incurred in depressions and expand their purchases. Better quality food is substituted for lesser quality eaten during depressions and clothing demand increases. Furniture, entertainment, and luxury items are purchased. Industries are stimulated as the revival expands across the economy. Optimism endues and loans are provided for business enterprise expansion. Optimism is reenforced by an increase in the volume of goods ordered.

Prices begin to rise, but tend to lag in the revival, and rising prices create a stronger incentive for obtaining larger supplies to sell at wider profit margins. Eager bidding allows suppliers to exact higher prices. Mr. Mitchell observed that (1) retail prices rose less than wholesale prices of the same commodities; (2) wholesale prices of finished goods lag behind the prices of partially manufactured goods in the same commodities; (3) wholesale consumer goods prices rose less than wholesale producers' goods prices; and (4) wholesale prices of raw materials responded to changes in business conditions with greater accuracy and certainty than whole prices of raw farm or forest products[5] Men control more completely the production of coal, iron, copper, and zinc more than the production of beef, pork, mutton, and wool to meet the increasing demand.

Workers traditionally think of making a living, rather than making money. The prices of labor rise less in a revival than wholesale commodity prices. Mitchell attributes some of the lag in wages to nonexistent or weak trade unions.[6] Despite a lagging wage, working-class members are better off as business conditions improve. Interest rates lag in a revival. In fact, discount rates are usually lower in the first year of a revival than the rates were in the last year of a business depression. Bank loans increase in a revival and bankers often have liberal reserves. During a recovery from a depression, the ratio of capital liabilities to total liabilities falls due to depositors' inflows.

The net effect of rising prices and lagging wages and interest costs are increased profits.[7] Supplemental costs rise slowly with the physical volume of business. Wages, freight costs, prices of prime and supplemental rise slower than prices such that net profits rise with business volume. Profitability increases vary greatly across industries, due to relative differences in industry prime, supplemental, labor, and transportation cost ratios. Mitchell turns his attention to the stock market, and states plainly that the market price of a business enterprise rests primarily on the capitalized value of its

---

[5] Mitchell, *Business Cycles*, 1963, p.13.
[6] Mitchell, *Business Cycles*, 1963, p. 17.
[7] Mitchell, *Business Cycles*, 1963, p. 20.

current and prospective profits. That is, stock prices "vary roughly" with the rate of profits.[8] In 1913, as Mitchell wrote his *Business Cycles* monograph, railroads were the one group of business enterprises with data existed on stock prices and profits.[9] "Dividend smoothing" was noted in 1913 as Mr. Mitchell noted that dividends had been kept more stable than net income. Interest rates at which stock prices are capitalized are subject to variations. Further complications, known in 1913, included stock manipulation, speculation, and contests for control. Mr. Mitchell's further observations included that low-priced stocks rose more than high-priced stocks; common stocks rose more than preferred stocks; and irregular dividend-paying stocks rose more rapidly than stable dividend-paying stocks.[10] Business revival conditions lead to increases to business expansion in size and the creation of new enterprises. New investment never ceases entirely, but falls to very low level in a depression, and becomes large again after the recovery is well established. The creation of new enterprises increases demand for buildings, machinery, and furnishings, which further increases the demand for materials, labor, equipment, and loans. Increases in prices, volume of trade, and profits make optimists of entrepreneurs and every convert to optimism makes new converts, further favoring business expansion and further price increases. Workers now demand, and employers conceded to higher wages, resulting in higher family income that widens the market for consumer goods. Higher wages increase labor costs of retail and wholesale commodities. Interest rates rise for similar reasons and increase the cost of production. The increases in wages and interest rates are why prosperity does not continue indefinitely. Mr. Mitchell refers to prosperity as "The Business Equilibrium."[11] It is the increasing costs of business that disrupt business equilibrium.

2.1.1 Mitchell's Early Business Cycles Analysis: Prosperity Breeding Crisis

Prosperity is not maintained because of the slow but sure increases in business costs. Once firms reach full capacity of existing mines, factories, stores, and railroads, then new enterprises are built to accommodate additional

---

[8] Mitchell, *Business Cycles*, 1963. p. 22.

[9] Mitchell, *Business Cycles*, 1963. p. 22.

[10] Mitchell, *Business Cycles*, 1963, p. 23. See also W. C. Mitchell, "The Prices of American Stocks: 1890–1909", *Journal of Political Economy* 18 (1910), 345–380, and his "The Prices of Preferred and Common Stocks, 1890–1909", *Journal of Political Economy* 18 (1910), 513–524.

[11] Mitchell *Business Cycles*, 1963. pp. 25–27.

orders. Rent, interest, depreciation, insurance, and office salaries, supplemental charges, increase. New construction of plants carries high interest costs. Businesses often close unprofitable goods production and rid themselves of unskillful management, antiquated equipment, and weak financial backers. The return of prosperity leads owners to reopen these enterprises and these reopening bid up the prices of labor and materials, which lessens the profitability of all well-equipped, located, financed, and managed firms. Prime costs increase in revival activities, labor, and materials. Full prosperity forces enterprises to hire more marginal talent, men too old, boys too young, or "trouble makers," which reduce the efficiency of the work force (Mitchell, 1941, p. 32). Prosperity leads to the employment of the relatively inefficient reserve of labor and increased overtime of existing, and potentially tired labor, working from 8 to 12 hours a day. The quality of output declines and the quantity of damaged goods increases. Material costs rise and materials in 1900 constituted two-thirds of all total costs. Bank loan costs increased with the interest rate. The increasing labor, materials, and interest costs lessen profits.

The rising interest rates in prosperity create tension in the money market because the demand for short-term loans rises at a rapid rate. Prosperity and the quantity of gold in monetary use have an interesting relationship. The factors lessening the quantity of gold in prosperity include increases in the cost of gold mining supplies and lessens the efficiency of labor. More gold is used in jewelry than for coinage in prosperity. If prosperity increases imports more than exports, then gold may be exported to trading partners. The factors increasing the quantity of gold in prosperity include investors want speculative securities promising higher rates of returns and it is easier to raise cash for developing new mines. Prosperity encourages the sale of securities to foreign capitalists, which can offset the increase of imports on the balance of payments.[12] Mr. Mitchell notes only a slight correspondence between the average quantity of bank notes and fluctuations in business activity in the 1890 to 1910 time period.[13] Selling prices cannot advance indefinitely because of an inadequate quantity of money.[14] An increase in business initially causes a rise in profits which tax the productive capacity of existing industrial equipment. The expectations of future profits induce bidding for materials, labor, and loans, increasing business costs. The decrease in bank reserves makes banks less interested in expanding loans. Increases in costs lead to the diminished expectations of prospective profits, even as

---

[12] Mitchell, *Business Cycles*, 1963. p. 50.
[13] Mitchell, *Business Cycles*, 1963. p. 51.
[14] Mitchell, *Business Cycles*, 1963. p. 54.

realized profits may be reaching their maximum level, and diminished profit expectations can turn prosperity into a crisis.[15] An aggressive businessman may borrow on credit and use leverage (other people's money) to engage in greater production and trade in prosperity. Rising profits enable greater use of credit. The increased interest rate reduced the capitalized value of current and future profits. Increasing interest rates reduce both bond and stock prices. Prosperity eventually turns to liquidation as expectations of future profits are reduced. When the demand for outstanding credit becomes the general phase of business, then prosperity turns into crisis.

2.1.2   Mitchell's Early Business Cycles Analysis: Crisis

The conditions that created prosperity will lead to a downward revision of credits, creating a crisis, which begins liquidation. External events, such as wars, political disorders, the collapse of a large financial institution engaged in speculative behavior, crop failures, crisis in foreign countries, or uncertainty regarding the monetary standard can start the process of liquidation. Mr. Mitchell says that while there is no general rule concerning the conditions on which debtors are forced to pay off their debts begin, violent price fluctuations of important materials can threaten losses to merchants or manufacturers, and these trades are often the first trades to lose credit.[16] Contractors providing industrial equipment are likely to be victims of debt payment demands as interest rates rise as the bond market becomes stringent. Banks may give notice to enterprises that their maturing debt will not be renewed or extended. The debtor must then raise funds, by seeking payment from his debtors or offer liberal inducements to settle accounts now yet due. The debtor may have to offer goods at "sale prices" or sell securities to raise the necessary cash. The debtor who successfully raises cash to pay off his debt and avoid bankruptcy may have forced his debtors, who paid him, into similar cash problems, injuring the market for other enterprises. An apprehensive creditor can be sufficient with a debtor in trouble may strengthen the movement toward liquidation. The start of liquidation can be difficult to stop. The demands for bank loans are increased not only by debtors being pushed for payments but also by enterprises to seek to build cash positions to meet future demands for their repayments of loans.

Banks may be reluctant to increase loans because their reserves were reduced by the preceding prosperity. Large reserves are maintained by banks

---

[15] Mitchell, *Business Cycles*, 1963. p. 63.
[16] Mitchell, *Business Cycles*, 1963. p. 72.

for their prestige.[17] The risk of bad debts increases with the demand for loans and banks holding the paper of bankrupt firms will suffer delays or loss on collections of these loans. The rising interest rates of prosperity give rise to possible liquidations as prospective profits fall and enterprise creditworthiness is questioned. The leading banks play a major role in whether rising interest rates that turn prosperity in a crisis will turn the crisis into a panic. Can banks maintain their reserves and mitigate the crisis by effective means of relief? The Panic of 1907 is a typical bank panic, brought on by bank failures. The U.S. had endured panics, indeed depressions, in 1893 and 1897. In months leading up to the panic of 1907, interest rates and uncertainty in the investment market caused a slackening of new construction. The demand for copper fell and its price fell from 26 cents a pound to only 20 cents a pound in July 1907. Subsequent price drops to the price of copper to 12 cents in October. Cooper mining stock prices fell substantially as a result of the copper price decline.[18] A prominent capitalist, Mr. F.A. Heinze, organized a pool to bolster the price of the United Copper Company. Mr. Heinze was one of many large owners of copper stocks who used the securities as collateral for bank loans. On October 14th, the copper pool of investors drove the price of United Copper Company stock from 37 to 60, but the price increase was only temporary. By October 16th, the price of United Copper Company had fallen to 10. Gross & Kleeberg failed, alleging that Mr. Heinze's brother did not take the stock purchased for his account. On October 17th, Otto, Heinze & Company trading was suspended.[19] Mr. Heinze was President of the Mercantile National Bank, and he was thought to exercise "control" over its operations. He was suspected to have taken advantage of the price decline of copper to obtain large loans upon the security of the stocks that had fallen so great in value. Bank depositors became alarmed and began to withdraw their accounts. Close business associates of Mr. Heinze controlled seven other banks and suspicion spread to these banks. These eight banks had $71.4 million dollars of deposits and $21.8 million dollars of capital and surplus on October 12th.[20] These eight banks believed that they could have difficulties in meeting depositor demands for cash and they appealed to the clearing house for support. The clearing house pledged its aid but required that Mr. Heinze and Messrs. C.W. Morse, E.R., and O.P. Thomas, his alleged

---

[17] Mitchell, *Business Cycles*, 1963. p. 74.
[18] Mitchell, *Business Cycles*, 1963. p. 75.
[19] Ibid..
[20] Mitchell, *Business Cycles*, 1963. p. 76.

associates, withdraw from control of the banks. By October 20th, it appeared that the panic had been averted.[21]

On October 21st, the President of the Knickerbocker Trust Company was interested in certain Morse enterprises. There were issues with unfavorable clearing house balances and shortly thereafter the National Bank of Commerce announced that it would no longer act as the clearing agent for the Knickerbocker Trust Company. On October 22, 1907, there was a run on the Knickerbocker Trust Company such that after three hours, it suspended operations after paying out $8 million of accounts. The Knickerbocker Trust Company was the third largest trust company in the U.S., with deposits of $62 million. Its failure caused widespread panic and led to runs on the Trust Company of America and the Lincoln Trust Company, with deposits of $64 million and $22.4 million, respectively. Several Westinghouse companies failed that same week and the Pittsburgh Stock Exchange closed. On October 24th, several runs began on banks and trust companies in Manhattan, Brooklyn, and Providence.[22] The New York bank run led out of state banks to call in loans outstanding with stockbrokers and timid depositors sought to withdraw their accounts. Businessmen prepared to maintain as large a cash balance as possible for possible emergencies and to take advantage of opportunistic buying at bargain prices. The Secretary of the Treasury deposited $35 million in national banks, with a larger share being placed in New York, to the threatened trust companies. To prevent further collapse of stock prices on the New York Stock Exchange, the NYSE, a pool was formed to lend $25 million on call on October 24th and $10 million on the 25th. The clearing house began to issue clearing-house loan certificates on October 26th. The money of the Treasury and the pool to help the NYSE was a mere fraction of the money ultimately used to prevent a collapse of the U.S. financial system.

The panic spread from New York such that two-thirds of all U.S. cities with more than 25,000 inhabitants had their banks suspend cash payments.[23] The amount of money in The Treasury went from $329 million on September 30, 1907, to $272 million on October 31, 1907, to $261 million on November

---

[21] Ibid..

[22] Mitchell *Business Cycles*, 1963. p. 77. Many economists were writing on business crises during the 1927–1939 period, but the publication date of Business Cycles assures its place in the history of business cycles research. Joseph A. Schumpeter, "The General Economist", in *Wesley Clair Mitchell: The Economic Scientist*, Arthur F. Burns, Editor (New York: National Bureau of Economic Research, 1952), pp. 331–332.

[23] Mitchell *Business Cycles*, 1963. p. 79. The U.S. population was approximately 96.2 million people in 1907. Its 2020 population is approximately 332.5 million. Thus, a 1907 city of 25,000 would be equivalent to a current city of 86,409. Source: https://en.wikipedia.org/wiki/List_of_countries_by_population_in_1907.

30, 1907, to \$270 million on December 31, 1907.[24] The corresponding average of 40 common stock prices on the NYSE were 197, 171.5, 159, and 167%, respectively. The "grand average" of common stock prices fell 15.6% over the four months, or 45.69% annualized.[25] Mr. Mitchell's statement that the "panic wrought" seems obvious. Business failures exceeded 3100 firms quarterly during the 1907–1908 time period, rising from 3138 firms failed in the first quarter of 1907 to 3635 failed firms in the fourth quarter of 1907 to 4909 failed firms in the first quarter of 1908 to 3524 failed firms in the fourth quarter of 1908. Business failures had quarterly average liabilities of \$10,228 in the first quarter of 1907, to \$22,379 in the fourth quarter of 1907, to \$12,099 in the fourth quarter of 1908 (Mitchell, 1941, p. 98).[26] Wholesale prices fell from 127 in January 1907 to 121 in December 1908 during the panic of 1907. Mr, Mitchell noted that it was very difficult to data when the crisis of 1907 began, with money markets having severe stringency in 1906, stock prices falling in January 1907, crashing in March 1907, and prices of raw materials falling in February 1907. The Panic of 1907 can be dated from October 22, 1907, with the collapse of the Knickerbocker Trust Company.[27] Failures of large business enterprises ushered in the panics of 1893 and 1907. Mr. Mitchell stated that the "Elasticity of lending power is more needed than the elasticity of currency."[28] Mr. Mitchell further stated that small, independent banks had no adequate means for putting available funds where they were most needed.[29]

2.1.3 Mitchell's Early Business Cycles Analysis: Business Depression

The Depressions of 1893 and 1907 were followed by increases in business activity. The impaired confidence that caused the preceding crises was replaced by optimism. The bursts of business activity following the panics passed quickly and renewed discouragement reigned. The decline in new orders began several months before the crisis. The lack of new orders will limit expansion. In 1894 and 1908, new orders were not sufficient to support the reopening of business enterprises, many of them mills. The lack of new orders blights the hope of a quick restoration of a prosperity following a severe

---

[24] The amount of money in circulation did not change (Mitchell, 1941, p. 84).
[25] Mitchell, *Business Cycles*, 1963. p. 87.
[26] Mitchell, *Business Cycles*, 1963. p. 98.
[27] Mitchell, *Business Cycles*, 1963. p. 123.
[28] Mitchell, *Business Cycles*, 1963. p. 126.
[29] Mitchell, *Business Cycles*, 1963. p. 127.

crisis. The confidence of the return of expectations of profitable prices and profits, and a large volume of business activity is not restored.[30] Workingmen are discharged during a crisis and consumer demand fell. Food expenditures are seriously reduced and even more sharply reduced are expenditures for clothing, furniture, fuel, and amusements. Accumulated savings are drawn down and personal property may be pawned off. Mr. Mitchell stated that in general, current business conditions lessen demand for raw materials and partially finished goods.[31] Manufacturers try to maintain as much employment as possible within a skeleton organization. The first lull in business activity allows an opportunity to overhaul plants and bring equipment back to the highest levels of efficiency. In the early stages of depression, very few new construction contracts are started. As more workers are discharged, consumer demands fall more, and there is less demand for raw materials. The lowest point in the physical volume of industrial behind raw production usually comes in the first or second year after a severe crisis.[32] As the crisis continues, prices continue to fall. Wholesale prices fell for four years after the crisis of 1893. The lowest point of commodity prices is reached toward the close of the subsequent depression, not during the crisis. Retail prices lag wholesale prices of the same goods. Manufactured commodities prices lag the raw materials from which they were made. Prices of labor fall less than wholesale commodity prices. Interest rates on long-term loans fall at a slow pace but for a longer period of time than wages. High-grade bond prices rise because of the fall of long-term interest rates whereas common stocks fall because of diminished (current) earnings and dull prospects of future earnings.[33] Preferred sticks fall, but less than common stocks.

Mr. Mitchell pointed out in his business depression chapter that the quantity of money did not contract consistently in the months of depression during the 1890 to 1910 time period. The gold currency rose in early 1897, late 1908, mid 1910–1911, and 1903–1904. The belief that gold currency contracts regularly with the volume of trade is not supported by the data.[34] Similar monetary patterns were reported in England, France, and Germany. The failure of the money supply to contract promptly when crisis turns to

[30] Mitchell, *Business Cycles*, 1963. p. 131.

[31] Mitchel, *Business Cycles*, 1963. p. 132.

[32] Mitchell, *Business Cycles*, 1963. p. 133. See Mr. Dorfman's discussion of Mr. Mitchell, his interest in crises and his 1905 course at Columbia on "Economic Crises and Depression", in Joseph Dorfman, "Professional Sketch", in *Wesley Clair Mitchell: The Economic Scientist*, Arthur F. Burns, Editor (New York: National Bureau of Economic Research, 1952), pp. 130–131.

[33] Mitchell, *Business Cycles*, 1963. p. 136.

[34] Mitchell, *Business Cycles*, 1963. p. 137.

depression results in monetary redundancy, or idle cash residing in banks.[35] The closest statement of Mr. Mitchell regarding the Quantity Theory of Money is found in the business depression chapter.

> In so far, the quantity of money is a factor in accelerating the adjustment of costs to selling prices that ultimately restores the prospects of profits and ushers in a period of expanding trade and rising prices. Hence such an increase in the world's production of gold as has been going in recent years tends to cut short and to mitigate depressions as well as to prolong and intensify prosperity. By thus altering both the intensity and the relative duration of these two phases of business cycles, it tends to give an upward direction to those long-period movements of the price curve in which the years if depression and prosperity are averaged. [36]

The decline in orders in depressions and the accompanying decline in selling prices put severe pressure on managers in business enterprises to cut expenses. Wholesale prices fell faster than retail prices; producer goods prices fell faster than consumer goods prices; and raw materials prices fell faster than manufacturing goods prices. Interest rates fell faster than wholesale prices and loan costs fell in proportion to prices of products. Wages decline in periods of severe depression. Mr. Mitchell pointed out that there was strong evidence that the efficiency of labor becomes much greater in depression than in prosperity.[37] The weeding out of less desirable workers instills the threat of layoffs in other workers and drives men to do his best. In depressions, the surviving business enterprises are those that achieve lower production costs on average during the period.[38] Supplemental costs are irrelevant in depressions as selling prices do not cover total costs in depressions. Although Mr. Mitchell does not explicitly make the statement at this point, profits become negative in depressions. Depressions eliminate small wastes in business enterprises. Business volume reaches its lowest point in the first or second year of depression. The quantity of goods produced starts to rise in the second or third year of depression. Goods increase and are transported by railroads and sold by merchants. First, the accumulated stocks of goods of the preceding prosperity are eventually sold. Manufacturers reduce their stocks of raw materials and fill orders with goods on hand. Once their current inventory is substantially reduced, then current purchases and production increase. Second, consumer demand eventually picks up as clothing and furniture is worn out and must be

---

[35] Mitchell, *Business Cycles*, 1963. p. 138.
[36] Mitchell, *Business Cycles*, 1963. pp. 138–139.
[37] Mitchell, *Business Cycles*, 1963. p. 139.
[38] Mitchell, *Business Cycles*, 1963. p. 140.

replaced.[39] Third, the population increases in depressions at about the same rate as other phases of the business cycle, further increasing demand. Mitchell uses German data to support the population statement as the U.S. data is uncertain.[40] Finally, and most importantly, demand for new construction in the latter stages of depression. Savings continue and the money-seeking fresh investments often goes to the purchase of property that the "embarrassed" owners are forced to sell.[41] Liquid cash creates investments that represent a redistribution of ownership. Small and large capitalists can take advantage of very low interest rates to borrow long term and the more enterprising spirits can build for themselves. Building is more efficient because materials are cheap, and labor is efficient. Technical improvements occur as the depression wears on and there is an incentive to invest in new equipment. When new orders begin to increase, business enterprises begin improvements in existing facilities and there are organizers of new ventures. Both sets of investments use cheaper construction costs to have their plants ready for operation by the time a revival of activity is recognized.[42] The physical volume of business reaches higher levels than those reached at the close of the preceding prosperity. Liquidations cease. Depression eventually breeds revival with prime cost, labor, materials, and interest, reductions. Expected profits increase and in the money economy, prospective profits are the great incentive to activity.[43] Prices and trade volume continue to fall even as the physical volume of business has begun to rise. Prices fall at a slower rate in the latter stages of depression than in the earlier stages. As business enterprises sell off their inventory and their heavy fixed charges are paid off, enterprises can live within their incomes. Mr. Mitchell summarizes his theory of business cycles as prosperity breeds crisis, which evolves to depression, and depression eventually paves the way to a return to prosperity.[44]

2.1.4 Mitchell's Early Business Cycles Analysis: Wider Aspects of Business Cycles

The revival of economic activity starts from depression and a low level of process compared to prosperity. Drastic business cost reductions, narrow profit margins, and liberal bank reserves are accompanied by an expansion

---

[39] Mitchell, *Business Cycles*, 1963. p. 143.
[40] Ibid.
[41] Mitchell, *Business Cycles*, 1963. p. 144.
[42] Mitchell, *Business Cycles*, 1963. p. 145.
[43] Mitchell, *Business Cycles*, 1963. p. 146.
[44] Mitchell, *Business Cycles*, 1963. p. 147.

in the physical volume of trade. Exceptional harvests and heavy government purchases of supplies may further increase demand in the home market. Active enterprises purchase more materials from other firms and employ more labor, use more borrowed money, and make higher profits. Prices lag the recovery. Newly employed labor, machinery, and starting old equipment and prices start to rise. Prices of raw materials rise first, and retail prices, which lag behind wholesale prices, eventually rise. Wages and interest rates often rise more than proportionally. Large profits often result from divergent price fluctuations and larger sales. Business optimism and the increase in profits leads to a marked expansion of investment, further driving up prices.

Business costs are driven up in business revivals and higher interest rates, rent, and salaries and the lessening efficiency of labor serve to drive costs higher than selling prices. The supply of funds fails to keep up with demand and there is a "scarcity of capital." Businessmen face the prospect of declining profits. Rising interest rates reduce the capitalized values of business enterprises. Profits start to fall. Prosperity starts a liquidation, which ultimately turns into crisis.[45]

Liquidation increases rapidly as businesses settle their maturing obligations. Liquidation generates a crisis. Making profits gives way to maintaining solvency. The volume of new orders falls dramatically, and expansion becomes contraction. If banks can meet credit needs and some business enterprise bankruptcy issues, then there is no panic. However, if businesses cannot borrow funds, and depositors are refused payment in full, then the alarm turns into a panic.[46]

Falling consumer demand, employee layoffs, the gradual exhaustion of savings, and reductions in family incomes, combined with a fall in trade and prices lead to a depression. Profits and prospective profits are reduced. Depression is overcome with the subsequent reduction in business costs that eventually spurs a business revival.[47]

The practitioner reader of Mr. Mitchell's *Business Cycles* (1913) must understand the business cycle movements from prosperity to crisis to business depression. One notes Mr, Mitchell's emphasis on the entrepreneur's seeking of corporate profits and the role of expectations and hard work in their achievement. Mr, Milton Friedman, a student of Mr, Mitchell at Columbia University, while appreciating the smooth, casual-sounding exposition of Mr.

---

[45] Mitchell, *Business Cycles*, 1963. pp. 156–157.
[46] Mitchell, *Business Cycles*, 1963. p. 158.
[47] Mitchell, *Business Cycles*, 1963. Pp. 158–161.

Mitchell's business cycle phases, nevertheless thought numerous significant theoretical insights underlie the text.[48]

2.2   Mr. Mitchell and His Business Cycles and Unemployment

It is an interesting note to Mr. Mitchell that the first NBER Studies in Business Cycles volume was *Business Cycles and Unemployment* (NBER, 1923), which addressed a public policy issue that brought together the titans of industry, including Owen Young, Chairman of the Board of the General Electric Company, Joseph Defrees, former President of the U.S. Chamber of Commerce, Mathew Moll, Vice President of the American Federation of Labor, and Clarence Wolley, President of The American Radiator Company, with Mr. Mitchell, and Mr. Herbert Hoover, the Secretary of Commerce. The President's Conference on Unemployment in September 1921 addressed relief to the four to five million unemployed Americans from the business slump of 1920–1921. Secretary Hoover wrote the Foreword for the volume. Hoover's Foreword stressed that unemployment was the greatest national waste and that the commission acknowledged the suffering associated with the inability of jobseekers to obtain employment. Some firms showed progress during the period of national recession, "the recent period of national disaster," in Secretary Hoover's words, and successfully achieved stability, whereas the ignorance of determinable facts accounted for disasters to many other firms. Mr. Mitchell and the Committee defined business cycles as changes in business conditions that were characterized by an upward movement to a boom, followed by a downward movement into depression."[49] As in his *Business Cycles* (1913), Mr. Mitchell began his business cycle analysis when business is recovering from a recession or depression. Characterized by an increasing manufacturing volume, rising stock exchange prices, business expansion, and increased demand for credit. Commodity prices rise as do interest rates, and credit becomes strained. Stock prices fall and general business conditions increase unevenly. Speculative buying overwhelms transportation and credit, which shakes public confidence. A widespread cancellation of orders is followed by a liquidation of inventories and an irregular fall in prices. During the period of depression, there is a widespread period of depression, there is widespread unemployment.

---

[48] Milton Friedman, "The Economic Theorist", in *Wesley Clair Mitchell: The Economic Scientist*, Arthur Burns, Editor, New York: National Bureau of Economic Research, Inc. 1952), pp. 237–282.
[49] Wesley Clair Mitchell, *Business Cycles and Unemployment* (NBER, 1923), p. xii.

The business cycle which ended in the depression of 1921 was unusual in its amount of preceding expansion and in its severity of unemployment and amount of unemployment. Thus, business cycles and fluctuations must be examined.[50] Mr. Mitchell discussed a tale of two businessmen in December 1919, who go to see their bank. The two manufacturers of silk had different perspectives of the post-war boom. The first businessman decided that the current boom was beginning to appear to be unsafe and he decided not to expand his operations and told his banker that he would sell his goods as quickly as possible. The second silk manufacturer decided that brisk business led to a scarcity of raw materials and that he should expand his inventory to maintain his trade. The second businessman asked the bank to grant him a loan given that his firm was in good financial shape, as characterized by the "two to one ratio" of quick assets, defined as total current assets less inventory, exceeded twice his current liabilities. Mr. Mitchell tells the reader that almost immediately following the bank visits, prosperity turned to depression in the silk industry and raw silk and finished produce prices fell significantly. The second silk manufacturer had a reduced value of his inventory that made him unable to liquidate his loan and his business was virtually bankrupt.[51] Silk wholesale prices increased until 1920 and in February 1920, silk manufacturers discussed its great demand and its shortage of raw goods, expecting prices to rise. Insurance companies discovered that the silk that they had insured was beyond safe limits and announced an excess supply of silk, which led to all prices of silk falling at once, and manufacturers could not liquidate their inventories. Mr. Mitchell and the Committee used the silk industry as a striking example of incomplete information as to inventory goods in transit, and speculative buying that is duplicated in many industries and leads to great problems for bankers.[52]

Mr. Mitchell stressed the need for facts regarding general business conditions, and probable future trends of general business conditions. The businessman must know current facts about his industry and his relative position within the industry; enough information about his firm to render proper policy judgment, including the attitude of his banker to loan extensions.[53] The Committee further discussed remedies for control of bank credit, control

---

[50] Mitchell, *Business Cycles and Unemployment*, 1923, pp. xii-xiii.
[51] Mitchell, *Business Cycles and Unemployment*, 1923, p. xv.
[52] Mitchell, *Business Cycles and Unemployment*, 1923, pp. xiv -xvii.
[53] Mitchell, *Business Cycles and Unemployment*, 1923, p. xviii.

of inflation by the Federal Reserve System, control of businessmen and business expansion, construction of public works in depressing unemployment, creating unemployment reserve funds, and Federal and state unemployment bureaus.[54] Information was to be increased in the *Survey of Current Business*, published by the Department of Commerce, where the series and services were to be maintained and expanded. Information must be increased to the Department of Commerce and bankers regarding inventory, shipments, prices, and sales volumes. Second, the Committee recommended that statistical analysis be increased and standardized by the Bureau of Labor Statistics. Greater analysis was possible in five-year, rather than two-year, statistical collection of data in the Census of Manufacturers, by the Department of Commerce. Third, general research into economic forces and trends must be expanded, with more integration with businesses. Fourth, control of bank credit expansion requires a large fund of knowledge of business activities.[55] Borrowing of banks from the Federal Reserve System is a last resort and was a new business activity in the depression of 1921. Fifth, the Federal Reserve System must control inflation by preventing excessive expansion of credit in upward periods. The automatic check on expansion is the legal minimum bank reserve against current liabilities, but bankers must realize their responsibilities in issuing additional credits to the community. The accumulation of U.S. gold in the First World War led to "excess gold" which could become the basis of a disastrous expansion of domestic credit. Prosperity should be maintained by credit, not destroyed by inflation.[56] Businessmen must control the expansions of their businesses, such that a strong financial condition allows the business to maintain steady employment of workers. Public and private construction must be controlled in boom periods, by postponing or ceasing construction work and reserves built up for construction during periods of depression. Here Mr. Mitchell and the Presidential Commission discuss public goods. Businessmen must have sufficient data for construction activities.[57] Public utilities must be regulated such that utilities and railroads finance new construction or improvements in times of depression, when costs are low. The Committee's ninth recommendation was for sufficient unemployment reserves to be created to stabilize employment and spending in time

---

[54] Mitchell, *Business Cycles and Unemployment*, 1923, p. xix.

[55] Mitchell, *Business Cycles and Unemployment*, 1923, p. xxiv.

[56] Mitchell, *Business Cycles and Unemployment*, 1923, p. xxvi.

[57] Mitchell, *Business Cycles and Unemployment*, 1923, p. xxviii. Joseph A. Schumpeter, "The General Economist", in *Wesley Clair Mitchell: The Economic Scientist*, Arthur F. Burns, Editor (New York: National Bureau of Economic Research, 1952), pp. 324–325.

of depression. The Committee, in 1921, found that the cooperative unemployment reserve fund lacking, confined by trade unions and efforts of few individual firms. The tenth, and final recommendation was for a national system of employment bureaus to be created. The employment bureaus' reports will provide reports on the demand for labor and become another measure of business conditions.[58]

2.3 Mitchell's Business Cycles Analysis at the NBER: Volume 1

Mr. Mitchell became the Director of Research at the National Bureau of Economic Research (NBER) in 1920. In 1927, Mr. Mitchell published the first of many NBER Studies in Business Cycles, entitled *Business Cycles: The Problem and Its Setting*.[59] The initial studies of commercial crises were made up of divergent fluctuations in many processes, leading every investigator to find evidence to support the hypothesis he favored.[60] Statistics has confirmed many of the theories of business cycles. Data on fluctuations in pig iron production, clearing bank checks, transporting freight, declaring dividends, and creating "general business conditions," in addition to wholesale prices, the volume of trade, and physical production "indexes" have been published. An inquiry into business cycles should begin with the individual series being studied objectively, seeking to find what these processes are, how they effect and interact with each other, and what whole story they make up. Mr. Mitchell stated that the best way to learn about the processes is to profit by the earlier work on business cycles; most researchers find clues in some single economic process. Mitchell starts with the Mississippi Bubble and the South Seas Scheme in France and England in 1720. Commercial crises emerged in 1763, 1772, 1783, and 1793. By 1815, progressive changes in economic organizations were better equipping men to deal with crises, and Adam Smith and Ricardo were developing political economy. Smith, J.S. Mill, and A. Marshall wrote of principles which hold "in the long run" or create a "normal state."[61] Mitchell wrote of Simonde de Sismondi, a Swiss, who observed economic fluctuations in England around the Napoleonic Wars; 1816 being depressed; 1817–1818 being great in industrial activity and 1820 seeing a

---

[58] Mitchell, *Business Cycles and Unemployment*, 1923, p. xxvi.
[59] Wesley C. Mitchell, *Business Cycles: The Problem and its Setting*. National Bureau of Economics Research, 1927.
[60] Wesley C. Mitchell, *Business Cycles*, 1927, p. 1.
[61] Wesley C. Mitchell, *Business Cycles*, 1927, p. 4.

return to depression. Sismondi noted that businessmen only observed prices (not knowing customers' purchasing power or tastes and consumption) and price expectations determine whether he expands or reduces prices.[62] "The needs of laboring men are limited of necessity." When production methods improve, economic institutions keep men busy and increase the volume of products offered for sale. Luxury goods are often made in foreign lands, and everyone would be better off if workers had sufficient incomes to provide a base for home demand.[63] Modern machinery growth has "over-produced" the capacity of society to consume; hence, the under-consumption theory of cycles was developed. When profits fall to a very low level, business failures rise and there is a loss of confidence. If workers lack the wages to buy goods, then over-stocking creates low expectations of profits, leading to a crisis.[64] J.S. Mill sought the fundamental cause of commercial fluctuations in psychology, fair trade breeds optimism, then recklessness, then disaster. Such disasters breed pessimism and stagnation. Depression ends when men's spirits recover, finding out that things are not as bad as they feared (Mitchell, 1927, p. 9).[65] Jevons sought weather and its control over crips and harvests. Mill and Walker discussed the "periodicity of crises." Juglar's 1899 book was a "book of facts on fluctuations."

Mitchell listed the current theories of business cycles:

1. Weather

W.S. Jevons studied the 1721–1878 time period, finding 16 crises in 157 years; 10.466 years for an average business cycle which was very similar to the 10.45 years for sunspots. Henry Moore's analysis of rainfall amounts shows 33-year and 8-year cycles of crop yields and business cycles, The eight-year cycle is confirmed by the time that Venus comes into the path of solar radiations to the Earth. Hunting observed that a low death rate breeds prosperity and health depended on the weather.

2. Uncertainty

C. Hardy builds on price expectations for production. Speculative purchases that producers hold when they are ready to sell goods.

---

[62] Wesley C. Mitchell, *Business Cycles*, 1927, pp. 5–6.
[63] Wesley C. Mitchell, *Business Cycles*, 1927, p. 7.
[64] Wesley C. Mitchell, *Business Cycles*, 1927, pp. 8–9.
[65] Wesley C. Mitchell, *Business Cycles*, 1927, p. 9.

3. Emotions in Business Decisions

Pigou held that business fluctuations are caused by businessmen's confidence. Optimism breeds prosperity but errors in expectations create a day of judgment.

4. Innovation, Promotion, and Progress

Schumpeter championed the concepts that business conditions are based on errors created by uncertainty and nourished by mass psychology. Scientific discoveries by a few men create innovation and their new forms of economic organization enhances the development of new products, seeking to new markets, exploiting new resources, and shifting trade routes. As innovation slows and enterprises cannot get capital, then depression develops. Depression eventually gives way to men regaining confidence. They borrow for new projects, raising interest rates, prices of industrial equipment, and payrolls. General activity increases until goods flood the market and creates a new crisis. Few men can innovate, and these highly endowed individuals achieve success.

5. Savings and Investment

Depressions lead to falling savings of entrepreneurs and wages decrease; landlords are unaffected, as are salaried workers and their savings are enhanced by a lower cost of living during a depression. Savings decline less than investing, and increases loan capital. Consumption rises in a prosperity. Goods eventually flood the market.

6. Construction Work

George Hull advanced the theory that enterprises build and equip houses, stores, factories, docks, and railroads. Construction accounts for 77% of industrial product.

7. Generalized Over-Production

Demand rises during depression, increasing employment and stimulating consumer demand, and encouraging newer orders for equipment. Prosperity cannot continue indefinitely.

8. Banking Operations.

Alvin Hansen, I. Fisher, and Hawtrey held an expansionary monetary policy lowers the interest rate and expands trade. Dealers give large orders to producers, increasing output and incomes. Rising incomes raise prices, retail demand, and prices. Businesses borrow more freely, and interest rates rise until interest rates equal the profit rate, and the inducement to increase goods is reduced.

9. Promotion and the Flow of Income

Emil Lederer held that depression begins with a decline in physical trade and prices, the cost of living falls faster than wage cuts. Consumers can buy more. Business profits fall because wages, rents, and interest charges lag behind falling selling prices. A business revival reverses prices, raising the volume of trade, quickening the circulation of money and credit. The gold supply increases, disproportionally of production and income. Over-production and prosperity turns into depression.

10. The Role of Profit-Making

Veblen held that prosperity has rising prices and profits, caused by an increased supply of gold or government purchases. Increased investment to exploit profits pushes up prices, confirmed by J.M. Clark.

Mr. Mitchell listed the theories of business cycles that prevailed before 1927.[66]

The emergence of joint-stock companies in England in 1600, with the establishment of the East Indian Company (EIC), known also as "The Company," with the consent of Queen Elizabeth, to trade in the Indian Ocean region and later China, England rose to dominant world trade. It is estimated that The Company accounted for one-half of world trade in the 1750–1815 time period. Financial crises were recorded in England during the 1558 to 1720 time period by Mr. William Scott, of St. Andrews.[67] These financial crises occurred every 5.5 years, but only 5 of the 29 crises were considered depressions during the 163 years. Mr. Scott associated twelve of the crises as being proceeded by "depressed trade," not prosperity. With the emergence of the Quant—Stock companies in England in 1600, with the

---

[66] Wesley C. Mitchell, *Business Cycles*, 1927, pp. 12–32.
[67] Wesley C. Mitchell, *Business Cycles*, 1927, pp. 76–77.

date of the establishment of the East Indian Company (EIC) known also as "The Company" by decree of Queen Elizabeth to trade in the Indian Ocean region and later China, England rose to dominate world trade. It is estimated that the Company accounted for one-half of World trade in the 1750–1815 period.

Financial crises were recorded in England during the 1558–1720 time period, by Dr. William Scott (of St. Andrews pp. 76–77). Scott's financial crisis occurs with famines, plague, wars, civil wars, or large governmental actions. Financial crises occur about every 5.5 years. Scott reports only 5 depressions followed the 29 crises during the 163 years. Scott listed 12 of 30 crises preceded by "depressed trade," not prosperity.[68]

Mitchell makes the point that Scott's British crises did not follow the pattern of modern business cycles (Mitchell, 1927, p. 80). England suffered financial crisis in 1745, 1972, and 1783 following military conflicts with "The Pretender and his Highlanders" the end of the Seven Year War, and the end of the American Revolution.[69] Mitchell addressed the issue of the labor force in the U.S., in 1920, Some 39.4% of the approximate 100-million-person population, made up of 72% men, 12% teenagers, aged 15–19, and 16% adult women. Employment during depressions was most reduced in manufacturing, railroads, mining construction and secondary in finance, wholesale trade, and transportation. In 1920, corporations owned 32% of American manufacturing establishments that employed 87% of wage earners and produced 88% of value-produced. In the Census of 1920, 345, 600 corporations filed tax returns reporting $126,000,000,000 of aggregate gross income.[70] Mitchell pointed out that parent, or holding, companies owned all or large parts of corporations, noting the growing power of financial alliances (mergers), involving the exchange of common stocks.

Mitchell noted that an investor could reduce his risks by spreading his stock holdings among numerous enterprises.[71] "A business enterprise can serve the community by making goods only on condition that, over a number of years, its operations yield a profit. Issues of social and business reforms and legislature add little to understanding business cycles (p. 105). Finally, in Chapter 2 Mr. Mitchell dismisses the Irving Fisher (restatement of the Quantity Theory of Money with regard to business cycles stating that we need a far more discriminating statement of the relations among prices, volume of trade, the quantity and velocity of money and circulating medium, taking into

---

[68] Wesley C. Mitchell, *Business Cycles,* 1927, p. 78.
[69] Wesley C. Mitchell, *Business Cycles,*1927, p. 81.
[70] Wesley C. Mitchell, *Business Cycles,*1927, p. 102.
[71] Wesley C. Mitchell, *Business Cycles,* 1927, p. 103.

account the relations produced by depression revival, prosperity and recession.[72] Corporate profits are the most volatile type of income.[73] To prosper, and survive, business enterprises must make profits on average. Profit making is the central process among the activities of a business economy.[74] Business cycles are among the unplanned results of business enterprises.

In Chapter 3, Mr. Mitchell discusses the time series modeling of U.S. data and the logistic (or Gompertz) trend curves of Simon Kuznets. The logistic curves are on a secondary business cycle nature, not the long-run Kondratieff (analysis) curve of British wholesale prices that rise from 1789 to 1814, fall to 1849, rise to 1873, fall to 1896, and rise to 1920. The first curve began in the late 1780s crested 1810–1817, troughed in 1844–1851, and lasted 50–60 years. The second long-run curve began in 1844–1851, crested in 1870 1875, troughed in 1890–1896, and lasted 40–50 years. The half-curve started in 1890–1896, and crested in 1914 - 1920 (Mitchell, 1927, p. 298).[75] The Kondratieff curves are statistically probable, but the author offers no economic explanation or hypothesis to account for them (p. 228) The Juglar 22–24 year secondary curves exist.

In Chapter 3, Mr. Mitchell further discussed efforts to estimate a business barometer. Much of this effort has been led by Warren Persons, of Harvard. Professor Persons had been modeling time series and constructing a business barometer for the Harvard Economic Service, during the 1916–1928 time period. Mr. Persons was one of the first economic forecasters and he also served as founding editor of the *Review of Economic Statistics,* which became the *Review of Economics and Statistics.* We will discuss the general business conditions index of Mr. Persons in Chapter 3. Persons was concerned that many of the economic time series in this modeling work had standard deviations such as bank cleanings and call-loan rates, several times as large as the standard deviation of bank reserves, the wholesale price index, and National Bank reserves. Mr. Mitchell suggested that the plotting of time series, with secular and seasonal trends removed, reveals that the time series will not reach peaks and throughs at the same time, but the peaks and throughs are distributed over several months, and perhaps as long as a year.[76] Cyclical changes in certain economic processes lead or lag the corresponding changes in other economic time series. The time intervals of the leads and lags that were constant.

---

[72] Wesley C. Mitchell, *Business Cycles,* 1927, p. 139.
[73] Wesley C. Mitchell, *Business Cycles,* 1927, p. 145.
[74] Wesley C. Mitchell, *Business Cycles,* 1927, p. 183.
[75] Wesley C. Mitchell, *Business Cycles,* 1927, p. 228.
[76] Wesley C. Mitchell, *Business Cycles,* 1927, p. 280.

Mitchell reminds his readers that a leading aim of statistical research is to determine the time sequence in which economic time series pass through business cycles and identify the average time periods by which the series lead or lag other time series.[77] Correlation Coefficients are estimated to identify the lead and lag periods of the economic variables. Mitchell's statement that the correlation coefficients of the time series may be relatively unchanged with its various lags is consistent with the estimated autocorrelation functions and cross correlation functions of many time series. Mitchell asks the reader to consider causal relations of variable leads and lags. Moreover, Mr. Mitchell argues that the theorist should not only consider one-way, or one direction, causality.[78] Mitchell quotes the Irving Fisher modeling results that the highest correlation coefficient between monthly change in the wholesale price index of the Bureau of Labor Statistics with the Persons' index of physical volume of trade was 0.727 for a seven-month lag in the volume of trade. Fisher conceived that the hypothesis that a given price change in one month upon the volume of trade is distributed in accordance with a probability curve. When professor Fisher produced his best fit, the monthly volume of trade lagged. Monthly price changes have a logarithmic time axis by 9.5 months, and probably error points between 5 and 18 months. Thus, Fisher held that monthly price changes and the Persons' Index of physical volume of trade had a correlation coefficient of 0.941 from August 1915 to March 1923 period. Mitchell further states that if a significant relationship is shown to exist between price changes and the volume of trade, but also a be between changes in volume of trade and subsequent changes in prices. Now known as "feedback," then the statistician would come closer to presenting the complicated relations in economic theory.[79] Mitchell stated the separate coefficients should be computed for periods of revival, recession, prosperity, and depression.[80]

Mitchell proceeds in Chapter 3 to discuss the estimation of "Indexes of Business Conditions" discussing works of Beveridge (1910), who modeled the U.K. economy, 1856–1907, and its bank rate, employment, foreign trade, marriage ratio, industrial production and consumption of beer. Beveridge could not trace the "pulse of the nation to a single significant factor or cause.[81] The second business conditions index that Mr. Mitchell addresses is the Persons' "Index of General Business Conditions" in which professor

[77] Wesley C. Mitchell, *Business Cycles*, 1927, p. 281.
[78] Wesley C. Mitchell, *Business Cycles*, 1927, p. 285.
[79] Wesley C. Mitchell, *Business Cycles*, 1927, p. 287.
[80] Wesley C. Mitchell, *Business Cycles*, 1927, p. 289.
[81] Wesley C. Mitchell, *Business Cycles*, 1927, p. 291.

Persons reduced series fluctuations relative to their respective standard deviations. Mr. Persons estimated correlation coefficient to access concurrent and lagged relationships among time series and the period of lags during 1875–1913 time period. Finally, Mr. Persons created three indexes of time series by averaging 13-time series. These indexes were "an index of speculation," composed work of railroad bond yield, industrial and railroad stock prices, and New York bank clearings; "an index of physical productivity and commodity prices combined, composed of pig iron production non-New York bank clearing, the Bradstreet price index, and New York bank reserves and "an index of the new financial; situation in New York" composed of 2–3 month, 4–6 month paper rates and loan and bank deposits of New York banks (p. 293) The Persons' index was created to forecast business changes. The index of speculation preceded the index of physical productivity and commodity prices, which preceded the index of financial conditions.[82] AT&T, the American Telephone and Telegraph Company, developed a variation of the Persons' model.

Mr. Mitchell reviewed 11 economic/ forecasting models in Chapter 3 and concluded that none of the indexes give an adequate picture of business cycles.[83] Business cycles are composed of a large number of time series that differ widely in amplitude and timing. Mitchell reminds the reader that index numbers are an indispensable tool in studying the arrays of price changes condensed into a single set of averages.[84] Mitchell suggested that rather than start with a single purpose and criticizing the existing indexes in their ill-adapted use, it is probably more useful to start with the methods and data (time series) employed, and consider what the results mean and how the results might be used.[85] Mr. Mitchell proceeds to "pop the hood" of the Persons' "General Business Index" and states that a forecasting sequence or model cannot be expected to properly use all available information to consider it a "general" model. It is difficult to find many economic time series with "regular" leads and lags to forecast reliably. The only relevant criteria are the forecasting results, Curve C variables, money rates, lagged Carve B variables, business variables, by four months, on average during the 1903–1914 time period. Curve B variables lagged Curve A variables, speculative variables, by an average of eight months. Curve C variables, rates, lagged Curve A variables, speculation, by an average of 12 months. To complete the analysis

---

[82] Wesley C. Mitchell, *Business Cycles,* 1927, p. 294.
[83] Wesley C. Mitchell, *Business Cycles,* 1927, p. 309.
[84] Ibid..
[85] Wesley C. Mitchell, *Business Cycles,* 1927, p. 312. this point will be discussed in Chapter 4, Burns and Mitchell, 1946.

Mr. Mitchell recommends that it is necessary to find the average period that speculative variables (A) in one cycle lag behind the money rates variables (C) in the preceding cycle.[86] Moreover, Mr. Mitchell stated that the irregular nature of the business indexes makes it difficult to count the number of business cycles in a given time period. All the business indexes correctly identified major crises in 1882, 1893, 1907, 1917, and 1920. However, minor business crises are not easily identified in all indexes nor are their durations consistent. The business indexes do not agree on the crest or trough of a given cycle nor agree on turning periods, not points, Mitchell reported that the Snyder's Clearing Index was more accurate than Fickey's, AT&T, and Persons' index of trade, ranks in order of accuracy. Lags lasted longer at crest than troughs.[87] The business cycles, crest to crest averaged 42–43 months (p. 341).[88] Mitchell noted that the general business indexes had differences in amplitude, but saw no reason to question the relative severity of the "deepest depressions."[89] The general business indexes identify troughs better than crests.[90] Finally, Mr. Mitchell commented that the National Bureau of Economic Research collected economic statistical data for the U.S., France, Germany, and Great Britain. The best U.S. data are wholesale prices, foreign trade, banking railroads, and money and securities markets data.[91]

Is there a "normal state of trade"? Mr. Mitchell says no. The economic histories of England, China, Sweden, Australia, and most other nations, from 1790 to 1925, show incessant business fluctuations .[92] Mitchell lists 32 recessions in the U.S. between 1790 and 1925 and 13 of these are considered severe enough to be business depressions.[93] The average term of the cycle is about 3 years in the U.S., and 4 years in England. There have 1.5 years of prosperity per year of depression in the U.S., as opposed to 1.11 years in England in the 1790–1925 period, and 1.18 in France and Germany in the mid 1850s-1860s to 1925.

In conclusion, Mr. Mitchell noted that counting from crisis to crisis widened the times of cycles relative to counting from recession to recession. Mr. Mitchell could not confirm that long holes are multipliers of shorter cycles. There appears to be no periodicity of crises. There is no regularity

---

[86] Wesley C. Mitchell, *Business Cycles,* 1927, p. 325.
[87] Wesley C. Mitchell, *Business Cycles,* 1927, p. 337.
[88] Wesley C. Mitchell. *Business Cycles,* 1927, p. 341.
[89] Wesley C. Mitchell, *Business Cycles,* 1927, p. 345.
[90] Wesley C. Mitchell, *Business Cycles,* 1927, p. 350.
[91] Wesley C. Mitchell, *Business Cycles,* 1927, p. 358.
[92] Wesley C. Mitchell, *Business Cycles,* 1927, p. 376.
[93] Wesley C. Mitchell, *Business Cycles,* 1927, p. 387.

in length to business cycles. The average duration of business cycles was 5.2 years in 1796–1822, 3.5 years in 1822–1960, 5.5 years in 1860–1888, and 3.2 years in 1888–1923. Mr. Mitchell concludes that business cycles are fluctuations in the economic activities of organized communities where business restricts activities to be of a commercial nature.[94] Cycles do not occur with regularity.[95] Business cycles may be confused with changes in business condition occurring between dates of "crises." Business cycles affect major activities of the business community, not minor parts of the community. Cycles do not include recurring fluctuations every year and "long waves" and the less established secondary trends. Mr. Mitchell's tentative working plan was to identify features characteristic of all or most cycles, minimizing particular cycles, and develop the "normal" features of business cycles.[96]

2.4   Summary and Conclusions of Mr. Mitchell and His Business Cycles and His Business Cycles

Mr. Mitchell in writing his *Business Cycles* (1913) and *Business Cycles: The Problems and its Settings* (1927) put forth the phases of the business cycle and laid the groundwork on how the NBER would conduct much of its business cycle research from its inception in 1920 until 1992. Mr. Mitchell was trained in traditional (classical) economics. His emphasis on empiricism and economic description and analysis of business conditions and cycles from 1862 to 1927 were discussed in this chapter. In later chapters, we review the analysis of Mr. Burns and Mr. Mitchell in 1938 and 1946 of real-world business cycles. In fact, the Leading Economic Indicators, LEI, the signaling indicator of economic conditions, created by continues to be widely followed to the current period. Why should investors and participants in the labor force examine the LEI? The LEI time series is highly statistically significant in the forecasting of real GDP growth and employment in the U.S., 1959–2021.

---

[94] Wesley C. Mitchell, *Business Cycles,* 1927, p. 468.
[95] Ibid..
[96] Wesley C. Mitchell, *Business Cycles,* 1927, p. 469.

3

Measuring Business Activity: An Introductions to the Contributions of Mr. Persons, Mr. Schumpeter, Mr. Haberler, and Mr. Eckstein

How does one measure business activity? Can one construct a general business barometer to measure economic activity? In 1919, Warren Persons joined the Harvard faculty and became head of the "Harvard Economic Service" and the founding editor of the *Review of Economics and Statistics*. In these capacities, Mr. Persons created and maintained an "economic barometer," which measured economic activity in the U.S. economy. In this chapter, we introduce the reader to several major contributions of Mr. Persons; his five-article set of papers in the *Review of Economic Statistics*, now known as *The Review of Economics and Statistics* in 1919 on "An Index of General Business Conditions."[1] This five-paper set was an early formulation of economic variables that Mr. Persons associated with business conditions. Professors Joseph Schumpeter, Gottfried Haberler, and Otto Eckstein, all of Harvard University, wrote major works on business cycles that are reviewed in this chapter.

The five-paper set of Mr. Persons in 1919 estimated "An Index of General Business Conditions," for the 1903–1914 period. Mr. Persons would develop the Harvard Economic Service into commercial venture that generated great interest by economists throughout the world, including Lord Keynes,

---

[1] The reader is specifically referred to the Persons articles. I. "The Index: A Statement of Results", Warren M. Persons, *The Review of Economics and Statistics* 1 (2) (April 1919), pp. 111–117; III. "Application of the Method to the Data, (A) The Individual Series", Warren M. Persons, *The Review of Economics and Statistics* 1 (2) (April 1919), pp. 139–181; and IV. "Application of the Method to the Data, (B) The Groups of Series", Warren M. Persons, *The Review of Economics and Statistics* 1 (2) (April 1919), pp. 182–205.

© The Author(s), under exclusive license to Springer Nature
Switzerland AG 2022
J. B. Guerard, *The Leading Economic Indicators and Business Cycles in the United States*, https://doi.org/10.1007/978-3-030-99418-1_3

However, the service lost subscripts when it failed to forecast the 1929 depression.[2] Mr. Persons left Harvard in 1928 to become a consulting economist. In 1931, Mr. Persons published a massive business fluctuations analysis, *Forecasting Business Cycles* (New York, Wiley, 1931).

3.1   Mr. Persons and the General Business Conditions Index

Mr. Persons concluded in his introduction to the Wiley book that the acute business depression in November 1930 would end, and the inevitable business upturn would be in progress by February or March 1931, and normal business activities should not be present before the end of 1931 or the first quarter of 1932.[3] In November 1930 and January 1931, Mr. Persons was forecasting a "V-shaped" recovery.

If one wants to follow the development of Mr. Persons and his economic barometer, then it is necessary to begin with his *American Economic Review* (1916) paper presented at the American Statistical Association meeting in San Francisco, August 1915.[4] In this paper, Mr. Persons constructed a model of U.S. business activity based on annual data for the 1879–1913 period. Mr. Persons selected the 1879–1913 period because of its "relative homogeneity" of monetary and business conditions and yet it contained sub-periods of prosperity and depression. As the reader saw in Chapter 1, prices fell from 1879 to 1896 and then rose from 1897 to 1913. This period contained the depression of 1893 and Panic of 1907.[5]

Mr. Persons estimated an (ordinary) Least Squares (LS) line to model annual data.[6] Mr. Persons illustrated his LS line on Bank Clearing (BC) data to estimate the secular trend of the time series.

$y = BC\hat{x}$

Mr. Persons calculated the Pearson coefficient of correlation between bank clearings and wholesale prices. The correlation coefficient for bank clearings preceding wholesale prices was 0.818. The concurrent correlation coefficient

[2] The reader is referred to Walter Friedman. "The Harvard Economic Service and the Problems of Forecasting." *History of Political Economy* 41 (1) (2009), for a thorough discussion of the initial success and subsequent failure of the Harvard Economic Service, HES.

[3] Warren M. Persons, *Forecasting Business Cycles* (New York, Wiley, 1931), p. 19.

[4] Warren M. Persons, "Construction of a Business Barometer Based Upon Annual Data", *The American Economic Review (AER)* 6 (4) (December 1916), pp. 739–769.

[5] Persons, *AER*, 1916, p. 747.

[6] *Persons, AER*, 1916, pp. 752–753.

Table 3.1 The persons correlation coefficients of wholesale prices, 1879–1913

| Series | Wholesale prices | | | |
	0	1	2	3
Gross receipts of railroads	0.945	0.856	0.748	0.637
Net earnings of railroads	0.862	0.839	0.803	0.811
Coal produced	0.931	0.88	0.795	0.731
U.S. exports	0.783	0.786	0.772	0.328
U.S. imports	0.861	0.754	0.578	0.445
Pig-iron produced	0.756	0.738	0.631	0.617
Immigration	0.789	0.626	0.494	–
Price of pig-iron	0.763	0.739	0.637	0.576

Table 3.2 The persons correlation coefficients on first differences of wholesale prices and time series, 1879–1913

Series	-1 (Lead)	0	1 (Lag)
Gross receipts of railroads	0.273	0.66	0.074
Net earnings of railroads	−0.095	0.546	0.177
Coal produced		0.545	0.037
U.S. exports		0.456	0.111
U.S. imports	−0.261	0.621	0.213
Pig iron produced	−0.314	0.408	0.212
Price of pig iron	−0.221	0.713	0.246
Immigration	0.17	0.615	0.046

was 0.758, and the correlation coefficient of a wholesale price preceding clearings of 0.575.[7] Mr. Persons noted that a Pearsonian coefficient one of 0.45 was considered "significant," one of 0.60 "high," and a correlation coefficient of 0.75 or 0.80 was "very high." Mr. Persons noted that the correlation coefficient reliability depended upon its size and the number of items on which it was computed.[8] Bank clearings led wholesale prices by one year. Persons calculated contemporary and correlation Correlation coefficients of eight economic time series with wholesale prices for the 1879–1913 period, see Table 3.1.

Persons then calculated contemporary and one-year lead and lagged correlation coefficients of eight economic time series with wholesale prices for the 1879–1913 period, see Table 3.2.

The four variables with significant one-year lags reported in Table 3.3, (1) shares sold on the NYSE and their average price of shares sold on

[7] *Persons, AER*, 1916, p. 753.
[8] Persons, *AER*, 1916, p. 754.

Table 3.3 The persons correlation coefficients with business barometer, 1879–1913

Series	Lag	Cyclical	First difference
1. Gross receipts of railroads		0.939	0.795
2. Net earnings of railroads	0	0.885	0.781
3. Coal produced	0	0.951	0.847
4. U.S. exports	0	0.8	0.516
5. U.S. imports	0	0.877	0.83
6. Pig iron produced	0	0.865	0.828
7. Price of pig iron	0	0.785	0.696
8. Immigration	0	0.835	0.778
9. Relative wholesale prices	0	0.945	0.782
Shares sold on NYSE	1	0.4	0.521
Avg price of shares sold	1	0.766	0.504
Correct clearing index	1	0.795	0.524
New railroad mileage	1	0.525	0.224
Percentage business failures	1	−0.755	−0.308
Average 5 series	1	0.86	0.51

the NYSE (2) correct bank clearings, (3) new railroad mileage, and (4) percentage of business failures, preceded the business barometer and are useful for forecasting business cycles. Thus, in 1916, Mr. Persons established the framework for his forecasting variable selection.[9] The nine-time series in the business barometer fluctuate concurrently with wholesale prices. Mr. Person concluded his 1916 analysis with the statement that intelligent use of fundamental statistics will be the basis of using the five series preceding the business barometer in forecasting business conditions.[10]

In 1919, Mr. Persons assumed the Editorship of *The Review of Economics and Statistics* (*REStat*) and published a five-article series in the first volume of *REStat* that held that it is possible to both measure general business prosperity and depression and forecast the sequence of the business cycle.[11] Mr. Persons started with 50 time series of data and found 20 time series with cyclical fluctuations connected with business activity. Five groups of the 20 time series were constructed to "epitomize" the business situation. These five groups of series produced wave patterns that had consecutive movements.

---

[9] Persons, *AER*, 1916, pp. 763–766.

[10] Persons, *AER*, 1916, p. 769.

[11] Warren M. Persons, "The Index: A Statement of Results", *The Review of Economics and Statistics* 1 (2) (April 1919), p. 111.

Group	Time Series
I	Ten American railroad bond yields
	Twenty railroad stock price averages
	The average price of industrial stocks
II	New York City bank clearings
	Building Permits in 20 cities
	Number of shares sold on the NYSE
III	Tonnage of pig iron produced
	Bank clearings outside of NYC
	U.S. imports
	Unfilled orders of the United States Steel Corporation
	Bradstreet's number of business failures
IV	Bradstreet index of commodity prices
	Gross earnings of ten railroads
	Wholesale price index
	NYC clearing house bank reserves
V	NYC Clearing House Banks' average loans
	NYC clearing house Banks' average deposits
	Interest Rate of 60–90 day
	NT Commercial paper
	Dividend payments by industrial corporations

Group I leads Group II by two to four months. Group II precedes Group III by two to four months. Group III precedes Group IV by two to four months, and Group IV precedes group V by four to six months. The entire series of movements covered 14–16 months.[12] The prices of securities reached its peak at the same time that capital was at its minimum. The value of building permits and general activity in the financial center (Group II) reached its peak four months later. Two months following the peak of Group II, the general business conditions of Group III comprised pig iron productions outside NYC bank clearings, imports, and unfilled orders of the United States Steel Corporation reaches its maximum.[13] Two months later, railroad gross earnings and commodity prices reach their maximum and bank reserves a minimum, Group IV.

Four months later, bank rates reach their maximum whereas loans and deposits reach their minimum. Mr. Persons assessed the maximum and minimum levels of the five groups and their leads and lags relative to the Panic of 1907. Persons constructed three groups of bimonthly, not monthly, time series that presented a clearer picture of the series movements than the five groups.

---

[12] Persons, "The Index: A Statement of Results", *REStat*, 1919, p. 112.

[13] Persons, ibid.

Group A created an "index of speculation" consisting of 10 railroad bond yields, prices of industrial stocks and prices of 20 railroad stocks, and NY bank clearings.

Group B created an "index of physical productivity and commodity?," consisting of outside NYC bank clearings, pig iron production, Bradstreet's prices, Bureau of Labor wholesale prices, and NY bank reserves.

Group C, an "index of the financial situation in New York," consisted of the 60–90 day commercial paper rate, the four- to six-month paper rate, loans of New York banks, and deposits of New York banks.[14] Each time series is decomposed into its secular trend, as specified in Persons (1916); seasonal variation within the year; cyclical fluctuations, removing the secular trend and seasonal variation, and dividing by the time series standard deviation, and the residual component. The cyclical fluctuations can be viewed as percentage deviations of the original series with corrections for trends and seasonality.[15]

The Bradstreet index is aggregate of the price per pound of selected staple commodities.[16] Mr. Persons reported the correlation coefficients of the twenty time series cyclical fluctuations relative to the Bradstreet index of wholesale prices. The Group I time series have correlation coefficients of exceeding 0.60 for the six to ten months preceding the Bradstreet wholesale price index—negative correlations for yields, positive for stock prices.[17] The corresponding Group II correlation coefficients exceed 0.50–0.60 for four to six months preceding the Bradstreet index. Group III time series have correlation coefficients exceeding 0.60–0.70 for two to four months preceding the Bradstreet wholesale price index. The Group IV absolute correlation coefficients exceed 0.70 for two months following the Bradstreet index. Group V correlation coefficients are in the 0.60–0.80 range for four- to six-month lags of the whole Bradstreet wholesale price index.[18] Mr. Persons, by 1919, had constructed and published a major group of time series for business cycle forecasting. Mr. Persons published a non-technical guide to the general business conditions index in *REStat* in 1920.[19]

---

[14] Persons, "The Index: A Statement of Results", *REStat*, 1919, p. 114.

[15] Persons, "The Index: A Statement of Results", *REStat*, 1919, p. 115.

[16] Warren M. Persons, "Application of the Method to the Data, (A) The Individual Series", *The Review of Economics and Statistics* 1 (2) (April 1919), p. 139.

[17] Warren M. Persons, "Application of the Method to the Data, (B) The Groups of Series", *The Review of Economics and Statistics* 1 (2) (April 1919), p. 182.

[18] Ibid.

[19] Warren M. Persons, "A Non-Technical Explanation of the Index of General Business Conditions", *The Review of Economics and Statistics* 2 (February 1920), pp. 39–48. The reader may be particularly interested in the statement by Mr. Persons on p. 40.

"The past is not exactly like the present and future; it is only more or less similar. A statistical measure based upon the past may be used in the present and future only in so far as the underlying

The application of the Persons approach to forecasting business cycles was done by the Harvard Economic Service (HES), a forecasting agency housed within the Economics Department. The service sold subscriptions for $100 per year that modeled a monthly review of economic statistics and a weekly newsletter on general economic conditions. Friedman (2009) wrote that by 1924 the HES sold 2400 subscriptions and employed a staff of 43 persons. It was well-known for the 1920s that Wesley Clair Mitchell, Irving Fisher, and Warren Persons were leading researchers on economic fluctuations. Lord Keynes, Frederich Hayek, and Corrando Gini expressed great interest in the HES, although interest in the HES waned quickly. First, the HES did not produce income, losing $13,700 in revenues of $68,500 in 1923.[20]The failure to forecast the 1923–1924 recession led to many subscription cancelations. The HES subscriptions fell to 1567 by 1927. The HES established working relationships with the London–Cambridge Economic service and institutes in Berlin, Vienna, Warsaw, and the Canadian Economic Service (Friedman, 2009, pp. 74–75) despite a correct forecast of the 1921 recession, the HES missed the 1923 recession, leading to the subscription decrease.[21] In 1928, the first international conference for economic forecasting was held at the London School of Economics and the London Cambridge Economic Service served as the host and the HES and most of its correspondent services attended. The participants agreed to share information needed and the desirability of standardizing methods.[22]

The HES model missed 1923 and its model was revised in 1923, 1926, and 1927 such that Curve A (speculation) included industrial and railroad stock prices. Curve B (business) kept bank clearings outside of New York City and the wholesale price index. Curve C was an index of short-term money rates. In January 1928, the HES became the Harvard Economic Society, Inc., a Massachusetts corporation, and was still run by many of the Harvard personnel, and the ultimate control of the corporation rested with Harvard University.[23] In summer 1928, Harvard President Lawrence Lowell

---

economic conditions of the past are similar to those of the present and future. An index of general business conditions can be safely used in forecasting general business conditions only when the present is shown to be similar to the past in all essential elements or when allowance is made for such differences as occur. Therefore, for forecasting on the basis of the indices of general business conditions obtained from the data of the past, a supplementary economic analysis is necessary.".

The past is the proxy for the future is embedded in every forecast.

[20] Walter Friedman. "The Harvard Economic Service and the Problems of Forecasting." *History of Political Economy (HOPE)* 41 (1) (2009), p. 67.

[21] Friedman, *HOPE*, pp. 74–75.

[22] Friedman, *HOPE*, p. 75.

[23] Friedman, *HOPE*, p. 80.

helped Charles Bullock, the HES head, to secure a grant from the Rocke-feller Foundation to help finance a five-year plan. The Harvard Economic Society, Inc. became a wholly separate entity from Harvard University, and the "gentlemen's agreement" with Harvard on many personnel issues was "canceled."

In summer of 1928, Mr. Persons left Harvard and his editorship at the *Review of Economic Statistics*, to become Vice President of the National Investors Corporation. Mr. Persons also established "Warren M. Persons and Associates, consulting economists and engineers," in New York and acquired AT&T, American Tobacco Company, and Philko Radio as clients.[24] Mr. W. L. Crum became editor of *The Review of Economic Statistics* in 1928 and the stock market was reaching its highest levels. Mr. Crum and the HES did not forecast the 1929 stock market crash and the depression. Further-more, the HES predicted a rapid recovery from the stock market crash and predicted that 1930 would be a fairly good year.[25] A short-term recession, much like 1921, with its extended recovery, was predicted. Mr. Persons now a consulting economist, would agree, as the reader will shortly see.

Mr. Persons published an interesting text, *Forecasting Business Cycles* (New York: Wiley, 1931). The book was written (completed) in November 1930. The perspective of Mr. Persons was sustained recoveries accompanied the depressed economic conditions of 1885, 1894, 1908, and 1921, with busi-ness remaining at a low trough for often 5–7 months. Sharp recoveries, often referred to as "V-Shaped" recoveries in January 1879 and January 1915. Mr. Persons listed the leading obstacles to the recovery of business in 1930–1931 as: (1) a worldwide depression with large stocks of goods, excess production capacity, declining prices, declining foreign trade, political unrest, and unem-ployment; (2) large international government debt with principal and interest payments, requiring the recovery of foreign trade in commodities or interna-tional loans; (3) large volumes of installment contracts and drastic declines in new installment purchasing; (4) the large volume of stock issues in 1928–1929 being carried as bank loans on securities; and (5) the collapse of pools that stabilized the control over rubber, silk, wool, coffee, copper, sugar, wheat, and other commodity prices.[26]

Secondly, Mr. Persons held that the U.S. depression of 1896 existed only in America, because of the collapse of farm products and the "free-silver" movement of the Bryan presidential campaign. Three worldwide depressed periods, 1875–1878, 1913–1915, and 1921–1922 might be compared to

---

[24] Friedman, *HOPE*, p. 81.

[25] Friedman, HOPE, p. 82.

[26] Persons, *Forecasting Business Cycles* (New York, Wiley, 1931), pp. 8–9.

the 1930 depressed conditions. The passage of the Resumption Act of 1875 restored payments on January 1, 1879. In the 1875–1878 period, deflation caused a great decline in business, which was alleviated by the restoration of specie payments in 1879 and business expansion occurred. The economic conditions of 1879 did not resemble 1930.[27] The depression of 1893–1894 was unlike 1930, crop failures and monetary conditions, such as the Sherman Silver Purchase Law and free-silver proposals led to a steady outflow of gold and reserves to restore the gold reserve for greenbacks. The uncertainty of the maintenance of the gold standard makes the depression of 1893–1894 unlike 1930. Finally, the depressions of 1970–1908 and 1920–1924 had similar characteristics to the depression of 1930. The maximum length of the business trough was seven months; the maximum length of sub-normal business was 25 months, and the intervals of recovery to normal ranged from 12 to 14 months. Mr. Persons thus stated that "recovery should begin in the next month or two and normal business should be attained toward the end of 1931."[28] Factors expediting recovery are (1) current low money rates, (2) improved national credit with the Fed, and (3) improved international credit with the Bank for international settlements.[29] Mr. Persons did not forecast the depression of 1930 lasting longer than early 1932.

In Chapter 7, *Forecasting Business Cycles,* Mr. Persons presents monthly data from his nine-time series of data in his (1919) model for the 1875–1930 period. We will model these data as in an Appendix to this chapter to a time series mode to forecast real GNP, 1875–1930. Our statistical modeling will report that only stock prices are statistically significant in forecasting real GNP. The other variables in the Persons general business conditions index are not statistically significant during the 1875–1930 period. The Persons business barometer forecasting variables are of marginal value for researchers and practitioners in much of the 1920s and 1930s. The real question that remains

---

[27] Persons, Forecasting Business Cycles, pp. 12–13.
[28] Persons, *Forecasting Business Cycles,* p. 17.
[29] Persons Forecasting Business Cycles, p. 18.

after almost 100 years is whether The Great Depression was forecastable.[30] Mr. Persons passed in October 1937.[31]

3.2   Mr. Schumpeter and His Business Cycles

Mr. Joseph Schumpeter of Harvard University published a two-volume, *Business Cycles* (New York: McGraw-Hill Books Company, 1939). Mr. Schumpeter discussed events as either extra-economic or non-extra-economic disturbers of economic life.[32] An external force such as the Tokyo earthquake does not allow one to draw a line between the event and the working of the economic system. Wars, dangers of wars, revolutions, and social unrest are Schumpeter's external factors. Crop variations due to weather conditions or plagues can be classed as external factors like earthquakes. Innovation and the opening of new markets, such as by Columbus, create economic and social changes that can be that external factors unless the formation of new companies to exploit the new opportunities, the exports of the new countries, and the settling of the new countries can be an economic process. Technical progress in industry, whether it is in invention or machinery, accounted for great growth in the U.S. in the nineteenth century. Technical progress could not be divorced from economic progress.[33] Business fluctuations in foreign countries can be external factors. Migration is clearly an internal factor. Schumpeter stated that an entire U.S. economic history of business fluctuations could be written using only external factors.[34] The greenback period and World War I were external events changing U.S. economic history.

Schumpeter held that statistical and historical facts can be important in building knowledge of a phenomenon more than to verify a theory drawn

---

[30] Kathryn M. Dominguez, Ray C. Fair and Matthew D. Shapiro, "Forecasting the Great Depression: Harvard versus Yale", Cowles Foundation Paper 710, *The American Economic Review* 78 (1988), pp. 595–612. Dominguez, Fair, and Shapiro (DFS) analyzed the Persons' general business conditions data and found it of little forecasting value. DFS applied Vector Autoregressive (VAR) models and could not forecast the depression. They concluded that The Great Depression was not forecastable. The studies of the decrease in the money supply and the Great Depression, in which the money supply fell by one-third from August 1929—March 1933, reported in Milton Friedman and Anna Schwartz, *A Monetary History of the United States, 1867–1960*, Princeton, NJ: Princeton University Press, 1963), does not imply the money supply drop was forecastable.

[31] "Warren Persons, Statistics Expert: Harvard Economics Professor Dies–Formerly Served on Dartmouth Faculty". *New York Times*. March 14, 1937.

[32] Joseph A. Schumpeter, *Business Cycles* (New York: McGraw-Hill Books Company, 1939), p. 7. Mr. Schumpeter, in his introduction to his *Business Cycles*, acknowledged the pioneering work of the HES and Professor (Robert A.) Gordon, then of the University of California, whose work the reader saw in Chapter 1.

[33] Schumpeter, *Business Cycles*, pp. 9–10.

[34] Schumpeter, *Business Cycles*, p. 12.

from other sources. Schumpeter discusses nonsense education and spurious verification in his Chapter 2. A low interest rate almost always precedes a business boom and a high interest rate almost always precedes a slump, yet the interest rate is not a causal factor of the business cycle, due to other variables, such as demand. Even if our proposition is correct, Schumpeter held that statistics could not prove it to be so.[35] No single factor accounts for all crises, booms, and depressions.[36]

Schumpeter is very well-known for his theory of how the economic system generates evolution (1939, Chapter 3). Changing tastes and changes in quality and quantity of the factors of production are internal factors changing the economic system.[37] Mr. Schumpeter held innovation is an internal factor because the turning of an existing factor of production into new uses is purely economic process and a matter of business behavior in a capitalistic society.[38] Mr. Schumpeter acknowledged the interactions of changing tastes growth, and innovation, but stated innovation is the outstanding fact in the economic history of a capitalistic society.[39] Changes in the economic process by innovation and effects are referred to as "Economic Evolution." Mr. Schumpeter defined innovation as the selling up of a new production function.[40] In the case of a new product, or organization (a merger), new markets can open and create higher output of product.

Mr. Schumpeter held that major innovations (and some minor innovations) require construction of new plant and equipment, or rebuilding existing facilities, and innovation changes the production function.[41] Most new firms are founded with an idea and a definite purpose. Firms can become obsolete and do not last forever.[42] Mr. Schumpeter assumed that innovation is associated with new men.[43] New production functions rarely grow from old businesses. Innovations tend to come in bunches in certain sectors, and in certain conditions.[44] Innovations, particularly large innovations, disrupt the existing system and enforce a process of adaption. Secondly, industrial change is rarely harmonious with all firms and sectors moving in unison. Evolution is

---

[35] Schumpeter, *Business Cycles*, p. 33.
[36] Schumpeter, *Business Cycles*, p. 34.
[37] Schumpeter, *Business Cycles*, pp. 72–73.
[38] Schumpeter, *Business Cycles*, p. 86.
[39] Ibid.
[40] Schumpeter, *Business Cycles*, p. 87.
[41] Schumpeter, *Business Cycles*, p. 94.
[42] Schumpeter, *Business Cycles*, p. 95.
[43] Schumpeter, *Business Cycles*, p. 96.
[44] Schumpeter, *Business Cycles*, pp. 100–101.

lopsided and discontinuous.[45] The entrepreneur is the individual who carries out the innovation. Mr. Schumpeter likens the entrepreneur and manager relationship of the firm to the workman (or farmer) and the landowner.[46] The entrepreneur will generally be found among the heads of the firms, mostly among the owners. The entrepreneur is generally the founder of the firm and of an industrial family. The entrepreneur often provides the capital for innovation. Schumpeter holds that the capitalist bears the risk, not necessarily the entrepreneur. Indeed, entrepreneurs are not a social class. The entrepreneur profits occur when his receipts exceed his costs. The entrepreneur's profits fall in a competitive economy. The bulk of private fortunes in a capitalistic society results from innovation.[47]

Schumpeter, as we denoted before, discussed the role of outside factors in affecting economic events. The French Wars of 1792 and specie payment suspension, the Peace of Amiens, and the trade war with America in 1809–1812 are politically created "disturbances" for the observed worldwide fluctuations.[48] Mr. Schumpeter, as a native Austrian, had personal insights into the fall and rise of Germany in the 1920s and 1930s, and its impact on worldwide fluctuations.[49] Mr. Schumpeter asks the most important question: are there business community fluctuations that are observable given an invariable institutional and natural framework?[50] If we disregard wars, revolutions, institutional changes, harvests, weather and disease, and other "outside factors," can we see that a businessman ordering a new machine is working for a direct outcome of the capitalist machine and that same businessman than lobbying for an increase of import duty on his product is doing a separate function?

Mr. Schumpeter introduces his reader to cycles, which means the sequence of values of economic quantities in historic time which may not increase or decrease monotonically, and secondly, "fluctuations" in the data that are not independent in every time series but display instantaneous (concurrent) of

---

[45] Schumpeter, *Business Cycles*, p. 102.

[46] Ibid.

[47] Schumpeter, *Business Cycles*, p. 106.

[48] Joseph A. Schumpeter, "An Analysis of Economic Change", *Review of Economic Statistics* 17 (May 1935), pp, 2–10. Reprinted in American Economic Association, *Readings in Business Cycle Theory*, G. Haberler, Editor (Homewood, Ill: Richard D. Irwin, Inc. 1951), pp. 1–2.

[49] Ibid.

[50] Joseph A. Schumpeter, "An Analysis of Economic Change", *Review of Economic Statistics* 17 (May 1935), pp, 2–10. Reprinted in American Economic Association, *Readings in Business Cycle Theory*, G. Haberler, Editor (Homewood, Ill: Richard D. Irwin, Inc. 1951), p. 3.

lagged associations with other time series.[51] Mr. Schumpeter discusses the Marshallian concept of equilibrium in a particular industry if there is no tendency for the industry to expand or contract its output or the factors of production it employs. Aggregate equilibrium exists in an economy if business receipts (in current dollars) equals the sum of business costs, including the profits of businessmen to keep them producing their output.[52] General equilibrium exists if every household and firm is individually in a state of Professor Walras.

Mr. Schumpeter defined growth as changes in economic data occurring continuously such that the system absorbs changes without an observed disturbance. People improve their means by creating changes in technology of production, new markets, and new commodities. Innovations are changes in production functions that cannot be decomposed into infinitesimal state.[53] Industrial change is due to the effect of outside factors, the non-cyclical elements of growth, and innovation, according to Mr. Schumpeter. Business cycle research must be a historical one and the solutions to its problems must be found in industrial and commercial history.

Mr. Schumpeter opens his discussion of prosperity and depression by stating that there are no definite dates when the first cycle arose out of a state of perfect equilibrium. Economic booms occurred in the U.S., or the U.K., with railroad booms. In these periods, expenditures rose in a sequence of credit creation. Expenditures often increase more than output and non-innovating sectors of the economic system must adapt.[54] This occurrence must be obvious to all observers as a period of what is business prosperity. The products or services reach their new markets, displacing other goods and services, now obsolete, creating liquidation, readjustment, and absorption.

There are errors and misbehaviors that are observable during this period as the capitalistic system struggles to reach a new equilibrium. Downturns result from the instability revenue receipts, the repayment of bank loans, and is in accordance with statistical evidence. Secondary movements or "waves" occur because businessmen act upon the rate of change that they observe. Mr. Schumpeter holds that cyclical movements lie between neighborhoods of

---

[51] Joseph A. Schumpeter, "An Analysis of Economic Change", *Review of Economic Statistics* 17 (May 1935), pp, 2–10. Reprinted in American Economic Association, *Readings in Business Cycle Theory*, G. Haberler, Editor (Homewood, Ill: Richard D. Irwin, Inc. 1951), p. 5.

[52] Ibid.

[53] Joseph A. Schumpeter, "An Analysis of Economic Change", *Review of Economic Statistics*, Vol. 17 (May 1935), pp, 2–10. Reprinted in American Economic Association, *Readings in Business Cycle Theory*, G. Haberler, Editor (Homewood, Ill: Richard D. Irwin, Inc. 1951), p. 7.

[54] Joseph A. Schumpeter, "An Analysis of Economic Change", *Review of Economic Statistics* 17 (May 1935), pp, 2–10. Reprinted in American Economic Association, *Readings in Business Cycle Theory*, G. Haberler, Editor (Homewood, Ill: Richard D. Irwin, Inc. 1951), p. 8.

equilibrium, and there are only two phases in the simplest model of economic growth. Depressive forces gather momentum on the way back from prosperity, owing to the breakdown of secondary waves. The system outruns the first neighborhood of equilibrium, which ignites forces starting movement to the next period of prosperity. In 1935, Mr. Schumpeter acknowledges the four phases of the business cycle, prosperity, recession, depression, and revival. Mr. Schumpeter does not agree that cycles can be counted from peak-to-peak or trough-to-trough but must begin after the revival and at the beginning of prosperity.[55] The failure to view cycles in this manner is too wrong because the forces at work in revival care are entirely different from the forces in prosperity. Innovations, according to Mr. Schumpeter, cluster in time. An example is the emergence of the motor-car industry after social resistance to change, fundamentally reward untried, were overcome. One can innovate in the same manner, or do similar things run different directions, producing a cluster. Competitive capitalism creates the system where historically every business cycle can be associated with a distinct industry or a few industries, which Mr. Schumpeter did not believe that it was possible to develop formal methods to approximate the general or absolute lengths of the four phases of the business cycle, even after the identification of the outside factors, Mr. Schumpeter stated that his economic growth and innovation analysis accounted for the waves of prosperity rising from a neighborhood of equilibrium, to their tapering off into depressions, but also for the up-swings and down-swings due not to outside factors. Mr. Schumpeter discussed the three-cycle schema of economics. Historic knowledge of what happened and the way it happened reveals the first "Long wave" of a period between 54 and 60 years, the Kondratieff Cycles.[56] Within the Kondratieff cycle, there are phases. One starts from equilibrium, prosperity is a phase of innovation, in which entrepreneurs borrow from banks and bid away factors of production from other industries.[57] The bidding activity holds down the increase in finished goods from its potential output. The rising prices stimulate speculative activity that assumes prices will rise indefinitely. Recession is when the innovation ceases and the "fruits of innovation are being reaped."[58] Output

---

[55] Joseph A. Schumpeter, "An Analysis of Economic Change", *Review of Economic Statistics* 17 (May 1935), pp, 2–10. Reprinted in American Economic Association, *Readings in Business Cycle Theory*, G. Haberler, Editor (Homewood, Ill: Richard D. Irwin, Inc. 1951), p. 10.

[56] Joseph A. Schumpeter, "An Analysis of Economic Change", *Review of Economic Statistics* 17 (May 1935), pp, 2–10. Reprinted in American Economic Association, *Readings in Business Cycle Theory*, G. Haberler, Editor (Homewood, Ill: Richard D. Irwin, Inc. 1951), p. 13.

[57] Rendigs Fels, *American Business Cycles, 1865–1897* (Chapel Hill: The University of North Carolina Press, 1959, p. 26.

[58] Rendigs Fels, *American Business Cycles, 1865–1897* (Chapel Hill: The University of North Carolina Press, 1959, p. 27. One of the real questions that the reader should ask is to corporate profits led,

of finished goods rises rapidly, and prices fall. Liquidation results from the speculation emerging in the prosperity phase. Innovators repay bank debt and obsolete firms are driven out of existence. Depression means abnormal liquidation. Such liquidations carry the economy below its equilibrium and creates falling prices. Falling prices in the Juglar cycles of 9–10 years with price spirals, panics, and falling output. Output does not fall in Kondratieff cycles. Revival is a return to equilibrium with rising prices and output. The Industrial Revolution drives the first wave from 1783 to 1842. The age of steel and steam and the "railroadization" of the world between 1842 and 1897 is a second wave. Railroad construction and its associated work is the driver of economic change and economic fluctuations. The Third Long Wave rose about 1897. Two Complete Kondratieff units contain six cycles of 9–10 years of cyclical movements, known as Juglar Cycles; within each Juglar cycle are three cycles of approximately 40 months known as Kitchin cycles.[59]

3.3   Mr. Haberler and Prosperity and Depression

Mr. Gottfried Haberler was an Austrian-born economist, educated at the University of Vienna. Mr. Haberler worked under Ludig von Mises and is best known for his *The Theory of International Trade* (Geneva: The League of Nations, 1935, the English edition) and *Prosperity and Depression* (Cambridge, MA: Harvard University Press, 1937).[60] Mr. Haberler and Mr. Schumpeter were Austrians who taught at Harvard for many years until Mr. Schumpeter's passing. In 1963, in the 4th edition of his *Prosperity and Depression*, Mr. Haberler included a rather lengthy introduction to his original 1937 thesis. Mr. Haberler asked two questions that are keys to the reader's understanding of business cycles and their relevance to daily life: (1) Why are some depressions mild and others become malignant? and (2) Why have postwar recessions been so benign? Mr. Haberler asks in his preface to the fourth edition if it is luck, a change in the bend structure of the economy creating a mild set of recession trends, or good policy? Postwar depressions

---

trial, or are coincidental with the business. The evidence is mixed, with corporate profits being in the Leading Economic Indicators (LEI) of 1950 and 1957 and a coincidental indicator of the 1961 and 1975 indicators.

[59] Schumpeter, *Business Cycles*, 1939, p. 216.

[60] In 1957, Mr. Haberler was appointed Galen L. Stone Professor of international trade emeritus at Harvard University, and in 1963 he was made President of the American Economic Association. He also served as president of the International Economic Association. After leaving Harvard, he was a Resident Scholar at the American Enterprise Institute. Source: https://mises.org/library/prosperity-and-depression.

averaged to months and a real GNP decrease of 2, 5%, whereas 22 peace time recessions averaged 30 months from 1854 to 1963. Real GNP fell 31.5% during the Great Depression and even sharper during May 1937 to June 1938 period. The Great Depression officially lasted 43 months, August 1929 to March 1933, but the depression of 1937–1938 meant that the U.S. economy was characterized by severe depression from 1929 to 1939.[61] Mr. Haberler attributed the relative mildness of postwar recessions attributing to profound and lasting changes in economic institutions and policies, the creation of the Federal Deposit Insurance Corporation, FDIC, insuring bank deposits greatly strengthened the financial structure.[62] The scope of government had doubled, to 20% of GDP, in 1963, and the transfer of payments for the social network created built-in stabilizers. Government spending on pensions and unemployment benefits keep depressions milder than what would have been the case in their absence.[63] Fed monetary policy had been used with greater energy and promptness in the 1945–1963 period than had been the case in the interwar period. Mr. Haberler laments that economics had not yet been successful at predicting business turning points.[64] Mr. Haberler labeled the NBER—Leading Economic Indicator, LEI, in 1963 as experimental and cannot be claimed to reliably forecast business cycles.[65] Mr. Haberler stated that the anti-depression fiscal and monetary policies had been an important means of stabilizing the economy. The business cycle had not been abolished as Mr. Haberler concluded that there had been inflation resulting from excessive pushes for wage increases in excess of productivity increase.[66] Monetary expansion created inflation and let the balance of payments deteriorate. Mr. Haberler held that the postwar policy of compromise led to inflation, permitting prices and unemployment to rise and growth to slow.[67] Wage discipline such that wage increases rose no more than labor productivity would be preferred. The price level would be stable unemployment lower, GNP growth faster, and the balance of payments could get back to equilibrium.[68] Real incomes and real wagers would be higher and rise faster. The business cycle would still be present, and its swing would vary about a steeper rising trend.

---

[61] Gottfried Haberler, *Prosperity and Depression* (Cambridge: Harvard University Press, 1937). The author used the Haberler, *Prosperity and Depression* (New York: Atheneum, 1963, reprinted edition), pp. viii–ix. All page numbers will refer to the 1963 edition.

[62] Haberler, *Prosperity and Depression*, 1963, p. x.

[63] Haberler, *Prosperity and Depression, p. xi.*

[64] *Haberler, Prosperity and Depression*, p. xiii.

[65] *Haberler, Prosperity and Depression*, p. x.

[66] *Haberler, Prosperity and Depression*, p. xv.

[67] *Haberler, Prosperity and Depression*, p. xvi.

[68] *Haberler*, ibid.

3.3.1 Mr. Haberler and the Prosperity and Depression Phases

Let us now explore *Prosperity and Depression* monograph; Mr. Haberler's seminal treatment of business cycles and fluctuations. The book won the David A. Wells award with its publication as the best work of the Harvard Department of Economics. Mr. Haberler stated his belief that in a competitive business economy, the expected price and marginal costs of the expected volume of the activity must equate, regardless of recession or depression conditions. As the reader learned in Chapter 2, Wesley Clair Mitchell stated that production costs rose during prosperity and declined in times of depression. The cost reductions during a depression prepare the business community for revival.[69]

The rise in wages and interest rates curtails expansion in the Hawtrey (1913) monetary approach to business cycles. Efficiency falls during the revival and prosperity and rises in recessions and depressions. Mr. Haberler also restated the positions of Mr. Mitchell, Mr. Pigou, and Mr. Taussig that "error theories," the forecast errors, incomplete knowledge, and the forecasting difficulties of managers responsible for estimating future demand and inefficient expansion and contraction of demand. Mr. Haberler also restated the Irving Fisher (1911) theories that "over-indebtedness" and deflation create depressions. That is, once depression has started, prices fall because demand falls. The fall in prices leads to diminished profit margins and a contraction of credit, further drops in demand and hoarding. The existence of large debts intensifies deflation, leading to distressed selling.[70] Easy money with low interest rates is a leading cause of "over-borrowing."

Mr. Haberler defined depression as a state of affairs in which real income consumed, or the volume of production per head, is falling and there are idle resources, particularly unused labor.[71] Prosperity is a state of affairs in which real income consumed and produced are rising or high, and there are no idle resources or (very few) unemployed workers.[72] Mr. Haberler reminds the reader that real income consumed or produced, and the rate of unemployment can be measured by his 1963 edition. A crisis is a turn from prosperity to depression. Mr. Haberler does make excellent points (in 1937) when he stated that the unemployment rate in the manufacturing sector was higher

[69] *Haberler, Prosperity and Depression*, pp. 107–108.
[70] Haberler, *Prosperity and Depression*, pp. 113–114.
[71] Haberler, *Prosperity and Depression*, p. 259. The reader sees that Mr. Haberler embraces the best of Wesley Clair Mitchell, and the Fisher-Hawtrey monetary approaches to prosperity and depression.
[72] Ibid.

than in the agricultural sector. Farmers work harder and may lose wives and children under bad economic conditions, Moreover, technical progress can lead to unemployed workers.[73] Fluctuations in profits (and losses) are frequently discussed in business cycles, but (reported) corporate profits need not reflect economic profits as a mixture of interest, rent, and monopoly gains.[74] As with Mr. Schumpeter, Mr. Haberler stated the magnitude of fluctuations, but the explanation of the "external" causes of the fluctuations, such as bad harvests, diseases, strikes, lock-outs, earthquakes, and sudden destruction of international trade may not be considered in the business cycle, in a technical sense.[75] Mr. Haberler also stated that there are two regular features of the cycle: (1) cyclical ups and downs of production and employment are accompanied by movements in the money value of production and transactions; and (2) cyclical fluctuations are more marked with the production of producers' goods than the production of consumer goods. The first feature is well-known as the Quantity Theory of Money. It can be rash to conclude that monetary forces (monetary theory) are the compelling cause of cyclical expansion and contraction of production and employment.

The process of expansion starts at the bottom of depreciation, as it did in Mr. Mitchell's analysis. There are unemployed resources. The supply of labor may be almost completely elastic in the upward direction; that is, an increasing demand can be satisfied at the same wage or one slightly higher. The supply of other factors is also elastic. The start of new production allows new investment opportunities to be opened and large sums of money may be invested.

If the recovery starts because of new money being injected into the economy, then producers of materials increase production drawing on idle funds or borrowing from banks or new stock or bond issues. The demand for consumers' goods rise and idle money is put into use and generates income.[76] As expansion continues, total demand grows. A sustained and rapid increase in output due to or accompanied by the increase in money leads to increases in prices, production costs, and commodity prices, even with an elastic labor supply. Profits rise because overhead (fixed) costs are spread over greater units of output and wages lag behind prices. Optimism is created from resign prices, wages, and profits. Entrepreneurs undertake capital investment and may borrow more freely from the capital markets.

---

[73] Haberler, *Prosperity and Depression*, pp. 260–261.
[74] Haberler, *Prosperity and Depression*, p. 263.
[75] Haberler, *Prosperity and Depression*, pp. 264–265.
[76] Haberler, *Prosperity and Depression*, p. 286.

Technical improvements are "waiting to be made" particularly at the end of depression and are often profitable at certain price-to-cost ratios.[77] The more durable the investment opportunity, the more important is the expected expectations factor on the investment. Mr. Haberler put the expansion process into more technical terms. The initial expansion is due to the difference between the natural or money rate of interest. Prices and profits rise and the natural, or equilibrium, rate of interest is forced up.[78] If one starts the expansion process once full employment is reached, then the labor supply, other factors of production, and goods supply in general become more inelastic and monetary increases produce higher prices, production costs, and smaller increments to output.

3.3.2 Mr. Haberler and His the Expansion and Contraction Phases

We noted previously that Mr. Haberler started his initial analysis at a period of depression. What happens as the economy reaches full employment and there are no idle resources to employ? Output only grows at the same pace in a revival at full employment with increased capital stock, increased working population, and improved methods of production. Monetary increases at a full employment level lead to smaller increases in output and larger increases in factor and commodity prices (Haberler, 1963, p. 288).[79] One industry can grow only at the expense of another industry, as it attracts workers and raw materials by offering higher wages and paying higher prices once full employment is reached. Continued monetary expansion produces a tendency for producers' goods industries to increase relative to consumer goods industries, although the condition will not last long.

Mr. Haberler monetary approach to business cycle expansion is a "Wicksellian process" which is driven by the natural equilibrium rate of interest exceeding the monetary rate of interest.[80] Mr. Haberler states his definitions of terms necessary to explain expansions (and contractions). Gross investment is defined as net investment plus reinvestment. Disinvestment is capital consumption which must be replaced; hence, reinvestment maintains the capital stock; gross investment is essentially the production of producer goods. Investment is determined by the supply of investible funds, including

---

[77] Ibid.
[78] Haberler, *Prosperity and Depression*, p. 287.
[79] Haberler, *Prosperity and Depression*, p. 288.
[80] Haberler, *Prosperity and Depression*, p. 289.

amortization quotas, new savings, and inflation. Amortization quotas are usually a continuous process, whereas the replacement of the means of production is not continuous. It is during an expansion that additions to the capital stock occur and the supply of amortization and the demand side replacement must equal. In a period of expansion, the volume of investment exceeds the volume of savings and the difference is financed by inflation. Savings is defined as income-less consumption expenditures.[81] Mr. Haberlener reminds the reader that savings are function of earned income more than the interest rate. The third source of investible funds, inflation, operates through the interest rate. A higher interest rate creates a greater temptation to dishoard increasing the supply of funds (ceteris paribus).[82] The reader immediately recognizes dishoarding as a liquidity preference.

In an expansion, new investment opportunities emerge and entrepreneurs borrow money to finance investment. Aggregate demand has increased and the demand for goods increase has been shifted to the right. The shift of aggregate supply to the right in an expansion leads to the optimism previously discussed in Mr. Mitchell (Chapter 2). Expansion can create frozen credits to thaw and previous bad debts to the repaid. Optimism and bad debt repayments tend to make lenders lend at lower interest rates. A period of rising demand and dishoarding of funds can occur with both rising demands for credit and rising prices and falling interest rates as it did in 1933–1936.[83] If demand is expected to rise in the future, then the increased output requires heavy investments in the future. Capitalistic production and the principle of acceleration lead to greater fluctuation in the production of capital goods. Acceleration in new machinery comes about only after production with existing resources has peaked and new investment is deemed necessary.

Savings, in an expansion, means a fall in the demand for consumers' goods and a rise in the supply of investible goods. In summary, the more people save in an expansion, the slower the expansion ceteris paribus.[84] The less than save, the more rapid the expansion. Aggregate demand increases produce profits which are the most important source in the supply of investible funds during the expansion. When the boom arrives, there is a shortage of materials and manpower, increasing costs and slowing expansion. The ratio of expenditures to income increases in the latter stages of the boom.

The contraction process may start from full employment, with gradual decreases in aggregate demand. Prices start to fall and profits turn to losses.

---

[81] Haberler, *Prosperity and Depression*, pp. 295–296.
[82] Haberler, Prosperity and Depression, p. 299.
[83] Haberler, *Prosperity and Depression*, p. 302.
[84] Haberler, *Prosperity and Depression*, p. 317.

Wages and other businesses costs are not as flexible, and decreases in stocks and orders exceed the decreases in sales. New investment and reinvestment declines. Banks may restrict credit and call-in loans. Obviously, there can be a run on the bank or gold hoarding. Decreases in total demand lead to decreases in production and reductions in the production of finished goods. Pessimism develops with the demand curve shifting to the left.[85] A reduction of central bank money is an invariable feature of event depression.[86] Industrial and commercial firms increase their liquidity during a contraction. Firms strengthen their cash reserves and reduce debt with banks. It is difficult to get bank credit in a contraction and firms might not be able to renew loans. Second, as prices and profits fall, firms may delay or postpone reinvestment of capital. Firm cash hoarding can provoke a contraction.

If the means of production are fixed the process of contraction leads to a more rapid decrease in the demand for producers' goods than the decrease in the demand for finished goods. If consumer demand falls to a certain level, when production falls, there are excessive stocks of producers' goods.[87] Mr. Haberler reminds us that expectations, expected future demands, increase the demand for equipment and investment. In a contraction consumers and producers reduce spending and production of producers' goods and consumers' goods are decreased, leading to a decreased demand for investible funds. The money supply shrinks, further reducing income and expenditures.[88]

3.3.3   Mr. Haberler on Crisis and Revival

In Chapter 11 of *Prosperity and Depression,* Mr. Haberler discusses the point where prosperity starts to turn into a contraction, the upper turning point, or crisis. When a contraction ends and an expansion begins, the lower turning point is a revival.[89] A deliberate contraction of the money supply can lead to a downturn. Central banks normally restrict credit to restore external equilibrium or stop a drain on its internal reserves. An expansion of domestic money leads to higher prices at home relative to abroad, and higher domestic prices lead to capital outflows and the loss of foreign markets. Central banks could contract the money supply for fears of a prolonged expansion, whether

---

[85] Haberler, *Prosperity and Depression,* pp. 326–327.
[86] Haberler, *Prosperity and Depression,* p. 330.
[87] Haberler, *Prosperity and Depression,* p. 345.
[88] Haberler, *Prosperity and Depression,* p. 344.
[89] Haberler, *Prosperity and Depression,* p. 345.

justified or not.[90] The tightening of credit and the supply of funds have a depressing influence on the public, limit the expansion, and bring in the contraction. Further deflationary pressures as demand falls and wages diminish and sales of liquidated stock go to repay bank loans.[91] The coming crisis impacts subsidiary industries and a further fall in demand. If output is reduced due to rising costs, the interest rate rises, and banks restrict credit, then further contraction occurs. An inelastic money supply creates a limited expansion in that an increase in demand for investible funds may not evoke (create) a proportional increase in the money supply and leads to an increase in the interest rate. A continued expansion leads to a growing inelastic money supply.[92] Non-monetary forces, such as "bottle-necks," increasing scarcity of some production factors, lead to a rise in prices and a reduction in expansion. Labor costs can rise due to a decrease in the efficiency of workers which occurs in an expansion, which Mr. Haberler attributes to Mr. Mitchell.[93] Mr. Haberler notes the asymmetry between turning points. An expansion "can always" be stopped by banks restricting credit; however, a contraction cannot always be ended by making credit cheap and the money supply plentiful. Aggregate demand may be so low that no interest rate leads to a revival of investment and an increased total demand for goods.[94] Mr. Haberler noted that the imposition of a tariff will often stimulate capital investment in the protected industry and raise demand. The reduction in imports leads to increased gold and foreign exchange, easing credit, increased foreign demand for domestic products. Individual dishoarding can increase consumer spending. Government action in the form of public works can increase expenditures and total demand.[95] The further a contraction goes, the supply of labor recovers its elasticity; that is, an increased demand for labor is satisfied by a constant, or slightly rising, wage. Depressing factors are mitigated by the free flow of resources as demand revives.[96] An extended contraction produces falling prices and a lack of confidence and uncertainty of the future. New investments can be made in a contraction that reduces production costs. There can also be an increase in replacement demand. In a contraction, improvements and replacements can be made when prices are

[90] Haberler, *Prosperity and Depression*, p. 349.
[91] Haberler, *Prosperity and Depression*, pp. 350–351.
[92] Haberler, *Prosperity and Depression*, p. 356.
[93] Haberler, *Prosperity and Depression*, p. 373.
[94] Haberler, *Prosperity and Depression*, p. 380.
[95] Haberler, *Prosperity and Depression*, p. 384.
[96] Haberler, *Prosperity and Depression*, p. 386.

very low.[97] Wages eventually fall and Mr. Haberler noted that it is very dangerous for a government to maintain a policy of keeping wages up.[98]

3.4 Econometric Modelling and Mr. Eckstein and His DRI Model

Econometric models of economies were constructed by Jan Tinbergen in the 1930s. In the 1950s, Lawence Klein and his colleagues at the University of Michigan and the Wharton School built models of the U.S. and the economies of Japan and other countries. These equations grew from nine variables into hundreds of variables and equations. These modeling efforts have continued to the present time. There are many celebrated econometricians who built models and several economists created very successful consulting practices and companies as a result of the econometric models.

In this section, we introduce the reader to the DRI model of the U.S. for several reasons. Mr. Eckstein, the Paul M. Warburg Professor of Economics at Harvard, traced the development of econometric models and the DRI model in particular. First, the creator of the DRI model, Professor Otto Eckstein, of Harvard, built a very sophisticated model that was used by many corporations. The initial DRI model (1971) had 300 equations. The third generation DRI model discussed in this section, as documented by Otto Eckstein, *The DRI Model of the United States* (New York Data Resources, Inc., 1983), contained an estimated 800 equations. The model was re-estimated each July after the national income accounts data are finalized. The initial DRI model of 1968–1972 was rebuilt and substantially enhanced after the OPEC oil shock of 1974.[99] The economy of the U.S. changed with the 1973 recessions. Writing in 1983, Mr. Eckstein discussed the enhancements in the third generation DRI model. The first enhancement was modeling the sectoral flow of funds, balance sheets, and financial interactions. Simultaneous equations were used for nonfinancial sources and uses of funds and balance sheet items. Sources of cash flow included cash flows from operations, sale of financial assets, new equity issues, and accumulation of debt.[100] External funds needed are estimated by the differences between sources and uses of funds, the outlays for financial and physical assets (i.e., capital investment). Near the peak of the business cycle, firms are (still) spending on capital investment, whereas their

---

[97] Haberler, *Prosperity and Depression*, p. 395.
[98] Haberler, *Prosperity and Depression*, p. 405.
[99] Otto Eckstein, *The DRI Model of the United States* (New York Data Resources, Inc., 1983), Preface.
[100] Otto Eckstein, *The DRI Model of the United States*, p. 8.

internal cash flow starts to decline and the firm's balance sheet deteriorates sharply.[101] Short-term debt is increased relative to long-term debt and the firm becomes more subject to business fluctuations. In the falling economy, interest rates rise, the firm's cost of capital increases, and the firm must reduce its business spending and capital investment. Mr. Eckstein points out that after the lower business cycle turning point, business completes the reduction of capital spending, and falling interest rates and costs of capital create the condition for future growth.

The flow of funds argument is precisely what the reader read in the business cycles of Mr. W. C. Mitchell (1913). Corporate profits and real net worth determine long-term business spending growth.[102] The DRI model contained equations for mortgage market activities. A second DRI model innovation traced inflationary pressures from raw material to semi-finished goods to wholesale and retail prices. The DRI model had better costs of materials.

A third innovation of the DRI model calculated utilization rates of manufacturing, and production was estimated from an input–output component within the model. Vendor performance data increased the explanatory power of the wholesale price equation.[103] Furthermore, a Cobb–Douglas production model with labor, capital energy, and R&D inputs calculated aggregate supply, which affects wages, productivity, prices, and the unemployment rate.

A fourth innovation was the "supply side economies" analysis of the relationship of taxes and aggregate supply. Mr. Eckstein wrote that the DRI model have previously integrated tax rates into the supply of capital and its impact on potential output, but by the 1980s the effects were significant and large enough to make a significant difference in raising income per capita ("living standards").[104] DRI incorporated an inventory behavior model, using the expected sales and stock of inventories as in the Metzler inventory-business cycle model.

The sixth enhancement was the modeling of "errors in expectations" that specifically used adaptive expectations and distributed lag models. These models addressed errors made by businesses created by false expectations of markets prices and profits.[105] This model innovation better explained business spending in the recession of 1973 and 1974 and the 1976 inventory cycle.

---

[101] Otto Eckstein, *The DRI Model of the United States*, p. 9.
[102] Otto Eckstein, *The DRI Model of the United States*, p. 9.
[103] Otto Eckstein, *The DRI Model of the United States*, p. 11.
[104] Otto Eckstein, *The DRI Model of the United States*, p. 12.
[105] Otto Eckstein, *The DRI Model of the United States*, p. 13.

The seventh DRI model enhancement was based on inflation and unemployment raising their savings rate. Uncertainty of consumers regarding future incomes plays a role in creating volatile consumer spending.[106] Credit and (the University of Michigan) consumer sentiment indexes enhance estimations of income and financial risk because of income volatility. The income tax rate deductions and the fiscal multipliers are reduced by the volatility measures.

Finally, the eighth DRI model enhancement was a more detailed U.S., foreign trade model, created by the 1971–1973 global economic boom and the world energy impact that created the subsequent boom. The U.S. economy dominates the world economy and the DRI model measured the impact of its trading partners and the U.S. imports and exports.[107] Mr. Eckstein wrote that the DRI model was reflecting new data and forecasting and simulation experiences. The DRI model contained 781 equations, 174 exogeneous variables, 375 stochastic equations, and 406 non stochastic equations. The stochastic equations were primarily in the financial section of the model, with the flow of funds in households, nonfinancial corporations, and mortgage markets; and industry production, investment, and employment section; and final GNP demand equations for consumption, business fixed investment, government spending, and foreign trade.[108]

The DRI model became more "cyclical" with a better inventory–production–price relationship, making the model more reflective of the 1973–1974 recession, more sensitive to inflation, and more reflective of financial conditions effecting business spending and the business cycle. Mr. Eckstein noted that fiscal multipliers were more modest and cyclical because of higher inflation and subsequent higher interest rates.[109] The reader is of the 2021 discussions of these issues with regard to COVID stimulus payments. In the Phillips curve, the trade-off between inflation and unemployment becomes, in the short-term, insensitive to higher inflation rates, the trade-off being 0.70 for a one-year curve going from 7 to 6%, whereas the trade-off was 3.2 going from 4 to 3%, reflecting the 1960s economic conditions.[110]

The initial forecasting record of the third generation DRI model was good in 1976–1979, but weaker in the early 1980s because of the more rigid monetary policy shift of October 1979 and the imposition of consumer credit

[106] Otto Eckstein, *The DRI Model of the United States*, pp. 13–14.
[107] Otto Eckstein, The DRI Model of the United States, p. 14.
[108] Otto Eckstein, *The DRI Model of the United States*, p. 16.
[109] Ibid.
[110] Otto Eckstein, *The DRI Model of the United States*, p. 21.

controls in 1980 that created larger forecasting errors, including the premature forecasting of the 1981 recession.[111] DRI published a comparison of
its model forecasts during the 1977:Q4–1983:Q3, which reported that DRI
model forecasts produced lower root mean squared forecasting errors than
ARIMA models, usually about 20–25% lower, particularly in nominal GDP
consumption, fixed business investment, and stocks.[112]

3.4.1   Mr. Eckstein: The DRI Model and the Business Cycle

Mr. Eckstein commented that theoretical analysis of business cycles reached
its peak in the works of Hicks, Duesenberry, and Matthews. Economic theory
has advanced no strong theory about the origins of cyclical behavior. Econometric models, however, represent cyclical behavior and can be used to reach
conclusions about the nature and origins of business cycles and fluctuations.[113] The DRI model recognized that business cycles can originate from
(1) stock-flow or nonlinear adjustment processes, which can produce damped
or explosive oscillations; (2) exogenous shocks acting on a nonlinear system;
individual error term coefficients; and (3) responses to the financial system to
monetary policy creating credit and real cycles.[114]

Over half of the DRI model equations represent the supply side; the
financial sector supplies funds to business fixed investment and residential
construction; the level and composition of unemployment are determined by
the supply of labor; and it is necessary to isolate supply and demand functions in many models. The DRI model specifically addressed light supply
equations: (1) labor; (2) physical capital; energy; R&D; the aggregate production function; the determination of industrial capacities, and efficient energy
use.[115] The supply of labor depends upon the participation rate and is
measured by the unemployment rate and real wages and the personal tax
rate. The supply of physical capital is determined by equations for producers'

---

[111] Otto Eckstein, *The DRI Model of the United States*, p. 25.

[112] Otto Eckstein, *The DRI Model of the United States*, p. 27.

[113] Otto Eckstein, *The DRI Model of the United States*, p. 51. The reader s referred to James S.
Duesenberry, *Business Cycles and Economic Growth* (New York: McGraw-Hill Book Company, Inc.,
1958) and James S. Duesenberry, Otto Eckstein, and Gary Fromm, "A Simulation of the United
State Economy in Recession", *Econometrica* 28 (1960); reprinted in Robert A. Gordon and Lawrence
R. Klein, Editors, *Readings in Business Cycles* (Homewood, Illinois: Richard D. Irwin, Inc. 1965),
pp. 237–77.

[114] Ibid.

[115] Otto Eckstein, *The DRI Model of the United States*, p. 60.

durable equipment and nonresidential construction.[116] The supply of energy is exogeneous, both quantity and the price of energy from foreign sources are exogeneous (p. 64). The supply of materials, industry capacity, measures the supply of steel, oil, chemicals, and other inputs to production. The supply of R&D incorporates government and private industrials R&D outlays. The supply of R&D investment affects the growth of potential GNP.[117]

The DRI model estimates a potential GDP equation of fuel, worker hours, and manufacturing capacity utilization in step one. The residuals of the Cobb–Douglas based production function along with personal tax rates to reflect total factor productivity. Potential output is defined to be a manufacturing week slightly more than 40 h and a capacity utilitzation rate of 87%.[118] Mr. Eckstein used the DRI model and its supply multipliers to simulate output growth. A real government spending increase in 1966, accommodated by monetary policies to hold nominal interest rates constant, boosts real GNP because of increased demand. Increased income increases consumption and higher economic activity induces additional investment. However, by the fourth year, the stimulus investment is reduced because of the government deficit and inflation rates that increase interest rates and partially "crowd out" private investment. Inflation continues and the supply multiplier, reaches its maximum value (0.58) in year four.[119] The supply multiplier is larger with an investment tax credit, rising through six years and reaching 1.47. Whereas a reduction in the corporate tax rate produces a smaller supply multiplier, 0.52, in year six.[120]

Consumer expenditures on (non-auto) durable goods are a function of real permanent income, real disposable income, the real worth of households, and the real interest rate on consumer installment credit.[121] Real disposable income is the most important determinant of consumer spending and the most volatile consumption category is durables, autos, furniture, and appliances with income elasticities exceeding 2.1 in the second quarter of increase in real disposable income.[122]

Business fixed investment is determined by the real stock of producers' equipment, capacity utilization rate, and the ratio of interest payments to the

[116] Otto Eckstein, *The DRI Model of the United States*, p. 61.
[117] Otto Eckstein, *The DRI Model of the United States*, p. 65.
[118] Otto Eckstein, *The DRI Model of the United States*, p. 69.
[119] Otto Eckstein, *The DRI Model of the United States*, p. 71.
[120] Otto Eckstein, *The DRI Model of the United States*, p. pp. 71–72.
[121] Otto Eckstein, *The DRI Model of the United States*, p. 101.
[122] Otto Eckstein, *The DRI Model of the United States*, p. 107.

cash flow of corporations.[123] Real nonfarm inventory is determined by industrial capacity utilization, real sales, expected sales, and defense contracts.[124] The unemployment rate less than the full employment rate using the Council of Economic Advisers estimates is a function of potential GNP to actual real GNP.[125] Publicly reported profits are determined by the level of GNP, the capacity utilization rate, changes energy costs, and foreign exchange earnings associated with changing exchange rates (p. 189).

Mr. Eckstein and Mr. Allan Sinai presented their analysis of business cycles in the post-WWII period based on their econometric time modeling with the DRI model.[126] The reader was introduced to the formulation of the DRI model in the previous section. The post-WWII period was influenced by the Korean War, the Vietnam War, and the battle with inflation during the 1966 to 1979 period.

Mr. Eckstein and Mr. Sinai classified postwar business cycles into five categories: (1) the traditional booms, where the economy rose because aggregate demand rose faster than its balanced growth path and pushed the economy to its productive ceiling; (2) negative demand shocks, where sudden aggregate demand declines caused negative cyclical movements; (3) supply shocks, where the supply of key materials is disrupted; (4) price shocks (imposition of wage and price controls); and (5) credit crunches, where tight monetary policy lessened the availability of credit and there was sharp rise in interest rates. The recessions were generally preceded by booms; six of the eight recessions followed booms which were caused by the Korean War, the Vietnam War. Two involved adjustments in consumer durable goods, a worldwide boom following the collapse of fixed exchange rates in 1971, and one in 1978 was created by excessive monetary policy that produced negative real rates of interest.[127] The recession of 1948 involved the conversion of a wartime to peacetime economy and in 1960 to President Eisenhower's balanced Federal

---

[123] Otto Eckstein, *The DRI Model of the United States*, p. 133.

[124] Otto Eckstein, *The DRI Model of the United States*, pp. 147–148.

[125] Otto Eckstein, *The DRI Model of the United States*, p. 218.

[126] At the moment of his untimely (and early) death, Mr. Eckstein and Mr. Allen Sinai were presenting the DRI analysis of postwar business cycles in Gordon (1986). Very few economists were both well published and well versed in business as Mr. Eckstein. See Karen D. Arenson, Otto Eckstein: Educator who Led in Economic Forecasting, *New York Times*, March 23, 1984.

[127] Otto Eckstein and Allen Sinai, "The Mechanisms of the Business Cycle in the Postwar Era", in Robert J. Gordon, Editor, *The American Business Cycle: Continuity and Change* (Chicago: The University of Chicago Press, 1986), pp. 39–42.

budget.[128] Three recessions were severe: 1957–1988, 1973–1975, and 1981–1982. Price controls collapsed in 1973 and the movement to flexible exchange rates "created" a truly global economy. The recession of 1981–1982 was significantly worsened by the monetary policy decisions to fight inflation with severe credit restraints. To understand the postwar business cycles, the DRI model was simulated for the 1966–1983 Q2 period. The substitution of actual values for all exogenous variables in the DRI model removed cyclical "noise" in the simulations and the "no noise" condition reduced DRI model cyclicality by 15.06% during the 1966–1983Q2, its largest simulation reduction from the model's history. Had there been no OPEC oil shocks, the DRI model cyclically would have been reduced by 10%.[129] A new "crude oil price" was created to establish a more stable path for oil prices. Had the Federal Reserve not engaged in alternatively tight money (1966), easy (1968), tight money (1969–1970), easier money with wage and price controls (1971–1972), tight money (1973–1974), easy (1975–1976) and "too easy" (1977–1978), and exceedingly tight (1980–1981), the DRI mode cyclicality would have been reduced by 7.9%. Finally, if real personal consumption expenditures on durable goods, gross fixed private nonresidential investment housing starts, and total changes in real business inventories were held at their trend values, then these terms addressed as "autonomous real final demands" the cyclicality of the DRI model would have been reduced by 11.5%. Thus, the real oil shocks, the monetary policy of the Federal Reserve, and the experiment with wage and price controls, and the "no noise" (or perfect foresight) conditions would have made a more effective DRI for the cast of the economy.[130]

3.5 Summary and Conclusions to the Contributions of Mr. Persons, Schumpeter, Haberler, and Eckstein

In this chapter, we introduced the reader to the business cycles analyses of Mr. Warren Persons, who built models to develop a general business conditions index during the 1916–1932 time period. His models failed to forecast The

---

[128] Otto Eckstein and Allen Sinai, "The Mechanisms of the Business Cycle in the Postwar Era", in Robert J. Gordon, Editor, *The American Business Cycle: Continuity and Change* (Chicago: The University of Chicago Press, 1986), p. 46.

[129] Otto Eckstein and Allen Sinai, "The Mechanisms of the Business Cycle in the Postwar Era", in Robert J. Gordon, Editor, *The American Business Cycle: Continuity and Change* (Chicago: The University of Chicago Press, 1986), p. 103.

[130] Ibid.

Great Depression and failed to forecast its length and severity. His models were of marginal value to economists as only his stock price variables were statistically associated with real GDP growth during the 1875 to 1930 period. Mr. Joseph Schumpeter wrote a massive two-volume monograph, *Business Cycles*, in 1939. His book stressed non-business factors, exogenous factors, which can cluster innovations and drive economic growth, creating business fluctuations. Mr. Gottfried Haberler published his *Prosperity and Depression* in 1937, winning the David Wells Award at Harvard, The Haberler integrated the Wesley Clair Mitchell and Irving Fisher-Hawtrey monetary theories of the business cycle. Mr. Otto Eckstein developed an econometric model to forecast the direction of real GDP growth and created a great commercial success, the Data Resources (DRI) Model. Is the model perfect? No. Was the model better than a naïve, no-change forecast, we shall see in Chapter 6. The reader is introduced to several of the great (non-NBER) research monographs of business cycles in this chapter. There are some books that the reader must read to understand topics currently being debated.

4

Mr. Burns and Mr. Mitchell on *Measuring Business Cycles*

In Chapter 2, we introduced the reader to Wesley Clair Mitchell, the first Director of the National Bureau of Economic Research, NBER, and a pioneer of U.S. business cycle research. The reader hopefully followed the Mitchell development of the prosperity, crisis, and business depression phases of business cycles in his *Business Cycles* (1913) Mr. Mitchell continued his business cycles research as Director of Research at the NBER was maintained in his *Business Cycles: The Problem and Its Setting* (Mitchell & Gay, 1927). Additionally, Chapter 2 highlighted the Presidential Conference (1923) on business cycles and unemployment. The reader in 2022 may well be struck by so many recommendations and topics of discussion in 1923 that are relevant in the COVID resources of the U.S. government. There should be little question that unemployment in 2020–2021 is as great, if not greater, an issue than it was in the depression of 1929.

Let us proceed to the work of Mr. Mitchell and his co-author and successor as Director of the NBER, Mr. Arthur Burns. The reader immediately recognizes that Mr. Burns was Chairman of the Federal Reserve System in the 1970s. Mr. Burns, in this chapter, works with Mr. Mitchell to develop an NBER monograph on Business cycles, *Measuring Business Cycles*, NBER, 1946. In this chapter, we work through the Burns and Mitchell (Burns & Mitchell, 1946) NBER volume which updated business cycle research for the 1854–1933 time period. The large 450-plus page *Business Cycles: The Problem and Its Setting*, evolves into the larger 550-plus page *Measuring Business Cycles*

J. B. Guerard, *The Leading Economic Indicators and Business Cycles in the United States*, https://doi.org/10.1007/978-3-030-99418-1_4

(Burns & Mitchell, 1946).[1] We now see even more statistical analysis in the Burns and Mitchell monograph.

Mr. Burns and Mr. Mitchell, denoted BM in this chapter, define business cycles as fluctuations in aggregate economic activity of nations that work in business enterprises. Business cycles consist of expansions, followed by general recessions, contractions, and revivals, merging into expansions in the next cycle. The business cycle sequence of changes (phases) are recurrent, but not periodic, lasting from one to ten-twelve years, and are not divisible into even smaller cycles. Burns and Mitchell define "business enterprise" as a measure of individual initiative and competition. The reader is reminded that Mr. Mitchell in his 1913 and 1927 monographs assumed that competition was present in the U.S. and that business enterprise as discussed by Clark (1917) was the predominant form of business organization. BM further ask if business cycles fade when certain nations limit competition. Did business cycles disappear in Facist Italy, Nazi Germany, and Soviet Russia?[2] Economic activities mean specific acts performed by individuals or by millions of people in broad categories of actions, such as the production, exchange, and distribution of wealth. BM point out that bankruptcies rise when general economic activities are still expanding and thus it is necessary to know precisely what each economic time series represents and its bearing upon the economic activity as a whole.[3] Business cycle researchers must identify cycles of historic record and BM RD and study their characteristics. BM stress that systematic factual research may not be a stage of "inductive verification," a step to be taken after a "theory" has been advanced, as much as theorists have been handicapped incomplete and often badly twisted or confused knowledge of the facts. No business cycle researcher should restrict himself to a single hypothesis. BM examine time series that record the fluctuations of specific processes from month to month, quarter to quarter, or year to year, as annual data is not adequate.[4] Furthermore, the longest records of business fluctuations in economic activities are the contemporary opinions, writings, of journalists, reporting on the condition of trade and prosperity and depression.

Mr. Burns and Mr. Mitchell present a sketch of the statistical analysis which has two parts. The first part seeks to determine how each economic process behaves during the periods of the business cycle. Every time series is broken into segments that occur within the general business activity in

[1] Arthur F. Burns and Wesley C. Mitchell, *Measuring Business Cycles* (New York: National Bureau of Economic Research, Inc., 1946).
[2] BM, *Measuring Business Cycles*, p. 5.
[3] Ibid.
[4] BM, *Measuring Business Cycles*, p. 10.

a particular country.[5] Burns and Mitchell analyze over 1000 time series of data to get a comprehensive picture of what happens during a business cycle. Most economic time series exhibit fluctuations, but the cyclical fluctuations may vary greatly in relationships in time to business cycles. The Burns and Mitchell business cycle research is based upon business cycle periods supplemented by studies of the cycles particular to each time series.[6]

Every economic time series has its seasonality removed and is broken into segments relative to the reference trough of the relevant country. The BM "reference cycle," or "reference cycle segment," is the segment of each time series that spans between successive reference troughs. In the King's English, Mitchell, and Burns and Mitchell break each time series into movements within the phases of business cycles, knowing that no two business cycles effect all time series equally. BM then average the monthly values of the time series during each reference cycle and convert it to a percentage of the base.[7] These percentages are referred to as business cycle relatives of "reference-cycle relatives." Burns and Mitchell then refer to the cyclical movement of a particular time series its "specific cycles." Burns and Mitchell compute the monthly average values of each time series during each business cycle and convert the data into "specific-cycle relatives."

BM illustrate their specific-cycle relative process on Coke production data, 1914–1933. The first trough-to-trough business cycle is November 1914 to May 1919 The average coke production (4,246,000 tons is the base). The second specific cycle of coke production is May 1919 to July 1921 (with a monthly average figure of 3,565,000 tons). "Specific-cycle relatives" are referred to as "S" tables whereas "reference-cycle relatives" are referred to as "R" tables. The dates of cycles yield measures of the duration of business cycles and expansions and contractions of each time series.[8] The dates of each series cyclical turn yield duration measured of specific cycles. BM compare the turning dates of specific cycles with the reference dates to determine the number of months by which the troughs and peaks in each time series proceed or follow the reference troughs and peaks.

Mr. Burns and Mr. Mitchell measured how individual time series moved from troughs-to-peaks peaks-to-troughs and averaged the monthly averages of these three individual time series movements to the general business movements to access the cyclical movements, the "specific cycles" of each time series. Their great volume of 1946 measured some 970 time series in the

[5] BM, *Measuring Business Cycles*, p. 21.
[6] BM, *Measuring Business Cycles*, p. 23.
[7] BM, *Measuring Business Cycles*, p. 24.
[8] BM, *Measuring Business Cycles*, p. 26.

U.S., 700-plus of these U.S. time series were monthly. The reference troughs and peaks of each time series are marked off. The relative dates of movements of each time series to the reference cycles of the general (the U.S., and three countries, Great Britain, Germany, and France) is noted in the Burns and Mitchell timing and duration of specific cycles (the "S" tables) and the average months of loads and lags of expansionary, contractionary, and full cycles of each time series, for each full circle, are produced. The percentage of the duration of specific cycles is a key output of the Mr. Burns and Mitchell output tables and methodology. Three-month average values of each time series is used to construct amplitude of each specific cycle. The three-month averages of the series centered on the initial trough, the peak, and the terminal trough of each series, in each cycle.

The lengths of the specific-cycle rises and falls are expressed as percentages to the full cycle. The Burns and Mitchell methodology computing series cycle relatives as percentages of the values during the specific or relative cycle is referred to as the "inter-cycle" portions of the secular trends, a term proposed by Mr. Persons noted in Chapter 3, as the reader remembers. Secular movements are measured for each time series by calculating percentage change values in each time series in the contractionary-to-expansionary phase and the expansionary-to-contractionary phase from the preceding phase. Total and per month averages are calculated for each time series relative to its preceding time series movements in the preceding cycle.[9] The time series relative movements during it specific cycles are reported in nine stages. The first stage contains the three-month average values centered on the initial trough. Stage five covers the three-month values centered on the peak, and stage mine the three months centered on the terminal trough. Stages two through four cover the first third, the middle third, and the final third periods of the expansion. Stages six through eight cover the first third, middle third, and final third of the contraction.[10] The nine stages of each time series, in each time series, show the behavior of the different processes from stage to stage of the business cycle. Mr. Burns and Mitchell stated that the nine stages reference table put their business cycle concept and its schedule of reference dates to a critical test. The troughs and peaks are taken from the standard list of reference dates instead of turning points of specific cycles, and the values reported are in terms of (percentiles) of reference-cycle relatives rather than specific-cycle relatives.[11]

---

[9] BM, *Measuring Business Cycles*, pp. 28–29.
[10] Ibid.
[11] BM, *Measuring Business Cycles*, p. 30–31.

A third table, "R3", measured how the time series average specific-cycle and average reference-cycle patterns conformed. The "Conformity to Business Cycles" table reported how each series conformed in monthly intervals and average changes per month relative to reference-cycle relatives during expansions and contractions of each cycle. The "index of conformity" measures the direction of movements and magnitudes of each series. The index on conformity averages for each cycle are *averaged for each set of cycles. Mr. Burns and Mitchell compute the deviations from the average* values. The deviations represent how individual cycles are clustered about the means of the cycles.[12] The Burns and Mitchell duration lines represent the average leads and lags of each series over all the cycles. Burns and Mitchell stated that the elimination of random movements from the original data would probably enhance the time series conformity to business cycles. The use of only annual data could obscure cyclical fluctuations.[13] The use of monthly and quarterly data necessitates the identification and removal of seasonal fluctuations.

Mr. Burns and Mitchell identified 27 trough-to-peak-to-trough business cycles in the U.S., from December 1854 to May 1938. The reader, when seeing the original NBER monograph, notes full business cycles in which the periods of contraction exceed one-half the time period of the full cycle, (1) the recession with a trough in December 1870; (2) the recession with a trough in March 1879 (a 99-month full cycle); (3) the recession with a trough of June 1894; (4) the recession with a trough of June 1897; (5) a recession with a trough of August 1904 (44 months) (6) the recession with a trough of September 1921; (7) and the depression of 1929–1933 with a trough of March 1933, with 45 months of contraction and 63 months of the full cycle.[14] When authors discuss the moderation of postwar recessions, they are often referring to the Burns and Mitchell monograph. The Burns and Mitchell trough-to-peak-to-trough reference dates were determined with referencing the Willard Thorp NBER Business Annuals. Burns and Mitchell reference the Federal Reserve Board index of production as a time series reference series. The reference dates are the culmination of the concept of cyclical expansions and contractions in "general business activity."[15]

Mr. Burns and Mitchell stated that the business cycle consists of many economic time series having roughly concurrent fluctuations, and that their reference dates should mark the turning points of business cycles. If that were to be the case, then every period scored as an expansion should be a reference

---

[12] BM, *Measuring Business Cycles*, p. 42–43.
[13] Ibid.
[14] BM, *Measuring Business Cycles*, p. 78.
[15] BM, *Measuring Business Cycles*, pp. 94–95.

expansion, and every contractionary period should be stored as a reference contraction. Mr. Burns and Mitchell examined 46 series of monthly and quarterly data and scored each series as a "t" for an expansion and all "-" for a contraction. The 46 series reported the "Directions of Movements in Successive References Phases 1854–1933," and 22 series had no tendency to lead or lag; their net score was "0". The tables (21 and 22) clearly support the hypothesis that many business activities in the U.S. have shared a common rhythm and that our reference-cycle chronology exposes and expresses this rhythm. [16] The chief time series not conforming to the reference-cycles bank clearings (in and outside New York City) pig iron production, total wholesale prices, pig iron wholesale prices, the index of railroad stock prices, and the number of Dun's business failures, inverted.[17]

One can also calculate the even diffusion ("diffusion of business cycles") of business where the proportion of rises (during reference expansions) exceed the proposition of declines during corresponding contractions. Most economists studying business cycles agree that the violent contractions of 1907–1908, 1920–1921, and 1929–1933 are "business cycle movements" (Burns & Mitchell, 1946, p. 107). Mr. Burns and Mitchell did find evidence of two "extra" cyclical movements suggested by Mr. Persons. Mr. Frickey studied the 1866–1914 period and concluded that short-term fluctuations permeate the whole structure of the U.S. industrial and commercial life (Burns & Mitchell, 1946, p. 111).[18] Mr. Burns and Mitchell reported finding no evidence of Mr. Frickey's "extra cyclical phase."[19]

Mr. Burns and Mitchell sought to compare the dates of each time series specific cycles of peaks and troughs with the reference dates in each country (Burns & Mitchell, 1946, p. 116).[20] The number of months that the turns on the specific cycles lead or lag the reference turns, can tell of the timing the series has with regard to the business cycle. Mr. Burns and Mitchell discussed "standardized the data" by subtracting the averages of the leads or lags for peaks and troughs and calculating their respective standard deviations.[21] All time series were analyzed on the number of "positives" basis for conforming to the general reference cycle. To minimize the bias of establishing a specific-cycle turn, the time series must meet two criteria:

---

[16] BM, *Measuring Business Cycles*, pp. 100–101.
[17] BM, *Measuring Business Cycles*, p. 101.
[18] BM, *Measuring Business Cycles*, p. 111.
[19] BM, *Measuring Business Cycles*, p. 113.
[20] BM, *Measuring Business Cycles*, p. 116.
[21] BM, *Measuring Business Cycles*, pp. 116–117.

(1) There is no other reference turn between the specific-cycle turn, S, and the reference turn, R, including S; and

(2) There is no other specific-cycle turn in the interval between S and R (including the month of R).[22]

A third criteria was adopted if rules (1) and (2) presented a possible problem. If the specific-cycle turn, S, met (1) and (2) criteria, and another possible S on the opposite side of R met only criteria (1), then S will be treated as a corresponding return if it did not deviate from R by more than three months. In general, Mr. Burns and Mitchell accepted a conformity score of 50 higher as being indicative of "close" conformity.

Mr. Burns and Mitchell discussed the duration of specific cycles. Expansion is from the midpoint of the date of the initial trough to the midpoint of the date of the initial peak. Contraction is the interval from the midpoint of the peak to the midpoint of the initial trough. The duration of the full cycle is found by summing the lengths of expansions and contractions.[23] The original economic time series are in different units, dollars, persons, tons, percentages, and miles. To create a consistent unit to express the expansion from trough-to-peak and from peak-to-trough, Mr. Burns and Mitchell calculated the amplitudes of different series as a percentile of the average monthly value of each series during the cycle.[24]

Mr. Burns and Mr. Mitchell further described specific cycle patterns in terms of the mounting or subsiding waves from trough-to-crest or crest-to-trough with the introduction of their nine-point charts of specific cycles of a given economic time series. They continued their bituminous coal production, 1907–1938, analysis. In each specific cycle, there are nine averages. The first average is the three months centered on the initial trough. The expansion period is subdivided into three parts, the first third, middle third, and last third of the expansion process. Stage five contains the three-month average centered on the peak. Stages six through eight contain averages of the first third, middle third, and last third of the contraction. The ninth stage contains the average centered about the terminal trough.[25] The nine-stage averages were presented for the eight specific stages of the coal production data in Table 4.[26] Stages II–IV, the expansionary period, were considerably longer

[22] BM, *Measuring Business Cycles*, p. 118.

[23] BM, *Measuring Business Cycles*, p. 113.

[24] BM, *Measuring Business Cycles*, p. 131.

[25] BM, *Measuring Business Cycles*, pp. 144–145.

[26] BM, *Measuring Business Cycles*, p. 145.

than stages VI–VIII, the contractionary period, for bituminous coal production during the 1907–1938 period. Finally, Mr. Burns and Mr. Mitchell presented in Table 5, average monthly rates of change in the nine stages from trough-to-peak and peak-to-trough.[27]

A graphical presentation of the averages of Table 4 were created for each time series, for each specific cycle, and then averaged. The slopes of the specific-cycles charts correspond to the averages in Table 5, the monthly rates of change data. Thus, Mr. Burns and Mitchell created a chart summarizing the leading features of the specific returns of a time series, which could be created for their 700 series. The slopes of the time series of specific cycles varied greatly with coal production, postal receipts, railroad bond yields "topping out" at an amplitude of the 110–120, whereas pig iron production, call monthly rates and shares traded topped out in the 150–170 range.[28]

A final set of charts standardized the amplitude peak. Reference charts were created similar to Tables 4 and 5 with NBER cycle dates added. Two conformity calculations are added. The first conformity calculation compares rates of changes in contractions with the previous reference-cycle expansions. A conformity index of + 100 reports that the time series corresponds to the full (reference) business cycle whether the cycle goes from peak-to-peak or trough-to-trough. The second calculation actor reports whether the average rate of change in the time series contraction is larger or smaller than the average rate of change in the reference expansion.[29] Mr. Burns and Mr. Mitchell developed these conformity measures to identify the leads and lags of the economic time series. Average shares traded led reference peaks by over 10 months and led reference troughs by 4.6 months. Railroad bond yields trailed reference peaks by 7.8 months and troughs by 11.8 months.[30] Mr. Burns and Mr. Mitchell stressed that if a series has mild erratic fluctuations, then monthly time series may be better spotted in monthly rather than quarterly data, and it may be easier to trace the sequence of revivals and recessions (Burns & Mitchell, 1946, p. 269).

In Chapter 7, Mr. Burns and Mr. Mitchel address the topic of trend-adjusted data and business cycles. Reporting trend results on a subset of their 800 time series, only railroad bond yields, electrical output, pig iron production, deflated bank clearings, the Frickey's clearings data, and the AT&T index the authors concluded that tread-adjustments made "most time series look alike" than unadjusted data. Mr. Burns and Mr. Mitchell stated that any investigation variables played in the past business cycle process, and their

---

[27] BM, *Measuring Business Cycles*, p. 150.

[28] BM, *Measuring Business Cycles*, pp. 154–157.

[29] BM, *Measuring Business Cycles*, p. 180–181.

[30] BM, *Measuring Business Cycles*, p. 226.

probable role in future business cycles cannot remove secular trends without sacrificing their main research premise. One should not limit business cycle research to time series that fluctuate in unison.[31] With respect to smoothing data, Mr. Burns and Mr. Mitchell tested the Macaulay smoothing algorithms and reported that smoothing methods did not help deflated clearings, pig iron production, railroad stock prices, and call money rates predict business cycle turning points with a higher degree of certainty than raw data.[32] Thus, the use of secular trends and smoothing were reflected.

In Chapter 9, Mr. Burns and Mr. Mitchell illustrate the large variability of cyclical time series in the U.S. during the 1857–1933 period. The seven-time series represented the production of durable (pig iron production and freight car orders), the money market (call money rates and railroad bond yields), the stock market (shares traded and railroad stock prices, and deflated bank clearings) the volume of payments, only pig iron production and share trading had specific cycles producing a one-to-one correspondence to business cycles. The seven series did not have consistent lead or lag relations at reference troughs.[33] The Burns and Mitchell averages suggested that stock prices, shares traded, and freight orders led business cycle revivals and recessions and bond yields tend to lag in revivals and recessions.[34] Deflated lank clearing and pig iron production led in revivals and lagged in recessions.[35] Mr. Burns and Mr. Mitchell reported correlation coefficients of the seven economic series on specific-cycle measures (the duration of full cycles and time, amplitude of full cycles and time, and per-month amplitude of full cycles and time) and their correlation coefficients never exceeded 0.16, judged to "unimpressive." The only interesting observation concerning the amplitudes of the seven economic series during the 1885–1915 and 1915–1931 periods that Mr. Burns and Mr. Mitchell made was that the call money rate series had a "significant" decrease in amplitude which they attributed to the Federal Reserve System.[36] In their conclusion of statistical tests, Mr. Burns and Mr. Mitchell found no significant evidence that secular or structural changes effected the cyclical behavior of the seven economic series in the U.S. or on the duration of business cycles in their four countries.[37] More importantly, Mr. Burns and Mr. Mitchell did

---

[31] BM, *Measuring Business Cycles*, p. 307.
[32] BM, *Measuring Business Cycles*, p. 359.
[33] BM, *Measuring Business Cycles*, p. 376.
[34] BM, *Measuring Business Cycles*, p. 380.
[35] Ibid.
[36] BM, *Measuring Business Cycles*, pp. 407–408.
[37] BM, *Measuring Business Cycles*, pp. 412–413.

not find the Schumpeter position that industry history produced a "Kondratieff cycle" that contained six "Juglar cycles" of 9–10 years which can be subdivided into three Kitchin cycles of 40 months.[38]

4.1   Comments on Measuring Business Cycles

The publication of the Burns and Mitchell *Measuring Business Cycles*, the second studies in Business Cycles of the NBER, was not without comments and criticisms.[39] One of the great economic exchanges of methodology came about as a result of the Mr. Tjalling Koopmans article in *The Review of Economics Statistics* (*REStat*) in 1947 and its rejoinder in *REStat* by Mr. Rutledge Vining in 1949.[40] Mr. Koopmans of the famed Cowles Foundation, discussed the NBER development of cyclical fluctuations in economic variables and the search for possible changes in these variables over time in cycles. Mr. Koopmans, in his "Measurement with Theory" commented on the empirical development of Mr. Burns and Mr. Mitchell, likening their work to the contribution of Johannes Kepler in measuring the positions of planets and their orbits. Mr. Koopmans began by stating that Mr. Kepler was an outstanding success due to his "strike out for new models and hypotheses if needed to account for the observations obtained. He was able to find simple

---

[38] BM, *Measuring Business Cycles*, pp. 440–441.

[39] Mr. John M. Clark authored a final interpretation of Mr. Mitchell and his business cycles that is still convincing. Mr. Mitchell, Mr. Clark asserted, emphasized the "how" and not "why" of his analytical description of business cycles; there is no causal relationship modeling. The description is both empirical and in accord with reason, as we noted in Chapter 2 with the note on Mr. Clark's discussion of Mr. Mitchell and his "money economy" in John Maurice Clark, "Theory of Business Cycles", in *Wesley Clair Mitchell: The Economic Scientist*, Arthur F. Burns, Editor (New York: National Bureau of Economic Research, 1952), pp. 198–203. See also Adolf A. Berle, "Wesley Clair Mitchell: The Economic Scientist", *Journal of the American Statistical Association* 48 (1953), pp. 169–175 and F.A. Hayek, "Wesley Clair Mitchell, 1874–1948", *Journal of the Royal Statistical Association*, Series A, 111 (1948), pp. 254–255. Mr. Hayek appreciated Mr. Mitchell's efforts in the development of a different approach than the traditional economics, directed by Professor James L. Laughlin, at the University of Chicago, his theses advisor, which was more in the spirit of empirical science, and for which he drew largely on the inspiration of Veblen, Dewey, and the German Historical School. Mr. Hayek credited Mr. Mitchell in his development of "institutional economics." See also Simon Kuznets, "Wesley Clair Mitchell, 1874–1948: An Appreciation" *Journal of the American Statistical Association* 44 (1949), pp. 126–131. The reader should note that Mr. Kuznets won the Nobel Prize in Economic Sciences in 1971 and Mr. Hayek won the Nobel Prize in 1974.

[40] Tjalling C. Koopmans, "Measurement without Theory", *The Review of Economic Statistics* 29 (1947); reprinted in Robert A. Gordon and Lawrence R. Klein, Editors, *Reading in Business Cycles* (Homewood, Illinois: Richard D. Irwin, Inc., 1965), pp. 186–203. Rutledge Vining, on the Choice of Variables to be Studied "Koopmans on the Choice of Variables to Be Studied and the Methods of Measurements", *The Review of Economic Statistics* 31 (1949);); reprinted in Robert A. Gordon and Lawrence R. Klein, Editors, *Reading in Business Cycles* (Homewood, Illinois: Richard D. Irwin, Inc., 1965), pp. 204–217.

'laws' which were in accord with past observations and permitted the prediction of future observations."[41] Mr. Koopmans stated that Mr. Kepler's work was great for large data gathering, scrutinizing of facts which precedes, independently, the formulation of theories and their testing by further facts. Mr. Koopmans held that Mr. Burns and Mr. Mitchell were more consistently empiricist than Kepler, yet unlike Kepler, who predicted circular motion once observations "spoke decisively" for the elliptical orbit, Mr. Burns and Mr. Mitchell did not reveal what explanations of cyclical fluctuations, if any, they believe. There was no hypotheses to the work of Mr. Burns and Mr. Mitchell; hence, no theory.[42] While Mr. Koopmans stated that Mr. Burns and Mr. Mitchell promised additional work and theory. Mr. Koopmans believed that a fuller utilization of economic theory, its concepts and hypotheses, as a part of observation and measurement promised to be the shortest road to understanding cyclical fluctuations.

Mr. Koopmans comments were directed to several major points: (1) the 1927 NBER volume, which the reader was introduced to in Chapter 2, is the guide to the vast data in the 1946 Burns and Mitchell volume, without a single demand or supply schedule or other equation of behavior or technical laws of production, being explicitly or implicitly present in the book; (2) the seven American economic time series selected by Mr. Burns and Mr. Mitchell (in their Chapters 8–12 previously discussed) are not chosen for any notable reason, but simply to show, the variability among the variables, and (3) the Burns and Mitchell methodology divorces the study of fluctuation from the levels and trends of around which the variables fluctuate. These three comments and objections created the discussion between measurement and hypothesis generation through theory economic measurement, and hypothesis testing and prediction.[43] In the King's English, it is the Cowler Foundation methodology versus the NBER empirical methodology. Mr. Koopmans stated that predictions of the effects of stated hypothetical measures of economic policy on the level and movements of economic variables were the most important objective of the analysis of economic fluctuations.[44] Mr. Koopmans discussed the development of structural equations, as one builds and estimates in simultaneous equation models. The specification of a system of structural equations is required to decide if the particular

---

[41] Tjalling C. Koopmans, "Measurement without Theory", The Review of Economic Statistics 29 (1947); reprinted in Robert A. Gordon and Lawrence R. Klein, Editors, *Reading in Business Cycles* (Homewood, Illinois: Richard D. Irwin, Inc., 1965), pp. 186–187.

[42] Koopmans, *REStat* (1947); reprinted in Gordon and Klein, 1965, p. 187.

[43] Koopmans, *REStat* (1947); reprinted in Gordon and Klein, 1965, p. 190.

[44] Koopmans, *REStat* (1947); reprinted in Gordon and Klein, 1965, pp. 193–194.

equation is sufficiently detailed to permit its identification. The reader immediately remembers that Mr. Eckstein and his DRI model of the U.S. economy
were introduced in Chapter 3. The stability of the system over time is an
issue for Mr. Koopmans. An observed regularity is subject to unknown reliability if it is not traced to an underlying behavioral pattern.[45] Mr. Koopmans
summarized his assessment of the Burns and Mitchell methodology that there
is no awareness of identification and measurement of economic variables as
a prerequisite to prediction. Mr. Koopmans commented on the Burns and
Mitchell use of previously published scientific topics to be tested in the
cyclical behavior chapter rather than the testing of possible arguments for
cyclical and secular changes in duration, amplitude and timing of reference
cycles within the seven tested American variables selected for testing. The
comments by Mr. Koopmans are as relevant in 2022 as they were in 1947.
First, Mr. Burns and Mr. Mitchell selected a set of economic variables in
1938 in an NBER study that we will discuss in Chapter 5, that were variables "of interest" in leading business cycles. Second, in Chapter 5 we review
the variables identified by Geoffrey Moore, in 1950, to be one of the first
sets of NBER leading economic indicators. In Chapter 6, we further discuss
the notes of Mr. Victor Zarnowitz regarding the consistency of the NBER
LEI during the 1950–1989 period. Finally, we will discuss the test by Mr.
Alan Auerbach in 1982 that statistically confirmed the validity of the NBER
economic variables in modeling the unemployment rate and the FRB index
of industrial production, 1949–1977, in the U.S. economy.[46]

Mr. Koopmans final summary was that the Burns and Mitchell *Measuring
Business Cycles* was empiricist in outlook and showed great perseverance in
handling vast amounts of data, In the second half of the Burns and Mitchell
book, theoretical and practical tests of cyclical movements are reported.
However, the lack of theory restricts the benefits of modern application of
statistical inference.[47]

Mr. Rutledge Vining, in his rejoinder to Mr. Koopmans, in his 1949
REStat piece, cast doubt in his mind that Mr. Koopmans would accept
research not using the Cowles Foundation methodology.[48] Mr. Vining argued
that Mr. Koopmans commented that without a theoretical framework having
his specified form, that statistical data cannot be used efficiently. Mr. Vining
asked what is the role of theory in quantitative research? Mr. Vining offered

[45] Koopmans, *REStat* (1947); reprinted in Gordon and Klein, 1965, p. 195.
[46] Alan J. Auerbach, "Measurement without Theory: Thirty-Five Years Later", *The Review of Economics and Statistics* 64 (1982), pp. 589–595.
[47] Koopmans, *REStat* (1947); reprinted in Gordon and Klein, 1965, p. 203.
[48] Koopmans, *REStat* (1947); reprinted in Gordon and Klein, 1965, pp. 204–205.

three points in defense of empiricism. First, Mr. Vining stated that Mr. Koopmans held too narrow the variation of the concept as to whether economics was a science of variation of an argument in political philosophy. Mr. Vining argued that the Burns and Mitchell book and its exploratory work did not proceed without the guidance of tentative hypotheses. Second, Mr. Vining questioned the position that research is to be evaluated from the point of view of social action. Third, modern statistical estimation and its extraction of maximum information is literally besides the point in deriving hypotheses. Exploratory research characterizes a great part of developing fields of knowledge.[49] Not all empirical work will find formal mathematics of immediate use. Mr. Koopmans assertion that the Cowles Foundation methodology was the best and simplest means to account for events in space and time of understanding cyclical fluctuations seemed to Mr. Vining to be an extraordinary statement in the present state of knowledge.[50] Mr. Vining discussed the problem of a tadpole and its transparent tail being researched by a biologist at the University of Virginia without the use of modern statistics. The photographic analysis of Mr. Speidel, the UVA biologist, contained hypotheses that he had in mind. Mr. Vining further quoted the eminent British statistician, Mr. M. G. Kendall, who stated that the problem of sampling theory was to inform the investigator as to the limits within his descriptive measures could be believed.[51] Does statistical development and estimation take place at the expense of important practical work? Mr. Vining concluded his rejoinder with comments that he would prefer to have Mr. Burns and Mr. Mitchell judge his research as the "Commissar of Research" than Mr. Koopmans, who would ask "Where are your different equations?", "Where is your argument showing that the best use has been made of the available data in relation to the most important aspects of the phenomena studied?" and "Where is your assurance that in what you have done you have wasted, no information?" Mr. Vining saw no need in his point in presenting his research to Mr. Koopmans as the Commissar.[52] The replies by both M. Koopmans and Mr. Vining satisfied neither party to the argument on research and empirical methodologies. As we stated earlier in this section, the economic variables recommended by Mr. Burns and Mr. Mitchell were not tested in 1938 and those of Mr. Moore and Mr. Zarnowitz were tested by themselves and Mr. Auerbach (1982), who

---

[49] Koopmans, *REStat* (1947); reprinted in Gordon and Klein, 1965, pp. 206–207.
[50] Koopmans, *REStat* (1947); reprinted in Gordon and Klein, 1965, p. 201.
[51] Koopmans, *REStat* (1947); reprinted in Gordon and Klein, 1965, pp. 206–207.
[52] Koopmans, *REStat* (1947); reprinted in Gordon and Klein, 1965, pp. 215–216.

reported statistical significance of the NBER "Measurement without Theory" approach for the 1949–1977 period.[53]

4.2   Mr. Burns on Mr. Mitchell and the Progress on Business Cycle Research

Mr. Burns, in 1951, shortly after the passing of Mr. Mitchell, at a Conference of Business Cycles, and in the introduction to Mitchell on What Happens During Business Cycles (Burns, 1951) stated that Mr. Mitchell continued to ask "Does economic life actually proceed in recurrent fluctuations having similar characteristics?"; and if so, "What processes are continuous and brought about?" Mr. Burns stated that about 90% of the 800 economic time series in Burns and Mitchell (1946) moved with aggregate activity.

Business cycles are not merely fluctuations in aggregate economic activity, but are fluctuations are widely diffused over the economy within industries, its commercial dealings, and its tangles of finance. The economy of the western world is a system of closely interrelated parts. Understanding business cycles requires the student to understand capitalism itself; and the workings of an economic system organized largely in a network of free enterprises searching for profit. Business cycles are concerned with the entire system, including the formation and disappearance of firms, prices, output, employment, costs, and profits. Mr. Mitchell discussed the merchandising of securities as well as commodities, the money supply and its turnover, and the fiscal operations of government. True to his education (with Mr. Dewey), Mr. Mitchell sought to integrate the psychological, institutional, and technological aspects within business aggregates. He explored the obstacles to the mutual adjustment of economic quantities in a disturbed environment.[54]

---

[53] See Geoffrey H. Moore, *Business Cycles, Inflation, and Forecasting* (Cambridge, MA: Ballinger, 1983, The National Bureau of Economic of variables Research, Studies in Business Cycles, No. 24), pp. 369–393. Mr, Moore reported that the eight economic variables of the 1950 list of the Leading Group led the peaks of business peaks by 12 months during the 1948–1975 periods and led business cycle troughs by 2 months during the corresponding periods. The Leading Group correctly identified 89% of the turning peaks in peaks and (only) 71% of the turning points in troughs. Mr. Alan Auerbach reported that the components of the Index of Leading Indicators, IEI, reduced the root mean square forecasting errors RMSE) of the Federal Reserve Index of Industrial Production and the Unemployment Rate during the 1949–1977 period relative to not using the leading indicators. Alan J. Auerbach, 'The Index of Leading Indicators: "Measurement without Theory," Thirty-Five Years Later', *The Review of Economics and Statistics* 64 (1982), 589–595.

[54] Arthur F. Burns, *Mitchell on What Happens During Business Cycles* (New York: National Bureau of Economic Research, Inc. 1951), pp. 3–5. Mr. Burns wrote in his introduction to the *Business Cycles: The Problem and Its Setting*, the 1951 edition, that when Mr. Mitchell published in 1913, he anchored a theory of fluctuations to an array of empirical observations unprecedentedly full for its

Between 1927 and the appearance of *Measuring Business Cycles* in 1946, Mr. Mitchell sought to integrate numerous studies of special aspects of cyclical fluctuations by the NBER staff with his own and other investigators' results; and develop a model of business cycles from carefully screened observations, to use it in explaining how the cycles of experience are developed and how to account for the outstanding differences among them. Serious students of Mr. Mitchell will notice that orders for investment goods tend to lead the tides in aggregate activity, that private construction is more closely related to business cycles than public construction, that call money rates or even commercial paper rates greatly overstate the fluctuations in the rates of interest at which bank customers ordinarily borrow, and that interest rates in New York tend to move before non-New York City rates and more widely used. The student will also note that the number of business failures lags behind the liabilities, that bond prices tend to lead stock prices which themselves lead the turns in aggregate activity, that bank deposits appear to be comparatively steady during depressions, and that imports conform closely to business cycles while exports do not. Grocery sales fail to show the regular response to business cycles characteristic of retail trade at large, etc., and how peculiar the cyclical behavior of smaller sectors of activity can be. Business cycles are complex phenomena.[55]

Large as are the variations in the cyclical timing of economic processes, the differences in amplitude of fluctuation are more impressive still. In high grade bond yields, for example, rise and fall is typically only about 10 percent of their average value during a business cycle. On the other hand, stocks of industrial equipment are remarkably steady, expanding usually during contractions as well as expansions of business cycles. The amplitude of the index of wholesale prices, excluding war episodes, is nearly twice as large; the amplitude of factory employment four or five times as large, of machine tool orders over twenty times as large. The proportions among economic quantities keep changing over a business cycle. Business cycles charts must contain

---

time. World War I had ushered in a new era of economic statistics, able theorists were elaborating new hypotheses, and statistical analysts were rapidly fashioning new devices for disentangling economic movements. It was from this perspective that Mr. Mitchell launched in 1922 a fresh investigation of business cycles; hence, his *Business Cycles: The Problem and Its Setting*, the first major instalment of Mitchell's investigation, was published in 1927.

[55] Arthur F. Burns, *Mitchell on What Happens During Business Cycles* (New York: National Bureau of Economic Research, Inc. 1951), pp. 6–8. The reader recalls the comments of Mr. Milton Friedman, from Chapter 2, when he stated that although he appreciated the smooth, casual-sounding exposition of Mr. Mitchell's business cycle phases, he nevertheless thought numerous significant theoretical insights underlie the text. Milton Friedman, "The Economic Theorist", in *Wesley Clair Mitchell: The Economic Scientist*, Arthur Burns, Editor, New York: National Bureau of Economic Research, Inc. 1952), pp. 237–282. In fact, Mr. Friedman wrote an Appendix to develop his version of the mathematical business cycle underlying Mr. Mitchell's *Business Cycles* (1913), pp. 275–282.

numerous lines that indicate the wide differences among the rates at which, and also some of the differences in the times at which, various elements in the economy expand and contract. For, unless these divergencies in cyclical behavior can be identified, we have no suggestion of the basic business-cycle problem.[56] It is necessary to see how an economic system of interrelated parts develops internal stresses during expansions, stresses that bring on recessions, and how the uneven contractions of its varied parts pave the way for revivals.

Mr. Burns continued on Mr. Mitchell's observations on business cycles; from bottom of a depression production characteristically rises in the first segment of expansion Employment and money income rise, as do commodity prices, imports, domestic trade, security transactions. Most economic series rise except bond yields and bankruptcies. In the second stage the broad advance continues until bond market trading declines. Bond prices join bond sales in the next stage; in other words, long-term interest rates, which initially fell during the first half of expansion—begin to rise. Prosperity has reached its zenith. Share trading and stock prices move downward; the liabilities of business failures, which hitherto have been receding, move up again; security issues and construction contracts drop; the turnover of bank deposits slackens; and bank debits in New York City become smaller.[57] Eventually the liabilities of business failures begin declining, which signifies that the liquidation of distressed business firms has passed its worst phase. These favorable developments are reinforced when trading and prices revive; business incorporations, security issues, and construction contracts move upward; money begins to turn over more rapidly; even total money payments expand.

Before long the expansion spreads to production, employment, prices, money incomes, and domestic trade. This is already the initial stage of general expansion. The percentages suggest that the deviations from type are not so numerous as to destroy the value of a generalized sketch of business cycles. The check to the dominant movement of business activity, whether it be expansion or contraction, is investment expenditure activities.[58]

Mr. Burns makes observations in 1951 that will become the statements precede the Mr. Geoffrey Moore and Mr. Victor Zarnowitz analysis of postwar business cycles: The arrays of individual turning points at business-cycle troughs are more dispersed and skewed toward leads than are the arrays at peaks. (1) expansions of aggregate activity average longer than contractions; and (2) expansions are also more vigorous, so that the trough from which a given expansion starts is ordinarily above the level from which the

---

[56] Arthur F. Burns, *Mitchell on What Happens During Business Cycles*, p. 9.

[57] Arthur F. Burns, *Mitchell on What Happens During Business Cycles*, p. 10.

[58] Arthur F. Burns, *Mitchell on What Happens During Business Cycles*, p. 12.

preceding expansion started.[59] Mr. Burns further asserted that (1) in the first segment of expansion the rate of improvement is more rapid than at any other stage of the cycle; (2) a sharp and general retardation of the advance occurs in the second segment of the expansion; (3) the third stage of the expansion, the advance is slower than it was at the beginning of expansion; (4) in the final stage of expansion, the business tide becomes full of warnings signs. Contractions follow a different pattern. The fall accelerates somewhat in the second segment of contraction, whereas the rise is much retarded in the second segment of expansion. The third stage brings a moderate retardation of the decline, whereas it brought a moderate reacceleration of the advance. The closing stages of expansion and contraction are similar in that the rate of change becomes slower; but this retardation is more pronounced in a contraction than at the end of expansion.[60] Finally, Mr. Burns asserted that the notions often suggested by the picturesque phrasing beloved of writers upon "booms and busts"—that prosperity grows at a dizzier pace the longer it lasts, and that slumps gather momentum as they proceed—are wrong if the Burns and Mitchell measures are right.[61]

Mr. Burns presented a 26-variable set of time series characteristic of the "comprehensive" series during a business cycle. These series ranged from NYSE bonds sold, railroad bond issues, business failures, common stock issues, and prices to pig iron production, employment, corporate profits, to railroad bond yields. The charts presented by Mr. Burns included movements within the trough-to-peak to trough sub-periods, as presented in the specific-cycle charts and the percent of confirming movements within expansions and contractions. Mr. Burns, reported that the largest amplitude time series, the most volatile of the 26 comprehensive series, were net profits of business enterprises, and investing capital, producing investment goods, and trading in securities.[62]

With this analysis, Mr. Burns had completed the task of updating Mr. Mitchell's 1927 business cycle text.

Mr. Burns invited Mr. Jacob Marschak, of the Cowles Foundation and The University of Chicago, to comment on his writing.[63] Mr. Marschak, an

---

[59] Arthur F. Burns, *Mitchell on What Happens During Business Cycles*, p. 12–13.

[60] Ibid.

[61] Arthur F. Burns, *Mitchell on What Happens During Business Cycles*, pp. 14–15.

[62] Arthur F. Burns, *Mitchell on What Happens During Business Cycles*, p. 11.

[63] Mr. Marschak studied at the University of Berlin and the University of Heidelberg. He emigrated to England in the 1930s and taught at the Oxford Institute of Statistics. Mr. Marschak emigrated in 1940 to the U.S. After teaching at the New School for Social Research in New York City. In 1943 he went to University of Chicago where he led the Cowles Commission. He followed the commission's move to Yale University. In 1946, Mr. Marschak was President of the Econometric

eminent econometrician, and head of the Cowles Commission, challenged the statement by Mr. Burns and Mr. Mitchell on several statements and hypotheses.

First, Mr. Marschak addressed the statement by Mr. Burns and Mr. Mitchell that the business cycle consists of many economic time series having roughly concurrent fluctuations, and that their reference dates should mark the turning points of business cycles. Every period scored as an expansion should be a reference expansion, and every contractionary period should be stored as a reference contraction. Mr. Marschak asked "Is that is common to all economic variables has the following properties: (1) each interval lasts from 2 to 12 years and overlaps its successor by 3 months; (2) each interval contains, for each variable, exactly 3 turning points, of which 2 are near the ends of the interval; (3) the time lag between two nearest peaks (troughs) for any two variables retains its sign (+,−, 0) throughout the sequence of intervals; (4) this time lag is zero for a large proportion of pairs of variables. The style of Mitchell's presentation does not make it easy to discuss whether this translation is faithful."[64] Mr. Marschak wanted a mathematical statement on business cycles or a more complete definition of business cycles. To the author, Mr. Marschak implies that he wants to see a Davis (1937) time series model of business cycles to be estimated.

Second, in response to Mr. Mitchell and his need for using knowledge of human behavior and institutions, Mr. Marschak questioned whether he used it, or intended to use it, in the most efficient way. Mr. Marschak stated that after "a frankly mechanical, though time consuming, manipulation of the 800 observed series, he interprets the results—the lags, the comparative statistical estimates. Amplitudes—often to state that 'none of the findings seems surprising'" (Chapter 7). Mr. Marschak differentiated between economic identities and verifiable economic relationships, commenting that sometimes the check is performed on mere identities and is therefore essentially a check on the consistency of data as opposed to the empirical results were checked not against identities but against verifiable implications of plausible human behavior. Mr. Marschak stated that Mr. Mitchell genuinely underestimated the logical intricacy of the economic system. Mr. Marschak continued his comments with a butter and milk consumption example and its implied demand and supply curve.[65]

Society and later became an Honorary Fellow of the Royal Statistical Society and a Distinguished Fellow of the American Economic Association.

[64] Arthur F. Burns, *Mitchell on What Happens During Business Cycles*, pp. 15–16.

[65] Arthur F. Burns, *Mitchell on What Happens During Business Cycles*, p. 19.

In our case, for example, one sees the importance of bringing in additional time series, viz., butter and milk prices (their ratio should fall with rising income if the hypothesis is correct); one sees how the data on family budgets and the production records of dairies, both commercial and experimental, might be used. This is not all. If we succeed in formulating our findings in terms of numerically specified human responses, e.g., if the demands for milk and butter are expressed as numerical functions of Behavior of consumers at high total income.[66]

Third, Mr. Marschak questioned Mr. Mitchell's general attitude toward economic facts and policies. It seems to me that a wave pattern that can describe American business cycles at a time when public expenditures equaled a tenth of national income is unlikely to have much predictive value for a time when public expenditures equal a fifth or a fourth of national income; nor can it help to predict how a given change in public expenditures or wages might affect national income. Mr. Marschak continued that in his opinion, Mr. Mitchell, effects of changes in these or similar parameters appear negligible, and that Mr. Mitchell is not particularly concerned with how policies have affected or can affect the course of economic time series; nor is it clear how his analysis might help to answer such questions of economic efficiency in the real economy.[67]

The author takes issue with Mr. Marschak on the third comment, particularly one remembers the 1923 President Commission on business cycles and unemployment. Mr. Mitchell and Mr. Hoover, then Secretary of Commerce, made ten recommendations to enhance information to try to alleviate the suffering and inefficiency to society of unemployment. Mr. Joseph Schumpeter, while declaring Mr. Mitchell an institutional economist, Mr. Schumpeter said that the relationship between institutional economics and laissez-faire liberalism, was not relevant to Mr. Mitchell because his work with the Bureau of Labor Statistics, the War Industries Board of the First World War and the Presidential Commission on Unemployment, and President Hoover's Research Commission on Social Trends (1929–1933) noted the government and industry must work together to solve problems, often dealing with the issues of business fluctuations and cycles.[68]

Mr. Burns in his reply to Mr. Marschak first quoted the Mitchell definition of business cycles, as defined on p. 3 of *Measuring Business Cycles*, to address the definition of a business cycle. Furthermore, Mr. Burns discussed

---

[66] Arthur F. Burns, *Mitchell on What Happens During Business Cycles*, p. 20.

[67] Arthur F. Burns, *Mitchell on What Happens During Business Cycles*, p. 25.

[68] Joseph A. Schumpeter, "The General Economist", in *Wesley Clair Mitchell: The Economic Scientist*, Arthur F. Burns, Editor (New York: National Bureau of Economic Research, 1952), pp. 322–329.

the timing and agreement of lead and lags among economic variables in business fluctuations.[69] Mr. Burns addressed the issues of whether business cycles occurred in non-capitalist countries and are there consistencies in business cycles through U.S. history. Mr. Burns also asked if the NBER volumes of Mr. Mitchell added to the knowledge of business fluctuations and whether his findings could be properly tested.

To Mr. Burns, Mr. Marschak stated that a number of mechanisms could generate the phenomena set out in the business cycle definition, and he specifies a "mechanism" which he believes Mitchell had in mind. But Mr. Marschak is quite wrong in the hypothesis be attributes to Mitchell. Mr. Mitchell saw the essence of the business cycle in a systematic divergence of the movements of different parts of the economy, not in the movements of some composite curve. The notion that "there exists a variable (called 'general business activity') whose value at any point of time depends, apart from random influences, upon one or more of its preceding values" does not belong to Mitchell's universe of thought. Mr. Mitchell viewed each stage of the business situation as evolving into its successor, thus, the relations existing at any one time among the parts of our interdependent system shaped the general direction of activities at later times. Nor did Mitchell believe that, "apart from random influences, each observable economic variable is certain, possibly lagged function of the general business activity."[70]

Mr. Burns and Mr. Mitchell's *Measuring Business Cycles* points out that numerous activities, some of large significance, move independently of business cycle and most activities move in varying degrees of conformity with a reference scale of business cycles, and therefore with each other. To "general business activity." It simply means that the business cycle is a special kind of fluctuation in aggregate activity, rather than a "general business activity" index. Mr. Mitchell was interested in analyzing the diffusion of economic activities through the study of the economic variables. Mr. Burns stated that this study required tracing the causal relations among specific activities, and the National Bureau's elaborate statistical apparatus, the NBER reference scale of business cycles and the various measures of specific and reference cycles was devised to arrange facts so as to facilitate such inquiries. Mr. Burns commented that Mr. Marschak has not grasped this fact, laboring under the impression that Mr. believes that each economic variable bears to the "nebulous congeries"—general business activity.[71] Mr. Burns stated that there was no "general business activity" index has been constructed or

[69] Ibid.
[70] Arthur F. Burns, *Mitchell on What Happens During Business Cycles*, pp. 25–26.
[71] Arthur F. Burns, *Mitchell on What Happens During Business Cycles*, pp. 27.

has there been any such design or any such statistical construction in the National Bureau's scheme. Finally, Mr. Burns countered Mr. Marschak on estimating supply and demand functions on commodities such as butter and milk, commenting:

> As far as I can see, Marschak's principal complaint here is that Mitchell has not worked out numerous demand and supply schedules. Marschak writes with enthusiasm of what could be accomplished with these schedules: "If the system of economic relationships valid under old institutions and technologies was properly estimated, and if the assumed change in institution or technology is well defined, the resulting change in the prices and quantities can be estimated in advance." It is easy to agree with Marschak that if Mitchell had attained results of this character, his work would be much more significant than it is. But I do not think it would be easy to supply concrete instances of outstanding success in Marschak's direction by others. Marschak is describing a goal that may be attained someday, not one that has already been reached.[72]

4.3   Summary and Conclusions of the Mr. Burns and Mr. Mitchell Business Cycle Research

Mr. Burns and Mr. Mitchell built upon the initial Mitchell volumes on business cycles (1913, 1923, and 1927), to develop a framework to analyze 800 monthly series of economic data relative to their specific cycles, reference cycles, and amplitude and confirmatory movements within expansions and contractions. The Burns and Mitchell Measuring Business Cycles is a seminal treatment of economic variables with business cycles. Mr. Moore builds upon the Burns and Mitchell framework and pushes forward lists of the leading economic time series. We will discuss Mr. Auerbach will statistically verify the predictive power of the Burns and Mitchell and Moore LEI during 1949–1977 in Chapter 5 and verify the LEI for the 1959–2020 period in Chapter 7.

References

Auerbach, A. J. (1982). Measurement without theory: Thirty-five years late. *The Review of Economics and Statistics, 64*, 589–595.

---

[72] Arthur F. Burns, *Mitchell on What Happens During Business Cycles*, p. 30.

Burns, A. F. (1951). *Mitchell on what happens during business cycles*. National Bureau of Economic Research, Inc.

Burns, A. F., & Mitchell, W. C. (1946). *Measuring business cycles*. National Bureau of Economic Research, Inc.

Clark, J. M. (2017). Business acceleration and the law of demand: A technical factor in economic cycles. *Journal of Political Economy, 25*, 217–235.

Davis, H. T. (1941). *The analysis of economic time series*. The Principia Press of Trinity University. A Revised Edition of the original 1937 text.

Mitchell, W. C., & Gay, E. F. (1927). *Business cycles: The problem and its setting* (Vol. 1). National Bureau of Economic Research New York.

5

Mr. Geoffrey Moore and NBER Business Cycle Research

Wesley Clair Mitchell passed in 1948 shortly after the publication of Burns and Mitchell's *Measuring Business Cycles* appeared in print. The book created great discussion and debate as we noted in the previous chapter. In 1961, Mr. Geoffrey H. Moore edited The NBER two-volume monograph *Business Cycle Indicator*. The Moore NBER volumes, the tenth of the NBER Studies in Business Cycles series, was a significant contribution to the business cycle literature. Mr. Moore would make remarkable and substantial contributions for over 30 years to NBER business cycle research.[1] The *Business Cycle Indicators* first volume contained a set of papers written during the past 5–15 years on current business conditions and indicators. The volume featured articles by Arthur Burns, the second NBER Director of Research, Thor Hultgren, the author of an NBER monograph on American transportation during business cycles and many (seven) articles by Mr. Moore, and several by Victor Zarnowitz, who would do joint esearch with Mr. Moore until his passing. Mr. Zarnowitz and his research will be the subject of the next chapter.

---

[1] In 1991, Mr. Moore was Director of the Center for International Business Cycle research at the Graduate School of Business, Columbia University. He was Director-at-Large at the NBER and a National Bureau staff member from 1939–1979, later serving as Director-Emeritus. Mr. Moore was Commissioner of Labour Statistics from 1969 to 1973. A graduate of Rutgers, Mr. Moore earned his Ph.D. from Harvard University. See Pami Dua, *Business Cycles and Economic Growth: An Analysis Using Leading Indicators* (Oxford: Oxford University Press, 2004), a collection of LEI studies dedicated to Mr. Moore.

© The Author(s), under exclusive license to Springer Nature Switzerland AG 2022
J. B. Guerard, *The Leading Economic Indicators and Business Cycles in the United States*, https://doi.org/10.1007/978-3-030-99418-1_5

5.1   Mr. Moore and his *Business Cycles Indicators* (1961)

Mr. Moore edited a two-volume set of collected NBER studies of the 1938–1960 period under the title, *Business Cycle Indicators: Contributions to the Analysis of Current Business Conditions* (Princeton, NJ: Princeton University Press, a study by the National Bureau of Economic Research, 1961). Hereafter, we will refer to this volume as Moore, BCI, 1961. Mr. More suggested that the reader read the articles chapter-by-chapter to grasp the depth of NBER research over a 20-year span. Mr. Moore discussed why he included the ten essays of Part One on the selection, testing, and interpretation of business cycle indicators. These essays showed how NBER conducted its research to develop its indicators and underline of importance of continuing the program if further progress is to be made.[2] Part One of the first volume contained chapters written by Mr. Solomon Fabricant, Mr. Arthur F. Burns, several by Mr. Moore, and a reprint of May 28, 1938, NBER Bulletin 69, "Statistical Indicators of Revivals," by Mr. Wesley Clair Mitchell and Mr. Arthur F. Burns. Mr. Mitchell and Mr. Burns proposed a set of 71 series and how they lead or lagged business cycle revivals. These time series were among the 487 time series discussed in the previous chapter in the Burns and Mitchell *Measuring Business Cycles* (1946). Part Two of the first volume contained several essays on behavior of particular types or related groups of indicators. These studies supported the types of indicators discussed in Part One.[3] The book Mr. Moore explained, did no more than explore one or two approaches to the problem of business forecasting.[4] Parts Two and Three essays provided information on three port-World War II business cycles, 1946–1949, 1949–1959, and 1954–1958. The second volume provided the actual data used in the essays. This is an enormous gift to researchers and practitioners, even if typing of the data is required!

In 1950, Mr. Arthur Burns was writing about completing the Wesley Mitchell book, *What Happens during Business Cycles* and examining the 97% of the 600-time series modeled in the Burns-Mitchell (1946) monograph that had undergone cyclical movements. The distribution of turning points peaked in 1920, 1923, 1929, 1932, and 1936–1937 for the economic time series analyzed during the 1919–1939 time period. Mr. Burns noted that few readers could be so naive to believe that most economic activities reach

---

[2] Moore, *Business Cycle Indicators: Contributions to the Analysis of Current Business Conditions, BCI,* p. xxiv.

[3] Ibid.

[4] Moore, *BCI,* p. xxix.

like turns at the same time and there was a wide dispersion of cyclical peaks and troughs.[5] Burns quoted Mr. Mitchell's observation that business cycles consist of numerous contractions in an expansionary period and numerous expansions in a predominately contraction period.[6] Indeed, there are numerous expansions and contractions within the sustained expansionary and contractionary periods.

If the economic activity is depressed and moderate spending, by either the government, business firms, or consumers pick up, then the enhanced spending can spur industries depending on their capacity, generating increases in incomes, both of men employed and the number of hours worked.

The impact of consumer spending may be spotty and may not drive an overall expansion. Will there need to be new construction activities and will construction projects be longer term in nature? As Mr. Mitchell stated in his 1913 text discussed in the previous chapter, a business recession starts while aggregate activity is increasing, and recovery starts while aggregate activity is still contracting. Second, recession or recovery spreads slowly over the economic system. Mr. Burns lists the 26 "Comprehensive" series during a business cycle that Mr. Mitchell identified and listed the series typical directions of secondary movements in periods of expansion and contraction. That is, in Table 2.1, Mr. Burns listed the sign of the series movements over the three troughs of an expansion period and the time series movements during the three peaks of a contractionary period.[7] Mr. Burns furthermore listed the percent of conforming movements during the stages when the series is said to rise or fall, and the amplitude of the movements during the stages when the series is said to rise or fall. It should be necessary for the reader for several examples to be presented. Common stock prices (and shares sold) rise in the first and to be presented. Common stock prices (and shares sold) rise in the first and middle troughs of an expansionary period.

Stock prices fall in the final stage of an expansion and fall in the first and middle stages of peaks within a contractionary period. Stock prices rise 94% of the stage when the series rise and fall to 82% of the stages when stock prices are said to fall. Stock prices rise 26.8% when stock prices are said to

---

[5] Moore, *BCI*, p.15. I am citing the page number od the essay in the Moore (1961) book, rather than the traditional author, book type to save the reader from additional irritation of seeing 5–8 essays cited. This is a monograph for practitioners. The Moore book could be purchased for $16.28 on January 22, 2022, on www.alibris.com.
  https://www.alibris.com/Business-Cycle-Indicators-Geoffrey-H-Moore/book/861052?matches=7.

[6] Moore, *BCI*, p.18. The manuscript itself was Arthur F. Bruns, "New Facts on Business Cycles", with minor revisions, originally published in in *Thirtieth Annual Report of the National Bureau of Economic Research*, May 1950, pp. 3–31.

[7] Moore, *BCI*, p. 28.

be rising and fall 20.2% when stock prices are said to be falling. New York City bank clearing has similar phases of the business cycle, as do stock prices, but have 100% confirming movements where when the series is rising and 89% confirming movements when the bank clearing at said to be falling. The respective amplitudes of movements are 30.8 and 26.6 in rising and falling series. Corporate profits rise from all troughs in an expansion and fall from all peaks in a contraction. The 100% confirming movements when the series is said to be rising or falling are associated with the greatest amplifier of any economic time comprehensive series as profits rise 168.8% when profits rise, and fall 174.6% when profits are said to fall. Department store sales follow the identical phases of the business cycle as corporate profits and yet the corresponding amplitudes are 17.6 and 9.1, respectively.[8]

The greatest amplitude following corporate profits is pig iron production, 54.2 and 44.9, respectively, and the corporate security issues previously discussed. The lowest amplitude among the 26 comprehensive time series is railroad bond yields, which rise in the middle to last stage of expansions and fall during most stages of contractions with 74% conforming movements when the time series is rising and 65% conforming movements when railroad bond yields are falling. The corresponding amplitudes are 3.7 and 6.2, respectively.[9]

Mr. Burns states that at the bottom of a depression, productivity rises in the first segment of the expansion, as do employment and income and so do imports, domestic trade, commodity prices, and security transactions. In the second stage of the recovery, the general economic activity rises and the bond market starts to decline in trading. Bond price and bond sales decline in the third stage and long-term interest rates start to rise. In the final stage of an expansion, the financial sector declines; stock prices and trading decline, business failure liabilities start to rise; construction contracts fall and bank deposits turnover falls and New York City bank clearings become smaller. Production, employment, prices, incomes, and corporate profits decline. Business failure liabilities and interest rates rise. By the middle of the contraction, bond sales and prices rise and the liabilities of business failures start to fall. Share trading and prices revive, business incorporation, security issues, and construction contracts move upward. Before long, Mr. Burns reminds us, production, employment incomes, and trade increase. The initial stage of general expansion has started. The reader is immediately reminded of the Mitchell Business Cycle phases of his 1913 book. As bond yields decline,

---

[8] Moore, *BCI*, p. 28.
[9] Ibid.

stock prices rise for stronger firms.[10] Mr. Burns specifically addresses the cyclical behavior of corporate profits. An initial look appears to lead the reader that profits tend to continue prosperity and depression until the end of the phases. Mr. Burns quotes Thor Hultgren who observed that the proportion and firms experiencing an expansion of profits begin to decline before the peak of economic activity and increase long before the trough. Profits foreshadow, or lead, economic activity.[11] In prosperity, unit (labor) costs rise, and profit margins start to fall (narrow). The squeeze on profit becomes more widespread as the business expansions continue. Secondly, increasing optimism leads to forecast errors in judgment.

Aggregate profits are rising, but the proportion of firms generating profits begins to decline. Mr. Burns highlighted corporate profits because of their extraordinary wide fluctuations, as noted previously in their respective amplitudes when profits are rising and falling (M, p. 33).[12] Mr. Burns dutifully notes that the very time series that wondered underlie his observation have such great variability in their respective duration, in their relative lengths of business cycle phases, and their respective amplitudes, that contractions like 1929–1933 can be long in duration and deep in magnitude while other contractions, like 1926–1927, can be mild and brief. Mr. Burns held that it is vital to recognize the dynamic changes in economic organization and the random and episodic factors that make each business cycle unique.[13] Mr. Burns hoped that his findings enhance knowledge of business cycles and may be helpful in predicting reversals in the direction of economic activity, i.e., business turning points.[14]

In 1937, the NBER recognized 21 indicators of cyclical revivals, with 7 leading series, leading economic activity by 4.2 to 7.8 months. These series included the Dow Jones Industrial Average stock prices, liabilities of business failures, innertube production, railroad operating income, paper production, non-New York City bank clearings, and residual building floor space contracts. The 14 remaining series had shorter leads or lags and included steel ingot production pig iron production, wholesale prices, FRB industrial production, factory employment, departments store sales, and ton–miles of railroad freight.[15]

---

[10] Moore, *BCI*, pp. 28–29.
[11] Moore, *BCI*, p. 32.
[12] Moore, *BCI*, p. 33.
[13] Moore, *BCI*, p. 34.
[14] Ibid.
[15] Moore, *BCI*, p. 43.

Moore returned to Arthur Burns' position that a large group of time series could be summarized by its distribution of peaks and troughs and the percentage of series expanding. These series appear to have merit for identifying business cycles. Mr. Mitchell and Mr. Burns did not regard this list of indicators as a forecasting machine, but as a "registering device" to interpret the general drift of business fluctuations.[16] The list of indicators requires judgment, facing these data with real-world complexities and their uncertainties, as noted previously with their volatilities.[17] The question addressed is, what series have been reliable indicators of cyclical revivals and recessions?

Mitchell and Burns stated several disclaimers: first that the reference dates, the dates of cyclical peaks, may not be correct and not all turning points may be correctly identified. Secondly, there may be issues in the original data and in perfect seasonal variation modeling.[18] The data of the 71 series, out of the original 487 time series, were the best judgments that could be formed on the statistical evidence. While most contractions lasted between ten to fourteen months, the long contraction of the 1870s of 65 months, discussed in Chapter 1, and the "Great Depression" of 1929–1933 lasted 45 months. Mr. Mitchell and Mr. Burns could not forecast the end date for the recession occurring when they wrote their May 1938 NBER report.[19]

Mr. Mitchell and Mr. Burns listed their requirements for an ideal statistical indicator of cyclical revivals and recessions.

1. The modeling period should cover 50 years or longer under a variety of conditions;
2. The series should lead cyclical revival centers by a 3- to 6-month time interval. Six months is preferred, and the lead time should be in variant;
3. The time series should sweep smoothly upward from each trough and sweep smoothing downward from each peak, showing no erratic movements;
4. The time series movements should be pronounced and recognizable, and its relative amplitude should be consistent;

---

[16] Moore, *BCI*, p. 162. Wesley Clair Mitchell and Arthur F. Burns, "Statistical Indicators of Cyclical Revivals", in Geoffrey H. Moore, Editor, *Business Cycle Indicators: Contributions to the Analysis of Current Business Conditions* (Princeton, NJ: Princeton University Press, a study by the National Bureau of Economic Research, 1961), pp. 162–183.

[17] Moore, *BCI*, pp. 162–163.

[18] Moore, *BCI*, pp. 163.

[19] Moore, *BCI*, pp. 165–167.

5. The time series should be related to general business activity such that it establishes confidence that its past behavior in business cycles will be as its past behavior.[20]

Mitchell and Burns identified 71 time series of revivals and recessions, and 49 that led to two-thirds of the business revivals that occurred within the months covered by the data, many 1919–1932. The average lead or lag time refers to the average timing of the specific-cycle revivals in each series relative to the reference dates of the business cycle revivals.

The most useful indicators of business cycle revivals met the following criteria:

1. Longer average leads at past revivals;
2. These lead times were uniform in occurrence and length;
3. The closer its specific cycles came to a one-to-one correspondence to business cycles;
4. Specific cycles were loosely defined;
5. Less intense is its erratic movements in comparison with amplitudes at specific cycles;
6. Fewer changes in monthly directions;
7. Fewer seasonal effects;
8. The larger the number of past revivals covered by the time series;
9. The more distant irregularities in conformity to business cycle revivals occurred;
10. The broader the range of activities; and
11. The more stable the economic significance of the process is represented.

The best revival indicators, based on average lead in 1938, were

1. Total Liabilities of Business Failures (9 months average lead);
2. Dow Jones Industrial Average Stock Prices (7 months),;
3. Passenger car production (6 months);
4. Inner Tube Production (6 monthss);
5. Total Railroad Operating Income (5 months);
6. Total, Paper Production (5 months);
7. Truck Production (5 months);
8. Ton–Miles of Freight Hauled (4 months);
9. Wholesale prices (4 months); and

---

[20] Moore, *BCI*, pp. 165–166.

10. Index of Industrial Production and the Pig Iron Production (3 months).[21]

Mr. Mitchell and Mr. Burns reminded the reader that cyclical depressions can contain "double bottoms" as was in case in July 1932 and March 1933. Many of the Mitchell-Burns' leading indicators failed in the fall of 1932, pointing upward in an aborted 1932 upturn (Moore, 1961, pp.182–183).[22]

Mr. Moore, in 1950, listed seven series as leading indicators for reference-cycle patterns of 1919–1938. These time series were (1) residential building contracts, floor space, (2) the FRB industrial production index, (3) railroad locomotive shipments, (4) liabilities of business failures, (5) refined copper stocks, (6) NYSE bond sales, and (7) agricultural marketing index (Moore, 1961, pp.192–193). Mr. Moore viewed corporate profits over the 1919–1938 period as a coincidental indicator, at troughs. Mr. Moore reports that three times as many time series lead than lag, stating that it is easier to identify indicators of revivals than recessions.[23]

In judging the recession of 1948–49, Mr. Moore identified the leading indicators as: (1) Commercial and industrial building contracts, (2) residual building Contracts, (3) new incorporations, (4) industrial stock prices, (5) basic commodity price index, and (6) durable goods new order. The coincident group was composed of (1) freight car loadings, (2) unemployment, (3) corporate profits, (4) Gross National Product (GNP), (5) wholesale prices, (6) nonagricultural employment, (7) bank clearings outside of New York City, and (8) the industrial production index. The Lagging group included (1) retail sales, personal income, and manufacturing inventories.[24] Thus, Mr. Moore and the NBER established the Leading Group of economic indicators, now known as the Leading Economic Indicators, or LEI.

---

[21] Moore, *BCI*, pp. 172–174.

[22] Moore, *BCI*, pp. 182–183.

[23] Moore, *BCI*, pp. 215–217. Geoffrey H. Moore, "Statistical Indicators Of Cyclical Revivals and Recessions", in Geoffrey H. Moore, Editor, *Business Cycle Indicators: Contributions to the Analysis of Current Business Conditions* (Princeton, NJ: Princeton University Press, a study by the National Bureau of Economic Research, 1961), pp. 184–260.

[24] Moore, *BCI*, pp. 256.

5.2   Mr. Moore and his *Business Cycles, Inflation, and Forecasting* (1983)

What is a recession? How severe were they in the initial postwar period? Recessions are contractionary periods.[25] Contractions reflect a fall in aggregate economic activity, as we discussed in Chapter 1. The fall in economic activity, such as manufacturing output, corporate profits, and the slowing down of growth, is not sufficient to qualify as a contractionary period, Mr. Moore used three kinds of historical comparisons for determining contractions; the first is the duration of the contraction in aggregate economic activity, similar to previous contractions. Second, the depth of the contraction, the similar decreases in economic activities, such as measures of real GNP, industrial production, employment, and unemployment, to previous contractions must be reported. Third, a set of diffusion indexes is constructed to report the movement among different sectors and industries are compared to previous contractions.[26] One then estimates the peak of the business cycle. One seeks to estimate the month when aggregate economic activity reached its maximum level (and the general contraction began).[27] Mr. Moore discussed using seasonally adjusted data to determine aggregate activity, referring to these series as the NBER "roughly coincident indicators". These data included current and constant dollar GDP, total business sales, the index of industrial production, the unemployment rate, personal income, and bank debits outside New York City.[28] Thus, one must reach a consensus based on the dimensions of economic contractions discussed above.

5.3   What is a Recession?

In June 1980, the NBER Committee on Business Cycle Dating issued a statement identifying January 1980 as the latest peak of business activity, although real GNP had not peaked, and continued to increase in 1980Q1. What information was the NBER Committee using for its decisions? The reader will remember that we discussed in Chapter 4 the Burns and Mitchell *Measuring Business Cycles* NBER (1946) monograph, the Mitchell and Burns (1938) list of 71 time series that were consistent in economic recoveries and the best

---

[25] Geoffrey H. Moore, *Business Cycles, Inflation, and Forecasting* (Cambridge, MA: Ballinger Publishing Company, for the National Bureau of Economic Research, Inc., 1983), p. 3.

[26] Moore, *Business Cycles, Inflation, and Forecasting*, pp. 5–6.

[27] Moore, *Business Cycles, Inflation, and Forecasting*, p. 7.

[28] Ibid.

subset of 21 "most trustworthy" indicators. Mr. Burns and Mr. Moore created the Leading Economic Indicators, LEI, lead economic activity. That is, the LEI should precede economic activity, such as real GNP, unemployment, and industrial production. The LEI analysis concentrated on which variables were recommended when forecasting the economy. The NBER LEI components of 1950, 1960, 1966, and 1975 had been developed. These lists were prepared by Mr. Moore (1950 and 1960), Mr. Moore and Shinkin (1966), and Mr. Zarnowitz and Boschan (1975).[29] Is there consistency among the lists? Yes, and no. The average workweek of production current dollars of workers in manufacturing is the only variable included in all five LEI lists. New orders time series makes all five lists; new orders in durable goods are the 1950, 1960, and 1966 components whereas new orders in consumer goods and materials, in constant dollars, are the LEI component on the 1975 list. Stock prices are included in all lists, but the Dow Jones Industrial Average is the stock price time series in the 1950 list, whereas the Standard and Poor's 500 stock price index is included in the 1960, 1966, and 1975 LEI lists. The money supply is present on two lists, with M1, in constant dollars, on the 1975 list. Several economic time series make two lists: the layoff rate in manufacturing (1960 and 1975); corporate profits after taxes, in current dollars, and current liabilities of business failures are among the LEI components on the 1950 and 1960 lists; and building permits for new private housing, and contracts and orders for plant and equipment, in constant dollars, are among the LEI component on the 1975 list. The year 1979 was one of very little growth and the NBER monthly indicators of macroeconomic activity declined in early 1980. Based on the data available through April 1980, January 1980 was declared the peak of the cycle. The Federal Reserve Bank softened and shortly thereafter eliminated credit controls and private borrowing increased quickly and strongly and falling interest rates improved consumer expectations. The recessionary trough was reached in May 1980; it was a short-lived recession. The monetary growth exploded in the summer and fall of 1980, driving interest rates above 20 percent.[30] The recession of 1980 was very mild, particularly in its impact on unemployment, primarily due to the growing importance of services industries, thought to be more recession-proof than manufacturing industries.[31] Mr. Moore wrote in March 1981 that the most available data suggested that July 1980, was the through of business activity and that real GNP would have declined for only one quarter. Mr. Moore stressed that the NBER, "for good reasons, never

[29] Zarnowitz, *Business Cycles*, pp. 334–336.
[30] Moore, *Business Cycles, Inflation, and Forecasting*, pp. 12–17.
[31] Moore, *Business Cycles, Inflation, and Forecasting*, pp. 16–17.

agreed with the popular notion that a recession requires as a minimum two consecutive quarterly declines in real GNP"![32] Furthermore, the recession of 1980 may have have had the dimensions of business cycle contractions discussed previously, notable duration. The reader is left with the thought that the declaration of a recession in 1980, coinciding with a political election in November 1980, might not be so coincidental. Mr. Moore stated his definition of a recession, which is total output, income, employment, and trade declined from six months to a year and is marked by widespread contractions in many sectors of the economy.[33]

Between 1834 and 1980, the 34 official NBER recessions averaged 19 months and the recessions of 1873–1879, lasting 65 months, and August 1929–March 1933, lasting 43 months were the longest. The shortest recession was January–July 1980, lasting six months. In his analysis of recessions and depressions of 1920–1982, Mr. Moore listed the Great Depression (1933), two major depressions (1921 and 1938), five sharp recessions (1924, 1949, 1954, 1958, and 1975), and five mild recessions (1927, 1945, 1961, 1970, and 1980).[34]

5.3.1 Mr. Moore and His Leading Group Indicators

Mr. Moore created the first Leading, Roughly Coincidental, and Lagging Groups of economic variables in 1950.[35] These eight Leading Group variables were:

1. Liabilities of business failures;
2. Dow Jones Index of industrial common stock prices;
3. New orders, durable goods;
4. Residential building contracts, floor space;
5. Commercial and industrial building contracts, floor space;
6. Average workweek, manufacturing;
7. New incorporations;

---

[32] Moore, *Business Cycles, Inflation, and Forecasting*, p. 16.

[33] Moore, *Business Cycles, Inflation, and Forecasting*, p. 19.

[34] Moore, *Business Cycles, Inflation, and Forecasting*, p. 21.

[35] Geoffrey H. Moore, *Statistical Indicators of Cyclical Revivals and Recessions*, Occasional Paper 31. New York: National Bureau of Economic Research, 1950, Table 12. Reprinted in Moore, *Business Cycles, Inflation, and Forecasting*, p. 374. The new incorporations variable was added to the leading list reflecting research of Mr. Victor Zarnowitz. See Victor Zarnowitz, "Cyclical Aspects of Incorporations and the Formation of New Business Enterprises", in Geoffrey H. Moore, Editor, *Business Cycle Indicators: Contributions to the Analysis of Current Business Conditions* (Princeton, NJ: Princeton University Press, a study by the National Bureau of Economic Research, 1961), pp. 162–183.

8. Wholesale price index, 28 basic commodities.

The eight Roughly Coincidental Group variables were:

1. Employment in nonagricultural establishments;
2. Unemployment;
3. Corporate profits after taxes
4. Bank debits outside of New York City;
5. Freight car loadings;
6. Industrial production price index, industrial commodities.

The five Lagging Group variables were:

1. Personal income;
2. Retail sales;
3. Consumer installment debt;
4. Bank rates on business loans;
5. Manufacturers' inventories, book value.

The Leading Group of indicators of 1950 led the peaks of business cycles by 15 months (the peak of November 1948), 13 months (the peak of July 1953), 9 months (the peak of April 1960), 8 months (the peak of 1969), and 6 months (the peak of November 1973), for an average lead time of 12 months during the 1948–1975 period. The Leading Group of 1950 indictors led the troughs by only 2 months during the 1948–1975 period. This is impressive.[36]Mr. Moore stated that the 12 indicators used by the Department of Commerce in 1978 had turned down before each business cycle peak and had risen before every business trough since 1948. Moreover, the 142 peaks and troughs of the 12 variables led to the business cycle peaks and troughs in 92 percent of the instances between 1948 and 1975.[37] The Lagging Group of 1950 indicators lagged peaks by 3 months and troughs by 4 months. Mr. Moore stated three conclusions: (1) the systematic consequences in the movements of different economic variables had persisted over many years of business cycles, but the changes in the way the economy worked were of such a complex nature that the riddle of the business cycle had not been solved; and (2) the tests of the ability to identify turning points revealed the Leading Group was the most sensitive to timing and skipped more cycles, registering a turning point when no business cycle turn occurred; and (3) the

---

[36] Moore, *Business Cycles, Inflation, and Forecasting*, p. 340.
[37] Ibid.

"quality" of the indicators deteriorated during the 1948–1975 period.[38] The leading indicators led to new private housing starts, residential fixed investment, contracts and orders of plant and equipment, business construction expenditures, the average workweek, the S&P 500 stock prices, and industrial production during the 1967–1977 period.[39]

5.3.2 Unemployment

The average workweek has been a leading indicator since 1937 in a study by Mr. Burns and Mr. Mitchell. Recessions and recoveries do not affect all aspects of the labor market at the same time. The average workweek has been a leading indicator on every composite NBER Leading Economic Indicator constructed.[40] It is cheaper for employers to change the length of the workweek, including paying overtime, than change the number of employees. Furthermore, the number of people unemployed for fifteen weeks or more will lag the turns in the number of persons unemployed by the time lag.[41] The average workweek variable leads employment turns by 1–6 months and unemployment turns by 2 to 11 months.[42]

5.3.3 The Money Supply and Stock Prices

Monetary economists since Irving Fisher (1911) and R.G. Hawtrey (1913) held that changes in the money supply stimulated economic activity. In more recent times, Friedman and Schwartz (1963), Sprinkel (1963, 1964), and Abdullah and Rangazas (1988) reported that changes in the money supply lead to economic activity. In Chapter 7 of his *Business Cycles, Inflation, and Forecasting*, Mr. Moore discussed stock prices and business cycles. In general, the level of stock prices at the peak of the boom was higher than at the bottom of the business cycle contractions.[43] This relationship does not guarantee that the knowledge of business cycle turns does not allow an investor to forecast significant downturns in stock prices.[44] Significant stock market declines

---

[38] Moore, *Business Cycles, Inflation, and Forecasting*, pp. 375–383.

[39] Moore, *Business Cycles, Inflation, and Forecasting*, pp. 343–345.

[40] Moore, *Business Cycles, Inflation, and Forecasting*, p. 105.

[41] See Phoebus Dhrymes, *Introductory Econometrics* (New York: Springer, 2017, Revised Edition) for an LEI analysis of unemployment using the fifteen weeks data.

[42] Moore, *Business Cycles, Inflation, and Forecasting*, pp. 105–107.

[43] Moore, *Business Cycles, Inflation, and Forecasting*, p. 143–144.

[44] Moore, *Business Cycles, Inflation, and Forecasting*, p. 143.

in 1962 and 1966 were not associated with business cycle contractions.[45] Stock market returns, as measured by the S&P 500 Index, were + 35% in expansions and + 4% in contractions associated with business cycle peaks, 1948–1970.[46] Stock prices decline faster than business activity and recover earlier than business activity, as a whole. In King's English, stock prices are and have been on the NBER lists of LEI since 1950, and, as the reader remembers from Chapter 3, stock prices were a variable in the economic barometer of Mr. Persons.

We test and report time series modeling and forecasting results to support the particular aspect of the Sprinkel findings that changes in the money supply provide liquidity to drive up stock prices. Why is this question interesting at this point in time? In the midst of the current pandemic, the money supply has increased to accommodate government relief while maintaining very low interest rates. The stock market has behaved in the manner as the readers of Friedman and Schwartz and Sprinkel would have expected. The positive relationship between the money supply and stock prices is verified for February 1964 to September 2020 time period. In this replication case study, we apply the Hendry and Doornik automatic time series PCGive (AutoMetrics) methodology to the money supply and stock price series. The Autometrics system substantially reduces the regression sum of squares measures relative to traditional variations on the random walk with drift model. The reader is referred to the Appendix on regression, time series modeling, and causality testing of the Book. Our results are greatly supportive of the significance of the money supply leading stock prices during the 1963 to 2020 time period.

We report statistically significant saturation variables in these data, 1964 to the present, as tested in September 2020. We tested univariate and bivariate models using the money supply and report highly significant forecast error reductions. Our chapter supports the continued statistical significance of the money supply in leading stock prices.

Our data is downloaded from The Conference Board Leading Economic Indicators database, monthly from February 1964 to September 2020. An ARIMA (1, 1, 0) model is cursory estimated as an illustration. In Table 5.1 that follows (we use a table to illustrate the results so that the reader can view the relevant statistics), we present the initial results for the simple AR(1) model for the S&P 500 Index and another one from the application of Autometrics (model I) using many indicator variables that capture such structural breaks. Note the implications for residual diagnostics, as the

---

[45] Ibid.

[46] Moore, *Business Cycles, Inflation, and Forecasting*, pp 143–146.

Table 5.1 Estimated *Autometrics* Time Series Model of Stock Prices, 1991–September 2020

	Coefficients	t-SE	t-HACSE	t-HCSE
DLSP500_1	0.11694	2.9750	2.3062	2.3165
Constant	0.0070803	4.6671	5.0326	4.3405
DLM1_2	0.39352	3.2009	3.8762	**3.9706**
I:326	0.099873	4.0409	63.673	55.410
I:401	0.086133	3.4733	33.759	28.559
I:416	−0.084526	−3.4137	−34.180	−37.136
I:419	0.093065	3.7671	72.977	66.544
I:431	0.063161	2.5535	36.242	30.385
I:442	−0.059054	−2.3874	−34.599	−28.979
I:447	−0.10367	−4.1910	−48.967	−45.977
I:453	−0.12952	−5.2340	−57.727	−56.661
I:462	−0.063800	−2.5747	−27.628	−23.202
I:463	−0.11592	−4.6627	−30.843	−28.802
I:465	−0.060412	−2.4454	−48.350	−43.620
I:470	−0.077276	−3.1270	−51.671	−47.693
I:529	−0.076502	−3.0924	−44.133	−41.940
I:535	−0.066975	−2.7011	−22.732	−20.699
I:538	−0.22533	−9.0585	−70.220	−59.604
I:539	−0.088073	−3.2900	−6.4461	−6.8578
I:542	−0.099748	−3.9108	−17.390	−18.714
I:544	0.11754	4.7177	32.424	27.893
I:548	0.057785	2.3275	25.299	25.150
I:557	−0.076628	−3.0982	−40.893	−40.655
I:572	−0.12565	−5.0828	−82.489	**−78.360**
I:675	−0.21843	−8.8379	−153.30	−132.09

ARCH 1–1 test: F(1,355) = 0.0011669 [0.9728]
Normality test: Chi^ 2(2) = 4.7880 [0.0913]
Hetero test: F(4,330) = 2.4100 [0.0491]*
RESET23 test: F(2,330) = 2.6486 [0.0723]

inclusion of the indicator functions makes the model congruent and consistent with the assumptions behind the *general-to-specific* approach, discussed in the Appendix on regression, time series, and casual modelling following Chapter 11. The results are highly illustrative. First, as expected, a simple AR(1) model simply produces the well-known result that the first differencing of the series is suggested and that anything else that remains after differencing must be modelled separately.

We calculated a partial autocorrelation function for the S&P 500 Index during 1964 to 1990 and its calculated coefficients indicated that an AR(3) process could be estimated for the 1991 to September 2020 time period. An estimated cross-correlogram function for SP500 Index and M1 indicated

Table 5.2 Performance Summary for Models for levels of the S&P 500 Index and the Money Supply, M1, 1991–2020

Estimated Model	RSS	ARCH (p-value)	Normality (p-value)	Heteroscedasticity (p-value)
AR(1)	0.459	0.000	0.000	0.053
AR(1) with Large Residuals	0.295	0.000	0.001	0.002
AR(3)	0.456	0.130	0.000	0.108
AR(3) with Large Residuals	0.308	0.130	0.002	0.000
AR(3) and lagged M1	0.202	0.973	0.091	0.049

that six periods of lags of M1 could be estimated for the 1991 to September 2020 time period. An Autometrics-estimated model of the SP500 Index with M1, modelled with large residuals, substantially the RSS from 0.459 to 0.308 (Model I), see Table 5.2. The model residuals of the AR(3) and six M1 lags, with large residuals, were plagued by non-normality and heteroscedasticity.

The *Autometrics* estimations of IIS saturation variables produce significant RSS reduction as well as reducing heteroscedasticity and non-normality, as can be seen by the increased *p*-values, indicating non-statistically significant residuals, a congruent model. There is a statistically significant AR(1) coefficient and a positive and statistically significant two-period lag on the M1 variable.

The money supply leads to stock prices, as reported by Sprinkel in 1963 and 1964.

The money supply leads to stock prices, as reported by Sprinkel in 1963 and 1964, with the lowest RSS produced by the *Autometrics* IIS variables. The impulse-indictor estimated variables produce the lowest RSS and a two-period lead of M1 on stock prices. See Table 5.2.

5.4   Mr. Moore and the Mildness and Shortness of Postwar Recessions

In March 1984, the NBER Research Conference on Business Cycles met in Puerto Rico, and Robert Gordon's 1986 volume is an outstanding contribution to the business cycles literature. In keeping with the spirit of this monograph, we incorporate only three papers of Gordon, *The American Business Cycle: Continuity and Change* (Chicago: University of Chicago Press, 1986). The papers by Mr. Otto Eckstein and Mr. Allen Sinai, Mr. Robert

J. Gordon and Mr. John Veitch, and Mr. Victor Zarnowitz and Mr. Geoffrey Moore. In this chapter, we discuss Zarnowitz and Moore's work.

Mr. Zarnowitz and Mr. Moore remind the reader that business cycle work goes back to the eighteenth century in Britain and the U.S. when modern industrialization and economic growth began. Zarnowitz and Moore discussed the three types of changes: the long-term or secular trends; the episodic changes; and the cyclical changes. The third type of change is the so-called "cycle of cycles" that economists have modeled for over 100 years. The long-wave Kondratieff associated with large movements in prices, wars, and major innovations. The 48–60 year cycle does not show up in production or consumption, according to Zarnowitz and Moore.[47] The Kuznets cycle of 15–25 yearss is associated with the construction of holdings and infrastructure, population growth, urban development, and business formation. Zarnowitz and Moore have more confidence in data to support the Kuznets cycles.[48] The Juglar cycles are 7–10 years and are well researched in the literature. The Kitchin cycle, 3–4 years, is a minor business cycle associated with inventory investment. Zarnowitz and Moore discussed the long-term secular cycle pre and post-World War II. In 1846–1945, mean expansions lasted 30 months and contractions lasted 20 months; in 1945–1982, expansions lasted 45 months and contractions only 11 months. The time of recessions and depressions fell from 45% in 1846–1945 to only 20% from 1945 to 1982. Many of the mildest recessions occurred in the post-WWII period which Zarnowitz and Moore referred to as more "slow downs" than recessions.[49] The moderation of business cycles in the post-WWII period occurred throughout the industrialized world. Zarnowitz and Moore suggest that the higher rates of real growth facilitated capital formation, international trade, and development and were associated with less cyclical instability.[50] Perhaps built-in stabilizers, such as taxes and transfer payments, helped stabilize the economy.

Employment in agriculture fell from 48% in 1869 to 21% in 1929 to 4% in 1970 (p. 536). Rising industrialization increased nonagricultural employment which is less recessionary prone than the declining industries. A notable drop in the sensitivity of employment to cyclical fluctuations in aggregate demand prevailed 1945–1982. Between 1903 and 1981, Zarnowitz and

---

[47] Robert J. Gordon, *The American Business Cycle: Continuity and Change* (Chicago: The University of Chicago Press, 1986) National Bureau of Economic Research, Studies in Business Cycles, Volume 25, p. 522. Hereafter, referred to as Gordon, *ABC*, 1986. Yes, Robert J. Gordon is the son of Robert A. Gordon.

[48] Ibid.

[49] Gordon, *ABC*, p. 525.

[50] Gordon, *ABC*, p. 533.

Moore reported that relatively high real growth periods had average lower money supply and price growth rates than periods of lower real growth (p. 553). Zarnowitz and Moore concluded in 1986:

1. Post-WWII business cycles had much longer expansions and much shorter contractions than from 1846 to 1945. The expansions to contractions ratio of 1846–1945 was 1.50 times whereas the ratio rose to 4.00 in the 1945–1982 time period.
2. No association was found in Post-WWII between inflation and relative durations of business cycle phases.
3. Business cycles have been less severe than before, when indicated employment income and production measurements. Changes in employment and increased labor force participation enhanced the moderation of the Post-WWII business cycles
4. In the past, lower long-term growth was associated with higher variability of the standard deviation of real GNP growth rates. No Post-WWII relationship is found.
5. Post-WWII contractions were associated with higher inflation, not present in expansionary periods
6. Post-WWII long-term interest rates lagged behind shorter-term interest rates and conformed less to cycles.
7. Zarnowitz and Moore reported no change in the records of timing among the groups of indicators.[51]

5.5   Mr. Moore and his *Leading Indicators for the 1990s*

In 1991, as Director of the Center for International Business Cycle Research, CIBCR, at the Graduate School of Business at Columbia University, and Director-at-Large of the National Bureau of Economic Research, Mr. Moore advocated separating the 11 *Business Conditions Digest (BCD)* of 1989 into two lists: (1) a short-leading list, including the index of net change in business population, the layoff rate, the National Association of Purchasing Management (NAPM) inventory change survey, the NAPM vendor performance, industrial materials prices growth rate, domestic nonfinancial debt growth rate (in constant dollars), the average workweek in manufacturing, initial claims of unemployment, new orders for consumer goods (in 1982

---

[51] Gordon, *ABC*, p. 571–572.

$), contracts and orders for plant and equipment (in 1982 $), and the S&P 500 stock price index; and a long-leading list, composed of the Dow Jones Index of bond prices, the ratio of price to unit labor costs in manufacturing, new housing permits (numbers), and the Money supply, M2 (in 1982 $). The short-leading list of economic variables leads the business cycle by 6 months. The long-leading list of economic variables leads the business cycle by 11 months.[52]

Mr. Moore included the index of net change in business population, or a new index of net business formation, calculated as the net of Dun & Bradstreet new business starts less the Dun & Bradstreet number of business failures.[53] The net change index-led business cycle (CIBCR) peaks by a median of 8 months during 1948–1989 period and corresponding troughs by 2 months. Mr. Moore included the new layoff series because a previous layoff series had been discontinued and it led business cycles by an average of six months.[54] Mr. Moore included the NAPM inventory change series because the series led business cycle (CIBCR) peaks by a median of 8 months during the 1948–1989 period and troughs by 2 months.[55] Mr. Moore included the NAPM vendor performance series because the series led business cycle (CIBCR) peaks by a median of 10 months during the 1948–1989 period and troughs by 5 months.[56]

The new industrial materials price index series because the six-month smoothed series led business cycle (CIBCR) peaks by a median of 11 months during the 1948–1986 period and troughs by 3 months.[57]

The new measures of the growth of debt series because the six-month smoothed series led business cycle (CIBCR) peaks by a median of 8 months during the 1948–1982 period and troughs by 2 months.[58] The 12 proposed new leading economic indicators time series that Mr. Moore, in 1991, series led business cycle (CIBCR) peaks by a median of 12 months during the 1948–1989 period and troughs by 3 months, on average. The new leading

---

[52] Geoffrey H. Moore, *Leading Indicators for the 1990s* (Homewood, Illinois: Dow Jones-Irwin, 1990), pp. 2–3. See also Geoffrey H. Moore, "New Developments in the Leading Indicators", in Kajal Lahiri and Geoffrey H. Moore, *Leading Economic Indicators: New Approaches and Forecasting Records* (New York: Cambridge University Press, 1991), pp. 141–146.

[53] Geoffrey H. Moore, *Leading Indicators for the 1990s*, pp. 16–17.

[54] Moore, *Leading Indicators for the 1990s*, pp. 19–21. Mr. John Cullity co-authored the chapter with Mr. Moore.

[55] Moore, *Leading Indicators for the 1990s*, pp.36–38.

[56] Moore, *Leading Indicators for the 1990s*, pp. 41–44. Mr. Philip Klein co-authored the chapter with Mr. Moore.

[57] Moore, *Leading Indicators for the 1990s*, pp. 45–50.

[58] Moore, *Leading Indicators for the 1990s*, pp. 45–50. Mr. Victor Zarnowitz co-authored the chapter with Mr. Moore.

proposed economic indicators correctly predicted 73 percent of business cycle turns, a consistency criticized level.[59]

The Moore *Leading Indicators for the 1990s* (Homewood, Illinois: Dow Jones-Irwin, 1990) book was an outstanding 150-page monograph for practitioners because each series was a chapter. Mr. Moore was an outstanding researcher and a great explainer of technical deals to a non-technical audience.

5.6   Mr. Moore and Mr. Lahiri and Their *Leading Economic Indicators* (1991)

In May 1987, Mr. Kajal Lahiri and Mr. Moore hosted a conference on the Leading Economic Indicators at the State University of New York at Albany.[60] The reader must now ask, what is the record of the NBER in its LEI approach to forecasting business cycles? Mr. McNees, in his analysis of the turning points of the 1973–1975, 1980, and 1981–1982 recessions, held that forecasters recognized the peaks of the 1973 and 1981 recessions, as they were occurring, but missed the 1980 recession. There were few warnings, though, that a recession had begun. Forecasters did not recognize the fact that the 1973 and 1981 recessions would be the most severe of the (then) post-World War II period.[61] Mr. Herman Stekler held it is necessary to develop rules for identifying turning points in the predictor of business cycles to analyze the forecasting record of the LEI. Such rules would be used for identifying turning in real-time.[62] It is useful to identify the number of months that the predictor is below the peak. Monthly changes identify too many false turning points in peaks and troughs. If one used three months up or down to identify peaks and troughs, the number of false turns during the 1948–1985 period fall from 37, for peaks, and 17, for troughs on a one-month basis, to only

---

[59] Moore, *Leading Indicators for the 1990s*, pp. 67–70. Mr. John Cullity co-authored the chapter with Mr. Moore.

[60] Kajal Lahiri and Geoffrey H. Moore, *Leading Economic Indicators: New Approaches and Forecasting Records* (New York: Cambridge University Press, 1991). Hereafter, *LM LEI*.

[61] *LM LEI*, pp. 165–166. Stephen K. McNees, "Forecasting Cyclical Turning Points: The Record in the Past Three Recessions", in Kajal Lahiri and Geoffrey H. Moore, *Leading Economic Indicators: New Approaches and Forecasting Records* (New York: Cambridge University Press, 1991), pp. 151–168.

[62] Herman K. Stekler, "Turning Point Predictions, Errors, and Forecasting Procedures", in *LM LEI* (1991), pp. 169–181. The Stekler paper is based upon Mr. Stekler's research with S. S. Alexander. See S. S. Alexander, "Rate of Change Approaches to Forecasting- Diffuse Indexes and First Differences", *Economic Journal* 68 (1958), 288–301 and S.S. Alexander and Herman K. Stekler, "Forecasting Industrial Production-Leading Series versus Autoregressions" *Journal of Political Economy* 67 (1957), 402–409.

12 for peaks and 6 for troughs, on a three-month basis.[63] The use of three consecutive months of advance or decline further reduces the number of false turns to 7 for peaks and 1 for troughs.[64]

Mr. Diebold and Mr. Rudebusch address real-time analysis of the Department of Commerce composite index of leading indicators (ICI), to predict turning points since 1968.[65] Diebold and Rudebusch test a sequential probability recursion (SPR) rule during the December 1968–December 1986 and reported that the real-time ex ante data SPR model outperforms naïve models in forecasting turning points for peaks, particularly at longer horizons. The deterioration of ex ante data in the SPR model for predicting troughs is more severe, leading to mixed results.[66] There was no indication that the turning point probabilities increased with the age of the expansion or contraction in the post-World War II period.[67]

5.7 Mr. Zarnowitz and his Tribute to Mr. Moore: The Ms. Dua Volume

Ms. Pami Dua (2004) edited a collection of papers to honor Geoffrey Moore upon his passing in 2000 and addressed the current state of business cycle research. Mr. Zarnowitz (2004) updated his Post-WWII research and shed light on the "recovery-boom-slowdown-recession" nature of 1991–2001. Mr. Zarnowitz noted 14 peak-to-peak growth cycles during the 1948–2000 time period that averaged 44.5 months. For the peak-to-peak (P to P) periods, trough-to-peak (T to P) periods averaged over 26 months, whereas peak-to-trough (P to T) averaged 18.4 months. The 1983–1987 and 1989–1991 growth cycles were the longest, with P to P periods of 52 and 72 months, respectively.

Furthermore, the P to T contractions were about the same duration as the T to P recoveries and booms. Mr. Zarnowitz noted the "V-shaped" recoveries (Dua, 2004, pp. 45–49). The NBER business cycles largest P to P

---

[63] *LM LEI*, pp. 170–171.

[64] Mr. Stekler raises two concerns that Harry Markowitz frequently voices for financial research: is the researcher uses data not available at the time of the decision? Mr. Stekler stated that the turning point results above use the latest version of the Index of Leading Series which may have been constructed on the basis of its ability to detect cyclical turns that already occurred. Second, the analysis does not handle preliminary or missing data.

[65] LMLEI, p. 231. Francis X. Diebold and Glenn D. Rudebusch, "Turning Point Prediction with the Composite Leading Index", in in Kajal Lahiri and Geoffrey H. Moore, *Leading Economic Indicators: New Approaches and Forecasting Records* (New York: Cambridge University Press, 1991), pp. 231–256.

[66] *LM LEI*, p. 245.

[67] *LM LEI*, p. 246.

post-WWII were 1960–1969, 1981–7/1990, and 7/1990–3/2001, in which peak-to-peak months totaled 116, 108, and 128, respectively. Furthermore, the T to P months were 106, 92, and 20, respectively, of the NBER business cycles. Let us re-examine the position and see why these results appear to be so different.

First, Mr. Zarnowitz discussed his phase average trend (PAT) which provided a basis for establishing a "growth cycle" base, created with fluctuations in de trended measures of total economic activity.[68] Zarnowitz stated that real GDP is an imperfect measure of total economic activity because of poor estimates of depreciation. Real Net Domestic Product (NDP) excludes the depreciation estimates. Deprecation is real, as Victor noted, and represented the portion of capital that needs to be replaced.[69] The depreciation problem makes the dating of business cycles more difficult. The four coincidental indicators, including nonfarm employment, real personal income, less transfer payments, real manufacturing, retail and wholesale trade sales, and the index of industrial production, best define the business cycle.

Second, real GDP growth is highly volatile.[70] Zarnowitz noted that real GDP growth became more stable for the mid-1980s to 2000 time period and NDP growth volatility is reduced. The greater stability probably resulted from regulatory changes stabilizing the supply for residential investment reduction and elimination of trade barriers and adoption of "just in time" computer-based inventory and ordering management systems [71] The Conference Board Coincidental Index serves as the benchmark. The Zarnowitz analysis of the 1948–2001 stages of U.S. expansion and contraction, based on the PAT is dominated by months of recovery and rise, 13.8 and 39.0, respectively, whereas months of slowdown, downturn, and decline are 8.1, 4.9, and 5.5, respectively.

Investment spending is the most cyclical component of total demand. It is a prime mover in the recovery, boom, slowdown, and recession phases Business investment rose throughout the 1992–1999 period and fell in 2000–2001. New information and technology spending dominated investment between 1991 and 2000. Residential investment was strong during the 1991–2001 period. Consumer spending, personal consumption rose during the expansion of the 1990s, falling in 2000.

---

[68] Pami Dua, *Business Cycles and Economic Growth: An Analysis Using Leading Indicators* (Oxford: Oxford University Press, 2004), p. 45. Hereafter, referred to as Dua, *BCEG* (2004).

[69] Dua, *BCEG* (2004), p. 47.

[70] Dua, *BCEG* (2004), p. 50.

[71] Dua, *BCEG* (2004), p. 54.

Mr. Zarnowitz concluded his 2004 anatomy of U.S. growth and business cycles:

1. Common fluctuations of real income, sales, and employment identify and date the business cycle better than any single time series, including quarterly GDP.
2. Smooth upward trends and shorter fluctuations character business cycles.
3. Trends should be estimated to allow interactions with business cycles and deviations from trends of growth are useful in divisions of business expansions and contractions.
4. Recessions are preceded by slowdowns or growth cycle contractor and the LEI anticipate these slowdowns
5. Expansions start from recoveries which extend from troughs back to the trend. Many of these recoveries are "V-Shaped," or very fast.
6. Business investment drove the expansion of the 1990s and was driven by new technological investing. The decline in business investment led to the 2000–2001 slowdown and recession.
7. Residential investment rose in the 1990s driven by low inflation and interest rates.
8. Real personal consumption expanded throughout the 1990s, for services, cyclical, and durable goods.
9. The real investment of firms was driven by low inflation and interest rates.
10. The Federal Reserve monetary policy stabilized the economy after the stock market crash of 1987. The Fed policy of monetary accommodation did little to moderate the stock market boom of the 1990s.
11. The reduction of government deficits of 1993–1997 and the surpluses of 1998–2000 contributed to a larger expansion and lower interest rates. However, the increased military spending following the "9/11" attack and decreased tax revenues reduced the surpluses and created growing deficits.
12. The main factor of positive growth over the long run is the improved growth of labor productivity as measured by output per hour. The increase in productivity was due to technological innovation and progress.[72]

---

[72] Dua, *BCEG* (2004), pp. 78–80.

5.8   Summary and Conclusions

The NBER LEI research advanced greatly under the direction of Mr. Geoffrey Moore, whose NBER business cycle volumes of 1961 and 1983 established models, with its accompanying data, that could be verified. Statistical significance is reported in forecasting real GDP, the Federal Reserve Index of Industrial Production, and the unemployment rate, using data known at the point. The evidence on forecasting turning points, particularly those of business cycle troughs is not particularly good. The Moore CIBCR volume of 1991 and his NBER volume of 1991, with the Zarnowitz *Business Cycles* (NBER, 1992) monograph reviewed in the next chapter created newer versions of the LEI that have been verified in forecasting the unemployment rate and real GDP.

6

Mr. Victor Zarnowitz and Economic Forecasting, and NBER Business Cycle Research

Business cycles are one of the earliest research areas of study at the NBER. The reader was introduced to the works of Wesley Clair Mitchell, Arthur Burns, and Geoffrey Moore in Chapters 2, , 4, and 5, respectively. Victor Zarnowitz follows in that great tradition of business cycle research. In this chapter, we introduce the reader to Victor's works, from his forecasting analysis with Jacob Mincer in 1969, through his seminal NBER University of Chicago Press (1992) monograph, to his 1998 forecasting work with Montgomery, Tsay, and Tiao (1998), and conclude with his 2004–2006 analysis of the Leading Economic Indicators, LEI, for which he became both well-known and famous. Victor asked very hard questions: if the LEI were so statistically significant, why weren't they better at forecasting turning points? If the econometrics models, including the DRI model, introduced in the previous chapter, were so well constructed and estimated, then why were many of the forecasting results not statistically significant in real-time analysis? The reader will be introduced to a small portion of Mr. Zarnowitz's work. The point that this author must leave with the reader is that the Zarnowitz versions of the LEI were not perfect, but highly statistically significant. The benchmarks that Mr. Zarnowitz established in his modeling were substantial benchmarks to meet (and beat).[1] The reader should be convinced that Victor Zarnowitz created, estimated, presented, and maintained outstanding

---

[1] Victor Zarnowitz, *Business cycles: Theory, history, indicators, and forecasting* (Chicago, The University of Chicago Press, 1992). The benchmarks that Mr. Zarnowitz developed and tested in Chapters 5 and 7 are most challenging; very few economists and models have consistently beat these benchmarks.

© The Author(s), under exclusive license to Springer Nature Switzerland AG 2022
J. B. Guerard, *The Leading Economic Indicators and Business Cycles in the United States*, https://doi.org/10.1007/978-3-030-99418-1_6

research and databases that are highly statistically significant in economic forecasting in our daily lives.

Victor Zarnowitz should be judged by most academically minded researchers as an intellectual giant in the proud NBER tradition of Mitchell, Burns, and Moore. *His Business Cycles: Theory, Histon, Indicators and Forecasting* is one that all practitioners should read for its testing methodologies. One reads Wesley Clair Mitchell because he was the first Director at the National Bureau of Economic Research and because his 1913, 1927, and 1946 volumes discussed in Chapters 2 and 4 are considered classical treatments of business cycles. One reads Geoffrey Moore because his two-volume NBER set on business cycle indicators is an outstanding summary of what was understood regarding business cycles in 1961. The Moore (1961) volumes contained essays by NBER researchers who were most influential at that time and the data that can still be tested, as we did in the previous chapter. The second volume of Moore should be appreciated by researchers who need to know "what people know and when did they know it"? The Moore (1983) monograph is an exceptionally readable volume on the LEI and its real-world applications.[2] Practitioners should read Victor Zarnowitz because his business cycles book chapters are written to discuss and evaluate real-world economic forecasting. Mr. Zarnowitz understood that used economic forecasts to create financial plans for investments, dividends, debt issues, and employment decisions. Would a reasonable businessman undertake a large capital investment project if real growth, the real GDP was expected to decline? Would not the businessman wait until a recession or possibly, a depression, and build new plants and acquire new equipment when prices, including labor costs and financing costs, had fallen? In Chapter 14 of his 1992 NBER monograph Mr. Zarnowitz compared the Data Resources, Inc. Econometric Model (DRI) to other econometric models and reported that although the econometric models produced more accurate forecasts than naive, no-change models, the econometric services forecasts were lowly correlated with actual changes in GNP during the 1970–1975 period. DRI's correlation was sometimes higher, and other times lower than other econometric forecasting services; however, DRI's forecast correlations with actual GNP changes increased for the two-year-ahead for cast relative to its one year ahead forecast, which we address later in this chapter.[3]

Mr. Zarnowitz worked until he was 89 and worked in his office several days a week including several weeks before his death. Victor created the economic

---

[2] Victor Zarnowitz, *Business cycles: Theory, history, indicators, and forecasting* (Chicago, The University of Chicago Press, 1992).

[3] Victor Zarnowitz, *Business cycles*, pp. 432–434.

research department at the Conference Board, a non-profit organization, in 1997. The Conference Board developed Leading Economic Indicators (LEI) for many countries and maintained the U.S. LEI time series and components. In our next chapter, we report that the effectiveness of the TCB LEI is forecasting real GDP and changes in the unemployment rate. One cannot stress too strongly how important these time series are in U.S. financial management and global economic interactions. The U.S., as the world's most dominant economy, as measured by real gross Domestic Product and/or real GNP, is the economy that often leads to the global expansions and attempts to moderate the world's recessions or business slowdowns. One cannot overstate the importance of U.S. investment in driving the U.S. and world economies. As we discussed in Chapter 3, real investment is a key driver of U.S. growth, which often drives global growth.

6.1 Forecast Rationality

Much of forecasting analysis, measurement, and relative accuracy were developed in Theil (1966) and Mincer and Zarnowitz (1969). Theil discussed several aspects of the quality of forecasts. Theil (p. 29) discussed the issue of turning points, or one-sided movements, correctly. Theil produced a two-by-two dichotomy of turning point forecasting. The Theil turning point analysis is well-worth reviewing. A turning point is correctly predicted; that is, a turning point is predicted and an actual turning point occurs (referred as "i"). In a second case, a turning point is predicted, but does not occur ("ii"). In the third case, a turning point actually occurs, but was not predicted ("iii"); the turning point is incorrectly predicted. In the fourth and final case, a turning point is not predicted and not recorded. Thus, "i" and "iv" are regarded as forecast successes and "ii" and "iii" are regarded as forecast failures. The Theil turning point table is written as:

Actual Turning Points		Predicted Turning Points
	Turning Point	No Turning Point
Turning Point	i	iii
No Turning Point	ii	iv

The Theil turning point failure measures:

$$\phi_1 = \frac{iii}{i + ii}; \phi_2 = \frac{iii}{i + iii}$$

Small values of ϕ_1 and ϕ_2 indicate successful turning point forecasting. The turning point errors are often expressed graphically, where (Chart 6.1):

Regions A and D represent over-estimates of changes whereas regions B and C represent under-estimates of changes. The 45° line represents the line of perfect forecasts. Elton, Gruber, Brown, and Goetzmann (2007) make extensive use of the Theil graphical chart in their analysis of analysts' forecasts of earnings per share.

A line of perfect forecasting is shown in Chart 6.2, where U = 0.
A line of maximum inequality is shown in Chart 6.3, where U = 1.
The forecasters in Chart 6.3 are very bad (the worst possible).

Theil (1966, p. 30) analyzed the relationship between predicted and actual values of individual i.

$$P_i = +\beta A_i, \beta > 0 \tag{6.1}$$

Perfect forecasting requires that $\alpha = 0$ and $\beta = 1$. An alternative representation of Eq. (6.1) can be represented by the now-familiar inequality

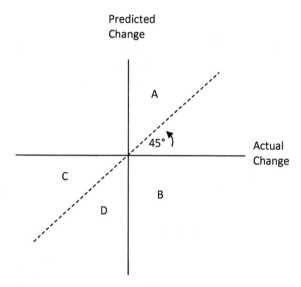

Chart 6.1 The relationship between Predicted Change and Actual Change should be represented by a line with a Positive Slope when the Turning Point is Correctly Forecast

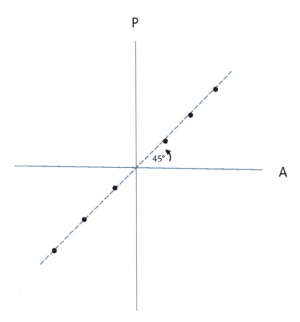

Chart 6.2 The relationship between Predicted and Actual Values should be represented by a line with a Positive Slope when the Value Correctly Forecast

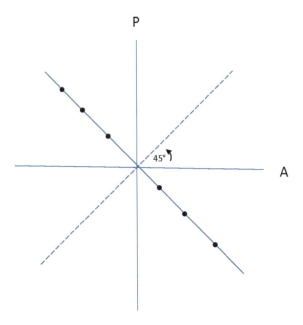

Chart 6.3 A Negative slope relationship between Predicted and Actual Values reports an Incorrect Forecast

coefficient, now known as Theil's U, or Theil Inequality coefficient, TIC.

$$\mu = \frac{\sqrt{\frac{1}{T}\sum(P_i - A_i)^2}}{\sqrt{\frac{1}{T}\sum P_i^2} + \sqrt{\frac{1}{T}\sum A_i^2}} \tag{6.2}$$

If U = 0, then $P_i = A_i$ for all I, and there is perfect forecasting. If U = 1, then the TIC reaches its "maximum in equality" and this represents very bad forecasting. Theil broke down the numerator of μ into sources or proportions of inequality.

$$\frac{1}{T}\sum(P_i - A_i)^2 = (\overline{P} - \overline{A})^2 + (S_P - S_A)^2 + 2(1 - r)S_P S_A \tag{6.3}$$

where $\overline{P}$ = mean of predicted values,
$\overline{A}$ = mean of actual values,
S_p = standard deviation of predicted values,
S_A = standard deviation of actual values,
and r = correlation coefficient of predicted and actual values.
Let D represent the denominator of Eq. (6.2).

$$U_M = \frac{\overline{P} - \overline{A}}{D};$$

$$U_S = \frac{S_P - S_A}{D};$$

$$U_C = \frac{\sqrt{2(1 - r)S_P S_A}}{D}$$

$$U_M^2 + U_S^2 + U_C^2 = U^2 \tag{6.4}$$

The term U_M is a measure of forecast bias. The term U_S represents the variance proportion and U_C represents the covariance proportion. U_M is bounded within plus and minus 1; that is, $U_M = 1$ indicates no variation of P and A or perfect correlation with slope of 1.

$$U^M = \frac{U^2 M}{U^2}; U^S = \frac{U_S^2}{U^2}; U^C = \frac{U_C^2}{U^2}$$

Theil refers to U^M, U^S, and U^C as partial coefficients of inequality due to unequal central tendency, unequal variation, and imperfect correlation, respectively.

$$U^M + U^S + U^C = 1 \qquad (6.5)$$

Theil (1966, p. 39) decomposes Eq. (6.3) into:

$$\frac{1}{T}\sum(P_i - A_i)^2 = (\overline{P} - \overline{A})^2 + (S_P - S_A)^2 + \left(1 - r^2\right)S_A^2 \qquad (6.6)$$

If a forecast is unbiased, then $E(\overline{P}) = E(\overline{A})$ and, in the regression of

$$A_i = P_i + U_i$$

where U_i = regression error term, the slope of A on P is $\frac{rS_A}{S_P}$.

$$U^2 = U_M^2 + U_R^2 + U_D^2$$

where $U_R^2 = \left(\frac{S_P - rS_A}{D}\right)^2$;

$$U_D^2 = \left(\frac{\sqrt{(1-r^2)}S_A}{D}\right)^2.$$

U_R is inequality due to an incorrect regression slope and U_D is inequality due to non-zero regression error terms (disturbances).

$U^R = \frac{U_R^2}{U^2}$ and $U^D = \frac{U_D^2}{U^2}$

The U^R term is the regression proportion of inequality. The U^D term is the disturbance proportion of inequality.

$$U^M + U^R + U^D = 1$$

The modern version of the Theil Inequality Coefficient, ITC, is written as the Theil U as

$$U = \sqrt{\frac{\sum_{t=1}^{T-1}\left(\frac{F_{t+1} - Y_t - Y_{t+1} + Y_t}{Y_t}\right)^2}{\sum_{t=1}^{T-1}\left(\frac{Y_{t+1} - Y_t}{Y_t}\right)^2}} \qquad (6.7)$$

or

$$U = \sqrt{\frac{\sum_{t=1}^{T-1}(FPE_{t+1} - APE_{t+1})^2}{\sum_{t=1}^{T-1}(APE_{t+1})^2}}$$

where $FPE_{t+1} = \frac{F_{t+1}-Y_t}{Y_t}$

and $APE_{t+1} = \frac{Y_{t+1}-Y_t}{Y_t}$

where F = forecast and A = Actual values.

where FPE is the forecast relative change and APE is the actual relative change.

6.2   Absolute and Relative Forecast Accuracy

Mincer and Zarnowitz (1969) built upon the Theil Inequality Coefficient (TIC) analysis and discussed absolute and relative forecasting accuracy in a more intuitive manner.

The line of perfect, LPF, is of course, where $P = A$, as was the case with Theil. Mincer and Zarnowitz (1969) write the mean square error of forecast, M_P, as

$$M_P = E(A - P)^2 \tag{6.8}$$

where E denotes expected value.

Let us return for the actual-predicted value regression analysis:

$$A_t = P_t + u_t \tag{6.9}$$

which is estimated with an ordinary least squares regression of

$$A_t = a + \beta P_t + v_t \tag{6.10}$$

It is necessary for the forecast error, u_t, to be uncorrelated with forecast values, P_t, for the regression slope β to equal unity (1.0). The residual variance in the regression $\sigma^2(v)$ equals the variance of the forecast error $\sigma^2(u)$. Forecasts are efficient if $\sigma^2(u) = \sigma^2(v)$. If the forecast is unbiased, $\alpha = 0$, and $\sigma^2(v) = \sigma^2(u) = M_P$.

Mincer and Zarnowitz (1969) discuss economic forecasts in terms of predictions of changes (not absolute levels). The mean square error is:

$$(A_t - A_{t-1}) - (P_t - A_{t-1}) = A_t - P_t = u_t \tag{6.11}$$

The relevant Mincer-Zarnowitz regression slope is:

$$\beta_\Delta = \frac{cov(A_t - A_{t-1}, P_t - A_{t-1})}{\sigma^2(P_t - A_{t-1})}$$

If the level forecast is efficient, then $\beta = 1$ $(cov\ (u_t,\ P_t) = 0)$. The $\beta_\Delta = 1$ and only if $cov\ (u, A_{t-1} = 0)$. The extrapolative value of A_{t-1} must be incorporated into the forecasts. Underestimation of change occurs when the predicted change $(P_t - A_{t-1})$ is of the same size, but smaller size, than the actual change $(A_t - A_{t-1})$.

$$E|P_t - A_{t-1}| < E|A_t - A_{t-1}| \qquad (6.12)$$

or

$$E(P_t - A_{t-1})^2 < E(A_t - A_{t-1})^2$$

$$\left[E(P_t) - E(A_{t-1})\right]^2 + \sigma^2(P_t - A_{t-1}) < \left[E(A_t) - E(A_{t-1})\right]^2$$
$$+ \sigma^2(A_t - A_{t-1})^2 \qquad (6.13)$$

Underestimation of changes occurs if

$$E(P_t) < E(A_t), \quad \text{when} A_t \text{and} P_t > A_{t-1},$$

$$E(P_t) < E(A_t), \quad \text{when} A_t \text{and} P_t < A_{t-1}$$

and / or

$$\sigma^2(P_t - A_{t-1}) < \sigma^2(A_t - A_{t-1}) \qquad (6.14)$$

In Eq. 6.16, when predictions of changes are efficient, $\beta_\Delta = 1$, then $\sigma^2(A_t - A_{t-1}) = \sigma^2(P_t - A_{t-1}) + \sigma^2(U_t)$.

Mincer and Zarnowitz (1969) decomposed the mean square error to create an index of forecasting quality, R_M. The index of forecasting quality is the ratio of the mean square error of forecast and the mean square error of extrapolation, the relative mean square error. If forecasts are "good" and are superior to extrapolated values, then $0 < R_M < 1$. If $R_M > 1$, then the forecast is inferior.

$$R_M = \frac{M_P}{M_X} = \frac{1 - \frac{U_X}{M_X}}{1 - \frac{U_P}{M_P}} \cdot \frac{M_P^C}{M_X^C} = g R M^C \qquad (6.15)$$

If x is a best, unbiased, and efficient extrapolation then $M_X^C = M_X$ and $g = \frac{M_P}{M^C P} > 1$ and $RM^C \leq RM$. Mincer and Zarnowtiz found that autoregressive extrapolations were not optimal, however, $RM^C < RM$ in twelve of

18 cases. Mincer and Zarnowitz found that inefficiency was primarily due to bias.

Mincer and Zarnowitz put for the r a theory that if RM_C, the forecast is superior relative to an extrapolative forecast benchmark, then "useful autonomous information enhanced the forecast." Autoregressive extrapolations showed substantial improvement over naïve (average) models, and while not optimal, were thus more efficient. A small number of lags produced satisfactory extrapolative benchmarks.

6.3 Extending the Mincer-Zarnowitz Forecasting Benchmark

The Mincer-Zarnowitz approach was important, only because of its no-change benchmarks, but (benchmark method of forecast) because of its use of an extrapolative forecast which should incorporate the history of the series. Mincer and Zarnowitz concluded that the underestimation of changes reflects the conservative prediction of growth rates in series with upward trends.

Granger and Newbold (1986) addressed two aspects of Mincer and Zarnowitz. First in the Mincer and Zarnowitz forecast efficiency regression:

$$X_t = a + \beta f_t + e_t \qquad (6.16)$$

A forecast is efficient if $\alpha = 0$ and $\beta = 1$. However, the forecast, f_t, must be uncorrelated with the error term, e_t. Granger and Newbold question this assumption in practical applications. Second, it is essential that the e_t, the error term be white noise-suboptimal forecasts (whether one-step-ahead or k-step-ahead), is not white noise. For a forecast to be optimal, the expected squared error must have zero mean and be uncorrelated with the predictor series. Unless the error term series takes on the value "zero" with probability of one, the predictor series will have a smaller variance than the real series. Second, random walk series appear to give reasonable predictors of another independent random walk series.

Granger and Newbold (1977, 1986) re-state the forecast and realization problem. The series to be analyzed and forecasted has a fixed mean and variance

$$E(x_t) = \mu_x$$

$$E(x--\mu_x)^2 = \sigma_x^2$$

The predictor series, f_2, has mean, f_x, variance σ_x^2, and a correlation ρ with x. The expected squared forecast error is:

$$E(x_t - f_t)^2 = (\mu_f - \mu_x)^2 + (\sigma_f - \rho\sigma_x)^2 + \left(1 - \rho^2\right)\sigma_x^2 \qquad (6.17)$$

A large correlation, ρ, minimizes the expected squared error. If

$$\mu_f = \mu_x \text{ and } \sigma_f = \rho\sigma_x,$$

then for optimal forecasts, the variance of the predictor series is less than the variance of the actual series. The population correlation coefficient is a measure of forecast quality. Granger and Newbold (1986) stated that it is "trivially easy" to obtain a predictor series "highly correlated" with the level of any economic time series.

Granger and Newbold (1986) restated Theil's decomposition of average squared forecast errors. Defining:

$$D_N^2 = \frac{1}{T}\sum_{t=1}^{T}(x_t - f_t)^2 = \left(\bar{f} - \bar{x}\right)^2 + (s_f - s_x)^2 + 2(1 - r)s_f s_x \qquad (6.18)$$

and

$$D_N^2 = \left(\bar{f} - \bar{x}\right)^2 + (s_f - rs_x)^2 + \left(1 - r^2\right)s_x^2 \qquad (6.19)$$

If $\bar{f}$ and $\bar{x}$ are sample means of the predictor and predicted series, s_f and s_x are the respective sample standard deviations, and r is the sample correlation coefficient of x and f.

$$U^m = \frac{\left(\bar{f} - \bar{x}\right)^2}{D_N^2}, \quad U^s = \frac{(s_f - s_x)^2}{D_N^2},$$

$$U^c = 2(1 - r)s_f s_x/D_N^2.$$

As with Theil, $U^M + U^s + U^c = 1$.
If x is a first-order autoregressive process,

$$x_t = ax_{t-1} + e_t$$

An optimal forecast, $f_t = ax_{t-1}$, produces $U^m = 0$, and $U^s + U^c = 1$. A high correlation between predictor and predicted series will most likely not be achieved. The standard deviation of the forecast series is less than the actual series and U^s is substantially different from zero. Granger and Newbold suggest testing for randomness of forecast errors.

One of the most important aspects of forecast accuracy is forecast rationality. Clements and Hendry (1998) discuss rationality in several levels. "Weak" rationality is associated with the concept of biasedness. A test of unbiasedness is generally written in the form:

$$A_t = \alpha + \beta P_t + \varepsilon_t \qquad (6.20)$$

where A_t = Actual value at time t,
P_t = Predicted value (Forecast) at time t,
ε_t = Error term at time t.

In Eq. (6.1), we have only assumed a one-step-ahead forecast horizon. One can replace t with $t + k$ to address the issues of k = Period ahead periods. Unbiasedness is defined in Eq. (6.1) with the null hypothesis that $\alpha = 0$ and $\beta = 1$. The requirement for unbiasedness is that $E(\varepsilon_t) = 0$. In expectational terms:

$$E[A_t] = \alpha + \beta E[P_t] \qquad (6.21)$$

One expects $\beta = 1$ and $\alpha = 0$, a sufficient, but not necessary condition for unbiasedness. "Strong" rationality or efficiency requires that the forecast errors are uncorrelated with other data or information available at the time of the forecast (Clements & Hendry, 1998).

The reader has been introduced to the Mincer and Zarnowitz benchmarks for forecasting. First, the use of a no-change model, in which last period's value is used as the forecast for the current period forecast, has a long and well-recognized history (Theil, 1966; Mincer & Zarnowitz, 1969). Second, one can establish several criteria for forecast accuracy. The forecast error, e_t, is equal to the actual value, A_t, less the forecasted value, F_t. One can seek to produce and use forecasts that have the lowest errors on the following measurements:

$$\text{Mean Error} = \frac{\sum_{t=1}^{T} e_T}{T};$$

$$\text{MAPE} = \text{Mean Absolute Percentage Error} = \frac{\sum_{t=1}^{T} |e_t|}{T};$$

and

$$\text{Mean Squared Forecast Error} = \text{MSFE} = \sum_{t=1}^{T} e_t^2$$

There are obviously advantages and disadvantages to these measures. First, in the mean error, small positive and negative values may "cancel" out implying that the forecasts are "perfect," Makridakis and Hibon (2000) remind us that the mean error is only useful in determining whether the forecaster over-forecasts, producing positive forecast errors; that is, the forecaster has a positive forecast bias. The MAPE, mean absolute percentage error, is the most commonly used forecast error efficiency criteria (Makridakis et al., 1982). The MAPE recognizes the need for the forecast to be as close as possible to the realized value. Thus, the sign of the forecast error, whether positive or negative, is not the primary concern. Finally, the mean squared forecast error is assuming a quadratic loss function, that is, a large positive forecast error is not preferred to a large negative forecast error. In this monograph, we examine the implications of the three primary measures of forecast accuracy. We are concerned with two types of forecasts; the economy (the U.S. and the World, particularly the Euro zone) and analysts forecasts of corporate earnings per share. Why? We believe, and will demonstrate, that a reasonable economic forecast of the direction of the economic strength is significant in allowing an asset manager or an investor to participate in economic growth. Second, we find that firms achieving the highest growth in *eps* generate the highest stockholder returns during the 1980–2009 period, moreover, we will demonstrate that the securities that achieve the highest *eps* growth and hence returns are not those forecast to have the highest *eps*, but are not that have the highest *eps* forecast revisions and that it is equally important for analysts to agree on the *eps* revisions. That is, the larger the number of analysts that raise their respective *eps* forecasts, the highest will be stockholder returns. We address these forecasting models and issues in Chapter 9.

The purpose of this monograph is to introduce the reader to a variety of financial techniques and tools to produce forecasts, test for forecasting accuracy, and demonstrate the effectiveness of financial forecasts in stock selection, portfolio construction and management, and portfolio attribution. We believe that financial markets are very near to being efficient, but statistically significant excess returns can be earned. Let us discuss several aspects to forecast accuracy; forecast rationality, turning point analysis, and absolute and relative accuracy.

6.4   Mr. Zarnowitz, the NBER, and Business Cycle Research in 1992

Mr. Zarnowitz in Chapter 5 of his *Business Cycles Theory, History, Indicators and Forecasting* (Chicago: University of Chicago Press, 1992) revised his commentary on 50 years of NBER research written in 1972. Mr. Zarnowitz reminded the reader of the NBER Directors of Research or its Presidents, that created or support NBER research on business cycles.[4] Mr. Mitchell, Mr. Burns, Mr. Solomon, and Mr. Moore are the first four names on the Zarnowitz list. The reader now sees why this monograph addresses the author of chapters two through five. These authors left research monographs that created much of the literature on U.S. business cycle research. The NBER studies of Simon Kuznets, Jacob Mincer, noted in this chapter, and Milton Friedman and his colleagues, are included in the Zarnowitz NBER business cycle literature reviews. This author is well aware that a 300–400-page monograph, including current data the 1959–2021 and its accompanying research, cannot possibly properly address 70 years of research. However, it is the purpose of this monograph to make the reader aware of the first four gentlemen named by Mr. Zarnowitz and try to educate the reader as to the continuing importance of economic measurement (without theory) and the relevant and statistical significance of the Leading Economic Indicators, LEI, and their relevance in portfolio selection. We end the discussions of Mr. Moore and Mr. Zarnowitz and their empirical work with the essays to Mr. Moore in the Dua (2004) volume.[5]

The business cycle research will continue, as the U.S. economy re-emerges from the present COVID pandemic, whenever that will be, and the application of portfolio selection put forth by Harry Markowitz in 1952, 1956, and 1959, advanced by William F. (Bill) Sharpe in 1963 and 1964, and revisited in Guerard, Markowitz, and Xu (2013, 2014, 2019, and 2020, and 2021) and presented in Chapter 9, should provide a solid intellectual foundation for the reader and the supporting statistically significant evidence of the risk-return trade-off during the 1962–2021 period. The worlds of Mitchell,

[4] Victor Zarnowitz, *Business cycles: Theory, history, indicators, and forecasting* (Chicago, The University of Chicago Press, 1992), pp. 164–165.

[5] Pami Dua, *Business cycles and economic growth: An analysis using leading indicators* (Oxford University Press, New Delhi: Oxford University Press, 2004). The reader is referred to the contributions of Victor Zarnowitz, Andrew Filardo, John Guerard, Herman Stekler, Lawrence Klein, and the Pami Dua set of articles on forecasting the Indian economy, particularly Victor Zarnowitz, "The Autonomy of Recent US Growth and Business Cycles", *Business Cycles and Economic Growth: An Analysis Using Leading Indicators*, pages 44–82. See also Zarnowitz, V., Ozyildirim, A., "On the measurement of business cycles and growth cycles", *Indian Economic Review*, (2001) pages 37–54. Econometric modelling and forecasting work began with Klein (1950) and was enhanced by the works of Granger and Newbold (1986), Clements and Hendry.

Moore, Zarnowitz, and Markowitz are very relevant in our daily lives. The NBER leadership hoped that its research into the accumulation of economic knowledge would aid other students (researchers), and laymen (practitioners) in wrestling with business cycles (Mr. Burns, as quoted in Zarnowitz (1992).[6] "Mr. Burns believed that this strategy promised to improve the long-run analysis of economic conditions, economic forecasting, and economic policies. Researchers address the issues of consumption, fixed business investment, and the monetary accommodation to finance economic growth have been key topics of NBER research."[7] It is very clear that exogenous factor, world wars, and disease can accelerate or retard economic expansion and growth. Mr. Zarnowitz repeated his claim that business cycle's peaks and troughs are not caused by favorable or unfavorable external forces. There is nothing either explosive or fundamentally unstable in economic cycles. There is a self-limiting nature to the U.S. economy.[8]

American Capitalism is quite capable of sustaining its growth in the long run. Mr. Zarnowitz commented extensively in Chapter 5 regarding the formulation, estimation, and interpretation of mathematical (and econometric models) of the U.S. in the 1930s, as the reader saw in Chapter 3. There are cross-influences in the theory measurements of econometric models and post-Keynesian analysis.[9] The accelerator and multiplier analysis of the late-1930s and 1940s led to the Hicks (1950) theory of the trade cycle. The econometric monetary of the post-Keynesian and the monetary tests and responses of Mr. Friedman and his colleagues (1963 to the current period) to the Keynesians resurrected Irving Fisher (1911) and the Quantity Theory of Money. Can the econometric models and business cycle simulations generate movements resembling the observed U.S. business fluctuations of the 1972–2021 period? Mr. Zarnowitz went further to discuss the role of money and U.S. monetary policy and the growth of real income.[10] Each money supply "shock" may overshoot and initially drive down interest rates, stimulating investment spending, income, and prices. The money stock, Mr. Zarnowitz tells us, is largely autonomous, and monetary changes are largely exogenous, and not formally "causally" related to business cycles. Mr. Zarnowitz is very clear to state in his research that monetary policy is an independent force determining movements of income within business cycles. Mr. Zarnowitz also explicitly rejects the hypothesis that investment is the main motive of

---

[6] Zarnowitz, *Business cycles*, p. 166.
[7] *Zarnowitz, Business cycles*, pp. 167–168.
[8] *Zarnowitz, Business cycles*, p. 169.
[9] *Zarnowitz, Business cycles*, p. 171.
[10] Zarnowitz, *Business cycles*, p. 175.

business cycles. Thus, Mr. Zarnowitz does not embrace the Fisherian "dance of the dollar" theory of business cycles, and tells the reader that it is clearly different than the business cycle research of Wesley Clair Mitchell.[11] Mr. Zarnowitz reminds the reader that Mr. Mitchell attached great importance to the role of money in economic cycles, as we saw in his 1923 monograph. Mr. Zarnowitz concluded chapter 5 on the 50 years NBER research with three sobering propositions: (1) both monetary and fiscal policies have significant effects on aggregate spending and neither set of policies are dominant at all times; (2) the combined monetary and fiscal policy variables account for the systematic component of changes in total spending and economic fluctuations; and (3) business cycle research, analysis, and forecasting can benefit from econometric models, but the inadequate knowledge of data and the body of experts analyzing it limit the potential usefulness of models at the present date.[12]

Is there a more important topic than business cycles and economic growth? In the long run, Mr. Zarnowitz believed that economic growth is "real" in that it can be measured by increasing in physical output and wealth per capita. Human and Capital productivity can be measured.[13] Growth cycles are movements in aggregate economic activity in comprehensive indicators adjusted for their long-term trends. Secular trends refer to market activities that occur over the long run and are not seasonal or cyclical, such as a type of industry that is sensitive to the business cycle. Firms with rising revenues in periods of prosperity and expansion and are lower in periods of depression and contraction are cyclical. Durable goods and consumer durable goods are highly sensitive to the business cycle. Consumer durable goods is a sector with consumers having a discretionary income that and its sales are highly sensitive to the business cycle. The airline industry is cyclical in that people with disposable income take vacations and use air travel. Conversely, in economic downturns, people with means may be less willing to travel. Secular growth is most meaningful for the longest periods of time where the stable trend fits the data well.[14] Cyclical bias can occur if one measures the business cycle trend, from a business cycle trough to a business cycle peak, which over-estimates growth." Economic growth is underestimated when measuring growth from a peak to a trough year. Over the very long run, trends dominate the business cycle, and there is little cyclical bias. Growth has been historically pervasive and persistent in that almost all business expansions have total output

---

[11] *Zarnowitz, Business cycles*, p. 176.

[12] *Zarnowitz, Business cycles*, p. 178.

[13] *Zarnowitz, Business cycles*, pp. 202–203.

[14] Zarnowitz, *Business cycles*, p. 204.

and employment growth above the peak of the previous cycle (excepting the 1933–1937 expansion, which followed the great contraction of 1929–1933 Zarnowitz, 1992, p. 204).[15] Recoveries are often faster from severe depressions than from mild declines. Mr. Zarnowitz characterized severe depressions as those of 1873–1879, 1893–1897, 1907–1908, 1920–1921, 1929–1933, and 1937–1938. Vigorous or "V-Shaped" recoveries were 1889–1882, 1897–1899, 1908–1910, 1921–1923, 1938–1945, 1949–1953, and 1961–1969.[16] Mr. Zarnowitz held that 33 complete business cycles occurred in the U.S. between 1834 and 1975, and most cycles were mild. Only nine expansions lasted longer than 3 years and 5 expansions were associated with wars. About one-half the expansions lasted for two years or less. Contractions have been much shorter, with 25 (85%) not exceeding two years and 11 (33%) did not exceed one year. Mr. Zarnowitz stated that few peacetime cycles resulted in disruptions of the secular trend of the U.S. economy.[17] Many NBER economists list four periods of relative low economic stability; 1892–1899, 1973–1923,1929–1948, and 1969–1980, with average growth rates in real GDP of 3.1, 2.4, 2.5, and 2.7%, respectively, and corresponding standard deviations of 6.8, 8.0, 9.4, and 3.1%, respectively; during the 1882–1980 period. High stability periods of the 1882–1980 period contained 12 complete cycles with a 4.0 percent growth in real GNP and a 4.4% standard deviation. The 10 complete cycles of the low stability period produced annual average growth rates of 2.6 with a 7.4% standard deviation.

Growth is lessened by periods of prolonged unemployment and high inflation. Underutilization of capacity reduces investment and pushes down the potential full-employment output curve. Bad tax policies distort resource allocation and hinder savings and productive investment. Fostering speculation lessens growth. All in all, growth has been substantial during the 1882–1980 period and even the "low" stability years (47 of them) produced an average annual growth in real GNP of 2.6 percent.[18] Finally, post-WWII business cycles have been very mild relative to historical standards. The U.S. business cycle moderated in the post-WWII period. Since 1948, expansions have lasted 48 months whereas business contractions lasted only 10 months, on average.[19] The LEI tends to turn down in anticipation of business slowdowns as well as contractions. The 1974–1975 recession, the most severe post-WWII recession, occurred in all nations (of the trading world) and

---

[15] Ibid.

[16] Zarnowitz, *Business cycles*, p. 205.

[17] Ibid.

[18] Zarnowitz, *Business cycles*, pp. 206–208.

[19] *Zarnowitz, Business cycles*, p. 214.

was quickly followed by a rapid expansionary period in 1976–1977 and a brief slowdown in 1979 and a substantial recession in 1980. In the NBER Peak-Trough-Peak (Three Trend Adjusted Indexes), the High-to-Low drops of October 1873–May 1879 (−33.6%), January 1893–June 1894 (-37.3%), and January 1920–July 1921 (38.7%) periods were the three worst peak-to-trough declines in economic activity during the 1873–1929 period.[20] Mr. Zanowitz summarizes his chapter 7 on "Business Cycles and Growth" as:

1. Severe depressions reduce economic growth strongly for some time; whereas vigorous expansions, which often follow, enhance growth in shorter periods. Furthermore, in reviewing the years of relative stable growth and unstable growth with their relative standard deviations of 4.4 and 7.4%, respectively; the stable growth rates exceed the unstable growth rates, 4.0 to 2.6%, respectively. Mr. Zarnowitz suggests that growth was higher when stability was greater.
2. Business cycles changed with the Great Depression and WWII in the 1929–1945 period. Recessions became milder with shorter periods and duration and smaller amplitudes, probably due to structural and institutional changes.
3. The mildness of post-WWII economic fluctuations has led to a revival in growth cycles. Growth cycles are symmetric in duration, as opposed to business cycles, and are characterized by longer expansions and shorter contractions. Trade and financial transactions (integration of markets) have linked growth cycles in the market-oriented economies.
4. Expansions and contraction in the early NBER years, 1882–1980, were approximately equal in length. Mr. Zarnowitz suggested that incomplete data for 1834–1929 may underestimate expansions because of general economic activity contractions, and not just below-average growth.[21]

6.4.1 Mr. Zarnowitz and the Lists of Leading Indicators, 1950–1989

We discussed in Chapter 4 the Burns and Mitchell *Measuring Business Cycles* NBER (1946) monograph and in Chapter 5, the Mitchell and Burns (1938) list of 71 time series that were consistent in economic recoveries and the best subset of 21 "most trustworthy" indicators. Mr. Zarnowitz continued the Mr. Moore approach to LEI analysis which concentrated on what variables were

[20] *Zarnowitz, Business cycles*, pp. 225–226.
[21] Zarnowitz, *Business cycles*, pp. 230–231.

recommended when forecasting the economy. In Chapter 11, Mr. Zarnowitz listed the 35 economic variables included in the five NBER LEI components of 1950, 1960, 1966, 1975, and 1989. These lists were prepared by Mr. Moore (1950 and 1960), Mr. Moore and Shinkin (1966), Mr. Zarnowitz and Boschan (1975), and Mr. Hertzberg and Beckman (1989).[22] Is there consistency among the lists? Yes, and no. The average workweek of production current dollars of workers in manufacturing is the only variable included in all five LEI lists. New orders time series makes all five lists; new orders in durable goods are the 1950, 1960, and 1966 components whereas new orders in consumer goods and materials, in constant dollars, are the LEI component on the 1975 and 1989 lists. Stock prices are included in all five lists, but the Dow Jones Industrial Average is the stock price time series in the 1950 list, whereas the Standard and Poor's 500 stock price index is included in the 1960, 1966, 1975, and 1989 LEI lists. The money supply is present on two lists, with M1, in constant dollars, on the 1975 list and M2, in constant dollars, on the 1989 list. Several economic time series make two lists: the layoff rate in manufacturing (1960 and 1975); corporate profits after taxes, in current dollars, and current liabilities of business failures are among the LEI components on the 1950 and 1960 lists; and building permits for new private housing, and contracts and orders for plant and equipment, in constant dollars, are among the LEI component on the 1975 and 1989 lists. Thus, about the average workweek, stock prices, and new orders are the most commonly used variables. Approximately one-third of the economic variables were unchanged from the previous list, while one-third of the LEI changes involved substitutions of time series within the same group of 12 groups of variables. Approximately 25% of the economic time series were deleted from each list of LEI components.[23]

6.4.2 Econometric Model Simulations and Business Cycles

Mr. Zarnowitz began analyzing the relationship between econometric modeling and business cycle research in the 1960s and by 1972, was discussing the role of simulations within large-scale models of the economy and implications for forecasting GNP and real GNP. Mr. Lawrence Klein,

---

[22] Zarnowitz, *Business cycles*, pp. 334–336.

[23] Ibid. Business failures research was reported in Victor Zarnowitz and Lionel J. Lerner, "Cyclical changes in business failures and corporate profits", in Geoffrey H. Moore, Editor, *Business cycle indicators: Contributions to the analysis of current business conditions* (Princeton, NJ: Princeton University Press, a study by the National Bureau of Economic Research, 1961), pp. 350–385.

the creator and Nobel Prize laureate of econometric models at The Wharton School, built one of the first and best-known models of the U.S. economy, the "Wharton Model" in 1950. Mr. Klein used his model to estimate consumption investment and income determination in the U.S. during 1921–1941. In Chapter Nine of Mr. Zarnowitz's *Business Cycles*, Mr. Zarnowitz discusses and compares the Wharton Model, the OBE, the Office of Business Economics of the Department of Commerce, the Federal Reserve Board-MIT- Penn Model, FMP, and Brookings models. These four econometric models were viewed for the 1948Q3 (quarter three) to 1969Q1 period, although Mr. Zarnowitz noted (with regret) that not all four models were actively modeled throughout the period. The Brookings model was only for the 1957–1965 period.[24] Mr. Zarnowitz does the reader a great service with his comparison of the leading series, by model, of these four models. All four models used nonfarm residential investment in the models. Changes in nonfarm inventories, corporate profits before taxes and inventory adjustments, and the average work week were present in these four models. The reader immediately notes that much of our discussion in the works of Mitchell, Persons, Moore, and Zarnowitz (earlier in this chapter), dealt with these variables. New orders, unfilled orders, private housing starts, and demand deposits, were the other leading series in the models.[25] GNP, real GNP, consumption, personal income, employment, and the employment rate were the "coincidental series" in the econometric models. The lagging time series were the government bill, Moody's corporate bond yields, wages, and investment in nonresidential structures and durable equipment.[26]

Mr. Zarnowitz measured the accuracy of the econometric models identifying turning points in the economy. Mr. Zarnowitz used "inferred" turning points to assess the predictive ability of these models. The Wharton model leads in accuracy of prediction; See also turning points in its actual simulation number of the 1949–1961 period, with its simulations identifying 64, 61, and 57% of the three-quarter, two-quarter, and one-quarter ahead turning points, respectively. The corresponding numbers for the OBE model

---

[24] Zarnowitz, *Business cycles*, pp. 265–267. The creators of the Brookings Model and later the DRI Model, discussed in the previous chapter, studied the role of active government in stabilizing the US economy in mild and severe recessions in the 1957–1959 period, see James Duesenberry, Otto Eckstein, and Gary Fromm, "A simulation of the United States economy in recession", *Econometrica*, Vol. 28 (1960), reprinted in the American Economic Association, *Readings in Business Cycles*, Robert A. Gordon and Lawrence R. Klein, Editors (Homewood, Ill: Richard D. Irwin, Inc, 1965). See also James S. Duesenberry, *Business cycles and economic growth* (New York: McGraw-Hill Book Company, 1958), Chapters 11–12 and Elmer C. Bratt, *Business cycles and forecasting* (Homewood, Ill: Richard D. Irwin, Inc, 1961).

[25] Zarnowitz, *Business cycles*, p. 268.

[26] Ibid.

for the 1954–1961 period were 58, 60, and 64 percent, respectively. Finally, the FMP Model only simulated 38, 44, and 45% of the turning points for the 1957–1961 period. The Wharton Model did the best job at forecasting the leading series 80% of all turning points and 88% of the coincidental series, including GNP and real GNP series. The forecasting of real GNP has been a test of econometric models for the past 50 years. The Wharton Model correctly simulated expansionary turning points by 6.4 models and contractionary turning points by 3.6 months. The corresponding numbers for the FMP Model, which forecast the leading series turning points only 33% and forecast expansionary periods by 3.7 months, and contractionary periods by 4.8 months, on average, during the 1957–1961 period, were not all accurate as the Wharton Model. The model accuracies did not increase over the forecast periods from one, two, …, to six quarters ahead.[27] Mr. Zarnowitz argued that the econometric models lacked fluctuations in the control series for the aggregates, like GNP, that generated cyclical movements. That is the models lacked mechanisms to cause simulated aggregates, GNP, to fluctuate in the absence of shocks in exogenous events of relationships with endogenous variables.[28] The econometric models showed only residual cyclical elements, much weaker than observed in the estimation periods of the models. The lack of fluctuations in the projected exogenous variables is an "unrealistic" feature of the econometric models that lead to the disappointing forecasting results regarding turning point forecasts.[29]

Mr. Zarnowitz argued that there is greater difficulty in predicting one or two quarters ahead than predicting one and two years-ahead.[30] Mr. Zarnowitz argued that there is a greater need for detailed (and accurate) forecasts in the 4–8 quarter ahead periods. The large econometric models, often estimating over 800 equations and variables, as we noted with Mr. Eckstein and the DRI model, could legitimately be compared with the econometric models in forecasting accuracy. Forecasting studies of the econometric model series are compared to the vector autoregressive models of Mr. Sims, who later won the Nobel Prize in economics, and the Bayesian vector autoregressive models of Mr. Litterman. Mr. Zarnowitz reported that the econometric model forecasts of the Chase, DRI, Wharton, and the Prudential Insurance Company model, among other models, produced mean absolute errors (MAE) of 1.4, 1.6, 1.0, 0.90, and 1.7 percent, respectively, when forecasting

---

[27] Zarnowitz, *Business cycles*, pp. 273–275.

[28] *Zarnowitz, Business cycles*, p. 380.

[29] Ibid. In its New York Times obituary in 2006, The Times noted Mr. Zarnowitz's emphasis on the accuracy of turning point forecasting.

[30] Zarnowitz, *Business cycles*, p. 527.

the growth rate of GNP during the 1953–1976, 1956–1963, 1963–1976, 1969–1976, and the 1977–1984 period, respectively.[31] An extrapolative prediction, a benchmark, using the average percentage change of the past four years, is the benchmark that economic growth and business cycles have been studied for many years.[32] The analysis of rising and falling economic activity has been measured by the GNP and GDP since 1927. The question still remains, what is a business cycle?

6.5   Mr. Zarnowitz and The Major Market Economies during the Post-World War II Period

Mr. Zarnowitz discussed international business cycles during the 1948–1990 period. World War II devasted the economies of Continental Europe and the Far East and the physical wealth and capital of once rich nations lay in ruins and in dire need of reconstruction. Human capital was much better preserved because educated and skilled people retained their high productive potential skills. There was a huge backlog of effective demand. Monetary, fiscal, and political reforms enabled both the defeated nations and the nations liberated by the Allies to make a relatively smooth transition from closed war economies to open market economies, and from totalitarian and oppressive to democratic and free social systems. Foreign aid, mainly from the U.S., was also made available to friends and former foes. The result of this historically rare, perhaps unique, combination of circumstances was that France, Italy, West Germany, and Japan came soon to enjoy extraordinarily high rates of real economic growth. Of course, the initial activity levels were very low, which helps explain the long persistence of very high and only gradually declining growth rates, but the progress achieved in the 1950s and 1960s was spectacular, particularly in the case of West Germany and Japan. As long as the steep upward trends in employment and output (much of it exported) continued, real growth in continental Europe and the Far East, the benefits of high growth were augmented by those of high cyclical stability.

West Germany had its first postwar recession in 3/1966–5/1967; Japan in 11/1973–2/1975; France in 4/1958–4/1959; and Italy in 10/1963–3/1965.

---

[31] Ibid.

[32] See Guerard, John B., Jr. 2001. "A note on the forecasting effectiveness of the U.S. leading economic indicators." Indian Economic Review, Vol. 36, pp. 251–268, and Phoebus Dhrymes, Introductory Econometrics (New York: Springer, 2017).

Meanwhile, Canada and the U.K., the U.S., and Australia, and other countries that suffered much smaller direct wartime damages, had less need for domestic reconstruction, and thus slower growth rates, and earlier and more frequent recessions. Economic growth slowed markedly everywhere during the 1970s and 1980s, and recessions became both more common and more severe. They spread worldwide in 1947–1975 after the oil embargo and huge increases in the OPEC cartel oil prices, and again in 1980–1982 after new price shocks and strong counter-inflationary policy moves in the U.S.. However, the index for Japan shows only a brief decline in late 1980; its growth after the mid-1970s was much slower than before but also remarkably steady. The index for France shows frequent but only short and shallow declines throughout, except in 1958–1959 and 1974–1975.[33]

6.5.1 Estimated Dimensions of Business Cycles in Eight Countries

There is no NBER-type international reference chronology of business cycle peaks and troughs for the post-World War II period. Perhaps the main reason for the belief that recessions have been generally replaced by were retardations of growth in most countries. But maybe expectation, but it is not a well-established fact. What is certainly true is that contractions of total output and employment have been short, few, and far between developed and developing countries that achieved high average rates of real growth. The so-identified declines last several (as a rule, six or more) months and have amplitudes of several or more percentage points (as a rule, at least U). They presumably reflect business contractions. The open dots mark shorter and/or smaller declines that do not qualify as recessions but may be associated with significant retardations in general economic activity. However. substantial business slowdowns can occur without any noticeable decreases in the levels of the index series, particularly in places and times of very high overall growth. The charts show some important similarities between the country indexes, notably the concentration of long expansions in the 1960s and l980s, of mild recessions or slowdowns in mid- or late-1960s, and of more severe contractions in mid-1970s and early l980s. But the differences are even more pronounced,

---

[33] Victor Zarnowitz, "What is a business cycle?" NBER Working Paper Series, Working Paper No. 3863, October 1991, pp 33–38. The data, collected and processed by the Center for International Business Cycle Research (CIBCR) at Columbia University Business School, are composite indexes of coincident indicators, which combine monthly and quarterly measures of aggregate activity (total output, industrial production, employment, real sales, inverted unemployment) and have trends made equal to those of the corresponding series for real CNP or GDP.

and they were primarily related to the longer growth trends. The main point here is that high growth helps to reduce the frequency and depth of business contractions. Thus, periods of rapid, recession-free growth were observed for West Germany and Italy before 1962; for France in most of the 1960s and again after 1985; for Japan before 1973; for Canada between 1961 and 1981; and for Australia between 1961 and 1973. The economies of the U.S. and U.K. had relatively low rates of real growth and most cyclical variability. In sharp contrast, Japan had both the fastest growth and least cyclicality; indeed, one can say that business cycles, as we know them, were essentially absent there. CIBCR data suggests that the postwar business cycles were shorter and more numerous in the U.S. than in any other of the developed countries. In 1955–1990, the longest common period covered, the numbers of complete peak-to-peak cycles in the indexes were as follows: U.S., 6; U.K. and Italy, 5 each; France and Australia, 4 each; Canada and West Germany, 3 each; and Japan, 2.[34] Comparisons between fewer countries over longer periods yield generally consistent results. Further, the inspection of the charts suggests that the greater frequency of U.S. cycles was mainly due to the shorter durations of U.S. expansions. On the whole, it was the expansions that differed greatly across the countries in both length and amplitude, whereas the contractions varied much less in both dimensions. Cyclical rises in the U.S. index were on average much shorter than the rises in the foreign indexes, and also much smaller in percentage terms than the indexes for the other countries, with the sole exception of the U.K.. As for the cyclical declines in the U.S. index, they were on average considerably deeper than the declines in the other indexes, but not particularly long. The entries on mean durations and mean amplitudes quantify the impression from the charts that expansions differed greatly across the countries (even apart from the extreme cases of West Germany and Japan), while contractions differed only moderately.

A comprehensive assessment of how business cycles in different countries compare would require an analysis of the performance of many individual indicators, which is not possible here. However, Mr. Zarnowitz examined the industrial production and employment components of the coincident indexes under consideration and find that a few general observations deserve to be made. The industrial production indexes cover sectors of high cyclical sensitivity (manufacturing everywhere, mining and/or public utilities in most countries). Therefore, they have at least as many specific cycles as the coincident indexes (which cover less sensitive sectors and processes as well), often significantly more. Thus, the industrial production series for Japan (mining

---

[34] Victor Zarnowitz, "What is a business cycle?", pp. 35–36.

and manufacturing) shows clearly seven expansions and six contractions in the period 1953–1990. In the U.S., although nonfarm employment has a much broader coverage than industrial production, the cyclical profiles of the two indicators are quite similar. In Japan, total employment of "regular workers had only one cyclical contraction (4/1975–5/1976) between 1954 and l990. In the U.K., employment in production industries followed a gradual downward trend since 1966, and the same applies to West German employment in manufacturing and mining from 1971 until mid-1984 as well as to French nonfarm employment between mid-1974 and mid-1985. This stands in contrast to the U.S., where an upward trend in employment prevailed throughout.[35] It is well-known that, after having stayed very low in the earlier postwar years, unemployment in Western Europe increased rapidly (quadrupled) between 1970 and 1985, from well below to well above the U.S. levels. Yet, despite the downtrends in employment and clear cyclical movements around them, business cycles apparently remained milder in Europe than here. This suggests that the persistent rise in European unemployment was largely noncyclical in nature, which is consistent with most recent hypotheses. There are no tested hypotheses, let alone accepted knowledge, on why the U.S. economy may be subject to more frequent and deeper recessions than Japan, West Germany, or France.

Investment in human and physical capital produces advances in knowledge, technological progress, and increased rates of growth in factor productivity, output, and real income. What is desired, therefore, is higher maintained rates (and shares in total output) of savings and investment in real terms. As a practical outcome, there is considerable consensus that the most successful economies are those that have the highest average long-term rates of capital investment. The U.S. had for some time now relatively low shares of private saving and total productive investment, hence it is widely and variously urged to perform better in this respect, as its main competitors in Europe and the Far East do. Fluctuations in business and consumer capital outlays have long been recognized to be a major source of cyclical instability in .aggregate demand. Investment can be both high and stable, provided it is a part of, and a response to growth in aggregate demand that is sufficient to keep the economy near full employment. As the classical long-run version of the accelerator theory has it, net investment is in the end only justified by growth in the demand for the product of the new capital. Increases in real capital, physical and human, generate improvements in productivity that can reduce costs and prices. This is particularly important in the competitive

---

[35] Victor Zarnowitz, "What is a business cycle?", pp. 36–38.

world of open economies. In sum, higher rates of saving, investment, and growth can coexist with, and may favor, greater cyclical stability.[36]

6.5.2 Growth Cycles

In countries where growth persisted at high rates and business contractions occurred rarely and remained mild for a considerable time, even mere slow-downs cause much public concern and indeed are often treated as actual recessions are treated elsewhere. This is so because the slowdowns are themselves of significant duration, result in some rise in unemployment and weak business conditions generally, and are usually associated with abso-lute declines in some more cyclically sensitive activities and sectors. In the 1960s, when confidence about the long-lasting era of high growth and rising prosperity reached its peak, business cycles seemed increasingly obsolete, and interest shifted to growth cycles, that is, fluctuations around the upward trend in a nation's economic activity expressed in real terms.[37]

The concept of growth cycles is an old one, as illustrated by the fact that early indexes of general business conditions and trade were more often than not available only in form of percentage deviations from estimated trend or "normal" curves. Implicitly, the idea of growth cycles has also long been popular with textbook authors who refer vaguely to business cycles being fluc-tuations around the trend and stress the transitory nature of departures of the actual from the potential (full employment) output. But it is very important to distinguish clearly between business cycles and growth cycles because the two differ qualitatively and not just in degree. A slow expansion is still an expansion; the problems posed by a contraction are quite distinct. Moreover, trends interact with cycles, vary over time, and are difficult to isolate and measure.

In spite of these difficulties, much interesting work has been done in the last twenty years on the postwar growth cycles in many countries, particularly by Mintz at the NBER and by Moore and his associates at the CIBCR.[38]

The chronology of growth cycles is derived from the observed consensus of the corresponding turning points in series of deviations from trend just as the chronology of business cycles is derived from the consensus of turning points in series of levels. In both cases, the same basic set of data is used, the main

---

[36] Victor Zarnowitz, "What is a business cycle?", pp. 39–40.
[37] I. Mintz, I. 1974. "Dating United States growth cycles". *Explorations in Economic Research* 1(1) 1974: 1—113.
[38] Victor Zarnowitz, "What is a business cycle?", pp. 40–41.

comprehensive measures of GNP or GDP, personal income, sales, employment, and industrial production (all deflated or in physical units). Growth cycles include both types of slowdowns, hence are much more numerous than business cycles that are defined by the presence of absolute decreases in aggregate activity (recessions). In the trend-adjusted indicator series, all major retardations are reflected in specific-cycle declines that make up growth-cycle contractions; some of these movements descend into the negative region, others stop short of it. Slowdowns occur either in the late stages of business expansions or they interrupt long expansions. As a result, expansions are shorter and contractions longer in growth cycles than in business cycles. Growth cycles are more nearly symmetrical and less variable than business cycles with respect to both durations and amplitudes of their phases. Growth-cycle peaks tend to occur before the corresponding business-cycle peaks, while the troughs of the matching growth cycles and business cycles tend to be roughly coincident.[39]

Mr. Zarnowitz stated that business cycles vary greatly in duration and intensity, less in diffusion. They are not only diverse but also evolving. What they have in common is not their overall dimensions but the make-up, features, and interaction of their many constituent processes. Thus, in each cycle, whether long or short, large or small, production, employment, real incomes, and real sales tend to expand and contract together in many industries and regions, though at uneven rates. Economic variables, e.g., hours worked per week, real new orders for manufactured goods, and change in prices of industrial raw materials, rise and fall correspondingly but earlier with variable leads. Some economic variables, such as inventory-sales ratios, real business loans outstanding, and change in unit labor cost also rise in business expansions and fall in contractions but somewhat later, with variable lags. These sequential movements usually recur in each successive cycle. They all are significantly persistent and pervasive. Systematic differences exist not only in the timing of cyclical movements in different variables but also in their relative size and conformity or coherence (i.e., correlation with business cycles). Among the earliest and most important observations in this area is that activities relating to durable (producer and consumer) goods have particularly large and well-conforming cyclical fluctuations. Other variables long and rightly viewed as highly cyclical are business profits, investment in plant, equipment, and inventories, and cost and volume of bank credit used to finance such investments. More than any other sector of the modern economy, manufacturing has historically been central to both economic

---

[39] Victor Zarnowitz, "What is a business cycle?", pp. 42–43. These arguments were first raised by Mr. Burns and Mr. Mitchell in their *Measuring business cycles*, as reviewed in Chapter 4.

growth and fluctuations. Mining, construction, transportation, communication, and public utilities have varying but significant degrees of cyclical sensitivity. Other nonfarm sectors, which produce largely services rather than goods tend to be much less responsive to business cycles. Employment in service industries broadly defined (including government) followed a strong and smooth upward trend. Agriculture, which underwent a long and strong downward trend in employment and a huge secular rise in productivity, is but weakly cyclical, except for prices. In sum, business cycles, which developed in the age of industrialization, still affect most strongly industries producing goods, especially durables.[40]

The cyclical variables are endogenous; generated by the system of relationships within which they interact. In order for them to be primarily responsible for the business cycles, Mr. Zarnowitz held that the system must have the required dynamics in form of some essential nonlinearities or leads and lags or both. Such elements are undoubtedly important, but we are still far from understanding well how they work, and hence how far the endogenous models can go in explaining business cycles.[41]

6.5.3 Mr. Zarnowitz and Exogenous Business Cycle Variables: Money

Recent theories view economic fluctuations as resulting mainly from changes in observable exogenous factors (variables) or unobservable random shocks (errors). Here the cyclical variables are no longer seen as the central part of a system that can produce self-sustaining cycles. Important policy variables such as the monetary base, tax rates, and federal government spending have been traditionally treated as exogenous, although this cannot be strictly true, since they are clearly influenced by the economy as well as influencing it. Money supply variables are of even more mixed nature in this regard. The extent to which a central bank controls the stock of money or (which is more relevant) its rate of growth depends on factors that vary across countries and over time. In the U.S., narrowly and broadly defined monetary aggregates normally trend upward in both expansions and contractions, though often at reduced rates before downturns. Long absolute declines in Ml or M2 are rare and as a rule associated with business depressions or stagnations. Monetary growth rates tend to lead at business cycle peaks and troughs but by intervals that are highly variable and on average long, as we discussed in Chapter 5

[40] Victor Zarnowitz, "What is a Business Cycle?", pp. 43–44.
[41] Victor Zarnowitz, "What is a business cycle?", p. 45.

with Mr. Friedman and Ms. Schwartz 1963. Cyclical changes in the deposit-reserve ratio and, particularly, the deposit-currency ratio, which reflect the chain of influence that runs from business activity to money, contribute on average strongly to the patterns of movement in money growth during business cycles (Cagan 1965; Plosser 1991). Money shows a systematic tendency to grow faster in business expansions than in contractions, and so does the domestic nonfinancial credit, but the stability of monetary relationships in the cyclical context is subject to much doubt and debate (B. Friedman 1986; Meltzer 1986). Certainly, there is more regularity in the long-term relation between money growth and changes in the price level, and in the procyclical behavior of interest rates and the income velocity of money (allowing for its long trends). For all of this, there is no denying that business cycles have important monetary and financial aspects. A six-variable, four-lag quarterly vector autoregressive (VAR) model applied to postwar and earlier U.S. data by Mr. Zarnowitz and Mr. Braun (1990), discussed earlier in this chapter, reported that the rate of change in real GNP was significantly affected by lagged rates of change in the monetary aggregates (base, Ml, and particularly M2) but much more strongly yet by lagged values of short-term interest rates. However, the influence of changes in the planned volume of fixed and inventory investment and purchases of durable goods proved to be strong as well.[42]

6.5.4 Mr. Zarnowitz, Business Cycles and Expectational Shocks

In the original monetarist theory, money supply was treated as the main exogenous factor driving the business cycle. In the more recent equilibrium version with rational expectations, the anticipated money growth can influence only prices, not output; that is, only unanticipated money shocks have real effects. Tests of this hypothesis have produced evidence that is mixed but mostly unfavorable in the sense of not confirming the importance of the .distinction between the effects of the anticipated and unanticipated components of monetary change. Full exogeneity of money is one extreme and unrealistic assumption: full endogeneity of money is another, at the opposite end of the spectrum. The latter view posits that changes in inside money accommodate the money stock to the level of economic activity; it is accepted both in some Keynesian disequilibrium models and the real business cycle (RBC) models in which fluctuations are strictly equilibrium phenomena.

---

[42] Victor Zarnowitz, "What is a business cycle?", pp. 45–47.

154 J. B. Guerard

In the RBC model, stochastic oscillations in the economy's real growth path are caused by a mixture of transitory and permanent shocks to productivity (Kydland and Prescott 1982). There is a long gestation lag in the production of capital goods, which imparts some persistence to output movements. As productivity gains fluctuate, so do real wages (or, more accurately, real returns on the work effort) to which labor supply responds very elastically. But the cyclical sensitivity of real wages is low, and tests of the hypothesis of high intertemporal substitution of leisure are mostly negative. To explain booms and busts, sufficiently large and frequent shocks to productivity would be necessary, yet the evidence for them is hard to find.[43]

That a variety of factors can and do serve as proximate causes of business cycles is an old idea embodied in the synthetic theories of Mitchell, Schumpeter, and very explicitly Pigou (1927).[44] Evidence from recent macroeconometric models supports this concept. Unlike the early Keynesian models dominated by demand factors and fiscal policy, the present models give considerable attention to supply factors as well, and actually have monetary policy matter more than fiscal. In large multi-sector models, the distinction between demand and supply shocks is rather blurred anyway.

Since the incisive and detailed analysis of the monetary history of the U.S. by Friedman and Schwartz (1963) the monetarist interpretation of business cycle developments gained and still retains a wide acceptance, despite critical countercurrents within the profession. It is simply very difficult to deny that strong restrictive monetary measures designed to combat inflation have contributed to subsequent economic downturns at least in some well-known episodes Similarly, the shift to a policy of lower money growth and sharply higher interest rates, first signaled in October 1979, was followed by the Volcker disinflation and the recessions of 1980 and 1981–1982. In each case, however, these monetary shocks were accompanied by changes in factors unrelated to monetary policy that must have also contributed to the recessions that followed (fiscal stringencies in 1920 and 1936–1937; an oil shock and financial deregulation in the late 1970s, fall in money velocity in the early 1980s).[45] So monetary and real disturbances (or unusual developments) coincided, and their effects are difficult to disentangle.

[43] Victor Zarnowitz, "What is a business cycle?", p. 47.
[44] Victor Zarnowitz, "What is a business cycle?", p. 48.
[45] Victor Zarnowitz, "What is a business cycle?", p. 49.

6.5.5 What is a Business Cycle: Some General Conclusions

Mr. Zarnowitz stated eight general conclusions to his NBER working paper, entitled "What is a business cycle?" These conclusions are:

1. A business cycle includes a downturn and contraction followed by an
   A business cycle includes a downturn and contraction followed by an upturn and expansion in aggregate economic activity, which ideally should be represented by comprehensive and reliable measures of total employment, output, real income, and real expenditures. But nominal income aggregates and price indexes can serve as good criteria, provided that the fluctuations extend to a broad class of sufficiently flexible prices, as was the case in the now rather distant past.

2. A business cycle is pervasive in the sense that it consists of co-movements and interactions of many variables. The regularity, magnitude, and timing of the fluctuations vary across the variables, and these differences are in part systematic. Thus, most activities are procyclical, mildly or strongly, but some are countercyclical. Some variables tend to have approximately coincident timing, others tend to lead, and still others tend to lag. These patterns may or may not be symmetrical, e.g., timing may be systematically different at peaks and troughs.

3. A business cycle is at least national in scope, that is, it involves most industries and regions of a country, though again with variations in intensity and timing. It can attain much larger dimensions when transmitted across countries through channels of international trade and finance.

4. A business cycle lasts as a rule several years and so is sufficiently persistent for serially correlated as well as intercorrelated movements in many variables to develop sequentially in the downward as well as upward direction. The movements tend to cumulate before reversing themselves.

5. In most but not all business cycles, prices in general move procyclically, at least apart from their long trends (in the last half-century. upward). This indicates a long and large role for the fluctuations of, and disturbances to, aggregate demand. These can be of real, monetary, or expectational origin and may well involve interactions between any or all such factors. But supply shifts are also part and parcel of business cycles, and they may be dominant in some, as in oil in the 1970s. The cyclical instability of profits, investment, and credit has a long history and is well-documented.

6. Business cycles have varied greatly over the past 200 years in length, spread, and size. They included vigorous and weak expansions, long

and short; mild and severe contractions, again some long, some short; and many moderate fluctuations of close-to-average duration (about 3–5 years). But since the 1930s, the U.S. suffered no major depression. Business expansions have become longer, recessions shorter and milder. The probable reasons include the shift of employment to the production of services, automatic stabilizers, some financial reforms and avoidance of crises, greater weight and some successes of governmental actions and policies, and higher levels of public confidence.

7. The postwar recessions were much fewer and generally milder still in France, Italy, and, particularly, West Germany and Japan. These countries also had much higher average rates of real economic growth than the U.S., especially in the early reconstruction phase of the post-1945 era. In the 1970s and 1980s, growth decreased everywhere and the recessions became more frequent and serious. All this suggests that countries and periods with stronger growth trends are less vulnerable to cyclical instability.

8. In sum, business cycles make up a class of varied, complex, and evolving phenomena of both history and economic dynamics. Theories or models that try to reduce them to a single causal mechanism or shock seem to me altogether unlikely to succeed.[46]

6.6   Summary and Conclusions

Mr. Zarnowitz continued the NBER analysis of business cycles in the tradition of Mr. Mitchell, Mr. Burns, and Mr. Moore, his frequent co-author. Mr. Zarnowitz included econometric model testing in his testing, reporting that econometric models, while often beating naïve, no-change models, failed to identify turning points. Mr. Zarnowitz, in his NBER monograph, *Business Cycles: Theory, History, Indictors, and Forecasting*, parts III and IV, verified the statistical significance on the LEI in forecasting, particularly real GDP. Mr. Zarnowitz continued the analysis of Mr, Moore and reported that the NBER LEI continued to be less than satisfactory in predicting turning points in business cycles. In measuring econometric model forecasting performance, Mr. Zarnowitz reported that the large-scale macroeconomic models were not accurate in forecasting turning points. In the next chapter, we test and report the efficiency of the LEI in modeling and forecasting real GDP and the unemployment rate. Practitioners and businessmen using the LEI in forecasting are well-advised to read the works of Mr. Zarnowitz.

---

[46] Victor Zarnowitz, "What is a business cycle?", pp. 59–61.

Appendix 6.1: Exponential Smoothing

The simplest forecast of a time series can be estimated from an arithmetic mean of the data, see Davis and Nelson (1937). If one defines f as frequencies, or occurrences of the data, and x as the values of the series, then the arithmetic mean is

$$A = \frac{f_1 x_1 + f_2 x_2 + f_3 x_3 + \ldots + f_t x_t}{T} \tag{6.22}$$

where $T = f_1 + f_2 + f_3 + \ldots + f_t$

$$A = \frac{f_i x_i}{T}$$

Alternatively,

$$\frac{f_i(x_i - x)}{T}$$

$$A = x + \frac{f_i(x_i - x)}{T} \tag{6.23}$$

The first moment, mean, is:

$$A = \frac{f_i x_i}{T} = \frac{m_1}{m_0}$$

$$m_0 = \sum f_i = T, \; m_1 = \sum f_i x_i$$

If $x = 0$, then

$$\sigma^2 = \frac{f_i x_i^2}{T} - A^2$$

$$\sigma^2 = \frac{m_2}{m_0} - \frac{m_1^2}{m_0^2} = \left(m_0 m_2 - m_1^2 \right) m_0^2 \tag{6.24}$$

Time series models often involve trend, cycle seasonal, and irregular components [Brown (1963)]. An upward-moving or increasing series over time could be modeled as

$$x_t = a + bt \tag{6.25}$$

where a is the mean and b is the trend or rate at which the series increases over time, t. Brown (1963, p. 61) uses the closing price of IBM common stock as his example of an increasing series. One could use a quadrant term, c. If c is positive, then the series

$$x_t = a + bt + ct^2 \tag{6.26}$$

trend is changing toward an increasing trend; whereas, a negative c denotes a decreasing rate of trend, from upward to downward.

In an exponential smoothing model, the underlying process is locally constant, $x_t = a$, plus random noise, ε_t.

$$x_t = ae_t \tag{6.27}$$

The average value of $\varepsilon = 0$.

A moving average can be estimated over a portion of the data:

$$M_t = \frac{x_1 + x_{t-1} + \ldots + x_{t-N} + 1}{N} \tag{6.28}$$

where M_t is the actual average of the most recent N observations.

$$M_t = M_{t-1} + \frac{x_t - x_{t-N}}{N} \tag{6.29}$$

An exponential smoothing forecast builds upon the moving average concept.

$$s_t(x) = ax_t + (1 - a)\, s_{t-1}(x)$$

where α = smoothing constant, which is similar to the fraction $\frac{1}{T}$ in a moving average.

$$s_t(x) = ax_t + (1 - a)[ax_{t-1} + (1 - a)\, s_{t-2}(x)]$$
$$= \sum_{ko}^{t-1} (1-)^k x_{t-k} + (1-)^t x_o \tag{6.30}$$

$s_t(x)$ is a linear combination of all past observations. The smoothing constant must be estimated. In a moving average process, the N most recent observations are weighted (equally) by 1/N and the average age of the data is:

$$k = \frac{0 + 1 + 2 + \ldots + N - 1}{N} = \frac{N - 1}{2}$$

A N-period moving average is equivalent to an exponential smoothing model having an average age of the data. The one-period forecast for an exponential smoothing model is:

$$F_{t+1} = F_t + a(y_t - F_t) \qquad (6.31)$$

where α is the constant, $0 < \alpha < 0.3$.

Intuitively, if α is near zero, then the forecast is very close to the previous value's forecast. Alternatively,

$$F_{t+1} = ay_t + (1 - a)F_t \qquad (6.32)$$

$$F_{t+1} = ay_t + a(1 - a) \, y_{t-1} + (1 - a)2F_{t-1}$$

Makridakis, Wheelwright, and Hyndman (1998) express F_{t-1} in terms of F_{t-2} and, over time,

$$\begin{aligned}
F_{t-1} = {} & ay_t + a(1 - a) \, y_{t-1} \\
& + a(a - a)^2 y_{t-2} + a(1 - a)^3 y_{t-3} \\
& + a(1 - a)^4 y_{t-4} + a(1 - a)^5 y_{t-5} + \ldots \\
& + a(1 - a)^{t-1} y_t + (1 - a)^t F_1 \qquad (6.33)
\end{aligned}$$

Different values of α produce different mean-squared errors. If one sought to minimize the mean absolute percentage error, the adaptive exponential smoothing can be rewritten as:

$$F_{t+1} = ay_t + (1 - a)F_t \qquad (6.34)$$

$$\alpha t + 1 = \left| \frac{A_t}{M_t} \right|$$

where $A_t = \beta E_t + (1 - \beta)A_{t-1}$

$$M_t = \beta |E_t| + (1 - \beta)M_{t-1}$$

$$E_t = y_t - F_t$$

A_t is a smoothed estimate of the forecast error and a weighted average of A_{t-1} and the last forecast error, E_t.

One of the great forecasting models is the Holt (1957) model that allowed forecasting of data with trends. Holt's linear exponential smoothing forecast is:

$$L_t = ay_t + (1 - a)(L_{t-1} + b_{t-1}) \qquad (6.35)$$

$$b_t = \beta(L_t - -L_{t-1}) + (1 - \beta)b_{t-1}$$

$$F_{t+m} = L_t + b_t m$$

L_t is the level of the series at time t, and b_t is the estimate of the slope of the series at time t. The Holt model forecast should be better forecasts than adaptive exponential smoothing models, which lack trends. Makridakis, Wheelwright, and Hyndman (1998) remind the reader that the Holt model is often referred to as "double exponential smoothing." If $\alpha = \beta$, then the Holt model is equal to Brown's double exponential smoothing model.

The Holt (1957) and Winters (1960) seasonal model can be written as:

(Level) $L_t = \alpha \frac{y_t}{S_{t-s}} + (1 - a)(L_{t-1} + b_{t-1})$

(Trend) $b_t + \beta(L_t - L_{t-1}) + (a - \beta) b_{t-1}$

(Seasonal) $s_t = \gamma + (a - \gamma)s_{t-s}$

(Forecast) $F_{t+m} = (L_t + b_t m)S_{t-s+m}$

Seasonality is the number of months or quarters, Lt is the level of the series, b_t is the trend of the series, and s_t is the seasonal component.

References

Clemen, R. T., & Guerard, J. B. (1989). Econometric GNP forecasts: Incremental information relative to naive extrapolation. *International Journal of Forecasting, 5,* 417–426.

Clements, M. P., & Hendry, D. F. (1998). *Forecasting economic time series.* Cambridge University Press.

Davis, H. T. (1941). *The analysis of economic time series (Cowles Foundation monograph #6).* Principia Press.

Dhrymes, P. J. (2017). *Introductory econometrics.* Springer.

Diebold, F. X., & Mariano, R. S. (1995). Comparing predictive accuracy. *Journal of Business and Economic Statistics, 13*, 253–263.

Elton, E. J., Gruber, M. J. Brown, S. J., & Goetzman, W. N. (2007). *Modern Portfolio theory and investment analysis* (7th ed.). John Wiley & Sons, Inc.

Gordon, R. J. (1986). *The American business cycle*. University of Chicago Press.

Granger, C. W. J., & Newbold, P. (1977). *Forecasting economic time series*. Academic Press.

Granger, C. W. J., & Newbold, P. (1986). *Forecasting economic time series* (2nd ed.). Academic Press, Inc.

Guerard, J. B., Jr. (2004). The forecasting effectiveness of the U.S. leading economic indicators: Further evidence and initial G7 results. In P. Dua (Ed.), *Business cycles and economic growth: An analysis using leading indicators* (pp. 174–187). Oxford University Press.

Guerard, J. B., Jr. (2001). A note on the forecasting effectiveness of the U.S. leading economic indicators. *Indian Economic Review, 36*, 251–268.

Gunst, R. F., & Mason, R. L. (1980). *Regression analysis and its application*. Marcel Dekker Inc.

Hahn, F., & Solow, R. (1995). *A critical essay on modern macroeconomic theory*. MIT Press.

Harberler, G. (1937). *Prosperity and depression*. League of Nations, Geneva. Reprinted 1963. Atheneum.

Klein, L. (1950). *Economic fluctuations in the United States*, 1941. Wiley & Sons.

Makridakis, S., Andersen, A., Carbone, R., Fildes, R., Hibon, M., et al. (1982). The accuracy of extrapolation (time series) methods: Results of a forecasting competition. *Journal of Forecasting, 1*, 111–153.

Makridakis, S., & Hibon, M. (2000). The M3-competition: Results, conclusions and implications. *International Journal of Forecasting, 16*, 451–476.

Makridakis, S., Wheelwright, S. C., Hyndman, R. J. (1998). *Forecasting: Methods and applications*. John Wiley & Sons, 3rd edition. Chapters 5, 6.

Mansfield, E. (1994). *Statistics for business and economics* (5th ed.). W.W. Norton & Company.

Mincer, J., & Zarnowitz, V. (1969). The Evaluation of Economic Forecasts. In Mincer, J. (Ed.), *Economic forecasts and expectations*, Columbia University Press.

Montgomery, A. L., Zarnowitz, V., Tsay, R., & Tiao, G. C. (1998). Forecasting the U.S. unemployment rate. *Journal of the American Statistical Association, 93*, 478–493.

Nelson, C. R., & Plosser, C. I. (1982). Trends and random walks in macroeconomic time series. *Journal of Monetary Economics, 10*, 139–162.

Nelson, C. R. (1973). *Applied time series analysis for managerial forecasting*. Holden-Day Inc.

Theil, H. (1966). *Applied economic forecasting*. Amsterdam, North-Holland.

Zarnowitz, V. (2004). The autonomy of recent US growth and business cycles. In P. Dua (Ed.), *Business cycles and economic growth: An analysis using leading indicators* (pp. 44–82). Oxford University Press.

Zarnowitz, V. (2001). The old and the new in the U.S. economic expansion. The Conference Board. EPWP #01–01.

Zarnowitz, V., & Ozyildirim, A. (2001). On the measurement of business cycles and growth cycles. *Indian Economic Review, 36*, 34–54.

Zarnowitz, V. (1992). *Business cycles: Theory, history, indicators, and forecasting.* University of Chicago Press.

Zarnowitz, V. (1991). What is a business cycle? NBER Working Paper Series, Number 3683.

7

Regression and Time Series Modeling of Real GDP, the Unemployment Rate, and the Impact of Leading Economic Indicators on Forecasting Accuracy

In this chapter, we evaluate the forecasting efficiency of the Leading Economic Indicators, LEI. We apply ordinary least square and robust regression methodologies to test the efficiency of the LEI and its components on several well-studied macroeconomics series, real GDP and the unemployment rate. We model changes in the unemployment rate as a function of changes in the leading economic indicators and weekly unemployment claims time series for the 1959–2020 time period. report that the OxMetrics and AutoMetrics system substantially reduce regression sum of squares measures relative to a traditional variation on the random walk with drift model. The modeling process of including the Leading Economic Indicator in forecasting real GDP and the unemployment rate. Victor Zarnowitz and his colleagues Montgomery, Tsay, and Tiao, produced the seminal forecasting study of the unemployment rate in 1998 and we update the forecasting the unemployment rate using recent time series analysis. Our forecasting results are more statistically significant. A similar conclusion is found for the impact of the LEI and weekly unemployment claims series leading the unemployment rate series. We report statistically significant breaks in these data. We tested univariate and best bivariate models over 60-day and 120-day rolling window periods and report highly forecast error reductions. The adaptive averaging autoregressive model ADA-AR and the newly proposed, adaptive learning forecast, ADL, produced the smallest root mean square errors and lowest mean absolute errors.

© The Author(s), under exclusive license to Springer Nature
Switzerland AG 2022
J. B. Guerard, *The Leading Economic Indicators and Business Cycles in the United States*, https://doi.org/10.1007/978-3-030-99418-1_7

Linear regression analysis is well known and taught in most universities in the student's sophomore year and in a one-term course in an MBA program. Simple linear regression is taught usually with one dependent variable and one independent variable, hypothesized to be associated with the dependent variable. The example of consumption is a function of disposable income is a very good and commonly used example in many econometric textbooks. In this chapter, we test whether the unemployment rate is associated with weekly unemployment claims. That is, if weekly unemployment claims increase, then one would expect the unemployment rate to rise in the future. We also test if an increase in the leading economic indicators, LEI, is announced, then economic activity is expected to increase, and the Gross Domestic Product, the market value of goods and services in our economy should rise in the future. Multiple regression is used when the student or researcher wants to test if more than one variable is associated with the dependent variable. We will test the hypothesis that the unemployment rate is a function of both the weekly unemployment claims and the leading economic indicator data. Regression analysis is used in Chapter 9 to test how fundamental data, such as earnings book value, cash flow, and sales, expectations data, such as analysts' forecasts, forecast revisions, and the direction of forecast revisions, and price momentum data are associated with stock returns over the 1996–2020 time period. In our linear regression models, we specifically address the problems of outliers and the correlation among our independent variables, the issue of multicollinearity. We must have well-conditioned regression models. The author assumes that the reader is several years past that his or her statistics course time and could benefit from the Regression and Time Series Appendix following Chapter 11, the conclusions of this monograph. Time series modeling has evolved from the Box and Jenkins (1970) approach for the identification, estimation, and forecasting of stationary (or series transformed to stationarity) series, through the analysis of the series autocorrelation and partial autocorrelation functions, to the world of Clive Granger (2001) and causality testing, to current applications of automatic time series modeling and forecasting of Hendry and Doornik (2014) to the approaches suggested via the M-competitions, reported in Makridakis et al. (1984) and Makridakis and Hibon (2000) and the very successful Theta method (Nikolopoulos & Thomakos, 2019). In this chapter, we introduce the reader to What paths should a practitioner seek to follow in analyzing time series models and using time series model forecasts?

One of the most important problems for a practitioner is the efficient use of information in forecasting. Clements and Hendry (2005) presented four themes that complemented the topics previously introduced. The four themes help the reader systematically address modern forecasting analysis and evaluation:

1. the use of more information, including forecast combinations and use of leading indicators;
2. the use of less information produced by parsimonious estimation of forecasting model and breaks;
3. transformed information via differencing, intercept corrections; and collinearity analysis; and
4. the role of evaluation information in forecasting with historical forecast comparisons and forecast encompassing.

Clements and Hendry remind us that forecasting is littered with forecast failures and criticize the naïve extrapolation models out-performance of econometric models in several out-of-sample financial forecasting competitions due to structural breaks. What we seek to do in this chapter is to re-examine relationships between real GDP forecasting and the unemployment rate, and the leading economic indicators. We use SAS for traditional simple linear and multiple regression modelling. The SAS software is one of the most widely used statistical packages in industry to estimate regression and time series (ARIMA) models. Practitioners use SAS to do model (and follow) these time series. One could say that such series can be thought of as random walks with drift. We will show that traditionally analyzed series, such as the (US) real GDP and the unemployment rate, can be effectively modeled by the leading economic indicators with the OxMetrics software, see Hendry and Doornik (2014) and Castle and Hendry (2019). There are significant breaks in these data. We will further show that the use of leading economic indicators is indeed significant in providing performance enhancements in forecasting, even without accounting for the presence of breaks.

7.1 Estimating an Ordinary Least Square Regression Line

In simple regression analysis, one seeks to measure the statistical association between two variables, X and Y. Regression analysis is generally used to measure how changes in the independent variable, X, influence changes in the dependent variable, Y. Regression analysis shows a statistical association or correlation among variables, rather than a causal relationship among variables. In this chapter, we address the relationship between the

U.S. unemployment rate, the Leading Economic Indicator (LEI) and Weekly Unemployment Claims, a component of the LEI.

The case of simple, linear, least-squares regression may be written in the form:

$$Y = \alpha + \beta X + \varepsilon \qquad (7.1)$$

where Y, the dependent variable, is a linear function of X, the independent variable. The parameters α and β characterize the population regression line and ε is the randomly distributed error term. The regression estimates of α and β will be derived from the principle of least squares. In applying least squares, the sum of the squared regression errors will be minimized; our regression errors equal the actual dependent variable minus the estimated value from the regression line. If Y represents the actual value and $\hat{Y}$ the estimated value, their difference is the error term, e. Least square regression minimizes the sum of the squared error terms. The simple regression line will yield an estimated value of Y, $\hat{Y}$ by the use of the sample regression:

$$\hat{Y} = \hat{a} + \hat{b}X \qquad (7.2)$$

In the estimation Eq. (7.2), a is the least-squares estimate of α and b is the estimate of β. Thus, a and b are the regression constants that must be estimated. The least-squares regression constants (or statistics) a and b are unbiased and efficient (smallest variance) estimators of α and β. The error term, $\hat{e}_i$, is the difference between the actual and estimated dependent variable value for any given independent variable values, X_i.

$$\hat{e}_i = Y_i - \hat{Y}_i \qquad (7.3)$$

The regression error term, $\hat{e}_i$, is the least-squares estimate of ε_i, the actual error term.[1]

---

[1] The reader is referred to an excellent statistical reference, such as Irwin Miller and J.E. Freund, *Probability and Statistics for Engineers* (Englewood Cliffs, NJ: Prentice-Hall, 1965), S. Makridakis, S.C. Wheelwright, and R. J. Hyndman, *Forecasting: Methods and Applications* (New York: John Wiley & Sons, 1998), Third Edition, G.S. Maddala and K. Lahiri, *Introduction to Econometrics* (New York: John Wiley & Sons, 2009), Fourth Edition, and P.J. Dhrymes, *Introductory Econometrics* (New York: Springer, 2017), Second Edition.

To minimize the error terms, the least-squares technique minimizes the sum of the squared error terms of the N observations,

$$\sum_{i=1}^{N} \hat{e}_i^2 \tag{7.4}$$

Thus, least squares regression minimizes:

$$\sum_{i=1}^{N} \hat{e}_i^2 = \sum_{i=1}^{N} [Y_i - \hat{Y}_i]^2 = \sum_{i=1}^{N} [Y_i - (\hat{a} + \hat{b}X_i)]^2 \tag{7.5}$$

To assure that a minimum is reached, the partial derivatives of the squared error terms function

$$\sum_{i=1}^{N} = [Y_i - (a + bX_i)]^2$$

will be taken with respect to a and b.

$$\frac{\partial \sum_{i=1}^{N} \hat{e}_i^2}{\partial \hat{a}} = 2 \sum_{i=1}^{N} \left(Y_i - \hat{a} - \hat{b}X_i \right)(-1)$$

$$= -2 \left(\sum_{i=1}^{N} Y_i - \sum_{i=1}^{N} \hat{a} - \hat{b} \sum_{i=1}^{N} X_i \right)$$

$$\frac{\partial \sum_{i=1}^{N} e_i^2}{\partial \hat{b}} = 2 \sum_{i=1}^{N} \left(Y_i - \hat{a} - \hat{b}X_i \right)(-X_i)$$

$$= -2 \left(\sum_{i=1}^{N} Y_i X_i - \hat{a} \sum_{i=1}^{N} X_i - \hat{b} \sum_{i=1}^{N} X_i^2 \right)$$

The partial derivatives will then be set equal to zero.
Rewriting these equations, one obtains the normal equations:

$$\sum_{i=1}^{N} Y_i = \sum_{i=1}^{N} \hat{a} + \hat{b} \sum_{i=1}^{N} X_i$$

$$\sum_{i=1}^{N} Y_i X_i = \hat{a} \sum_{i=1}^{N} X_i + \hat{b} \sum_{i=1}^{N} X_i^2 \qquad (7.6)$$

Solving the normal equations simultaneously for a and b yields the least squares regression estimates:

$$\hat{a} = \frac{\left(\sum_{i=1}^{N} X_i^2\right)\left(\sum_{i=1}^{N} Y_i\right) - \left(\sum_{i=1}^{N} X_i Y_i\right)}{N\left(\sum_{i=1}^{N} X_i^2\right) - \left(\sum_{i=1}^{N} X_i\right)^2}$$

$$\hat{b} = \frac{N\left(\sum_{i=1}^{N} X_i Y_i\right) - \left(\sum_{i=1}^{N} X_i\right)\left(\sum_{i=1}^{N} Y_i\right)}{N\left(\sum_{i=1}^{N} X_i^2\right) - \left(\sum_{i=1}^{N} X_i\right)^2} \qquad (7.7)$$

The coefficient of determination, R^2, is the percentage of the variance of the dependent variable explained by the independent variable. The coefficient of determination cannot exceed 1 nor be less than zero. In the case of $R^2 = 0$, the regression line is $Y = \overline{Y}$ and no variation in the dependent variable is explained. If the dependent variable pattern continues as in the past, the model with time as the independent variable should be of good use in forecasting.

One can test whether the a and b coefficients are statistically different from zero, the generally accepted null hypothesis. A t-test is used to test the two null hypotheses:

$$H_{o_1} : a = 0$$
$$H_{A_1} : a \text{ ne } 0$$
$$H_{o_2} : \beta = 0$$
$$H_{A_2} : \beta \text{ ne } 0$$

where ne denotes not equal.

The H_o represents the null hypothesis while H_A represents the alternative hypothesis. To reject the null hypothesis, the calculated t-value must exceed the critical t-value given in the t-tables in the statistics texts.

7.2   Estimating Multiple Regression Lines

It may well be that several economic variables influence the variable that one is interested in forecasting. For example, the change in the unemployment rate as a function of changes in the Leading Economic Indicators or weekly unemployment claims. Multiple regression is an extremely easy statistical tool for researchers and management to employ due to the great proliferation of computer software. We use SAS and OxMetrics in this Appendix. The general form of the two-independent variable multiple regression is:

$$Y_t = \beta_1 + \beta_2 X_{2t} + \beta_3 X_{3t} + \varepsilon_t, \quad t = 1, \ldots, N \quad (7.8)$$

In matrix notation multiple regression can be written:

$$Y = X\beta + \varepsilon \quad (7.9)$$

Multiple regression requires unbiasedness, the expected value of the error term is zero, and the X's are fixed and independent of the error term. The error term is an identically and independently distributed normal variable. Least squares estimation of the coefficients yields:

$$\hat{\beta} = (\hat{\beta}_1, \hat{\beta}_2, \hat{\beta}_3)$$
$$Y = X\hat{\beta} + e \quad (7.10)$$

Multiple regression, using the least squared principle, minimizes the sum of the squared error terms:

$$\sum_{i=1}^{N} \hat{e}_1^2 = \hat{e}'\hat{e}$$
$$= (Y - X\hat{\beta})'(Y - X\hat{\beta}) \quad (7.11)$$

To minimize the sum of the squared error terms, one takes the partial derivative of the squared errors with respect to $\hat{\beta}$ and the partial derivative and set equal to zero.

$$\partial \frac{(\hat{e}'\hat{e})}{\partial \beta} = -2X'Y + 2X'X\hat{\beta} = 0$$
$$\hat{\beta} = (X'X)^{-1}X'Y \quad (7.12)$$

Alternatively, one could solve the normal equations for the two-variable to determine the regression coefficients.

$$\Sigma Y = \hat{\beta}_1 N + \hat{\beta}_2 \Sigma X_2 + \hat{\beta}_3 \Sigma X_3$$
$$\Sigma X_2 Y = \hat{\beta}_1 \Sigma X_2 + \hat{\beta}_2 X_2^2 + \hat{\beta}_3 \Sigma X_3^2$$
$$\Sigma X_3 Y = \hat{\beta}_1 \Sigma X_3 + \hat{\beta}_2 \Sigma X_2 X_3 + \hat{\beta}_3 \Sigma X_3^2 \qquad (7.13)$$

When we solved the normal equations (7.13), to find the a and b that minimized the sum of our squared error terms in simple linear regression, and when we solved the two variable normal equations, Eq. (7.13) to find the multiple regression estimated parameters, we made several assumptions. First, we assumed that the error term is independently and identically distributed; i.e., a random variable with an expected value, or mean of zero, and a finite, and constant, standard deviation. The error term should not be a function of time nor should the error term be a function of the size of the independent variable (s), a condition known as heteroscedasticity. One may plot the residuals as a function of the independent variable (s) to be certain that the residuals are independent of the independent variables. The error term should be a normally distributed variable. That is, the error terms should have an expected value of zero and 67.6% of the observed error terms should fall within the mean value plus or minus one standard deviation of the error terms (the so-called "Bell Curve" or normal distribution). Ninety-five percent of the observations should fall within the plus or minus two standard deviation levels, the so-called 95% confidence interval. The presence of extreme, or influential, observations may distort estimated regression lines and the corresponding estimated residuals. Another problem in regression analysis is the assumed independence of the independent variables in Eq. (7.8). Significant correlations may produce estimated regression coefficients that are "unstable" and have the "incorrect" signs. Let us spend some time discussing two problems discussed in this section, the problems of influential observations, commonly known as outliers, and the correlation among independent variables, known as multicollinearity.

There are several methods that one can use to identify influential observations or outliers. First, we can plot the residuals and 95% confidence intervals and examine how many observations have residuals falling outside these limits. One should expect no more than 5% of the observations to fall outside of these intervals. One may find that one or two observations may distort a regression estimate even if there are 100 observations in the database. The estimated residuals should be normally distributed, and the ratio of the residuals divided by their standard deviation, known as standardized residuals, should be a normal variable. We showed, in Eq. (7.12), that in multiple regression:

$$\hat{\beta} = (X'X)X'Y$$

The residuals of the multiple regression line is given by:

$$\hat{e} = Y' - \hat{\beta}X$$

7.3 Influential Observations and Possible Outliers and the Application of Robust Regression

The standardized residual concept can be modified such that the reader can calculate a variation on that term to identify influential observations. If we delete observation i in a regression, we can measure the impact of observation i on the change in estimated regression coefficients and residuals. Belsley et al. (1980) showed that the estimated regression coefficients change by an amount, DFBETA, where:

$$DFBETA_i = \frac{(X'X)^{-1}X'\hat{e}_i}{1 - h_i} \tag{7.14}$$

where:

$$h_i = X_i(X'X)^{-1}X'_i$$

The h_i or "hat," term is calculated by deleting observation i. The corresponding residual is known as the studentized residual, sr, and defined as:

$$sr_i = \frac{\hat{e}_i}{\hat{\sigma}\sqrt{1 - h_i}} \tag{7.15}$$

where $\hat{\sigma}$ is the estimated standard deviation of the residuals. A studentized residual that exceeds 2.0 indicates a potential influential observation (Belsley et al., 1980). Another distance measure has been suggested by Cook (1977), which modifies the studentized residual, to calculate a scaled residual known as the Cook distance measure, CookD. As the researcher or modeler deletes observations, one needs to compare the original matrix of the estimated residuals with the modified variance matrix. The COVRATIO calculation performs this calculation, where:

$$\text{COVRATIO} = \frac{1}{[\frac{n-p-1}{n-p} + \frac{\hat{e}_i*}{(n-p)}]^p (1-h_i)} \tag{7.16}$$

where n = number of observations,
p = number of independent variables,
and $\hat{e}_i*$ = deleted observations.

If the absolute value of the deleted observation is > 2, then the COVRATIO calculation approaches:

$$1 - \frac{3p}{n} \tag{7.17}$$

A calculated COVRATIO that is larger than $\frac{3p}{n}$ indicates an influential observation. The DFBETA, studentized residual, CookD, and COVRATIO calculations may be performed within SAS. See Appendix A for the Belsley et al. (1980) influential observations and outlier analysis. The identification of influential data is an important component of regression analysis. One may create variables for use in multiple regression that make use of the influential data, or outliers, to which they are commonly referred.

The modeler can identify outliers, or influential data, and re-run the ordinary least squares regressions on the re-weighted data, a process referred to as robust (ROB) regression. In ordinary least squares, OLS, all data is equally weighted. The weights are 1.0. In robust regression one weights the data universally with its OLS residual; i.e., the larger the residual, the smaller the weight of the observation in the robust regression. In robust regression, several weights may be used. We will report the Huber (1973), Beaton-Tukey (1974), and Tukey MM-estimate with 99% efficiency, discussed in Maronna et al. (2019) weighting schemes.

In the Huber (1973) robust regression procedure, one uses the following calculation to weigh the data:

$$w_i = \left(1 - \left(\frac{|\hat{e}_i|}{\sigma_i}\right)^2\right)^2 \tag{7.18}$$

where $\hat{e}_i$ = residual i,

σ_i = standard deviation of residual.

and w_i = weight of observation i.

The intuition is that the larger the estimated residual, the smaller the weight. A second robust re-weighting scheme is calculated from the Beaton-Tukey bisquare criteria where:

$$
w_i = \left(1 - \left(\frac{\frac{|\hat{e}_i|}{\sigma_e}}{4.685}\right)^2\right)^2, \quad \text{if } \frac{|\hat{e}_i|}{\sigma_e} > 4.685;
$$

$$
1, \quad \text{if } \frac{|\hat{e}_i|}{\sigma_e} < 4.685.
$$

(7.19)

The second major problem is one of multicollinearity, the condition of correlation among the independent variables. If the independent variables are perfectly correlated in multiple regression, then the $(X'X)$ matrix of Eq. (7.30), cannot be inverted and the multiple regression coefficients have multiple solutions. In reality, highly correlated independent variables can produce unstable regression coefficients due to an unstable $(X'X)^{-1}$ matrix. Belsley et al. advocate the calculation of a condition number, which is the ratio of the largest latent root of the correlation matrix relative to the smallest latent root of the correlation matrix. A condition number exceeding 30.0 indicates severe multicollinearity.

7.4 Estimating Simple and Multiple Regression Models in SAS

In this section, we estimate real-world regression models with the SAS software. The author has used SAS and finds it easy and effective for student use. We will estimate regression models to identify variables associated with the U.S. unemployment rate. We revisit the approaches used in the seminal paper of Montgomery, Zarnowitz, Tsay, and Tiao (Montgomery et al., 1998), hereafter denoted as MZTT, on forecasting the U.S. unemployment rate using weekly unemployment claims as an input to the transfer function model.[2]

---

[2] Mr. Zarnowitz, retired from the University of Chicago, and spent his "retirement" working on enhancing and maintaining the LEI time series. Victor, the subject of our Chapter 6, was Director of Research at The Conference Board, for many of these years.

The Conference Board's components of the composite leading indicators for the year 2018 reflect the work and variables shown in Levanon et al. (2015) which continued work of Burns and Mitchell (1938, 1946), Moore (1961), and Zarnowitz (1992). The Conference Board index of leading indicators, in November 2019, is composed of:

Average weekly hours, manufacturing
Average weekly initial claims for unemployment insurance
Manufacturers' new orders, consumer goods and materials
ISM® Index of New Orders
Manufacturers' new orders, nondefense capital goods excluding aircraft orders
Building permits, new private housing units
Stock prices, 500 common stocks
Leading Credit Index™
Interest rate spread, 10-year Treasury bonds less federal funds.[3]

Monthly Data (Click on series to chart data).
G0M910 - LEI - Composite index of 10 leading indicators (2016 = 100).
A0M001 - Average weekly hours, mfg. (hours).
A0M005 - WkUNCL-Average weekly initial claims, unemploy. insurance (thous.)
A0M008 - Mfrs' new orders, consumer goods and materials (mil. 1982 $).
A0M033 - Mfrs' new orders, nondefense capital goods excl. aircraft (mil. chain 1982 $).
A0M029 - Building permits for new private housing units (thous.)
U0M019 - Index of stock prices, 500 common stocks, NSA (1941–43 = 10).
A0M106 - Money supply, M2 (bil. chain 2012 $) (LEI comp. until Apr '90).
U0M107 - Leading Credit Index™ (std. dev.)
U0M129 - Interest rate spread, 10-year Treasury bonds less federal funds.
U0M083 - Consumer expectations, NSA (Copyright, Univ. of Michigan) (LEI comp. until Dec '77).
A0M125 - Avg. consumer expectations for business conditions (std. dev.)
G0M920 - Composite index of 4 coincident indicators (2016 = 100).
G0M930 - Composite index of 7 lagging indicators (2016 = 100).
A0M043 - UER-Civilian unemployment rate (pct.)

---

[3] The one change with the first edition of Guerard and Schwartz (2007) is the exclusion of the money supply.

A0M044 - Unemployment rate 15 weeks and over (pct.)

A0M052 - Personal income (AR bil. chain 2012 $).

A0M051 - Personal income less transfer payments (AR bil. chain 2012 $).

A0Q055 - **GDP Known**-Gross domestic product (AR bil. Chain 2012 $).

7.4.1 Estimating OLS and Robust Regression Real GDP Models in SAS

What do the LEI lead? In this section, we address the question of do the LEI lead real GDP, as put forth by Auerbach (1982) and Zarnowitz (1992) and Guerard (2001, 2004), and Guerard et al. (2020), and the unemployment rate. We test whether the LEI and or weekly unemployment claims lead the unemployment rate during the 2959 to 2018 period. We then address the impact of COVID-19 on unemployment claims and the unemployment rate using the 1959–2019 and 1959 to 11/2020 period using the TCB LEI database.

We first test whether the LEI leads real GDP, 1959 to 2018. Guerard (2004) reported that four periods of LEI led real GDP in the post-WWII period. In Estimation One, we report a statistically significant one-period lag in the LEI leads real GDP during the 1959–2018 period. The estimated LEI coefficient is positive, 0.301, and highly statistically significant with a t-statistic of 13.43.[4]

---

[4] Geoffrey Moore passed in 2000. Pami Dua edited a collection of papers to honor Moore, entitled *Business Cycles and Economic Growth* (Oxford University Press, India, 2004). The reader is referred to papers in the volume by Victor Zarnowitz, John Guerard, Lawrence Klein, and S. Ozmucur, and D. Ivanova and Kajal Lahiri. The Conference Board index of leading indicators was composed of the following variables in 2001; Average weekly hours (mfg.); Average weekly initial claims for unemployment insurance; Manufacturers' new orders for consumer goods and materials; Vendor performance; Manufacturers' new orders of non-defense capital goods; Building permits of new private housing units; Index of stock prices; Money supply; Interest rate spread; and the Index of consumer expectations. The reader is referred to Zarnowitz (1992) for his seminal development of underlying economic assumption and theory of the LEI and business cycles. Thomakos and Guerard (2004) reported that he U.S. leading indicators lead real GDP, as one should expect, and the transfer function model produced lower forecast errors than the univariate model, and a naive benchmark, the no-change model. The model forecast errors are not statistically different (the t-value of the paired differences of the univariate and TF models is 0.91). The multiple regression models indicate statistical significance in the U.S. composite index of leading economic indicators for the 1978-March 2002 period. One does not find that the transfer function model forecast errors are (statistically) significantly lower than univariate ARIMA model (RWD) errors in a rolling one-period-ahead analysis.

Estimation One: OLS RGDP and the LEI 1959–2018
The REG Procedure
Model: MODEL1
Dependent Variable: DLRGDP

Number of observations read	239
Number of observations used	237
Number of observations with missing values	2

Analysis of variance

Source	DF	Sum of squares	Mean square	F Value	Pr > F
Model	1	0.00688	0.00688	180.28	<0.0001
Error	235	0.00896	0.00003815		
Corrected Total	236	0.01584			

Root MSE	0.00618	**R-square**	0.4341
Dependent mean	0.00747	**Adj R-square**	0.4317
Coeff var	82.72054		

Parameter estimates

Variable	DF	Parameter estimate	Standard error	t Value	Pr > |t|
Intercept	1	0.00578	0.00042043	13.75	<0.0001
DLLEIL1	1	0.30074	0.02240	13.43	<0.0001

OLS RGDP and the LEI 1959–2018
The REG Procedure
Model: MODEL1
Dependent Variable: DLRGDP

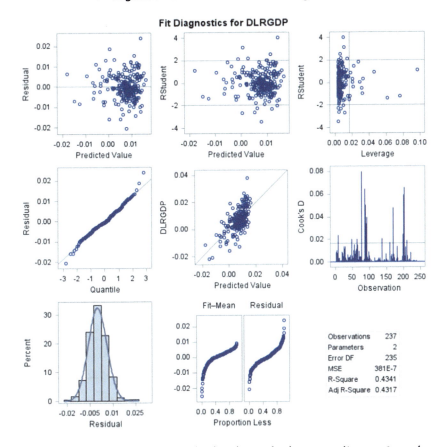

Fit Diagnostics for DLRGDP

Observations	237
Parameters	2
Error DF	235
MSE	381E-7
R-Square	0.4341
Adj R-Square	0.4317

Several observations of standardized residuals, exceeding $+2$ and are less than -2, and several large Cook's D observations suggest influential observations (leverage) possible outlier issues in the real GDP regression. Let

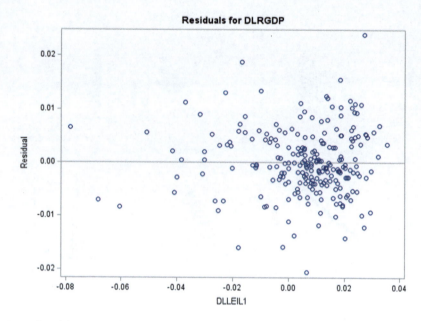

We should proceed to use the additional Belsley et al. (1980) regression diagnostics to identify influential observations and potential outliers.

The REG Procedure
Model: MODEL1
Dependent Variable: DLRGDP

Output statistics

Obs	Residual	RStudent	Hat Diag H	Cov Ratio	DFFITS	DFBETAS Intercept	DLLEIL1
1	–	–	–	–	–	–	–
2	–	–	–	–	–	–	–
3	−0.0102	−1.6612	0.0059	0.9911	−0.1282	−0.0827	−0.0688
4	−0.000934	−0.1514	0.0062	1.0147	−0.0120	−0.0115	0.0068
5	0.0124	2.0195	0.0050	0.9792	0.1437	0.1082	0.0579
6	−0.0112	−1.8231	0.0046	0.9851	−0.1244	−0.1244	0.0372
7	−0.001872	−0.3031	0.0043	1.0121	−0.0199	−0.0196	0.0025
8	−0.0207	−3.4286	0.0042	0.9183	−0.2235	−0.2093	−0.0123
9	−0.001064	−0.1723	0.0042	1.0126	−0.0112	−0.0105	−0.0006
10	0.003302	0.5364	0.0097	1.0159	0.0530	0.0215	0.0399
11	0.004680	0.7612	0.0110	1.0148	0.0805	0.0285	0.0633
12	0.005290	0.8607	0.0106	1.0130	0.0892	0.0329	0.0693
13	0.004703	0.7641	0.0087	1.0123	0.0714	0.0323	0.0512
14	−0.002944	−0.4776	0.0071	1.0138	−0.0405	−0.0220	−0.0259
15	0.004677	0.7581	0.0042	1.0079	0.0493	0.0469	0.0005
16	−0.005065	−0.8213	0.0043	1.0071	−0.0542	−0.0484	−0.0089
17	−0.002518	−0.4088	0.0094	1.0167	−0.0398	−0.0167	−0.0295
18	−0.002037	−0.3307	0.0091	1.0168	−0.0316	−0.0137	−0.0231

Output statistics

Obs	Residual	RStudent	Hat Diag H	Cov Ratio	DFFITS	DFBETAS Intercept	DLLEIL1
19	0.0103	1.6741	0.0065	0.9913	0.1355	0.0801	0.0803
20	−0.004843	−0.7859	0.0064	1.0097	−0.0631	−0.0379	−0.0369
21	0.0104	1.7001	0.0055	0.9896	0.1268	0.0872	0.0618
22	−0.001114	−0.1807	0.0071	1.0155	−0.0153	−0.0083	−0.0097
23	0.002954	0.4794	0.0080	1.0147	0.0430	0.0210	0.0295
24	−0.007822	−1.2718	0.0060	1.0007	−0.0984	−0.0632	−0.0531
25	0.0109	1.7812	0.0087	0.9903	0.1665	0.0752	0.1193
26	0.001067	0.1730	0.0065	1.0149	0.0140	0.0083	0.0083
27	0.0120	1.9663	0.0051	0.9811	0.1411	0.1045	0.0593
28	0.0102	1.6634	0.0081	0.9931	0.1499	0.0726	0.1035
29	0.0115	1.8867	0.0078	0.9863	0.1677	0.0833	0.1139
30	−0.008243	−1.3415	0.0068	1.0000	−0.1106	−0.0632	−0.0678
31	0.005869	0.9537	0.0078	1.0086	0.0843	0.0764	−0.0570
32	0.004376	0.7099	0.0061	1.0104	0.0558	0.0535	−0.0313
33	0.001698	0.2749	0.0042	1.0122	0.0179	0.0174	−0.0012
34	−0.005841	−0.9475	0.0044	1.0053	−0.0628	−0.0624	0.0117
35	−0.002845	−0.4616	0.0075	1.0144	−0.0402	−0.0207	−0.0267
36	−0.003362	−0.5450	0.0059	1.0120	−0.0420	−0.0272	−0.0224
37	0.008797	1.4321	0.0065	0.9976	0.1156	0.0687	0.0682
38	0.008355	1.3580	0.0043	0.9971	0.0893	0.0805	0.0128
39	−0.001718	−0.2783	0.0048	1.0127	−0.0193	−0.0153	−0.0066
40	−0.006691	−1.0868	0.0056	1.0041	−0.0818	−0.0553	−0.0411
41	0.008518	1.3847	0.0043	0.9965	0.0905	0.0884	−0.0081
42	−0.005726	−0.9289	0.0045	1.0056	−0.0621	−0.0535	−0.0141
43	0.005542	0.9016	0.0102	1.0119	0.0915	0.0771	−0.0700
44	−0.008273	−1.3463	0.0067	0.9998	−0.1102	−0.1037	0.0667
45	−0.001204	−0.1958	0.0130	1.0215	−0.0225	−0.0177	0.0185
46	0.003079	0.5019	0.0164	1.0232	0.0648	0.0481	−0.0558
47	0.002158	0.3494	0.0042	1.0118	0.0228	0.0222	−0.0018
48	**−0.0159**	**−2.6206**	**0.0050**	**0.9567**	**−0.1858**	**−0.1848**	**0.0735**
49	**0.0154**	**2.5346**	**0.0064**	**0.9616**	**0.2040**	**0.1218**	**0.1198**
50	−0.007086	−1.1525	0.0079	1.0051	−0.1027	−0.0508	−0.0700
51	−0.001759	−0.2850	0.0051	1.0131	−0.0205	−0.0151	−0.0086
52	−0.006928	−1.1249	0.0047	1.0025	−0.0775	−0.0623	−0.0253
53	0.004872	0.7919	0.0092	1.0125	0.0764	0.0325	0.0562
54	0.009253	1.5089	0.0089	0.9981	0.1431	0.0629	0.1038
55	−0.001913	−0.3101	0.0064	1.0142	−0.0248	−0.0150	−0.0144
56	0.001107	0.1801	0.0136	1.0222	0.0211	0.0060	0.0176
57	0.0108	1.7720	0.0098	0.9917	0.1762	0.0706	0.1330
58	0.006043	0.9810	0.0053	1.0056	0.0715	0.0706	−0.0321
59	−0.008463	−1.3775	0.0069	0.9993	−0.1149	−0.1071	0.0717
60	0.008473	1.3815	0.0102	1.0026	0.1406	0.1183	−0.1078
61	−0.007372	−1.2039	0.0152	1.0116	−0.1496	−0.1132	0.1272
62	0.003237	0.5271	0.0142	1.0207	0.0634	0.0488	−0.0532
63	−0.007370	−1.2050	0.0176	1.0140	−0.1613	−0.1174	0.1407
64	0.005568	0.9227	0.0459	1.0495	0.2024	0.1162	−0.1929
65	−0.005709	−0.9395	0.0325	1.0347	−0.1723	−0.1073	0.1608
66	−0.000544	−0.0880	0.0042	1.0128	−0.0057	−0.0054	−0.0002
67	0.004454	0.7233	0.0080	1.0121	0.0648	0.0317	0.0445
68	0.002779	0.4505	0.0057	1.0126	0.0340	0.0229	0.0172
69	0.009323	1.5202	0.0085	0.9974	0.1405	0.0649	0.0996
70	−0.005426	−0.8817	0.0082	1.0102	−0.0804	−0.0381	−0.0562
71	−0.006504	−1.0572	0.0072	1.0063	−0.0901	−0.0484	−0.0581
72	−0.001917	−0.3105	0.0046	1.0124	−0.0211	−0.0174	−0.0062

Output statistics

Obs	Residual	RStudent	Hat Diag H	Cov Ratio	DFFITS	DFBETAS Intercept	DLLEIL1
73	0.000447	0.0725	0.0063	1.0149	0.0058	0.0035	0.0033
74	0.006544	1.0642	0.0083	1.0072	0.0973	0.0459	0.0682
75	0.007911	1.2859	0.0051	0.9996	0.0925	0.0682	0.0392
76	−0.007854	−1.2760	0.0042	0.9989	−0.0833	−0.0775	−0.0060
77	−0.002068	−0.3350	0.0049	1.0126	−0.0236	−0.0235	0.0089
78	0.0239	4.0095	0.0105	0.8924	0.4123	0.1546	0.3185
79	0.002717	0.4401	0.0042	1.0112	0.0287	0.0276	−0.0010
80	0.004102	0.6650	0.0047	1.0095	0.0457	0.0369	0.0147
81	−0.000460	−0.0747	0.0082	1.0168	−0.0068	−0.0061	0.0047
82	−0.001130	−0.1834	0.0082	1.0166	−0.0167	−0.0149	0.0116
83	0.003666	0.5946	0.0062	1.0118	0.0471	0.0450	−0.0268
84	0.002946	0.4794	0.0133	1.0202	0.0557	0.0437	−0.0461
85	0.003697	0.6018	0.0137	1.0194	0.0709	0.0552	−0.0589
86	−0.008354	−1.3994	0.0619	1.0573	−0.3594	−0.1933	0.3469
87	−0.006979	−1.1333	0.0046	1.0022	−0.0773	−0.0773	0.0231
88	0.005954	0.9678	0.0080	1.0086	0.0867	0.0424	0.0595
89	**0.0187**	**3.0948**	**0.0108**	**0.9410**	**0.3237**	**0.2685**	**−0.2529**
90	**−0.0138**	**−2.2504**	**0.0044**	**0.9706**	**−0.1496**	**−0.1489**	**0.0304**
91	**0.0130**	**2.1328**	**0.0148**	**0.9851**	**0.2617**	**0.1994**	**−0.2214**
92	**−0.009170**	**−1.5014**	**0.0168**	**1.0063**	**−0.1962**	**−0.1446**	**0.1697**
93	**−0.0161**	**−2.6546**	**0.0115**	**0.9615**	**−0.2862**	**−0.2336**	**0.2276**
94	−0.001179	−0.1910	0.0046	1.0129	−0.0130	−0.0130	0.0039
95	−0.006542	−1.0634	0.0075	1.0064	−0.0922	−0.0843	0.0608
96	−0.006582	−1.0683	0.0043	1.0031	−0.0698	−0.0682	0.0063
97	−0.001671	−0.2717	0.0120	1.0201	−0.0299	−0.0097	−0.0241
98	0.006857	1.1185	0.0139	1.0120	0.1330	0.0366	0.1111
99	0.003375	0.5500	0.0159	1.0222	0.0699	0.0165	0.0599
100	0.005588	0.9101	0.0125	1.0141	0.1024	0.0319	0.0833
101	0.005200	0.8460	0.0108	1.0134	0.0884	0.0321	0.0691
102	0.006178	1.0033	0.0060	1.0059	0.0777	0.0498	0.0419
103	0.000272	0.0441	0.0047	1.0133	0.0030	0.0024	0.0010
104	0.001398	0.2264	0.0043	1.0125	0.0149	0.0146	−0.0018
105	−0.001653	−0.2679	0.0063	1.0143	−0.0213	−0.0130	−0.0123
106	0.0000737	0.0119	0.0045	1.0131	0.0008	0.0007	0.0002
107	0.005541	0.8990	0.0049	1.0066	0.0632	0.0487	0.0238
108	−0.000785	−0.1271	0.0043	1.0128	−0.0083	−0.0076	−0.0011
109	0.000183	0.0296	0.0046	1.0132	0.0020	0.0017	0.0006
110	−0.004106	−0.6655	0.0044	1.0092	−0.0443	−0.0386	−0.0092
111	0.000443	0.0717	0.0046	1.0132	0.0049	0.0040	0.0014
112	−0.002244	−0.3634	0.0042	1.0117	−0.0237	−0.0223	−0.0008
113	−0.001597	−0.2586	0.0046	1.0126	−0.0175	−0.0146	−0.0048
114	0.002184	0.3537	0.0044	1.0119	0.0235	0.0206	0.0045
115	−0.001209	−0.1958	0.0050	1.0133	−0.0139	−0.0105	−0.0055
116	0.007672	1.2466	0.0047	1.0000	0.0859	0.0691	0.0280
117	−0.000228	−0.0369	0.0049	1.0135	−0.0026	−0.0026	0.0010
118	0.002830	0.4587	0.0053	1.0121	0.0334	0.0240	0.0150
119	−0.003017	−0.4887	0.0045	1.0110	−0.0328	−0.0280	−0.0080
120	0.004835	0.7838	0.0043	1.0077	0.0517	0.0461	0.0085
121	0.002607	0.4222	0.0042	1.0113	0.0275	0.0262	0.0001
122	0.003084	0.4999	0.0055	1.0120	0.0371	0.0364	−0.0178
123	0.004177	0.6778	0.0068	1.0115	0.0562	0.0526	−0.0348
124	−0.003779	−0.6125	0.0046	1.0100	−0.0418	−0.0418	0.0125
125	0.005542	0.8991	0.0049	1.0065	0.0629	0.0627	−0.0229
126	−0.000886	−0.1435	0.0055	1.0140	−0.0107	−0.0105	0.0052

Output statistics

Obs	Residual	RStudent	Hat Diag	Cov	DFFITS	DFBETAS	
			H	Ratio		Intercept	DLLEIL1
127	−0.003335	−0.5407	0.0059	1.0121	−0.0418	−0.0403	0.0224
128	−0.002880	−0.4730	0.0315	1.0393	−0.0852	−0.0535	0.0793
129	0.002001	0.3290	0.0334	1.0425	0.0612	0.0378	−0.0572
130	0.001540	0.2493	0.0044	1.0125	0.0166	0.0166	−0.0036
131	−0.006373	−1.0353	0.0064	1.0059	−0.0833	−0.0498	−0.0489
132	−0.004595	−0.7448	0.0043	1.0081	−0.0488	−0.0446	−0.0057
133	0.005219	0.8462	0.0043	1.0068	0.0557	0.0550	−0.0080
134	−0.000874	−0.1416	0.0068	1.0153	−0.0117	−0.0067	−0.0072
135	−0.000430	−0.0697	0.0053	1.0139	−0.0051	−0.0036	−0.0023
136	0.001553	0.2516	0.0045	1.0126	0.0169	0.0144	0.0042
137	−0.0123	−2.0131	0.0104	0.9848	−0.2064	−0.0779	−0.1592
138	−0.003798	−0.6157	0.0049	1.0102	−0.0431	−0.0335	−0.0159
139	−0.002663	−0.4314	0.0042	1.0112	−0.0281	−0.0268	0.0000
140	0.002729	0.4423	0.0058	1.0128	0.0338	0.0222	0.0177
141	−0.001372	−0.2224	0.0061	1.0143	−0.0174	−0.0109	−0.0097
142	0.000533	0.0865	0.0086	1.0173	0.0081	0.0037	0.0058
143	−0.005062	−0.8214	0.0059	1.0087	−0.0633	−0.0410	−0.0337
144	−0.000514	−0.0834	0.0071	1.0157	−0.0070	−0.0038	−0.0045
145	−0.005677	−0.9211	0.0046	1.0060	−0.0629	−0.0515	−0.0190
146	−0.002027	−0.3284	0.0051	1.0128	−0.0235	−0.0233	0.0097
147	0.002721	0.4408	0.0046	1.0116	0.0301	0.0301	−0.0090
148	−0.000844	−0.1366	0.0042	1.0127	−0.0089	−0.0084	−0.0003
149	0.007014	1.1428	0.0113	1.0088	0.1222	0.1002	−0.0967
150	0.005067	0.8225	0.0065	1.0093	0.0666	0.0394	0.0395
151	−0.000969	−0.1570	0.0051	1.0135	−0.0112	−0.0084	−0.0046
152	0.001935	0.3133	0.0043	1.0121	0.0207	0.0184	0.0034
153	−0.003379	−0.5476	0.0050	1.0110	−0.0388	−0.0295	−0.0153
154	0.005007	0.8127	0.0066	1.0095	0.0661	0.0387	0.0396
155	−0.000717	−0.1164	0.0089	1.0175	−0.0110	−0.0049	−0.0080
156	−0.000968	−0.1568	0.0049	1.0133	−0.0110	−0.0086	−0.0040
157	0.002407	0.3898	0.0042	1.0115	0.0254	0.0242	0.0001
158	0.000383	0.0621	0.0045	1.0131	0.0042	0.0036	0.0010
159	0.006290	1.0208	0.0045	1.0041	0.0685	0.0684	−0.0167
160	0.0133	2.1716	0.0075	0.9764	0.1883	0.1722	−0.1242
161	0.002598	0.4209	0.0043	1.0114	0.0276	0.0272	−0.0034
162	−0.000094	−0.0152	0.0042	1.0129	−0.0010	−0.0009	−0.0001
163	0.003552	0.5756	0.0048	1.0106	0.0399	0.0316	0.0138
164	0.009467	1.5405	0.0042	0.9926	0.1003	0.0959	−0.0006
165	−0.008043	−1.3087	0.0068	1.0007	−0.1079	−0.0616	−0.0661
166	0.0110	1.7977	0.0042	0.9855	0.1173	0.1142	−0.0086
167	−0.000600	−0.0973	0.0087	1.0174	−0.0091	−0.0080	0.0066
168	0.004361	0.7084	0.0088	1.0132	0.0668	0.0585	−0.0483
169	0.000373	0.0609	0.0210	1.0302	0.0089	0.0062	−0.0080
170	0.0111	1.8350	0.0280	1.0084	0.3114	0.2011	−0.2869
171	−0.008566	−1.3935	0.0056	0.9976	−0.1047	−0.1022	0.0523
172	0.005191	0.8479	0.0186	1.0214	0.1169	0.0838	−0.1028
173	−0.001079	−0.1748	0.0050	1.0134	−0.0124	−0.0094	−0.0049
174	−0.006185	−1.0051	0.0075	1.0074	−0.0871	−0.0454	−0.0574
175	−0.003484	−0.5645	0.0042	1.0101	−0.0369	−0.0342	−0.0028
176	−0.003227	−0.5230	0.0053	1.0116	−0.0382	−0.0377	0.0173
177	−0.002715	−0.4398	0.0043	1.0112	−0.0289	−0.0261	−0.0040
178	0.005257	0.8535	0.0067	1.0091	0.0701	0.0658	−0.0426
179	0.004074	0.6615	0.0082	1.0132	0.0603	0.0286	0.0421
180	−0.002830	−0.4599	0.0109	1.0178	−0.0482	−0.0174	−0.0377

Obs	Residual	RStudent	Hat Diag H	Cov Ratio	DFFITS	DFBETAS Intercept	DLLEIL1
				Output statistics			
181	−0.009351	−1.5272	0.0117	1.0005	−0.1663	−0.0554	−0.1331
182	−0.005547	−0.9018	0.0089	1.0106	−0.0855	−0.0376	−0.0620
183	−0.001702	−0.2759	0.0061	1.0141	−0.0217	−0.0135	−0.0121
184	−0.000110	−0.0178	0.0052	1.0139	−0.0013	−0.0009	−0.0006
185	−0.001455	−0.2361	0.0078	1.0160	−0.0210	−0.0104	−0.0143
186	−0.002984	−0.4833	0.0042	1.0108	−0.0315	−0.0298	−0.0007
187	0.001347	0.2180	0.0042	1.0124	0.0142	0.0135	0.0002
188	−0.000652	−0.1056	0.0043	1.0128	−0.0069	−0.0068	0.0007
189	0.003602	0.5837	0.0049	1.0106	0.0409	0.0318	0.0150
190	−0.002607	−0.4224	0.0052	1.0123	−0.0305	−0.0302	0.0131
191	−0.000760	−0.1234	0.0082	1.0167	−0.0112	−0.0100	0.0078
192	0.004195	0.6803	0.0057	1.0103	0.0514	0.0501	−0.0260
193	−0.002778	−0.4501	0.0050	1.0119	−0.0318	−0.0317	0.0125
194	−0.000079	−0.0128	0.0046	1.0133	−0.0009	−0.0009	0.0003
195	0.000824	0.1335	0.0054	1.0139	0.0099	0.0097	−0.0047
196	0.005734	0.9335	0.0116	1.0128	0.1009	0.0822	−0.0804
197	−0.002316	−0.3785	0.0217	1.0296	−0.0563	−0.0388	0.0505
198	0.008884	1.4585	0.0226	1.0134	0.2219	0.1513	−0.2001
199	0.000369	0.0606	0.0297	1.0394	0.0106	0.0067	−0.0098
200	−0.007139	−1.2036	0.0761	1.0782	−0.3453	−0.1779	0.3356
201	0.006499	1.1078	0.0970	1.1053	0.3632	0.1784	−0.3552
202	0.001903	0.3108	0.0211	1.0294	0.0456	0.0317	−0.0408
203	−0.007743	−1.2592	0.0064	1.0014	−0.1011	−0.0607	−0.0590
204	−0.001886	−0.3061	0.0083	1.0162	−0.0281	−0.0132	−0.0197
205	−0.009949	−1.6245	0.0100	0.9961	−0.1629	−0.0642	−0.1237
206	−0.002895	−0.4696	0.0073	1.0141	−0.0404	−0.0214	−0.0263
207	0.0000473	0.007654	0.0042	1.0128	0.0005	0.0005	−0.0000
208	−0.003335	−0.5404	0.0043	1.0104	−0.0356	−0.0319	−0.0057
209	−0.0143	−2.3429	0.0071	0.9697	−0.1975	−0.1083	−0.1252
210	−0.003972	−0.6443	0.0061	1.0112	−0.0505	−0.0317	−0.0281
211	−0.009538	−1.5524	0.0047	0.9927	−0.1064	−0.0865	−0.0332
212	0.007104	1.1543	0.0056	1.0028	0.0865	0.0846	−0.0429
213	−0.000385	−0.0623	0.0043	1.0129	−0.0041	−0.0037	−0.0005
214	−0.003885	−0.6295	0.0043	1.0095	−0.0413	−0.0375	−0.0055
215	−0.004048	−0.6562	0.0048	1.0097	−0.0456	−0.0456	0.0160
216	−0.005702	−0.9248	0.0043	1.0055	−0.0607	−0.0597	0.0074
217	0.000645	0.1044	0.0043	1.0128	0.0069	0.0062	0.0009
218	−0.006594	−1.0702	0.0042	1.0030	−0.0698	−0.0652	−0.0042
219	0.000337	0.0545	0.0042	1.0128	0.0035	0.0034	−0.0000
220	−0.002510	−0.4069	0.0055	1.0127	−0.0302	−0.0210	−0.0145
221	−0.0119	−1.9354	0.0046	0.9815	−0.1314	−0.1091	−0.0372
222	0.002779	0.4505	0.0057	1.0126	0.0340	0.0229	0.0172
223	0.000637	0.1032	0.0065	1.0151	0.0084	0.0049	0.0050
224	−0.003608	−0.5846	0.0047	1.0103	−0.0400	−0.0326	−0.0123
225	0.000954	0.1545	0.0044	1.0128	0.0103	0.0090	0.0020
226	−0.001515	−0.2453	0.0043	1.0124	−0.0161	−0.0146	−0.0022
227	−0.004014	−0.6504	0.0042	1.0092	−0.0424	−0.0401	−0.0012
228	−0.005081	−0.8239	0.0043	1.0071	−0.0542	−0.0535	0.0078
229	0.000723	0.1171	0.0052	1.0137	0.0085	0.0084	−0.0037
230	−0.003882	−0.6291	0.0043	1.0095	−0.0411	−0.0402	0.0037
231	−0.001883	−0.3049	0.0042	1.0120	−0.0199	−0.0191	0.0007
232	−0.000081	−0.0130	0.0044	1.0130	−0.0009	−0.0009	0.0002
233	−0.004329	−0.7020	0.0051	1.0095	−0.0503	−0.0374	−0.0209
234	−0.004126	−0.6686	0.0044	1.0091	−0.0442	−0.0392	−0.0077

Output statistics							
Obs	Residual	RStudent	Hat Diag	Cov	DFFITS	DFBETAS	
			H	Ratio		Intercept	DLLEIL1
235	−0.001697	−0.2748	0.0046	1.0125	−0.0186	−0.0156	−0.0051
236	−0.001722	−0.2792	0.0063	1.0143	−0.0222	−0.0136	−0.0127
237	−0.001291	−0.2092	0.0056	1.0139	−0.0158	−0.0106	−0.0079
238	−0.003530	−0.5722	0.0053	1.0111	−0.0419	−0.0299	−0.0191
239	−0.004158	−0.6740	0.0047	1.0094	−0.0465	−0.0373	−0.0154

Sum of residuals	0
Sum of squared residuals	0.00896
Predicted residual SS (press)	0.00914

The observations in BOLD denote influential observations and potential outliers. We report the RStudent, cov ratio, DFFITS, and DFBETAS for the real GDP and LEI regression discussed in the Appendix.

We first now test whether the LEI leads real GDP, 1959 to 2018 by four periods by estimating an OLS regression.

Estimation Two: OLS RGDP and Four Lags in the LEI 1959–2018
The REG Procedure
Model: MODEL1
Dependent Variable: DLRGDP

Number of observations read	239
Number of observations used	234
Number of observations with missing values	5

Analysis of variance					
Source	DF	Sum of squares	Mean square	F value	Pr > F
Model	4	0.00699	0.00175	46.72	<0.0001
Error	229	0.00857	0.00003741		
Corrected Total	233	0.01556			

Root MSE	0.00612	**R-square**	0.4493
Dependent mean	0.00745	**Adj R-square**	0.4397
Coeff var	82.07022		

Parameter estimates

Variable	DF	Parameter estimate	Standard error	T value	Pr > |t|
Intercept	1	0.00565	0.00042857	13.19	<0.0001
DLLEIL1	1	0.26192	0.03103	8.44	<0.0001
DLLEIL2	1	0.04344	0.03825	1.14	0.2574
DLLEIL3	1	0.02165	0.03792	0.57	0.5687
DLLEIL4	1	-0.00444	0.03074	-0.14	0.8854

In the OLS regression, Estimation Two, only the first period lag is statistically significant. However, there are again outlier issues, as we see in the regression diagnostics.

OLS RGDP and the LEI 1959–2018
The REG Procedure
Model: MODEL1
Dependent Variable: DLRGDP

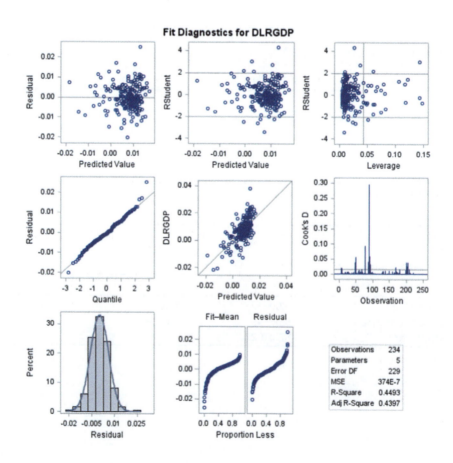

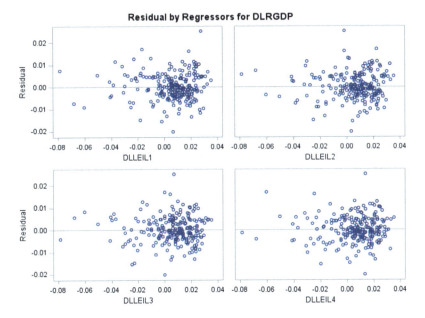
Residual by Regressors for DLRGDP

We estimate a robust regression using the Tukey Bisquare for whether the LEI leads real GDP, 1959 to 2018 in Estimation Three. The estimated robust LEI coefficient is positive, 0.293 and highly statistically significant with a *p*-value of 0.000. Robust regression confirms that the LEI, lagged one-period, leads real GDP in the 1959–2018 period.

Estimation Three: ROB Tukey Bisquare RGDP and the LEI 1959–2018
The ROBUSTREG Procedure

Model information	
Data set	WORK.RERGDP
Dependent variable	DLRGDP
Number of independent variables	1
Number of observations	237
Missing values	2
Method	M Estimation

Parameter estimates

Parameter	DF	Estimate	Standard error	95% confidence	Limits	Chi-square	Pr > Chi-square
Intercept	1	0.0057	0.0004	0.0049	0.0065	198.69	<0.0001
DLLEIL1	1	0.2925	0.0216	0.2502	0.3348	183.56	<0.0001
Scale	1	0.0055					

Diagnostics

Obs	Mahalanobis distance	Robust MCD distance	Leverage	Standardized robust residual	Outlier
6	0.0551	0.4350		−3.7245	*
43	1.4380	2.4460	*	−0.2364	
44	1.6942	2.7912	*	0.5334	
59	1.6107	2.6786	*	−1.3593	
60	1.5382	2.5811	*	0.5662	
61	1.7778	2.9037	*	−1.3634	
62	3.1371	4.7346	*	0.9459	
63	2.5856	3.9918	*	−1.0840	
76	1.2138	1.1257		4.3831	*
82	1.4658	2.4835	*	0.5154	
83	1.4937	2.5211	*	0.6507	
84	3.6886	5.4775	*	−1.5933	
87	1.2485	2.1909		3.3728	*
89	1.5828	2.6411	*	2.3311	
90	1.7221	2.8287	*	−1.6884	
91	1.3098	2.2734	*	−2.9330	
126	2.5354	3.9242	*	−0.5696	
127	2.6246	4.0443	*	0.3130	
147	1.2931	2.2509	*	1.2576	
167	1.9895	3.1889	*	0.0348	
168	2.3683	3.6991	*	1.9728	
170	1.8446	2.9938	*	0.9123	
194	1.3154	2.2809	*	1.0249	
195	2.0285	3.2414	*	−0.4539	
196	2.0842	3.3164	*	1.5755	
197	2.4519	3.8117	*	0.0217	
198	4.1176	6.0553	*	−1.3844	
199	4.6803	6.8131	*	1.0731	
200	1.9951	3.1964	*	0.3121	

Diagnostics summary

Observation type	Proportion	Cutoff
Outlier	0.0127	3.0000
Leverage	0.1097	2.2414

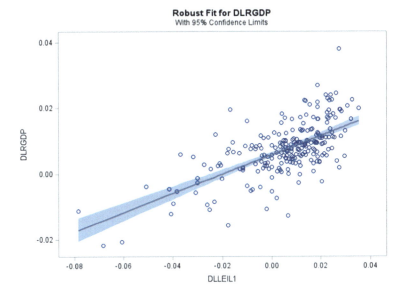

Robust Fit for DLRGDP
With 95% Confidence Limits

Goodness-of-fit	
Statistic	Value
R-Square	0.3171
AICR	239.9393
BICR	247.5348
Deviance	0.0072

We estimate a robust regression using the Tukey Bisquare for whether four lags in the LEI leads real GDP, 1959 to 2018 in Estimation Four. The estimated robust LEI coefficient is positive, 0.256 and highly statistically significant with a p-value of 0.000. Only the first lag of LEI is statistically significant in the real GDP regressions for the 1959–2018 period. Robust regression confirms that the LEI, lagged one-period, leads real GDP.

Estimation Four: ROB Tukey MM Bisquare RGDP and the LEI 1959–2018
The ROBUSTREG Procedure

Model information	
Data set	WORK.RERGDP
Dependent variable	DLRGDP
Number of independent variables	4
Number of observations	234
Missing values	5

Model information	
Method	MM estimation

Number of observations read	239
Number of observations used	234
Missing values	5

Profile for the initial LTS estimate	
Total number of observations	234
Number of squares minimized	177
Number of coefficients	5
Highest possible breakdown value	0.2479

MM profile	
Chi function	Tukey
K1	7.0410
Efficiency	0.9900

Parameter estimates

Parameter	DF	Estimate	Standard error	95% confidence	Limits	Chi-square	Pr > Chi-square
Intercept	1	0.0056	0.0004	0.0048	0.0064	183.26	<0.0001
DLLEIL1	1	0.2559	0.0303	0.1966	0.3153	71.37	<0.0001
DLLEIL2	1	0.0478	0.0373	−0.0253	0.1209	1.64	0.1997
DLLEIL3	1	0.0119	0.0369	−0.0605	0.0843	0.10	0.7474
DLLEIL4	1	0.0050	0.0302	−0.0542	0.0642	0.03	0.8696
Scale	0	0.0059					

Diagnostics

Obs	Mahalanobis distance	Robust MCD dstance	Leverage	Standardized robust residual	Outlier
1	2.3265	3.3589	*	−1.9716	
3	0.9838	1.4873		−3.4534	*
26	2.2523	3.3931	*	0.7172	
27	2.2082	3.3588	*	0.7481	
28	2.2015	3.3739	*	0.4064	
40	2.2845	3.3454	*	−0.2405	
42	2.3135	4.1655	*	0.6725	

Diagnostics					
Obs	Mahalanobis distance	Robust MCD dstance	Leverage	Standardized robust residual	Outlier
43	2.3648	4.3430	*	−2.6511	
44	2.7451	4.7941	*	2.8065	
53	2.3513	3.5771	*	0.7318	
54	2.3775	3.7669	*	−1.5208	
55	2.3621	3.5556	*	1.3960	
59	3.3092	4.7950	*	0.8619	
60	3.2574	5.0904	*	−0.7649	
61	4.0501	7.3154	*	0.4370	
62	4.1686	8.0608	*	1.0260	
63	3.7681	6.5966	*	0.4597	
73	2.2670	3.3730	*	4.2611	*
74	2.5349	3.8011	*	0.3014	
75	2.5259	3.7270	*	0.7162	
76	2.4645	3.5960	*	−0.2660	
81	4.0572	5.6731	*	−1.6246	
82	5.1458	8.2637	*	−0.6019	
83	5.2419	8.8661	*	1.3448	
84	5.6738	9.2779	*	2.9267	
85	3.3022	4.8749	*	−2.1916	
86	3.6036	5.2138	*	2.0490	
87	2.6810	4.0540	*	−1.5193	
88	2.1615	3.5022	*	−2.5799	
89	1.9651	4.0938	*	0.0435	
90	2.1221	3.9596	*	−1.0972	
91	1.9611	3.5229	*	−0.9577	
92	2.2634	3.8899	*	−0.0400	
93	2.3403	4.1127	*	1.1944	
123	2.9847	4.2255	*	−0.7043	
124	3.1846	4.6856	*	0.3900	
125	3.8470	6.4972	*	0.7211	
126	3.6974	7.1303	*	−0.8045	
127	3.6217	6.3701	*	−0.8092	
145	3.0071	4.6589	*	1.1570	
146	2.9323	4.5341	*	−0.1546	
147	2.5951	4.2206	*	0.2873	
165	2.4867	3.6997	*	1.9088	
166	2.8496	5.0397	*	−1.0858	
167	3.5200	5.7266	*	0.8348	
168	4.2429	7.0599	*	0.2092	
169	3.2347	5.3881	*	−0.9045	
170	3.1433	5.2830	*	−0.6839	
174	2.6028	4.1028	*	0.9439	

Diagnostics

Obs	Mahalanobis distance	Robust MCD dstance	Leverage	Standardized robust residual	Outlier
175	2.5240	3.9329	*	−0.4148	
176	2.4099	3.8782	*	−1.5962	
193	2.2734	3.4702	*	1.5778	
194	2.6394	4.1142	*	0.1338	
195	4.2767	6.0908	*	−1.2959	
196	4.8731	7.0264	*	1.1890	
197	5.1237	8.7792	*	0.9245	
198	5.7863	11.0390	*	−0.6817	
199	5.6941	10.5817	*	−0.1375	
200	3.6094	6.0519	*	−1.6534	

Diagnostics summary

Observation type	Proportion	Cutoff
Outlier	0.0085	3.0000
Leverage	0.2479	3.3382

Goodness-of-fit

Statistic	Value
R-square	0.4000
AICR	232.8038
BICR	251.4834
Deviance	0.0078

We estimate a robust regression using the Tukey Bisquare for whether four lags in the LEI leads real GDP, 1959 to 2018 in Estimation Four. The estimated robust LEI coefficient is positive, 0.256 and highly statistically significant with a p-value of 0.000. Robust regression confirms that the LEI, lagged one-period, leads real GDP. We report support for the LEI in leading real GDP, as reported by Auerbach (1982), Guerard (2001, 2004), and Guerard et al. (2020) in the 1959–2018 period.[5]

---

[5] Mr. Zarnowitz should be smiling as we report continued post-publication, out-of-sample modeling of the LEI.

7.4.2 Estimating OLS and Robust Regression Models of the Unemployment Rate in SAS

In this section, we invite the reader to think about the current COVID period and its possible impact on the U.S. unemployment rate. The unemployment rate has been linked to traditional business cycles Burns & Mitchell, 1946; Harberler, 1937; (Keynes, 1936; Klein, 1950; Mitchell, 1923; Samuelson, 1948; and Zarnowitz, 1992). It was generally agreed that during an expansion, employment, production, prices, money, wages, interest rates, and profits are usually rising, while the reverse occurs during a contraction. In the late 1990s, Mr. Victor Zarnowitz, the subject of our Chapter 6, joined a "dream team" of economists and econometricians to forecast the U.S. unemployment rate. Professors Montgomery, Zarnowitz, Tsay, and Tiao (Montgomery et al., 1998), hereafter denoted as MZTT, published a seminal paper on forecasting the U.S. unemployment rate. Based on monthly observations in the period of 1959 to 1993, MZTT demonstrated that time series models are useful in predicting 1-month to 5-month ahead unemployment rates and they compared the out-sample prediction performance of a range of models. More than 20 years have passed since the MZTT publication and it is useful and necessary to re-exam models post-publication, as well as to investigate the impact of new phenomena since, including the financial crisis of 2008. We pay special attention to the relationship between the U.S unemployment rate and the lagged U.S. weekly unemployment claim, as well as the U.S. Leading Economic Indicator (LEI) series constructed by The Conference Board and its weekly unemployment claims, WkUNCL, component.

MZTT modeled the change in the U.S. unemployment rate as a function of the weekly unemployment claims time series, 1948–1993. MZTT reported that nonlinear models, such as TAR reduced forecasting errors by as much as 28%, being more effective in periods of economic contraction and rising unemployment. One would expect that an increase in weekly unemployment claims should lead to an increase in the U.S. unemployment rate. One would expect that an increase in the U.S. Leading Economic Indicator (LEI) time series should lead to a decrease in the U.S. unemployment rate.

We replicate and extend the MZTT analysis. We report that the U.S. LEI is negatively and statistically highly significantly associated with the change in the U.S. unemployment rate during the 1959–2020 time period. This is particularly true for a one-month lag in the LEI. This is true during the COVID pandemic. We also report that the U.S. weekly unemployment claims time series, reported on Thursday mornings, is positively and highly statistically significantly associated with the U.S. unemployment rate during the 1959–2020 time period, particularly for lags one and three-month variables. We estimate several equations of the weekly unemployment claims and the composite leading indicator for the whole sample period from 1959 to 2020 and the results obtained verify the previous ones, as to that both variables lead unemployment.

We pay special attention to the relationship of U.S. unemployment rate (UER) and the (one period) lagged U.S. weekly unemployment claims (WkUNCL), as well as the (one period) lagged U.S. Leading Economic Indicator (LEI) series. We use the model of unemployment rate as a function of the LEI. As the LEI increases, the general economic activity should increase, and the unemployment rate should decrease. There should be a negative coefficient on the LEI variable in the unemployment regression model. We use The Conference Board (TCB) Leading Economic Indicator (LEI) database for the January 1959–December 2018 time period for our initial estimates. In Estimation Five, we estimate the unemployment rate as a function of the LEI. The LEI coefficient is negative as expected, $-.0097$, and highly statistically significant, having a t-statistic of -3.59.

Estimation Five: The Unemployment Rate and LEI OLS Model, 1959–2018
The REG Procedure
Model: MODEL1
Dependent Variable: UER

Number of observations read	719
Number of observations used	718
Number of observations with missing values	1

Analysis of variance

Source	DF	Sum of squares	Mean square	F value	Pr > F
Model	1	31.70383	31.70383	12.85	0.0004
Error	716	1766.00382	2.46649		
Corrected Total	717	1797.70765			

Root MSE	1.57050	**R-Square**	0.0176
Dependent mean	5.99819	**Adj R-Sq**	0.0163
Coeff var	26.18298		

Parameter estimates

Variable	DF	Parameter estimate	Standard error	t Value	Pr > |t|
Intercept	1	6.64530	0.18977	35.02	< 0.0001
LEIL1	1	−0.00965	0.00269	−3.59	0.0004

REG Procedure and its Diagnostics
Model: MODEL1 Dependent Variable: UER

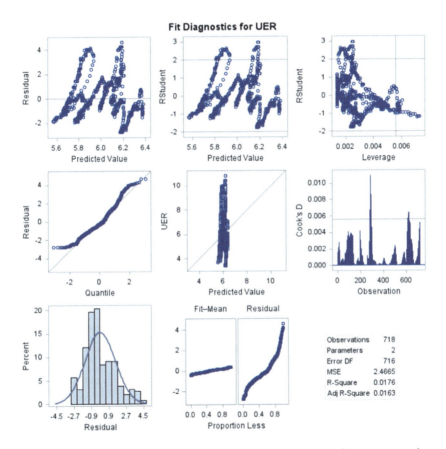

Fit Diagnostics for UER

Several observations of standardized residuals, exceeding +2 and are less than −2, and several large Cook's D observations suggest influential observations (leverage) possible outlier issues.

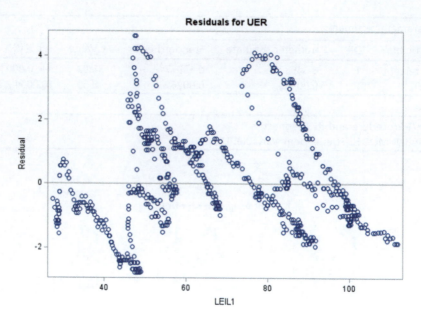

Several observations of standardized residuals, exceeding +2 and are less than −2, and several large Cook's D observations suggest influential observations (leverage) possible outlier issues.

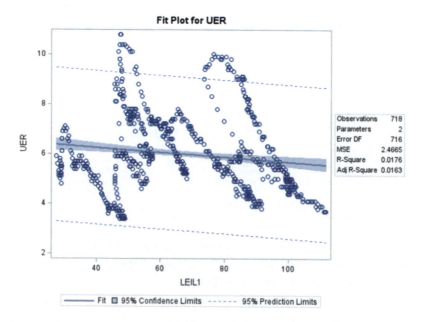

We should proceed to use the additional Belsley et al. (1980) regression diagnostics to identify influential observations and potential outliers. We report the RStudent, cov ratio, DFFITS, and DFBETAS for the UER and LEI regression discussed in the Appendix.

Dependent Variable: UER
Output Statistics

Obs	Residual	RStudent	Hat Diag H	Cov Ratio	DFFITS	DFBETAS Intercept	LEIL1
1	.	.	.	.	.	.	.
2	-0.4828	-0.3081	0.0061	1.0086	-0.0241	-0.0236	0.0211
3	-0.7789	-0.4972	0.0060	1.0081	-0.0385	-0.0378	0.0337
4	-1.1751	-0.7502	0.0059	1.0071	-0.0577	-0.0566	0.0504
5	-1.2741	-0.8135	0.0058	1.0068	-0.0624	-0.0612	0.0545
6	-1.3722	-0.8761	0.0058	1.0065	-0.0669	-0.0656	0.0584
7	-1.2712	-0.8116	0.0058	1.0068	-0.0619	-0.0607	0.0539
8	-1.1702	-0.7471	0.0058	1.0070	-0.0569	-0.0557	0.0495
9	-0.8712	-0.5561	0.0058	1.0078	-0.0424	-0.0416	0.0369
10	-0.6712	-0.4284	0.0058	1.0081	-0.0327	-0.0320	0.0285
11	-0.5722	-0.3652	0.0058	1.0083	-0.0279	-0.0274	0.0243
12	-1.0741	-0.6857	0.0058	1.0074	-0.0526	-0.0516	0.0459
13	-1.1683	-0.7458	0.0057	1.0070	-0.0565	-0.0554	0.0492
14	-1.5683	-1.0015	0.0057	1.0057	-0.0759	-0.0744	0.0660
15	-0.9683	-0.6181	0.0057	1.0075	-0.0469	-0.0459	0.0407
16	-1.1693	-0.7464	0.0057	1.0070	-0.0567	-0.0555	0.0493
17	-1.2683	-0.8097	0.0057	1.0067	-0.0614	-0.0601	0.0534
...							
33	0.3558	0.2270	0.0052	1.0079	0.0164	0.0159	-0.0140
34	0.1558	0.0994	0.0052	1.0080	0.0072	0.0070	-0.0061
35	-0.2393	-0.1527	0.0051	1.0078	-0.0109	-0.0106	0.0093
36	-0.3355	-0.2140	0.0050	1.0077	-0.0151	-0.0147	0.0129
37	-0.5326	-0.3397	0.0049	1.0074	-0.0239	-0.0232	0.0202
38	-0.8326	-0.5312	0.0049	1.0070	-0.0373	-0.0362	0.0316
39	-0.7287	-0.4649	0.0048	1.0071	-0.0324	-0.0314	0.0274
40	-0.7278	-0.4643	0.0048	1.0070	-0.0323	-0.0313	0.0272
41	-0.8258	-0.5268	0.0048	1.0068	-0.0365	-0.0353	0.0307
42	-0.8258	-0.5268	0.0048	1.0068	-0.0365	-0.0353	0.0307
43	-0.9268	-0.5913	0.0048	1.0066	-0.0411	-0.0397	0.0346
44	-0.6249	-0.3986	0.0048	1.0071	-0.0276	-0.0267	0.0232
45	-0.7229	-0.4612	0.0047	1.0070	-0.0318	-0.0307	0.0267
46	-0.9220	-0.5882	0.0047	1.0066	-0.0404	-0.0390	0.0339
47	-0.6210	-0.3961	0.0047	1.0071	-0.0272	-0.0262	0.0228
48	-0.8171	-0.5212	0.0046	1.0067	-0.0354	-0.0342	0.0296
49	-0.6162	-0.3930	0.0046	1.0070	-0.0267	-0.0257	0.0222
50	-0.4133	-0.2636	0.0045	1.0072	-0.0178	-0.0171	0.0148
51	-0.6104	-0.3893	0.0045	1.0069	-0.0261	-0.0251	0.0216
52	-0.6075	-0.3874	0.0044	1.0068	-0.0258	-0.0248	0.0213

Output Statistics

Obs	Residual	RStudent	Hat Diag H	Cov Ratio	DFFITS	DFBETAS Intercept	LEIL1
....							
104	-2.4110	-1.5388	0.0028	0.9990	-0.0818	-0.0731	0.0582
105	-2.4061	-1.5357	0.0028	0.9990	-0.0807	-0.0717	0.0568
106	-2.2042	-1.4064	0.0027	1.0000	-0.0736	-0.0652	0.0515
107	-2.3033	-1.4698	0.0027	0.9995	-0.0767	-0.0679	0.0536
108	-2.4004	-1.5319	0.0027	0.9989	-0.0794	-0.0701	0.0551
109	-2.4965	-1.5934	0.0026	0.9983	-0.0819	-0.0718	0.0562
110	-2.3955	-1.5288	0.0026	0.9989	-0.0784	-0.0687	0.0537
111	-2.4936	-1.5915	0.0026	0.9983	-0.0812	-0.0710	0.0553
112	-2.6926	-1.7191	0.0026	0.9971	-0.0875	-0.0764	0.0594
214	1.5556	0.9915	0.0021	1.0021	0.0451	0.0360	-0.0258
215	1.6556	1.0554	0.0021	1.0018	0.0480	0.0383	-0.0274
216	1.6604	1.0584	0.0020	1.0017	0.0477	0.0375	-0.0266
217	1.3653	0.8700	0.0020	1.0027	0.0388	0.0301	-0.0211
218	1.4653	0.9338	0.0020	1.0023	0.0416	0.0323	-0.0227
219	1.2682	0.8081	0.0020	1.0029	0.0358	0.0276	-0.0192
220	1.0759	0.6855	0.0019	1.0034	0.0299	0.0225	-0.0153
221	0.8769	0.5586	0.0019	1.0038	0.0243	0.0182	-0.0124
238	-0.2894	-0.1843	0.0017	1.0044	-0.0075	-0.0050	0.0030
239	-0.1894	-0.1206	0.0017	1.0044	-0.0049	-0.0032	0.0020
240	-0.0923	-0.0588	0.0017	1.0045	-0.0024	-0.0016	0.0010
241	-0.1923	-0.1224	0.0017	1.0044	-0.0050	-0.0034	0.0020
242	-0.1952	-0.1243	0.0017	1.0045	-0.0051	-0.0035	0.0021
243	-0.2961	-0.1886	0.0017	1.0044	-0.0078	-0.0053	0.0033
244	-0.2913	-0.1855	0.0017	1.0044	-0.0076	-0.0051	0.0031
245	-0.5009	-0.3190	0.0017	1.0042	-0.0133	-0.0092	0.0058
246	-0.3980	-0.2535	0.0017	1.0043	-0.0105	-0.0072	0.0045
247	-0.4009	-0.2554	0.0017	1.0043	-0.0106	-0.0074	0.0047
248	-0.1058	-0.0674	0.0018	1.0046	-0.0028	-0.0020	0.0013
249	-0.2077	-0.1323	0.0018	1.0045	-0.0056	-0.0040	0.0026
250	-0.1106	-0.0704	0.0018	1.0046	-0.0030	-0.0022	0.0014
251	-0.2154	-0.1372	0.0018	1.0046	-0.0059	-0.0043	0.0029
252	-0.1222	-0.0778	0.0019	1.0047	-0.0034	-0.0025	0.0017
253	0.1740	0.1108	0.0019	1.0047	0.0048	0.0037	-0.0025
254	0.1730	0.1102	0.0019	1.0047	0.0048	0.0037	-0.0025
255	0.1711	0.1090	0.0019	1.0047	0.0048	0.0037	-0.0025
256	0.7585	0.4832	0.0020	1.0042	0.0218	0.0173	-0.0123

Output Statistics

Obs	Residual	RStudent	Hat Diag H	Cov Ratio	DFFITS	DFBETAS Intercept	LEIL1
257	1.3431	0.8560	0.0022	1.0029	0.0401	0.0329	-0.0242
258	1.4363	0.9155	0.0023	1.0027	0.0435	0.0362	-0.0269
259	1.6392	1.0450	0.0022	1.0020	0.0494	0.0408	-0.0302
260	1.5431	0.9836	0.0022	1.0023	0.0461	0.0378	-0.0278
261	1.3460	0.8578	0.0022	1.0029	0.0399	0.0325	-0.0238
262	1.3508	0.8609	0.0021	1.0028	0.0396	0.0319	-0.0231
263	1.3537	0.8627	0.0021	1.0028	0.0394	0.0316	-0.0227
264	1.0547	0.6720	0.0021	1.0036	0.0306	0.0245	-0.0176
265	1.3518	0.8615	0.0021	1.0028	0.0395	0.0318	-0.0230
266	1.2460	0.7940	0.0022	1.0032	0.0369	0.0301	-0.0220
267	1.2421	0.7916	0.0022	1.0032	0.0371	0.0305	-0.0225
268	1.0440	0.6652	0.0022	1.0037	0.0311	0.0254	-0.0187
269	1.3469	0.8584	0.0021	1.0029	0.0398	0.0324	-0.0236
270	1.3431	0.8560	0.0022	1.0029	0.0401	0.0329	-0.0242
271	1.0392	0.6622	0.0022	1.0038	0.0313	0.0258	-0.0191
272	1.2354	0.7873	0.0023	1.0033	0.0375	0.0312	-0.0233
273	1.4334	0.9137	0.0023	1.0028	0.0437	0.0366	-0.0274
274	1.7267	1.1009	0.0024	1.0018	0.0535	0.0453	-0.0343
275	2.1238	1.3547	0.0024	1.0001	0.0663	0.0564	-0.0429
276	2.3218	1.4814	0.0024	0.9991	0.0729	0.0622	-0.0474
277	2.4209	1.5448	0.0024	0.9986	0.0762	0.0651	-0.0497
278	2.7161	1.7340	0.0025	0.9969	0.0865	0.0745	-0.0573
279	2.8180	1.7993	0.0025	0.9962	0.0893	0.0767	-0.0588
280	3.1161	1.9907	0.0025	0.9942	0.0993	0.0855	-0.0658
281	3.2161	2.0549	0.0025	0.9935	0.1025	0.0883	-0.0679
282	3.4132	2.1817	0.0025	0.9921	0.1096	0.0948	-0.0732
283	3.6103	2.3087	0.0026	0.9905	0.1167	0.1014	-0.0786
284	3.6103	2.3087	0.0026	0.9905	0.1167	0.1014	-0.0786
285	3.9074	2.5003	0.0026	0.9880	0.1273	0.1111	-0.0865
286	4.2112	2.6966	0.0025	0.9852	0.1360	0.1180	-0.0914
287	4.6122	2.9563	0.0025	0.9812	0.1488	0.1289	-0.0997
288	4.6141	2.9575	0.0025	0.9812	0.1482	0.1280	-0.0987
289	4.2180	2.7009	0.0025	0.9851	0.1341	0.1151	-0.0883
290	4.2267	2.7063	0.0024	0.9849	0.1316	0.1114	-0.0843
291	4.1315	2.6447	0.0023	0.9857	0.1272	0.1067	-0.0801
292	4.0382	2.5844	0.0022	0.9865	0.1224	0.1013	-0.0752
293	3.9421	2.5222	0.0022	0.9874	0.1184	0.0972	-0.0716

Output Statistics

Obs	Residual	RStudent	Hat Diag H	Cov Ratio	DFFITS	DFBETAS Intercept	LEIL1
294	3.9489	2.5265	0.0021	0.9872	0.1167	0.0945	-0.0687
295	3.2556	2.0799	0.0021	0.9928	0.0947	0.0754	-0.0541
296	3.3604	2.1473	0.0020	0.9920	0.0967	0.0761	-0.0540
297	3.0624	1.9557	0.0020	0.9941	0.0877	0.0687	-0.0485
298	2.6682	1.7028	0.0020	0.9967	0.0754	0.0581	-0.0405
299	2.3749	1.5150	0.0019	0.9983	0.0661	0.0500	-0.0342
300	2.1788	1.3895	0.0019	0.9993	0.0601	0.0449	-0.0304
301	1.8846	1.2015	0.0018	1.0006	0.0514	0.0377	-0.0250
302	1.6904	1.0774	0.0018	1.0013	0.0456	0.0327	-0.0213
303	1.6952	1.0805	0.0018	1.0013	0.0453	0.0319	-0.0205
304	1.5962	1.0172	0.0017	1.0017	0.0425	0.0299	-0.0191
305	1.2991	0.8277	0.0017	1.0026	0.0344	0.0239	-0.0151
306	1.1029	0.7026	0.0017	1.0031	0.0290	0.0199	-0.0124
307	1.4048	0.8952	0.0017	1.0022	0.0368	0.0250	-0.0154
308	1.4068	0.8964	0.0017	1.0022	0.0367	0.0247	-0.0151
309	1.2068	0.7688	0.0017	1.0028	0.0315	0.0212	-0.0130
310	1.3068	0.8326	0.0017	1.0025	0.0341	0.0230	-0.0141
311	1.1087	0.7063	0.0017	1.0031	0.0289	0.0193	-0.0117
...							
554	-0.2888	-0.1842	0.0044	1.0071	-0.0123	0.0075	-0.0101
555	-0.4840	-0.3087	0.0045	1.0071	-0.0208	0.0129	-0.0173
556	-0.4879	-0.3111	0.0044	1.0070	-0.0208	0.0128	-0.0172
557	-0.5830	-0.3719	0.0045	1.0070	-0.0251	0.0155	-0.0209
580	-1.1782	-0.7517	0.0046	1.0059	-0.0512	0.0320	-0.0428
581	-1.2821	-0.8180	0.0045	1.0055	-0.0553	0.0343	-0.0460
582	-1.0811	-0.6897	0.0046	1.0061	-0.0467	0.0291	-0.0389
583	-0.9830	-0.6271	0.0045	1.0063	-0.0423	0.0262	-0.0352
584	-1.0840	-0.6915	0.0045	1.0060	-0.0465	0.0288	-0.0387
585	-0.9898	-0.6314	0.0044	1.0061	-0.0419	0.0257	-0.0347
601	1.9037	1.2136	0.0017	1.0004	0.0504	-0.0069	0.0220
602	2.3882	1.5233	0.0016	0.9979	0.0615	-0.0047	0.0234
603	2.7766	1.7720	0.0016	0.9956	0.0703	-0.0020	0.0236
604	3.0641	1.9564	0.0015	0.9937	0.0762	0.0020	0.0217
605	3.4660	2.2146	0.0015	0.9907	0.0865	0.0015	0.0253
606	3.5689	2.2809	0.0015	0.9899	0.0894	0.0004	0.0272
607	3.5747	2.2846	0.0016	0.9899	0.0903	-0.0018	0.0296
608	3.6805	2.3528	0.0016	0.9890	0.0938	-0.0042	0.0329

Output Statistics

Obs	Residual	RStudent	Hat Diag H	Cov Ratio	DFFITS	DFBETAS Intercept	LEIL1
609	3.8882	2.4868	0.0016	0.9873	0.1004	-0.0076	0.0382
610	4.0940	2.6196	0.0017	0.9855	0.1069	-0.0106	0.0429
611	3.9979	2.5576	0.0017	0.9864	0.1050	-0.0120	0.0437
612	4.0056	2.5626	0.0017	0.9863	0.1068	-0.0154	0.0473
613	3.9133	2.5031	0.0018	0.9872	0.1058	-0.0183	0.0496
614	3.9181	2.5063	0.0018	0.9872	0.1070	-0.0204	0.0518
615	4.0181	2.5708	0.0018	0.9863	0.1098	-0.0209	0.0532
616	4.0317	2.5797	0.0019	0.9863	0.1133	-0.0269	0.0595
617	3.7355	2.3887	0.0020	0.9889	0.1058	-0.0264	0.0568
618	3.5365	2.2605	0.0020	0.9906	0.1003	-0.0254	0.0541
619	3.5375	2.2611	0.0020	0.9906	0.1005	-0.0258	0.0545
620	3.6384	2.3261	0.0020	0.9898	0.1036	-0.0269	0.0565
621	3.6413	2.3280	0.0020	0.9898	0.1044	-0.0281	0.0577
622	3.5461	2.2668	0.0020	0.9906	0.1027	-0.0292	0.0582
623	3.9471	2.5253	0.0021	0.9872	0.1147	-0.0329	0.0652
624	3.4539	2.2075	0.0021	0.9914	0.1018	-0.0313	0.0597
625	3.2625	2.0845	0.0022	0.9929	0.0981	-0.0326	0.0596
626	3.1635	2.0209	0.0022	0.9936	0.0953	-0.0319	0.0581
627	3.1693	2.0247	0.0023	0.9937	0.0967	-0.0340	0.0603
628	3.2780	2.0946	0.0024	0.9930	0.1021	-0.0382	0.0656
629	3.1780	2.0304	0.0024	0.9937	0.0990	-0.0371	0.0636
630	3.2828	2.0978	0.0024	0.9930	0.1035	-0.0400	0.0675
631	3.1818	2.0329	0.0024	0.9937	0.1000	-0.0384	0.0651
632	3.1867	2.0360	0.0025	0.9937	0.1013	-0.0402	0.0669
633	3.1809	2.0323	0.0024	0.9937	0.0998	-0.0381	0.0647
634	2.9770	1.9013	0.0024	0.9951	0.0925	-0.0344	0.0592
635	2.7828	1.7767	0.0024	0.9964	0.0876	-0.0339	0.0572
636	2.6838	1.7133	0.0024	0.9970	0.0847	-0.0330	0.0554
637	2.4876	1.5876	0.0025	0.9982	0.0792	-0.0316	0.0525
638	2.4896	1.5889	0.0025	0.9983	0.0796	-0.0321	0.0530
639	2.3944	1.5280	0.0026	0.9988	0.0774	-0.0321	0.0523
640	2.3992	1.5311	0.0026	0.9989	0.0785	-0.0335	0.0538
641	2.3973	1.5299	0.0026	0.9989	0.0781	-0.0329	0.0532
642	2.3983	1.5305	0.0026	0.9989	0.0783	-0.0332	0.0535
643	2.3944	1.5280	0.0026	0.9988	0.0774	-0.0321	0.0523
644	2.2963	1.4652	0.0026	0.9994	0.0746	-0.0313	0.0507
660	0.9407	0.5997	0.0032	1.0050	0.0339	-0.0173	0.0255

Output Statistics

Obs	Residual	RStudent	Hat Diag H	Cov Ratio	DFFITS	DFBETAS Intercept	LEIL1
661	0.8407	0.5359	0.0032	1.0052	0.0303	-0.0155	0.0228
662	0.9427	0.6009	0.0032	1.0050	0.0342	-0.0175	0.0257
663	0.9475	0.6040	0.0033	1.0051	0.0347	-0.0181	0.0264
664	0.5562	0.3545	0.0034	1.0059	0.0208	-0.0112	0.0160
665	0.5571	0.3551	0.0034	1.0059	0.0209	-0.0112	0.0161
666	0.3620	0.2307	0.0035	1.0062	0.0137	-0.0075	0.0107
667	0.4687	0.2988	0.0036	1.0062	0.0181	-0.0100	0.0142
668	0.4735	0.3019	0.0037	1.0063	0.0185	-0.0104	0.0146
669	0.1764	0.1125	0.0038	1.0066	0.0069	-0.0039	0.0055
670	-0.0178	-0.0113	0.0039	1.0067	-0.0007	0.0004	-0.0006
671	0.0851	0.0543	0.0039	1.0067	0.0034	-0.0020	0.0027
672	-0.1110	-0.0708	0.0040	1.0068	-0.0045	0.0026	-0.0036
673	-0.006191	-0.003947	0.0041	1.0069	-0.0003	0.0001	-0.0002
674	-0.2052	-0.1309	0.0041	1.0069	-0.0084	0.0050	-0.0068
675	-0.2052	-0.1309	0.0041	1.0069	-0.0084	0.0050	-0.0068
676	-0.3004	-0.1915	0.0042	1.0069	-0.0124	0.0074	-0.0102
677	-0.1956	-0.1247	0.0043	1.0071	-0.0082	0.0049	-0.0067
678	-0.3917	-0.2498	0.0044	1.0070	-0.0165	0.0101	-0.0136
679	-0.4869	-0.3105	0.0044	1.0070	-0.0208	0.0128	-0.0172
680	-0.5888	-0.3755	0.0044	1.0068	-0.0250	0.0153	-0.0207
681	-0.6888	-0.4393	0.0044	1.0067	-0.0292	0.0179	-0.0242
682	-0.6898	-0.4399	0.0044	1.0067	-0.0292	0.0179	-0.0241
683	-0.6859	-0.4375	0.0045	1.0068	-0.0293	0.0181	-0.0243
684	-0.6821	-0.4350	0.0045	1.0068	-0.0294	0.0183	-0.0245
685	-0.7840	-0.5001	0.0045	1.0066	-0.0336	0.0208	-0.0280
686	-0.7869	-0.5019	0.0044	1.0066	-0.0336	0.0207	-0.0278
687	-0.6879	-0.4387	0.0044	1.0067	-0.0293	0.0180	-0.0242
688	-0.6879	-0.4387	0.0044	1.0067	-0.0293	0.0180	-0.0242
689	-0.9830	-0.6271	0.0045	1.0063	-0.0423	0.0262	-0.0352
690	-0.7850	-0.5007	0.0045	1.0066	-0.0336	0.0208	-0.0279
...							
706	-1.5367	-0.9812	0.0055	1.0056	-0.0731	0.0487	-0.0632
707	-1.5232	-0.9727	0.0058	1.0060	-0.0745	0.0505	-0.0650
708	-1.5193	-0.9702	0.0059	1.0061	-0.0749	0.0511	-0.0655
709	-1.5116	-0.9654	0.0061	1.0063	-0.0757	0.0521	-0.0665
710	-1.5048	-0.9612	0.0063	1.0065	-0.0764	0.0529	-0.0674
711	-1.4981	-0.9569	0.0064	1.0067	-0.0771	0.0538	-0.0682

Output Statistics

Obs	Residual	RStudent	Hat Diag H	Cov Ratio	DFFITS	DFBETAS Intercept	LEIL1
712	-1.6952	-1.0831	0.0065	1.0061	-0.0877	0.0614	-0.0778
713	-1.7904	-1.1440	0.0066	1.0058	-0.0935	0.0658	-0.0831
714	-1.5894	-1.0154	0.0067	1.0066	-0.0832	0.0586	-0.0740
715	-1.6836	-1.0758	0.0068	1.0064	-0.0891	0.0632	-0.0795
716	-1.6769	-1.0716	0.0070	1.0066	-0.0899	0.0641	-0.0805
717	-1.8720	-1.1966	0.0071	1.0060	-0.1013	0.0726	-0.0909
718	-1.8653	-1.1924	0.0073	1.0062	-0.1023	0.0737	-0.0920
719	-1.8682	-1.1942	0.0072	1.0061	-0.1019	0.0732	-0.0915

Sum of Residuals	0
Sum of Squared Residuals	1766.00382
Predicted Residual SS (PRESS)	1775.08809

BOLD denotes influential observations

There is clearly a need for a robust regression estimate of the UER and LEI relationship.

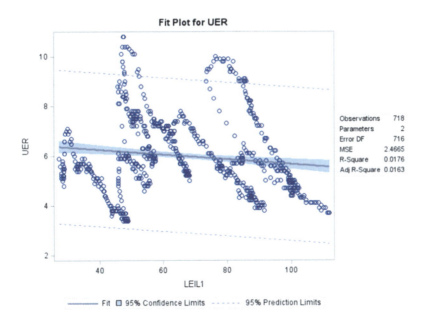

7.4.2.1   Estimation Six: The Unemployment Rate and WkUNCL OLS Model, 1959–2018

In Estimation Six, we estimate the unemployment rate as a function of the WkUNCL. The WkUNCL coefficient is positive as expected, 0.015, and highly statistically significant, having a t-statistic of 38.94.

Estimation Six: The REG Procedure
Model: MODEL1
Dependent Variable: UER

Number of observations read	719
Number of observations used	718
Number of observations with missing values	1

Analysis of variance

Source	DF	Sum of squares	Mean square	F value	Pr > F
Model	1	1221.11584	1221.11584	1516.36	<0.0001
Error	716	576.59181	0.80530		
Corrected total	717	1797.70765			

Root MSE	0.89738	**R-square**	0.6793
Dependent mean	5.99819	**Adj R-Sq**	0.6788
Coeff var	14.96089		

Parameter estimates

Variable	DF	Parameter estimate	Standard error	t Value	Pr > |t|
Intercept	1	0.81165	0.13734	5.91	<0.0001
WkUNCLL1	1	0.01507	0.00038698	38.94	<0.0001

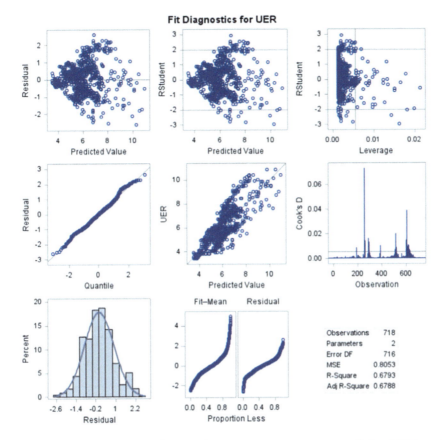

Fit Diagnostics for UER

There is clearly a need for a robust regression estimate of the UER and WkUNCL relationship for the 1959–2018 period, just as there was for the LEI variable.

In Estimation Seven, we estimate the unemployment rate as a function of the WkUNCL and the LEI. The LEI coefficient is negative as expected, −.010, and highly statistically significant, having a t-statistic of −6.74. The WkUNCL coefficient is positive as expected, 0.015, and highly statistically significant, having a t-statistic of 40.18. The OLS regression estimate is highly statistically significant, with an estimated F-statistic of 827.98, and an adjusted R-squared of 0.698.

Estimation Seven: MZTT 1959–2018 The Unemployment Rate and LEI WkUNCL OLS Model
The REG Procedure
Model: MODEL1
Dependent Variable: UER

Number of observations read	719
Number of observations used	718
Number of observations with missing values	1

Analysis of variance

Source	DF	Sum of squares	Mean square	F value	Pr > F
Model	2	1255.55443	627.77721	827.92	<0.0001
Error	715	542.15322	0.75826		
Corrected total	717	1797.70765			

Root MSE	0.87078	**R-square**	0.6984
Dependent mean	5.99819	**Adj R-Sq**	0.6976
Coeff var	14.51737		

Parameter estimates

Variable	DF	Parameter estimate	Standard error	t Value	Pr > |t|
Intercept	1	1.48018	0.16613	8.91	<0.0001
LEIL1	1	−0.01006	0.00149	−6.74	<0.0001
WkUNCLL1	1	0.01509	0.00037551	40.18	<0.0001

We proceed to use the additional Belsley et al. (1980) regression diagnostics to identify influential observations and potential outliers. We report the RStudent, cov ratio, DFFITS, and DFBETAS.

Output statistics

Obs	Residual	RStudent	Hat Diag H	Cov Ratio	DFFITS	DFBETAS Intercept	LEIL1	WkUNCLL1
1								
2	0.2566	0.2954	0.0065	1.0104	0.0239	0.0192	−0.0202	−0.0063
3	0.0798	0.0919	0.0066	1.0108	0.0075	0.0062	−0.0062	−0.0023
4	0.0836	0.0963	0.0072	1.0114	0.0082	0.0073	−0.0064	−0.0035
5	0.1898	0.2186	0.0076	1.0117	0.0191	0.0175	−0.0146	−0.0092
6	0.0631	0.0727	0.0075	1.0118	0.0063	0.0058	−0.0048	−0.0030

Output statistics

Obs	Residual	RStudent	Hat Diag H	Cov Ratio	DFFITS	DFBETAS Intercept	LEIL1	WkUNCLL1
7	−0.007862	−0.009054	0.0071	1.0114	−0.0008	−0.0007	0.0006	0.0003
8	0.001118	0.001288	0.0069	1.0112	0.0001	0.0001	−0.0001	−0.0000
9	−0.1223	−0.1408	0.0062	1.0104	−0.0112	−0.0090	0.0093	0.0030
10	0.3870	0.4456	0.0067	1.0101	0.0366	0.0316	−0.0295	−0.0135
11	−0.1190	−0.1370	0.0060	1.0102	−0.0106	−0.0079	0.0091	0.0018
12	−1.2320	−1.4200	0.0059	1.0016	−0.1091	−0.0627	0.0951	−0.0064
...								
122	−0.5220	−0.6012	0.0066	1.0093	−0.0489	−0.0460	0.0189	0.0389
123	−0.5276	−0.6076	0.0065	1.0092	−0.0492	−0.0463	0.0189	0.0392
124	−0.3848	−0.4432	0.0070	1.0105	−0.0373	−0.0351	0.0137	0.0304
125	−0.3365	−0.3876	0.0072	1.0108	−0.0330	−0.0310	0.0118	0.0271
126	−0.2289	−0.2637	0.0073	1.0113	−0.0225	−0.0212	0.0082	0.0185
127	−0.3753	−0.4322	0.0067	1.0102	−0.0356	−0.0336	0.0136	0.0285
128	−0.5171	−0.5954	0.0063	1.0090	−0.0473	−0.0446	0.0190	0.0369
129	−0.2924	−0.3367	0.0064	1.0102	−0.0269	−0.0254	0.0108	0.0211
130	−0.2220	−0.2557	0.0066	1.0106	−0.0208	−0.0197	0.0082	0.0166
131	−0.5080	−0.5850	0.0063	1.0092	−0.0467	−0.0441	0.0190	0.0365
132	−0.6202	−0.7141	0.0060	1.0081	−0.0554	−0.0523	0.0235	0.0423
133	−0.4148	−0.4774	0.0054	1.0087	−0.0352	−0.0330	0.0159	0.0256
134	−0.5935	−0.6828	0.0042	1.0065	−0.0443	−0.0404	0.0234	0.0274
135	−0.5092	−0.5857	0.0040	1.0068	−0.0371	−0.0334	0.0205	0.0216
136	−0.4510	−0.5186	0.0037	1.0068	−0.0318	−0.0282	0.0185	0.0171
137	−1.3533	−1.5578	0.0027	0.9967	−0.0814	−0.0473	0.0568	0.0022
138	−0.7087	−0.8149	0.0030	1.0044	−0.0448	−0.0346	0.0296	0.0139
139	−0.4925	−0.5662	0.0031	1.0060	−0.0317	−0.0255	0.0206	0.0115
140	−0.1698	−0.1951	0.0034	1.0075	−0.0114	−0.0097	0.0071	0.0052
141	−0.007538	−0.008664	0.0032	1.0074	−0.0005	−0.0004	0.0003	0.0002
142	−0.4129	−0.4746	0.0028	1.0060	−0.0250	−0.0168	0.0171	0.0039
143	−0.0833	−0.0958	0.0027	1.0069	−0.0050	−0.0033	0.0035	0.0006
...								
250	−0.7281	−0.8368	0.0021	1.0034	−0.0384	−0.0047	0.0168	−0.0148
251	−1.0881	−1.2515	0.0024	1.0001	−0.0620	−0.0007	0.0263	−0.0313
252	−1.2395	−1.4265	0.0029	0.9986	−0.0769	0.0059	0.0318	−0.0456
253	−1.1381	−1.3099	0.0033	1.0003	−0.0755	0.0106	0.0301	−0.0492
254	−0.9249	−1.0638	0.0029	1.0024	−0.0574	0.0034	0.0246	−0.0334
255	−0.9631	−1.1079	0.0030	1.0020	−0.0606	0.0042	0.0260	−0.0360
256	−0.6855	−0.7885	0.0037	1.0054	−0.0483	0.0074	0.0203	−0.0326
257	**−1.8636**	**−2.1571**	**0.0106**	**0.9954**	**−0.2232**	**0.1012**	**0.0625**	**−0.1988**
258	**−2.8282**	**−3.2986**	**0.0171**	**0.9764**	**−0.4353**	**0.2307**	**0.1005**	**−0.4056**
259	**−2.3205**	**−2.6968**	**0.0150**	**0.9890**	**−0.3332**	**0.1709**	**0.0806**	**−0.3076**
260	**−1.6682**	**−1.9296**	**0.0106**	**0.9993**	**−0.1999**	**0.0907**	**0.0559**	**−0.1781**
261	−1.2738	−1.4697	0.0078	1.0029	−0.1300	0.0501	0.0416	−0.1105
262	−0.7347	−0.8459	0.0057	1.0069	−0.0639	0.0192	0.0231	−0.0506
263	0.1056	0.1214	0.0034	1.0075	0.0070	−0.0005	−0.0032	0.0043
264	0.0465	0.0534	0.0029	1.0071	0.0029	0.0000	−0.0014	0.0015
265	0.3586	0.4121	0.0029	1.0064	0.0223	0.0006	−0.0111	0.0117
266	0.1907	0.2192	0.0031	1.0071	0.0122	0.0001	−0.0061	0.0066
267	−0.0336	−0.0386	0.0035	1.0078	−0.0023	0.0001	0.0011	−0.0014
268	0.0867	0.0997	0.0029	1.0071	0.0054	0.0003	−0.0028	0.0027
269	0.3656	0.4202	0.0029	1.0064	0.0228	0.0009	−0.0117	0.0118
270	0.2409	0.2769	0.0032	1.0071	0.0156	−0.0000	−0.0079	0.0087
271	−0.2985	−0.3432	0.0037	1.0074	−0.0209	0.0017	0.0100	−0.0131
272	−0.1342	−0.1543	0.0038	1.0079	−0.0095	0.0008	0.0046	−0.0061

Output statistics

Obs	Residual	RStudent	Hat Diag H	Cov Ratio	DFFITS	DFBETAS Intercept	LEIL1	WkUNCLL1
273	−0.0720	−0.0828	0.0041	1.0084	−0.0053	0.0007	0.0025	−0.0036
274	−0.2829	−0.3256	0.0057	1.0095	−0.0246	0.0060	0.0103	−0.0188
275	−0.1333	−0.1535	0.0066	1.0107	−0.0125	0.0036	0.0049	−0.0099
276	−0.2069	−0.2383	0.0076	1.0117	−0.0209	0.0070	0.0078	−0.0173
277	−0.4624	−0.5332	0.0092	1.0123	−0.0514	0.0199	0.0175	−0.0442
278	−0.3244	−0.3741	0.0100	1.0138	−0.0377	0.0151	0.0126	−0.0327
279	−0.0488	−0.0563	0.0092	1.0135	−0.0054	0.0021	0.0019	−0.0046
280	−0.0948	−0.1094	0.0109	1.0152	−0.0115	0.0048	0.0037	−0.0101
281	−0.4504	−0.5205	0.0135	1.0168	−0.0608	0.0283	0.0177	−0.0549
282	−0.2399	−0.2772	0.0134	1.0175	−0.0323	0.0149	0.0095	−0.0291
283	−0.2103	−0.2432	0.0145	1.0187	−0.0295	0.0139	0.0085	−0.0268
284	0.2000	0.2309	0.0121	1.0162	0.0255	−0.0111	−0.0081	0.0226
285	−0.4067	−0.4710	0.0178	1.0214	−0.0634	0.0320	0.0168	−0.0586
286	−0.7378	−0.8568	0.0226	1.0242	−0.1301	0.0709	0.0302	−0.1226
287	0.1143	0.1324	0.0191	1.0236	0.0185	−0.0096	−0.0046	0.0172
288	0.8314	0.9616	0.0142	1.0147	0.1154	−0.0545	−0.0330	0.1047
289	1.5895	1.8359	0.0081	0.9982	0.1659	−0.0575	−0.0611	0.1385
290	1.9772	2.2848	0.0065	0.9889	0.1847	−0.0544	−0.0723	0.1474
291	1.9441	2.2459	0.0062	0.9894	0.1776	−0.0515	−0.0691	0.1409
292	1.9930	2.3021	0.0057	0.9878	0.1736	−0.0472	−0.0680	0.1350
293	1.6300	1.8814	0.0066	0.9960	0.1529	−0.0505	−0.0544	0.1248
294	2.0730	2.3945	0.0050	0.9853	0.1698	−0.0428	−0.0661	0.1287
295	1.8779	2.1660	0.0036	0.9882	0.1305	−0.0164	−0.0569	0.0855
296	2.4476	2.8283	0.0027	0.9738	0.1473	0.0063	−0.0716	0.0739
297	1.6729	1.9282	0.0036	0.9922	0.1156	−0.0165	−0.0484	0.0767
298	1.6832	1.9394	0.0027	0.9912	0.1018	−0.0004	−0.0465	0.0547
299	1.5351	1.7677	0.0025	0.9936	0.0881	0.0041	−0.0402	0.0425
300	1.5563	1.7920	0.0022	0.9930	0.0839	0.0120	−0.0394	0.0319
301	1.4932	1.7188	0.0020	0.9938	0.0760	0.0192	−0.0360	0.0192
302	1.5844	1.8241	0.0018	0.9921	0.0773	0.0308	−0.0362	0.0055
303	1.7463	2.0115	0.0018	0.9891	0.0843	0.0399	−0.0381	−0.0029
304	1.5719	1.8096	0.0017	0.9922	0.0757	0.0327	−0.0340	0.0013
305	0.9143	1.0511	0.0018	1.0014	0.0452	0.0103	−0.0193	0.0116
306	0.8949	1.0286	0.0017	1.0015	0.0429	0.0137	−0.0181	0.0061
307	1.1184	1.2861	0.0018	0.9990	0.0539	0.0146	−0.0222	0.0105
308	1.1597	1.3336	0.0017	0.9985	0.0555	0.0160	−0.0226	0.0094
309	0.5101	0.5861	0.0021	1.0048	0.0267	0.0012	−0.0100	0.0117
370	−0.5948	−0.6833	0.0014	1.0036	−0.0256	−0.0061	−0.0007	0.0019
371	−0.8845	−1.0165	0.0015	1.0013	−0.0389	−0.0005	−0.0006	−0.0084
372	−0.5214	−0.5990	0.0014	1.0041	−0.0224	−0.0051	−0.0005	0.0012
373	−0.8005	−0.9199	0.0014	1.0021	−0.0348	−0.0021	−0.0007	−0.0054
374	−0.9453	−1.0865	0.0014	1.0007	−0.0413	−0.0015	−0.0006	−0.0078
375	−0.9437	−1.0846	0.0014	1.0007	−0.0408	−0.0041	−0.0004	−0.0046
...								
502	−1.2007	−1.3821	0.0034	0.9995	−0.0801	0.0025	−0.0554	0.0266
503	−1.2233	−1.4081	0.0032	0.9991	−0.0800	0.0017	−0.0542	0.0266
504	−1.7569	−2.0248	0.0028	0.9899	−0.1070	0.0246	−0.0753	0.0077
505	−1.6510	−1.9019	0.0026	0.9917	−0.0973	0.0282	−0.0664	−0.0027
506	−1.5383	−1.7715	0.0026	0.9936	−0.0897	0.0207	−0.0604	0.0035
507	−1.9478	−2.2460	0.0026	0.9858	−0.1144	0.0488	−0.0725	−0.0277
508	−2.0811	−2.4011	0.0026	0.9829	−0.1237	0.0607	−0.0720	−0.0448
509	−2.3259	−2.6863	0.0027	0.9770	−0.1402	0.0735	−0.0764	−0.0606
510	−2.1848	−2.5219	0.0028	0.9806	−0.1343	0.0733	−0.0730	−0.0614

Output statistics								
Obs	Residual	RStudent	Hat Diag H	Cov Ratio	DFFITS	DFBETAS		
						Intercept	LEIL1	WkUNCLL1
511	−1.9983	−2.3048	0.0027	0.9848	−0.1192	0.0614	−0.0651	−0.0501
512	−1.7470	−2.0133	0.0027	0.9900	−0.1050	0.0553	−0.0562	−0.0465
513	−1.6506	−1.9015	0.0027	0.9918	−0.0988	0.0519	−0.0524	−0.0440
514	−2.0415	−2.3564	0.0038	0.9849	−0.1460	0.0960	−0.0586	−0.1002
515	−2.4178	−2.7974	0.0054	0.9772	−0.2066	0.1478	−0.0665	−0.1648
516	−1.8070	−2.0844	0.0042	0.9903	−0.1360	0.0923	−0.0514	−0.0985
517	−1.0617	−1.2214	0.0027	1.0007	−0.0641	0.0348	−0.0316	−0.0318
518	−1.1432	−1.3154	0.0029	0.9998	−0.0706	0.0399	−0.0340	−0.0373
519	−0.9209	−1.0590	0.0026	1.0021	−0.0544	0.0279	−0.0288	−0.0235
520	−1.0925	−1.2572	0.0033	1.0008	−0.0719	0.0442	−0.0350	−0.0415
521	−1.3072	−1.5052	0.0036	0.9983	−0.0900	0.0578	−0.0434	−0.0549
522	−0.8827	−1.0152	0.0029	1.0028	−0.0549	0.0305	−0.0308	−0.0249
523	−0.6967	−0.8010	0.0027	1.0042	−0.0417	0.0209	−0.0246	−0.0154
524	−0.7554	−0.8685	0.0026	1.0037	−0.0445	0.0215	−0.0261	−0.0156
525	−0.8902	−1.0238	0.0028	1.0026	−0.0541	0.0285	−0.0309	−0.0223
526	−1.1075	−1.2743	0.0031	1.0004	−0.0706	0.0411	−0.0377	−0.0356
527	−0.8798	−1.0119	0.0030	1.0029	−0.0555	0.0319	−0.0298	−0.0275
528	−0.4972	−0.5715	0.0027	1.0055	−0.0297	0.0148	−0.0173	−0.0110
529	−1.0789	−1.2414	0.0032	1.0010	−0.0706	0.0427	−0.0376	−0.0374
530	−0.7596	−0.8735	0.0029	1.0039	−0.0472	0.0260	−0.0268	−0.0209
531	−1.0136	−1.1662	0.0033	1.0018	−0.0669	0.0410	−0.0353	−0.0363
532	−1.0413	−1.1983	0.0035	1.0017	−0.0711	0.0453	−0.0360	−0.0416
533	−1.1495	−1.3234	0.0039	1.0008	−0.0830	0.0557	−0.0391	−0.0538
534	−0.7021	−0.8075	0.0035	1.0050	−0.0479	0.0305	−0.0251	−0.0273
535	−0.7784	−0.8954	0.0036	1.0044	−0.0535	0.0341	−0.0289	−0.0298
536	−0.5993	−0.6891	0.0031	1.0053	−0.0386	0.0222	−0.0227	−0.0175
537	−0.5375	−0.6179	0.0031	1.0057	−0.0345	0.0195	−0.0210	−0.0147
538	−0.5610	−0.6451	0.0031	1.0056	−0.0362	0.0201	−0.0230	−0.0141
539	−0.4608	−0.5297	0.0030	1.0060	−0.0289	0.0136	−0.0197	−0.0072
540	−0.3531	−0.4059	0.0030	1.0065	−0.0222	0.0091	−0.0158	−0.0032
541	−0.2772	−0.3186	0.0031	1.0069	−0.0176	0.0069	−0.0129	−0.0019
542	−0.4089	−0.4701	0.0032	1.0065	−0.0266	0.0110	−0.0197	−0.0033
543	−0.1933	−0.2222	0.0033	1.0073	−0.0128	0.0054	−0.0096	−0.0015
544	−0.1011	−0.1162	0.0035	1.0076	−0.0069	0.0022	−0.0053	0.0001
545	−0.1534	−0.1764	0.0035	1.0076	−0.0104	0.0036	−0.0081	−0.0001
546	−0.0478	−0.0550	0.0036	1.0079	−0.0033	0.0011	−0.0026	0.0001
547	−0.1845	−0.2122	0.0037	1.0078	−0.0129	0.0044	−0.0102	0.0003
548	−0.3534	−0.4064	0.0038	1.0073	−0.0251	0.0093	−0.0199	−0.0004
549	−0.2498	−0.2873	0.0039	1.0077	−0.0179	0.0061	−0.0143	0.0006
550	−0.1307	−0.1503	0.0040	1.0081	−0.0095	0.0032	−0.0077	0.0003
551	−0.1402	−0.1612	0.0041	1.0082	−0.0103	0.0032	−0.0083	0.0008
552	−0.0592	−0.0681	0.0042	1.0084	−0.0044	0.0013	−0.0036	0.0005
553	−0.1456	−0.1675	0.0044	1.0085	−0.0111	0.0033	−0.0091	0.0012
554	−0.2171	−0.2497	0.0044	1.0084	−0.0166	0.0061	−0.0138	0.0005
555	0.0194	0.0223	0.0047	1.0090	0.0015	−0.0003	0.0012	−0.0003
556	−0.2984	−0.3433	0.0045	1.0082	−0.0230	0.0075	−0.0190	0.0019
557	−0.2109	−0.2426	0.0046	1.0086	−0.0166	0.0044	−0.0136	0.0026
558	−0.4130	−0.4751	0.0046	1.0079	−0.0322	0.0097	−0.0266	0.0037
559	−0.3426	−0.3941	0.0047	1.0083	−0.0272	0.0078	−0.0225	0.0038
560	−0.4581	−0.5271	0.0047	1.0078	−0.0364	0.0106	−0.0302	0.0048
561	−0.2269	−0.2610	0.0049	1.0089	−0.0184	0.0047	−0.0153	0.0033
562	−1.4635	−1.6872	0.0051	0.9974	−0.1214	0.0752	−0.0962	−0.0380
563	−0.6614	−0.7611	0.0047	1.0065	−0.0524	0.0207	−0.0440	0.0003

Output statistics

Obs	Residual	RStudent	Hat Diag H	Cov Ratio	DFFITS	DFBETAS Intercept	LEIL1	WkUNCLL1
564	−0.3299	−0.3796	0.0050	1.0086	−0.0269	0.0070	−0.0224	0.0048
565	−0.5148	−0.5924	0.0050	1.0078	−0.0420	0.0107	−0.0349	0.0077
566	−0.1126	−0.1296	0.0055	1.0096	−0.0096	0.0016	−0.0078	0.0028
567	−0.1930	−0.2221	0.0055	1.0095	−0.0165	0.0027	−0.0134	0.0049
568	−0.2609	−0.3002	0.0055	1.0093	−0.0222	0.0042	−0.0183	0.0060
569	−0.4816	−0.5542	0.0052	1.0082	−0.0401	0.0087	−0.0332	0.0092
570	−0.8798	−1.0129	0.0048	1.0048	−0.0707	0.0242	−0.0595	0.0055
571	−0.4052	−0.4663	0.0051	1.0084	−0.0333	0.0072	−0.0273	0.0075
572	−0.5898	−0.6787	0.0048	1.0071	−0.0472	0.0128	−0.0392	0.0075
573	−0.7012	−0.8071	0.0048	1.0063	−0.0563	0.0135	−0.0463	0.0110
574	−0.8450	−0.9727	0.0048	1.0051	−0.0676	0.0172	−0.0558	0.0120
575	−0.7334	−0.8441	0.0048	1.0060	−0.0585	0.0145	−0.0482	0.0108
576	−1.0240	−1.1790	0.0046	1.0030	−0.0805	0.0249	−0.0668	0.0087
577	−0.7461	−0.8587	0.0048	1.0059	−0.0593	0.0171	−0.0493	0.0081
578	−0.7656	−0.8812	0.0047	1.0057	−0.0607	0.0155	−0.0500	0.0105
579	−0.9798	−1.1280	0.0046	1.0035	−0.0770	0.0226	−0.0637	0.0097
580	−0.6007	−0.6913	0.0049	1.0071	−0.0485	0.0098	−0.0395	0.0114
581	−0.9099	−1.0474	0.0047	1.0043	−0.0717	0.0192	−0.0590	0.0112
582	−0.5142	−0.5917	0.0048	1.0076	−0.0412	0.0084	−0.0335	0.0096
583	−0.5385	−0.6196	0.0047	1.0073	−0.0425	0.0103	−0.0348	0.0079
584	−0.6033	−0.6942	0.0047	1.0069	−0.0477	0.0109	−0.0389	0.0096
585	−0.6104	−0.7023	0.0045	1.0067	−0.0473	0.0122	−0.0386	0.0076
586	−0.5178	−0.5958	0.0045	1.0072	−0.0398	0.0086	−0.0320	0.0082
587	−0.7532	−0.8666	0.0042	1.0053	−0.0563	0.0164	−0.0457	0.0062
588	−0.6418	−0.7383	0.0040	1.0059	−0.0468	0.0162	−0.0377	0.0015
589	−0.7876	−0.9061	0.0038	1.0046	−0.0562	0.0217	−0.0447	−0.0017
590	−0.7523	−0.8654	0.0036	1.0047	−0.0523	0.0169	−0.0411	0.0020
591	−0.6494	−0.7468	0.0035	1.0053	−0.0440	0.0152	−0.0341	−0.0002
592	−1.1054	−1.2721	0.0033	1.0007	−0.0736	0.0335	−0.0546	−0.0127
593	−0.6411	−0.7372	0.0032	1.0052	−0.0420	0.0179	−0.0310	−0.0059
594	−0.4898	−0.5632	0.0031	1.0060	−0.0316	0.0137	−0.0229	−0.0052
595	−0.5528	−0.6357	0.0033	1.0058	−0.0363	0.0188	−0.0253	−0.0105
596	−0.7844	−0.9023	0.0037	1.0045	−0.0549	0.0351	−0.0327	−0.0282
597	−0.9825	−1.1308	0.0039	1.0028	−0.0710	0.0474	−0.0389	−0.0414
598	−1.1216	−1.2919	0.0050	1.0022	−0.0916	0.0664	−0.0398	−0.0666
599	−1.0504	−1.2099	0.0054	1.0034	−0.0888	0.0641	−0.0315	−0.0694
600	−1.3329	−1.5384	0.0081	1.0024	−0.1390	0.1035	−0.0332	−0.1218
601	−1.4052	−1.6242	0.0107	1.0039	−0.1686	0.1254	−0.0285	−0.1545
602	−1.3060	−1.5108	0.0128	1.0075	−0.1719	0.1272	−0.0222	−0.1606
603	−1.7433	−2.0249	0.0183	1.0055	−0.2762	0.2058	−0.0254	−0.2640
604	−1.6841	−1.9575	0.0199	1.0083	−0.2792	0.2064	−0.0200	−0.2684
605	−0.6198	−0.7170	0.0152	1.0175	−0.0890	0.0650	−0.0077	−0.0844
606	−0.5063	−0.5856	0.0151	1.0181	−0.0725	0.0531	−0.0066	−0.0687
607	−0.2513	−0.2904	0.0135	1.0176	−0.0340	0.0249	−0.0036	−0.0320
608	0.3948	0.4555	0.0104	1.0139	0.0467	−0.0338	0.0061	0.0430
609	0.6300	0.7270	0.0103	1.0124	0.0742	−0.0541	0.0108	0.0681
610	1.1257	1.2992	0.0089	1.0060	0.1228	−0.0890	0.0206	0.1107
611	1.2968	1.4962	0.0076	1.0025	0.1313	−0.0942	0.0248	0.1160
612	1.7499	2.0198	0.0059	0.9930	0.1555	−0.1088	0.0365	0.1306
613	1.9430	2.2432	0.0050	0.9882	0.1583	−0.1084	0.0437	0.1267
614	1.7851	2.0604	0.0055	0.9920	0.1537	−0.1081	0.0418	0.1260
615	1.8866	2.1783	0.0055	0.9899	0.1625	−0.1142	0.0442	0.1331
616	2.1376	2.4695	0.0049	0.9837	0.1725	−0.1200	0.0562	0.1340

Output statistics

Obs	Residual	RStudent	Hat Diag H	Cov Ratio	DFFITS	DFBETAS Intercept	LEIL1	WkUNCLL1
617	1.9668	2.2704	0.0045	0.9872	0.1529	−0.1050	0.0533	0.1150
618	1.7723	2.0445	0.0045	0.9912	0.1376	−0.0945	0.0483	0.1033
619	1.8050	2.0823	0.0044	0.9905	0.1388	−0.0950	0.0496	0.1033
620	1.8879	2.1787	0.0045	0.9889	0.1462	−0.1005	0.0522	0.1093
621	1.6752	1.9325	0.0052	0.9937	0.1392	−0.0990	0.0473	0.1089
622	1.9257	2.2222	0.0042	0.9878	0.1442	−0.0980	0.0564	0.1031
623	2.4007	2.7754	0.0040	0.9763	0.1762	−0.1181	0.0709	0.1229
624	2.2200	2.5636	0.0034	0.9803	0.1490	−0.0931	0.0687	0.0906
625	2.1769	2.5132	0.0032	0.9811	0.1417	−0.0854	0.0713	0.0781
626	1.8712	2.1582	0.0036	0.9883	0.1294	−0.0834	0.0615	0.0799
627	2.3117	2.6700	0.0029	0.9775	0.1435	−0.0791	0.0791	0.0655
628	2.4253	2.8027	0.0030	0.9747	0.1529	−0.0854	0.0874	0.0684
629	1.9346	2.2319	0.0036	0.9871	0.1348	−0.0873	0.0694	0.0795
630	2.1105	2.4364	0.0035	0.9831	0.1454	−0.0927	0.0779	0.0818
631	2.0925	2.4152	0.0034	0.9833	0.1408	−0.0872	0.0768	0.0753
632	2.1835	2.5210	0.0033	0.9811	0.1449	−0.0875	0.0824	0.0724
633	2.2046	2.5455	0.0032	0.9805	0.1438	−0.0853	0.0806	0.0711
634	1.9071	2.1996	0.0033	0.9873	0.1265	−0.0774	0.0681	0.0674
635	1.9243	2.2193	0.0030	0.9867	0.1223	−0.0690	0.0711	0.0545
636	2.0275	2.3389	0.0028	0.9842	0.1237	−0.0625	0.0754	0.0439
637	2.0351	2.3476	0.0026	0.9839	0.1210	−0.0531	0.0774	0.0304
638	1.9904	2.2957	0.0027	0.9850	0.1196	−0.0548	0.0764	0.0328
639	2.0885	2.4097	0.0026	0.9827	0.1240	−0.0484	0.0824	0.0211
640	2.1026	2.4261	0.0027	0.9824	0.1261	−0.0495	0.0850	0.0206
641	1.8381	2.1190	0.0029	0.9883	0.1134	−0.0551	0.0734	0.0339
642	1.9507	2.2497	0.0028	0.9859	0.1186	−0.0532	0.0784	0.0288
643	1.8668	2.1522	0.0028	0.9877	0.1138	−0.0538	0.0735	0.0325
644	1.8774	2.1645	0.0027	0.9874	0.1132	−0.0494	0.0747	0.0260
645	1.5623	1.7994	0.0027	0.9934	0.0937	−0.0410	0.0612	0.0222
646	1.3953	1.6065	0.0029	0.9963	0.0867	−0.0435	0.0559	0.0277
647	1.5423	1.7762	0.0027	0.9937	0.0929	−0.0386	0.0622	0.0181
648	1.2067	1.3889	0.0033	0.9994	0.0796	−0.0467	0.0485	0.0355
649	2.0489	2.3637	0.0027	0.9836	0.1225	−0.0415	0.0841	0.0104
650	1.7922	2.0657	0.0027	0.9891	0.1078	−0.0353	0.0750	0.0067
651	1.6656	1.9190	0.0028	0.9916	0.1009	−0.0306	0.0710	0.0024
652	1.6590	1.9114	0.0028	0.9917	0.1006	−0.0348	0.0703	0.0082
653	1.6807	1.9365	0.0028	0.9913	0.1026	−0.0310	0.0726	0.0018
654	1.6264	1.8737	0.0028	0.9924	0.1000	−0.0329	0.0712	0.0048
655	1.5224	1.7534	0.0028	0.9942	0.0937	−0.0273	0.0670	−0.0003
656	1.3963	1.6076	0.0029	0.9962	0.0861	−0.0262	0.0617	0.0010
657	1.6206	1.8671	0.0030	0.9926	0.1022	−0.0227	0.0740	−0.0105
658	1.8987	2.1897	0.0032	0.9874	0.1249	−0.0154	0.0899	−0.0293
659	1.0214	1.1750	0.0031	1.0015	0.0651	−0.0231	0.0479	0.0037
660	1.2433	1.4312	0.0033	0.9989	0.0819	−0.0166	0.0609	−0.0124
661	0.8204	0.9436	0.0032	1.0037	0.0534	−0.0177	0.0401	0.0005
662	1.1789	1.3569	0.0033	0.9997	0.0777	−0.0180	0.0582	−0.0092
663	1.1100	1.2774	0.0033	1.0007	0.0737	−0.0197	0.0559	−0.0059
664	0.8790	1.0112	0.0035	1.0034	0.0601	−0.0129	0.0458	−0.0093
665	0.8257	0.9498	0.0035	1.0039	0.0564	−0.0134	0.0432	−0.0073
666	0.8585	0.9877	0.0037	1.0038	0.0604	−0.0094	0.0458	−0.0140
667	0.9278	1.0677	0.0038	1.0032	0.0660	−0.0119	0.0508	−0.0140
668	1.1531	1.3277	0.0041	1.0009	0.0852	−0.0090	0.0644	−0.0258
669	0.8124	0.9348	0.0041	1.0047	0.0600	−0.0075	0.0458	−0.0170

Output statistics

Obs	Residual	RStudent	Hat Diag H	Cov Ratio	DFFITS	DFBETAS Intercept	LEIL1	WkUNCLL1
670	0.7557	0.8696	0.0044	1.0054	0.0576	−0.0049	0.0435	−0.0193
671	0.9960	1.1467	0.0046	1.0033	0.0780	−0.0033	0.0580	−0.0299
672	0.6447	0.7417	0.0045	1.0064	0.0496	−0.0050	0.0380	−0.0161
673	0.9186	1.0576	0.0048	1.0043	0.0733	−0.0037	0.0552	−0.0280
674	0.6744	0.7761	0.0047	1.0064	0.0535	−0.0036	0.0406	−0.0196
675	0.4255	0.4894	0.0044	1.0077	0.0326	−0.0049	0.0256	−0.0088
676	0.5960	0.6859	0.0048	1.0071	0.0479	−0.0033	0.0365	−0.0176
677	0.7463	0.8591	0.0050	1.0061	0.0609	−0.0037	0.0464	−0.0232
678	0.6439	0.7411	0.0052	1.0072	0.0537	−0.0019	0.0406	−0.0220
679	0.5640	0.6492	0.0054	1.0078	0.0476	−0.0018	0.0361	−0.0196
680	0.5268	0.6064	0.0054	1.0081	0.0448	−0.0007	0.0335	−0.0194
681	0.3635	0.4183	0.0053	1.0088	0.0306	−0.0011	0.0231	−0.0126
682	0.4952	0.5700	0.0055	1.0084	0.0425	0.0003	0.0314	−0.0194
683	0.5068	0.5834	0.0056	1.0085	0.0439	0.0002	0.0326	−0.0199
684	0.4671	0.5376	0.0056	1.0087	0.0404	−0.0006	0.0304	−0.0177
685	0.3454	0.3976	0.0055	1.0091	0.0297	−0.0005	0.0223	−0.0129
686	0.1689	0.1944	0.0052	1.0093	0.0140	−0.0009	0.0108	−0.0053
687	0.4475	0.5150	0.0055	1.0086	0.0382	−0.0004	0.0286	−0.0168
688	0.4399	0.5063	0.0055	1.0086	0.0375	−0.0005	0.0281	−0.0164
689	0.2385	0.2745	0.0057	1.0097	0.0209	0.0002	0.0155	−0.0096
690	0.2554	0.2939	0.0054	1.0093	0.0216	−0.0009	0.0165	−0.0088
691	0.4244	0.4885	0.0057	1.0090	0.0371	0.0001	0.0276	−0.0169
692	0.4993	0.5749	0.0060	1.0088	0.0445	0.0008	0.0329	−0.0211
693	0.5707	0.6570	0.0059	1.0083	0.0506	0.0005	0.0376	−0.0235
694	0.7035	0.8103	0.0065	1.0079	0.0653	0.0045	0.0467	−0.0344
695	0.2491	0.2868	0.0061	1.0100	0.0225	0.0006	0.0166	−0.0109
696	0.4718	0.5433	0.0064	1.0095	0.0437	0.0025	0.0316	−0.0225
697	0.5346	0.6157	0.0064	1.0091	0.0495	0.0019	0.0363	−0.0248
698	0.5131	0.5909	0.0067	1.0095	0.0486	0.0024	0.0355	−0.0250
699	0.3387	0.3901	0.0068	1.0105	0.0324	0.0017	0.0236	−0.0168
700	0.1819	0.2094	0.0068	1.0109	0.0173	0.0005	0.0129	−0.0086
701	0.1699	0.1957	0.0070	1.0112	0.0165	0.0008	0.0121	−0.0085
702	0.2177	0.2507	0.0072	1.0113	0.0214	0.0012	0.0157	−0.0113
703	0.1799	0.2073	0.0073	1.0114	0.0177	0.0006	0.0132	−0.0091
704	0.3146	0.3625	0.0074	1.0111	0.0313	0.0013	0.0232	−0.0162
705	−0.0141	−0.0162	0.0072	1.0115	−0.0014	−0.0000	−0.0011	0.0007
706	−0.2303	−0.2652	0.0069	1.0109	−0.0221	0.0007	−0.0172	0.0099
707	0.1444	0.1664	0.0081	1.0123	0.0150	0.0007	0.0112	−0.0080
708	0.0579	0.0667	0.0080	1.0122	0.0060	0.0001	0.0045	−0.0030
709	0.0750	0.0864	0.0082	1.0124	0.0078	0.0001	0.0060	−0.0039
710	0.1726	0.1989	0.0086	1.0127	0.0185	0.0005	0.0140	−0.0096
711	0.3184	0.3671	0.0091	1.0129	0.0353	0.0017	0.0263	−0.0191
712	0.0671	0.0773	0.0091	1.0134	0.0074	0.0002	0.0056	−0.0039
713	0.0762	0.0879	0.0095	1.0138	0.0086	0.0004	0.0064	−0.0047
714	0.2184	0.2518	0.0093	1.0134	0.0244	0.0009	0.0185	−0.0131
715	0.1350	0.1557	0.0095	1.0138	0.0153	0.0005	0.0116	−0.0081
716	0.2944	0.3396	0.0102	1.0140	0.0344	0.0020	0.0257	−0.0192
717	0.1688	0.1948	0.0105	1.0147	0.0201	0.0013	0.0149	−0.0114
718	0.2211	0.2552	0.0109	1.0150	0.0267	0.0018	0.0198	−0.0153
719	0.1125	0.1298	0.0104	1.0147	0.0133	0.0007	0.0100	−0.0074

Sum of residuals	5.29421E−12
Sum of squared residuals	542.15322
Predicted residual SS (press)	546.78206

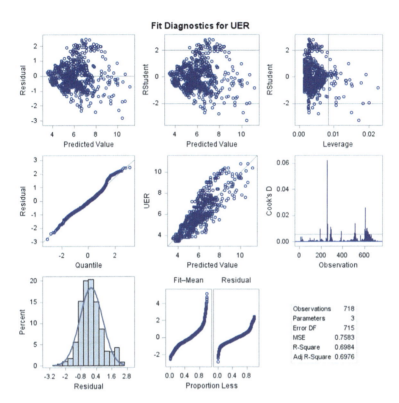

The Belsley et al. (1980) regression diagnostics clearly a need for a robust regression estimate of the UER and LEI, WkUNCL multiple regression relationship.

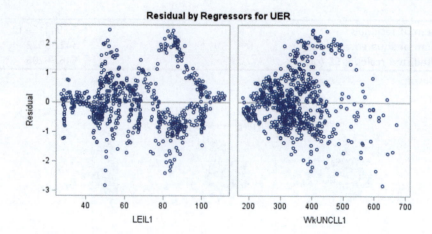

Residual by Regressors for UER

There is a need to estimate a multiple regression model for the unemployment rate as a function of LEI and WkUNCL with a 1959–2018 period.

The first-difference of the UER variable, DUE, is modeled as a function of the first-difference of the of the logarithmically-transformed LEI variable, DLLEIL1.

Estimation Eight: The DUE and DLLEI Model, 1959–2018
The REG Procedure
Model: MODEL1
Dependent Variable: DUE

Number of observations read	719
Number of observations used	717
Number of observations with missing values	2

Analysis of variance

Source	DF	Sum of squares	Mean square	F value	Pr > F
Model	1	3.32233	3.32233	121.01	<0.0001
Error	715	19.63092	0.02746		
Corrected total	716	22.95325			

Root MSE	0.16570	**R-Square**	0.1447
Dependent mean	−0.00307	**Adj R-Sq**	0.1435
Coeff Var	−5400.24848		

Parameter estimates

Variable	DF	Parameter estimate	Standard error	*t* Value	Pr > |t|
Intercept	1	0.01600	0.00643	2.49	0.0130
DLLEIL1	1	−9.68726	0.88064	−11.00	<0.0001

The estimation reports a negative and highly statistically significant coefficient on the LEI.

MZTT 1959–2018 Regressions and TF Models
The REG Procedure
Model: MODEL1
Dependent Variable: DUE

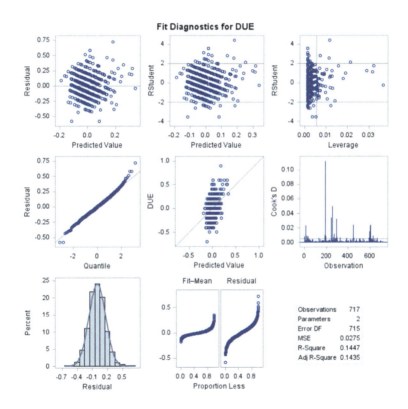

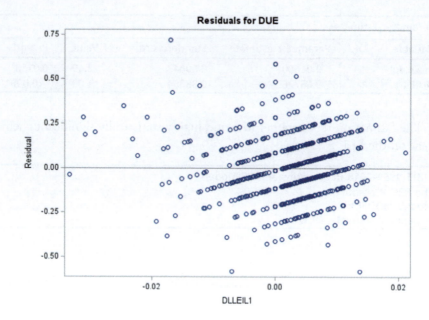

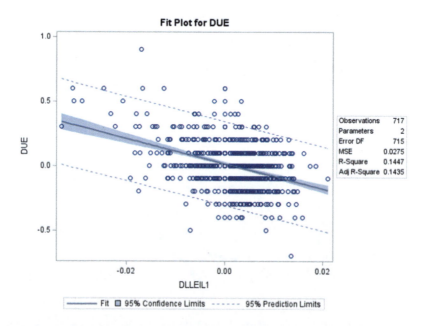

The first difference of the UER variable, DUE, is modeled as a function of the first difference of the logarithmically transformed LEI variable, DLLEIL1.

MZTT 1959–2018 Regressions and TF Models
The REG Procedure
Model: MODEL1
Dependent Variable: DUE

Number of observations read	719
Number of observations used	717
Number of observations with missing values	2

Analysis of variance

Source	DF	Sum of squares	Mean square	F value	Pr > F
Model	1	3.32233	3.32233	121.01	<0.0001
Error	715	19.63092	0.02746		
Corrected total	716	22.95325			

Root MSE	0.16570	R-Square	0.1447
Dependent mean	−0.00307	Adj R-Sq	0.1435
Coeff var	−5400.24848		

Parameter estimates

Variable	DF	Parameter estimate	Standard error	t Value	Pr > |t|
Intercept	1	0.01600	0.00643	2.49	0.0130
DLLEIL1	1	−9.68726	0.88064	−11.00	< 0.0001

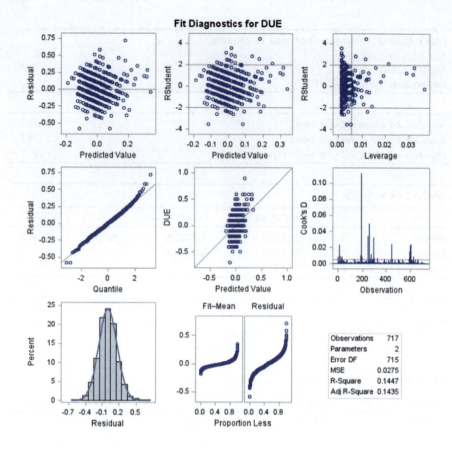

Fit Diagnostics for DUE

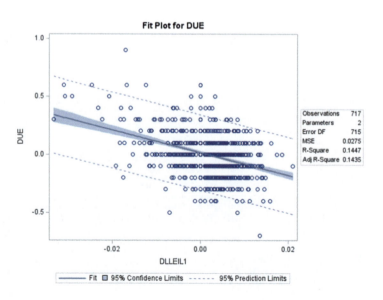

Fit Plot for DUE

In Estimation Nine, we estimate change in the unemployment rate as a function of the DLOG WkUNCL. The DLWkUNCL coefficient is positive as expected, 0.820, and statistically significant, having a t-statistic of 6.64.

Estimation Nine: the DUE DLWkUNCL Regression Model, 1959–2018
The REG Procedure
Model: MODEL1
Dependent Variable: DUE

Number of observations read	719
Number of observations used	717
Number of observations with missing values	2

Analysis of variance

Source	DF	Sum of squares	Mean square	F value	Pr > F
Model	1	1.26454	1.26454	41.69	<0.0001
Error	715	21.68871	0.03033		
Corrected total	716	22.95325			

Root MSE	0.17417	R-Square	0.0551
Dependent mean	−0.00307	Adj R-Sq	0.0538
Coeff var	−5676.23415		

Parameter Estimates

Variable	DF	Parameter Estimate	Standard Error	t Value	Pr > |t|
Intercept	1	−0.00271	0.00650	−0.42	0.6776
DLWkUNCLL1	1	0.81960	0.12694	6.46	<0.0001

The REG Procedure
Model: MODEL1
Dependent Variable: DUE

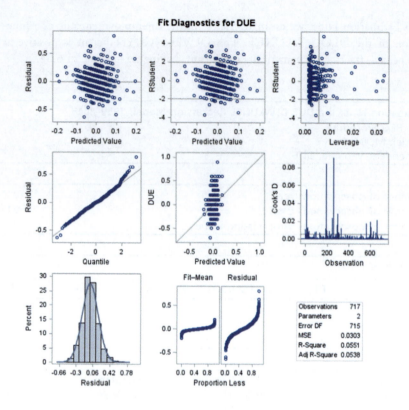

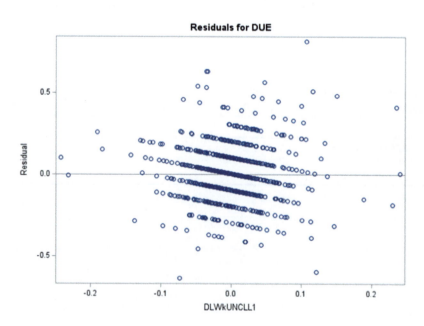

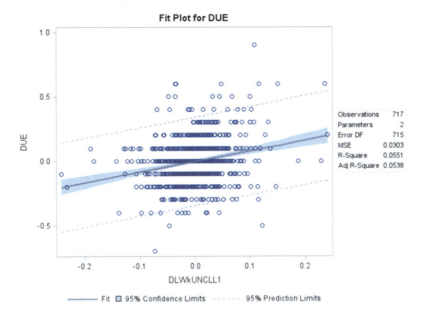

Fit Plot for DUE

Observations	717
Parameters	2
Error DF	715
MSE	0.0303
R-Square	0.0551
Adj R-Square	0.0538

—— Fit ☐ 95% Confidence Limits ----- 95% Prediction Limits

   In Estimation Ten, we estimate change in the unemployment rate, DUE, as a function of the DLOG WkUNCL and DLOG LEI. The DLWkUNCL coefficient is positive as expected, 0.082, and insignificant, having a t-statistic of 0.55. The DLLEIL1 coefficient is negative as expected, -9.344, and highly significant, having a t-statistic of -8.67. The overall regression is highly statistically significant, producing a F-statistic of 60.60.

Estimation Ten: the DUE DLWkUNCL DLLEI Regression Model, 1959–2018
The REG Procedure
Model: MODEL1
Dependent Variable: DUE

Number of observations read	719
Number of observations used	717
Number of observations with missing values	2

Analysis of variance

Source	DF	Sum of squares	Mean square	F value	Pr > F
Model	2	3.33075	1.66537	60.60	<0.0001
Error	714	19.62250	0.02748		
Corrected total	716	22.95325			

Root MSE	0.16578	R-Square	0.1451
Dependent mean	−0.00307	Adj R-Sq	0.1427
Coeff var	−5402.87061		

Parameter estimates

Variable	DF	Parameter estimate	Standard error	t Value	Pr > |t|
Intercept	1	0.01536	0.00653	2.35	0.0190
DLLEIL1	1	−9.34393	1.07763	−8.67	<0.0001
DLWkUNCLL1	1	0.08177	0.14778	0.55	0.5802

MZTT 1959–2018 Regressions and TF Models
The REG Procedure
Model: MODEL1
Dependent Variable: DUE

Output statistics

Obs	Residual	RStudent	Hat Diag H	Cov Ratio	DFFITS	DFBETAS Intercept	DLLEIL1	DLWkUNCLL1
1	–	–	–	–	–	–	–	–
2	–	–	–	–	–	–	–	–
3	−0.1767	−1.0695	0.0065	1.0059	−0.0862	−0.0144	−0.0734	−0.0251
4	−0.2729	−1.6540	0.0073	1.0001	−0.1422	−0.0413	−0.0517	0.0659
5	−0.0773	−0.4669	0.0032	1.0065	−0.0264	−0.0189	0.0078	0.0194
6	−0.0497	−0.2997	0.0028	1.0067	−0.0160	−0.0070	−0.0113	−0.0079
7	0.1137	0.6867	0.0036	1.0058	0.0412	0.0172	0.0229	0.0317
8	0.1154	0.6969	0.0022	1.0044	0.0326	0.0199	0.0154	0.0187
9	0.2437	1.4767	0.0070	1.0021	0.1244	0.0457	0.0240	0.1028
10	0.1906	1.1536	0.0066	1.0053	0.0942	0.0588	−0.0576	−0.0828
11	0.0407	0.2471	0.0127	1.0168	0.0280	0.0062	0.0087	0.0254
12	−0.5916	−3.6158	0.0093	0.9599	−0.3507	−0.1269	−0.0134	−0.2719
13	0.1017	0.6235	0.0328	1.0365	0.1147	0.0216	−0.0002	−0.0919
14	−0.4169	−2.5265	0.0016	0.9793	−0.1014	−0.0919	0.0067	−0.0259
15	0.5876	3.5790	0.0030	0.9549	0.1973	0.1616	−0.1113	−0.1400
16	−0.2573	−1.5607	0.0088	1.0028	−0.1470	−0.0451	−0.0358	−0.1269
17	−0.0801	−0.4836	0.0019	1.0052	−0.0212	−0.0179	0.0027	0.0104
18	0.2787	1.6877	0.0048	0.9970	0.1169	0.0474	0.0413	0.0968
19	0.1159	0.6995	0.0019	1.0041	0.0309	0.0205	0.0135	0.0154
20	0.0812	0.4902	0.0024	1.0056	0.0242	0.0161	0.0044	0.0150
21	−0.0893	−0.5402	0.0076	1.0106	−0.0471	−0.0105	−0.0280	−0.0423
22	0.5874	3.5779	0.0029	0.9548	0.1932	0.1605	−0.1079	−0.1342
23	−0.0203	−0.1225	0.0037	1.0079	−0.0074	−0.0037	−0.0022	−0.0057
24	0.4821	2.9262	0.0019	0.9708	0.1290	0.1010	0.0101	0.0610
25	−0.0146	−0.0879	0.0017	1.0059	−0.0037	−0.0036	0.0015	0.0014
26	0.3466	2.1000	0.0042	0.9900	0.1371	0.0425	0.1014	0.0978
27	0.009178	0.0556	0.0086	1.0129	0.0052	0.0010	0.0031	0.0047
28	0.2220	1.3465	0.0099	1.0065	0.1343	0.0420	0.0153	−0.0922
29	0.1785	1.0795	0.0046	1.0039	0.0732	0.0190	0.0608	0.0391

Output statistics

Obs	Residual	RStudent	Hat Diag H	Cov Ratio	DFFITS	DFBETAS Intercept	DLLEIL1	DLWkUNCLL1
30	−0.1168	−0.7057	0.0039	1.0060	−0.0439	−0.0202	−0.0144	0.0179
31	0.2137	1.2930	0.0053	1.0025	0.0948	0.0299	0.0485	−0.0257
32	−0.3880	−2.3520	0.0033	0.9845	−0.1362	−0.0608	−0.0727	−0.1026
33	0.2441	1.4795	0.0083	1.0033	0.1352	0.0317	0.0627	−0.0506
34	−0.2188	−1.3224	0.0025	0.9993	−0.0657	−0.0433	−0.0122	−0.0409
...								
191	0.4592	2.7972	0.0098	0.9815	0.2779	0.1314	−0.0938	0.1419
192	0.4154	2.5348	0.0154	0.9929	0.3173	0.1292	−0.1144	0.1631
193	0.7160	4.4016	0.0123	0.9381	0.4911	0.2562	−0.3029	0.1113
194	−0.1022	−0.6179	0.0051	1.0077	−0.0441	−0.0289	0.0212	−0.0131
195	0.4670	2.8366	0.0041	0.9750	0.1818	0.1409	−0.1283	−0.1334
196	0.1427	0.8620	0.0028	1.0039	0.0453	0.0406	−0.0312	−0.0128
197	0.3116	1.8880	0.0050	0.9942	0.1333	0.0400	0.0827	−0.0154
198	−0.1514	−0.9141	0.0023	1.0030	−0.0439	−0.0295	−0.0085	0.0165
199	−0.1553	−0.9380	0.0022	1.0027	−0.0437	−0.0249	−0.0260	−0.0138
200	−0.1083	−0.6554	0.0064	1.0089	−0.0528	−0.0216	−0.0041	0.0356
201	0.003875	0.0234	0.0014	1.0056	0.0009	0.0008	0.0001	0.0001
202	0.0250	0.1509	0.0015	1.0057	0.0059	0.0050	0.0012	−0.0005
203	−0.0317	−0.1914	0.0036	1.0077	−0.0115	−0.0061	−0.0018	0.0061
204	−0.0719	−0.4343	0.0029	1.0063	−0.0234	−0.0169	0.0050	0.0160
205	−0.2526	−1.5275	0.0032	0.9977	−0.0872	−0.0550	0.0042	0.0562
206	−0.0816	−0.4937	0.0077	1.0110	−0.0434	−0.0050	−0.0393	−0.0221
207	0.0221	0.1335	0.0058	1.0100	0.0102	0.0028	0.0058	−0.0022
208	0.1192	0.7198	0.0030	1.0051	0.0396	0.0185	0.0224	0.0279
209	−0.2805	−1.6964	0.0027	0.9949	−0.0890	−0.0447	−0.0493	−0.0596
210	0.2539	1.5388	0.0076	1.0019	0.1351	0.0219	0.1043	0.1120
211	0.2026	1.2233	0.0015	0.9994	0.0469	0.0414	0.0062	0.0106
212	0.0776	0.4684	0.0034	1.0067	0.0272	0.0102	0.0200	0.0070
213	−0.1786	−1.0780	0.0015	1.0008	−0.0420	−0.0345	−0.0114	−0.0040
214	0.1534	0.9281	0.0055	1.0061	0.0688	0.0162	0.0532	0.0522
215	0.0835	0.5041	0.0015	1.0047	0.0197	0.0188	0.0029	0.0025
216	0.0783	0.4729	0.0032	1.0065	0.0270	0.0129	0.0118	−0.0068
217	−0.2220	−1.3422	0.0035	1.0001	−0.0791	−0.0384	−0.0273	0.0290
218	0.0764	0.4624	0.0084	1.0118	0.0426	0.0109	0.0182	0.0386
219	−0.1704	−1.0342	0.0127	1.0125	−0.1171	−0.0121	−0.0794	−0.1086
220	−0.0571	−0.3499	0.0312	1.0361	−0.0628	−0.0161	0.0125	0.0563
221	−0.2008	−1.2136	0.0027	1.0007	−0.0626	−0.0355	−0.0244	−0.0431
222	0.2342	1.4159	0.0029	0.9986	0.0758	0.0348	0.0490	0.0472
223	−0.2422	−1.4647	0.0033	0.9985	−0.0845	−0.0496	−0.0058	0.0490
224	0.0831	0.5015	0.0016	1.0048	0.0201	0.0183	−0.0015	0.0048
225	−0.1646	−0.9937	0.0021	1.0022	−0.0461	−0.0267	−0.0267	−0.0198
226	0.002626	0.0158	0.0016	1.0058	0.0006	0.0006	−0.0001	−0.0002
227	0.001457	0.008786	0.0014	1.0056	0.0003	0.0003	−0.0000	−0.0000
228	−0.3798	−2.2997	0.0017	0.9839	−0.0945	−0.0822	0.0032	0.0339
229	0.000443	0.002670	0.0015	1.0057	0.0001	0.0001	0.0000	0.0000
...								
245	−0.3918	−2.3899	0.0156	0.9960	−0.3004	−0.1271	0.1246	−0.1393
246	0.1497	0.9151	0.0263	1.0277	0.1503	0.0542	−0.0702	−0.1453
247	−0.0699	−0.4222	0.0037	1.0071	−0.0256	−0.0172	0.0066	−0.0118
248	0.1984	1.1999	0.0048	1.0029	0.0831	0.0624	−0.0613	−0.0078
249	−0.1508	−0.9103	0.0023	1.0030	−0.0434	−0.0396	0.0228	0.0012
250	0.0347	0.2097	0.0040	1.0081	0.0133	0.0108	−0.0107	−0.0069
251	−0.2039	−1.2335	0.0049	1.0027	−0.0862	−0.0637	0.0614	0.0033

Output statistics

Obs	Residual	RStudent	Hat Diag H	Cov Ratio	DFFITS	DFBETAS Intercept	DLLEIL1	DLWkUNCLL1
252	−0.0382	−0.2312	0.0079	1.0120	−0.0207	−0.0139	0.0175	0.0046
253	0.2130	1.2880	0.0039	1.0012	0.0809	0.0645	−0.0582	−0.0098
254	−0.0304	−0.1835	0.0037	1.0078	−0.0113	−0.0089	0.0077	0.0081
255	−0.0504	−0.3042	0.0026	1.0064	−0.0154	−0.0141	0.0103	0.0048
256	0.3509	2.1483	0.0245	1.0097	0.3406	0.1803	−0.3218	−0.1228
257	0.2748	1.6937	0.0398	1.0333	0.3448	0.1153	−0.1620	0.1499
258	−0.0549	−0.3330	0.0107	1.0146	−0.0346	−0.0166	0.0141	−0.0157
259	0.2434	1.4708	0.0020	0.9972	0.0665	0.0473	0.0141	−0.0203
260	−0.0346	−0.2089	0.0053	1.0093	−0.0152	−0.0076	0.0011	0.0112
261	−0.1543	−0.9325	0.0043	1.0049	−0.0615	−0.0362	0.0109	0.0467
262	0.0820	0.4955	0.0042	1.0075	0.0324	0.0150	0.0073	−0.0166
263	0.0488	0.2960	0.0107	1.0147	0.0308	0.0139	−0.0112	−0.0281
264	−0.2945	−1.7814	0.0025	0.9934	−0.0898	−0.0740	0.0352	0.0602
265	0.2306	1.3950	0.0040	1.0001	0.0890	0.0724	−0.0720	−0.0431
266	−0.2255	−1.3669	0.0084	1.0048	−0.1260	−0.0852	0.1146	0.0574
267	−0.0920	−0.5560	0.0042	1.0071	−0.0360	−0.0280	0.0257	0.0031
268	−0.1739	−1.0503	0.0029	1.0025	−0.0565	−0.0411	0.0131	0.0389
269	0.3394	2.0544	0.0022	0.9887	0.0960	0.0546	0.0571	0.0382
270	−0.0908	−0.5485	0.0045	1.0075	−0.0369	−0.0290	0.0297	0.0106
271	−0.3922	−2.3783	0.0042	0.9848	−0.1537	−0.1192	0.1075	0.0091
272	0.1095	0.6620	0.0053	1.0077	0.0482	0.0367	−0.0412	−0.0217
273	0.1456	0.8791	0.0024	1.0034	0.0432	0.0391	−0.0247	−0.0032
274	0.1460	0.8846	0.0088	1.0098	0.0833	0.0510	−0.0601	0.0041
275	0.3239	1.9612	0.0033	0.9914	0.1125	0.0922	−0.0698	−0.0001
276	0.1434	0.8660	0.0025	1.0036	0.0436	0.0366	−0.0181	0.0083
277	0.0613	0.3703	0.0025	1.0061	0.0185	0.0136	−0.0012	0.0093
278	0.1859	1.1252	0.0065	1.0055	0.0913	0.0654	−0.0793	−0.0324
279	0.1256	0.7582	0.0016	1.0034	0.0307	0.0258	0.0029	−0.0078
280	0.2420	1.4628	0.0027	0.9979	0.0759	0.0608	−0.0270	0.0213
281	0.0803	0.4850	0.0031	1.0064	0.0271	0.0151	0.0071	0.0195
282	0.1259	0.7608	0.0043	1.0061	0.0502	0.0402	−0.0414	−0.0243
283	0.1242	0.7505	0.0035	1.0054	0.0446	0.0372	−0.0330	−0.0104
284	−0.0116	−0.0698	0.0039	1.0081	−0.0043	−0.0033	0.0026	0.0034
285	0.2167	1.3120	0.0068	1.0038	0.1083	0.0486	−0.0037	0.0766
286	0.3588	2.1801	0.0094	0.9937	0.2125	0.0254	0.1662	0.1808
287	0.4080	2.4735	0.0030	0.9817	0.1350	0.1046	−0.0552	−0.0983
288	0.0302	0.1822	0.0051	1.0092	0.0130	0.0078	−0.0045	−0.0109
289	−0.3256	−1.9803	0.0122	1.0001	−0.2204	−0.0871	0.0572	0.1960
290	0.1625	0.9849	0.0095	1.0098	0.0967	0.0086	0.0820	0.0182
291	−0.0194	−0.1170	0.0039	1.0081	−0.0073	−0.0023	−0.0058	−0.0028
292	0.0180	0.1087	0.0064	1.0106	0.0087	0.0014	0.0075	0.0031
293	−0.0436	−0.2634	0.0055	1.0095	−0.0196	−0.0045	−0.0153	−0.0146
294	0.1185	0.7164	0.0054	1.0075	0.0529	0.0145	0.0333	−0.0063
295	−0.5823	−3.5511	0.0057	0.9582	−0.2681	−0.0810	−0.1364	0.0756
296	0.1803	1.0904	0.0044	1.0036	0.0722	0.0340	0.0133	−0.0399
297	−0.2860	−1.7338	0.0070	0.9986	−0.1458	−0.0342	−0.0884	−0.1294
298	−0.3046	−1.8444	0.0043	0.9943	−0.1213	−0.0480	−0.0523	0.0393
299	−0.1910	−1.1556	0.0053	1.0039	−0.0846	−0.0185	−0.0700	−0.0243
300	−0.1432	−0.8648	0.0024	1.0034	−0.0422	−0.0258	−0.0145	0.0104
301	−0.2093	−1.2652	0.0037	1.0012	−0.0771	−0.0291	−0.0484	0.0024
302	−0.1092	−0.6598	0.0038	1.0062	−0.0408	−0.0166	−0.0207	0.0086
303	0.0712	0.4298	0.0028	1.0062	0.0227	0.0110	0.0131	−0.0001
304	−0.0997	−0.6018	0.0016	1.0043	−0.0238	−0.0201	−0.0040	−0.0077

Output statistics

Obs	Residual	RStudent	Hat Diag H	Cov Ratio	DFFITS	DFBETAS Intercept	DLLEIL1	DLWkUNCLL1
305	−0.2713	−1.6443	0.0070	0.9998	−0.1377	−0.0295	−0.0928	−0.1196
306	−0.1464	−0.8839	0.0022	1.0031	−0.0417	−0.0263	−0.0151	0.0081
321	0.0101	0.0612	0.0055	1.0097	0.0046	0.0014	0.0026	0.0039
322	0.0145	0.0878	0.0017	1.0059	0.0036	0.0027	0.0013	0.0014
323	−0.0987	−0.5954	0.0015	1.0042	−0.0230	−0.0223	0.0039	0.0056
324	0.0179	0.1081	0.0019	1.0061	0.0047	0.0040	−0.0007	−0.0023
325	−0.2681	−1.6202	0.0017	0.9949	−0.0661	−0.0522	−0.0159	0.0083
326	0.5194	3.1571	0.0028	0.9660	0.1684	0.1268	−0.0497	−0.1180
327	0.0144	0.0868	0.0017	1.0059	0.0036	0.0026	0.0014	0.0015
328	−0.1028	−0.6203	0.0020	1.0046	−0.0279	−0.0196	−0.0079	−0.0154
329	0.1292	0.7800	0.0022	1.0039	0.0370	0.0210	0.0211	0.0193
330	0.0154	0.0929	0.0015	1.0056	0.0036	0.0032	0.0003	−0.0004
331	−0.1366	−0.8251	0.0026	1.0039	−0.0417	−0.0235	−0.0174	0.0080
332	−0.1159	−0.6995	0.0015	1.0037	−0.0272	−0.0268	0.0064	0.0007
333	0.0929	0.5617	0.0066	1.0096	0.0459	0.0130	0.0226	0.0408
334	0.0165	0.0995	0.0017	1.0059	0.0041	0.0036	−0.0004	−0.0016
335	−0.0964	−0.5823	0.0034	1.0062	−0.0340	−0.0256	0.0159	0.0261
336	−0.2825	−1.7081	0.0022	0.9942	−0.0801	−0.0659	0.0180	0.0471
337	0.0446	0.2689	0.0019	1.0059	0.0119	0.0076	0.0058	0.0014
338	−0.0138	−0.0830	0.0021	1.0063	−0.0038	−0.0035	0.0019	0.0020
339	0.0591	0.3567	0.0026	1.0063	0.0183	0.0087	0.0124	0.0056
340	−0.2967	−1.7954	0.0031	0.9938	−0.1002	−0.0777	0.0456	0.0742
341	−0.001124	−0.006778	0.0014	1.0057	−0.0003	−0.0002	−0.0000	−0.0000
342	−0.0851	−0.5137	0.0015	1.0046	−0.0200	−0.0182	0.0001	0.0046
343	−0.0692	−0.4173	0.0018	1.0053	−0.0178	−0.0142	−0.0015	0.0060
344	−0.0731	−0.4411	0.0019	1.0053	−0.0193	−0.0126	−0.0096	−0.0079
345	−0.0852	−0.5142	0.0015	1.0046	−0.0199	−0.0181	−0.0001	0.0042
346	0.1454	0.8780	0.0025	1.0035	0.0440	0.0299	0.0031	−0.0221
347	−0.1848	−1.1158	0.0016	1.0006	−0.0446	−0.0403	0.0027	0.0142
348	−0.1462	−0.8828	0.0021	1.0031	−0.0407	−0.0373	0.0184	−0.0018
349	−0.0182	−0.1098	0.0021	1.0062	−0.0050	−0.0037	−0.0006	−0.0026
350	0.007937	0.0480	0.0058	1.0101	0.0037	0.0011	0.0021	0.0032
351	0.0610	0.3685	0.0037	1.0073	0.0223	0.0125	0.0012	−0.0136
352	−0.2699	−1.6321	0.0023	0.9953	−0.0784	−0.0598	0.0074	0.0440
353	0.1967	1.1882	0.0018	1.0000	0.0501	0.0388	0.0109	0.0231
354	−0.1736	−1.0479	0.0017	1.0013	−0.0436	−0.0311	−0.0191	−0.0131
355	0.0426	0.2569	0.0019	1.0058	0.0111	0.0079	0.0038	−0.0013
356	0.1798	1.0864	0.0036	1.0029	0.0657	0.0326	0.0197	0.0503
357	−0.1985	−1.1995	0.0024	1.0006	−0.0591	−0.0501	0.0245	0.0384
358	0.0164	0.0989	0.0027	1.0069	0.0052	0.0040	−0.0016	−0.0036
359	−0.0716	−0.4322	0.0019	1.0054	−0.0190	−0.0153	0.0002	0.0083
360	−0.001935	−0.0117	0.0014	1.0056	−0.0004	−0.0004	−0.0000	−0.0001
361	0.1122	0.6769	0.0014	1.0037	0.0255	0.0232	0.0023	−0.0007
362	−0.2008	−1.2124	0.0015	0.9995	−0.0463	−0.0454	0.0077	0.0091
363	−0.2217	−1.3414	0.0053	1.0020	−0.0980	−0.0367	−0.0363	−0.0829
364	0.1414	0.8539	0.0025	1.0037	0.0431	0.0380	−0.0238	−0.0003
365	0.001924	0.0116	0.0028	1.0070	0.0006	0.0005	−0.0003	−0.0004
366	0.0535	0.3230	0.0027	1.0065	0.0170	0.0122	−0.0020	0.0084
367	−0.1329	−0.8026	0.0024	1.0039	−0.0395	−0.0287	0.0000	−0.0210
368	−0.0567	−0.3424	0.0030	1.0067	−0.0187	−0.0165	0.0136	0.0072
369	0.1145	0.6908	0.0017	1.0039	0.0282	0.0253	−0.0030	−0.0106
370	−0.0167	−0.1006	0.0016	1.0057	−0.0040	−0.0037	0.0004	−0.0007
371	0.0506	0.3058	0.0043	1.0082	0.0201	0.0104	0.0017	0.0144

Obs	Residual	RStudent	Hat Diag H	Cov Ratio	DFFITS	DFBETAS Intercept	DLLEIL1	DLWkUNCLL1
372	0.004238	0.0256	0.0053	1.0095	0.0019	0.0012	−0.0010	−0.0016
373	−0.0197	−0.1190	0.0031	1.0073	−0.0067	−0.0037	−0.0017	−0.0048
374	−0.1300	−0.7849	0.0018	1.0034	−0.0330	−0.0324	0.0143	0.0042
375	−0.1278	−0.7718	0.0026	1.0043	−0.0395	−0.0352	0.0248	0.0228
376	0.1870	1.1297	0.0026	1.0014	0.0574	0.0497	−0.0310	−0.0370
377	−0.0475	−0.2867	0.0028	1.0067	−0.0152	−0.0108	0.0018	−0.0076
378	−0.2147	−1.2970	0.0017	0.9988	−0.0535	−0.0527	0.0215	0.0181
379	0.2842	1.7177	0.0015	0.9933	0.0667	0.0662	−0.0165	−0.0031
380	0.1412	0.8528	0.0027	1.0038	0.0440	0.0394	−0.0283	−0.0075
381	0.0526	0.3186	0.0083	1.0121	0.0291	0.0186	−0.0224	−0.0013
382	−0.1304	−0.7897	0.0088	1.0105	−0.0744	−0.0498	0.0678	0.0329
383	0.1486	0.9003	0.0086	1.0094	0.0837	0.0510	−0.0583	0.0070
384	−0.0820	−0.4974	0.0122	1.0155	−0.0552	−0.0329	0.0469	0.0087
385	−0.0208	−0.1256	0.0080	1.0122	−0.0113	−0.0077	0.0102	0.0052
386	0.0789	0.4780	0.0087	1.0120	0.0447	0.0301	−0.0410	−0.0231
387	0.1498	0.9048	0.0034	1.0042	0.0528	0.0330	−0.0019	0.0320
388	−0.1638	−0.9892	0.0027	1.0028	−0.0518	−0.0441	0.0277	−0.0032
389	0.2969	1.7982	0.0047	0.9953	0.1230	0.0485	0.0455	−0.0493
390	0.0489	0.2954	0.0030	1.0068	0.0161	0.0103	0.0002	−0.0095
391	−0.0977	−0.5898	0.0023	1.0051	−0.0285	−0.0244	0.0113	0.0180
392	0.1761	1.0640	0.0031	1.0026	0.0597	0.0244	0.0413	0.0104
393	−0.002628	−0.0159	0.0019	1.0062	−0.0007	−0.0005	−0.0002	−0.0004
394	0.1595	0.9633	0.0025	1.0028	0.0483	0.0242	0.0310	0.0107
395	−0.0310	−0.1873	0.0018	1.0059	−0.0079	−0.0077	0.0034	0.0009
396	0.2815	1.7024	0.0022	0.9943	0.0804	0.0569	0.0118	0.0458
...								
455	0.2090	1.2619	0.0015	0.9990	0.0484	0.0455	−0.0029	−0.0102
456	0.0552	0.3330	0.0025	1.0063	0.0167	0.0082	0.0111	0.0054
457	−0.1193	−0.7205	0.0028	1.0048	−0.0383	−0.0229	−0.0089	−0.0261
458	−0.0532	−0.3212	0.0028	1.0066	−0.0170	−0.0112	−0.0004	0.0096
459	0.1144	0.6913	0.0051	1.0074	0.0496	0.0141	0.0321	−0.0041
460	−0.0708	−0.4274	0.0018	1.0053	−0.0183	−0.0123	−0.0088	−0.0062
461	−0.2073	−1.2526	0.0024	1.0001	−0.0620	−0.0386	−0.0190	−0.0403
462	0.1438	0.8680	0.0022	1.0032	0.0405	0.0286	0.0062	−0.0156
463	−0.0497	−0.3000	0.0036	1.0074	−0.0179	−0.0064	−0.0133	−0.0112
464	−0.002087	−0.0126	0.0041	1.0084	−0.0008	−0.0003	−0.0006	−0.0001
465	0.1023	0.6179	0.0044	1.0070	0.0409	0.0156	0.0206	0.0337
466	−0.1456	−0.8792	0.0029	1.0039	−0.0477	−0.0294	−0.0047	0.0252
467	−0.0814	−0.4913	0.0015	1.0047	−0.0191	−0.0170	−0.0012	0.0036
468	0.1050	0.6335	0.0016	1.0041	0.0254	0.0205	0.0061	0.0090
469	−0.0821	−0.4956	0.0015	1.0046	−0.0190	−0.0164	−0.0034	−0.0002
470	−0.0180	−0.1087	0.0020	1.0062	−0.0048	−0.0037	−0.0004	−0.0024
471	0.1820	1.0999	0.0037	1.0029	0.0674	0.0222	0.0524	0.0216
472	−0.4040	−2.4475	0.0016	0.9809	−0.0989	−0.0960	0.0299	0.0358
473	0.0759	0.4580	0.0024	1.0058	0.0226	0.0205	−0.0134	−0.0127
474	0.1369	0.8265	0.0024	1.0038	0.0409	0.0212	0.0256	0.0211
475	−0.0852	−0.5148	0.0049	1.0080	−0.0360	−0.0214	0.0090	−0.0186
476	0.0198	0.1197	0.0025	1.0066	0.0059	0.0047	−0.0014	−0.0038
477	0.0988	0.5968	0.0035	1.0062	0.0352	0.0267	−0.0179	−0.0271
478	−0.1666	−1.0077	0.0056	1.0056	−0.0757	−0.0557	0.0631	0.0510
479	−0.1717	−1.0371	0.0031	1.0028	−0.0576	−0.0471	0.0318	−0.0049
480	0.0165	0.0997	0.0017	1.0059	0.0041	0.0031	0.0015	0.0015
481	−0.0942	−0.5684	0.0014	1.0043	−0.0215	−0.0193	−0.0026	−0.0030

Output statistics

Output statistics

Obs	Residual	RStudent	Hat Diag H	Cov Ratio	DFFITS	DFBETAS Intercept	DLLEIL1	DLWkUNCLL1
482	0.0724	0.4368	0.0018	1.0052	0.0184	0.0166	−0.0032	0.0045
483	−0.1559	−0.9426	0.0046	1.0051	−0.0641	−0.0373	0.0136	0.0502
484	0.0842	0.5082	0.0015	1.0046	0.0198	0.0196	−0.0051	−0.0013
485	−0.1056	−0.6373	0.0014	1.0039	−0.0241	−0.0230	0.0013	−0.0019
486	0.1384	0.8352	0.0019	1.0032	0.0362	0.0238	0.0181	0.0078
487	0.0200	0.1207	0.0026	1.0067	0.0061	0.0047	−0.0016	−0.0040
488	−0.0866	−0.5230	0.0029	1.0060	−0.0284	−0.0139	−0.0149	−0.0202
489	0.008072	0.0487	0.0023	1.0065	0.0023	0.0020	−0.0008	−0.0015
490	−0.1164	−0.7026	0.0015	1.0037	−0.0275	−0.0263	0.0041	−0.0032
491	0.0188	0.1134	0.0019	1.0060	0.0049	0.0042	−0.0006	−0.0023
492	−0.0619	−0.3734	0.0018	1.0054	−0.0157	−0.0112	−0.0062	−0.0005
493	0.0688	0.4155	0.0030	1.0065	0.0227	0.0095	0.0162	0.0063
494	0.1329	0.8028	0.0041	1.0056	0.0513	0.0176	0.0347	0.0388
495	−0.1783	−1.0778	0.0038	1.0031	−0.0664	−0.0546	0.0511	0.0190
496	−0.1056	−0.6382	0.0055	1.0080	−0.0474	−0.0193	−0.0095	0.0271
497	0.1940	1.1711	0.0015	0.9999	0.0450	0.0413	0.0007	0.0090
498	−0.1209	−0.7312	0.0065	1.0085	−0.0591	−0.0418	0.0492	0.0136
499	0.0135	0.0816	0.0022	1.0064	0.0038	0.0024	0.0017	0.0022
500	0.0408	0.2462	0.0026	1.0066	0.0125	0.0107	−0.0059	0.0016
501	−0.2805	−1.6970	0.0035	0.9956	−0.1006	−0.0790	0.0577	−0.0098
502	0.0185	0.1116	0.0022	1.0064	0.0052	0.0043	−0.0011	−0.0031
503	−0.1090	−0.6599	0.0072	1.0096	−0.0561	−0.0395	0.0504	0.0276
504	−0.0981	−0.5941	0.0079	1.0107	−0.0530	−0.0230	0.0045	−0.0365
505	0.1435	0.8698	0.0103	1.0114	0.0887	0.0564	−0.0794	−0.0272
506	−0.0668	−0.4036	0.0054	1.0090	−0.0298	−0.0222	0.0248	0.0196
507	−0.0313	−0.1896	0.0076	1.0118	−0.0166	−0.0093	0.0077	−0.0062
508	−0.0605	−0.3669	0.0106	1.0144	−0.0380	−0.0239	0.0338	0.0109
509	−0.2172	−1.3153	0.0066	1.0036	−0.1075	−0.0765	0.0929	0.0351
510	0.2174	1.3134	0.0017	0.9987	0.0545	0.0399	0.0212	0.0206
511	0.0410	0.2478	0.0042	1.0082	0.0160	0.0128	−0.0128	−0.0095
512	0.2616	1.5811	0.0020	0.9957	0.0710	0.0683	−0.0382	−0.0142
513	0.0622	0.3753	0.0022	1.0058	0.0175	0.0167	−0.0105	−0.0059
514	0.1059	0.6426	0.0133	1.0160	0.0746	0.0390	−0.0493	0.0129
515	0.1088	0.6578	0.0053	1.0078	0.0482	0.0276	−0.0123	0.0253
516	0.2463	1.4896	0.0031	0.9980	0.0836	0.0535	−0.0037	−0.0529
517	0.0622	0.3766	0.0088	1.0126	0.0355	0.0160	−0.0090	−0.0308
518	−0.0164	−0.0992	0.0015	1.0057	−0.0039	−0.0037	0.0006	−0.0005
519	0.0782	0.4719	0.0031	1.0064	0.0263	0.0117	0.0153	−0.0010
520	0.2245	1.3590	0.0059	1.0024	0.1046	0.0270	0.0681	0.0891
521	−0.0496	−0.2997	0.0035	1.0074	−0.0178	−0.0065	−0.0132	−0.0110
522	0.0788	0.4763	0.0039	1.0072	0.0300	0.0144	0.0072	−0.0146
523	0.009590	0.0579	0.0021	1.0063	0.0026	0.0023	−0.0007	−0.0015
524	−0.1586	−0.9587	0.0036	1.0040	−0.0579	−0.0484	0.0452	0.0302
525	−0.006031	−0.0364	0.0017	1.0060	−0.0015	−0.0012	−0.0003	−0.0007
526	−0.0510	−0.3075	0.0024	1.0062	−0.0150	−0.0127	0.0053	−0.0035
527	0.1738	1.0495	0.0019	1.0015	0.0461	0.0448	−0.0239	−0.0164
528	0.1435	0.8668	0.0025	1.0036	0.0435	0.0299	0.0018	−0.0226
529	−0.2205	−1.3335	0.0039	1.0007	−0.0837	−0.0394	−0.0264	−0.0657
530	0.1100	0.6638	0.0023	1.0046	0.0317	0.0266	−0.0101	−0.0196
531	−0.0411	−0.2482	0.0024	1.0063	−0.0121	−0.0094	0.0018	−0.0051
532	0.0718	0.4332	0.0017	1.0051	0.0180	0.0168	−0.0044	0.0028
533	0.0494	0.2979	0.0023	1.0062	0.0143	0.0124	−0.0057	0.0024
534	0.2867	1.7348	0.0035	0.9951	0.1028	0.0403	0.0652	−0.0000

Obs	Residual	RStudent	Hat Diag H	Cov Ratio	DFFITS	DFBETAS Intercept	DLLEIL1	DLWkUNCLL1

Output statistics

Obs	Residual	RStudent	Hat Diag H	Cov Ratio	DFFITS	Intercept	DLLEIL1	DLWkUNCLL1
535	−0.0385	−0.2326	0.0029	1.0070	−0.0127	−0.0053	−0.0092	−0.0050
536	−0.0790	−0.4771	0.0026	1.0058	−0.0243	−0.0187	0.0060	0.0160
537	0.0499	0.3009	0.0022	1.0060	0.0141	0.0080	0.0083	0.0032
538	−0.007934	−0.0479	0.0046	1.0088	−0.0032	−0.0008	−0.0027	−0.0012
539	−0.1160	−0.7005	0.0035	1.0056	−0.0414	−0.0183	−0.0197	0.0094
540	−0.007808	−0.0472	0.0038	1.0080	−0.0029	−0.0010	−0.0020	−0.0002
541	0.0688	0.4155	0.0030	1.0065	0.0227	0.0095	0.0162	0.0063
542	−0.0235	−0.1418	0.0045	1.0087	−0.0096	−0.0025	−0.0079	−0.0052
543	0.2660	1.6092	0.0033	0.9966	0.0921	0.0348	0.0697	0.0392
544	−0.0802	−0.4851	0.0055	1.0088	−0.0360	−0.0091	−0.0250	0.0008
545	0.003401	0.0205	0.0015	1.0057	0.0008	0.0007	0.0001	0.0002
546	0.0749	0.4525	0.0031	1.0065	0.0254	0.0103	0.0179	0.0054
547	−0.0768	−0.4632	0.0018	1.0051	−0.0196	−0.0137	−0.0087	−0.0073
548	−0.0679	−0.4100	0.0023	1.0058	−0.0198	−0.0108	−0.0117	−0.0103
549	0.0255	0.1535	0.0016	1.0057	0.0062	0.0052	0.0007	−0.0013
550	0.1530	0.9243	0.0025	1.0031	0.0465	0.0228	0.0311	0.0169
551	−0.0850	−0.5128	0.0015	1.0047	−0.0202	−0.0183	0.0006	0.0055
552	0.0531	0.3206	0.0022	1.0060	0.0151	0.0086	0.0085	0.0022
553	−0.0293	−0.1771	0.0036	1.0077	−0.0106	−0.0036	−0.0083	−0.0047
554	0.1294	0.7819	0.0035	1.0052	0.0467	0.0183	0.0302	0.0339
555	−0.1615	−0.9769	0.0061	1.0063	−0.0764	−0.0420	0.0246	0.0652
556	−0.0580	−0.3504	0.0037	1.0074	−0.0213	−0.0132	0.0019	−0.0125
557	−0.0656	−0.3959	0.0021	1.0057	−0.0182	−0.0138	−0.0004	0.0085
558	−0.1264	−0.7629	0.0017	1.0035	−0.0315	−0.0292	0.0064	−0.0059
559	0.0511	0.3084	0.0022	1.0060	0.0144	0.0083	0.0081	0.0024
560	−0.1063	−0.6414	0.0014	1.0039	−0.0242	−0.0236	0.0028	0.0001
561	0.1428	0.8622	0.0019	1.0030	0.0377	0.0268	0.0113	−0.0066
562	−0.0995	−0.6104	0.0331	1.0369	−0.1129	−0.0110	−0.0371	−0.1065
563	0.0337	0.2048	0.0158	1.0201	0.0259	0.0111	−0.0124	−0.0246
564	−0.0532	−0.3219	0.0056	1.0094	−0.0241	−0.0131	0.0058	0.0197
565	−0.2151	−1.2992	0.0016	0.9987	−0.0520	−0.0519	0.0185	0.0128
566	0.1637	0.9891	0.0036	1.0037	0.0592	0.0328	0.0059	−0.0341
567	−0.1150	−0.6940	0.0016	1.0038	−0.0280	−0.0279	0.0103	0.0076
568	0.0104	0.0630	0.0017	1.0059	0.0026	0.0019	0.0009	0.0011
569	−0.1725	−1.0425	0.0032	1.0028	−0.0590	−0.0498	0.0397	0.0070
570	−0.0771	−0.4663	0.0050	1.0084	−0.0332	−0.0181	0.0043	−0.0203
571	0.0817	0.4943	0.0081	1.0113	0.0445	0.0267	−0.0293	−0.0397
572	−0.0652	−0.3935	0.0028	1.0064	−0.0210	−0.0173	0.0101	−0.0032
573	−0.2325	−1.4054	0.0028	0.9987	−0.0748	−0.0655	0.0497	0.0442
574	−0.1161	−0.7007	0.0015	1.0037	−0.0272	−0.0266	0.0055	−0.0009
575	0.0662	0.3994	0.0021	1.0057	0.0184	0.0176	−0.0108	−0.0068
576	−0.1372	−0.8285	0.0022	1.0036	−0.0393	−0.0310	0.0047	−0.0167
577	0.2232	1.3484	0.0015	0.9981	0.0530	0.0452	0.0077	−0.0073
578	−0.1513	−0.9143	0.0038	1.0045	−0.0566	−0.0462	0.0436	0.0344
579	−0.1266	−0.7642	0.0017	1.0035	−0.0319	−0.0289	0.0054	−0.0077
580	0.1174	0.7093	0.0037	1.0058	0.0430	0.0301	−0.0162	−0.0337
581	−0.1563	−0.9439	0.0027	1.0031	−0.0489	−0.0386	0.0154	−0.0158
582	0.1973	1.1925	0.0030	1.0012	0.0655	0.0523	−0.0324	−0.0476
583	0.0638	0.3851	0.0019	1.0055	0.0169	0.0152	−0.0047	0.0034
584	−0.1241	−0.7490	0.0019	1.0038	−0.0331	−0.0320	0.0172	0.0131
585	0.0268	0.1621	0.0033	1.0074	0.0093	0.0079	−0.0066	−0.0017
586	−0.0800	−0.4839	0.0064	1.0097	−0.0389	−0.0279	0.0337	0.0253
587	−0.0762	−0.4604	0.0034	1.0067	−0.0268	−0.0206	0.0129	−0.0057

Output statistics

Obs	Residual	RStudent	Hat Diag H	Cov Ratio	DFFITS	DFBETAS Intercept	DLLEIL1	DLWkUNCLL1
588	0.1948	1.1785	0.0051	1.0035	0.0842	0.0627	−0.0647	−0.0119
589	−0.1147	−0.6936	0.0062	1.0085	−0.0549	−0.0396	0.0465	0.0157
590	−0.2205	−1.3391	0.0122	1.0090	−0.1486	−0.0912	0.1372	0.1013
591	0.0740	0.4477	0.0080	1.0114	0.0401	0.0274	−0.0360	−0.0162
592	−0.2719	−1.6512	0.0108	1.0037	−0.1729	−0.1046	0.1417	0.0184
593	0.3352	2.0309	0.0044	0.9914	0.1351	0.1070	−0.1102	−0.0782
594	0.1018	0.6156	0.0058	1.0084	0.0469	0.0349	−0.0407	−0.0206
595	0.1295	0.7822	0.0031	1.0048	0.0439	0.0342	−0.0195	0.0103
596	0.0684	0.4162	0.0184	1.0223	0.0570	0.0304	−0.0482	−0.0064
597	−0.1346	−0.8148	0.0081	1.0096	−0.0735	−0.0497	0.0645	0.0226
598	0.1616	0.9844	0.0199	1.0205	0.1403	0.0749	−0.1232	−0.0250
599	−0.0298	−0.1839	0.0481	1.0548	−0.0414	−0.0196	0.0406	0.0201
600	0.1887	1.1575	0.0328	1.0325	0.2132	0.1030	−0.1900	−0.0390
601	0.2063	1.2657	0.0321	1.0305	0.2304	0.1150	−0.2163	−0.0731
602	0.2867	1.7476	0.0181	1.0097	0.2373	0.1333	−0.2206	−0.0801
603	0.2288	1.3885	0.0106	1.0068	0.1435	0.0815	−0.0982	0.0177
604	0.1192	0.7243	0.0148	1.0170	0.0887	0.0526	−0.0835	−0.0378
605	0.4155	2.5218	0.0048	0.9825	0.1753	0.1129	−0.0768	−0.1473
606	0.1230	0.7425	0.0016	1.0035	0.0295	0.0231	0.0100	0.0055
607	0.0625	0.3775	0.0025	1.0061	0.0187	0.0102	0.0099	−0.0003
608	0.1644	0.9936	0.0034	1.0035	0.0584	0.0324	0.0077	−0.0319
609	0.2839	1.7189	0.0044	0.9962	0.1141	0.0309	0.0942	0.0514
610	0.2613	1.5798	0.0025	0.9962	0.0785	0.0451	0.0330	−0.0135
611	−0.0641	−0.3865	0.0020	1.0056	−0.0172	−0.0131	−0.0016	0.0067
612	0.0856	0.5172	0.0038	1.0069	0.0318	0.0141	0.0128	−0.0104
613	−0.0169	−0.1018	0.0033	1.0075	−0.0059	−0.0025	−0.0034	0.0004
614	0.0417	0.2516	0.0033	1.0072	0.0144	0.0057	0.0101	0.0092
615	0.0847	0.5108	0.0016	1.0047	0.0202	0.0202	−0.0065	−0.0037
616	0.1508	0.9140	0.0091	1.0098	0.0874	0.0076	0.0774	0.0268
617	−0.2672	−1.6149	0.0017	0.9949	−0.0661	−0.0515	−0.0174	0.0067
618	−0.2041	−1.2325	0.0014	0.9992	−0.0465	−0.0456	0.0063	0.0037
619	−0.003774	−0.0228	0.0015	1.0057	−0.0009	−0.0009	0.0002	0.0001
620	0.0956	0.5770	0.0014	1.0042	0.0217	0.0211	−0.0020	−0.0001
621	0.0167	0.1008	0.0026	1.0068	0.0052	0.0027	0.0027	0.0034
622	−0.0543	−0.3279	0.0027	1.0064	−0.0170	−0.0113	−0.0006	0.0093
623	0.3967	2.4031	0.0016	0.9817	0.0950	0.0929	−0.0249	−0.0293
624	−0.4321	−2.6208	0.0029	0.9786	−0.1414	−0.0768	−0.0482	0.0457
625	−0.1125	−0.6799	0.0038	1.0060	−0.0418	−0.0141	−0.0311	−0.0086
626	−0.1068	−0.6446	0.0021	1.0046	−0.0296	−0.0205	−0.0077	−0.0170
627	0.0566	0.3422	0.0039	1.0077	0.0215	0.0122	−0.0007	−0.0145
628	0.1837	1.1110	0.0045	1.0036	0.0749	0.0195	0.0623	0.0357
629	−0.1205	−0.7279	0.0039	1.0059	−0.0455	−0.0215	−0.0143	−0.0356
630	0.1397	0.8435	0.0018	1.0031	0.0361	0.0246	0.0164	0.0041
631	−0.1255	−0.7577	0.0022	1.0040	−0.0357	−0.0333	0.0206	0.0176
632	0.0400	0.2411	0.0018	1.0058	0.0103	0.0071	0.0044	0.0006
633	−0.0804	−0.4860	0.0050	1.0083	−0.0346	−0.0266	0.0294	0.0181
634	−0.2605	−1.5752	0.0028	0.9966	−0.0831	−0.0738	0.0559	0.0177
635	−0.1472	−0.8885	0.0022	1.0031	−0.0421	-0.0270	−0.0136	0.0101
636	−0.1014	−0.6120	0.0025	1.0051	−0.0305	−0.0259	0.0136	0.0200
637	−0.1695	−1.0234	0.0020	1.0018	−0.0463	−0.0363	0.0009	0.0218
638	0.005458	0.0329	0.0015	1.0057	0.0013	0.0011	0.0002	0.0003
639	−0.0583	−0.3521	0.0021	1.0058	−0.0160	−0.0116	−0.0026	0.0056
640	0.0380	0.2295	0.0020	1.0060	0.0102	0.0064	0.0054	0.0030

Output statistics

Obs	Residual	RStudent	Hat Diag H	Cov Ratio	DFFITS	DFBETAS Intercept	DLLEIL1	DLWkUNCLL1
641	−0.0407	−0.2454	0.0026	1.0066	−0.0125	−0.0090	0.0009	−0.0064
642	−0.003482	−0.0210	0.0018	1.0061	−0.0009	−0.0008	0.0003	0.0004
643	−0.0595	−0.3592	0.0027	1.0064	−0.0189	−0.0168	0.0127	0.0042
644	−0.0923	−0.5570	0.0016	1.0045	−0.0225	−0.0210	0.0041	0.0086
645	−0.3473	−2.1027	0.0025	0.9883	−0.1058	−0.0971	0.0707	0.0375
646	0.0354	0.2140	0.0035	1.0075	0.0127	0.0049	0.0086	0.0088
647	−0.1015	−0.6132	0.0031	1.0058	−0.0344	−0.0270	0.0170	0.0255
648	0.1771	1.0723	0.0071	1.0066	0.0909	0.0268	0.0373	0.0808
649	0.1270	0.7709	0.0134	1.0154	0.0900	0.0409	−0.0441	−0.0850
650	−0.2727	−1.6483	0.0016	0.9944	−0.0657	−0.0515	−0.0213	−0.0054
651	−0.1722	−1.0399	0.0016	1.0012	−0.0414	−0.0334	−0.0104	0.0019
652	0.0727	0.4389	0.0017	1.0051	0.0181	0.0169	−0.0042	0.0029
653	−0.0715	−0.4314	0.0017	1.0051	−0.0177	−0.0145	−0.0023	0.0043
654	0.0155	0.0936	0.0017	1.0059	0.0039	0.0029	0.0014	0.0014
655	−0.2036	−1.2297	0.0018	0.9996	−0.0519	−0.0492	0.0181	0.0234
656	−0.1055	−0.6366	0.0014	1.0039	−0.0240	−0.0231	0.0018	−0.0011
657	0.0610	0.3682	0.0026	1.0063	0.0188	0.0110	0.0060	−0.0058
658	0.0714	0.4312	0.0033	1.0067	0.0247	0.0129	0.0070	−0.0102
659	−0.3350	−2.0356	0.0100	0.9969	−0.2044	−0.0482	−0.0802	−0.1867
660	−0.1060	−0.6407	0.0051	1.0076	−0.0460	−0.0188	−0.0112	0.0242
661	−0.1206	−0.7286	0.0040	1.0060	−0.0461	−0.0214	−0.0147	−0.0364
662	0.1093	0.6602	0.0033	1.0057	0.0380	0.0283	−0.0160	−0.0289
663	0.0339	0.2045	0.0024	1.0065	0.0101	0.0053	0.0062	0.0054
664	−0.3221	−1.9497	0.0031	0.9914	−0.1084	−0.0476	−0.0663	−0.0012
665	−0.005992	−0.0361	0.0015	1.0057	−0.0014	−0.0013	−0.0000	−0.0003
666	−0.1620	−0.9783	0.0026	1.0028	−0.0496	−0.0351	0.0023	0.0287
667	0.1531	0.9250	0.0030	1.0036	0.0508	0.0211	0.0367	0.0258
668	0.0380	0.2296	0.0026	1.0066	0.0117	0.0083	−0.0006	−0.0068
669	−0.2872	−1.7362	0.0016	0.9932	−0.0696	−0.0547	−0.0217	−0.0229
670	−0.1540	−0.9298	0.0020	1.0026	−0.0420	−0.0290	−0.0118	0.0098
671	0.1162	0.7013	0.0020	1.0041	0.0312	0.0266	−0.0060	−0.0165
672	−0.1800	−1.0874	0.0031	1.0024	−0.0609	−0.0275	−0.0352	−0.0437
673	0.1364	0.8234	0.0022	1.0035	0.0384	0.0286	0.0011	−0.0181
674	−0.2069	−1.2493	0.0015	0.9991	−0.0478	−0.0446	0.0008	−0.0077
675	−0.0199	−0.1204	0.0033	1.0075	−0.0070	−0.0037	−0.0020	−0.0052
676	−0.0628	−0.3793	0.0034	1.0070	−0.0221	−0.0145	0.0038	0.0157
677	0.1332	0.8037	0.0017	1.0032	0.0330	0.0245	0.0122	0.0021
678	−0.1752	−1.0580	0.0017	1.0012	−0.0431	−0.0364	−0.0028	0.0121
679	−0.0683	−0.4124	0.0017	1.0052	−0.0172	−0.0122	−0.0075	−0.0035
680	−0.1328	−0.8017	0.0026	1.0042	−0.0413	−0.0370	0.0270	0.0228
681	−0.1166	−0.7038	0.0015	1.0037	−0.0277	−0.0260	0.0033	−0.0048
682	−0.0220	−0.1331	0.0032	1.0074	−0.0076	−0.0062	0.0048	0.0053
683	0.0222	0.1337	0.0016	1.0057	0.0053	0.0042	0.0017	0.0008
684	0.0211	0.1275	0.0018	1.0060	0.0054	0.0038	0.0024	0.0022
685	−0.1344	−0.8116	0.0019	1.0034	−0.0358	−0.0348	0.0188	0.0083
686	−0.0468	−0.2825	0.0025	1.0063	−0.0140	−0.0110	0.0030	−0.0054
687	0.0788	0.4762	0.0041	1.0074	0.0304	0.0230	−0.0197	−0.0235
688	−0.0155	−0.0936	0.0015	1.0057	−0.0037	−0.0037	0.0011	0.0005
689	−0.2667	−1.6122	0.0017	0.9950	−0.0672	−0.0528	−0.0129	0.0144
690	0.1623	0.9803	0.0025	1.0026	0.0488	0.0359	−0.0027	0.0247
691	0.0160	0.0965	0.0025	1.0066	0.0048	0.0038	−0.0013	−0.0031
692	0.0235	0.1416	0.0016	1.0057	0.0056	0.0048	0.0006	−0.0011
693	0.0840	0.5071	0.0015	1.0046	0.0197	0.0194	−0.0045	−0.0002

Output statistics

Obs	Residual	RStudent	Hat Diag H	Cov Ratio	DFFITS	DFBETAS Intercept	DLLEIL1	DLWkUNCLL1
694	−0.0918	−0.5544	0.0042	1.0072	−0.0361	−0.0249	0.0169	0.0295
695	−0.3094	−1.8718	0.0025	0.9921	−0.0942	−0.0579	−0.0280	−0.0623
696	0.1059	0.6393	0.0022	1.0047	0.0297	0.0258	−0.0101	−0.0177
697	0.1304	0.7875	0.0021	1.0037	0.0363	0.0215	0.0202	0.0171
698	−0.0587	−0.3540	0.0018	1.0055	−0.0152	−0.0107	−0.0056	0.0007
699	−0.1878	−1.1337	0.0014	1.0002	−0.0428	−0.0390	−0.0036	0.0018
700	−0.0709	−0.4281	0.0023	1.0058	−0.0206	−0.0114	−0.0119	−0.0112
701	−0.0957	−0.5777	0.0018	1.0046	−0.0246	−0.0226	0.0070	0.0118
702	0.0221	0.1330	0.0015	1.0057	0.0052	0.0044	0.0009	−0.0004
703	0.0379	0.2285	0.0025	1.0065	0.0113	0.0058	0.0071	0.0058
704	0.1124	0.6785	0.0014	1.0037	0.0257	0.0236	0.0013	−0.0026
705	−0.1828	−1.1044	0.0030	1.0021	−0.0607	−0.0286	−0.0337	−0.0432
706	−0.1178	−0.7112	0.0019	1.0040	−0.0310	−0.0247	−0.0021	−0.0142
707	0.1168	0.7070	0.0069	1.0091	0.0591	0.0192	0.0171	−0.0310
708	0.0181	0.1091	0.0024	1.0066	0.0053	0.0030	0.0027	0.0032
709	0.0549	0.3315	0.0026	1.0064	0.0170	0.0080	0.0116	0.0063
710	0.0474	0.2863	0.0020	1.0059	0.0128	0.0086	0.0048	−0.0015
711	0.0487	0.2936	0.0023	1.0062	0.0141	0.0095	0.0027	−0.0054
712	−0.1905	−1.1504	0.0017	1.0004	−0.0478	−0.0358	−0.0159	−0.0204
713	−0.0699	−0.4216	0.0019	1.0054	−0.0183	−0.0146	−0.0007	0.0072
714	0.1916	1.1571	0.0016	1.0001	0.0459	0.0403	0.0026	0.0138
715	−0.0637	−0.3845	0.0019	1.0055	−0.0166	−0.0110	−0.0083	−0.0042
716	0.0473	0.2853	0.0025	1.0064	0.0143	0.0096	0.0014	−0.0070
717	−0.1715	−1.0357	0.0017	1.0014	−0.0423	−0.0347	−0.0057	0.0098
718	0.0447	0.2696	0.0019	1.0059	0.0119	0.0077	0.0057	0.0010
719	−0.0433	−0.2613	0.0022	1.0061	−0.0122	−0.0104	0.0034	−0.0033

Sum of residuals	0
Sum of squared residuals	19.62250
Predicted residual SS (press)	19.63220

Fit Diagnostics for DUE

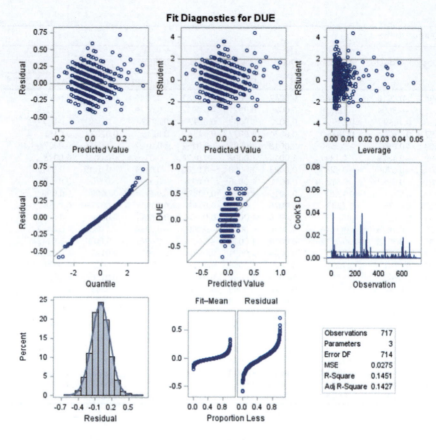

We report statistically significant modeling results of the U.S. unemployment rate whether we model the unemployment rate, or the change in the unemployment rate with respect to the LEI and WkUNCL variables, regardless of their transformations.[6] The reader notes the effectiveness of using SAS for simple linear regression, multiple OLS regression, and robust regression.

7.5 Estimating Robust Regression Simple and Multiple Regression Model in SAS

The robust regression model using the Tukey Bisquare weighting for the UER and LEI variable is shown in Estimation 11 for the 1959 -2018 period.

---

[6] The author appreciates several conversations with Dr. Jennifer Castle, of the University of Oxford and OxMetrics on this topic. The author is solely responsible for any errors remaining in the manuscript.

Estimation 11: The Robust regression UER and DLLEI Model, 1959–2018
The ROBUSTREG Procedure

Model Information	
Data set	WORK.REMZTT
Dependent variable	DUE
Number of independent variables	1
Number of observations	717
Missing values	2
Method	MM estimation

Number of observations read	719
Number of observations used	717
Missing values	2

Profile for the initial LTS estimate	
Total number of observations	717
Number of squares minimized	538
Number of coefficients	2
Highest possible breakdown value	0.2510

MM profile	
Chi function	Tukey
K1	7.0410
Efficiency	0.9900

Parameter estimates

Parameter	DF	Estimate	Standard error	95% confidence	Limits	Chi-square	Pr > Chi-square
Intercept	1	0.0137	0.0063	0.0014	0.0260	4.76	0.0291
DLLEIL1	1	−9.2343	0.8667	−10.9330	−7.5356	113.52	<0.0001
Scale	0	0.1614					

Diagnostics

Obs	Mahalanobis distance	Robust MCD distance	Leverage	Standardized robust residual	Outlier
10	1.2897	1.9431		−3.5895	*
11	2.7207	3.1684	*	0.5028	
13	0.2800	0.6561		3.6331	*
20	0.2800	0.6561		3.6331	*
22	0.2800	0.6561		3.0134	*
31	2.0239	2.2802	*	1.4618	
132	1.7874	2.5775	*	1.1675	
175	1.5741	2.3056	*	−0.6056	
179	1.8727	2.6862	*	0.5135	
183	2.4700	3.4475	*	−0.9661	
185	1.9438	2.7768	*	−0.1347	
186	1.6879	2.4506	*	−0.6514	
187	2.8540	3.9369	*	1.3580	
188	2.8967	3.9913	*	−0.5181	
189	2.0434	2.9037	*	2.9235	
190	2.6691	3.7013	*	2.6718	
191	2.7118	3.7556	*	4.5136	*
243	2.7829	3.8463	*	−2.3313	
246	1.5456	2.2693	*	1.2648	
249	1.5741	2.3056	*	−1.2253	
250	2.1003	2.9762	*	−0.1977	
254	3.7784	5.1151	*	2.2254	
255	4.7028	6.2933	*	1.8535	
256	2.2567	3.1756	*	−0.2606	
264	1.9438	2.7768	*	−1.3741	
272	2.2994	3.2300	*	0.9615	
276	1.7590	2.5412	*	1.1790	
288	2.3652	2.7153	*	0.9794	
293	1.6541	1.8090		−3.6444	*
324	0.1893	0.0580		3.2023	*
379	2.2140	3.1212	*	0.3762	
380	2.0149	2.8675	*	−0.7830	
381	2.2567	3.1756	*	0.9787	
382	2.7402	3.7919	*	−0.4552	
383	1.8727	2.6862	*	−0.1061	
384	1.8870	2.7043	*	0.5078	
444	3.0247	4.1544	*	−1.8090	
496	1.8443	2.6500	*	−0.7143	
501	1.7021	2.4687	*	−0.6571	
503	2.3847	3.3387	*	0.9272	
505	1.9296	2.7587	*	−0.1290	
506	2.4416	3.4113	*	−0.3350	

Diagnostics

Obs	Mahalanobis distance	Robust MCD distance	Leverage	Standardized robust residual	Outlier
507	1.8016	2.5956	*	−1.3168	
512	2.8682	3.9550	*	0.7327	
586	1.6025	2.3418	*	1.2419	
587	1.7590	2.5412	*	−0.6800	
588	1.9154	2.7406	*	−1.3626	
589	1.9438	2.7768	*	0.4849	
590	2.5838	3.5925	*	−1.6316	
592	1.5314	2.2512	*	0.6509	
594	3.4655	4.7163	*	0.4923	
595	2.0576	2.9219	*	−0.8002	
596	3.5793	4.8613	*	1.0662	
597	5.0298	6.7101	*	−0.1371	
598	4.6601	6.2389	*	1.2510	
599	4.4325	5.9489	*	1.3425	
600	3.2380	4.4263	*	1.8232	
601	2.5411	3.5381	*	1.4839	
602	2.7687	3.8281	*	0.7727	
614	2.2087	2.5159	*	0.9165	

Diagnostics summary

Observation type	Proportion	Cutoff
Outlier	0.0098	3.0000
Leverage	0.0753	2.2414

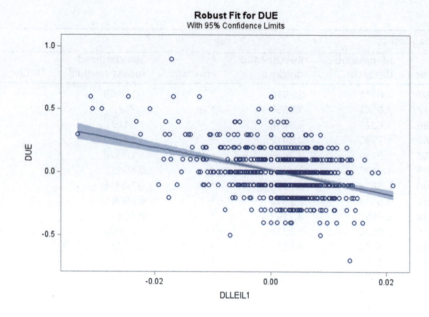

Robust Fit for DUE
With 95% Confidence Limits

Goodness-of-fit	
Statistic	Value
R-Square	0.1163
AICR	697.8581
BICR	707.4878
Deviance	18.0823

The robust regression model using the Tukey Bisquare weighting for the UER and LEI variable is shown in Estimation 12 for the 1959–2018 period.

Estimation 12: The Robust regression UER and DLWkUNCL Model, 1959–2018
The ROBUSTREG Procedure

Model information	
Data set	WORK.REMZTT
dependent variable	DUE
Number of independent variables	1
Number of observations	717
Missing values	2
Method	MM Estimation

Number of observations read	719
Number of observations used	717
Number of observations with missing values	2

Parameter information

Parameter	Effect
Intercept	Intercept
DLWkUNCLL1	DLWkUNCLL1

Summary statistics

Variable	Q1	Median	Q3	Mean	Standard deviation	MAD
DLWkUNCLL1	−0.0312	−0.00240	0.0280	−0.00044	0.0513	0.0442
DUE	−0.1000	0	0.1000	−0.00307	0.1790	0.1483

Profile for the initial LTS estimate

Total number of observations	717
Number of squares minimized	538
Number of coefficients	2
Highest possible breakdown value	0.2510

MM profile

Chi function	Tukey
K1	7.0410
Efficiency	0.9900

Parameter estimates

Parameter	DF	Estimate	Standard error	95% confidence	Limits	Chi-square	Pr > Chi-square
Intercept	1	−0.0055	0.0062	−0.0177	0.0067	0.79	0.3750
DLWkUNCLL1	1	0.7501	0.1229	0.5091	0.9910	37.23	< 0.0001
Scale	0	0.1629					

Diagnostics

Obs	Mahalanobis distance	Robust MCD distance	Leverage	Standardized robust residual	Outlier
7	1.9647	2.3897	*	1.4141	
9	2.6824	3.2424	*	0.0165	
10	2.3801	2.8832	*	−3.5963	*
11	4.7383	5.5741	*	0.5409	
13	0.6934	0.7685		3.8839	*
14	2.2183	2.6909	*	−1.7160	
20	0.6583	0.7268		3.8756	*
26	2.4428	2.8469	*	1.2269	
80	2.4701	2.8793	*	0.0053	
86	3.5701	4.1861	*	0.8791	
97	3.6849	4.4334	*	−0.8342	
100	2.2556	2.6244	*	1.1827	
132	2.6161	3.1636	*	1.2602	
135	4.7029	5.6429	*	0.1534	
136	2.1776	2.5318	*	1.1643	
140	2.1344	2.5913	*	0.1459	
161	1.8809	2.2901	*	−1.0222	
163	2.0645	2.3974	*	−0.0905	
179	2.4972	3.0223	*	0.6743	
187	2.0096	2.4430	*	2.0175	
189	2.2807	2.7651	*	3.1816	*
190	2.9340	3.5413	*	3.0273	*
191	2.1110	2.5635	*	5.0637	*
193	0.6856	0.7592		3.2681	*
216	1.9784	2.4059	*	0.1828	
217	1.9764	2.4036	*	−1.6588	
218	4.5257	5.3215	*	−0.1233	
230	2.0723	2.4066	*	−0.7027	
243	2.8677	3.4625	*	−1.8693	
244	3.7007	4.3414	*	1.5240	
254	0.9409	1.1732		3.4980	*
255	4.6054	5.5270	*	2.6326	
256	2.3236	2.8160	*	0.1013	
261	2.3765	2.7681	*	0.5972	
283	1.9589	2.3828	*	1.4155	
287	2.6788	3.1272	*	−1.7875	
293	1.4170	1.6281		−3.9276	*
324	0.9255	1.0442		3.3247	*
403	2.0040	2.3255	*	0.5092	
405	1.9709	2.2861	*	1.1154	
420	2.2631	2.7442	*	−0.4985	
502	2.1481	2.6075	*	−0.4713	

Diagnostics

Obs	Mahalanobis distance	Robust MCD distance	Leverage	Standardized robust residual	Outlier
512	2.0876	2.5357	*	1.3851	
515	2.2185	2.5804	*	0.5599	
560	4.4864	5.3857	*	−1.0235	
561	2.7783	3.2454	*	0.6921	
598	1.9589	2.3828	*	2.6435	
647	2.5130	2.9303	*	1.2435	
657	2.2475	2.7257	*	−2.3369	

Diagnostics summary

Observation type	Proportion	Cutoff
Outlier	0.0139	3.0000
Leverage	0.0600	2.2414

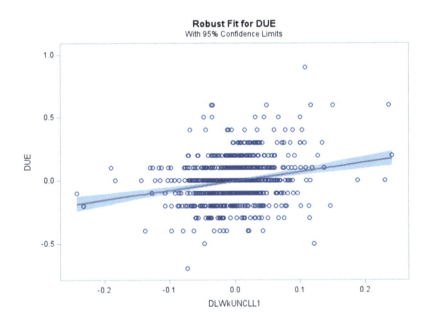

Robust Fit for DUE
With 95% Confidence Limits

Goodness-of-fit	
Statistic	Value
R-Square	0.0419
AICR	744.3017
BICR	753.7989
Deviance	19.6441

In Estimation 13, we estimate change in the unemployment rate, DUE, as a function of the DLOG WkUNCL and DLOG LEI. The DLWkUNCLL1 coefficient is positive as expected, 0.100, and insignificant, having a p-value 0.485. The DLLEIL1 coefficient is negative as expected, -8.82, and highly significant, having a p-value 0.000. The overall regression is highly statistically significant, producing a F-statistic of 60.60.

Estimation 13: The Robust regression UER and DLLEI DLWkUNCL Models, 1959–2018
The ROBUSTREG Procedure

Model information	
Data set	WORK.REMZTT
dependent variable	DUE
Number of independent variables	2
Number of observations	717
Missing values	2
Method	MM estimation

Profile for the initial LTS estimate	
Total number of observations	717
Number of squares minimized	538
Number of coefficients	3
Highest possible breakdown value	0.2150

MM profile	
Chi function	Tukey
K1	7.0410
Efficiency	0.9900

Parameter estimates

Parameter	DF	Estimate	Standard error	95% confidence	Limits	Chi-square	Pr > Chi-square
Intercept	1	0.0130	0.0064	0.0005	0.0255	4.12	0.0423
DLLEIL1	1	-8.8200	1.0545	-10.8869	-6.7531	69.95	<0.0001
DLWkUNCLL1	1	0.1003	0.1440	-0.1820	0.3826	0.49	0.4860
Scale	0	0.1611					

Diagnostics

Obs	Mahalanobis distance	Robust MCD distance	Leverage	Standardized robust residual	Outlier
9	2.8417	3.7196	*	0.2633	
10	2.3822	3.2345	*	-3.6486	*
11	4.7383	6.1169	*	0.6057	
13	1.0822	1.4549		3.6665	*
14	2.3009	3.0472	*	-1.5841	
20	1.0407	1.4049		3.6654	*
22	0.6240	0.9185		3.0039	*
25	2.2717	2.8749	*	0.0507	
26	2.4615	3.1302	*	1.3632	
31	2.2196	2.8140	*	1.4886	
59	2.4640	3.0947	*	0.7822	
80	2.5072	3.1843	*	-0.1019	
86	3.7905	4.8404	*	0.5321	
97	3.8370	5.0260	*	-0.5701	
100	2.2850	2.8955	*	1.1054	
107	2.6136	3.2578	*	-0.2763	
132	2.6386	3.6330	*	1.1182	
135	4.9232	6.4200	*	0.5349	
136	2.8742	3.6966	*	0.6102	
140	2.4296	3.1343	*	0.4725	
151	2.1659	2.7613	*	-0.6421	
161	2.9879	3.7472	*	-0.3394	
179	2.5532	3.5458	*	0.4684	
183	4.2073	5.5581	*	-0.8798	
185	1.9440	2.8289	*	-0.1351	
186	2.1929	3.0361	*	-0.6166	
187	2.8889	4.1094	*	1.3477	
188	3.0105	4.2297	*	-0.4986	
189	2.4493	3.4532	*	2.8926	
190	3.1693	4.4226	*	2.6309	
191	2.7939	3.9758	*	4.5030	*
216	2.2402	2.8953	*	0.4774	

Diagnostics

Obs	Mahalanobis distance	Robust MCD distance	Leverage	Standardized robust residual	Outlier
217	2.8411	3.5765	*	−1.0727	
218	4.6219	5.9278	*	−0.3613	
229	2.4196	3.0375	*	0.1626	
243	3.1843	4.4592	*	−2.3768	
244	4.2194	5.3897	*	0.9490	
250	2.1652	3.1029	*	−0.1851	
254	4.0690	5.6139	*	2.2675	
255	5.2443	7.2465	*	1.7946	
256	2.5811	3.6481	*	−0.2946	
261	2.5812	3.2866	*	0.3133	
264	2.2433	3.1486	*	−1.3479	
272	2.3027	3.3161	*	0.9592	
276	1.9192	2.7445	*	1.2004	
284	2.3955	2.9763	*	2.2069	
287	2.7867	3.5467	*	−2.0177	
288	2.4156	3.0437	*	0.9689	
293	1.7490	2.1768		−3.6355	*
324	1.0165	1.2888		3.2338	*
379	2.2168	3.1951	*	0.3789	
380	2.3006	3.2292	*	−0.7561	
381	2.2663	3.2674	*	0.9742	
382	2.7797	3.9402	*	−0.4448	
383	2.1687	3.0485	*	−0.0785	
384	2.2843	3.1822	*	0.5416	
405	2.3119	2.9565	*	0.7678	
420	2.3887	3.1403	*	−0.3057	
444	3.3386	4.6238	*	−1.7763	
496	1.9099	2.7581	*	−0.7033	
501	2.0356	2.8600	*	−0.6298	
502	2.1577	2.9853	*	−0.5812	
503	2.5255	3.5682	*	0.9497	
505	2.1147	3.0361	*	−0.1525	
506	2.5671	3.6283	*	−0.3158	
507	1.9372	2.7753	*	−1.3012	
512	2.9174	4.1468	*	0.7190	
515	2.3076	2.9284	*	0.3904	
560	4.7630	6.1916	*	−0.6066	
561	3.2077	4.0973	*	0.2276	
569	2.1837	2.8376	*	0.5341	
588	2.7772	3.7603	*	−1.3132	
589	2.1691	3.0657	*	0.5102	
590	2.6008	3.7068	*	−1.6276	

| Diagnostics | | | | | |
Obs	Mahalanobis distance	Robust MCD distance	Leverage	Standardized robust residual	Outlier
594	3.4894	4.9038	*	0.5026	
595	2.1865	3.1137	*	−0.7830	
596	3.6421	5.0966	*	1.0844	
597	5.7845	7.8305	*	−0.0644	
598	4.7436	6.5766	*	1.2748	
599	4.6859	6.4544	*	1.3831	
600	3.4586	4.8071	*	1.8570	
601	2.5637	3.6696	*	1.4768	
602	3.0962	4.2937	*	0.8093	
614	2.3429	2.9324	*	0.8982	
647	2.9374	3.7540	*	0.8070	
657	2.4803	3.2194	*	−2.0744	

| Diagnostics summary | | |
Observation type	Proportion	Cutoff
Outlier	0.0098	3.0000
Leverage	0.1130	2.7162

| Goodness-of-fit | |
Statistic	Value
R-Square	0.1167
AICR	701.4232
BICR	715.8575
Deviance	18.0660

7.6   Estimating Automatic Time Series Models and Forecasting

Let us consider the US real GDP as can be represented by an autoregressive integrated moving average (ARIMA) model. The data is differenced to create a process that has a (finite) mean and variance that do not change over time and the covariance between data points of two series depends upon the distance between the data points, not on the time itself—a transformation to stationarity. Thus, it is assumed that the raw data, with or without a logarithmic transformation, form an integrated (non-stationary) process, and the characteristics of such a process can concisely be modeled as follows:

$$\varphi(B)(1 - B)^d X_t = \theta(B)\varepsilon_t \tag{7.20}$$

where $\varphi(B)$ and $\theta(B)$ are the autoregressive and moving average polynomials in the backward operator B, of orders p and q, ε_t is a white noise error term, and d is an integer representing the order of the data differencing. In economic time series, a first-difference of the data is normally performed.[7] The application of the differencing operator, d, produces a stationary autoregressive moving average ARMA(p,q) model when all parameters are constant across time. Many economics series can be modeled with a simple subset of the class of ARIMA(p, d, q) models, particularly the random walk with drift and a moving average term such as below:

$$\Delta X_t = \mu + \varepsilon_t + \theta\varepsilon_{t-1} \tag{7.21}$$

This type of model and economic time series behavior is not new and practitioner estimation techniques were presented to graduate students in Nelson (1982) and Granger and Newbold (1977).

7.6.1   Automatic Time Series Model Selection Using OxMetrics

Automatic time series models have been discussed in Hendry and Krolzig (2001a, 2001b, 2005), Hendry and Nielsen (2007), and Hendry and Doornik (2014). Hendry sets the tone for automatic modeling, in his OxMetrics system, by contrasting how statistically based his PCGive and AutoMetrics work in contrast to the "data mining" and "garbage in, garbage out" routines, citing their forecasting efficiency and performance. If one starts with a large number of predictors, or candidate explanatory variables, say N, then the general model can be written:

$$y_t = \sum_{i=1}^{n} \gamma_i Z_{it} + u_t \tag{7.22}$$

---

[7] Box and Jenkins, *Time Series Analysis*. Chapter 6; C.W.J. Granger and Paul Newbold, *Forecasting Economic Time Series*. Second Edition (New York: Academic Press, 1986), pp. 109–110, 115–117, 206.

while the (conditional) data generating processes is assumed to be given by:

$$y_t = \sum_{i=1}^{n} \hat{\beta}_i Z_{(i),t} + \epsilon_t \qquad (7.23)$$

where $\epsilon_t \cong IN(0, \sigma_e^2)$ for any $n \le N$. One must select the relevant regressors where $\beta_j \ne 0$ in (7.5). Hendry and his colleagues refer to Eq. (7.4) as the most general, statistical model that can be postulated, given the availability of data and previous empirical and theoretical research as the general unrestricted model (GUM). The Hendry general-to-specific modeling process is referred to as Gets. One seeks to identify all relevant variables, the relevant lag structure, and cointegrating relations, forming near orthogonal variables. The general unrestricted model, GUM, with lags of all variables can then be written:

$$y_t = \beta_0 + \sum_{i=1}^{s} x_i y_{t-i} + \sum_{j=1}^{N} \sum_{i=1}^{s} \beta_{j,i} z_{j,t-i} + \varepsilon_t \qquad (7.24)$$

where $\varepsilon_t \sim IN(0, \sigma_e^2)$. Furthermore, outliers and shifts for T observations can be modeled with impulse-indicator saturation variables, denoted IIS, see Doornik and Hendry (2015) and Hendry and Doornik (2014, Chapter 7):

$$
\begin{aligned}
y_t = {} & \sum_{i=1}^{N} \sum_{j=0}^{s} \beta_{i,j} u_{i,t-j} + \sum_{i=1}^{N} \sum_{j=0}^{s} \theta_{i,j} u_{i,t-j}^2 \\
& + \sum_{i=1}^{N} \sum_{j=0}^{s} \gamma_{i,j} u_{i,tj}^3 + \sum_{i=1}^{N} \sum_{j=0}^{s} k_{i,j} e^{-|u_{i,t-j}|} \\
& + \sum_{j=1}^{s} \lambda_j y_{t-j} + \sum_{i=1}^{T} \delta_i 1_{(i=T)} + \varepsilon_t
\end{aligned}
\qquad (7.25)
$$

where nonlinearity is introduced by the $u_{i,j}^2$, $u_{i,t}^3$, and $u_{i,j} \exp(-|u_{i,t}|)$.

Automatic modeling seeks to eliminate irrelevant variables. One can consider the orthogonal regressor case in which one ranks the variables by their t-statistics, highest to lowest, and defines m to be the smallest, but statistically significant t-statistic, t_m^2, and discards all variables with t-statistics below the m largest t-values. We seek to select a model of the form:

$$y_t = \sum_{r=1}^{m} \delta_r Z_{\{r\},t} + n_t \qquad (7.26)$$

where $Z_{\{r\},t}$ is a subset of the initial N variables.[8]

One progresses from the general unrestricted model to the "final" model in (8) by establishing that model residuals are approximately normal, homoscedastic, and independent. Model reduction proceeds by checking whether the least significant variable can be eliminated given a critical value of c_α (establishing the simplified equation is congruent, if so). Congruence must be maintained at each step as the least significant variables are examined. The last, non-rejected model is referred to as the terminal equation. Selected model regressors have coefficients that are large relative to their estimated standard errors; since the estimators obtained by the initial model (5) are unbiased, the selected estimators are upward biased conditional on retaining $Z_{(j),t}$. The unselected variables will have downward biased estimators. By omitting irrelevant variables, the selection model does not "overfit" the model and the relevant (retained) variables have estimated standard errors close to those from fitting Eq. (7.25). The automatic time series modeling program (PCGets) or AutoMetrics) is efficient, but Hendry and Nielsen (2007) state that the largest selection bias can arise from strongly correlated regressors. AutoMetrics deals with outliers and breaks in its automatic time series modeling. AutoMetrics applies indicator-indicator saturation variables (IIS) to all marginal models which can be postulated as follows:

$$z_t = \sum_{j=1}^{s} \Pi_j X_{t-j} + \sum_{i=1}^{T} \rho_{i,\alpha_t} 1_{i=t} + V_t \qquad (7.27)$$

$$y_t = \mu_0 + \beta^1 z_t + \sum_{i=1}^{m} b_{i,\alpha_t} 1_{(i=t_1)} + \varepsilon_t \qquad (7.28)$$

where there are m significant indicators, including impulse-indicator saturation, IIS, and step-indicator saturation, SIS, differenced impulse indicator saturation, DIIS, and trend saturation, TIS variables.

---

[8] In the selection process, one tests the null hypothesis that the parameter in front of a variable is zero. The relevant t-statistic from a two-sided test is used.

7.6.2 Automatic Time Series Modeling of Real GDP Using Leading Economic Indicators (LEI), 1959–2020

The Conference Board's components of the composite leading index for the year 2002 reflected the work and variables shown in Zarnowitz (1992) list, which continued work of the Burns and Mitchell (1938, 1946), and Moore (1961).[9] The Conference Board composite index of leading economic indicators, LEI, is an equally weighted index in which its components are standardized to produce constant variances. Let us now examine the effectiveness of changes in the LEI to be statistically associated with future changes (growth) in real GDP over the 1959–2020Q3 period. The present (September 2016) ten components of The Conference Board Leading Economic Index® for the U.S. include:

1. Average weekly hours, manufacturing
2. Average weekly initial claims for unemployment insurance
3. Manufacturers' new orders, consumer goods, and materials
4. ISM® Index of New Orders
5. Manufacturers' new orders, nondefense capital goods excluding aircraft orders
6. Building permits, new private housing units
7. Stock prices, 500 common stocks
8. Leading Credit Index™
9. Interest rate spread, 10-year Treasury bonds less federal funds
10. Average consumer expectations for business conditions.

Let us now fit the unemployment time series model with OxMetrics using a traditional AR1 model for the 1959–2020Q3.

---

[9] The author is very grateful to conversations with Mr. Zarnowitz on this topic while we were Associate Editors of the *International Journal of Forecasting*., an Elsevier peer-reviewed journal.

```
Modelling real GDP OxMetrics Estimation(14) by OLS
The dataset is: C:\JBG\JGResearch\MZTT 122020\TCB LEI US Data 1959 2020 known.csv

        The estimation sample is: 2 - 247

                    Coefficient  Std.Error  t-value  t-prob Part.R^2
GDP Known_1            0.968159    0.01396     69.4  0.0000   0.9519
Constant               92.3114      29.82      3.10  0.0022   0.0379
Trend                  2.31018      0.9478     2.44  0.0155   0.0239

sigma                  154.284   RSS                 5784263.02
R^2                   0.998994   F(2,243) =    1.206e+05 [0.000]**
Adj.R^2               0.998985   log-likelihood        -1587.09
no. of observations        246   no. of parameters            3
mean(GDP Known)        10021.1   se(GDP Known)           4843.5
When the log-likelihood constant is NOT included:
AIC                    10.0897   SC                     10.1325
HQ                     10.1069   FPE                    24093.8
When the log-likelihood constant is included:
AIC                    12.9276   SC                     12.9703
HQ                     12.9448   FPE                    411510.

AR 1-2 test:       F(2,241)  =    6.6939 [0.0015]**
ARCH 1-1 test:     F(1,244)  =   52.524  [0.0000]**
Normality test:    Chi^2(2)  =   506.53  [0.0000]**
Hetero test:       F(4,241)  =    6.5819 [0.0000]**
Hetero-X test:     F(5,240)  =    5.2439 [0.0001]**
RESET23 test:      F(2,241)  =   10.026  [0.0001]**
```

The residuals of the AR(1) Model are not random, violating normality, and RESET, polynomial function parameters. The Chi-squared score of the Estimation (14) model residuals has exceeded the score consistent with residuals being normally distributed at the 10% level.

Let us now fit the unemployment time series model with OxMetrics addressing large outliers, 1959–2020Q3. The estimated large outliers occur only in 2020.

```
Real GDP OxMetrics Modelling Estimation (15) by OLS
The dataset is: C:\JBG\JGResearch\MZTT 122020\TCB LEI US Data 1959 2020 known.csv

        The estimation sample is: 2 - 247

                    Coefficient  Std.Error  t-value  t-prob Part.R^2
GDP Known_1            1.00313   0.0009685     1036.  0.0000   0.9998
Constant               34.1261      10.64      3.21  0.0015   0.0408
I:246                 -1801.99      73.06     -24.7  0.0000   0.7154
I:247                  1192.66      72.88      16.4  0.0000   0.5253

sigma                  72.3727   RSS                 1267550.14
R^2                   0.999779   F(3,242) =    3.657e+05 [0.000]**
Adj.R^2               0.999777   log-likelihood        -1400.37
no. of observations        246   no. of parameters            4
mean(GDP Known)        10021.1   se(GDP Known)           4843.5
When the log-likelihood constant is NOT included:
AIC                    8.57979   SC                     8.63678
HQ                     8.60274   FPE                    5322.98
When the log-likelihood constant is included:
AIC                    11.4177   SC                     11.4747
HQ                     11.4406   FPE                    90913.6

AR 1-2 test:       F(2,240)  =   16.990  [0.0000]**
ARCH 1-1 test:     F(1,244)  =   17.942  [0.0000]**
Normality test:    Chi^2(2)  =   56.546  [0.0000]**
Hetero test:       F(2,241)  =    4.1280 [0.0173]*
Hetero-X test:     F(2,241)  =    4.1280 [0.0173]*
RESET23 test:      F(2,240)  =    1.9166 [0.1493]
```

The large residuals of the RealGDP AR(1) Model with estimated large residuals are not random. It may be surprising that large residuals are not identified for the Global Financial Crisis of 2007–2008. The least squares model fit in OxMetrics Estimation (15) is inadequate.

The application of impulse indicator saturation (IIS), differenced (DIIS), and trend saturation variables (TIS) in the Hendry OxMetrics methodology applied to real GDP is reported in Estimation (16).

```
Real GDP OxMetrics Modelling Estimation(16) by OLS
The dataset is: C:\JBG\JGResearch\MZTT 122020\TCB LEI US Data 1959 2020 known.csv
        The estimation sample is: 2 - 247

                Coefficient  Std.Error  t-value  t-prob Part.R^2
GDP Known_1        0.987992   0.001825     541.  0.0000   0.9992
DI:78              88.2196      33.35      2.65  0.0087   0.0304
DI:89              92.0866      33.35      2.76  0.0062   0.0331
DI:92             -140.126      47.42     -2.95  0.0035   0.0377
DI:166             85.8602      33.66      2.55  0.0114   0.0283
DI:221            -134.808      33.35     -4.04  0.0001   0.0683
DI:246            -1484.39      33.38     -44.5  0.0000   0.8986
I:65              -125.115      47.35     -2.64  0.0088   0.0304
I:86              -201.355      47.39     -4.25  0.0000   0.0749
I:93              -313.240      67.45     -4.64  0.0000   0.0882
I:128             -157.632      47.66     -3.31  0.0011   0.0468
I:129             -119.243      47.62     -2.50  0.0130   0.0273
I:197             -167.210      51.01     -3.28  0.0012   0.0460
I:245             -356.174      49.41     -7.21  0.0000   0.1890
T1:124            -1.80747     0.4814     -3.75  0.0002   0.0594
T1:165            47.1223       9.398      5.01  0.0000   0.1013
T1:168           -59.5877      11.91     -5.00  0.0000   0.1010
T1:178            17.3253       4.489      3.86  0.0001   0.0626
T1:197            190.784      22.16      8.61  0.0000   0.2495
T1:199           -321.575      32.85     -9.79  0.0000   0.3005
T1:202            126.697      13.35      9.49  0.0000   0.2876
T1:244            346.095      38.25      9.05  0.0000   0.2686
T1:245           -344.177      37.88     -9.09  0.0000   0.2702

sigma                47.1602  RSS                    495971.583
log-likelihood       -1284.96
no. of observations      246  no. of parameters            23
mean(GDP Known)      10021.1  se(GDP Known)            4843.5
When the log-likelihood constant is NOT included:
AIC                  7.79593  SC                      8.12367
HQ                   7.92790  FPE                     2432.03
When the log-likelihood constant is included:
AIC                  10.6338  SC                      10.9615
HQ                   10.7658  FPE                     41537.8

AR 1-2 test:      F(2,221)  =   1.7101 [0.1832]
ARCH 1-1 test:    F(1,244)  =   1.3444 [0.2474]
Normality test:   Chi^2(2)  =   0.22907 [0.8918]
Hetero test:      F(28,209) =   1.6643 [0.0241]*
RESET23 test:     F(2,221)  =   0.15345 [0.8578]
```

The application of impulse indicator (IIS), differenced indicator (DIIS), and trend indicator saturation variables (TIS) variables in the Hendry OxMetrics methodology, we obtain normally distributed residuals and our model is more adequately fit, see the real GDP OxMetrics Estimation (16) estimation and its RSS compared to the AR1 real GDP in Estimation (14). The real GDP OxMetrics RSS falls from 1,267,550 to 495,972.

The application of impulse (IIS) saturation, the differenced step (DIIS), and trend saturation variables (TIS) variables and the four-period lagged leading economic indicator, LEI, variable in the Hendry OxMetrics methodology for real GDP is reported in OxMetrics Estimation (17).

```
Real GDP Modelling Estimation(17) by OLS
The dataset is: C:\JBG\JGResearch\MZTT 122020\TCB LEI US Data 1959 2020 known.csv

        The estimation sample is: 2 - 247


                 Coefficient  Std.Error  t-value  t-prob Part.R^2
GDP Known_1         0.534609    0.03696     14.5  0.0000   0.4979
Trend              26.8723       2.247      12.0  0.0000   0.4041
LEI_1              32.6986       2.423      13.5  0.0000   0.4633
LEI_2             -16.1939       2.939     -5.51  0.0000   0.1258
DI:89             159.083       33.28       4.78  0.0000   0.0977
DI:165            -88.7931      24.30      -3.65  0.0003   0.0595
DI:170             81.4111      24.48       3.33  0.0010   0.0498
DI:220             73.5550      24.23       3.04  0.0027   0.0418
DI:246           -829.007       41.08     -20.2   0.0000   0.6587
I:164              99.7842      35.16       2.84  0.0050   0.0368
I:179             111.140       35.68       3.11  0.0021   0.0440
I:209            -172.136       41.82      -4.12  0.0001   0.0743
I:212             120.169       39.23       3.06  0.0025   0.0426
T1:47              -3.43263      0.9077    -3.78  0.0002   0.0635
T1:76            -118.194       23.41      -5.05  0.0000   0.1078
T1:77             121.325       25.47       4.76  0.0000   0.0971
T1:88            -164.191       47.81      -3.43  0.0007   0.0529
T1:89             230.043       57.66       3.99  0.0001   0.0702
T1:92             -80.2734      13.76      -5.83  0.0000   0.1388
T1:124              6.69430      1.167      5.74  0.0000   0.1349
T1:147            -29.0833       2.558    -11.4   0.0000   0.3799
T1:169             22.6145       2.604      8.69  0.0000   0.2634
T1:181            -16.2017       3.043     -5.32  0.0000   0.1184
T1:197             91.0526      16.52       5.51  0.0000   0.1258
T1:199            -81.3793      18.53      -4.39  0.0000   0.0837
T1:208             99.9100      24.27       4.12  0.0001   0.0744
T1:210           -158.343       36.52      -4.34  0.0000   0.0818
T1:212             73.0491      21.17       3.45  0.0007   0.0534
T1:220            -91.7159      28.43      -3.23  0.0015   0.0470
T1:221             76.1462      25.64       2.97  0.0033   0.0401
T1:243            294.833       22.37      13.2   0.0000   0.4514
T1:245           -286.667       21.35     -13.4   0.0000   0.4607

sigma                34.1073  RSS                  245457.565
log-likelihood    -1185.32
no. of observations     243  no. of parameters            32
mean(GDP Known)    10105.3   se(GDP Known)           4813.09
When the log-likelihood constant is NOT included:
AIC                  7.18119  SC                       7.64118
HQ                   7.36647  FPE                      1316.50
When the log-likelihood constant is included:
AIC                 10.0191   SC                      10.4791
HQ                  10.2043   FPE                     22485.1

AR 1-2 test:      F(2,209)  =  0.82946 [0.4377]
ARCH 1-1 test:    F(1,241)  =  1.0000 [0.3183]
Normality test:   Chi^2(2)  =  4.2978 [0.1166]
Hetero test:      F(49,189) =  1.1926 [0.2025]
RESET23 test:     F(2,209)  =  1.5045 [0.2245]
```

The application of iOxMetrics to estimate IIS, DIIS, and TIS saturation variables (TIS) variables and the four-period lagged leading economic indicator, LEI, variable in the Hendry OxMetrics methodology, produces normally distributed residuals and our model is more adequately fit, see the real GDP OxMetrics EQ(17) estimation. The Residual Sum of Square, RSS, falls from 495,972 to 245,458. The reader notes that the net two LEI variable estimated coefficients are positive, as expected. As the Leading Economic Indicators increase, then real GDP should rise. The OxMetrics solution produces a more economically efficient solution than the four-quarter modeling result of Guerard (2001 and 2004) of real GDP.

The application of impulse (I) saturation, the step (S), and trend saturation variables (TIS) variables and the four-period lagged DLOG-transformed leading economic indicator, LEI, variable in the Hendry OxMetrics methodology, produces normally distributed residuals and our model is more adequately fit, see the DLOG real GDP OxMetrics Estimation (18).

```
Estimation(18) Modelling DLGDP Known by OLS
       The dataset is: C:\JBG\JGResearch\CFRM UW\TCB LEI US DLOG Data1959 2020
known.csv
       The estimation sample is: 6 - 247

                    Coefficient  Std.Error  t-value  t-prob Part.R^2
DLG0M910_1            0.295206    0.01835     16.1   0.0000   0.5305
DI:24               -0.00941042   0.003583    -2.63  0.0092   0.0292
DI:29                0.00993252   0.003583     2.77  0.0060   0.0325
DI:48               -0.0157320    0.003588    -4.39  0.0000   0.0775
DI:76               -0.0125296    0.004138    -3.03  0.0027   0.0385
DI:77               -0.0193424    0.004148    -4.66  0.0000   0.0867
DI:89                0.0161703    0.003587     4.51  0.0000   0.0815
DI:91                0.0170264    0.004137     4.12  0.0001   0.0689
DI:92                0.0119543    0.004138     2.89  0.0042   0.0352
DI:246              -0.0495642    0.004135   -12.0   0.0000   0.3855
I:8                 -0.0219919    0.005117    -4.30  0.0000   0.0746
T1:189               0.000100417  1.704e-05    5.89  0.0000   0.1317
T1:244              -0.000107151  1.151e-05   -9.31  0.0000   0.2747

sigma             0.00506660  RSS              0.00587853827
R^2               0.817413    log-likelihood        942.288
no. of observations      242  no. of parameters          13
mean(Y)           0.00717236  se(Y)               0.0112308

AR 1-2 test:     F(2,227)   =    1.3609 [0.2585]
ARCH 1-1 test:   F(1,240)   =   0.73059 [0.3935]
Normality test:  Chi^2(2)   =    1.1270 [0.5692]
Hetero test:     F(22,218)  =   0.74088 [0.7940]
Hetero-X test:   F(24,216)  =   0.71625 [0.8325]
RESET23 test:    F(2,227)   =   0.54158 [0.5826]
Model saved to C:\JBG\JGResearch\CFRM UW\Original MZTT Regressions\Model DLRGDP AR1
IIS DIIS TIS Saturation with DLLEI L4 Variables 1959 2020.pdf
Model saved to C:\JBG\JGResearch\CFRM UW\Original MZTT Regressions\Model DLRGDP AR1
IIS DIIS TIS Saturation with DLLEI L4 Variables 1959 2020.pdf.gwg
```

The application of impulse (IIS) saturation, the differenced indicator impulse (DIIS), and trend saturation variables (TIS) variables and the four-period lagged leading economic indicator, LEI, variable in the Hendry OxMetrics methodology, produces normally distributed residuals and our model is more adequately fit, see the real GDP OxMetrics Estimation(18) estimation. The reader notes that only one DLOG LEI variable is statistically significant. As the Leading Economic Indicators increase, then real GDP should rise. The OxMetrics solution produces a more economically efficient solution than the four-quarter modeling result of Guerard (2001 and 2004) of real GDP.

7.7 Automatic Time Series Modeling of the Unemployment Rate Using Leading Economic Indicators (LEI)

Economic theory indicates that an appropriate level of unemployment is the key to economic development. A high unemployment rate leads to human suffering and many other negative societal consequences, while an extremely low unemployment rate leads to an increase in labor cost and subsequent inflation. One of the certain missions of government monetary policy is to control the unemployment rate at the ideal level while controlling inflation. Hence it is vital to be able to accurately forecast the unemployment rate in the near and long-term future, based on limited current information of the economy.

We continue revisiting the MZTT analysis by applying the Hendry OxMetrics system for automatic time series modelling and forecasting. Based on the success of OxMerics in modelling real GDP data, the reader should anticipate a similar result for modelling the unemployment rate. Indeed, we report that the U.S. LEI is negatively and statistically highly significantly associated with the change in the U.S. unemployment rate during the 1959–2020 time period. This is particularly true for a one-month lag in the LEI. This is true during the COVID pandemic. We also report that the U.S. weekly unemployment claims time series, reported on Thursday mornings, is positively and highly statistically significantly associated with the U.S. unemployment rate during the 1959–2020 time period, particularly for lags one and three-month variables. We estimate several equations of the weekly unemployment claims and the composite leading indicator for the whole sample period from 1959 to 2020 and the results obtained verify the previous ones, as to that both variables lead to unemployment.

```
Ox Professional version 8.10 (Windows_64/U) (C) J.A. Doornik, 1994-2019


---- PcGive 15.10 session started at 11:48:22 on  7-11-2020 ----

UER OxMetrics Estimation (19) Modelling UER by OLS
The    dataset    is:  C:\JBG\JGResearch\Palgrave  Business  Cycles\2020Q3\LEI   UER
11072020.csv

        The estimation sample is: 2 - 741

                    Coefficient  Std.Error  t-value  t-prob Part.R^2
UER_1                  0.965395   0.009621    100.   0.0000   0.9318
Constant               0.196670    0.06389    3.08   0.0022   0.0127
Trend               3.20747e-05  7.522e-05   0.426   0.6699   0.0002

sigma                  0.435504  RSS               139.782007
R^2                    0.932308  F(2,737) =     5075 [0.000]**
Adj.R^2                0.932124  log-likelihood       -433.385
no. of observations         740  no. of parameters           3
mean(UER)             5.98986  se(UER)               1.67161

AR 1-2 test:      F(2,735)  =    2.5994 [0.0750]
ARCH 1-1 test:    F(1,738)  =    0.20134 [0.6538]
Normality test:   Chi^2(2)  =    61482. [0.0000]**
Hetero test:      F(4,735)  =    2.2288 [0.0643]
Hetero-X test:    F(5,734)  =    2.1242 [0.0607]
RESET23 test:     F(2,735)  =    10.980 [0.0000]**
Model    saved    to   C:\JBG\JGResearch\Palgrave  Business  Cycles\2020Q3\LEI   UER
11072020_files\Model UER AR1 LS.pdf
Model    saved    to   C:\JBG\JGResearch\Palgrave  Business  Cycles\2020Q3\LEI   UER
11072020_files\Model UER AR1 LS.pdf.gwg
```

The residuals of the UER AR(1) Model are not random. The least squares model fit in OxMetrics Estimation (19) is inadequate. The Chi-squared score of the residuals has exceeded the score consistent with residuals being normally distributed at the 10% level.

Let us now fit the unemployment time series model with OxMetrics addressing large outliers. The estimated large outliers occur in 2020, to no reader's surprise. See Estimation (20).

```
UER OxMetrics Estimation(20) Modelling UER by OLS

The dataset is: C:\JBG\JGResearch\Palgrave Business Cycles\2020Q3\LEI UER 11072020.csv

        The estimation sample is: 2 - 741


                    Coefficient  Std.Error  t-value  t-prob Part.R^2
UER_1                0.984549    0.004340    227.    0.0000  0.9859
Constant             0.0851295   0.02690     3.17    0.0016  0.0134
I:735               10.2829      0.1939      53.0    0.0000  0.7928
I:737               -2.07963     0.1964     -10.6    0.0000  0.1324
I:739               -1.72753     0.1946     -8.88    0.0000  0.0968

sigma                0.193629    RSS                 27.5567291
R^2                  0.986655    F(4,735) =   1.359e+04 [0.000]**
Adj.R^2              0.986583    log-likelihood        167.435
no. of observations       740   no. of parameters         5
mean(UER)            5.98986     se(UER)               1.67161

AR 1-2 test:        F(2,733)  =    33.129 [0.0000]**
ARCH 1-1 test:      F(1,738)  =    10.080 [0.0016]**
Normality test:     Chi^2(2)  =    306.98 [0.0000]**
Hetero test:        F(2,734)  =    82.754 [0.0000]**
Hetero-X test:      F(2,734)  =    82.754 [0.0000]**
RESET23 test:       F(2,733)  =    25.082 [0.0000]**
Model    saved    to    C:\JBG\JGResearch\Palgrave    Business    Cycles\2020Q3\LEI    UER
11072020_files\Model UER AR1 Large Residuals.pdf
Model    saved    to    C:\JBG\JGResearch\Palgrave    Business    Cycles\2020Q3\LEI    UER
11072020_files\Model UER AR1 Large Residuals.pdf.gwg
```

The residuals of the AR(1) Model are not random, violating normality and RESET, polynomial function parameters. The model fit in Estimation (20) is inadequate, despite identifying large outliers in 2020Q2 and 2020Q3. The Chi-squared score of the Estimation (20) model residuals has exceeded the score consistent with residuals being normally distributed at the 10 percent level.

When we allow OxMetrics to estimate IIS, DIIS, and TIS saturation variables in the Hendry OxMetrics methodology, we obtain normally distributed residuals and our model is adequately fit, see the UER OxMetrics Estimation (21) estimation.

UER OxMetrics Estimation(21) Modelling UER by OLS
The dataset is: C:\JBG\JGResearch\Palgrave Business Cycles\2020Q3\LEI UER 11072020.csv

The estimation sample is: 2 - 741

	Coefficient	Std.Error	t-value	t-prob	Part.R^2
UER_1	0.997229	0.0008978	1111.	0.0000	0.9994
I:3	-0.384481	0.1437	-2.68	0.0076	0.0103
I:11	-0.483927	0.1437	-3.37	0.0008	0.0163
I:13	-0.385589	0.1437	-2.68	0.0075	0.0104
I:14	0.613302	0.1437	4.27	0.0000	0.0259
I:21	0.615242	0.1437	4.28	0.0000	0.0261
I:23	0.516905	0.1437	3.60	0.0003	0.0185
I:31	-0.380601	0.1437	-2.65	0.0083	0.0101
I:34	-0.381987	0.1437	-2.66	0.0080	0.0102
I:74	-0.385867	0.1437	-2.69	0.0074	0.0104
I:87	0.0105308	0.1436	0.0733	0.9416	0.0000
I:90	0.0105308	0.1436	0.0733	0.9416	0.0000
I:91	0.0105308	0.1436	0.0733	0.9416	0.0000
I:100	0.0105308	0.1436	0.0733	0.9416	0.0000
I:103	0.0105308	0.1436	0.0733	0.9416	0.0000
I:104	0.0105308	0.1436	0.0733	0.9416	0.0000
I:132	0.409699	0.1436	2.85	0.0045	0.0117
I:142	0.415242	0.1437	2.89	0.0040	0.0120
I:188	0.415242	0.1437	2.89	0.0040	0.0120
I:190	0.616628	0.1437	4.29	0.0000	0.0262
I:191	0.618290	0.1437	4.30	0.0000	0.0263
I:192	0.919953	0.1437	6.40	0.0000	0.0564
I:194	0.522447	0.1438	3.63	0.0003	0.0189
I:209	0.220507	0.1437	1.53	0.1255	0.0034
I:227	-0.381155	0.1437	-2.65	0.0082	0.0102
I:247	0.315796	0.1437	2.20	0.0283	0.0070
I:255	0.617459	0.1437	4.30	0.0000	0.0262
I:256	0.619122	0.1437	4.31	0.0000	0.0264
I:268	0.319953	0.1437	2.23	0.0263	0.0072
I:273	0.321062	0.1438	2.23	0.0258	0.0072
I:277	0.323833	0.1438	2.25	0.0246	0.0073
I:279	0.324941	0.1438	2.26	0.0242	0.0074
I:286	0.428821	0.1439	2.98	0.0030	0.0128
I:288	-0.370070	0.1439	-2.57	0.0103	0.0096
I:294	-0.672010	0.1439	-4.67	0.0000	0.0309
I:297	-0.374504	0.1438	-2.60	0.0094	0.0098
I:325	0.518567	0.1437	3.61	0.0003	0.0187
I:597	0.416905	0.1437	2.90	0.0038	0.0121
I:599	0.518845	0.1437	3.61	0.0003	0.0187
I:600	0.520230	0.1437	3.62	0.0003	0.0188
I:601	0.521616	0.1438	3.63	0.0003	0.0189
I:602	0.423001	0.1438	2.94	0.0034	0.0125
I:604	0.424941	0.1438	2.95	0.0032	0.0126
I:622	0.426050	0.1438	2.96	0.0032	0.0126
I:623	-0.472842	0.1439	-3.29	0.0011	0.0155
I:663	-0.481433	0.1437	-3.35	0.0009	0.0161
I:734	0.909699	0.1436	6.33	0.0000	0.0553
I:735	10.3122	0.1436	71.8	0.0000	0.8827
I:736	-1.35926	0.1442	-9.43	0.0000	0.1148
I:737	-2.16314	0.1441	-15.0	0.0000	0.2476
I:738	-0.869239	0.1439	-6.04	0.0000	0.0505
I:739	-1.77173	0.1439	-12.3	0.0000	0.1812
I:740	-0.476721	0.1438	-3.32	0.0010	0.0158
I:741	-0.978107	0.1438	-6.80	0.0000	0.0633

sigma	0.143591	RSS	14.1235451
log-likelihood	414.744		
no. of observations	740	no. of parameters	55
mean(UER)	5.98986	se(UER)	1.67161

AR 1-2 test:	$F(2,683)$	=	4.1410 [0.0163]*
ARCH 1-1 test:	$F(1,738)$	=	1.1487 [0.2842]
Normality test:	**Chi^2(2)**	=	**1.7943 [0.4077]**
Hetero test:	$F(2,683)$	=	4.6304 [0.0101]*
RESET23 test:	$F(2,683)$	=	2.9548 [0.0528]

Model saved to C:\JBG\JGResearch\Palgrave Business Cycles\2020Q3\LEI UER
11072020_files\Model UER AR1 IIS.pdf
Model saved to C:\JBG\JGResearch\Palgrave Business Cycles\2020Q3\LEI UER
11072020_files\Model UER AR1 IIS.pdf.gwg

Normality of errors is achieved in Estimation (21) with the IIS, SIS, and TIS estimated saturation variables. The Residual sum of squares has fallen from 139.78 with the AR1 model to 14.12. The OxMetrics Estimation (21) is an acceptable representation of the UER time series.

When we apply the impulse (IIS) saturation, the differenced indicator step (DIIS), and trend saturation variables (TIS) variables in the Hendry OxMetrics methodology, we obtain normally distributed residuals and our model is more adequately fit, see the UER OxMetrics Estimation (22) estimation.

```
UER OxMetrics Estimation(22) Modelling UER by OLS
The dataset is: C:\JBG\JGResearch\Palgrave Business Cycles\2020Q3\LEI UER 11072020.csv

        The estimation sample is: 2 - 741
```

	Coefficient	Std.Error	t-value	t-prob	Part.R^2
UER_1	0.876395	0.008377	105.	0.0000	0.9439
I:14	0.779566	0.1271	6.13	0.0000	0.0546
I:32	0.255197	0.1204	2.12	0.0344	0.0069
I:43	0.392532	0.1224	3.21	0.0014	0.0155
I:46	0.514656	0.1262	4.08	0.0001	0.0249
I:53	-0.273810	0.1179	-2.32	0.0205	0.0082
I:66	-0.322366	0.1178	-2.74	0.0064	0.0114
I:70	-0.323045	0.1179	-2.74	0.0063	0.0114
I:74	-0.411362	0.1181	-3.48	0.0005	0.0183
I:188	0.375289	0.1206	3.11	0.0019	0.0147
I:193	-0.493717	0.1275	-3.87	0.0001	0.0225
I:221	0.325258	0.1243	2.62	0.0091	0.0104
I:222	-0.316031	0.1258	-2.51	0.0122	0.0096
I:227	-0.337714	0.1200	-2.81	0.0050	0.0120
I:234	0.429905	0.1208	3.56	0.0004	0.0191
I:263	-0.325220	0.1255	-2.59	0.0098	0.0102
I:288	-0.270773	0.1260	-2.15	0.0320	0.0070
I:325	0.521928	0.1166	4.47	0.0000	0.0298
I:352	0.250573	0.1199	2.09	0.0370	0.0067
I:381	-0.230542	0.1181	-1.95	0.0513	0.0058
I:395	0.252107	0.1179	2.14	0.0328	0.0070
I:449	-0.250036	0.1165	-2.15	0.0322	0.0070
I:451	-0.355727	0.1164	-3.06	0.0023	0.0141
I:471	-0.387921	0.1161	-3.34	0.0009	0.0169
I:591	-0.273094	0.1195	-2.29	0.0226	0.0080
I:737	-1.03182	0.1340	-7.70	0.0000	0.0835
I:739	-1.01499	0.1334	-7.61	0.0000	0.0817
S1:16	-0.298216	0.1465	-2.04	0.0422	0.0063
S1:21	0.895949	0.2199	4.07	0.0001	0.0249
S1:23	0.918645	0.2092	4.39	0.0000	0.0288
S1:37	-0.362127	0.09863	-3.67	0.0003	0.0203
S1:47	-0.421862	0.07816	-5.40	0.0000	0.0428
S1:74	0.107972	0.04328	2.49	0.0129	0.0095
S1:131	-0.385991	0.04731	-8.16	0.0000	0.0928
S1:177	-0.117715	0.04416	-2.67	0.0079	0.0108
S1:189	-0.424540	0.1966	-2.16	0.0312	0.0071
S1:196	0.365767	0.07720	4.74	0.0000	0.0333
S1:208	-0.326279	0.07686	-4.25	0.0000	0.0269
S1:221	-0.191561	0.09035	-2.12	0.0344	0.0069
S1:254	-0.539449	0.09595	-5.62	0.0000	0.0463
S1:256	0.358341	0.1157	3.10	0.0020	0.0145
S1:258	0.201815	0.09621	2.10	0.0363	0.0067
S1:283	-0.233599	0.09767	-2.39	0.0171	0.0087
S1:286	0.409035	0.09214	4.44	0.0000	0.0294
S1:293	0.723292	0.1281	5.65	0.0000	0.0467
S1:294	-0.702477	0.1633	-4.30	0.0000	0.0276
S1:306	0.250496	0.1204	2.08	0.0378	0.0066
S1:401	0.0855031	0.03413	2.51	0.0125	0.0095
S1:434	-0.373222	0.1174	-3.18	0.0016	0.0153
S1:435	0.378560	0.1170	3.24	0.0013	0.0158
S1:502	-0.318608	0.03930	-8.11	0.0000	0.0917
S1:740	0.475763	0.1164	4.09	0.0000	0.0250
T1:9	0.637548	0.1138	5.60	0.0000	0.0460
T1:10	-0.581051	0.1195	-4.86	0.0000	0.0350
T1:19	-0.425653	0.09466	-4.50	0.0000	0.0301

T1:24	0.721285	0.1638	4.40	0.0000	0.0289
T1:25	-0.240353	0.1110	-2.16	0.0308	0.0071
T1:49	-0.0377874	0.007908	-4.78	0.0000	0.0339
T1:187	-0.100768	0.05601	-1.80	0.0725	0.0049
T1:191	0.123400	0.05678	2.17	0.0301	0.0072
T1:233	-0.0384347	0.007241	-5.31	0.0000	0.0415
T1:263	0.0836272	0.03805	2.20	0.0283	0.0074
T1:266	-0.513973	0.1659	-3.10	0.0020	0.0145
T1:267	0.724688	0.1993	3.64	0.0003	0.0199
T1:269	-0.842397	0.1852	-4.55	0.0000	0.0308
T1:270	0.549938	0.1234	4.46	0.0000	0.0296
T1:294	0.442910	0.1339	3.31	0.0010	0.0165
T1:295	-0.424343	0.1395	-3.04	0.0024	0.0140
T1:304	-0.435657	0.1395	-3.12	0.0019	0.0148
T1:305	0.435101	0.1336	3.26	0.0012	0.0160
T1:352	-0.121564	0.05588	-2.18	0.0300	0.0072
T1:354	0.340109	0.1640	2.07	0.0385	0.0066
T1:355	-0.227902	0.1151	-1.98	0.0481	0.0060
T1:376	-0.304800	0.05821	-5.24	0.0000	0.0404
T1:377	0.310480	0.05537	5.61	0.0000	0.0461
T1:579	-0.0287408	0.003631	-7.92	0.0000	0.0878
T1:595	-0.0993416	0.02030	-4.89	0.0000	0.0355
T1:599	0.141783	0.02018	7.03	0.0000	0.0705
T1:620	-0.507148	0.1258	-4.03	0.0001	0.0244
T1:621	1.32388	0.2569	5.15	0.0000	0.0392
T1:622	-1.02160	0.1950	-5.24	0.0000	0.0405
T1:624	0.197132	0.05653	3.49	0.0005	0.0183
T1:661	0.422074	0.1213	3.48	0.0005	0.0183
T1:662	-0.774660	0.2349	-3.30	0.0010	0.0164
T1:663	0.347375	0.1187	2.93	0.0035	0.0130
T1:732	-0.947770	0.1185	-8.00	0.0000	0.0894
T1:733	-8.56757	0.2591	-33.1	0.0000	0.6268
T1:734	19.8793	0.2709	73.4	0.0000	0.8922
T1:735	-10.3681	0.1454	-71.3	0.0000	0.8865

sigma	0.115192	**RSS**		8.638275
log-likelihood	596.651			
no. of observations	740	no. of parameters		89
mean(UER)	5.98986	se(UER)	1.67161	

AR 1-2 test:	F(2,649)	=	4.1407 [0.0163]*
ARCH 1-1 test:	F(1,738)	=	0.41390 [0.5202]
Normality test:	**Chi^2(2)**	=	**0.18537 [0.9115]**
Hetero test:	F(78,627)	=	0.68428 [0.9813]
RESET23 test:	F(2,649)	=	1.3256 [0.2664]

Model saved to C:\JBG\JGResearch\Palgrave Business Cycles\2020Q3\LEI UER 11072020_files\Model UER AR1 IIS SIS TIS.pdf
Model saved to C:\JBG\JGResearch\Palgrave Business Cycles\2020Q3\LEI UER 11072020_files\Model UER AR1 IIS SIS TIS.pdf.gwg

The Residual Sum of Square, RSS, falls from 14.12 to 8.63 in Estimation (22).

When we apply the impulse (IIS) saturation, the differenced indicator step (DIIS), and trend saturation variables (TIS) variables with the one-period lagged LEI variable in Estimation (23) we obtain normally distributed residuals and our model is more adequately fit, see the UER OxMetrics Estimation (23) estimation. The Residual Sum of Square, RSS, falls from 8.63 to 6.68. The reader notes that the LEI variable estimated coefficient is negative, as expected. As the Leading Economic Indicators increase, then the unemployment rate should fall.

```
UER OxMetrics Estimation (23) Modelling UER by OLS
The dataset is: C:\JBG\JGResearch\Palgrave Business Cycles\2020Q3\LEI UER 11072020.csv
```

The estimation sample is: 2 - 741

	Coefficient	Std.Error	t-value	t-prob	Part.R^2
UER_1	0.546415	0.02153	25.4	0.0000	0.5001
Constant	291.493	37.92	7.69	0.0000	0.0840
Trend	-0.382204	0.05112	-7.48	0.0000	0.0799
LEI_1	-0.0524908	0.004226	-12.4	0.0000	0.1933
I:24	-0.230072	0.1083	-2.13	0.0339	0.0070
I:31	-0.371475	0.1084	-3.43	0.0006	0.0179
I:45	-0.378490	0.1102	-3.44	0.0006	0.0180
I:47	-0.327582	0.1101	-2.98	0.0030	0.0136
I:58	0.272069	0.1045	2.60	0.0094	0.0104
I:66	-0.278819	0.1043	-2.67	0.0077	0.0110
I:70	-0.271086	0.1044	-2.60	0.0096	0.0104
I:74	-0.323243	0.1047	-3.09	0.0021	0.0146
I:177	-0.287349	0.1043	-2.75	0.0061	0.0116
I:188	0.377232	0.1061	3.55	0.0004	0.0192
I:270	-0.408508	0.1095	-3.73	0.0002	0.0211
I:435	0.318932	0.1037	3.07	0.0022	0.0145
I:471	-0.262076	0.1036	-2.53	0.0116	0.0098
I:587	0.250967	0.1055	2.38	0.0177	0.0087
I:596	-0.301059	0.1049	-2.87	0.0042	0.0126
I:735	6.82678	0.3112	21.9	0.0000	0.4276
I:737	-1.14448	0.1252	-9.14	0.0000	0.1149
I:739	-0.816471	0.1221	-6.68	0.0000	0.0649
S1:10	0.605520	0.1076	5.63	0.0000	0.0469
S1:12	0.343610	0.1265	2.72	0.0068	0.0113
S1:13	-0.744499	0.1450	-5.14	0.0000	0.0393
S1:14	0.529544	0.1253	4.23	0.0000	0.0270
S1:16	-0.293185	0.08832	-3.32	0.0010	0.0168
S1:20	-0.547046	0.1140	-4.80	0.0000	0.0345
S1:21	0.330324	0.1447	2.28	0.0228	0.0080
S1:22	-0.451915	0.1093	-4.13	0.0000	0.0258
S1:32	0.275755	0.1083	2.55	0.0111	0.0100
S1:33	0.259962	0.1080	2.41	0.0163	0.0089
S1:44	-0.225297	0.05241	-4.30	0.0000	0.0279
S1:52	0.165362	0.04903	3.37	0.0008	0.0174
S1:77	0.346970	0.04382	7.92	0.0000	0.0887
S1:131	-0.494345	0.04965	-9.96	0.0000	0.1334
S1:139	-0.339948	0.08244	-4.12	0.0000	0.0257
S1:141	-0.202813	0.07840	-2.59	0.0099	0.0103
S1:165	0.145345	0.03619	4.02	0.0001	0.0244
S1:192	0.783665	0.1403	5.59	0.0000	0.0462
S1:193	-0.496643	0.1183	-4.20	0.0000	0.0266
S1:196	0.256547	0.07271	3.53	0.0004	0.0190
S1:208	-0.315545	0.07195	-4.39	0.0000	0.0290
S1:233	-0.296552	0.1103	-2.69	0.0074	0.0111
S1:234	0.329199	0.1122	2.93	0.0035	0.0132
S1:263	-0.269537	0.09886	-2.73	0.0066	0.0114
S1:267	-0.386120	0.08631	-4.47	0.0000	0.0301
S1:288	-0.759730	0.2148	-3.54	0.0004	0.0191
S1:293	0.508982	0.1157	4.40	0.0000	0.0292
S1:294	-0.556878	0.1448	-3.85	0.0001	0.0225
S1:295	0.449759	0.1212	3.71	0.0002	0.0209
S1:323	0.329059	0.1117	2.95	0.0033	0.0133
S1:338	0.273408	0.05075	5.39	0.0000	0.0431
S1:450	0.630075	0.2079	3.03	0.0025	0.0141
S1:553	0.136968	0.05155	2.66	0.0081	0.0108
S1:561	0.207741	0.05159	4.03	0.0001	0.0246
S1:615	0.320456	0.08123	3.95	0.0001	0.0236
S1:621	-0.322258	0.1126	-2.86	0.0043	0.0126
T1:13	0.0715930	0.01313	5.45	0.0000	0.0442

```
T1:187          -0.341477    0.02318    -14.7   0.0000   0.2520
T1:192           0.366428    0.02388     15.3   0.0000   0.2678
T1:225           0.212157    0.06119      3.47  0.0006   0.0183
T1:226          -0.235913    0.05969     -3.95  0.0001   0.0237
T1:253          -0.679358    0.07677     -8.85  0.0000   0.1084
T1:254           0.737311    0.08243      8.94  0.0000   0.1105
T1:270          -0.142180    0.01360    -10.5   0.0000   0.1450
T1:286           0.571330    0.1136       5.03  0.0000   0.0378
T1:288          -0.448181    0.1127      -3.98  0.0001   0.0240
T1:303          -0.0424522   0.01233     -3.44  0.0006   0.0181
T1:323          -0.674863    0.1443      -4.68  0.0000   0.0329
T1:324           1.00239     0.2304       4.35  0.0000   0.0285
T1:325          -0.317966    0.1069      -2.97  0.0030   0.0136
T1:376          -0.301476    0.05858     -5.15  0.0000   0.0395
T1:377           0.279795    0.06120      4.57  0.0000   0.0314
T1:393          -0.326233    0.06085     -5.36  0.0000   0.0427
T1:394           0.348407    0.05766      6.04  0.0000   0.0536
T1:449          -0.367481    0.1057      -3.48  0.0005   0.0184
T1:451           0.364783    0.1059       3.44  0.0006   0.0181
T1:507          -0.100037    0.01988     -5.03  0.0000   0.0378
T1:510           0.0799097   0.02053      3.89  0.0001   0.0230
T1:570           0.275813    0.05551      4.97  0.0000   0.0369
T1:571          -0.260236    0.05721     -4.55  0.0000   0.0311
T1:590          -0.0740667   0.01026     -7.22  0.0000   0.0749
T1:601           0.0359921   0.01232      2.92  0.0036   0.0131
T1:621           0.743363    0.1268       5.86  0.0000   0.0507
T1:622          -0.777967    0.1397      -5.57  0.0000   0.0459
T1:626           0.0978210   0.02225      4.40  0.0000   0.0291
T1:661           0.346537    0.1077       3.22  0.0014   0.0158
T1:662          -0.623966    0.2090      -2.99  0.0029   0.0137
T1:663           0.263958    0.1072       2.46  0.0140   0.0093
T1:704          -0.0407574   0.008367    -4.87  0.0000   0.0355
T1:711           0.0327275   0.009889     3.31  0.0010   0.0167
T1:732          -0.890431    0.1109      -8.03  0.0000   0.0910
T1:733          -2.08216     0.3742      -5.56  0.0000   0.0459
T1:734           3.60793     0.3965       9.10  0.0000   0.1139
T1:737          -0.254771    0.1088      -2.34  0.0195   0.0084

sigma                0.10191    RSS                    6.6883333
R^2                  0.996761   F(95,644) =     2086 [0.000]**
Adj.R^2              0.996283   log-likelihood          691.311
no. of observations      740   no. of parameters            96
mean(UER)            5.98986    se(UER)              1.67161

AR 1-2 test:      F(2,642)  =     4.2621 [0.0145]*
ARCH 1-1 test:    F(1,738)  =  0.0022536 [0.9622]
Normality test:   Chi^2(2)  =     3.4241 [0.1805]
Hetero test:      F(88,623) =    0.88083 [0.7686]
RESET23 test:     F(2,642)  =     2.0975 [0.1236]
```

Estimation (23) is an acceptable representation of the unemployment rate in the U.S., 1959–11/2020.

When we apply the impulse (IIS) saturation, the differenced indicator step (DIIS), and trend saturation variables (TIS) and the twelve-periods of lagged leading economic indicator, LEI, variable in the Hendry OxMetrics methodology, we obtain normally distributed residuals and our model is more adequately fit, see the UER OxMetrics Estimation (24) estimation. The Regression Sum of Square, RSS, rises from 6.68 to 7.91. The reader notes that the LEI variable estimated coefficient is negative, as expected. The lagged Leading Economic Indicators coefficients are not always negative and the increasing RSS shows that USER OxMetrics is not optimal.

```
UER OxMetrics Estimation (24) Modelling by OLS
The dataset is: C:\JBG\JGResearch\Palgrave Business Cycles\2020Q3\LEI UER 11072020.csv

        The estimation sample is: 13 - 741

                 Coefficient  Std.Error  t-value  t-prob  Part.R^2
UER_1              0.816220    0.01587     51.4    0.0000   0.8046
Trend              0.00669369  0.0007230    9.26   0.0000   0.1178
LEI_1             -0.0550260   0.007926    -6.94   0.0000   0.0698
LEI_3              0.0471806   0.01201      3.93   0.0001   0.0235
LEI_6             -0.0410286   0.008715    -4.71   0.0000   0.0334
LEI_11             0.0473930   0.01408      3.37   0.0008   0.0174
LEI_12            -0.0406443   0.01213     -3.35   0.0009   0.0172
I:14               0.761380    0.1251       6.08   0.0000   0.0545
I:17               0.322259    0.1190       2.71   0.0069   0.0113
I:21               0.514766    0.1159       4.44   0.0000   0.0298
I:23               0.390466    0.1166       3.35   0.0009   0.0172
I:47              -0.435324    0.1302      -3.34   0.0009   0.0171
I:73               0.309381    0.1126       2.75   0.0062   0.0116
I:154              0.197740    0.1123       1.76   0.0787   0.0048
I:168             -0.258599    0.1125      -2.30   0.0219   0.0082
I:177             -0.234299    0.1128      -2.08   0.0382   0.0067
I:193             -0.617381    0.1272      -4.85   0.0000   0.0354
I:208             -0.319287    0.1143      -2.79   0.0054   0.0120
I:216             -0.332919    0.1215      -2.74   0.0063   0.0116
I:222             -0.187883    0.1158      -1.62   0.1053   0.0041
I:227             -0.316377    0.1141      -2.77   0.0057   0.0118
I:234              0.316791    0.1132       2.80   0.0053   0.0121
I:235             -0.277188    0.1131      -2.45   0.0145   0.0093
I:255              0.336628    0.1271       2.65   0.0083   0.0108
I:263             -0.350114    0.1165      -3.01   0.0028   0.0139
I:268              0.260961    0.1182       2.21   0.0276   0.0075
I:270             -0.334303    0.1206      -2.77   0.0057   0.0118
I:283             -0.289363    0.1179      -2.45   0.0144   0.0093
I:288             -0.437493    0.1160      -3.77   0.0002   0.0217
I:294             -0.612145    0.1264      -4.84   0.0000   0.0353
I:306              0.410282    0.1169       3.51   0.0005   0.0188
I:325              0.571200    0.1120       5.10   0.0000   0.0389
I:351             -0.278376    0.1120      -2.49   0.0132   0.0095
I:377             -0.317220    0.1119      -2.83   0.0047   0.0124
I:405             -0.227114    0.1121      -2.03   0.0431   0.0064
I:435              0.402637    0.1115       3.61   0.0003   0.0199
I:449             -0.231008    0.1116      -2.07   0.0388   0.0066
I:451             -0.397159    0.1122      -3.54   0.0004   0.0192
I:471             -0.237611    0.1124      -2.11   0.0349   0.0069
I:622              0.830964    0.1572       5.29   0.0000   0.0417
I:734             -4.31732     0.1250     -34.5    0.0000   0.6502
I:736             -8.12166     0.2271     -35.8    0.0000   0.6658
I:737             -7.34991     0.2293     -32.1    0.0000   0.6154
I:738             -3.75565     0.1648     -22.8    0.0000   0.4471
I:739             -2.11415     0.1889     -11.2    0.0000   0.1633
I:740              1.00149     0.1836       5.46   0.0000   0.0443
S1:28              0.722376    0.1927       3.75   0.0002   0.0214
S1:30              0.814422    0.2484       3.28   0.0011   0.0165
S1:32              0.691235    0.1939       3.57   0.0004   0.0194
S1:45             -0.531346    0.1553      -3.42   0.0007   0.0179
```

```
S1:60          0.108731    0.04221     2.58   0.0102   0.0102
S1:131        -0.319819    0.04588    -6.97   0.0000   0.0704
S1:295         0.314227    0.07914     3.97   0.0001   0.0240
S1:306        -0.158957    0.04822    -3.30   0.0010   0.0166
S1:318         0.103422    0.03634     2.85   0.0046   0.0125
S1:604         0.181414    0.05777     3.14   0.0018   0.0151
S1:621         0.365089    0.1167      3.13   0.0018   0.0150
S1:623        -0.357156    0.1144     -3.12   0.0019   0.0150
S1:648         0.162699    0.04301     3.78   0.0002   0.0218
S1:662         0.416811    0.1153      3.62   0.0003   0.0200
S1:663        -0.388324    0.1150     -3.38   0.0008   0.0174
S1:712        -0.184447    0.04758    -3.88   0.0001   0.0229
T1:27         -0.294073    0.1114     -2.64   0.0085   0.0107
T1:32          0.324968    0.1115      2.91   0.0037   0.0131
T1:42          0.0917000   0.02814     3.26   0.0012   0.0163
T1:49         -0.0728004   0.02452    -2.97   0.0031   0.0135
T1:186        -0.295628    0.1136     -2.60   0.0095   0.0104
T1:187         0.506349    0.2413      2.10   0.0362   0.0068
T1:188        -0.511841    0.1715     -2.98   0.0030   0.0137
T1:191         0.455030    0.05652     8.05   0.0000   0.0917
T1:197        -0.164541    0.01895    -8.68   0.0000   0.1051
T1:216         0.196945    0.06819     2.89   0.0040   0.0128
T1:217        -0.182505    0.06597    -2.77   0.0058   0.0118
T1:253        -0.287147    0.05940    -4.83   0.0000   0.0351
T1:255         0.769432    0.1772      4.34   0.0000   0.0285
T1:256        -0.480083    0.1276     -3.76   0.0002   0.0216
T1:269        -0.0395719   0.01118    -3.54   0.0004   0.0191
T1:284         0.0671472   0.01362     4.93   0.0000   0.0365
T1:294        -0.0337779   0.009579   -3.53   0.0005   0.0190
T1:538        -0.0191958   0.003144   -6.11   0.0000   0.0549
T1:552         0.0236104   0.004369    5.40   0.0000   0.0435
T1:589         0.223249    0.1171      1.91   0.0569   0.0056
T1:590        -0.588118    0.2273     -2.59   0.0099   0.0103
T1:591         0.363055    0.1170      3.10   0.0020   0.0148
T1:732        -5.23974     0.05776   -90.7    0.0000   0.9276
T1:734         7.41626     0.08206    90.4    0.0000   0.9271
T1:739        -2.18126     0.03282   -66.5    0.0000   0.8731

sigma          0.111021  RSS                 7.91303129
R^2            0.996158  F(86,642) =     1935 [0.000]**
Adj.R^2        0.995643  log-likelihood   614.287
no. of observations   729  no. of parameters    87
mean(UER)      5.99973  se(UER)         1.68195

AR 1-2 test:    F(2,640)  =   4.5895 [0.0105]*
ARCH 1-1 test:  F(1,727)  =   0.18294 [0.6690]
Normality test: Chi^2(2)  =   2.6650 [0.2638]
Hetero test:    F(72,650) =   0.83191 [0.8350]
RESET23 test:   F(2,640)  =   3.4507 [0.0323]*
Model   saved   to   C:\JBG\JGResearch\Palgrave   Business   Cycles\2020Q3\LEI   UER
11072020_files\Model UER AR1 LEIL12 IIS SIS TIS.pdf
Model   saved   to   C:\JBG\JGResearch\Palgrave   Business   Cycles\2020Q3\LEI   UER
11072020_files\Model UER AR1 LEIL12 IIS SIS TIS.pdf.gwg
```

The higher lags of the LEI variable alternate in signs and the one-period lag produces a lower RSS.

The application of impulse (IIS) saturation, the differenced indicator impulse (DIIS), and trend saturation variables (TIS) variables and one-period of lagged leading economic indicator, LEI, variable and Weekly Unemployment Claims (WkUNCL) time series in the Hendry OxMetrics methodology, we obtain normally distributed residuals and our model is more adequately fit, see the UER OxMetrics Estimation (25) estimation. The Residual Sum of Square, RSS, rises from 6.68 to 6.16.

```
UER OxMetrics Estimation (25) Modelling UER by OLS
The dataset is: C:\JBG\JGResearch\Palgrave Business Cycles\2020Q3\LEI UER 11072020.csv

       The estimation sample is: 13 - 741

                  Coefficient  Std.Error   t-value   t-prob  Part.R^2
UER_1              0.587949     0.02230     26.4     0.0000   0.5290
WkUNCL 1           0.00179660   0.0001511   11.9     0.0000   0.1858
Trend             -0.380823     0.1478      -2.58    0.0102   0.0106
Constant           286.409      109.5        2.62    0.0091   0.0109
LEI_1             -0.0325899    0.003296    -9.89    0.0000   0.1364
I:14               0.676524     0.1178       5.74    0.0000   0.0506
I:17               0.275647     0.1119       2.46    0.0140   0.0097
I:22              -0.436997     0.1268      -3.45    0.0006   0.0188
I:32               0.461905     0.1079       4.28    0.0000   0.0287
I:43               0.257000     0.1078       2.38    0.0174   0.0091
I:46               0.268675     0.1078       2.49    0.0129   0.0099
I:66              -0.301968     0.1056      -2.86    0.0044   0.0130
I:70              -0.293822     0.1058      -2.78    0.0057   0.0123
I:75               0.300341     0.1067       2.81    0.0050   0.0126
I:142              0.284350     0.1063       2.67    0.0077   0.0114
I:177             -0.289734     0.1056      -2.74    0.0062   0.0120
I:188              0.322453     0.1091       2.96    0.0032   0.0139
I:190              0.312563     0.1079       2.90    0.0039   0.0134
I:192              0.353928     0.1135       3.12    0.0019   0.0155
I:193             -0.512800     0.1194      -4.29    0.0000   0.0289
I:217              0.187 119    0. 1077      1.74    0.08 29   0.0048
I:221              0.259 260    0. 1096      2.37    0.0183   0.0090
I:234              0.341 608    0. 1066      3.20    0.00 14   0.0163
I:247              0.236 534    0. 1073      2.21    0.02 78   0.0078
I:252              0.226 020    0. 1105      2.05    0.04 13   0.0067
I:257             -0.340 081    0. 1188      -2.86    0.00 44   0.0131
I:263             -0.451 113    0. 1343      -3.36    0.00 08   0.0179
I:267             -0.229 067    0. 1101      -2.08    0.03 79   0.0069
I:217              0.187119     0.1077       1.74    0.0829   0.0048
I:221              0.259260     0.1096       2.37    0.0183   0.0090
I:234              0.341608     0.1066       3.20    0.0014   0.0163
I:247              0.236534     0.1073       2.21    0.0278   0.0078
I:252              0.226020     0.1105       2.05    0.0413   0.0067
I:257             -0.340081     0.1188      -2.86    0.0044   0.0131
```

I:263	-0.451113	0.1343	-3.36	0.0008	0.0179
I:267	-0.229067	0.1101	-2.08	0.0379	0.0069
I:270	-0.447234	0.1081	-4.14	0.0000	0.0269
I:286	0.348923	0.1076	3.24	0.0012	0.0167
I:294	-0.673975	0.1113	-6.06	0.0000	0.0560
I:735	7.91026	0.1906	41.5	0.0000	0.7356
I:739	-1.05758	0.1283	-8.24	0.0000	0.0988
S1:20	-0.489817	0.1075	-4.56	0.0000	0.0325
S1:23	0.298609	0.1060	2.82	0.0050	0.0126
S1:30	0.554428	0.07386	7.51	0.0000	0.0834
S1:46	-0.122340	0.03916	-3.12	0.0019	0.0155
S1:73	0.298872	0.04371	6.84	0.0000	0.0702
S1:132	-0.148611	0.06544	-2.27	0.0235	0.0083
S1:151	0.165462	0.06033	2.74	0.0063	0.0120
S1:226	0.178735	0.06348	2.82	0.0050	0.0126
S1:264	0.348380	0.09686	3.60	0.0003	0.0205
S1:295	0.622912	0.08026	7.76	0.0000	0.0887
S1:323	0.234684	0.1093	2.15	0.0321	0.0074
S1:324	-0.735251	0.1463	-5.03	0.0000	0.0392
S1:325	0.296822	0.1102	2.69	0.0072	0.0116
T1:30	0.0468194	0.01300	3.60	0.0003	0.0205
T1:128	-0.0358872	0.005232	-6.86	0.0000	0.0706
T1:151	0.0397925	0.005524	7.20	0.0000	0.0773
T1:188	-0.248350	0.02573	-9.65	0.0000	0.1309
T1:192	0.272830	0.03042	8.97	0.0000	0.1150
T1:204	-0.0486586	0.01454	-3.35	0.0009	0.0178
T1:213	0.0891594	0.02353	3.79	0.0002	0.0227
T1:217	-0.0620323	0.01738	-3.57	0.0004	0.0202
T1:252	-0.220315	0.03330	-6.62	0.0000	0.0661
T1:255	0.345149	0.05609	6.15	0.0000	0.0576
T1:259	-0.307797	0.06282	-4.90	0.0000	0.0373
T1:262	0.138841	0.04210	3.30	0.0010	0.0173
T1:295	0.0778517	0.01332	5.84	0.0000	0.0523
T1:304	-0.402782	0.1170	-3.44	0.0006	0.0188
T1:305	0.545428	0.1578	3.46	0.0006	0.0189
T1:307	-0.194741	0.06151	-3.17	0.0016	0.0159
T1:316	0.0290265	0.008453	3.43	0.0006	0.0187
T1:357	-0.0260645	0.003217	-8.10	0.0000	0.0959
T1:392	-0.0592402	0.009557	-6.20	0.0000	0.0584
T1:400	0.142552	0.03192	4.47	0.0000	0.0312
T1:404	-0.329023	0.1081	-3.04	0.0024	0.0147
T1:405	0.271160	0.08758	3.10	0.0020	0.0153
T1:433	-0.439302	0.1107	-3.97	0.0001	0.0248
T1:434	0.773832	0.2168	3.57	0.0004	0.0202
T1:435	-0.343481	0.1189	-2.89	0.0040	0.0133
T1:448	-0.242848	0.1188	-2.04	0.0413	0.0067
T1:449	0.726000	0.2372	3.06	0.0023	0.0149
T1:450	-0.819434	0.2358	-3.47	0.0005	0.0191
T1:451	0.332062	0.1147	2.90	0.0039	0.0134
T1:469	0.305808	0.1146	2.67	0.0078	0.0114
T1:470	-0.628684	0.2158	-2.91	0.0037	0.0135
T1:471	0.325654	0.1123	2.90	0.0039	0.0134
T1:494	-0.192197	0.07979	-2.41	0.0163	0.0093
T1:495	0.229452	0.09049	2.54	0.0115	0.0103
T1:502	-0.269148	0.1128	-2.39	0.0174	0.0091
T1:503	0.308935	0.1246	2.48	0.0134	0.0098
T1:507	-0.205319	0.05286	-3.88	0.0001	0.0238

T1:510	0.103903	0.02862	3.63	0.0003	0.0209
T1:536	0.0192190	0.002941	6.53	0.0000	0.0645
T1:595	-0.232053	0.07157	-3.24	0.0012	0.0167
T1:596	0.167796	0.07483	2.24	0.0253	0.0081
T1:608	0.0563033	0.01298	4.34	0.0000	0.0295
T1:620	-0.410378	0.1185	-3.46	0.0006	0.0190
T1:621	1.09896	0.2268	4.85	0.0000	0.0365
T1:622	-0.763798	0.1431	-5.34	0.0000	0.0440
T1:626	0.107946	0.02628	4.11	0.0000	0.0265
T1:643	-0.0614637	0.02625	-2.34	0.0195	0.0088
T1:647	0.267770	0.1176	2.28	0.0231	0.0083
T1:648	-0.232220	0.1076	-2.16	0.0313	0.0075
T1:656	0.306777	0.1099	2.79	0.0054	0.0124
T1:657	-0.358541	0.1257	-2.85	0.0045	0.0130
T1:661	0.541862	0.1500	3.61	0.0003	0.0207
T1:662	-0.816900	0.2273	-3.59	0.0004	0.0204
T1:663	0.344055	0.1164	2.96	0.0032	0.0139
T1:676	-0.0113826	0.005908	-1.93	0.0545	0.0060
T1:711	-0.273425	0.1091	-2.51	0.0125	0.0100
T1:712	0.533897	0.2214	2.41	0.0162	0.0093
T1:713	-0.301099	0.1362	-2.21	0.0274	0.0078
T1:718	0.0472086	0.02251	2.10	0.0364	0.0071
T1:732	-0.959673	0.1171	-8.20	0.0000	0.0979
T1:733	3.50024	0.3286	10.7	0.0000	0.1549
T1:735	-4.40927	0.4965	-8.88	0.0000	0.1130
T1:737	1.66494	0.2210	7.53	0.0000	0.0840
T1:739	0.572695	0.1930	2.97	0.0031	0.0140

sigma	0.10338	RSS		6.6155155
R^2	0.996788	F(109,619) =	1762	[0.000]**
Adj.R^2	0.996222	log-likelihood		679.566
no. of observations	729	no. of parameters		110
mean(A0M043)	5.99973	se(A0M043)		1.68195

AR 1-2 test:	F(2,617)	=	4.2170 [0.0152]*
ARCH 1-1 test:	F(1,727)	=	0.11784 [0.7315]
Normality test:	**Chi^2(2)**	**=**	**0.35944 [0.8355]**
Hetero test:	F(112,584)=		0.96057 [0.5953]
RESET23 test:	F(2,617)	=	0.55195 [0.5761]

Model saved to C:\JBG\JGResearch\Palgrave Business Cycles\2020Q3\LEI UER 11072020_files\Model UER AR1 LEIL1 WkunclL1 IIS SIS TIS.pdf
Model saved to C:\JBG\JGResearch\Palgrave Business Cycles\2020Q3\LEI UER 11072020_files\Model UER AR1 LEIL1 WkunclL1 IIS SIS TIS.pdf.gwg

The reader notes that the LEI variable estimated coefficient is negative, and the weekly unemployment variable is positive, as expected. The estimated residuals are normally distributed and the UER OxMetrics Estimation (25) is a preferred estimation.

The estimation of IIS, DIIS, and TIS saturation variables and twelve-periods of lagged leading economic indicator, LEI, variable and Weekly Unemployment Claims (WkUNCL) time series in the Hendry OxMetrics methodology, produces an estimated models with normally distributed residuals. The model, reported in Estimation (26), is more adequately fit.

```
UER OxMetrics Estimation(26) Modelling UER by OLS
The dataset is: C:\JBG\JGResearch\TCB MZTT 1959 2020.csv
```

The estimation sample is: 13 - 741

	Coefficient	Std.Error	t-value	t-prob	Part.R^2
UER_1	0.921307	0.007293	126.	0.0000	0.9614
Trend	-0.000874548	0.0003432	-2.55	0.0111	0.0100
LEI_2	-0.0202502	0.003734	-5.42	0.0000	0.0439
LEI_5	0.0128916	0.004029	3.20	0.0014	0.0157
WkUNCL_1	0.00170038	3.565e-05	47.7	0.0000	0.7804
WkUNCL_4	-0.000780162	4.538e-05	-17.2	0.0000	0.3159
WkUNCL_5	0.000417559	4.657e-05	8.97	0.0000	0.1116
DI:31	0.231472	0.07683	3.01	0.0027	0.0140
DI:53	0.240194	0.07672	3.13	0.0018	0.0151
DI:74	0.289495	0.07672	3.77	0.0002	0.0218
DI:131	-0.231182	0.08859	-2.61	0.0093	0.0105
DI:132	-0.301288	0.08859	-3.40	0.0007	0.0178
DI:143	0.212391	0.08862	2.40	0.0168	0.0089
DI:144	0.270911	0.08860	3.06	0.0023	0.0144
DI:154	-0.202484	0.07672	-2.64	0.0085	0.0108
DI:169	-0.204119	0.07671	-2.66	0.0080	0.0109
DI:191	0.342367	0.1103	3.11	0.0020	0.0148
DI:192	0.638741	0.1585	4.03	0.0001	0.0248
DI:208	0.201022	0.07672	2.62	0.0090	0.0106
DI:211	0.174327	0.08860	1.97	0.0496	0.0060
DI:212	0.177007	0.08860	2.00	0.0462	0.0062
DI:218	0.193226	0.07672	2.52	0.0120	0.0098
DI:222	0.269343	0.07678	3.51	0.0005	0.0189
DI:227	0.193883	0.07671	2.53	0.0117	0.0099
DI:235	0.300325	0.07674	3.91	0.0001	0.0234
DI:245	-0.196712	0.07674	-2.56	0.0106	0.0102
DI:248	0.229428	0.07675	2.99	0.0029	0.0138
DI:295	-0.409681	0.07674	-5.34	0.0000	0.0426
DI:306	-0.241609	0.07671	-3.15	0.0017	0.0153
DI:317	-0.154893	0.07671	-2.02	0.0439	0.0063
DI:325	-0.402322	0.07672	-5.24	0.0000	0.0412
DI:375	-0.164817	0.07672	-2.15	0.0321	0.0072
DI:406	-0.231520	0.07672	-3.02	0.0026	0.0140
DI:450	-0.246498	0.07672	-3.21	0.0014	0.0159
DI:581	-0.158606	0.07671	-2.07	0.0391	0.0066
DI:592	-0.236179	0.07672	-3.08	0.0022	0.0146
DI:596	0.165538	0.07677	2.16	0.0314	0.0072
DI:623	0.412385	0.07673	5.37	0.0000	0.0432
DI:649	0.202539	0.07672	2.64	0.0085	0.0108
DI:664	-0.272934	0.07675	-3.56	0.0004	0.0194
DI:735	0.919113	0.1085	8.47	0.0000	0.1008
DI:736	7.13848	0.1079	66.1	0.0000	0.8723
I:13	0.440506	0.1660	2.65	0.0081	0.0109
I:15	0.932459	0.1298	7.19	0.0000	0.0747
I:22	0.556903	0.1185	4.70	0.0000	0.0333
I:24	0.522629	0.1296	4.03	0.0001	0.0248
I:33	0.274590	0.1133	2.42	0.0156	0.0091
I:44	0.378949	0.1197	3.17	0.0016	0.0154
I:47	0.331479	0.1231	2.69	0.0073	0.0112
I:48	-0.267656	0.1251	-2.14	0.0327	0.0071
I:51	-0.275586	0.1168	-2.36	0.0186	0.0086
I:67	-0.246501	0.1097	-2.25	0.0250	0.0078
I:71	-0.245369	0.1096	-2.24	0.0255	0.0078
I:193	1.18533	0.1973	6.01	0.0000	0.0534
I:195	0.242673	0.1106	2.19	0.0286	0.0075

```
I:210            0.246666    0.1106     2.23   0.0260   0.0077
I:256            0.577928    0.1120     5.16   0.0000   0.0399
I:257            0.395322    0.1124     3.52   0.0005   0.0189
I:264           -0.616509    0.1715    -3.59   0.0004   0.0198
I:289           -0.261446    0.1098    -2.38   0.0176   0.0088
I:353            0.263597    0.1090     2.42   0.0159   0.0091
I:436            0.409600    0.1087     3.77   0.0002   0.0217
I:452           -0.364358    0.1088    -3.35   0.0009   0.0172
I:472           -0.357662    0.1089    -3.28   0.0011   0.0166
I:497            0.242278    0.1089     2.22   0.0265   0.0077
I:509           -0.321887    0.1094    -2.94   0.0034   0.0134
I:543            0.234834    0.1090     2.15   0.0317   0.0072
I:678           -0.221274    0.1089    -2.03   0.0426   0.0064
I:714            0.240931    0.1092     2.21   0.0277   0.0075
I:738           -4.66310     0.1527    -30.5   0.0000   0.5929
T1:17            0.147544    0.04286    3.44   0.0006   0.0182
T1:24           -0.252306    0.1159    -2.18   0.0298   0.0074
T1:25            0.255199    0.1068     2.39   0.0172   0.0088
T1:37           -0.351837    0.09575   -3.67   0.0003   0.0207
T1:38            0.358306    0.1028     3.48   0.0005   0.0186
T1:45           -0.166375    0.04990   -3.33   0.0009   0.0171
T1:48            0.182825    0.05624    3.25   0.0012   0.0162
T1:52           -0.0523997   0.02213   -2.37   0.0182   0.0087
T1:196           0.144294    0.04054    3.56   0.0004   0.0194
T1:197          -0.145107    0.04153   -3.49   0.0005   0.0187
T1:234           0.00731190  0.003014   2.43   0.0155   0.0091
T1:262          -0.500468    0.1394    -3.59   0.0004   0.0197
T1:263           0.648337    0.1830     3.54   0.0004   0.0192
T1:267          -0.687917    0.1659    -4.15   0.0000   0.0262
T1:268           0.844189    0.1890     4.47   0.0000   0.0302
T1:270          -0.793267    0.1705    -4.65   0.0000   0.0327
T1:271           0.490655    0.1075     4.56   0.0000   0.0315
T1:293          -0.00746525  0.001973  -3.78   0.0002   0.0219
T1:735           0.288968    0.03223    8.96   0.0000   0.1116
T1:740          -0.287283    0.03200   -8.98   0.0000   0.1119
```

```
sigma                0.108486   RSS                  7.53228744
R^2                  0.996344   F(89,640) =       1960 [0.000]**
Adj.R^2              0.995836   log-likelihood         633.629
no. of observations       730   no. of parameters          90
mean(UER)            5.99863    se(UER)            1.68106
```

```
AR 1-2 test:      F(2,638)  =   2.2730 [0.1038]
ARCH 1-1 test:    F(1,728)  =   1.7539 [0.1858]
Normality test:   Chi^2(2)  =   1.8503 [0.3965]
Hetero test:      F(107,592)=   0.65487 [0.9963]
RESET23 test:     F(2,638)  =   0.52386 [0.5925]
```
Model saved to C:\JBG\JGResearch\Palgrave Business Cycles\Model UER LEI and Wkuncl L12
IIS DIIS TIS 1959 2020.pdf
Model saved to C:\JBG\JGResearch\Palgrave Business Cycles\Model UER LEI and Wkuncl L12
IIS DIIS TIS 1959 2020.pdf.gwg

In Estimation (26), Autometrics retains only 2 and 5 months lag in the LEI and 1,4, and 5-month lags in the WKUNCL time series in the U.S. unemployment model, a result reported in Dhrymes (2017). The net estimated LEI coefficients are negative and the net weekly unemployment claims are positive, as expected. However, the RSS rises from 6.61 to 7.53. Hence, the OxMetrics estimated Eq. (7.25), with one-period lags of the LEI and WKUNCL time series are optimal. What is the real advantage of an automatic time series system such as Autometrics? The researcher can estimate naïve AR(1) models, with and without outliers. One can then apply Autometrics for model validation and /or obtain a better estimate, one with normal residuals. Second, the researcher can select a larger number of lags and Auto-metrics will retain the statistically significant variables.[10] The author should ask the reader a most important question: what more should a practitioner need than SAS and OxMetrics to estimate regression and time series models?

7.8 Forecasting the Unemployment Series with Leading Indicators and Adaptive Learning

Our analysis so far evolved around the idea that automatic time series modeling can help to both uncover the underlying relationships that economics presume exist among variable of interest to practitioners and to account for the subtle nuances that come from the presence of outliers and structural breaks. However, once a practitioner is satisfied that the relationship under consideration is there one is tempted (if not usually required) to produce a forecast about the future path of the series that enters as the dependent variable. Thus, a forecasting exercise is certainly the natural next step and, it might be argued, is possibly more straightforward to benchmark. With the latter statement we mean something well understood in the literature of forecasting: an explanatory variable that has significant presence in the fit of a model should usually help in reducing the mean-squared measure of out-of-sample forecasts even when the model used is relatively simpler to the model used for the in-sample fit. In this section we present the results of a rolling window forecasting exercise where we illustrate the practical usefulness of our previous analysis across two themes: first, we show that the inclusion of either of our two previous leading indicator variables (the composite leading indicator and the weekly unemployment claims) are useful in providing either on-par performance or performance enhancements compared to standard benchmarks (in the context of linear forecasting models as linear were the in-sample fit models before); second, we show that the use of adaptive learning forecasting, a new method recently proposed by Kyriazi et al. (2019), helps to improve even more the forecasting enhancements of the first theme.

Our forecasting exercise is structured in a simple, and practically relevant, fashion: we use the monthly unemployment data and two rolling

---

[10] Guerard et al. (2020) reported that the LEI time series was an useful input in the real GDP time series and changes in the U.S. unemployment rate models estimated with Autometrics during the 1959–2018 period. The Autometrics algorithm of the OxMetrics package has been developed in Hendry (1986, 2000), Castle and Shepard (2009), Hendry and Nielsen (2007), Castle, Doornik, and Hendry (2013), Hendry and Doornik (2014), and Castle, Clements, and Hendry (2015), and Castle and Hendry (2019).

windows of 60 and 120 months and a number of standard models, univariate and bivariate, to evaluate the forecasting performance on the unemployment series. The forecasts are computed on models based on the differenced data and then the differencing operation is reversed for the forecast evaluation against the actual values of the unemployment rate. We summarize our results in the table that follows and evaluate the forecasts with their (root) mean-squared error, mean absolute error, and the test statistics of the Mincer-Zarnowitz evaluating regression.[11] For easier readability we provide results for the best univariate and best bivariate models (in terms of their root mean-squared error rankings relative to the naïve benchmark), the adaptive averaging autoregressive model ADA-AR (Singer & Feder, 1999)—which is not included in the individual model ranking—as well as the best adaptive learning forecast ADL—the latter is computed by the combination of the best two models (which might be different if the best two models are not the top univariate and top bivariate that we report, e.g. we might have that two univariate models are the top ones) (Table 7.1).

The results from the table tell a consistent story all along. Let's point out the salient points of our forecasting exercise:

i. All models easily beat the no-change, naïve, benchmark, by about 25% to 30%, so that the unemployment rate is clearly forecastable.
ii. The autoregressive models are extremely tough to beat, by a wide margin, within the class of linear models
iii. Autoregressive adaptive averaging tends to work and occasionally improve forecast efficiency but cannot solely be relied upon, especially on the presence of bivariate models and adaptive learning forecasts.
iv. The impact of the bivariate models, that account for the explanatory variables, is clearly present in the larger rolling window—not an unsurprising result as the estimation of parameters requires a relatively larger sample.[12]

The reader is referred to Guerard, Thomakos, and Kyrizai (2019) for plots of the rolling window estimates, and associated p-values, from the VAR(AIC) model using the 120-months rolling window: we can that the correct signs are present in the estimates and that the p-values indicate the explanatory

---

[11] For details on the evaluation approach of these tables see Kyriazi et al. (2019).

[12] In the interest of completion on the performance of the bivariate models, and given that only two appear (BMA and VAR(AIC)) we report the evaluation values for the BMA on the 120-month rolling window for the composite leading indicator (RMSE $= 0.754$, MAE $= 0.760$, $d_0 = 0.112$, $d_1 = 0.981$ and $p_F = 0.001$) and for the VAR(AIC) for the 60-month rolling window for the weekly unemployment claims VAR(p) (RMSE $= 0.769$, MAE $= 0.785$, $d_0 = 0.182$, $d_1 = 0.969$ and $p_F = 0.000$).

Table 7.1 Forecasting performance comparison, US unemployment rate, 1959–2018

Model	RMSE	MAE	d_0	d_1	p_F
Composite leading indicator, 60 months rolling window					
AR(4)	0.746	0.730	0.067	0.988	0.037
BMA	0.747	0.748	0.098	0.983	0.001
ADA-AR	0.740	0.721	0.044	0.992	0.200
ADL	0.728	0.722	0.079	0.986	0.007
Composite leading indicator, 120 months rolling window					
AR(4)	0.734	0.729	0.089	0.986	0.009
VAR(AIC)	0.702	0.714	0.025	0.996	0.674
ADA-AR	0.742	0.728	0.070	0.989	0.043
ADL	0.699	0.717	0.036	0.994	0.431
Weekly unemployment claims, 60 months rolling window					
AR(2)	0.746	0.731	0.067	0.989	0.031
BMA	0.774	0.765	0.134	0.976	0.000
ADA-AR	0.740	0.722	0.068	0.988	0.026
ADL	0.744	0.727	0.072	0.987	0.018
Weekly unemployment claims, 120 months rolling window					
AR(4)	0.725	0.714	0.078	0.986	0.007
VAR(AIC)	0.711	0.720	0.109	0.981	0.000
ADA-AR	0.729	0.715	0.059	0.990	0.052
ADL	0.701	0.702	0.091	0.984	0.000

Notes:

a. RMSE and MAE are the root mean-squared and the mean absolute forecast errors relative to the naïve (no-change) model

b. d_0 and d_1 are the estimates from the Mincer-Zarnowitz regression of the actual value on the forecast and under the forecast efficiency assumption these estimates should not differ significantly from 0 and 1 respectively.

c. p_F is the p-value of the joint F-test for the null hypothesis of $d_0 = 0$ and $d_1 = 1$, computed using a HAC covariance matrix.

d. AR(p) is a univariate autoregressive model of order p, BMA is the bivariate trend-stationary Theta model, ADA-AR is the adaptive averaging AR model, VAR(AIC) is the bivariate vector autoregressive model of order selected by the AIC and ADL is the adaptive learning forecast.

power of the associated variables, the composite leading indicator and the weekly unemployment claims—we note that the results of the plots tally very well with the results from the forecasting exercise in that the relationship is stronger with the weekly unemployment claims than with the leading indicator.

v .The composite leading indicator tends to produce more efficient forecasts in terms of larger p_F values, even though the weekly unemployment claims tend to produce slightly better forecasting performance.

vi .The adaptive learning forecast provides RMSE improvements in all cases but one (where is one par with the best model) as it was designed to do, and thus is the top performing forecast in the table—whose efficiency is either better overall or better from the worst of its two component forecasts. It would be interesting to see how adaptive learning performs if the input models that the method uses have one or more of the nonlinear models used by the MZTT study.

7.9   Concluding Remarks and Extensions

In this chapter, we applied the SAS and OxMetrics Hendry and Doornik automatic time series PCGive (OxMetrics) methodology to several well-studied macroeconomics series, real GDP and the unemployment rate. We report that the OxMetrics and AutoMetrics system substantially reduced the residual sum of squares measures relative to a traditional variation on the random walk with drift model. The modeling process of including the Leading Economic Indicator in forecasting real GDP has been addressed before, but our results are more statistically significant. A similar conclusion is found for the impact of the LEI and weekly unemployment claims series leading the unemployment rate series. Breaks in time series must be estimated. We complemented the OxMetrics analysis with an application of the rolling window forecasting analysis which produced additional validation of the LEI and weekly unemployment claims series and the unemployment time series. We provided results for the best univariate and best bivariate models, in terms of their root mean-squared error rankings relative to the naïve benchmark, and the adaptive averaging autoregressive model ADA-AR and the adaptive learning forecast, ADL, produced the smallest root mean square errors and lowest mean absolute errors. Such results should excite practitioners!

Appendix: OxMetrics Modeling in the COVID Period

What has been the impact of the COVID period on the unemployment rate in the U.S.? We offer a set of OxMetrics automatic time series models to answer that question, using TCB LEI data, as the data became known in January 2020, the author subscribed to the TCB database, as Director of Quantitative Research at McKinley Capital Management, in Anchorage, Alaska. Let us compare the AR1 and "optimal" automatic time series model estimated with OxMetrics in this Chapter.

```
Ox Professional version 8.10 (Windows_64/U) (C) J.A. Doornik, 1994-2019

---- PcGive 15.10 session started at 6:54:41 on 1-03-2021 ----

Appendix 7 Estimation (1) Modelling UER AR1 by OLS 1959 - 2019
        The dataset is: C:\JBG\JGResearch\Univ Washington CFRM\LEI UER WkUNCL.csv
        The estimation sample is: 2 - 731

                   Coefficient  Std.Error  t-value  t-prob Part.R^2
UER_1                 0.995585   0.004154     240.   0.0000   0.9875
Constant              0.0321253  0.02745      1.17   0.2422   0.0019
Trend              -2.51544e-05  3.141e-05   -0.801  0.4235   0.0009

sigma                 0.17849  RSS                  23.1612975
R^2                   0.987549  F(2,727) =   2.883e+04 [0.000]**
Adj.R^2               0.987515  log-likelihood         223.63
no. of observations       730  no. of parameters           3
mean(UER)             5.96014  se(UER)               1.59744
When the log-likelihood constant is NOT included:
AIC                  -3.44234  SC                     -3.42347
HQ                   -3.43506  FPE                  0.0319897
When the log-likelihood constant is included:
AIC                  -0.604466  SC                    -0.585590
HQ                   -0.597183  FPE                   0.546366

AR 1-2 test:      F(2,725)  =    32.348 [0.0000]**
ARCH 1-1 test:    F(1,728)  =    48.528 [0.0000]**
Normality test:   Chi^2(2)  =    52.234 [0.0000]**
Hetero test:      F(4,725)  =     9.9857 [0.0000]**
Hetero-X test:    F(5,724)  =     8.7045 [0.0000]**
RESET23 test:     F(2,725)  =     0.12553 [0.8820]
```

The AR1 model fails all OxMetrics diagnostics tests. The model is not adequately fitted for the 1959–2019 period (Chart 7.1).

Let us now re-estimate the preferred OxMetrics Automatic Time Series Model of UER in 1959–2018 with IIS, DIIS, TIS, LEI, and WkUNCL, lagged one-period for the 1959–2019 period.

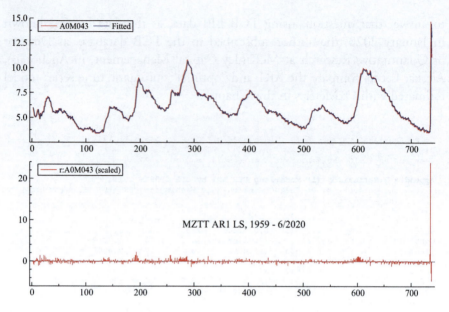

Chart 7.1 Residuals indicate that the model is not adequately estimated

Appendix 7 Estimation (2) Modelling UER with the OxMerics of 1959- 2019.

Robust standard errors

	Coefficients	SE	HACSE	HCSE
UER_1	0.85488	0.012581	0.015093	0.012783
Trend	0.0018025	0.00037709	0.00042823	0.00038342
LEI_6	-0.011594	0.0022090	0.0025124	0.0022732
WkUNCL_1	0.0025801	0.00015417	0.00017797	0.00016743
WkUNCL_4	-0.00080785	0.00018747	0.00021363	0.00018974
WkUNCL_9	0.00043224	0.00014552	0.00014766	0.00014064
DI:14	-0.37509	0.081988	0.0078721	0.015692
DI:15	0.24436	0.082597	0.013962	0.018823
DI:17	-0.16760	0.071017	0.0041577	0.0083903
DI:21	-0.35983	0.070993	0.027904	0.073428
DI:23	-0.23913	0.071052	0.040599	0.10702
DI:26	0.17237	0.071018	0.017301	0.045381
DI:31	0.26327	0.070990	0.015918	0.042143
DI:33	0.28397	0.082051	0.038180	0.078624
DI:34	0.22446	0.082102	0.038320	0.078662
DI:38	-0.19024	0.071001	0.031902	0.084634
DI:43	-0.19411	0.070979	0.017033	0.045067
DI:46	-0.23048	0.070986	0.011679	0.030594
DI:48	-0.17183	0.070992	0.0019055	0.0024554
DI:50	0.17689	0.070993	0.0068019	0.017225
DI:59	0.17139	0.071012	0.020042	0.052760
DI:66	0.18079	0.070988	0.011362	0.029836
DI:71	-0.20469	0.071038	0.0043805	0.0087623
DI:74	0.28437	0.070995	0.0033602	0.0080577
DI:95	-0.14055	0.071016	0.018905	0.049683
DI:131	-0.21463	0.082006	0.018717	0.037841
DI:132	-0.28424	0.082001	0.018708	0.037834
DI:166	0.18888	0.070991	0.0018075	0.0014483
DI:169	-0.20235	0.071001	0.014643	0.038345
DI:178	-0.19546	0.070992	0.0038030	0.0090493
DI:193	0.76763	0.14063	0.032776	0.060971
DI:208	0.21169	0.071004	0.011316	0.029149
DI:222	0.24618	0.071498	0.026838	0.065509
DI:227	0.16592	0.071332	0.027895	0.070818
DI:235	0.30459	0.071091	0.010996	0.026560
DI:238	-0.13201	0.071067	0.0075195	0.016886
DI:248	0.21643	0.071437	0.017290	0.039350
DI:257	0.26489	0.072029	0.033792	0.074714
DI:264	-0.27095	0.072386	0.013864	0.024537
DI:269	0.35028	0.083642	0.017352	0.030356
DI:270	0.37959	0.083728	0.017240	0.030562
DI:289	-0.18890	0.071026	0.0075020	0.019222
DI:296	0.22485	0.071312	0.023355	0.060283
DI:305	-0.22197	0.081984	0.011254	0.023086
DI:306	-0.34766	0.081982	0.011394	0.023083
DI:308	0.13954	0.071040	0.010880	0.027436
DI:311	-0.16999	0.071102	0.021665	0.056005
DI:325	-0.40176	0.070998	0.037521	0.099026
DI:346	0.13193	0.070985	0.0086559	0.022774
DI:352	-0.22715	0.071048	0.0060454	0.012540
DI:356	0.17120	0.070991	0.0018969	0.0024180
DI:363	-0.17166	0.071021	0.016849	0.044024
DI:378	-0.22173	0.071038	0.020382	0.053192
DI:388	-0.17497	0.071066	0.045054	0.12034
DI:406	-0.24308	0.071186	0.0065450	0.0088587
DI:418	0.15464	0.070988	0.022100	0.058582

DI:436	0.28289	0.071026	0.035773	0.094449
DI:451	0.28643	0.071069	0.020420	0.053224
DI:461	-0.14227	0.070997	0.0088298	0.023175
DI:496	-0.19069	0.070995	0.019188	0.050476
DI:529	-0.15780	0.071008	0.022409	0.059064
DI:577	0.13803	0.070992	0.0020213	0.0037727
DI:592	-0.23605	0.070999	0.0049809	0.012151
DI:677	0.21664	0.071017	0.013512	0.035259
DI:706	-0.12947	0.071009	0.0096733	0.024994
DI:713	-0.17885	0.071003	0.0037906	0.0088266
I:143	0.24649	0.10202	0.012010	0.018802
I:189	0.24184	0.10384	0.016948	0.028832
I:191	0.22189	0.10570	0.018250	0.026460
I:193	-0.57639	0.22348	0.058048	0.10561
I:245	-0.34711	0.10283	0.016695	0.020786
I:256	0.53119	0.10500	0.023920	0.031582
I:295	-0.51443	0.10320	0.026100	0.024515
I:472	-0.34064	0.10092	0.0094537	0.010311
I:509	-0.26623	0.10142	0.014229	0.014750
I:597	-0.25063	0.10262	0.020920	0.021999
I:623	0.59767	0.11081	0.015805	0.033965
I:649	0.21103	0.10286	0.017796	0.024913
I:664	-0.36231	0.10162	0.015588	0.017583
T1:111	-0.0064843	0.0017389	0.0013140	0.0017246
T1:132	0.0064641	0.0020272	0.0012827	0.0020670
T1:189	-0.11767	0.027201	0.012288	0.019338
T1:193	0.27013	0.055860	0.024933	0.036010
T1:197	-0.16145	0.032101	0.014931	0.020686
T1:217	0.16731	0.056118	0.038328	0.066487
T1:218	-0.15816	0.054378	0.037844	0.064647
T1:254	0.067673	0.026180	0.024330	0.026184
T1:257	-0.10716	0.041138	0.038913	0.038888
T1:263	0.097660	0.040443	0.031015	0.027988
T1:267	-0.12478	0.042077	0.023227	0.024346
T1:271	0.066970	0.018464	0.010164	0.011100
T1:528	-0.0035839	0.00047804	0.00046893	0.00048906
T1:604	0.14744	0.062046	0.047731	0.058015
T1:605	-0.14986	0.065631	0.049199	0.060719
T1:621	0.12862	0.049662	0.019474	0.037050
T1:623	-0.23422	0.074073	0.025625	0.051332
T1:626	0.11463	0.031405	0.013219	0.022932
T1:657	0.073872	0.041306	0.036697	0.045441
T1:658	-0.078190	0.039988	0.035802	0.044024

	Coefficients	t-SE	t-HACSE	t-HCSE
UER_1	0.85488	67.950	56.641	66.876
Trend	0.0018025	4.7801	4.2093	4.7012
LEI_6	-0.011594	-5.2486	-4.6148	-5.1003
WkUNCL_1	0.0025801	16.735	14.497	15.410
WkUNCL_4	-0.00080785	-4.3092	-3.7816	-4.2578
WkUNCL_9	0.00043224	2.9703	2.9273	3.0735
DI:14	-0.37509	-4.5749	-47.648	-23.903
DI:15	0.24436	2.9585	17.502	12.982
DI:17	-0.16760	-2.3600	-40.311	-19.976
DI:21	-0.35983	-5.0684	-12.895	-4.9004
DI:23	-0.23913	-3.3656	-5.8900	-2.2345
DI:26	0.17237	2.4272	9.9633	3.7984
DI:31	0.26327	3.7086	16.539	6.2470
DI:33	0.28397	3.4609	7.4376	3.6117
DI:34	0.22446	2.7340	5.8576	2.8535
DI:38	-0.19024	-2.6794	-5.9633	-2.2478
DI:43	-0.19411	-2.7348	-11.396	-4.3072
DI:46	-0.23048	-3.2469	-19.735	-7.5337

DI:48	-0.17183	-2.4204	-90.177	-69.981
DI:50	0.17689	2.4917	26.006	10.269
DI:59	0.17139	2.4135	8.5516	3.2485
DI:66	0.18079	2.5468	15.913	6.0594
DI:71	-0.20469	-2.8814	-46.728	-23.361
DI:74	0.28437	4.0055	84.629	35.292
DI:95	-0.14055	-1.9791	-7.4344	-2.8289
DI:131	-0.21463	-2.6173	-11.468	-5.6720
DI:132	-0.28424	-3.4663	-15.194	-7.5128
DI:166	0.18888	2.6605	104.50	130.41
DI:169	-0.20235	-2.8499	-13.819	-5.2771
DI:178	-0.19546	-2.7533	-51.397	-21.600
DI:193	0.76763	5.4586	23.420	12.590
DI:208	0.21169	2.9814	18.707	7.2624
DI:222	0.24618	3.4432	9.1729	3.7580
DI:227	0.16592	2.3260	5.9479	2.3429
DI:235	0.30459	4.2845	27.700	11.468
DI:238	-0.13201	-1.8575	-17.555	-7.8174
DI:248	0.21643	3.0296	12.517	5.5001
DI:257	0.26489	3.6775	7.8387	3.5454
DI:264	-0.27095	-3.7431	-19.544	-11.042
DI:269	0.35028	4.1878	20.186	11.539
DI:270	0.37959	4.5336	22.018	12.420
DI:289	-0.18890	-2.6596	-25.180	-9.8270
DI:296	0.22485	3.1530	9.6275	3.7298
DI:305	-0.22197	-2.7075	-19.723	-9.6151
DI:306	-0.34766	-4.2407	-30.512	-15.062
DI:308	0.13954	1.9642	12.825	5.0860
DI:311	-0.16999	-2.3908	-7.8464	-3.0353
DI:325	-0.40176	-5.6587	-10.708	-4.0571
DI:346	0.13193	1.8586	15.242	5.7932
DI:352	-0.22715	-3.1972	-37.574	-18.114
DI:356	0.17120	2.4116	90.257	70.804
DI:363	-0.17166	-2.4171	-10.188	-3.8993
DI:378	-0.22173	-3.1213	-10.879	-4.1685
DI:388	-0.17497	-2.4620	-3.8835	-1.4540
DI:406	-0.24308	-3.4148	-37.140	-27.440
DI:418	0.15464	2.1784	6.9972	2.6397
DI:436	0.28289	3.9829	7.9078	2.9951
DI:451	0.28643	4.0302	14.027	5.3815
DI:461	-0.14227	-2.0039	-16.113	-6.1390
DI:496	-0.19069	-2.6860	-9.9384	-3.7779
DI:529	-0.15780	-2.2222	-7.0415	-2.6716
DI:577	0.13803	1.9443	68.291	36.587
DI:592	-0.23605	-3.3247	-47.391	-19.426
DI:677	0.21664	3.0505	16.033	6.1442
DI:706	-0.12947	-1.8232	-13.384	-5.1799
DI:713	-0.17885	-2.5189	-47.181	-20.262
I:143	0.24649	2.4162	20.524	13.110
I:189	0.24184	2.3288	14.269	8.3877
I:191	0.22189	2.0993	12.158	8.3858
I:193	-0.57639	-2.5792	-9.9296	-5.4578
I:245	-0.34711	-3.3756	-20.791	-16.699
I:256	0.53119	5.0589	22.207	16.820
I:295	-0.51443	-4.9850	-19.710	-20.985
I:472	-0.34064	-3.3752	-36.032	-33.035
I:509	-0.26623	-2.6250	-18.711	-18.049
I:597	-0.25063	-2.4424	-11.981	-11.393
I:623	0.59767	5.3937	37.815	17.597
I:649	0.21103	2.0515	11.858	8.4707
I:664	-0.36231	-3.5654	-23.243	-20.606
T1:111	-0.0064843	-3.7290	-4.9348	-3.7599
T1:132	0.0064641	3.1887	5.0394	3.1272

```
T1:189          -0.11767      -4.3260      -9.5761      -6.0852
T1:193           0.27013       4.8358      10.834        7.5014
T1:197          -0.16145      -5.0294     -10.813       -7.8049
T1:217           0.16731       2.9813       4.3651       2.5164
T1:218          -0.15816      -2.9085      -4.1793      -2.4465
T1:254           0.067673      2.5849       2.7815       2.5845
T1:257          -0.10716      -2.6048      -2.7538      -2.7556
T1:263           0.097660      2.4147       3.1488       3.4894
T1:267          -0.12478      -2.9655      -5.3723      -5.1254
T1:271           0.066970      3.6269       6.5891       6.0334
T1:528          -0.0035839    -7.4970      -7.6427      -7.3281
T1:604           0.14744       2.3762       3.0889       2.5413
T1:605          -0.14986      -2.2833      -3.0459      -2.4680
T1:621           0.12862       2.5899       6.6048       3.4715
T1:623          -0.23422      -3.1620      -9.1404      -4.5629
T1:626           0.11463       3.6501       8.6714       4.9987
T1:657           0.073872      1.7884       2.0130       1.6257
T1:658          -0.078190     -1.9554      -2.1840      -1.7761
```

Model saved to C:\JBG\JGResearch\Univ Washington CFRM\XCG 1959 2019\Model UER AR1 IIS
DIIS TIS LEI112 WkUNCLL12.pdf
Model saved to C:\JBG\JGResearch\Univ Washington CFRM\XCG 1959 2019\Model UER AR1 IIS
DIIS TIS LEI112 WkUNCLL12.pdf.gwg

```
sigma                  0.100376  RSS                   6.246704
log-likelihood         685.901
no. of observations         719  no. of parameters           99
mean(UER)              5.96871   se(UER)               1.60769
When the log-likelihood constant is NOT included:
AIC                   -4.47042   SC                   -3.84009
HQ                    -4.22707   FPE                   0.0114626
When the log-likelihood constant is included:
AIC                   -1.63255   SC                   -1.00222
HQ                    -1.38919   FPE                   0.195775
```

```
AR 1-2 test:      F(2,618)   =    1.0635 [0.3459]
ARCH 1-1 test:    F(1,717)   = 0.054216 [0.8159]
Normality test:   Chi^2(2)   =  0.72955 [0.6944]
Hetero test:      F(159,545)=  0.49774 [1.0000]
RESET23 test:     F(2,618)   =    1.2886 [0.2764]
```

BOLD Notes the Statistically Significant AR1 and LEI Coefficients and the WkUNCL Component Variables

The AR1 RSS is 23.161 and the OxMetrics model of this chapter, reported in the Appendix Estimation (2) produces an RSS of only 6.25, with clean residuals! One observes the expected negative coefficient on the LEI variable in the unemployment rate equation and the weekly unemployment claims lagged variables have predominately positive coefficients. The initial OxMetrics model produces an adequately fitted model for the 1959–2019 period.

The TCB LEI data for 1959–2020 became known in January 2021. The AR1 model of the unemployment rate and the preferred OxMetrics Automatic Time Series Model of UER in 1959–2018 re-estimated with IIS, DIIS, TIS, LEI, and WkUNCL, lagged one-period for 1959–2020. The initial AR1 model is reported in the Appendix Estimation (3).

```
Appendix 7 Estimation (3) Modelling UER by OLS, 1959 -2020

        The dataset is: C:\JBG\JGResearch\Univ Washington CFRM\LEI UER WkUNCL.csv
        The estimation sample is: 13 - 741

                     Coefficient  Std.Error  t-value  t-prob Part.R^2
UER_1                   0.966259   0.009651    100.   0.0000  0.9325
Trend                3.42129e-05  7.702e-05    0.444  0.6570  0.0003
Constant               0.192907    0.06476     2.98  0.0030  0.0121

sigma                  0.436328  RSS                 138.217505
R^2                    0.932881  F(2,726) =     5045 [0.000]**
Adj.R^2                0.932697  log-likelihood        -428.299
no. of observations         729  no. of parameters           3
mean(UER)               5.99739  se(UER)              1.68188
When the log-likelihood constant is NOT included:
AIC                    -1.65461  SC                   -1.63572
HQ                     -1.64732  FPE                  0.191166
When the log-likelihood constant is included:
AIC                     1.18326  SC                    1.20216
HQ                      1.19055  FPE                   3.26501
I:736 [    1 -  742] saved to LEI UER WkUNCL.csv
I:738 [    1 -  742] saved to LEI UER WkUNCL.csv
I:740 [    1 -  742] saved to LEI UER WkUNCL.csv

AR 1-2 test:      F(2,724)  =    3.1499 [0.0434]*
ARCH 1-1 test:    F(1,727)  =   0.20376 [0.6518]
Normality test:   Chi^2(2)  =   64199. [0.0000]**
Hetero test:      F(4,724)  =    2.2186 [0.0654]
Chow test:        F(218,508)=   16.592 [0.0000]** for break after 523


Summary of Autometrics search
initial search space      2^6  final search space       2^5
no. estimated models        5  no. terminal models        1
test form                LR-F  target size        Small:0.01
large residuals         0.005  presearch reduction      lags
backtesting              GUM0  tie-breaker                SC
diagnostics p-value       0.1  search effort        standard
time                     0.08  Autometrics version      2.0a
```

The AR1 model fails all OxMetrics diagnostics tests. The model is not adequately fitted for the 1959–2020 period.

Let us now re-estimate the preferred OxMetrics Automatic Time Series Model of UER in 1959–2018 with IIS, DIIS, TIS, LEI, and WkUNCL, lagged one-period for the 1959–2020 period.

Appendix 7 Estimation (4) Modelling UER with the OxMerics of 1959- 2020.

Robust standard errors

	Coefficients	SE	HACSE	HCSE
UER_1	0.83339	0.0097388	0.012302	0.010887
Trend	-0.0033954	0.00039337	0.00043073	0.00038428
LEI_1	-0.0058106	0.0020007	0.0020786	0.0019870
WkUNCL_1	0.0020021	3.2142e-05	1.5984e-05	1.5374e-05
DI:14	-0.47923	0.075131	0.024927	0.064519
DI:24	0.22765	0.075452	0.034070	0.089303
DI:26	0.15676	0.074847	0.0053966	0.013161
DI:31	0.25121	0.074833	0.015932	0.041349
DI:33	0.25816	0.086454	0.022827	0.046108
DI:34	0.21455	0.086452	0.022751	0.046102
DI:44	0.17222	0.074849	0.051053	0.13433
DI:47	0.24725	0.075378	0.0086139	0.0093184
DI:59	0.17637	0.074818	0.025027	0.066142
DI:66	0.18451	0.074813	0.010376	0.027467
DI:74	0.28768	0.074817	0.0045858	0.011454
DI:193	0.37563	0.075211	0.023671	0.065059
DI:208	0.20833	0.074859	0.014544	0.036061
DI:227	0.18586	0.074817	0.023767	0.062849
DI:255	-0.27405	0.074822	0.049975	0.13215
DI:257	0.27387	0.074849	0.0073981	0.018240
DI:260	-0.26330	0.10899	0.018886	0.024946
DI:264	-0.27349	0.074831	0.013976	0.036343
DI:461	-0.15232	0.074835	0.0036185	0.0086286
DI:465	0.11719	0.074841	0.0062291	0.016043
DI:471	0.23789	0.074810	0.022884	0.060558
DI:496	-0.17971	0.074816	0.0073385	0.019078
DI:520	0.14003	0.074820	0.0016735	0.0014605
DI:529	-0.14762	0.074814	0.015550	0.040980
DI:542	-0.14378	0.074811	0.035134	0.092906
DI:576	-0.14702	0.074810	0.0033324	0.0087384
DI:592	-0.23942	0.074818	0.015718	0.041159
DI:666	-0.13336	0.074812	0.0035371	0.0092171
DI:671	0.14903	0.074812	0.0013005	0.0026758
DI:677	0.22439	0.074820	0.0023466	0.0047022
DI:713	-0.18231	0.074814	0.0089661	0.023530
DI:729	-0.13724	0.074816	0.0023867	0.0053266
DI:736	6.1990	0.083398	0.042334	0.038838
DI:738	-2.7861	0.10303	0.035984	0.033168
DI:739	-2.3854	0.11852	0.043506	0.040246
DI:740	-2.0464	0.097737	0.029678	0.027214
I:22	0.50176	0.11573	0.031150	0.062681
I:71	-0.21380	0.10714	0.019261	0.018854
I:131	-0.26572	0.10793	0.019426	0.021389
I:132	-0.16743	0.10947	0.023360	0.028486
I:143	0.25706	0.10815	0.016709	0.023456
I:155	0.19082	0.10785	0.011319	0.021378
I:222	0.24597	0.10740	0.019134	0.022781
I:235	0.38962	0.10924	0.018610	0.030459
I:245	-0.32859	0.10744	0.013683	0.021757
I:261	-0.56575	0.15882	0.038413	0.050712
I:287	0.28965	0.10793	0.028640	0.025501
I:295	-0.39634	0.10795	0.031242	0.026755
I:296	0.35453	0.10725	0.024835	0.021795
I:307	0.33096	0.10671	0.012769	0.014860
I:326	0.51869	0.10680	0.011763	0.015480
I:436	0.42924	0.10798	0.0099799	0.019055

I:534	0.19425	0.10703	0.014605	0.014887
I:597	-0.23044	0.10712	0.018902	0.017864
I:658	0.18841	0.10781	0.022775	0.022889
I:664	-0.38406	0.10737	0.019883	0.020055
I:735	0.93986	0.10843	0.018978	0.023016
T1:20	-0.051115	0.030722	0.027685	0.037360
T1:24	0.055219	0.022099	0.023786	0.026679
T1:44	-0.066418	0.020313	0.018549	0.017685
T1:49	0.39117	0.13208	0.044005	0.038064
T1:50	-0.52664	0.17749	0.029776	0.026271
T1:52	0.45564	0.16342	0.027783	0.027050
T1:53	-0.26239	0.099709	0.028333	0.027571
T1:128	-0.053169	0.011672	0.0095514	0.011815
T1:132	0.052589	0.012602	0.0097616	0.012704
T1:165	0.080836	0.033007	0.012028	0.024756
T1:168	-0.40585	0.13288	0.036430	0.099014
T1:169	0.35506	0.11491	0.032063	0.087559
T1:177	-0.34485	0.11041	0.033260	0.068683
T1:178	0.39644	0.12170	0.033729	0.069782
T1:182	-0.13462	0.031867	0.0088305	0.021895
T1:192	0.12799	0.021618	0.010789	0.022591
T1:197	-0.087236	0.019213	0.012710	0.021263
T1:209	0.022358	0.0067520	0.0065482	0.0080879
T1:233	-0.013396	0.0034714	0.0028594	0.0037318
T1:267	-0.31620	0.10337	0.026228	0.037201
T1:268	0.62045	0.16545	0.025764	0.038900
T1:270	-0.79143	0.16413	0.022883	0.033334
T1:271	0.49340	0.10110	0.022178	0.030881
T1:350	0.21752	0.10856	0.016885	0.023949
T1:351	-0.65662	0.23775	0.015562	0.023148
T1:352	0.79941	0.25557	0.0064995	0.0068856
T1:353	-0.53591	0.19318	0.0047439	0.0070370
T1:355	0.47229	0.18099	0.018217	0.053610
T1:356	-0.35334	0.14603	0.023880	0.069188
T1:360	0.23024	0.088516	0.016131	0.033585
T1:362	-0.44296	0.16441	0.039502	0.080391
T1:363	0.27460	0.11411	0.040820	0.074722
T1:375	0.074283	0.061374	0.029993	0.054892
T1:377	-0.44622	0.16199	0.057264	0.096469
T1:378	0.38167	0.12240	0.045633	0.068069
T1:386	0.22883	0.13078	0.038214	0.049509
T1:387	-0.52931	0.22676	0.035768	0.062198
T1:388	0.27112	0.11864	0.026205	0.049322
T1:404	0.33524	0.11864	0.038938	0.065884
T1:405	-0.67703	0.22469	0.037140	0.076210
T1:406	0.35981	0.12424	0.030512	0.052891
T1:417	0.17789	0.11582	0.033026	0.064184
T1:418	-0.31920	0.16429	0.033493	0.067392
T1:420	0.19486	0.080840	0.018175	0.039247
T1:424	-0.059240	0.023931	0.0090347	0.017555
T1:448	0.22980	0.11433	0.016087	0.029246
T1:449	-0.68799	0.24011	0.015917	0.027792
T1:450	1.0124	0.25918	0.0054144	0.0049737
T1:451	-0.96222	0.24125	0.023132	0.040150
T1:452	0.41722	0.11738	0.024935	0.043246
T1:466	-0.011481	0.0039601	0.0024373	0.0035166
T1:581	-0.0087932	0.0018301	0.0015522	0.0017370
T1:621	-0.38757	0.11152	0.031932	0.036893
T1:622	0.87816	0.21784	0.077685	0.074007
T1:623	-0.48079	0.11418	0.070453	0.070288
T1:648	0.15317	0.049017	0.049219	0.063130
T1:649	-0.15080	0.047187	0.046387	0.059879
T1:734	0.65345	0.021103	0.015574	0.014810

| T1:739 | −0.65201 | 0.020635 | 0.014990 | 0.014202 |

	Coefficients	t-SE	t-HACSE	t-HCSE
UER_1	0.83339	85.573	67.743	76.550
Trend	−0.0033954	−8.6315	−7.8830	−8.8358
LEI_1	−0.0058106	−2.9043	−2.7954	−2.9243
WkUNC1_1	0.0020021	62.290	125.26	130.23
DI:14	−0.47923	−6.3786	−19.225	−7.4278
DI:24	0.22765	3.0172	6.6820	2.5492
DI:26	0.15676	2.0944	29.048	11.911
DI:31	0.25121	3.3569	15.767	6.0752
DI:33	0.25816	2.9861	11.310	5.5991
DI:34	0.21455	2.4818	9.4307	4.6539
DI:44	0.17222	2.3009	3.3734	1.2821
DI:47	0.24725	3.2801	28.704	26.533
DI:59	0.17637	2.3573	7.0474	2.6666
DI:66	0.18451	2.4663	17.783	6.7176
DI:74	0.28768	3.8452	62.734	25.116
DI:193	0.37563	4.9944	15.869	5.7738
DI:208	0.20833	2.7829	14.324	5.7771
DI:227	0.18586	2.4842	7.8200	2.9572
DI:255	−0.27405	−3.6628	−5.4839	−2.0738
DI:257	0.27387	3.6590	37.019	15.015
DI:260	−0.26330	−2.4158	−13.942	−10.555
DI:264	−0.27349	−3.6548	−19.568	−7.5253
DI:461	−0.15232	−2.0354	−42.096	−17.653
DI:465	0.11719	1.5659	18.814	7.3047
DI:471	0.23789	3.1799	10.395	3.9283
DI:496	−0.17971	−2.4021	−24.489	−9.4197
DI:520	0.14003	1.8715	83.674	95.877
DI:529	−0.14762	−1.9732	−9.4936	−3.6023
DI:542	−0.14378	−1.9219	−4.0923	−1.5476
DI:576	−0.14702	−1.9653	−44.119	−16.825
DI:592	−0.23942	−3.2000	−15.232	−5.8169
DI:666	−0.13336	−1.7826	−37.702	−14.468
DI:671	0.14903	1.9921	114.60	55.696
DI:677	0.22439	2.9991	95.623	47.720
DI:713	−0.18231	−2.4369	−20.334	−7.7480
DI:729	−0.13724	−1.8343	−57.500	−25.765
DI:736	6.1990	74.331	146.43	159.61
DI:738	−2.7861	−27.041	−77.425	−83.999
DI:739	−2.3854	−20.127	−54.831	−59.272
DI:740	−2.0464	−20.937	−68.951	−75.194
I:22	0.50176	4.3357	16.108	8.0049
I:71	−0.21380	−1.9956	−11.101	−11.340
I:131	−0.26572	−2.4618	−13.678	−12.423
I:132	−0.16743	−1.5294	−7.1673	−5.8775
I:143	0.25706	2.3769	15.384	10.959
I:155	0.19082	1.7692	16.858	8.9259
I:222	0.24597	2.2902	12.855	10.797
I:235	0.38962	3.5667	20.936	12.792
I:245	−0.32859	−3.0583	−24.014	−15.103
I:261	−0.56575	−3.5622	−14.728	−11.156
I:287	0.28965	2.6837	10.113	11.358
I:295	−0.39634	−3.6714	−12.686	−14.814
I:296	0.35453	3.3055	14.275	16.267
I:307	0.33096	3.1016	25.918	22.272
I:326	0.51869	4.8566	44.097	33.508
I:436	0.42924	3.9753	43.011	22.527
I:534	0.19425	1.8148	13.300	13.048
I:597	−0.23044	−2.1512	−12.192	−12.900
I:658	0.18841	1.7475	8.2726	8.2315
I:664	−0.38406	−3.5771	−19.316	−19.150

I:735	0.93986	8.6678	49.523	40.836
T1:20	-0.051115	-1.6638	-1.8463	-1.3682
T1:24	0.055219	2.4987	2.3215	2.0698
T1:44	-0.066418	-3.2698	-3.5806	-3.7557
T1:49	0.39117	2.9617	8.8892	10.277
T1:50	-0.52664	-2.9672	-17.687	-20.046
T1:52	0.45564	2.7881	16.400	16.844
T1:53	-0.26239	-2.6316	-9.2610	-9.5170
T1:128	-0.053169	-4.5552	-5.5666	-4.5003
T1:132	0.052589	4.1730	5.3873	4.1396
T1:165	0.080836	2.4490	6.7205	3.2653
T1:168	-0.40585	-3.0542	-11.140	-4.0989
T1:169	0.35506	3.0900	11.074	4.0551
T1:177	-0.34485	-3.1233	-10.368	-5.0209
T1:178	0.39644	3.2574	11.754	5.6811
T1:182	-0.13462	-4.2244	-15.245	-6.1485
T1:192	0.12799	5.9203	11.863	5.6653
T1:197	-0.087236	-4.5404	-6.8634	-4.1028
T1:209	0.022358	3.3113	3.4144	2.7644
T1:233	-0.013396	-3.8590	-4.6850	-3.5897
T1:267	-0.31620	-3.0590	-12.056	-8.5000
T1:268	0.62045	3.7501	24.082	15.950
T1:270	-0.79143	-4.8220	-34.586	-23.743
T1:271	0.49340	4.8806	22.247	15.977
T1:350	0.21752	2.0037	12.882	9.0825
T1:351	-0.65662	-2.7618	-42.194	-28.366
T1:352	0.79941	3.1280	123.00	116.10
T1:353	-0.53591	-2.7742	-112.97	-76.157
T1:355	0.47229	2.6094	25.926	8.8098
T1:356	-0.35334	-2.4197	-14.796	-5.1070
T1:360	0.23024	2.6012	14.273	6.8555
T1:362	-0.44296	-2.6942	-11.214	-5.5100
T1:363	0.27460	2.4065	6.7271	3.6750
T1:375	0.074283	1.2103	2.4767	1.3533
T1:377	-0.44622	-2.7546	-7.7923	-4.6255
T1:378	0.38167	3.1181	8.3639	5.6071
T1:386	0.22883	1.7497	5.9882	4.6221
T1:387	-0.52931	-2.3342	-14.798	-8.5101
T1:388	0.27112	2.2852	10.346	5.4969
T1:404	0.33524	2.8257	8.6098	5.0884
T1:405	-0.67703	-3.0132	-18.229	-8.8838
T1:406	0.35981	2.8962	11.793	6.8029
T1:417	0.17789	1.5359	5.3865	2.7716
T1:418	-0.31920	-1.9430	-9.5303	-4.7364
T1:420	0.19486	2.4104	10.721	4.9649
T1:424	-0.059240	-2.4755	-6.5569	-3.3745
T1:448	0.22980	2.0100	14.285	7.8574
T1:449	-0.68799	-2.8653	-43.222	-24.755
T1:450	1.0124	3.9060	186.98	203.55
T1:451	-0.96222	-3.9885	-41.597	-23.965
T1:452	0.41722	3.5545	16.732	9.6477
T1:466	-0.011481	-2.8993	-4.7106	-3.2649
T1:581	-0.0087932	-4.8047	-5.6651	-5.0624
T1:621	-0.38757	-3.4754	-12.137	-10.505
T1:622	0.87816	4.0313	11.304	11.866
T1:623	-0.48079	-4.2107	-6.8243	-6.8403
T1:648	0.15317	3.1248	3.1120	2.4262
T1:649	-0.15080	-3.1957	-3.2508	-2.5183
T1:734	0.65345	30.965	41.958	44.123
T1:739	-0.65201	-31.597	-43.495	-45.911

BOLD Denotes Statistically Significant Coefficients on the AR1 and LEI and Its WkUNCL Components

```
sigma                  0.105795   RSS                     6.81631162
R^2                    0.99669    F(119,609) =   1541 [0.000]**
Adj.R^2                0.996043   log-likelihood          668.667
no. of observations         729   no. of parameters           120
mean(UER)              5.99739    se(UER)                 1.68188
When the log-likelihood constant is NOT included:
AIC                   -4.34314    SC                     -3.58731
HQ                    -4.05151    FPE                     0.0130350
When the log-likelihood constant is included:
AIC                   -1.50526    SC                     -0.749429
HQ                    -1.21364    FPE                     0.222632


AR 1-2 test:      F(2,607)   =     2.1504 [0.1173]
ARCH 1-1 test:    F(1,727)   =     0.41450 [0.5199]
Normality test:   Chi^2(2)   =     0.89062 [0.6406]
Hetero test:      F(157,541)=     0.85068 [0.8884]
RESET23 test:     F(2,607)   =     1.0927 [0.3360]
```

Model saved to C:\JBG\JGResearch\Univ Washington CFRM\XCG 1959 2019\Model UER AR1 IIS DIIS TIS LEI11 WkUNCLL1 N741.pdf
Model saved to C:\JBG\JGResearch\Univ Washington CFRM\XCG 1959 2019\Model UER AR1 IIS DIIS TIS LEI11 WkUNCLL1 N741.pdf.gwg

(Chart 7.2) The AR1 RSS is 138.21 and the OxMetrics model of this chapter, reported in the Appendix Estimation (4), produces an RSS of only

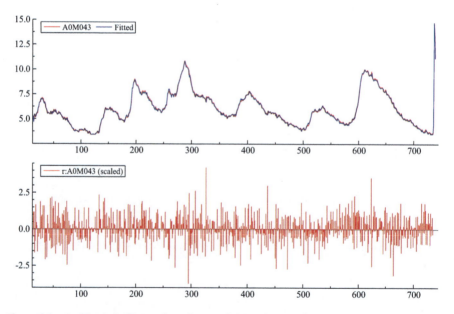

Chart 7.2 Residuals indicate that the model is adequately estimated

6.82, with clean residuals. Note the great RSS rise during 2020. One observes the expected negative coefficient on the LEI variable in the unemployment rate equation and the weekly unemployment claims lagged variables have predominately positive coefficients. The initial OxMetrics model produces an adequately fitted model for the 1959–2019 period.

```
NOTE ERRORS ARE CLEAN with LEI and WkUNL with Lags to 12!
RSS from 138.22.16 to 5.89. Time Period: 1959-2020.
```

Appendix 7 Estimation (5) Modelling UER by OLS with LEI and WkUNCL, Lags to 12

```
The dataset is: C:\JBG\JGResearch\Univ Washington CFRM\LEI UER WkUNCL.csv
The estimation sample is: 13 - 742
```

```
Robust standard errors
              Coefficients            SE          HACSE           HCSE
UER_1            0.51867       0.024475       0.024455       0.025611
Constant          1624.8         234.75         192.07         183.12
Trend            -2.1929        0.31728        0.25963        0.24757
LEI_2          -0.025952      0.0029114      0.0028707      0.0029763
WkUNCL_1       0.0014813     9.5735e-05     4.7811e-05     5.9361e-05
WkUNCL_2      0.00081458     0.00014364     7.7952e-05     8.9312e-05
WkUNCL_6       0.0013461     0.00015188     0.00012782     0.00012307
WkUNCL_9      0.00084001     0.00017490     0.00019229     0.00019345
DI:14           -0.41523       0.070343       0.017853       0.045818
DI:17           -0.22196       0.070344      0.0065730       0.013286
DI:22            0.53868        0.10267       0.011066       0.023087
DI:23            0.71694        0.14999       0.027905       0.049768
DI:24            -3.3857        0.40876        0.23278        0.31620
DI:25            -3.0634        0.37656        0.20880        0.28426
DI:26            -2.5182        0.34466        0.18651        0.25355
DI:27            -2.1786        0.31008        0.16007        0.21879
DI:28            -1.7370        0.27467        0.13483        0.18449
DI:29            -1.2441        0.23690        0.10737        0.14757
DI:30           -0.95275        0.19633       0.077059        0.10812
DI:31           -0.43501        0.15374       0.050556       0.071559
DI:32           -0.42544        0.10319       0.020810       0.032092
DI:57            0.21977        0.10409       0.042343       0.033288
DI:58            0.38396        0.15363       0.083567       0.065865
DI:59            0.78023        0.19543        0.12371       0.097768
DI:60            0.90969        0.23378        0.16259        0.12945
DI:61             1.2144        0.26968        0.20105        0.16040
DI:62             1.2741        0.30401        0.23876        0.19108
DI:63             1.4882        0.33677        0.27564        0.22079
DI:64             1.6166        0.36859        0.31170        0.25008
DI:65             1.6170        0.39924        0.34688        0.27842
DI:66             1.8138        0.42849        0.38145        0.30580
DI:67             1.7051        0.45742        0.41507        0.33302
DI:68             1.8847        0.48496        0.44774        0.35877
DI:69             2.1110        0.51215        0.47977        0.38437
DI:70             2.3367        0.53911        0.51078        0.40981
DI:71             2.2791        0.56551        0.54096        0.43480
DI:72             2.5603        0.59052        0.57034        0.45827
DI:73             2.6588        0.61545        0.59892        0.48185
DI:74             3.0625        0.63976        0.62657        0.50466
DI:75           -0.23155        0.10128       0.026429       0.021629
DI:129           0.25210       0.097413       0.030896       0.031037
DI:130           0.41558        0.13608       0.065053       0.062672
DI:131           0.37888        0.16494        0.10072       0.095075
DI:132           0.41646        0.18739        0.13502        0.12576
DI:133           0.81533        0.20622        0.16961        0.15678
DI:134           0.66623        0.18468        0.13290        0.12067
DI:135           0.50130        0.16155       0.098403       0.087517
DI:136           0.37854        0.13411       0.064989       0.056917
DI:137           0.21162       0.097090       0.032617       0.028898
DI:194          -0.19754       0.074098      0.0055254      0.0071029
DI:222           0.20061       0.070283       0.018627       0.045611
DI:263           0.19994       0.075850       0.015648       0.029002
DI:471           0.19953       0.070163       0.026472       0.069336
DI:677           0.17706       0.070198       0.016498       0.043164
DI:736            7.1216        0.23661        0.11225        0.13687
DI:737            3.4161        0.29882        0.14095        0.16825
I:24              4.7075        0.48623        0.26851        0.37973
I:44             0.28106        0.10534       0.019686       0.033150
I:48            -0.36255        0.11670       0.035817       0.057255
I:53             0.41201        0.10490       0.045326       0.035827
```

I:75	3.2074	0.68701	0.67967	0.54909
I:143	0.20275	0.10250	0.027915	0.031451
I:211	0.21543	0.10234	0.032391	0.035243
I:235	0.40345	0.10935	0.032494	0.036826
I:326	0.39668	0.10316	0.029204	0.034983
I:378	-0.29485	0.10173	0.014959	0.021517
I:406	-0.23651	0.10232	0.028534	0.025973
I:436	0.36233	0.10085	0.019062	0.017889
I:450	-0.25770	0.10015	0.014565	0.013359
I:452	-0.36916	0.10015	0.013821	0.013239
I:509	-0.30378	0.10105	0.016723	0.018167
I:554	0.21543	0.10093	0.025229	0.018282
I:588	0.27166	0.10245	0.028988	0.029506
I:597	-0.29523	0.10383	0.019071	0.019086
I:735	0.91553	0.10882	0.022755	0.039768
T1:45	-0.36001	0.084781	0.040458	0.078614
T1:46	0.42981	0.096570	0.048696	0.089371
T1:52	-0.063255	0.015090	0.012182	0.014081
T1:132	-0.57985	0.062505	0.076406	0.071978
T1:133	0.56982	0.063036	0.076586	0.072684
T1:165	0.13574	0.031579	0.012340	0.020543
T1:168	-0.35739	0.11764	0.038161	0.073238
T1:169	0.23350	0.093423	0.035973	0.062425
T1:187	-0.096620	0.048023	0.025992	0.049592
T1:189	-0.19421	0.081267	0.036430	0.083968
T1:192	0.66215	0.14739	0.041387	0.10645
T1:193	-0.42952	0.15191	0.029778	0.072416
T1:196	0.55490	0.13711	0.056639	0.064438
T1:197	-0.51505	0.10156	0.056695	0.065079
T1:217	0.13242	0.034612	0.035224	0.038835
T1:219	-0.091210	0.035671	0.036721	0.038321
T1:235	-0.17636	0.070478	0.065451	0.065351
T1:236	0.16193	0.069385	0.064289	0.065059
T1:254	-0.53444	0.080500	0.048084	0.098443
T1:255	0.61166	0.089737	0.054666	0.11133
T1:262	-0.27498	0.068954	0.038998	0.063221
T1:264	0.26338	0.092935	0.039486	0.077808
T1:267	-0.59319	0.15108	0.035903	0.055576
T1:268	0.68577	0.16639	0.031243	0.065938
T1:270	-0.30870	0.076401	0.028532	0.059845
T1:274	0.11919	0.024160	0.013146	0.022350
T1:293	0.52460	0.11136	0.036205	0.049531
T1:294	-0.85617	0.21259	0.081497	0.11768
T1:295	0.39464	0.11891	0.089394	0.11930
T1:305	-0.47272	0.10989	0.069117	0.088402
T1:306	0.56044	0.14899	0.065543	0.084698
T1:308	-0.11653	0.054545	0.029389	0.036452
T1:324	-0.075815	0.030594	0.039546	0.039021
T1:326	0.071211	0.027319	0.036201	0.034200
T1:375	-0.050068	0.0092539	0.0060220	0.0088572
T1:382	0.075829	0.019912	0.012095	0.020275
T1:388	-0.090938	0.021264	0.016275	0.024124
T1:395	0.034748	0.013175	0.012836	0.014881
T1:410	0.026714	0.010116	0.0087893	0.010083
T1:420	0.055726	0.016759	0.012421	0.017413
T1:425	-0.058222	0.011239	0.0082901	0.011574
T1:510	-0.020937	0.0018287	0.0020453	0.0019240
T1:545	0.020685	0.0022575	0.0027640	0.0024124
T1:591	-0.26654	0.057056	0.044529	0.048869
T1:592	0.22995	0.057791	0.044337	0.048808
T1:621	-0.36503	0.10816	0.030403	0.039146
T1:622	0.99649	0.21221	0.041388	0.052922
T1:623	-0.63938	0.12455	0.031656	0.045904

T1:629	0.059445	0.013584	0.0099907	0.011000
T1:662	0.41623	0.10506	0.028744	0.042591
T1:663	-0.70159	0.20330	0.038835	0.053292
T1:664	0.27426	0.10374	0.025593	0.034442
T1:712	-0.16673	0.051709	0.046040	0.060647
T1:713	0.16478	0.053745	0.047815	0.063326
T1:735	0.37004	0.039868	0.022120	0.026657
T1:739	1.8177	0.32622	0.26015	0.24718

	Coefficients	t-SE	t-HACSE	t-HCSE
UER_1	0.51867	21.192	21.210	20.252
Constant	1624.8	6.9215	8.4597	8.8731
Trend	-2.1929	-6.9115	-8.4461	-8.8578
LEI_2	-0.025952	-8.9140	-9.0404	-8.7197
WkUNCL_1	0.0014813	15.473	30.982	24.954
WkUNCL_2	0.00081458	5.6709	10.450	9.1206
WkUNCL_6	0.0013461	8.8630	10.531	10.937
WkUNCL_9	0.00084001	4.8027	4.3684	4.3422
DI:14	-0.41523	-5.9029	-23.259	-9.0627
DI:17	-0.22196	-3.1554	-33.769	-16.707
DI:22	0.53868	5.2465	48.678	23.332
DI:23	0.71694	4.7799	25.692	14.406
DI:24	-3.3857	-8.2830	-14.544	-10.708
DI:25	-3.0634	-8.1351	-14.671	-10.777
DI:26	-2.5182	-7.3062	-13.501	-9.9317
DI:27	-2.1786	-7.0257	-13.610	-9.9571
DI:28	-1.7370	-6.3240	-12.883	-9.4152
DI:29	-1.2441	-5.2517	-11.587	-8.4307
DI:30	-0.95275	-4.8527	-12.364	-8.8123
DI:31	-0.43501	-2.8295	-8.6045	-6.0791
DI:32	-0.42544	-4.1229	-20.444	-13.257
DI:57	0.21977	2.1114	5.1902	6.6021
DI:58	0.38396	2.4994	4.5947	5.8296
DI:59	0.78023	3.9923	6.3071	7.9803
DI:60	0.90969	3.8912	5.5949	7.0274
DI:61	1.2144	4.5033	6.0405	7.5711
DI:62	1.2741	4.1909	5.3362	6.6677
DI:63	1.4882	4.4190	5.3989	6.7404
DI:64	1.6166	4.3860	5.1866	6.4645
DI:65	1.6170	4.0503	4.6617	5.8079
DI:66	1.8138	4.2330	4.7550	5.9312
DI:67	1.7051	3.7277	4.1080	5.1202
DI:68	1.8847	3.8863	4.2094	5.2532
DI:69	2.1110	4.1220	4.4001	5.4923
DI:70	2.3367	4.3343	4.5747	5.7018
DI:71	2.2791	4.0301	4.2130	5.2416
DI:72	2.5603	4.3356	4.4890	5.5868
DI:73	2.6588	4.3202	4.4394	5.5181
DI:74	3.0625	4.7869	4.8877	6.0684
DI:75	-0.23155	-2.2862	-8.7613	-10.706
DI:129	0.25210	2.5879	8.1596	8.1225
DI:130	0.41558	3.0538	6.3883	6.6310
DI:131	0.37888	2.2971	3.7616	3.9851
DI:132	0.41646	2.2224	3.0844	3.3116
DI:133	0.81533	3.9537	4.8072	5.2004
DI:134	0.66623	3.6075	5.0129	5.5212
DI:135	0.50130	3.1030	5.0943	5.7280
DI:136	0.37854	2.8226	5.8247	6.6508
DI:137	0.21162	2.1796	6.4880	7.3229
DI:194	-0.19754	-2.6659	-35.751	-27.811
DI:222	0.20061	2.8542	10.770	4.3981
DI:263	0.19994	2.6360	12.778	6.8941
DI:471	0.19953	2.8437	7.5372	2.8777

DI:677	0.17706	2.5222	10.732	4.1020
DI:736	7.1216	30.099	63.445	52.033
DI:737	3.4161	11.432	24.236	20.303
I:24	4.7075	9.6816	17.532	12.397
I:44	0.28106	2.6681	14.277	8.4782
I:48	-0.36255	-3.1067	-10.122	-6.3322
I:53	0.41201	3.9277	9.0900	11.500
I:75	3.2074	4.6686	4.7191	5.8413
I:143	0.20275	1.9780	7.2632	6.4466
I:211	0.21543	2.1051	6.6511	6.1127
I:235	0.40345	3.6894	12.416	10.956
I:326	0.39668	3.8455	13.583	11.339
I:378	-0.29485	-2.8984	-19.710	-13.703
I:406	-0.23651	-2.3115	-8.2886	-9.1061
I:436	0.36233	3.5929	19.008	20.255
I:450	-0.25770	-2.5732	-17.693	-19.290
I:452	-0.36916	-3.6861	-26.710	-27.884
I:509	-0.30378	-3.0061	-18.165	-16.722
I:554	0.21543	2.1344	8.5388	11.784
I:588	0.27166	2.6516	9.3713	9.2069
I:597	-0.29523	-2.8433	-15.481	-15.468
I:735	0.91553	8.4134	40.234	23.022
T1:45	-0.36001	-4.2463	-8.8983	-4.5795
T1:46	0.42981	4.4508	8.8264	4.8093
T1:52	-0.063255	-4.1918	-5.1923	-4.4922
T1:132	-0.57985	-9.2768	-7.5890	-8.0559
T1:133	0.56982	9.0396	7.4402	7.8397
T1:165	0.13574	4.2983	11.000	6.6074
T1:168	-0.35739	-3.0379	-9.3654	-4.8799
T1:169	0.23350	2.4994	6.4910	3.7405
T1:187	-0.096620	-2.0119	-3.7173	-1.9483
T1:189	-0.19421	-2.3897	-5.3309	-2.3128
T1:192	0.66215	4.4926	15.999	6.2202
T1:193	-0.42952	-2.8274	-14.424	-5.9313
T1:196	0.55490	4.0472	9.7971	8.6114
T1:197	-0.51505	-5.0713	-9.0846	-7.9142
T1:217	0.13242	3.8257	3.7592	3.4097
T1:219	-0.091210	-2.5570	-2.4838	-2.3801
T1:235	-0.17636	-2.5023	-2.6945	-2.6986
T1:236	0.16193	2.3337	2.5187	2.4889
T1:254	-0.53444	-6.6390	-11.115	-5.4289
T1:255	0.61166	6.8161	11.189	5.4944
T1:262	-0.27498	-3.9878	-7.0511	-4.3494
T1:264	0.26338	2.8340	6.6700	3.3849
T1:267	-0.59319	-3.9264	-16.522	-10.673
T1:268	0.68577	4.1216	21.950	10.400
T1:270	-0.30870	-4.0405	-10.819	-5.1583
T1:274	0.11919	4.9333	9.0668	5.3328
T1:293	0.52460	4.7107	14.490	10.592
T1:294	-0.85617	-4.0274	-10.506	-7.2751
T1:295	0.39464	3.3187	4.4146	3.3079
T1:305	-0.47272	-4.3018	-6.8395	-5.3474
T1:306	0.56044	3.7617	8.5507	6.6169
T1:308	-0.11653	-2.1364	-3.9650	-3.1968
T1:324	-0.075815	-2.4781	-1.9171	-1.9429
T1:326	0.071211	2.6067	1.9671	2.0822
T1:375	-0.050068	-5.4104	-8.3141	-5.6528
T1:382	0.075829	3.8082	6.2695	3.7400
T1:388	-0.090938	-4.2766	-5.5877	-3.7696
T1:395	0.034748	2.6373	2.7070	2.3350
T1:410	0.026714	2.6406	3.0394	2.6493
T1:420	0.055726	3.3250	4.4863	3.2003
T1:425	-0.058222	-5.1802	-7.0231	-5.0305

```
T1:510          -0.020937      -11.449      -10.236      -10.882
T1:545           0.020685        9.1628       7.4836       8.5744
T1:591          -0.26654        -4.6715      -5.9857      -5.4542
T1:592           0.22995         3.9789       5.1864       4.7112
T1:621          -0.36503        -3.3751     -12.007      -9.3249
T1:622           0.99649         4.6958      24.077       18.829
T1:623          -0.63938        -5.1336     -20.198     -13.929
T1:629           0.059445        4.3762       5.9500       5.4039
T1:662           0.41623         3.9617      14.480        9.7728
T1:663          -0.70159        -3.4509     -18.066     -13.165
T1:664           0.27426         2.6438      10.716        7.9631
T1:712          -0.16673        -3.2243      -3.6213      -2.7491
T1:713           0.16478         3.0660       3.4462       2.6021
T1:735           0.37004         9.2816      16.728       13.882
T1:739           1.8177          5.5720       6.9872       7.3538


sigma                0.0991424  RSS                    5.88770531
R^2                  0.997142   F(130,599) =   1608 [0.000]**
Adj.R^2              0.996522   log-likelihood         723.54
no. of observations       730  no. of parameters         131
mean(UER)            5.99863    se(UER)                1.68106
When the log-likelihood constant is NOT included:
AIC                 -4.46127    SC                    -3.63704
HQ                  -4.14328    FPE                    0.0115931
When the log-likelihood constant is included:
AIC                 -1.62340    SC                    -0.799166
HQ                  -1.30540    FPE                    0.198004


AR 1-2 test:     F(2,597)   =   0.94150 [0.3906]
ARCH 1-1 test:   F(1,728)   =   1.4837 [0.2236]
Normality test:  Chi^2(2)   =   0.46182 [0.7938]
Hetero test:     F(128,549) =   0.91178 [0.7355]
RESET23 test:    F(2,597)   =   0.80208 [0.4489]
```

Model saved to C:\JBG\JGResearch\Univ Washington CFRM\XCG 1959 2019\Model UER AR1 IIS DIIS TIS LEI112 WkUNCLL12.pdf
Model saved to C:\JBG\JGResearch\Univ Washington CFRM\XCG 1959 2019\Model UER AR1 IIS DIIS TIS LEI112 WkUNCLL12.pdf.gwg

How did the OxMetrics automatic time series model do in modeling unemployment rate in the U.S. in the COVID period? Very well indeed! The pre-COVID AR1—OxMetrics RSS reduction 23.16 to 6.25 in January 2020 becomes 138.22 to 6.82 in January 2021! OxMetrics proved itself quite well in the author's mind. We will see the reader-enhanced modeling in the November 2021 period in Chapter 10.

References

Auerbach, A. J. (1982). The index of leading indicators: "Measurement without theory," thirty-five years later. *The Review of Economics, and Statistics, 64*, 589–595.

Beaton, A. E., & Tukey, J. W. (1974). The fitting of power series, meaning polynomials, illustrated on bank-spectroscopic data. *Technometrics, 16*, 147–185.

Belsley, D. A., Kuh, E., & Welsch, R. E. (1980). *Regression diagnostics: Identifying influential data and sources of collinearity.* John Wiley & Sons. Chapter 2.

Box, G. E. P., & Jenkins, G. (1970). *Time series analysis: Forecasting and control.* Holden-Day.

Burns, A. F., & Mitchell, W. C. (1946). *Measuring business cycles*. NBER.

Castle, J., & Shepard, N. (2009). *The methodology and practice of econometrics*. Oxford University Press.

Castle, J., Doornik, J. A., & Hendry, D. F. (2013). Model selection in equations with many 'small' effects. *Oxford Bulletin of Economics and Statistics, 75*, 6–22.

Castle, J., Clements, M. P., & Hendry, D. F. (2015). Robust approaches to forecasting. *International Journal of Forecasting, 31*, 99–112.

Castle, J. L., & Hendry, D. F. (2019). *Modelling our changing world*. Palgrave.

Clements, M. P., & Hendry, D. F. (2005). Evaluating a model by forecast performance. *Oxford Bulletin of Economics and Statistics, 67*, 931–956.

Cook, R. D. (1977). *Detection of influential observation in linear regression*. Technometrics.

Dhrymes, P. (2017). *Introductory econometrics*. Springer, Revised Edition.

Doornik, J. A., & Hendry, D. F. (2015). Statistical model selection with big data. *Cogent Economics & Finance, 3*, 1–15.

Efron, B., Hastie, T., Johnstone, J., & Tibshirani, R. (2004). Least angle regression. *The Annals of Statistics, 32*, 407–499.

Granger, C. W. J. (2001). *Essays in econometrics*. In E. Ghysels, N. R. Swanson, & M. W. Watson (Eds.). Cambridge University Press.

Granger, C. W. J., & Newbold, P. (1977). *Forecasting economic time series*. Academic Press Inc.

Guerard, J. B., Jr. (2001). A note on the forecasting effectiveness of the U.S. leading economic indicators. *Indian Economic Review, 36*, 251–268.

Guerard, J. B., Jr. (2004). The forecasting effectiveness of the U.S. leading economic indicators: Further evidence and initial G7 results. In P. Dua (Ed.), *Business cycles and economic growth: An analysis using leading indicators* (pp. 174–187). Oxford University Press.

Guerard, J. B., Jr., & Schwartz, E. (2007). *Quantitative corporate finance*. Kluwer.

Guerard, J. B., Jr., Xu, G., & Wang, Z. (2019). *Portfolio and investment analysis with SAS: Financial modeling techniques for optimization*. SAS Press.

Guerard, J. B., Jr., Thomakos, D. D., & Kyrizai, F. S. (2020). Automatic time series modelling and forecasting: A replication case study of forecasting real GDP, the unemployment rate, and the impact of leading economic indicators. *Cogent Economics and Finance, 8*(1), 1759483.

Gunst, R. F., & Mason, R. L. (1980). *regression analysis and its application*. Marcel Dekker Inc.

Hahn, F., & Solow, R. (1995). *A critical essay on modern macroeconomic theory*. MIT Press.

Harberler, G. (1937). *Prosperity and depression*. League of Nations, Geneva. Reprinted 1963. Atheneum, New York.

Hastie, T., Tibshirani, R., Friedman, J. (2016). *The elements of statistical learning: Data mining, inference, and prediction*, 2nd ed, 11th printing. Springer.

Hendry, D. F. (1986). Using PC-give in econometrics teaching. *Oxford Bulletin of Economics and Statistics, 48*, 87–98.

Hendry, D. F. (2000). *Econometrics: Alchemy or science?* Oxford University Press.

Hendry, D. F., & Nielsen, B. (2007). *Econometric modeling: A likelihood Approach.* Princeton University Press.

Hendry, D. F., & Doornik, J. A. (2014). *Empirical model discovery and theory evaluation.* MIT Press.

Hendry, D. F., & Krolzig, H. M. (2005). The properties of automatic gets modelling. *The Economic Journal, 115*, c32–c61.

Huber, P. J. (1973). Robust regression: Asymptotics, conjectures, and Monte Carlo. *Annals of Statistics, 1*, 799–821.

Keynes, J. (1936). *The general theory of employment, interest, and money.* Macmillan.

Klein, L. (1950). *Economic fluctuations in the United States, 1941.* Wiley & Sons.

Krolzig, H.-M., & Hendry, D. F. (2001a). Computer automation of general-to-specific model selection procedures. *Journal of Economic Dynamics & Control, 25*, 831–866.

Krolzig, H. M., & Hendry, D. F. (2001b). Computer automation of general-to-specific model selection procedures. *Journal of Economic Dynamics and Control, 25*, 831–866.

Kyriazi, F. S., Thomakos, D. D., & Guerard, J. B. (2019). Adaptive learning forecasting with applications in forecasting agricultural prices. *International Journal of Forecasting*, forthcoming.

Levanon, G., Manini, J.-C., Ozyildirim, A., Schaitkin, B., & Tanchua, J. (2015). Using financial indicators to predict turning points in the business cycle: The case of the leading economic index for the united states. *International Journal of Forecasting, 31*(2), 426–445.

Makridakis, S., Anderson, A., Carbone, R., Fildes, R., Hibon, M., Newton, J., Parzen, E., & Winkler, R. (1984). *The forecasting accuracy of major time series methods.* Wiley.

Makridakis, S., & Hibon, M. (2000). The M3-competition: Results, conclusions and implications. *International Journal of Forecasting, 16*, 451–476.

Makridakis, S., Wheelwright, S. C., & Hyndman, R. J. (1998). *Forecasting: Methods and applications.* John Wiley & Sons, 3rd ed. Chapters 5, 6.

Mansfield, E. (1994). *Statistics for business and economics* (5th ed.). W.W. Norton & Company.

Maronna, R. A., Martin, R. D., & Yohai, V. J. (2006). *Robust statistics: Theory and methods with R.* Wiley.

Maronna, R. A., Martin, R. D., Yohai, V. J., & Salibian-Barrera, M. (2019). *Robust statistics: Theory and methods with R* (2nd ed.). Wiley.

Miller, I., & Freund, J. E. (1965). *Probability and statistics for engineers.* Prentice-Hall.

Mincer, J., & Zarnowitz, V. (1969). The evaluation of economic forecasts. In J. Mincer (Ed.), *Economic forecasts and expectations.* Columbia University Press.

Mitchell, W. C. (1923). *Business cycles and unemployment.* National Bureau of Economic Research.

Mitchell, W. C., & Burns, A. F. (1938). Statistical indicators of cyclical revivals. *Bulletin* 69. NBER. Reprinted as Chapter 6, in G. H. Moore, *Business cycle indicators* (Vol. 1, pp. 162–183), Princeton University Press, 1961.

Montgomery, A. L., Zarnowitz, V., Tsay, R., & Tiao, G. C. (1998). Forecasting the U.S. unemployment rate. *Journal of the American Statistical Association, 93*, 478–493.

Moore, G. H. (1961). *Business cycle indicators,* (Vol. 1). Princeton University Press.

Nelson, C. R., & Plossner, C. I. (1982). Trends and random walks in macroeconomic time series: Some evidence and implications. *Journal of Monetary Economics, 10*, 139–162.

Nikolopoulos, K. I., & Thomakos, D. D. (2019). *Forecasting with the theta method*. Wiley.

Samuelson, P. (1948). *Economics*. McGraw-Hill.

Singer, A. C., & Feder, M. (1999). Universal linear prediction by model order weighting. *IEEE Transactions on Signal Processing, 47*, 2685–2699.

Zarnowitz, V. (1992). *Business cycles: Theory, history, indicators, and forecasting*. University of Chicago Press.

8

Granger Causality Testing and LEI Forecasting of Quarterly Mergers and the Unemployment Rate

In this chapter we examine, in the context of a data-specific case study, the automatic time series approach to modeling and forecasting time series. The time series modeling approach has evolved from the Box and Jenkins (1970) approach for the identification, estimation, and forecasting of stationary (or series transformed to stationarity) series, through the analysis of the series autocorrelation and partial autocorrelation functions, to the world of Clive Granger (2001) and causality testing, to current applications of automatic time series modeling and forecasting of Tsay (1988, 1989), implemented in the Scientific Computing Associates (DCA) program, and Vinod (2014), in his R-program. The reader is reminded of our statistical Appendix. What paths should a practitioner seek to follow in analyzing time series models and using time series model forecasts?

Vinod (2014) reminds the reader that causality modeling and testing is quite old. Koopmans (1950) was the first to propose that the right-hand side (RHS) variables in an econometric regression be "exogenous" in the sense of having independent or self-dependent data generating process (DGP) being "approximately causal" for the left-hand side (LHS) variable. Granger causality in Econometrics texts, Vinod (2008), refers to Granger (1969) who proposed tools for the detection of causal paths between two or more economic time series. Roughly speaking, we say that the Granger's causal path $X_i \overset{Gr}{\to} X_j$ holds if variable X_i helps to predict variable X_j. The idea can be formulated in terms of mean square error (MSE) of forecasting h steps ahead based on the information set $I_{nf,t}$, at time t. For example, we say that X_i

J. B. Guerard, *The Leading Economic Indicators and Business Cycles in the United States*, https://doi.org/10.1007/978-3-030-99418-1_8

Granger-causes X_j if the MSEs satisfy the inequality:

$$\text{MSE}_h(I_{\text{nf},t}, \text{ with } x_i) < \text{MSE}_h(I_{\text{nf},t}, \text{ without } x_i), \qquad (8.1)$$

where we have spelled out the condition on the information set that forecasting MSE should be smaller when X_i is included compared to the MSE based on information without the benefit of related X_i variable.

Any statistical test based on lags and leads of effects is subject to the famous fallacy called "post hoc ergo propter hoc." The ancients were aware that a rooster crowing at sunrise before the sun rises was not the cause of the sunrise. Since Granger causality focuses on time precedence, it remains subject to the fallacy, although it obviously remains useful when used with care.

8.1   Causal Analysis for Economic Policy

Assume we have $t = 1, 2, \dots T$ observations. Consider a model having X_j on the left-hand side (LHS) and X_i plus a set of variables combined into generic X_k on the RHS:

$$X_{jt} = f(X_{it}, X_{kt}) + \in_{j|ik}, \qquad (8.2)$$

where we use generic symbols f to denote a possibly nonlinear function and $\in_{j|ik}$ to denote unobserved shocks or errors. We use nonlinear non-parametric kernel regressions to estimate the conditional expectation functions. The specification (2) implies the causal path (RHS → LHS) or $(X_i \rightarrow X_j)$.

We also consider a model for the opposite causal path, $(X_j \rightarrow X_i)$ obtained by flipping X_j with X_i:

$$X_{it} = f(X_{jt}, X_{kt}) + \in_{i|jk}, . \qquad (8.3)$$

By analogy with Granger causality, but avoiding the time-precedence requirement, the data support the causal path $(X_i \rightarrow X_j)$, provided the model (2) has a superior fit (smaller forecasting MSE) compared to the model (3). Theorem 1 in Vinod (2019) extends Granger's intuition to develop computational methods for assessing causal paths and their strength indices. There are at least three coequal empirical criteria, denoted by Cr1, Cr2, and Cr3, which quantify the empirical support for the causal path $(X_i \rightarrow X_j)$.

The criterion Cr1 evaluates finite sample implications of consistency of conditional expectation functions of flipped kernel regressions. The true unknown errors $\in_{j|ik}$ should be orthogonal to the regressors with probability limit satisfying:

$$plim_{T\to\infty}(\in_{j|ik} X_{it})/T = 0 \qquad (8.4)$$

Koopmans (1950) formulated the consistency requirement of Eq. (8.4) as exogeneity of X_i, and went on to require that each RHS variable should "approximately cause" the LHS variable. We plug observable residuals into the (consistency) exogeneity condition (4), yielding two sets of T multiplications $\in_{j|ik} X_{it}$ and $\in_{i|jk} X_{jt}$, where we replace the true unknown errors $\in_{.|..}$ by corresponding residuals $e_{.|...}$.

Our Cr1 assumes that closeness to zero of these observable expressions reveals relative speeds of convergence. The criterion Cr2 checks which flip has "lower" absolute values of residuals. We use asymmetric generalized partial correlation coefficients from Vinod (2014) as our third criterion Cr3.

Since it is not possible to prove why one criterion should dominate others, we use the "preponderance of evidence" standard by constructing a unanimity index $ui \in [-100, 000]$. We simply use a weighted sum of the three criteria denoted by ui. Given a 5% threshold, say, (or $\tau = 5$), the index allows us to propose the following decision rules:

Rule 1: If $(ui < -\tau)$, the causal path is: $X_i \to X_j$.
Rule 2: If $(ui > +\tau)$, the causal path is: $X_j \to X_i$.
Rule 3: If $(|ui| \leq -\tau)$, we obtain bi-directional causality: $X_i \leftrightarrow X_j$, that is, the variables are jointly dependent.

Complete computational details for using these decision rules on any given data set are a part of an open-source and free software package called "generalCorr," Vinod (2017), in a computer language called R. It is readily available in an open forum for further checking and development. The R package comes with three vignettes that provide theoretical details about the algorithms used, as well as examples.

8.2   Regression Modeling of Quarterly Mergers, Stock Prices, and the LEI

This section develops traditional regression modeling of mergers, stock prices, and LEI during the 1975–2018 time period. Mergers are highly statistically associated, contemporaneously, with both stock prices and the LEI, in the initial ordinary least squares regression (OLS) analysis reported in Table

Table 8.1 OLS and Robust regression analysis of mergers, stock prices, and the LEI quarterly data, 1975 Q1 to 2018 Q4

Regression	Constant	SP500	LEI	R-Squared	F
OLS	477.9	1.332		0.825	818.3
(t)	−9.25	(28.61)			
	−2685		55.149	0.837	899.9
	(−18.27)		(30.00)		
	−1365.6	0.636	31.252	0.868	575.5
	(−5.59)	(6.42)	(7.67)		
Robust (OIF)	438.8	1.383		0.805	
	(8.99)	(20.51)			
	−2604.5		54.365	0.648	
	(−16.26)		(27.19)		
	−1318.7	0.666	30.382	0.851	
	(−5.38)	(6.61)	(7.42)		

8.1. The relationship among mergers, stock mergers, and industrial production has been empirically modeled by Nelson (1959, 1966), Melicher et al. (1983), Guerard (1985), Golbe and White (1993), and Vinod and Guerard (2020).

A multiple regression model of the quarterly data finds both stock prices and the LEI have the expected positive coefficients and are highly statistically significant, with both stock prices and LEI variables having t-statistics exceeding 6.40, and an adjusted R-squared of 0.868. Moreover, the SAS application of the robust regression modeling of Maronna et al. (2019), addressing outlier issues, reports that stock prices and the LEI variable coefficients are positive and highly statistically significant. The robust regression statistics are reported in Table 8.1. The robust regression modeling diagnostics of the 99% efficiency OIF estimate of mergers as a function of the contemporaneous S&P 500 stock price index series is shown in Table 8.2. It reports both Mahalanobis distance and its robust version called minimum covariance determinant (MCD-distance).

Mergers are statistically associated with contemporaneous stock prices.

The robust regression modeling diagnostics of the 99% efficiency estimate of mergers as a function of four-period lags of the S&P 500 stock prices series is shown in Table 8.3.

The large p-values for regression coefficients associated with (2, 3, 4)-period lags of stock prices (SP500) reported in Table 8.4 show that those lags are not significant in explaining mergers, whereas lag-1 stock price variable, L1SP500 has a p-value less than 0.05, suggesting significant explanatory evidence.

Table 8.2 FactSet Mergerstat 1975–2018

Model: MODEL1
Dependent Variable: Mergers

Profile for the Initial LTS Estimate

Total Number of Observations	176
Number of Squares Minimized	132
Number of Coefficients	2
Highest Possible Breakdown Value	0.2557

MM Profile

Chi Function	Tukey
K1	7.0410
Efficiency	0.9900

Parameter Estimates

Parameter	DF	Estimate	Standard Error	95% Confidence Limits		Chi-Square	Pr > ChiSq
Intercept	1	438.7779	48.7570	343.2158	534.3399	80.99	<.0001
SP500	1	1.3833	0.0457	1.2937	1.4729	915.22	<.0001

Diagnostics

Obs	Mahalanobis Distance	Robust MCD Distance	Leverage	Standardized Robust Residual	Outlier
101	0.8261	1.3020		3.1042	*
162	1.7567	2.2491	*	-0.4051	
167	1.8394	2.3332	*	-0.8262	
168	1.9653	2.4614	*	-1.5607	
169	2.1356	2.6346	*	-1.7372	
170	2.2307	2.7315	*	-2.6267	
171	2.3140	2.8163	*	-3.3079	*
172	2.5569	3.0635	*	-3.5206	*
173	2.6113	3.1188	*	-3.4382	*
174	2.6844	3.1932	*	-2.7848	
175	2.8928	3.4053	*	-3.5000	*
176	2.4195	2.9236	*	-2.8476	

Diagnostics Summary

Type	Proportion	Cutoff
Outlier	0.0284	3.0000
Leverage	0.0625	2.2414

Goodness-of-Fit

Statistic	Value
R-Square	0.8049
AICR	202.3846
BICR	208.8762
Deviance	29682350

Table 8.3 Mergers explained by Stock Prices with 4-period Lags

Data Set	WORK.QMERGERS
Dependent Variable	Mergers
Number of Independent Variables	4
Number of Observations	172
Missing Values	4
Method	MM-Estimation

The ROBUSTREG Procedure

MM Profile

Efficiency   0.9900

Parameter Estimates

Parameter	DF	Estimate	Standard Error	95% Confidence Limits		Chi-Square	Pr > ChiSq
Intercept	1	440.8733	51.2495	340.4261	541.3206	74.00	<.0001
L1SP500	1	0.9667	0.4931	0.0003	1.9331	3.84	0.0499
L2SP500	1	0.1433	0.7528	-1.3321	1.6187	0.04	0.8491
L3SP500	1	0.1140	0.7569	-1.3696	1.5976	0.02	0.8803
L4SP500	1	0.1952	0.5059	-0.7964	1.1868	0.15	0.6996
Scale	0	418.5720					

Diagnostics

Obs	Mahalanobis Distance	Robust MCD Distance	Leverage	Standardized Robust Residual	Outlier
49	1.5644	3.3557	*	-0.5230	
51	1.5786	3.6535	*	-0.5573	
92	2.3158	5.7556	*	-0.1169	
93	3.0624	6.7710	*	0.8097	
94	3.1981	7.8304	*	1.5528	
95	2.4511	5.4119	*	1.4050	
97	1.6365	3.3882	*	2.9200	
98	1.7089	3.6919	*	2.3695	
101	2.6625	7.3217	*	1.0058	
102	3.4834	10.0949	*	0.8633	
103	3.6105	10.3693	*	-0.1852	
104	4.3179	11.4367	*	0.4439	
105	3.8547	8.6968	*	0.5040	
106	3.7901	10.1589	*	0.4703	
107	2.8489	7.3740	*	0.3658	
108	3.3279	9.5254	*	0.7882	
109	3.3916	9.7277	*	1.0028	
110	2.7798	7.8797	*	1.4645	
111	2.3402	5.1640	*	1.0795	
112	2.3483	5.4864	*	1.6032	
113	1.9912	4.3654	*	2.0224	
124	1.4330	3.4124	*	1.6146	
125	1.8293	4.7925	*	1.6095	
127	2.0034	3.7249	*	0.3292	
128	1.9193	4.3071	*	0.1075	
129	1.8937	4.4007	*	-0.4626	
130	3.0998	8.8132	*	-0.5906	
131	3.0834	8.2722	*	-0.4325	
132	3.7461	10.6050	*	-1.2982	
133	5.7717	15.7629	*	-0.6607	
134	5.8923	16.1756	*	0.1121	

(continued)

Table 8.3 (continued)

135	6.4110	17.5382	*	0.1643	
136	3.6573	9.1898	*	0.3275	
137	2.6910	6.3351	*	0.9000	
138	1.6469	3.4199	*	0.6988	
139	1.6858	4.1814	*	0.8512	
140	1.5918	3.9163	*	1.1040	
141	2.1804	5.9520	*	0.8763	
143	1.8276	3.9254	*	0.3303	
144	2.3493	6.4426	*	0.5754	
145	2.4574	6.4028	*	0.3169	
146	3.0906	8.3165	*	0.0715	
147	2.6485	5.5535	*	0.3173	
148	3.0326	6.2098	*	1.1063	
149	2.5082	6.1299	*	-0.3742	
150	2.4891	4.8178	*	-0.8499	
151	2.1363	4.7772	*	-0.1883	
159	1.8804	3.4577	*	-0.1732	
160	3.4747	9.0612	*	0.0492	
161	3.8120	8.9474	*	-0.6629	
162	4.0076	10.5361	*	-0.9371	
163	2.4489	4.5000	*	-0.6087	
164	2.3064	5.4183	*	-1.2273	
166	2.4356	3.4181	*	-2.1824	
169	3.0924	5.0707	*	-3.0225	*
170	3.2253	4.9896	*	-2.4432	
171	3.2707	4.8971	*	-2.8241	
172	3.2222	5.5129	*	-3.7737	*

Diagnostics Summary

Observation Type	Proportion	Cutoff
Outlier	0.0116	3.0000
Leverage	0.3372	3.3382

Table 8.4 Causal paths between mergers and LEI, SP500 and Unemployment at lag value specified in the "lag" column

	Cause	Response	Strength	Corr.	p-value	Lag
1	LEI	Mergers	100	0.9172	0	1
2	SP500	Mergers	100	0.9057	0	1
3	UnEmp	Mergers	31.496	-0.4383	0	1
4	LEI	Mergers	100	0.9167	0	2
5	SP500	Mergers	100	0.9062	0	2
6	UnEmp	Mergers	31.496	-0.427	0	2
7	LEI	Mergers	100	0.9121	0	3
8	SP500	Mergers	100	0.9056	0	3
9	UnEmp	Mergers	31.496	-0.4092	0	3
10	LEI	Mergers	100	0.9059	0	4
11	SP500	Mergers	100	0.9027	0	4
12	UnEmp	Mergers	31.496	-0.3918	0	4

8.3 Time Series Model Selection and Granger Causality Modeling

Vinod and Guerard (2020) applied the Vinod (2008) Granger causality to report causality findings of the LEI on quarterly mergers during the 1975–2018 time period. The application of decision rules mentioned in our introductory section produces evidence that both stock prices and the LEI cause quarterly mergers during the 1975–2018 time period. See Table 8.4. Stock prices and LEI cause mergers at lag values one through four.

As reported in Table 8.4, the Vinod causality modeling decision rules produce evidence that both stock prices and the LEI cause quarterly mergers during the 1975–2018 time period. The software allows us to choose control variables so that the effect of control variables is removed from both flipped variables before choosing the direction of the path. Let us return to the problem of time series modelling and forecasting the unemployment rate, examined in the previous chapter.

We revisit the approaches used in the seminal paper of Montgomery, Zarnowitz, Tsay, and Tiao (Montgomery et al., 1998), hereafter denoted as MZTT, on forecasting the U.S. unemployment rate. Based on monthly observations in the period (RC 1948 to 1993), they demonstrated that time series models are useful in predicting 1-month to 5-month ahead unemployment rates and they compared the out-sample prediction performance of a range of models. More than 20 years have passed and it is useful and necessary to re-exam these models *post publication*, as well as investigate new phenomenon aroused since, including the financial crisis of 2018. We pay special attention to the relationship of the U.S unemployment rate and the lagged U.S. weekly unemployment claim, as well as the U.S. Leading Economic Indicator (LEI) series.

Because of its importance, there is an extensive literature on forecasting unemployment rate. MZTT modelled the U.S. unemployment rate as a function of the weekly unemployment claims time series, 1948–1993. MZTT reported that nonlinear models, such as TAR reduced forecasting errors by as much as 28%, being more effective in periods of economic contraction and rising unemployment. The majority of the reduced forecasting error occurs in the first quarter following the forecasting origin while one-third of the forecasting error occurs in the second quarter. The transfer function modeling using unemployment claims in MZTT did not reduce the forecasting error. Thomakos and Guerard (2004) re-examined several sets of transfer function modeling sets, including the MZTT U.S. unemployment rate, weekly unemployment claims, and LEI relationships during the 1952–1998 time period.

Thomakos and Guerard reported leading indicator and the initial unemployment claims provided RMSE reductions of 7.6 and 8.6%, respectively, over the no-change model. The RMSE reduction reductions were not statistically significant. The coefficients of the TF and VAR models were generally statistically significant and of the correct sign in the Thomakos and Guerard rolling regressions.

Vinod and Guerard (2020) applied the transfer function methodology of the Scientific Computing Associates (SCA) and its Chen and Lee (1990) test for Granger causality to report Granger-causal relationships in which LEI lad the U.S. unemployment rate. Vinod and Guerard (2020) modeled The Conference Board database for the 1959–2018 time period to establish the casual relationship in which LEI led the U.S. employment rate. Several sets of regression and time series-based models have established that transfer functions with LEI and weekly unemployment claims data were highly statistically significant for modelling the MZTT unemployment rate data. Vinod and Guerard (2020) reported LEI transfer function Granger causality findings for the unemployment rate time series during the 1959–2018 time period, but only concurrent statistical association between time series during the 1959–1993 time period. The authors reported that the weekly unemployment claims transfer function for the unemployment rate time series produced concurrent statistical association between the time series during both the 1959–1993 and 1959–2018 time periods. The 1994–2018 time period was one of economic growth, despite the Global Finance Crisis of 2008–2009. This result is important because the authors did not find the MZTT result that economic contractions and rising unemployment were primarily periods of RMSE reductions.

Following MTZZ, we employ the SARIMA and transfer function modeling using the leading economic indicators and one of its components, weekly unemployment claims, to forecast the U.S. unemployment rate. We report that the SARIMA and the LEI-based transfer function models significantly outperform the no-change models. The U.S. unemployment rate was approaching a 60-year low during 2018. Moreover, the U.S. Leading Economic Indicators (LEI) time series was at an all-time high. There have been statistically significant relationships among the unemployment rate, weekly unemployment claims, and the LEI time series, reported in MZTT, Guerard et al. (2020), and Vinod and Guerard (2020). These time series have been addressed before, but our results are more statistically significant using more recently developed time series modelling techniques and software. The MZTT results are validated, post-publication, and additional time series modeling enhances the statistical significance of the seminal study results.

Our results are very consistent with the forecasting analysis of Guerard et al. (2020) and Vinod and Guerard (2020).

8.4   Granger Causality Testing in the SCA System

One can use the SCA system, see Liu (1999), and test for causality, as an application of the Chen and Lee (1990) test, one finds statistically significant association in the DUE, DLEI relationship with the 4-month DLEI lags, see Table 8.5.

Moreover, the use of SCA system produces univariate DUE time series results that the four-lag of DLEI data are statistically significant, with an R-squared of 0.188. DLEI lags of 2 and 3 are statistically significant at the 5% level, lag one is significant at the 10% level, and the application of the Tsay (1988) outlier procedure reduces the RSS from 0.161 to 0.113, see Table 8.6.

Let us use SCA for causality testing, we start with enhanced modelling of transfer functions of the unemployment rate as a function of the TCB LEI variable, We then apply the Chen and Lee (1990) test, to establish statistically significant causality in the DUE, DLEI relationship with both 4-month DLEI lags (Tables 8.7, 8.8 and 8.9).

The Ashley Granger Schmalensee (AGS, 1980) approach assumes the pre-whitening of the input and output prior to model construction. The pre-whitening must occur before the period of testing. That is, we must pre-whiten the input and output and estimate the cross-correlations of the pre-whitened residuals. We show the estimated cross-correlations of pre-whitened input, the TCB LEI, and the unemployment rate in Fig. 8.1, for the 60 months of the 1995–2000 time period. The data represents post-sample of Montgomery, Zarnowitz, Tsay, and Tiao (MZTT, 1998). The estimated cross-correlations in which the LEI lead the unemployment rate, the right side of Fig. 8.1 are negative, as one would expect; that is, the lags in the LEI data lead the unemployment rate with negative coefficients. The higher the LEI, the lower should be the unemployment rate for 1995–2000. We estimated monthly pre-whitened cross-correlations of the 60 months of inputs and output during the 1995–2020 time period. Finally, in Fig. 8.2, we show the pre-whitened correlations of inputs of LEI and the unemployment rate during the entire 1995–1/2020 post-sample MZTT time period. We repeat the pre-whitening AGS procedure using monthly data of the weekly unemployment claims and the unemployment rate. The reader expects to see a set of positive estimated cross-correlations in which

Table 8.5 Summary for univariate time series model for the U.S. Unemployment rate

```
-------------------------------------------------------------------
```

VARIABLE TYPE OF ORIGINAL DIFFERENCING

      VARIABLE OR CENTERED

DUE   RANDOM   ORIGINAL   NONE

DLEI   RANDOM   ORIGINAL   NONE

```
-------------------------------------------------------------------
```


PARAMETER LABEL	VARIABLE NAME	NUM./ DENOM.	FACTOR	ORDER	CONS-TRAINT	VALUE	STD ERROR	T VALUE
1	DLEI	NUM.	1	1	NONE	-.0402	.0171	-2.35
2	DLEI	NUM.	1	2	NONE	-.0629	.0183	-3.45
3	DLEI	NUM.	1	3	NONE	-.0464	.0182	-2.55
4	DLEI	NUM.	1	4	NONE	-.0321	.0171	-1.88
5	DUE	D-AR	1	1	NONE	-.0807	.0376	-2.15


```
EFFECTIVE NUMBER OF OBSERVATIONS . .           710
R-SQUARE . . . . . . . . . . . . . .         0.188
RESIDUAL STANDARD ERROR. . . . . .   0.161307E+00
(-2)*LOG LIKELIHOOD FUNCTION . . . . -0.575818E+03
AIC. . . . . . . . . . . . . . . . . -0.563818E+03
SIC. . . . . . . . . . . . . . . . . -0.536427E+03
--
```

THE CRITICAL VALUE FOR SIGNIFICANCE TESTS OF ACF AND ESTIMATES IS 1.960

SUMMARY FOR UNIVARIATE TIME SERIES MODEL -- UTSMODEL

```
-------------------------------------------------------------------
```
VARIABLE TYPE OF ORIGINAL DIFFERENCING
     VARIABLE OR CENTERED

NS   RANDOM   ORIGINAL   NONE
```
-------------------------------------------------------------------
```

PARAMETER LABEL	VARIABLE NAME	NUM./ DENOM.	FACTOR	ORDER	CONS-TRAINT	VALUE	STD ERROR	T VALUE
1	CNST	1	0	NONE	.0193	.0060	3.20	

```
TOTAL NUMBER OF OBSERVATIONS . . . .      711
EFFECTIVE NUMBER OF OBSERVATIONS . .      711
RESIDUAL STANDARD ERROR. . . . . . . 0.160581E+00
--
```

the weekly unemployment claims lead the unemployment rate; that is, the lags in the weekly unemployment claims data lead the unemployment rate. The estimated cross-correlations in which the weekly unemployment claims data lead the unemployment rate, the right side of Fig. 8.3 are positive, as one would expect. The higher the monthly date of weekly unemployment

Table 8.6 Summary for univariate time series model with outliers—TFM1

VARIABLE	TYPE OF VARIABLE	ORIGINAL OR CENTERED	DIFFERENCING
DUE	RANDOM	ORIGINAL	NONE
DLEI	RANDOM	ORIGINAL	NONE

PARAMETER LABEL	VARIABLE NAME	NUM./ DENOM.	FACTOR	ORDER	CONS-TRAINT	VALUE	STD ERROR	T VALUE
1	DLEI	NUM.	1	1	NONE	-.0233	.0148	-1.57
2	DLEI	NUM.	1	2	NONE	-.0628	.0154	-4.08
3	DLEI	NUM.	1	3	NONE	-.0490	.0154	-3.18
4	DLEI	NUM.	1	4	NONE	-.0154	.0149	-1.04

SUMMARY OF OUTLIER DETECTION AND ADJUSTMENT

TIME	ESTIMATE	T-VALUE	TYPE
11	-0.458	-5.47	TC
14	0.783	6.72	AO
17	0.268	3.21	TC
21	0.597	6.26	TC
22	-0.449	-3.44	AO
31	-0.380	-3.92	TC
32	0.396	3.00	AO
34	-0.238	-2.02	AO
43	0.306	2.71	AO
46	0.323	2.86	AO
66	-0.259	-2.29	AO
70	-0.260	-2.30	AO
74	-0.353	-3.13	AO
132	0.370	4.58	TC
140	0.338	4.12	TC
144	-0.277	-2.42	AO
177	-0.257	-2.28	AO
188	0.315	2.79	AO
190	0.566	6.20	TC
192	0.511	4.20	AO
193	-0.302	-2.58	AO
194	0.285	2.48	AO
197	-0.231	-2.85	TC
209	0.228	2.82	TC
216	-0.269	-2.38	AO
222	-0.257	-2.27	AO
227	-0.380	-3.36	AO
234	0.361	3.19	AO
235	-0.266	-2.35	AO
247	0.269	2.38	AO
255	0.587	6.35	TC
257	-0.358	-3.85	TC
263	-0.254	-2.68	TC
264	0.505	3.86	AO
268	0.335	2.93	AO
270	-0.295	-2.61	AO
273	0.340	4.18	TC
279	0.216	2.62	TC

Table 8.6 (continued)

284	0.325	3.92	TC
288	-0.455	-3.97	AO
294	-0.620	-5.49	AO
296	-0.359	-4.44	TC
306	0.356	3.15	AO
319	-0.259	-2.29	AO
324	-0.272	-2.41	AO
325	0.535	4.74	AO
335	-0.278	-2.46	AO
339	-0.260	-2.30	AO
378	0.263	3.26	TC
395	0.202	2.47	TC
400	0.202	2.45	TC
405	-0.298	-2.62	AO
435	0.414	3.67	AO
450	0.278	2.98	TC
451	-0.525	-4.03	AO
471	-0.337	-2.98	AO
508	-0.259	-2.30	AO
511	0.262	3.25	TC
542	0.330	2.92	AO
591	-0.273	-2.42	AO
592	0.183	2.27	TC
599	0.203	2.51	TC
608	0.278	3.44	TC
622	0.448	3.97	AO
623	-0.450	-3.98	AO
633	-0.242	-3.00	TC
644	-0.308	-2.72	AO
649	-0.269	-2.39	AO
663	-0.338	-2.99	AO
688	-0.298	-2.64	AO
694	-0.279	-2.47	AO
713	0.259	2.29	AO

MAXIMUM NUMBER OF OUTLIERS IS REACHED

** THE OUTLIER(S) AFTER TIME PERIOD 710 OCCURS WITHIN THE
   LAST FIVE OBSERVATIONS OF THE SERIES. THE IDENTIFIED TYPE
   AND THE ESTIMATE OF THE OUTLIER(S) MAY NOT BE RELIABLE

TOTAL NUMBER OF OBSERVATIONS.   715
EFFECTIVE NUMBER OF OBSERVATIONS.   711
RESIDUAL STANDARD ERROR (WITHOUT OUTLIER ADJUSTMENT). . 0.162276E+00
RESIDUAL STANDARD ERROR (WITH OUTLIER ADJUSTMENT) . . . 0.112951E+00
--

claims, the higher should be the unemployment rate for 1995–2000. We show a similar (positive) estimated cross-correlation function in Fig. 8.4 for the 1995–1/2020 time period with unemployment claims data. Figures 8.3 and 8.4 specifically substantiate the initial MZTT modeling results.

Table 8.7 SCA transfer function modelling of the U.S. unemployment rate
VARIABLES ARE DUE, DLEI.

TIME PERIOD ANALYZED . . . . 1 TO 715
EFFECTIVE NUMBER OF OBSERVATIONS (NOBE). . .   715

SERIES	NAME	MEAN	STD. ERROR
1	DUE	-0.0029	0.1791
2	DLEI	0.1175	0.4798

NOTE: THE APPROX. STD. ERROR FOR THE ESTIMATED CORRELATIONS BELOW
  IS (1/NOBE**.5) = 0.03740

SAMPLE CORRELATION MATRIX OF THE SERIES

 1.00
-0.35 1.00

SUMMARIES OF CROSS CORRELATION MATRICES USING +,-,., WHERE
  + DENOTES A VALUE GREATER THAN 2/SQRT(NOBE)
  - DENOTES A VALUE LESS THAN -2/SQRT(NOBE)
  . DENOTES A NON-SIGNIFICANT VALUE BASED ON THE ABOVE CRITERION

BEHAVIOR OF VALUES IN (I,J)TH POSITION OF CROSS CORRELATION MATRIX OVER
ALL OUTPUTTED LAGS WHEN SERIES J LAGS SERIES I

       1   2

1 +++++++++.+- ------------
1 ....-   ------.-....

2 ----........ +++++++++++++
2 ......++.+++ +..........-

CROSS CORRELATION MATRICES IN TERMS OF +,-,.

LAGS 1 THROUGH 6

   +-   +-   +-   +-   +-   +-
   -+   -+   -+   -+   .+   .+

LAGS 7 THROUGH 12

   +-   +-   +-   .-   +-   --
   .+   .+   .+   .+   .+   .+

LAGS 13 THROUGH 18

(continued)

Table 8.7 (continued)

```
 .-   .-   .-   .-   .-   .-
 .+   ..   ..   ..   ..   ..
```

LAGS 19 THROUGH 24

```
 ..   .-   ..   ..   ..   -.
 +.   +.   ..   +.   +.   + -
--
```

STEPAR VARIABLES ARE DUE,DLEI. @
ARFITS ARE 1 to 4. rccm 1 to 4.

TIME PERIOD ANALYZED . . . . 1 TO 715
EFFECTIVE NUMBER OF OBSERVATIONS (NOBE). . .   715

SERIES	NAME	MEAN	STD. ERROR
1	DUE	-0.0029	0.1791
2	DLEI	0.1175	0.4798

NOTE: THE APPROX. STD. ERROR FOR THE ESTIMATED CORRELATIONS BELOW
    IS (1/NOBE**.5) =   0.03740

SAMPLE CORRELATION MATRIX OF THE SERIES

```
 1.00
-0.35  1.00
```

SUMMARIES OF CROSS CORRELATION MATRICES USING +,-,., WHERE
    + DENOTES A VALUE GREATER THAN 2/SQRT(NOBE)
    - DENOTES A VALUE LESS THAN -2/SQRT(NOBE)
    . DENOTES A NON-SIGNIFICANT VALUE BASED ON THE ABOVE CRITERION

BEHAVIOR OF VALUES IN (I,J)TH POSITION OF CROSS CORRELATION MATRIX OVER
ALL OUTPUTTED LAGS WHEN SERIES J LAGS SERIES I

```
        1         2

1  +++++++++.+-  ------------
1  ...........-  ------.-....


2  ----........  ++++++++++++
2  ......++.+++  +..........-
```

CROSS CORRELATION MATRICES IN TERMS OF +,-,.

LAGS 1 THROUGH 6

```
 + -   + -   + -   + -   + -   + -
 - +   - +   - +   - +   .+   .+
```

(continued)

Table 8.7 (continued)

LAGS 7 THROUGH 12

```
+-   +-   +-   .-   +-   --
.+   .+   .+   .+   .+   .+
```

LAGS 13 THROUGH 18

```
.-   .-   .-   .-   .-   .-
.+   ..   ..   ..   ..   ..
```

LAGS 19 THROUGH 24

```
..   .-   ..   ..   ..   -.
+.   +.   ..   +.   +.   +-
```

DETERMINANT OF S(0) = 0.644754E-02

NOTE: S(0) IS THE SAMPLE COVARIANCE MATRIX OF W(MAXLAG+1),...,W(NOBE)

AUTOREGRESSIVE FITTING ON LAG(S) 1

SUMMARIES OF CROSS CORRELATION MATRICES USING +,-,., WHERE
    + DENOTES A VALUE GREATER THAN 2/SQRT(NOBE)
    - DENOTES A VALUE LESS THAN -2/SQRT(NOBE)
    . DENOTES A NON-SIGNIFICANT VALUE BASED ON THE ABOVE CRITERION

BEHAVIOR OF VALUES IN (I,J)TH POSITION OF CROSS CORRELATION MATRIX OVER
ALL OUTPUTTED LAGS WHEN SERIES J LAGS SERIES I

```
          1         2

1  .+++++....+-  +--.--.-.-.
1  .-.........-  --...-.....

2  +......+.++.  -+++.+..+.+.
2  ........+..  ............
```

CROSS CORRELATION MATRICES IN TERMS OF +,-,.

LAGS 1 THROUGH 6

```
.+   +-   +-   +-   +.   +-
+-   .+   .+   .+   ..   .+
```

LAGS 7 THROUGH 12

```
.-   ..   .-   ..   +-   -.
..   +.   .+   +.   ++   ..
```

LAGS 13 THROUGH 18

```
.-   --   ..   ..   ..   .-
..   ..   ..   ..   ..   ..
```

(continued)

Table 8.7   (continued)

LAGS 19 THROUGH 24

```
..   .-  ..  ..  ..  -.
..   ..  ..  +.  ..  ..
```

AUTOREGRESSIVE FITTING ON LAG(S) 1 2

SUMMARIES OF CROSS CORRELATION MATRICES USING +,-,., WHERE
  + DENOTES A VALUE GREATER THAN 2/SQRT(NOBE)
  - DENOTES A VALUE LESS THAN -2/SQRT(NOBE)
  . DENOTES A NON-SIGNIFICANT VALUE BASED ON THE ABOVE CRITERION

BEHAVIOR OF VALUES IN (I,J)TH POSITION OF CROSS CORRELATION MATRIX OVER
ALL OUTPUTTED LAGS WHEN SERIES J LAGS SERIES I

```
       1        2

1  ..++.......-  .+......-...
1  ...........-  .-.-.-....

2  ...+...+..+.  .-+.....+...
2  .........+..  ............
```

CROSS CORRELATION MATRICES IN TERMS OF +,-,.

LAGS 1 THROUGH 6

```
..   .+  +.  +.  ..  ..
..   .-  .+  +.  ..  ..
```

LAGS 7 THROUGH 12

```
..   ..  .-  ..  ..  -.
..   +.  .+  ..  +.  ..
```

LAGS 13 THROUGH 18

```
..   .-  ..  ..  .-  ..
..   ..  ..  ..  ..  ..
```

LAGS 19 THROUGH 24

```
..   .-  ..  ..  ..  -.
..   ..  ..  +.  ..  ..
```

AUTOREGRESSIVE FITTING ON LAG(S) 1 2 3

SUMMARIES OF CROSS CORRELATION MATRICES USING +,-,., WHERE
  + DENOTES A VALUE GREATER THAN 2/SQRT(NOBE)
  - DENOTES A VALUE LESS THAN -2/SQRT(NOBE)
  . DENOTES A NON-SIGNIFICANT VALUE BASED ON THE ABOVE CRITERION

BEHAVIOR OF VALUES IN (I,J)TH POSITION OF CROSS CORRELATION MATRIX OVER

(continued)

Table 8.7   (continued)

ALL OUTPUTTED LAGS WHEN SERIES J LAGS SERIES I

       1   2

1 ...+.......- ....-...
1 ....- ....

2 ...+......+. ....+...
2 ....

CROSS CORRELATION MATRICES IN TERMS OF +,-,.

LAGS 1 THROUGH 6

.. .. .. +. .. ..
.. .. .. +. .. ..

LAGS 7 THROUGH 12

.. .. .- .. .. -.
.. .. .+ .. +. ..

LAGS 13 THROUGH 18

.. ..
.. ..

LAGS 19 THROUGH 24

.. .. -.
.. ..

AUTOREGRESSIVE FITTING ON LAG(S) 1 2 3 4

SUMMARIES OF CROSS CORRELATION MATRICES USING +,-,., WHERE
  + DENOTES A VALUE GREATER THAN 2/SQRT(NOBE)
  - DENOTES A VALUE LESS THAN -2/SQRT(NOBE)
  . DENOTES A NON-SIGNIFICANT VALUE BASED ON THE ABOVE CRITERION

BEHAVIOR OF VALUES IN (I,J)TH POSITION OF CROSS CORRELATION MATRIX OVER
ALL OUTPUTTED LAGS WHEN SERIES J LAGS SERIES I

       1   2

1 ....- ....
1 ....- ....

2 ....+.....+. ....+...
2 ....+.. ....

(continued)

Table 8.7   (continued)

CROSS CORRELATION MATRICES IN TERMS OF +,-,.

LAGS 1 THROUGH 6

```
 ..   ..   ..   ..   ..   ..
 ..   ..   ..   ..   +.   ..
```

LAGS 7 THROUGH 12

```
 ..   ..   ..   ..   ..   -.
 ..   ..   .+   ..   +.   ..
```

LAGS 13 THROUGH 18

```
 ..   ..   ..   ..   ..   ..
 ..   ..   ..   ..   ..   ..
```

LAGS 19 THROUGH 24

```
 ..   ..   ..   ..   ..   -.
 ..   ..   ..   +.   ..   ..
```

8.5   Rolling Forecast Windows Modeling Efficiency

In economic forecasting, many authors stress the importance of input-sample and out-of-sample, or post-sample, modeling. We endorse that rationale which drives the AGS procedure. We estimated 60 months of cross-correlations of the pre-whitened LEI and weekly unemployment claims data with the unemployment rate for the entire 1959 to 2020 time period. We show the initial five-year period of the estimated cross-correlations of LEI input and outputs of the 1959–1965 and 1959–1/2020 time periods in Figs. 8.1 through 8.4.

Both figures show negative estimated cross-correlations for the period when lags of the LEI series lead the unemployment rate. We show the initial five-year period of the estimated cross-correlations of monthly data of unemployment claims input and outputs of the 1959–1/2020 time periods in Figs. 8.3 and 8.4. Both figures show positive cross-correlations for the period when lags of the unemployment claims data lead the unemployment rate time series.

More importantly, the respective input estimated cross-correlations are shown in Figs. 8.5 and 8.6, respectively, for the entire 1959–12/2020 time period, including most of the year of COVID, 2020. The LEI data input continues to produce estimated negative cross-correlations and the weekly unemployment claims data input continues to produce estimated positive cross-correlations, as we expected.

Table 8.8 Stepwise autoregression summary

```
--------------------------------------------------------------------
    I RESIDUAL  I EIGENVAL.I CHI-SQ  I          I SIGNIFICANCE
LAG I VARIANCES I OF SIGMA I  TEST   I   AIC    I OF PARTIAL AR COEFF.
----+-----------+----------+---------+----------+---------------------
  1 I .279E-01  I .267E-01 I 340.10 I  -5.514 I . -
    I .148E+00  I .149E+00 I        I         I . +
----+-----------+----------+---------+----------+---------------------
  2 I .257E-01  I .253E-01 I 136.90 I  -5.696 I + -
    I .129E+00  I .130E+00 I        I         I . +
----+-----------+----------+---------+----------+---------------------
  3 I .251E-01  I .248E-01 I  43.44 I  -5.747 I + -
    I .124E+00  I .124E+00 I        I         I . +
----+-----------+----------+---------+----------+---------------------
  4 I .247E-01  I .243E-01 I  18.65 I  -5.762 I + .
    I .123E+00  I .124E+00 I        I         I + .
--------------------------------------------------------------------


NOTE:  CHI-SQUARED CRITICAL VALUES WITH   4   DEGREES OF FREEDOM ARE

              5 PERCENT:   9.5    1 PERCENT:  13.3


NOTE:  THE PARTIAL AUTOREGRESSION COEFFICIENT MATRIX FOR LAG L IS THE
       ESTIMATED PHI(L) FROM THE FIT WHERE THE MAXIMUM LAG USED IS L
       (I.E. THE LAST COEFFICIENT MATRIX). THE ELEMENTS ARE
       STANDARDIZED BY DIVIDING EACH BY ITS STANDARD ERROR.
--


  MTSMODEL ARMA12. SERIES ARE DUE,DLEI. @
  MODEL IS (1-PHI*B)SERIES=C+(1-TH1*B)NOISE.


SUMMARY FOR MULTIVARIATE ARMA MODEL -- ARMA12

VARIABLE   DIFFERENCING

  DUE
  DLEI

  PARAMETER      FACTOR      ORDER    CONSTRAINT

  1        C    CONSTANT      0        CC
  2        PHI  REG AR        1        CPHI
  3        TH1  REG MA        1        CTH1
--


  CAUSALTEST MODEL ARMA12. OUTPUT PRINT(CORR). alpha .01


SUMMARY OF THE TIME SERIES

SERIES    NAME           MEAN       STD DEV    DIFFERENCE ORDER(S)

  1     DUE           -0.0029       0.1791
  2     DLEI           0.1175       0.4798


------------------------
```

(continued)

Table 8.8 (continued)

```
ERROR COVARIANCE MATRIX
-----------------------

                1           2
    1        .032113
    2       -.030341      .230366

ITERATIONS TERMINATED DUE TO:
  MAXIMUM NUMBER OF ITERATIONS  10 REACHED
  TOTAL NUMBER OF ITERATIONS IS   14

MODEL SUMMARY WITH MAXIMUM LIKELIHOOD PARAMETER ESTIMATES

----- CONSTANT VECTOR (STD ERROR) -----

     0.052  (    0.016  )
    -0.138  (    0.044  )

----- PHI MATRICES -----

ESTIMATES OF   PHI( 1 ) MATRIX AND SIGNIFICANCE

    -1.377    -.531       - -
     6.484    2.414       + +

STANDARD ERRORS

      .263     .064
      .782     .204

----- THETA MATRICES -----

ESTIMATES OF   THETA( 1 ) MATRIX AND SIGNIFICANCE

    -1.323    -.475       - -
     6.300    2.112       + +

STANDARD ERRORS

      .264     .066
      .780     .209


-----------------------
ERROR COVARIANCE MATRIX
-----------------------

                1           2
    1        .025766
    2       -.004718      .125043
```

The Granger causality and Forecasting Tables, reported here as initially reported in Kyriazi et al. (2019) for agricultural prices, tell a compelling story of verified Granger causality and Root Mean Square Error (RMSE) forecasting errors substantially lower than AR(1) and Sample Mean Forecasts that are often used as forecasting benchmarks of the unemployment rate. See Tables 8.10 and 8.11.

We report that robust regression (RR) with one, two, and three period lags and the adaptive learning models with the LEI input significantly reduce

Table 8.9 Summary of final parameter estimates and their standard errors

PARAMETER NUMBER	PARAMETER DESCRIPTION	FINAL ESTIMATE	ESTIMATED STD. ERROR
1	CONSTANT (1)	0.052124	0.016013
2	CONSTANT (2)	-0.138469	0.044296
3	AUTOREGRESSIVE (1, 1, 1)	-1.377163	0.263322
4	AUTOREGRESSIVE (1, 1, 2)	-0.530786	0.064085
5	AUTOREGRESSIVE (1, 2, 1)	6.484085	0.782178
6	AUTOREGRESSIVE (1, 2, 2)	2.413705	0.204443
7	MOVING AVERAGE (1, 1, 1)	-1.322794	0.263844
8	MOVING AVERAGE (1, 1, 2)	-0.475195	0.065672
9	MOVING AVERAGE (1, 2, 1)	6.300207	0.780190
10	MOVING AVERAGE (1, 2, 2)	2.111769	0.209422

```
-------------------------------------
CORRELATION MATRIX OF THE PARAMETERS
-------------------------------------

         1     2     3     4     5     6     7     8     9    10
  1    1.00
  2    -.73  1.00
  3    -.33  -.36  1.00
  4    -.41  -.21   .85  1.00
  5    -.30  -.40   .77   .76  1.00
  6    -.18  -.48   .77   .49   .88  1.00
  7    -.33  -.37  1.00   .85   .79   .78  1.00
  8    -.40  -.24   .88   .98   .78   .55   .88  1.00
  9    -.30  -.40   .78   .76  1.00   .87   .79   .78  1.00
 10    -.18  -.47   .76   .49   .87   .99   .77   .52   .86  1.00
```

```
THE RESIDUAL COVARIANCE MATRIX IS SET TO FULL MATRIX
ALL ELEMENTS IN THE MATRIX PARAMETERS ARE ALLOWED TO BE ESTIMATED
-2*(LOG LIKELIHOOD AT FINAL ESTIMATES UNDER H5 ) IS  -0.26704472E+04


THE RESIDUAL COVARIANCE MATRIX IS SET TO DIAGONAL MATRIX
ALL ELEMENTS IN THE MATRIX PARAMETERS ARE ALLOWED TO BE ESTIMATED
-2*(LOG LIKELIHOOD AT FINAL ESTIMATES UNDER H5*) IS  -0.26876968E+04


THE RESIDUAL COVARIANCE MATRIX IS SET TO FULL MATRIX
THE (2,1)TH ELEMENTS IN THE MATRIX PARAMETERS ARE SET TO ZERO
-2*(LOG LIKELIHOOD AT FINAL ESTIMATES UNDER H4 ) IS  -0.26703238E+04


THE RESIDUAL COVARIANCE MATRIX IS SET TO DIAGONAL MATRIX
THE (2,1)TH ELEMENTS IN THE MATRIX PARAMETERS ARE SET TO ZERO
-2*(LOG LIKELIHOOD AT FINAL ESTIMATES UNDER H4*) IS  -0.26660243E+04


THE RESIDUAL COVARIANCE MATRIX IS SET TO FULL MATRIX
THE (1,2)TH ELEMENTS IN THE MATRIX PARAMETERS ARE SET TO ZERO
-2*(LOG LIKELIHOOD AT FINAL ESTIMATES UNDER H3 ) IS  -0.26014689E+04


THE RESIDUAL COVARIANCE MATRIX IS SET TO DIAGONAL MATRIX
THE (1,2)TH ELEMENTS IN THE MATRIX PARAMETERS ARE SET TO ZERO
```

(continued)

Table 8.9 (continued)

```
-2*(LOG LIKELIHOOD AT FINAL ESTIMATES UNDER H3*) IS  -0.25922485E+04


THE RESIDUAL COVARIANCE MATRIX IS SET TO FULL MATRIX
THE (2,1)TH ELEMENTS IN THE MATRIX PARAMETERS ARE SET TO ZERO
THE (1,2)TH ELEMENTS IN THE MATRIX PARAMETERS ARE SET TO ZERO
-2*(LOG LIKELIHOOD AT FINAL ESTIMATES UNDER H2 ) IS  -0.25870429E+04


THE RESIDUAL COVARIANCE MATRIX IS SET TO DIAGONAL MATRIX
THE (2,1)TH ELEMENTS IN THE MATRIX PARAMETERS ARE SET TO ZERO
THE (1,2)TH ELEMENTS IN THE MATRIX PARAMETERS ARE SET TO ZERO
-2*(LOG LIKELIHOOD AT FINAL ESTIMATES UNDER H1 ) IS  -0.25733307E+04


CAUSALITY TEST BETWEEN VARIABLES    DUE    AND    DLEI

P, PP, Q, QQ, NP, NAR, NSAR, NMA, NSMA:
   1     0    1    0    0    4    0    4    0

-2*(LOG LIKELIHOOD) UNDER H5,H5*,H4,H4*,H3,H3*,H2,H1 ARE:
   1    -0.26704472E+04
   2    -0.26876968E+04
   3    -0.26703238E+04
   4    -0.26660243E+04
   5    -0.26014689E+04
   6    -0.25922485E+04
   7    -0.25870429E+04
   8    -0.25733307E+04

-2*(LOG LIKELIHOOD) UNDER H1,H2,H3,H3*,H4,H4*,H5,H5* ARE:
  -0.25733306E+04
  -0.25870430E+04
  -0.26014690E+04
  -0.25922485E+04
  -0.26703237E+04
  -0.26660242E+04
  -0.26704473E+04
  -0.26876968E+04
  LR1 TO LR10:  68.97827148437500 0.1235351562500000 14.42602539062500 83.28076171875000
13.71240234375000     83.40429687500000     9.220458984375000     4.299560546875000     -
17.24951171875000 97.11669921875000
  DDF1    TO    DDF10:    2.000000000000000    2.000000000000000    2.000000000000000
2.000000000000000     1.000000000000000    4.000000000000000    1.000000000000000
1.000000000000000 1.000000000000000 5.000000000000000
  CHI1    TO    CHI10:    9.210340416679674    9.210340416679674    9.210340416679674
9.210340416679674     6.634896640840623     13.27670418742523     6.634896640840623
6.634896640840623 6.634896640840623 15.08627252353956
  T1  TO  T10:    59.7679329  -9.08680534  5.21568489  74.0704193  7.07750559  70.1275940
2.58556223 -2.33533621 -23.8844090 82.0304260
  IT1 TO IT10:  1 -1 1 1 1 1 1 -1 -1 1
  I1 TO I6:  1 3 1 3 3 3

RESULT BASED ON THE BACKWARD PROCEDURE ( Y:DUE    , X: DLEI   )
          DUE <<= DLEI    (Y IS STRONGLY CAUSED BY X)

RESULT BASED ON THE FORWARD PROCEDURE  ( Y:DUE    , X: DLEI   )
          DUE <<= DLEI    (Y IS STRONGLY CAUSED BY X)

Thus, the application of the Chen and Lee (1990) test, reported in Table 8.9, leads one
to find causality in the DUE, DLEI relationship with both 4-month DLEI lags for the
entire 1959-2018 time period.
```

the RMSE relative to AR(1) and naïve forecasts of the unemployment rate, 1995–January 2020 and 1995–November 2020.

We report that robust regression (RR) with one, two, and three period lags and the adaptive learning models with the TCB unemployment claims input significantly reduce the RMSE relative to AR(1) and naïve forecasts

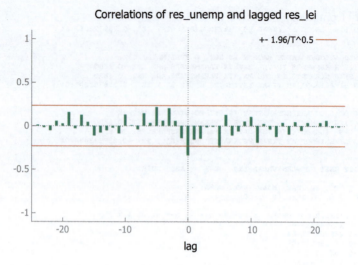

Fig. 8.1 Cross-correlation of pre-whitened unemployment and LEI, 1959–1965

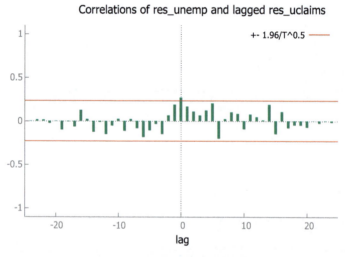

Fig. 8.2 Cross-correlation of pre-whitened unemployment and weekly unemployment claims, 1959–1965

of the unemployment rate, 1995–January 2020 and 1995–November 2020. See Table 8.11. The RMSE is substantially reduced for the COVID period, whether the period commences in 1959 or in the post-sample, 1995–2020, time period.

We also verified Granger causality and Root Mean Square Error (RMSE) forecasting errors substantially lower than AR(1) and Sample Mean Forecasts

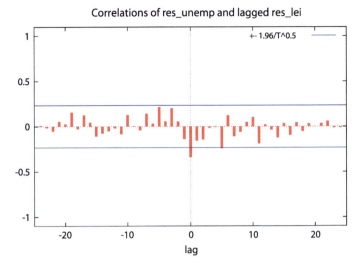

Fig. 8.3 Cross-correlation of pre-whitened unemployment and LEI, 1959-1/2020

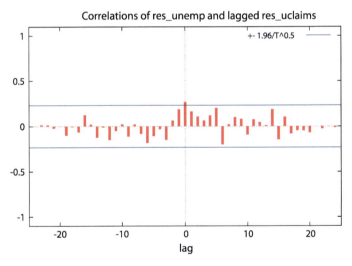

Fig. 8.4 Cross-correlation of pre-whitened unemployment and weekly unemploy-ment claims, 1959-1/2020

that are often used as forecasting benchmarks of the unemployment rate for the 3/1964–11/2020 period, with the LEI input. See Table 8.12.

We report that robust regression (RR) with one and three period lags, the neural network models, and the adaptive learning models with the LEI input significantly reduce the RMSE relative to AR(1) and naïve forecasts of the unemployment rate, 1959–January 2020.

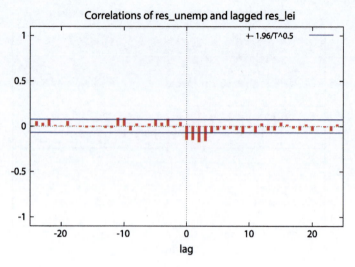

Fig. 8.5 Cross-correlation of pre-whitened unemployment and LEI, 1959-12/2020

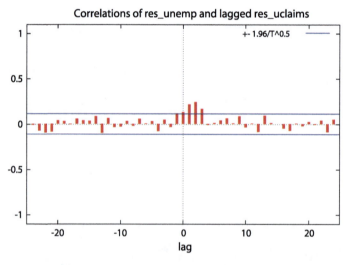

Fig. 8.6 Cross-correlation of pre-whitened unemployment and weekly unemployment claims, 1959-12/2020

8.5.1 Rolling Windows and Real GDP with the LEI and Money Supply

Zarnowitz was concerned that seeming endless revisions to the LEI data could cast doubt as to whether the U.S. LEI data, as reported, was statistically significant. Victor Zarnowitz and his team at The Conference Board created

Table 8.10 TCB LEI as an input to forecasting the unemployment rate in the U.S., 1959–2020 and 1995–2020

	Jan1995–Jan2020						Jan1995–Nov2020					
	RMSE	MAE	d0	d1	t-pv	F-pv	RMSE	MAE	d0	d1	t-pv	F-pv
Sample Mean Forecast	0.837	0.820	0.148	0.973	0.002	0.004	0.305	0.574	0.551	0.909	0.017	0.035
Naive Forecast	1.000	1.000	0.082	0.986	0.000	0.002	1.000	1.000	3.486	0.418	0.001	0.003
Naive-Drift Forecast	1.009	1.011	0.084	0.985	0.000	0.001	1.025	1.016	3.549	0.408	0.001	0.002
Moving Average (SMA) Forecast	0.768	0.766	0.079	0.986	0.026	0.074	0.434	0.731	1.382	0.765	0.076	0.205
Linear Trend Forecast	0.869	0.851	0.220	0.961	0.000	0.000	0.322	0.631	0.744	0.875	0.019	0.046
Theta Forecast #1	0.836	0.833	0.074	0.987	0.034	0.095	2.749	1.975	5.200	0.133	0.000	0.000
Theta Forecast with SMA	0.776	0.774	0.087	0.985	0.028	0.080	2.185	1.591	4.948	0.175	0.000	0.000
Bivariate Theta Forecast	0.849	0.850	0.079	0.986	0.028	0.074	0.510	0.700	1.751	0.707	0.066	0.170
AR(1) Forecast	0.798	0.752	0.023	0.997	0.625	0.783	8.740	4.232	5.858	0.029	0.000	0.000
AR(p) Forecast	0.932	0.878	0.122	0.979	0.025	0.047	22.419	10.116	5.980	0.010	0.000	0.000
SES Forecast	0.745	**0.749**	0.125	0.979	0.001	0.002	1.011	0.947	3.496	0.415	0.001	0.002
Auto-ARIMA Forecast	0.798	0.785	0.129	0.978	0.009	0.018	2.486	1.587	5.150	0.144	0.000	0.000
ARIMA(1,1,0) Forecast	0.836	0.834	0.074	0.987	0.036	0.100	3.028	2.120	5.293	0.118	0.000	0.000
VAR(1) Forecast	0.796	0.798	0.174	0.970	0.000	0.000	0.729	0.804	2.674	0.554	0.017	0.053
VAR(p) Forecast	0.795	0.780	0.156	0.974	0.005	0.005	0.759	0.855	2.792	0.538	0.015	0.050
Differences-VAR(1) Forecast	0.871	0.876	0.061	0.989	0.110	**0.253**	0.475	0.697	1.579	0.736	0.078	**0.197**
Differences-VAR(p)	0.831	0.811	0.075	0.986	0.047	0.139	0.898	0.982	3.219	0.463	0.003	0.009
Robust Regression with 1 lag Forecast	**0.750**	0.757	0.058	0.991	0.219	**0.215**	**0.291**	**0.521**	0.427	0.934	0.092	**0.223**
Robust Regression with lags 1 to 3 Forecast	**0.728**	**0.719**	0.044	0.993	0.311	**0.466**	**0.305**	**0.541**	0.515	0.917	0.075	**0.187**
Robust Regression with lag 3 Forecast	**0.736**	**0.727**	0.065	0.989	0.110	0.185	**0.305**	**0.536**	0.498	0.920	0.064	**0.168**
Adaptive AR Forecast	0.752	**0.738**	0.042	0.993	0.227	**0.474**	11.911	5.576	5.914	0.020	0.000	0.000
Adaptive Learning Forecast—no smoothing	**0.729**	**0.721**	0.044	0.993	0.299	**0.455**	**0.305**	0.542	0.517	0.917	0.076	**0.190**

(continued)

Table 8.10 (continued)

| | Jan1995–Jan2020 | | | | | | Jan1995–Nov2020 | | | | | |
	RMSE	MAE	d0	d1	t-pv	F-pv	RMSE	MAE	d0	d1	t-pv	F-pv
Adaptive Learning Forecast—smoothing	0.843	0.816	0.061	1.001	0.908	0.000	**0.306**	**0.577**	0.539	0.923	0.106	0.118

Note **BOLD** denotes the five most effective forecasting models

Table 8.11 TCB unemployment claims as an input to forecasting the unemployment rate in the U.S., 1959–2020 and 1995–2020

	Jan1995–Jan2020						Jan1995–Nov2020					
	RMSE	MAE	d0	d1	t-pv	F-pv	RMSE	MAE	d0	d1	t-pv	F-pv
Sample Mean Forecast	0.837	0.820	0.148	0.973	0.002	0.004	0.305	0.574	0.551	0.909	0.017	0.035
Naive Forecast	1.000	1.000	0.082	0.986	0.000	0.002	1.000	1.000	3.486	0.418	0.001	0.003
Naive-Drift Forecast	1.009	1.011	0.084	0.985	0.000	0.001	1.025	1.016	3.549	0.408	0.001	0.002
Moving Average (SMA) Forecast	**0.768**	0.766	0.079	0.986	0.026	0.074	0.434	0.731	1.382	0.765	0.076	**0.205**
Linear Trend Forecast	0.869	0.851	0.220	0.961	0.000	0.000	0.322	0.631	0.744	0.875	0.019	0.046
Theta Forecast #1	0.836	0.833	0.074	0.987	0.034	0.095	2.749	1.975	5.200	0.133	0.000	0.000
Theta Forecast with SMA	0.776	0.774	0.087	0.985	0.028	0.080	2.185	1.591	4.948	0.175	0.000	0.000
Bivariate Theta Forecast	0.849	0.842	0.076	0.987	0.027	0.078	0.278	0.566	0.394	0.937	0.020	0.062
AR(1) Forecast	0.798	**0.752**	0.023	0.997	0.625	0.783	8.740	4.232	5.858	0.029	0.000	0.000
AR(p) Forecast	0.932	0.878	0.122	0.979	0.025	0.047	22.419	10.116	5.980	0.010	0.000	0.000
SES Forecast	**0.745**	**0.749**	0.125	0.979	0.001	0.002	1.011	0.947	3.496	0.415	0.001	0.002
Auto-ARIMA Forecast	0.798	0.785	0.129	0.978	0.009	0.018	2.486	1.587	5.150	0.144	0.000	0.000
ARIMA(1,1,0) Forecast	0.836	0.834	0.074	0.987	0.036	0.100	3.028	2.120	5.293	0.118	0.000	0.000
VAR(1) Forecast	0.867	0.837	0.217	0.962	0.000	0.000	**0.281**	**0.533**	0.295	0.957	0.000	0.000
VAR(p) Forecast	0.809	0.805	0.167	0.973	0.000	0.000	0.304	0.539	0.310	0.959	0.028	**0.071**
Differences-VAR(1) Forecast	0.871	0.867	0.059	0.990	0.106	0.247	**0.289**	0.592	0.326	0.950	0.160	**0.239**
Differences-VAR(p) Forecast	0.793	0.787	0.065	0.988	0.080	0.215	0.313	**0.551**	0.453	0.927	0.048	**0.140**
Robust Regression with 1 lag Forecast	0.831	0.819	0.118	0.980	0.010	0.013	0.319	0.594	0.710	0.883	0.051	**0.148**
Robust Regression with lags 1 to 3 Forecast	**0.749**	**0.761**	0.061	0.990	0.160	0.285	0.963	0.937	3.388	0.434	0.001	0.005
Robust Regression with lag 3 Forecast	0.818	0.793	0.117	0.980	0.006	0.011	**0.297**	**0.531**	0.423	0.933	0.008	0.006
Adaptive AR Forecast	**0.752**	**0.738**	0.042	0.993	0.227	0.474	11.911	5.576	5.914	0.020	0.000	0.000
Adaptive Learning Forecast—no smoothing	**0.749**	**0.762**	0.062	0.990	0.149	0.267	**0.297**	**0.531**	0.424	0.933	0.011	0.008

(continued)

Table 8.11 (continued)

	Jan1995–Jan2020						Jan1995–Nov2020					
	RMSE	MAE	d0	d1	t-pv	F-pv	RMSE	MAE	d0	d1	t-pv	F-pv
Adaptive Learning Forecast—smoothing	0.842	0.818	0.077	0.998	0.791	0.000	**0.298**	**0.550**	0.443	0.940	0.023	0.070

Note **BOLD** denotes the five most effective forecasting models

Table 8.12 MZTT data, 1964.03–2020.11 unemployment is a function of LEI

	RMSE	MAE	d0	d1	t-pv	F-pv
Mean	0.7976	0.7851	0.1437	0.9754	0.0006	0.0013
Naive	1.0000	1.0000	0.1314	0.9780	0.0000	0.0000
Naive-D	1.0082	1.0103	0.1341	0.9775	0.0000	0.0000
SMA	0.7583	0.7553	0.1160	0.9804	0.0001	0.0002
LT	0.8402	0.8214	0.2467	0.9582	0.0000	0.0000
UR1	0.8456	0.8455	0.1142	0.9808	0.0000	0.0000
UR1-A	1.3514	1.3783	0.2155	0.9640	0.0000	0.0000
UR2	1.3091	1.3094	0.2512	0.9579	0.0000	0.0000
TS1	0.7650	0.7581	0.1245	0.9791	0.0001	0.0004
TS1-BC1	0.7682	0.7609	0.1265	0.9788	0.0001	0.0003
TS1-BC2	0.7644	0.7577	0.1239	0.9792	0.0001	0.0004
TS2	2.7716	1.1488	0.8498	0.8584	0.0841	0.2246
TS2-BC1	2.7658	1.1499	0.8477	0.8587	0.0832	0.2226
TS2-BC2	2.3806	1.1183	0.6598	0.8897	0.0580	0.1546
TS-DBL	0.9994	1.0012	0.1330	0.9777	0.0000	0.0000
BUR-L	1.0090	1.0172	0.1472	0.9758	0.0000	0.0000
BUR-RR	1.0142	1.0230	0.1491	0.9755	0.0000	0.0000
BUR-D	0.8471	0.8477	0.1093	0.9817	0.0000	0.0000
BCT	0.8612	0.8547	0.0905	0.9846	0.0000	0.0001
BMA	0.7499	0.7497	0.1086	0.9818	0.0004	0.0014
BMA-BC	0.7527	0.7535	0.1105	0.9815	0.0004	0.0012
AR(1)	0.7741	0.7471	0.0352	0.9946	0.2739	**0.4430**
AR(2)	0.7558	0.7417	0.0566	0.9908	0.0579	0.1432
AR(3)	0.7528	0.7390	0.0689	0.9884	0.0169	0.0552
AR(4)	0.7528	0.7359	0.0824	0.9863	0.0063	0.0209
AR(p)	0.8834	0.8519	0.1246	0.9800	0.0009	0.0014
SES	0.7534	0.7450	0.1573	0.9743	0.0000	0.0000
HB	0.7638	0.7535	0.1721	0.9714	0.0000	0.0000
Auto-ARIMA	0.7822	0.7727	0.1596	0.9738	0.0000	0.0000
ARIMA(1,1,0)	0.8468	0.8465	0.1148	0.9807	0.0000	0.0000
VAR(1)	0.7586	0.7502	0.1426	0.9766	0.0000	0.0000
VAR(p)	0.7583	0.7547	0.1294	0.9789	0.0005	0.0007
D-VAR(1)	0.8701	0.8738	0.1024	0.9829	0.0001	0.0003
D-VAR(p)	0.8216	0.8119	0.1167	0.9804	0.0004	0.0015
RobLM(1)	0.7166	0.7278	0.0380	0.9944	0.2294	0.3480
RobLM(1:3)	0.7118	0.7164	0.0161	0.9978	0.6369	**0.7530**
RobLM(3)	0.7354	0.7308	0.0679	0.9896	0.0324	0.0336
NN1	0.8185	0.7749	−0.0227	1.0048	0.5630	**0.8089**
NN2	0.8117	0.7793	−0.0731	1.0162	0.0381	0.0326
TF	0.7313	0.7332	0.0185	0.9983	0.7629	**0.3931**

(continued)

Table 8.12 (continued)

	RMSE	MAE	d0	d1	t-pv	F-pv
ADA-AR	0.7441	0.7264	0.0581	0.9905	0.0455	0.1217
ADL1-NS	0.7314	0.7328	0.0188	0.9983	0.7539	**0.3878**
ADL2-NS	0.7314	0.7328	0.0188	0.9983	0.7539	0.3878
ADL1	0.7579	0.7595	−0.0162	1.0086	0.1319	0.0000

a Vintage (real-time) LEI time series.[1] Dhrymes (2017) reported evidence that the time series of real GDP was plagued by structural breaks using Autometrics with the OxMetrics software.[2] Dhrymes (2017) examined analysis of the Vintage Conference Board data for the 1/2003 to 3/2016 time period. Dhrymes reported that the real-time (vintage) LEI continued to be statistically significant with a one-quarter lead at the 1% level, producing a t-statistic of 3.90, out-of-sample, post-publication. The Conference Board Vintage LEI and the traditional LEI both lead U.S. RGDP for the 2003–March 2016 time period.

If one takes one last look at the Kyriazi et al. (2019) 10-year rolling windows modeling of Real GDP with the LEI and constant dollar (1982 $) money supply, M2, We report that robust regression (RR) with one and three period lags, the neural network models, and the adaptive learning models with LEI and M2 inputs significantly reduce the RMSE relative to AR(1) and naïve forecasts of the unemployment rate, 1959–November 2020, see Tables 8.13 and 8.14.

We report in Table 8.13 that robust regression (RR) with one and three period lags, the neural network models, and the adaptive learning models with the LEI input significantly reduce the MSE relative to AR(1) and naïve forecasts of the Real GDP, 1995–November 2020.

We report in Table 8.14 that robust regression (RR) with one and three period lags, the neural network models, and the adaptive learning models with the M2 input significantly reduce the RMSE relative to AR(1) and naïve forecasts of the Real GDP, 1995–November 2020.

---

[1] The authors are indebted to Ataman Ozyildirim of The Conference Board for providing the Vintage data.

[2] In a recent study of U.S. GDP and GDP growth, Castle et al. (2015) reported for the 2000 -2011 period that an AR(1) model was difficult to beat; however, the non-smooth robust model of four principal components (R1PC1-4) was better than the AR(1) forecasts in the 2007–2011 period. Papilias and Thomakos (2017) in the IJF reports the effectiveness of using a sophisticated version of exponential smoothing, EXSSA, exponential smoothing of covariance eigenvalues on real U.S. DGP, quarterly, 1950 – 2014. The EXSSA AR(1) reduced the out-of-sample forecasting errors relative to AR(1) and the Castle et al. (2015) time series procedures.

Table 8.13 The LEI and real GDP, 1995–11/2020 the 10-year rolling windows approach

	RMSE	MAE	d0	d1	t-pv	F-pv
Mean	0.6841	0.7801	0.0138	−2.0104	0.0213	0.0269
Naive	1.0000	1.0000	0.0045	−0.3676	0.0000	0.0000
Naive-D	1.0115	1.0157	0.0045	−0.3570	0.0000	0.0000
SMA	0.7470	0.8399	0.0064	−0.7093	0.0262	0.0826
LT	0.7021	0.7927	0.0078	−1.0243	0.0307	0.0950
UR1	1.2284	1.0594	0.0043	−0.3844	0.0000	0.0000
UR1-A	1.1936	1.2060	0.0040	−0.2549	0.0000	0.0000
UR2	0.9707	1.1557	0.0058	−0.6448	0.0002	0.0009
TS1	1.1739	1.0212	0.0048	−0.4766	0.0000	0.0000
TS1-BC1	1.1776	1.0300	0.0047	−0.4709	0.0000	0.0000
TS1-BC2	1.1794	1.0249	0.0048	−0.4735	0.0000	0.0000
TS2	1.3583	1.3638	0.0042	−0.2935	0.0000	0.0000
TS2-BC1	1.3616	1.3711	0.0042	−0.2918	0.0000	0.0000
TS2-BC2	1.3622	1.3635	0.0042	−0.2960	0.0000	0.0000
TS-DBL	1.0063	0.9754	0.0049	−0.4454	0.0000	0.0000
BUR-L	1.0387	1.0424	0.0042	−0.3714	0.0000	0.0000
BUR-RR	1.0457	1.0545	0.0046	−0.3760	0.0000	0.0000
BUR-D	0.8641	0.9151	0.0065	−0.7997	0.0005	0.0020
BCT	1.1270	1.0170	0.0064	−0.5998	0.0000	0.0000
BMA	0.8364	0.8831	0.0076	−1.0218	0.0000	0.0001
BMA-BC	0.8393	0.8918	0.0074	−0.9849	0.0000	0.0002
AR(1)	1.0906	0.9811	0.0039	−0.4559	0.0000	0.0000
AR(2)	1.2413	1.0346	0.0039	−0.4185	0.0000	0.0000
AR(p)	1.1397	1.0921	0.0040	−0.4895	0.0000	0.0000
SES	1.0378	0.9531	0.0055	−0.6135	0.0000	0.0000
HB	1.0367	0.9521	0.0054	−0.5995	0.0000	0.0000
Auto-ARIMA	1.0290	0.9572	0.0053	−0.5745	0.0000	0.0000
ARIMA(1,1,0)	1.2585	1.0666	0.0043	−0.3744	0.0000	0.0000
VAR(1)	0.8824	0.8684	0.0079	−1.0782	0.0000	0.0000
VAR(p)	0.9007	0.9430	0.0068	−0.9405	0.0000	0.0000
D-VAR(1)	0.8499	0.9196	0.0065	−0.7601	0.0049	0.0183
D-VAR(p)	0.7965	0.9950	0.0060	−0.5942	0.0192	0.0529
RobLM(1)	0.7011	0.7913	0.0244	−3.3152	0.0294	**0.0898**
RobLM(1:3)	0.7213	0.7868	0.0199	−2.6998	0.0364	**0.1007**
RobLM(3)	0.6777	0.7618	0.0087	−0.8629	0.0215	0.0569
NN1	0.6997	0.9363	−0.0155	1.9180	0.5206	0.0041
NN2	0.7009	0.8379	0.0080	−0.5342	0.2895	0.0041
TF	0.8000	0.8686	0.0106	−1.5678	0.0035	0.0131
ADA-AR	1.3028	1.0581	0.0038	−0.3937	0.0000	0.0000

(continued)

Table 8.13   (continued)

	RMSE	MAE	d0	d1	t-pv	F-pv
ADL1-NS	0.6845	0.7686	0.0139	−2.0837	0.1208	**0.2882**
ADL2-NS	0.6845	0.7688	0.0140	−2.0908	0.1203	**0.2877**
ADL1	0.6826	0.7619	0.0130	−1.9875	0.1586	**0.3606**
ADL2	0.6827	0.7617	0.0130	−1.9916	0.1584	**0.3605**

Dhrymes (2017) reported SCA causality findings of LEI leading the real GDP, 1959–2018. We extend the period through much of COVID. Thomakos and Guerard (2022) applied traditional Granger frequency and time series models and report statistically significant causality testing of LEI and real GDP and the unemployment rate during the 1995–11/2020 and the 1959–11/2020 periods.

8.6   Summary and Conclusions

We applied the econometric causality testing methodologies of Clive Granger and his colleagues to corporate mergers and the unemployment rate, reporting statistically significant causality findings using the LEI and its components, stock prices and weekly unemployment claims. This chapter builds upon the regression and time series modeling in the previous chapter where we established the basis model for real GDP and the unemployment rate. We report Granger causality results of the unemployment rate, using both the SCA system, based on the modeling of Mr. Ruey Tsay and his colleagues, and the rolling window analysis of Kyriazi, Thomakos, and Guerard. We verified Granger causality and Root Mean Square Error (RMSE) forecasting errors substantially lower than the AR(1) and Sample Mean Forecasts that are often used as forecasting benchmarks of the unemployment rate. In Chapter 10, we will use the latest reported TCB data to validate the forecasting efficiency of our models.

Table 8.14 The money supply and real GDP, 1995–11/2020 the 10-year rolling windows approach

	RMSE	MAE	d0	d1	t-pv	F-pv
Mean	0.6841	0.7801	0.0138	−2.0104	0.0213	0.0269
Naive	1.0000	1.0000	0.0045	−0.3676	0.0000	0.0000
Naive-D	1.0115	1.0157	0.0045	−0.3570	0.0000	0.0000
SMA	0.7470	0.8399	0.0064	−0.7093	0.0262	0.0826
LT	0.7021	0.7927	0.0078	−1.0243	0.0307	0.0950
UR1	1.2284	1.0594	0.0043	−0.3844	0.0000	0.0000
UR1-A	1.1936	1.2060	0.0040	−0.2549	0.0000	0.0000
UR2	0.9707	1.1557	0.0058	−0.6448	0.0002	0.0009
TS1	1.1739	1.0212	0.0048	−0.4766	0.0000	0.0000
TS1-BC1	1.1776	1.0300	0.0047	−0.4709	0.0000	0.0000
TS1-BC2	1.1794	1.0249	0.0048	−0.4735	0.0000	0.0000
TS2	1.3583	1.3638	0.0042	−0.2935	0.0000	0.0000
TS2-BC1	1.3616	1.3711	0.0042	−0.2918	0.0000	0.0000
TS2-BC2	1.3622	1.3635	0.0042	−0.2960	0.0000	0.0000
TS-DBL	1.0063	0.9754	0.0049	−0.4454	0.0000	0.0000
BUR-L	1.0387	1.0424	0.0042	−0.3714	0.0000	0.0000
BUR-RR	1.0457	1.0545	0.0046	−0.3760	0.0000	0.0000
BUR-D	0.8641	0.9151	0.0065	−0.7997	0.0005	0.0020
BCT	1.1270	1.0170	0.0064	−0.5998	0.0000	0.0000
BMA	0.8364	0.8831	0.0076	−1.0218	0.0000	0.0001
BMA-BC	0.8393	0.8918	0.0074	−0.9849	0.0000	0.0002
AR(1)	1.0906	0.9811	0.0039	−0.4559	0.0000	0.0000
AR(2)	1.2413	1.0346	0.0039	−0.4185	0.0000	0.0000
AR(p)	1.1397	1.0921	0.0040	−0.4895	0.0000	0.0000
SES	1.0378	0.9531	0.0055	−0.6135	0.0000	0.0000
HB	1.0367	0.9521	0.0054	−0.5995	0.0000	0.0000
Auto-ARIMA	1.0290	0.9572	0.0053	−0.5745	0.0000	0.0000
ARIMA(1,1,0)	1.2585	1.0666	0.0043	−0.3744	0.0000	0.0000
VAR(1)	0.8824	0.8684	0.0079	−1.0782	0.0000	0.0000
VAR(p)	0.9007	0.9430	0.0068	−0.9405	0.0000	0.0000
D-VAR(1)	0.8499	0.9196	0.0065	−0.7601	0.0049	0.0183
D-VAR(p)	0.7965	0.9950	0.0060	−0.5942	0.0192	**0.0529**
RobLM(1)	0.7011	0.7913	0.0244	−3.3152	0.0294	**0.0898**
RobLM(1:3)	0.7231	0.7985	0.0200	−2.6660	0.0303	**0.0846**
RobLM(3)	0.6777	0.7618	0.0087	−0.8629	0.0215	**0.0569**
NN1	0.6997	0.9363	−0.0155	1.9180	0.5206	0.0041
NN2	0.7009	0.8379	0.0080	−0.5342	0.2895	0.0041
TF	0.8000	0.8686	0.0106	−1.5678	0.0035	0.0131
ADA-AR	1.3028	1.0581	0.0038	−0.3937	0.0000	0.0000

(continued)

Table 8.14 (continued)

	RMSE	MAE	d0	d1	t-pv	F-pv
ADL1-NS	0.6845	0.7686	0.0139	−2.0837	0.1208	**0.2882**
ADL2-NS	0.6845	0.7688	0.0140	−2.0908	0.1203	0.2877
ADL1	0.6826	0.7619	0.0130	−1.9875	0.1586	**0.3606**
ADL2	0.6827	0.7617	0.0130	−1.9916	0.1584	**0.3605**

References

Ashley, R. A. (2003). Statistically significant forecasting improvements: How much out-of-sample data is likely necessary? *International Journal of Forecasting, 19*, 229–240.

Ashley, R. (1998). A new technique for postsample model selection and validation. *Journal of Economic Dynamics and Control, 22*, 647–665.

Ashley, R., Granger, C. W. J., & Schmalensee, R. (1980). Advertising and aggregate consumption: An analysis of causality. *Econometrica, 48*, 149–167.

Box, G. E. P., & Jenkins, G. M. (1970). *Time series analysis: Forecasting and control*. Holden-Day.

Burns, A. F., & Mitchell, W. C. (1946). *Measuring business cycles*. NBER.

Castle, J., & Shepard, N. (2009). *The methodology and practice of econometrics*. Oxford University Press.

Castle, J., Doornik, J. A., & Hendry, D. F. (2013). Model selection in equations with many 'small' effects. *Oxford Bulletin of Economics and Statistics, 75*, 6–22.

Castle, J., Clements, M. P., & Hendry, D. F. (2015). Robust approaches to forecasting. *International Journal of Forecasting, 31*, 99–112.

Castle, J., & Hednry, D. F. (2019). *Modelling our changing world*. Palgrave.

Chen, C., & Lee, C. J. (1990). A VARMA test on the Gibson paradox. *Review of Economics and Statistics, 72*, 96–107.

Chen, C., & Liu, L.-M. (1993a). Joint estimation of model parameters and outliers in time series. *Journal of the American Statistical Association, 88*, 284–297.

Chen, C., & Liu, L.-M. (1993b). Forecasting time series with outliers. *Journal of Forecasting, 12*, 13–35.

Clemen, R. T., & Guerard, J. B. (1989). Econometric GNP forecasts: Incremental information relative to naive extrapolation. *International Journal of Forecasting, 5*, 417–426.

Clements, M. P., & Hendry, D. F. (1998). *Forecasting economic time series*. Cambridge University Press.

Dhrymes, P. J. (2017). *Introductory econometrics*. Springer.

Diebold, F. X., & Rudebusch, G. D. (1999). *Business cycles: Durations, dynamics and forecasting*. Princeton University Press.

Diebold, F. X., & Mariano, R. S. (1995). Comparing predictive accuracy. *Journal of Business and Economic Statistics, 13*, 253–263.

Golbe, D. L., & White, L. J. (1993). Catch a wave: The time series behaviour of mergers. *The Review of Economics and Statistics, 75*, 493–499.

Gordon, R. J. (1986). *The American business cycle*. University of Chicago Press.

Granger, C. W. J. (1969). Investigating Casual relations by economic models and cross-spectral methods. *Econometrica, 37*, 424–438.

Granger, C. W. J. (1980). Testing for causality: A personal viewpoint. *Journal of Economic Dynamics and Control, 2*, 329–352.

Granger, C. W. J. (2001). *Essays in econometrics* (2 Vols, E. Ghysels, N. R. Swanson, & M. W. Watson, Eds.). Cambridge University Press.

Granger, C. W. J., & Newbold, P. (1977). *Forecasting economic time series*. New York Academic Press.

Guerard, J. B. (1985). Mergers, stock prices, and industrial production: An empirical test of the nelson hypothesis. In *Time series analysis: Theory and practice* (7, O. D. Anderson, Ed.). Amsterdam North-Holland Publishing Company.

Guerard, J. B., and McDonald, J. B. (1995). Mergers in the United States: A case study in robust time series. In *Advances in financial planning and forecasting* (C. F. Lee, Ed.). JAI Press.

Guerard, J., Thomakos, D., & Kyriazi, F. (2020). Automatic time series modeling and forecasting: A replication case study of forecasting real GDP, the unemployment rate and the impact of leading economic indicators. *Cogent Economics & Finance*, 8(1): 1759483.

Hamilton, J. R. (1994). *Time series analysis*. Princeton.

Hendry, D. F. (1986). Using PC-give in econometrics teaching. *Oxford Bulletin of Economics and Statistics, 48*, 87–98.

Hendry, D. F. (2000). *Econometrics: Alchemy or science?* Oxford University Press.

Hendry, D. F., & Doornik, J. A. (2014). *Empirical model discovery and theory evaluation*. MIT Press.

Hendry, D. F., & Krolzig, H. M. (2005). The properties of automatic gets modelling. *The Economic Journal, 115*, c32–c61.

Koopmans, T. C. (1947). Measure without theory. *The review of economic statistics* reprinted in R. Gordon & L. Klein, *Readings in business cycles*. Richard A. Irwin, Inc, 1965.

Koopmans, T. C. (1950). When is an equation system complete for statistical purposes. Tech. Report, Yale University. http://cowles.econ.yale.edu/P/cm/m10/m10-17.pdf

Krolzig, H.-M. (2001). Business cycle measurement in the presence of structural change: international evidence. *International Journal of Forecasting, 17*, 349–368.

Krolzig, H.-M., & Hendry, D. F. (2001). Computer automation of general-to-specific model selection procedures. *Journal of Economic Dynamics & Control*, 831–866.

Kyriazi, F. S., Thomakos, D. D., & Guerard, J. B. (2019). Adaptive learning forecasting with applications in forecasting agricultural prices. *International Journal of Forecasting, 35*(4): 1356–1369.

Liu, L.-M. (1999). *Forecasting and time series analysis using the SCA statistical system.* Scientific Computing Associates. Chicago, Illinois.

Maronna, R. A., Martin, R. D., Yohai, V. J., & Salibian-Barrera, M. (2019). *Robust statistics: Theory and methods (with R).* Wiley.

Melicher, R., Ledolter, J., & D'Antonio, L. J. (1983). A time series analysis of aggregate merger activity. *Review of Economics and Statistics, 65,* 423–430.

McCracken, M. (2000). Robust out-of-sample inference. *Journal of Econometrics, 39,* 195–223.

Mincer, J., & Zarnowitz, V. (1969). The evaluation of economic forecasts. In J. Mincer (Ed.), *Economic forecasts and expectations.* Columbia University Press.

Mitchell, W. C. (1913). *Business cycles.* Burt Franklin reprint.

Mitchell, W. C. (1951). *What happens during business cycles: A progress report.* NBER.

Montgomery, A. L., Zarnowitz, V., Tsay, R. S., & Tiao, G. C. (1998). Forecasting the US unemployment rate. *Journal of the American Statistical Association, 93,* 478–493.

Moore, G. H. (1961). *Business cycle indicators.* (2 Vols). Princeton University Press.

Nelson, C. R., & Plosser, C. I. (1982). Trends and random walks in macroeconomic time series. *Journal of Monetary Economics, 10,* 139–162.

Nelson, C. R. (1973). *Applied time series analysis for managerial forecasting.* Holden-Day Inc.

Nelson, R. L. (1959). *Merger movements in American industry 1895–1954.* Princeton University Press.

Nelson, R. L. (1966). Business cycle factors in the choice between internal and external growth. In W. W. Alberts & J. E. Segall (Eds.), *The corporate merger.* The University of Chicago Press.

Papilias, F., & Thomakos, D. D. (2017). EXSSA: SSA-based reconstruction of time series via exponential smoothing of covariance eigenvalues. *International Journal of Forecasting, 33,* 214–229.

Swanson, N. R. (1998). Money and output viewed through a rolling window. *Journal of Monetary Economics, 41*(1998), 455–473.

Theil, H. (1966). *Applied economic forecasting.* North-Holland.

Tsay, R. S. (1988). Outliers, level shifts, and variance changes in time series. *Journal of Forecasting, 7,* 1–20.

Tsay, R. S. (1989). Testing and modeling threshold autoregressive processes. *Journal of the American Statistical Association, 84,* 231–249.

Tsay, R. S. (2010). *Analysis of financial time series* (3rd ed.). Wiley.

Tsay, R. S., & Chen, R. (2019). *Nonlinear time series analysis.* Wiley.

Thomakos, D., & Guerard, J. (2004). Naïve, ARIMA, transfer function, and VAR models: A comparison of forecasting performance. *The International Journal of Forecasting, 20,* 53–67.

Thomakos, D., & Guerard, J. (2022). Causality testing and forecasting of the US unemployment rate [Unpublished Working Paper, University of Athens].

Vinod, H. D. (2008). *Hands-on intermediate econometrics using R: Templates for extending dozens of practical examples.* World Scientific. ISBN 10-981-281-885-5. http://www.worldscibooks.com/economics/6895.html

Vinod, H. D. (2014). Matrix algebra topics in statistics and economics using R. In M. B. Rao & C. R. Rao (Eds.), *Handbook of statistics: Computational statistics with R* (Vol. 34, Ch. 4, pp. 143–176). Elsevier Science.

Vinod, H. D. (2017). *Causal paths and exogeneity tests in generalCorr package for air pollution and monetary policy.* A vignette accompanying the package "generalCorr" of R. https://cloud.r-project.org/web/packages/generalCorr/vignettes/generalCorr-vignette3.pdf

Vinod, H. D. (2019). New exogeneity tests and causal paths. In H. D. Vinod & C. R. Rao (Eds.), *Handbook of statistics: Conceptual econometrics using R* (Vol. 41, Ch. 2, pp. 33–64). Elsevier. https://doi.org/10.1016/bs.host.2018.11.011

Vinod, V. D., & Guerard, J. B., Jr. (2020). Causality studies of real GDP, unemployment, and leading indicators In J. B. Guerard Jr. & W. T. Ziemba (Eds.), *Handbook of applied investment research.* World Scientific Publishing, Inc.

Vining, R. (1949). Koopmans on the choice of variables to be studied and on methods of measurement. *The review of economics and statistics,* reprinted in R. Gorgon & L. Klein, *Readings in business cycles.* Richard A. Irwin, Inc, 1965.

West, K., & McCracken, M. (1998). Regression-based tests of predictive ability. *International Economic Review, 39,* 817–840.

Zarnowitz, V. (2004). The autonomy of recent US growth and business cycles. In P. Dua (Ed.), *Business cycles and economic growth: An analysis using leading indicators* (pp. 44–82). Oxford University Press.

Zarnowitz, V. (2001). *The old and the new in the U.S. economic expansion.* The Conference Board. EPWP #01-01.

Zarnowitz, V., & Ozyildirim, A. (2001). On the measurement of business cycles and growth cycles. *Indian Economic Review, 36,* 34–54.

Zarnowitz, V. (1992). *Business cycles: Theory, history, indicators, and forecasting.* University of Chicago Press.

9

Active Management in Portfolio Selection and Management Within Business Cycles and Present-Day COVID

The purpose of this study is to document the existence and effectiveness of variables reported as financial anomalies in portfolio selection during 1976 through 2020. Portfolio selection concerns all adults in our world. How can one provide opportunities for our children? Are these opportunities dependent upon the phases of the business cycles? Portfolio selection was pioneered by Harry Markowitz (1952, 1959) and William Sharpe, who shared the 1991 Nobel Prize in Economic Sciences. In this chapter, we create optimal portfolios, to maximize returns for a given level of risk, or minimize risk for a given level of return, as Markowitz taught us to do in his seminal 1959 monograph, *Portfolio Selection*, and his work in the past 25 years, including Bloch et al. (1993), Guerard (2014, 2015), and Guerard et al. (2013, 2021). In this chapter, we report portfolio selection, construction, and management results for the 1974–1990, 2002–2018, and 2001–2020 time periods that should educate the reader that Markowitz analysis is for everyone at all times. We create optimal portfolios to assess the predictive power of financial anomalies. We have both an overall boom period for our analysis and several significant recessions, 1975, 1991, and 2007–2008. How have the portfolio selection models performed?

This chapter is composed of six sections. The first section addresses the development of Markowitz, Sharpe, and Elton and Gruber optimal portfolios. The second section addresses the implementation of optimal portfolios. We address what we knew in 1991 through 2003 with regard to reported fundamental data, earnings forecasting, composite modeling of earnings forecasting and fundamental variables, and what risk models were available for creating and monitoring the effectiveness of optimized portfolios. It presents a brief literature review of the fundamental variables used in modeling stock returns from 1991 to 2003, including the earnings forecasting models and fundamentally based stock selection models. The third section examines Markowitz optimization and the use of BARRA and Axioma Risk Models used in the analysis. The fourth section asks if a bottom-up stock picker's world has changed post-2003 or post-Global Financial Crisis periods by estimating models of stock selection. The fifth section presents that active portfolios are not dependent upon NBER recessions. The sixth section presents summaries and conclusions as well as thoughts regarding future research and testing.

9.1   The Risk-Return Trade-Off Work of Markowitz, Sharpe, and Elton and Gruber

Markowitz (1991) acknowledges a great intellectual debt to Professor James Tobin of Yale University. Tobin, in his 1958 seminal article on liquidity preference, analyzed the risk-return trade-off of two assets, cash, and a monetary asset, consuls. A consul is a (perpetual) bond that pays a current yield of r (per year). The expected yield on cash is zero. The investor expectations of the rate on consuls change with market conditions. If the investor expects the rate on consuls to be r_e at the end of the year, then the capital gain (or loss) on the consul is given by g, where:

$$g = \frac{r}{r_e} - 1 \qquad (9.1)$$

An investor divides his (or her) balance between A_1 of cash and A_2 in consuls. If the current rate plus the expected capital gain exceeds zero, then the investor invests all his resources in consuls. If $r + g$ is expected to be less than zero, then the investor invests exclusively in cash. Tobin expressed a critical level of the current rate, r_c, where:

$$r_c = \frac{r_e}{1 + r_e} \qquad (9.2)$$

If the current rate exceeds r_c, then all funds are invested in consuls; however, if r is less than r_c, then all funds are invested in cash.

An investor is fully invested such that $A_1 + A_2 = 1$. The return on the portfolio, R, is:

$$R = A_2(r + g), \text{ where } 0 \leq A_2 \leq 1. \tag{9.3}$$

If g is a random variable with an expected value of zero, then

$$E(R) = \mu_r = A_2 r. \tag{9.4}$$

The mean value of the portfolio return is μ_r and the standard deviation is a measure of portfolio dispersion, σ_R. A high standard deviation portfolio offers the investor a chance of large returns, as well as an equal chance of large losses. The standard deviation of the portfolio depends exclusively upon the standard deviation of consuls, and the percentage of assets invested in consuls.

$$\sigma_R = A_2 \sigma_g \text{ where } 0 \leq A_2 \leq 1. \tag{9.5}$$

The ratio of expected return relative to risk can be written as:

$$\mu_R = \frac{r}{\sigma_g} \sigma_R, \quad 0 \leq \sigma_R \leq \sigma_g \tag{9.6}$$

Tobin discusses the indifference of pairs (μ_R, σ_R) of risk and returns that lie on the utility indifference curve I_1. Points on the I_2 indifference curve dominate points of the I_1 indifference curve. For a given level of risk, an investor prefers more returns to lesser returns. Risk-averters will accept more risk only if they are compensated with higher expected returns, see Fig. 9.2.

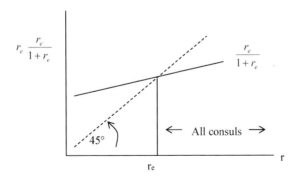

Fig. 9.1 Cash or bonds

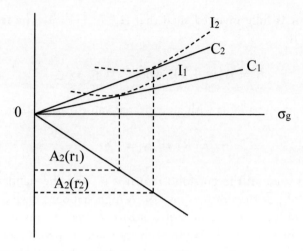

Fig. 9.2 Mr. Tobin and the risk-return trade-off

There is a risk premium on stocks relative to the risk-free rate, as reflected in the 90-day Treasury bill yield, R_R. If investors can borrow and lend at the risk-free asset (with unlimited funds), then one can invest x percent of the portfolio in risky assets with expected return, R_A, and $(1-x)$ percent of the portfolio in the risk-free asset. The expected return of the combined portfolio is:

$$E(R_P) = (1 - x)\ R_F + x\ E\ (R_A) \tag{9.7}$$

The risk of the combined portfolio, as measured by its standard deviation is given by:

$$\sigma_p = \left[(1 - x)^2\sigma_F^2 + x^2\sigma_A^2 + 2x(1 - x)\sigma_A\sigma_F\rho_{FA}\right]^{1/2} \tag{9.8}$$

where ρ_{FA} = correlation coefficient between risky and risk-free assets.
The standard deviation of the risk-free rate, σ_F, is assumed to be zero.

$$\sigma_v = (x^2\sigma_A^2)^{1/2} = X\ \sigma_A \tag{9.9}$$

The percentage invested in the risk-free asset, X, can be found by:

$$\frac{\sigma\rho}{\sigma A} = x \tag{9.10}$$

The expected return of the combined portfolio, shown in Eq. (9.7), may be written using Eq. (9.10) as:

$$E(R_\rho) = \left(1 - \frac{\sigma\rho}{\sigma_A}\right)R_F + \frac{\sigma\rho}{\sigma_A} \tag{9.11}$$

$$E(R_\rho) = R_F + \left(\frac{R_A - R_F}{\sigma_A}\right)\sigma_\rho. \tag{9.12}$$

Graphically, see Fig. 9.3, one sees Eq. (9.12) as the risk-return trade-off between risky and risk-free assets.

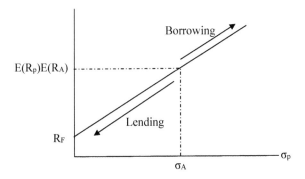

Fig. 9.3 Mr. Tobin and landing and borrowing

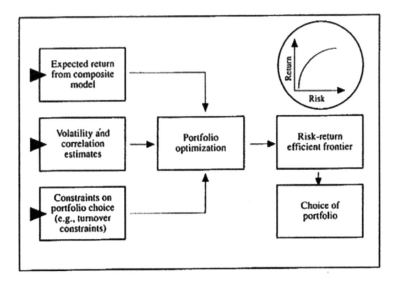

Fig. 9.4 Mr. Markowitz and optimal portfolio selection

Let us examine the question of optimal weighting of risky and risk-free assets, given a two asset portfolio. In Eq. (9.15), we saw the expected return of a two asset portfolio,

$$E(R_\rho) = (1 - x)R_F + XE(R_A).$$

The standard deviation of the two asset portfolio was shown in Eq. (9.8),

$$\sigma_\rho = \left[(1 - x)^2 \sigma_F^2 + x^2 \sigma_A^2 + 2(1 - x)(x)\sigma_A \sigma_F \rho_{FA} \right]^{1/2}$$

We must take the derivative of Eq. (9.16) with respect to our decision variable, the percentage invested in the risky asset, and settle derivative to zero.

$$\frac{\partial \sigma_\rho}{\partial x} = 1/2 \left[\frac{2X\sigma_A^2 - 2\sigma_F^2 + 2_F^2 X + 2\sigma_A \sigma_F \rho_{FA} - 4X\sigma_A \sigma_F \rho_{AF}}{X^2 \sigma_A^2 + (1 - X)^2 \sigma_F^2 + 2X(1 - X)\rho_{FA}\sigma_A \sigma_F \rho_{FA}\sigma_A \sigma_F} \right]$$

$$X = \frac{\partial \sigma \rho}{\partial x} = 0 = \frac{\sigma_F^2 - \rho_{FA}\sigma_A \sigma_F}{\sigma_A^2 + \sigma_F^2 - 2\sigma_A \sigma_F \rho_{FA}} \tag{9.13}$$

The Tobin presentation of the risk-return trade-off is quite relevant for common stocks and forms the basis of much of the Markowitz (1959) presentation. When one owns stocks, one is paid a dividend and earns stock price appreciation. That is, an investor buys stock when he or she expects its stock price to rise and compensates the investor for bearing the risk of the stock's price movements. Investors have become aware in recent years that not all price movements are in positive directions. One can calculate returns on stocks with several different methods.

Let us now examine a three stock portfolio construction process.

$$E(Rp) = \sum_{i=1}^{N} x_i E(R_i) \tag{9.14}$$

$$\sigma_p^2 = \sum_{i=1}^{N} \sum_{j=1}^{N} x_i x_j \sigma_{ij} \tag{9.15}$$

$$E(Rp) = x_1 E(R_1) + x_2 E(R_2) + x_3 E(R_3)$$

let $x_3 = 1 - x_1 - x_2$

$$E(Rp) = x_1 E(R_1) + x_2 E(R_2) + (1 - x_1 - x_2) E(R_3)$$

$$
\begin{aligned}
\sigma_p^2 &= x_1^2\sigma_1^2 + x_2^2\sigma_2^2 + \sigma_3^2 x_3^2 + 2x_1 x_2 \sigma_{12} + 2x_1 x_3 \sigma_{23} + 2x_2 x_3 \sigma_{23} \\
&= x_1^2\sigma_1^2 + x_2^2\sigma_2^2 + (1 - x_1 - x_2)^2 \sigma_3^2 + 2x_1 x_2 \sigma_{12} + 2x_1(1 - x_1 - x_2)\sigma_{13} \\
&\quad + 2x_2(1 - x_1 - x_2)\sigma_{23} \\
&= x_1^2\sigma_1^2 + x_2^2\sigma_2^2 + (1 - x_1 - x_2)(1 - x_1 - x_2)\sigma_3^2 + 2x_1 x_2 \sigma_{12} + 2x_1 \sigma_{13} \\
&\quad - 2x_1^2\sigma_{13} - 2x_1 x_2 \sigma_{13} + 2x_2\sigma_{23} - 2x_1 x_2\sigma_{23} - 2x_2^2\sigma_{23} \\
&= x_1^2\sigma_1^2 + x_2^2\sigma_2^2 + (1 - 2x_1 - 2x_2 + 2x_1 x_2 + x_1^2 + x_2^2)\sigma_3^2 + 2x_1 x_2 \sigma_{12} \\
&\quad + 2x_1 \sigma_{13} - 2x_1^2\sigma_{13} - 2x_1 x_2 \sigma_{13} + 2x_2 \sigma_{23} - 2x_1 x_2 \sigma_{23} - 2x_2^2\sigma_{23}
\end{aligned}
$$
$$(9.16)$$

$$
\frac{\partial\sigma_p^2}{\partial x_1} = 2x_1(\sigma_1^2 + \sigma_3^2 - 2\sigma_{13}) + x_2(2\sigma_3^2 + 2\sigma_{12} - 2\sigma_{13} - 2\sigma_{23})
$$
$$
- 2\sigma_3^2 + 2\sigma_{13} = 0
$$

$$
\frac{\partial\sigma_p^2}{\partial x_2} = 2x_2(\sigma_2^2 + \sigma_3^2 - 2\sigma_{23}) + x_1(2\sigma_3^2 + 2\sigma_{12} - 2\sigma_{13} - 2\sigma_{23})
$$
$$
- 2\sigma_3^2 + 2\sigma_{23} = 0
$$

9.1.1 Markowitz Optimization Analysis

The basis form of the Markowitz portfolio optimization analysis can be expressed graphically as by Harry in Bloch et al. (1993). What are the decision variables in Markowitz optimization analysis? One can vary the period of volatility calculation, such as using five years of monthly data in calculating the covariance matrix, as was done in Bloch et al. (1993), or one year of daily returns to calculate a covariance matrix, as was done in Guerard et al. (1993), or data to calculate factor returns as in the Barra or Axioma risk models, and discussed in Menchero et al. (2010) or Blin et al. (2021).

The goal in investment research is to operate as closely to the Efficient Frontier as possible. The Efficient Frontier, shown in Fig. 9.5, depicts the maximum return for a given level of risk.

In Bloch et al. (1993), Markowitz and his research department estimated Efficient Frontiers for Japanese-only securities for the 1974–1990 period. The

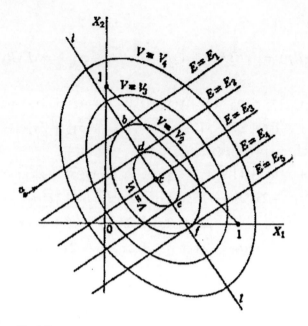

Fig. 9.5 The critical line

Bloch et al. Efficient Frontier is shown in Fig. 9.5. The upper bounds on security weights is a decision variable in which an increase in the upper bound allows the investment manager to exercise more asset selection power and possibly shift out the Efficient Frontier, as shown in Fig. 9.6, from Bloch

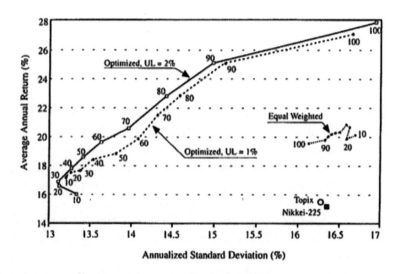

Fig. 9.6 Observed risk-return trade-off, Japan (WLRR,4Q,4), TCR = 2%

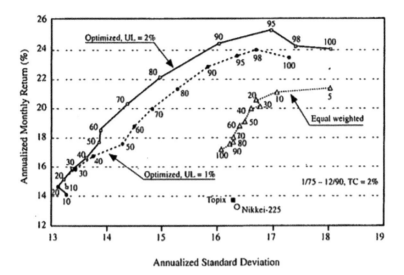

Fig. 9.7 Observed risk-return trade-off, TSE Section 1, standard composite model

et al. (1993), in which the upper bound on security weights increases from one percent to two percent.

The "Public" model trade-off curve, or Efficient Frontier, is shown in Fig. 9.3 and the corresponding "Proprietary" model is shown in Fig. 9.7.

9.1.1.1 A General Form of Portfolio Optimization

The general four-asset linear programming has been written by Martin (1955) as:

$$x_1 + x_2 + x_3 + x_4 = 1 \tag{9.17}$$

$$x_1 > 0, \quad I = 1, \dots, 4$$

$$E = x_1 \mu_1 + x_2 \mu_2 + x_3 \mu_3 + x_4 \mu_4 \tag{9.18}$$

E = expected returns

$$V = x_1^2 \sigma_{11} + x_2^2 \sigma_{12} + 2x_1 x_2 \sigma_{12} + 2x_1 x_3 \sigma_{13}$$
$$+ 2x_1 x_4 \sigma_{14} + x_2^2 \sigma_{33} + 2x_3 x_4 \sigma_{34} + x_4^2 \sigma_{44} \tag{9.19}$$

$$\phi = V + \lambda_1 \left(\sum_{i=1}^{4} x_i \mu_i - E \right) + \lambda_2 \left(\sum_{i=1}^{4} x_i - 1 \right) \tag{9.20}$$

$$\frac{\partial \phi}{\partial x_1} = x_1 \sigma_{11} + x_2 \sigma_{12} + x_3 \sigma_{13} + x_4 \sigma_{14} + \tfrac{1}{2} \lambda_1 \mu_1 + \tfrac{1}{2} \lambda_2 = 0$$

$$\vdots$$

$$\frac{\partial \phi}{\partial x_1} = x_1 \sigma_{14} + x_2 \sigma_{24} + x_3 \sigma_{34} + x_4 \sigma_{44} + \tfrac{1}{2} \lambda_4 \mu_4 + \tfrac{1}{2} \lambda_2 = 0$$

The four-asset optimization problem is expressed in a six-equation format by Martin (1955). All partial derivatives are set equal to zero as we did with Markowitz (1959) and the security weights sum to one. The Martin framework can be applied to any number of assets, if one can properly calculate the covariance among the stocks. The reader is reminded in Markowitz (1959) that one thousand stocks require (1000 X 999)/2 estimated covariances. These calculations are not trivial. The investor is fully invested. The portfolio expected returns are a weighted sum of security expected returns and security weights.

The final set of Markowitz four-asset optimization equations may be written as:

$$x_1 \sigma_{11} + x_2 \sigma_{12} + x_3 \sigma_{13} + x_4 \sigma_{14} + \tfrac{1}{2} \lambda_1 \mu_1 + \tfrac{1}{2} \lambda_2 = 0$$

$$x_1 \sigma_{12} + x_2 \sigma_{22} + x_3 \sigma_{23} + x_4 \sigma_{24} + \tfrac{1}{2} \lambda_1 \mu_2 + \tfrac{1}{2} \lambda_2 = 0$$

$$x_1 \sigma_{13} + x_2 \sigma_{23} + x_3 \sigma_{33} + x_4 \sigma_{34} + \tfrac{1}{2} \lambda_1 \mu_3 + \tfrac{1}{2} \lambda_2 = 0$$

$$x_1 \sigma_{14} + x_2 \sigma_{24} + x_3 \sigma_{34} + x_4 \sigma_{44} + \tfrac{1}{2} \lambda_1 \mu_4 + \tfrac{1}{2} \lambda_2 = 0$$

$$x_1 \mu_1 + x_2 \mu_2 + x_3 m \mu + x_4 \mu_4 = E$$

$$x_1 + x_2 + x_3 + x_4 = 1$$

The Martin (1995) model can be applied to 4 or 3000 assets, provided one can invert the covariance matrix.

Markowitz (1959, pp. 282–283) discusses the Rational Mean theory of investing as Latane (1959) is doing at the same time. In the long run, the expected return of the natural logarithm, Ln, of $1 + R$, the portfolio return, is represented by:

$$Ln(1 + R) = Ln(1 + E) - \frac{1/2V}{(1 + E)^2} \qquad (9.21)$$

where

$E = \text{expt } (R)$
$V = \text{variance } (R)$.

The portfolio that maximizes (9.12) must minimize the variance, V, for a given level of return, and will maximize return in the long run. The maximizing return is the Geometric Mean. Support for the establishment of the Geometric Mean investment criterion is found empirically in Young and Trent (1969) and Levy and Markowitz (1979).

$$GM = \sqrt[n]{\Pi(1 + R)} \qquad (9.22)$$

where Π stands for the product. Thus, one multiplies one plus the portfolio return for n periods and takes the nth root of the cumulative wealth ratio. The mean-variance approximation of Eq. (9.12) worked very well in approximating the GM for the 1, 4, 8, 16, and 32 stock portfolios in Young and Trent for the 1953–1960 period using 233 stocks.

Levy and Markowitz found that the mean-variance approximation worked very well for 149 investment companies during 1958–1967. Does the investor only need to be concerned with mean and variance? What about skewness, the third moment, and Kurtosis, the fourth moment?

Is skewness good for an investment manager? Skewness is helpful, if skewness is positive, which has been the case historically. This is a huge literature on skewness but is it sficient to say that the market rewards positive skewness, see Arditti (1967), Arditti and Levy (1975), Stone (1983), and Stone and Guerard (2010). In Arditti (1967), returns are positively associated with variances; the higher the variance, the higher must be the return. However, for skewness, as skewness rises, the market requires lower returns because skewness (positive skewness) is desirable. Across all securities in the S&P Composite Index from 1946 to 1963, Arditti (p. 26) found:

$$\text{Returns} = .1044 + .4221 \text{ Variance} - .1677 \text{ Skewness}$$
$$(\text{s.e.}) \quad (.0074)(.0831) \quad\quad\quad (.0435)$$

The final form of the Martin (1955) representation of Markowitz can be found in Elton (2007) later shown in this chapter.

Modern-day Markowitz analysis, as illustrated in Elton (2007), continues to use Lagrangian multipliers. One seeks to the ratio of portfolio excess return, defined as the expected return of the portfolio less the risk-free rate, divided by the portfolio standard deviation.

$$\theta = \frac{E(R_p) - R_F}{\sigma_p} \tag{9.23}$$

subject to $\sum_{i=1}^{N} w_i = 1$.
We can rewrite (9.24) as

$$\theta = \frac{\sum_{i=1}^{N} w_i (E(R_i) - R_F)}{\left[\sum_{i=1}^{N} w_i^2 \sigma_i^2 + \sum_{i=1}^{N} \sum_{j=1}^{N} w_i w_j \sigma_{ij}\right]^{1/2}} \tag{9.24}$$

$$i \neq j$$

To maximize the portfolio selection problem in (9.9), one again takes the partial derivatives and set them equal to 0.

$$\frac{\partial \theta}{\partial w_1} = 0, \quad \frac{\partial \theta}{\partial w_2} = 0, \quad \ldots, \quad \frac{\partial \theta}{\partial w_N} = 0$$

$$\frac{\partial \theta}{\partial w_i} = -(\lambda w_1 \sigma_{1i} + \lambda w_2 \sigma_{2i} + \lambda w_3 \sigma_{3i} + \cdots + \lambda x_i \sigma_i^2$$
$$+ \cdots \lambda w_{N-1} \sigma_{N-1i} + E(R_i) - R_F = 0 \tag{9.25}$$

In Eq. (9.15), we may define λw to be z, such that

$$E(R_i) - R_F = z_i \sigma_{1i} + z_2 \sigma_{2i} + \cdots + z_{N-1} \sigma_{N-1} + z_N \sigma_{Ni} \tag{9.26}$$

Thus, Elton, Gruber, Brown, and Goetzmann solve a set of simultaneous equations where:

$$E(R_i) - R_F = z_i\sigma_1^2 + z_2\sigma_{12} + z_3\sigma_3 + \cdots + z_N\sigma_{1N}$$
$$E(R_2) - R_F = z_i\sigma_{12} + z_2\sigma_2^2 + z_3\sigma_3^2 + \cdots + z_N\sigma_{2N} \qquad (9.27)$$
$$E(R_3) - R_F = z_i\sigma_{13} + z_2\sigma_{23} + z_3\sigma_{23} + \cdots + z_N\sigma_{3N}$$

$$w_k = \frac{z_k}{\sum_{i-1}^{N} z_i} \qquad (9.28)$$

Sharpe (1963) developed the Diagonal Model that reduced the computing time of the RAND QP (quadratic programming) code on the IBM 7090 computer from 33 minutes to 30 seconds for a 100-stock example. In the Diagonal Model, Sharpe modeled stock returns are related through common relationships of an underlying factor or index. Sharpe specifically suggested variables such as the level of the stock market, Gross National Product (GNP), or a price index.[1]

Markowitz measured risk as the portfolio standard deviation, its measure of dispersion, or total risk. The Sharpe (1964), Lintner (1965), and Mossin (1966) development of the Capital Asset Pricing Model (CAPM) held that investors are compensated for bearing not total risk, but rather market risk, or systematic risk, as measured by the stock beta. An investor is not compensated for bearing risk that may be diversified away from the portfolio. The beta is the slope of the market model, in which the stock return is regressed as a function of the market return.

The CAPM holds that the return to a security is a function of the security beta.

$$R_{jt} = R_F + b_j[E(R_{Mt}) - R_F] + e_j \qquad (9.29)$$

where

R_{jt} = expected security return at time t;

---

[1] Harry Markowitz (1959) anticipated the Diagonal Model in footnote 1, page 100, of chapter four where the return of a security can be expressed as a function of the value of an index. Given that Sharpe's Diagonal Model paper had four references, three of which were Markowitz publications, one can clearly understand that modern portfolio theory was developed in large part to the interactions of these great thinkers. It is little wonder they shared the Noble Prize. Elton and Gruber (1980) and Elton et al. (2007) brought the correlation coefficients and covariances and beta relationships to a far greater audience, MBA students. The Elton and Gruber texts are excellent books (the first and seventh editions) that greatly enhanced multi-factor risk explanations, particularly in integrating stock betas.

$E(R_{Mt})$ = expected return on the market at time t;
R_F = risk-free rate;
β_j = security beta; and
e_j = randomly distributed error term.

Let us examine the Capital Asset Pricing Model beta, its measure of systematic risk, from the Capital Market Line equilibrium condition.

$$\beta_j = \frac{\text{Cov}(R_j, R_M)}{\text{Var}(R_M)} \qquad (9.30)$$

$$E(R_j) = R_F + \left[\frac{E(R_M) - R_F}{\sigma_M^2}\right]\text{Cov}(R_j, R_M)$$

$$= R_F + [E(R_M) - R_F]\frac{\text{Cov}(R_j, R_M)}{\text{Var}(R_M)}$$

$$E(R_j) = R_F + [E(R_M) - R_F]\beta_j \qquad (9.31)$$

The Security Market Line, SML, shown in Eq. (9.31), is the linear relationship between return and systematic risk, as measured by beta.

9.1.2 Multi-Beta Risk Control Models

pirical tests of the CAPM often resulted in unsatisfactory results. That is, the average estimated market risk premium was too small, relative to the theoretical market risk premium and the average estimated risk-free rate exceeded the known risk-free rate. Thus low-beta scks appeared to earn more than was expected and high-beta stocks appeared to earn less than was expected [Black et al., 1972)]. The equity world appeared more risk-neutral than one would have expected during the 1931–1965 period. There could be many issues with estimating betas using ordinary least squares. Roll (1969, 1977) and Sharpe (1971) identified and tested several issues with beta estimations. Bill Sharpe estimated characteristic lines, the line of stock or mutual fund return versus the market return, using ordinary least squares (OLS) and the mean absolute deviation (MAD) for the 30 stocks of the Dow Jones Industrial Average stocks versus the Standard and Poor's 425 Index (S&P 425) for the 1965–1970 period and 30 randomly selected mutual funds over the 1964–1970 period versus the S&P 425. Sharpe found little difference in the

OLS and MAD betas and concluded that the MAD estimation gains may be "relatively modest".

Phaps more than one beta should be estimated. Farrell (1974, 1997) estimated a four "factor" model extra-market covariance model.[2] Farrell took an initial universe of 100 stocks in 1974 (due to computer limitations), and ran market models to estimate betas and residuals from the market model:

$$R_{j_t} = a_j + b_j R_{M_t} + e_j \tag{9.32}$$

$$e_{j_t} = R_{j_t} - \hat{a}_j - \hat{b}_j R_{MT} \tag{9.33}$$

The residuals of Eq. (9.33) should be independent variables. That is, after removing the market impact by estimating a beta, the residual of IBM should be independent of Dow, Merck, or Dominion Resources. The residuals should be independent, of course, in theory. Farrell (1974) examined the correlations among the security residuals of Eq. (9.33) and found that the residuals of IBM and Merck were highly correlated, but the residuals of IBM and D (then Virginia Electric & Power) were not correlated. Farrell used a statistical technique known as Cluster Analysis to create clusters, or groups, of securities, having highly correlated market model residuals. Farrell found four clusters of securities based on his extra-market covariance. The clusters contained securities with highly correlated residuals that were uncorrelated with residuals of securities in the other clusters. Farrell referred to his clusters as "Growth Stocks" (electronics, office equipment, drug, hospital supply firms and firms with above-average earnings growth), "Cyclical Stocks" (Metals, machinery, building supplies, general industrial firms, and other companies with above-average exposure to the business cycle), "Stable Stocks" (banks, utilities, retailers, and firms with below-average exposure to the business cycle), and "Energy Stocks" (coal, crude oil, and domestic and international oil firms).

Bernell Stone published his dissertation at MIT on capital market equilibrium in 1970, by MIT Press. Mr. Stone (1974) developed a two-factor index model which modeled equity returns as a function of an equity index and long-term debt returns. Both equity and debt returns had significant betas. In recent years, Stone et al. (2002, 2010) have developed a portfolio algorithm to generate portfolios that have similar stock betas (systematic risk), market capitalizations, dividend yield, and sales growth cross sections, such

---

[2] The reader is referred to Mr. Farrrell's 1997 text on investment analysis which presents an excellent overview of the CAPM and multi-factor portfolio selection analysis.

that one can access the excess returns of the analysts' forecasts, forecast revisions, and breadth model, as one moves from low (least preferred) to high (most preferred) securities with regard to your portfolio construction variable (i.e., CTEF or a composite model of value and analysts' forecasting factors). In the Stone et al. (2010) work, the ranking on forecasted return and grouping into fractile portfolios produces a set of portfolios ordered on the basis of predicted return score. This return cross section will almost certainly have a wide range of forecasted return values. However, each portfolio in the cross section will almost never have the same average values as the control variables. To produce a cross-sectional match on any of the control variables, we must reassign stocks. For instance, if we were trying to make each portfolio in the cross section have the same average beta value, we could move a stock with an above-average beta value into a portfolio whose average beta value is below the population average. At the same time, we could shift a stock with a below-average beta value into the above-average portfolio from the below-average portfolio. The reassignment problem can be formulated as a mathematical assignment program (MAP). Using the MAP produces a cross-sectional match on beta or any other control variable. All (fractile) portfolios should have explanatory controls equal to their population average value.

Given a cross section of rank-ordered portfolios, the objective of the assignment program is the objective is not just to match each portfolio in the cross section on the portfolio average value of beta but to find that particular match that preserves as much as possible a wide range of well-ordered return forecasts while preserving within-portfolio homogeneity of forecasted return subject to the constraints that:

- the portfolio average value of each control variable equals the population mean,
- the initial size (number of securities) of each portfolio be preserved,
- each security be fully assigned,
- there are no short sales.

The crucial constraints are the control matching restrictions. Preserving initial portfolio size and full use of each security are technical constraints that go with full use of the sample. Prohibiting short sales prevents one return observation from canceling out other return observations.

P = number of rank-based portfolios in the cross section
p= 1 is the portfolio with the smallest value of the rank ordering variable
$p = P$ is the portfolio with the largest value of the rank ordering variable

S = total number of securities being assigned to portfolios
s = security subscript
X_{ps} = the fraction of security s assigned to portfolio p
V = representative control variable
VTARGET = target average value of a representative control variable.[3]

The advance start that is input to the mathematical assignment program (MAP) is a set of P rank-based fractile portfolios. The linear objective function is a trade-off between preserving as much as possible a measure of cross-portfolio range while minimizing the shifting of stocks away from the original rank-order portfolio. Preserving range and minimizing cross-portfolio mixing are two aspects of statistical power. They are complementary measures in that optimizing one tends to optimize the other. To reflect the relative importance of these two measures, we define a trade-off parameter Φ that defines a relative weighting, where $0 < \Phi < 1$, reflected by a weighting parameter Φ. Thus, the objective function can be written:

$$\text{Maximize: OBJECTIVE FUNCTION} = \Phi[\text{RANGE}]$$
$$- (1 - \Phi[\text{SHIFTING}])$$

Let D_{ps} be the squared difference in the numerical rank of between portfolio p and the natural portfolio rank of security s in the initial range-based partitioning. The set of D_{ps} can be scaled such that large shifts are much worse than small ones. If FS_s denotes the value of the forecast score for stock s, then the objective function above can be written in terms of assignment variables as:

$$\text{Maximize } \Phi[\Sigma_S X_{Ps} FS_s - \Sigma_5 X_{1s} FS_s]$$
$$- (1 - \Phi)\left[\Sigma_p \Sigma_s X_{Ps} D_{Ps}\right] \qquad (9.34)$$

The MAP can be solved for a range of trade-off values by varying Φ from zero to 1. However, experience shows that the solutions are robust to variation in the trade-off Φ. Because these two attributes of statistical power are complementary objectives, minimizing cross-fractile shifting generally preserves the range in the starting fractile portfolios. Note that the Stone et al. analysis represents a multi-surface programming problem in the spirit of the Sharpe Responsiveness Model. This result should not be surprising as Bill

---

[3] In this study, the target average value is always the ex ante sample average value.

Sharpe and Bernell Stone developed linear programming models of portfolio construction as far back as 1973.

Let V_s denote the security s value of a representative control variable. Let VTARGET denote the target value of this representative control variable for all P portfolios in the cross section. The representative control constraint can be expressed as:

$$\sum_s X_{ps} V_j = \text{VTARGET}_j \quad p = 1, \ldots, P-1. \tag{9.35}$$

We impose two generic data usage constraints. The first says that each security must be fully assigned to one or more portfolios, i.e.:

$$\sum_p X_{ps} = 1 \quad s = 1, \ldots, S \tag{9.36}$$

The second security assignment constraint keeps the number of securities in each matched portfolio the same as the number of securities in the corresponding fractile of the starting rank-order partitioning of the distribution of V1. Let F_p denote the number of securities in fractile p. Then this restriction is:

$$\sum_s X_{ps} = F_p \quad p = 1, \ldots, P \tag{9.37}$$

The no short-sale restriction and the natural limitation that no security can be used more than once requires:

$$0 \leq X_{ps} \leq 1 \tag{9.38}$$

The substance of the reassignment process is well understood by knowing input and output. The input is a cross section formed by ranking stocks into fractile portfolios, which is the focus of most cross-sectional return analyses in past work on cross-sectional return dependencies. The output is a cross section of fractile portfolios that are matched on a specified set of explanatory controls. Optimization arises in finding the particular reassignment that maximizes a trade-off between preserving the widest possible range of well-ordered portfolio values of forecasted return and also ensuring preservation of within-portfolio homogeneity of forecasted return. The original input cross section is transformed by the optimal reassignment of stocks to produce a new cross section that is matched on the average values of a set of explanatory controls.[4] Stone and Guerard (2010) tested the hypothesis that a composite model of earnings, book value, cash flow, and sales-based value-investing strategies produced superior returns even after correcting for risk, growth, and other return impact variables. We will report the MAP portfolio selection results later in this chapter.

In 1976, Ross published his "Arbitrage Theory of Capital Asset Pricing," which held that security returns were a function of several (4–5) economic factors. Ross and Roll (1980) empirically substantially the need for 4–5 factors to describe the return generating process. The Stone, Farrell, and Chen, Ross, and Roll multi-factor models used 4–5 factors to describe equity security risk. The models used different statistical approaches and economic models to control for risk. Asset managers create portfolios for clients, investors, who seek to maximize expected portfolio returns relative to risk. The purpose of this section has been to introduce the reader to Capital Market Theory, beta estimations, and the relevance of multi-factor risk control models.

9.1.3   The BARRA Model: The Primary Institutional Risk Model

Barr Rosenberg and Walt McKibben (1973) estimated the determinants of security betas and standard deviations. This estimation formed the basis of the Rosenberg extra-market component study (1974), in which security specific risk could be modeled as a function of financial descriptors, or known financial characteristics of the firm. Rosenberg and McKibben found that the financial characteristics that were statistically associated with beta during the 1954–1970 period were:

1. Latest annual proportional change in earnings per share;
2. Liquidity, as measured by the quick ratio;
3. Leverage, as measured by the senior debt-to-total assets ratio;
4. Growth, as measured by the growth in earnings per share;
5. Book-to-Price ratio;
6. Historic beta;
7. Logarithm of stock price;
8. Standard deviation of earnings per share growth;

---

[4] Given our sample data, a decision about the number of portfolios to be formed, and an initial rank-ordering into fractile portfolios, we are maximizing the statistical power to test for return dependencies for portfolio observations that belong to a well-defined subsurface of an overall multivariate cross-sectional return dependency.

9. Gross plant per dollar of total assets;
10. Share turnover.

Rosenberg and McKibben used 32 variables and a 578-firm sample to estimate the determinants of betas and standard deviations. For betas, Rosenberg
and McKibben found that the positive and statistically significant determinants of beta were the standard deviation of eps growth, share turnover, the
price-to-book multiple, and the historic beta. Rosenberg et al. (1975), Rosenberg and Marathe (1979), Rudd and Rosenberg (1979, 1980), and Rudd and
Clasing (1982) expanded upon the initial Rosenberg MFM framework.

In 1975, Barr Rosenberg and his associates introduced the BARRA
US Equity Model, often denoted USE1. We spend a great deal of time
on the BARRA USE1 and USE3 models because 70 of the 100 largest
investment managers use the BARRA USE3 Model.[5] The BARRA USE1
Model predicted risk, which required the evaluation of the firm's response
to economic events, which were measured by the company's fundamentals. There were six descriptors, or risk indexes, in the BARRA model.
These descriptors were composite variables primarily based on the statistically significant variables in Rosenberg and McKibben (1973). Rudd and
Clasing (1982) is an excellent reference for how the BARRA equity model
is constructed. BARRA is a proprietary model; that is, the composite models'
weights are not disclosed. Thus, there were nine factors in the Index of
Market Variability, including the historic beta estimate, historic sigma estimate, share turnover for 3 months, trading volume, the log of the common
stock price, and a historical alpha estimate, and cumulative range over one
year, but without coefficients, one cannot reproduce the model. One can
correlate an investment manager's variables with the risk indexes, as we will
discuss later in the chapter. The Index of Earnings Variability included the
variance of earnings, variance of cash flow, and the covariability of earnings and price. The Index of Low Valuation and Unsuccess included the
growth in earnings per share, recent earnings change, relative strength (a price
momentum variable), the book-to-price ratio, dividend cuts, and the return
of equity. The Index of Immaturity and Smallness included the log of total
assets, the log of market capitalization, and net plant/common equity. The
Index of Growth Orientation included the dividends-to-earnings ratio (the
payout ratio), dividend yield, growth in total assets, the earnings-to-price
(ep) multiple, and the typical ep ratio over the past five years. The Graham
and Dodd low P/E investment manager would "load up" on The Index of

---

[5] According to BARRA online advertisements.

Growth Orientation, and would offer investors positive asset selection (good stock picking) only if the portfolio weights differed from weights on the "Growth" Index components. The Index of Financial Risk" included leverage at market and book values, debt-to-assets ratio, and cash flow-to-current liabilities ratio.[6]

There were 39 industry variables in the BARRA USE1 model. How is the data manipulated and /or normalized to be used in the BARRA USE1 model? First, raw data is normalized by subtracting a mean and dividing through by the variable standard deviation; however, the mean subtracted is the market capitalization weighted mean for each descriptor for all securities in the S&P 500. Rudd and Clasing remind us that the capitalization weighted value for S&P 500 stocks is zero. The relevant variable standard deviation is not the universe standard deviation of each variable, but the standard deviation of the variables for companies with market capitalizations exceeding $50 million. A final transformation occurs when the normalized descriptor is scaled such that its value is one standard deviation above the S&P 500 mean. Every month the monthly stock return in the quarter are regressed as a function of the normalized descriptors. If the firm is typical of the S&P 500 firms, then most of the scaled descriptor values and coefficients should be approximately zero. The monthly residual risk factors are calculated by regressing residual returns (the stock excess return less the predicted beta times the market excess return) versus the six risk indexes and the industry dummy variables.

The statistically significant determinants of the security systematic risk became the basis of the BARRA E1 Model risk indexes. The domestic BARRA E3 (USE3, or sometimes denoted USE3) model, with some 15 years of research and evolution, uses 13 sources of factor, or systematic, exposures. The sources of extra-market factor exposures are volatility, momentum, size, size non-linearity, trading activity, growth, earnings yield, value, earnings variation, leverage, currency sensitivity, dividend yield, and non-estimation universe. The BARRA USE3 descriptors are included in the appendix to this chapter.

How does USE3 differ from USE1? There are many changes; of importance to many readers, the USE3 uses analysts' predictions of the current year and one-year-ahead earnings per share in the earnings yield index which is used in conjunction with the historic and twelve-month trailing earnings-to-price multiples. The analysts' standard deviation of forecasts is a component of the earnings variability component. Momentum, book-to-market (denoted as "value") and dividend yield are now separate risk indexes.

---

[6] See Rudd and Clasing (1982, p. 115), for the USE1 descriptors.

The total excess return for a multiple-factor model, referred to as the MFM, in the Rosenberg methodology for security j, at time t, dropping the subscript t for time, may be written:

$$E(R_j) = \sum_{k=1}^{K} \beta_{jk} \tilde{f}_k + \tilde{e} \tag{9.39}$$

The non-factor, or asset-specific, return on security j, is the residual risk of the security, after removing the estimated impacts of the K factors. The term, f, is the rate of return on factor k. A single factor model, in which the market return is the only estimated factor, is obviously the basis of the Capital Asset Pricing Model. Accurate characterization of portfolio risk requires an accurate estimate of the covariance matrix of security returns. A relatively simple way to estimate this covariance matrix is to use the history of security returns to compute each variance, covariance, and security beta. The use of beta, the covariance of security and market index returns, is one method of estimating a reasonable cost of equity funds for firms. However, the approximation obtained from simple models may not yield the best possible cost of equity. The simple, single index beta estimation approach suffers from two major drawbacks:

- Estimating a covariance matrix for the Russell 3,000 stocks requires a great deal of data;
- It is subject to estimation error. Thus, one might expect a higher correlation between DuPont and Dow than between DuPont and IBM, given that DuPont and Dow are both chemical firms.

Taking this further, one can argue that firms with similar characteristics, such as firms in their line of business, should have returns that behave similarly. For example, DuPont and IBM will all have a common component in their returns because they would all be affected by news that affects the stock market, measured by their respective betas. The degree to which each of the three stocks responds to this stock market component depends on the sensitivity of each stock to the stock market component.

Investors look at the variance of their total portfolios to provide a comprehensive assessment of risk. To calculate the variance of a portfolio, one needs to calculate the covariances of all the constituent components. Without the framework of a multiple-factor model, estimating the covariance of each asset

with every other asset is computationally burdensome and subject to significant estimation errors. Let us examine the risk structure of the BARRA
MFM.

$V(I,j) = \text{Covariance } [r(\tilde{i}), r(\tilde{j})].$

where $V(i,j)$ = asset covariance matrix, and

i,j = individual stocks.

$$V = \begin{bmatrix} V(1,1) & V(1,2) & \cdots & V(1,N) \\ V(2,1) & V(2,2) & \cdots & V(2,N) \\ V(3,1) & V(3,2) & \cdots & V(3,N) \\ \vdots & \vdots & & \vdots \\ V(N,1) & V(N,2) & \cdots & V(N,N) \end{bmatrix}$$

The BARRA MFM simplifies these calculations dramatically, replacing
individual company profiles with categories defined by common characteristics (factors). The specific risk is assumed to be uncorrelated among the assets
and only the factor variances and covariances are calculated during model
estimation. Let us briefly review how Barr Rosenberg initially estimated the
BARRA factor structure.

$$\tilde{r} = X\tilde{f} + \tilde{u}$$

$\tilde{r}$ = vector of excess returns,

X = exposure matrix,

$\tilde{f}$ = vector of factor returns, and

$\tilde{u}$ = vector of specific returns.

$$\begin{bmatrix} \tilde{r}(1) \\ \tilde{r}(2) \\ \vdots \\ \tilde{r}(N) \end{bmatrix} = \begin{bmatrix} X(1,1) & X(1,2) & \cdots & X(1,K) \\ X(2,1) & X(2,2) & \cdots & X(2,K) \\ \vdots & \vdots & \cdots & \vdots \\ X(N,1) & X(N,2) & \cdots & X(N,K) \end{bmatrix} \begin{bmatrix} \tilde{f}(1) \\ \tilde{f}(2) \\ \vdots \\ \tilde{f}(K) \end{bmatrix} + \begin{bmatrix} \tilde{u}(1) \\ \tilde{u}(2) \\ \vdots \\ \tilde{u}(N) \end{bmatrix}$$

The multiple-factor risk model significantly reduces the number of calculations. For example, in the U.S. Equity Model (USE3), 65 factors capture
the risk characteristics of equities. This reduces the number of covariance
and variance calculations; moreover, since there are fewer parameters to
determine, they can be estimated with greater precision. The BARRA risk

management system begins with the MFM equation:

$$\tilde{r}_i = X\tilde{f} + \tilde{u} \qquad (9.40)$$

where

$\tilde{r}_i$ = excess return on asset I,
X = exposure coefficient on the factor,
$\tilde{f}$ = factor return, and
$\tilde{u}$ = specific return.

Substituting this relation in the basic equation, we find that:

$$\text{Risk} = \text{Var}(\tilde{r}_j) \qquad (9.41)$$

$$= \text{Var}\left(X\tilde{f} + \tilde{u}\right) \qquad (9.42)$$

Using the matrix algebra formula for variance, the risk equation becomes:

$$\text{Risk} = XFX^T + \Delta \qquad (9.43)$$

where

X = exposure matrix of companies upon factors,
F = covariance matrix of factors,
X^T = transpose of X matrix, and
Δ = diagonal matrix of specific risk variances.

This is the basic equation that defines the matrix calculations used in risk analysis in the BARRA equity models.[7] Investment managers seek to maximize portfolio return for a given level of risk. For many managers, risk is measured by the BARRA risk model. In 2008, MSCI BARRA introduced the BARRA Global Equity Model, Version 2. Jose Menchero and his colleagues at BARRA authored the "Global Equity Risk Modeling" article in this volume.

---

[7] Markowitz discusses the MFM formulation in his second monograph, *Mean-Variance Analysis in Portfolio Choice and Capital Markets* (New Hope, PA: Frank J. Fabozzi Associates, 2000), Chapter 3, pp. 45–47. The Markowitz (1987, 2000) Mean-Variance Analysis volume requires great patience and thought on the part of the reader, as noted by Bill Sharpe in his foreword to the 2000 edition.

Menchero et al. (2010) estimated an eight-risk index model in the spirit of the Rosenberg USE3 model.

9.2   Implementing Optimal Portfolio Selection

We report a "one-button" approach to portfolio construction and management that is consistent with the teachings of Harry Markowitz and William F. Sharpe, the creators of Modern Portfolio Theory, MPT. On the FactSet platform, we pull down FactSet Fundamentals financial data and the I/B/E/S earnings history and create fundamental ratios and data, run robust regression to implement a statistically significant stock selection model, create portfolios, and assess the portfolios over time (i.e., backtest the strategies). We report the expected returns modeling work of Ed Elton, Martin Gruber, and Mustafa Gultekin; William Ziemba and Sandra Schwartz; and John Guerard continues to drive stock returns. What do we add to an extensive anomaly literature? We test portfolio anomalies in a post-publication setting. We report three results: (1) many of the reported financial anomalies published between 1993 and 2003 maintained their statistical significance active (or excess) returns; (2) the anomalies are greater in non-U.S. markets than in the U.S.; and (3) transactions costs do not destroy the excess returns. The authors report highly statistically significant excess returns above transactions costs and data mining corrections adjustments in U.S. and non-U.S. stocks during the 2003–2020 time period modeled with the FactSet Research Systems Inc.

9.2.1   What We Knew in 1991 Tests of Fundamental Data

In 1991, Harry Markowitz developed an equity research group, DPOS, at Daiwa Securities Trust Company in Jersey City, NJ. Financial modeling used traditional fundamental variables, such as earnings-to-price, book value-to-price, cash flow-to-price, sales-to-price, cash flow-to-price, small size, institutional holdings, earnings forecasts, revisions, recommendations, and breadth, earnings surprises, dividend yield variables identified in Dimson (1988) and Jacobs and Levy (1988), and on-going conversations with William (Bill) Ziemba as anomalies.[8]

---

[8] Bloch et al. (1993), Ziemba and Schwartz (1993), and Chan et al. (1991) specifically addressed many of the earlier reported non-U.S. anomalies and/or compared U.S. and non-U.S. anomalies.

Benjamin Graham and David Dodd, in their classical *Security Analysis* (1934), are presently considered by many, including Warren Buffet, the preeminent financial contributors to the theory of stock valuation. In Chapter 17, "The Theory of Common-Stock Investment," Graham and Dodd discussed their explanation for the departure of the public from rational common valuation during the 1927–1929 period. Graham and Dodd attributed much of the valuation departures to the instability of intangibles and the dominant importance of intangibles (p. 301). Investment in the pre-war (World War I) was confined to common stocks with stable dividends and fairly stable earnings, which would lead to stable market levels (p. 303). Graham and Dodd hold that the function of (security) analysis is to search for weakness in pre-war conditions such as improperly stated earnings, a poor current condition of its balance sheet, or debt growing too rapidly (p. 303). Moreover, new competition, deteriorating management, and/or market share must condemn the common stock from the possible valuation of a "cautious investor." Graham and Dodd attributed speculation on future prospects or expectations. They taught their students at Columbia Universitythat buying common stock could be viewed as taking a share in the business (p. 305). In the "new-era theory of common stock valuation, (1) dividend rate had little bearing upon value; (2) there was no relationship between earning power and asset value; and (3) past earnings were significant only to the extent that they indicated what changes in earnings might occur in the future" (p. 307). Graham and Dodd chastised 1927–1929 investors for valuation analysis that emphasized: (1) "the value of a common stock depends on what it can earn in the future; (2) good common stocks will prove sound and profitable investments; and (3) good common stocks are those which have shown a rising trend of earnings" (p. 309). The new-era investment theory was held to be the equivalent of pre-war speculation. Graham and Dodd attributed much of the speculation to the work of Edgar Smith and his *Common Stocks as Long-Term Investments* (1924) text. Graham and Dodd held that Smith postulated that stocks increased in value more than was justified as a result of reinvestment earnings capitalization. That is, if a company earned nine percent, paid dividends of six percent, and added three percent to surplus (retained earnings), then good management should lead the stock value to increase with its book value, with the three percent compounded. Graham and Dodd assaulted the new-era investment theory for paying 20–40 times earnings. Smith, with his reinvestment of surplus earnings theory built up asset values and thus created the growth of common-stock values

(Graham & Dodd, p. 313). Average earnings, as advocated by Williams previously noted, ceased to be a dependable measure of future earnings, and there is a danger of projecting trends into the future.

Bloch et al. (1993) built fundamental-based stock selection models for Japanese and U.S. stocks. What did we know in 1991? The DPOS Group was well-versed in the low PE or high earnings-to-price, EP, high book value-to-price, high cash flow-to-price, high sales-to-price, net current asset value, and the earnings forecasting models in Graham and Dodd (1934), Graham et al. (1962), Elton and Gruber (1972a, 1972b), Latane et al. (1975), Jacobs and Levy (1988), and Dimson (1988).[9] DPOS built stock selection models and created Markowitz Mean-variance Efficient Frontiers for U.S. and Japanese stock markets. The investable stock universe was the first section, nonfinancial Tokyo Stock Exchange common stocks from January 1975 to December 1990 in Japan, and the U.S. investable universe was the 1,000 largest market-capitalized common stocks from November 1975 to December 1990.

Eight factors were used in the quarterly, cross-sectional regressions in Japan and the U.S. Bloch et al. (1993) estimated Eq. (9.43) to assess empirically the relative explanatory power of each of the eight variables in the equation to estimate the determinants of total stock returns, TR. We refer to this model as REG8.

$$TR = w_0 + w_1 EP + w_2 BP + w_3 CP + w_4 SP + w_5 REP$$
$$+ w_6 RBP + w_7 RCP + w_8 RSP + e_t \qquad (9.44)$$

where

EP = [earnings per share]/[price per share] = earnings-price ratio;
BP = [book value per share]/[price per share] = book-price ratio;
CP = [cash flow per share]/[price per share] = cash flow-price ratio;
SP = [net sales per share]/[price per share] = sales-price ratio;
REP = [current EP ratio]/[average EP ratio over the past five years];

---

[9] Nerlove (1968) reported the statistical significance of the growth sales and earnings in association with stock returns. The major papers on the combination of value ratios for the prediction of stock returns (including at least CP and/or SP) include those of Jacobs and Levy (1988), Chan et al. (1991), Fama and French (1992, 1995), Bloch et al. (1993). Lakonishok et al. (1994) and Haugen and Baker (1996) later produced highly cited variable testing which confirmed that fundamental variables enhanced portfolio returns over the long-run. Our point is this brief survey of anomalies is to acknowledge that Jacobs and Levy, Chan et al. (1991), Bloch et al. (1993), and Ziemba and Schwartz (1993), were correct in their Berkeley Program in Finance and Q-Group presentations of the early 1990s on the inefficiencies of stock markets.

RBP = [current BP ratio]/[average BP ratio over the past five years];
RCP = [current CP ratio]/[average CP ratio over the past five years]; and
RSP = [current SP ratio]/[average SP ratio over the past five years];

Given concerns about both outlier distortion and multicollinearity, Bloch et al. (1993) tested the relative explanatory and predictive merits of alternative regression estimation procedures: OLS; robust regression using the Beaton and Tukey (1974) bisquare criterion to mitigate the impact of outliers; the presence of highly correlated variables latent root regression to address the issue of the highly correlated variables, known as multicollinearity (see Gunst et al., 1976); and weighted latent roots, denoted WLRR, a combination of robust and latent roots. Bloch et al. (1993) used the estimated regression coefficients to construct a rolling horizon return forecast. The predicted returns and predictions of risk parameters were used as inputs for a mean-variance optimizer (see Markowitz, 1959, 1987) to create mean-variance efficient portfolios in financial markets in both Japan and the U.S. The DPOS analysis found that a series of Markowitz (1952, 1959, 1976) mean-variance efficient portfolios produced statistically significant excess returns. First, they compared OLS and robust regression techniques, inputting the expected return forecasts produced by each method into a mean-variance optimizer. The robust regression-constructed composite model portfolio produced higher Sharpe ratios and geometric means than the OLS-constructed composite model portfolio in both Japan and the U.S., indicating that controlling for both outliers and multicollinearity is important. Second, Bloch et al. (1993) quantified the survivor bias (including dead companies in the database) and found that it was not statistically significant in either Japan or the U.S. for the period tested. Third, they investigated period-to-period portfolio revision and found that tighter turnover and rebalancing triggers led to higher portfolio returns for value-based strategies.

Mr. Markowitz and Mr. Sharpe shared the Nobel Prize in Economics in 1991. New York University (NYU) hosted a seminar to honor Mr. Markowitz and the paper presented by Mr. Markowitz was published in *Japan & the World Economy*; an economics journal edited at NYU.[10] We reproduce the original Markowitz presentation in Table 9.1, because the table specifically reports that the robust regression models, to address outliers, produce higher out-of-sample geometric means and Sharpe Ratios than did ordinary least

---

[10] Mr. Martin Gruber, a Nomura Chaired Professor at NYU, refereed the piece by Mr. Markowitz. Mr. Gruber, previously noted in this chapter as the author of a widely used MBA portfolio selection and investment text.

Table 9.1 Mr. Markowitz and DPOS Japanese and U.S. simulations

D-POS, Japan. Simulation results; sorted by geometric mean. Let UL = 2.0 TCR = 2.0 PM = −1 PPar = 0.90 Begin = 7412 End = 9012

SID	OP	TOV	RP	Rtri	ERET	GM	Shrp
900869	3	10.00	1	25.0	PROPRIETARY	25.60	0.89
900867	3	10.00	0	0.0	PROPRIETARY	25.39	0.89
900868	. 3	10.00	1	20.0	PROPRIETARY	25.32	0.87
900860	3	15.00	1	25.0	PROPRIETARY	24.28	0.84
900853	3	15.00	0	0.0	PROPRIETARY	24.19	0.85
900858	3	10.00	1	25.0	PROPRIETARY	24.04	0.85
900852	3	12.50	0	0.0	PROPRIETARY	23.94	0.85
900855	3	10.00	1	20.0	PROPRIETARY	23,93	0.86
900856	3	12.50	1	20.0	PROPRIETARY	23.90	0.84
900854	3	17.50	0	0.0	PROPRIETARY	23.89	0.84
900859	3	12.50	1	25.0	PROPRIETARY	23.89	0.83
900857	3	15.00	1	20.0	PROPRIETARY	23.81	0.82
900819	3	10.00	0	0.0	REGR(WLRR,4Q,4)	22.74	0.83
900820	3	10.00	1	25.0	REGR(WLRR,4Q,4)	22.68	0.82
900944	3	10.00	0	0.0	BPR^x	22.43	0.78
900908	3	10.00	1	20.0	REGR(LRR,4Q,9.1)	22.23	0.75
900874	3	10.00	0	0.0	REGR(OLS,4Q,8)	22.16	0.79
900878	3	10.00	0	0.0	REG R(OLS,4Q,9,1)	22,16	0.79
900903	3	10.00	0	0.0	REGR(OLS,4Q,8)	22.16	0.79
900914	3	10.00	0	0.0	REGR(OLS,4Q,9.1)	22.16	0.79
900841	3	10.00	1	25.0	REGR(WLRR,1Q,4)	22.00	0.79
900817	3	10.00	0	0.0	REGR(LRR,4Q14)	21.99	0.76
900983	3	10.00	1	20.0	REGR(WLRR,4Q,9.1)	21.93	0.75
900984	3	10.00	1	20.0	REGR(WLRR,4Q,9.i)	21.86	0.75
900794	3	15.00	1	20.0	REGR(WLRR,1Q,4)	21.84	0.76
900818	3	10.00	1	25.0	REGR(LRR,4Q,4)	21.84	0.75
900877	3	10.00	0	0.0	REGR(WLRR,4Q,8)	21.84	0.78
900906	3	10.00	0	0.0	REGR(WLRR,4Q,8)	21.84	0.78
900985	3	12.50	1	20.0	REGR(WLRR,4Q,9.1)	21.84	0.75
900913	3	10.00	0	0.0	REGR(WLRR,4Q,9.2)	21.83	0.77
900793	3	12.50	1	20.0	REGR(WLRR,1Q,4)	21.78	0.78
900791	3	12.50	0	0.0	REGR(WLRR,1Q,4)	2.1.75	0.79
900792	3	15.00	0	0.0	REGR(WLRR,1Q,4)	21.68	0.77
900982	3	10.00	1	20.0	REGR(WLRR,4Q,9.1)	21.66	0.75
900842	3	10.00	1	25.0	REGR(WLRR,10,4)	21.55	0.79
900766	3	10.00	1	20.0	REGR(WLRR, 1 Q,4)	21.49	0.78
900810	3	15.00	0	0.0	REGR(WLRR, 1 Q,4)	' 21.47	0.76

(continued)

Table 9.1 (continued)

D-POS, Japan. Simulation results; sorted by geometric mean. Let UL = 2.0 TCR = 2.0 PM = −1 PPar = 0.90 Begin = 7412 End = 9012

SID	OP	TOV	RP	Rtri	ERET	GM	Shrp
900901	3	10.00	0	0.0	REGR(LRR,4Q,9.1)	21.45	0.72
900813	3	10.00	0	0.0	REGR(OLS,4Q,4)	21.42	0.78
900840	3	10.00	1	25.0	REGR(WLRR,1Q,4)	21.41	0.76
900838	3	10.00	1	25.0	REGR(WLRR,1Q,4)	21.40	0.76
900909	3	10.00	1	20.0	REGR(WLRR,4Q,9.1)	21.40	0.75
900910	3	10.00	0	0.0	REGRtLRR,40,9.2)	21.34	0.75
900816	3	10.00	1	25.0	REGR(ROB,4Q,4)	21.30	0.76
900839	3	10.00	1	25.0	REGR(WLRR,1Q,4)	21.30	0.75
900912	3	10.00	0	0.0	REGR(LRR,4Q,9.2)	21.29	0.71
900765	3	10.00	0	0.0	REGR(WLRR,1Q,4)	21.24	0.76
900815	3	10.00	0	0.0	REGR(ROB,4Q,4)	21.23	0.76
900902	3	10.00	0	0.0	REGR(WLRR,4Q,9.1)	21.16	0.74
900986	3	15.00	1	20.0	REGR(WLRR,4Q,9.1)	21,09	0.72
900954	3	10.00	0	0.0	REGR(OLS,4Q,4)	20.91	0.72
900876	3	10.00	0	0,0	REGR(LRR,4Q$_f$8)	20.90	0.74
900905	3 -	10.00	0	0.0	REGR(LRR,4Q,8)	20.90	0.74
900911	3	10.00	0	0.0	REGR{ROB,4Q,9.2)	20.66	0.72
900907	3	10.00	1	20.0	REGR(ROB,4Q,9.1)	20.36	0.74
900763	3	10.00	0	0.0	REGR(LRR,1Q,4)	20.21	0.71
900875	3	10.00	0	0.0	REGR(ROB,4Q,8)	20.15	0.71
900904	3	10.00	0	0.0	REGR(ROB,4Q,8)	20.15	0.71
900787	3	12.50	0	0.0	REGR(LRR,1Q,4)	20.08	0.71
900900	3	10.00	0	0.0	REGR(ROB,4Q,9.1)	20.07	0.72
900781	3	12.50	1	20.0	REGR(OLS,IQ,4)	19.96	0.71
900788	3	15.00	0	0.0	REGR(LRR,1Q,4)	19.92	0.70
900764	3	10.00	1	20.0	REGR(LRR,1Q,4)	19.88	0.70
900790	3	15.00	1	20.0	REGR(LRR,1Q,4)	19.81	0.70
900789	3	12.50	1	20.0	REGR(LRR, 1 Q,4)	19.78	0.70
900779	3	12.50	0	0.0	REGR(OLS,IQ$_5$4)	19.77	0.67
900786	3	15.00	1	20.0	REGR(ROB,IQ,4)	19.76	0.71
900780	3	15.00	0	0.0	REGR(OLS, 1Q,4)	19.72	0.69
900784	3	15.00	0	0.0	REGR(R0B,1Q,4)	19.67	0.71
900782	3	15.00	1	20.0	REGR(OLS, 1 Q,4)	19.41	0.69
900759	3	10.00	0	0.0	REGR(OLS,IQ,4)	19.40	0.67
900785	3	12.50	1	20.0	REGR(ROB,IQ,4)	19.33	0.69
900760	3	10.00	1	20.0	REGR(OLS,IQ,4)	19.31	0.66

(continued)

Table 9.1 (continued)

D-POS, Japan. Simulation results; sorted by geometric mean. Let UL = 2.0 TCR = 2.0 PM = −1 PPar = 0.90 Begin = 7412 End = 9012

SID	OP	TOV	RP	Rtri	ERET	GM	Shrp
900783	3	12.50	0	0.0	REGR(ROB, 1Q,4)	19.10	0.69
900761	3	10.00	0	0.0	REGR(ROB,IQ,4)	19.03	0.68
900931	3	10.00	0	0.0	CPR	19.01	0.68
900762	3	10.00	1	20.0	REGR(ROB,IQ,4)	19.00	0.67
900932	3	10.00	0	0.0	SPR	18.63	0.61
900716	3	10.00	1	20.0	benchmark	17.25	0.60
900927	3	10.00	0	0.0	EPR	16.82	0.57
900826	6	20.00	3	25.0	PROPRIETARY	24.63	0.84
900709	6	20.00	3	20.0	PROPRIETARY	23,61	0.81
900710	6	20.00	3	25.0	PROPRIETARY	23.44	0.82
900733	6	25.00	1	20.0	PROPRIETARY	23,34	0.80
900773	6	17.50	3	20.0	PROPRIETARY	23.26	0.78
900707	6	20.00	3	20.0	PROPRIETARY	23.08	0.79
900847	6	20.00	0	0.0	PROPRIETARY	22.62	0.81
901030	6	20.00	3	20.0	BPR	22.42	0.78
900796	6	20.00	3	20.0	REGR(OLS,2S,4)	22.33	0.79
901047	6	20.00	3	20.0	BPR	22.20	0.77
900770	6	22.50	0	0.0	REGR(OLS,IS,4)	22.17	0.77
900795	6	20.00	0	0.0	REGR{OLS,2S,4)	22.14	0.79
900749	6	20.00	3	25.0	REGR(OLS,IS,4)	22.03	0.78
900800	6	20.00	3	20.0	REGR(LRR,2S,4)	21.98	0.76
900849	6	20.00	0	0.0	REGR(LRR,3S,4)	21.98	0.77
900748	6	20.00	3	20.0	REGRCOLS, 1 S,4)	21.80	0.77
900754	6	20.00	3	20.0	REGR(LRR,12,4)	21.68	0.74
900747	6	20.00	0	0.0	REGR(OLS,IS,4)	21.65	0.77
900802	6	20.00	3	20.0	REGR(WLRR,2S,4)	21.60	0.79
901029	6	20.00	0	0.0	BPR	21.59	0.76
900755	6	20.00	3	25.0	REGR(LRR,1S,4)	21.52	0.74
900799	6	20.00	0	0.0	REGR(LRR,2S,4)	21.51	0.77
901046	6	20.00	0	0.0	BPR	21.49	0.76
900801	6	20.00	0	0.0	REGR(WLRRi2S,4)	21.40	0.79
900769	6	17.50	0	0.0	REGRCOLS, IS,4)	21.34	0.76
900778	6	22.50	3	20,0	REGRCWLRR, 1S,4)	21.30	0.79
900772	6	22.50	0	0,0	REGRCLRR, IS,4)	21.26	0.72
900753	6	20.00	0	0.0	REGRCLRR, 1 S,4)	21.20	0.72
900756	6	20.00	0	0.0	REGRCWLRR,IS,4)	21.10	0.77

(continued)

Table 9.1 (continued)

D-POS, Japan. Simulation results; sorted by geometric mean. Let UL = 2.0 TCR = 2.0 PM = −1 PPar = 0.90 Begin = 7412 End = 9012

SID	OP	TOV	RP	Rtri	ERET	GM	Shrp
900757	6	20.00	3	20.0	REGRCWLRR,IS,4)	21.06	0.78
900758	6	20.00	3	25.0	REGRCWLRR, IS,4)	21.02	0.78
900777	6	17.50	3	20.0	REGRCWLRR, IS,4)	20.95	0.78
900771	6	17,50	0	0.0	REGRCLRR,IS,4)	20.93	0.71
900848	6	20.00	0	0.0	REGRCROB.3S.4)	20.74	0.76
900776	6	22.50	3	20.0	REGR(ROB,IS,4)	20.37	0.76
900797	6	20.00	0	0.0	REGR(ROB,22,4)	20.24	0.75
900798	6	20.00	3	20.0	REGR(ROB,2S,4)	20,12	0.76
900752	6	20.00	3	25.0	REGR(RpB,IS,4)	19.56	0.73
900751	6	20.00	3	20.0	REGR(ROB,IS,4)	19.35	0.73
900750	6	20.00	0	0.0	REGR(ROB,IS,4)	19.29	0.72
900775	6	17.50	3	20.0	REGR(ROB,IS,4)	19.26	0.72
901049	6	20.00	3	20.0	CPR	18.99	0.68
901051	6	20.00	3	20.0	SPR	18.69	0.61
901048	6	20.00	0	0.0	CPR	18.65	0.67
901050	6	20.00	0	0.0	SPR	17.87	0.59
901045	6	20.00	3	20.0	EPR	17.55	0.59
901044	6	20.00	0	0,0	EPR	17.34	0.59

SID = simulation ID; OP = period of re-optimization; TOV = turnover constraint; Rtri = rebalancing trigger; ERET = model description; GM = geometric mean; Shrp = Sharpe ratio. *REGR (technique, period, equation)*

Technique=

OLS for ordinary least-squares regression analysis,

LRR for latent root regression,

ROB for robust regression,

WLRR for weighted latent root regression;

Period=

IS for one-period semi-annual analysis,

2S for two-period semi-annual analysis,

3S for three-period semi-annual analysis,

IQ for one-period quarterly analysis,

4Q for four-period quarterly analysis;

Equation = 4; TRR $=a_0 + a_1$EPR $+a_2$BPR $+ a_3$CPR $+ a_4$SPR $+a_5$REPR $+ a_6$RPBR $+a_7$RCPR $+a_8$RSPR $+e_t$

8; TRR $=a_0 + a_1$EPR $+a_2$BPR $+a_3$CPR $+a_4$SPR $+e_t$

9.1; TRR $=a_0 + a_1$EPR $+a_2$BPR $+a_3$CPR $+a_4$SPR $+a_5$REPR(2) $+a_6$RPBR(2) $+a_7$RCPR(2) $+a_8$RSPR(3) $+e_t$,

where (2) denotes 2-year averages of relative variables.

9.2; TRR $=a_0 + a_1$EPR $+a_2$BPR $+a_3$CPR $+a_4$SPR $+a_5$REPR(3) $+a_6$RPBR(3) $+a_7$RCPR(3) $+ a_8$RSPR(3) $+ e_t$,

where (3) denotes 3-year averages of relative variables

squares modeling. The results are consistent with what the reader was shown in Chapter 7.

The Bloch et al. (1993) results will be expanded later in this chapter for the 2001–2018 period.

Finally, Markowitz and Xu (1994) developed a test for data mining.[11] In addition to testing the hypothesis of data mining, the test can also be used to estimate and assess the expected differences between the best test model and the average of simulated policies. We will refer to the eight-factor model as REG8, or the Markowitz model, in this analysis.

9.2.2 What We Learned After 1993

Models to enhance the Bloch et al. (1993) work were in development as the paper was published.

Elton and Gruber (1972a, 1972b), Latane et al. (1975), Jacobs and Levy (1988) reported that historic earnings and the "low P/E" approach enhanced returns in stock valuation models. We will show with the Institutional Brokerage Estimation Services (I/B/E/S) that earnings expectations provide greater insight into stock selection than historical earnings.

Earnings forecasting and price momentum models were developed to enhance the REG8 model. Studies of the effectiveness of corporate earnings forecasting variables reported in Cragg and Malkiel (1968), Elton (1981), De Bondt and Thaler (1989), Wheeler (1994), and Guerard and Stone (1992) were reprinted in Bruce and Epstein (1994).[12] Analysts' forecasts of earnings per share (eps), eps revision, and the direction of eps forecast revisions were incorporated into the Institutional Broker Estimation Services

---

[11] Bloch et al. (1993) wrote their manuscript in 1991. At the time of the original estimation of eight-factor regression model, the international Institutional Estimation Brokerage Service (I/B/E/S) was only four years old, having started in 1987, and did not have sufficient data for model building and testing such that the models with earnings forecasts could pass the Markowitz and Xu (1994) Data Mining Corrections test.

[12] The Bruce and Epstein (1994) and Brown (2000) works contain much of the rich history of earnings forecasting and resulting excess returns. Researchers such as Elton, Gruber, and Gultekin, who developed I/B/E/S database and published the initial research (1981 and 1984) and Hawkins et al. (1984). The Elton et al. (1981) paper is one of the most influential analyses in earnings forecasting and security analysis. Guerard et al. (1993) employed Toyo Keizai earnings forecasts in Japan because of the limitations of the non-U.S. I/B/E/S database. The Toyo Keizai earnings forecasts enhanced portfolio returns by over 200 basis points annually. The GPRD team was well aware of the return-enhancement of I/B/E/S forecasts in U.S. stocks, see Guerard and Stone (1992). The Guerard and Stone research was sponsored by the Institute for Quantitative Research in Finance, the "Q-Group", circa 1985. Womack (1996) Guerard et al. (1997), Guerard et al. (2015), and Ball and Ghysels (2018), are among the thousands of studies of analysts' forecasting efficiency and how analysts' forecasts enhance portfolio returns.

(I/B/E/S) in-print database in July 1972. The I/B/E/S database has computer-readable data from January 1976, domestically, and January 1987.[13] In 1993, the best and longest source of Japanese earnings forecasts was the Toyo Keizai database source. We present evidence in this section that the I/B/E/S database has been a source of highly statistically significant excess returns. We refer the reader to Brown (2000) which contains about 570 abstracts of I/B/E/S studies. Guerard et al. (1997) reported that analysts' forecast variables enhanced portfolio returns over the long-run. By 1997, we knew that CTEF, a composite model of earnings forecasts, revisions, and breadth, the agreement among analysts' revisions, was highly statistically significantly correlated with stock returns. Guerard and Mark (2003) published that CTEF, and a nine-factor model, denoted REG9, composed of REG8 plus CTEF was also highly (statistically) significantly correlated with stock returns. By 2003, Guerard and Mark were pushing CTEF, REG8, and REG9 for stock selection modeling using the BARRA risk model. In 1975, Barr Rosenberg and his associates introduced the BARRA U.S. Equity Model, often denoted USE1.[14] There were 39 industry variables in the BARRA USE1 model. How is the data manipulated and/or normalized to be used in the BARRA USE1 model? First, raw data is normalized by subtracting a mean and dividing through by the variable standard deviation; however, the mean subtracted is the market capitalization weighted mean for each descriptor for

---

[13] The newly-created non-U.S. I/B/E/S database did not have enough data in 1991–1994 to pass the Markowitz-Xu data mining test for its use in Japan.

[14] The BARRA USE1 Model predicted risk, which required the evaluation of the firm's response to economic events, which were measured by the company's fundamentals. There were six descriptors, or risk indexes, in the BARRA model. These descriptors were composite variables primarily based on the statistically significant variables in Rosenberg and McKibben (1973). Rosenberg and Marathe (1979), Rudd and Rosenberg (1979), and Rudd and Clasing (1982) are excellent references for how the BARRA equity model is constructed. BARRA is a proprietary model; that is, the composite model weights are not disclosed. Thus, there were nine factors in the Index of Market Variability, including the historic beta estimate, historic sigma estimate, share turnover for three months, trading volume, the log of the common stock price, and a historical alpha estimate, and cumulative range over one year. Without coefficients, one cannot reproduce the model. One can correlate an investment manager's variables with the risk indexes, as we will discuss later in the chapter. The Index of Earnings Variability included the variance of earnings, variance of cash flow, and the coverability of earnings and price. The Index of Low Valuation and Unsuccess included the growth in earnings per share, recent earnings change, relative strength (a price momentum variable), the book-to-price ratio, dividend cuts, and the return of equity. The Index of Immaturity and Smallness included the log of total assets, the log of market capitalization, and net plant/common equity. The Index of Growth Orientation included the dividends-to-earnings ratio (the payout ratio), dividend yield, growth in total assets, the earnings-to-price (ep) multiple, and the typical ep ratio over the past five years. The Graham and Dodd low P/E investment manager would "load up" on The Index of Growth Orientation and would offer investors positive asset selection (good stock picking) only if the portfolio weights differed from weights on the "Growth" Index components. The Index of Financial Risk included leverage at market and book values, debt-to-assets ratio, and cash flow-to-current liabilities ratio.

all securities in the S&P 500.[15] The monthly residual risk factors are calculated by regressing residual returns (the stock excess return less the predicted beta times the market excess return) versus the six risk indexes and the industry dummy variables.[16] The domestic BARRA E3 (USE3 or sometimes denoted USE3) model, with some 15 years of research and evolution, uses 13 sources of factor or systematic exposures. The sources of extra-market factor exposures are volatility, momentum, size, size non-linearity, trading activity, growth, earnings yield, value, earnings variation, leverage, currency sensitivity, dividend yield, and the non-estimation universe.[17]

There was an extensive body of literature on the impact of price momentum variables on the cross section of stock returns. Price momentum, or the non-random character of stock market prices, has been studied since Bachelier in 1900, but the availability of much of the early, pre-1964 research was made far more accessible in Cootner (1964).[18] Later, and in both U.S. and international stock market analyses, Guerard (2014) used the Fama

---

[15] The relevant variable standard deviation is not the universe standard deviation of each variable, but the standard deviation of the variables for companies with market capitalizations exceeding $50 million. A final transformation occurs when the normalized descriptor is scaled such that its value is one standard deviation above the S&P 500 mean. Every month the monthly stock return in the quarter is regressed as a function of the normalized descriptors. If the firm is typical of the S&P 500 firms, then most of the scaled descriptor values and coefficients should be approximately zero.

[16] See Rudd and Clasing (1982, p. 115), for the USE1 descriptors.

[17] There is an equally extensive body of literature on the impact of price momentum variables on the cross-section of stock returns. Price momentum, or the non-random character of stock market prices, have been studied since Bachelier in 1900 but the availability of much of the early, pre-1964 research was made far more accessible in Cootner (1964). Guerard and Mark (2003) did not use price momentum in their stock selection model. The BARRA risk model contained a price momentum factor risk premium and thus one might not expect the momentum to be significant with a risk model incorporating the variable. Influential recent researchers such as Conrad and Kaul (1993), Jagadeesh and Titman (1993), Conrad and Kaul (1998), and Lo et al. (2000) extended the technical analysis and price momentum literature. Most importantly for our analysis, Conrad and Kaul (1998) reported the mean-reversion of stock returns in the very short run, one week or one month, and the medium-term persistence of momentum to drive stock prices higher in the 3, 6, 9, 12, and 18-month time horizons over the 1926–1988 and 1926–1989 periods. Jagadeesh and Titman (1993) constructed portfolios based on six-months of positive price momentum, held the portfolios for six months, and earned excess returns of 12.01% over the 1965–1989 period. Medium-term momentum is an important and persistent risk premium. In the very long-run, 24 and 36-months in Conrad and Kaul (1998) momentum returns become very negative. Lo et al. (2000) produced a definitive study of technical analysis over the 1962–1996 period and found that technical patterns produced incremental returns, particularly for NASDAQ stocks. Price momentum and technical analysis variables enhanced portfolio returns over the long-run, although the majority of the academic studies did not use the BARRA model, which dominated the asset management industrial use.

[18] The classic Cootner-edited volume reprinted the works of Bachelier (translated), Kendall, Osborne, Working, Cowles, Granger, Fama, Mandelbrot, and Samuelson among others. It is interesting to note that these researchers published in economics, business, statistical, operations research, and industrial management journals. The Cootner volume papers reported evidence of efficient and inefficient markets. The reader is referred to Lo et al. (2000) for a definitive (but dated) test of price momentum in the U.S.

and French (1998) PM122 variable, defined as $P(t-2)/P(t-12)$, in their stock selection model, to create a ten-factor stock selection model for the U.S. expected returns. Guerard, Markowitz, and Xu referred to the 10-factor model as the USER model.[19] Guerard et al. (2013) and Guerard and Mark (2020) applied the 10-factor model to global stocks, referring to the model as GLER or REG10. See Eq. (9.45).

$$TR_{t+1} = a_0 + a_1 EP_t + a_2 BP_t + a_3 CP_t + a_4 SP_t + a_5 REP_t + a_6 RBP_t$$
$$+ a_7 RCP_t + a_8 RSP_t + a_9 CTEF_t + a_{10} PM_t + e_{t+1}, \qquad (9.45)$$

where

EP = [earnings per share]/[price per share] = earnings-price ratio;
BP = [book value per share]/[price per share] = book-price ratio;
CP = [cash flow per share]/[price per share] = cash flow-price ratio;
SP = [net sales per share]/[price per share] = sales-price ratio;
REP = [current EP ratio]/[average EP ratio over the past five years];
RBP = [current BP ratio]/[average BP ratio over the past five years];
RCP = [current CP ratio]/[average CP ratio over the past five years];
RSP = [current SP ratio]/[average SP ratio over the past five years];
CTEF = consensus earnings per share I/B/E/S forecast, revisions and breadth;
PM122 = price momentum; and
e = randomly distributed error term.

Guerard, Markowitz, et al. (2013) and Guerard, Rachev, et al. (2013) estimated the ten-factor model for all global stocks included in the FactSet database over the period January 1997–December 2011. Bloch et al. (1993) used the Beaton-Tukey bisquare robust regression weighting scheme, as part of their regression analysis, which they denoted WLRR. The Beaton-Tukey bisquare is one of several schemes analyzed in Andrews et al. (1972). The Andrews et al. (1972) volume reported that most robust regression modeling techniques produce similar median forecasting errors, which are substantially lower than the OLS median forecasting errors. Guerard and Mark (2020) updated the GLER model simulation period to the 1996–2016 time period. The GLER model produced highly statistically significant active

---

[19] Brush and Boles (1983) and Brush (2001) tested a PM121 price momentum variable, defined as $P(t-1)/P(t-12)$. The Brush PM121 model was useful in the U.S., market but not useful in Japan.

returns and better stock selections than the USER model over the corresponding period.[20] The earnings forecasting model, CTEF, continued to produce statistically significant Active Returns and Specific Returns (stock selection) during the 1996–2016 period. The I/B/E/S database continues to be a great source of statistically significant excess returns for stocks.

The identification of influential data is an important component of regression analysis. The modeler can identify outliers, or influential data, and re-run the ordinary least squares regressions on the re-weighted data, a process referred to as robust (ROB) regression. In ordinary least squares (OLS), all data is equally weighted. The weights are 1.0. In robust regression, the larger is the OLS residual, the smaller is the weight of the observation in the robust regression. In robust regression, several weights may be used. The authors have tested 7–8 weighting functions and Guerard et al. (2019) reported finding no statistically significant differences in simulated portfolios using the robust regression-weighted GLER model with the Beaton-Tukey bisquare, Huber, Hampel, Fair, and Tukey and Yohai Optimal Influence Function (OIF) weightings. The Huber and Tukey bisquare weightings are derived upon bounded loss functions and have smooth psi-functions that produce a unique solution, see Huber (1981) and Maronna et al. (2019), and Maronna (2019). The starting point, OLS estimates in Bloch et al. (1993) influences the number of iterations, but not the final result, see Maronna et al. (2006) and Maronna et al. (2019).[21]

Testing and reporting on financial anomalies in October 2018, we find that many of the Jacobs and Levy, Levy, Bloch, Guerard, Markowitz, Todd, and Xu, Ziemba and Schwartz, Chan, Hamao, and Lakonishok, and Haugen and Baker variables have continued to produce statistically significant Active and Specific Returns in the post-publication period, 2003–2018 (and later) periods. The forecasted earnings acceleration variable has produced statistically significant Active and Specific Returns in the Post-Global Financial Crisis Period. The composite model of earnings, price momentum, and fundamental data is a consistent source of alpha in the U.S. and international markets. Excess returns are greater in international stocks than in U.S. stocks. The recent literature on financial anomalies is summarized in Fama and French (2008), Levy (2012), Guerard et al. (2013, 2014, 2015), Jacobs and Levy (2017), Chu et al. (2017), and Bartram and Grinblatt (2021).

---

[20] That is, global stock selection models outperformed domestic stock selection models. Thus, U.S. investors should prefer global portfolios in order to maximize portfolio returns.

[21] John Guerard thanks Doug Martin for a detailed conversation regarding this point.

9.2.3 Markowitz Risk Modeling with Barra and Axioma Risk Models: Constructing Mean-Variance Efficient Frontiers

The Markowitz (1952, 1959) portfolio construction approach seeks to identify the efficient frontier, the point at which returns are maximized for a given level of risk or risk is minimized for a given level of return. The portfolio expected return, $E(R_p)$, is calculated by taking the sum of the security weights multiplied by their respective expected returns. The portfolio standard deviation is the sum of the weighted covariances.

$$E(R_p) = \sum_{i=1}^{N} x_i E(R_i) = \sum_{i=1}^{N} x_i \mu_i \qquad (9.46)$$

$$\sigma_p^2 = \sum_{i=1}^{N} \sum_{j=1}^{N} x_i x_j c_{ij} \qquad (9.47)$$

where μ is the expected return vector, C is the variance–covariance matrix, and x is the portfolio weights.

The efficient frontier can be traced out by

$$\text{minimize}_{\{x_i \geq 0, x_i \leq \overline{u}\}} x^T C x - \lambda \mu^T x \qquad (9.48)$$

where λ is the risk-returntrade-off parameter and $\overline{u}$ is the fixed upper bound. Bloch (1993) created efficient frontiers using a purely full historical covariance matrix.

In early 2010, the author was Director of Quantitative Research at McKinley Capital Management, in Anchorage, Alaska. The founder of the firm, Mr. Robert B. Gillam, was greatly influenced by Mr. Markowitz when he earned his MBA at UCLA. Mr, Markowitz was teaching at UCLA, at that time. Mr. Robert A. Gillam, the McKinley Capital Chief Investment Officer, at that time, wanted to test (and compare) various risk models at that time. The result was the creation of the McKinley Capital "Horse Race" where a set of expected returns was shared with Barra, APT, FinAnalytica, and Axioma, among others. The goal was to assess the benefits of various risk models in creating risk-returntrade-offs with their respective construction methodologies of portfolio betas and risk measures. In the initial McKinley Capital

Horse Race, Barra, APT, and FinAnalytica produced portfolios for comparison.[22] A follow-up to the initial Barra Horse Race portfolio was published in Miller et al. (2014). The reader will note that as the risk-aversion level increases, the total managed portfolio return decreases. There is a historic risk-return trade-off for 1998–2009, just as there was for 1974–1990 in the U.S. equity market. The USER model in Table 9.2 is the same model as REG10, the 10-factor model for stock selection. The Miller et al. (2014) Barra risk model-developed trade-off analysis reveals several "by products" of quantitative modeling of stock returns: (1) as your risk tolerance increases, or your risk-aversion decreases, your managed portfolio returns increase and these increases are associated with smaller market-capitalized stocks; i.e., the small stock effect, shown with the increasing negative size coefficients in Table 9.2. Asset selection, AS, increases wit risk tolerance and is highly statistically significant, as evidenced by the t-statistics on asset selection for US portfolios for all stocks with Compustat, CRSP, and I/B/E/S eps forecasts during the 1998–2010 time period. Managed returns, TManaged, and Asset Selection, AssetSel (AS), is higher in the robust regression-weighted portfolios, USER, than in the equally weighted portfolios, EQ. Regression modeling of outliers and multicollinearity works to enhance the Information Ratios, IRs, of the portfolios. The IR is the portfolio excess return divided by its tracking error, a variation of the Treynor Ratio, which is the portfolio excess return divided by the portfolio beta (Fig. 9.8).

The reader should note the consistency of stock selection models of expected returns and their use in constructing optimal portfolios during the 1991–2010 period. However, our story has not ended. When one spends 15 years as Director of Quantitative Research in Anchorage, Alaska, where the sun rises between 8 and 10 AM, and sets between 3 and 5 PM, for four months of the year, there are plenty of opportunities to estimate portfolio trade-off curves without missing much sunlight.[23]

---

[22] The reader is referred to Guerard, Gultekin, and Saxena, *Quantitative Corporate Finance* (New York: Springer, Third Edition, 2022), Chapter 15, for a history of the McKinley Capital Management Horse Races.

[23] The author thanks, again, as he did in his *Quantitative Corporate Finance* text, his McKinley Capital young quantitative analysts, Sundaram Chettiappan, Eli Krauklis, Manish Kumar, and Ziwei (Elaine) Wang, who worked with the author at McKinley Capital for many years and together we "crunched" thousands of trade-off curves in SAS.

Table 9.2 BARRA-estimated USER, EQ efficient frontiers, 1998.01–2007.12

RAL	Model	TManaged	STD	TActive	t-Active	AssetSel (AS)	t-AS	RskI	t-RskI	IR	Size
0.01	EQ	12.480	19.962	8.663	2.475	7.445	3.164	4.468	1.545	0.783	-1.176
0.01	USER	13.263	20.844	9.446	2.720	8.265	3.300	3.555	1.370	0.860	-1.220
0.02	EQ	10.993	20.193	7.176	2.267	6.526	2.980	3.759	1.458	0.717	-1.042
0.02	USER	12.517	20.494	8.700	2.779	7.490	3.281	3.214	1.394	0.879	-1.050
0.03	EQ	10.612	20.155	6.796	2.230	6.270	2.945	3.564	1.440	0.703	-0.990
0.03	USER	11.651	20.578	7.835	2.660	6.956	3.220	2.901	1.330	0.839	-0.980
0.05	EQ	9.155	19.992	5.339	2.054	5.300	2.848	2.640	1.280	0.650	-0.787
0.05	USER	9.355	20.346	5.539	2.360	5.742	3.226	2.014	1.234	0.745	-0.764
0.09	EQ	7.839	19.982	4.022	1.878	4.101	2.578	2.115	1.282	0.594	-0.582
0.09	USER	8.170	20.161	4.353	2.194	5.214	3.342	1.610	1.147	0.694	-0.598
0.15	EQ	6.540	19.979	2.723	1.575	3.265	2.408	1.629	1.233	0.498	-0.421
0.15	USER	7.122	19.800	3.305	1.967	4.358	3.197	1.349	1.169	0.622	-0.477
0.20	EQ	5.814	19.848	1.997	1.322	2.822	2.294	1.369	1.184	0.418	-0.356
0.20	USER	6.617	19.641	2.801	1.824	4.007	3.174	1.191	1.143	0.577	-0.416

where

RAL = Risk-Aversion Level,

TManaged = Total Managed Return,

TActive = Total Active Return,

AssetSel = Asset Selection,

IR = Information Ratio,

Size, MOM, EY, Value, Growth are BARRA Multi-Factor Risk Exposures,

EQ = EQ-WT(EP, BP, CP, SP, REP, RBP, RCP, RSP, PM, CTEF),

USER = WLRR-WT(EP, BP, CP, SP, REP, RBP, RCP, RSP, PM, CTEF)

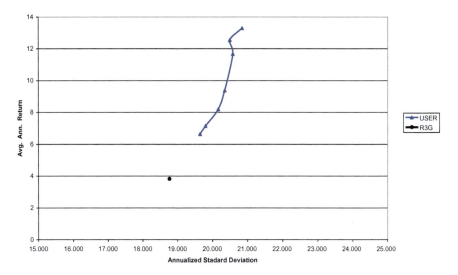

Fig. 9.8 The Barra-estimated trade-off curve of the USER Model, 1998–2007

9.2.4   The Stone Mathematical Assignment Program Trade-off Curve

In the Stone et al. (2010) work discussed earlier, the ranking on forecasted return and grouping into fractile portfolios produces a set of portfolios ordered on the basis of predicted return score. This return cross section will almost certainly have a wide range of forecasted return values. If one was trying to make each portfolio in the cross section have the same average beta value, we could move a stock with an above-average beta value into a portfolio whose average beta value is below the population average. At the same time, one could shift a stock with a below-average beta value into the above-average portfolio from the below-average portfolio. The reassignment problem can be formulated as a mathematical assignment program (MAP). Using the MAP produces a cross-sectional match on beta or any other control variable. All (fractile) portfolios should have explanatory controls equal to their population average value. What did the 30-portfolio trade-off curve look like for various controls?

For simplicity, we report only portfolios 1, the lowest, and 30, the highest, forecast score (FS) portfolios.

Second, we report only about two-thirds of the reported control variables; Beta-only; size-only; BP-only; Beta, Size, and BP (the Fama-French [1992] three-factor model); and two more complicated models. The first complicated model takes the Fama-French model and adds financial leverage, FL,

EP, and Dividend Yield, DP variables. The second complicated model adds DP, historical sales growth for the past 5 years, SAG5, and sustainable growth for 3 years, assuming only internal financing, SUS3.

The reader notes in Table 9.3 that there is an 8.8% spread of portfolio 30 return, P30, composed of the highest FS stocks, less portfolio 1 return, P1, composed of the lowest FS stocks, using no constraints. The FS, Forecast Score, model works. This is an alternative IC estimation. The implementation of a Beta-only contain lowers the Portfolio 1 return, composed of the lowest beta stocks, and raises the P30 – P1 spread to 12.12%. Beta is a useful portfolio constraint. The implementation of a Size-only contain does not change the Portfolio 1 return, composed of the lowest size stocks, and slightly reduces the P30 – P1 spread to 8.56%. Size is a useful portfolio constraint. The beta, Size, and BP constraint, the basis of the three-factor Fama-French (1992) model does not reduce the P30 -P1 spread relative to the no constraints model. The Beta, Size, BP, FL, EP, DP Constraints model picks better P30 stocks, increasing the P30 to 21.40% and reducing the P1 return to 0.30%, producing a P30 – P1 spread of 21.10%. The Beta, Size, DP, FL, SAG5, SUS3 Constraints model picks better P30 stocks, increasing the P30 to 25.92% and reducing the P1 return to 8.59%, producing a P30 – P1 spread of 17.33%. The Stone P30 portfolios exhibit pronounced positive skewness. That is the highest ranked stocks produce higher returns that one would expect from a normal distribution. Positive skewness is an investor's friend. Second, the Sharpe Ratios of the P30 portfolios rise, indicating higher returns relative to risk for the P30 portfolios as one adds additional constraints. The Stone MAP results are highly statistically significant, from the F-statistical of the portfolio return to forecasted scores regressions.

9.3   The Existence and Continued Persistence of Financial Anomalies, 2003–2108

The McKinley Capital Horse Races were held during the 2010–2018 time period. Guerard et al. (2015) reported three levels of testing investment strategies.[24] The first level is the information coefficient (IC) of a strategy

---

[24] The first level is the information coefficient, IC, of a strategy in which the subsequent ranked returns are regressed as a function of the ranked financial strategy. The regression coefficient is the IC which is a randomly distributed variable to test the statistical significance of the individual variable or composite model strategies. The second level of investment testing is to estimate, with transaction costs, the Markowitz efficient frontier, by varying either the lambda or the targeted tracking error. The third level of testing is to apply the Markowitz and Xu (1994) Data Mining Corrections, DMC, to test whether the strategy is statistically different from any model that could have been used.

Table 9.3 The Stone MAP trade-off curve

Universe: The intersection of Compustat and CRSP companies with five years of data

Test period: January 1967–December 2004		Portfolio 1 (Lowest)			
Constraints	Forecast Score	Annualized Risky Return (%)	Annualized Risky STD (%)	Skewness	Sharpe Ratio
No Constraints	2.98	10.29	8.96	0.80	0.10
Beta-only Constraint	4.21	7.77	7.36	−0.25	0.09
Size-only Constraint	3.28	10.31	8.90	0.91	0.10
Beta, Size, BP Constraints	5.40	9.88	7.32	−0.41	0.11
Beta, Size, BP, FL, EP, DP Constraints	10.42	0.30	6.50	−0.42	0.00
Beta, Size, DP, FL, SAG5, SUS3 Constraints	2.03	8.59	6.82	−0.39	0.03

Portfolio Constraints	Forecast Score	Portfolio 30 (Highest)				Annualized Risky Return P30−P1 (%)
		Annualized Risky Return (%)	Annualized Risky STD (%)	Skewness	Sharpe Ratio	
No Constraints	96.59	19.12	10.61	2.31	0.15	8.83
Beta-only Constraint	95.94	19.89	9.55	1.59	0.17	12.12
Size-only Constraint	96.28	18.87	10.55	2.33	0.15	8.56
Beta, Size, BP Constraints	94.82	18.56	9.34	1.62	0.17	8.68
Beta, Size, BP, FL, EP, DP Constraints	93.65	21.40	8.92	1.79	0.20	21.1
Beta, Size, DP, FL, SAG5, SUS3 Constraints	94.59	25.92	9.43	1.55	0.33	17.33

where
Beta = Regression slope of 3 years of monthly returns versus the CRSP value-weighted index,
Size = Stock Market Capitalization,
BP = Book-to-Price Ratio,
FL = Financial Leverage, Total Debt / Total Assets
EP = Earnings-to-Price Ratio,
DP = Dividend Yield,
SAG5 = Average annual historical sales growth of 5 years,
SUS3 = Three years of sustainable growth, using internal financing.

in which the subsequent ranked returns are regressed as a function of the ranked financial strategy. The regression coefficient is the IC which is a randomly distributed variable to test the statistical significance of the individual variable or composite model strategies. The second level of investment testing is to estimate, with transactions costs, the Markowitz efficient frontier by varying either the lambda or the targeted tracking error. The third level of testing is to apply the Markowitz and Xu (1994) Data Mining Corrections (DMC) to test whether the strategy is statistically different from any model that could have been used. Moreover, the regression coefficient of the DMC test indicates how much excess returns could be continued, holding everything else constant. We seek to maximize the Geometric Mean (GM), Information Ratios (IRs), and Sharpe Ratios (ShRs). We rank our variables, low to high, and 99 is preferred.

One must use transaction costs in one's portfolio construction and management in the industry. Our portfolio optimization models employ a piecewise linear transaction cost model by ITG, specifically the Non-Discretionary ITG ACE Optimal 0.7 Trade Urgency model. In the unlikely event that a security is not covered by the model, we assume a conservative default buy and sell cost of 150 basis points. We refer the reader to the white paper *ITG ACE – Agency Cost Estimator: A Model Description* (2007) for a detailed review of the transaction cost model methodology. We will review some basic definitions here. "Non-Discretionary" estimates are calibrated to observed transaction costs for a subset of the ITG Peer Group Database that do not exhibit opportunistic characteristics. Non-discretionary trades will typically have higher transaction costs than discretionary trades. "ITG ACE Optimal" strategies are determined by creating a trade-off between minimizing expected cost and standard deviation of cost with respect to trade urgency. The trade urgency range is between 0 and 1, with 0.7 reflecting an aggressive strategy that weighs minimizing risk (standard deviation of estimated trade cost) above minimizing transaction cost. The model described here is used to estimate transaction costs during each rebalance period throughout the portfolio construction process for all our model portfolios.[25]

Moreover, the regression coefficient of the DMC test indicates how much excess returns could be continued into the future, holding everything else constant.

[25] The FactSet Portfolio Analytics System is used as the calculation engine behind our performance attribution results. Transaction costs generated from the ITG model described above are used to determine the "Risk Transaction Effect" calculated by FactSet. Factor returns and exposures from the Axioma Risk Models are used to calculate the "Risk Factors Effect," "Risk Factors Effect T-Stat," and "Compounded Factor Impact" columns produced by FactSet. The portfolio's Total Effect is calculated using FactSet's Daily Valuation method, a CFA Institute/PPS transactions-based performance calculation methodology shown below:

The initial data used in this analysis is the Morgan Stanley Capital International (MSCI) Index-constituents data for the All Country World (ACW) Index, the MSCI Non-U.S. (XUS) Index, the MSCI Japanese (JP) Index,

---

This total effect can be further decomposed into four underlying effects as previously highlighted in Tables 2 and 3.

The statistical significance of two of these effects, factor and stock specific, are also presented as T-Stats.

Risk Factors Effect: The overall excess return explained by the active exposures to the factors in the risk model. It is calculated by compounding the calculation period results for the sum of each factor's Active Exposure multiplied by its Factor Return. This effect can be further decomposed down to individual risk model factors.

Risk Stock Specific Effect: The portion of the active return that is not explained by the risk model, often referred to as stock selection skill:

Risk Total Effect – Risk Factors Effect

Risk Total Effect: The overall active performance of the portfolio gross of transaction costs. It is equal to:

Risk Stock Specific Effect + Risk Factors Effect

At the asset level, this can be expressed by the following formula:

$$r_i = r_f + \epsilon_i = \sum_{k=1}^{K} x_{i,k} f_k + \epsilon_i \qquad (9.50)$$

r_i: Standalone asset total return
r_f: Standalone factors effect
ϵ_i: Asset specific returns
$x_{i,k}$: Asset raw factor exposure to factor k
f_k: Raw factor return of factor k

Risk Transaction Effect: The performance impact of fees, trading costs, and execution price relative to close price.

Risk Stock Specific & Factors Effect T-Stat: Tests whether the average return is statistically different than zero.

The calculation is as follows:

(Average Return – 0)/(Model Standard Deviation/Square Root of the number of periods)

To calculate cumulative effects over time, FactSet applies compounding algorithms to standalone effects. Our portfolios use the Residual Free – Portfolio Cumulative compounding algorithm with attribution effects, also known as the GRAP Method or the Frongello Method. The results will produce a total effect that equals the difference between the geometrically linked portfolio and benchmark total returns.

$$e_{i'} = (e_{i-1'})(1 + BR_i/100) + (e_i)(1 + PR_{i-1'}/100) \qquad (9.51)$$

where

$e_{i'}$ = cumulative attribution effect through period i
$e_{i-1'}$ = cumulative attribution effect in period i–1
BR_i = benchmark return in period i
e_i = attribution effect in period i
$PR_{i-1'}$ = cumulative portfolio return through period i–1

All portfolio attribution results are annualized by taking the arithmetic difference of the annualized portfolio and annualized benchmark returns. This method produces annualized attribution effects

MSCI China A-Shares Index, MSCI Emerging Markets (EM) Index, and the Russell 3000 (R3) Index, for the 12/2001–11/2018 period. In a second analysis, we require stocks to be covered by at least two analysts on the Institutional Brokerage Estimate Services (I/B/E/S) universe in the ACW and CH analyses. McKinley Capital Management (MCM) maintains a factor database of approximately 70 factors since 1999. We show that CTEF, the most statistically significant model used for stock selection published in 1997, has been one of the two to three most dominant variables in the MCM in all MSCI universes up until September 2019; please see the Appendix of Guerard and Markowitz.[26] We test five sets of expected returns, CTEF, REG8, REG9, and REG10, for the six index-constituent universes. We use data only as it is known (or more exactly, our portfolios are tested out-of-sample).

We report an Alpha Tester set of non-U.S. stock results in Table 1. The CTEF variable, REG8, REG9, and REG10 models produced statistically significant Active Returns for 12/2002–11/2018. The FactSet Alpha Tester analysis as a default equals weights stocks according to the variable fractile (such as quintiles in our reported results). The Bloch et al. (1993) universes, the R1000, and (MSCI) Japan-only universes report the REG8 model produced over 200 basis points, annualized returns over the benchmark, without Markowitz Mean-Variance optimization or transactions costs. The XUs and EM Alpha Testers report statistically significant stock selection in XUS and EM universes for CTEF and REG10 variables; in fact, in the EM universe, CTEF, REG8, REG9, and REG10 are statistically significant. The Alpha Tester analysis is a similar (alternative) test to the Information Coefficients, ICs, reported in Guerard (2015) in Level I testing.

The authors used familiar simulation conditions, assuming 8% monthly turnover, 35 basis point threshold positions, an upper bound in Mean-Variance optimization of 4% on security weights, and ITG transactions

---

while maintaining their additive property so that:

$$\text{Annualized Stock Specific Effect} + \text{Annualized Factors Effect}$$
$$+ \text{Annualized Transaction Effect} = \text{Annualized Total Effect} \qquad (9.52)$$

$$[(EMV + ACCRe) - (BMV + ACCRb)$$
$$-(FEE + PRCH - SALE - INC - CPN - PRIN)]/(BMV + ACCRb) \qquad (9.49)$$

[26] The models discussed in Guerard and Markowitz (2019), written for 84,000 Certified Financial Planners, stressed that the models identified by the authors well before 2003–11/2018 were highly statistically significant post-publication. The models that passed the Markowitz-Xu (1994) Data Mining Corrections test in 1994 and 1997 continued to be statistically significant for another 25 years.

costs.[27] We use the Mean-Variance (MV) optimization techniques. Our portfolios simulations reported in Table 9.3 use the Axioma Fundamental Risk Model. The optimizations use the ITG transactions costs curves discussed in Borkovec et al. (2010). ITG transactions costs have been taken out of the portfolio returns reported in Table 9.3. The financial anomalies of EP, BP, CP, SP, CTEF, and PM are reflected in Table 9.3 reporting REG10 results. The CTEF-optimized portfolios outperform in 70 and 77% of the years, respectively. Financial anomalies, as published in 1993 and 2003, continue to outperform with slightly reduced winning percentages from 83% in 1993 to 77% in 2018. Is that and should that be enough for investors? The excess returns reported in Table 9.4, particularly for targeted tracking errors of six and eight percent should satisfy investors who seek to maximize the Geometric Mean and the utility of terminal wealth.[28] Several more results should be pointed to our readers in Table 9.4, where models within stock universes are ranked by Specific returns: (1) CTEF is highly statistically significant in non-U.S., EM, and China A-Shares universes; (2) REG8 is statistically significant in all stock universes; (3) REG10 Active Returns dominate in non-U.S., EM, and China A-Shares portfolios.

In the MSCI All Country World ex-U.S. universe, during the 12/2002–11/2018 period, the ranked EP and CTEF variables produced highly statistically significant Active Returns (Risk Total Effect) and Specific Returns, see Table 9.3. Modern robust statistics minimize a scale measure of residuals insensitive to large residuals such as the median of the absolute residuals, see Maronna et al. (2019). The least median squares (LMS) estimator was introduced by Hampel (1971) and Rousseeuw (in press). When we use a very large efficiency measure such as 99%, large outliers have virtually no influence

---

[27] ITG estimates our transactions costs to be about 60 basis points, each-way, for 2011–2015.

[28] Fama (1991) hypothesized that anomalies could not be effectively tested because of changing asset pricing models and the number of factors in multi-factor models. Barillas and Shanken (2018) addressed the issue of changing risk models and factors. We have addressed these issues in two previous studies and are currently addressing a third issue. First, in Guerard and Mark (2003), we based what BARRA USE models were known at that time; there was no look-ahead bias in risk models. Second, in Guerard and Mark (2018) we used the Boolean signal portfolio construction process in which we buy attractively-ranked stocks and sell when they fall through pre-determined levels (buy stocks with CTEF or REG10 scores of at least 85 and higher, where 0 is least preferred and 99 is most preferred and sell at 70, holding in equally-weighted portfolios). The Boolean signal tests re-enforced the mean-variance portfolio results. The mean-variance portfolios, with a specified upper bound on stock weights and positive holdings for long-only portfolios produced very reasonable (possible) weights. We do not believe the Brennan-Lo (2011) footnote that repeats the impossible mean-variance optimized portfolios tales told by Wall Street portfolio managers. The Axioma attribution of the Boolean signal portfolios attributed all Active Returns to stock selection in the CTEF model and the majority of the REG10 model Active Returns were due to Specific Returns or asset selection. Finally, we test are testing whether it makes a difference as to whether we use a (1) mean-variance tracking error at risk model, stressing systematic risk minimization; (2) a mean-variance model without factors (MVM59), using only total risk; or (3) a mean-variance model using only systematic risk.

Table 9.4 An anomalies-based risk-return trade-off curve, 2001–2018

Portfolio dashboard mean-variance optimization AXIOMA fundamental risk model 1/2002–11/2018

Portfolios	Sharpe ratio	Info ratio	Risk stock specific effect	Risk stock specific effect T-stat	Risk factors Effect	Risk factors Effect T-stat	Risk total effect	Risk transaction effect	Total effect	Earnings yield	Growth	Medium-term momentum
R3000_REG9_8TE	0.68	0.38	3.01	2.04	0.06	0.55	3.07	−1.20	1.88	0.29	−0.15	−0.21
R3000_REG8_6TE	0.60	0.18	1.86	1.66	−0.88	−0.24	0.98	−0.94	0.04	−0.31	−0.15	−0.28
R3000_CTEF_8TE	0.75	0.52	1.61	1.36	3.30	2.24	4.92	−2.26	2.65	1.81	0.07	1.41
R3000_REG8_8TE	0.51	0.06	1.77	1.36	−1.53	−0.50	0.24	−1.28	−1.03	−0.74	−0.18	−0.41
R3000_REG9_6TE	0.64	0.25	1.35	1.14	0.15	0.55	1.50	−1.12	0.38	0.43	−0.13	−0.15
R3000_CTEF_6TE	0.71	0.42	0.35	0.57	2.59	2.26	2.95	−1.55	1.39	1.66	0.06	1.07
R3000_CTEF_4TE	0.72	0.42	−0.02	0.20	2.03	2.73	2.02	−0.92	1.10	1.29	0.03	0.72
R3000_REG9_4TE	0.62	0.12	0.02	0.05	0.31	0.67	0.33	−0.55	−0.22	0.53	−0.11	−0.02
R3000_REG8_4TE	0.58	0.02	−0.06	−0.05	−0.11	0.17	−0.17	−0.45	−0.62	0.10	−0.11	−0.19
R3000_REG10_8TE	0.53	0.08	−0.42	−0.14	0.85	0.86	0.43	−1.96	−1.54	0.61	−0.17	0.28
R3000_REG10_4TE	0.62	0.12	−0.17	−0.17	0.52	0.89	0.35	−0.81	−0.46	0.71	−0.16	0.18
R3000_REG10_6TE	0.53	−0.01	−0.88	−0.62	0.53	0.68	−0.35	−1.33	−1.68	0.67	−0.17	0.18
R1000_REG8_6TE	0.69	0.30	2.52	2.07	−0.55	0.16	1.97	−0.88	1.10	0.08	−0.09	−0.28
R1000_REG8_8TE	0.58	0.13	2.36	1.57	−1.40	−0.18	0.96	−1.10	−0.15	−0.03	−0.11	−0.39
R1000_REG8_4TE	0.71	0.27	0.81	1.00	0.44	0.84	1.25	−0.43	0.82	0.31	−0.07	−0.21
R1000_REG9_8TE	0.58	0.15	1.25	0.99	0.07	0.59	1.32	−1.15	0.17	0.55	−0.15	−0.25
R1000_CTEF_4TE	0.75	0.44	0.63	0.89	1.53	2.34	2.16	−0.69	1.47	1.18	0.01	0.62
R1000_REG10_6TE	0.66	0.19	0.75	0.68	0.41	0.70	1.16	−0.95	0.20	0.75	−0.09	0.19
R1000_CTEF_6TE	0.73	0.39	0.47	0.66	2.23	2.04	2.70	−1.00	1.70	1.62	0.03	0.91
R1000_CTEF_8TE	0.72	0.40	0.29	0.57	2.89	2.09	3.18	−2.08	1.10	1.72	0.05	1.21

Portfolio dashboard mean-variance optimization AXIOMA fundamental risk model 1/2002–11/2018

Portfolios	Sharpe ratio	Info ratio	Risk stock specific effect	Risk stock specific effect T-stat	Risk factors Effect	Risk factors Effect T-stat	Risk total effect	Risk transaction effect	Total effect	Earnings yield	Growth	Medium-term momentum
R1000_REG9_6TE	0.61	0.13	0.54	0.46	0.31	0.71	0.85	−1.04	−0.19	0.57	−0.16	−0.15
R1000_REG9F_4TE	0.67	0.19	0.10	0.21	0.73	1.16	0.83	−0.74	0.10	0.57	−0.07	−0.03
R1000_REG10_8TE	0.58	0.09	−0.15	0.02	0.62	0.75	0.47	−0.86	−0.39	0.84	−0.08	0.46
R1000_REG10_4TE	0.66	0.14	−0.34	−0.29	1.01	1.41	0.66	−0.76	−0.10	0.71	−0.08	0.23
ALLXUS_CTEF_6TE	0.85	1.45	9.35	6.89	5.58	6.80	14.93	−4.16	10.77	0.69	−0.18	3.25
ALLXUS_CTEF_8TE	0.91	1.44	11.51	6.60	5.24	5.27	16.74	−4.98	11.76	0.70	−0.26	4.08
ALLXUS_CTEF_4TE	0.70	1.26	6.40	5.77	4.66	7.71	11.05	−3.07	7.98	0.67	−0.10	2.05
ALLXUS_REG10_6TE	0.65	1.21	4.16	3.53	7.23	6.53	11.39	−4.27	7.12	0.36	0.08	2.22
ALLXUS_REG10_4TE	0.49	1.07	2.66	3.09	4.67	5.85	7.33	−3.06	4.26	0.36	0.09	1.27
ALLXUS_REG10_8TE	0.70	1.14	4.41	2.98	8.72	6.12	13.13	−4.88	8.26	0.44	0.08	2.87
ALLXUS_REG8_8TE	0.39	0.45	5.53	2.93	5.29	4.65	10.82	−5.44	5.38	−0.18	0.42	0.85
ALLXUS_REG8_6TE	0.44	0.61	2.61	0.59	5.33	4.68	7.94	−4.34	3.60	0.34	0.11	0.15
ALLXUS_REG9_8TE	0.60	0.93	1.03	−0.78	10.85	7.01	11.89	−4.75	7.14	0.66	0.08	0.95
ALLXUS_REG9_6TE	0.56	0.95	1.34	−0.84	8.59	7.25	9.93	−3.92	6.01	0.63	0.06	0.65
ALLXUS_REG8_4TE	0.44	0.82	2.89	−0.89	3.09	3.95	5.98	−3.42	2.56	0.30	0.11	−0.21
ALLXUS_REG9_4TE	0.48	1.02	1.39	−2.08	5.06	6.62	6.45	−2.88	3.56	0.50	0.06	0.43
EM_REG8_4TE	0.51	0.31	3.99	2.38	1.79	2.11	5.78	−2.05	3.73	0.25	0.26	−0.85
EM_REG9_4TE	0.55	0.49	3.45	2.20	3.28	3.60	6.73	−2.11	4.63	0.43	0.16	−0.19
EM_CTEF_8TE	0.59	0.61	3.54	2.18	5.76	3.64	9.30	−3.58	5.72	0.87	−0.02	2.69

(continued)

Table 9.4 (continued)

Portfolio dashboard mean-variance optimization AXIOMA fundamental risk model 1/2002–11/2018

Portfolios	Sharpe ratio	Info ratio	Risk stock specific effect	Risk stock specific effect T-stat	Risk factors Effect	Risk factors Effect T-stat	Risk total effect	Risk transaction effect	Total effect	Earnings yield	Growth	Medium-term momentum
EM_CTEF_4TE	0.58	0.72	3.20	2.16	3.84	4.42	7.04	-2.10	4.94	0.63	-0.09	1.51
EM_CTEF_6TE	0.60	0.65	3.67	2.13	4.67	4.02	8.34	-2.75	5.59	0.80	-0.06	2.13
EM_REG9_8TE	0.51	0.30	3.40	1.73	5.09	3.31	8.50	-3.62	4.88	0.38	0.21	0.25
EM_REG8_6TE	0.44	0.06	3.30	1.64	2.32	2.17	5.63	-2.79	2.83	0.13	0.32	-0.99
EM_REG10_4TE	0.54	0.45	2.25	1.58	4.06	4.24	6.31	-1.92	4.39	0.44	0.17	0.53
EM_REG9_6TE	0.48	0.22	2.62	1.54	4.37	3.49	6.99	-2.80	4.19	0.41	0.18	-0.09
EM_REG8_8TE	0.43	0.10	3.37	1.36	2.59	2.27	5.96	-3.52	2.44	0.00	0.41	-0.78
EM_REG10_6TE	0.52	0.33	1.33	1.07	5.63	4.17	6.96	-2.96	4.00	0.41	0.23	0.93
EM_REG10_8TE	0.49	0.24	0.30	0.59	6.34	3.68	6.64	-3.54	3.10	0.39	0.24	1.32
JAPAN_REG8_8TE	0.56	0.54	5.64	4.00	-0.18	0.44	5.46	-2.24	3.26	-0.39	0.28	-0.75
JAPAN_REG8_6TE	0.54	0.51	4.73	3.74	-0.23	0.20	4.50	-1.49	3.04	-0.34	0.25	-0.72
JAPAN_REG8_4TE	0.50	0.46	2.75	2.88	0.17	0.63	2.92	-0.79	2.17	-0.16	0.18	-0.58
JAPAN_REG9_8TE	0.42	0.28	2.14	1.65	0.74	1.34	2.87	-2.00	0.95	-0.05	0.22	-0.44
JAPAN_REG9_4TE	0.44	0.31	1.54	1.59	0.55	1.45	2.09	-0.82	1.32	0.05	0.13	-0.33
JAPAN_REG9_6TE	0.41	0.25	1.83	1.50	0.44	1.04	2.27	-1.35	0.98	-0.03	0.19	-0.44
JAPAN_REG10_8TE	0.38	0.19	0.23	0.44	1.48	1.98	1.71	-1.80	-0.01	-0.02	0.19	0.11
JAPAN_REG10_6TE	0.37	0.16	-0.13	0.14	1.40	2.01	1.26	-1.48	-0.16	0.03	0.19	0.07
JAPAN_CTEF_8TE	0.35	0.15	-0.93	-0.01	2.20	2.50	1.28	-6.73	-5.40	0.56	-0.25	1.29
JAPAN_CTEF_6TE	0.12	0.09	-0.90	-0.18	2.32	3.13	1.42	-3.87	-2.38	0.56	-0.18	1.19

Portfolio dashboard mean-variance optimization AXIOMA fundamental risk model 1/2002–11/2018

Portfolios	Sharpe ratio	Info ratio	Risk stock specific effect	Risk stock specific effect T-stat	Risk factors Effect	Risk factors Effect T-stat	Risk total effect	Risk trans-action effect	Total effect	Earnings yield	Growth	Medium-term momentum
JAPAN_CTEF_4TE	0.30	0.19	−0.82	−0.38	1.96	3.97	1.13	−1.35	−0.17	0.53	−0.13	0.96
JAPAN_REG10_4TE	0.35	0.07	−0.97	−0.76	1.39	2.70	0.42	−1.06	−0.58	0.08	0.11	0.08
CHINAA_CTEF_4TE	0.60	**1.23**	7.12	**6.75**	2.22	6.32	9.35	−1.74	7.68	**0.34**	−0.08	0.55
CHINAA_CTEF_6TE	0.59	**1.05**	7.30	**5.16**	2.54	5.31	9.84	−2.39	7.52	**0.34**	−0.12	0.78
CHINAA_CTEF_8TE	0.57	**0.95**	7.19	**4.87**	2.75	4.98	9.94	−2.61	7.40	**0.35**	−0.13	0.89
CHINAA_REG10_4TE	0.51	**0.87**	4.62	**4.43**	2.31	5.60	6.93	−1.78	5.19	**0.22**	0.19	−0.06
CHINAA_REG9_4TE	0.44	**0.54**	3.45	**3.41**	1.42	3.77	4.88	−1.66	3.24	**0.17**	0.19	−0.51
CHINAA_REG10_6TE	0.52	**0.72**	4.77	**3.31**	3.06	5.51	7.84	−2.51	5.39	**0.28**	0.24	−0.05
CHINAA_REG8_4TE	0.42	0.47	3.17	**3.29**	1.29	3.29	4.47	−1.65	2.83	**0.12**	0.20	−0.74
CHINAA_REG10_8TE	0.50	**0.63**	4.38	**2.89**	3.18	5.05	7.56	−2.79	4.83	**0.30**	0.26	−0.01
CHINAA_REG8_6TE	0.41	0.39	3.45	**2.67**	1.49	2.84	4.94	−2.41	2.58	**0.11**	0.28	−0.91
CHINAA_REG8_8TE	0.41	0.37	3.65	**2.56**	1.64	2.75	5.30	−2.67	2.67	**0.10**	0.33	−0.91
CHINAA_REG9_8TE	0.41	0.38	3.40	**2.40**	1.76	3.06	5.16	−2.63	2.57	**0.18**	0.27	−0.55
CHINAA_REG9_6TE	0.42	0.42	3.18	**2.37**	1.82	3.52	5.01	−2.37	2.69	**0.18**	0.24	−0.58

REG8 = OIF99 Regression(EP,BP,CP,SP,REP,RBP,RCP,RSP)
REG9 = OIF99 Regression(EP,BP,CP,SP,REP,RBP,RCP,RSP,CTEF)
REG10 = OIF99 Regression(EP,BP,CP,SP,REP,RBP,RCP,RSP,CTEF,PM71)
BOLD IRs exceed 0.50
BOLD Risk Stock Specific T-Stat is statistically significant

on the regression estimates. FactSet uses the R system for robust regression modeling. The larger the efficiency, the larger the bias under contamination, and there can be a trade-off between normal efficiency and contamination by outlier bias.[29]

The role of historical and forecasted earnings in the non-U.S. universe is well documented, as in Guerard (2015). The CTEF portfolio Geometric Means, Sharpe Ratios, and IRs are followed by REG8, REG9, and REG10, see Table 9.4. The CTEF, REG8, and REG9 variables produced statistically significant portfolio Active Total returns and Stock Specific returns in the non-U.S. universe. The CTEF, REG8, REG9, and REG10 Mean-Variance portfolios produce statistically significant portfolio Active and Specific returns. If one uses the largest 5000 market-capitalized non-U.S. stocks for the corresponding period, the CTEF, REG8, REG9, and REG10 Mean-Variance portfolios produce statistically significant portfolio Active and Specific Returns. However, only CTEF produces higher Specific Returns than in the index-constituent universe. The risk index Returns for the size and value factors create higher Active Returns in the larger non-U.S. universe for the 2002–11/2018 time period. In the Russell 3000 (R3) universe, only the ranked CTEF portfolios produced statistically significant portfolio Active and Specific Returns. The R3 EP, REG8, REG9, and REG10 Mean-Variance portfolios did not produce consistently statistically significant portfolio Active returns and significant Stock Specific Returns for the 1/2003–11/2018 time period. Only the REG8 and REG9 produced statistically significant stock selection at 6 and 8% targeted tracking errors, respectively. In the Russell 1000 (R1) universe, only the ranked CTEF portfolios produced statistically significant portfolio Active Returns. The important result of the empirical update is that CTEF, REG8, REG9, and REG10 Mean-Variance portfolios produce statistically significant portfolio Active Returns and significant Stock Specific Returns for the 12/2002–11/2018 time period in foreign markets.[30]

---

[29] The SAS robustreg procedure uses an 85% efficiency default level as a result of Maronna et al. (2006). We use 99% because of research conversations with Doug Martin, the publication of Maronnaet al. (2019) and the resulting higher portfolio simulation Sharpe Ratios.

[30] Before closing the discussion of Mean-Variance analysis, it is important to respond to Brennan and Lo (2012) whose article on portfolio optimization will be regarded as a modern classic. In a footnote, Brennan and Lo repeat comments of practitioners who claim the MV analysis produces absurd solutions. It is our experience, with our variables, that this is not a valid claim. A simple test was performed for the January 2003–December 2016 period. We produce monthly ranked CTEF variables for the Russell 3000 (R3) and World Investable ex-U.S. (XUS) index constituents. We prefer higher-ranked stocks, 85–99, and sell those with lower scores such as 70. The R3 and XUS model correctly rank-order stocks; that is, to buy R3 stocks exceeding 85, hold them in equally-weighted portfolios until their monthly CTEF score falls below 70, produced an annualized Active Return of 6.88%, composed of highly-statistically significant stock selection (Specific Returns). A similar test to buy XUS stocks exceeding 85, hold them in equally-weighted portfolios until their monthly CTEF

Fig. 9.9 Large Cap U.S. Stock Portfolios

No U.S. portfolio should be run with a tracking error of less than 6% if one wants to outperform the market.[31] Moreover, as reported by Guerard (2015) and Beheshti (2015), the CTEF and REG9 Efficient Frontier portfolios produced with the Axioma Statistical Risk Model outperform the Axioma Fundamental Risk Model Efficient Frontier portfolios. See Figs. 9.9–9.14.

We have shown how forecasted earnings acceleration produces highly statistically significant stock selection in Non-U.S. and U.S. stock universes. CTEF, REG8, REG9, and REG10 models optimized portfolios produce higher Active and Specific Returns in Non-U.S. stocks, whereas only CTEF consistently produces statistically significant Specific Returns in the U.S. The

score falls below 70, produced annualized Active Returns of 8.15%, see Table 30.11. We refer to the "buy, hold, sell" test as the Boolean Signal test. The Boolean Signal "buy at 85 and sell at 70" XUS and R3 portfolios are analyzed in the Axioma attribution system and produce highly statistically significant Active Returns and Specific Returns for the 2003–2016 period as well as the 2012–2016 post-Global Financial Crisis period. In fact, in the post-GFC period, all ranked CTEF Active returns are Specific returns. In the 2003–2016 time period, all R3 ranked CTEF Active Returns (6.88%) are Specific Returns (7.24%); whereas the majority of Non-U.S. ranked CTEF Active Returns (8.15%) are Specific Returns (5.02%). We believe that the Boolean Signal test confirms the validity of MV application. The world is changing; As bottom-up quantitative stock pickers, we report that MV models that were statistically significant for 1990–2001 in Guerard and Mark (2003) continue to be statistically significant in 1996–2016, 2003–2017, and the post-Global Financial Crisis period. Models cannot be perfect but they can, and for practitioners, should be statistically significant.

[31] Another means to analyze the updated non-U.S. and R3 portfolios is to directly compare Information Ratios, Sharpe Ratios, and Draw Downs, DD. Drawdowns do not vary as much as one might expect from varying targeted tracking errors. In non-U.S. portfolios, the Sharpe Ratios and IRs are maximized at a targeted 6% level with CTEF and 8% with REG9. In the U.S., the maximum TE of 8% maximizes the Sharpe Ratios and Information Ratios.

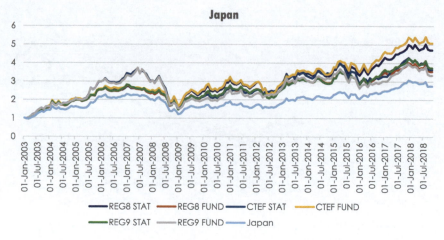

Fig. 9.10 MSCI Japan Stock Portfolios

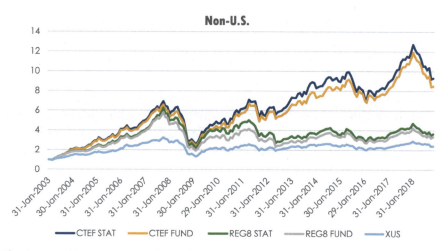

Fig. 9.11 MSCI Non-U.S. Stock Portfolios

non-U.S. CTEF and REG9 models outperform in 80% of the years, post-publication of 2003. The U.S. CTEF and REG9 models outperform in 60% of the years.

The authors modified the Domowitz and Moghe (2018) "Donut" strategy to accommodate the five largest market-capitalized stocks within the MSCI Non-U.S., Global, and Russell 3000 index constituents to become the "holes" in the donut. We optimize the portfolios such that the sum of the market-capitalized weights of the top five stocks are within two percent of the sum of the respective stock benchmark weights. The remaining stocks are optimized within a traditional Markowitz Mean-Variance within three percent of the

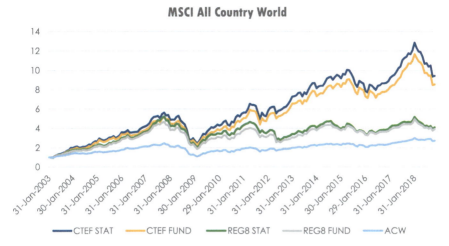

Fig. 9.12   MSCI All World (Global) Stock Portfolios

Fig. 9.13   Russell 3000 U.S. Stock Portfolios

index weights. Donuts are not an optimal solution compared to traditional optimization; however, there is no less possibility of portfolio implementation shortfall. The reader is referred to Table 9.5.

The CTEF and REG9 Efficient Frontier Donut portfolios produced with the Axioma Statistical Risk Model outperform the Axioma Fundamental Risk Model Efficient Frontier Donut portfolios. See Fig. 9.15. In the real world of asset management, it may well be better to be near-optimal in portfolio construction and its implementation than optimal in portfolio construction

Emerging Markets

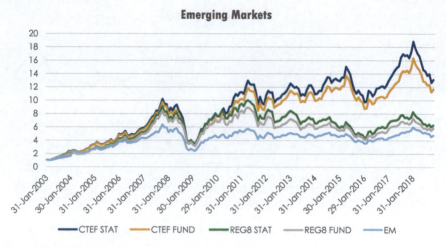

Fig. 9.14 MSCI Emerging Markets Stock Portfolios

and avoid needless debate regarding the relative risk of large benchmark weight stocks.

9.3.1 Portfolio Selection Through Much of COVID

Has COVID affected portfolio selection? Let us construct portfolio selection models for January 2001–December 2020 to initially address this issue. The FactSet data, commercially available, is used in this analysis is for two universes: (1) Russell 3000 (R3) Index constituents, for the January 2000–December 2020 time period; and (2) MSCI ex USA stocks Index constituents, for the January 2000–December 2020 time period.[32] The U.S.

---

[32] In 2010, Stone and Guerard presented an update to the Guerard and Takano model at the CRSP Forum. The Japanese stock returns were from the Tokyo Stock Exchange from January 1975 through December 2005. The database used for both stock returns and financial statement data is the PACAP Research Center database of University of Rhode Island. The Stone and Guerard universe used all securities in the United States covered by the Center for Research in Security Prices (CRSP) database and had Compustat data on the Wharton Research Data Services (WRDS) files, 1980–2005.

In contrast to many stock return forecast models, the intent here is not to forecast either overall stock return or even the numerical value of excess return. Here excess return refers to the difference between realized return in a month and the fair return for both time and risk. Stone and Guerard (2010) referred to realized excess return as alpha performance. The forecast objective is to predict an attribute of the distribution of the excess return component, namely the relative rank-ordering on alpha performance for an entire sample of stocks. The concern is the ability to use the stock return forecast, FS, to enhance portfolio performance relative to passive strategies. The overall JP Guerard et al. (1992) model is highly statistically significant, with an overall t-statistic of 19.7 on the FS variable with respect to realized return. The overall U.S. Guerard et al. (1992) model is highly statistically significant, with an overall t-statistic of 18.1 on the Forecasted Score (FS) variable with respect to realized return. For an overall perspective, the R-squared of the 30 fractile portfolios is

Table 9.5 Donuts and portfolio selection (Donut portfolio analysis time period: 12/2002–11/2018)

Portfolios	Risk stock specific effect	Risk stock specific effect t-stat	Risk factors effect	Risk factors effect T-stat	Risk total effect	Risk transaction effect	Total effect	Earnings yield	Growth	Medium-term momentum
ACW_DONUT_CTEF_STAT_6TE	4.43	3.65	3.00	3.11	7.42	7.42	3.46	0.69	−0.11	2.67
EM_DONUT_CTEF_STAT_6TE	1.82	1.94	4.37	3.94	6.19	6.19	3.25	0.59	−0.03	2.09
XUS_DONUT_CTEF_STAT_6TE	3.14	3.27	4.18	3.73	7.32	7.32	2.76	0.72	−0.13	2.63
EM_DONUT_CTEF_FUND_6TE	1.49	1.76	4.00	4.01	5.49	5.49	2.66	0.60	−0.03	2.00
ACW_DONUT_CTEF_FUND_6TE	3.93	3.17	2.19	2.66	6.12	6.12	2.36	0.66	−0.16	2.53
XUS_DONUT_CTEF_FUND_6TE	2.46	2.72	3.82	3.48	6.28	6.28	1.94	0.72	−0.18	2.48
EM_DONUT_REG9_STAT_6TE	0.27	0.79	4.57	3.76	4.83	4.83	1.68	0.27	0.25	0.06
EM_DONUT_REG9_FUND_6TE	0.31	0.71	3.82	3.60	4.14	4.14	1.22	0.27	0.20	−0.03
XUS_DONUT_REG9_STAT_6TE	0.51	0.58	2.85	2.87	3.35	3.35	−0.68	0.21	0.06	0.30
ACW_DONUT_REG9_STAT_6TE	−0.50	−0.21	2.78	2.47	2.29	2.29	−1.22	0.15	0.01	0.42
XUS_DONUT_REG9_FUND_6TE	0.18	0.51	2.30	2.39	2.48	2.48	−1.38	0.19	0.06	0.23
ACW_DONUT_REG9_FUND_6TE	−0.57	−0.27	2.34	2.29	1.77	1.77	−1.43	0.17	−0.03	0.29
R3000_DONUT_CTEF_STAT_6TE	0.38	0.54	3.39	2.33	3.78	−1.84	1.94	1.53	0.00	1.27
R3000_DONUT_CTEF_FUND_6TE	0.56	0.74	2.71	2.22	3.27	−1.52	1.74	1.49	0.04	1.06
R3000_DONUT_REG9_STAT_6TE	2.43	1.79	0.19	0.59	2.62	−1.85	0.77	0.23	−0.17	−0.25
R3000_DONUT_REG9_FUND_6TE	1.23	1.06	0.40	0.68	1.63	−1.43	0.20	0.36	−0.14	−0.14

BOLD Denotes Statistically Significant at 5% Level

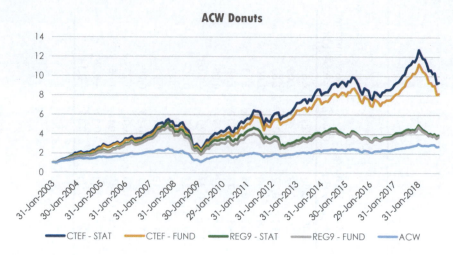

Fig. 9.15 ACW Donuts

and global portfolio selection problem can be solved by the "one button" approach within FactSet, see Beheshti et al. (2021). We report the factor ICs within the Russell 3000 in Table 9.6, MSCI ex USA (XUS) in Table 9.7, and a larger global universe composed of the Russell 3000 and non-US, XUS, index constituents, some 5000–5500 stocks, in Table 9.8. In the U.S. Russell 3000 universe, the REG10, I/B/E/S forecasted earnings yield FY1 and FY2, denoted FEP1 and FEP2, CTEF, EP, and REG9 factor produce the largest, and highly statistically significant Information Coefficients, ICs. Within the MSCI ex USA, XUS, universe, the dividend yield, DP, CTEF, REG10, and breadth of analysts' forecasts, BR1 and BR2, and relative dividend yield, RDP, produce the largest, and highly statistically significant Information Coefficients, ICs.

Within the Russell 3000 and appended XUS universe, the larger global universe, the REG10, CTEF, REG9, and the I/B/E/S FEP1 and FEP2 factors produce the largest, and highly statistically significant Information Coefficients, ICs. We report an executive summary of the top six factors within each respective universe in Table 9.9. The REG10, CTEF, and REG9 variables produce the largest, and highly statistically significant Information Coefficients, ICs within these universes. Robust regression modeling, using

---

93% in Japan and 42% in the U.S. However, the Guerard and Takano model has quite volatile in the U.S., performing extremely well in 1980–1985 ($t = 15.31$), 1991–1995 ($t = 5.12$), and 2001–2005 ($t = 22.5$). However, the Guerard and Takano model performed very poorly in the U.S. "Bubble Period", 1996–2000 ($t = -5.24$), even worse than in Japan, and was insignificant in the 1986–1990 period. Guerard reported these results in the *Journal of Investing* 25th Anniversary issue.

Table 9.6 Monthly ICs of US Factors within the Rissell 3000 Index Constituents

Factor	Universe Return 1	2	3	4	5	Excess vs. Bench 1	2	3	4	5	IC	Pooled IC T-Stat	Alpha 1	2	3	4	5
REG10	11.61	9.27	9.39	8.87	4.94	2.24	-0.25	-0.24	-0.29	-3.75	0.041	5.75	3.28	3.26	2.09	2.74	35.68
FEP1	11.27	10.09	7.30	7.16	3.82	1.51	0.38	-2.11	-1.71	-4.00	0.041	5.77	5.44	4.51	1.10	6.73	25.64
FEP2	12.33	9.96	8.50	6.26	4.80	2.70	0.28	-1.13	-2.75	-3.35	0.039	5.65	4.58	5.02	1.50	4.54	18.31
CTEF	11.45	10.63	6.80	8.00	4.38	1.82	0.96	-2.33	-1.00	-4.38	0.037	5.27	8.33	3.12	2.23	1.09	-0.56
EP	12.80	9.70	8.64	7.55	3.56	3.51	-0.13	-0.95	-1.52	-4.53	0.036	5.32	0.16	3.71	2.76	3.02	36.82
REG9	12.13	10.05	9.66	6.13	7.18	2.90	0.27	0.03	-2.94	-1.92	0.035	5.28	-1.01	2.23	2.25	3.46	10.95
CP	11.67	10.03	10.73	6.37	4.48	2.37	0.31	1.00	-2.66	-3.99	0.033	5.08	-8.27	3.83	3.47	3.55	26.59
REG8	11.36	10.97	9.47	7.04	7.46	2.17	1.27	-0.20	-2.24	-1.64	0.030	4.95	-3.50	2.25	1.93	5.59	11.44
RDP	9.69	9.73	7.10	9.42	#N/A	0.31	-0.16	-2.15	0.77	#N/A	0.024	3.26	-0.96	3.75	5.81	6.81	#N/A
DP	9.91	8.74	7.36	9.07	#N/A	-0.07	-0.75	-1.47	0.38	#N/A	0.023	2.93	0.29	4.40	3.49	6.64	#N/A
PM71	10.06	9.19	9.76	7.95	4.03	0.69	-0.32	0.22	-1.29	-4.32	0.023	4.36	13.65	3.40	2.58	2.04	41.01
SP	11.01	11.50	8.95	8.01	7.03	1.70	1.78	-0.56	-1.51	-1.76	0.022	4.17	-5.64	2.90	4.77	1.74	10.88
BR1	10.54	8.93	7.85	7.71	9.16	1.16	-0.50	-1.45	-1.45	-0.18	0.022	4.26	7.99	2.42	0.08	0.08	0.40
BR2	10.42	9.78	6.72	8.06	9.45	1.09	0.26	-2.51	-1.18	0.15	0.022	4.13	7.71	2.58	-0.37	-0.04	0.40
RV2	9.71	10.75	7.83	6.29	7.61	0.47	0.19	-1.05	-2.91	-1.15	0.015	2.87	4.24	3.82	2.15	1.18	-2.05
RV1	9.43	12.37	8.91	7.07	8.20	0.25	0.80	-0.33	-1.91	-0.61	0.010	2.10	3.43	4.47	1.74	0.74	-0.88
BP	7.81	10.42	9.35	9.56	8.65	-0.98	0.78	-0.19	-0.06	-0.54	0.006	2.24	5.97	4.36	1.84	2.27	6.59

Factor	T-Stat Alpha 1	2	3	4	5	Beta 1	2	3	4	5	Sharpe Ratio 1	2	3	4	5
REG10	**0.28**	0.68	0.69	0.82	0.89	2.15	1.46	1.30	1.34	1.91	0.650	0.619	0.521	0.344	-0.067
FEP1	**0.70**	1.74	0.57	1.11	0.76	1.86	1.10	1.10	1.66	2.59	0.577	0.659	0.511	0.287	0.019
FEP2	**0.42**	1.64	0.78	1.03	0.77	2.27	1.20	1.08	1.41	2.28	0.515	0.661	0.537	0.268	0.037
CTEF	**2.95**	0.97	0.58	0.17	-0.05	1.25	1.34	1.43	1.76	2.08	0.764	0.565	0.388	0.255	0.106
EP	**0.01**	0.91	1.41	0.89	1.03	2.61	1.19	1.02	1.33	2.59	0.522	0.677	0.606	0.314	-0.002
REG9	**-0.05**	0.40	0.75	0.81	1.41	3.06	1.53	1.25	1.25	1.51	0.557	0.549	0.504	0.298	0.036
CP	**-0.26**	0.84	1.54	1.21	1.05	3.84	1.31	1.08	1.16	1.95	0.465	0.628	0.634	0.328	-0.013
REG8	**-0.12**	0.34	0.70	0.92	1.56	3.42	1.57	1.22	1.22	1.51	0.493	0.564	0.514	0.323	0.042

(continued)

Table 9.6 (continued)

Factor	T-Stat Alpha					Beta					Sharpe Ratio				
	1	2	3	4	5	1	2	3	4	5	1	2	3	4	5
RDP	-0.08	1.78	2.09	0.91	#N/A	2.01	0.86	0.91	1.92	#N/A	0.533	0.667	0.524	0.262	#N/A
DP	0.03	1.81	1.49	0.90	#N/A	1.58	0.99	1.14	1.92	#N/A	0.559	0.626	0.513	0.261	#N/A
PM71	2.12	1.43	0.90	0.25	0.53	1.33	1.05	1.17	1.72	5.21	0.527	0.604	0.578	0.427	-0.019
SP	-0.17	0.50	1.64	0.79	1.44	4.08	1.60	1.16	1.10	1.39	0.369	0.549	0.584	0.422	0.047
BR1	2.89	0.69	0.01	0.01	0.05	1.34	1.40	1.59	1.78	1.65	0.639	0.484	0.373	0.310	0.234
BR2	2.89	0.70	-0.08	-0.01	0.05	1.31	1.40	1.60	1.78	1.75	0.634	0.475	0.371	0.283	0.278
RV2	0.95	1.33	0.73	0.30	-0.15	1.67	1.23	1.17	1.38	2.40	0.469	0.677	0.397	0.408	0.157
RV1	0.96	1.07	0.58	0.14	-0.07	1.58	1.23	1.25	1.50	2.25	0.417	0.652	0.449	0.376	0.195
BP	0.15	0.93	0.72	0.95	1.30	4.16	1.40	1.18	1.21	1.42	0.301	0.537	0.474	0.418	0.212

Factor	Information Ratio					% > Bench- mark					% Total Turnover				
	1	2	3	4	5	1	2	3	4	5	1	2	3	4	5
REG10	0.39	0.27	0.07	-0.18	-0.51	51.20	48.11	47.08	47.08	48.45	51.27	97.27	102.27	89.29	43.61
FEP1	0.28	0.21	-0.09	-0.14	-0.37	51.89	50.17	45.02	50.52	47.42	28.98	51.91	46.52	29.17	15.83
FEP2	0.25	0.27	-0.05	-0.24	-0.38	50.17	50.17	45.36	47.08	48.11	30.67	57.11	54.04	33.97	15.65
CTEF	0.53	0.19	-0.10	-0.23	-0.41	56.01	48.80	41.24	46.05	39.18	78.91	125.70	136.56	130.97	77.27
EP	0.22	0.23	0.06	-0.22	-0.35	55.33	48.45	48.11	47.77	49.48	22.44	38.11	34.27	21.77	11.99
REG9	0.30	0.16	0.02	-0.30	-0.43	52.92	46.39	46.05	44.67	48.80	38.24	77.07	80.69	68.54	32.40
CP	0.19	0.21	0.18	-0.27	-0.42	55.33	46.39	52.58	43.30	47.77	18.74	35.22	36.28	24.88	12.51
REG8	0.22	0.18	0.02	-0.25	-0.42	51.55	50.52	48.80	45.36	51.89	28.83	58.34	62.67	52.90	25.11
RDP	0.14	0.03	-0.04	-0.13	#N/A	46.39	47.08	45.36	50.17	#N/A	16.55	24.58	30.74	3.87	#N/A
DP	0.06	0.10	0.04	-0.13	#N/A	45.36	46.39	50.86	50.17	#N/A	9.27	14.29	20.79	3.97	#N/A
PM71	0.17	0.10	0.09	0.00	-0.35	54.64	47.77	49.48	49.14	44.33	66.03	113.22	120.32	111.16	60.09
SP	0.10	0.19	0.16	-0.22	-0.44	49.14	52.92	47.77	41.58	49.14	13.50	26.53	30.33	26.39	13.35
BR1	0.41	0.06	-0.11	-0.15	-0.32	56.01	49.48	42.96	45.36	47.42	69.01	98.37	103.72	92.10	60.95
BR2	0.40	0.04	-0.11	-0.20	-0.24	53.61	51.20	40.89	44.33	49.48	66.91	101.82	104.55	92.89	61.28
RV2	0.14	0.30	-0.16	-0.11	-0.31	48.80	51.91	48.23	41.58	44.33	149.67	256.85	195.71	172.23	97.23
RV1	0.03	0.14	-0.08	-0.12	-0.27	47.42	53.85	47.65	45.33	46.39	152.07	270.55	162.67	180.42	95.48

Factor	Information Ratio					% > Bench-mark					% Total Turnover				
	1	2	3	4	5	1	2	3	4	5	1	2	3	4	5
BP	0.00	0.13	−0.08	−0.13	−0.27	45.02	51.20	46.39	50.17	49.14	20.67	40.05	41.30	32.67	15.87

Source FactSet Research Systems, Inc.
Note **Factors**: Model Name: Client:/Jg_research/JG_US_SCORES; Date Range: 12/31/1996 To 2/26/2021; Return Type/Horizon: Weighted/1-Month

Table 9.7 Monthly ICs of Non–US Factors within the MSCI ex USA Index Consitiuents

Factor	Universe Return					Excess vs. Bench					IC	Pooled IC T-Stat	Alpha				
	1	2	3	4	5	1	2	3	4	5			1	2	3	4	5
DP	7.17	−2.40	3.71	−8.97	−4.75	1.66	−7.58	−2.20	−13.96	−9.81	0.041	4.97	12.86	4.66	2.93	1.32	6.57
CTEF	11.61	7.12	7.88	−0.40	−5.59	5.89	1.37	2.40	−5.71	−10.76	0.035	4.71	13.34	5.02	1.47	0.98	1.69
REG10	8.21	−0.15	−5.43	1.62	−1.68	2.98	−5.69	−10.66	−4.15	−6.64	0.032	4.59	11.25	5.69	3.59	1.71	1.22
BR2	11.46	5.15	5.03	4.48	−5.66	5.51	−0.25	−0.41	−0.91	−10.72	0.030	4.25	10.67	5.12	2.09	1.46	2.76
BR1	8.81	6.78	4.36	3.64	−6.52	3.04	1.30	−1.17	−1.68	−11.59	0.027	4.09	9.58	5.88	2.39	0.67	3.29
RDP	5.74	6.72	0.80	−3.51	−4.70	0.42	1.07	−4.92	−8.62	−9.66	0.026	3.85	13.26	3.35	3.12	3.98	6.56
REG9	11.86	−2.11	−2.72	−3.22	−0.49	6.49	−7.41	−7.95	−8.38	−5.67	0.026	4.12	11.27	5.57	2.28	1.49	2.75
PM71	2.95	5.95	3.67	−2.05	4.23	−2.62	−0.02	−1.94	−7.13	−0.84	0.022	3.85	15.19	4.35	1.45	1.10	12.22
CP	3.86	−1.72	3.66	1.08	−4.64	−1.19	−7.23	−1.90	−4.66	−9.39	0.022	3.51	14.14	4.25	2.44	2.01	4.49
RV2	9.43	4.17	6.77	4.46	−6.96	3.84	−1.49	1.03	−0.88	−11.82	0.022	3.48	9.67	3.91	2.76	1.88	5.63
RV1	8.88	2.50	8.07	4.54	−6.94	3.33	−3.17	2.33	−0.82	−11.83	0.021	3.36	8.68	4.12	2.59	1.85	5.15
REG8	8.45	−7.85	0.25	1.67	−1.01	3.12	−12.62	−5.30	−3.57	−6.16	0.020	3.55	11.03	5.64	3.27	1.42	2.97
EP	−0.60	3.92	2.38	0.54	−0.36	−5.57	−1.27	−3.16	−5.16	−5.58	0.020	3.35	13.32	3.12	1.43	2.26	7.99
FEP2	10.46	7.78	6.67	5.95	0.94	5.51	2.30	0.82	0.12	−4.60	0.019	3.61	16.34	3.58	2.14	0.60	5.34
FEP1	9.60	7.34	7.17	0.99	−2.09	4.47	1.77	1.34	−4.41	−7.51	0.018	3.52	14.12	3.83	1.75	1.34	6.04
SP	5.33	−4.18	2.79	−1.90	−1.84	0.36	−9.62	−3.14	−6.91	−7.00	0.009	2.12	17.03	4.26	2.75	2.14	2.17
BP	0.89	−0.29	−3.01	3.00	−0.70	−4.11	−5.49	−8.15	−2.57	−5.95	−0.001	N/A	20.08	3.22	2.58	1.44	4.66

Beta

Factor	1	2	3	4	5
DP	1.53	1.33	1.12	1.04	0.93
CTEF	1.21	1.20	1.08	1.15	1.19
REG10	1.05	1.71	1.25	1.03	0.97
BR2	1.24	1.01	1.14	1.21	1.24
BR1	1.24	1.01	1.15	1.22	1.24
RDP	1.65	1.52	1.01	0.91	0.98
REG9	0.91	2.04	1.23	1.10	0.97
PM71	2.45	0.98	0.92	1.01	1.27

T-Stat Alpha

Factor	1	2	3	4	5
DP	**3.71**	2.67	1.81	0.80	1.20
CTEF	**5.56**	3.11	0.71	0.38	0.66
REG10	**2.00**	2.16	2.13	1.04	0.63
BR2	**5.41**	2.63	0.91	0.57	1.06
BR1	**5.53**	2.82	1.10	0.27	1.21
RDP	**2.44**	2.00	2.57	2.42	1.16
REG9	**1.46**	2.10	1.21	1.09	1.40
PM71	**3.14**	2.95	1.04	0.34	0.96

Sharpe Ratio

Factor	1	2	3	4	5
DP	0.654	0.516	0.418	0.275	0.114
CTEF	0.714	0.540	0.351	0.193	0.208
REG10	0.625	0.548	0.414	0.266	0.094
BR2	0.777	0.497	0.326	0.200	0.241
BR1	0.729	0.511	0.347	0.180	0.285
RDP	0.482	0.455	0.489	0.445	0.123
REG9	0.559	0.476	0.378	0.305	0.182
PM71	0.637	0.523	0.389	0.281	0.146

Factor	T-Stat Alpha					Beta					Sharpe Ratio				
	1	2	3	4	5	1	2	3	4	5	1	2	3	4	5
CP	1.95	2.24	1.83	1.50	1.26	1.87	1.14	0.99	0.91	1.23	0.505	0.479	0.436	0.365	0.107
RV2	3.73	2.58	1.78	0.72	1.17	1.22	0.96	0.98	1.16	1.65	0.596	0.483	0.411	0.245	0.269
RV1	4.19	2.82	1.63	0.65	1.15	1.17	0.96	1.01	1.22	1.59	0.564	0.482	0.414	0.260	0.273
REG8	1.30	2.05	1.67	1.04	1.55	2.11	1.22	1.10	0.95	0.91	0.506	0.470	0.403	0.304	0.208
EP	1.34	1.26	0.98	1.69	2.09	2.09	1.19	1.00	0.88	1.12	0.439	0.402	0.396	0.408	0.264
FEP2	2.40	1.75	1.76	0.38	1.75	1.90	1.22	0.95	0.86	1.17	0.444	0.394	0.421	0.285	0.351
FEP1	2.12	2.17	1.47	0.75	1.72	1.77	1.12	0.95	0.92	1.31	0.441	0.428	0.409	0.298	0.339
SP	1.88	1.95	1.74	1.39	1.07	1.88	1.19	1.14	1.01	0.95	0.467	0.427	0.415	0.340	0.236
BP	1.82	1.42	1.49	1.07	2.74	2.05	1.16	1.07	1.02	0.96	0.394	0.372	0.388	0.346	0.375

Factor	Information Ratio					% > Bench-mark					% Total Turnover				
	1	2	3	4	5	1	2	3	4	5	1	2	3	4	5
DP	0.82	0.61	0.30	-0.16	-0.16	55.67	53.95	53.61	48.11	46.74	18.19	32.69	32.57	23.52	11.98
CTEF	1.09	0.70	0.15	-0.19	-0.14	59.79	53.95	47.08	45.36	45.36	82.88	129.09	135.91	123.70	65.45
REG10	0.80	0.67	0.28	-0.13	-0.42	56.36	51.89	45.02	47.77	48.45	49.46	95.03	102.72	92.68	47.36
BR2	1.26	0.57	0.13	-0.14	-0.03	67.35	50.52	48.11	44.33	45.36	74.02	114.05	118.42	105.80	59.12
BR1	1.22	0.59	0.19	-0.20	0.06	61.51	55.67	41.58	44.67	44.67	71.97	111.67	117.49	104.29	58.23
RDP	0.48	0.34	0.43	0.37	-0.13	49.83	53.26	48.11	49.83	47.77	27.10	54.09	58.43	40.35	16.48
REG9	0.66	0.49	0.22	-0.05	-0.28	56.01	51.89	47.77	51.20	53.26	36.72	74.79	81.35	70.32	33.23
PM71	0.67	0.50	0.17	0.02	-0.02	51.55	50.52	51.20	47.77	45.36	64.19	115.57	124.10	115.21	63.08
CP	0.55	0.51	0.33	0.07	-0.24	45.36	50.52	58.08	51.20	46.05	18.06	34.10	36.26	28.33	16.25
RV2	0.82	0.45	0.23	-0.08	0.12	56.70	52.58	49.83	50.02	46.39	141.45	151.13	142.29	138.74	86.69
RV1	0.78	0.46	0.26	-0.03	0.12	57.39	52.23	48.45	46.39	46.39	137.34	152.58	137.32	135.43	83.28
REG8	0.55	0.45	0.30	-0.07	-0.23	52.58	51.20	48.45	52.23	52.92	31.30	63.75	70.58	61.28	29.66
EP	0.45	0.33	0.20	0.14	0.02	48.45	50.17	51.89	49.48	48.80	21.36	40.22	42.78	32.38	17.30
FEP2	0.48	0.35	0.26	-0.21	0.17	57.73	54.98	51.55	46.05	49.83	24.71	49.92	52.10	38.32	17.75
FEP1	0.46	0.40	0.23	-0.12	0.19	56.36	53.26	54.64	47.08	50.52	23.81	47.21	49.11	36.43	18.29
SP	0.44	0.40	0.38	0.09	-0.17	52.23	45.02	53.95	49.83	51.55	12.92	26.65	29.77	25.84	12.65

(continued)

Table 9.7 (continued)

Factor	Information Ratio					% > Bench- mark					% Total Turnover				
	1	2	3	4	5	1	2	3	4	5	1	2	3	4	5
BP	0.33	0.21	0.24	0.11	0.21	47.42	49.48	49.48	49.14	54.30	18.46	37.02	38.81	31.62	14.64

Source FactSet Research Systems, Inc.
Note **Factors**: Model Name: Client:/Jg_research/JG_XUS_SCORES; Date Range: 12/31/1996 To 2/26/2021; Return Type/Horizon: Weighted/1-Month

Table 9.8 Monthly ICs of Global Factors within the Russell 3000 and MSCI ex USA Index Consitiunents

Factor	Universe Return					Excess vs. Bench					Pooled Information Coefficient	Pooled IC T-Stat	Alpha				
	1	2	3	4	5	1	2	3	4	5			1	2	3	4	5
REG10	11.18	9.37	13.18	3.24	-2.06	4.50	2.06	5.67	-3.64	-8.03	0.035	6.32	6.40	4.55	3.26	2.69	8.23
CTEF	11.65	7.16	8.32	5.69	4.40	4.27	-0.02	1.48	-1.19	-2.07	0.032	6.02	10.63	5.25	2.34	0.54	-1.00
REG9	15.37	5.50	7.68	0.86	2.03	8.69	-1.57	0.28	-5.55	-4.60	0.029	5.74	4.30	4.15	2.82	2.69	4.00
FEP1	10.43	9.16	7.02	7.53	4.45	3.44	1.85	-0.29	0.69	-2.17	0.030	5.85	8.25	4.71	2.27	4.74	5.95
FEP2	11.06	9.08	7.64	5.86	5.68	4.23	1.89	0.24	-1.16	-1.05	0.029	5.78	8.41	4.84	2.81	3.15	5.24
DP	18.59	0.77	4.57	10.05	6.03	10.53	-5.85	-2.11	3.00	-0.88	0.022	5.06	4.34	4.53	8.77	6.04	1.78
EP	11.59	3.60	5.62	1.39	3.48	5.03	-3.08	-1.57	-5.48	-3.21	0.026	5.44	3.83	3.57	3.09	3.11	13.19
CP	4.45	10.92	4.28	3.29	0.22	-1.93	3.54	-2.35	-3.75	-6.02	0.025	5.31	1.47	4.06	3.77	3.48	11.23
REG8	17.81	4.31	8.84	-0.25	0.88	10.87	-2.48	1.48	-6.66	-5.77	0.024	5.25	1.84	3.91	2.87	3.01	5.81
BR2	11.25	7.24	5.53	6.28	6.81	3.92	0.42	-1.45	-0.62	0.21	0.021	4.96	9.33	4.35	1.60	0.89	0.90
RDP	10.28	13.12	3.67	11.10	1.86	3.32	5.55	-3.12	3.93	-4.49	0.017	4.36	3.50	3.51	7.08	8.83	2.96
BR1	9.36	7.17	5.75	5.12	9.30	2.17	0.29	-1.26	-1.68	2.60	0.021	4.94	9.28	3.16	2.36	0.62	1.38
PM71	7.26	9.02	6.91	7.57	4.67	0.11	1.62	-0.23	0.55	-1.28	0.021	4.92	12.52	4.36	2.66	1.66	10.09
RV2	9.56	11.45	5.84	3.11	8.09	2.58	3.74	-0.89	-3.65	1.71	0.013	3.91	7.28	7.10	1.92	1.86	0.62
SP	13.04	5.65	7.14	4.35	0.67	6.24	-1.15	-0.24	-2.55	-5.62	0.014	4.07	2.60	3.98	4.16	2.52	5.09
RV1	9.57	13.03	2.81	3.58	8.48	2.58	5.22	-3.71	-3.18	2.05	0.011	3.48	6.39	7.20	1.39	1.57	0.93
BP	5.46	6.21	5.87	5.69	7.28	-0.79	-0.50	-1.16	-1.30	0.15	0.003	1.76	6.08	3.93	2.74	2.59	5.35

Factor	T-Stat Alpha					Beta					Sharpe Ratio				
	1	2	3	4	5	1	2	3	4	5	1	2	3	4	5
REG10	0.85	1.27	1.52	1.22	0.88	1.93	1.37	1.18	1.14	1.36	0.694	0.627	0.517	0.343	-0.018
CTEF	4.64	2.35	0.92	0.13	-0.20	1.19	1.22	1.28	1.50	1.61	0.792	0.610	0.395	0.254	0.148
REG9	0.35	1.03	1.25	1.21	1.27	2.48	1.41	1.19	1.10	1.18	0.602	0.561	0.494	0.320	0.091
FEP1	1.37	2.29	1.61	1.58	0.65	1.79	1.09	1.01	1.25	1.89	0.567	0.599	0.507	0.322	0.137
FEP2	1.09	2.01	1.93	1.33	0.68	2.09	1.20	1.00	1.12	1.68	0.528	0.585	0.536	0.308	0.148
DP	0.85	2.39	1.70	1.23	0.65	1.45	1.04	1.24	1.60	1.20	0.670	0.626	0.343	0.366	0.225

(continued)

Table 9.8 (continued)

Factor	T-Stat Alpha					Beta					Sharpe Ratio				
	1	2	3	4	5	1	2	3	4	5	1	2	3	4	5
EP	0.34	1.10	1.96	1.65	1.33	2.31	1.20	0.98	1.09	1.71	0.533	0.601	0.558	0.379	0.095
CP	0.10	1.30	2.25	1.94	1.23	2.70	1.25	1.04	1.02	1.47	0.524	0.613	0.598	0.378	0.035
REG8	0.12	0.92	1.41	1.19	1.73	2.78	1.42	1.16	1.07	1.17	0.553	0.563	0.501	0.333	0.111
BR2	4.97	1.64	0.52	0.22	0.20	1.15	1.26	1.37	1.55	1.50	0.747	0.481	0.398	0.263	0.287
RDP	0.55	2.13	1.47	1.73	1.08	1.74	0.91	0.99	1.69	1.24	0.572	0.625	0.352	0.383	0.303
BR1	5.05	1.32	0.64	0.14	0.37	1.14	1.25	1.45	1.56	1.40	0.728	0.487	0.418	0.264	0.284
PM71	3.68	2.58	1.30	0.30	0.36	1.09	0.97	1.09	1.54	3.56	0.628	0.618	0.537	0.400	0.050
RV2	2.42	2.57	0.87	0.69	0.08	1.44	1.12	1.09	1.26	2.05	0.546	0.566	0.434	0.383	0.212
SP	0.17	1.05	1.98	1.57	1.51	2.80	1.41	1.15	1.04	1.14	0.446	0.537	0.555	0.423	0.124
RV1	2.65	2.50	0.61	0.45	0.13	1.38	1.16	1.13	1.32	1.94	0.515	0.530	0.414	0.388	0.238
BP	0.34	1.20	1.41	1.62	2.05	2.92	1.30	1.11	1.10	1.17	0.375	0.513	0.469	0.421	0.290

Factor	Information Ratio					% > Bench-mark					% Total Turnover				
	1	2	3	4	5	1	2	3	4	5	1	2	3	4	5
REG10	0.72	0.57	0.32	-0.05	-0.48	52.23	58.42	53.95	48.45	46.74	50.39	96.14	102.70	90.66	44.89
CTEF	0.95	0.62	0.11	-0.14	-0.31	62.54	57.73	45.02	48.11	46.05	80.56	127.45	137.51	128.75	72.84
REG9	0.58	0.43	0.28	-0.12	-0.39	53.95	55.67	54.98	51.55	46.74	37.53	75.40	81.21	69.35	32.67
FEP1	0.52	0.44	0.21	-0.01	-0.21	58.08	56.70	52.92	50.52	46.74	26.80	49.79	47.36	31.81	16.51
FEP2	0.49	0.46	0.28	-0.11	-0.23	57.39	56.70	51.20	48.11	47.42	28.19	54.11	53.36	35.63	16.20
DP	0.53	0.46	0.06	0.12	-0.25	54.98	49.48	49.48	58.08	46.05	12.96	21.77	62.35	45.44	9.62
EP	0.45	0.43	0.30	0.01	-0.22	51.89	51.20	52.92	49.14	47.77	21.99	39.08	37.67	26.00	14.11
CP	0.45	0.49	0.44	-0.02	-0.35	46.39	53.95	59.45	46.05	45.70	18.43	34.65	36.24	26.15	13.94
REG8	0.49	0.43	0.29	-0.10	-0.33	51.89	52.23	52.92	51.55	47.42	29.86	60.66	65.86	55.94	26.87
BR2	0.97	0.30	0.12	-0.10	-0.09	61.17	52.58	43.99	46.74	47.08	70.22	105.67	109.50	98.06	60.63
RDP	0.45	0.29	-0.04	0.18	-0.08	54.30	53.95	49.83	58.76	48.11	20.88	36.84	75.16	33.01	16.54

Factor	Information Ratio					% > Bench-mark					% Total Turnover				
	1	2	3	4	5	1	2	3	4	5	1	2	3	4	5
BR1	0.93	0.31	0.20	−0.10	−0.11	60.82	52.58	44.33	43.30	51.55	70.09	103.44	107.69	97.40	60.36
PM71	0.50	0.42	0.29	0.14	−0.21	55.33	51.55	49.14	48.80	45.02	65.19	114.20	121.76	112.83	61.25
RV2	0.53	0.40	0.05	0.06	−0.10	58.08	57.39	47.42	44.33	50.52	146.34	149.83	173.69	141.19	93.24
SP	0.33	0.41	0.42	0.05	−0.33	51.89	49.83	54.98	46.05	50.86	13.23	26.56	30.06	26.14	13.06
RV1	0.47	0.34	0.02	0.08	−0.07	58.08	55.67	45.02	44.67	49.83	147.53	143.67	195.98	136.71	90.99
BP	0.22	0.31	0.19	0.10	−0.07	45.02	53.95	52.58	54.64	54.64	19.69	38.79	40.25	32.30	15.39

Source FactSet Research Systems, Inc.
Note **Factors**: Model Name: Client:/Jg_research/JG_GL_SCORES; Date Range: 12/31/1996 To 2/26/2021; Return Type/Horizon: Weighted/1-Month

Table 9.9 Top Six Factors within Stock Universes

US Universe	Quintile Excess Returns						
Factor	1	2	3	4	5	IC	t (IC)
REG10	2.24	−0.25	−0.24	−0.29	−3.75	0.041	5.75
FEP1	1.51	0.38	−2.11	−1.71	−4.00	0.041	5.77
FEP2	2.70	0.28	−1.13	−2.75	−3.35	0.039	5.65
CTEF	1.82	0.96	−2.33	−1.00	−4.38	0.037	5.27
EP	3.51	−0.13	−0.95	−1.52	−4.53	0.036	5.32
REG9	2.90	0.27	0.03	−2.94	−1.92	0.035	5.28
XUS Universe							
Factor	1	2	3	4	5	IC	t (IC)
DP	1.66	−7.58	−2.20	−13.96	−9.81	0.041	4.97
CTEF	5.89	1.37	2.40	−5.71	−10.76	0.035	4.71
REG10	2.98	−5.69	−10.66	−4.15	−6.64	0.032	4.59
BR2	5.51	−0.25	−0.41	−0.91	−10.72	0.030	4.25
BR1	3.04	1.30	−1.17	−1.68	−11.59	0.027	4.09
RDP	0.42	1.07	−4.92	−8.62	−9.66	0.026	3.85
GL Universe							
Factor	1	2	3	4	5	IC	t (IC)
REG10	4.50	2.06	5.67	−3.64	−8.03	0.035	6.32
CTEF	4.27	−0.02	1.48	−1.19	−2.07	0.032	6.02
REG9	8.69	−1.57	0.28	−5.55	−4.60	0.029	5.74
FEP1	3.44	1.85	−0.29	0.69	−2.17	0.030	5.85
FEP2	4.23	1.89	0.24	−1.16	−1.05	0.029	5.78
DP	10.53	−5.85	−2.11	3.00	−0.88	0.022	5.06

Source FactSet Research Systems, Inc.
Note Date Range: 12/31/1996 To 2/26/2021

RobStatTM, in R, and CTEF gives investors the best chance in win in terms of stock selection in global portfolio selection.

Given the authors are examining the very large, 5000–5500 stock global stock universe, the question of "investability" must be considered. The authors create XUS and global portfolios over the 2001–2020 time period using an extremely conservative, equally active weighted two percent portfolio construction strategy (EAW2), in which no stock weight can deviate more than two percent from its benchmark weight. In the XUS portfolio, the authors use the MSCI All Country World ex USA benchmark weights. In the global portfolio, the authors use the MSCI All Country World benchmark weights. The authors have reported EAW2 and more traditional Mean-Variance (MV) portfolios, with four percent maximum stock weights in Guerard et al. (2013, 2014, 2019). Quarterly turnover is constrained to 20%. We report the EAW2 portfolio selection here to ensure "investability" across the globe. In Table 9.10, we report portfolios created with targeted tracking errors of two, four, and six percent, respectively. We also report "Donut" portfolios with the Domowitz and Moghe (2018), where the weights of the five largest stocks in the universe must be weighted such that the sum of their portfolio weights cannot deviate by more than two percent of their sum of their benchmark weights. Donuts help ensure an investable portfolio.

The reader sees in Tables 9.10 and 9.11 that the XUS portfolio and Global (GL) Sharpe Ratios and Information rise as targeted tracking errors rise, from two percent to six percent, a result noted in Guerard (2015) and in the higher risk-return "pick parameter" levels of Bloch et al. (1993) and Guerard et al. (1992). There has a risk-return trade-off in US, XUS, and GL stock markets during the past twenty (and 45) years, and true stock-pickers with quantitative stock selection models that are enhanced with smaller-capitalized stocks having positive exposures to medium-term momentum, growth, and value risk factors have outperformed the stock universes on the basis of risk and return. There is still a risk-return trade-off, including COVID! The CTEF portfolios produce over 400 basis points of excess returns, over transactions costs of 150 basis points, each way, in the six percent Donut portfolios, reported in Table 9.10, for the 2001–2020 period. The REG10 portfolios produce in the 224–250 basis point range of excess returns, over transactions costs of 150 basis points, each way, in the six percent targeted tracking error Donut portfolios.

In the global portfolios, the REG9 portfolios produce in the 190–210 basis point range of excess returns, over transactions costs of 150 basis points, each way, in the six percent Donut portfolios.[33] What factors drive factor returns? In the CTEF and REG9 portfolios, earnings yield, value and size premiums enhance portfolio return. The REG9 portfolios produce in the 290–300 basis point range of excess returns, over transactions costs of 150 basis points, each way, in the six percent Donut portfolios. The Russell 3000 stocks create a small-stock concentration in the appended global stock universe. Why would we recommend such a universe? Because we want to earn Active portfolio Returns!

We do not replicate the Markowitz Mean-Variance (1959) optimization with total variance, used in Guerard et al. (1992) and Bloch et al. (1993)

---

[33] The discriminating reader will see the differences in the reported Sharpe Ratios, Information Ratios, and excess returns of the CTEF and REG10 portfolios reported here and those reported in Markowitz et al. (2021). The differences are due to the authors using the Axioma Worldwide 4 model here, with its profitability factor, introduced in 2018, and the Axioma Worldwide 2 model used in Markowitz et al. (2021), as well as using EAW2 versus the MV four percent weighting constraints. Commercially available risk models change, and in the marketplace, these changes may often change the stock selection component of the portfolio active returns.

Table 9.10 Portfolio Dashboard of Non-US Portfokios

Portfolios	Sharpe Ratio	Information Ratio	Risk Stock Specific Effect	Risk Stock Specific Effect T-Stat	Risk Factors Effect	Risk Factors Effect T-Stat	Risk Total Effect	Risk Transaction Effect	Total Effect
XUS_CTEF_QTR_EAW2_2TE	#REF!	#REF!	0.81	1.75	3.03	6.27	3.84	-2.27	1.57
XUS_CTEF_QTR_EAW2_2TE_DONUT	#REF!	#REF!	0.64	1.54	2.96	6.40	3.60	-2.09	1.51
XUS_REG8_QTR_EAW2_2TE	#REF!	#REF!	0.24	0.53	1.16	2.79	1.40	-1.48	-0.08
XUS_REG8_QTR_EAW2_2TE_DONUT	#REF!	#REF!	-0.07	-0.01	1.28	3.01	1.21	-1.40	-0.20
XUS_REG9_QTR_EAW2_2TE	#REF!	#REF!	0.34	0.75	1.70	3.73	2.04	-1.58	0.46
XUS_REG9_QTR_EAW2_2TE_DONUT	#REF!	#REF!	0.12	0.39	1.89	4.04	2.02	-1.57	0.45
XUS_REG10_QTR_EAW2_2TE	0.28	0.22	-0.27	0.21	2.98	5.67	2.71	-1.73	0.98
XUS_REG10_QTR_EAW2_2TE_DONUT	0.28	0.23	-0.45	-0.15	3.14	6.06	2.69	-1.71	0.99
XUS_CTEF_QTR_EAW2_4TE	0.42	0.53	1.50	1.64	5.14	5.68	6.64	-3.26	3.38
XUS_CTEF_QTR_EAW2_4TE_DONUT	0.41	0.53	0.97	1.27	5.56	5.89	6.53	-3.31	3.22
XUS_REG8_QTR_EAW2_4TE	0.39	0.09	1.05	0.84	1.90	3.10	2.94	-1.85	1.09
XUS_REG8_QTR_EAW2_4TE_DONUT	0.28	0.13	0.30	0.26	2.34	3.36	2.64	-1.72	0.92
XUS_REG9_QTR_EAW2_4TE	0.25	0.05	-0.89	-0.50	3.29	3.47	2.40	-2.06	0.34
XUS_REG9_QTR_EAW2_4TE_DONUT	0.23	0.02	-2.29	-0.92	5.49	3.58	3.20	-3.08	0.12
XUS_REG10_QTR_EAW2_4TE	0.29	0.16	-1.91	-0.54	5.13	4.67	3.22	-2.17	1.05
XUS_REG10_QTR_EAW2_4TE_DONUT	0.30	0.20	-2.10	-0.85	5.50	5.22	3.39	-2.15	1.25
XUS_CTEF_QTR_EAW2_6TE	0.52	0.66	1.56	1.73	6.74	6.04	8.30	-3.12	5.18
XUS_CTEF_QTR_EAW2_6TE_DONUT	0.47	0.57	0.37	1.01	7.04	5.82	7.41	-3.12	4.29
XUS_REG8_QTR_EAW2_6TE	0.30	0.13	0.81	0.69	2.17	2.87	2.98	-1.74	1.24
XUS_REG8_QTR_EAW2_6TE_DONUT	0.28	0.11	0.36	0.45	2.39	2.91	2.75	-1.73	1.02
XUS_REG9_QTR_EAW2_6TE	0.34	0.21	0.41	0.63	3.47	3.77	3.88	-1.94	1.94
XUS_REG9_QTR_EAW2_6TE_DONUT	0.34	0.23	0.31	0.54	3.78	4.02	4.09	-2.01	2.08
XUS_REG10_QTR_EAW2_6TE	0.35	0.28	-0.97	0.12	5.64	4.91	4.67	-2.43	2.24
XUS_REG10_QTR_EAW2_6TE_DONUT	0.36	0.33	-1.59	-0.33	6.51	5.44	4.92	-2.50	2.43

Compounded Factor Impact

Portfolios	Dividend Yield	Earnings Yield	Exchange Rate Sensitivity	Growth	Leverage	Liquidity	Market Sensitivity	Medium-Term Momentum
XUS_CTEF_QTR_EAW2_2TE	0.09	0.36	-0.01	0.03	-0.09	-0.05	0.08	1.31
XUS_CTEF_QTR_EAW2_2TE_DONUT	0.09	0.33	-0.01	0.02	-0.08	-0.04	0.09	1.24
XUS_REG8_QTR_EAW2_2TE	0.44	0.58	0.05	-0.08	-0.10	0.02	-1.29	-0.35
XUS_REG8_QTR_EAW2_2TE_DONUT	0.43	0.54	0.06	-0.06	-0.09	0.02	-1.23	-0.30
XUS_REG9_QTR_EAW2_2TE	0.41	0.64	0.01	-0.09	-0.11	0.07	-0.86	-0.43
XUS_REG9_QTR_EAW2_2TE_DONUT	0.32	0.62	0.02	-0.08	-0.10	0.07	-0.84	-0.40
XUS_REG10_QTR_EAW2_2TE	0.31	0.57	-0.02	0.03	-0.03	-0.10	0.04	0.39
XUS_REG10_QTR_EAW2_2TE_DONUT	0.30	0.54	-0.02	0.04	-0.01	-0.09	0.04	0.38
XUS_CTEF_QTR_EAW2_4TE	-0.06	0.56	-0.04	-0.03	-0.11	-0.14	0.05	2.84
XUS_CTEF_QTR_EAW2_4TE_DONUT	-0.10	0.53	-0.04	-0.03	-0.10	-0.14	0.08	2.84
XUS_REG8_QTR_EAW2_4TE	0.73	0.79	-0.01	0.11	-0.11	-0.17	0.20	-2.24
XUS_REG8_QTR_EAW2_4TE_DONUT	0.70	0.72	0.00	0.10	-0.11	-0.14	0.23	-2.10
XUS_REG9_QTR_EAW2_4TE	0.71	1.19	-0.01	0.09	-0.22	-0.21	0.37	-1.60
XUS_REG9_QTR_EAW2_4TE_DONUT	1.10	1.72	0.00	0.17	-0.26	-0.28	0.55	-2.44
XUS_REG10_QTR_EAW2_4TE	0.42	0.79	-0.05	0.02	-0.03	-0.17	0.05	1.17
XUS_REG10_QTR_EAW2_4TE_DONUT	0.40	0.74	-0.04	0.03	0.01	-0.16	0.11	1.13
XUS_CTEF_QTR_EAW2_6TE	-0.18	0.60	-0.04	-0.06	-0.04	-0.17	0.51	3.38
XUS_CTEF_QTR_EAW2_6TE_DONUT	-0.16	0.58	-0.04	-0.08	-0.01	-0.17	0.35	3.29
XUS_REG8_QTR_EAW2_6TE	0.85	0.81	0.01	0.16	-0.23	-0.15	0.47	-2.54
XUS_REG8_QTR_EAW2_6TE_DONUT	0.83	0.77	0.01	0.13	-0.23	-0.13	0.45	-2.46
XUS_REG9_QTR_EAW2_6TE	0.62	1.09	0.02	0.08	-0.22	-0.18	0.57	-1.53
XUS_REG9_QTR_EAW2_6TE_DONUT	0.56	0.96	0.00	0.07	-0.19	-0.16	0.62	-1.38
XUS_REG10_QTR_EAW2_6TE	0.38	0.79	-0.06	-0.05	0.01	-0.17	0.40	1.32
XUS_REG10_QTR_EAW2_6TE_DONUT	0.33	0.72	-0.06	-0.03	0.03	-0.15	0.51	1.26

(continued)

Table 9.10 (continued)

Portfolios	Compounded Factor Impact								
	Profitability	Size	Value	Volatility	Market	Local	Industry	Country	Currency
XUS_CTEF_QTR_EAW2_2TE	-0.30	0.62	0.61	-0.07	0.13	0.07	-0.39	0.34	0.28
XUS_CTEF_QTR_EAW2_2TE_DONUT	-0.28	0.55	0.59	-0.04	0.12	0.06	-0.29	0.34	0.29
XUS_REG8_QTR_EAW2_2TE	0.94	1.90	-0.50	0.07	0.01	-1.18	0.55	0.09	0.10
XUS_REG8_QTR_EAW2_2TE_DONUT	0.88	1.84	-0.44	0.05	0.00	-1.02	0.53	0.08	0.09
XUS_REG9_QTR_EAW2_2TE	0.93	1.87	-0.33	0.12	0.00	-1.17	0.54	0.10	0.10
XUS_REG9_QTR_EAW2_2TE_DONUT	0.89	1.88	-0.30	0.11	0.00	-1.04	0.57	0.09	0.10
XUS_REG10_QTR_EAW2_2TE	-0.46	0.87	1.71	-0.33	0.15	-0.05	-0.73	0.37	0.24
XUS_REG10_QTR_EAW2_2TE_DONUT	-0.42	0.83	1.70	-0.28	0.14	-0.05	-0.60	0.39	0.25
XUS_CTEF_QTR_EAW2_4TE	-0.12	1.14	0.91	-1.43	0.17	0.21	-0.16	0.37	0.98
XUS_CTEF_QTR_EAW2_4TE_DONUT	-0.13	1.07	0.91	-1.27	0.18	0.19	0.33	0.26	0.99
XUS_REG8_QTR_EAW2_4TE	-0.74	1.78	3.46	-2.39	0.03	0.03	-1.83	1.74	0.52
XUS_REG8_QTR_EAW2_4TE_DONUT	-0.74	1.60	3.41	-2.19	0.02	0.03	-1.42	1.72	0.49
XUS_REG9_QTR_EAW2_4TE	-0.91	2.13	3.99	-2.38	-0.03	0.01	-2.03	1.80	0.40
XUS_REG9_QTR_EAW2_4TE_DONUT	-1.38	2.99	6.13	-3.33	-0.06	-0.02	-2.41	2.50	0.51
XUS_REG10_QTR_EAW2_4TE	-0.72	1.77	3.20	-2.07	0.30	-0.04	-1.25	0.69	1.03
XUS_REG10_QTR_EAW2_4TE_DONUT	-0.65	1.60	3.09	-1.81	0.25	-0.06	-0.79	0.68	0.98
XUS_CTEF_QTR_EAW2_6TE	-0.11	1.41	0.92	-1.88	0.15	0.25	0.47	0.09	1.48
XUS_CTEF_QTR_EAW2_6TE_DONUT	-0.16	1.34	1.01	-1.77	0.16	0.24	0.77	0.19	1.48
XUS_REG8_QTR_EAW2_6TE	-1.03	2.22	4.21	-3.35	0.02	0.00	-1.80	1.94	0.57
XUS_REG8_QTR_EAW2_6TE_DONUT	-0.99	2.00	4.24	-3.25	0.00	0.02	-1.44	1.91	0.51
XUS_REG9_QTR_EAW2_6TE	-0.98	2.12	3.88	-2.95	-0.03	0.01	-1.53	2.07	0.45
XUS_REG9_QTR_EAW2_6TE_DONUT	-0.91	1.90	3.76	-2.64	-0.04	-0.02	-1.12	1.87	0.51
XUS_REG10_QTR_EAW2_6TE	-0.74	1.95	3.24	-2.21	0.21	-0.08	-1.13	0.74	1.04
XUS_REG10_QTR_EAW2_6TE_DONUT	-0.75	1.84	3.26	-2.12	0.18	-0.06	-0.56	1.09	1.01

Source FactSet Research Systems, Inc.
Note Time Period: December 2001–December 2021

Table 9.11 Global Portfolio Dashboard, 2001–2021

Portfolios	Sharpe Ratio	Information Ratio	Risk Stock Specific Effect	Risk Stock Specific Effect T-Stat	Risk Factors Effect	Risk Factors Effect T-Stat	Risk Total Effect	Risk Transaction Effect	Total Effect
GL_CTEF_QTR_EAW2_2TE	0.41	0.38	0.40	1.32	3.41	6.06	3.81	−1.96	1.85
GL_CTEF_QTR_EAW2_2TE_DONUT	0.42	0.39	0.48	1.44	3.38	6.18	3.85	−1.96	1.89
GL_REG8_QTR_EAW2_2TE	0.32	0.07	0.48	0.75	1.47	2.89	1.95	−1.58	0.37
GL_REG8_QTR_EAW2_2TE_DONUT	0.33	0.09	0.55	0.83	1.57	3.01	2.12	−1.65	0.47
GL_REG9_QTR_EAW2_2TE	0.35	0.13	0.20	0.60	2.22	3.67	2.42	−1.68	0.74
GL_REG9_QTR_EAW2_2TE_DONUT	0.36	0.16	0.32	0.85	2.25	3.80	2.57	−1.67	0.90
GL_REG10_QTR_EAW2_2TE	0.31	0.02	−4.06	−2.09	7.73	4.86	3.67	−3.57	0.10
GL_REG10_QTR_EAW2_2TE_DONUT	0.33	0.09	−1.69	−1.63	3.90	5.16	2.20	−1.79	0.41
GL_CTEF_QTR_EAW2_4TE	0.49	0.41	1.24	1.45	5.49	4.90	6.73	−3.70	3.03
GL_CTEF_QTR_EAW2_4TE_DONUT	0.50	0.46	1.63	1.76	5.51	5.06	7.15	−3.87	3.28
GL_REG8_QTR_EAW2_4TE	0.32	0.04	−0.38	−0.20	2.34	2.71	1.96	−1.65	0.31
GL_REG8_QTR_EAW2_4TE_DONUT	0.32	0.04	−0.09	−0.04	2.06	2.70	1.97	−1.61	0.36
GL_REG9_QTR_EAW2_4TE	0.36	0.12	−0.37	−0.16	3.25	3.45	2.87	−1.86	1.01
GL_REG9_QTR_EAW2_4TE_DONUT	0.39	0.18	0.34	0.31	2.98	3.61	3.32	−1.84	1.47
GL_REG10_QTR_EAW2_4TE	0.33	0.06	−4.26	−1.75	7.25	4.63	2.99	−2.53	0.46
GL_REG10_QTR_EAW2_4TE_DONUT	0.35	0.11	−2.51	−1.33	5.18	4.73	2.66	−1.85	0.81
GL_CTEF_QTR_EAW2_6TE	0.64	0.57	4.39	3.00	5.66	4.62	10.05	−4.65	5.39
GL_CTEF_QTR_EAW2_6TE_DONUT	0.63	0.59	3.96	2.90	5.57	4.71	9.53	−4.16	5.37
GL_REG8_QTR_EAW2_6TE	0.32	0.03	0.78	0.47	1.14	2.06	1.92	−1.64	0.28
GL_REG8_QTR_EAW2_6TE_DONUT	0.32	0.03	0.52	0.36	1.38	2.16	1.91	−1.62	0.29
GL_REG9_QTR_EAW2_6TE	0.48	0.27	2.58	1.75	2.49	3.21	5.07	−2.18	2.89
GL_REG9_QTR_EAW2_6TE_DONUT	0.49	0.29	2.52	1.72	2.69	3.40	5.21	−2.20	3.00
GL_REG10_QTR_EAW2_6TE	0.40	0.19	−2.21	−0.80	5.95	4.56	3.74	−2.05	1.69
GL_REG10_QTR_EAW2_6TE_DONUT	0.40	0.19	−2.36	−0.80	6.26	4.57	3.90	−2.25	1.65

(continued)

Table 9.11 (continued)

Compounded Factor Impact

Portfolios	Dividend Yield	Earnings Yield	Exchange Rate Sensitivity	Growth	Leverage	Liquidity	Market Sensitivity	Medium-Term Momentum
GL_CTEF_QTR_EAW2_2TE	0.09	0.42	0.00	0.02	-0.02	-0.09	0.09	1.57
GL_CTEF_QTR_EAW2_2TE_DONUT	0.10	0.42	-0.01	0.02	0.00	-0.08	0.08	1.52
GL_REG8_QTR_EAW2_2TE	0.40	0.61	-0.03	0.08	-0.01	-0.11	0.02	-1.63
GL_REG8_QTR_EAW2_2TE_DONUT	0.41	0.62	-0.02	0.07	0.00	-0.11	0.02	-1.68
GL_REG9_QTR_EAW2_2TE	0.33	0.74	0.00	0.05	0.01	-0.13	0.04	-1.19
GL_REG9_QTR_EAW2_2TE_DONUT	0.33	0.73	0.00	0.04	0.02	-0.13	0.03	-1.18
GL_REG10_QTR_EAW2_2TE	0.60	1.48	-0.07	0.15	0.05	-0.27	0.13	1.01
GL_REG10_QTR_EAW2_2TE_DONUT	0.29	0.72	-0.03	0.06	0.05	-0.13	0.05	0.49
GL_CTEF_QTR_EAW2_4TE	-0.06	0.82	0.05	-0.08	-0.13	-0.17	-0.12	3.68
GL_CTEF_QTR_EAW2_4TE_DONUT	-0.07	0.76	0.07	-0.07	-0.10	-0.13	-0.20	3.54
GL_REG8_QTR_EAW2_4TE	0.50	0.97	-0.02	0.13	-0.14	-0.12	0.07	-2.85
GL_REG8_QTR_EAW2_4TE_DONUT	0.48	0.92	-0.02	0.10	-0.11	-0.12	0.05	-2.76
GL_REG9_QTR_EAW2_4TE	0.33	1.12	-0.01	0.18	-0.08	-0.20	0.22	-2.13
GL_REG9_QTR_EAW2_4TE_DONUT	0.31	1.05	-0.01	0.17	-0.06	-0.19	0.22	-2.03
GL_REG10_QTR_EAW2_4TE	0.27	1.23	-0.08	0.00	-0.01	-0.28	0.42	1.74
GL_REG10_QTR_EAW2_4TE_DONUT	0.19	0.87	-0.05	0.01	0.04	-0.21	0.32	1.20
GL_CTEF_QTR_EAW2_6TE	-0.47	0.86	0.12	-0.22	-0.15	-0.16	-0.36	4.83
GL_CTEF_QTR_EAW2_6TE_DONUT	-0.36	0.79	0.09	-0.19	-0.05	-0.11	-0.22	4.41
GL_REG8_QTR_EAW2_6TE	0.62	0.83	0.01	0.15	-0.15	-0.12	0.18	-3.29
GL_REG8_QTR_EAW2_6TE_DONUT	0.66	0.83	0.01	0.13	-0.09	-0.14	0.24	-3.16
GL_REG9_QTR_EAW2_6TE	0.15	1.07	-0.03	0.17	-0.15	-0.22	0.39	-2.13
GL_REG9_QTR_EAW2_6TE_DONUT	0.14	1.04	-0.02	0.15	-0.14	-0.23	0.41	-2.08
GL_REG10_QTR_EAW2_6TE	0.14	0.94	-0.01	-0.06	0.05	-0.21	0.56	1.49
GL_REG10_QTR_EAW2_6TE_DONUT	0.14	1.00	0.01	-0.07	0.05	-0.28	0.60	1.54

Compounded Factor Impact

Portfolios	Profitability	Size	Value	Volatility	Market	Local	Industry	Country	Currency
GL_CTEF_QTR_EAW2_2TE	−0.33	1.32	0.86	−0.65	0.06	0.08	−0.61	0.46	0.14
GL_CTEF_QTR_EAW2_2TE_DONUT	−0.29	1.28	0.83	−0.60	0.06	0.07	−0.61	0.42	0.16
GL_REG8_QTR_EAW2_2TE	−0.57	1.78	2.95	−1.32	0.01	0.00	−1.42	0.63	0.07
GL_REG8_QTR_EAW2_2TE_DONUT	−0.55	1.79	2.97	−1.28	0.01	0.00	−1.44	0.67	0.09
GL_REG9_QTR_EAW2_2TE	−0.63	1.84	2.97	−1.00	0.02	0.00	−1.47	0.53	0.11
GL_REG9_QTR_EAW2_2TE_DONUT	−0.59	1.78	2.90	−0.92	0.02	0.01	−1.45	0.54	0.12
GL_REG10_QTR_EAW2_2TE	−1.32	3.72	5.70	−1.96	0.16	−0.09	−2.81	0.96	0.28
GL_REG10_QTR_EAW2_2TE_DONUT	−0.61	1.78	2.75	−0.88	0.08	−0.04	−1.33	0.49	0.17
GL_CTEF_QTR_EAW2_4TE	−0.48	2.83	1.61	−2.89	0.10	0.11	−0.96	0.73	0.45
GL_CTEF_QTR_EAW2_4TE_DONUT	−0.42	2.67	1.52	−2.73	0.09	0.10	−0.81	0.77	0.53
GL_REG8_QTR_EAW2_4TE	−0.96	3.19	5.25	−4.09	−0.03	−0.01	−1.30	1.29	0.45
GL_REG8_QTR_EAW2_4TE_DONUT	−0.89	2.93	4.97	−3.89	−0.04	0.00	−1.39	1.34	0.46
GL_REG9_QTR_EAW2_4TE	−0.92	3.12	4.93	−3.32	−0.06	−0.01	−1.48	1.23	0.33
GL_REG9_QTR_EAW2_4TE_DONUT	−0.84	2.86	4.56	−3.21	−0.06	0.00	−1.45	1.27	0.40
GL_REG10_QTR_EAW2_4TE	−1.10	3.89	5.66	−3.98	0.15	−0.07	−2.21	0.75	0.86
GL_REG10_QTR_EAW2_4TE_DONUT	−0.74	2.67	4.01	−2.79	0.10	−0.05	−1.60	0.56	0.65
GL_CTEF_QTR_EAW2_6TE	−0.43	3.24	1.66	−4.52	−0.02	0.12	−0.88	1.01	1.02
GL_CTEF_QTR_EAW2_6TE_DONUT	−0.32	2.80	1.50	−3.91	0.02	0.15	−0.90	0.88	0.99
GL_REG8_QTR_EAW2_6TE	−1.04	3.68	6.21	−5.97	−0.02	0.02	−1.87	1.38	0.51
GL_REG8_QTR_EAW2_6TE_DONUT	−1.04	3.48	6.02	−5.58	−0.03	0.02	−1.95	1.51	0.51
GL_REG9_QTR_EAW2_6TE	−0.94	3.39	5.14	−4.67	−0.06	−0.01	−1.52	1.41	0.52
GL_REG9_QTR_EAW2_6TE_DONUT	−0.91	3.21	5.00	−4.46	−0.06	−0.01	−1.46	1.62	0.48
GL_REG10_QTR_EAW2_6TE	−0.71	3.12	4.48	−3.84	0.05	−0.05	−1.45	0.88	0.57
GL_REG10_QTR_EAW2_6TE_DONUT	−0.69	3.15	4.64	−3.95	0.05	−0.04	−1.53	1.06	0.58

Source FactSEt Research Systems, Inc.

in this analysis. Markowitz (2021) reported those results. The Markowitz MV optimization is a very difficult benchmark to dominate for portfolio construction. We report an EAW2 portfolio construction analysis with the expectations of generating significant active returns in a very large investable global portfolio over the next 2–15 years.

9.4   Summary and Conclusions

In this chapter we surveyed 70 years of portfolio selection through the works of Nobel Prize laureates James Tobin, Harry Markowitz, and William Sharpe. We reported the effectiveness of stock selection modeling in creating expected returns models for portfolio selection during the 1974–1990, 1998–2018, and 2001–2020 time periods. We reproduced how fundamental variables and earnings forecasting models continue to produce statistically significant asset selection in domestic and global stocks, 2003–11/2018. Regression models of fundamental factors and earnings forecasting factors continue to enhance portfolio returns. Momentum enhances portfolio returns primarily in non-U.S. equity markets. We report that the Markowitz mean-variance optimization is particularly efficient for producing efficient frontiers using a forecasted earnings acceleration model, CTEF, and a composite, robust regression based ten-factor model, REG10. Have markets and stock selection models changed since Bloch (1993) and Guerard and Mark (2003) published their studies? No. CTEF, REG9, and REG10 still dominate most other models. The risk models have changed evolved during the 1993–2018 period; the Axioma model has been introduced and Barra evolved and APT was sold to Sungard. The authors believe that financial anomalies exist and persist. Have the financial anomalies persisted through COVID? Yes, they have through December 2020. We report most of our results produced by the FactSet Research Systems, Inc., platform. Are markets efficient? No, not completely, but significant databases and computers are required to outperform.

References

Andrews, D. F., Bickel, P. J., Hampel, F. R., Huber, P. J., Rogers, W. H., & Tukey, J. W. (1972). *Robust estimates of location.* Princeton University Press.
Arditti, F. D. (1967). Risk and return and the required return on equity. *Journal of Finance, 21,* 19–37.

Arditti, F. D., & Levy, H. (1975). Portfolio efficiency analysis in three moments: The multiperiod case. *Journal of Finance*. American Finance Association.

Asness, C., Moskowitz, T., & Pedersen, L. (2013). Value and momentum everywhere. *Journal of Finance, 68*, 929–985.

Ball, R. T., & Ghysels, E. (2018). Automated earnings forecasts: Beat analysts or combine and conquer? *Management Science*.

Barillas, F., & Shanken, J. (2018). Comparing asset pricing models. *Journal of Finance, 73*, 715–755.

Bartram, S., & Grinblatt, M. (2021). Global market inefficiencies. *Journal of Financial Economics, 139*(1), 234–259.

Basu, S. (1977). Investment performance of common stocks in relation to their price earnings ratios: A test of market efficiency. *Journal of Finance, 32*, 663–682.

Baumol, W. J. (1963). An expected gain-confidence limit criteria for portfolio selection. *Management Science, 10*, 174–182.

Beheshti, B. (2015). A note on the integration of the alpha alignment factor and earnings forecasting models in producing more efficient Markowitz frontiers. *International Journal of Forecasting, 31*, 582–585.

Beaton, A. E., & Tukey, J. W. (1974). The Fitting of power series, meaning polynomials, illustrated on bank-spectroscopic data. *Technometrics, 16*, 147–185.

Belsley, D. A., Kuh, E., & Welsch, R. E. (1980). *Regression diagnostics: Identifying influential data and sources of collinearity*. Wiley.

Black, F., Jensen, M., & Scholes, M. S. (1972). The capital asset pricing model: Some empirical findings. In M. Jensen (Ed.), *Studies in the theory of capital markets*. Praeger Publishers.

Blin, J. M., Bender, S., & Guerard, J. B., Jr. (1997). Earnings forecasts, revisions and momentum in the Estimation of efficient market-neutral Japanese and U.S. portfolios. In A. Chen (Ed.), *Research in Finance* (Vol. 15).

Blin, J. M., Guerard, J. B., Jr., & Mark, A. (2021, March). The risks you know—and those you don't. *Wilmott* (112), 16–37.

Bloch, M., Guerard, J. B., Jr., Markowitz, H. M., Todd, P., & Xu, G.-L. (1993). A comparison of some aspects of the U.S. and Japanese equity markets. *Japan and the World Economy, 5*, 3–26.

Bloch, M., Guerard, J. B., Jr., Markowitz, H. M., Todd, P., & Xu, G.-L. (1993). A comparison of some aspects of the U.S. and Japanese equity markets. *Japan and the World Economy, 5*, 3–26.

Borkovec, M., Domowitz, I., Kiernan, B., & Serbin, V. (2010). Portfolio optimization and the cost of trading. *Journal of Investing, 19*, 63–76.

Brennan, T. J., & Lo, A. (2010). Impossible frontiers. *Management Science, 56*, 905–923.

Brown, L. D. (2000). *Annotated bibliography. I/B/E/S/*. New York.

Brush, J. (2001). *Price momentum: A twenty-year research effort*. Columbine Newsletter.

Bruce, B., & Epstein, C. B. (1994). *The handbook of corporate earnings analysis*. Probus Publishing Company.

Chan, L. K. C., Hamao, Y., & Lakonishok, J. (1991). Fundamentals and stock returns in Japan. *Journal of Finance, 46*, 1739–1764.

Chu, Y., Hirschleifer, D., & Ma, L. (2017). *The casual effect of limits on arbitrage on asset pricing models* (NBER Working Paper 24144). http://www.nber.org/papers/w24144

Conrad, J., & Kaul, G. (1989). Mean reversion in short-horizon expected returns. *Review of Financial Studies, 2*, 225–240.

Conrad, J., & Kaul, G. (1993). Long-term market overreaction or biases in compound returns. *Journal of Finance, 59*, 39–63.

Conrad, J., & Kaul, G. (1998). An anatomy of trading strategies. *Review of Financial Studies, 11*, 489–519.

Connor, G., Goldberg, L., & Korajczyk, R. A. (2010). *Portfolio risk analysis*. Princeton University Press.

Cootner, P. (1964). *The random character of stock market prices*. MIT Press.

Cragg, J. G., & Malkiel, B. G. (1968). The consensus and accuracy of some predictions of the growth of corporate earnings. *Journal of Finance*. American Finance Association.

De Bondt, W. F. M., & Thaler, R. H. (1989). Anomalies: A mean-reverting walk down wall street. *Journal of Economic Perspectives*.

Dimson, E. (1988). *Stock market anomalies*. Cambridge University Press.

Domowitz, I., & Moghe, A. (2018). Donuts: A picture of optimization applied to fundamental portfolios. *Journal of Portfolio Management, 44*, 103–113.

Elton, E., & Gruber, M. J. (1972a). Earnings estimates and the accuracy of expectational data. *Management Science, 18*, B-367–B-481.

Elton, E. J., & Gruber, M. J. (1972b). *Security analysis and portfolio analysis*. Prentice-Hall Inc.

Elton, E. J., & Gruber, M. J. (1980). *Modern portfolio theory and investment analysis*. Wiley.

Elton, E. J., Gruber, M. J., & Gultekin, M. (1981). Expectations and share prices. *Management Science, 27*, 975–987.

Elton, E. J., Gruber, M. J., Brown, S. J., & Goetzman, W.N. (2007). *Modern portfolio theory and investment analysis* (7th ed.). Wiley.

Fama, E. F. (1965). Portfolio analysis in a stable Paretian Market. *Management Science, 11*, 404–419.

Fama, E. F. (1976). *Foundations of finance*. Basis Books.

Fama, E. F. (1991). Efficient capital markets II. *Journal of Finance, 46*, 1575–1617.

Fama, E. F., & French, K. R. (1992). Cross-sectional variation in expected stock returns. *Journal of Finance, 47*, 427–465.

Fama, E. F., & French, K. R. (2008). Dissecting anomalies. *Journal of Finance, 63*, 1653–1678.

Farrell, J. L., Jr. (1974). Analyzing covariance of returns to determine homogeneous stock groupings. *Journal of Business, 47*, 186–207.

Farrell, J. L., Jr. (1997). *Portfolio management: Theory and applications*. McGraw-Hill/Irwin.

Grinold, R., & Kahn, R. (1999). *Active portfolio management*. McGraw-Hill/Irwin.

Graham, B., & Dodd, D. (1934). *Security analysis: Principles and technique* (1st ed.). McGraw-Hill Book Company.

Graham, B., Dodd, D., & Cottle, S. (1962). *Security analysis: Principles and technique* (4th ed.). McGraw-Hill Book Company.

Graham, B. (1973). *The intelligent investor*. Harper & Row.

Guerard, J. B., Jr., Gultekin, M., & Stone, B. K. (1997). The role of fundamental data and analysts' earnings breadth, forecasts, and revisions in the creation of efficient portfolios. In A. Chen (Ed.), *Research in finance* (Vol. 15).

Guerard, J. B., Jr., & Mark, A. (2003). The optimization of efficient portfolios: The case for an r&d quadratic term. In A. Chen (Ed.), *Research in finance* 20.

Guerard, J., & Mark, A. (2020). Earnings forecasts and revisions, price momentum, and fundamental data: Further explorations of financial anomalies. *Handbook of Financial Econometrics, Mathematics, Statistics, and Machine Learning*.

Guerard, J. B., Jr., & Mark, A. (2020). Earnings forecasts and revisions, price momentum, and fundamental data: Further explorations of financial anomalies. In C. F. Lee (Ed.), *Handbook of financial econometrics*. World Scientific Handbook in Financial Economics.

Guerard, J. B., Jr., & Markowitz, H. M. (2018). The existence and persistence of financial anomalies: What have you done for me lately? *Financial Planning Review*. https://doi.org/10.1002/cfp2.1022

Guerard, J. B., Jr., Markowitz, H. M., & Xu, G.-L. (2013). Global stock selection modeling and efficient portfolio construction and management. *Journal of Investing, 22*(2013), 121–128.

Guerard, J. B., Jr., Markowitz, H. M., & Xu, G. (2014). The role of effective corporate decisions in the creation of efficient portfolios. *IBM Journal of Research and Development, 58*(4), Paper 11.

Guerard, J. B., Jr., Markowitz, H. M., & Xu, G. (2015). Earnings forecasting in a global stock selection model and efficient portfolio construction and management. *International Journal of Forecasting, 31*, 550–560.

Guerard, J. B., Jr., Rachev, R. T., & Shao, B. (2013). Efficient global portfolios: Big data and investment universes. *IBM Journal of Research and Development, 57*(5), Paper 11.

Guerard, J. B., Jr., & Stone, B. K. (1992). Composite forecasting of annual corporate earnings. In A. Chen (Ed.), *Research in finance* (Vol. 10).

Guerard, J., & Takano, M., Yamane, Y. (1993). The development of efficient portfolios in Japan with particular emphasis on sales and earnings forecasting. *Annals of Operations Research*.

Guerard, J. B., Jr., Xu, G., & Markowitz, H. M. (2021). A further analysis of robust regression modeling and data mining corrections testing in global stocks. *Annals of Operations Research, 303*(2021), 175–195

Gunst, R. F., Webster, J. T., & Mason, R. L. (1976). A comparison of least squares and latent root regression estimators. *Technometrics, 18*, 75–83.

Hampel, F. R. (1971). A general qualitative definition of robustness. *Annals of Mathematical Statistics, 42,* 1887–1896.

Harvey, C. R., Lin, Y., & Zhu, H. (2016). …the cross-section of expected returns. *Review of Financial Studies, 291,* 5–69.

Haugen, R. A., & Baker, N. (1996). Communality in the determinants of expected results. *Journal of Financial Economics, 41,* 401–440.

Haugen, R. A., & Baker, N. (2010). Case closed. In J. B. Guerard (Ed.), *The Handbook of portfolio construction: Contemporary applications of Markowitz techniques.* Springer.

Hawkins, E. H., Chamberlain, S. C., & Daniel, W. E. (1984). Earnings expectations and security prices. *Financial Analysts Journal, 405,* 24–38.

Hirshleifer, D. S. (2001). Investor psychology and asset pricing. *Journal of Finance, 64,* 1533–1597.

Hirschleifer, D. S. (2014). Behavioral finance. *Annual Review of Economics, 7,* Submitted. https://doi.org/10.1146/annurev-financial-092214-043752

Hochbaum, D. S. (2018, October 19). Machine learning and data mining with combinatorial optimization algorithms. *INFORMS TutOrials in Operations Research,* 109–129.

Hirschleifer, D., Hon, K., & Teoh, S. H. (2012). The accrual anomaly: Risk or mispricing? *Management Science, 57,* 1–16.

Hong, H., Kubik, J. D., & Solomon, A. (2000). Security analysts' career concerns and the herding of earnings forecasts. *Rand Journal of Economics, 31,* 121–144.

Hong, H., & Kubik, J. D. (2003). Analyzing the analysts: Career concerns and biased earnings Forecasts. *Journal of Finance, 58,* 313–351.

Huber, P. (1981). *Robust statistics.* Wiley.

ITG. (2007). *ITG ACE – Agency cost estimator: A model description.*

Jacobs, B. I., & Levy, K. (1988). Disentangling equity return regularities: New insights and investment opportunities. *Financial Analysts Journal, 44,* 18–43.

Jacobs, B. I., & Levy, K. (2017). *Equity management: The art and science of modern quantitative investing* (2nd ed.). McGraw-Hill.

Jagadeesh, N., & Titman, S. (1993). Returns to buying winners and selling losers: Implications for stock market efficiency. *Journal of Finance, 48,* 65–91.

Kim, H. K., & Swanson, N. R. (2018). Mining big data using parsimonious factor, machine learning, variable selection, and shrinkage methods. *International Journal of Forecasting, 34,* 339–434.

Konno, H., & Yamazaki, H. (1991). Mean—Absolute deviation portfolio optimization and its application to the Toyko stock market. *Management Science, 37,* 519–537.

Korajczyk, R. A., & Sadka, R. (2004). Are momentum profits robust to trading costs? *Journal of Finance, 59,* 1039–1082.

Kuhn, M., & Johnson, K. (2013). *Applied predictive modeling.* Springer.

Lakonishok, J., Shleifer, A., & Vishny, R. W. (1994). Contrarian investment, extrapolation and risk. *Journal of Finance, 49,* 1541–1578.

Latane, H. A. (1959). Criteria for choice among risky ventures. *Journal of Political Economy, 67*, 144–155.

Latane, H. A., & Jones, C. P. (1977). Standardized unexpected earnings—A progress report. *Journal of Finance, 32*, 1457–1465.

Latane, H. A., Tuttle, D., & Jones, C. P. (1975). *Security analysis and portfolio management*. Ronald Press.

Leamer, E. E. (1973). Multicollinearity: A Bayesian interpretation. *Review of Economics and Statistics., 1973*(55), 371–380.

Leamer, E. E. (1978). *Specification searches: Ad hoc inference with nonexperimental data*. Wiley.

Levy, H. (1999). *Introduction to investments* (2nd ed.). South-Western College Publishing.

Levy, H., & Duchin, R. (2010). Markowitz's mean-variance rule and the Talmudic diversification recommendation. In J. B. Guerard (Ed.), *The handbook of portfolio construction: Contemporary applications of Markowitz techniques*. Springer.

Levy, H. (2012). *The capital asset pricing model in the 21st century*. Cambridge University Press.

Levy, H., & Markowitz, H. M. (1979). Approximating expected utility by a function of mean and variance. *The American Economic Review*.

Lintner, J. (1965). The valuation of risk assets and the selection of risky investments in stock portfolios and capital budgets. *Review of Economics and Statistics, 47*, 51–68.

Lo, A. W., Mamaysky, H., & Wang, J. (2000). Foundations of technical analysis: Computational algorithms, statistical inference, and empirical implementation. *Journal of Finance, 60*(2000), 1705–1764.

Lo, A. (2017). *Adaptive markets*. Princeton University Press.

Malkiel, B. (1996). *A random walk down wall street* (6th ed.). W. W. Norton.

Markowitz, H. M. (1952). Portfolio selection. *Journal of Finance, 7*, 77–91.

Markowitz, H. M. (1959). *Portfolio selection: Efficient diversification of investment*. Cowles Foundation Monograph No.16. Wiley.

Markowitz, H. (1987). *Mean-variance analysis in portfolio choice and capital markets*. Basil Blackwell.

Markowitz, H. M. (1976). Investment in the long run: New evidence for an old rule. *Journal of Finance, 31*, 1273–1286.

Markowitz, H. M. (1991). Foundations of Portfolio theory. *The Journal of Finance*.

Markowitz, H. M., Guerard, J. B., Jr., Xu, G., & Bijan, B. (2021). Financial anomalies in portfolio construction and management. *Journal of Portfolio Management, 47*(6), 51–64.

Markowitz, H. M., & Xu, G. (1994). Data mining corrections. *Journal of Portfolio Management, 21*, 60–69.

Maronna, R. A., Martin, R. D., Yohai, V. J., & Salibian-Barrera, M. (2019). *Robust statistics; Theory and methods (with R)*. Wiley.

Maronna, R. A., Martin, R. D., & Yojai, V. J. (2006). *Robust statistics: Theory and methods*. Wiley.

Martin, A. D., Jr. (1955). Mathematical programming of portfolio selections. *Mabagement Science, 1*, 152–166.

Menchero, J., Morozov, A., & Shepard, P. (2010). Global equity modeling. In J. B. Guerard (Ed.), *The handbook of portfolio construction: Contemporary applications of Markowitz techniques.* Springer.

Miller, W., Xu, G., & Guerard, J. B., Jr. (2014). Portfolio construction and management in the BARRA aegis system: A case study using the user Data. *Journal of Investing, 23*, 111–120.

Mossin, J. (1966). Equilibrium in a capital asset market. *Econometrica, 34*, 768–783.

Mueller, P. (1993). Empirical tests of biases in equity portfolio optimization. In S. A. Zenios (Ed.), *Financial optimization.* Cambridge University Press.

Ramnath, S., Rock, S., & Shane, P. (2008). The financial analyst forecasting literature: A taxonomy with suggestions for further research. *International Journal of Forecasting, 24*, 34–75.

Rosenberg, B. (1974). Extra-market components of covariance in security returns. *Journal of Financial and Quantitative Analysis, 9*, 263–274.

Rosenberg, B., Hoaglet, M., Marathe, V., & McKibben, W. (1975). *Components of covariance in security returns* (Working paper no. 13, Research Program in Finance). Institute of Business and Economic Research, University of California. Berkeley.

Rosenberg, B., & Marathe, V. (1979). Tests of capital asset pricing hypotheses. In H. Levy (Ed.), *Research in finance* (Vol. 1).

Rosenberg, B., & McKibben, W. (1973). The reduction of systematic and specific risk in common stocks. *Journal of Financial and Quantitative Analysis, 8*, 317–333.

Ross, S. A. (1976). The arbitrage theory of capital asset pricing. *Journal of Economic Theory, 13*, 341–360.

Roll, R. (1969). Bias in fitting the sharpe model to time series data. *The Journal of Financial and Quantitative.*

Roll, R. (1977). A crtique of the asset pricing theory's tests. Part I: On pat and potential testability of the theory. *Journal of Financial Economics.*

Ross, S. A., & Roll, R. (1980). An empirical investigation of the arbitrage pricing theory. *Journal of Finance, 352*, 1071–1103.

Rousseeuw, P. J. (in press). Multivariate estimation with high. Breakdown Point. In Proceedings of the fourth Pannonian symposium on mathematical statistics and probability, Bad Tatzmanns-dorf, Austria, September 4–9, 1983.

Rudd, A., & Rosenberg, B. (1979). Realistic portfolio optimization. In E. Elton & M. J. Gruber (Eds.), *Portfolio theory, 25 years after.* North-Holland.

Rudd, A., & Rosenberg, B. (1980). The 'Market Model' in investment management. *Journal of Finance, 35*, 597–607.

Rudd, A., & Clasing, H. K. (1982). *Modern portfolio theory: The principles of investment management.* Dow-Jones Irwin.

Sharpe, W. F. (1963). A simplified model for portfolio analysis. *Management Science, 9*, 277–293.

Sharpe, W. F. (1964). Capital asset prices: A theory of market equilibrium under conditions of risk. *Journal of Finance, 19*, 425–442.

Sharpe, W. F. (1971). Mean-absolute deviation characteristic lines for securities and portfolios. A simplified model for portfolio analysis. *Management Science, 18*, B1–B13.

Sharpe, W. F. (2012). *William F. Sharpe: Selected works*. World Scientific Publishing Company.

Stone, B. K., & Guerard, J. B., Jr. (2010). Methodologies for isolating and assessing the portfolio performance potential of stock market return forecast models with an illustration. In J. B. Guerard (Ed.), *The handbook of portfolio construction: Contemporary applications of Markowitz techniques*. Springer.

Stone, B. K., Guerard, J. B., Jr., Gultekin, M., & Adams, G. (2002). *Socially responsible investment screening* (Working Paper). Marriott Scholl of Management, Brigham Young University.

Wheeler, L. B. (1994). Changes in consensus earnings estimates and their impact on stock returns. In B. Bruce & C. B. Epstein (Eds.), *The handbook of corporate earnings analysis*. Probus.

Womack, K. L. (1996). Do brokerage analysts' recommendations have investment value? *Journal of Finance, 51*, 137–167.

Young, W. E., & Trent, R. (1969). Mathematics. *Journal of Financial and Quantitative Analysis*. Published 1 June.

Ziemba, W. T., & Schwartz, S. L. (1993). *The Japanese futures, options, and warrants markets*. Probus Chicago.

10

Testing and Forecasting the Unemployment Rate with the Most Current Data, TCB LEI, Data as of 11/05/2021

In this chapter we examine, in the context of a data-specific case study, the automatic time series approach to modeling and forecasting time series. The author asked his (good) friends and former colleagues of Victor Zarnowitz at The Conference Board for an updated version of the TCB LEI database. We specifically wanted to re-estimate the regression and time series models with the addition of U.S. data in the first 11 months of 2021. Will the reader see notable differences in the model estimates? Are the LEI and Weekly Unemployment time series still statistically significant in the SAS regression analysis in modeling the U.S. unemployment rate? Are the regression outliers of 2020 found in the 1959–11/2020 database still the regression outliers of the 1959–11/2021 period? Are the LEI and Weekly Unemployment time series still statistically significant in the OxMetrics time series modeling analysis of the U.S. unemployment rate? Do we still find statistically significant impulse indicator response (IIS), differenced impulse indicator response (DIIS) and trend impulse indicator response (TIS) saturation variables? A very quick answer to these questions is "Yes."

Let us re-estimate SAS OLS and robust regression models using the updated, TCB LEI database as of November 5, 2021. We use the unemployment, UER, rate of persons unemployed 15 weeks and over, as modeled in Dhrymes (2017) with the TCB database. We refer to the Dhrymes (PJD) analysis of the unemployment rate. We discussed the potential difference in the traditional unemployment rate and the 15-week unemployment rate analyses in Chapter 5 with Mr. Moore. We estimate an unemployment rate

© The Author(s), under exclusive license to Springer Nature
Switzerland AG 2022
J. B. Guerard, *The Leading Economic Indicators and Business Cycles in the United States*, https://doi.org/10.1007/978-3-030-99418-1_10

regression model first using the LEI variable. We DLOG the variables and estimate an OLS regression with a one-period lag in the transformed LEI variable, denoted DLLEIL1. We estimate an unemployment rate regression model second using the WkUNCL variable. We DLOG the variables and estimate an OLS regression with a one-period lag in the transformed variable, denoted WkUNCLL1.

10.1 OLS Modeling of the PJD Unemployment Rate, TCB LEI 11052021 in 1959–11/2021

Let us estimate SAS OLS and robust regression models using the TCB LEI database as of November 5, 2021. We estimate an OLS regression with a one-period lag in the transformed LEI and WkUNCL variables, in simple linear regressions and multiple regressions. The regressions of DUE are expected to produce negative and statistically significant coefficients on DLLEIL1 variable and positive and statistically significant coefficients on the WkUNCLL1 variable.

Let us start with the estimation of the full period, 1/1959–11/2021 PJD UER, LEI, and WkUNCL correlation matrix. The correlation coefficients of the UER and LEI (G0M910) is positive, rather than negative, as expected. The correlation coefficients of the UER and WkUNCL (A0M005) are positive, as expected.

PJD UER (A0M044) and the LEI (G0M910)
The CORR Procedure
3 Variables: G0M910 A0M005 A0M044

Simple statistics

Variable	N	Mean	Std dev	Sum	Minimum	Maximum
G0M910	753	70.54090	22.82135	53,117	28.20000	117.50000
A0M005	753	360.68021	211.21179	271,592	179.90000	4181
A0M044	753	1.96069	1.12487	1476	0.40000	5.90000

Pearson correlation coefficients, $N = 753$
Prob > |r| under H0: Rho = 0

	G0M910	A0M005	A0M044
G0M910	1.00000	0.11116	0.24387
		0.0023	<0.0001

Pearson correlation coefficients, $N = 753$
Prob $> |r|$ under H0: Rho $= 0$

	G0M910	A0M005	A0M044
A0M005	0.11116	1.00000	0.26133
	0.0023		<0.0001
A0M044	0.24387	0.26133	1.00000
	<0.0001	<0.0001	

Palgrave DUE DLLEI DLWkUNCL PJD 110521
The CORR Procedure
Variables: A0M044 G0M910 A0M005

Simple statistics

Variable	N	Mean	Std dev	Sum	Minimum	Maximum
A0M044	753	1.96069	1.12487	1476	0.40000	5.90000
G0M910	753	70.54090	22.82135	53,117	28.20000	117.50000
A0M005	753	360.68021	211.21179	271,592	179.90000	4181

Pearson correlation coefficients, $N = 753$
Prob $> |r|$ under H0: Rho $= 0$

	A0M044	G0M910	A0M005
A0M044	1.00000	0.24387	0.26133
		<0.0001	<0.0001
G0M910		1.00000	0.11116
	<0.0001		<0.0023
A0M005	0.26133	0.11116	1.00000
	<0.0001	<0.0023	

Palgrave **DUE DLLEI DLWkUNCL PJD 110521**
The CORR Procedure
Variables: DUE DLLEI DLWkUNCL

Simple statistics

Variable	N	Mean	Std dev	Sum	Minimum	Maximum
DUE	752	0.0002660	0.16039	0.20000	−0.80000	3.00000
DLLEI	752	0.00190	0.00809	1.42712	−0.07900	0.03052
DLWkUNCL	752	0.0002111	0.11147	0.15875	−0.60267	2.52262

Pearson correlation coefficients, N = 752
Prob > |r| under H0: Rho = 0

	DUE	DLLEI	DLWkUNCL
DUE	1.00000	−0.03275	−0.03261
		0.3699	0.3719
DLLEI	−0.03275	1.00000	−0.63304
			<0.0001
DLWkUNCL	−0.03261	−0.63304	1.00000
	0.3719	<0.0001	

Is the LEI still statistically significant in the regression analysis in modeling the U.S. unemployment rate? Yes, logged first-difference of the LEI (DLLEI) variable has a negative as expected, coefficient, −0.649. The coefficient is not statistically significant, having an estimated t-statistic of only −0.90.

Palgrave DUE DLLEIL PJD 110521
The REG Procedure
Model: MODEL1
Dependent Variables: DUE

Number of observations read	753
Number of observations used	752
Number of observations with missing values	1

Analysis of variance

Source	DF	Sum of squares	Mean square	F value	Pr > F
Model	1	0.02072	0.02072	0.81	0.3699
Error	750	19.29923	0.02573		
Corrected Total	751	19.31995			

Root MSE	0.16041	R-square	0.0011
Dependent mean	0.00026596	Adj R-square	−0.0003
Coeff var	60,315		

Parameter estimates

Variable	DF	Parameter estimate	Standard error	t value	Pr > |t|
Intercept	1	0.00150	0.00601	0.25	0.8032
DLLEI	1	−0.64930	0.72364	−0.90	0.3699

We are interested in the lagged DLLEI relation in this chapter. We want to test if the DLLEIL1 variable leads the DUE variable.

Palgrave DUE DLLEIL1 PJD 110521
The REG Procedure
Model: MODEL1
Dependent Variables: DUE

Number of observations read	753
Number of observations used	751
Number of observations with missing values	2

Analysis of variance

Source	DF	Sum of squares	Mean square	F value	Pr > F
Model	1	0.06542	0.06542	2.55	0.1107
Error	749	19.21437	0.02565		
Corrected Total	750	19.27979			

Root MSE	0.16017	**R-square**	0.0034
Dependent mean	0.00053262	**Adj R-square**	0.0021
Coeff var	30,071		

Parameter estimates

Variable	DF	Parameter estimate	Standard error	t value	Pr > |t|
Intercept	1	0.00272	0.00600	0.45	0.6503
DLLEIL1	1	−1.15381	0.72253	−1.60	0.1107

Is the LEI still statistically significant in the OLS regression analysis in modeling the U.S. unemployment rate? No, the logged first-difference of the LEI (DLLEI) variable with a one-month lag (DLLEIL1) is negatively, but not statistically associated, at the 10% level, with the change (DUE) in the unemployment rate, with an estimated t-statistic of −1.60 in the ordinary least square regression. The OLS estimated DLLEIL1 coefficient is negative, −1.154, and statistically significant at the 11% level. However, we must identify influential observations and use robust regression techniques to fit outliers, if appropriate. The SAS regression diagnostics of the DUE and DLLEIL1 simple linear regression model indicates with the large residuals, studentized regression residuals, RStudent, and Cook's D measures that OLS analysis is not sufficient, and we should proceed to estimate a robust regression line for the DUE and DLLEIL1 variables.

Palgrave DUE DLLEIL1 PJD 110521
The REG Procedure
Model: MODEL1
Dependent Variable: DUE

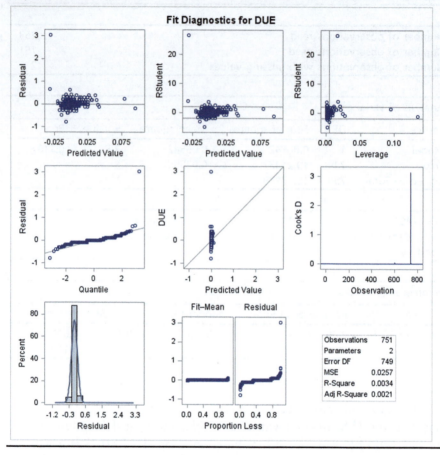

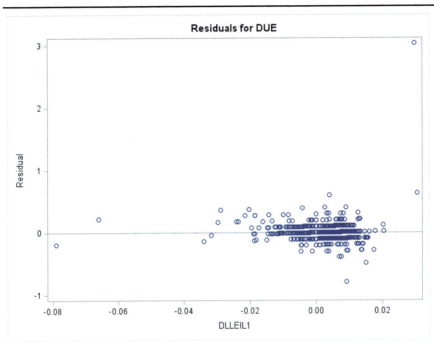

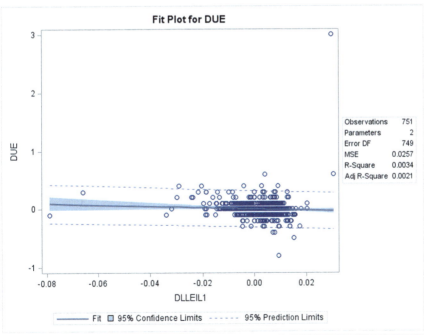

We should proceed to use the additional Belsley, Kuh, and Welsch (1980) regression diagnostics that we used in Chapter 7 to identify influential observations and potential outliers. We report the RStudent, cov ratio, DFFITS, and DFBETAS discussed in Chapter 7.

The REG Procedure
Model: MODEL1
Dependent Variable: DUE

Output statistics

Obs	Residual	RStudent	Hat diag H	Cov ratio	DFFITS	DFBETAS	
						Intercept	DLLEIL1
1	–	–	–	–	–	–	–
2	–	–	–	–	–	–	–
3	−0.0905	−0.5657	0.0029	1.0047	−0.0303	−0.0151	−0.0222
4	−0.2827	−1.7728	0.0062	1.0005	−0.1402	−0.0348	−0.1243
5	−0.0988	−0.6167	0.0014	1.0030	−0.0229	−0.0209	−0.0043
6	0.005180	0.0324	0.0018	1.0045	0.0014	0.0010	0.0007
7	−0.0988	−0.6170	0.0014	1.0030	−0.0229	−0.0210	−0.0042
8	0.001195	0.007463	0.0014	1.0041	0.0003	0.0003	0.0001
9	−0.006640	−0.0415	0.0019	1.0046	−0.0018	−0.0017	0.0010
10	−0.002723	−0.0170	0.0014	1.0041	−0.0006	−0.0006	0.0001
11	0.0933	0.5831	0.0019	1.0037	0.0255	0.0239	−0.0140
12	−0.1106	−0.6914	0.0029	1.0043	−0.0372	−0.0308	0.0273
13	0.0208	0.1305	0.0083	1.0110	0.0119	0.0022	0.0109
14	−0.0988	−0.6173	0.0014	1.0030	−0.0229	−0.0210	−0.0041
15	0.1973	1.2330	0.0014	1.0000	0.0462	0.0462	−0.0106
16	−0.1105	−0.6906	0.0028	1.0043	−0.0369	−0.0307	0.0269
17	−0.1988	−1.2427	0.0014	0.9999	−0.0461	−0.0423	−0.0083
18	0.0973	0.6075	0.0014	1.0031	0.0228	0.0228	−0.0052
19	0.1012	0.6317	0.0014	1.0030	0.0234	0.0215	0.0042
20	−0.002723	−0.0170	0.0014	1.0041	−0.0006	−0.0006	0.0001
21	0.1011	0.6317	0.0014	1.0030	0.0234	0.0215	0.0041
22	0.3011	1.8846	0.0014	0.9946	0.0699	0.0642	0.0123
23	−0.002723	−0.0170	0.0014	1.0041	−0.0006	−0.0006	0.0001
24	−0.1066	−0.6658	0.0019	1.0034	−0.0290	−0.0273	0.0157
25	0.3011	1.8846	0.0014	0.9946	0.0699	0.0642	0.0123
26	0.1049	0.6556	0.0018	1.0033	0.0278	0.0201	0.0140
27	0.1011	0.6313	0.0014	1.0030	0.0234	0.0215	0.0040
28	0.2124	1.3294	0.0039	1.0019	0.0831	0.0319	0.0674
29	0.1085	0.6780	0.0026	1.0040	0.0345	0.0186	0.0240
30	−0.0916	−0.5724	0.0025	1.0044	−0.0289	−0.0158	−0.0200
31	0.3119	1.9548	0.0037	0.9962	0.1192	0.0478	0.0954
32	−0.2991	−1.8718	0.0014	0.9947	−0.0692	−0.0641	−0.0106
33	−0.0847	−0.5301	0.0052	1.0071	−0.0381	−0.0114	−0.0329
34	−0.0992	−0.6192	0.0014	1.0030	−0.0229	−0.0213	−0.0033
35	−0.0886	−0.5537	0.0035	1.0054	−0.0329	−0.0138	−0.0260
36	−0.0853	−0.5334	0.0049	1.0068	−0.0374	−0.0117	−0.0319
37	−0.0958	−0.5985	0.0017	1.0034	−0.0245	−0.0188	−0.0111
38	0.000717	0.004474	0.0014	1.0040	0.0002	0.0002	0.0000
39	−0.0891	−0.5568	0.0033	1.0052	−0.0322	−0.0141	−0.0250
40	−0.0993	−0.6204	0.0014	1.0030	−0.0228	−0.0214	−0.0029
41	0.004025	0.0251	0.0016	1.0043	0.0010	0.0008	0.0004
42	−0.1027	−0.6415	0.0014	1.0030	−0.0241	−0.0241	0.0055
43	−0.006091	−0.0380	0.0018	1.0045	−0.0016	−0.0015	0.0008

Output statistics

Obs	Residual	RStudent	Hat diag H	Cov ratio	DFFITS	DFBETAS	
						Intercept	DLLEIL1
44	0.004005	0.0250	0.0016	1.0043	0.0010	0.0008	0.0004
45	0.003966	0.0248	0.0016	1.0043	0.0010	0.0008	0.0004
46	--0.0994	-0.6207	0.0014	1.0030	-0.0228	-0.0214	-0.0028
47	0.1006	0.6283	0.0014	1.0030	0.0231	0.0217	0.0028
48	0.0105	0.0654	0.0032	1.0059	0.0037	0.0017	0.0028
49	0.1006	0.6280	0.0013	1.0030	0.0231	0.0217	0.0027
50	0.007042	0.0440	0.0022	1.0049	0.0021	0.0013	0.0013
51	-0.0930	-0.5813	0.0022	1.0040	-0.0272	-0.0168	-0.0170
52	0.006879	0.0430	0.0022	1.0049	0.0020	0.0012	0.0012
53	0.1100	0.6873	0.0030	1.0044	0.0378	0.0180	0.0282
54	-0.0964	-0.6023	0.0016	1.0033	-0.0240	-0.0192	-0.0097
55	0.003531	0.0220	0.0016	1.0043	0.0009	0.0007	0.0004
56	0.1035	0.6464	0.0016	1.0031	0.0257	0.0207	0.0102
57	-0.0996	-0.6222	0.0013	1.0030	-0.0228	-0.0216	-0.0022
58	0.009585	0.0599	0.0029	1.0056	0.0032	0.0016	0.0024
59	0.006423	0.0401	0.0021	1.0048	0.0018	0.0012	0.0011
60	-0.0997	-0.6226	0.0013	1.0030	-0.0228	-0.0217	-0.0021
61	0.1033	0.6453	0.0016	1.0031	0.0255	0.0207	0.0097
62	-0.0967	-0.6040	0.0016	1.0033	-0.0238	-0.0194	-0.0090
63	0.009203	0.0575	0.0028	1.0055	0.0030	0.0015	0.0022
64	-0.0998	-0.6230	0.0013	1.0030	-0.0228	-0.0217	-0.0019
65	0.006119	0.0382	0.0020	1.0047	0.0017	0.0011	0.0010
66	0.1061	0.6625	0.0020	1.0035	0.0296	0.0197	0.0171
67	0.005985	0.0374	0.0020	1.0047	0.0017	0.0011	0.0010
68	-0.0941	-0.5877	0.0020	1.0037	-0.0261	-0.0175	-0.0148
69	0.005856	0.0366	0.0020	1.0046	0.0016	0.0011	0.0009
70	-0.0914	-0.5710	0.0026	1.0044	-0.0292	-0.0156	-0.0205
71	0.0973	0.6075	0.0014	1.0031	0.0228	0.0228	-0.0052
72	-0.0943	-0.5890	0.0019	1.0037	-0.0259	-0.0177	-0.0144
73	-0.0916	-0.5722	0.0026	1.0044	-0.0290	-0.0158	-0.0201
74	0.1083	0.6769	0.0025	1.0040	0.0341	0.0187	0.0235
75	-0.1000	-0.6244	0.0013	1.0030	-0.0228	-0.0219	-0.0014
76	0.008188	0.0512	0.0025	1.0052	0.0026	0.0014	0.0017
77	-0.0973	-0.6077	0.0015	1.0032	-0.0235	-0.0199	-0.0077
78	0.1027	0.6412	0.0015	1.0031	0.0248	0.0210	0.0080
79	-0.1974	-1.2335	0.0015	1.0001	-0.0476	-0.0404	-0.0153
80	0.1026	0.6409	0.0015	1.0031	0.0247	0.0210	0.0079
81	0.002595	0.0162	0.0015	1.0042	0.0006	0.0005	0.0002
82	-0.0948	-0.5921	0.0018	1.0036	-0.0254	-0.0180	-0.0133
83	0.0104	0.0648	0.0031	1.0058	0.0036	0.0017	0.0028
84	0.007649	0.0478	0.0024	1.0050	0.0023	0.0013	0.0015
85	-0.0924	-0.5776	0.0023	1.0041	-0.0279	-0.0164	-0.0183
86	0.002383	0.0149	0.0015	1.0041	0.0006	0.0005	0.0002
87	0.002360	0.0147	0.0015	1.0041	0.0006	0.0005	0.0002
88	0.007376	0.0461	0.0023	1.0050	0.0022	0.0013	0.0014
89	-0.0977	-0.6102	0.0015	1.0031	-0.0233	-0.0202	-0.0067
90	-0.1077	-0.6731	0.0021	1.0036	-0.0311	-0.0283	0.0190
91	-0.005239	-0.0327	0.0017	1.0044	-0.0013	-0.0013	0.0006
92	-0.005245	-0.0327	0.0017	1.0044	-0.0013	-0.0013	0.0006
93	-0.005250	-0.0328	0.0017	1.0044	-0.0013	-0.0013	0.0006
94	-0.005256	-0.0328	0.0017	1.0044	-0.0013	-0.0013	0.0006
95	-0.005261	-0.0329	0.0017	1.0044	-0.0013	-0.0013	0.0006
96	-0.002723	-0.0170	0.0014	1.0041	-0.0006	-0.0006	0.0001
97	-0.005267	-0.0329	0.0017	1.0044	-0.0013	-0.0013	0.0006
98	0.004893	0.0306	0.0018	1.0045	0.0013	0.0009	0.0006

Obs	Residual	RStudent	Hat diag H	Cov ratio	DFFITS	DFBETAS	
						Intercept	DLLEIL1
99	−0.0103	−0.0646	0.0028	1.0055	−0.0034	−0.0029	0.0025
100	0.004893	0.0306	0.0018	1.0045	0.0013	0.0009	0.0006
101	−0.1002	−0.6257	0.0013	1.0030	−0.0229	−0.0221	−0.0008
102	0.007332	0.0458	0.0023	1.0050	0.0022	0.0013	0.0014
103	0.004762	0.0297	0.0018	1.0044	0.0012	0.0009	0.0006
104	0.1047	0.6541	0.0018	1.0033	0.0274	0.0202	0.0134
105	0.009565	0.0598	0.0029	1.0056	0.0032	0.0016	0.0024
106	−0.000281	−0.001752	0.0013	1.0040	−0.0001	−0.0001	−0.0000
107	0.002146	0.0134	0.0014	1.0041	0.0005	0.0004	0.0001
108	0.004542	0.0284	0.0017	1.0044	0.0012	0.0009	0.0006
109	0.006893	0.0431	0.0022	1.0049	0.0020	0.0012	0.0013
110	−0.000331	−0.002068	0.0013	1.0040	−0.0001	−0.0001	−0.0000
111	0.002045	0.0128	0.0014	1.0041	0.0005	0.0004	0.0001
112	−0.1003	−0.6267	0.0013	1.0030	−0.0229	−0.0222	−0.0005
113	0.002016	0.0126	0.0014	1.0041	0.0005	0.0004	0.0001
114	0.004349	0.0272	0.0017	1.0044	0.0011	0.0008	0.0005
115	0.001968	0.0123	0.0014	1.0041	0.0005	0.0004	0.0001
116	−0.000385	−0.002401	0.0013	1.0040	−0.0001	−0.0001	−0.0000
117	−0.007403	−0.0462	0.0021	1.0047	−0.0021	−0.0019	0.0012
118	0.008944	0.0559	0.0027	1.0054	0.0029	0.0015	0.0021
119	0.006526	0.0408	0.0021	1.0048	0.0019	0.0012	0.0011
120	−0.1004	−0.6271	0.0013	1.0030	−0.0229	−0.0222	−0.0003
121	−0.002723	−0.0170	0.0014	1.0041	−0.0006	−0.0006	0.0001
122	−0.000426	−0.002662	0.0013	1.0040	−0.0001	−0.0001	−0.0000
123	0.001856	0.0116	0.0014	1.0041	0.0004	0.0004	0.0001
124	0.0996	0.6218	0.0013	1.0030	0.0227	0.0221	0.0002
125	0.004098	0.0256	0.0017	1.0043	0.0010	0.0008	0.0005
126	−0.009543	−0.0596	0.0026	1.0053	−0.0030	−0.0026	0.0021
127	−0.009584	−0.0599	0.0026	1.0053	−0.0030	−0.0026	0.0021
128	−0.009625	−0.0601	0.0026	1.0053	−0.0031	−0.0026	0.0021
129	−0.005033	−0.0314	0.0016	1.0043	−0.0013	−0.0012	0.0006
130	−0.000413	−0.002576	0.0013	1.0040	−0.0001	−0.0001	−0.0000
131	−0.009666	−0.0604	0.0026	1.0053	−0.0031	−0.0026	0.0022
132	−0.007375	−0.0461	0.0020	1.0047	−0.0021	−0.0019	0.0012
133	−0.009737	−0.0608	0.0026	1.0053	−0.0031	−0.0027	0.0022
134	0.0831	0.5201	0.0054	1.0074	0.0384	0.0261	−0.0333
135	−0.0123	−0.0766	0.0034	1.0061	−0.0045	−0.0035	0.0035
136	0.0901	0.5629	0.0027	1.0045	0.0292	0.0248	−0.0207
137	−0.0124	−0.0775	0.0035	1.0062	−0.0046	−0.0036	0.0036
138	0.0973	0.6075	0.0014	1.0031	0.0228	0.0228	−0.0052
139	−0.002723	−0.0170	0.0014	1.0041	−0.0006	−0.0006	0.0001
140	0.0997	0.6227	0.0013	1.0030	0.0227	0.0220	0.0006
141	−0.000301	−0.001880	0.0013	1.0040	−0.0001	−0.0001	−0.0000
142	−0.002723	−0.0170	0.0014	1.0041	−0.0006	−0.0006	0.0001
143	0.0949	0.5925	0.0017	1.0034	0.0241	0.0235	−0.0107
144	0.2973	1.8604	0.0014	0.9949	0.0698	0.0698	−0.0159
145	0.0141	0.0883	0.0046	1.0073	0.0060	0.0020	0.0051
146	0.002045	0.0128	0.0014	1.0041	0.0005	0.0004	0.0001
147	0.009111	0.0569	0.0028	1.0054	0.0030	0.0015	0.0021
148	0.1067	0.6664	0.0021	1.0036	0.0307	0.0194	0.0188
149	0.001939	0.0121	0.0014	1.0041	0.0005	0.0004	0.0001
150	0.004235	0.0264	0.0017	1.0044	0.0011	0.0008	0.0005
151	0.0996	0.6219	0.0013	1.0030	0.0227	0.0220	0.0003
152	0.001883	0.0118	0.0014	1.0041	0.0004	0.0004	0.0001
153	−0.000426	−0.002662	0.0013	1.0040	−0.0001	−0.0001	−0.0000

Output statistics

Output statistics

Obs	Residual	RStudent	Hat diag H	Cov ratio	DFFITS	DFBETAS	
						Intercept	DLLEIL1
154	0.001856	0.0116	0.0014	1.0041	0.0004	0.0004	0.0001
155	0.004111	0.0257	0.0017	1.0043	0.0010	0.0008	0.0005
156	0.001811	0.0113	0.0014	1.0041	0.0004	0.0004	0.0001
157	0.0108	0.0673	0.0033	1.0060	0.0039	0.0017	0.0030
158	0.008404	0.0525	0.0026	1.0052	0.0027	0.0014	0.0018
159	−0.0895	−0.5595	0.0032	1.0050	−0.0316	−0.0144	−0.0241
160	0.006002	0.0375	0.0020	1.0047	0.0017	0.0011	0.0010
161	−0.0962	−0.6010	0.0016	1.0033	−0.0242	−0.0191	−0.0101
162	0.003741	0.0234	0.0016	1.0043	0.0009	0.0007	0.0004
163	0.003705	0.0231	0.0016	1.0043	0.0009	0.0007	0.0004
164	0.005793	0.0362	0.0019	1.0046	0.0016	0.0011	0.0009
165	0.0120	0.0752	0.0037	1.0064	0.0046	0.0018	0.0037
166	0.009774	0.0611	0.0030	1.0056	0.0033	0.0016	0.0025
167	−0.0924	−0.5774	0.0023	1.0041	−0.0280	−0.0163	−0.0184
168	−0.0925	−0.5780	0.0023	1.0041	−0.0279	−0.0164	−0.0182
169	0.009423	0.0589	0.0028	1.0055	0.0031	0.0016	0.0023
170	−0.0947	−0.5915	0.0019	1.0036	−0.0255	−0.0179	−0.0135
171	0.001270	0.007928	0.0014	1.0041	0.0003	0.0003	0.0001
172	−0.1047	−0.6541	0.0016	1.0031	−0.0262	−0.0257	0.0107
173	−0.008727	−0.0545	0.0024	1.0050	−0.0027	−0.0023	0.0017
174	−0.002723	−0.0170	0.0014	1.0041	−0.0006	−0.0006	0.0001
175	−0.1047	−0.6542	0.0016	1.0031	−0.0262	−0.0257	0.0107
176	0.0892	0.5575	0.0029	1.0048	0.0303	0.0250	−0.0224
177	−0.0129	−0.0806	0.0037	1.0063	−0.0049	−0.0038	0.0039
178	−0.008865	−0.0554	0.0024	1.0051	−0.0027	−0.0024	0.0018
179	−0.004777	−0.0298	0.0016	1.0043	−0.0012	−0.0012	0.0005
180	−0.1089	−0.6805	0.0024	1.0038	−0.0334	−0.0293	0.0223
181	0.0848	0.5304	0.0046	1.0066	0.0361	0.0259	−0.0305
182	−0.0111	−0.0694	0.0030	1.0057	−0.0038	−0.0031	0.0029
183	−0.009056	−0.0566	0.0024	1.0051	−0.0028	−0.0024	0.0019
184	0.0930	0.5812	0.0020	1.0037	0.0258	0.0240	−0.0146
185	−0.0177	−0.1107	0.0058	1.0085	−0.0085	−0.0056	0.0075
186	−0.009199	−0.0575	0.0025	1.0052	−0.0029	−0.0025	0.0019
187	−0.0158	−0.0987	0.0049	1.0076	−0.0069	−0.0049	0.0059
188	−0.0137	−0.0858	0.0040	1.0067	−0.0054	−0.0041	0.0044
189	0.0772	0.4840	0.0089	1.0111	0.0459	0.0269	−0.0423
190	0.0746	0.4678	0.0108	1.0130	0.0489	0.0272	−0.0458
191	−0.0166	−0.1036	0.0053	1.0080	−0.0075	−0.0052	0.0065
192	0.1786	1.1195	0.0080	1.0074	0.1006	0.0609	−0.0919
193	0.2758	1.7331	0.0099	1.0046	0.1730	0.0986	−0.1609
194	0.2876	1.8016	0.0035	0.9975	0.1064	0.0832	−0.0836
195	0.1949	1.2180	0.0017	1.0004	0.0496	0.0483	−0.0220
196	0.3924	2.4608	0.0021	0.9887	0.1127	0.1030	−0.0680
197	0.2118	1.3256	0.0037	1.0017	0.0804	0.0325	0.0641
198	0.2045	1.2783	0.0017	1.0000	0.0530	0.0397	0.0251
199	0.1068	0.6674	0.0022	1.0036	0.0310	0.0194	0.0192
200	−0.0909	−0.5681	0.0027	1.0046	−0.0298	−0.0153	−0.0214
201	0.0996	0.6222	0.0013	1.0030	0.0227	0.0220	0.0004
202	−0.1980	−1.2378	0.0014	1.0000	−0.0468	−0.0412	−0.0121
203	0.1066	0.6659	0.0021	1.0036	0.0306	0.0194	0.0185
204	0.001902	0.0119	0.0014	1.0041	0.0004	0.0004	0.0001
205	−0.0958	−0.5985	0.0017	1.0034	−0.0245	−0.0188	−0.0110
206	−0.1868	−1.1689	0.0042	1.0033	−0.0761	−0.0272	−0.0630
207	−0.0848	−0.5303	0.0051	1.0071	−0.0381	−0.0114	−0.0328
208	−0.2983	−1.8667	0.0014	0.9948	−0.0701	−0.0626	−0.0165

Output statistics

Obs	Residual	RStudent	Hat diag H	Cov ratio	DFFITS	DFBETAS	
						Intercept	DLLEIL1
209	−0.0983	−0.6139	0.0014	1.0031	−0.0231	−0.0206	−0.0054
210	0.2061	1.2885	0.0020	1.0002	0.0577	0.0382	0.0334
211	0.001656	0.0103	0.0014	1.0041	0.0004	0.0003	0.0001
212	0.1082	0.6758	0.0025	1.0039	0.0337	0.0188	0.0230
213	−0.0984	−0.6145	0.0014	1.0031	−0.0230	−0.0207	−0.0051
214	0.003729	0.0233	0.0016	1.0043	0.0009	0.0007	0.0004
215	−0.000580	−0.003621	0.0013	1.0040	−0.0001	−0.0001	0.0000
216	0.007931	0.0495	0.0024	1.0051	0.0024	0.0014	0.0016
217	−0.0922	−0.5759	0.0024	1.0042	−0.0283	−0.0162	−0.0189
218	−0.1027	−0.6415	0.0014	1.0030	−0.0241	−0.0241	0.0055
219	−0.0943	−0.5894	0.0019	1.0037	−0.0258	−0.0177	−0.0143
220	−0.0882	−0.5515	0.0037	1.0055	−0.0334	−0.0135	−0.0266
221	0.001391	0.008684	0.0014	1.0041	0.0003	0.0003	0.0001
222	−0.0966	−0.6032	0.0016	1.0033	−0.0239	−0.0193	−0.0093
223	0.005417	0.0338	0.0019	1.0046	0.0015	0.0010	0.0008
224	−0.1027	−0.6415	0.0014	1.0030	−0.0241	−0.0241	0.0055
225	0.1033	0.6455	0.0016	1.0031	0.0255	0.0207	0.0098
226	−0.1007	−0.6289	0.0013	1.0030	−0.0230	−0.0225	0.0004
227	−0.000711	−0.004437	0.0013	1.0040	−0.0002	−0.0002	0.0000
228	−0.0987	−0.6165	0.0014	1.0030	−0.0229	−0.0209	−0.0044
229	−0.1007	−0.6290	0.0013	1.0030	−0.0230	−0.0225	0.0005
230	−0.0107	−0.0672	0.0029	1.0056	−0.0036	−0.0030	0.0027
231	−0.0967	−0.6039	0.0016	1.0033	−0.0238	−0.0194	−0.0091
232	0.007250	0.0453	0.0023	1.0049	0.0022	0.0013	0.0014
233	−0.0889	−0.5558	0.0034	1.0053	−0.0325	−0.0140	−0.0253
234	−0.0988	−0.6171	0.0014	1.0030	−0.0229	−0.0210	−0.0042
235	0.003129	0.0195	0.0015	1.0042	0.0008	0.0006	0.0003
236	−0.1047	−0.6538	0.0016	1.0031	−0.0261	−0.0257	0.0106
237	0.1050	0.6562	0.0018	1.0033	0.0279	0.0201	0.0143
238	0.001143	0.007135	0.0014	1.0041	0.0003	0.0002	0.0000
239	−0.1008	−0.6295	0.0013	1.0030	−0.0230	−0.0225	0.0006
240	−0.0105	−0.0653	0.0028	1.0055	−0.0035	−0.0029	0.0025
241	−0.002723	−0.0170	0.0014	1.0041	−0.0006	−0.0006	0.0001
242	−0.008555	−0.0534	0.0023	1.0050	−0.0026	−0.0023	0.0017
243	0.0953	0.5954	0.0016	1.0033	0.0238	0.0234	−0.0096
244	−0.0930	−0.5810	0.0022	1.0040	−0.0273	−0.0168	−0.0171
245	−0.0242	−0.1519	0.0099	1.0126	−0.0152	−0.0086	0.0141
246	−0.0949	−0.5925	0.0018	1.0036	−0.0253	−0.0181	−0.0132
247	−0.0106	−0.0661	0.0029	1.0056	−0.0036	−0.0029	0.0026
248	−0.0106	−0.0665	0.0029	1.0056	−0.0036	−0.0030	0.0026
249	−0.008696	−0.0543	0.0024	1.0050	−0.0026	−0.0023	0.0017
250	0.0913	0.5703	0.0024	1.0042	0.0277	0.0245	−0.0183
251	−0.0148	−0.0927	0.0045	1.0071	−0.0062	−0.0045	0.0052
252	−0.0150	−0.0935	0.0045	1.0072	−0.0063	−0.0045	0.0053
253	0.0870	0.5438	0.0037	1.0056	0.0332	0.0254	−0.0266
254	−0.004792	−0.0299	0.0016	1.0043	−0.0012	−0.0012	0.0005
255	0.0931	0.5817	0.0019	1.0037	0.0257	0.0240	−0.0144
256	0.1699	1.0689	0.0147	1.0145	0.1304	0.0667	−0.1244
257	−0.0395	−0.2495	0.0245	1.0277	−0.0396	−0.0178	0.0385
258	−0.0182	−0.1140	0.0061	1.0088	−0.0089	−0.0059	0.0079
259	0.3017	1.8884	0.0014	0.9946	0.0709	0.0633	0.0167
260	0.1061	0.6630	0.0020	1.0035	0.0297	0.0196	0.0173
261	0.2061	1.2883	0.0020	1.0002	0.0576	0.0382	0.0332
262	−0.0918	−0.5739	0.0025	1.0043	−0.0286	−0.0160	−0.0195
263	0.1059	0.6616	0.0020	1.0035	0.0294	0.0197	0.0167

Output statistics

Obs	Residual	RStudent	Hat diag H	Cov ratio	DFFITS	DFBETAS	
						Intercept	DLLEIL1
264	−0.002723	−0.0170	0.0014	1.0041	−0.0006	−0.0006	0.0001
265	−0.009187	−0.0574	0.0025	1.0052	−0.0029	−0.0025	0.0019
266	−0.0158	−0.0986	0.0049	1.0076	−0.0069	−0.0049	0.0059
267	−0.1115	−0.6970	0.0032	1.0046	−0.0393	−0.0316	0.0299
268	−0.0983	−0.6141	0.0014	1.0031	−0.0230	−0.0206	−0.0053
269	0.001656	0.0103	0.0014	1.0041	0.0004	0.0003	0.0001
270	0.0907	0.5668	0.0025	1.0043	0.0284	0.0246	−0.0194
271	−0.1115	−0.6973	0.0032	1.0046	−0.0394	−0.0317	0.0301
272	0.0884	0.5525	0.0032	1.0051	0.0313	0.0251	−0.0240
273	−0.009437	−0.0590	0.0025	1.0052	−0.0030	−0.0026	0.0021
274	−0.0185	−0.1161	0.0063	1.0090	−0.0092	−0.0060	0.0082
275	−0.009570	−0.0598	0.0026	1.0053	−0.0030	−0.0026	0.0021
276	0.0927	0.5790	0.0020	1.0038	0.0261	0.0241	−0.0154
277	−0.007329	−0.0458	0.0020	1.0047	−0.0021	−0.0019	0.0012
278	0.2857	1.7901	0.0042	0.9984	0.1168	0.0858	−0.0967
279	0.2042	1.2768	0.0017	1.0000	0.0524	0.0399	0.0239
280	0.0903	0.5643	0.0026	1.0044	0.0289	0.0247	−0.0202
281	0.1973	1.2330	0.0014	1.0000	0.0462	0.0462	−0.0106
282	0.0926	0.5785	0.0021	1.0038	0.0262	0.0241	−0.0155
283	0.0879	0.5493	0.0034	1.0053	0.0320	0.0252	−0.0249
284	0.0996	0.6222	0.0013	1.0030	0.0227	0.0220	0.0004
285	0.1878	1.1750	0.0034	1.0024	0.0687	0.0541	−0.0536
286	0.3067	1.9206	0.0021	0.9950	0.0889	0.0558	0.0546
287	0.2020	1.2624	0.0014	0.9998	0.0477	0.0420	0.0124
288	0.1996	1.2476	0.0013	0.9998	0.0456	0.0442	0.0007
289	0.006601	0.0412	0.0021	1.0048	0.0019	0.0012	0.0012
290	0.0180	0.1126	0.0066	1.0093	0.0092	0.0021	0.0082
291	0.0109	0.0680	0.0033	1.0060	0.0039	0.0017	0.0030
292	−0.2871	−1.7986	0.0041	0.9982	−0.1155	−0.0423	−0.0950
293	0.2061	1.2889	0.0020	1.0002	0.0579	0.0382	0.0336
294	−0.0852	−0.5330	0.0049	1.0069	−0.0375	−0.0117	−0.0320
295	−0.0876	−0.5478	0.0039	1.0058	−0.0342	−0.0132	−0.0277
296	−0.2920	−1.8285	0.0024	0.9962	−0.0903	−0.0512	−0.0607
297	−0.1985	−1.2405	0.0014	1.0000	−0.0464	−0.0418	−0.0100
298	−0.0880	−0.5502	0.0037	1.0056	−0.0337	−0.0134	−0.0270
299	−0.1882	−1.1774	0.0037	1.0026	−0.0714	−0.0289	−0.0570
300	−0.0945	−0.5903	0.0019	1.0036	−0.0257	−0.0178	−0.0139
301	−0.0905	−0.5655	0.0029	1.0047	−0.0304	−0.0150	−0.0222
302	−0.1886	−1.1800	0.0035	1.0025	−0.0700	−0.0294	−0.0551
303	−0.0928	−0.5795	0.0023	1.0040	−0.0276	−0.0166	−0.0177
304	−0.1007	−0.6291	0.0013	1.0030	−0.0230	−0.0225	0.0005
305	0.003210	0.0200	0.0015	1.0042	0.0008	0.0006	0.0003
306	−0.1949	−1.2181	0.0018	1.0005	−0.0521	−0.0371	−0.0270
307	0.001189	0.007421	0.0014	1.0041	0.0003	0.0003	0.0000
308	−0.000772	−0.004820	0.0013	1.0040	−0.0002	−0.0002	0.0000
309	−0.1008	−0.6294	0.0013	1.0030	−0.0230	−0.0225	0.0006
310	−0.002723	−0.0170	0.0014	1.0041	−0.0006	−0.0006	0.0001
311	−0.0988	−0.6173	0.0014	1.0030	−0.0229	−0.0210	−0.0041
312	0.003080	0.0192	0.0015	1.0042	0.0008	0.0006	0.0003
313	−0.0950	−0.5936	0.0018	1.0035	−0.0252	−0.0182	−0.0128
314	0.1030	0.6434	0.0015	1.0031	0.0251	0.0208	0.0089
315	0.002985	0.0186	0.0015	1.0042	0.0007	0.0006	0.0003
316	0.002957	0.0185	0.0015	1.0042	0.0007	0.0006	0.0003
317	−0.1027	−0.6415	0.0014	1.0030	−0.0241	−0.0241	0.0055
318	0.002929	0.0183	0.0015	1.0042	0.0007	0.0006	0.0002

Output statistics							
Obs	Residual	RStudent	Hat diag H	Cov ratio	DFFITS	DFBETAS	
						Intercept	DLLEIL1
319	0.002901	0.0181	0.0015	1.0042	0.0007	0.0006	0.0002
320	0.002874	0.0179	0.0015	1.0042	0.0007	0.0006	0.0002
321	−0.0990	−0.6183	0.0014	1.0030	−0.0229	−0.0211	−0.0037
322	0.1010	0.6307	0.0014	1.0030	0.0233	0.0216	0.0037
323	−0.1009	−0.6300	0.0013	1.0029	−0.0230	−0.0226	0.0008
324	0.000964	0.006017	0.0014	1.0040	0.0002	0.0002	0.0000
325	−0.0972	−0.6072	0.0015	1.0032	−0.0235	−0.0198	−0.0079
326	0.2009	1.2559	0.0014	0.9998	0.0464	0.0430	0.0072
327	−0.0991	−0.6188	0.0014	1.0030	−0.0229	−0.0212	−0.0035
328	−0.1009	−0.6302	0.0013	1.0029	−0.0230	−0.0226	0.0009
329	0.1027	0.6415	0.0015	1.0031	0.0248	0.0209	0.0082
330	0.1027	0.6414	0.0015	1.0031	0.0248	0.0210	0.0081
331	−0.0955	−0.5968	0.0017	1.0034	−0.0247	−0.0186	−0.0116
332	−0.002723	−0.0170	0.0014	1.0041	−0.0006	−0.0006	0.0001
333	0.1008	0.6298	0.0014	1.0030	0.0232	0.0216	0.0034
334	−0.1992	−1.2448	0.0014	0.9999	−0.0459	−0.0427	−0.0067
335	0.0973	0.6075	0.0014	1.0031	0.0228	0.0228	−0.0052
336	−0.0974	−0.6083	0.0015	1.0032	−0.0234	−0.0199	−0.0075
337	0.004334	0.0271	0.0017	1.0044	0.0011	0.0008	0.0005
338	−0.002723	−0.0170	0.0014	1.0041	−0.0006	−0.0006	0.0001
339	−0.0957	−0.5978	0.0017	1.0034	−0.0246	−0.0187	−0.0113
340	0.1008	0.6293	0.0014	1.0030	0.0232	0.0216	0.0032
341	−0.000981	−0.006125	0.0013	1.0040	−0.0002	−0.0002	0.0000
342	−0.0992	−0.6198	0.0014	1.0030	−0.0228	−0.0213	−0.0031
343	−0.0975	−0.6091	0.0015	1.0032	−0.0234	−0.0200	−0.0072
344	0.002448	0.0153	0.0015	1.0041	0.0006	0.0005	0.0002
345	0.000711	0.004442	0.0014	1.0040	0.0002	0.0002	0.0000
346	−0.0959	−0.5989	0.0017	1.0034	−0.0244	−0.0188	−0.0109
347	0.000681	0.004252	0.0014	1.0040	0.0002	0.0001	0.0000
348	−0.007832	−0.0489	0.0021	1.0048	−0.0023	−0.0021	0.0014
349	−0.1010	−0.6309	0.0013	1.0029	−0.0231	−0.0227	0.0012
350	0.000681	0.004252	0.0014	1.0040	0.0002	0.0001	0.0000
351	0.005743	0.0359	0.0019	1.0046	0.0016	0.0011	0.0009
352	−0.0977	−0.6100	0.0015	1.0031	−0.0233	−0.0201	−0.0068
353	0.0990	0.6180	0.0013	1.0030	0.0226	0.0223	−0.0012
354	−0.0977	−0.6102	0.0015	1.0031	−0.0233	−0.0201	−0.0068
355	0.003937	0.0246	0.0016	1.0043	0.0010	0.0008	0.0004
356	−0.002723	−0.0170	0.0014	1.0041	−0.0006	−0.0006	0.0001
357	0.000593	0.003702	0.0014	1.0040	0.0001	0.0001	0.0000
358	0.000583	0.003643	0.0014	1.0040	0.0001	0.0001	0.0000
359	−0.0994	−0.6209	0.0014	1.0030	−0.0228	−0.0215	−0.0027
360	0.000565	0.003525	0.0013	1.0040	0.0001	0.0001	0.0000
361	−0.001082	−0.006758	0.0013	1.0040	−0.0002	−0.0002	0.0000
362	−0.0994	−0.6211	0.0013	1.0030	−0.0228	−0.0215	−0.0026
363	−0.004358	−0.0272	0.0016	1.0042	−0.0011	−0.0011	0.0004
364	−0.007643	−0.0477	0.0021	1.0048	−0.0022	−0.0020	0.0013
365	−0.001080	−0.006744	0.0013	1.0040	−0.0002	−0.0002	0.0000
366	−0.1060	−0.6622	0.0018	1.0033	−0.0280	−0.0268	0.0142
367	0.1956	1.2228	0.0016	1.0002	0.0483	0.0477	−0.0184
368	−0.2077	−1.2986	0.0021	1.0003	−0.0597	−0.0545	0.0363
369	0.1006	0.6282	0.0014	1.0030	0.0231	0.0217	0.0027
370	−0.002723	−0.0170	0.0014	1.0041	−0.0006	−0.0006	0.0001
371	−0.006029	−0.0376	0.0018	1.0045	−0.0016	−0.0015	0.0008
372	−0.001068	−0.006670	0.0013	1.0040	−0.0002	−0.0002	0.0000
373	−0.002723	−0.0170	0.0014	1.0041	−0.0006	−0.0006	0.0001

Output statistics

Obs	Residual	RStudent	Hat diag H	Cov ratio	DFFITS	DFBETAS	
						Intercept	DLLEIL1
374	−0.004377	−0.0273	0.0016	1.0042	−0.0011	−0.0011	0.0004
375	−0.006038	−0.0377	0.0018	1.0045	−0.0016	−0.0015	0.0008
376	−0.001064	−0.006641	0.0013	1.0040	−0.0002	−0.0002	0.0000
377	−0.007707	−0.0481	0.0021	1.0048	−0.0022	−0.0020	0.0014
378	−0.002723	−0.0170	0.0014	1.0041	−0.0006	−0.0006	0.0001
379	0.0973	0.6075	0.0014	1.0031	0.0228	0.0228	−0.0052
380	0.0923	0.5765	0.0021	1.0039	0.0266	0.0242	−0.0162
381	−0.0196	−0.1225	0.0069	1.0096	−0.0102	−0.0065	0.0091
382	−0.0164	−0.1024	0.0052	1.0079	−0.0074	−0.0051	0.0064
383	0.1817	1.1383	0.0061	1.0054	0.0895	0.0587	−0.0792
384	−0.1238	−0.7765	0.0096	1.0108	−0.0765	−0.0439	0.0710
385	0.0848	0.5304	0.0046	1.0066	0.0361	0.0259	−0.0305
386	0.0829	0.5185	0.0056	1.0075	0.0387	0.0262	−0.0338
387	0.0936	0.5849	0.0019	1.0036	0.0252	0.0238	−0.0133
388	−0.008195	−0.0512	0.0022	1.0049	−0.0024	−0.0022	0.0015
389	0.1082	0.6761	0.0025	1.0040	0.0338	0.0188	0.0231
390	0.2063	1.2899	0.0020	1.0003	0.0584	0.0380	0.0345
391	−0.1027	−0.6415	0.0014	1.0030	−0.0241	−0.0241	0.0055
392	0.1098	0.6862	0.0030	1.0044	0.0374	0.0181	0.0277
393	−0.000946	−0.005907	0.0013	1.0040	−0.0002	−0.0002	0.0000
394	0.1044	0.6518	0.0017	1.0032	0.0269	0.0203	0.0125
395	−0.002723	−0.0170	0.0014	1.0041	−0.0006	−0.0006	0.0001
396	0.1955	1.2220	0.0016	1.0003	0.0485	0.0478	−0.0189
397	0.0937	0.5855	0.0018	1.0036	0.0251	0.0238	−0.0131
398	0.1061	0.6629	0.0020	1.0035	0.0297	0.0196	0.0172
399	0.000790	0.004931	0.0014	1.0040	0.0002	0.0002	0.0000
400	−0.0922	−0.5764	0.0024	1.0042	−0.0282	−0.0162	−0.0187
401	0.3059	1.9154	0.0020	0.9949	0.0851	0.0570	0.0485
402	0.2059	1.2872	0.0020	1.0002	0.0570	0.0384	0.0322
403	−0.0976	−0.6095	0.0015	1.0031	−0.0233	−0.0201	−0.0070
404	0.000681	0.004252	0.0014	1.0040	0.0002	0.0001	0.0000
405	−0.0959	−0.5993	0.0017	1.0034	−0.0244	−0.0188	−0.0108
406	−0.001034	−0.006459	0.0013	1.0040	−0.0002	−0.0002	0.0000
407	−0.0994	−0.6205	0.0014	1.0030	−0.0228	−0.0214	−0.0029
408	0.2073	1.2965	0.0023	1.0005	0.0619	0.0370	0.0399
409	−0.1878	−1.1751	0.0038	1.0028	−0.0726	−0.0285	−0.0586
410	−0.0962	−0.6006	0.0016	1.0033	−0.0242	−0.0190	−0.0103
411	−0.0962	−0.6008	0.0016	1.0033	−0.0242	−0.0190	−0.0102
412	−0.1044	−0.6518	0.0016	1.0031	−0.0257	−0.0254	0.0097
413	0.1054	0.6584	0.0019	1.0034	0.0285	0.0199	0.0153
414	−0.001105	−0.006902	0.0013	1.0040	−0.0003	−0.0002	0.0000
415	0.002115	0.0132	0.0014	1.0041	0.0005	0.0004	0.0001
416	−0.1027	−0.6415	0.0014	1.0030	−0.0241	−0.0241	0.0055
417	0.1053	0.6578	0.0019	1.0034	0.0283	0.0200	0.0150
418	−0.0963	−0.6018	0.0016	1.0033	−0.0241	−0.0191	−0.0099
419	0.002035	0.0127	0.0014	1.0041	0.0005	0.0004	0.0001
420	0.003591	0.0224	0.0016	1.0043	0.0009	0.0007	0.0004
421	0.0129	0.0807	0.0041	1.0068	0.0052	0.0019	0.0043
422	0.0957	0.5979	0.0015	1.0033	0.0235	0.0233	−0.0088
423	−0.0996	−0.6221	0.0013	1.0030	−0.0228	−0.0216	−0.0022
424	−0.0858	−0.5366	0.0047	1.0066	−0.0367	−0.0120	−0.0310
425	0.004893	0.0306	0.0018	1.0045	0.0013	0.0009	0.0006
426	−0.0982	−0.6131	0.0014	1.0031	−0.0231	−0.0205	−0.0057
427	0.1078	0.6737	0.0024	1.0039	0.0330	0.0189	0.0220
428	−0.0982	−0.6135	0.0014	1.0031	−0.0231	−0.0206	−0.0055

Obs	Residual	RStudent	Hat diag H	Cov ratio	DFFITS	DFBETAS	
						Intercept	DLLEIL1
429	0.006199	0.0387	0.0020	1.0047	0.0017	0.0011	0.0010
430	0.1032	0.6445	0.0015	1.0031	0.0253	0.0208	0.0094
431	−0.1939	−1.2123	0.0020	1.0007	−0.0543	−0.0359	−0.0314
432	−0.0998	−0.6233	0.0013	1.0030	−0.0228	−0.0217	−0.0018
433	−0.0955	−0.5962	0.0017	1.0035	−0.0248	−0.0185	−0.0119
434	−0.001274	−0.007954	0.0013	1.0040	−0.0003	−0.0003	0.0000
435	−0.1027	−0.6415	0.0014	1.0030	−0.0241	−0.0241	0.0055
436	0.1958	1.2240	0.0015	1.0002	0.0480	0.0475	−0.0174
437	0.0973	0.6075	0.0014	1.0031	0.0228	0.0228	−0.0052
438	−0.3042	−1.9039	0.0015	0.9946	−0.0746	−0.0739	0.0271
439	−0.001272	−0.007943	0.0013	1.0040	−0.0003	−0.0003	0.0000
440	0.0958	0.5985	0.0015	1.0033	0.0235	0.0232	−0.0085
441	−0.0955	−0.5964	0.0017	1.0034	−0.0248	−0.0185	−0.0118
442	0.000158	0.000989	0.0013	1.0040	0.0000	0.0000	0.0000
443	0.0958	0.5986	0.0015	1.0033	0.0235	0.0232	−0.0085
444	−0.002723	−0.0170	0.0014	1.0041	−0.0006	−0.0006	0.0001
445	−0.001283	−0.008011	0.0013	1.0040	−0.0003	−0.0003	0.0000
446	−0.1245	−0.7811	0.0101	1.0113	−0.0790	−0.0447	0.0736
447	0.1104	0.6901	0.0032	1.0046	0.0388	0.0178	0.0295
448	0.000173	0.001079	0.0013	1.0040	0.0000	0.0000	0.0000
449	0.003046	0.0190	0.0015	1.0042	0.0007	0.0006	0.0003
450	0.007304	0.0456	0.0023	1.0050	0.0022	0.0013	0.0014
451	−0.0956	−0.5972	0.0017	1.0034	−0.0247	−0.0186	−0.0115
452	−0.004141	−0.0259	0.0015	1.0042	−0.0010	−0.0010	0.0004
453	0.000112	0.000701	0.0013	1.0040	0.0000	0.0000	0.0000
454	0.000105	0.000658	0.0013	1.0040	0.0000	0.0000	0.0000
455	−0.0985	−0.6151	0.0014	1.0031	−0.0230	−0.0207	−0.0049
456	0.004291	0.0268	0.0017	1.0044	0.0011	0.0008	0.0005
457	−0.001325	−0.008272	0.0013	1.0040	−0.0003	−0.0003	0.0000
458	0.004241	0.0265	0.0017	1.0044	0.0011	0.0008	0.0005
459	0.0125	0.0778	0.0039	1.0066	0.0049	0.0019	0.0040
460	0.002746	0.0171	0.0015	1.0042	0.0007	0.0006	0.0002
461	−0.001360	−0.008488	0.0013	1.0040	−0.0003	−0.0003	0.0000
462	−0.0946	−0.5908	0.0019	1.0036	−0.0256	−0.0179	−0.0138
463	0.1040	0.6497	0.0016	1.0032	0.0264	0.0205	0.0116
464	−0.0894	−0.5585	0.0032	1.0051	−0.0319	−0.0143	−0.0245
465	−0.000067	−0.000419	0.0013	1.0040	−0.0000	−0.0000	−0.0000
466	−0.0935	−0.5840	0.0021	1.0039	−0.0267	−0.0171	−0.0161
467	−0.1001	−0.6251	0.0013	1.0030	−0.0229	−0.0220	−0.0011
468	0.0999	0.6239	0.0013	1.0030	0.0228	0.0219	0.0011
469	−0.0988	−0.6170	0.0014	1.0030	−0.0229	−0.0210	−0.0042
470	−0.002723	−0.0170	0.0014	1.0041	−0.0006	−0.0006	0.0001
471	0.008965	0.0560	0.0027	1.0054	0.0029	0.0015	0.0021
472	−0.2014	−1.2590	0.0013	0.9998	−0.0462	−0.0458	0.0044
473	−0.004014	−0.0251	0.0015	1.0042	−0.0010	−0.0010	0.0003
474	0.1037	0.6478	0.0016	1.0032	0.0260	0.0206	0.0108
475	−0.1105	−0.6904	0.0028	1.0042	−0.0368	−0.0307	0.0268
476	0.0999	0.6236	0.0013	1.0030	0.0228	0.0220	0.0010
477	−0.000144	−0.000900	0.0013	1.0040	−0.0000	−0.0000	−0.0000
478	−0.1105	−0.6905	0.0028	1.0043	−0.0369	−0.0307	0.0269
479	−0.007920	−0.0495	0.0022	1.0048	−0.0023	−0.0021	0.0014
480	−0.000121	−0.000755	0.0013	1.0040	−0.0000	−0.0000	−0.0000
481	0.001169	0.007298	0.0014	1.0041	0.0003	0.0002	0.0000
482	−0.005315	−0.0332	0.0017	1.0044	−0.0014	−0.0013	0.0006
483	0.003749	0.0234	0.0016	1.0043	0.0009	0.0007	0.0004

Output statistics

Obs	Residual	RStudent	Hat diag H	Cov ratio	DFFITS	DFBETAS Intercept	DLLEIL1
484	−0.001433	−0.008945	0.0013	1.0040	−0.0003	−0.0003	0.0000
485	−0.002723	−0.0170	0.0014	1.0041	−0.0006	−0.0006	0.0001
486	0.1037	0.6478	0.0016	1.0032	0.0260	0.0206	0.0107
487	−0.0989	−0.6175	0.0014	1.0030	−0.0229	−0.0210	−0.0040
488	−0.0989	−0.6176	0.0014	1.0030	−0.0229	−0.0211	−0.0040
489	−0.000178	−0.001113	0.0013	1.0040	−0.0000	−0.0000	−0.0000
490	−0.002723	−0.0170	0.0014	1.0041	−0.0006	−0.0006	0.0001
491	0.001083	0.006764	0.0014	1.0041	0.0003	0.0002	0.0000
492	0.003593	0.0224	0.0016	1.0043	0.0009	0.0007	0.0004
493	0.007311	0.0457	0.0023	1.0050	0.0022	0.0013	0.0014
494	−0.0965	−0.6027	0.0016	1.0033	−0.0240	−0.0193	−0.0095
495	−0.0102	−0.0637	0.0028	1.0054	−0.0034	−0.0028	0.0024
496	0.008474	0.0529	0.0026	1.0053	0.0027	0.0015	0.0019
497	−0.000249	−0.001556	0.0013	1.0040	−0.0001	−0.0001	−0.0000
498	−0.0151	−0.0947	0.0046	1.0073	−0.0064	−0.0046	0.0054
499	−0.000228	−0.001423	0.0013	1.0040	−0.0001	−0.0001	−0.0000
500	0.0923	0.5765	0.0021	1.0039	0.0266	0.0242	−0.0162
501	−0.1103	−0.6891	0.0028	1.0042	−0.0364	−0.0305	0.0262
502	0.002305	0.0144	0.0015	1.0041	0.0005	0.0005	0.0002
503	−0.0153	−0.0959	0.0047	1.0074	−0.0066	−0.0047	0.0056
504	−0.0116	−0.0727	0.0032	1.0059	−0.0041	−0.0033	0.0032
505	0.0805	0.5044	0.0068	1.0089	0.0417	0.0265	−0.0374
506	−0.0105	−0.0658	0.0029	1.0055	−0.0035	−0.0029	0.0026
507	0.0842	0.5264	0.0049	1.0069	0.0370	0.0260	−0.0316
508	−0.1200	−0.7518	0.0071	1.0084	−0.0637	−0.0399	0.0575
509	−0.0148	−0.0928	0.0045	1.0071	−0.0062	−0.0045	0.0052
510	0.1013	0.6329	0.0014	1.0030	0.0236	0.0214	0.0046
511	0.0905	0.5656	0.0026	1.0044	0.0286	0.0246	−0.0198
512	0.0946	0.5906	0.0017	1.0034	0.0244	0.0236	−0.0113
513	0.0959	0.5991	0.0015	1.0032	0.0234	0.0232	−0.0083
514	−0.0247	−0.1551	0.0103	1.0130	−0.0158	−0.0089	0.0147
515	0.1889	1.1816	0.0030	1.0020	0.0652	0.0532	−0.0488
516	0.1056	0.6599	0.0019	1.0034	0.0289	0.0198	0.0159
517	0.1056	0.6596	0.0019	1.0034	0.0288	0.0199	0.0158
518	−0.002723	−0.0170	0.0014	1.0041	−0.0006	−0.0006	0.0001
519	0.1083	0.6765	0.0025	1.0040	0.0339	0.0187	0.0233
520	0.1014	0.6331	0.0014	1.0030	0.0236	0.0214	0.0047
521	0.006763	0.0422	0.0021	1.0048	0.0020	0.0012	0.0012
522	0.1067	0.6666	0.0021	1.0036	0.0308	0.0194	0.0188
523	−0.1000	−0.6248	0.0013	1.0030	−0.0228	−0.0219	−0.0012
524	−0.008077	−0.0504	0.0022	1.0049	−0.0024	−0.0021	0.0015
525	−0.000042	−0.000265	0.0013	1.0040	−0.0000	−0.0000	−0.0000
526	0.0919	0.5742	0.0022	1.0040	0.0270	0.0243	−0.0170
527	−0.004068	−0.0254	0.0015	1.0042	−0.0010	−0.0010	0.0004
528	0.2053	1.2837	0.0019	1.0001	0.0554	0.0389	0.0294
529	−0.1041	−0.6499	0.0015	1.0031	−0.0254	−0.0252	0.0090
530	−0.000049	−0.000304	0.0013	1.0040	−0.0000	−0.0000	−0.0000
531	−0.005397	−0.0337	0.0017	1.0044	−0.0014	−0.0013	0.0006
532	0.0959	0.5992	0.0015	1.0032	0.0234	0.0232	−0.0083
533	−0.006750	−0.0422	0.0019	1.0046	−0.0019	−0.0017	0.0010
534	0.1093	0.6832	0.0028	1.0043	0.0363	0.0183	0.0263
535	0.1066	0.6657	0.0021	1.0036	0.0305	0.0195	0.0185
536	−0.0988	−0.6168	0.0014	1.0030	−0.0229	−0.0210	−0.0043
537	0.005144	0.0321	0.0018	1.0045	0.0014	0.0010	0.0007
538	0.0103	0.0642	0.0031	1.0058	0.0036	0.0017	0.0027

Obs	Residual	RStudent	Hat diag H	Cov ratio	DFFITS	DFBETAS	
						Intercept	DLLEIL1
539	−0.0912	−0.5696	0.0027	1.0045	−0.0295	−0.0155	−0.0209
540	0.009999	0.0625	0.0030	1.0057	0.0034	0.0016	0.0026
541	0.008608	0.0538	0.0026	1.0053	0.0028	0.0015	0.0019
542	−0.0927	−0.5794	0.0023	1.0040	−0.0276	−0.0166	−0.0177
543	0.1072	0.6696	0.0022	1.0037	0.0317	0.0192	0.0202
544	−0.2868	−1.7972	0.0042	0.9983	−0.1168	−0.0419	−0.0965
545	0.0997	0.6227	0.0013	1.0030	0.0227	0.0220	0.0006
546	0.008134	0.0508	0.0025	1.0052	0.0025	0.0014	0.0017
547	−0.0979	−0.6116	0.0014	1.0031	−0.0232	−0.0203	−0.0062
548	−0.0968	−0.6043	0.0015	1.0033	−0.0238	−0.0194	−0.0089
549	0.1032	0.6446	0.0015	1.0031	0.0254	0.0208	0.0094
550	0.1044	0.6518	0.0017	1.0032	0.0269	0.0203	0.0125
551	−0.0992	−0.6195	0.0014	1.0030	−0.0229	−0.0213	−0.0032
552	0.005456	0.0341	0.0019	1.0046	0.0015	0.0010	0.0008
553	−0.0923	−0.5766	0.0024	1.0042	−0.0281	−0.0163	−0.0186
554	0.1030	0.6435	0.0015	1.0031	0.0252	0.0208	0.0090
555	−0.0970	−0.6058	0.0015	1.0032	−0.0237	−0.0196	−0.0084
556	−0.1073	−0.6704	0.0020	1.0035	−0.0302	−0.0279	0.0178
557	0.004139	0.0258	0.0017	1.0043	0.0011	0.0008	0.0005
558	−0.2061	−1.2888	0.0018	1.0001	−0.0549	−0.0523	0.0283
559	0.006389	0.0399	0.0021	1.0047	0.0018	0.0012	0.0011
560	0.0973	0.6075	0.0014	1.0031	0.0228	0.0228	−0.0052
561	0.005192	0.0324	0.0018	1.0045	0.0014	0.0010	0.0007
562	−0.0106	−0.0665	0.0029	1.0056	−0.0036	−0.0030	0.0026
563	0.001807	0.0113	0.0014	1.0041	0.0004	0.0004	0.0001
564	−0.0960	−0.5994	0.0017	1.0034	−0.0244	−0.0189	−0.0107
565	−0.1027	−0.6415	0.0014	1.0030	−0.0241	−0.0241	0.0055
566	0.2062	1.2895	0.0020	1.0003	0.0582	0.0381	0.0341
567	−0.1027	−0.6415	0.0014	1.0030	−0.0241	−0.0241	0.0055
568	−0.000495	−0.003091	0.0013	1.0040	−0.0001	−0.0001	−0.0000
569	−0.1083	−0.6767	0.0023	1.0037	−0.0322	−0.0288	0.0206
570	−0.1095	−0.6840	0.0025	1.0040	−0.0346	−0.0298	0.0239
571	0.0950	0.5935	0.0016	1.0034	0.0240	0.0235	−0.0103
572	−0.007238	−0.0452	0.0020	1.0047	−0.0020	−0.0019	0.0012
573	−0.006121	−0.0382	0.0018	1.0045	−0.0016	−0.0016	0.0008
574	−0.1039	−0.6487	0.0015	1.0031	−0.0251	−0.0250	0.0084
575	−0.003859	−0.0241	0.0015	1.0042	−0.0009	−0.0009	0.0003
576	−0.006138	−0.0383	0.0018	1.0045	−0.0016	−0.0016	0.0008
577	0.001829	0.0114	0.0014	1.0041	0.0004	0.0004	0.0001
578	−0.006135	−0.0383	0.0018	1.0045	−0.0016	−0.0016	0.0008
579	0.0961	0.6004	0.0015	1.0032	0.0233	0.0231	−0.0078
580	0.002964	0.0185	0.0015	1.0042	0.0007	0.0006	0.0003
581	−0.006131	−0.0383	0.0018	1.0045	−0.0016	−0.0016	0.0008
582	−0.002723	−0.0170	0.0014	1.0041	−0.0006	−0.0006	0.0001
583	−0.006141	−0.0384	0.0018	1.0045	−0.0016	−0.0016	0.0008
584	−0.005007	−0.0313	0.0016	1.0043	−0.0013	−0.0012	0.0005
585	−0.008454	−0.0528	0.0023	1.0050	−0.0025	−0.0023	0.0016
586	−0.009639	−0.0602	0.0026	1.0053	−0.0031	−0.0026	0.0021
587	−0.009680	−0.0605	0.0026	1.0053	−0.0031	−0.0026	0.0022
588	0.0868	0.5425	0.0038	1.0057	0.0335	0.0255	−0.0270
589	−0.0145	−0.0908	0.0043	1.0070	−0.0060	−0.0044	0.0050
590	−0.0146	−0.0916	0.0044	1.0071	−0.0061	−0.0044	0.0051
591	−0.0160	−0.0999	0.0050	1.0077	−0.0071	−0.0049	0.0061
592	0.0802	0.5021	0.0070	1.0091	0.0422	0.0266	−0.0380
593	0.0899	0.5616	0.0027	1.0046	0.0294	0.0248	−0.0211

Output statistics

Obs	Residual	RStudent	Hat diag H	Cov ratio	DFFITS	DFBETAS	
						Intercept	DLLEIL1
594	0.0873	0.5460	0.0036	1.0055	0.0327	0.0254	−0.0260
595	0.0898	0.5609	0.0028	1.0046	0.0296	0.0248	−0.0213
596	0.1693	1.0652	0.0153	1.0151	0.1326	0.0671	−0.1267
597	0.0843	0.5275	0.0048	1.0068	0.0368	0.0259	−0.0313
598	0.2723	1.7129	0.0126	1.0076	0.1938	0.1031	−0.1833
599	−0.1420	−0.8988	0.0276	1.0289	−0.1514	−0.0661	0.1477
600	0.3638	2.3017	0.0208	1.0097	0.3357	0.1568	−0.3248
601	0.1627	1.0275	0.0219	1.0223	0.1539	0.0710	−0.1492
602	0.3737	2.3536	0.0115	0.9995	0.2539	0.1386	−0.2388
603	0.2808	1.7613	0.0067	1.0011	0.1444	0.0923	−0.1292
604	0.2759	1.7335	0.0098	1.0045	0.1726	0.0985	−0.1604
605	0.4004	2.5101	0.0013	0.9873	0.0921	0.0872	0.0087
606	0.6019	3.7940	0.0014	0.9665	0.1431	0.1267	0.0358
607	0.006423	0.0401	0.0021	1.0048	0.0018	0.0012	0.0011
608	0.004843	0.0302	0.0018	1.0045	0.0013	0.0009	0.0006
609	0.4078	2.5585	0.0024	0.9877	0.1252	0.0720	0.0833
610	0.1077	0.6729	0.0024	1.0038	0.0328	0.0190	0.0217
611	0.1032	0.6445	0.0015	1.0031	0.0253	0.0208	0.0094
612	0.1090	0.6813	0.0027	1.0042	0.0356	0.0184	0.0254
613	0.008888	0.0555	0.0027	1.0054	0.0029	0.0015	0.0020
614	0.004475	0.0279	0.0017	1.0044	0.0012	0.0009	0.0005
615	0.0973	0.6075	0.0014	1.0031	0.0228	0.0228	−0.0052
616	0.0158	0.0988	0.0054	1.0081	0.0073	0.0021	0.0063
617	−0.0971	−0.6064	0.0015	1.0032	−0.0236	−0.0197	−0.0082
618	0.001486	0.009277	0.0014	1.0041	0.0003	0.0003	0.0001
619	−0.1027	−0.6415	0.0014	1.0030	−0.0241	−0.0241	0.0055
620	−0.2013	−1.2583	0.0013	0.9998	−0.0461	−0.0456	0.0039
621	0.0000712	0.000444	0.0013	1.0040	0.0000	0.0000	0.0000
622	0.1042	0.6511	0.0017	1.0032	0.0267	0.0204	0.0121
623	−0.004110	−0.0257	0.0015	1.0042	−0.0010	−0.0010	0.0004
624	0.008332	0.0521	0.0025	1.0052	0.0026	0.0014	0.0018
625	−0.0891	−0.5567	0.0033	1.0052	−0.0323	−0.0141	−0.0250
626	−0.2027	−1.2671	0.0014	0.9998	−0.0475	−0.0475	0.0109
627	0.006752	0.0422	0.0021	1.0048	0.0020	0.0012	0.0012
628	−0.0920	−0.5748	0.0024	1.0042	−0.0285	−0.0161	−0.0192
629	0.0973	0.6075	0.0014	1.0031	0.0228	0.0228	−0.0052
630	0.005262	0.0329	0.0018	1.0045	0.0014	0.0010	0.0007
631	−0.002723	−0.0170	0.0014	1.0041	−0.0006	−0.0006	0.0001
632	0.1026	0.6406	0.0015	1.0031	0.0247	0.0210	0.0078
633	−0.0107	−0.0667	0.0029	1.0056	−0.0036	−0.0030	0.0026
634	−0.3081	−1.9289	0.0022	0.9950	−0.0905	−0.0816	0.0568
635	−0.0947	−0.5918	0.0018	1.0036	−0.0254	−0.0180	−0.0134
636	−0.1014	−0.6332	0.0013	1.0029	−0.0232	−0.0230	0.0021
637	−0.0974	−0.6085	0.0015	1.0032	−0.0234	−0.0200	−0.0074
638	−0.1001	−0.6251	0.0013	1.0030	−0.0228	−0.0220	−0.0011
639	−0.0949	−0.5925	0.0018	1.0036	−0.0253	−0.0181	−0.0132
640	0.001191	0.007435	0.0014	1.0041	0.0003	0.0003	0.0001
641	−0.005330	−0.0333	0.0017	1.0044	−0.0014	−0.0013	0.0006
642	0.0986	0.6157	0.0013	1.0030	0.0226	0.0224	−0.0021
643	−0.2079	−1.3003	0.0022	1.0003	−0.0607	−0.0549	0.0377
644	−0.000106	−0.000663	0.0013	1.0040	−0.0000	−0.0000	−0.0000
645	−0.1080	−0.6745	0.0022	1.0036	−0.0315	−0.0285	0.0196
646	0.002516	0.0157	0.0015	1.0042	0.0006	0.0005	0.0002
647	−0.2001	−1.2507	0.0013	0.9998	−0.0457	−0.0440	−0.0021
648	0.0960	0.5994	0.0015	1.0032	0.0234	0.0232	−0.0082

Obs	Residual	RStudent	Hat diag H	Cov ratio	DFFITS	DFBETAS	
						Intercept	DLLEIL1
649	−0.0975	−0.6090	0.0015	1.0032	−0.0234	−0.0200	−0.0072
650	0.003756	0.0235	0.0016	1.0043	0.0009	0.0007	0.0004
651	−0.1001	−0.6254	0.0013	1.0030	−0.0229	−0.0220	−0.0010
652	−0.005304	−0.0331	0.0017	1.0044	−0.0014	−0.0013	0.0006
653	0.003720	0.0232	0.0016	1.0043	0.0009	0.0007	0.0004
654	−0.0989	−0.6175	0.0014	1.0030	−0.0229	−0.0210	−0.0040
655	−0.1014	−0.6335	0.0013	1.0029	−0.0232	−0.0230	0.0023
656	−0.1002	−0.6256	0.0013	1.0030	−0.0229	−0.0220	−0.0009
657	0.003642	0.0227	0.0016	1.0043	0.0009	0.0007	0.0004
658	−0.0926	−0.5786	0.0023	1.0041	−0.0277	−0.0165	−0.0179
659	−0.002723	−0.0170	0.0014	1.0041	−0.0006	−0.0006	0.0001
660	−0.0915	−0.5715	0.0026	1.0044	−0.0291	−0.0157	−0.0203
661	−0.2027	−1.2671	0.0014	0.9998	−0.0475	−0.0475	0.0109
662	0.0985	0.6153	0.0013	1.0030	0.0226	0.0224	−0.0023
663	0.004721	0.0295	0.0018	1.0044	0.0012	0.0009	0.0006
664	−0.2916	−1.8260	0.0025	0.9963	−0.0921	−0.0504	−0.0635
665	−0.1015	−0.6339	0.0013	1.0029	−0.0233	−0.0231	0.0024
666	−0.0966	−0.6035	0.0016	1.0033	−0.0239	−0.0193	−0.0092
667	0.005766	0.0360	0.0019	1.0046	0.0016	0.0011	0.0009
668	−0.0967	−0.6039	0.0016	1.0033	−0.0238	−0.0194	−0.0091
669	−0.1015	−0.6340	0.0013	1.0029	−0.0233	−0.0231	0.0025
670	−0.0943	−0.5894	0.0019	1.0037	−0.0258	−0.0177	−0.0143
671	−0.000341	−0.002130	0.0013	1.0040	−0.0001	−0.0001	−0.0000
672	−0.0992	−0.6193	0.0014	1.0030	−0.0229	−0.0213	−0.0033
673	0.004371	0.0273	0.0017	1.0044	0.0011	0.0009	0.0005
674	−0.1027	−0.6415	0.0014	1.0030	−0.0241	−0.0241	0.0055
675	−0.1015	−0.6342	0.0013	1.0029	−0.0233	−0.0231	0.0025
676	−0.0980	−0.6122	0.0014	1.0031	−0.0231	−0.0204	−0.0060
677	0.1020	0.6368	0.0014	1.0030	0.0241	0.0212	0.0062
678	−0.0981	−0.6124	0.0014	1.0031	−0.0231	−0.0204	−0.0059
679	−0.0958	−0.5982	0.0017	1.0034	−0.0245	−0.0187	−0.0112
680	−0.007356	−0.0459	0.0020	1.0047	−0.0021	−0.0019	0.0012
681	−0.1027	−0.6415	0.0014	1.0030	−0.0241	−0.0241	0.0055
682	−0.002723	−0.0170	0.0014	1.0041	−0.0006	−0.0006	0.0001
683	0.000755	0.004711	0.0014	1.0040	0.0002	0.0002	0.0000
684	0.001897	0.0118	0.0014	1.0041	0.0004	0.0004	0.0001
685	−0.1039	−0.6488	0.0015	1.0031	−0.0252	−0.0250	0.0085
686	0.0892	0.5573	0.0030	1.0048	0.0303	0.0250	−0.0225
687	−0.001561	−0.009748	0.0013	1.0040	−0.0004	−0.0004	0.0000
688	−0.002723	−0.0170	0.0014	1.0041	−0.0006	−0.0006	0.0001
689	−0.1992	−1.2453	0.0014	0.9999	−0.0459	−0.0428	−0.0063
690	0.0961	0.6003	0.0015	1.0032	0.0233	0.0231	−0.0079
691	0.000748	0.004667	0.0014	1.0040	0.0002	0.0002	0.0000
692	−0.0993	−0.6199	0.0014	1.0030	−0.0228	−0.0213	−0.0031
693	0.0973	0.6075	0.0014	1.0031	0.0228	0.0228	−0.0052
694	0.000727	0.004538	0.0014	1.0040	0.0002	0.0002	0.0000
695	−0.1050	−0.6560	0.0016	1.0032	−0.0266	−0.0260	0.0115
696	−0.000424	−0.002648	0.0013	1.0040	−0.0001	−0.0001	−0.0000
697	0.003004	0.0188	0.0015	1.0042	0.0007	0.0006	0.0003
698	−0.0948	−0.5919	0.0018	1.0036	−0.0254	−0.0180	−0.0134
699	−0.0982	−0.6132	0.0014	1.0031	−0.0231	−0.0205	−0.0056
700	0.001789	0.0112	0.0014	1.0041	0.0004	0.0004	0.0001
701	−0.001597	−0.009974	0.0013	1.0040	−0.0004	−0.0004	0.0000
702	−0.0982	−0.6135	0.0014	1.0031	−0.0231	−0.0205	−0.0055
703	0.1040	0.6495	0.0016	1.0032	0.0263	0.0205	0.0115

Output statistics

Obs	Residual	RStudent	Hat diag H	Cov ratio	DFFITS	DFBETAS Intercept	DLLEIL1
704	−0.000497	−0.003105	0.0013	1.0040	−0.0001	−0.0001	−0.0000
705	0.000607	0.003792	0.0014	1.0040	0.0001	0.0001	0.0000
706	−0.1005	−0.6277	0.0013	1.0030	−0.0229	−0.0223	−0.0001
707	0.0116	0.0723	0.0036	1.0063	0.0043	0.0018	0.0034
708	−0.0973	−0.6075	0.0015	1.0032	−0.0235	−0.0198	−0.0077
709	0.003784	0.0236	0.0016	1.0043	0.0010	0.0007	0.0004
710	−0.0963	−0.6012	0.0016	1.0033	−0.0242	−0.0191	−0.0101
711	0.004780	0.0299	0.0018	1.0044	0.0013	0.0009	0.0006
712	0.1015	0.6342	0.0014	1.0030	0.0237	0.0214	0.0051
713	−0.1974	−1.2339	0.0015	1.0001	−0.0475	−0.0404	−0.0151
714	0.0973	0.6075	0.0014	1.0031	0.0228	0.0228	−0.0052
715	0.1047	0.6538	0.0017	1.0033	0.0273	0.0202	0.0133
716	−0.0954	−0.5957	0.0017	1.0035	−0.0249	−0.0184	−0.0120
717	−0.000632	−0.003948	0.0013	1.0040	−0.0001	−0.0001	0.0000
718	0.004564	0.0285	0.0017	1.0044	0.0012	0.0009	0.0006
719	−0.1038	−0.6481	0.0015	1.0030	−0.0250	−0.0249	0.0082
720	0.0973	0.6075	0.0014	1.0031	0.0228	0.0228	−0.0052
721	−0.1027	−0.6415	0.0014	1.0030	−0.0241	−0.0241	0.0055
722	0.0962	0.6011	0.0015	1.0032	0.0232	0.0231	−0.0076
723	−0.001684	−0.0105	0.0014	1.0040	−0.0004	−0.0004	0.0000
724	−0.0986	−0.6156	0.0014	1.0031	−0.0230	−0.0208	−0.0047
725	−0.002723	−0.0170	0.0014	1.0041	−0.0006	−0.0006	0.0001
726	−0.003758	−0.0235	0.0015	1.0042	−0.0009	−0.0009	0.0003
727	−0.001687	−0.0105	0.0014	1.0040	−0.0004	−0.0004	0.0000
728	0.002440	0.0152	0.0015	1.0041	0.0006	0.0005	0.0002
729	−0.004785	−0.0299	0.0016	1.0043	−0.0012	−0.0012	0.0005
730	−0.003755	−0.0234	0.0015	1.0042	−0.0009	−0.0009	0.0003
731	−0.005826	−0.0364	0.0018	1.0044	−0.0015	−0.0015	0.0008
732	−0.1007	−0.6286	0.0013	1.0030	−0.0230	−0.0224	0.0003
733	−0.004792	−0.0299	0.0016	1.0043	−0.0012	−0.0012	0.0005
734	0.003475	0.0217	0.0016	1.0043	0.0009	0.0007	0.0003
735	−0.003753	−0.0234	0.0015	1.0042	−0.0009	−0.0009	0.0003
736	−0.1939	−1.3017	0.1345	1.1533	−0.5132	−0.1664	0.5106
737	0.2212	1.4527	0.0950	1.1017	0.4707	0.1610	−0.4674
738	0.6325	4.0252	0.0180	0.9782	0.5450	0.0245	0.5245
739	3.0315	26.6223	0.0170	0.2689	3.4976	0.1869	3.3576
740	0.1206	0.7559	0.0082	1.0094	0.0686	0.0126	0.0627
741	−0.4853	−3.0540	0.0049	0.9829	−0.2143	−0.0670	−0.1828
742	−0.7919	−5.0302	0.0025	0.9404	−0.2498	−0.1403	−0.1692
743	−0.1952	−1.2204	0.0018	1.0005	−0.0513	−0.0376	−0.0253
744	−0.1921	−1.2012	0.0024	1.0012	−0.0591	−0.0337	−0.0396
745	0.001496	0.009341	0.0014	1.0041	0.0003	0.0003	0.0001
746	0.1025	0.6404	0.0015	1.0031	0.0246	0.0210	0.0077
747	−0.002723	−0.0170	0.0014	1.0041	−0.0006	−0.0006	0.0001
748	−0.1881	−1.1771	0.0037	1.0027	−0.0715	−0.0288	−0.0571
749	−0.1863	−1.1659	0.0044	1.0035	−0.0778	−0.0266	−0.0651
750	0.2125	1.3299	0.0039	1.0019	0.0834	0.0319	0.0678
751	−0.3947	−2.4750	0.0019	0.9883	−0.1066	−0.0751	−0.0565
752	−0.1928	−1.2053	0.0023	1.0010	−0.0573	−0.0345	−0.0366
753	−0.3938	−2.4698	0.0020	0.9885	−0.1110	−0.0730	−0.0647

Sum of residuals	0
Sum of squared residuals	19.21437
Predicted residual SS (press)	19.63220

Yes, we see very large studentized residuals, RStudent, and large cov Ratio, DFBETAS and DFFITS variables for observation 738–742, the March–July 2020 period. A year past the start of COVID, the influential variables indicate it is appropriate to estimate robust regressions for the DUE and DLLEIL1 relationship.

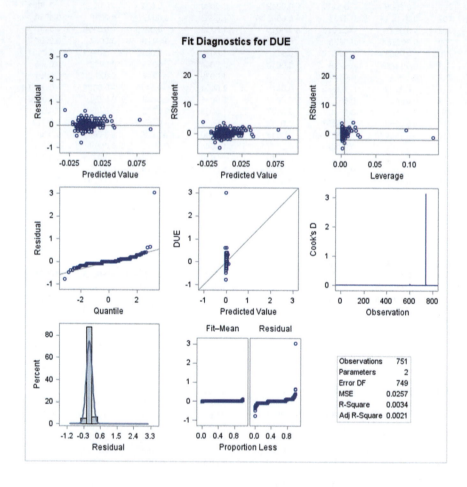

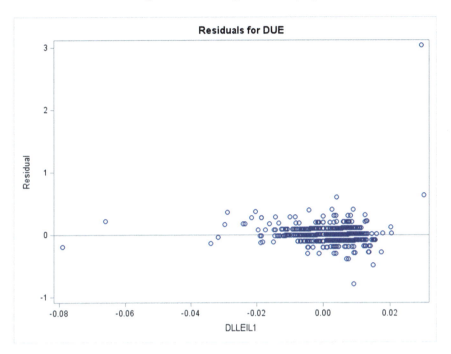

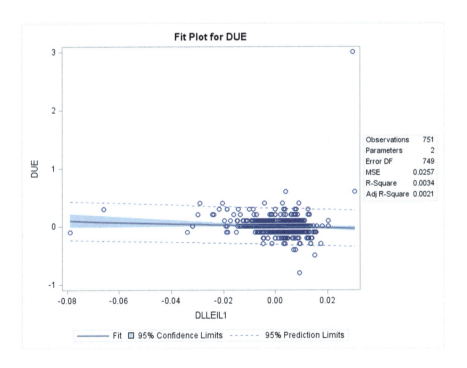

Is the weekly unemployment claims variable, WkUNCL, still statistically significant in the regression analysis in modeling the U.S. unemployment rate? No, the logged first-difference of the WkUNCL (DLWkUNCL) variable has a negative, rather than the positive coefficient expected, coefficient, −0.047. The coefficient is not statistically significant, having an estimated t-statistic of only −0.89. We are interested in the lagged DLWkUNCL relation in this chapter. We want to test if the DLWkUNCL variable leads the DUE variable.

Palgrave DUE DLWkUNCLL1 PJD 110521
The REG Procedure
Model: MODEL1
Dependent Variable: DUE

Number of observations read	753
Number of observations used	752
Number of observations with missing values	1

Analysis of variance

Source	DF	Sum of squares	Mean square	F value	Pr > F
Model	1	0.02054	0.02054	0.80	0.3719
Error	750	19.29940	0.02573		
Corrected Total	751	19.31995			

Root MSE	0.16041	**R-square**	0.0011
Dependent mean	0.00026596	**Adj R-square**	−0.0003
Coeff var	60,316		

Parameter estimates

Variable	DF	Parameter estimate	Standard error	t value	Pr > |t|
Intercept	1	0.00027586	0.00585	0.05	0.9624
DLWkUNCL	1	−0.04692	0.05251	−0.89	0.3719

Is the weekly unemployment variable, WkUNCL, still statistically significant in the OLS regression analysis in modeling the U.S. unemployment rate? No, the logged first-difference of the WkUNCL (DLWkUNCL) variable with a one-month lag (DLWkUNCL1) is negatively, not positively statistically associated, with the change (DUE) in the unemployment rate. The DLWkUNCL1with an estimated t-statistic of -1.86 in the ordinary least square regression. The OLS estimated DLWkUNCLL1 coefficient is negative, -0.98, and statistically significant at the 6% level. However, we must identify influential observations and use robust regression techniques to fit outliers, if appropriate.

Palgrave DUE DLWkUNCLL1 PJD 110521
The REG Procedure
Model: MODEL1
Dependent Variable: DUE

Number of observations read	753
Number of observations used	751
Number of observations with missing values	2

Analysis of variance

Source	DF	Sum of squares	Mean square	F value	Pr > F
Model	1	0.08911	0.08911	3.48	0.0626
Error	749	19.19068	0.02562		
Corrected Total	750	19.27979			

Root MSE	0.16007	R-square	0.0046
Dependent mean	0.00053262	Adj R-square	0.0033
Coeff var	30,053		

Parameter estimates

Variable	DF	Parameter estimate	Standard error	t value	Pr > |t|
Intercept	1	0.00055755	0.00584	0.10	0.9240
DLWkUNCLL1	1	−0.09772	0.05240	−1.86	0.0626

Palgrave DUE DLWkUNCLL1 PJD 110521
The REG Procedure
Model: MODEL1
Dependent Variable: DUE

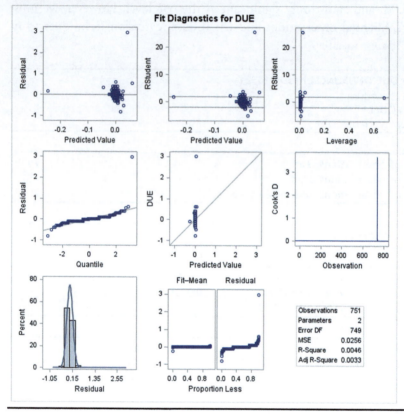

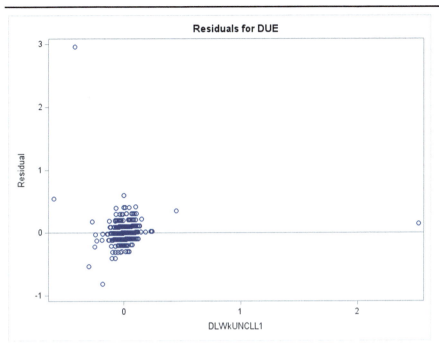

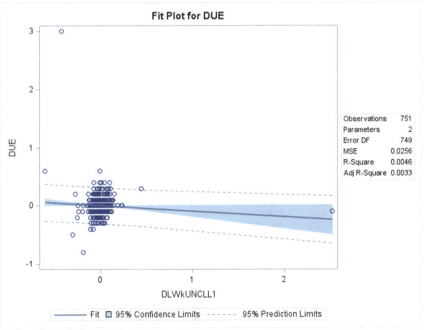

The SAS regression diagnostics of the DUE and DLWkUNCL1 simple linear regression model indicates with the large residuals, studentized regression residuals, RStudent, and Cook's D measures that OLS analysis is not sufficient, and we should proceed to estimate a robust regression line for the DUE and DLWkUNCL1 variables.

Palgrave DUE DLWkUNCLL1 PJD 110521
The REG Procedure
Model: MODEL1
Dependent Variable: DUE

Output statistics

Obs	Residual	RStudent	Hat diag H	Cov ratio	DFFITS	DFBETAS Intercept	DLWkUNCLL1
1	–	–	–	–	–	–	–
2	–	–	–	–	–	–	–
3	−0.1032	−0.6450	0.0014	1.0030	−0.0243	−0.0236	0.0058
4	−0.3101	−1.9429	0.0023	0.9950	−0.0943	−0.0711	0.0620
5	−0.1058	−0.6614	0.0016	1.0032	−0.0268	−0.0242	0.0117
6	0.000194	0.001212	0.0013	1.0040	0.0000	0.0000	0.0000
7	−0.0962	−0.6010	0.0015	1.0033	−0.0236	−0.0219	−0.0088
8	0.001714	0.0107	0.0014	1.0041	0.0004	0.0004	0.0001
9	0.009240	0.0578	0.0024	1.0051	0.0028	0.0021	0.0019
10	−0.007633	−0.0477	0.0019	1.0046	−0.0021	−0.0017	0.0011
11	0.1128	0.7059	0.0033	1.0047	0.0408	0.0257	0.0317
12	−0.0887	−0.5545	0.0029	1.0048	−0.0300	−0.0202	−0.0221
13	−0.0243	−0.1526	0.0077	1.0104	−0.0134	−0.0056	0.0122
14	−0.0987	−0.6166	0.0014	1.0030	−0.0228	−0.0225	−0.0038
15	0.1959	1.2253	0.0015	1.0001	0.0471	0.0448	−0.0146
16	−0.0895	−0.5596	0.0027	1.0045	−0.0291	−0.0204	−0.0207
17	−0.2036	−1.2733	0.0014	0.9998	−0.0483	−0.0465	0.0130
18	0.1065	0.6656	0.0019	1.0034	0.0289	0.0243	0.0156
19	0.1012	0.6323	0.0014	1.0030	0.0234	0.0231	0.0036
20	0.003550	0.0222	0.0015	1.0042	0.0009	0.0008	0.0003
21	0.1073	0.6710	0.0020	1.0035	0.0302	0.0245	0.0177
22	0.2961	1.8542	0.0015	0.9950	0.0709	0.0678	−0.0209
23	0.005312	0.0332	0.0017	1.0044	0.0014	0.0012	0.0007
24	−0.0975	−0.6094	0.0014	1.0031	−0.0231	−0.0222	−0.0062
25	0.2985	1.8692	0.0013	0.9947	0.0685	0.0683	−0.0060
26	0.1025	0.6404	0.0014	1.0030	0.0243	0.0234	0.0065
27	0.1081	0.6757	0.0022	1.0036	0.0315	0.0246	0.0195
28	0.1872	1.1713	0.0030	1.0020	0.0646	0.0429	−0.0484
29	0.1000	0.6251	0.0013	1.0030	0.0229	0.0228	0.0012
30	−0.1067	−0.6668	0.0018	1.0032	−0.0280	−0.0244	0.0137
31	0.2926	1.8327	0.0019	0.9956	0.0791	0.0670	−0.0421
32	−0.2964	−1.8560	0.0015	0.9950	−0.0725	−0.0677	−0.0259
33	−0.1102	−0.6889	0.0024	1.0038	−0.0336	−0.0252	0.0223
34	−0.0964	−0.6025	0.0015	1.0032	−0.0235	−0.0220	−0.0083
35	−0.1083	−0.6773	0.0020	1.0035	−0.0304	−0.0248	0.0177
36	−0.1004	−0.6276	0.0013	1.0030	−0.0229	−0.0229	−0.0002
37	−0.1032	−0.6452	0.0014	1.0030	−0.0243	−0.0236	0.0059
38	0.000872	0.005450	0.0014	1.0040	0.0002	0.0002	0.0000
39	−0.1023	−0.6396	0.0014	1.0030	−0.0237	−0.0234	0.0039
40	−0.1033	−0.6453	0.0014	1.0030	−0.0243	−0.0236	0.0059

Output statistics

Obs	Residual	RStudent	Hat diag H	Cov ratio	DFFITS	DFBETAS	
						Intercept	DLWkUNCLL1
41	−0.001952	−0.0122	0.0014	1.0040	−0.0004	−0.0004	0.0001
42	−0.0947	−0.5919	0.0017	1.0035	−0.0245	−0.0216	−0.0116
43	0.000534	0.003334	0.0013	1.0040	0.0001	0.0001	0.0000
44	−0.000877	−0.005480	0.0013	1.0040	−0.0002	−0.0002	0.0000
45	0.000113	0.000703	0.0013	1.0040	0.0000	0.0000	0.0000
46	−0.1021	−0.6382	0.0014	1.0029	−0.0236	−0.0233	0.0034
47	0.1008	0.6296	0.0014	1.0030	0.0232	0.0230	0.0027
48	−0.002230	−0.0139	0.0014	1.0040	−0.0005	−0.0005	0.0001
49	0.1029	0.6428	0.0015	1.0030	0.0246	0.0235	0.0073
50	−0.000589	−0.003679	0.0013	1.0040	−0.0001	−0.0001	0.0000
51	−0.1034	−0.6459	0.0014	1.0030	−0.0244	−0.0236	0.0061
52	−0.005010	−0.0313	0.0016	1.0042	−0.0012	−0.0011	0.0005
53	0.1014	0.6337	0.0014	1.0030	0.0235	0.0231	0.0041
54	−0.1025	−0.6405	0.0014	1.0030	−0.0238	−0.0234	0.0042
55	−0.001916	−0.0120	0.0014	1.0040	−0.0004	−0.0004	0.0001
56	0.0988	0.6176	0.0013	1.0030	0.0226	0.0226	−0.0013
57	−0.0978	−0.6114	0.0014	1.0031	−0.0230	−0.0223	−0.0055
58	−0.002144	−0.0134	0.0014	1.0040	−0.0005	−0.0005	0.0001
59	−0.001515	−0.009464	0.0013	1.0040	−0.0003	−0.0003	0.0000
60	−0.1027	−0.6416	0.0014	1.0030	−0.0239	−0.0234	0.0046
61	0.1079	0.6744	0.0021	1.0036	0.0311	0.0246	0.0190
62	−0.1066	−0.6661	0.0017	1.0032	−0.0278	−0.0244	0.0135
63	−0.005295	−0.0331	0.0016	1.0043	−0.0013	−0.0012	0.0005
64	−0.0980	−0.6122	0.0014	1.0031	−0.0230	−0.0223	−0.0053
65	−0.004962	−0.0310	0.0016	1.0042	−0.0012	−0.0011	0.0005
66	0.0986	0.6159	0.0013	1.0030	0.0226	0.0225	−0.0019
67	−0.002801	−0.0175	0.0014	1.0041	−0.0007	−0.0006	0.0001
68	−0.0994	−0.6213	0.0013	1.0030	−0.0228	−0.0227	−0.0023
69	−0.006571	−0.0411	0.0017	1.0044	−0.0017	−0.0015	0.0008
70	−0.1000	−0.6247	0.0013	1.0030	−0.0228	−0.0228	−0.0012
71	0.1009	0.6305	0.0014	1.0030	0.0232	0.0230	0.0030
72	−0.0956	−0.5974	0.0016	1.0033	−0.0240	−0.0218	−0.0099
73	−0.1048	−0.6549	0.0015	1.0031	−0.0257	−0.0239	0.0094
74	0.0962	0.6013	0.0014	1.0032	0.0229	0.0220	−0.0065
75	−0.0985	−0.6155	0.0014	1.0030	−0.0229	−0.0225	−0.0042
76	−0.004916	−0.0307	0.0015	1.0042	−0.0012	−0.0011	0.0005
77	−0.1005	−0.6279	0.0013	1.0030	−0.0229	−0.0229	−0.0001
78	0.0935	0.5847	0.0017	1.0035	0.0243	0.0214	−0.0116
79	−0.2002	−1.2521	0.0013	0.9998	−0.0457	−0.0457	−0.0013
80	0.1022	0.6385	0.0014	1.0030	0.0240	0.0233	0.0058
81	0.006459	0.0404	0.0019	1.0046	0.0018	0.0015	0.0009
82	−0.1130	−0.7067	0.0031	1.0044	−0.0392	−0.0259	0.0295
83	−0.004920	−0.0307	0.0015	1.0042	−0.0012	−0.0011	0.0005
84	0.001147	0.007165	0.0014	1.0040	0.0003	0.0003	0.0000
85	−0.1033	−0.6458	0.0014	1.0030	−0.0244	−0.0236	0.0061
86	0.006422	0.0401	0.0019	1.0046	0.0017	0.0015	0.0009
87	−0.002012	−0.0126	0.0014	1.0040	−0.0005	−0.0005	0.0001
88	−0.0185	−0.1157	0.0050	1.0076	−0.0082	−0.0042	0.0070
89	−0.1023	−0.6395	0.0014	1.0030	−0.0237	−0.0234	0.0039
90	−0.0937	−0.5856	0.0019	1.0036	−0.0253	−0.0214	−0.0134
91	0.000750	0.004686	0.0014	1.0040	0.0002	0.0002	0.0000
92	0.001763	0.0110	0.0014	1.0041	0.0004	0.0004	0.0001
93	−0.002678	−0.0167	0.0014	1.0041	−0.0006	−0.0006	0.0001
94	0.000878	0.005484	0.0014	1.0040	0.0002	0.0002	0.0000

Output statistics

Obs	Residual	RStudent	Hat diag H	Cov ratio	DFFITS	DFBETAS	
						Intercept	DLWkUNCLL1
95	0.001917	0.0120	0.0014	1.0041	0.0004	0.0004	0.0001
96	0.002135	0.0133	0.0014	1.0041	0.0005	0.0005	0.0001
97	0.004527	0.0283	0.0016	1.0043	0.0011	0.0010	0.0005
98	−0.006109	−0.0382	0.0017	1.0044	−0.0016	−0.0014	0.0007
99	0.0179	0.1118	0.0051	1.0078	0.0080	0.0041	0.0069
100	−0.002279	−0.0142	0.0014	1.0040	−0.0005	−0.0005	0.0001
101	−0.0944	−0.5902	0.0017	1.0035	−0.0247	−0.0215	−0.0121
102	−0.0119	−0.0744	0.0028	1.0055	−0.0039	−0.0027	0.0028
103	−0.006126	−0.0383	0.0017	1.0044	−0.0016	−0.0014	0.0007
104	0.1039	0.6495	0.0016	1.0031	0.0256	0.0237	0.0097
105	−0.009594	−0.0600	0.0023	1.0049	−0.0028	−0.0022	0.0018
106	0.001136	0.007100	0.0014	1.0040	0.0003	0.0003	0.0000
107	0.0000307	0.000192	0.0013	1.0040	0.0000	0.0000	0.0000
108	−0.008643	−0.0540	0.0021	1.0047	−0.0025	−0.0020	0.0015
109	0.006667	0.0417	0.0019	1.0046	0.0018	0.0015	0.0010
110	−0.000194	−0.001213	0.0013	1.0040	−0.0000	−0.0000	−0.0000
111	−0.009428	−0.0589	0.0022	1.0049	−0.0028	−0.0022	0.0018
112	−0.1009	−0.6306	0.0013	1.0029	−0.0230	−0.0230	0.0008
113	0.000779	0.004865	0.0014	1.0040	0.0002	0.0002	0.0000
114	−0.001994	−0.0125	0.0014	1.0040	−0.0005	−0.0005	0.0001
115	−0.002625	−0.0164	0.0014	1.0041	−0.0006	−0.0006	0.0001
116	0.001460	0.009118	0.0014	1.0041	0.0003	0.0003	0.0001
117	0.000139	0.000866	0.0013	1.0040	0.0000	0.0000	0.0000
118	−0.004141	−0.0259	0.0015	1.0042	−0.0010	−0.0009	0.0003
119	−0.003533	−0.0221	0.0014	1.0041	−0.0008	−0.0008	0.0002
120	−0.1009	−0.6304	0.0013	1.0029	−0.0230	−0.0230	0.0007
121	0.007403	0.0463	0.0020	1.0047	0.0021	0.0017	0.0012
122	−0.003140	−0.0196	0.0014	1.0041	−0.0007	−0.0007	0.0002
123	−0.000306	−0.001913	0.0013	1.0040	−0.0001	−0.0001	−0.0000
124	0.0946	0.5913	0.0016	1.0033	0.0236	0.0216	−0.0096
125	−0.002153	−0.0134	0.0014	1.0040	−0.0005	−0.0005	0.0001
126	−0.000934	−0.005832	0.0013	1.0040	−0.0002	−0.0002	0.0000
127	0.004425	0.0277	0.0016	1.0043	0.0011	0.0010	0.0005
128	0.004037	0.0252	0.0016	1.0042	0.0010	0.0009	0.0004
129	−0.001390	−0.008687	0.0013	1.0040	−0.0003	−0.0003	0.0000
130	−0.002848	−0.0178	0.0014	1.0041	−0.0007	−0.0006	0.0001
131	0.002174	0.0136	0.0014	1.0041	0.0005	0.0005	0.0001
132	0.002954	0.0185	0.0015	1.0041	0.0007	0.0007	0.0002
133	0.005267	0.0329	0.0017	1.0044	0.0014	0.0012	0.0006
134	0.1125	0.7038	0.0032	1.0046	0.0401	0.0257	0.0308
135	0.002283	0.0143	0.0014	1.0041	0.0005	0.0005	0.0001
136	0.1029	0.6428	0.0015	1.0030	0.0246	0.0235	0.0073
137	0.0230	0.1439	0.0075	1.0102	0.0125	0.0052	0.0114
138	0.0885	0.5533	0.0027	1.0046	0.0287	0.0203	−0.0204
139	−0.003063	−0.0191	0.0014	1.0041	−0.0007	−0.0007	0.0002
140	0.0945	0.5904	0.0016	1.0034	0.0237	0.0216	−0.0099
141	0.002582	0.0161	0.0014	1.0041	0.0006	0.0006	0.0002
142	0.0101	0.0631	0.0026	1.0053	0.0032	0.0023	0.0022
143	0.1008	0.6300	0.0014	1.0030	0.0232	0.0230	0.0029
144	0.2982	1.8670	0.0014	0.9947	0.0687	0.0682	−0.0082
145	−0.006993	−0.0437	0.0018	1.0045	−0.0019	−0.0016	0.0009
146	−0.002702	−0.0169	0.0014	1.0041	−0.0006	−0.0006	0.0001
147	−0.005268	−0.0329	0.0016	1.0043	−0.0013	−0.0012	0.0005
148	0.1028	0.6422	0.0015	1.0030	0.0245	0.0234	0.0071

Output statistics

Obs	Residual	RStudent	Hat diag H	Cov ratio	DFFITS	DFBETAS	
						Intercept	DLWkUNCLL1
149	−0.003569	−0.0223	0.0014	1.0041	−0.0008	−0.0008	0.0002
150	0.002087	0.0130	0.0014	1.0041	0.0005	0.0005	0.0001
151	0.0987	0.6168	0.0013	1.0030	0.0226	0.0225	−0.0016
152	0.001707	0.0107	0.0014	1.0041	0.0004	0.0004	0.0001
153	0.008222	0.0514	0.0022	1.0049	0.0024	0.0019	0.0015
154	−0.006866	−0.0429	0.0018	1.0045	−0.0018	−0.0016	0.0009
155	−0.003061	−0.0191	0.0014	1.0041	−0.0007	−0.0007	0.0002
156	−0.003942	−0.0246	0.0015	1.0041	−0.0009	−0.0009	0.0003
157	−0.007261	−0.0454	0.0018	1.0045	−0.0019	−0.0017	0.0010
158	−0.000084	−0.000525	0.0013	1.0040	−0.0000	−0.0000	−0.0000
159	−0.1026	−0.6410	0.0014	1.0030	−0.0238	−0.0234	0.0044
160	−0.000967	−0.006038	0.0013	1.0040	−0.0002	−0.0002	0.0000
161	−0.1000	−0.6251	0.0013	1.0030	−0.0229	−0.0228	−0.0010
162	0.000658	0.004109	0.0013	1.0040	0.0002	0.0002	0.0000
163	0.008823	0.0551	0.0023	1.0050	0.0027	0.0020	0.0017
164	−0.004044	−0.0253	0.0015	1.0041	−0.0010	−0.0009	0.0003
165	−0.0109	−0.0684	0.0025	1.0052	−0.0035	−0.0025	0.0024
166	−0.000481	−0.003005	0.0013	1.0040	−0.0001	−0.0001	−0.0000
167	−0.1024	−0.6400	0.0014	1.0030	−0.0237	−0.0234	0.0040
168	−0.1034	−0.6465	0.0014	1.0030	−0.0244	−0.0236	0.0063
169	0.000720	0.004501	0.0013	1.0040	0.0002	0.0002	0.0000
170	−0.1080	−0.6750	0.0020	1.0034	−0.0299	−0.0247	0.0168
171	−0.003955	−0.0247	0.0015	1.0041	−0.0009	−0.0009	0.0003
172	−0.0976	−0.6101	0.0014	1.0031	−0.0231	−0.0223	−0.0059
173	0.004186	0.0262	0.0016	1.0043	0.0010	0.0010	0.0004
174	−0.001795	−0.0112	0.0013	1.0040	−0.0004	−0.0004	0.0000
175	−0.0987	−0.6168	0.0014	1.0030	−0.0228	−0.0225	−0.0038
176	0.1004	0.6272	0.0013	1.0030	0.0230	0.0229	0.0019
177	0.004089	0.0256	0.0016	1.0043	0.0010	0.0009	0.0004
178	−0.003169	−0.0198	0.0014	1.0041	−0.0007	−0.0007	0.0002
179	−0.002997	−0.0187	0.0014	1.0041	−0.0007	−0.0007	0.0002
180	−0.0949	−0.5931	0.0017	1.0034	−0.0244	−0.0216	−0.0112
181	0.1119	0.7000	0.0031	1.0044	0.0388	0.0255	0.0292
182	0.006826	0.0427	0.0019	1.0046	0.0019	0.0016	0.0011
183	0.000867	0.005415	0.0014	1.0040	0.0002	0.0002	0.0000
184	0.0981	0.6133	0.0014	1.0030	0.0226	0.0224	−0.0027
185	−0.007429	−0.0464	0.0019	1.0045	−0.0020	−0.0017	0.0011
186	0.000274	0.001714	0.0013	1.0040	0.0001	0.0001	0.0000
187	0.004919	0.0307	0.0017	1.0043	0.0013	0.0011	0.0006
188	−0.001470	−0.009186	0.0013	1.0040	−0.0003	−0.0003	0.0000
189	0.1095	0.6845	0.0025	1.0039	0.0340	0.0250	0.0230
190	0.1044	0.6525	0.0016	1.0031	0.0262	0.0238	0.0108
191	0.0108	0.0677	0.0028	1.0055	0.0036	0.0025	0.0026
192	0.2141	1.3408	0.0037	1.0016	0.0821	0.0489	0.0659
193	0.3100	1.9426	0.0026	0.9952	0.0986	0.0708	0.0685
194	0.3061	1.9175	0.0018	0.9947	0.0820	0.0699	0.0426
195	0.1960	1.2256	0.0015	1.0001	0.0470	0.0448	−0.0144
196	0.4004	2.5119	0.0013	0.9873	0.0921	0.0917	0.0078
197	0.1939	1.2130	0.0017	1.0004	0.0497	0.0444	−0.0225
198	0.1956	1.2231	0.0015	1.0002	0.0474	0.0447	−0.0160
199	0.0992	0.6198	0.0013	1.0030	0.0226	0.0226	−0.0006
200	−0.1101	−0.6883	0.0024	1.0038	−0.0335	−0.0252	0.0221
201	0.0999	0.6243	0.0013	1.0030	0.0228	0.0228	0.0009
202	−0.2019	−1.2628	0.0014	0.9998	−0.0465	−0.0461	0.0058

Obs	Residual	RStudent	Hat diag H	Cov ratio	DFFITS	DFBETAS	
						Intercept	DLWkUNCLL1
203	0.0933	0.5828	0.0018	1.0035	0.0245	0.0213	−0.0121
204	−0.005550	−0.0347	0.0016	1.0043	−0.0014	−0.0013	0.0006
205	−0.1064	−0.6648	0.0017	1.0032	−0.0275	−0.0243	0.0130
206	−0.2008	−1.2556	0.0013	0.9998	−0.0459	−0.0458	0.0010
207	−0.1074	−0.6711	0.0019	1.0033	−0.0289	−0.0245	0.0154
208	−0.2972	−1.8611	0.0015	0.9949	−0.0711	−0.0679	−0.0209
209	−0.0976	−0.6099	0.0014	1.0031	−0.0231	−0.0223	−0.0060
210	0.2049	1.2818	0.0017	1.0000	0.0523	0.0468	0.0234
211	0.000334	0.002088	0.0013	1.0040	0.0001	0.0001	0.0000
212	0.0978	0.6113	0.0014	1.0030	0.0226	0.0223	−0.0034
213	−0.1010	−0.6311	0.0013	1.0029	−0.0231	−0.0230	0.0010
214	0.003197	0.0200	0.0015	1.0042	0.0008	0.0007	0.0002
215	0.000742	0.004637	0.0013	1.0040	0.0002	0.0002	0.0000
216	−0.005310	−0.0332	0.0016	1.0043	−0.0013	−0.0012	0.0005
217	−0.1061	−0.6629	0.0017	1.0032	−0.0271	−0.0242	0.0123
218	−0.0907	−0.5670	0.0024	1.0042	−0.0279	−0.0207	−0.0187
219	−0.0907	−0.5671	0.0024	1.0042	−0.0279	−0.0207	−0.0187
220	−0.1233	−0.7727	0.0071	1.0083	−0.0655	−0.0284	0.0591
221	0.003308	0.0207	0.0015	1.0042	0.0008	0.0008	0.0003
222	−0.0984	−0.6149	0.0014	1.0030	−0.0229	−0.0224	−0.0044
223	−0.006447	−0.0403	0.0017	1.0044	−0.0017	−0.0015	0.0008
224	−0.0987	−0.6170	0.0014	1.0030	−0.0228	−0.0225	−0.0037
225	0.1001	0.6258	0.0013	1.0030	0.0229	0.0228	0.0014
226	−0.1020	−0.6371	0.0014	1.0029	−0.0235	−0.0233	0.0030
227	−0.000558	−0.003483	0.0013	1.0040	−0.0001	−0.0001	0.0000
228	−0.1029	−0.6429	0.0014	1.0030	−0.0240	−0.0235	0.0051
229	−0.0993	−0.6208	0.0013	1.0030	−0.0228	−0.0227	−0.0025
230	−0.002435	−0.0152	0.0014	1.0041	−0.0006	−0.0006	0.0001
231	−0.0923	−0.5770	0.0021	1.0039	−0.0264	−0.0210	−0.0159
232	−0.0110	−0.0686	0.0026	1.0052	−0.0035	−0.0025	0.0024
233	−0.1062	−0.6637	0.0017	1.0032	−0.0273	−0.0243	0.0126
234	−0.0998	−0.6235	0.0013	1.0030	−0.0228	−0.0228	−0.0016
235	0.001517	0.009476	0.0014	1.0041	0.0004	0.0003	0.0001
236	−0.0956	−0.5975	0.0016	1.0033	−0.0239	−0.0218	−0.0099
237	0.0951	0.5942	0.0015	1.0033	0.0234	0.0217	−0.0087
238	−0.003817	−0.0238	0.0015	1.0041	−0.0009	−0.0009	0.0003
239	−0.0995	−0.6218	0.0013	1.0030	−0.0228	−0.0227	−0.0021
240	0.004412	0.0276	0.0016	1.0043	0.0011	0.0010	0.0005
241	0.000793	0.004955	0.0014	1.0040	0.0002	0.0002	0.0000
242	0.001516	0.009472	0.0014	1.0041	0.0004	0.0003	0.0001
243	0.1002	0.6258	0.0013	1.0030	0.0229	0.0228	0.0014
244	−0.1009	−0.6304	0.0013	1.0029	−0.0230	−0.0230	0.0007
245	0.0138	0.0861	0.0036	1.0063	0.0052	0.0031	0.0041
246	−0.1191	−0.7460	0.0052	1.0064	−0.0540	−0.0274	0.0466
247	0.005432	0.0339	0.0017	1.0044	0.0014	0.0012	0.0007
248	0.003146	0.0197	0.0015	1.0042	0.0008	0.0007	0.0002
249	0.001534	0.009582	0.0014	1.0041	0.0004	0.0003	0.0001
250	0.0988	0.6175	0.0013	1.0030	0.0226	0.0225	−0.0014
251	0.003643	0.0228	0.0015	1.0042	0.0009	0.0008	0.0003
252	0.003306	0.0207	0.0015	1.0042	0.0008	0.0008	0.0003
253	0.1024	0.6400	0.0014	1.0030	0.0242	0.0234	0.0063
254	−0.003833	−0.0239	0.0015	1.0041	−0.0009	−0.0009	0.0003
255	0.1000	0.6249	0.0013	1.0030	0.0228	0.0228	0.0011
256	0.2041	1.2767	0.0016	0.9999	0.0507	0.0466	0.0199

Output statistics

Obs	Residual	RStudent	Hat diag H	Cov ratio	DFFITS	DFBETAS	
						Intercept	DLWkUNCLL1
257	0.0225	0.1408	0.0073	1.0100	0.0121	0.0051	0.0109
258	0.0110	0.0690	0.0028	1.0055	0.0037	0.0025	0.0027
259	0.2962	1.8551	0.0014	0.9950	0.0707	0.0678	−0.0201
260	0.0911	0.5695	0.0021	1.0039	0.0262	0.0208	−0.0160
261	0.1923	1.2029	0.0019	1.0007	0.0526	0.0440	−0.0289
262	−0.1075	−0.6719	0.0019	1.0033	−0.0291	−0.0246	0.0157
263	0.0875	0.5471	0.0029	1.0048	0.0297	0.0200	−0.0220
264	−0.004270	−0.0267	0.0015	1.0042	−0.0010	−0.0010	0.0003
265	−0.000796	−0.004972	0.0013	1.0040	−0.0002	−0.0002	0.0000
266	0.000416	0.002597	0.0013	1.0040	0.0001	0.0001	0.0000
267	−0.0972	−0.6072	0.0015	1.0032	−0.0232	−0.0222	−0.0068
268	−0.1055	−0.6593	0.0016	1.0031	−0.0265	−0.0241	0.0110
269	−0.000174	−0.001089	0.0013	1.0040	−0.0000	−0.0000	−0.0000
270	0.1013	0.6333	0.0014	1.0030	0.0235	0.0231	0.0040
271	−0.0970	−0.6060	0.0015	1.0032	−0.0233	−0.0221	−0.0072
272	0.0999	0.6244	0.0013	1.0030	0.0228	0.0228	0.0009
273	0.001446	0.009034	0.0014	1.0041	0.0003	0.0003	0.0001
274	0.006538	0.0409	0.0019	1.0046	0.0018	0.0015	0.0010
275	0.002747	0.0172	0.0015	1.0041	0.0007	0.0006	0.0002
276	0.1029	0.6434	0.0015	1.0030	0.0247	0.0235	0.0075
277	0.003834	0.0240	0.0015	1.0042	0.0009	0.0009	0.0004
278	0.3013	1.8870	0.0014	0.9946	0.0699	0.0689	0.0117
279	0.1974	1.2343	0.0014	1.0000	0.0459	0.0451	−0.0087
280	0.1035	0.6470	0.0015	1.0031	0.0252	0.0236	0.0088
281	0.2046	1.2798	0.0016	0.9999	0.0517	0.0467	0.0221
282	0.0993	0.6205	0.0013	1.0030	0.0227	0.0227	−0.0004
283	0.1013	0.6329	0.0014	1.0030	0.0234	0.0231	0.0038
284	0.0949	0.5930	0.0016	1.0033	0.0235	0.0217	−0.0091
285	0.2092	1.3092	0.0024	1.0005	0.0642	0.0477	0.0428
286	0.3058	1.9153	0.0018	0.9947	0.0808	0.0699	0.0405
287	0.1950	1.2195	0.0016	1.0003	0.0481	0.0446	−0.0183
288	0.1919	1.2007	0.0020	1.0008	0.0533	0.0439	−0.0303
289	−0.0140	−0.0877	0.0034	1.0060	−0.0051	−0.0032	0.0040
290	−0.005412	−0.0338	0.0016	1.0043	−0.0014	−0.0012	0.0006
291	−0.001374	−0.008584	0.0013	1.0040	−0.0003	−0.0003	0.0000
292	−0.3025	−1.8941	0.0014	0.9945	−0.0702	−0.0692	0.0122
293	0.2030	1.2696	0.0015	0.9998	0.0487	0.0463	0.0150
294	−0.1064	−0.6651	0.0017	1.0032	−0.0276	−0.0243	0.0131
295	−0.1077	−0.6732	0.0019	1.0034	−0.0294	−0.0246	0.0162
296	−0.3077	−1.9278	0.0019	0.9947	−0.0844	−0.0705	0.0465
297	−0.1932	−1.2085	0.0019	1.0007	−0.0532	−0.0441	−0.0297
298	−0.1068	−0.6673	0.0018	1.0033	−0.0281	−0.0244	0.0139
299	−0.2029	−1.2689	0.0014	0.9998	−0.0474	−0.0464	0.0100
300	−0.1041	−0.6509	0.0015	1.0030	−0.0250	−0.0238	0.0079
301	−0.1045	−0.6532	0.0015	1.0030	−0.0254	−0.0239	0.0087
302	−0.2057	−1.2866	0.0016	0.9999	−0.0520	−0.0470	0.0222
303	−0.1035	−0.6468	0.0014	1.0030	−0.0245	−0.0236	0.0064
304	−0.0991	−0.6195	0.0014	1.0030	−0.0228	−0.0226	−0.0029
305	0.005979	0.0374	0.0018	1.0045	0.0016	0.0014	0.0008
306	−0.2037	−1.2741	0.0014	0.9998	−0.0485	−0.0466	0.0135
307	0.000853	0.005328	0.0014	1.0040	0.0002	0.0002	0.0000
308	−0.001260	−0.007873	0.0013	1.0040	−0.0003	−0.0003	0.0000
309	−0.0928	−0.5800	0.0020	1.0038	−0.0260	−0.0212	−0.0151
310	0.001402	0.008757	0.0014	1.0041	0.0003	0.0003	0.0001

Output statistics

Obs	Residual	RStudent	Hat diag H	Cov ratio	DFFITS	DFBETAS	
						Intercept	DLWkUNCLL1
311	−0.0955	−0.5966	0.0016	1.0033	−0.0240	−0.0218	−0.0101
312	−0.004845	−0.0303	0.0015	1.0042	−0.0012	−0.0011	0.0004
313	−0.1055	−0.6591	0.0016	1.0031	−0.0264	−0.0241	0.0109
314	0.0977	0.6104	0.0014	1.0030	0.0226	0.0223	−0.0036
315	0.002975	0.0186	0.0015	1.0042	0.0007	0.0007	0.0002
316	−0.002103	−0.0131	0.0014	1.0040	−0.0005	−0.0005	0.0001
317	−0.0967	−0.6040	0.0015	1.0032	−0.0234	−0.0220	−0.0079
318	−0.001718	−0.0107	0.0013	1.0040	−0.0004	−0.0004	0.0000
319	−0.000831	−0.005192	0.0013	1.0040	−0.0002	−0.0002	0.0000
320	−0.004185	−0.0261	0.0015	1.0042	−0.0010	−0.0010	0.0003
321	−0.0942	−0.5886	0.0018	1.0035	−0.0249	−0.0215	−0.0125
322	0.1005	0.6283	0.0013	1.0030	0.0231	0.0229	0.0023
323	−0.1015	−0.6344	0.0013	1.0029	−0.0233	−0.0232	0.0021
324	−0.003478	−0.0217	0.0014	1.0041	−0.0008	−0.0008	0.0002
325	−0.1024	−0.6397	0.0014	1.0030	−0.0237	−0.0234	0.0039
326	0.1948	1.2181	0.0016	1.0003	0.0485	0.0445	−0.0192
327	−0.0993	−0.6203	0.0013	1.0030	−0.0228	−0.0226	−0.0026
328	−0.0977	−0.6108	0.0014	1.0031	−0.0230	−0.0223	−0.0057
329	0.1009	0.6306	0.0014	1.0030	0.0232	0.0230	0.0031
330	0.0984	0.6149	0.0013	1.0030	0.0226	0.0225	−0.0022
331	−0.1042	−0.6511	0.0015	1.0030	−0.0251	−0.0238	0.0080
332	0.0000995	0.000621	0.0013	1.0040	0.0000	0.0000	0.0000
333	0.1075	0.6719	0.0021	1.0035	0.0305	0.0245	0.0181
334	−0.2029	−1.2690	0.0014	0.9998	−0.0474	−0.0464	0.0101
335	0.0947	0.5916	0.0016	1.0033	0.0236	0.0216	−0.0095
336	−0.1041	−0.6507	0.0015	1.0030	−0.0250	−0.0238	0.0078
337	−0.001831	−0.0114	0.0014	1.0040	−0.0004	−0.0004	0.0000
338	−0.002485	−0.0155	0.0014	1.0041	−0.0006	−0.0006	0.0001
339	−0.1013	−0.6331	0.0013	1.0029	−0.0232	−0.0231	0.0017
340	0.0950	0.5939	0.0016	1.0033	0.0234	0.0217	−0.0088
341	0.000289	0.001806	0.0013	1.0040	0.0001	0.0001	0.0000
342	−0.1021	−0.6377	0.0014	1.0029	−0.0235	−0.0233	0.0032
343	−0.1033	−0.6454	0.0014	1.0030	−0.0243	−0.0236	0.0059
344	0.000289	0.001803	0.0013	1.0040	0.0001	0.0001	0.0000
345	−0.001951	−0.0122	0.0014	1.0040	−0.0004	−0.0004	0.0001
346	−0.1051	−0.6566	0.0016	1.0031	−0.0260	−0.0240	0.0100
347	−0.002461	−0.0154	0.0014	1.0041	−0.0006	−0.0006	0.0001
348	0.001697	0.0106	0.0014	1.0041	0.0004	0.0004	0.0001
349	−0.0972	−0.6073	0.0015	1.0032	−0.0232	−0.0222	−0.0068
350	0.006215	0.0388	0.0018	1.0045	0.0017	0.0014	0.0009
351	−0.006962	−0.0435	0.0018	1.0045	−0.0018	−0.0016	0.0009
352	−0.1046	−0.6537	0.0015	1.0031	−0.0255	−0.0239	0.0089
353	0.1017	0.6356	0.0014	1.0030	0.0237	0.0232	0.0048
354	−0.1003	−0.6266	0.0013	1.0030	−0.0229	−0.0229	−0.0005
355	−0.002792	−0.0174	0.0014	1.0041	−0.0007	−0.0006	0.0001
356	0.005281	0.0330	0.0017	1.0044	0.0014	0.0012	0.0006
357	−0.003913	−0.0244	0.0015	1.0041	−0.0009	−0.0009	0.0003
358	−0.005002	−0.0313	0.0016	1.0042	−0.0012	−0.0011	0.0005
359	−0.1037	−0.6480	0.0014	1.0030	−0.0246	−0.0237	0.0069
360	0.000144	0.000901	0.0013	1.0040	0.0000	0.0000	0.0000
361	−0.001092	−0.006820	0.0013	1.0040	−0.0002	−0.0002	0.0000
362	−0.1012	−0.6326	0.0013	1.0029	−0.0231	−0.0231	0.0015
363	0.006966	0.0435	0.0020	1.0046	0.0019	0.0016	0.0011
364	0.001969	0.0123	0.0014	1.0041	0.0005	0.0004	0.0001

Output statistics

Obs	Residual	RStudent	Hat diag H	Cov ratio	DFFITS	DFBETAS	
						Intercept	DLWkUNCLL1
365	−0.004467	−0.0279	0.0015	1.0042	−0.0011	−0.0010	0.0004
366	−0.0957	−0.5983	0.0016	1.0033	−0.0239	−0.0218	−0.0096
367	0.2037	1.2740	0.0015	0.9999	0.0499	0.0465	0.0180
368	−0.2003	−1.2525	0.0013	0.9998	−0.0457	−0.0457	−0.0011
369	0.0973	0.6080	0.0014	1.0031	0.0226	0.0222	−0.0044
370	0.001018	0.006358	0.0014	1.0040	0.0002	0.0002	0.0000
371	0.006610	0.0413	0.0019	1.0046	0.0018	0.0015	0.0010
372	−0.007234	−0.0452	0.0018	1.0045	−0.0019	−0.0017	0.0010
373	0.004629	0.0289	0.0016	1.0043	0.0012	0.0011	0.0005
374	0.000231	0.001444	0.0013	1.0040	0.0001	0.0001	0.0000
375	−0.002417	−0.0151	0.0014	1.0041	−0.0006	−0.0006	0.0001
376	−0.003386	−0.0212	0.0014	1.0041	−0.0008	−0.0008	0.0002
377	0.004347	0.0272	0.0016	1.0043	0.0011	0.0010	0.0004
378	−0.001317	−0.008229	0.0013	1.0040	−0.0003	−0.0003	0.0000
379	0.1000	0.6250	0.0013	1.0030	0.0228	0.0228	0.0011
380	0.1011	0.6317	0.0014	1.0030	0.0233	0.0231	0.0034
381	0.005332	0.0333	0.0017	1.0044	0.0014	0.0012	0.0007
382	0.000663	0.004143	0.0013	1.0040	0.0002	0.0002	0.0000
383	0.2068	1.2935	0.0019	1.0001	0.0569	0.0472	0.0316
384	−0.0946	−0.5913	0.0017	1.0035	−0.0246	−0.0216	−0.0117
385	0.1003	0.6269	0.0013	1.0030	0.0230	0.0229	0.0018
386	0.0996	0.6222	0.0013	1.0030	0.0227	0.0227	0.0002
387	0.1054	0.6588	0.0017	1.0032	0.0274	0.0240	0.0131
388	0.002572	0.0161	0.0014	1.0041	0.0006	0.0006	0.0002
389	0.0925	0.5784	0.0019	1.0037	0.0250	0.0212	−0.0134
390	0.1941	1.2138	0.0017	1.0004	0.0495	0.0444	−0.0220
391	−0.1038	−0.6487	0.0015	1.0030	−0.0247	−0.0237	0.0071
392	0.0973	0.6083	0.0014	1.0031	0.0226	0.0222	−0.0043
393	0.002091	0.0131	0.0014	1.0041	0.0005	0.0005	0.0001
394	0.0982	0.6136	0.0014	1.0030	0.0226	0.0224	−0.0026
395	0.000313	0.001956	0.0013	1.0040	0.0001	0.0001	0.0000
396	0.2032	1.2707	0.0015	0.9998	0.0490	0.0464	0.0157
397	0.1020	0.6372	0.0014	1.0030	0.0239	0.0233	0.0053
398	0.0960	0.6002	0.0015	1.0032	0.0230	0.0219	−0.0069
399	−0.000182	−0.001134	0.0013	1.0040	−0.0000	−0.0000	−0.0000
400	−0.1035	−0.6469	0.0014	1.0030	−0.0245	−0.0236	0.0065
401	0.2979	1.8656	0.0014	0.9948	0.0688	0.0681	−0.0096
402	0.1974	1.2343	0.0014	1.0000	0.0459	0.0451	−0.0087
403	−0.0994	−0.6211	0.0013	1.0030	−0.0228	−0.0227	−0.0024
404	0.005720	0.0357	0.0018	1.0045	0.0015	0.0013	0.0007
405	−0.1106	−0.6918	0.0025	1.0039	−0.0345	−0.0253	0.0235
406	0.001719	0.0107	0.0014	1.0041	0.0004	0.0004	0.0001
407	−0.1105	−0.6908	0.0024	1.0038	−0.0342	−0.0253	0.0230
408	0.1966	1.2295	0.0014	1.0001	0.0464	0.0449	−0.0118
409	−0.2077	−1.2996	0.0019	1.0001	−0.0569	−0.0475	0.0313
410	−0.0976	−0.6096	0.0014	1.0031	−0.0231	−0.0222	−0.0061
411	−0.1030	−0.6436	0.0014	1.0030	−0.0241	−0.0235	0.0053
412	−0.0970	−0.6061	0.0015	1.0032	−0.0233	−0.0221	−0.0072
413	0.0989	0.6183	0.0013	1.0030	0.0226	0.0226	−0.0011
414	−0.002081	−0.0130	0.0014	1.0040	−0.0005	−0.0005	0.0001
415	−0.001529	−0.009551	0.0013	1.0040	−0.0004	−0.0003	0.0000
416	−0.0964	−0.6026	0.0015	1.0032	−0.0235	−0.0220	−0.0083
417	0.0955	0.5967	0.0015	1.0032	0.0232	0.0218	−0.0080
418	−0.1013	−0.6329	0.0013	1.0029	−0.0232	−0.0231	0.0016

Output statistics

Obs	Residual	RStudent	Hat diag H	Cov ratio	DFFITS	DFBETAS	
						Intercept	DLWkUNCLL1
419	0.003818	0.0239	0.0015	1.0042	0.0009	0.0009	0.0003
420	−0.004242	−0.0265	0.0015	1.0042	−0.0010	−0.0010	0.0003
421	−0.005526	−0.0345	0.0016	1.0043	−0.0014	−0.0013	0.0006
422	0.1107	0.6925	0.0028	1.0042	0.0364	0.0252	0.0262
423	−0.1047	−0.6545	0.0015	1.0031	−0.0256	−0.0239	0.0092
424	−0.1047	−0.6542	0.0015	1.0031	−0.0256	−0.0239	0.0091
425	0.002438	0.0152	0.0014	1.0041	0.0006	0.0006	0.0002
426	−0.0966	−0.6034	0.0015	1.0032	−0.0235	−0.0220	−0.0080
427	0.0933	0.5834	0.0018	1.0035	0.0244	0.0213	−0.0120
428	−0.0985	−0.6155	0.0014	1.0030	−0.0229	−0.0225	−0.0042
429	−0.002912	−0.0182	0.0014	1.0041	−0.0007	−0.0007	0.0001
430	0.0970	0.6063	0.0014	1.0031	0.0227	0.0222	−0.0050
431	−0.1988	−1.2430	0.0014	0.9999	−0.0460	−0.0454	−0.0074
432	−0.1027	−0.6417	0.0014	1.0030	−0.0239	−0.0234	0.0046
433	−0.1017	−0.6355	0.0013	1.0029	−0.0233	−0.0232	0.0025
434	0.002480	0.0155	0.0014	1.0041	0.0006	0.0006	0.0002
435	−0.0983	−0.6141	0.0014	1.0031	−0.0229	−0.0224	−0.0047
436	0.1989	1.2439	0.0013	0.9999	0.0455	0.0454	−0.0024
437	0.1035	0.6470	0.0015	1.0031	0.0252	0.0236	0.0088
438	−0.2961	−1.8545	0.0015	0.9951	−0.0730	−0.0677	−0.0274
439	−0.002047	−0.0128	0.0014	1.0040	−0.0005	−0.0005	0.0001
440	0.1024	0.6398	0.0014	1.0030	0.0242	0.0233	0.0062
441	−0.1055	−0.6595	0.0016	1.0031	−0.0265	−0.0241	0.0110
442	0.001232	0.007697	0.0014	1.0040	0.0003	0.0003	0.0000
443	0.1015	0.6342	0.0014	1.0030	0.0236	0.0231	0.0043
444	0.000463	0.002894	0.0013	1.0040	0.0001	0.0001	0.0000
445	−0.003814	−0.0238	0.0015	1.0041	−0.0009	−0.0009	0.0003
446	−0.0977	−0.6103	0.0014	1.0031	−0.0230	−0.0223	−0.0059
447	0.1000	0.6247	0.0013	1.0030	0.0228	0.0228	0.0010
448	0.003341	0.0209	0.0015	1.0042	0.0008	0.0008	0.0003
449	−0.008897	−0.0556	0.0021	1.0048	−0.0026	−0.0020	0.0016
450	−0.004499	−0.0281	0.0015	1.0042	−0.0011	−0.0010	0.0004
451	−0.1012	−0.6323	0.0013	1.0029	−0.0231	−0.0231	0.0014
452	−0.002312	−0.0144	0.0014	1.0040	−0.0005	−0.0005	0.0001
453	−0.001520	−0.009496	0.0013	1.0040	−0.0003	−0.0003	0.0000
454	0.002131	0.0133	0.0014	1.0041	0.0005	0.0005	0.0001
455	−0.1017	−0.6356	0.0013	1.0029	−0.0233	−0.0232	0.0025
456	−0.001107	−0.006918	0.0013	1.0040	−0.0003	−0.0003	0.0000
457	0.004172	0.0261	0.0016	1.0043	0.0010	0.0010	0.0004
458	−0.005606	−0.0350	0.0016	1.0043	−0.0014	−0.0013	0.0006
459	−0.005943	−0.0371	0.0017	1.0043	−0.0015	−0.0014	0.0007
460	−0.000189	−0.001182	0.0013	1.0040	−0.0000	−0.0000	−0.0000
461	0.003229	0.0202	0.0015	1.0042	0.0008	0.0007	0.0003
462	−0.1042	−0.6513	0.0015	1.0030	−0.0251	−0.0238	0.0081
463	0.1014	0.6334	0.0014	1.0030	0.0235	0.0231	0.0040
464	−0.1042	−0.6510	0.0015	1.0030	−0.0251	−0.0238	0.0079
465	0.005187	0.0324	0.0017	1.0044	0.0013	0.0012	0.0006
466	−0.1058	−0.6613	0.0016	1.0032	−0.0268	−0.0242	0.0117
467	−0.1020	−0.6376	0.0014	1.0029	−0.0235	−0.0233	0.0032
468	0.1008	0.6300	0.0014	1.0030	0.0232	0.0230	0.0028
469	−0.1012	−0.6323	0.0013	1.0029	−0.0231	−0.0231	0.0014
470	0.002605	0.0163	0.0014	1.0041	0.0006	0.0006	0.0002
471	−0.001866	−0.0117	0.0014	1.0040	−0.0004	−0.0004	0.0001
472	−0.2019	−1.2624	0.0014	0.9998	−0.0464	−0.0461	0.0056

Output statistics

Obs	Residual	RStudent	Hat diag H	Cov ratio	DFFITS	DFBETAS	
						Intercept	DLWkUNCLL1
473	−0.002374	−0.0148	0.0014	1.0041	−0.0005	−0.0005	0.0001
474	0.1007	0.6291	0.0013	1.0030	0.0231	0.0230	0.0025
475	−0.0930	−0.5816	0.0020	1.0037	−0.0258	−0.0212	−0.0146
476	0.0953	0.5958	0.0015	1.0033	0.0233	0.0218	−0.0082
477	−0.005220	−0.0326	0.0016	1.0043	−0.0013	−0.0012	0.0005
478	−0.1030	−0.6436	0.0014	1.0030	−0.0241	−0.0235	0.0053
479	0.003070	0.0192	0.0015	1.0042	0.0007	0.0007	0.0002
480	0.000406	0.002537	0.0013	1.0040	0.0001	0.0001	0.0000
481	−0.000156	−0.000976	0.0013	1.0040	−0.0000	−0.0000	−0.0000
482	0.001786	0.0112	0.0014	1.0041	0.0004	0.0004	0.0001
483	−0.007959	−0.0497	0.0020	1.0046	−0.0022	−0.0018	0.0012
484	−0.000072	−0.000450	0.0013	1.0040	−0.0000	−0.0000	−0.0000
485	0.0000860	0.000537	0.0013	1.0040	0.0000	0.0000	0.0000
486	0.0989	0.6180	0.0013	1.0030	0.0226	0.0226	−0.0012
487	−0.1048	−0.6552	0.0015	1.0031	−0.0257	−0.0240	0.0095
488	−0.0970	−0.6059	0.0015	1.0032	−0.0233	−0.0221	−0.0073
489	−0.003995	−0.0250	0.0015	1.0041	−0.0010	−0.0009	0.0003
490	0.000712	0.004451	0.0013	1.0040	0.0002	0.0002	0.0000
491	−0.003422	−0.0214	0.0014	1.0041	−0.0008	−0.0008	0.0002
492	−0.001935	−0.0121	0.0014	1.0040	−0.0004	−0.0004	0.0001
493	−0.001779	−0.0111	0.0013	1.0040	−0.0004	−0.0004	0.0000
494	−0.0968	−0.6047	0.0015	1.0032	−0.0234	−0.0221	−0.0076
495	0.000984	0.006148	0.0014	1.0040	0.0002	0.0002	0.0000
496	−0.008955	−0.0560	0.0021	1.0048	−0.0026	−0.0020	0.0016
497	0.000595	0.003718	0.0013	1.0040	0.0001	0.0001	0.0000
498	0.002683	0.0168	0.0014	1.0041	0.0006	0.0006	0.0002
499	0.001770	0.0111	0.0014	1.0041	0.0004	0.0004	0.0001
500	0.1027	0.6418	0.0014	1.0030	0.0244	0.0234	0.0070
501	−0.0965	−0.6028	0.0015	1.0032	−0.0235	−0.0220	−0.0082
502	−0.004168	−0.0260	0.0015	1.0042	−0.0010	−0.0010	0.0003
503	−0.000265	−0.001656	0.0013	1.0040	−0.0001	−0.0001	−0.0000
504	0.0102	0.0635	0.0026	1.0053	0.0033	0.0023	0.0023
505	0.1029	0.6429	0.0015	1.0030	0.0246	0.0235	0.0073
506	−0.002773	−0.0173	0.0014	1.0041	−0.0006	−0.0006	0.0001
507	0.1085	0.6785	0.0023	1.0037	0.0322	0.0247	0.0206
508	−0.0968	−0.6050	0.0015	1.0032	−0.0233	−0.0221	−0.0076
509	0.001684	0.0105	0.0014	1.0041	0.0004	0.0004	0.0001
510	0.1004	0.6277	0.0013	1.0030	0.0230	0.0229	0.0021
511	0.0980	0.6122	0.0014	1.0030	0.0226	0.0224	−0.0031
512	0.1002	0.6262	0.0013	1.0030	0.0229	0.0229	0.0016
513	0.0995	0.6216	0.0013	1.0030	0.0227	0.0227	−0.0000
514	0.009861	0.0616	0.0025	1.0052	0.0031	0.0022	0.0021
515	0.2074	1.2979	0.0020	1.0002	0.0588	0.0473	0.0347
516	0.0938	0.5863	0.0017	1.0035	0.0241	0.0214	−0.0111
517	0.0883	0.5520	0.0027	1.0046	0.0289	0.0202	−0.0207
518	0.000737	0.004605	0.0013	1.0040	0.0002	0.0002	0.0000
519	0.0960	0.5999	0.0015	1.0032	0.0230	0.0219	−0.0070
520	0.1054	0.6588	0.0017	1.0032	0.0274	0.0240	0.0131
521	0.001282	0.008009	0.0014	1.0040	0.0003	0.0003	0.0000
522	0.0929	0.5809	0.0018	1.0036	0.0247	0.0212	−0.0127
523	−0.1036	−0.6473	0.0014	1.0030	−0.0245	−0.0237	0.0066
524	−0.001314	−0.008207	0.0013	1.0040	−0.0003	−0.0003	0.0000
525	0.001694	0.0106	0.0014	1.0041	0.0004	0.0004	0.0001
526	0.1029	0.6430	0.0015	1.0030	0.0246	0.0235	0.0074

Obs	Residual	RStudent	Hat diag H	Cov ratio	DFFITS	DFBETAS	
						Intercept	DLWkUNCLL1
527	−0.001012	−0.006323	0.0013	1.0040	−0.0002	−0.0002	0.0000
528	0.1949	1.2191	0.0016	1.0003	0.0482	0.0446	−0.0186
529	−0.0944	−0.5900	0.0018	1.0035	−0.0247	−0.0215	−0.0121
530	−0.004014	−0.0251	0.0015	1.0041	−0.0010	−0.0009	0.0003
531	0.003440	0.0215	0.0015	1.0042	0.0008	0.0008	0.0003
532	0.1014	0.6336	0.0014	1.0030	0.0235	0.0231	0.0041
533	0.002520	0.0157	0.0014	1.0041	0.0006	0.0006	0.0002
534	0.0959	0.5990	0.0015	1.0032	0.0230	0.0219	−0.0072
535	0.0992	0.6198	0.0013	1.0030	0.0226	0.0226	−0.0006
536	−0.1049	−0.6556	0.0015	1.0031	−0.0258	−0.0240	0.0096
537	−0.001458	−0.009107	0.0013	1.0040	−0.0003	−0.0003	0.0000
538	−0.001639	−0.0102	0.0013	1.0040	−0.0004	−0.0004	0.0000
539	−0.1054	−0.6590	0.0016	1.0031	−0.0264	−0.0241	0.0109
540	−0.004022	−0.0251	0.0015	1.0041	−0.0010	−0.0009	0.0003
541	−0.001777	−0.0111	0.0013	1.0040	−0.0004	−0.0004	0.0000
542	−0.0998	−0.6238	0.0013	1.0030	−0.0228	−0.0228	−0.0015
543	0.0993	0.6206	0.0013	1.0030	0.0227	0.0227	−0.0003
544	−0.3057	−1.9148	0.0016	0.9945	−0.0774	−0.0700	0.0332
545	0.1005	0.6278	0.0013	1.0030	0.0230	0.0229	0.0021
546	−0.002383	−0.0149	0.0014	1.0041	−0.0006	−0.0005	0.0001
547	−0.0998	−0.6235	0.0013	1.0030	−0.0228	−0.0228	−0.0016
548	−0.0992	−0.6197	0.0014	1.0030	−0.0228	−0.0226	−0.0028
549	0.0976	0.6097	0.0014	1.0031	0.0226	0.0223	−0.0039
550	0.0992	0.6200	0.0013	1.0030	0.0226	0.0226	−0.0005
551	−0.1022	−0.6389	0.0014	1.0030	−0.0236	−0.0233	0.0037
552	−0.002003	−0.0125	0.0014	1.0040	−0.0005	−0.0005	0.0001
553	−0.1006	−0.6289	0.0013	1.0030	−0.0230	−0.0230	0.0002
554	0.1029	0.6428	0.0015	1.0030	0.0246	0.0235	0.0073
555	−0.1091	−0.6823	0.0022	1.0036	−0.0318	−0.0250	0.0197
556	−0.0942	−0.5890	0.0018	1.0035	−0.0248	−0.0215	−0.0124
557	−0.004180	−0.0261	0.0015	1.0042	−0.0010	−0.0010	0.0003
558	−0.1985	−1.2416	0.0014	0.9999	−0.0461	−0.0453	−0.0083
559	−0.001820	−0.0114	0.0014	1.0040	−0.0004	−0.0004	0.0000
560	0.0998	0.6235	0.0013	1.0030	0.0228	0.0228	0.0006
561	−0.003094	−0.0193	0.0014	1.0041	−0.0007	−0.0007	0.0002
562	0.0219	0.1371	0.0070	1.0097	0.0115	0.0050	0.0103
563	−0.0145	−0.0908	0.0035	1.0062	−0.0054	−0.0033	0.0043
564	−0.1089	−0.6809	0.0021	1.0036	−0.0314	−0.0249	0.0191
565	−0.1009	−0.6303	0.0013	1.0029	−0.0230	−0.0230	0.0007
566	0.1932	1.2084	0.0018	1.0005	0.0509	0.0442	−0.0254
567	−0.1010	−0.6311	0.0013	1.0029	−0.0231	−0.0230	0.0010
568	0.000991	0.006190	0.0014	1.0040	0.0002	0.0002	0.0000
569	−0.0981	−0.6131	0.0014	1.0031	−0.0229	−0.0224	−0.0050
570	−0.0926	−0.5789	0.0020	1.0038	−0.0262	−0.0211	−0.0154
571	0.0918	0.5741	0.0020	1.0038	0.0256	0.0210	−0.0147
572	0.003151	0.0197	0.0015	1.0042	0.0008	0.0007	0.0002
573	−0.002410	−0.0151	0.0014	1.0041	−0.0006	−0.0005	0.0001
574	−0.0997	−0.6228	0.0013	1.0030	−0.0228	−0.0227	−0.0018
575	−0.000836	−0.005222	0.0013	1.0040	−0.0002	−0.0002	0.0000
576	0.003238	0.0202	0.0015	1.0042	0.0008	0.0007	0.0003
577	−0.002028	−0.0127	0.0014	1.0040	−0.0005	−0.0005	0.0001
578	−0.002266	−0.0142	0.0014	1.0040	−0.0005	−0.0005	0.0001
579	0.1017	0.6357	0.0014	1.0030	0.0237	0.0232	0.0048
580	−0.006219	−0.0389	0.0017	1.0044	−0.0016	−0.0014	0.0007

Output statistics

Output statistics

Obs	Residual	RStudent	Hat diag H	Cov ratio	DFFITS	DFBETAS	
						Intercept	DLWkUNCLL1
581	0.003681	0.0230	0.0015	1.0042	0.0009	0.0008	0.0003
582	−0.004573	−0.0286	0.0015	1.0042	−0.0011	−0.0010	0.0004
583	0.001983	0.0124	0.0014	1.0041	0.0005	0.0005	0.0001
584	−0.001304	−0.008144	0.0013	1.0040	−0.0003	−0.0003	0.0000
585	0.001511	0.009439	0.0014	1.0041	0.0004	0.0003	0.0001
586	−0.002595	−0.0162	0.0014	1.0041	−0.0006	−0.0006	0.0001
587	0.004072	0.0254	0.0016	1.0043	0.0010	0.0009	0.0004
588	0.1029	0.6432	0.0015	1.0030	0.0246	0.0235	0.0074
589	0.001993	0.0124	0.0014	1.0041	0.0005	0.0005	0.0001
590	−0.003309	−0.0207	0.0014	1.0041	−0.0008	−0.0008	0.0002
591	0.001069	0.006676	0.0014	1.0040	0.0002	0.0002	0.0000
592	0.1056	0.6603	0.0018	1.0033	0.0277	0.0241	0.0137
593	0.0982	0.6137	0.0013	1.0030	0.0226	0.0224	−0.0026
594	0.1002	0.6259	0.0013	1.0030	0.0229	0.0229	0.0015
595	0.1039	0.6494	0.0016	1.0031	0.0256	0.0237	0.0097
596	0.2077	1.2997	0.0021	1.0003	0.0596	0.0474	0.0360
597	0.1023	0.6393	0.0014	1.0030	0.0241	0.0233	0.0061
598	0.3070	1.9231	0.0020	0.9948	0.0853	0.0701	0.0484
599	−0.0978	−0.6111	0.0014	1.0031	−0.0230	−0.0223	−0.0056
600	0.4092	2.5691	0.0024	0.9876	0.1260	0.0937	0.0840
601	0.2060	1.2885	0.0018	1.0000	0.0548	0.0470	0.0281
602	0.4038	2.5335	0.0015	0.9872	0.0995	0.0924	0.0365
603	0.3081	1.9305	0.0022	0.9949	0.0900	0.0704	0.0560
604	0.3017	1.8894	0.0014	0.9946	0.0704	0.0690	0.0142
605	0.3927	2.4639	0.0018	0.9884	0.1059	0.0901	−0.0559
606	0.5993	3.7798	0.0013	0.9667	0.1380	0.1380	−0.0017
607	−0.003217	−0.0201	0.0014	1.0041	−0.0008	−0.0007	0.0002
608	−0.006590	−0.0412	0.0017	1.0044	−0.0017	−0.0015	0.0008
609	0.3991	2.5039	0.0013	0.9874	0.0915	0.0914	−0.0028
610	0.0960	0.6002	0.0015	1.0032	0.0230	0.0219	−0.0069
611	0.0962	0.6011	0.0015	1.0032	0.0229	0.0220	−0.0066
612	0.0938	0.5861	0.0017	1.0035	0.0242	0.0214	−0.0112
613	−0.004370	−0.0273	0.0015	1.0042	−0.0011	−0.0010	0.0004
614	0.001639	0.0102	0.0014	1.0041	0.0004	0.0004	0.0001
615	0.0994	0.6213	0.0013	1.0030	0.0227	0.0227	−0.0001
616	−0.003768	−0.0235	0.0014	1.0041	−0.0009	−0.0009	0.0003
617	−0.1023	−0.6393	0.0014	1.0030	−0.0236	−0.0234	0.0038
618	−0.000621	−0.003880	0.0013	1.0040	−0.0001	−0.0001	0.0000
619	−0.1010	−0.6312	0.0013	1.0029	−0.0231	−0.0230	0.0010
620	−0.2003	−1.2527	0.0013	0.9998	−0.0458	−0.0457	−0.0010
621	0.002430	0.0152	0.0014	1.0041	0.0006	0.0006	0.0002
622	0.0946	0.5913	0.0016	1.0033	0.0236	0.0216	−0.0096
623	−0.001623	−0.0101	0.0013	1.0040	−0.0004	−0.0004	0.0000
624	−0.005190	−0.0324	0.0016	1.0043	−0.0013	−0.0012	0.0005
625	−0.1028	−0.6426	0.0014	1.0030	−0.0240	−0.0235	0.0049
626	−0.1974	−1.2345	0.0014	1.0000	−0.0469	−0.0451	−0.0130
627	−0.007327	−0.0458	0.0018	1.0045	−0.0020	−0.0017	0.0010
628	−0.1006	−0.6288	0.0013	1.0030	−0.0230	−0.0230	0.0002
629	0.1056	0.6598	0.0017	1.0033	0.0276	0.0241	0.0135
630	−0.001639	−0.0102	0.0013	1.0040	−0.0004	−0.0004	0.0000
631	−0.001838	−0.0115	0.0014	1.0040	−0.0004	−0.0004	0.0001
632	0.0981	0.6130	0.0014	1.0030	0.0226	0.0224	−0.0028
633	−0.000986	−0.006162	0.0013	1.0040	−0.0002	−0.0002	0.0000
634	−0.2991	−1.8729	0.0014	0.9947	−0.0690	−0.0684	−0.0091

Output statistics

Obs	Residual	RStudent	Hat diag H	Cov ratio	DFFITS	DFBETAS	
						Intercept	DLWkUNCLL1
635	−0.1039	−0.6494	0.0015	1.0030	−0.0248	−0.0237	0.0073
636	−0.1039	−0.6492	0.0015	1.0030	−0.0248	−0.0237	0.0073
637	−0.1040	−0.6501	0.0015	1.0030	−0.0249	−0.0238	0.0076
638	−0.0998	−0.6234	0.0013	1.0030	−0.0228	−0.0228	−0.0016
639	−0.1039	−0.6495	0.0015	1.0030	−0.0248	−0.0237	0.0074
640	−0.000718	−0.004488	0.0013	1.0040	−0.0002	−0.0002	0.0000
641	0.004001	0.0250	0.0016	1.0042	0.0010	0.0009	0.0004
642	0.0975	0.6095	0.0014	1.0031	0.0226	0.0223	−0.0040
643	−0.1992	−1.2457	0.0014	0.9999	−0.0458	−0.0455	−0.0056
644	−0.002428	−0.0152	0.0014	1.0041	−0.0006	−0.0006	0.0001
645	−0.1003	−0.6271	0.0013	1.0030	−0.0229	−0.0229	−0.0004
646	0.002382	0.0149	0.0014	1.0041	0.0006	0.0005	0.0001
647	−0.2048	−1.2809	0.0015	0.9998	−0.0502	−0.0468	0.0183
648	0.1084	0.6779	0.0022	1.0037	0.0321	0.0247	0.0204
649	−0.1132	−0.7080	0.0031	1.0045	−0.0397	−0.0259	0.0301
650	−0.001276	−0.007972	0.0013	1.0040	−0.0003	−0.0003	0.0000
651	−0.1018	−0.6364	0.0014	1.0029	−0.0234	−0.0232	0.0028
652	0.001390	0.008686	0.0014	1.0041	0.0003	0.0003	0.0001
653	−0.002730	−0.0171	0.0014	1.0041	−0.0006	−0.0006	0.0001
654	−0.0995	−0.6217	0.0013	1.0030	−0.0228	−0.0227	−0.0022
655	−0.1023	−0.6395	0.0014	1.0030	−0.0237	−0.0234	0.0039
656	−0.1000	−0.6252	0.0013	1.0030	−0.0229	−0.0228	−0.0010
657	−0.004709	−0.0294	0.0015	1.0042	−0.0012	−0.0011	0.0004
658	−0.1060	−0.6624	0.0017	1.0032	−0.0270	−0.0242	0.0121
659	0.0107	0.0667	0.0027	1.0054	0.0035	0.0024	0.0025
660	−0.1084	−0.6779	0.0020	1.0035	−0.0306	−0.0248	0.0180
661	−0.1943	−1.2155	0.0018	1.0005	−0.0511	−0.0443	−0.0253
662	0.0945	0.5904	0.0016	1.0034	0.0237	0.0216	−0.0099
663	0.000359	0.002242	0.0013	1.0040	0.0001	0.0001	0.0000
664	−0.3037	−1.9020	0.0014	0.9945	−0.0723	−0.0695	0.0202
665	−0.0992	−0.6197	0.0014	1.0030	−0.0228	−0.0226	−0.0028
666	−0.1053	−0.6582	0.0016	1.0031	−0.0263	−0.0241	0.0106
667	0.000288	0.001799	0.0013	1.0040	0.0001	0.0001	0.0000
668	−0.1047	−0.6545	0.0015	1.0031	−0.0256	−0.0239	0.0092
669	−0.0995	−0.6215	0.0013	1.0030	−0.0228	−0.0227	−0.0022
670	−0.1034	−0.6464	0.0014	1.0030	−0.0244	−0.0236	0.0063
671	−0.003757	−0.0235	0.0014	1.0041	−0.0009	−0.0009	0.0003
672	−0.0975	−0.6090	0.0014	1.0031	−0.0231	−0.0222	−0.0063
673	−0.003898	−0.0244	0.0015	1.0041	−0.0009	−0.0009	0.0003
674	−0.1001	−0.6256	0.0013	1.0030	−0.0229	−0.0228	−0.0009
675	−0.0955	−0.5966	0.0016	1.0033	−0.0240	−0.0218	−0.0101
676	−0.1063	−0.6646	0.0017	1.0032	−0.0275	−0.0243	0.0129
677	0.0989	0.6177	0.0013	1.0030	0.0226	0.0226	−0.0013
678	−0.1029	−0.6433	0.0014	1.0030	−0.0241	−0.0235	0.0052
679	−0.1011	−0.6317	0.0013	1.0029	−0.0231	−0.0231	0.0012
680	−0.001166	−0.007283	0.0013	1.0040	−0.0003	−0.0003	0.0000
681	−0.0991	−0.6193	0.0014	1.0030	−0.0228	−0.0226	−0.0030
682	−0.003501	−0.0219	0.0014	1.0041	−0.0008	−0.0008	0.0002
683	−0.000996	−0.006221	0.0013	1.0040	−0.0002	−0.0002	0.0000
684	−0.000083	−0.000518	0.0013	1.0040	−0.0000	−0.0000	−0.0000
685	−0.1002	−0.6261	0.0013	1.0030	−0.0229	−0.0229	−0.0007
686	0.1035	0.6470	0.0015	1.0031	0.0252	0.0236	0.0088
687	−0.005372	−0.0336	0.0016	1.0043	−0.0013	−0.0012	0.0005
688	−0.000302	−0.001887	0.0013	1.0040	−0.0001	−0.0001	−0.0000

Output statistics

Obs	Residual	RStudent	Hat diag H	Cov ratio	DFFITS	DFBETAS	
						Intercept	DLWkUNCLL1
689	−0.2022	−1.2644	0.0014	0.9998	−0.0467	−0.0462	0.0070
690	0.1036	0.6473	0.0015	1.0031	0.0253	0.0236	0.0089
691	−0.004881	−0.0305	0.0015	1.0042	−0.0012	−0.0011	0.0004
692	−0.1010	−0.6309	0.0013	1.0029	−0.0231	−0.0230	0.0009
693	0.1003	0.6268	0.0013	1.0030	0.0230	0.0229	0.0017
694	−0.006150	−0.0384	0.0017	1.0044	−0.0016	−0.0014	0.0007
695	−0.0969	−0.6054	0.0015	1.0032	−0.0233	−0.0221	−0.0074
696	−0.004874	−0.0305	0.0015	1.0042	−0.0012	−0.0011	0.0004
697	0.000579	0.003614	0.0013	1.0040	0.0001	0.0001	0.0000
698	−0.1023	−0.6392	0.0014	1.0030	−0.0236	−0.0233	0.0038
699	−0.1024	−0.6397	0.0014	1.0030	−0.0237	−0.0234	0.0039
700	0.001717	0.0107	0.0014	1.0041	0.0004	0.0004	0.0001
701	−0.002229	−0.0139	0.0014	1.0040	−0.0005	−0.0005	0.0001
702	−0.1021	−0.6377	0.0014	1.0029	−0.0235	−0.0233	0.0033
703	0.1001	0.6257	0.0013	1.0030	0.0229	0.0228	0.0014
704	0.000489	0.003054	0.0013	1.0040	0.0001	0.0001	0.0000
705	0.003251	0.0203	0.0015	1.0042	0.0008	0.0007	0.0003
706	−0.0971	−0.6069	0.0015	1.0032	−0.0232	−0.0221	−0.0070
707	−0.0107	−0.0666	0.0025	1.0052	−0.0033	−0.0024	0.0023
708	−0.0998	−0.6235	0.0013	1.0030	−0.0228	−0.0228	−0.0016
709	−0.000885	−0.005530	0.0013	1.0040	−0.0002	−0.0002	0.0000
710	−0.1022	−0.6385	0.0014	1.0029	−0.0236	−0.0233	0.0035
711	−0.006136	−0.0383	0.0017	1.0044	−0.0016	−0.0014	0.0007
712	0.1014	0.6337	0.0014	1.0030	0.0235	0.0231	0.0041
713	−0.2023	−1.2650	0.0014	0.9998	−0.0468	−0.0462	0.0073
714	0.1003	0.6269	0.0013	1.0030	0.0230	0.0229	0.0018
715	0.0985	0.6154	0.0013	1.0030	0.0226	0.0225	−0.0020
716	−0.1029	−0.6429	0.0014	1.0030	−0.0240	−0.0235	0.0051
717	−0.002150	−0.0134	0.0014	1.0040	−0.0005	−0.0005	0.0001
718	−0.000512	−0.003197	0.0013	1.0040	−0.0001	−0.0001	−0.0000
719	−0.0995	−0.6215	0.0013	1.0030	−0.0228	−0.0227	−0.0022
720	0.1041	0.6506	0.0016	1.0031	0.0258	0.0237	0.0101
721	−0.1048	−0.6550	0.0015	1.0031	−0.0257	−0.0239	0.0094
722	0.1023	0.6395	0.0014	1.0030	0.0241	0.0233	0.0061
723	−0.000733	−0.004580	0.0013	1.0040	−0.0002	−0.0002	0.0000
724	−0.1030	−0.6437	0.0014	1.0030	−0.0241	−0.0235	0.0053
725	−0.001190	−0.007435	0.0013	1.0040	−0.0003	−0.0003	0.0000
726	0.0000750	0.000468	0.0013	1.0040	0.0000	0.0000	0.0000
727	0.001492	0.009323	0.0014	1.0041	0.0003	0.0003	0.0001
728	−0.004151	−0.0259	0.0015	1.0042	−0.0010	−0.0009	0.0003
729	0.000851	0.005314	0.0014	1.0040	0.0002	0.0002	0.0000
730	−0.002149	−0.0134	0.0014	1.0040	−0.0005	−0.0005	0.0001
731	0.000219	0.001366	0.0013	1.0040	0.0000	0.0000	0.0000
732	−0.1001	−0.6255	0.0013	1.0030	−0.0229	−0.0228	−0.0009
733	0.003867	0.0242	0.0015	1.0042	0.0010	0.0009	0.0004
734	−0.007736	−0.0483	0.0019	1.0046	−0.0021	−0.0018	0.0012
735	0.001333	0.008327	0.0014	1.0041	0.0003	0.0003	0.0001
736	**0.1460**	**1.6218**	**0.6832**	**3.1425**	**2.3814**	**0.0997**	**2.3791**
737	**0.3434**	**2.1757**	**0.0230**	**1.0134**	**0.3336**	**0.0796**	**0.3238**
738	**0.5405**	**3.4725**	**0.0403**	**1.0119**	**0.7115**	**0.1309**	**−0.6996**
739	**2.9581**	**25.5247**	**0.0205**	**0.2924**	**3.6944**	**0.9493**	**−3.5725**
740	**0.0884**	**0.5528**	**0.0027**	**1.0046**	**0.0288**	**0.0202**	**−0.0205**
741	**−0.5300**	**−3.3526**	**0.0111**	**0.9841**	**−0.3553**	**−0.1238**	**0.3333**
742	**−0.8183**	**−5.2131**	**0.0049**	**0.9382**	**−0.3641**	**−0.1914**	**0.3102**

Output statistics							
Obs	Residual	RStudent	Hat diag H	Cov ratio	DFFITS	DFBETAS	
						Intercept	DLWkUNCLL1
743	−0.2048	−1.2812	0.0015	0.9998	−0.0503	−0.0468	0.0185
744	−0.2076	−1.2990	0.0019	1.0001	−0.0567	−0.0475	0.0310
745	0.008254	0.0516	0.0022	1.0049	0.0024	0.0019	0.0015
746	0.1066	0.6661	0.0019	1.0034	0.0290	0.0243	0.0158
747	−0.007722	−0.0483	0.0019	1.0046	−0.0021	−0.0018	0.0012
748	−0.2112	−1.3217	0.0026	1.0006	−0.0675	−0.0484	0.0472
749	−0.2250	−1.4120	0.0080	1.0054	−0.1270	−0.0520	0.1160
750	0.1729	1.0854	0.0092	1.0089	0.1049	0.0400	−0.0970
751	−0.4081	−2.5613	0.0020	0.9873	−0.1138	−0.0937	0.0647
752	−0.2011	−1.2575	0.0013	0.9998	−0.0460	−0.0459	0.0023
753	−0.4106	−2.5779	0.0025	0.9875	−0.1282	−0.0944	0.0869

Sum of residuals	0
Sum of squared residuals	19.19068
Predicted residual SS (PRESS)	19.82684

Yes, we see very large studentized residuals, RStudent, and large cov Ratio, DFBETAS and DFFITS variables for observation 738–742, the March–July 2020 period. A year past the start of COVID, the influential variables indicate it is appropriate to estimate robust regressions for the DUE and DLWkUNCLL1 relationship.

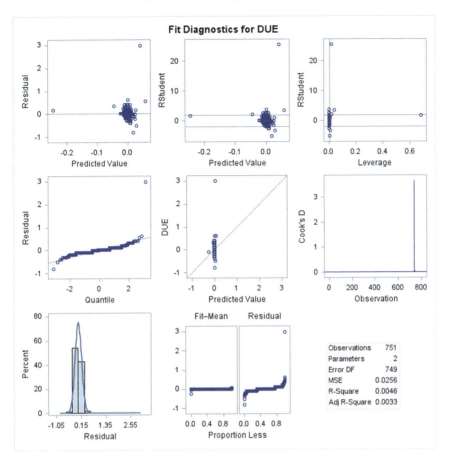

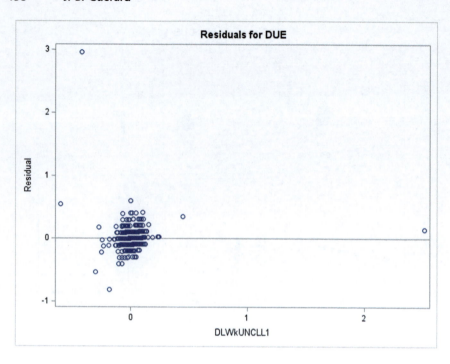

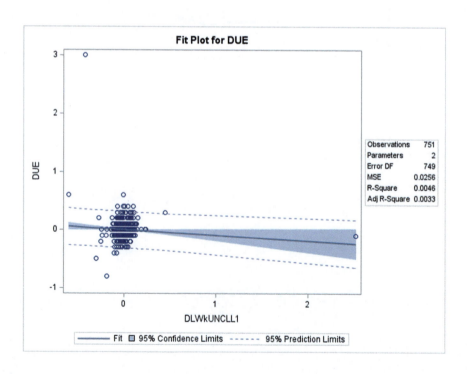

We want to estimate an OLS multiple regression line for the change in the unemployment rate as a function of the DLOG Leading Economic Indicator, LEI, and weekly unemployment claims variables for the 1959–11/2021 period. We expect to report a negative coefficient on the DLLEIL1 variable and a positive coefficient on the DLWkUNCLL1 variable.

Palgrave DUE DLLEIL1 DLWkUNCLL1 PJD 110521
The REG Procedure
Model: MODEL1
Dependent Variable: DUE

Number of observations read	753
Number of observations used	751
Number of observations with missing values	2

Analysis of variance

Source	DF	Sum of squares	Mean square	F value	Pr > F
Model	2	0.41924	0.20962	8.31	0.0003
Error	748	18.86055	0.02521		
Corrected Total	750	19.27979			

Root MSE	0.15879	R-square	0.0217
Dependent mean	0.00053262	Adj R-square	0.0191
Coeff Var	29,813		

Parameter estimates

Variable	DF	Parameter estimate	Standard error	t value	Pr > |t|
Intercept	1	0.00695	0.00606	1.15	0.2515
DLLEIL1	1	−3.34841	0.92539	−3.62	0.0003
DLWkUNCLL1	1	−0.25156	0.06715	−3.75	0.0002

We report a negative coefficient on the DLLEIL1 variable, −3.438, that is highly statistically significant, having a t-statistic of −3.62. We negative coefficient on the DLWkUNCLL1 variable, −0.252, that is highly statistically significant, having a t-statistic of −3.75. The weekly unemployment claims variable has the incorrect sign on its coefficient. Let us examine the OLS regression diagnostics.

Palgrave DUE DLLEIL1 DLWkUNCLL1 PJD 110521
The REG Procedure
Model: MODEL1
Dependent Variable: DUE

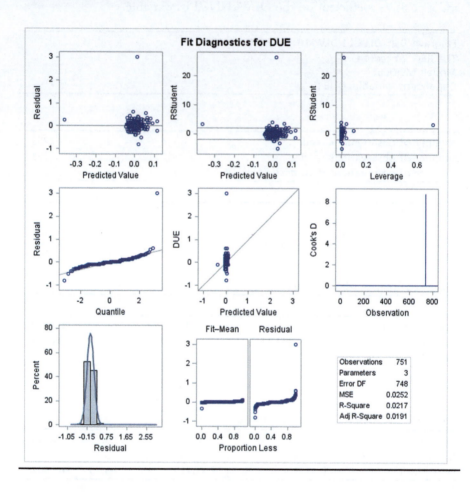

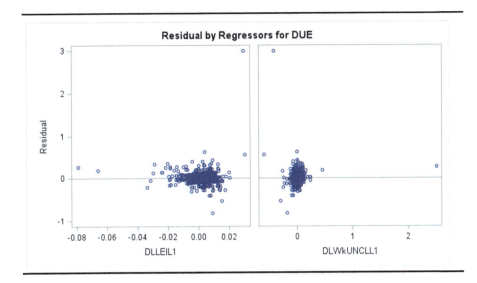

The reader sees that the Belsley et al. (1980) regression diagnostics indicate that the OLS estimated multiple regression line is not sufficient.

Palgrave DUE DLLEIL1 DLWkUNCLL1 PJD 110521
The REG Procedure
Model: MODEL1
Dependent Variable: DUE

Number of observations read	753
Number of observations used	751
Number of observations with missing values	2

Analysis of variance

Source	DF	Sum of squares	Mean square	F value	Pr > F
Model	2	0.41924	0.20962	8.31	0.0003
Error	748	18.86055	0.02521		
Corrected Total	750	19.27979			

Root MSE	0.15879	R-square	0.0217
Dependent mean	0.00053262	Adj R-square	0.0191
Coeff Var	29,813		

Parameter estimates

Variable	DF	Parameter estimate	Standard error	t value	Pr > |t|
Intercept	1	0.00695	0.00606	1.15	0.2515
DLLEIL1	1	−3.34841	0.92539	−3.62	0.0003
DLWkUNCLL1	1	−0.25156	0.06715	−3.75	0.0002

Palgrave DUE DLLEIL1 DLWkUNCLL1 PJD 110521
The REG Procedure
Model: MODEL1
Dependent Variable: DUE

Output statistics

Obs	Residual	RStudent	Hat diag H	Cov ratio	DFFITS	DFBETAS		
						Intercept	DLLEIL1	DLWkUNCLL1
1	–	–	–	–	–	–	–	–
2	–	–	–	–	–	–	–	–
3	−0.0784	−0.4941	0.0033	1.0063	−0.0284	−0.0110	−0.0214	−0.0101
4	−0.2732	−1.7281	0.0065	0.9985	−0.1395	−0.0282	−0.1113	−0.0277
5	−0.1090	−0.6865	0.0017	1.0038	−0.0281	−0.0251	0.0038	0.0118
6	0.0179	0.1129	0.0023	1.0063	0.0054	0.0029	0.0035	0.0024
7	−0.0842	−0.5308	0.0020	1.0049	−0.0236	−0.0153	−0.0110	−0.0130
8	0.0103	0.0647	0.0016	1.0056	0.0026	0.0020	0.0010	0.0010
9	0.006900	0.0435	0.0024	1.0064	0.0021	0.0016	−0.0002	0.0010
10	−0.0252	−0.1586	0.0028	1.0068	−0.0084	−0.0070	0.0048	0.0060
11	0.1161	0.7323	0.0034	1.0052	0.0426	0.0243	0.0042	0.0281
12	−0.0993	−0.6260	0.0033	1.0057	−0.0358	−0.0252	0.0116	−0.0120
13	0.000149	0.000945	0.0095	1.0137	0.0001	0.0000	0.0000	−0.0000
14	−0.0908	−0.5723	0.0016	1.0043	−0.0226	−0.0177	−0.0078	−0.0077
15	0.1840	1.1600	0.0019	1.0005	0.0507	0.0476	−0.0241	−0.0259
16	−0.1010	−0.6368	0.0031	1.0055	−0.0355	−0.0259	0.0128	−0.0102
17	−0.2034	−1.2827	0.0014	0.9989	−0.0486	−0.0447	−0.0003	0.0099
18	0.1112	0.7005	0.0019	1.0040	0.0310	0.0228	0.0057	0.0164
19	0.1088	0.6853	0.0015	1.0037	0.0269	0.0213	0.0091	0.0088
20	0.003621	0.0228	0.0015	1.0055	0.0009	0.0008	0.0000	0.0002
21	0.1246	0.7855	0.0029	1.0045	0.0426	0.0205	0.0236	0.0310
22	0.2956	1.8662	0.0015	0.9916	0.0713	0.0657	−0.0015	−0.0173
23	0.008156	0.0514	0.0017	1.0058	0.0021	0.0017	0.0003	0.0009
24	−0.1103	−0.6950	0.0019	1.0040	−0.0306	−0.0288	0.0155	0.0043
25	0.3018	1.9054	0.0014	0.9909	0.0707	0.0634	0.0110	0.0022
26	0.1231	0.7761	0.0027	1.0043	0.0405	0.0190	0.0279	0.0237
27	0.1264	0.7968	0.0032	1.0047	0.0450	0.0204	0.0254	0.0339
28	0.2053	1.2964	0.0040	1.0013	0.0825	0.0335	0.0411	−0.0154
29	0.1271	0.8018	0.0036	1.0050	0.0479	0.0170	0.0379	0.0251
30	−0.0905	−0.5701	0.0026	1.0053	−0.0288	−0.0152	−0.0161	−0.0011
31	0.3180	2.0106	0.0038	0.9917	0.1243	0.0444	0.0890	0.0206
32	−0.2856	−1.8032	0.0019	0.9929	−0.0781	−0.0531	−0.0337	−0.0408
33	−0.0795	−0.5016	0.0052	1.0083	−0.0364	−0.0097	−0.0269	−0.0044
34	−0.0859	−0.5413	0.0019	1.0047	−0.0233	−0.0160	−0.0099	−0.0121
35	−0.0859	−0.5417	0.0035	1.0064	−0.0323	−0.0128	−0.0212	−0.0024
36	−0.0560	−0.3535	0.0073	1.0109	−0.0304	−0.0044	−0.0275	−0.0175
37	−0.0938	−0.5910	0.0017	1.0043	−0.0243	−0.0178	−0.0097	−0.0020

Output statistics

Obs	Residual	RStudent	Hat diag H	Cov ratio	DFFITS	DFBETAS Intercept	DLLEIL1	DLWkUNCLL1
38	0.006709	0.0423	0.0015	1.0055	0.0016	0.0014	0.0004	0.0004
39	−0.0719	−0.4537	0.0042	1.0074	−0.0294	−0.0089	−0.0241	−0.0131
40	−0.1041	−0.6556	0.0014	1.0037	−0.0247	−0.0232	0.0009	0.0052
41	0.009039	0.0569	0.0017	1.0057	0.0024	0.0017	0.0011	0.0005
42	−0.0919	−0.5789	0.0017	1.0044	−0.0241	−0.0194	−0.0028	−0.0106
43	−0.0139	−0.0877	0.0020	1.0060	−0.0039	−0.0037	0.0022	0.0012
44	0.0117	0.0740	0.0018	1.0058	0.0032	0.0021	0.0016	0.0010
45	0.0142	0.0894	0.0019	1.0059	0.0039	0.0025	0.0022	0.0015
46	−0.1013	−0.6383	0.0014	1.0037	−0.0236	−0.0220	−0.0009	0.0021
47	0.1061	0.6682	0.0014	1.0037	0.0253	0.0215	0.0062	0.0062
48	0.0270	0.1703	0.0040	1.0079	0.0107	0.0034	0.0087	0.0047
49	0.1113	0.7014	0.0017	1.0037	0.0288	0.0215	0.0104	0.0127
50	0.0213	0.1343	0.0028	1.0068	0.0071	0.0032	0.0051	0.0032
51	−0.0861	−0.5423	0.0023	1.0052	−0.0262	−0.0142	−0.0163	−0.0064
52	0.009451	0.0595	0.0022	1.0062	0.0028	0.0016	0.0015	0.0003
53	0.1349	0.8515	0.0048	1.0059	0.0590	0.0153	0.0498	0.0358
54	−0.0937	−0.5902	0.0016	1.0042	−0.0237	−0.0180	−0.0091	−0.0027
55	0.007699	0.0485	0.0016	1.0057	0.0020	0.0015	0.0008	0.0003
56	0.1095	0.6900	0.0017	1.0038	0.0283	0.0204	0.0128	0.0070
57	−0.0910	−0.5731	0.0016	1.0043	−0.0226	−0.0180	−0.0069	−0.0083
58	0.0247	0.1556	0.0035	1.0075	0.0093	0.0033	0.0073	0.0040
59	0.0171	0.1079	0.0024	1.0064	0.0053	0.0027	0.0035	0.0019
60	−0.1036	−0.6527	0.0014	1.0037	−0.0243	−0.0231	0.0011	0.0043
61	0.1323	0.8347	0.0039	1.0052	0.0524	0.0188	0.0355	0.0407
62	−0.1050	−0.6615	0.0017	1.0040	−0.0277	−0.0226	−0.0018	0.0092
63	0.0155	0.0975	0.0029	1.0069	0.0052	0.0024	0.0035	0.0010
64	−0.0917	−0.5776	0.0015	1.0042	−0.0226	−0.0183	−0.0063	−0.0078
65	0.007368	0.0464	0.0020	1.0060	0.0021	0.0013	0.0010	0.0001
66	0.1162	0.7326	0.0023	1.0042	0.0351	0.0190	0.0226	0.0126
67	0.0125	0.0790	0.0021	1.0061	0.0036	0.0021	0.0021	0.0009
68	−0.0790	−0.4977	0.0026	1.0057	−0.0255	−0.0122	−0.0177	−0.0127
69	0.002464	0.0155	0.0020	1.0060	0.0007	0.0005	0.0002	−0.0001
70	−0.0725	−0.4572	0.0036	1.0068	−0.0276	−0.0096	−0.0219	−0.0145
71	0.0968	0.6097	0.0014	1.0039	0.0229	0.0226	−0.0044	−0.0005
72	−0.0697	−0.4394	0.0036	1.0069	−0.0266	−0.0096	−0.0198	−0.0182
73	−0.0855	−0.5389	0.0027	1.0055	−0.0278	−0.0136	−0.0181	−0.0055
74	0.1168	0.7363	0.0027	1.0046	0.0385	0.0180	0.0264	0.0105
75	−0.0937	−0.5903	0.0014	1.0041	−0.0225	−0.0192	−0.0049	−0.0062
76	0.0135	0.0850	0.0026	1.0066	0.0043	0.0022	0.0027	0.0008
77	−0.0910	−0.5734	0.0016	1.0043	−0.0230	−0.0173	−0.0094	−0.0061
78	0.0935	0.5892	0.0017	1.0044	0.0245	0.0206	−0.0000	−0.0091
79	−0.1905	−1.2009	0.0016	0.9998	−0.0484	−0.0360	−0.0203	−0.0139
80	0.1156	0.7283	0.0020	1.0039	0.0323	0.0205	0.0170	0.0159
81	0.0265	0.1673	0.0031	1.0070	0.0093	0.0041	0.0059	0.0067
82	−0.1159	−0.7308	0.0031	1.0050	−0.0407	−0.0267	0.0037	0.0260
83	0.0198	0.1250	0.0034	1.0074	0.0073	0.0028	0.0054	0.0020
84	0.0275	0.1736	0.0035	1.0074	0.0102	0.0037	0.0080	0.0058
85	−0.0843	−0.5311	0.0025	1.0054	−0.0267	−0.0134	−0.0176	−0.0073
86	0.0258	0.1628	0.0030	1.0070	0.0090	0.0041	0.0055	0.0064
87	0.004055	0.0255	0.0015	1.0055	0.0010	0.0008	0.0003	0.0001
88	−0.0238	−0.1502	0.0050	1.0090	−0.0107	−0.0057	0.0014	0.0079
89	−0.0970	−0.6108	0.0015	1.0040	−0.0233	−0.0197	−0.0057	−0.0008
90	−0.1038	−0.6543	0.0022	1.0045	−0.0305	−0.0262	0.0116	−0.0043
91	−0.0109	−0.0686	0.0018	1.0058	−0.0029	−0.0028	0.0014	0.0007

Output statistics								
Obs	Residual	RStudent	Hat diag H	Cov ratio	DFFITS	DFBETAS		
						Intercept	DLLEIL1	DLWkUNCLL1
92	−0.008298	−0.0523	0.0017	1.0057	−0.0022	−0.0021	0.0009	0.0003
93	−0.0197	−0.1244	0.0023	1.0062	−0.0059	−0.0054	0.0037	0.0030
94	−0.0106	−0.0668	0.0018	1.0058	−0.0028	−0.0027	0.0013	0.0006
95	−0.007951	−0.0501	0.0017	1.0057	−0.0021	−0.0020	0.0009	0.0002
96	−0.000020	−0.000124	0.0014	1.0055	−0.0000	−0.0000	0.0000	−0.0000
97	−0.001247	−0.007852	0.0017	1.0058	−0.0003	−0.0003	0.0001	−0.0001
98	0.000858	0.005405	0.0018	1.0059	0.0002	0.0002	0.0001	−0.0000
99	0.0184	0.1159	0.0051	1.0091	0.0083	0.0040	0.0001	0.0056
100	0.0107	0.0675	0.0019	1.0059	0.0029	0.0019	0.0015	0.0007
101	−0.0839	−0.5284	0.0021	1.0050	−0.0242	−0.0156	−0.0097	−0.0145
102	−0.006984	−0.0440	0.0029	1.0069	−0.0024	−0.0014	−0.0004	0.0011
103	0.000433	0.002727	0.0018	1.0058	0.0001	0.0001	0.0000	−0.0000
104	0.1262	0.7955	0.0031	1.0045	0.0440	0.0188	0.0308	0.0287
105	0.005446	0.0343	0.0029	1.0070	0.0019	0.0009	0.0009	−0.0002
106	0.004495	0.0283	0.0014	1.0054	0.0011	0.0009	0.0002	0.0002
107	0.008691	0.0547	0.0016	1.0056	0.0022	0.0017	0.0008	0.0006
108	−0.006684	−0.0421	0.0021	1.0061	−0.0019	−0.0014	−0.0001	0.0008
109	0.0395	0.2496	0.0052	1.0090	0.0180	0.0045	0.0143	0.0137
110	0.000923	0.005814	0.0013	1.0054	0.0002	0.0002	0.0000	0.0000
111	−0.0160	−0.1005	0.0023	1.0063	−0.0049	−0.0039	0.0011	0.0030
112	−0.1010	−0.6359	0.0013	1.0037	−0.0232	−0.0222	0.0001	0.0006
113	0.0102	0.0645	0.0016	1.0056	0.0026	0.0019	0.0011	0.0009
114	0.009873	0.0622	0.0018	1.0058	0.0026	0.0018	0.0013	0.0006
115	0.001339	0.008430	0.0014	1.0055	0.0003	0.0003	0.0001	−0.0000
116	0.005025	0.0316	0.0014	1.0054	0.0012	0.0010	0.0002	0.0003
117	−0.0187	−0.1181	0.0024	1.0064	−0.0058	−0.0053	0.0039	0.0023
118	0.0177	0.1114	0.0029	1.0069	0.0060	0.0027	0.0042	0.0016
119	0.0122	0.0771	0.0022	1.0062	0.0036	0.0021	0.0021	0.0007
120	−0.1011	−0.6368	0.0013	1.0037	−0.0233	−0.0223	0.0002	0.0007
121	0.0135	0.0853	0.0022	1.0062	0.0040	0.0027	0.0009	0.0023
122	−0.006936	−0.0437	0.0015	1.0055	−0.0017	−0.0016	0.0003	0.0005
123	0.006982	0.0440	0.0015	1.0055	0.0017	0.0014	0.0006	0.0004
124	0.0872	0.5495	0.0018	1.0046	0.0231	0.0213	−0.0071	−0.0114
125	0.008735	0.0550	0.0017	1.0057	0.0023	0.0016	0.0010	0.0004
126	−0.0277	−0.1747	0.0035	1.0074	−0.0104	−0.0085	0.0082	0.0053
127	−0.0140	−0.0885	0.0026	1.0066	−0.0046	−0.0039	0.0028	0.0007
128	−0.0152	−0.0955	0.0027	1.0067	−0.0050	−0.0043	0.0032	0.0009
129	−0.0158	−0.0995	0.0020	1.0060	−0.0044	−0.0042	0.0025	0.0018
130	−0.006144	−0.0387	0.0014	1.0054	−0.0015	−0.0014	0.0002	0.0004
131	−0.0201	−0.1265	0.0029	1.0069	−0.0068	−0.0058	0.0049	0.0022
132	−0.0114	−0.0719	0.0021	1.0061	−0.0033	−0.0030	0.0018	0.0005
133	−0.0123	−0.0776	0.0026	1.0067	−0.0040	−0.0034	0.0024	0.0003
134	0.0856	0.5403	0.0054	1.0083	0.0399	0.0263	−0.0254	0.0023
135	−0.0273	−0.1722	0.0041	1.0080	−0.0110	−0.0086	0.0089	0.0044
136	0.0809	0.5103	0.0029	1.0059	0.0276	0.0235	−0.0195	−0.0078
137	0.0255	0.1612	0.0075	1.0116	0.0141	0.0054	0.0007	0.0103
138	0.0648	0.4090	0.0044	1.0078	0.0271	0.0193	−0.0169	−0.0224
139	−0.0134	−0.0844	0.0017	1.0057	−0.0035	−0.0034	0.0015	0.0015
140	0.0873	0.5500	0.0018	1.0046	0.0231	0.0212	−0.0069	−0.0115
141	0.008156	0.0514	0.0015	1.0056	0.0020	0.0016	0.0005	0.0007
142	0.0205	0.1289	0.0029	1.0069	0.0070	0.0038	0.0023	0.0050
143	0.0896	0.5643	0.0017	1.0045	0.0235	0.0229	−0.0111	−0.0050
144	0.2897	1.8289	0.0016	0.9922	0.0724	0.0717	−0.0268	−0.0232
145	0.0254	0.1600	0.0050	1.0089	0.0113	0.0030	0.0090	0.0030

Output statistics

Obs	Residual	RStudent	Hat diag H	Cov ratio	DFFITS	DFBETAS		
						Intercept	DLLEIL1	DLWkUNCLL1
146	0.001365	0.008594	0.0014	1.0055	0.0003	0.0003	0.0001	−0.0000
147	0.0153	0.0962	0.0029	1.0069	0.0052	0.0024	0.0034	0.0010
148	0.1288	0.8125	0.0035	1.0049	0.0482	0.0176	0.0369	0.0303
149	−0.001175	−0.007398	0.0015	1.0055	−0.0003	−0.0002	−0.0000	0.0000
150	0.0200	0.1263	0.0024	1.0064	0.0062	0.0033	0.0040	0.0034
151	0.0979	0.6164	0.0013	1.0038	0.0226	0.0218	−0.0009	−0.0018
152	0.0122	0.0771	0.0017	1.0057	0.0032	0.0023	0.0014	0.0013
153	0.0223	0.1406	0.0028	1.0068	0.0074	0.0039	0.0035	0.0054
154	−0.009905	−0.0624	0.0018	1.0058	−0.0027	−0.0023	0.0003	0.0012
155	0.006435	0.0405	0.0017	1.0057	0.0017	0.0012	0.0007	0.0002
156	−0.002508	−0.0158	0.0015	1.0055	−0.0006	−0.0005	−0.0000	0.0001
157	0.0150	0.0943	0.0033	1.0073	0.0055	0.0022	0.0037	0.0007
158	0.0266	0.1674	0.0035	1.0074	0.0099	0.0036	0.0078	0.0051
159	−0.0738	−0.4655	0.0039	1.0071	−0.0291	−0.0095	−0.0234	−0.0123
160	0.0173	0.1091	0.0023	1.0063	0.0053	0.0028	0.0035	0.0021
161	−0.0867	−0.5466	0.0019	1.0047	−0.0237	−0.0154	−0.0127	−0.0087
162	0.0149	0.0941	0.0020	1.0060	0.0042	0.0026	0.0023	0.0018
163	0.0358	0.2261	0.0045	1.0084	0.0152	0.0048	0.0107	0.0122
164	0.008785	0.0553	0.0020	1.0060	0.0025	0.0016	0.0012	0.0003
165	0.009118	0.0575	0.0038	1.0078	0.0035	0.0014	0.0020	−0.0003
166	0.0295	0.1861	0.0041	1.0080	0.0119	0.0037	0.0097	0.0062
167	−0.0818	−0.5156	0.0027	1.0056	−0.0266	−0.0126	−0.0185	−0.0092
168	−0.0847	−0.5340	0.0025	1.0054	−0.0267	−0.0136	−0.0174	−0.0070
169	0.0316	0.1992	0.0042	1.0081	0.0130	0.0038	0.0107	0.0074
170	−0.1027	−0.6475	0.0020	1.0044	−0.0292	−0.0209	−0.0059	0.0088
171	−0.004111	−0.0259	0.0015	1.0055	−0.0010	−0.0009	0.0000	0.0002
172	−0.1052	−0.6629	0.0016	1.0039	−0.0265	−0.0257	0.0087	0.0006
173	−0.0122	−0.0767	0.0024	1.0064	−0.0038	−0.0033	0.0022	0.0004
174	−0.0101	−0.0638	0.0016	1.0056	−0.0025	−0.0025	0.0009	0.0008
175	−0.1080	−0.6806	0.0016	1.0038	−0.0275	−0.0270	0.0110	0.0038
176	0.0720	0.4542	0.0038	1.0070	0.0280	0.0224	−0.0224	−0.0131
177	−0.0245	−0.1545	0.0040	1.0080	−0.0098	−0.0076	0.0077	0.0030
178	−0.0315	−0.1986	0.0038	1.0077	−0.0123	−0.0098	0.0098	0.0076
179	−0.0192	−0.1209	0.0022	1.0062	−0.0057	−0.0052	0.0034	0.0029
180	−0.1103	−0.6954	0.0024	1.0045	−0.0342	−0.0297	0.0187	0.0017
181	0.0889	0.5612	0.0047	1.0075	0.0384	0.0261	−0.0225	0.0039
182	−0.0123	−0.0775	0.0030	1.0071	−0.0043	−0.0035	0.0026	0.0002
183	−0.0217	−0.1366	0.0029	1.0069	−0.0074	−0.0063	0.0054	0.0029
184	0.0774	0.4878	0.0027	1.0057	0.0252	0.0222	−0.0176	−0.0128
185	−0.0681	−0.4314	0.0130	1.0165	−0.0495	−0.0285	0.0458	0.0368
186	−0.0236	−0.1488	0.0031	1.0070	−0.0083	−0.0070	0.0062	0.0036
187	−0.0308	−0.1941	0.0055	1.0094	−0.0145	−0.0103	0.0121	0.0049
188	−0.0412	−0.2602	0.0061	1.0099	−0.0204	−0.0144	0.0181	0.0121
189	0.0606	0.3835	0.0097	1.0132	0.0379	0.0230	−0.0328	−0.0107
190	0.0399	0.2528	0.0142	1.0182	0.0304	0.0172	−0.0286	−0.0148
191	−0.0178	−0.1125	0.0053	1.0093	−0.0082	−0.0056	0.0056	0.0002
192	0.1764	1.1159	0.0080	1.0071	0.1004	0.0604	−0.0734	−0.0040
193	0.2580	1.6351	0.0108	1.0041	0.1706	0.1007	−0.1488	−0.0494
194	0.2822	1.7827	0.0036	0.9949	0.1066	0.0840	−0.0744	−0.0164
195	0.1771	1.1166	0.0026	1.0016	0.0565	0.0498	−0.0368	−0.0335
196	0.3814	2.4124	0.0024	0.9833	0.1192	0.1076	−0.0800	−0.0448
197	0.2211	1.3960	0.0039	1.0001	0.0874	0.0296	0.0661	0.0218
198	0.2040	1.2862	0.0017	0.9991	0.0533	0.0395	0.0188	−0.0011
199	0.1201	0.7569	0.0027	1.0044	0.0390	0.0184	0.0275	0.0169

Obs	Residual	RStudent	Hat diag H	Cov ratio	DFFITS	DFBETAS Intercept	DLLEIL1	DLWkUNCLL1

Output statistics

Obs	Residual	RStudent	Hat diag H	Cov ratio	DFFITS	Intercept	DLLEIL1	DLWkUNCLL1
200	−0.0972	−0.6128	0.0029	1.0054	−0.0328	−0.0175	−0.0138	0.0065
201	0.1010	0.6364	0.0013	1.0037	0.0233	0.0219	0.0013	0.0015
202	−0.1968	−1.2410	0.0014	0.9993	−0.0470	−0.0402	−0.0109	−0.0025
203	0.1041	0.6562	0.0021	1.0044	0.0303	0.0193	0.0124	−0.0027
204	−0.006384	−0.0402	0.0016	1.0056	−0.0016	−0.0014	0.0001	0.0006
205	−0.1019	−0.6419	0.0018	1.0041	−0.0271	−0.0210	−0.0050	0.0065
206	−0.1612	−1.0184	0.0061	1.0060	−0.0796	−0.0151	−0.0703	−0.0439
207	−0.0724	−0.4567	0.0056	1.0088	−0.0342	−0.0079	−0.0279	−0.0096
208	−0.2854	−1.8016	0.0019	0.9929	−0.0782	−0.0521	−0.0371	−0.0391
209	−0.0865	−0.5447	0.0018	1.0046	−0.0232	−0.0159	−0.0106	−0.0108
210	0.2327	1.4696	0.0040	0.9994	0.0932	0.0306	0.0712	0.0659
211	0.008051	0.0507	0.0015	1.0055	0.0020	0.0016	0.0007	0.0005
212	0.1204	0.7594	0.0029	1.0046	0.0410	0.0178	0.0299	0.0157
213	−0.0955	−0.6017	0.0014	1.0040	−0.0227	−0.0193	−0.0057	−0.0029
214	0.0214	0.1351	0.0025	1.0065	0.0068	0.0035	0.0043	0.0040
215	0.002612	0.0164	0.0014	1.0054	0.0006	0.0006	0.0001	0.0001
216	0.0117	0.0739	0.0025	1.0065	0.0037	0.0019	0.0022	0.0005
217	−0.0905	−0.5702	0.0024	1.0051	−0.0280	−0.0154	−0.0155	−0.0016
218	−0.0816	−0.5140	0.0027	1.0056	−0.0266	−0.0155	−0.0082	−0.0183
219	−0.0573	−0.3615	0.0058	1.0093	−0.0276	−0.0065	−0.0211	−0.0226
220	−0.1233	−0.7791	0.0071	1.0088	−0.0660	−0.0274	0.0000	0.0461
221	0.0149	0.0941	0.0019	1.0059	0.0041	0.0027	0.0019	0.0021
222	−0.0836	−0.5265	0.0020	1.0050	−0.0239	−0.0144	−0.0136	−0.0115
223	0.001510	0.009515	0.0019	1.0059	0.0004	0.0003	0.0001	−0.0001
224	−0.1023	−0.6443	0.0014	1.0038	−0.0242	−0.0237	0.0040	−0.0005
225	0.1124	0.7085	0.0018	1.0038	0.0300	0.0203	0.0152	0.0109
226	−0.1047	−0.6595	0.0014	1.0037	−0.0245	−0.0240	0.0032	0.0044
227	−0.001114	−0.007013	0.0013	1.0054	−0.0003	−0.0002	0.0000	0.0000
228	−0.1013	−0.6381	0.0014	1.0038	−0.0239	−0.0218	−0.0018	0.0028
229	−0.0980	−0.6175	0.0014	1.0038	−0.0227	−0.0211	−0.0014	−0.0028
230	−0.0351	−0.2213	0.0046	1.0085	−0.0150	−0.0114	0.0126	0.0091
231	−0.0682	−0.4302	0.0038	1.0072	−0.0267	−0.0097	−0.0181	−0.0206
232	−0.004846	−0.0305	0.0027	1.0067	−0.0016	−0.0010	−0.0003	0.0006
233	−0.0813	−0.5129	0.0036	1.0065	−0.0307	−0.0115	−0.0222	−0.0065
234	−0.0936	−0.5894	0.0015	1.0041	−0.0225	−0.0187	−0.0064	−0.0052
235	0.0154	0.0968	0.0020	1.0060	0.0043	0.0027	0.0023	0.0020
236	−0.0999	−0.6292	0.0017	1.0041	−0.0256	−0.0233	0.0047	−0.0051
237	0.1044	0.6576	0.0018	1.0041	0.0280	0.0199	0.0106	−0.0007
238	−0.004126	−0.0260	0.0015	1.0055	−0.0010	−0.0009	0.0000	0.0002
239	−0.0987	−0.6215	0.0013	1.0038	−0.0228	−0.0214	−0.0009	−0.0022
240	−0.0166	−0.1046	0.0029	1.0069	−0.0057	−0.0048	0.0038	0.0011
241	−0.003475	−0.0219	0.0014	1.0054	−0.0008	−0.0008	0.0002	0.0000
242	−0.0185	−0.1168	0.0026	1.0066	−0.0060	−0.0053	0.0041	0.0020
243	0.0892	0.5620	0.0017	1.0045	0.0232	0.0228	−0.0107	−0.0058
244	−0.0796	−0.5016	0.0027	1.0057	−0.0261	−0.0121	−0.0186	−0.0113
245	−0.0325	−0.2053	0.0101	1.0141	−0.0207	−0.0120	0.0166	0.0029
246	−0.1320	−0.8333	0.0057	1.0070	−0.0632	−0.0347	0.0187	0.0521
247	−0.0144	−0.0904	0.0029	1.0069	−0.0049	−0.0041	0.0031	0.0006
248	−0.0204	−0.1285	0.0032	1.0071	−0.0072	−0.0060	0.0053	0.0021
249	−0.0189	−0.1191	0.0026	1.0066	−0.0061	−0.0054	0.0042	0.0020
250	0.0740	0.4665	0.0032	1.0064	0.0264	0.0222	−0.0202	−0.0136
251	−0.0313	−0.1973	0.0052	1.0091	−0.0143	−0.0104	0.0120	0.0055
252	−0.0325	−0.2051	0.0054	1.0093	−0.0151	−0.0109	0.0128	0.0061
253	0.0708	0.4468	0.0045	1.0077	0.0299	0.0228	−0.0246	−0.0122

Output statistics

Obs	Residual	RStudent	Hat diag H	Cov ratio	DFFITS	DFBETAS Intercept	DLLEIL1	DLWkUNCLL1
254	−0.0214	−0.1348	0.0024	1.0064	−0.0066	−0.0059	0.0041	0.0038
255	0.0824	0.5196	0.0023	1.0052	0.0248	0.0228	−0.0159	−0.0093
256	0.1257	0.7995	0.0202	1.0221	0.1148	0.0603	−0.1102	−0.0601
257	−0.0544	−0.3466	0.0252	1.0294	−0.0557	−0.0259	0.0470	0.0088
258	−0.0220	−0.1392	0.0061	1.0102	−0.0109	−0.0072	0.0080	0.0009
259	0.2977	1.8794	0.0015	0.9914	0.0717	0.0643	0.0048	−0.0127
260	0.0972	0.6128	0.0022	1.0048	0.0290	0.0195	0.0065	−0.0092
261	0.2001	1.2622	0.0021	0.9997	0.0578	0.0391	0.0172	−0.0126
262	−0.0932	−0.5875	0.0025	1.0051	−0.0294	−0.0163	−0.0146	0.0014
263	0.0873	0.5504	0.0029	1.0058	0.0299	0.0193	−0.0002	−0.0172
264	−0.0165	−0.1040	0.0019	1.0059	−0.0046	−0.0043	0.0022	0.0024
265	−0.0263	−0.1659	0.0033	1.0072	−0.0096	−0.0080	0.0074	0.0048
266	−0.0423	−0.2670	0.0069	1.0107	−0.0222	−0.0152	0.0199	0.0119
267	−0.1237	−0.7801	0.0036	1.0052	−0.0468	−0.0378	0.0361	0.0160
268	−0.1069	−0.6735	0.0016	1.0038	−0.0271	−0.0240	0.0017	0.0097
269	0.006742	0.0425	0.0015	1.0055	0.0016	0.0013	0.0005	0.0004
270	0.0788	0.4970	0.0029	1.0059	0.0268	0.0230	−0.0195	−0.0099
271	−0.1233	−0.7778	0.0036	1.0052	−0.0466	−0.0376	0.0357	0.0154
272	0.0685	0.4318	0.0043	1.0076	0.0285	0.0220	−0.0237	−0.0145
273	−0.0213	−0.1341	0.0029	1.0069	−0.0073	−0.0062	0.0053	0.0027
274	−0.0346	−0.2185	0.0070	1.0109	−0.0184	−0.0122	0.0157	0.0059
275	−0.0183	−0.1154	0.0028	1.0068	−0.0061	−0.0053	0.0042	0.0017
276	0.0887	0.5592	0.0021	1.0048	0.0255	0.0236	−0.0138	−0.0037
277	−0.009015	−0.0568	0.0020	1.0061	−0.0026	−0.0024	0.0013	0.0002
278	0.2642	1.6707	0.0055	0.9984	0.1247	0.0900	−0.1081	−0.0604
279	0.2079	1.3111	0.0017	0.9988	0.0544	0.0388	0.0241	0.0081
280	0.0833	0.5253	0.0028	1.0057	0.0276	0.0237	−0.0185	−0.0062
281	0.2063	1.3011	0.0016	0.9989	0.0527	0.0443	0.0039	0.0198
282	0.0791	0.4986	0.0026	1.0056	0.0253	0.0225	−0.0175	−0.0113
283	0.0705	0.4446	0.0042	1.0075	0.0290	0.0225	−0.0239	−0.0130
284	0.0882	0.5554	0.0017	1.0045	0.0229	0.0213	−0.0065	−0.0107
285	0.1908	1.2037	0.0034	1.0016	0.0706	0.0533	−0.0387	0.0059
286	0.3368	2.1309	0.0047	0.9906	0.1463	0.0408	0.1153	0.1079
287	0.1952	1.2309	0.0016	0.9995	0.0486	0.0429	0.0005	−0.0140
288	0.1805	1.1386	0.0024	1.0012	0.0554	0.0464	−0.0226	−0.0366
289	−0.0146	−0.0917	0.0034	1.0074	−0.0053	−0.0032	0.0001	0.0033
290	0.0406	0.2568	0.0080	1.0119	0.0231	0.0030	0.0207	0.0098
291	0.0304	0.1919	0.0044	1.0083	0.0128	0.0036	0.0106	0.0063
292	−0.2664	−1.6840	0.0053	0.9980	−0.1231	−0.0280	−0.1061	−0.0587
293	0.2279	1.4385	0.0033	0.9991	0.0834	0.0320	0.0624	0.0527
294	−0.0712	−0.4493	0.0055	1.0087	−0.0333	−0.0077	−0.0276	−0.0106
295	−0.0815	−0.5140	0.0040	1.0070	−0.0325	−0.0111	−0.0235	−0.0053
296	−0.2944	−1.8596	0.0024	0.9926	−0.0921	−0.0525	−0.0431	0.0075
297	−0.1757	−1.1083	0.0029	1.0020	−0.0594	−0.0288	−0.0338	−0.0425
298	−0.0802	−0.5057	0.0039	1.0069	−0.0317	−0.0109	−0.0234	−0.0067
299	−0.1707	−1.0777	0.0045	1.0039	−0.0727	−0.0201	−0.0604	−0.0317
300	−0.0923	−0.5816	0.0019	1.0046	−0.0254	−0.0168	−0.0120	−0.0021
301	−0.0817	−0.5148	0.0031	1.0061	−0.0287	−0.0120	−0.0205	−0.0077
302	−0.1792	−1.1309	0.0038	1.0026	−0.0694	−0.0244	−0.0522	−0.0179
303	−0.0856	−0.5393	0.0024	1.0053	−0.0265	−0.0139	−0.0168	−0.0065
304	−0.0975	−0.6143	0.0014	1.0039	−0.0227	−0.0209	−0.0017	−0.0033
305	0.0271	0.1708	0.0032	1.0071	0.0096	0.0041	0.0063	0.0069
306	−0.1922	−1.2121	0.0018	1.0000	−0.0521	−0.0353	−0.0242	−0.0054
307	0.008029	0.0506	0.0015	1.0055	0.0020	0.0016	0.0006	0.0006

Output statistics								
Obs	Residual	RStudent	Hat diag H	Cov ratio	DFFITS	DFBETAS		
						Intercept	DLLEIL1	DLWkUNCLL1
308	−0.003100	−0.0195	0.0013	1.0054	−0.0007	−0.0007	0.0001	0.0001
309	−0.0813	−0.5124	0.0024	1.0054	−0.0252	−0.0149	−0.0103	−0.0168
310	−0.001909	−0.0120	0.0014	1.0054	−0.0005	−0.0004	0.0001	−0.0000
311	−0.0826	−0.5202	0.0021	1.0051	−0.0240	−0.0147	−0.0117	−0.0142
312	−0.001149	−0.007240	0.0016	1.0056	−0.0003	−0.0002	−0.0000	0.0001
313	−0.0972	−0.6126	0.0018	1.0043	−0.0261	−0.0189	−0.0088	0.0023
314	0.1052	0.6626	0.0015	1.0038	0.0260	0.0206	0.0086	0.0024
315	0.0187	0.1178	0.0022	1.0062	0.0056	0.0032	0.0032	0.0031
316	0.005550	0.0350	0.0015	1.0056	0.0014	0.0011	0.0005	0.0002
317	−0.0969	−0.6104	0.0015	1.0040	−0.0237	−0.0214	0.0003	−0.0060
318	0.006461	0.0407	0.0015	1.0056	0.0016	0.0013	0.0006	0.0002
319	0.008664	0.0546	0.0016	1.0056	0.0022	0.0016	0.0009	0.0005
320	−0.000049	−0.000311	0.0015	1.0056	−0.0000	−0.0000	−0.0000	0.0000
321	−0.0798	−0.5026	0.0024	1.0054	−0.0247	−0.0139	−0.0126	−0.0163
322	0.1066	0.6719	0.0015	1.0037	0.0257	0.0214	0.0071	0.0064
323	−0.1041	−0.6556	0.0014	1.0037	−0.0242	−0.0238	0.0029	0.0035
324	−0.003772	−0.0238	0.0014	1.0055	−0.0009	−0.0008	0.0000	0.0002
325	−0.0956	−0.6024	0.0015	1.0041	−0.0234	−0.0190	−0.0071	−0.0016
326	0.1916	1.2081	0.0016	0.9998	0.0485	0.0442	−0.0066	−0.0189
327	−0.0930	−0.5861	0.0015	1.0041	−0.0225	−0.0186	−0.0064	−0.0060
328	−0.0944	−0.5947	0.0015	1.0041	−0.0227	−0.0198	−0.0034	−0.0065
329	0.1126	0.7096	0.0018	1.0038	0.0299	0.0206	0.0145	0.0118
330	0.1061	0.6684	0.0015	1.0038	0.0261	0.0207	0.0089	0.0038
331	−0.0955	−0.6014	0.0017	1.0043	−0.0249	−0.0184	−0.0091	−0.0001
332	−0.005261	−0.0331	0.0014	1.0054	−0.0013	−0.0012	0.0003	0.0001
333	0.1241	0.7825	0.0029	1.0045	0.0421	0.0207	0.0227	0.0307
334	−0.2027	−1.2776	0.0014	0.9989	−0.0477	−0.0445	−0.0006	0.0075
335	0.0807	0.5087	0.0022	1.0052	0.0238	0.0214	−0.0123	−0.0142
336	−0.1007	−0.6343	0.0015	1.0039	−0.0247	−0.0211	−0.0038	0.0035
337	0.0103	0.0646	0.0018	1.0058	0.0027	0.0019	0.0014	0.0006
338	−0.0119	−0.0750	0.0016	1.0057	−0.0030	−0.0030	0.0012	0.0012
339	−0.0885	−0.5578	0.0018	1.0046	−0.0239	−0.0159	−0.0124	−0.0067
340	0.0918	0.5784	0.0016	1.0043	0.0230	0.0212	−0.0032	−0.0087
341	0.000281	0.001772	0.0013	1.0054	0.0001	0.0001	−0.0000	0.0000
342	−0.1007	−0.6344	0.0014	1.0038	−0.0234	−0.0217	−0.0015	0.0016
343	−0.0989	−0.6230	0.0015	1.0039	−0.0239	−0.0204	−0.0048	0.0014
344	0.0102	0.0644	0.0016	1.0057	0.0026	0.0019	0.0011	0.0008
345	−0.000575	−0.003620	0.0014	1.0054	−0.0001	−0.0001	−0.0000	0.0000
346	−0.0987	−0.6217	0.0017	1.0042	−0.0255	−0.0197	−0.0069	0.0029
347	−0.001976	−0.0124	0.0014	1.0054	−0.0005	−0.0004	−0.0000	0.0001
348	−0.0160	−0.1007	0.0023	1.0063	−0.0049	−0.0044	0.0031	0.0014
349	−0.0933	−0.5878	0.0015	1.0041	−0.0228	−0.0194	−0.0040	−0.0076
350	0.0204	0.1283	0.0024	1.0064	0.0064	0.0036	0.0032	0.0042
351	0.001128	0.007106	0.0020	1.0060	0.0003	0.0002	0.0001	−0.0001
352	−0.1027	−0.6469	0.0015	1.0039	−0.0253	−0.0220	−0.0021	0.0055
353	0.1038	0.6537	0.0014	1.0037	0.0245	0.0221	0.0023	0.0053
354	−0.0917	−0.5774	0.0016	1.0042	−0.0228	−0.0176	−0.0087	−0.0059
355	0.006623	0.0417	0.0017	1.0057	0.0017	0.0013	0.0007	0.0002
356	0.008077	0.0509	0.0017	1.0058	0.0021	0.0017	0.0002	0.0009
357	−0.005968	−0.0376	0.0015	1.0055	−0.0014	−0.0014	0.0001	0.0004
358	−0.008798	−0.0554	0.0016	1.0056	−0.0022	−0.0020	0.0004	0.0009
359	−0.1055	−0.6643	0.0015	1.0037	−0.0253	−0.0238	0.0020	0.0067
360	0.004394	0.0277	0.0014	1.0054	0.0010	0.0009	0.0002	0.0002
361	−0.003568	−0.0225	0.0014	1.0054	−0.0008	−0.0008	0.0001	0.0001

Output statistics

Obs	Residual	RStudent	Hat diag H	Cov ratio	DFFITS	DFBETAS		
						Intercept	DLLEIL1	DLWkUNCLL1
362	−0.0992	−0.6248	0.0013	1.0038	−0.0230	−0.0212	−0.0022	−0.0003
363	0.007668	0.0483	0.0020	1.0060	0.0021	0.0017	0.0001	0.0010
364	−0.0147	−0.0928	0.0022	1.0062	−0.0044	−0.0040	0.0027	0.0011
365	−0.0122	−0.0772	0.0017	1.0057	−0.0032	−0.0030	0.0010	0.0014
366	−0.1041	−0.6559	0.0018	1.0041	−0.0279	−0.0257	0.0095	−0.0021
367	0.1992	1.2559	0.0016	0.9993	0.0502	0.0467	−0.0098	0.0075
368	−0.2206	−1.3919	0.0026	0.9988	−0.0708	−0.0630	0.0493	0.0303
369	0.0971	0.6117	0.0014	1.0039	0.0228	0.0214	−0.0002	−0.0036
370	−0.002897	−0.0182	0.0014	1.0054	−0.0007	−0.0007	0.0001	0.0000
371	0.001904	0.0120	0.0020	1.0060	0.0005	0.0004	−0.0001	0.0002
372	−0.0193	−0.1218	0.0023	1.0063	−0.0058	−0.0050	0.0026	0.0037
373	0.006399	0.0403	0.0016	1.0057	0.0016	0.0014	0.0001	0.0006
374	−0.009723	−0.0612	0.0016	1.0057	−0.0025	−0.0024	0.0011	0.0006
375	−0.0214	−0.1346	0.0025	1.0064	−0.0067	−0.0060	0.0044	0.0035
376	−0.009419	−0.0593	0.0015	1.0055	−0.0023	−0.0023	0.0006	0.0008
377	−0.008791	−0.0554	0.0021	1.0061	−0.0026	−0.0023	0.0013	0.0001
378	−0.008908	−0.0561	0.0015	1.0055	−0.0022	−0.0022	0.0007	0.0006
379	0.0945	0.5954	0.0014	1.0040	0.0225	0.0225	−0.0057	−0.0028
380	0.0827	0.5214	0.0024	1.0053	0.0255	0.0231	−0.0167	−0.0084
381	−0.0407	−0.2570	0.0081	1.0120	−0.0233	−0.0150	0.0207	0.0092
382	−0.0434	−0.2744	0.0072	1.0110	−0.0234	−0.0158	0.0211	0.0125
383	0.1667	1.0537	0.0068	1.0064	0.0871	0.0583	−0.0736	−0.0266
384	−0.1528	−0.9680	0.0120	1.0124	−0.1066	−0.0627	0.0986	0.0475
385	0.0591	0.3733	0.0065	1.0100	0.0302	0.0209	−0.0269	−0.0162
386	0.0515	0.3256	0.0083	1.0120	0.0298	0.0194	−0.0273	−0.0172
387	0.0978	0.6164	0.0019	1.0044	0.0269	0.0239	−0.0081	0.0043
388	−0.0148	−0.0931	0.0024	1.0064	−0.0045	−0.0041	0.0028	0.0010
389	0.1070	0.6742	0.0025	1.0047	0.0338	0.0187	0.0169	−0.0014
390	0.2054	1.2954	0.0020	0.9993	0.0587	0.0379	0.0256	−0.0020
391	−0.1153	−0.7264	0.0019	1.0038	−0.0313	−0.0296	0.0145	0.0154
392	0.1239	0.7818	0.0035	1.0051	0.0465	0.0168	0.0363	0.0186
393	0.005021	0.0316	0.0014	1.0055	0.0012	0.0011	0.0002	0.0003
394	0.1104	0.6953	0.0018	1.0039	0.0295	0.0200	0.0147	0.0070
395	−0.004711	−0.0297	0.0014	1.0054	−0.0011	−0.0011	0.0003	0.0001
396	0.1975	1.2451	0.0016	0.9994	0.0496	0.0470	−0.0123	0.0041
397	0.0893	0.5623	0.0019	1.0046	0.0245	0.0233	−0.0124	−0.0042
398	0.1099	0.6927	0.0020	1.0041	0.0314	0.0193	0.0167	0.0044
399	0.004209	0.0265	0.0014	1.0054	0.0010	0.0009	0.0002	0.0002
400	−0.0842	−0.5305	0.0026	1.0055	−0.0269	−0.0133	−0.0179	−0.0072
401	0.3143	1.9852	0.0022	0.9904	0.0925	0.0529	0.0565	0.0279
402	0.2126	1.3412	0.0021	0.9989	0.0613	0.0365	0.0357	0.0153
403	−0.0891	−0.5611	0.0017	1.0044	−0.0229	−0.0167	−0.0101	−0.0081
404	0.0191	0.1203	0.0023	1.0063	0.0058	0.0034	0.0028	0.0037
405	−0.1132	−0.7138	0.0025	1.0045	−0.0357	−0.0259	0.0032	0.0208
406	0.003808	0.0240	0.0014	1.0054	0.0009	0.0008	0.0001	0.0002
407	−0.1227	−0.7736	0.0029	1.0045	−0.0417	−0.0319	0.0165	0.0304
408	0.2149	1.3556	0.0024	0.9991	0.0670	0.0348	0.0432	0.0172
409	−0.1821	−1.1495	0.0039	1.0026	−0.0719	−0.0253	−0.0513	−0.0110
410	−0.0802	−0.5052	0.0023	1.0054	−0.0245	−0.0132	−0.0153	−0.0136
411	−0.0942	−0.5938	0.0016	1.0042	−0.0240	−0.0181	−0.0090	−0.0019
412	−0.1025	−0.6456	0.0016	1.0039	−0.0256	−0.0243	0.0062	−0.0020
413	0.1153	0.7268	0.0021	1.0041	0.0337	0.0193	0.0207	0.0121
414	−0.006180	−0.0389	0.0014	1.0054	−0.0015	−0.0014	0.0003	0.0003
415	0.004587	0.0289	0.0015	1.0055	0.0011	0.0009	0.0003	0.0001

Output statistics

Obs	Residual	RStudent	Hat diag H	Cov ratio	DFFITS	DFBETAS Intercept	DLLEIL1	DLWkUNCLL1
416	−0.0963	−0.6068	0.0015	1.0041	−0.0237	−0.0211	−0.0001	−0.0065
417	0.1061	0.6687	0.0019	1.0041	0.0288	0.0198	0.0124	0.0009
418	−0.0903	−0.5689	0.0017	1.0044	−0.0235	−0.0167	−0.0109	−0.0058
419	0.0181	0.1142	0.0022	1.0061	0.0053	0.0032	0.0028	0.0031
420	0.001885	0.0119	0.0016	1.0056	0.0005	0.0004	0.0001	−0.0000
421	0.0256	0.1617	0.0046	1.0085	0.0109	0.0031	0.0088	0.0035
422	0.1176	0.7415	0.0029	1.0047	0.0400	0.0233	0.0089	0.0273
423	−0.1087	−0.6847	0.0016	1.0037	−0.0272	−0.0253	0.0047	0.0104
424	−0.0684	−0.4319	0.0055	1.0088	−0.0321	−0.0072	−0.0273	−0.0126
425	0.0229	0.1441	0.0027	1.0066	0.0075	0.0035	0.0051	0.0044
426	−0.0835	−0.5259	0.0020	1.0049	−0.0237	−0.0149	−0.0120	−0.0130
427	0.1079	0.6803	0.0024	1.0046	0.0333	0.0188	0.0173	0.0001
428	−0.0886	−0.5583	0.0017	1.0044	−0.0229	−0.0167	−0.0096	−0.0090
429	0.0129	0.0811	0.0022	1.0062	0.0038	0.0022	0.0022	0.0009
430	0.1040	0.6551	0.0015	1.0038	0.0258	0.0206	0.0079	0.0009
431	−0.1768	−1.1149	0.0028	1.0019	−0.0594	−0.0265	−0.0428	−0.0322
432	−0.1040	−0.6549	0.0014	1.0037	−0.0244	−0.0233	0.0014	0.0046
433	−0.0888	−0.5595	0.0019	1.0046	−0.0241	−0.0159	−0.0126	−0.0063
434	0.005070	0.0319	0.0015	1.0055	0.0012	0.0011	0.0001	0.0003
435	−0.1011	−0.6366	0.0014	1.0038	−0.0239	−0.0231	0.0031	−0.0018
436	0.1874	1.1818	0.0017	1.0001	0.0492	0.0482	−0.0236	−0.0167
437	0.1036	0.6525	0.0015	1.0038	0.0254	0.0228	0.0000	0.0069
438	−0.2998	−1.8925	0.0016	0.9913	−0.0755	−0.0695	0.0120	−0.0140
439	−0.006577	−0.0414	0.0014	1.0054	−0.0016	−0.0015	0.0003	0.0004
440	0.0964	0.6072	0.0015	1.0041	0.0238	0.0230	−0.0063	0.0006
441	−0.0987	−0.6221	0.0018	1.0042	−0.0260	−0.0196	−0.0074	0.0034
442	0.006015	0.0379	0.0014	1.0055	0.0014	0.0012	0.0003	0.0004
443	0.0941	0.5931	0.0015	1.0042	0.0233	0.0229	−0.0076	−0.0017
444	−0.004324	−0.0272	0.0014	1.0054	−0.0010	−0.0010	0.0002	0.0001
445	−0.0112	−0.0703	0.0016	1.0056	−0.0028	−0.0027	0.0009	0.0012
446	−0.1627	−1.0322	0.0142	1.0142	−0.1241	−0.0706	0.1177	0.0668
447	0.1325	0.8359	0.0045	1.0058	0.0564	0.0154	0.0474	0.0311
448	0.0115	0.0724	0.0017	1.0057	0.0030	0.0022	0.0010	0.0014
449	−0.0117	−0.0736	0.0021	1.0062	−0.0034	−0.0027	0.0004	0.0018
450	0.0120	0.0756	0.0023	1.0063	0.0037	0.0020	0.0022	0.0006
451	−0.0879	−0.5540	0.0019	1.0047	−0.0240	−0.0156	−0.0128	−0.0072
452	−0.0156	−0.0982	0.0019	1.0059	−0.0043	−0.0041	0.0023	0.0019
453	−0.001203	−0.007574	0.0013	1.0054	−0.0003	−0.0003	−0.0000	0.0000
454	0.008176	0.0515	0.0015	1.0055	0.0020	0.0016	0.0005	0.0007
455	−0.0976	−0.6150	0.0014	1.0039	−0.0230	−0.0202	−0.0044	−0.0009
456	0.0120	0.0755	0.0019	1.0059	0.0033	0.0021	0.0017	0.0010
457	0.009278	0.0584	0.0017	1.0057	0.0024	0.0019	0.0005	0.0010
458	0.000259	0.001630	0.0017	1.0058	0.0001	0.0001	0.0000	−0.0000
459	0.0232	0.1464	0.0042	1.0082	0.0095	0.0030	0.0074	0.0027
460	0.009866	0.0621	0.0016	1.0057	0.0025	0.0019	0.0011	0.0007
461	0.006751	0.0425	0.0015	1.0056	0.0017	0.0014	0.0003	0.0006
462	−0.0927	−0.5844	0.0019	1.0045	−0.0254	−0.0170	−0.0117	−0.0018
463	0.1175	0.7408	0.0022	1.0040	0.0345	0.0198	0.0209	0.0168
464	−0.0774	−0.4883	0.0036	1.0067	−0.0295	−0.0104	−0.0228	−0.0098
465	0.0155	0.0979	0.0020	1.0060	0.0044	0.0029	0.0018	0.0026
466	−0.0936	−0.5900	0.0021	1.0047	−0.0270	−0.0170	−0.0125	0.0002
467	−0.1031	−0.6495	0.0014	1.0037	−0.0240	−0.0230	0.0012	0.0033
468	0.1042	0.6564	0.0014	1.0037	0.0245	0.0218	0.0039	0.0047
469	−0.0972	−0.6121	0.0014	1.0039	−0.0228	−0.0201	−0.0043	−0.0017

Output statistics

Obs	Residual	RStudent	Hat diag H	Cov ratio	DFFITS	DFBETAS Intercept	DLLEIL1	DLWkUNCLL1
470	0.001190	0.007495	0.0014	1.0055	0.0003	0.0003	−0.0000	0.0000
471	0.0236	0.1488	0.0033	1.0073	0.0086	0.0033	0.0066	0.0037
472	−0.2065	−1.3022	0.0014	0.9986	−0.0491	−0.0486	0.0106	0.0112
473	−0.0154	−0.0969	0.0019	1.0059	−0.0042	−0.0040	0.0022	0.0019
474	0.1149	0.7241	0.0020	1.0039	0.0321	0.0201	0.0180	0.0136
475	−0.1101	−0.6939	0.0028	1.0049	−0.0370	−0.0302	0.0206	−0.0005
476	0.0900	0.5669	0.0016	1.0043	0.0228	0.0214	−0.0053	−0.0094
477	−0.0115	−0.0723	0.0017	1.0057	−0.0030	−0.0028	0.0008	0.0014
478	−0.1357	−0.8565	0.0046	1.0057	−0.0585	−0.0442	0.0489	0.0364
479	−0.0127	−0.0800	0.0022	1.0062	−0.0038	−0.0034	0.0022	0.0006
480	0.003079	0.0194	0.0014	1.0054	0.0007	0.0007	0.0001	0.0001
481	0.005374	0.0338	0.0014	1.0055	0.0013	0.0011	0.0003	0.0002
482	−0.008443	−0.0532	0.0017	1.0057	−0.0022	−0.0021	0.0009	0.0003
483	−0.007226	−0.0455	0.0020	1.0060	−0.0020	−0.0016	−0.0001	0.0008
484	−0.001959	−0.0123	0.0013	1.0054	−0.0005	−0.0004	0.0000	0.0000
485	−0.005296	−0.0334	0.0014	1.0054	−0.0013	−0.0013	0.0003	0.0001
486	0.1103	0.6949	0.0017	1.0038	0.0289	0.0203	0.0138	0.0077
487	−0.1068	−0.6731	0.0016	1.0038	−0.0265	−0.0242	0.0023	0.0090
488	−0.0866	−0.5454	0.0018	1.0046	−0.0232	−0.0162	−0.0099	−0.0113
489	−0.008417	−0.0530	0.0015	1.0055	−0.0021	−0.0020	0.0004	0.0007
490	−0.003683	−0.0232	0.0014	1.0054	−0.0009	−0.0009	0.0002	0.0000
491	−0.003280	−0.0207	0.0014	1.0055	−0.0008	−0.0007	−0.0000	0.0002
492	0.007830	0.0493	0.0016	1.0057	0.0020	0.0015	0.0008	0.0004
493	0.0190	0.1199	0.0027	1.0066	0.0062	0.0029	0.0043	0.0024
494	−0.0791	−0.4987	0.0024	1.0055	−0.0246	−0.0129	−0.0153	−0.0146
495	−0.0247	−0.1556	0.0034	1.0073	−0.0090	−0.0075	0.0070	0.0038
496	0.003923	0.0247	0.0026	1.0067	0.0013	0.0007	0.0006	−0.0002
497	0.003193	0.0201	0.0014	1.0054	0.0007	0.0007	0.0001	0.0001
498	−0.0347	−0.2187	0.0057	1.0096	−0.0165	−0.0118	0.0143	0.0072
499	0.006279	0.0395	0.0015	1.0055	0.0015	0.0013	0.0003	0.0004
500	0.0869	0.5479	0.0022	1.0050	0.0257	0.0235	−0.0150	−0.0049
501	−0.1183	−0.7456	0.0030	1.0048	−0.0406	−0.0343	0.0283	0.0100
502	−0.001657	−0.0104	0.0015	1.0055	−0.0004	−0.0004	−0.0000	0.0001
503	−0.0428	−0.2703	0.0068	1.0106	−0.0224	−0.0153	0.0201	0.0125
504	−0.005221	−0.0329	0.0033	1.0074	−0.0019	−0.0014	0.0009	−0.0004
505	0.0533	0.3371	0.0089	1.0126	0.0319	0.0203	−0.0292	−0.0155
506	−0.0353	−0.2227	0.0046	1.0085	−0.0151	−0.0115	0.0126	0.0093
507	0.0783	0.4942	0.0050	1.0081	0.0351	0.0249	−0.0260	−0.0049
508	−0.1475	−0.9330	0.0093	1.0099	−0.0902	−0.0568	0.0827	0.0433
509	−0.0364	−0.2295	0.0058	1.0096	−0.0175	−0.0125	0.0152	0.0083
510	0.1074	0.6766	0.0015	1.0037	0.0261	0.0212	0.0082	0.0069
511	0.0696	0.4390	0.0038	1.0071	0.0271	0.0217	−0.0217	−0.0154
512	0.0871	0.5489	0.0019	1.0047	0.0237	0.0228	−0.0125	−0.0069
513	0.0892	0.5617	0.0017	1.0044	0.0229	0.0226	−0.0101	−0.0064
514	−0.0440	−0.2784	0.0113	1.0152	−0.0298	−0.0174	0.0262	0.0091
515	0.1894	1.1948	0.0030	1.0013	0.0659	0.0527	−0.0376	0.0009
516	0.1028	0.6479	0.0019	1.0043	0.0285	0.0197	0.0102	−0.0031
517	0.0884	0.5572	0.0027	1.0055	0.0292	0.0195	0.0001	−0.0161
518	−0.003619	−0.0228	0.0014	1.0054	−0.0009	−0.0008	0.0002	0.0000
519	0.1160	0.7315	0.0027	1.0046	0.0379	0.0181	0.0255	0.0096
520	0.1203	0.7580	0.0024	1.0041	0.0371	0.0207	0.0196	0.0241
521	0.0253	0.1595	0.0031	1.0071	0.0089	0.0036	0.0067	0.0050
522	0.1036	0.6530	0.0022	1.0045	0.0303	0.0193	0.0121	−0.0034
523	−0.1070	−0.6738	0.0015	1.0037	−0.0259	−0.0247	0.0040	0.0078

Output statistics

Obs	Residual	RStudent	Hat diag H	Cov ratio	DFFITS	DFBETAS		
						Intercept	DLLEIL1	DLWkUNCLL1
524	−0.0244	−0.1540	0.0030	1.0069	−0.0084	−0.0072	0.0062	0.0042
525	0.006621	0.0417	0.0015	1.0055	0.0016	0.0014	0.0004	0.0005
526	0.0864	0.5442	0.0023	1.0051	0.0261	0.0236	−0.0157	−0.0051
527	−0.0120	−0.0758	0.0017	1.0057	−0.0031	−0.0031	0.0015	0.0010
528	0.2048	1.2914	0.0019	0.9992	0.0557	0.0387	0.0222	−0.0012
529	−0.0950	−0.5985	0.0018	1.0043	−0.0251	−0.0211	0.0006	−0.0091
530	−0.008089	−0.0509	0.0015	1.0055	−0.0020	−0.0019	0.0004	0.0007
531	−0.004423	−0.0279	0.0017	1.0057	−0.0011	−0.0011	0.0004	−0.0000
532	0.0942	0.5933	0.0015	1.0041	0.0232	0.0229	−0.0075	−0.0018
533	−0.0107	−0.0675	0.0020	1.0060	−0.0030	−0.0028	0.0016	0.0005
534	0.1188	0.7488	0.0031	1.0048	0.0415	0.0175	0.0299	0.0119
535	0.1193	0.7522	0.0026	1.0043	0.0381	0.0186	0.0264	0.0162
536	−0.1066	−0.6718	0.0016	1.0038	−0.0265	−0.0241	0.0020	0.0089
537	0.0136	0.0854	0.0020	1.0060	0.0038	0.0023	0.0022	0.0012
538	0.0280	0.1764	0.0040	1.0079	0.0112	0.0035	0.0091	0.0053
539	−0.0860	−0.5419	0.0028	1.0056	−0.0285	−0.0136	−0.0184	−0.0047
540	0.0210	0.1327	0.0034	1.0073	0.0077	0.0030	0.0058	0.0025
541	0.0228	0.1437	0.0032	1.0071	0.0081	0.0032	0.0062	0.0034
542	−0.0761	−0.4798	0.0030	1.0062	−0.0265	−0.0110	−0.0198	−0.0134
543	0.1214	0.7655	0.0028	1.0045	0.0406	0.0182	0.0295	0.0184
544	−0.2741	−1.7323	0.0047	0.9967	−0.1186	−0.0328	−0.0956	−0.0373
545	0.1027	0.6471	0.0014	1.0037	0.0239	0.0219	0.0025	0.0033
546	0.0199	0.1251	0.0029	1.0068	0.0067	0.0030	0.0049	0.0025
547	−0.0911	−0.5736	0.0016	1.0043	−0.0227	−0.0175	−0.0087	−0.0066
548	−0.0861	−0.5423	0.0019	1.0047	−0.0235	−0.0153	−0.0124	−0.0098
549	0.1054	0.6642	0.0016	1.0038	0.0263	0.0206	0.0091	0.0025
550	0.1130	0.7121	0.0019	1.0039	0.0311	0.0199	0.0171	0.0104
551	−0.1011	−0.6366	0.0014	1.0038	−0.0236	−0.0219	−0.0013	0.0020
552	0.0131	0.0823	0.0020	1.0060	0.0037	0.0022	0.0022	0.0011
553	−0.0769	−0.4848	0.0030	1.0061	−0.0268	−0.0111	−0.0201	−0.0126
554	0.1185	0.7472	0.0022	1.0040	0.0351	0.0201	0.0204	0.0195
555	−0.1124	−0.7085	0.0022	1.0042	−0.0332	−0.0260	0.0041	0.0184
556	−0.1040	−0.6553	0.0021	1.0044	−0.0298	−0.0261	0.0111	−0.0037
557	0.003634	0.0229	0.0017	1.0057	0.0009	0.0007	0.0003	−0.0000
558	−0.2117	−1.3351	0.0019	0.9988	−0.0583	−0.0555	0.0306	0.0124
559	0.0162	0.1023	0.0023	1.0063	0.0050	0.0026	0.0032	0.0017
560	0.0939	0.5915	0.0014	1.0041	0.0224	0.0224	−0.0060	−0.0034
561	0.009488	0.0598	0.0019	1.0059	0.0026	0.0017	0.0013	0.0004
562	0.0278	0.1759	0.0071	1.0111	0.0149	0.0056	0.0018	0.0114
563	−0.0298	−0.1877	0.0042	1.0081	−0.0122	−0.0080	0.0050	0.0100
564	−0.1088	−0.6858	0.0021	1.0043	−0.0316	−0.0240	−0.0001	0.0149
565	−0.1077	−0.6788	0.0015	1.0036	−0.0261	−0.0261	0.0081	0.0057
566	0.2030	1.2800	0.0021	0.9995	0.0582	0.0384	0.0218	−0.0070
567	−0.1081	−0.6808	0.0015	1.0036	−0.0263	−0.0262	0.0084	0.0061
568	0.003498	0.0220	0.0014	1.0054	0.0008	0.0007	0.0001	0.0001
569	−0.1168	−0.7364	0.0025	1.0043	−0.0366	−0.0327	0.0240	0.0106
570	−0.1060	−0.6682	0.0026	1.0048	−0.0340	−0.0279	0.0156	−0.0039
571	0.0669	0.4221	0.0039	1.0072	0.0263	0.0201	−0.0183	−0.0200
572	−0.0105	−0.0662	0.0020	1.0061	−0.0030	−0.0028	0.0016	0.0004
573	−0.0216	−0.1360	0.0025	1.0064	−0.0068	−0.0061	0.0045	0.0035
574	−0.1079	−0.6800	0.0015	1.0037	−0.0268	−0.0266	0.0098	0.0047
575	−0.0110	−0.0691	0.0016	1.0057	−0.0028	−0.0028	0.0012	0.0008
576	−0.007092	−0.0447	0.0018	1.0058	−0.0019	−0.0018	0.0008	0.0001
577	0.002471	0.0156	0.0014	1.0054	0.0006	0.0005	0.0001	0.0000

Output statistics

Obs	Residual	RStudent	Hat diag H	Cov ratio	DFFITS	DFBETAS		
						Intercept	DLLEIL1	DLWkUNCLL1
578	−0.0213	−0.1339	0.0025	1.0064	−0.0066	−0.0060	0.0044	0.0034
579	0.0956	0.6023	0.0015	1.0041	0.0234	0.0229	−0.0064	−0.0005
580	−0.005024	−0.0316	0.0017	1.0057	−0.0013	−0.0011	−0.0001	0.0004
581	−0.005933	−0.0374	0.0018	1.0058	−0.0016	−0.0015	0.0006	−0.0000
582	−0.0173	−0.1089	0.0020	1.0060	−0.0049	−0.0045	0.0024	0.0027
583	−0.0103	−0.0651	0.0019	1.0059	−0.0028	−0.0027	0.0014	0.0005
584	−0.0155	−0.0977	0.0019	1.0059	−0.0043	−0.0041	0.0024	0.0017
585	−0.0183	−0.1151	0.0026	1.0065	−0.0058	−0.0052	0.0040	0.0019
586	−0.0323	−0.2035	0.0040	1.0079	−0.0130	−0.0102	0.0105	0.0078
587	−0.0152	−0.0960	0.0027	1.0067	−0.0050	−0.0043	0.0032	0.0009
588	0.0715	0.4509	0.0045	1.0077	0.0302	0.0230	−0.0247	−0.0116
589	−0.0346	−0.2185	0.0055	1.0093	−0.0162	−0.0117	0.0140	0.0074
590	−0.0486	−0.3072	0.0076	1.0114	−0.0270	−0.0179	0.0243	0.0176
591	−0.0412	−0.2604	0.0068	1.0106	−0.0215	−0.0147	0.0192	0.0111
592	0.0594	0.3753	0.0082	1.0118	0.0342	0.0220	−0.0303	−0.0132
593	0.0684	0.4314	0.0040	1.0073	0.0275	0.0216	−0.0224	−0.0156
594	0.0660	0.4167	0.0049	1.0082	0.0291	0.0218	−0.0248	−0.0149
595	0.0827	0.5214	0.0029	1.0059	0.0282	0.0238	−0.0193	−0.0062
596	0.1331	0.8464	0.0189	1.0205	0.1176	0.0621	−0.1109	−0.0519
597	0.0628	0.3967	0.0061	1.0096	0.0312	0.0219	−0.0273	−0.0144
598	0.2398	1.5237	0.0156	1.0105	0.1919	0.1059	−0.1794	−0.0837
599	−0.2138	−1.3763	0.0421	1.0403	−0.2887	−0.1318	0.2838	0.1697
600	0.3209	2.0522	0.0260	1.0136	0.3354	0.1657	−0.3196	−0.1498
601	0.1096	0.7007	0.0299	1.0329	0.1231	0.0596	−0.1193	−0.0635
602	0.3357	2.1356	0.0156	1.0015	0.2687	0.1495	−0.2551	−0.1375
603	0.2674	1.6925	0.0072	0.9997	0.1439	0.0943	−0.1202	−0.0380
604	0.2369	1.5036	0.0141	1.0092	0.1800	0.1027	−0.1709	−0.0994
605	0.3846	2.4327	0.0020	0.9825	0.1100	0.0951	−0.0342	−0.0643
606	0.6061	3.8551	0.0015	0.9478	0.1480	0.1214	0.0455	0.0275
607	0.0127	0.0803	0.0022	1.0062	0.0038	0.0022	0.0022	0.0009
608	−0.000525	−0.003305	0.0019	1.0059	−0.0001	−0.0001	−0.0000	0.0000
609	0.4227	2.6772	0.0030	0.9786	0.1474	0.0614	0.1102	0.0674
610	0.1145	0.7218	0.0025	1.0044	0.0361	0.0185	0.0232	0.0083
611	0.1018	0.6415	0.0015	1.0039	0.0253	0.0206	0.0063	−0.0015
612	0.1125	0.7092	0.0028	1.0048	0.0373	0.0181	0.0231	0.0042
613	0.0169	0.1067	0.0029	1.0069	0.0057	0.0026	0.0040	0.0014
614	0.0196	0.1234	0.0024	1.0063	0.0060	0.0032	0.0039	0.0031
615	0.0930	0.5858	0.0015	1.0041	0.0224	0.0224	−0.0066	−0.0042
616	0.0385	0.2431	0.0069	1.0107	0.0202	0.0033	0.0179	0.0093
617	−0.0951	−0.5990	0.0015	1.0041	−0.0234	−0.0187	−0.0075	−0.0020
618	0.005097	0.0321	0.0014	1.0055	0.0012	0.0010	0.0003	0.0002
619	−0.1081	−0.6810	0.0015	1.0036	−0.0263	−0.0262	0.0084	0.0062
620	−0.2022	−1.2750	0.0013	0.9988	−0.0468	−0.0458	0.0043	0.0020
621	0.008847	0.0557	0.0016	1.0056	0.0022	0.0018	0.0006	0.0008
622	0.1008	0.6351	0.0017	1.0041	0.0263	0.0202	0.0068	−0.0037
623	−0.0137	−0.0864	0.0018	1.0058	−0.0037	−0.0036	0.0018	0.0014
624	0.0132	0.0832	0.0026	1.0066	0.0042	0.0021	0.0027	0.0007
625	−0.0731	−0.4612	0.0041	1.0073	−0.0295	−0.0092	−0.0239	−0.0124
626	−0.1988	−1.2534	0.0014	0.9992	−0.0477	−0.0447	0.0031	−0.0082
627	0.003116	0.0196	0.0022	1.0062	0.0009	0.0006	0.0004	−0.0001
628	−0.0760	−0.4791	0.0032	1.0063	−0.0270	−0.0107	−0.0206	−0.0129
629	0.1088	0.6854	0.0018	1.0039	0.0289	0.0228	0.0039	0.0133
630	0.0134	0.0846	0.0020	1.0060	0.0038	0.0023	0.0022	0.0012
631	−0.0102	−0.0646	0.0016	1.0056	−0.0026	−0.0025	0.0009	0.0008

Output statistics

Obs	Residual	RStudent	Hat diag H	Cov ratio	DFFITS	DFBETAS Intercept	DLLEIL1	DLWkUNCLL1
632	0.1049	0.6611	0.0015	1.0038	0.0256	0.0208	0.0079	0.0026
633	−0.0311	−0.1963	0.0041	1.0080	−0.0126	−0.0099	0.0103	0.0068
634	−0.3186	−2.0133	0.0025	0.9903	−0.1010	−0.0903	0.0686	0.0359
635	−0.0924	−0.5822	0.0019	1.0045	−0.0251	−0.0169	−0.0117	−0.0023
636	−0.1116	−0.7034	0.0016	1.0037	−0.0285	−0.0274	0.0095	0.0121
637	−0.1005	−0.6332	0.0015	1.0039	−0.0246	−0.0210	−0.0039	0.0033
638	−0.0972	−0.6125	0.0014	1.0039	−0.0226	−0.0206	−0.0027	−0.0029
639	−0.0928	−0.5846	0.0018	1.0045	−0.0251	−0.0171	−0.0113	−0.0020
640	0.003991	0.0251	0.0014	1.0054	0.0009	0.0008	0.0002	0.0001
641	−0.002785	−0.0175	0.0017	1.0057	−0.0007	−0.0007	0.0002	−0.0001
642	0.0919	0.5790	0.0015	1.0041	0.0222	0.0219	−0.0057	−0.0065
643	−0.2186	−1.3791	0.0025	0.9989	−0.0689	−0.0618	0.0466	0.0247
644	−0.004175	−0.0263	0.0014	1.0054	−0.0010	−0.0009	0.0001	0.0002
645	−0.1216	−0.7667	0.0027	1.0044	−0.0399	−0.0351	0.0284	0.0176
646	0.0158	0.0996	0.0020	1.0060	0.0044	0.0028	0.0023	0.0022
647	−0.2103	−1.3259	0.0016	0.9986	−0.0535	−0.0500	0.0127	0.0227
648	0.1124	0.7085	0.0023	1.0043	0.0339	0.0233	0.0049	0.0196
649	−0.1244	−0.7844	0.0035	1.0051	−0.0465	−0.0320	0.0153	0.0355
650	0.009999	0.0630	0.0017	1.0057	0.0026	0.0018	0.0012	0.0007
651	−0.1028	−0.6474	0.0014	1.0037	−0.0238	−0.0229	0.0010	0.0029
652	−0.009429	−0.0594	0.0017	1.0057	−0.0025	−0.0024	0.0011	0.0004
653	0.006150	0.0387	0.0016	1.0056	0.0016	0.0012	0.0006	0.0002
654	−0.0930	−0.5861	0.0015	1.0041	−0.0225	−0.0185	−0.0066	−0.0057
655	−0.1078	−0.6791	0.0015	1.0036	−0.0260	−0.0256	0.0065	0.0073
656	−0.0982	−0.6187	0.0013	1.0038	−0.0227	−0.0210	−0.0020	−0.0020
657	0.000830	0.005225	0.0016	1.0057	0.0002	0.0002	0.0001	−0.0000
658	−0.0916	−0.5770	0.0023	1.0050	−0.0277	−0.0160	−0.0145	−0.0010
659	0.0219	0.1383	0.0031	1.0071	0.0077	0.0040	0.0027	0.0057
660	−0.0946	−0.5960	0.0026	1.0052	−0.0305	−0.0167	−0.0144	0.0031
661	−0.1909	−1.2037	0.0018	1.0000	−0.0511	−0.0399	−0.0072	−0.0239
662	0.0838	0.5283	0.0020	1.0049	0.0234	0.0213	−0.0098	−0.0131
663	0.0170	0.1072	0.0022	1.0062	0.0050	0.0028	0.0031	0.0022
664	−0.2829	−1.7866	0.0028	0.9940	−0.0939	−0.0436	−0.0648	−0.0263
665	−0.0998	−0.6288	0.0014	1.0038	−0.0232	−0.0222	0.0007	−0.0018
666	−0.1015	−0.6394	0.0016	1.0040	−0.0259	−0.0211	−0.0043	0.0052
667	0.0199	0.1251	0.0025	1.0065	0.0063	0.0031	0.0043	0.0030
668	−0.1002	−0.6313	0.0016	1.0040	−0.0252	−0.0206	−0.0050	0.0037
669	−0.1006	−0.6339	0.0013	1.0038	−0.0233	−0.0225	0.0013	−0.0009
670	−0.0900	−0.5674	0.0020	1.0047	−0.0252	−0.0160	−0.0132	−0.0041
671	−0.008278	−0.0521	0.0015	1.0055	−0.0020	−0.0019	0.0004	0.0007
672	−0.0886	−0.5584	0.0017	1.0044	−0.0229	−0.0170	−0.0086	−0.0099
673	0.005034	0.0317	0.0017	1.0057	0.0013	0.0010	0.0005	0.0000
674	−0.1058	−0.6666	0.0014	1.0037	−0.0252	−0.0252	0.0066	0.0035
675	−0.0904	−0.5697	0.0017	1.0044	−0.0235	−0.0184	−0.0050	−0.0107
676	−0.1082	−0.6817	0.0017	1.0039	−0.0283	−0.0245	0.0022	0.0117
677	0.1051	0.6622	0.0015	1.0037	0.0253	0.0210	0.0072	0.0035
678	−0.0996	−0.6272	0.0014	1.0039	−0.0237	−0.0208	−0.0037	0.0016
679	−0.0881	−0.5553	0.0018	1.0046	−0.0239	−0.0157	−0.0125	−0.0071
680	−0.0220	−0.1384	0.0026	1.0066	−0.0071	−0.0063	0.0050	0.0034
681	−0.1032	−0.6501	0.0014	1.0037	−0.0244	−0.0241	0.0046	0.0005
682	−0.0145	−0.0915	0.0018	1.0058	−0.0039	−0.0037	0.0018	0.0018
683	0.002010	0.0127	0.0014	1.0054	0.0005	0.0004	0.0001	0.0000
684	0.007677	0.0483	0.0015	1.0055	0.0019	0.0015	0.0007	0.0005
685	−0.1094	−0.6890	0.0016	1.0037	−0.0275	−0.0273	0.0110	0.0064

Output statistics

Obs	Residual	RStudent	Hat diag H	Cov ratio	DFFITS	DFBETAS Intercept	DLLEIL1	DLWkUNCLL1
686	0.0800	0.5046	0.0032	1.0062	0.0285	0.0237	−0.0207	−0.0078
687	−0.0160	−0.1006	0.0019	1.0059	−0.0044	−0.0041	0.0019	0.0024
688	−0.006294	−0.0396	0.0014	1.0055	−0.0015	−0.0015	0.0004	0.0002
689	−0.2010	−1.2674	0.0014	0.9989	−0.0469	−0.0435	−0.0025	0.0038
690	0.1003	0.6321	0.0016	1.0040	0.0249	0.0231	−0.0036	0.0045
691	−0.008010	−0.0504	0.0016	1.0056	−0.0020	−0.0018	0.0003	0.0007
692	−0.0980	−0.6171	0.0014	1.0039	−0.0228	−0.0206	−0.0032	−0.0013
693	0.0952	0.6000	0.0014	1.0040	0.0226	0.0225	−0.0053	−0.0020
694	−0.0113	−0.0714	0.0018	1.0058	−0.0030	−0.0027	0.0006	0.0014
695	−0.1041	−0.6560	0.0016	1.0039	−0.0266	−0.0253	0.0083	−0.0010
696	−0.0114	−0.0718	0.0017	1.0057	−0.0029	−0.0027	0.0008	0.0013
697	0.0126	0.0793	0.0018	1.0058	0.0034	0.0023	0.0017	0.0013
698	−0.0883	−0.5562	0.0020	1.0047	−0.0247	−0.0155	−0.0136	−0.0061
699	−0.0984	−0.6201	0.0014	1.0039	−0.0233	−0.0204	−0.0042	0.0003
700	0.0120	0.0756	0.0017	1.0057	0.0031	0.0022	0.0014	0.0013
701	−0.007989	−0.0503	0.0015	1.0055	−0.0019	−0.0019	0.0005	0.0005
702	−0.0978	−0.6159	0.0014	1.0039	−0.0232	−0.0202	−0.0046	−0.0005
703	0.1143	0.7201	0.0019	1.0039	0.0318	0.0200	0.0177	0.0125
704	0.002200	0.0139	0.0014	1.0054	0.0005	0.0005	0.0000	0.0001
705	0.0125	0.0788	0.0018	1.0058	0.0033	0.0024	0.0013	0.0016
706	−0.0917	−0.5775	0.0016	1.0042	−0.0228	−0.0186	−0.0055	−0.0086
707	0.008541	0.0538	0.0036	1.0076	0.0032	0.0014	0.0018	−0.0003
708	−0.0891	−0.5615	0.0017	1.0044	−0.0230	−0.0166	−0.0104	−0.0077
709	0.0111	0.0698	0.0018	1.0058	0.0029	0.0020	0.0015	0.0009
710	−0.0923	−0.5817	0.0017	1.0043	−0.0237	−0.0174	−0.0100	−0.0038
711	0.000462	0.002907	0.0018	1.0058	0.0001	0.0001	0.0000	−0.0000
712	0.1105	0.6961	0.0016	1.0037	0.0281	0.0211	0.0110	0.0105
713	−0.1959	−1.2352	0.0015	0.9994	−0.0477	−0.0392	−0.0136	−0.0031
714	0.0953	0.6004	0.0014	1.0040	0.0226	0.0225	−0.0052	−0.0020
715	0.1120	0.7059	0.0019	1.0039	0.0308	0.0198	0.0167	0.0087
716	−0.0916	−0.5771	0.0018	1.0045	−0.0244	−0.0169	−0.0113	−0.0037
717	−0.004986	−0.0314	0.0014	1.0054	−0.0012	−0.0011	0.0002	0.0002
718	0.0143	0.0902	0.0020	1.0060	0.0040	0.0025	0.0023	0.0015
719	−0.1071	−0.6750	0.0015	1.0037	−0.0264	−0.0262	0.0090	0.0038
720	0.1050	0.6616	0.0016	1.0038	0.0263	0.0228	0.0011	0.0086
721	−0.1179	−0.7428	0.0021	1.0039	−0.0337	−0.0309	0.0169	0.0189
722	0.0975	0.6141	0.0015	1.0040	0.0238	0.0230	−0.0052	0.0013
723	−0.004389	−0.0276	0.0014	1.0054	−0.0010	−0.0010	0.0002	0.0001
724	−0.1012	−0.6376	0.0014	1.0038	−0.0240	−0.0217	−0.0020	0.0028
725	−0.008580	−0.0540	0.0015	1.0055	−0.0021	−0.0021	0.0007	0.0005
726	−0.008328	−0.0525	0.0015	1.0056	−0.0021	−0.0021	0.0008	0.0004
727	0.001329	0.008370	0.0014	1.0054	0.0003	0.0003	−0.0000	0.0000
728	−0.001220	−0.007683	0.0015	1.0055	−0.0003	−0.0003	−0.0000	0.0000
729	−0.009312	−0.0587	0.0017	1.0057	−0.0024	−0.0024	0.0010	0.0004
730	−0.0140	−0.0885	0.0018	1.0058	−0.0037	−0.0036	0.0018	0.0015
731	−0.0140	−0.0879	0.0019	1.0059	−0.0039	−0.0037	0.0022	0.0012
732	−0.0998	−0.6285	0.0013	1.0038	−0.0230	−0.0218	−0.0004	−0.0009
733	−0.001568	−0.009879	0.0016	1.0057	−0.0004	−0.0004	0.0001	−0.0001
734	−0.007446	−0.0469	0.0019	1.0059	−0.0021	−0.0016	−0.0000	0.0009
735	−0.005077	−0.0320	0.0015	1.0055	−0.0012	−0.0012	0.0004	0.0001
736	0.2631	3.1772	0.7247	3.5035	5.1553	−0.1598	1.2347	4.6524
737	0.1853	1.2296	0.0987	1.1072	0.4068	0.1487	−0.3563	−0.0781
738	**0.5436**	**3.5213**	**0.0403**	**0.9958**	**0.7218**	**0.1214**	**0.0193**	**−0.5369**
739	**2.9858**	**26.4567**	**0.0228**	**0.1414**	**4.0455**	**0.5655**	**1.2914**	**−2.0522**

Obs	Residual	RStudent	Hat diag H	Cov ratio	DFFITS	DFBETAS		
						Intercept	DLLEIL1	DLWkUNCLL1
740	0.1323	0.8368	0.0086	1.0098	0.0777	0.0107	0.0643	0.0166
741	−0.5322	−3.3938	0.0111	0.9698	−0.3599	−0.1236	0.0127	0.2692
742	−0.8212	−5.2765	0.0049	0.9040	−0.3696	−0.1932	0.0272	0.2603
743	−0.1962	−1.2373	0.0018	0.9996	−0.0520	−0.0379	−0.0185	0.0021
744	−0.1944	−1.2261	0.0024	1.0004	−0.0605	−0.0346	−0.0283	0.0047
745	0.0280	0.1763	0.0034	1.0073	0.0103	0.0044	0.0061	0.0079
746	0.1266	0.7984	0.0031	1.0046	0.0446	0.0197	0.0279	0.0324
747	−0.0254	−0.1601	0.0029	1.0068	−0.0086	−0.0070	0.0049	0.0061
748	−0.1920	−1.2118	0.0037	1.0019	−0.0740	−0.0306	−0.0405	0.0079
749	−0.2220	−1.4049	0.0080	1.0042	−0.1265	−0.0474	−0.0072	0.0848
750	0.1689	1.0684	0.0093	1.0088	0.1035	0.0399	−0.0076	−0.0787
751	−0.4030	−2.5498	0.0020	0.9803	−0.1155	−0.0827	−0.0225	0.0356
752	−0.1794	−1.1315	0.0028	1.0016	−0.0595	−0.0271	−0.0428	−0.0255
753	−0.4070	−2.5759	0.0025	0.9802	−0.1291	−0.0855	−0.0162	0.0570

Sum of residuals	0
Sum of squared residuals	18.86055
Predicted residual SS (PRESS)	20.23701

The very large studentized residuals, RStudent, and large cov Ratio, DFBETAS and DFFITS variables for observation 738–742, the March–July 2020 period. A year past the start of COVID, the influential variables indicate it is appropriate to estimate robust multiple regressions for the DUE and DLLEIL1 and DLWkUNCLL1 relationship.

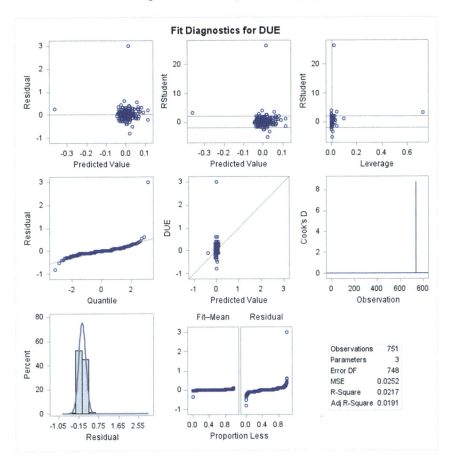

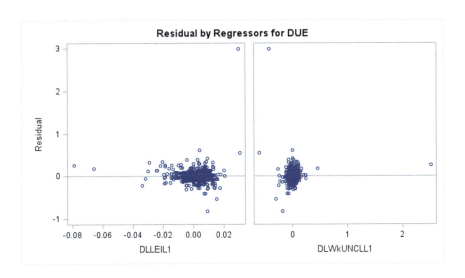

10.2 Robust Regression of the Modeling the PJD Unemployment Rate, TCB LEI 11052021

We can use SAS proc robustreg to estimate a robust regression line for the DUE AND DLLLEILI relationship. We will use the Huber weighting function in this application.

SAS M-Huber DUE DLLEIL1 Robust Regression PJD TCB 110521
The ROBUSTREG Procedure

Model information	
Data set	WORK.REMZTT
Dependent variable	DUE
Number of independent variables	1
Number of observations	751
Missing values	2
Method	M estimation

Number of observations read	753
Number of observations used	751
Missing values	2

Parameter estimates

Parameter	DF	Estimate	Standard error	95% confidence limits		Chi-square	Pr > Chi-square
Intercept	1	−0.0001	0.0035	−0.0070	0.0068	0.00	0.9787
DLLEIL1	1	−2.9796	0.4260	−3.8145	−2.1447	48.93	<0.0001
Scale	1	0.1099					

Diagnostics

Obs	Mahalanobis distance	Robust MCD Distance	Leverage	Standardized Robust residual	Outlier
2	1.9141	2.4706	*	−2.2571	
11	2.2869	3.0141	*	0.5541	
29	1.3343	1.6251		3.0745	*
132	1.7504	2.8728	*	0.5780	
175	1.3230	2.2496	*	−0.2380	
179	1.5701	2.6100	*	0.6176	
183	1.8375	2.9998	*	−0.3509	
185	1.6331	2.7018	*	−0.3060	
186	1.4122	2.3798	*	−0.2576	
187	2.3831	3.7955	*	0.4392	
188	2.6665	4.2087	*	0.3770	
189	1.7170	2.8242	*	−0.3244	
190	2.2393	3.5857	*	1.3806	

Diagnostics

Obs	Mahalanobis distance	Robust MCD Distance	Leverage	Standardized Robust residual	Outlier
191	2.5294	4.0089	*	2.2267	
194	0.7558	1.4225		3.5257	*
243	2.5359	4.0183	*	−0.5041	
249	1.5304	2.5521	*	−0.2835	
250	1.5441	2.5721	*	−0.2865	
251	1.3366	2.2695	*	0.6688	
254	3.1627	4.9323	*	1.1779	
255	4.1715	6.4032	*	−0.8630	
256	1.8928	3.0805	*	−0.3630	
264	1.6305	2.6980	*	−0.3055	
272	1.9285	3.1326	*	−0.3709	
276	1.4761	2.4730	*	2.4578	
288	1.9827	2.5706	*	0.4874	
379	2.0380	3.2923	*	−0.3949	
380	1.6965	2.7944	*	−0.3200	
381	1.9002	3.0914	*	1.4550	
382	2.4910	3.9528	*	−1.4041	
383	1.5701	2.6100	*	0.6176	
384	1.7788	2.9143	*	0.5718	
444	2.5670	4.0636	*	−1.4208	
496	1.5643	2.6016	*	−0.2909	
501	1.5847	2.6313	*	−0.2954	
503	2.0260	3.2747	*	0.5176	
505	1.6400	2.7119	*	0.6023	
506	2.0859	3.3621	*	−1.3152	
507	1.5327	2.5554	*	−0.2840	
512	2.5905	4.0980	*	−0.5161	
586	1.3604	2.3043	*	0.6636	
587	1.4977	2.5044	*	−0.2763	
588	1.5108	2.5235	*	−0.2792	
589	1.6538	2.7320	*	−0.3106	
590	2.0648	3.3313	*	0.5090	
594	3.2312	5.0322	*	1.1629	
595	1.6211	2.6843	*	0.6064	
596	2.9126	4.5676	*	2.1426	
597	4.4375	6.7911	*	−1.8312	
598	3.8243	5.8970	*	2.8524	
599	3.9318	6.0537	*	1.0092	
600	2.7623	4.3484	*	3.0854	*
601	2.0028	3.2410	*	2.3422	
602	2.5224	3.9986	*	2.2282	
603	0.0950	0.1821		3.7124	*
604	0.2580	0.0557		5.5678	*
607	0.8908	0.9784		3.8870	*
734	9.9944	14.8940	*	−3.0505	*
735	8.3830	12.5444	*	0.9422	
736	3.5362	4.8358	*	6.2871	*
737	3.4245	4.6729	*	28.0979	*
738	2.2638	2.9805	*	1.4589	
739	1.6356	2.0645		−4.1378	*
740	0.9201	1.0212		−7.0242	*
749	0.6249	0.5907		−3.4498	*
751	0.7171	0.7251		−3.4296	*

Diagnostics summary

Observation type	Proportion	Cutoff
Outlier	0.0173	3.0000
Leverage	0.0759	2.2414

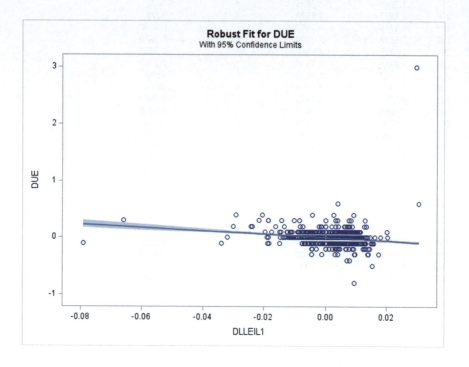

Goodness-of-fit

Statistic	Value
R-square	0.0284
AICR	729.2207
BICR	739.8780
Deviance	8.7785

The application of robust regression, SAS proc robustreg, with the Huber weighting function, produces a negative and highly statistically significant coefficient, −2.980, on the DLLEIL1 variable with its estimated probability of 0.0001. The simple linear robust regression of DUE as a function of the DLLEIL1 variable is reported, using the Huber weighting function. The reader notes the very large number of outliers identified.

We can use SAS proc robustreg to estimate a robust regression line for the DUE AND DLLLEILI relationship. We will use the Tukey Bisquare weighting function in this application.

SAS M-Bisquare Robust Regression
The ROBUSTREG Procedure

Model information	
Data set	WORK.REMZTT
Dependent variable	DUE
Number of independent variables	1
Number of observations	751
Missing values	2
Method	M estimation

Parameter estimates

Parameter	DF	Estimate	Standard error	95% confidence limits		Chi-square	Pr > Chi-square
Intercept	1	−0.0004	0.0036	−0.0075	0.0066	0.02	0.9004
DLLEIL1	1	−3.3374	0.4325	−4.1852	−2.4897	59.53	<0.0001
Scale	1	0.1048					

Diagnostics

Obs	Mahalanobis Distance	Robust MCD distance	Leverage	Standardized robust residual	Outlier
2	1.9141	2.4706	*	−2.3045	
11	2.2869	3.0141	*	0.6542	
29	1.3343	1.6251		3.2713	*
132	1.7504	2.8728	*	0.5677	
175	1.3230	2.2496	*	−0.2763	
179	1.5701	2.6100	*	0.6142	
183	1.8375	2.9998	*	−0.4089	
185	1.6331	2.7018	*	−0.3562	
186	1.4122	2.3798	*	−0.2993	
187	2.3831	3.7955	*	0.4046	
188	2.6665	4.2087	*	0.3316	
189	1.7170	2.8242	*	−0.3779	
190	2.2393	3.5857	*	1.3959	
191	2.5294	4.0089	*	2.2753	
194	0.7558	1.4225		3.6868	*

Diagnostics

Obs	Mahalanobis Distance	Robust MCD distance	Leverage	Standardized robust residual	Outlier
243	2.5359	4.0183	*	−0.5890	
249	1.5304	2.5521	*	−0.3298	
250	1.5441	2.5721	*	−0.3333	
251	1.3366	2.2695	*	0.6744	
254	3.1627	4.9323	*	1.1579	
255	4.1715	6.4032	*	−1.0106	
256	1.8928	3.0805	*	−0.4232	
264	1.6305	2.6980	*	−0.3556	
272	1.9285	3.1326	*	−0.4324	
276	1.4761	2.4730	*	2.5469	
284	0.7782	0.8142		3.1280	*
288	1.9827	2.5706	*	0.5758	
379	2.0380	3.2923	*	−0.4606	
380	1.6965	2.7944	*	−0.3726	
381	1.9002	3.0914	*	1.4833	
382	2.4910	3.9528	*	−1.5316	
383	1.5701	2.6100	*	0.6142	
384	1.7788	2.9143	*	0.5604	
399	0.6923	0.6890		3.1058	*
444	2.5670	4.0636	*	−1.5512	
496	1.5643	2.6016	*	−0.3385	
501	1.5847	2.6313	*	−0.3438	
503	2.0260	3.2747	*	0.4967	
505	1.6400	2.7119	*	0.5962	
506	2.0859	3.3621	*	−1.4272	
507	1.5327	2.5554	*	−0.3303	
512	2.5905	4.0980	*	−0.6030	
586	1.3604	2.3043	*	0.6683	
587	1.4977	2.5044	*	−0.3213	
588	1.5108	2.5235	*	−0.3247	
589	1.6538	2.7320	*	−0.3616	
590	2.0648	3.3313	*	0.4867	
594	3.2312	5.0322	*	1.1402	
595	1.6211	2.6843	*	0.6011	
596	2.9126	4.5676	*	2.1766	
597	4.4375	6.7911	*	−2.0334	
598	3.8243	5.8970	*	2.8958	
599	3.9318	6.0537	*	0.9596	
600	2.7623	4.3484	*	3.1695	*
601	2.0028	3.2410	*	2.4111	
602	2.5224	3.9986	*	2.2772	
603	0.0950	0.1821		3.9061	*

Diagnostics

Obs	Mahalanobis Distance	Robust MCD distance	Leverage	Standardized robust residual	Outlier
604	0.2580	0.0557		5.8565	*
607	0.8908	0.9784		4.1112	*
632	0.8051	1.4945		−3.0054	*
734	9.9944	14.8940	*	−3.4658	*
735	8.3830	12.5444	*	0.7664	
736	3.5362	4.8358	*	6.7015	*
737	3.4245	4.6729	*	29.5738	*
738	2.2638	2.9805	*	1.6025	
739	1.6356	2.0645		−4.2847	*
740	0.9201	1.0212		−7.3318	*
749	0.6249	0.5907		−3.5910	*
751	0.7171	0.7251		−3.5673	*

Diagnostics summary

Observation type	Proportion	Cutoff
Outlier	0.0213	3.0000
Leverage	0.0759	2.2414

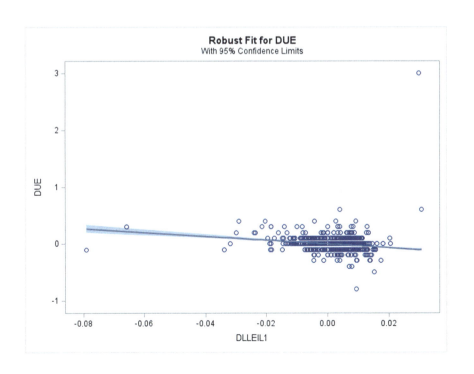

Goodness-of-fit	
Statistic	Value
R-square	0.0341
AICR	645.2622
BICR	655.9362
Deviance	7.0586

The application of robust regression, SAS proc robustreg, with the Bisquare weighting function, produces a negative and highly statistically significant coefficient, −2.980, on the DLLEIL1 variable with its estimated probability of 0.0001. The simple linear robust regression of DUE as a function of the DLLEIL1 variable is reported, using the Bisquare weighting function. The reader notes the very large number of outliers identified.

We can use SAS proc robustreg to estimate a robust regression line for the DUE AND DLLLEILI relationship. We will use the Hampel weighting function in this application.

SAS M-Hampel Robust Regression
The ROBUSTREG Procedure

Model information	
Data set	WORK.REMZTT
Dependent variable	DUE
Number of independent variables	1
Number of observations	751
Missing values	2
Method	M estimation

Parameter estimates

Parameter	DF	Estimate	Standard error	95% confidence limits		Chi-square	Pr > Chi-square
Intercept	1	0.0012	0.0038	−0.0062	0.0087	0.10	0.7469
DLLEIL1	1	−3.1772	0.4586	−4.0759	−2.2784	48.00	<0.0001
Scale	1	0.1084					

Diagnostics

Obs	Mahalanobis distance	Robust MCD distance	Leverage	Standardized robust residual	Outlier
2	1.9141	2.4706	*	−2.2700	
11	2.2869	3.0141	*	0.5870	

Diagnostics				
Obs	Mahalanobis distance	Robust MCD distance	Leverage	Standardized robust residual	Outlier
29	1.3343	1.6251		3.1295	*
132	1.7504	2.8728	*	0.5517	
175	1.3230	2.2496	*	−0.2697	
179	1.5701	2.6100	*	0.5945	
183	1.8375	2.9998	*	−0.3918	
185	1.6331	2.7018	*	−0.3433	
186	1.4122	2.3798	*	−0.2909	
187	2.3831	3.7955	*	0.4016	
188	2.6665	4.2087	*	0.3343	
189	1.7170	2.8242	*	−0.3632	
190	2.2393	3.5857	*	1.3585	
191	2.5294	4.0089	*	2.2125	
194	0.7558	1.4225		3.5563	*
243	2.5359	4.0183	*	−0.5575	
249	1.5304	2.5521	*	−0.3189	
250	1.5441	2.5721	*	−0.3222	
251	1.3366	2.2695	*	0.6499	
254	3.1627	4.9323	*	1.1394	
255	4.1715	6.4032	*	−0.9457	
256	1.8928	3.0805	*	−0.4049	
264	1.6305	2.6980	*	−0.3427	
272	1.9285	3.1326	*	−0.4134	
276	1.4761	2.4730	*	2.4625	
288	1.9827	2.5706	*	0.5149	
379	2.0380	3.2923	*	−0.4394	
380	1.6965	2.7944	*	−0.3583	
381	1.9002	3.0914	*	1.4390	
382	2.4910	3.9528	*	−1.4697	
383	1.5701	2.6100	*	0.5945	
384	1.7788	2.9143	*	0.5450	
444	2.5670	4.0636	*	−1.4878	
496	1.5643	2.6016	*	−0.3270	
501	1.5847	2.6313	*	−0.3318	
503	2.0260	3.2747	*	0.4863	
505	1.6400	2.7119	*	0.5779	
506	2.0859	3.3621	*	−1.3736	
507	1.5327	2.5554	*	−0.3194	
512	2.5905	4.0980	*	−0.5705	
586	1.3604	2.3043	*	0.6443	
587	1.4977	2.5044	*	−0.3111	
588	1.5108	2.5235	*	−0.3142	
589	1.6538	2.7320	*	−0.3482	
590	2.0648	3.3313	*	0.4771	
594	3.2312	5.0322	*	1.1231	
595	1.6211	2.6843	*	0.5824	
596	2.9126	4.5676	*	2.1216	
597	4.4375	6.7911	*	−1.9317	
598	3.8243	5.8970	*	2.8281	
599	3.9318	6.0537	*	0.9569	
600	2.7623	4.3484	*	3.0801	*
601	2.0028	3.2410	*	2.3375	
602	2.5224	3.9986	*	2.2142	
603	0.0950	0.1821		3.7582	*
604	0.2580	0.0557		5.6426	*
607	0.8908	0.9784		3.9471	*

Diagnostics

Obs	Mahalanobis distance	Robust MCD distance	Leverage	Standardized robust residual	Outlier
734	9.9944	14.8940	*	−3.2505	*
735	8.3830	12.5444	*	0.8233	
736	3.5362	4.8358	*	6.4206	*
737	3.4245	4.6729	*	28.5424	*
738	2.2638	2.9805	*	1.5044	
739	1.6356	2.0645		−4.1817	*
740	0.9201	1.0212		−7.1201	*
749	0.6249	0.5907		−3.4988	*
751	0.7171	0.7251		−3.4769	*

Diagnostics summary

Observation type	Proportion	Cutoff
Outlier	0.0173	3.0000
Leverage	0.0759	2.2414

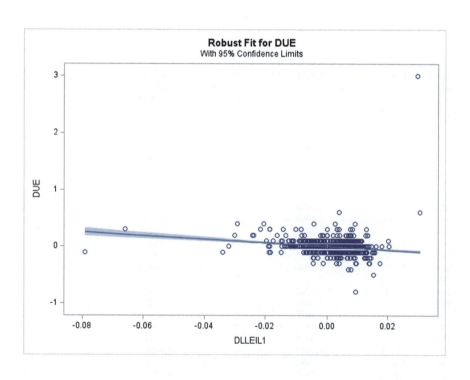

Goodness-of-fit	
Statistic	Value
R-square	0.0392
AICR	763.6684
BICR	773.6355
Deviance	8.9285

The application of robust regression, SAS proc robustreg, with the Hampel weighting function, produces a negative and highly statistically significant coefficient, −3.117, on the DLLEIL1 variable with its estimated probability of 0.001. The simple linear robust regression of DUE as a function of the DLLEIL1 variable is reported, using the Hampel weighting function. The reader notes the very large number of outliers identified.

We can use SAS proc robustreg to estimate a robust regression line for the DUE AND DLLLEILI relationship. We will use the Fair weighting function in this application.

SAS M-Fair Robust Regression
The ROBUSTREG Procedure

Model information	
Data set	WORK.REMZTT
Dependent variable	DUE
Number of independent variables	1
Number of observations	751
Missing values	2
Method	M estimation

Parameter	DF	Estimate	Standard error	95% confidence limits		Chi-square	Pr > Chi-square
Intercept	1	−0.0002	0.0035	−0.0070	0.0066	0.00	0.9527
DLLEIL1	1	−2.7248	0.4154	−3.5390	−1.9106	43.02	<0.0001
Scale	1	0.1130					

Obs	Mahalanobis distance	Robust MCD distance	Leverage	Standardized robust residual	Outlier
2	1.9141	2.4706	*	−2.2333	
11	2.2869	3.0141	*	0.4939	

| Obs | Diagnostics | | | | |
	Mahalanobis distance	Robust MCD distance	Leverage	Standardized robust residual	Outlier
132	1.7504	2.8728	*	0.5908	
175	1.3230	2.2496	*	−0.2106	
179	1.5701	2.6100	*	0.6260	
183	1.8375	2.9998	*	−0.3110	
185	1.6331	2.7018	*	−0.2711	
186	1.4122	2.3798	*	−0.2280	
187	2.3831	3.7955	*	0.4673	
188	2.6665	4.2087	*	0.4120	
189	1.7170	2.8242	*	−0.2875	
190	2.2393	3.5857	*	1.3802	
191	2.5294	4.0089	*	2.2084	
194	0.7558	1.4225		3.4393	*
243	2.5359	4.0183	*	−0.4473	
249	1.5304	2.5521	*	−0.2511	
250	1.5441	2.5721	*	−0.2538	
251	1.3366	2.2695	*	0.6716	
254	3.1627	4.9323	*	1.2000	
255	4.1715	6.4032	*	−0.7665	
256	1.8928	3.0805	*	−0.3218	
264	1.6305	2.6980	*	−0.2706	
272	1.9285	3.1326	*	−0.3288	
276	1.4761	2.4730	*	2.4139	
288	1.9827	2.5706	*	0.4345	
379	2.0380	3.2923	*	−0.3502	
380	1.6965	2.7944	*	−0.2835	
381	1.9002	3.0914	*	1.4464	
382	2.4910	3.9528	*	−1.3234	
383	1.5701	2.6100	*	0.6260	
384	1.7788	2.9143	*	0.5853	
444	2.5670	4.0636	*	−1.3382	
496	1.5643	2.6016	*	−0.2577	
501	1.5847	2.6313	*	−0.2617	
503	2.0260	3.2747	*	0.5370	
505	1.6400	2.7119	*	0.6123	
506	2.0859	3.3621	*	−1.2443	
507	1.5327	2.5554	*	−0.2515	
512	2.5905	4.0980	*	−0.4580	
586	1.3604	2.3043	*	0.6669	
587	1.4977	2.5044	*	−0.2447	
588	1.5108	2.5235	*	−0.2473	
589	1.6538	2.7320	*	−0.2752	
590	2.0648	3.3313	*	0.5294	

Diagnostics

Obs	Mahalanobis distance	Robust MCD distance	Leverage	Standardized robust residual	Outlier
594	3.2312	5.0322	*	1.1866	
595	1.6211	2.6843	*	0.6160	
596	2.9126	4.5676	*	2.1336	
597	4.4375	6.7911	*	−1.7032	
598	3.8243	5.8970	*	2.8405	
599	3.9318	6.0537	*	1.0499	
600	2.7623	4.3484	*	3.0478	*
601	2.0028	3.2410	*	2.3112	
602	2.5224	3.9986	*	2.2098	
603	0.0950	0.1821		3.6054	*
604	0.2580	0.0557		5.4068	*
607	0.8908	0.9784		3.7607	*
734	9.9944	14.8940	*	−2.7876	
735	8.3830	12.5444	*	1.0661	
736	3.5362	4.8358	*	6.0465	*
737	3.4245	4.6729	*	27.2602	*
738	2.2638	2.9805	*	1.3742	
739	1.6356	2.0645		−4.0573	*
740	0.9201	1.0212		−6.8514	*
749	0.6249	0.5907		−3.3697	*
751	0.7171	0.7251		−3.3517	*

Diagnostics summary

Observation type	Proportion	Cutoff
Outlier	0.0146	3.0000
Leverage	0.0759	2.2414

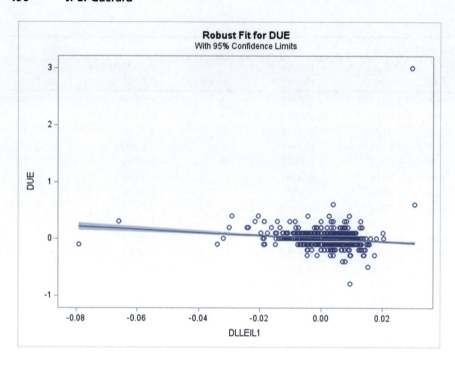

Goodness-of-fit	
Statistic	Value
R-square	0.0235
AICR	477.8056
BICR	489.5396
Deviance	6.0838

The application of robust regression, SAS proc robustreg, with the Fair weighting function, produces a negative and highly statistically significant coefficient, -2.980, on the DLLEIL1 variable with its estimated probability of 0.0001. The simple linear robust regression of DUE as a function of the DLLEIL1 variable is reported, using the Fair weighting function. The reader notes the very large number of outliers identified.

The reader recognizes that the Huber, Tukey Bisquare, Hampel, and Fair robust regression weighting schemes produce negative and highly statistically significant coefficients on the DLLEIL1 variable in the DUE regression equation. Our robust weighting functions lead the reader is see that for 1959–11/2021 the (DLOG) LEI variable led the (DUE) unemployment rate variable.

We can use SAS proc robustreg to estimate a robust regression line for the DUE AND DWkUNCLLI relationship for the 1959–11/2021 period. We will use the Huber weighting function in this application.

SAS M-Huber Robust Regression
The ROBUSTREG Procedure

Model information	
Data SET	WORK.REMZTT
Dependent variable	DUE
Number of independent variables	1
Number of observations	751
Missing values	2
Method	M estimation

Number of observations read	753
Number of observations used	751
Missing values	2

Parameter estimates

Parameter	DF	Estimate	Standard error	95% confidence limits		Chi-square	Pr > Chi-square
Intercept	1	−0.0054	0.0038	−0.0130	0.0021	2.02	0.1549
DLWkUNCLL1	1	0.0217	0.0344	−0.0456	0.0890	0.40	0.5278
Scale	1	0.1390					

Diagnostics

Obs	Mahalanobis distance	Robust MCD distance	Leverage	Standardized robust residual	Outlier
7	0.8966	2.3355	*	0.0235	
9	1.2264	3.1730	*	0.7373	
10	1.0883	2.8222	*	−0.6993	
11	2.1847	5.4888	*	0.0772	
14	1.0134	2.6320	*	−0.6980	
26	1.1292	2.8088	*	1.4979	
80	1.1417	2.8403	*	−0.6605	
86	1.6474	4.1246	*	0.0678	
97	1.6879	4.3449	*	0.0098	
100	1.0434	2.5907	*	0.0573	
132	1.1964	3.0967	*	0.7379	

Diagnostics					
Obs	Mahalanobis distance	Robust MCD distance	Leverage	Standardized robust residual	Outlier
135	2.1557	5.5328	*	0.0016	
136	1.0077	2.5000	*	0.7762	
140	0.9746	2.5335	*	0.0222	
163	0.9553	2.3671	*	0.0558	
179	1.1417	2.9578	*	0.7388	
187	0.9179	2.3895	*	0.7427	
189	1.0420	2.7048	*	0.0210	
190	1.3426	3.4680	*	1.4549	
191	0.9638	2.5062	*	2.1810	
216	0.9030	2.3517	*	−0.6961	
217	0.9019	2.3489	*	−0.6961	
218	2.0863	5.2391	*	−0.6441	
230	0.9586	2.3755	*	0.0558	
243	1.3116	3.3893	*	0.0163	
244	1.7071	4.2761	*	−0.6507	
255	2.1105	5.4181	*	0.0024	
256	1.0617	2.7548	*	0.0207	
261	1.0990	2.7320	*	0.7778	
283	0.8940	2.3289	*	1.4627	
287	1.2374	3.0835	*	0.0607	
403	0.9273	2.2959	*	−0.6642	
405	0.9119	2.2569	*	−0.6645	
420	1.0340	2.6843	*	0.7407	
502	0.9809	2.5496	*	0.0221	
512	0.9535	2.4801	*	0.0226	
515	1.0264	2.5477	*	0.7766	
560	2.0566	5.2810	*	0.0034	
561	1.2837	3.2009	*	0.0615	
598	0.8944	2.3300	*	2.9017	
604	0.0125	0.0270		4.3566	*
647	1.1618	2.8914	*	−0.6602	
657	1.0273	2.6673	*	0.0213	
705	0.9283	2.2986	*	0.0553	
734	22.6136	57.4816	*	−1.0740	
735	4.0288	10.2891	*	2.1276	
736	5.4054	13.6671	*	4.4505	*
737	3.7935	9.5741	*	21.6913	*
738	1.0154	2.5198	*	0.7764	
739	2.7077	6.8170	*	−3.5114	*
740	1.6256	4.0692	*	−5.6888	*
746	0.9773	2.4228	*	−1.3829	
747	2.2401	5.6296	*	−1.3609	

Diagnostics

Obs	Mahalanobis distance	Robust MCD distance	Leverage	Standardized robust residual	Outlier
748	2.4369	6.1294	*	1.5207	
751	0.9224	2.2836	*	−2.8229	

Diagnostics summary

Observation type	Proportion	Cutoff
Outlier	0.0067	3.0000
Leverage	0.0719	2.2414

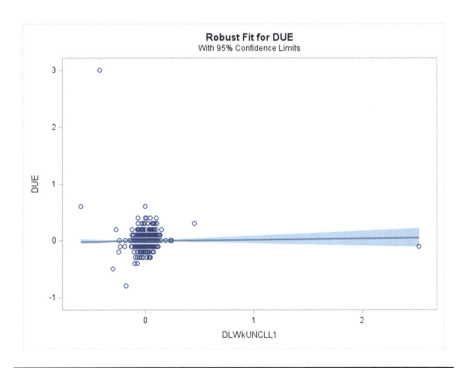

Goodness-of-fit

Statistic	Value
R-square	0.0004
AICR	514.9332
BICR	526.1755
Deviance	9.9073

The SAS robust regression of the DUE and DLWkUNCLL1 relationship is not statistically significant using the Huber weighting function. The coefficient is positive, 0.022, but its p-level is 0.528. It is nowhere statistically significant at the 10% level.

We can use SAS proc robustreg to estimate a robust regression line for the DUE AND DWkUNCLLI relationship for the 1959–11/2021 period. We will use the Tukey Bisquare weighting function in this application.

SAS M-Bisquare Robust Regression
The ROBUSTREG Procedure

Model information

Data set	WORK.REMZTT
Dependent variable	DUE
Number of independent variables	1
Number of observations	751
Missing values	2
Method	M estimation

Parameter estimates

Parameter	DF	estimate	Standard error	95% confidence limits		Chi-square	Pr > Chi-square
Intercept	1	−0.0060	0.0037	−0.0131	0.0012	2.69	0.1010
DLWkUNCLL1	1	0.0477	0.0328	−0.0166	0.1119	2.12	0.1458
Scale	1	0.1367					

Diagnostics

Obs	Mahalanobis distance	Robust MCD distance	Leverage	Standardized robust residual	Outlier
7	0.8966	2.3355	*	0.0089	
9	1.2264	3.1730	*	0.7274	
10	1.0883	2.8222	*	−0.7300	
11	2.1847	5.4888	*	0.1287	
14	1.0134	2.6320	*	−0.7270	
26	1.1292	2.8088	*	1.5504	
80	1.1417	2.8403	*	−0.6433	
86	1.6474	4.1246	*	0.1078	
97	1.6879	4.3449	*	−0.0219	
100	1.0434	2.5907	*	0.0843	
132	1.1964	3.0967	*	0.7286	
135	2.1557	5.5328	*	−0.0401	
136	1.0077	2.5000	*	0.8143	
140	0.9746	2.5335	*	0.0058	
163	0.9553	2.3671	*	0.0809	
179	1.1417	2.9578	*	0.7307	

Diagnostics

Obs	Mahalanobis distance	Robust MCD distance	Leverage	Standardized robust residual	Outlier
187	0.9179	2.3895	*	0.7394	
189	1.0420	2.7048	*	0.0032	
190	1.3426	3.4680	*	1.4543	
191	0.9638	2.5062	*	2.2004	
216	0.9030	2.3517	*	−0.7228	
217	0.9019	2.3489	*	−0.7227	
218	2.0863	5.2391	*	−0.6065	
230	0.9586	2.3755	*	0.0810	
243	1.3116	3.3893	*	−0.0073	
244	1.7071	4.2761	*	−0.6213	
255	2.1105	5.4181	*	−0.0383	
256	1.0617	2.7548	*	0.0025	
261	1.0990	2.7320	*	0.8178	
283	0.8940	2.3289	*	1.4717	
287	1.2374	3.0835	*	0.0918	
403	0.9273	2.2959	*	−0.6516	
405	0.9119	2.2569	*	−0.6522	
420	1.0340	2.6843	*	0.7349	
502	0.9809	2.5496	*	0.0056	
512	0.9535	2.4801	*	0.0067	
515	1.0264	2.5477	*	0.8150	
560	2.0566	5.2810	*	−0.0362	
561	1.2837	3.2009	*	0.0936	
598	0.8944	2.3300	*	2.9344	
604	0.0125	0.0270		4.4324	*
647	1.1618	2.8914	*	−0.6425	
657	1.0273	2.6673	*	0.0038	
705	0.9283	2.2986	*	0.0798	
734	22.6136	57.4816	*	−1.5668	
735	4.0288	10.2891	*	2.0812	
736	5.4054	13.6671	*	4.6421	*
737	3.7935	9.5741	*	22.1324	*
738	1.0154	2.5198	*	0.8146	
739	2.7077	6.8170	*	−3.5079	*
740	1.6256	4.0692	*	−5.7441	*
746	0.9773	2.4228	*	−1.3810	
747	2.2401	5.6296	*	−1.3319	
748	2.4369	6.1294	*	1.6012	
751	0.9224	2.2836	*	−2.8459	

Diagnostics summary

Observation type	Proportion	Cutoff
Outlier	0.0067	3.0000
Leverage	0.0719	2.2414

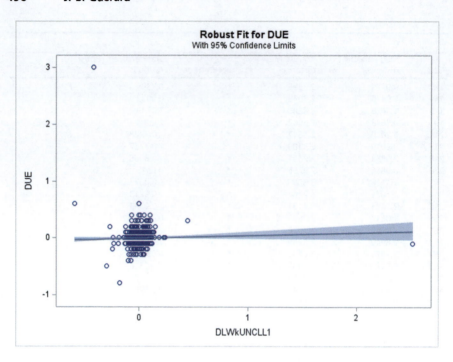

Goodness-of-fit	
Statistic	Value
R-square	0.0014
AICR	441.6976
BICR	453.1398
Deviance	8.2238

The SAS robust regression of the DUE and DLWkUNCLL1 relationship is not statistically significant using the Tukey Bisquare weighting function. The coefficient is positive, 0.048, but its p-level is 0.146. It is statistically significant at the 15% level; not at the 10% level used in economics.

SAS M-Hampel Robust Regression
The ROBUSTREG Procedure

Model information	
Data set	WORK.REMZTT
Dependent variable	DUE
Number of independent variables	1

Model information	
Number of observations	751
Missing values	2
Method	M estimation

Number of observations read	**753**
Number of observations used	**751**
Missing values	**2**

Parameter information	
Parameter	Effect
Intercept	Intercept
DLWkUNCLL1	DLWkUNCLL1

Summary statistics

Variable	Q1	Median	Q3	Mean	Standard deviation	MAD
DLWkUNCLL1	−0.0329	−0.00260	0.0276	0.000255	0.1115	0.0447
DUE	−0.1000	0	0	0.000533	0.1603	0.1483

Parameter estimates

Parameter	DF	Estimate	Standard error	95% confidence limits		Chi-square	Pr > Chi-sq
Intercept	1	−0.0041	0.0040	−0.0119	0.0037	1.08	0.2989
DLWkUNCLL1	1	0.0414	0.0356	−0.0285	0.1112	1.35	0.2459
Scale	1	0.1398					

Diagnostics

Obs	Mahalanobis distance	Robust MCD distance	Leverage	Standardized robust residual	Outlier
7	0.8966	2.3355	*	−0.0001	
9	1.2264	3.1730	*	0.7041	
10	1.0883	2.8222	*	−0.7216	
11	2.1847	5.4888	*	0.1015	
14	1.0134	2.6320	*	−0.7191	
26	1.1292	2.8088	*	1.4969	
80	1.1417	2.8403	*	−0.6480	
86	1.6474	4.1246	*	0.0838	
97	1.6879	4.3449	*	−0.0263	
100	1.0434	2.5907	*	0.0639	
132	1.1964	3.0967	*	0.7051	
135	2.1557	5.5328	*	−0.0417	

Diagnostics

Obs	Mahalanobis distance	Robust MCD distance	Leverage	Standardized robust residual	Outlier
136	1.0077	2.5000	*	0.7778	
140	0.9746	2.5335	*	−0.0027	
163	0.9553	2.3671	*	0.0610	
179	1.1417	2.9578	*	0.7069	
187	0.9179	2.3895	*	0.7143	
189	1.0420	2.7048	*	−0.0049	
190	1.3426	3.4680	*	1.4153	
191	0.9638	2.5062	*	2.1429	
216	0.9030	2.3517	*	−0.7155	
217	0.9019	2.3489	*	−0.7154	
218	2.0863	5.2391	*	−0.6168	
230	0.9586	2.3755	*	0.0611	
243	1.3116	3.3893	*	−0.0138	
244	1.7071	4.2761	*	−0.6293	
255	2.1105	5.4181	*	−0.0402	
256	1.0617	2.7548	*	−0.0056	
261	1.0990	2.7320	*	0.7808	
283	0.8940	2.3289	*	1.4301	
287	1.2374	3.0835	*	0.0703	
403	0.9273	2.2959	*	−0.6551	
405	0.9119	2.2569	*	−0.6556	
420	1.0340	2.6843	*	0.7104	
502	0.9809	2.5496	*	−0.0029	
512	0.9535	2.4801	*	−0.0020	
515	1.0264	2.5477	*	0.7784	
560	2.0566	5.2810	*	−0.0384	
561	1.2837	3.2009	*	0.0718	
598	0.8944	2.3300	*	2.8603	
604	0.0125	0.0270		4.3204	*
647	1.1618	2.8914	*	−0.6473	
657	1.0273	2.6673	*	−0.0045	
705	0.9283	2.2986	*	0.0601	
734	22.6136	57.4816	*	−1.4318	
735	4.0288	10.2891	*	2.0418	
736	5.4054	13.6671	*	4.4984	*
737	3.7935	9.5741	*	21.6076	*
738	1.0154	2.5198	*	0.7780	
739	2.7077	6.8170	*	−3.4567	*
740	1.6256	4.0692	*	−5.6377	*
746	0.9773	2.4228	*	−1.3685	
747	2.2401	5.6296	*	−1.3268	
748	2.4369	6.1294	*	1.5400	
751	0.9224	2.2836	*	−2.8005	

Diagnostics summary

Observation type	Proportion	Cutoff
Outlier	0.0067	3.0000
Leverage	0.0719	2.2414

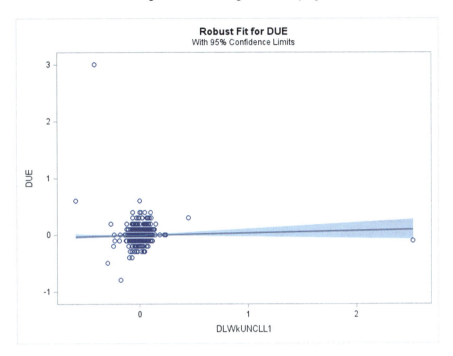

Robust Fit for DUE
With 95% Confidence Limits

Goodness-of-fit	
Statistic	Value
R-square	0.0014
AICR	512.6235
BICR	523.5656
Deviance	9.9796

The SAS robust regression of the DUE and DLWkUNCLL1 relationship is not statistically significant using the Hampel weighting function. The coefficient is positive, 0.041, but its p-level is 0.246. It is not statistically significant at the 10% level used in economics.

As a final SAS robust regression estimation, we use proc robustreg with the Fair weighting function to estimate the DUE and DLWkUNCLL1 relationship.

SAS M-Fair Robust Regression
The ROBUSTREG Procedure

Model information

Data set	WORK.REMZTT
Dependent variable	DUE
Number of independent variables	1
Number of observations	751
Missing values	2
Method	M estimation

Parameter estimates

Parameter	DF	Estimate	Standard error	95% confidence limits		Chi-square	Pr > Chi-sq
Intercept	1	−0.0049	0.0033	−0.0114	0.0016	2.18	0.1403
DLWkUNCLL1	1	0.0187	0.0298	−0.0397	0.0772	0.39	0.5297
Scale	1	0.1399					

Diagnostics

Obs	Mahalanobis distance	Robust MCD distance	Leverage	Standardized robust residual	Outlier
7	0.8966	2.3355	*	0.0216	
9	1.2264	3.1730	*	0.7312	
10	1.0883	2.8222	*	−0.6958	
11	2.1847	5.4888	*	0.0676	
14	1.0134	2.6320	*	−0.6947	
26	1.1292	2.8088	*	1.4810	
80	1.1417	2.8403	*	−0.6625	
86	1.6474	4.1246	*	0.0596	
97	1.6879	4.3449	*	0.0098	
100	1.0434	2.5907	*	0.0506	
132	1.1964	3.0967	*	0.7317	
135	2.1557	5.5328	*	0.0028	
136	1.0077	2.5000	*	0.7646	
140	0.9746	2.5335	*	0.0204	
163	0.9553	2.3671	*	0.0493	
179	1.1417	2.9578	*	0.7325	
187	0.9179	2.3895	*	0.7358	
189	1.0420	2.7048	*	0.0194	
190	1.3426	3.4680	*	1.4440	
191	0.9638	2.5062	*	2.1642	

Diagnostics

Obs	Mahalanobis distance	Robust MCD distance	Leverage	Standardized robust residual	Outlier
216	0.9030	2.3517	*	−0.6930	
217	0.9019	2.3489	*	−0.6930	
218	2.0863	5.2391	*	−0.6484	
230	0.9586	2.3755	*	0.0493	
243	1.3116	3.3893	*	0.0154	
244	1.7071	4.2761	*	−0.6540	
255	2.1105	5.4181	*	0.0035	
256	1.0617	2.7548	*	0.0191	
261	1.0990	2.7320	*	0.7660	
283	0.8940	2.3289	*	1.4507	
287	1.2374	3.0835	*	0.0535	
403	0.9273	2.2959	*	−0.6657	
405	0.9119	2.2569	*	−0.6659	
420	1.0340	2.6843	*	0.7341	
502	0.9809	2.5496	*	0.0203	
512	0.9535	2.4801	*	0.0208	
515	1.0264	2.5477	*	0.7649	
560	2.0566	5.2810	*	0.0043	
561	1.2837	3.2009	*	0.0542	
598	0.8944	2.3300	*	2.8798	
604	0.0125	0.0270		4.3225	*
647	1.1618	2.8914	*	−0.6622	
657	1.0273	2.6673	*	0.0197	
705	0.9283	2.2986	*	0.0489	
734	22.6136	57.4816	*	−1.0174	
735	4.0288	10.2891	*	2.1185	
736	5.4054	13.6671	*	4.4030	*
737	3.7935	9.5741	*	21.5281	*
738	1.0154	2.5198	*	0.7647	
739	2.7077	6.8170	*	−3.4973	*
740	1.6256	4.0692	*	−5.6571	*
746	0.9773	2.4228	*	−1.3795	
747	2.2401	5.6296	*	−1.3606	
748	2.4369	6.1294	*	1.5005	
751	0.9224	2.2836	*	−2.8094	

Diagnostics summary

Observation type	Proportion	Cutoff
Outlier	0.0067	3.0000
Leverage	0.0719	2.2414

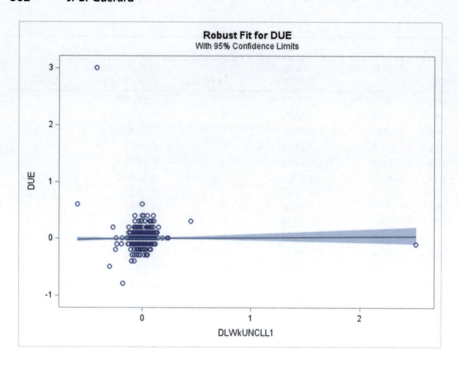

Goodness-of-fit	
Statistic	Value
R-square	0.0002
AICR	351.4483
BICR	363.6121
Deviance	6.8622

The SAS robust regression of the DUE and DLWkUNCLL1 relationship is not statistically significant using the Fair weighting function. The coefficient is positive, 0.018, but its p-level is 0.530. It is not statistically significant at the 10% level used in economics. In summary, for the 1959–11/2021 period, the use of SAS robust regression, with several weighting functions, does not produce statistically significant coefficients on the DLWkUNCLL1 variable in the DUE M-robust regressions.

10.3 Robust Regression Estimations of the DUE, DLLEIL1, and DkWkUNCLL1 Relationships Using M, S, and MM-Estimations

In this section we estimate a set of DUE, DLLEIL1, and DkWkUNCLL1 relationships using S, and MM-Estimations for the 1959–11/2021 period.

SAS S,MM-Tukey Robust Regression PJD TCB 110521
The ROBUSTREG Procedure

Model information	
Data set	WORK.REMZTT
Dependent variable	DUE
Number of independent variables	1
Number of observations	751
Missing values	2
Method	S estimation

S profile	
Total number of observations	751
Number of coefficients	2
Subset size	2
Chi function	Tukey
K0	7.0410
Breakdown value	0.0570
Efficiency	0.9900

Parameter estimates

Parameter	DF	Estimate	Standard error	95% confidence limits		Chi-square	Pr > Chi-square
Intercept	1	0.0010	0.0038	−0.0064	0.0084	0.07	0.7904
DLLEIL1	1	−3.2290	0.4761	−4.1621	−2.2960	46.01	<0.0001
Scale	0	0.1095					

Diagnostics summary		
Observation type	Proportion	Cutoff
Outlier	0.0173	3.0000

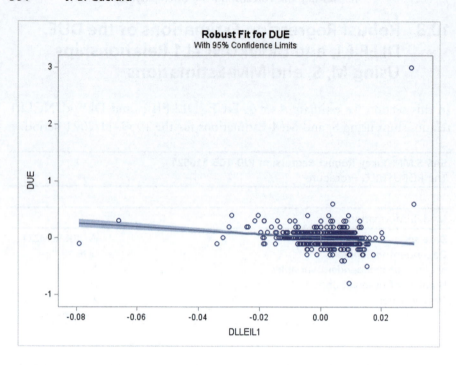

Goodness-of-fit	
Statistic	Value
R-square	0.0485
Deviance	0.0120

The Tukey S-estimation of the DLLEIL1 variable in the DUE equation supports the M-estimate regression that the DLOG transformation of the LEI leads the change in the unemployment rate. The S-estimate DLLEIL1 coefficient is negative, -3.229, and statistically significant with a p-level of 0.0001. Thus, an increase in the LEI leads to a reduction in the unemployment rate during the 1959–11/2021 period.

SAS S,MM-Tukey Robust Regression PJD TCB 110521
The ROBUSTREG Procedure

Model information	
Data set	WORK.REMZTT
Dependent variable	DUE
Number of independent variables	1
Number of observations	751
Missing values	2
Method	MM-estimation

Profile for the initial LTS estimate	
Total number of observations	751
Number of squares minimized	564
Number of coefficients	2
Highest possible breakdown value	0.2503

MM profile	
Chi function	Tukey
K1	7.0410
Efficiency	0.9900

Parameter estimates							
Parameter	DF	Estimate	Standard error	95% confidence limits		Chi-square	Pr > Chi-square
Intercept	1	0.0007	0.0037	−0.0066	0.0080	0.03	0.8547
DLLEIL1	1	−3.2650	0.4742	−4.1943	−2.3357	47.42	<0.0001
Scale	0	0.0974					

Diagnostics summary		
Observation type	Proportion	Cutoff
Outlier	0.0293	3.0000

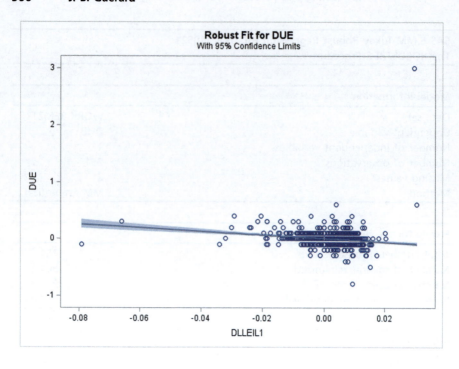

Goodness-of-fit	
Statistic	Value
R-square	0.0405
AICR	858.9176
BICR	868.5879
Deviance	8.1106

The Tukey MM-estimation of the DLLEIL1 variable in the DUE equation supports the M-estimate regression that the DLOG transformation of the LEI leads the change in the unemployment rate. The MM-estimate DLLEIL1 coefficient is negative, -3.229, and statistically significant with a p-level of 0.0001. Thus, the M, S, and MM-estimated robust regression models report that an increase in the LEI leads to a reduction in the unemployment rate during the 1959–11/2021 period.

SAS S,MM-Tukey Robust Regression PJD TCB 110521
The ROBUSTREG Procedure

Model information	
Data set	WORK.REMZTT
dependent variable	DUE
Number of independent variables	1
Number of observations	751
Missing values	2
Method	S estimation

S profile	
Total number of observations	751
Number of coefficients	2
Subset size	2
Chi function	Tukey
K0	7.0410
Breakdown value	0.0570
Efficiency	0.9900

Parameter estimates

Parameter	DF	Estimate	Standard error	95% confidence limits	Chi-square	Pr > Chi-square
Intercept	1	−0.0051	0.0037	−0.0124 0.0023	1.82	0.1768
DLWkUNCLL1	1	0.0464	0.0362	−0.0246 0.1174	1.64	0.2004
Scale	0	0.1121				

Diagnostics summary		
Observation type	Proportion	Cutoff
Outlier	0.0160	3.0000

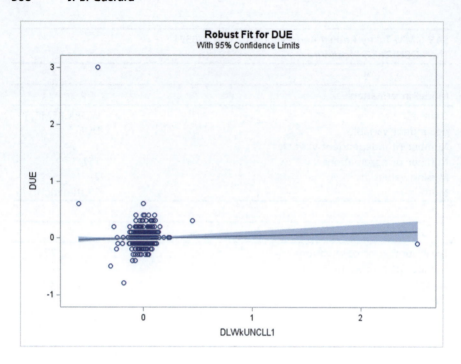

Goodness-of-fit	
Statistic	Value
R-square	0.0015
Deviance	0.0126

−0.0246	0.1174	1.64	0.2004

The S-estimate DLWkUNCLL1 coefficient is positive, 0.046, and is not statistically significant with a p-level of 0.2004.

SAS S,MM-Tukey Robust Regression PJD TCB 110521
The ROBUSTREG Procedure

Model information	
Data set	WORK.REMZTT
Dependent variable	DUE
Number of independent variables	1
Number of observations	751
Missing values	2
Method	MM-estimation

Summary statistics

Variable	Q1	Median	Q3	Mean	Standard deviation	MAD
DLWkUNCLL1	−0.0329	−0.00260	0.0276	0.000255	0.1115	0.0447
DUE	−0.1000	0	0	0.000533	0.1603	0.1483

Profile for the initial LTS estimate

Total number of observations	751
Number of squares minimized	564
Number of coefficients	2
Highest possible breakdown value	0.2503

MM profile

Chi function	Tukey
K1	7.0410
efficiency	0.9900

Parameter estimates

Parameter	DF	Estimate	Standard error	95% confidence limits		Chi-square	Pr > Chi-square
Intercept	1	−0.0052	0.0037	−0.0124	0.0020	2.01	0.1564
DLWkUNCLL1	1	0.3056	0.0661	0.1760	0.4352	21.36	<0.0001
Scale	0	0.0990					

Diagnostics summary

Observation type	Proportion	Cutoff
Outlier	0.0333	3.0000

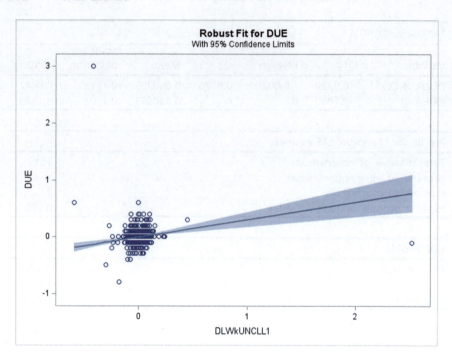

Goodness-of-fit	
Statistic	Value
R-square	0.0015
AICR	869.5162
BICR	879.2034
Deviance	8.4936

The MM-estimate DLWkUNCLL1 coefficient is positive, 0.306, and statistically significant with a p-level of 0.0001. Thus, only the MM-estimated robust regression models report that an increase in the weekly unemployment claims time series leads to an increase in the unemployment rate during the 1959–11/2021 period.

We perform two final robust regression exercises for the DUE and DLLEIL1 and DLWkUNCLL1 multiple regressions for the 1959–11/2021 period. We use S and MM-Tukey weighting functions to estimate the multiple regression models of the unemployment rate.

AS S,MM-Tukey Robust Regression PJD TCB 110521
The ROBUSTREG Procedure

Model information	
Data set	WORK.REMZTT
Dependent variable	DUE
Number of independent variables	2
Number of observations	751
Missing values	2
Method	S estimation

S profile	
Total number of observations	751
Number of coefficients	3
Subset size	3
Chi function	Tukey
K0	7.0410
Breakdown value	0.0570
Efficiency	0.9900

Parameter estimates

Parameter	DF	Estimate	Standard error	95% confidence limits		Chi-square	Pr > Chi-square
Intercept	1	0.0031	0.0038	−0.0044	0.0106	0.65	0.4211
DLLEIL1	1	−4.2106	0.5888	−5.3647	−3.0565	51.14	<0.0001
DLWkUNCLL1	1	−0.1424	0.0429	−0.2264	−0.0583	11.03	0.0009
Scale	0	0.1089					

Diagnostics

Obs	Mahalanobis distance	Robust MCD distance	Leverage	Standardized robust residual	Outlier
2	1.9634	2.9238	*	−2.2372	
9	1.2363	3.7184	*	0.9373	
10	1.2002	3.2125	*	−1.0521	
11	2.4771	6.0619	*	0.4426	
14	1.1525	3.0068	*	−1.0586	
25	1.1760	2.8766	*	1.1332	
26	1.4235	3.0865	*	2.1507	
29	1.3634	2.0043		3.1258	*
31	1.7100	2.7196	*	−0.4719	

Diagnostics

Obs	Mahalanobis distance	Robust MCD distance	Leverage	Standardized robust residual	Outlier
34	2.1193	2.8710	*	−0.3598	
59	1.3967	3.0843	*	1.2051	
80	1.1502	3.3080	*	−0.8468	
86	1.6668	4.8294	*	0.0703	
97	1.6881	5.0216	*	−0.0370	
100	1.0694	2.8790	*	0.1569	
107	1.7008	3.2275	*	0.3905	
132	1.7541	3.6968	*	0.5903	
135	2.1592	6.4168	*	−0.0378	
136	1.5118	3.6622	*	0.7433	
140	1.0927	3.1390	*	0.1142	
151	1.0470	2.7620	*	0.1661	
161	1.5479	3.4241	*	0.3126	
179	1.5816	3.4828	*	0.6387	
183	2.9596	4.9747	*	−0.6217	
186	1.8967	2.8978	*	−0.4090	
187	2.5023	3.9200	*	0.3517	
188	3.1081	4.4277	*	0.1951	
189	1.7180	3.3682	*	−0.3399	
190	2.2414	4.3090	*	1.3767	
191	2.6602	4.1423	*	2.1488	
194	0.9107	1.4234		3.4938	*
216	1.0026	2.9007	*	−0.8144	
217	1.8309	3.8333	*	−0.5339	
218	2.0863	5.9989	*	−0.7639	
229	1.3740	3.0255	*	−0.6341	
243	2.5642	4.5131	*	−0.5568	
244	1.8133	5.1960	*	−0.9315	
254	3.7616	5.3257	*	0.9541	
255	4.2274	7.2372	*	−0.9521	
256	1.9010	3.5429	*	−0.3920	
261	1.0991	3.1247	*	1.0190	
264	2.0370	2.9983	*	−0.4520	
272	2.0654	3.1647	*	−0.4634	
283	1.2544	2.7713	*	1.6218	
284	1.5870	2.9393	*	3.1275	*
287	1.2377	3.5346	*	0.1041	
288	2.2404	2.8926	*	0.6006	
379	2.2579	3.3256	*	−0.5138	
380	2.1048	3.0853	*	−0.4694	
381	2.0215	3.1320	*	1.3846	
382	2.8263	4.0644	*	−1.5729	

Diagnostics

Obs	Mahalanobis distance	Robust MCD distance	Leverage	Standardized robust residual	Outlier
383	1.9656	2.9009	*	0.4837	
384	2.2902	3.3939	*	0.4084	
405	1.0822	2.9342	*	−0.9661	
420	1.0847	3.2268	*	0.9889	
444	3.1123	4.4521	*	−1.6375	
501	2.0273	3.0132	*	−0.4468	
502	1.2246	2.9505	*	−0.1834	
503	2.3824	3.4351	*	0.3751	
505	1.6619	2.9591	*	0.5714	
506	2.4393	3.5131	*	−1.4755	
512	2.7381	4.2185	*	−0.6261	
515	1.0265	2.9074	*	1.0187	
560	2.0761	6.1862	*	0.0067	
561	1.4749	4.0724	*	−0.0633	
569	1.3778	2.9674	*	0.7127	
588	2.1750	3.4403	*	−0.4644	
589	2.0217	2.9571	*	−0.4506	
590	2.2760	3.3632	*	0.4000	
594	3.6345	5.1914	*	0.9810	
595	1.8992	2.7748	*	0.4943	
596	3.2729	4.6958	*	1.9888	
597	5.5329	7.8616	*	−2.2246	
598	4.3030	6.1108	*	2.6516	
599	4.6303	6.5091	*	0.7383	
600	3.2699	4.6501	*	2.9110	
601	2.0945	3.3404	*	2.2887	
602	3.0973	4.4474	*	2.0405	
603	0.7298	1.9788		3.6572	*
604	0.3234	0.3165		5.6330	*
607	1.1259	1.4290		3.9921	*
647	1.2780	3.5951	*	−0.9409	
657	1.1593	3.3147	*	0.1219	
734	23.2927	68.3354	*	−0.7032	
735	8.5442	14.0717	*	0.7640	
736	5.4074	15.6258	*	5.8725	*
737	4.0170	10.6577	*	28.1071	*
738	2.3272	3.4728	*	1.5239	
739	2.7096	7.8485	*	−4.4280	*
740	1.6317	4.7139	*	−7.2484	*
743	1.2382	2.9761	*	0.2310	
747	2.2444	6.3975	*	−1.6399	
748	2.4446	7.0970	*	1.9624	

Diagnostics					
Obs	Mahalanobis distance	Robust MCD distance	Leverage	Standardized robust residual	Outlier
749	0.7324	1.8529		−3.5322	*
751	0.9383	2.5442		−3.5370	*

Diagnostics summary		
Observation type	Proportion	cutoff
Outlier	0.0160	3.0000
Leverage	0.1172	2.7162

Goodness-of-fit	
Statistic	Value
R-square	0.0590
Deviance	0.0119

The S-estimate of the DUE equation produces a negative DLLEIL1 variable coefficient and highly statistically significant. The DLWkUNCLL1 coefficient is unexpected negative and statistically significant with a p-level of 0.0001. Thus, a change in the LEI time series significantly affects the unemployment rate during the 1959–11/2021 period.

SAS S,MM-Tukey Robust Regression PJD TCB 110521
The ROBUSTREG Procedure

Model information	
Data set	WORK.REMZTT
Dependent variable	DUE
Number of independent variables	2
Number of observations	751
Missing values	2
Method	MM-estimation

Number of coefficients	**3**
Highest possible breakdown value	**0.2503**

MM profile

Chi function	Tukey
K1	7.0410
Efficiency	0.9900

Parameter estimates

Parameter	DF	Estimate	Standard error	95% confidence limits		Chi-square	Pr > Chi-square
Intercept	1	0.0026	0.0038	−0.0048	0.0100	0.48	0.4877
DLLEIL1	1	−4.1944	0.5834	−5.3379	−3.0510	51.69	<0.0001
DLWkUNCLL1	1	−0.1404	0.0424	−0.2236	−0.0572	10.95	0.0009
Scale	0	0.0976					

Diagnostics

Obs	Mahalanobis distance	Robust MCD distance	Leverage	Standardized robust residual	Outlier
2	1.9634	2.9238	*	−2.4942	
9	1.2363	3.7184	*	1.0489	
10	1.2002	3.2125	*	−1.1714	
11	2.4771	6.0619	*	0.5003	
14	1.1525	3.0068	*	−1.1785	
20	0.3095	0.8440		3.1427	*
23	0.1808	0.1237		3.1781	*
25	1.1760	2.8766	*	1.2675	
26	1.4235	3.0865	*	2.4063	
29	1.3634	2.0043		3.4939	*
31	1.7100	2.7196	*	−0.5229	
34	2.1193	2.8710	*	−0.3996	
59	1.3967	3.0843	*	1.3476	
80	1.1502	3.3080	*	−0.9394	
86	1.6668	4.8294	*	0.0854	
97	1.6881	5.0216	*	−0.0394	
100	1.0694	2.8790	*	0.1807	
107	1.7008	3.2275	*	0.4378	
132	1.7541	3.6968	*	0.6630	
135	2.1592	6.4168	*	−0.0411	
136	1.5118	3.6622	*	0.8368	
140	1.0927	3.1390	*	0.1299	
142	0.4188	0.8276		3.0294	*
151	1.0470	2.7620	*	0.1880	
161	1.5479	3.4241	*	0.3508	
179	1.5816	3.4828	*	0.7170	
183	2.9596	4.9747	*	−0.6860	

Diagnostics

Obs	Mahalanobis distance	Robust MCD distance	Leverage	Standardized robust residual	Outlier
186	1.8967	2.8978	*	−0.4502	
187	2.5023	3.9200	*	0.3981	
188	3.1081	4.4277	*	0.2247	
189	1.7180	3.3682	*	−0.3752	
190	2.2414	4.3090	*	1.5414	
191	2.6602	4.1423	*	2.4047	
194	0.9107	1.4234		3.9060	*
216	1.0026	2.9007	*	−0.9067	
217	1.8309	3.8333	*	−0.5947	
218	2.0863	5.9989	*	−0.8457	
229	1.3740	3.0255	*	−0.7059	
243	2.5642	4.5131	*	−0.6170	
244	1.8133	5.1960	*	−1.0326	
254	3.7616	5.3257	*	1.0729	
255	4.2274	7.2372	*	−1.0579	
256	1.9010	3.5429	*	−0.4332	
257	0.3043	0.7553		3.1669	*
261	1.0991	3.1247	*	1.1436	
264	2.0370	2.9983	*	−0.4984	
272	2.0654	3.1647	*	−0.5120	
283	1.2544	2.7713	*	1.8147	
284	1.5870	2.9393	*	3.4939	*
287	1.2377	3.5346	*	0.1223	
288	2.2404	2.8926	*	0.6732	
379	2.2579	3.3256	*	−0.5679	
380	2.1048	3.0853	*	−0.5178	
381	2.0215	3.1320	*	1.5513	
382	2.8263	4.0644	*	−1.7497	
383	1.9656	2.9009	*	0.5463	
384	2.2902	3.3939	*	0.4626	
399	0.7916	0.9027		3.3486	*
405	1.0822	2.9342	*	−1.0724	
420	1.0847	3.2268	*	1.1066	
436	0.4395	1.2768		−3.0910	*
444	3.1123	4.4521	*	−1.8212	
501	2.0273	3.0132	*	−0.4925	
502	1.2246	2.9505	*	−0.2011	
503	2.3824	3.4351	*	0.4252	
505	1.6619	2.9591	*	0.6426	
506	2.4393	3.5131	*	−1.6411	
512	2.7381	4.2185	*	−0.6934	
515	1.0265	2.9074	*	1.1431	

Diagnostics

Obs	Mahalanobis distance	Robust MCD distance	Leverage	Standardized robust residual	Outlier
560	2.0761	6.1862	*	0.0087	
561	1.4749	4.0724	*	−0.0638	
569	1.3778	2.9674	*	0.8023	
588	2.1750	3.4403	*	−0.5116	
589	2.0217	2.9571	*	−0.4969	
590	2.2760	3.3632	*	0.4524	
594	3.6345	5.1914	*	1.1023	
595	1.8992	2.7748	*	0.5578	
596	3.2729	4.6958	*	2.2271	
597	5.5329	7.8616	*	−2.4741	
598	4.3030	6.1108	*	2.9680	
599	4.6303	6.5091	*	0.8325	
600	3.2699	4.6501	*	3.2573	*
601	2.0945	3.3404	*	2.5606	
602	3.0973	4.4474	*	2.2854	
603	0.7298	1.9788		4.0889	*
604	0.3234	0.3165		6.2933	*
607	1.1259	1.4290		4.4604	*
632	0.9411	1.4665		−3.2791	*
647	1.2780	3.5951	*	−1.0440	
657	1.1593	3.3147	*	0.1384	
734	23.2927	68.3354	*	−0.8185	
735	8.5442	14.0717	*	0.8595	
736	5.4074	15.6258	*	6.5686	*
737	4.0170	10.6577	*	31.3903	*
738	2.3272	3.4728	*	1.7050	
739	2.7096	7.8485	*	−4.9357	*
740	1.6317	4.7139	*	−8.0862	*
743	1.2382	2.9761	*	0.2601	
747	2.2444	6.3975	*	−1.8237	
748	2.4446	7.0970	*	2.1989	
749	0.7324	1.8529		−3.9387	*
751	0.9383	2.5442		−3.9437	*

Diagnostics summary

Observation type	Proportion	Cutoff
Outlier	0.0266	3.0000
Leverage	0.1172	2.7162

Goodness-of-fit	
Statistic	Value
R-square	0.0490
AICR	850.6291
BICR	865.1661
Deviance	8.0445

The MM-estimated DLLEIL1 is negative and statistically significant in both the S and MM-estimate robust regression models. The DLWkUNCLL1 coefficient is negative and statistically significant in the S and MM.

10.4   OLS Modeling of the PJD Unemployment Rate, TCB LEI 11052021 in 1999–11/2021

Is the LEI still statistically significant in the regression analysis in modeling the U.S. unemployment rate during the 1999–11/2021?

UER (A0M044) and the LEI (G0M910)			

Pearson correlation coefficients, N = 273
Prob > |r| under H0: Rho = 0

	G0M910	A0M005	A0M044
G0M910	1.00000	−0.07877	−0.46222
		0.1945	<0.0001
A0M005	−0.07877	1.00000	0.12533
	0.1945		0.0385
A0M044	0.46222	0.12533	1.00000
	<0.0001	0.0385	

Pearson correlation coefficients, N = 272
Prob > |r| under H0: Rho = 0

	DUE	DLLEI	DLWkUNCL
DUE	1.00000	0.04338	−0.05819
		0.4762	0.3390
DLLEI	0.04338	1.00000	−0.69979
	0.4762		<0.0001
DLWkUNCL	−0.05819	−0.69979	1.00000
	0.3390	<0.0001	

Palgrave PS DUE DLLEIL1 PJD 110521
The REG Procedure
Model: MODEL1
Dependent Variable: DUE

Number of observations read	273
Number of observations used	272
Number of observations with missing values	1

Analysis of variance

Source	DF	Sum of squares	Mean square	F value	Pr > F
Model	1	0.02663	0.02663	0.51	0.4762
Error	270	14.12807	0.05233		
Corrected Total	271	14.15471			

Root MSE	0.22875	**R-square**	0.0019
Dependent Mean	0.00441	**Adj R-square**	−0.0018
Coeff var	5184.98206		

Parameter estimates

Variable	DF	Parameter estimate	Standard error	t value	Pr > |t|
Intercept	1	0.00340	0.01394	0.24	0.8077
DLLEI	1	0.98924	1.38663	0.71	0.4762

No, the logged first-difference of the LEI (DLLEI) variable with a one-month lag (DLLEIL1) is positive and not statistically associated, at the 10% level with the change (DUE) in the unemployment rate, with an estimated t-statistic of 0.71. However, we must identify influential observations and use robust regression techniques to fit.

Output statistics

Obs	Residual	RStudent	Hat diag H	Cov ratio	DFFITS	DFBETAS	
						Intercept	DLLEIL1
1	–	–	–	–	–	–	–
2	–	–	–	–	–	–	–
3	−0.006404	−0.0279	0.0045	1.0120	−0.0019	−0.0016	−0.0008
4	−0.004469	−0.0195	0.0037	1.0112	−0.0012	−0.0012	−0.0000
5	−0.003987	−0.0174	0.0037	1.0112	−0.0011	−0.0011	0.0001
6	0.0936	0.4084	0.0045	1.0107	0.0273	0.0236	0.0113
7	−0.1054	−0.4599	0.0039	1.0098	−0.0287	−0.0272	−0.0064
8	−0.1054	−0.4599	0.0039	1.0098	−0.0287	−0.0272	−0.0064
9	−0.004938	−0.0215	0.0037	1.0113	−0.0013	−0.0013	−0.0002

Output statistics							
Obs	Residual	RStudent	Hat diag H	Cov ratio	DFFITS	DFBETAS	
						Intercept	DLLEIL1
10	−0.003987	−0.0174	0.0037	1.0112	−0.0011	−0.0011	0.0001
11	−0.005409	−0.0236	0.0039	1.0114	−0.0015	−0.0014	−0.0003
12	−0.006346	−0.0277	0.0044	1.0119	−0.0018	−0.0016	−0.0007
13	−0.007735	−0.0338	0.0059	1.0134	−0.0026	−0.0019	−0.0016
14	−0.1063	−0.4639	0.0044	1.0103	−0.0308	−0.0268	−0.0123
15	−0.001194	−0.005213	0.0058	1.0133	−0.0004	−0.0003	0.0002
16	−0.008169	−0.0357	0.0065	1.0140	−0.0029	−0.0020	−0.0019
17	−0.004911	−0.0214	0.0037	1.0113	−0.0013	−0.0013	−0.0001
18	0.000652	0.002851	0.0088	1.0164	0.0003	0.0002	−0.0002
19	−0.004919	−0.0214	0.0037	1.0113	−0.0013	−0.0013	−0.0001
20	0.0979	0.4271	0.0047	1.0109	0.0295	0.0273	−0.0139
21	−0.1012	−0.4418	0.0058	1.0119	−0.0337	−0.0288	0.0203
22	−0.005865	−0.0256	0.0041	1.0116	−0.0016	−0.0015	−0.0005
23	0.000723	0.003162	0.0089	1.0166	0.0003	0.0002	−0.0002
24	−0.000659	−0.002877	0.0065	1.0141	−0.0002	−0.0002	0.0002
25	0.1023	0.4480	0.0125	1.0187	0.0505	0.0316	−0.0424
26	−0.001072	−0.004678	0.0059	1.0135	−0.0004	−0.0003	0.0002
27	0.1009	0.4414	0.0093	1.0155	0.0429	0.0302	−0.0333
28	−0.0975	−0.4274	0.0131	1.0195	−0.0493	−0.0302	0.0418
29	0.000542	0.002368	0.0086	1.0162	0.0002	0.0002	−0.0002
30	0.0945	0.4122	0.0039	1.0102	0.0259	0.0243	0.0062
31	0.0985	0.4302	0.0054	1.0116	0.0318	0.0279	−0.0180
32	0.0970	0.4233	0.0041	1.0103	0.0272	0.0265	−0.0087
33	0.0965	0.4210	0.0039	1.0101	0.0262	0.0261	−0.0056
34	0.004232	0.0186	0.0185	1.0265	0.0026	0.0014	−0.0023
35	0.1991	0.8706	0.0062	1.0081	0.0688	0.0572	−0.0438
36	0.0929	0.4054	0.0051	1.0114	0.0291	0.0230	0.0153
37	0.0929	0.4055	0.0051	1.0114	0.0290	0.0230	0.0152
38	−0.003987	−0.0174	0.0037	1.0112	−0.0011	−0.0011	0.0001
39	0.0919	0.4014	0.0063	1.0127	0.0321	0.0222	0.0207
40	0.0945	0.4121	0.0039	1.0102	0.0259	0.0243	0.0063
41	−0.007530	−0.0329	0.0056	1.0131	−0.0025	−0.0018	−0.0014
42	0.0925	0.4038	0.0056	1.0119	0.0302	0.0227	0.0175
43	−0.1050	−0.4579	0.0038	1.0097	−0.0281	−0.0274	−0.0036
44	−0.001987	−0.008669	0.0049	1.0124	−0.0006	−0.0006	0.0003
45	−0.004988	−0.0218	0.0038	1.0113	−0.0013	−0.0013	−0.0002
46	0.0980	0.4278	0.0049	1.0110	0.0299	0.0274	−0.0147
47	−0.003485	−0.0152	0.0039	1.0114	−0.0009	−0.0009	0.0002
48	0.1930	0.8432	0.0050	1.0072	0.0597	0.0480	0.0305
49	−0.1035	−0.4514	0.0039	1.0098	−0.0281	−0.0279	0.0060
50	−0.004986	−0.0217	0.0038	1.0113	−0.0013	−0.0013	−0.0002
51	−0.002988	−0.0130	0.0041	1.0116	−0.0008	−0.0008	0.0003
52	0.0965	0.4210	0.0039	1.0100	0.0262	0.0261	−0.0056
53	−0.002483	−0.0108	0.0044	1.0120	−0.0007	−0.0007	0.0003
54	0.0915	0.3998	0.0069	1.0133	0.0334	0.0219	0.0229
55	0.0925	0.4040	0.0055	1.0118	0.0300	0.0227	0.0172
56	−0.1055	−0.4601	0.0039	1.0098	−0.0288	−0.0272	−0.0067
57	−0.006926	−0.0302	0.0049	1.0125	−0.0021	−0.0017	−0.0011
58	−0.008841	−0.0386	0.0075	1.0151	−0.0034	−0.0021	−0.0024
59	−0.1083	−0.4731	0.0067	1.0125	−0.0388	−0.0261	−0.0259
60	−0.008739	−0.0382	0.0074	1.0149	−0.0033	−0.0021	−0.0023
61	−0.008220	−0.0359	0.0065	1.0141	−0.0029	−0.0020	−0.0019
62	−0.1077	−0.4703	0.0058	1.0117	−0.0360	−0.0263	−0.0218
63	0.0923	0.4031	0.0058	1.0121	0.0307	0.0225	0.0185

Output statistics

Obs	Residual	RStudent	Hat diag H	Cov ratio	DFFITS	DFBETAS	
						Intercept	DLLEIL1
64	−0.3099	−1.3601	0.0097	1.0034	−0.1344	−0.0719	−0.1057
65	0.0951	0.4148	0.0037	1.0100	0.0254	0.0248	0.0027
66	−0.008043	−0.0351	0.0063	1.0138	−0.0028	−0.0019	−0.0018
67	−0.1058	−0.4615	0.0041	1.0100	−0.0294	−0.0271	−0.0088
68	−0.1062	−0.4634	0.0043	1.0102	−0.0305	−0.0269	−0.0117
69	0.0938	0.4092	0.0043	1.0106	0.0269	0.0237	0.0102
70	0.0934	0.4074	0.0047	1.0109	0.0278	0.0234	0.0127
71	−0.1053	−0.4593	0.0038	1.0098	−0.0285	−0.0272	−0.0057
72	−0.007042	−0.0307	0.0050	1.0126	−0.0022	−0.0017	−0.0011
73	−0.1079	−0.4711	0.0061	1.0119	−0.0368	−0.0262	−0.0230
74	0.0939	0.4095	0.0043	1.0105	0.0268	0.0238	0.0099
75	−0.1061	−0.4630	0.0043	1.0102	−0.0303	−0.0269	−0.0111
76	−0.1023	−0.4463	0.0046	1.0106	−0.0304	−0.0284	0.0135
77	−0.006550	−0.0286	0.0046	1.0121	−0.0019	−0.0016	−0.0009
78	−0.2027	−0.8854	0.0043	1.0059	−0.0580	−0.0558	0.0215
79	−0.007391	−0.0323	0.0054	1.0130	−0.0024	−0.0018	−0.0013
80	0.0960	0.4188	0.0037	1.0099	0.0256	0.0256	−0.0026
81	−0.006944	−0.0303	0.0049	1.0125	−0.0021	−0.0017	−0.0011
82	−0.001031	−0.004499	0.0060	1.0135	−0.0003	−0.0003	0.0002
83	−0.005679	−0.0248	0.0040	1.0115	−0.0016	−0.0015	−0.0004
84	−0.1065	−0.4648	0.0045	1.0105	−0.0314	−0.0268	−0.0137
85	−0.1040	−0.4536	0.0037	1.0097	−0.0277	−0.0277	0.0028
86	0.1927	0.8419	0.0054	1.0076	0.0618	0.0475	0.0345
87	−0.1040	−0.4536	0.0037	1.0097	−0.0277	−0.0277	0.0028
88	−0.004819	−0.0210	0.0037	1.0112	−0.0013	−0.0013	−0.0001
89	−0.1019	−0.4448	0.0050	1.0110	−0.0314	−0.0286	0.0158
90	−0.1015	−0.4430	0.0054	1.0115	−0.0327	−0.0287	0.0185
91	0.0969	0.4225	0.0040	1.0102	0.0268	0.0264	−0.0076
92	−0.002300	−0.0100	0.0046	1.0121	−0.0007	−0.0006	0.0003
93	−0.002718	−0.0119	0.0043	1.0118	−0.0008	−0.0007	0.0003
94	−0.1036	−0.4518	0.0038	1.0098	−0.0280	−0.0279	0.0055
95	−0.003563	−0.0155	0.0038	1.0114	−0.0010	−0.0010	0.0002
96	−0.002711	−0.0118	0.0043	1.0118	−0.0008	−0.0007	0.0003
97	−0.005687	−0.0248	0.0040	1.0115	−0.0016	−0.0015	−0.0004
98	−0.002713	−0.0118	0.0043	1.0118	−0.0008	−0.0007	0.0003
99	0.0964	0.4207	0.0038	1.0100	0.0261	0.0260	−0.0051
100	−0.006111	−0.0267	0.0043	1.0118	−0.0017	−0.0015	−0.0006
101	−0.002714	−0.0118	0.0043	1.0118	−0.0008	−0.0007	0.0003
102	−0.003987	−0.0174	0.0037	1.0112	−0.0011	−0.0011	0.0001
103	−0.002710	−0.0118	0.0043	1.0118	−0.0008	−0.0007	0.0003
104	−0.003134	−0.0137	0.0040	1.0115	−0.0009	−0.0009	0.0002
105	−0.001846	−0.008054	0.0050	1.0125	−0.0006	−0.0005	0.0003
106	−0.001404	−0.006126	0.0055	1.0130	−0.0005	−0.0004	0.0003
107	−0.001388	−0.006058	0.0055	1.0131	−0.0005	−0.0004	0.0003
108	0.0999	0.4367	0.0075	1.0136	0.0379	0.0292	−0.0269
109	0.000420	0.001835	0.0083	1.0159	0.0002	0.0001	−0.0001
110	0.000465	0.002034	0.0084	1.0160	0.0002	0.0001	−0.0001
111	0.000964	0.004217	0.0094	1.0171	0.0004	0.0003	−0.0003
112	0.1024	0.4487	0.0129	1.0191	0.0513	0.0317	−0.0434
113	0.0988	0.4313	0.0057	1.0119	0.0327	0.0281	−0.0195
114	0.0997	0.4357	0.0071	1.0133	0.0369	0.0290	−0.0256
115	0.0988	0.4315	0.0058	1.0119	0.0329	0.0282	−0.0198
116	0.2065	0.9124	0.0272	1.0292	0.1525	0.0703	−0.1418
117	0.1009	0.4411	0.0092	1.0154	0.0425	0.0301	−0.0329

Output statistics

Obs	Residual	RStudent	Hat diag H	Cov ratio	DFFITS	DFBETAS	
						Intercept	DLLEIL1
118	0.3054	1.3488	0.0226	1.0169	0.2052	0.1015	−0.1877
119	−0.0893	−0.3987	0.0488	1.0579	−0.0903	−0.0335	0.0868
120	0.4085	1.8230	0.0369	1.0207	0.3570	0.1467	−0.3387
121	0.2089	0.9289	0.0389	1.0415	0.1869	0.0753	−0.1778
122	0.4048	1.7910	0.0207	1.0045	0.2601	0.1333	−0.2357
123	0.3022	1.3276	0.0123	1.0068	0.1484	0.0933	−0.1242
124	0.3040	1.3393	0.0177	1.0121	0.1799	0.0979	−0.1601
125	0.3949	1.7313	0.0038	0.9891	0.1068	0.1031	0.0173
126	0.5943	2.6247	0.0040	0.9615	0.1666	0.1541	0.0472
127	−0.007403	−0.0323	0.0054	1.0130	−0.0024	−0.0018	−0.0014
128	−0.006813	−0.0297	0.0048	1.0123	−0.0021	−0.0017	−0.0010
129	0.3921	1.7210	0.0061	0.9916	0.1347	0.0957	0.0846
130	0.0921	0.4023	0.0060	1.0124	0.0314	0.0224	0.0196
131	0.0938	0.4093	0.0043	1.0106	0.0269	0.0238	0.0102
132	0.0916	0.4003	0.0068	1.0131	0.0330	0.0220	0.0223
133	−0.008324	−0.0363	0.0067	1.0143	−0.0030	−0.0020	−0.0020
134	−0.006676	−0.0291	0.0047	1.0122	−0.0020	−0.0017	−0.0009
135	0.0960	0.4188	0.0037	1.0099	0.0256	0.0256	−0.0026
136	−0.0109	−0.0477	0.0120	1.0197	−0.0053	−0.0025	−0.0044
137	−0.1061	−0.4629	0.0042	1.0101	−0.0302	−0.0269	−0.0109
138	−0.005559	−0.0242	0.0039	1.0115	−0.0015	−0.0014	−0.0004
139	−0.1040	−0.4536	0.0037	1.0097	−0.0277	−0.0277	0.0028
140	−0.2045	−0.8930	0.0037	1.0052	−0.0544	−0.0540	−0.0010
141	−0.005031	−0.0219	0.0038	1.0113	−0.0013	−0.0013	−0.0002
142	0.0934	0.4076	0.0046	1.0109	0.0277	0.0234	0.0124
143	−0.003469	−0.0151	0.0039	1.0114	−0.0009	−0.0009	0.0002
144	−0.008117	−0.0354	0.0064	1.0139	−0.0028	−0.0020	−0.0018
145	−0.1091	−0.4769	0.0080	1.0139	−0.0428	−0.0257	−0.0314
146	−0.2040	−0.8907	0.0037	1.0053	−0.0545	−0.0545	0.0055
147	−0.007526	−0.0328	0.0056	1.0131	−0.0025	−0.0018	−0.0014
148	−0.1080	−0.4717	0.0062	1.0121	−0.0373	−0.0262	−0.0237
149	0.0960	0.4188	0.0037	1.0099	0.0256	0.0256	−0.0026
150	−0.006970	−0.0304	0.0050	1.0125	−0.0021	−0.0017	−0.0011
151	−0.003987	−0.0174	0.0037	1.0112	−0.0011	−0.0011	0.0001
152	0.0940	0.4102	0.0042	1.0104	0.0265	0.0239	0.0089
153	−0.001018	−0.004444	0.0060	1.0135	−0.0003	−0.0003	0.0002
154	−0.3020	−1.3218	0.0049	0.9993	−0.0924	−0.0847	0.0453
155	−0.1070	−0.4669	0.0050	1.0109	−0.0330	−0.0266	−0.0167
156	−0.1045	−0.4557	0.0037	1.0096	−0.0277	−0.0276	−0.0003
157	−0.1060	−0.4623	0.0042	1.0101	−0.0299	−0.0270	−0.0100
158	−0.1050	−0.4579	0.0037	1.0097	−0.0281	−0.0274	−0.0035
159	−0.1069	−0.4667	0.0049	1.0108	−0.0328	−0.0266	−0.0164
160	−0.005449	−0.0238	0.0039	1.0114	−0.0015	−0.0014	−0.0003
161	−0.003013	−0.0131	0.0041	1.0116	−0.0008	−0.0008	0.0003
162	0.0955	0.4166	0.0037	1.0099	0.0254	0.0252	0.0003
163	−0.2020	−0.8827	0.0048	1.0065	−0.0614	−0.0565	0.0298
164	−0.004964	−0.0216	0.0037	1.0113	−0.0013	−0.0013	−0.0002
165	−0.1020	−0.4453	0.0048	1.0109	−0.0310	−0.0285	0.0151
166	−0.005944	−0.0259	0.0041	1.0117	−0.0017	−0.0015	−0.0006
167	−0.2050	−0.8950	0.0037	1.0052	−0.0549	−0.0535	−0.0067
168	0.0965	0.4209	0.0039	1.0100	0.0262	0.0260	−0.0055
169	−0.1059	−0.4622	0.0041	1.0101	−0.0298	−0.0270	−0.0098
170	−0.006407	−0.0279	0.0045	1.0120	−0.0019	−0.0016	−0.0008
171	−0.1050	−0.4578	0.0037	1.0097	−0.0281	−0.0274	−0.0034

Output statistics

Obs	Residual	RStudent	Hat diag H	Cov ratio	DFFITS	DFBETAS Intercept	DLLEIL1
172	−0.003023	−0.0132	0.0041	1.0116	−0.0008	−0.0008	0.0003
173	−0.006394	−0.0279	0.0045	1.0120	−0.0019	−0.0016	−0.0008
174	−0.1054	−0.4599	0.0039	1.0098	−0.0287	−0.0272	−0.0065
175	−0.1045	−0.4557	0.0037	1.0096	−0.0277	−0.0276	−0.0002
176	−0.1049	−0.4577	0.0037	1.0097	−0.0281	−0.0274	−0.0033
177	−0.006364	−0.0278	0.0044	1.0120	−0.0019	−0.0016	−0.0008
178	−0.1078	−0.4706	0.0059	1.0118	−0.0362	−0.0263	−0.0221
179	−0.003987	−0.0174	0.0037	1.0112	−0.0011	−0.0011	0.0001
180	−0.1082	−0.4726	0.0065	1.0124	−0.0382	−0.0261	−0.0251
181	−0.2040	−0.8907	0.0037	1.0053	−0.0545	−0.0545	0.0055
182	0.0955	0.4167	0.0037	1.0099	0.0254	0.0252	0.0001
183	−0.006768	−0.0295	0.0048	1.0123	−0.0020	−0.0017	−0.0010
184	−0.3081	−1.3499	0.0064	1.0003	−0.1083	−0.0747	−0.0704
185	−0.1044	−0.4556	0.0037	1.0096	−0.0277	−0.0276	−0.0001
186	−0.1063	−0.4637	0.0044	1.0103	−0.0307	−0.0269	−0.0120
187	−0.007158	−0.0312	0.0052	1.0127	−0.0023	−0.0018	−0.0012
188	−0.1062	−0.4635	0.0043	1.0102	−0.0306	−0.0269	−0.0118
189	−0.1044	−0.4555	0.0037	1.0096	−0.0277	−0.0276	−0.0001
190	−0.1071	−0.4676	0.0051	1.0110	−0.0335	−0.0265	−0.0177
191	−0.004877	−0.0213	0.0037	1.0112	−0.0013	−0.0013	−0.0001
192	−0.1053	−0.4594	0.0038	1.0098	−0.0285	−0.0272	−0.0058
193	−0.006637	−0.0290	0.0047	1.0122	−0.0020	−0.0017	−0.0009
194	−0.1040	−0.4536	0.0037	1.0097	−0.0277	−0.0277	0.0028
195	−0.1044	−0.4555	0.0037	1.0096	−0.0277	−0.0276	0.0000
196	−0.1057	−0.4613	0.0040	1.0100	−0.0294	−0.0271	−0.0085
197	0.0943	0.4112	0.0040	1.0103	0.0262	0.0241	0.0076
198	−0.1057	−0.4612	0.0040	1.0099	−0.0293	−0.0271	−0.0085
199	−0.1066	−0.4651	0.0046	1.0105	−0.0317	−0.0267	−0.0142
200	−0.002256	−0.009842	0.0046	1.0122	−0.0007	−0.0006	0.0003
201	−0.1040	−0.4536	0.0037	1.0097	−0.0277	−0.0277	0.0028
202	−0.003987	−0.0174	0.0037	1.0112	−0.0011	−0.0011	0.0001
203	−0.005286	−0.0230	0.0038	1.0114	−0.0014	−0.0014	−0.0003
204	−0.005713	−0.0249	0.0040	1.0115	−0.0016	−0.0015	−0.0005
205	−0.1036	−0.4517	0.0038	1.0098	−0.0280	−0.0279	0.0055
206	0.0990	0.4325	0.0061	1.0122	0.0338	0.0284	−0.0212
207	−0.004421	−0.0193	0.0037	1.0112	−0.0012	−0.0012	0.0000
208	−0.003987	−0.0174	0.0037	1.0112	−0.0011	−0.0011	0.0001
209	−0.2053	−0.8965	0.0038	1.0053	−0.0556	−0.0532	−0.0108
210	0.0964	0.4207	0.0038	1.0100	0.0261	0.0260	−0.0052
211	−0.005283	−0.0230	0.0038	1.0114	−0.0014	−0.0014	−0.0003
212	−0.1053	−0.4592	0.0038	1.0098	−0.0285	−0.0272	−0.0055
213	0.0960	0.4188	0.0037	1.0099	0.0256	0.0256	−0.0026
214	−0.005276	−0.0230	0.0038	1.0113	−0.0014	−0.0014	−0.0003
215	−0.1031	−0.4499	0.0040	1.0100	−0.0286	−0.0281	0.0082
216	−0.004846	−0.0211	0.0037	1.0112	−0.0013	−0.0013	−0.0001
217	−0.006126	−0.0267	0.0043	1.0118	−0.0017	−0.0016	−0.0006
218	−0.1070	−0.4669	0.0050	1.0109	−0.0330	−0.0266	−0.0167
219	−0.1057	−0.4610	0.0040	1.0099	−0.0292	−0.0271	−0.0081
220	−0.005672	−0.0247	0.0040	1.0115	−0.0016	−0.0015	−0.0004
221	−0.004407	−0.0192	0.0037	1.0112	−0.0012	−0.0012	0.0000
222	−0.1057	−0.4610	0.0040	1.0099	−0.0292	−0.0271	−0.0080
223	0.0935	0.4080	0.0045	1.0108	0.0275	0.0235	0.0119
224	−0.004818	−0.0210	0.0037	1.0112	−0.0013	−0.0013	−0.0001
225	−0.005231	−0.0228	0.0038	1.0113	−0.0014	−0.0014	−0.0003

Obs	Residual	RStudent	Hat diag H	Cov ratio	DFFITS	DFBETAS	
						Intercept	DLLEIL1
226	−0.1048	−0.4572	0.0037	1.0097	−0.0279	−0.0274	−0.0025
227	−0.009326	−0.0408	0.0084	1.0160	−0.0038	−0.0022	−0.0028
228	−0.1060	−0.4626	0.0042	1.0101	−0.0300	−0.0270	−0.0104
229	−0.006418	−0.0280	0.0045	1.0120	−0.0019	−0.0016	−0.0008
230	−0.1064	−0.4643	0.0045	1.0104	−0.0311	−0.0268	−0.0129
231	−0.006790	−0.0296	0.0048	1.0123	−0.0021	−0.0017	−0.0010
232	0.0944	0.4119	0.0040	1.0102	0.0259	0.0243	0.0067
233	−0.2060	−0.8996	0.0042	1.0056	−0.0581	−0.0525	−0.0196
234	0.0960	0.4188	0.0037	1.0099	0.0256	0.0256	−0.0026
235	0.0933	0.4069	0.0048	1.0110	0.0281	0.0233	0.0133
236	−0.1067	−0.4658	0.0047	1.0106	−0.0321	−0.0267	−0.0151
237	−0.004768	−0.0208	0.0037	1.0112	−0.0013	−0.0012	−0.0001
238	−0.006709	−0.0293	0.0047	1.0122	−0.0020	−0.0017	−0.0009
239	−0.1036	−0.4519	0.0038	1.0098	−0.0280	−0.0279	0.0053
240	0.0960	0.4188	0.0037	1.0099	0.0256	0.0256	−0.0026
241	−0.1040	−0.4536	0.0037	1.0097	−0.0277	−0.0277	0.0028
242	0.0964	0.4205	0.0038	1.0100	0.0261	0.0260	−0.0049
243	−0.004375	−0.0191	0.0037	1.0112	−0.0012	−0.0012	0.0000
244	−0.1055	−0.4604	0.0039	1.0099	−0.0289	−0.0271	−0.0072
245	−0.003987	−0.0174	0.0037	1.0112	−0.0011	−0.0011	0.0001
246	−0.003600	−0.0157	0.0038	1.0113	−0.0010	−0.0010	0.0002
247	−0.004374	−0.0191	0.0037	1.0112	−0.0012	−0.0012	0.0000
248	−0.005916	−0.0258	0.0041	1.0116	−0.0017	−0.0015	−0.0005
249	−0.003217	−0.0140	0.0040	1.0115	−0.0009	−0.0009	0.0002
250	−0.003601	−0.0157	0.0038	1.0113	−0.0010	−0.0010	0.0002
251	−0.002828	−0.0123	0.0042	1.0117	−0.0008	−0.0008	0.0003
252	−0.1048	−0.4569	0.0037	1.0097	−0.0279	−0.0274	−0.0021
253	−0.003214	−0.0140	0.0040	1.0115	−0.0009	−0.0009	0.0002
254	−0.006302	−0.0275	0.0044	1.0119	−0.0018	−0.0016	−0.0007
255	−0.003602	−0.0157	0.0038	1.0113	−0.0010	−0.0010	0.0002
256	−0.0699	−0.3490	0.2390	1.3227	−0.1956	−0.0439	0.1941
257	0.3244	1.5555	0.1685	1.1901	0.7003	0.1734	−0.6926
258	**0.5829**	**2.6159**	**0.0357**	**0.9934**	**0.5031**	**0.1126**	**0.4763**
259	**2.9832**	**22.3554**	**0.0337**	**0.1270**	**4.1771**	**0.9740**	**3.9420**
260	0.0873	0.3833	0.0172	1.0240	0.0508	0.0188	0.0450
261	**−0.5105**	**−2.2552**	**0.0110**	**0.9811**	**−0.2380**	**−0.1173**	**−0.1940**
262	**−0.8080**	**−3.6124**	**0.0062**	**0.9218**	**−0.2861**	**−0.2004**	**−0.1828**
263	−0.2068	−0.9035	0.0048	1.0062	−0.0627	−0.0517	−0.0300
264	−0.2080	−0.9092	0.0061	1.0075	−0.0715	−0.0505	−0.0452
265	−0.005563	−0.0243	0.0039	1.0115	−0.0015	−0.0014	−0.0004
266	0.0941	0.4103	0.0041	1.0104	0.0265	0.0240	0.0088
267	−0.003987	−0.0174	0.0037	1.0112	−0.0011	−0.0011	0.0001
268	−0.2094	−0.9169	0.0086	1.0099	−0.0856	−0.0491	−0.0648
269	−0.2101	−0.9206	0.0101	1.0114	−0.0931	−0.0484	−0.0742
270	0.1903	0.8332	0.0091	1.0115	0.0799	0.0443	0.0617
271	−0.4070	−1.7862	0.0050	0.9888	−0.1264	−0.1017	−0.0644
272	−0.2077	−0.9080	0.0058	1.0072	−0.0694	−0.0508	−0.0420
273	−0.4073	−1.7879	0.0053	0.9891	−0.1309	−0.1010	−0.0726

Sum of residuals	0
Sum of squared residuals	14.14963
Predicted residual SS (PRESS)	14.94205

The SAS regression diagnostics report the same large studentized residuals, RStudent, Cov ratio, DFFITS, and DFBETAS in the DUE and DLLEIL1 1999–11/2021 regressions as was reported in the 1959–11/2021. The same results are present in the simple linear regression model of DUE and DLWkUNCL1 and in the multiple regression models of DUE and the DLLEIL1 and DLWKuNCLL1 variables, not shown to conserve space. The application of robust regression is appropriate for the DUE, DLLEIL1, and DLWkUNCLL1 variables during the 1999–2021 period.

The application of robust regression is appropriate for the DUE, DLLEIL1, and DLWkUNCLL1 variables during the 1999–11/2021 period. The SAS robust regression analysis of the DUE and DLWkUNCLL1 relationship, using the Huber weighting function, reported the expected negative and highly statistically significant coefficient on the DLLEIL1 variable during the 1999–11/2021 period, as was the case for the 1959–11/2021 period.

SAS PS M-Huber DUE DLLEIL1 Robust Regression PJD TCB 110521
The ROBUSTREG Procedure

Model information	
Data set	WORK.REMZTT
Dependent variable	DUE
Number of independent variables	1
Number of observations	271
Missing values	2
Method	M estimation

Parameter ESTIMATES

Parameter	DF	Estimate	Standard error	95% confidence limits		Chi-square	Pr > Chi-square
Intercept	1	−0.0039	0.0062	−0.0161	0.0084	0.38	0.5373
DLLEIL1	1	−3.0361	0.6204	−4.2521	−1.8202	23.95	<0.0001
Scale	1	0.1183					

Diagnostics

Obs	Mahalanobis distance	Robust MCD distance	Leverage	Standardized robust residual	Outlier
16	1.1741	2.4940	*	−0.2438	
21	1.1905	2.5233	*	−0.2480	
23	1.5463	3.1579	*	0.5059	
25	1.2351	2.6028	*	0.5861	
26	1.5946	3.2440	*	−1.1978	

Diagnostics

Obs	Mahalanobis distance	Robust MCD distance	Leverage	Standardized robust residual	Outlier
27	1.1486	2.4485	*	−0.2372	
32	2.0015	3.9698	*	−0.4570	
107	1.1204	2.3982	*	−0.2299	
108	1.1309	2.4170	*	−0.2326	
109	1.2462	2.6227	*	−0.2624	
110	1.5776	3.2137	*	0.4979	
114	2.5180	4.8911	*	1.1011	
115	1.2198	2.5756	*	0.5901	
116	2.2611	4.4329	*	2.0130	
117	3.4906	6.6257	*	−1.6865	
118	2.9962	5.7440	*	2.6691	
119	3.0828	5.8985	*	0.9555	
120	2.1399	4.2167	*	2.8898	
121	1.5276	3.1246	*	2.2020	
122	1.9465	3.8717	*	2.0941	
123	0.1637	0.1079		3.4836	*
124	0.2952	0.1266		5.2088	*
127	0.8054	1.0366		3.6490	*
134	1.4958	2.2680	*	0.4444	
254	7.9708	14.6168	*	−2.8414	
255	6.6717	12.2996	*	0.8761	
256	2.9382	4.8407	*	5.8901	*
257	2.8482	4.6801	*	26.1624	*
258	1.9124	3.0110	*	1.3974	
259	1.4059	2.1076		−3.8070	*
260	0.8290	1.0787		−6.4926	*
269	0.5910	0.6542		−3.1714	*
271	0.6653	0.7867		−3.1522	*

Diagnostics summary

Observation type	Proportion	Cutoff
Outlier	0.0332	3.0000
Leverage	0.0959	2.2414

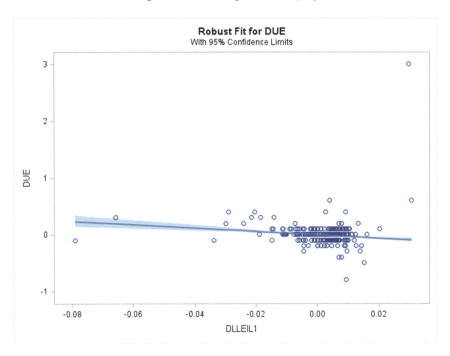

Goodness-of-fit	
Statistic	Value
R-square	0.0237
AICR	326.4605
BICR	335.0806
Deviance	4.5290

The SAS M-estimation robust regression analysis of the DUE and DLLEIL1 relationship, using the Huber weighting function, reported the expected negative and highly statistically significant coefficient on the DLLEIL1 variable during the 1999–11/2021 period, as was the case for the 1959–11/2021 period.

SAS PS M-Bisquare Robust Regression
The ROBUSTREG Procedure

Model information	
Data set	WORK.REMZTT
Dependent variable	DUE

Model information	
Number of independent variables	1
Number of observations	271
Missing values	2
Method	M estimation

Parameter estimates

Parameter	DF	Estimate	Standard error	95% confidence limits		Chi-square	Pr > Chi-square
Intercept	1	−0.0033	0.0061	−0.0154	0.0087	0.30	0.5847
DLLEIL1	1	−4.2494	0.6082	−5.4414	−3.0574	48.82	<0.0001
Scale	1	0.1090					

Diagnostics

Obs	Mahalanobis distance	Robust MCD distance	Leverage	Standardized robust residual	Outlier
16	1.1741	2.4940	*	−0.3890	
21	1.1905	2.5233	*	−0.3955	
23	1.5463	3.1579	*	0.3829	
25	1.2351	2.6028	*	0.5048	
26	1.5946	3.2440	*	−1.4714	
27	1.1486	2.4485	*	−0.3791	
32	2.0015	3.9698	*	−0.7130	
107	1.1204	2.3982	*	−0.3680	
108	1.1309	2.4170	*	−0.3721	
109	1.2462	2.6227	*	−0.4173	
110	1.5776	3.2137	*	0.3707	
114	2.5180	4.8911	*	0.9202	
115	1.2198	2.5756	*	0.5107	
116	2.2611	4.4329	*	1.9385	
117	3.4906	6.6257	*	−2.2137	
118	2.9962	5.7440	*	2.5684	
119	3.0828	5.8985	*	0.6991	
120	2.1399	4.2167	*	2.9036	
121	1.5276	3.1246	*	2.2256	
122	1.9465	3.8717	*	2.0616	
123	0.1637	0.1079		3.8055	*
124	0.2952	0.1266		5.6924	*
127	0.8054	1.0366		4.0567	*
134	1.4958	2.2680	*	0.6562	
254	7.9708	14.6168	*	−3.9677	*
255	6.6717	12.2996	*	0.2117	
256	2.9382	4.8407	*	6.7272	*

Diagnostics

Obs	Mahalanobis distance	Robust MCD distance	Leverage	Standardized robust residual	Outlier
257	2.8482	4.6801	*	28.7167	*
258	1.9124	3.0110	*	1.7370	
259	1.4059	2.1076		−3.9675	*
260	0.8290	1.0787		−6.9464	*
269	0.5910	0.6542		−3.3688	*
271	0.6653	0.7867		−3.3397	*

Diagnostics summary

Observation type	Proportion	Cutoff
Outlier	0.0369	3.0000
Leverage	0.0959	2.2414

Goodness-of-fit

Statistic	Value
R-square	0.0390
AICR	257.1846
BICR	265.8445
Deviance	3.0236

The application of robust regression is appropriate for the DUE, DLLEIL1, and DLWkUNCLL1 variables during the 1999–11/2021 period. The SAS robust regression analysis of the DUE and DLLELL1 relationship, using the Tukey Bisquare weighting function, reported the expected negative and highly statistically significant coefficient on the DLLEIL1 variable during the 1999–11/2021 period, as was the case for the 1959–11/2021 period. Similar results are found for the Hampel and Fair weighting functions, but not reported because of space limitations.

What do we find for the DUE and DLWkUNCLL1 robust regression modeling during the 1999–11/2021 period? We report nothing of statistical significance. The sign of the coefficients are often incorrect; negative. We report the Huber application of the M-estimation during the 1999–11/2021 period.

SAS PS M-Huber Robust Regression
The ROBUSTREG Procedure

Model information

Model information	
Data set	WORK.REMZTT
Dependent variable	DUE
Number of independent variables	1
Number of observations	271
Missing values	2
Method	M estimation

Parameter estimates

Parameter	DF	Estimate	Standard error	95% confidence limits		Chi-square	Pr > Chi-square
Intercept	1	−0.0083	0.0067	−0.0214	0.0048	1.53	0.2160
DLWkUNCLL1	1	−0.0068	0.0392	−0.0835	0.0700	0.03	0.8631
Scale	1	0.1359					

Diagnostics

Obs	Mahalanobis distance	Robust MCD distance	Leverage	Standardized robust residual	Outlier
22	0.6388	2.8025	*	0.0664	
25	0.5406	2.3814	*	0.8013	
32	0.6210	2.7261	*	0.0662	
35	0.6695	2.8026	*	0.7910	
80	1.3399	5.8060	*	0.0723	
81	0.8371	3.5208	*	0.0538	
118	0.5825	2.5611	*	3.0091	*
120	0.2565	1.1645		3.0063	*
121	0.5167	2.2792	*	2.2727	
123	0.4047	1.6684		3.0007	*
124	0.0086	0.0286		4.4757	*
127	0.0207	0.0231		3.0039	*
166	0.5356	2.3602	*	0.8013	
167	0.7577	3.1805	*	−0.6813	
177	0.6691	2.9320	*	0.0666	
225	0.6055	2.5286	*	0.0558	
254	14.7384	63.2067	*	−0.5496	
255	2.6254	11.3130	*	2.2906	
256	3.5235	15.0297	*	4.4458	*
257	2.4730	10.5289	*	22.1139	*

Diagnostics

Obs	Mahalanobis distance	Robust MCD distance	Leverage	Standardized robust residual	Outlier
258	0.6623	2.7718	*	0.7911	
259	1.7653	7.4972	*	−3.6331	*
260	1.0600	4.4756	*	−5.8345	*
263	0.5249	2.3143	*	0.0654	
266	0.6374	2.6652	*	−1.4161	
267	1.4605	6.1915	*	−1.4231	
268	1.5888	6.7411	*	1.5190	
271	0.6017	2.5121	*	−2.8874	

Diagnostics summary

Observation type	Proportion	Cutoff
Outlier	0.0332	3.0000
Leverage	0.0886	2.2414

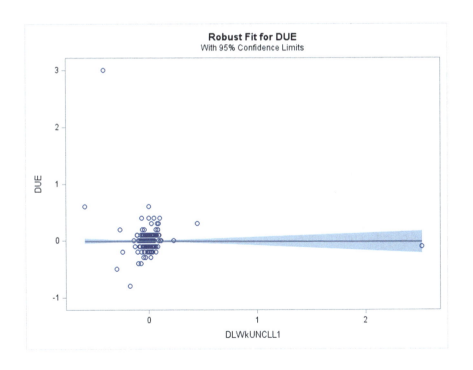

Goodness-of-fit	
Statistic	Value
R-square	0.0001
AICR	272.5300
BICR	281.4879
Deviance	4.9923

The SAS robust regression analysis of the DUE and DLWkUNCLL1 relationship, using the Huber weighting function, reported the expected positive coefficient negative, -0.007, with a p-level of 0.528, and not statistically significant coefficient during the 1999–11/2021 period, as was the case for the 1959–11/2021 period. Similar results were found with the M-estimates with Tukey Bisquare, Hampel, and Fair weighting function and are not reported.

10.5 Robust Regression of the Modeling the PJD Unemployment Rate, TCB LEI 11052021, 1999–11/2021

The SAS robust regression analysis of the DUE, DLEIL1, and DLWkUNCLL1 relationship during the 1999–11/2021 period, as was the case for the 1959–11/2021 period.

SAS PS S,MM-Tukey Robust Regression PJD TCB 110521
The ROBUSTREG Procedure

Model information	
Data set	WORK.REMZTT
Dependent variable	DUE
Number of independent variables	1
Number of observations	271
Missing values	2
Method	S estimation

S profile	
Total number of observations	271
Number of coefficients	2
Subset size	2
Chi function	Tukey

S profile	
K0	7.0410
Breakdown value	0.0570
Efficiency	0.9900

Parameter estimates

Parameter	DF	Estimate	Standard error	95% confidence limits		Chi-square	Pr > Chi-square
Intercept	1	−0.0044	0.0067	−0.0176	0.0087	0.44	0.5087
DLLEIL1	1	−3.3710	0.7144	−4.7712	−1.9707	22.26	<0.0001
Scale	0	0.1293					

Diagnostics summary

Observation type	Proportion	Cutoff
Outlier	0.0258	3.0000

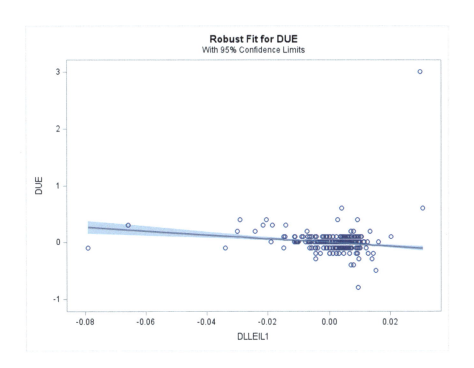

Robust Fit for DUE
With 95% Confidence Limits

Goodness-of-fit	
Statistic	Value
R-square	0.0574
Deviance	0.0167

SAS PS S,MM-Tukey Robust Regression PJD TCB 110521
The ROBUSTREG Procedure

Model information	
Data set	WORK.REMZTT
Dependent variable	DUE
Number of independent variables	1
Number of observations	271
Missing values	2
Method	MM-estimation

Profile for the initial LTS estimate	
Total number of observations	271
Number of squares minimized	204
Number of coefficients	2
Highest possible breakdown value	0.2509

MM profile	
Chi function	Tukey
K1	7.0410
Efficiency	0.9900

Parameter estimates							
Parameter	DF	Estimate	Standard error	95% confidence limits		Chi-square	Pr > Chi-square
Intercept	1	−0.0046	0.0064	−0.0172	0.0080	0.52	0.4726
DLLEIL1	1	−3.6620	0.7071	−5.0479	−2.2762	26.82	<0.0001
Scale	0	0.1037					

Diagnostics summary		
Observation type	Proportion	Cutoff
Outlier	0.0443	3.0000

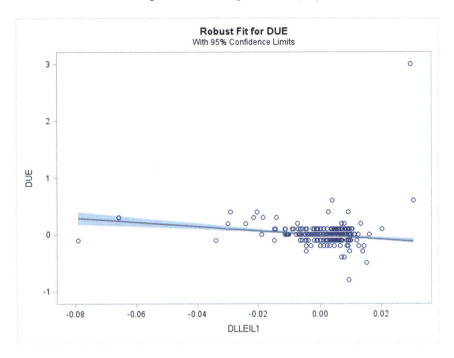

Goodness-of-fit	
Statistic	Value
R-square	0.0480
AICR	352.5818
BICR	360.3042
Deviance	3.7565

The SAS MM-estimation robust regression analysis of the DUE and DLLEIL1 relationship, using the Tukey Bisquare weighting function, reported the expected negative and highly statistically significant coefficient on the DLLEIL1 variable during the 1999–11/2021 period, as was the case for the 1959–11/2021 period.

SAS PS S,MM-Tukey Robust Regression PJD TCB 110521
The ROBUSTREG Procedure

Model information

Data set	WORK.REMZTT
Dependent variable	DUE
Number of independent variables	1
Number of observations	271
Missing values	2
Method	S estimation

S profile

Total number of observations	271
Number of coefficients	2
Subset size	2
Chi function	Tukey
K0	7.0410
Breakdown value	0.0570
Efficiency	0.9900

Parameter estimates

Parameter	DF	Estimate	Standard error	95% confidence limits		Chi-square	Pr > Chi-square
Intercept	1	−0.0074	0.0069	−0.0210	0.0061	1.15	0.2830
DLWkUNCLL1	1	0.0133	0.0418	−0.0685	0.0951	0.10	0.7498
Scale	0	0.1332					

Diagnostics summary

Observation type	Proportion	Cutoff
Outlier	0.0332	3.0000

Goodness-of-fit

Statistic	Value
R-square	0.0000
Deviance	0.0177

The SAS S-estimation robust regression analysis of the DUE and DLLEIL1 relationship, using the Tukey Bisquare weighting function, reported the expected positive, but not highly statistically significant coefficient on the DLWkUNCLL1 variable during the 1999–11/2021 period, as was the case for the 1959–11/2021 period.

SAS PS S,MM-Tukey Robust Regression PJD TCB 110521
The ROBUSTREG Procedure

Model information

Data set	WORK.REMZTT
Dependent variable	DUE
Number of independent variables	1
Number of observations	271
Missing values	2
Method	MM-estimation

Profile for the initial LTS estimate

Total number of observations	271
Number of squares minimized	204
Number of coefficients	2
Highest possible breakdown value	0.2509

MM profile

Chi function	Tukey
K1	7.0410
Efficiency	0.9900

Parameter estimates

Parameter	DF	Estimate	Standard error	95% confidence limits		Chi-square	Pr > Chi-square
Intercept	1	−0.0069	0.0065	−0.0195	0.0058	1.13	0.2875
DLWkUNCLL1	1	0.5806	0.1105	0.3640	0.7972	27.60	<0.0001
Scale	0	0.1046					

Diagnostics summary

Observation type	Proportion	Cutoff
Outlier	0.0480	3.0000

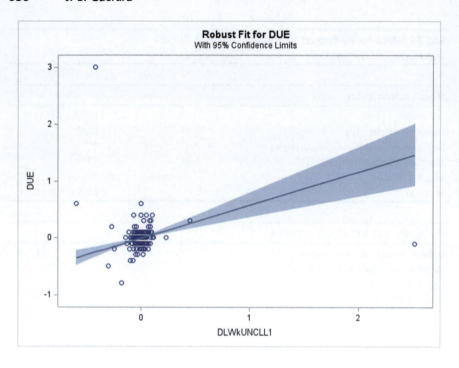

Goodness-of-fit	
Statistic	Value
R-square	0.0085
AICR	362.5106
BICR	370.2433
Deviance	3.9319

The SAS MM-estimation robust regression analysis of the DUE and DLLEIL1 relationship, using the Tukey Bisquare weighting function, reported the expected positive, but highly statistically significant coefficient on the DLWkUNCLL1 variable during the 1999–11/2021 period, as was the case for the 1959–11/2021 period.

We estimate two final S- and MM-estimates of the DUE multiple regressions of DLLEIL1 and DLWkUNCLL1 for the 1999–11/ 2021 period.

SAS PS S,MM-Tukey Robust Regression PJD TCB 110521
The ROBUSTREG Procedure

Model information

Data set	WORK.REMZTT
Dependent variable	DUE
Number of independent variables	2
Number of observations	271
Missing values	2
Method	S estimation

S profile

Total number of observations	271
Number of coefficients	3
Subset size	3
Chi function	Tukey
K0	7.0410
Breakdown value	0.0570
Efficiency	0.9900

Parameter estimates

Parameter	DF	Estimate	Standard error	95% confidence limits		Chi-square	Pr > Chi-square
Intercept	1	−0.0018	0.0067	−0.0149	0.0112	0.08	0.7831
DLLEIL1	1	−5.2092	0.9297	−7.0313	−3.3871	31.40	<0.0001
DLWkUNCLL1	1	−0.1843	0.0539	−0.2900	−0.0786	11.67	0.0006
Scale	0	0.1274					

Diagnostics

Obs	Mahalanobis distance	Robust MCD distance	Leverage	Standardized robust residual	Outlier
21	1.6514	2.9977	*	−0.4282	
22	0.8720	3.2515	*	−0.1428	
23	1.9762	3.4405	*	0.2572	
25	1.3156	3.1165	*	0.4685	
26	2.0268	3.5231	*	−1.3280	
32	2.2797	4.3493	*	−0.6113	
35	0.7001	3.1093	*	0.9284	
80	1.3568	6.9396	*	0.0661	
81	0.9345	4.3648	*	−0.0319	
89	0.9756	3.0740	*	0.6071	
108	1.7541	3.4737	*	−0.4488	
109	1.6540	2.9378	*	−0.4314	
110	1.8839	3.4020	*	0.2853	

Diagnostics

Obs	Mahalanobis distance	Robust MCD distance	Leverage	Standardized robust residual	Outlier
114	3.0814	5.2853	*	0.7151	
115	1.5511	2.7558	*	0.3828	
116	2.7628	4.7710	*	1.5945	
117	4.7293	8.0608	*	−2.1211	
118	3.6703	6.2407	*	2.1110	
119	3.9546	6.6365	*	0.4571	
120	2.7563	4.7024	*	2.3818	
121	1.7122	3.4481	*	1.9126	
122	2.5976	4.4913	*	1.6457	
123	0.4380	2.0440		3.1639	*
124	0.4049	0.5076		4.8861	*
127	1.1073	1.6635		3.5224	*
134	1.9138	2.8486	*	0.6228	
166	0.5807	2.9271	*	0.8863	
167	0.7996	3.8441	*	−0.7731	
177	0.8430	3.7866	*	0.1805	
225	1.1617	2.7442	*	0.3715	
254	15.0989	75.6567	*	−0.3520	
255	7.2591	14.8779	*	0.3227	
256	3.5851	17.1556	*	5.1010	*
257	2.9263	11.6463	*	24.1653	*
258	2.1336	3.7170	*	1.4629	
259	1.7814	8.5682	*	−3.7284	*
260	1.0670	5.1028	*	−6.1458	*
263	1.0258	3.4226	*	0.2943	
264	1.0009	2.9814	*	1.0909	
266	1.1815	2.8847	*	−1.1963	
267	1.5179	6.9666	*	−1.3342	
268	1.5948	7.7371	*	1.7304	

Diagnostics summary

Observation type	Proportion	Cutoff
Outlier	0.0258	3.0000
Leverage	0.1439	2.7162

Goodness-of-fit

Statistic	Value
R-square	0.0882
Deviance	0.0162

The SAS S-estimation robust regression analysis of the DUE and DLLEIL1 and WkUNCLL1 variables relationships, using the Tukey Bisquare weighting function, reported the expected negative, but highly statistically significant coefficient on the DLLEIL11 and the negative, but unexpected negative, but highly statistically significant coefficient on the

DLWkUNCLL1 variable during the 1999–11/2021 period, as was the case for the 1959–11/2021 period.

We estimate final MM-estimates of the DUE multiple regressions of DLLEIL1 and DLWkUNCLL1 for the 1999–11/ 2021 period.

SAS PS S,MM-Tukey Robust Regression PJD TCB 110521
The ROBUSTREG Procedure

Model information	
Data set	WORK.REMZTT
Dependent variable	DUE
Number of independent variables	2
Number of observations	271
Missing values	2
Method	MM-estimation

Profile for the initial LTS estimate	
Total number of observations	271
Number of squares minimized	204
Number of coefficients	3
Highest possible breakdown value	0.2509

MM profile	
Chi function	Tukey
K1	7.0410
Efficiency	0.9900

Parameter estimates

Parameter	DF	Estimate	Standard error	95% confidence limits		Chi-square	Pr > Chi-square
Intercept	1	−0.0024	0.0064	−0.0150	0.0102	0.14	0.7066
DLLEIL1	1	−5.2548	0.9017	−7.0222	−3.4875	33.96	<0.0001
DLWkUNCLL1	1	−0.1813	0.0521	−0.2835	−0.0792	12.11	0.0005
Scale	0	0.1040					

Diagnostics

Obs	Mahalanobis distance	Robust MCD distance	Leverage	Standardized robust residual	Outlier
21	1.6514	2.9977	*	−0.5235	

Diagnostics

Obs	Mahalanobis distance	Robust MCD distance	Leverage	Standardized robust residual	Outlier
22	0.8720	3.2515	*	−0.1756	
23	1.9762	3.4405	*	0.3131	
25	1.3156	3.1165	*	0.5716	
26	2.0268	3.5231	*	−1.6279	
32	2.2797	4.3493	*	−0.7541	
35	0.7001	3.1093	*	1.1486	
80	1.3568	6.9396	*	0.0770	
81	0.9345	4.3648	*	−0.0276	
89	0.9756	3.0740	*	0.7502	
108	1.7541	3.4737	*	−0.5476	
109	1.6540	2.9378	*	−0.5280	
110	1.8839	3.4020	*	0.3466	
114	3.0814	5.2853	*	0.8681	
115	1.5511	2.7558	*	0.4686	
116	2.7628	4.7710	*	1.9460	
117	4.7293	8.0608	*	−2.6068	
118	3.6703	6.2407	*	2.5744	
119	3.9546	6.6365	*	0.5503	
120	2.7563	4.7024	*	2.9114	
121	1.7122	3.4481	*	2.3383	
122	2.5976	4.4913	*	2.0117	
123	0.4380	2.0440		3.8822	*
124	0.4049	0.5076		5.9892	*
127	1.1073	1.6635		4.3221	*
134	1.9138	2.8486	*	0.7761	
152	0.7078	1.4012		−3.0672	*
166	0.5807	2.9271	*	1.0876	
167	0.7996	3.8441	*	−0.9353	
177	0.8430	3.7866	*	0.2234	
225	1.1617	2.7442	*	0.4688	
254	15.0989	75.6567	*	−0.5313	
255	7.2591	14.8779	*	0.3590	
256	3.5851	17.1556	*	6.2810	*
257	2.9263	11.6463	*	29.6153	*
258	2.1336	3.7170	*	1.8087	
259	1.7814	8.5682	*	−4.5437	*
260	1.0670	5.1028	*	−7.5092	*
263	1.0258	3.4226	*	0.3650	
264	1.0009	2.9814	*	1.3411	
266	1.1815	2.8847	*	−1.4504	
267	1.5179	6.9666	*	−1.6144	
268	1.5948	7.7371	*	2.1376	

Diagnostics

Obs	Mahalanobis distance	Robust MCD distance	Leverage	Standardized robust residual	Outlier
269	0.5933	1.9601		−3.6038	*
271	0.6920	2.7159		−3.6111	*

Diagnostics summary

Observation type	Proportion	Cutoff
Outlier	0.0369	3.0000
Leverage	0.1439	2.7162

Goodness-of-fit

Statistic	Value
R-square	0.0707
AICR	344.4279
BICR	356.1080
Deviance	3.6732

The SAS MM-estimation robust regression analysis of the DUE and DLLEIL1 and WkUNCLL1 variables relationships, using the Tukey Bisquare weighting function, reported the expected negative, but highly statistically significant coefficient on the DLLEIL11 and the negative, but unexpected negative, but highly statistically significant coefficient on the DLWkUNCLL1 variable during the 1999–11/2021 period, as was the case for the 1959–11/2021 period.

10.6 Automatic Time Series Modeling and Forecasting the PJD Unemployment Rate, the Application of OxMetrics to TCB LEI 11052021

Let us apply the OxMetrics automatic time series modeling and forecasting models to TCB LEI database as of November 5, 2021. Dhrymes (2017) used OxMetrics with TCB LEI data for the 1959–2015 period, using the methodology of the Hendry and Doornik (2014) and saturation variables. Castle and Hendry (2019) continued the analysis of breaks and saturation variables. The reader is referred to the "Appendix: The Theory and Estimation of Regression, Time Series Analysis, and Causality Modeling of the Unemployment Rate and the Leading Economic Indicators (LEI)," which assumes no knowledge of statistics and walks the reader through simple linear and multiple regression, traditional Box and Jenkins time series modeling, the Hendry and his colleagues and their methodology of time series model with breaks, saturation variables, and to Granger causality modeling.

The reader may be reminded to return to Chapter 7 to see how we developed the automatic time series modeling work of Hendry and Doornik (2014) and Castle and Doornik (2019). Normally, one starts with an AR1 model, a first autoregressive model in which the current value of the time series equals the value last period plus some random error term. An AR1 model is a benchmark, as could be a no-change model. We model the unemployment rate for those unemployed 15 weeks or more, denoted as UER. Dhrymes (2017) use OxMetrics in his forecasting chapter using the TCB LEI and weekly unemployment claims data to forecast real GDP. We model the UER with an AR1 model to serve as a benchmark.

```
Ox Professional version 8.20 (Windows_64/U) (C) J.A. Doornik, 1994-2019

---- PcGive 15.20 session started at 5:40:12 on 15-11-2021 ----
```

We model the UER with an estimated AR1 model to serve as a forecasting benchmark. The estimated AR1 is shown in Eq. (1) for the 1959–11/2021 period (Fig. 10.1).

```
EQ(1) Modelling A0M044 by OLS
    The dataset is: C:\JBG\JGResearch\Palgrave Business Cycles\JG TCBData 11052021.csv
        The estimation sample is: 1959(2) - 2021(9)

                    Coefficient  Std.Error  t-value  t-prob Part.R^2
A0M044_1               0.986886   0.005789     170.  0.0000   0.9749
Constant               0.0126840    0.01331    0.953  0.3409   0.0012
Trend               3.52009e-05  2.999e-05     1.17  0.2409   0.0018

sigma                  0.160055  RSS               19.1875524
R^2                    0.979835  F(2,749) =    1.82e+04 [0.000]**
Adj.R^2                0.979781  log-likelihood       312.305
no. of observations         752  no. of parameters         3
mean(A0M044)            1.96051  se(A0M044)           1.12561

AR 1-7 test:      F(7,742)  =      9.1274 [0.0000]**
ARCH 1-7 test:    F(7,738)  =      0.71651 [0.6581]
Normality test:   Chi^2(2)  =      3168.4 [0.0000]**
Hetero test:      F(4,747)  =      2.7767 [0.0261]*
Hetero-X test:    F(5,746)  =      2.2194 [0.0506]
RESET23 test:     F(2,747)  =      0.45354 [0.6356]
```

The estimated AR1 model, Eq. (1) produces a Residual Sum of Squares (RSS) is 19.19 and its sigma, standard error, is 0.161. The model error terms are non-random, see the Normality test criteria. The model is not adequately fitted.

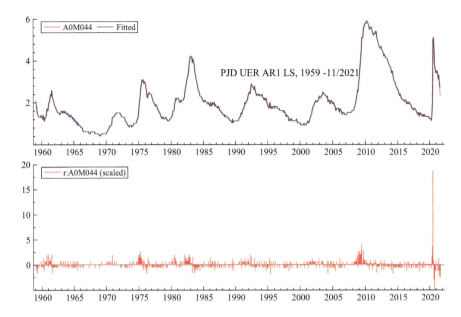

Fig. 10.1   Model UER AR1 LS

We model the UER with an estimated AR1 model and estimated impulse indicator saturation (IIS) variables is shown in Eq. (2) (Fig. 10.2).

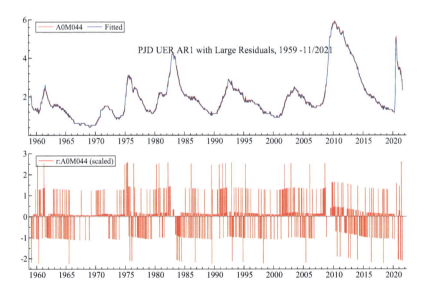

Fig. 10.2   Model UER AR1 large residuals

EQ(2) Modelling A0M044 by OLS
C:\JBG\JGResearch\Palgrave Business Cycles\JG TCBData 11052021.csv
The estimation sample is: 1959(2) - 2021(9)

	Coefficient	Std.Error	t-value	t-prob	Part.R^2
A0M044_1	0.993571	0.001448	686.	0.0000	0.9985
I:1959(4)	-0.288428	0.08484	-3.40	0.0007	0.0160
I:1960(10)	0.309001	0.08482	3.64	0.0003	0.0184
I:1961(1)	0.310287	0.08483	3.66	0.0003	0.0185
I:1961(7)	0.314787	0.08486	3.71	0.0002	0.0190
I:1961(8)	-0.283284	0.08488	-3.34	0.0009	0.0155
I:1970(12)	0.306429	0.08481	3.61	0.0003	0.0181
I:1975(1)	0.309001	0.08482	3.64	0.0003	0.0184
I:1975(2)	0.310929	0.08483	3.67	0.0003	0.0186
I:1975(4)	0.414144	0.08486	4.88	0.0000	0.0325
I:1976(4)	-0.283284	0.08488	-3.34	0.0009	0.0155
I:1980(7)	0.310287	0.08483	3.66	0.0003	0.0185
I:1982(2)	0.314144	0.08486	3.70	0.0002	0.0190
I:1982(5)	0.218001	0.08489	2.57	0.0104	0.0092
I:1982(9)	0.221216	0.08493	2.60	0.0094	0.0095
I:1982(10)	0.322502	0.08495	3.80	0.0002	0.0199
I:1982(11)	0.224431	0.08498	2.64	0.0084	0.0097
I:1982(12)	0.225716	0.08500	2.66	0.0081	0.0098
I:1983(4)	-0.272998	0.08502	-3.21	0.0014	0.0143
I:1983(5)	0.225073	0.08499	2.65	0.0083	0.0098
I:1983(8)	-0.274927	0.08499	-3.23	0.0013	0.0145
I:1992(5)	0.315430	0.08487	3.72	0.0002	0.0191
I:1992(6)	0.217359	0.08489	2.56	0.0107	0.0092
I:1995(6)	-0.287142	0.08485	-3.38	0.0008	0.0159
I:2004(4)	-0.285213	0.08486	-3.36	0.0008	0.0157
I:2008(10)	0.314787	0.08486	3.71	0.0002	0.0190
I:2008(12)	0.416073	0.08487	4.90	0.0000	0.0328
I:2009(1)	0.218644	0.08490	2.58	0.0102	0.0093
I:2009(2)	0.419930	0.08492	4.95	0.0000	0.0333
I:2009(3)	0.322502	0.08495	3.80	0.0002	0.0199
I:2009(4)	0.324431	0.08498	3.82	0.0001	0.0201
I:2009(5)	0.426359	0.08501	5.02	0.0000	0.0343
I:2009(6)	0.628931	0.08505	7.40	0.0000	0.0716
I:2009(9)	0.432788	0.08512	5.08	0.0000	0.0352
I:2011(10)	-0.265283	0.08516	-3.12	0.0019	0.0135
I:2014(4)	-0.277498	0.08495	-3.27	0.0011	0.0148
I:2020(5)	0.307072	0.08481	3.62	0.0003	0.0182
I:2020(6)	0.609001	0.08482	7.18	0.0000	0.0678
I:2020(7)	3.01286	0.08485	35.5	0.0000	0.6401
I:2020(9)	-0.467212	0.08512	-5.49	0.0000	0.0408
I:2020(10)	-0.770426	0.08506	-9.06	0.0000	0.1037
I:2021(7)	-0.378784	0.08493	-4.46	0.0000	0.0273
I:2021(9)	-0.382641	0.08489	-4.51	0.0000	0.0279

```
sigma                 0.0847977  RSS                 5.09817433
log-likelihood          810.647
no. of observations         752  no. of parameters          43
mean(A0M044)            1.96051  se(A0M044)            1.12561

AR 1-7 test:      F(7,702)  =   8.8206 [0.0000]**
ARCH 1-7 test:    F(7,738)  =   3.9163 [0.0003]**
Normality test:   Chi^2(2)  =   4.5044 [0.1052]
Hetero test:      F(2,707)  =  21.846 [0.0000]**
RESET23 test:     F(2,707)  =   6.8641 [0.0011]**
Model saved to C:\JBG\JGResearch\Palgrave Business Cycles\PJD TCB 112021\Model UER AR1
with IIS Saturation variables.pdf.
```

The estimated AR1 model and IIS, DIIS, and TIS variables, produces a much lower Residual Sum of Squares (RSS) is 5.10, than the AR1 benchmark, and its sigma, standard error, is 0.085, also far less than the AR1 model benchmark. The model error terms are non-random, see the Heteroscedasticity test criteria. The model is not adequately fitted.

We estimate a UER AR1 shown in Eq. (3) with impulse indicator saturation (IIS), differenced impulse indicator saturation variables (DIIS), and trend impulse indicator (TIS) saturation variables. We use the small (0.01) indicator level (Fig. 10.3).

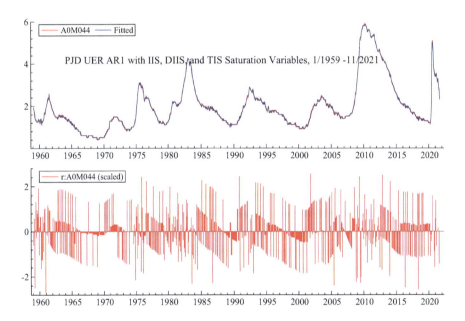

Fig. 10.3 Model UER AR1 with IIS, DIIS, and TIS saturation variables

```
EQ(3) Modelling A0M044 by OLS
      The dataset is: C:\JBG\JGResearch\Palgrave Business Cycles\JG TCBData
11052021.csv
      The estimation sample is: 1959(2) - 2021(9)
```

	Coefficient	Std.Error	t-value	t-prob	Part.R^2
A0M044_1	0.965859	0.005948	162.	0.0000	0.9748
DI:1960(2)	-0.142963	0.04941	-2.89	0.0039	0.0121
DI:1960(5)	-0.141256	0.04941	-2.86	0.0044	0.0119
DI:1960(10)	0.150209	0.04942	3.04	0.0025	0.0134
DI:1961(7)	0.294923	0.04941	5.97	0.0000	0.0497
DI:1965(6)	0.148337	0.04940	3.00	0.0028	0.0131
DI:1975(8)	-0.128392	0.04951	-2.59	0.0097	0.0098
DI:1976(4)	-0.225748	0.05706	-3.96	0.0001	0.0225
DI:1976(5)	-0.261357	0.05705	-4.58	0.0000	0.0299
DI:1980(9)	0.150569	0.04941	3.05	0.0024	0.0135
DI:1983(4)	-0.263128	0.04943	-5.32	0.0000	0.0399
DI:1989(6)	-0.147837	0.04940	-2.99	0.0029	0.0130
DI:1989(8)	-0.146130	0.04941	-2.96	0.0032	0.0127
DI:1994(10)	0.148503	0.04940	3.01	0.0027	0.0131
DI:1995(4)	0.194731	0.05705	3.41	0.0007	0.0168
DI:1995(5)	0.295869	0.05705	5.19	0.0000	0.0380
I:1961(1)	0.195277	0.07344	2.66	0.0080	0.0103
I:1970(12)	0.305437	0.07021	4.35	0.0000	0.0270
I:1980(7)	0.221088	0.07336	3.01	0.0027	0.0132
I:1982(2)	0.190029	0.07154	2.66	0.0081	0.0103
I:1986(2)	0.239918	0.07037	3.41	0.0007	0.0168
I:1991(6)	0.181542	0.07091	2.56	0.0107	0.0095
I:1991(12)	0.186312	0.07124	2.62	0.0091	0.0099
I:1992(5)	0.300933	0.07121	4.23	0.0000	0.0256
I:1992(6)	0.219203	0.07111	3.08	0.0021	0.0138
I:1992(12)	0.263951	0.07092	3.72	0.0002	0.0199
I:1998(4)	-0.207377	0.07017	-2.96	0.0032	0.0127
I:2002(12)	0.196360	0.07058	2.78	0.0055	0.0112
I:2004(4)	-0.303548	0.07094	-4.28	0.0000	0.0262
I:2008(10)	0.237842	0.07392	3.22	0.0014	0.0150
I:2009(6)	0.401398	0.07252	5.53	0.0000	0.0431
I:2009(9)	0.277587	0.07178	3.87	0.0001	0.0215
I:2011(10)	-0.258603	0.07303	-3.54	0.0004	0.0181
I:2014(4)	-0.240396	0.07059	-3.41	0.0007	0.0167
I:2020(7)	2.64798	0.08162	32.4	0.0000	0.6071
I:2020(9)	-0.229213	0.09035	-2.54	0.0114	0.0094
I:2020(10)	-0.589826	0.08467	-6.97	0.0000	0.0665
I:2021(4)	-0.288636	0.08000	-3.61	0.0003	0.0188
I:2021(5)	-0.339007	0.08444	-4.01	0.0001	0.0231
I:2021(7)	-0.434942	0.07630	-5.70	0.0000	0.0455
I:2021(9)	-0.307818	0.07169	-4.29	0.0000	0.0264
T1:1961(3)	0.0970221	0.01611	6.02	0.0000	0.0506
T1:1961(5)	-0.0864507	0.01471	-5.88	0.0000	0.0483
T1:1974(6)	-0.0397654	0.003999	-9.94	0.0000	0.1268
T1:1975(3)	0.100052	0.009875	10.1	0.0000	0.1310
T1:1975(9)	-0.0598178	0.006963	-8.59	0.0000	0.0978
T1:1979(3)	-0.00834765	0.002590	-3.22	0.0013	0.0150
T1:1980(9)	0.0400213	0.009620	4.16	0.0000	0.0248
T1:1981(2)	-0.0491372	0.009718	-5.06	0.0000	0.0362
T1:1982(9)	0.0535816	0.005285	10.1	0.0000	0.1311
T1:1983(6)	-0.0374106	0.003414	-11.0	0.0000	0.1499
T1:1992(3)	0.00893931	0.002516	3.55	0.0004	0.0182
T1:1992(11)	-0.00844819	0.002436	-3.47	0.0006	0.0174
T1:2004(3)	0.00422325	0.001528	2.76	0.0059	0.0111
T1:2005(12)	-0.252788	0.07509	-3.37	0.0008	0.0164
T1:2006(1)	0.500236	0.1442	3.47	0.0006	0.0174
T1:2006(2)	-0.255789	0.07428	-3.44	0.0006	0.0171
T1:2008(10)	-0.313885	0.04109	-7.64	0.0000	0.0789
T1:2008(11)	0.336992	0.04187	8.05	0.0000	0.0869

```
T1:2010(7)          -0.114645    0.03132    -3.66   0.0003    0.0193
T1:2010(9)           0.160808    0.04584     3.51   0.0005    0.0177
T1:2011(1)          -0.136761    0.03709    -3.69   0.0002    0.0196
T1:2011(4)           0.0917601   0.02535     3.62   0.0003    0.0189
T1:2012(2)          -0.0894700   0.02823    -3.17   0.0016    0.0145
T1:2012(5)           0.251056    0.08059     3.12   0.0019    0.0141
T1:2012(6)          -0.180727    0.05892    -3.07   0.0022    0.0136
T1:2020(3)          -0.331185    0.03172    -10.4   0.0000    0.1380
T1:2020(5)           0.589080    0.05752     10.2   0.0000    0.1335
T1:2020(8)          -0.302025    0.03868    -7.81   0.0000    0.0822
T1:2021(5)           0.191150    0.03901     4.90   0.0000    0.0341
T1:2021(7)          -0.147608    0.02948    -5.01   0.0000    0.0355


sigma                0.0698658  RSS                    3.32411631
R^2                  0.996090   log-likelihood            971.454
no. of observations       752   no. of parameters              71
mean(A0M044)          1.96051   se(A0M044)                1.12561



      AR 1-7 test:        F(7,674)   =    3.6761 [0.0007]**
      ARCH 1-7 test:      F(7,738)   =   0.70769 [0.6656]
      Normality test:     Chi^2(2)   =    2.1413 [0.3428]
      Hetero test:        F(84,641)  =   0.91028 [0.6996]
      RESET23 test:       F(2,679)   =   0.46273 [0.6298]
```

The estimated AR1 model and IIS, DIIS, and TIS saturation variables in Eq. (3) produces a much lower Residual Sum of Squares (RSS) is 3.32, the AR1 benchmark, and its sigma, standard error, is 0.069, also far less than the AR1 model benchmark. The model error terms are non-random, see the Autoregressive Error test criteria. The model is adequately fitted.

We model the UER, A0M044, with an AR1 model and a one-month lag in the LEI time series in Eq. (4) (Fig. 10.4).

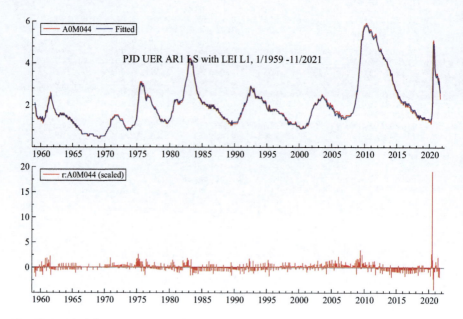

Fig. 10.4 Model UER AR1 LS with LEI L1

```
EQ(4) Modelling A0M044 by OLS
        The dataset is: C:\JBG\JGResearch\Palgrave Business Cycles\JG TCBData
11052021.csv
        The estimation sample is: 1959(2) - 2021(9)

                        Coefficient   Std.Error   t-value   t-prob Part.R^2
A0M044_1                 0.927950     0.008343       111.   0.0000   0.9430
Constant                 0.491496     0.05264       9.34    0.0000   0.1044
Trend                    0.00146196   0.0001549     9.44    0.0000   0.1064
G0M910_1                -0.0127966    0.001366     -9.37    0.0000   0.1050

sigma                    0.151518     RSS                 17.1723885
R^2                      0.981953     F(3,748) =    1.357e+04 [0.000]**
Adj.R^2                  0.98188      log-likelihood        354.025
no. of observations      752          no. of parameters       4
mean(A0M044)             1.96051      se(A0M044)           1.12561

AR 1-7 test:       F(7,741)   =    8.6250 [0.0000]**
ARCH 1-7 test:     F(7,738)   =    0.43409 [0.8810]
Normality test:    Chi^2(2)   =    3922.1 [0.0000]**
Hetero test:       F(6,745)   =    2.7518 [0.0119]*
Hetero-X test:     F(9,742)   =    2.4856 [0.0084]**
RESET23 test:      F(2,746)   =    2.3506 [0.0960]
```

The estimated AR1 model and the one-period lagged LEI, G0M910, variables in Eq. (4) produces a slightly Residual Sum of Squares (RSS) 17.12, the AR1 benchmark, and its sigma, standard error, is 0.152, also slightly less than the AR1 model benchmark. The model error terms are non-random, see the Autoregressive Error, Normality, and Heteroscedasticity test criteria. The model is not adequately fitted.

We model the UER with an AR1 model to serve as a forecasting benchmark. The estimated AR1 is shown in Eq. (5) with impulse indicator saturation (IIS), differenced impulse indicator saturation variables (DIIS), and trend impulse indicator (TIS) saturation variables, based on the small (0.01) indicator criteria, and a one-month lag in the LEI, G0M910, time series (Fig. 10.5).

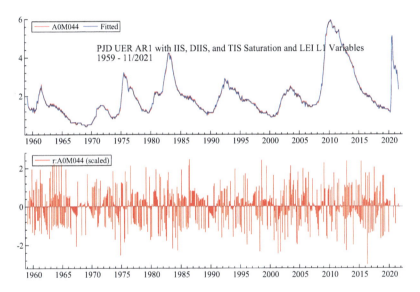

Fig. 10.5 Model UER AR1 with IIS, DIIS, and TIS saturation and LEI L1 variables

```
EQ(5) Modelling A0M044 by OLS
      The dataset is: C:\JBG\JGResearch\Palgrave Business Cycles\JG TCBData
11052021.csv
      The estimation sample is: 1959(2) - 2021(9)


                 Coefficient  Std.Error  t-value  t-prob  Part.R^2
A0M044_1           0.855660    0.01074     79.7   0.0000   0.9085
Constant         154.350      20.45        7.55   0.0000   0.0819
Trend             -0.202148    0.02720     -7.43  0.0000   0.0795
G0M910_1          -0.0182331   0.001147   -15.9   0.0000   0.2835
DI:1960(2)        -0.140730    0.04153     -3.39  0.0007   0.0176
DI:1960(5)        -0.133513    0.04154     -3.21  0.0014   0.0159
DI:1960(10)        0.273904    0.04905      5.58  0.0000   0.0465
DI:1960(11)        0.222279    0.04907      4.53  0.0000   0.0311
DI:1961(7)         0.265014    0.04160      6.37  0.0000   0.0597
DI:1965(6)         0.141817    0.04152      3.42  0.0007   0.0179
DI:1975(3)        -0.0938264   0.04156     -2.26  0.0243   0.0079
DI:1975(10)       -0.148123    0.04167     -3.55  0.0004   0.0194
DI:1976(4)        -0.177221    0.04941     -3.59  0.0004   0.0197
DI:1976(5)        -0.176277    0.05575     -3.16  0.0016   0.0154
DI:1977(9)         0.0908635   0.04152      2.19  0.0290   0.0074
DI:1978(8)        -0.0974375   0.04152     -2.35  0.0192   0.0085
DI:1980(4)         0.0995410   0.04153      2.40  0.0168   0.0089
DI:1980(6)        -0.153346    0.04153     -3.69  0.0002   0.0209
DI:1980(9)         0.129485    0.04154      3.12  0.0019   0.0150
DI:1982(1)        -0.130812    0.04154     -3.15  0.0017   0.0153
DI:1983(4)        -0.243844    0.04155     -5.87  0.0000   0.0511
DI:1985(9)        -0.0939817   0.04152     -2.26  0.0239   0.0080
DI:1986(9)         0.141584    0.04152      3.41  0.0007   0.0179
DI:1986(11)        0.0906727   0.04152      2.18  0.0293   0.0074
DI:1987(3)        -0.0939817   0.04152     -2.26  0.0239   0.0080
DI:1988(4)        -0.0930700   0.04152     -2.24  0.0253   0.0078
DI:1989(6)        -0.141247    0.04152     -3.40  0.0007   0.0178
DI:1989(8)        -0.136765    0.04153     -3.29  0.0010   0.0167
DI:1990(11)        0.147130    0.04153      3.54  0.0004   0.0193
DI:1991(6)         0.136191    0.04153      3.28  0.0011   0.0165
DI:1992(4)        -0.200972    0.04155     -4.84  0.0000   0.0353
DI:1993(8)        -0.0964918   0.04152     -2.32  0.0204   0.0084
DI:1994(6)        -0.0983151   0.04152     -2.37  0.0182   0.0087
DI:1994(10)        0.138163    0.04152      3.33  0.0009   0.0170
DI:1995(4)         0.178250    0.04797      3.72  0.0002   0.0211
DI:1995(5)         0.283669    0.04796      5.91  0.0000   0.0519
DI:1997(6)        -0.0964918   0.04152     -2.32  0.0204   0.0084
DI:2004(3)         0.182352    0.04153      4.39  0.0000   0.0293
DI:2006(1)        -0.150257    0.04152     -3.62  0.0003   0.0201
DI:2008(10)        0.143320    0.04805      2.98  0.0030   0.0137
DI:2008(11)       -0.140474    0.04813     -2.92  0.0036   0.0132
DI:2020(5)        -0.733345    0.05100    -14.4   0.0000   0.2445
DI:2020(6)        -1.44778     0.05118    -28.3   0.0000   0.5560
DI:2020(8)        -0.141507    0.04836     -2.93  0.0036   0.0132
I:1959(4)         -0.190815    0.06309     -3.02  0.0026   0.0141
I:1965(2)          0.128512    0.05903      2.18  0.0298   0.0074
I:1970(12)         0.238986    0.05972      4.00  0.0001   0.0245
I:1986(2)          0.217314    0.05922      3.67  0.0003   0.0206
I:1992(6)          0.214347    0.06077      3.53  0.0005   0.0191
I:1992(12)         0.276302    0.06188      4.47  0.0000   0.0303
I:1997(12)         0.144928    0.06031      2.40  0.0166   0.0090
I:2001(4)         -0.210513    0.05947     -3.54  0.0004   0.0192
I:2002(12)         0.180662    0.05952      3.04  0.0025   0.0142
I:2005(2)          0.134972    0.06002      2.25  0.0249   0.0079
I:2005(6)         -0.170726    0.05973     -2.86  0.0044   0.0126
```

I:2009(5)	0.182503	0.06059	3.01	0.0027	0.0140
I:2009(6)	0.428170	0.06048	7.08	0.0000	0.0727
I:2009(9)	0.294976	0.06067	4.86	0.0000	0.0357
I:2010(8)	-0.168417	0.06356	-2.65	0.0083	0.0109
I:2011(2)	-0.193792	0.06075	-3.19	0.0015	0.0157
I:2011(10)	-0.334565	0.06652	-5.03	0.0000	0.0381
I:2014(4)	-0.171348	0.06150	-2.79	0.0055	0.0120
I:2020(4)	-0.619482	0.06224	-9.95	0.0000	0.1342
I:2020(11)	0.263235	0.07027	3.75	0.0002	0.0215
I:2021(4)	-0.249932	0.07305	-3.42	0.0007	0.0180
I:2021(5)	-0.325085	0.07248	-4.49	0.0000	0.0305
I:2021(7)	-0.356459	0.07025	-5.07	0.0000	0.0387
T1:1960(8)	-0.0647249	0.01219	-5.31	0.0000	0.0423
T1:1960(12)	0.0936778	0.01411	6.64	0.0000	0.0645
T1:1961(8)	-0.0265626	0.004246	-6.26	0.0000	0.0577
T1:1970(10)	-0.0571254	0.01211	-4.72	0.0000	0.0336
T1:1970(12)	0.0583458	0.01247	4.68	0.0000	0.0331
T1:1974(8)	-0.0370736	0.004551	-8.15	0.0000	0.0941
T1:1975(6)	0.226085	0.04956	4.56	0.0000	0.0315
T1:1975(7)	-0.170697	0.05208	-3.28	0.0011	0.0165
T1:1976(4)	-0.135347	0.05110	-2.65	0.0083	0.0109
T1:1976(5)	0.119542	0.04568	2.62	0.0091	0.0106
T1:1979(10)	-0.0893300	0.03038	-2.94	0.0034	0.0133
T1:1979(11)	0.0903606	0.03105	2.91	0.0037	0.0131
T1:1981(8)	-0.0323065	0.003974	-8.13	0.0000	0.0937
T1:1982(9)	0.0529565	0.005029	10.5	0.0000	0.1479
T1:1983(8)	-0.0249456	0.002607	-9.57	0.0000	0.1253
T1:1991(8)	-0.0551916	0.01089	-5.07	0.0000	0.0387
T1:1991(11)	0.0637025	0.01282	4.97	0.0000	0.0372
T1:1993(3)	-0.131208	0.03442	-3.81	0.0002	0.0222
T1:1993(4)	0.122248	0.03237	3.78	0.0002	0.0218
T1:1998(3)	-0.0606341	0.02796	-2.17	0.0305	0.0073
T1:1998(5)	0.197427	0.08099	2.44	0.0151	0.0092
T1:1998(6)	-0.137934	0.05466	-2.52	0.0119	0.0099
T1:2004(3)	-0.130689	0.02696	-4.85	0.0000	0.0355
T1:2004(4)	0.133890	0.02721	4.92	0.0000	0.0365
T1:2008(9)	-0.0178999	0.003211	-5.57	0.0000	0.0464
T1:2010(3)	0.0623210	0.02187	2.85	0.0045	0.0126
T1:2010(5)	-0.0514930	0.02247	-2.29	0.0223	0.0082
T1:2011(9)	0.177662	0.05646	3.15	0.0017	0.0153
T1:2011(10)	-0.164187	0.06768	-2.43	0.0155	0.0091
T1:2012(2)	-0.0650301	0.03629	-1.79	0.0736	0.0050
T1:2012(5)	0.223935	0.07383	3.03	0.0025	0.0142
T1:2012(6)	-0.161526	0.05602	-2.88	0.0041	0.0128
T1:2013(12)	-0.166743	0.05963	-2.80	0.0053	0.0121
T1:2014(1)	0.259796	0.08410	3.09	0.0021	0.0147
T1:2014(3)	-0.0973684	0.02857	-3.41	0.0007	0.0178
T1:2018(1)	-0.0842701	0.02842	-2.97	0.0031	0.0136
T1:2018(3)	0.353275	0.09918	3.56	0.0004	0.0195
T1:2018(4)	-0.495617	0.1309	-3.78	0.0002	0.0219
T1:2018(5)	0.228212	0.06419	3.56	0.0004	0.0194
T1:2020(2)	-0.380518	0.01557	-24.4	0.0000	0.4831
T1:2020(6)	1.21850	0.06108	20.0	0.0000	0.3838
T1:2020(8)	-0.663091	0.1196	-5.54	0.0000	0.0459
T1:2020(9)	-0.374258	0.09277	-4.03	0.0001	0.0248
T1:2021(1)	0.337193	0.08559	3.94	0.0001	0.0237
T1:2021(2)	-0.214709	0.09256	-2.32	0.0207	0.0084
T1:2021(5)	0.277606	0.04794	5.79	0.0000	0.0499

```
sigma                    0.0587128  RSS                    2.20275611
R^2                      0.997685   F(112,639) =      2459 [0.000]**
Adj.R^2                  0.997279   log-likelihood         1126.18
no. of observations           752  no. of parameters          113
mean(A0M044)             1.96051    se(A0M044)             1.12561

AR 1-7 test:       F(7,632)   =     2.5320 [0.0142]*
ARCH 1-7 test:     F(7,738)   =     2.3354 [0.0231]*
Normality test:    Chi^2(2)   = 0.079877 [0.9608]
Hetero test:       F(143,578) =   0.70742 [0.9938]
RESET23 test:      F(2,637)   =    1.6295 [0.1968]
```

The estimated AR1 model and small IIS, DIIS, and TIS saturation variables in Eq. (5) produces a much lower Residual Sum of Squares (RSS) is 2.20, the AR1 benchmark, and its sigma, standard error, is 0.059, also far less than the AR1 model benchmark. The model error terms are essentially random, see the Autoregressive and ARCH Error test criteria. The model is adequately fitted.

We model the UER with estimated AR1 with a one-period lag in the weekly unemployment claims time series, A0M005, shown in Eq. (6) (Fig. 10.6).

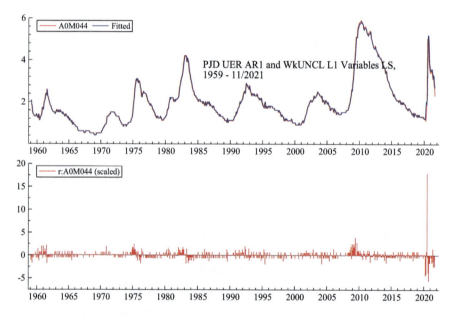

Fig. 10.6 Model UER AR1 LS with WkUNCL L1

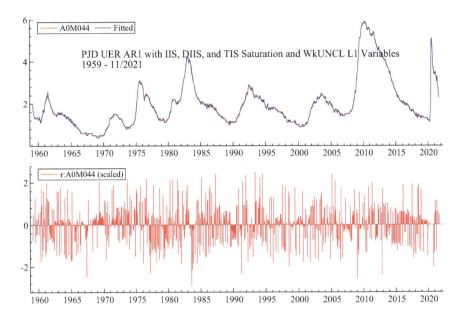

Fig. 10.7 Model UER AR1 with IIS, DIIS, and TIS saturation and WkUNCL L1 variables

```
EQ(6) Modelling A0M044 by OLS
      The dataset is: C:\JBG\JGResearch\Palgrave Business Cycles\JG TCBData
11052021.csv
      The estimation sample is: 1959(2) - 2021(9)

                   Coefficient  Std.Error  t-value  t-prob Part.R^2
A0M044_1             0.977415   0.005624    174.    0.0000   0.9758
Constant            -0.0450489   0.01431   -3.15    0.0017   0.0131
Trend              8.54468e-06  2.876e-05    0.297  0.7664   0.0001
A0M005_1           0.000239426  2.745e-05    8.72   0.0000   0.0923

sigma                0.152590  RSS                 17.4161047
R^2                  0.981696  F(3,748) =     1.337e+04 [0.000]**
Adj.R^2              0.981623  log-likelihood        348.726
no. of observations       752  no. of parameters           4
mean(A0M044)          1.96051  se(A0M044)            1.12561

AR 1-7 test:      F(7,741)  =    8.0905 [0.0000]**
ARCH 1-7 test:    F(7,738)  =    3.6550 [0.0007]**
Normality test:   Chi^2(2)  =   896.27 [0.0000]**
Hetero test:      F(6,745)  =   23.335 [0.0000]**
Hetero-X test:    F(9,742)  =   21.657 [0.0000]**
RESET23 test:     F(2,746)  =   0.56003 [0.5714]
```

The estimated AR1 model and one-period weekly unemployment claims variables (6) produces an equal Residual Sum of Squares (RSS) is 17.42, the AR1 benchmark, and its sigma, standard error, is 0.153, also slightly less than the AR1 model benchmark. The model error terms are non-random, see the Autoregressive, ARCH, Normality, and Heteroscdasticity Error test criteria. The model is adequately not fitted.

We model the UER with an AR1 model with small impulse indicator saturation (IIS), differenced impulse indicator saturation variables (DIIS) and trend impulse indicator (TIS) saturation variables and a one-month lag in the weekly unemployment claims, A0M005, time series in Eq. (7) (Fig. 10.7).

```
EQ(7) Modelling A0M044 by OLS
        The dataset is: C:\JBG\JGResearch\Palgrave Business Cycles\JG TCBData
11052021.csv
        The estimation sample is: 1959(2) - 2021(9)

                Coefficient  Std.Error  t-value  t-prob  Part.R^2
A0M044_1          0.918928    0.004881     188.   0.0000   0.9818
Constant         -0.574980    0.04022     -14.3   0.0000   0.2370
A0M005_1          0.00101811  5.374e-05    18.9   0.0000   0.3529
DI:1961(7)        0.296091    0.04342      6.82   0.0000   0.0660
DI:1963(8)        0.100788    0.04342      2.32   0.0206   0.0081
DI:1964(10)      -0.0932938   0.04341     -2.15   0.0320   0.0070
DI:1965(5)       -0.103380    0.04342     -2.38   0.0175   0.0085
DI:1965(7)       -0.138942    0.04342     -3.20   0.0014   0.0153
DI:1975(4)        0.247501    0.06257      3.96   0.0001   0.0232
DI:1975(5)        0.358486    0.08979      3.99   0.0001   0.0237
DI:1975(10)      -0.156097    0.04342     -3.60   0.0003   0.0193
DI:1976(5)       -0.135360    0.04342     -3.12   0.0019   0.0146
DI:1983(4)       -0.230310    0.04343     -5.30   0.0000   0.0410
DI:1986(1)       -0.154918    0.04342     -3.57   0.0004   0.0190
DI:1986(10)      -0.151323    0.04342     -3.49   0.0005   0.0181
DI:1989(6)       -0.138425    0.04342     -3.19   0.0015   0.0152
DI:1989(8)       -0.145469    0.04342     -3.35   0.0009   0.0168
DI:1994(10)       0.149018    0.04341      3.43   0.0006   0.0176
DI:1995(4)        0.201828    0.05014      4.03   0.0001   0.0240
DI:1995(5)        0.305175    0.05014      6.09   0.0000   0.0533
DI:2009(6)        0.342244    0.05020      6.82   0.0000   0.0660
DI:2009(7)        0.151909    0.05017      3.03   0.0026   0.0137
DI:2014(1)       -0.151638    0.04342     -3.49   0.0005   0.0182
DI:2015(4)       -0.0978010   0.04341     -2.25   0.0246   0.0077
DI:2016(5)       -0.135916    0.04342     -3.13   0.0018   0.0147
DI:2016(8)       -0.0946022   0.04341     -2.18   0.0297   0.0072
DI:2018(4)        0.144134    0.04342      3.32   0.0010   0.0165
DI:2019(1)       -0.0924642   0.04341     -2.13   0.0336   0.0068
DI:2020(4)       -0.481861    0.04896     -9.84   0.0000   0.1283
DI:2020(6)        0.845798    0.07031     12.0    0.0000   0.1803
DI:2020(7)        3.05658     0.1024      29.9    0.0000   0.5754
DI:2020(8)        2.77368     0.1382      20.1    0.0000   0.3798
DI:2020(9)        2.25400     0.1658      13.6    0.0000   0.2192
I:1959(4)        -0.168364    0.06761     -2.49   0.0130   0.0093
I:1959(12)       -0.175757    0.06710     -2.62   0.0090   0.0103
I:1960(3)         0.314754    0.06832      4.61   0.0000   0.0313
I:1970(12)        0.243801    0.06164      3.96   0.0001   0.0232
I:1975(6)         0.506763    0.1114       4.55   0.0000   0.0305
I:1976(4)        -0.223234    0.06190     -3.61   0.0003   0.0194
I:1982(2)         0.167989    0.06271      2.68   0.0076   0.0108
I:1988(5)         0.129804    0.06179      2.10   0.0360   0.0067
I:1990(12)       -0.207231    0.06227     -3.33   0.0009   0.0166
I:1991(7)        -0.144525    0.06245     -2.31   0.0210   0.0081
I:1992(5)         0.177986    0.06896      2.58   0.0101   0.0100
I:1992(12)        0.262798    0.06227      4.22   0.0000   0.0264
I:1993(9)         0.160465    0.06208      2.58   0.0100   0.0101
I:1998(4)        -0.190316    0.06167     -3.09   0.0021   0.0143
```

```
I:2001(4)        -0.178418       0.06187    -2.88   0.0041   0.0125
I:2002(12)        0.202785       0.06213     3.26   0.0012   0.0159
I:2004(4)        -0.361006       0.07314    -4.94   0.0000   0.0357
I:2005(6)        -0.155430       0.06329    -2.46   0.0143   0.0091
I:2006(2)         0.237859       0.06246     3.81   0.0002   0.0216
I:2008(11)       -0.398295       0.06431    -6.19   0.0000   0.0551
I:2009(9)         0.239464       0.06247     3.83   0.0001   0.0218
I:2010(8)        -0.188523       0.06226    -3.03   0.0026   0.0137
I:2011(2)        -0.162018       0.06215    -2.61   0.0093   0.0102
I:2011(8)         0.153084       0.06205     2.47   0.0139   0.0092
I:2011(10)       -0.239331       0.06207    -3.86   0.0001   0.0221
I:2012(6)         0.153585       0.06185     2.48   0.0133   0.0093
I:2012(7)        -0.141725       0.06187    -2.29   0.0223   0.0079
I:2013(1)        -0.0370343      0.06182    -0.599  0.5493   0.0005
I:2014(4)        -0.238312       0.06189    -3.85   0.0001   0.0220
I:2020(10)        1.56075        0.1892      8.25   0.0000   0.0937
I:2021(6)         0.590046       0.06594     8.95   0.0000   0.1085
I:2021(8)         0.208243       0.06627     3.14   0.0018   0.0148
T1:1959(10)       0.0586745      0.01584     3.71   0.0002   0.0204
T1:1960(3)       -0.0900598      0.01945    -4.63   0.0000   0.0315
T1:1960(9)        0.213545       0.04294     4.97   0.0000   0.0362
T1:1960(11)      -0.522209       0.09764    -5.35   0.0000   0.0417
T1:1960(12)       0.398371       0.07515     5.30   0.0000   0.0410
T1:1961(5)       -0.0426056      0.009515   -4.48   0.0000   0.0296
T1:1965(3)        0.00215218     0.0005376   4.00   0.0001   0.0238
T1:1980(3)        0.132627       0.02876     4.61   0.0000   0.0313
T1:1980(5)       -0.471624       0.09775    -4.82   0.0000   0.0342
T1:1980(6)        0.391054       0.09313     4.20   0.0000   0.0261
T1:1980(9)       -0.224831       0.08790    -2.56   0.0108   0.0098
T1:1980(10)       0.205547       0.07772     2.64   0.0084   0.0105
T1:1981(2)       -0.0392922      0.01462    -2.69   0.0074   0.0109
T1:1982(10)       0.00886875     0.002695    3.29   0.0011   0.0162
T1:1984(9)       -0.00334474     0.001281   -2.61   0.0092   0.0103
T1:1992(3)       -0.110987       0.03157    -3.52   0.0005   0.0184
T1:1992(5)        0.328995       0.09317     3.53   0.0004   0.0186
T1:1992(6)       -0.217558       0.06249    -3.48   0.0005   0.0181
T1:2004(1)       -0.175285       0.05368    -3.27   0.0011   0.0159
T1:2004(2)        0.221734       0.06753     3.28   0.0011   0.0161
T1:2004(7)       -0.236030       0.07355    -3.21   0.0014   0.0154
T1:2004(8)        0.225320       0.07264     3.10   0.0020   0.0144
T1:2004(12)      -0.0376141      0.01308    -2.88   0.0042   0.0124
T1:2008(8)       -0.184582       0.02997    -6.16   0.0000   0.0545
T1:2008(9)        0.188368       0.02982     6.32   0.0000   0.0572
T1:2015(9)       -0.00232524     0.0005941  -3.91   0.0001   0.0228
T1:2020(2)        2.11359        0.1189      17.8   0.0000   0.3245
T1:2020(4)       -4.00029        0.2273     -17.6   0.0000   0.3200
T1:2020(6)        1.88705        0.1090      17.3   0.0000   0.3131

sigma                0.0613955   RSS                   2.48027373
R^2                  0.997393    F(93,658) =        2707 [0.000]**
Adj.R^2              0.997025    log-likelihood        1081.56
no. of observations       752   no. of parameters          94
mean(A0M044)         1.96051     se(A0M044)            1.12561

AR 1-7 test:      F(7,651)  =    2.6430 [0.0106]*
ARCH 1-7 test:    F(7,738)  =    0.92277 [0.4880]
Normality test:   Chi^2(2)  =    0.40313 [0.8175]
Hetero test:      F(99,630) =    1.0390 [0.3865]
RESET23 test:     F(2,656)  =    1.6079 [0.2011]
```

Model saved to C:\JBG\JGResearch\Palgrave Business Cycles\PJD TCB 112021\Model UER AR1
with IIS, DIIS, and TIS Saturation and WkUNCL L1 Variables.pdf
Model saved to C:\JBG\JGResearch\Palgrave Business Cycles\PJD TCB 112021\Model UER AR1
with IIS, DIIS, and TIS Saturation and WkUNCL L1 Variables.pdf.gwg

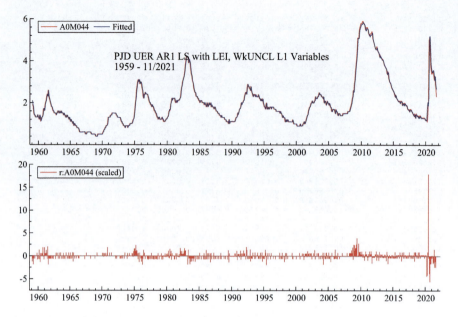

Fig. 10.8   Model UER AR1 LS with LEI, WkUNCL L1

The estimated AR1 model and small IIS, DIIS, and TIS saturation variables in Eq. (7) produces a much lower Residual Sum of Squares (RSS) is 2.48, the AR1 benchmark, and its sigma, standard error, is 0.061, also far less than the AR1 model benchmark. The model error terms are essentially random, see the Autoregressive Error test criteria. The model is adequately fitted.

We model the UER with an AR1 model and one-month lags in the weekly unemployment claims, A0M005, and weekly unemployment claims, A0M044, time series in Eq. (8) (Fig. 10.8).

```
EQ(8) Modelling A0M044 by OLS
      The dataset is: C:\JBG\JGResearch\Palgrave Business Cycles\JG TCBData
11052021.csv
      The estimation sample is: 1959(2) - 2021(9)

                 Coefficient  Std.Error  t-value  t-prob Part.R^2
A0M044_1          0.979218    0.005256     186.   0.0000   0.9789
Constant         -0.0292917    0.02003    -1.46   0.1440   0.0029
A0M005_1         0.000241620  2.732e-05    8.85   0.0000   0.0947
G0M910_1         -0.000239175 0.0002523   -0.948  0.3435   0.0012
```

```
sigma                    0.152507  RSS                    17.3972609
R^2                      0.981716  F(3,748) =       1.339e+04 [0.000]**
Adj.R^2                  0.981643  log-likelihood         349.133
no. of observations           752  no. of parameters            4
mean(A0M044)              1.96051  se(A0M044)             1.12561

AR 1-7 test:        F(7,741)  =     8.0209 [0.0000]**
ARCH 1-7 test:      F(7,738)  =     3.4919 [0.0011]**
Normality test:     Chi^2(2)  =    939.12 [0.0000]**
Hetero test:        F(6,745)  =    20.154 [0.0000]**
Hetero-X test:      F(9,742)  =    18.426 [0.0000]**
RESET23 test:       F(2,746)  =    0.54671 [0.5791]
Model saved to C:\JBG\JGResearch\Palgrave Business Cycles\PJD TCB 112021\Model UER AR1
LS with LEI, WkUNCL L1.pdf
Model saved to C:\JBG\JGResearch\Palgrave Business Cycles\PJD TCB 112021\Model UER AR1
LS with LEI, WkUNCL L1.pdf.gwg
```

The estimated AR1 model and the one-period lagged LEI, G0M910, and weekly unemployment claims, A0M005, variables in Eq. (8) produces an equal Residual Sum of Squares (RSS) 17.40, to the AR1 benchmark, and its sigma, standard error, is 0.153, also only less than the AR1 model benchmark. The model error terms are non-random, see the Autoregressive Error, Normality, and Heteroscedasticity test criteria. The model is not adequately fitted.

We model the UER with an AR1 model with impulse indicator saturation (IIS), differenced impulse indicator saturation variables (DIIS) and trend impulse indicator (TIS) saturation variables and a one-month lag in the weekly unemployment claims, A0M005, and weekly unemployment claims, A0M044, time series in Eq. (9). We use the small (0.01) criteria for identifying outliers (Fig. 10.9).

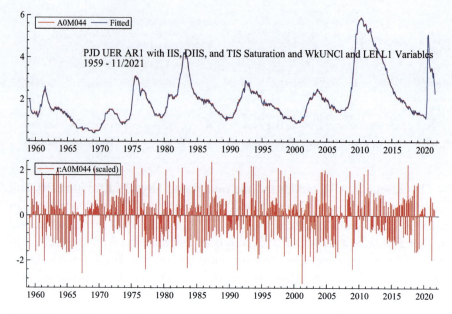

Fig. 10.9 Model UER AR1 with IIS, DIIS, and TIS saturation and WkUNCL LEI L1 variables

```
Summary of Autometrics search
initial search space      2^258   final search space         2^193
no. estimated models      4580    no. terminal models          20
test form                 LR-F    target size          Small:0.01
large residuals            no     presearch reduction         lags
backtesting               GUM0    tie-breaker                   SC
diagnostics p-value       0.01    search effort            standard
time                  35:53.04    Autometrics version           2

EQ(9) Modelling A0M044 by OLS
      The dataset is: C:\JBG\JGResearch\Palgrave Business Cycles\JG TCBData
11052021.csv

      The estimation sample is: 1959(2) - 2021(9)
```

	Coefficient	Std.Error	t-value	t-prob	Part.R^2
A0M044_1	0.919041	0.004552	202.	0.0000	0.9840
Constant	-0.591327	0.03807	-15.5	0.0000	0.2665
A0M005_1	0.00110324	4.842e-05	22.8	0.0000	0.4388
DI:1960(3)	0.162060	0.04384	3.70	0.0002	0.0202
DI:1961(7)	0.289211	0.04385	6.59	0.0000	0.0615
DI:1965(1)	-0.0994374	0.04382	-2.27	0.0236	0.0077
DI:1965(6)	0.147431	0.04382	3.36	0.0008	0.0168
DI:1975(10)	-0.157335	0.04382	-3.59	0.0004	0.0190
DI:1976(5)	-0.134519	0.04382	-3.07	0.0022	0.0140
DI:1978(8)	-0.104764	0.04382	-2.39	0.0171	0.0085
DI:1980(9)	0.122486	0.04383	2.79	0.0053	0.0116
DI:1981(7)	-0.0946844	0.04382	-2.16	0.0311	0.0070
DI:1982(1)	-0.144154	0.04382	-3.29	0.0011	0.0160
DI:1983(3)	0.144924	0.04382	3.31	0.0010	0.0162
DI:1986(1)	-0.155772	0.04382	-3.56	0.0004	0.0187
DI:1986(10)	-0.152220	0.04382	-3.47	0.0005	0.0179
DI:1989(6)	-0.137899	0.04382	-3.15	0.0017	0.0147

DI:1989(8)	-0.145877	0.04382	-3.33	0.0009	0.0164
DI:1992(4)	-0.199483	0.04382	-4.55	0.0000	0.0303
DI:1995(3)	-0.122929	0.04440	-2.77	0.0058	0.0114
DI:1995(6)	-0.216818	0.05060	-4.28	0.0000	0.0269
DI:1995(7)	-0.152106	0.05060	-3.01	0.0027	0.0134
DI:2009(7)	-0.161662	0.05061	-3.19	0.0015	0.0151
DI:2009(8)	-0.282492	0.05060	-5.58	0.0000	0.0448
DI:2012(11)	-0.122990	0.04383	-2.81	0.0052	0.0117
DI:2014(1)	-0.152060	0.04382	-3.47	0.0006	0.0178
DI:2015(4)	-0.0975579	0.04382	-2.23	0.0263	0.0074
DI:2016(5)	-0.136284	0.04382	-3.11	0.0020	0.0144
DI:2016(8)	-0.0953515	0.04382	-2.18	0.0299	0.0071
DI:2018(4)	0.162640	0.04438	3.66	0.0003	0.0198
DI:2020(4)	-0.501605	0.04933	-10.2	0.0000	0.1347
DI:2020(6)	0.995047	0.08805	11.3	0.0000	0.1613
DI:2020(7)	3.39062	0.1773	19.1	0.0000	0.3551
DI:2020(8)	3.26877	0.2625	12.5	0.0000	0.1893
DI:2020(9)	0.562567	0.08588	6.55	0.0000	0.0607
I:1959(4)	-0.193201	0.06667	-2.90	0.0039	0.0125
I:1959(12)	-0.163069	0.06381	-2.56	0.0108	0.0097
I:1960(5)	-0.228799	0.06514	-3.51	0.0005	0.0182
I:1960(10)	0.194348	0.06887	2.82	0.0049	0.0119
I:1970(12)	0.236205	0.06221	3.80	0.0002	0.0213
I:1975(4)	0.227659	0.06291	3.62	0.0003	0.0193
I:1976(4)	-0.225721	0.06243	-3.62	0.0003	0.0193
I:1982(12)	0.155134	0.06296	2.46	0.0140	0.0091
I:1983(5)	0.253401	0.06270	4.04	0.0001	0.0240
I:1988(5)	0.132572	0.06234	2.13	0.0338	0.0068
I:1990(12)	-0.211250	0.06267	-3.37	0.0008	0.0168
I:1991(7)	-0.145381	0.06267	-2.32	0.0206	0.0080
I:1991(12)	0.142537	0.06280	2.27	0.0235	0.0077
I:1992(6)	0.224002	0.06296	3.56	0.0004	0.0187
I:1992(12)	0.259530	0.06261	4.15	0.0000	0.0252
I:1998(4)	-0.176973	0.06236	-2.84	0.0047	0.0120
I:2002(12)	0.185754	0.06222	2.99	0.0029	0.0132
I:2004(4)	-0.252079	0.06231	-4.05	0.0001	0.0241
I:2005(6)	-0.180944	0.06233	-2.90	0.0038	0.0125
I:2006(2)	0.226637	0.06243	3.63	0.0003	0.0195
I:2008(11)	-0.378535	0.06450	-5.87	0.0000	0.0493
I:2009(6)	0.333167	0.06338	5.26	0.0000	0.0400
I:2010(8)	-0.181185	0.06274	-2.89	0.0040	0.0124
I:2011(2)	-0.155931	0.06266	-2.49	0.0131	0.0092
I:2011(8)	0.156967	0.06258	2.51	0.0124	0.0094
I:2011(10)	-0.237119	0.06259	-3.79	0.0002	0.0212
I:2012(6)	0.154257	0.06240	2.47	0.0137	0.0091
I:2012(7)	-0.142158	0.06241	-2.28	0.0231	0.0078
I:2014(4)	-0.247149	0.06229	-3.97	0.0001	0.0232
I:2020(9)	2.34022	0.3948	5.93	0.0000	0.0503
I:2021(6)	0.569563	0.06772	8.41	0.0000	0.0963
I:2021(8)	0.190660	0.06790	2.81	0.0051	0.0117
T1:1960(9)	0.112803	0.03437	3.28	0.0011	0.0160
T1:1960(11)	-0.388307	0.09194	-4.22	0.0000	0.0262
T1:1960(12)	0.293249	0.06540	4.48	0.0000	0.0294
T1:1961(11)	-0.0155844	0.003648	-4.27	0.0000	0.0268
T1:1965(7)	0.00281944	0.0005301	5.32	0.0000	0.0409
T1:1980(3)	0.142589	0.02885	4.94	0.0000	0.0355
T1:1980(5)	-0.433467	0.08579	-5.05	0.0000	0.0370
T1:1980(6)	0.289916	0.05754	5.04	0.0000	0.0368
T1:1992(6)	-0.00248665	0.001008	-2.47	0.0139	0.0091
T1:1994(9)	0.191797	0.04986	3.85	0.0001	0.0218
T1:1994(10)	-0.237233	0.06112	-3.88	0.0001	0.0222
T1:1995(3)	0.118223	0.03452	3.42	0.0007	0.0174
T1:1995(5)	-0.0704419	0.02200	-3.20	0.0014	0.0152
T1:2008(8)	-0.183683	0.02315	-7.93	0.0000	0.0866
T1:2008(9)	0.185380	0.02333	7.95	0.0000	0.0868
T1:2018(3)	-0.0390141	0.01415	-2.76	0.0060	0.0113
T1:2018(4)	0.0399902	0.01574	2.54	0.0113	0.0096
T1:2020(2)	2.27930	0.1093	20.8	0.0000	0.3956
T1:2020(4)	-4.20023	0.2050	-20.5	0.0000	0.3874
T1:2020(6)	1.88158	0.1087	17.3	0.0000	0.3110
T1:2021(2)	0.0370379	0.01452	2.55	0.0110	0.0097

562   J. B. Guerard

```
sigma                 0.0619638  RSS                 2.54943546
R^2                   0.997321   F(87,664) =     2841 [0.000]**
Adj.R^2               0.99697    log-likelihood      1071.22
no. of observations   752        no. of parameters        88
mean(A0M044)          1.96051    se(A0M044)          1.12561

AR 1-7 test:      F(7,657)  =    2.2182 [0.0311]*
ARCH 1-7 test:    F(7,738)  =    1.0223 [0.4139]
Normality test:   Chi^2(2)  =    1.2925 [0.5240]
Hetero test:      F(90,624) =    0.95938 [0.5865]
RESET23 test:     F(2,662)  =    2.9443 [0.0533]
Model saved to C:\JBG\JGResearch\Palgrave Business Cycles\PJD TCB 112021\Model UER AR1
with IIS, DIIS, and TIS Saturation and WkUNCL  LEI L1  Variables.pdf
Model saved to C:\JBG\JGResearch\Palgrave Business Cycles\PJD TCB 112021\Model UER AR1
with IIS, DIIS, and TIS Saturation and WkUNCL  LEI L1  Variables.pdf.gwg

Model UER AR1 with IIS, DIIS, and TIS Saturation and WkUNCL  LEI L1  Variables.pdf
saved to C:\JBG\JGResearch\Palgrave Business Cycles\PJD TCB 112021\Model UER AR1 with
IIS, DIIS, and TIS Saturation and WkUNCL  LEI L1  Variables.pdf
Model UER AR1 with IIS, DIIS, and TIS Saturation and WkUNCL  LEI L1  Variables.pdf
```

The estimated AR1 model and small IIS, DIIS, and TIS saturation variables in Eq. (7) produces a much lower Residual Sum of Squares (RSS) 2.54, than the AR1 benchmark, and its sigma, standard error, is 0.062, also far less than the AR1 model benchmark. The model error terms are essentially random, see the Autoregressive Error test criteria. The model is adequately fitted.

We model the UER with an AR1 model with impulse indicator saturation (IIS), differenced impulse indicator saturation variables (DIIS) and trend impulse indicator (TIS) saturation variables and twelve months of lags in the weekly unemployment claims, A0M044, and the LEI, G0M910, time series in Eq. (10). We use the standard (0.05) criteria for identifying outliers (Fig. 10.10).

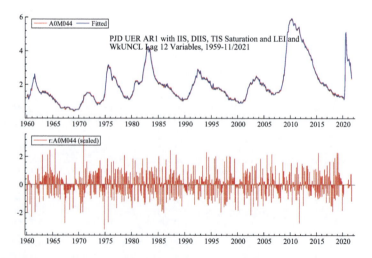

Fig. 10.10 Model UER AR1 with IIS, DIIS, and TIS saturation and WkUNCL L12 variables

```
Autometrics identification block search over regressors
no. initial regressors    2246  no. of observations        741
significance level         0.01  block method           standard
extension effort       standard  reduction effort       standard
block backtesting          GUM0  used in blocks         A,B,C1,D1
```

EQ(10) Modelling A0M044 by OLS
     The dataset is: C:\JBG\JGResearch\Palgrave Business Cycles\JG TCBData
11052021.csv
     The estimation sample is: 1960(1) - 2021(9)

	Coefficient	Std.Error	t-value	t-prob	Part.R^2
A0M044_1	0.769767	0.01357	56.7	0.0000	0.8405
A0M005_1	0.000800691	9.638e-05	8.31	0.0000	0.1015
G0M910_1	0.0221387	0.006685	3.31	0.0010	0.0176
G0M910_2	-0.0279371	0.007106	-3.93	0.0001	0.0247
G0M910_9	-0.0208180	0.002510	-8.30	0.0000	0.1012
Trend	0.00390414	0.0004290	9.10	0.0000	0.1194
DI:1960(3)	0.138695	0.03905	3.55	0.0004	0.0202
DI:1961(1)	0.245102	0.05625	4.36	0.0000	0.0301
DI:1961(2)	0.344187	0.08116	4.24	0.0000	0.0286
DI:19DI:1961(4)	0.687290	0.1200	5.73	0.0000	0.0509
DI:1961(5)	0.882954	0.1369	6.45	0.0000	0.0637
DI:1961(6)	0.920356	0.1527	6.03	0.0000	0.0561
DI:1962(10)	-0.0894186	0.03902	-2.29	0.0223	0.0085
DI:1963(5)	0.0836338	0.03903	2.14	0.0325	0.0075
DI:1963(8)	0.0908453	0.03902	2.33	0.0202	0.0088
DI:1964(11)	0.0978946	0.03904	2.51	0.0124	0.0102
DI:1965(1)	-0.0941717	0.03902	-2.41	0.0161	0.0094
DI:1965(7)	-0.126235	0.03904	-3.23	0.0013	0.0168
DI:1973(7)	-0.0939211	0.03903	-2.41	0.0164	0.0094
DI:1976(5)	-0.133079	0.03908	-3.41	0.0007	0.0186
DI:1980(10)	-0.117796	0.03911	-3.01	0.0027	0.0146
DI:1981(6)	0.156005	0.04894	3.19	0.0015	0.0164
DI:1984(6)	-0.0831718	0.03903	-2.13	0.0335	0.0074
DI:1986(2)	0.179124	0.04509	3.97	0.0001	0.0252
DI:1986(3)	0.103011	0.04506	2.29	0.0226	0.0085
DI:1986(9)	0.132673	0.03903	3.40	0.0007	0.0186
DI:1986(11)	0.0860534	0.03904	2.20	0.0279	0.0079
DI:1989(7)	0.174061	0.03905	4.46	0.0000	0.0315
DI:1992(3)	-0.114416	0.04792	-2.39	0.0173	0.0092
DI:1992(4)	-0.338601	0.05536	-6.12	0.0000	0.0577
DI:1992(5)	-0.166258	0.04800	-3.46	0.0006	0.0193
DI:1993(8)	-0.0961014	0.03907	-2.46	0.0142	0.0098
DI:1994(10)	0.141768	0.03903	3.63	0.0003	0.0211
DI:1995(5)	0.191649	0.03903	4.91	0.0000	0.0380
DI:2000(8)	0.0860967	0.03905	2.21	0.0278	0.0079
DI:2004(2)	-0.0951601	0.03903	-2.44	0.0151	0.0096
DI:2005(1)	-0.0985225	0.03905	-2.52	0.0119	0.0103
DI:2005(5)	0.0864219	0.03913	2.21	0.0276	0.0079
DI:2008(9)	-0.0927071	0.03913	-2.37	0.0181	0.0091
DI:2009(1)	-0.0964014	0.04000	-2.41	0.0162	0.0094
DI:2012(11)	-0.122420	0.03908	-3.13	0.0018	0.0158
DI:2013(11)	0.0977573	0.04510	2.17	0.0306	0.0076
DI:2013(12)	0.0985493	0.04513	2.18	0.0294	0.0077
DI:2016(5)	-0.140275	0.03943	-3.56	0.0004	0.0203
DI:2018(5)	-0.131199	0.03907	-3.36	0.0008	0.0181
DI:2020(4)	-0.325273	0.05473	-5.94	0.0000	0.0547
DI:2020(6)	0.570640	0.1124	5.07	0.0000	0.0404
DI:2020(7)	2.93600	0.1502	19.5	0.0000	0.3848
DI:2020(8)	1.87540	0.08896	21.1	0.0000	0.4211
DI:2020(9)	0.886785	0.05701	15.6	0.0000	0.2837
DI:2020(11)	-0.0846409	0.04096	-2.07	0.0392	0.0069
DI:2021(4)	-0.209460	0.04612	-4.54	0.0000	0.0327
DI:2021(5)	-0.381085	0.04664	-8.17	0.0000	0.0985
DI:2021(7)	-0.0950066	0.04053	-2.34	0.0194	0.0089
I:1960(5)	-0.231463	0.05602	-4.13	0.0000	0.0272

I:1960(10)	0.236529	0.05611	4.22	0.0000	0.0283
I:1961(7)	1.34995	0.1674	8.07	0.0000	0.0962
I:1975(4)	0.197868	0.05764	3.43	0.0006	0.0189
I:1975(10)	-0.290306	0.06095	-4.76	0.0000	0.0358
I:1979(3)	0.151497	0.05823	2.60	0.0095	0.0110
I:1980(5)	-0.161055	0.06031	-2.67	0.0078	0.0115
I:1980(6)	-0.265010	0.06107	-4.34	0.0000	0.0299
I:1983(4)	-0.346940	0.06057	-5.73	0.0000	0.0510
I:1990(12)	-0.226447	0.06579	-3.44	0.0006	0.0190
I:1992(12)	0.270714	0.05819	4.65	0.0000	0.0342
I:1995(4)	0.209471	0.05583	3.75	0.0002	0.0225
I:1998(4)	-0.148378	0.05578	-2.66	0.0080	0.0114
I:2004(4)	-0.265595	0.05813	-4.57	0.0000	0.0330
I:2006(2)	0.221575	0.05618	3.94	0.0001	0.0248
I:2008(11)	-0.211433	0.06020	-3.51	0.0005	0.0198
I:2009(9)	0.277039	0.06065	4.57	0.0000	0.0330
I:2012(6)	0.167932	0.05674	2.96	0.0032	0.0141
I:2014(4)	-0.168475	0.06053	-2.78	0.0055	0.0125
T1:1974(6)	-0.00987175	0.002480	-3.98	0.0001	0.0253
T1:1975(9)	0.0684125	0.01033	6.62	0.0000	0.0670
T1:1976(3)	-0.266580	0.05189	-5.14	0.0000	0.0414
T1:1976(4)	0.217224	0.04697	4.62	0.0000	0.0338
T1:1977(7)	-0.171014	0.06235	-2.74	0.0063	0.0122
T1:1977(8)	0.300315	0.1159	2.59	0.0098	0.0109
T1:1977(9)	-0.132629	0.06067	-2.19	0.0292	0.0078
T1:1979(3)	-0.0116792	0.004271	-2.73	0.0064	0.0121
T1:1980(5)	0.0228131	0.006256	3.65	0.0003	0.0213
T1:1981(5)	-0.144573	0.06174	-2.34	0.0195	0.0089
T1:1981(6)	0.155353	0.06830	2.27	0.0233	0.0084
T1:1981(12)	-0.210308	0.05552	-3.79	0.0002	0.0229
T1:1982(1)	0.167160	0.04858	3.44	0.0006	0.0190
T1:1983(4)	0.125053	0.01475	8.48	0.0000	0.1053
T1:1983(7)	-0.110678	0.01231	-8.99	0.0000	0.1168
T1:1986(6)	0.00338643	0.001049	3.23	0.0013	0.0168
T1:1990(9)	-0.136389	0.04968	-2.75	0.0062	0.0122
T1:1990(10)	0.175978	0.06137	2.87	0.0043	0.0133
T1:1991(3)	-0.132268	0.04282	-3.09	0.0021	0.0154
T1:1991(5)	0.287229	0.08624	3.33	0.0009	0.0178
T1:1991(6)	-0.220385	0.06179	-3.57	0.0004	0.0204
T1:1992(3)	0.0337073	0.007729	4.36	0.0000	0.0302
T1:1993(3)	-0.125642	0.03504	-3.59	0.0004	0.0206
T1:1993(4)	0.115419	0.03207	3.60	0.0003	0.0208
T1:2001(2)	0.0750250	0.03040	2.47	0.0139	0.0099
T1:2001(3)	-0.0731638	0.03192	-2.29	0.0222	0.0085
T1:2002(10)	-0.206157	0.06130	-3.36	0.0008	0.0182
T1:2002(11)	0.361594	0.1156	3.13	0.0018	0.0158
T1:2002(12)	-0.159835	0.06112	-2.61	0.0091	0.0111
T1:2004(7)	-0.115311	0.03490	-3.30	0.0010	0.0176
T1:2004(8)	0.118205	0.03390	3.49	0.0005	0.0195
T1:2008(10)	-0.136715	0.04995	-2.74	0.0064	0.0121
T1:2008(11)	0.155544	0.06318	2.46	0.0141	0.0098
T1:2009(3)	-0.218695	0.04713	-4.64	0.0000	0.0340
T1:2009(5)	0.673421	0.08824	7.63	0.0000	0.0870
T1:2009(6)	-0.485097	0.06336	-7.66	0.0000	0.0875

T1:2010(5)	0.104984	0.03166	3.32	0.0010	0.0177
T1:2010(7)	-0.229304	0.05596	-4.10	0.0000	0.0267
T1:2010(9)	0.180135	0.04218	4.27	0.0000	0.0290
T1:2011(1)	-0.0746353	0.01967	-3.80	0.0002	0.0230
T1:2011(8)	0.217488	0.04718	4.61	0.0000	0.0336
T1:2011(9)	-0.178488	0.04176	-4.27	0.0000	0.0290
T1:2013(12)	-0.141520	0.05407	-2.62	0.0091	0.0111
T1:2014(1)	0.244672	0.07924	3.09	0.0021	0.0154
T1:2014(3)	-0.110108	0.02971	-3.71	0.0002	0.0220
T1:2015(12)	-0.105978	0.04540	-2.33	0.0199	0.0088
T1:2016(1)	0.132798	0.05253	2.53	0.0117	0.0104
T1:2016(7)	-0.165315	0.06228	-2.65	0.0082	0.0114
T1:2016(8)	0.176049	0.06417	2.74	0.0063	0.0122
T1:2016(12)	-0.0439485	0.01212	-3.63	0.0003	0.0211
T1:2020(2)	1.58941	0.1962	8.10	0.0000	0.0970
T1:2020(4)	-2.96773	0.3263	-9.10	0.0000	0.1193
T1:2020(7)	1.73699	0.1477	11.8	0.0000	0.1845
T1:2020(11)	-0.431334	0.03343	-12.9	0.0000	0.2142
T1:2021(4)	0.140144	0.02857	4.91	0.0000	0.0379
T1:2021(7)	-0.0633002	0.02056	-3.08	0.0022	0.0153

```
sigma                 0.0551738   RSS                   1.85997479
R^2                   0.998039    F(129,611) =      2410 [0.000]**
Adj.R^2               0.997624    log-likelihood         1166.91
no. of observations        741   no. of parameters          130
mean(A0M044)           1.96815    se(A0M044)             1.13191

AR 1-7 test:      F(7,604)   =   1.9023 [0.0668]
ARCH 1-7 test:    F(7,727)   =   0.96396 [0.4565]
Normality test:   Chi^2(2)   =   5.0639 [0.0795]
Hetero test:      F(180,550)=   0.56830 [1.0000]
RESET23 test:     F(2,609)   =   1.0691 [0.3440]
Model saved to C:\JBG\JGResearch\Palgrave Business Cycles\PJD TCB 112021\Model UER AR1
with IIS, DIIS, and TIS Saturation and WkUNCL L12 Variables.pdf
Model saved to C:\JBG\JGResearch\Palgrave Business Cycles\PJD TCB 112021\Model UER AR1
with IIS, DIIS, and TIS Saturation and WkUNCL L12 Variables.pdf.gwg
```

The estimated AR1 model, small IIS, DIIS, and TIS saturation, and twelve months of lagged weekly unemployment claims variables in Eq. (10) produces a much lower Residual Sum of Squares (RSS) is 1.86, the AR1 benchmark, and its sigma, standard error, is 0.055, also far less than the AR1 model benchmark. The lagged LEI, G0M910, and weekly unemployment claims, A0M005, variables have the expected signs of the coefficients. The model error terms are essentially random. The model is adequately fitted.

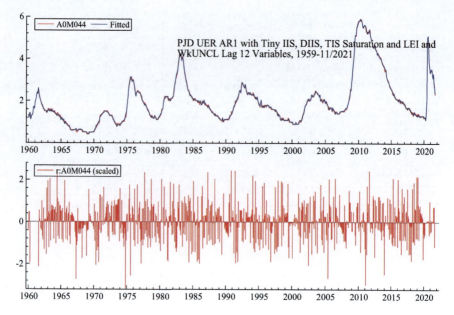

Fig. 10.11 Model UER AR1 with Tiny IIS, DIIS, and TIS saturation and WkUNCL L12 variables

We model the UER with an AR1 model with impulse indicator saturation (IIS), differenced impulse indicator saturation variables (DIIS) and trend impulse indicator (TIS) saturation variables and twelve months of lags in the weekly unemployment claims, A0M044, and the LEI, G0M910, time series in Eq. (11). We use the tiny (0.001) criteria for identifying outliers (Fig. 10.11).[1]

---

[1] See Castle, Doonik, and Hendry (2013) for support of the tiny criteria.

```
Summary of Autometrics search
initial search space      2^124   final search space       2^124
no. estimated models       2863   no. terminal models         20
test form                  LR-F   target size        Tiny:0.001
large residuals              no   presearch reduction       lags
backtesting                GUM0   tie-breaker                 SC
diagnostics p-value        0.01   search effort         standard
time                    3:31.70   Autometrics version        2.1
```

EQ(11) Modelling A0M044 by OLS
          The dataset is: C:\JBG\JGResearch\Palgrave Business Cycles\JG TCBData
11052021.csv
          The estimation sample is: 1960(1) - 2021(9)

	Coefficient	Std.Error	t-value	t-prob	Part.R^2
A0M044_1	0.775541	0.01382	56.1	0.0000	0.8348
A0M005_1	0.000836828	9.458e-05	8.85	0.0000	0.1116
G0M910_1	0.0182959	0.006683	2.74	0.0064	0.0119
G0M910_2	-0.0243087	0.007023	-3.46	0.0006	0.0189
G0M910_9	-0.0188992	0.002390	-7.91	0.0000	0.0912
Trend	0.00362609	0.0004231	8.57	0.0000	0.1055
DI:1961(1)	-1.04128	0.1592	-6.54	0.0000	0.0642
DI:1961(2)	-0.952650	0.1429	-6.66	0.0000	0.0666
DI:1961(3)	-0.870741	0.1251	-6.96	0.0000	0.0722
DI:1961(4)	-0.631971	0.1063	-5.95	0.0000	0.0537
DI:1961(5)	-0.447568	0.08466	-5.29	0.0000	0.0429
DI:1961(6)	-0.420986	0.05824	-7.23	0.0000	0.0774
DI:1963(8)	0.0913927	0.04022	2.27	0.0234	0.0082
DI:1964(11)	0.0977871	0.04023	2.43	0.0154	0.0094
DI:1965(1)	-0.0945161	0.04021	-2.35	0.0191	0.0088
DI:1973(7)	-0.0932539	0.04022	-2.32	0.0207	0.0086
DI:1976(5)	-0.131556	0.04024	-3.27	0.0011	0.0169
DI:1980(10)	-0.115689	0.04028	-2.87	0.0042	0.0131
DI:1981(6)	0.0883496	0.04024	2.20	0.0285	0.0077
DI:1986(2)	0.180275	0.04647	3.88	0.0001	0.0236
DI:1986(3)	0.103784	0.04644	2.23	0.0258	0.0080
DI:1986(9)	0.132863	0.04022	3.30	0.0010	0.0172
DI:1986(11)	0.0855218	0.04023	2.13	0.0339	0.0072
DI:1989(7)	0.175148	0.04025	4.35	0.0000	0.0295
DI:1992(3)	-0.120396	0.04934	-2.44	0.0150	0.0095
DI:1992(4)	-0.340456	0.05705	-5.97	0.0000	0.0541
DI:1992(5)	-0.165306	0.04947	-3.34	0.0009	0.0176
DI:1993(8)	-0.0969169	0.04026	-2.41	0.0164	0.0092
DI:1994(10)	0.141757	0.04022	3.52	0.0005	0.0195
DI:1995(5)	0.192635	0.04022	4.79	0.0000	0.0355
DI:2000(8)	0.0876365	0.04024	2.18	0.0298	0.0076
DI:2004(2)	-0.0948177	0.04023	-2.36	0.0187	0.0088
DI:2005(1)	-0.0972531	0.04024	-2.42	0.0159	0.0093
DI:2008(9)	-0.0911085	0.04032	-2.26	0.0242	0.0081
DI:2009(1)	-0.0971373	0.04050	-2.40	0.0168	0.0091
DI:2012(11)	-0.121714	0.04027	-3.02	0.0026	0.0145
DI:2016(5)	-0.125982	0.04026	-3.13	0.0018	0.0155
DI:2018(5)	-0.130995	0.04026	-3.25	0.0012	0.0167
DI:2020(4)	-0.348629	0.05523	-6.31	0.0000	0.0601
DI:2020(7)	2.25611	0.05910	38.2	0.0000	0.7005
DI:2020(8)	1.51164	0.06575	23.0	0.0000	0.4590
DI:2020(9)	0.751395	0.05527	13.6	0.0000	0.2288
DI:2021(4)	-0.217495	0.04755	-4.57	0.0000	0.0325
DI:2021(5)	-0.384399	0.04803	-8.00	0.0000	0.0932
DI:2021(7)	-0.0929922	0.04175	-2.23	0.0263	0.0079
I:1960(5)	1.02470	0.2754	3.72	0.0002	0.0217

I:1975(4)	0.191710	0.05931	3.23	0.0013	0.0165
I:1975(10)	-0.285050	0.06269	-4.55	0.0000	0.0321
I:1979(3)	0.146911	0.05903	2.49	0.0131	0.0098
I:1980(5)	-0.152383	0.06112	-2.49	0.0129	0.0099
I:1980(6)	-0.252743	0.06196	-4.08	0.0001	0.0260
I:1983(4)	-0.344297	0.06241	-5.52	0.0000	0.0466
I:1990(12)	-0.139159	0.05844	-2.38	0.0176	0.0090
I:1992(12)	0.273274	0.05996	4.56	0.0000	0.0323
I:1995(4)	0.207243	0.05752	3.60	0.0003	0.0204
I:1998(4)	-0.150230	0.05746	-2.61	0.0092	0.0109
I:2004(4)	-0.262404	0.05991	-4.38	0.0000	0.0299
I:2006(2)	0.223967	0.05788	3.87	0.0001	0.0235
I:2008(11)	-0.216208	0.06183	-3.50	0.0005	0.0193
I:2009(9)	0.277517	0.06197	4.48	0.0000	0.0312
I:2012(6)	0.159633	0.05764	2.77	0.0058	0.0122
I:2014(4)	-0.158273	0.06093	-2.60	0.0096	0.0107
T1:1974(6)	-0.00980702	0.002481	-3.95	0.0001	0.0245
T1:1975(9)	0.0658159	0.01050	6.27	0.0000	0.0594
T1:1976(3)	-0.240227	0.04942	-4.86	0.0000	0.0365
T1:1976(4)	0.189820	0.04251	4.47	0.0000	0.0310
T1:1979(3)	-0.00965405	0.002874	-3.36	0.0008	0.0178
T1:1980(5)	0.0138350	0.003850	3.59	0.0004	0.0203
T1:1981(12)	-0.161193	0.03901	-4.13	0.0000	0.0267
T1:1982(1)	0.135622	0.03995	3.39	0.0007	0.0182
T1:1983(4)	0.122828	0.01509	8.14	0.0000	0.0961
T1:1983(7)	-0.108010	0.01255	-8.61	0.0000	0.1062
T1:1986(6)	0.00324086	0.001028	3.15	0.0017	0.0157
T1:1991(6)	-0.0166361	0.003722	-4.47	0.0000	0.0311
T1:1992(3)	0.0226290	0.006524	3.47	0.0006	0.0189
T1:1993(3)	-0.114829	0.03576	-3.21	0.0014	0.0163
T1:1993(4)	0.106643	0.03278	3.25	0.0012	0.0167
T1:2001(2)	0.0787545	0.03083	2.55	0.0109	0.0104
T1:2001(3)	-0.0780556	0.03240	-2.41	0.0163	0.0092
T1:2002(10)	-0.202052	0.06311	-3.20	0.0014	0.0162
T1:2002(11)	0.363739	0.1191	3.05	0.0024	0.0148
T1:2002(12)	-0.165382	0.06297	-2.63	0.0088	0.0110
T1:2004(7)	-0.102971	0.03543	-2.91	0.0038	0.0134
T1:2004(8)	0.106351	0.03438	3.09	0.0021	0.0151
T1:2008(10)	-0.134622	0.04415	-3.05	0.0024	0.0147
T1:2008(11)	0.152527	0.04980	3.06	0.0023	0.0148
T1:2009(6)	-0.0304978	0.01194	-2.55	0.0109	0.0104
T1:2010(5)	0.106616	0.03226	3.30	0.0010	0.0172
T1:2010(7)	-0.210402	0.05216	-4.03	0.0001	0.0254
T1:2010(9)	0.125040	0.02613	4.78	0.0000	0.0354
T1:2013(12)	-0.145611	0.05436	-2.68	0.0076	0.0114
T1:2014(1)	0.253292	0.08015	3.16	0.0017	0.0158
T1:2014(3)	-0.116073	0.02905	-3.99	0.0001	0.0250
T1:2016(8)	0.0225949	0.007837	2.88	0.0041	0.0132
T1:2016(12)	-0.0272475	0.007546	-3.61	0.0003	0.0205
T1:2020(2)	1.68369	0.1922	8.76	0.0000	0.1097
T1:2020(4)	-3.76034	0.4129	-9.11	0.0000	0.1175
T1:2020(7)	1.19820	0.08641	13.9	0.0000	0.2358
T1:2020(11)	-0.324804	0.02912	-11.2	0.0000	0.1665
T1:2021(4)	0.126864	0.02943	4.31	0.0000	0.0290
T1:2021(7)	-0.0575866	0.02117	-2.72	0.0067	0.0117
DI:1960(2)	-0.143392	0.04022	-3.57	0.0004	0.0200
DI:1960(5)	-1.26218	0.2642	-4.78	0.0000	0.0353
DI:1960(6)	-1.26408	0.2525	-5.01	0.0000	0.0387
DI:1960(7)	-1.25547	0.2408	-5.21	0.0000	0.0418
DI:1960(8)	-1.34087	0.2286	-5.87	0.0000	0.0523
DI:1960(9)	-1.34397	0.2157	-6.23	0.0000	0.0587
DI:1960(10)	-1.11531	0.2028	-5.50	0.0000	0.0463
DI:1960(11)	-1.13866	0.1886	-6.04	0.0000	0.0553
DI:1960(12)	-1.27738	0.1739	-7.34	0.0000	0.0797
DI:1964(1)	0.0804419	0.04023	2.00	0.0460	0.0064
DI:1965(6)	0.140240	0.04021	3.49	0.0005	0.0191
DI:1970(12)	0.119583	0.04030	2.97	0.0031	0.0139
I:2009(5)	0.189520	0.06197	3.06	0.0023	0.0148
I:2009(6)	0.458263	0.06322	7.25	0.0000	0.0778
I:2011(8)	0.168149	0.05824	2.89	0.0040	0.0132
I:2011(10)	-0.169422	0.05843	-2.90	0.0039	0.0133
T1:2020(5)	1.13772	0.1976	5.76	0.0000	0.0505

```
sigma                0.0568646    RSS                    2.01451957
R^2                  0.997876     F(117,623) =      2501 [0.000]**
Adj.R^2              0.997477     log-likelihood         1137.34
no. of observations       741    no. of parameters          118
mean(A0M044)         1.96815      se(A0M044)             1.13191

AR 1-7 test:      F(7,616)  =    1.6920 [0.1081]
ARCH 1-7 test:    F(7,727)  =    0.89206 [0.5121]
Normality test:   Chi^2(2)  =    2.8733 [0.2377]
Hetero test:      F(157,576)=    0.69811 [0.9965]
RESET23 test:     F(2,621)  =    0.24266 [0.7846]
Model saved to C:\JBG\JGResearch\Palgrave Business Cycles\PJD TCB 112021\Model UER AR1
with Tiny IIS, DIIS, and TIS Saturation and LEI, WkUNCL L12 Variables.pdf
Model saved to C:\JBG\JGResearch\Palgrave Business Cycles\PJD TCB 112021\Model UER AR1
with Tiny IIS, DIIS, and TIS Saturation and LEI, WkUNCL L12 Variables.pdf.gwg
```

The estimated AR1 model, small IIS, DIIS, and TIS saturation, and twelve months of lagged weekly unemployment claims variables in Eq. (11) produces a much lower Residual Sum of Squares (RSS) is 2.01, the AR1 benchmark, and its sigma, standard error, is 0.057, also far less than the AR1 model benchmark. The lagged LEI, G0M910, and weekly unemployment claims, A0M005, variables have the expected signs of the coefficients. The model error terms are essentially random. The model is adequately fitted.

10.7 Automatic Time Series Modeling and Forecasting the PJD Unemployment Rate, the Application of OxMetrics to TCB LEI 11052021 to the MZTT Post-publication Period, 1999–11/2021

We model the UER with an estimated AR1 model to serve as a forecasting benchmark. The estimated AR1 is shown in Eq. (12) for the 1999–11/2021, the MZTT post-publication period. Harry Markowitz insists on modeling only data that "the little man inside the computer can see." He also believes that you should only test and verify models in the post-publication period. It does not good to verify models using techniques identified with the period in which the analysis was developed. In the opinions of the authors, this section of our chapter truly tests what we knew, and when we knew it (or could have known it). The application of the Hendry and Doornik (2014) system is appropriate since Mr. Hendry was publishing applications of his automatic time series methodology in (1980) and (1986) with PCGive. A component of the OxMetrics software used in this chapter.

```
PJD PS OxMetrics TCBData 11052021.csv loaded from C:\JBG\JGResearch\Palgrave Business
Cycles\PJD PS OxMetrics TCBData 11052021.csv


Ox Professional version 8.20 (Windows_64/U) (C) J.A. Doornik, 1994-2019

---- PcGive 15.20 session started at 6:15:30 on 16-11-2021 ----

EQ(12) Modelling A0M044 by OLS
        The dataset is: C:\JBG\JGResearch\Palgrave Business Cycles\PJD PS OxMetrics
TCBData 11052021.csv
        The estimation sample is: 1999-02-01 - 2021-09-01

                   Coefficient  Std.Error  t-value  t-prob Part.R^2
A0M044_1              0.986525   0.009981     98.8  0.0000   0.9732
Constant             0.0485242    0.03378     1.44  0.1520   0.0076
Trend             -7.33694e-05  0.0001820   -0.403  0.6872   0.0006

sigma                 0.228373  RSS            14.0294553
R^2                   0.974754  F(2,269) =      5193 [0.000]**
Adj.R^2               0.974566  log-likelihood    17.2402
no. of observations        272  no. of parameters       3
mean(A0M044)           2.52941  se(A0M044)        1.43198


AR 1-7 test:      F(7,262)  =    4.1437 [0.0002]**
ARCH 1-7 test:    F(7,258)  =   0.20862 [0.9833]
Normality test:   Chi^2(2)  =    3191.6 [0.0000]**
Hetero test:      F(4,267)  =    1.7257 [0.1446]
Hetero-X test:    F(5,266)  =    1.5417 [0.1771]
RESET23 test:     F(2,267)  =   0.46524 [0.6285]
Model saved to C:\JBG\JGResearch\Palgrave Business Cycles\PJD TCB 112021\PJD PS
TCBData 11052021\Model PS UER AR1 LS.pdf
Model saved to C:\JBG\JGResearch\Palgrave Business Cycles\PJD TCB 112021\PJD PS
TCBData 11052021\Model PS UER AR1 LS.pdf.gwg
```

The estimated AR1 model, Eq. (12) produces a Residual Sum of Squares (RSS) is 14.03 and its sigma, standard error, is 0.229. The model error terms are non-random, see the Normality test criteria. The model is not adequately fitted (Fig. 10.12).

We can estimate an AR1 model1 with large residuals within OxMetrics as we do in Eq. (13).

```
EQ(13) Modelling A0M044 by OLS
        The dataset is: C:\JBG\JGResearch\Palgrave Business Cycles\PJD PS OxMetrics
TCBData 11052021.csv
        The estimation sample is: 1999-02-01 - 2021-09-01

                   Coefficient  Std.Error  t-value  t-prob Part.R^2
A0M044_1              0.996753   0.002715     367.  0.0000   0.9980
I:2020-07-01          3.00649     0.1294     23.2  0.0000   0.6674
I:2020-10-01        -0.785064     0.1299    -6.04  0.0000   0.1196

sigma                 0.129283  RSS             4.49610200
log-likelihood         172.001
no. of observations        272  no. of parameters       3
mean(A0M044)           2.52941  se(A0M044)        1.43198


AR 1-7 test:      F(7,262)  =    8.2126 [0.0000]**
ARCH 1-7 test:    F(7,258)  =    12.468 [0.0000]**
Normality test:   Chi^2(2)  =    74.354 [0.0000]**
Hetero test:      F(2,267)  =    6.1627 [0.0024]**
Hetero-X test:    F(2,267)  =    6.1627 [0.0024]**
RESET23 test:     F(2,267)  =   0.84113 [0.4324]
Model saved to C:\JBG\JGResearch\Palgrave Business Cycles\PJD TCB 112021\PJD PS
TCBData 11052021\Model.pdf
Model saved to C:\JBG\JGResearch\Palgrave Business Cycles\PJD TCB 112021\PJD PS
TCBData 11052021\Model.pdf.gwg
```

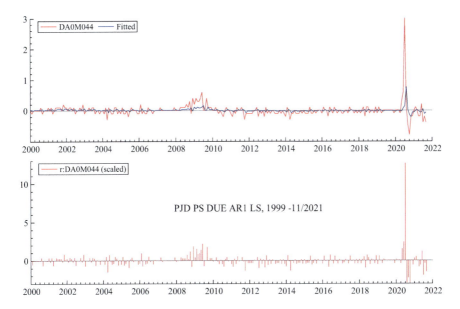

Fig. 10.12 Model DLGDP AR1 IIS DIIS TIS saturation variables

The estimated UER AR1 model with large-estimated residuals (both in 2020), Eq. (13), produces a Residual Sum of Squares (RSS) that is 4.50, substantially lower than the AR1 model, and its sigma, standard error, is 0.129, is significantly lower than the AR1 benchmark. However, the model error terms are non-random; see the Autoregressive Error, ARCH, and Normality test criteria. The model is not adequately fitted.

We estimate a UER AR1 shown in Eq. (14) with impulse indicator saturation (IIS), differenced impulse indicator saturation variables (DIIS), and trend impulse indicator (TIS) saturation variables. We use the small (0.01) indicator level. The model estimation period is again the MZTT post-publication period, 1999–11/2021.

```
EQ(14) Modelling AOM044 by OLS
        The dataset is: C:\JBG\JGResearch\Palgrave Business Cycles\PJD PS OxMetrics
TCBData 11052021.csv
        The estimation sample is: 1999-02-01 - 2021-09-01
```

	Coefficient	Std.Error	t-value	t-prob	Part.R^2
AOM044_1	0.965707	0.006427	150.	0.0000	0.9894
DI:2006-02-01	0.147462	0.05440	2.71	0.0072	0.0296
DI:2008-10-01	0.195747	0.05440	3.60	0.0004	0.0510
DI:2008-12-01	-2.18395	0.1959	-11.1	0.0000	0.3403
DI:2009-01-01	-2.00789	0.1777	-11.3	0.0000	0.3463
DI:2009-02-01	-1.62675	0.1580	-10.3	0.0000	0.3055
DI:2009-03-01	-1.33368	0.1360	-9.80	0.0000	0.2851
DI:2009-04-01	-1.03210	0.1104	-9.35	0.0000	0.2661
DI:2009-05-01	-0.622019	0.07755	-8.02	0.0000	0.2107
DI:2011-09-01	0.297004	0.07831	3.79	0.0002	0.0563
DI:2012-06-01	0.145759	0.05440	2.68	0.0079	0.0289
DI:2012-11-01	-0.149097	0.05440	-2.74	0.0066	0.0302
DI:2020-05-01	-0.726150	0.06444	-11.3	0.0000	0.3451
DI:2020-06-01	-2.17176	0.06682	-32.5	0.0000	0.8143
DI:2020-08-01	0.575249	0.06399	8.99	0.0000	0.2511
DI:2020-09-01	0.482107	0.06398	7.54	0.0000	0.1907
DI:2021-06-01	0.296571	0.05440	5.45	0.0000	0.1098
I:2004-04-01	-0.291579	0.07809	-3.73	0.0002	0.0547
I:2008-12-01	2.54807	0.2131	12.0	0.0000	0.3724
I:2009-09-01	0.437250	0.07778	5.62	0.0000	0.1159
I:2011-09-01	-0.292227	0.1126	-2.59	0.0100	0.0272
I T1:2004-02-01	0.0483234	0.01419	3.41	0.0008	0.0459
T1:2004-04-01	-0.0486187	0.01407	-3.46	0.0006	0.0472
T1:2011-09-01	0.00683436	0.001316	5.19	0.0000	0.1006
T1:2014-03-01	-0.00510147	0.001090	-4.68	0.0000	0.0833
T1:2020-03-01	-1.02970	0.03565	-28.9	0.0000	0.7758
T1:2020-05-01	2.22656	0.07896	28.2	0.0000	0.7674
T1:2020-07-01	-1.26862	0.05606	-22.6	0.0000	0.6800
T1:2021-02-01	0.274574	0.06373	4.31	0.0000	0.0715
T1:2021-03-01	-0.202754	0.05427	-3.74	0.0002	0.0547

```
sigma                0.0769241  RSS                   1.42607506
R^2                  0.995177   log-likelihood         328.168
no. of observations      272   no. of parameters          31
mean(AOM044)         2.52941   se(AOM044)             1.43198

AR 1-7 test:     F(7,234)  =  0.70246 [0.6700]
ARCH 1-7 test:   F(7,258)  =  0.44854 [0.8707]
Normality test:  Chi^2(2)  =  0.18720 [0.9106]
Hetero test:     F(28,228) =  0.88978 [0.6296]
RESET23 test:    F(2,239)  =  2.8104 [0.0622]
Model saved to C:\JBG\JGResearch\Palgrave Business Cycles\PJD TCB 112021\PJD PS
TCBData 11052021\Model PS UER AR1 IIS, DIIS, TIS Saturation Variables.pdf
Model saved to C:\JBG\JGResearch\Palgrave Business Cycles\PJD TCB 112021\PJD PS
TCBData 11052021\Model PS UER AR1 IIS, DIIS, TIS Saturation Variables.pdf.gwg
```

The estimated AR1 model, small IIS, DIIS, and TIS saturation variables in Eq. (14) produces a much lower Residual Sum of Squares (RSS) is 1.42, the AR1 benchmark, and its sigma, standard error, is 0.077, also far less than the AR1 model benchmark. The model error terms essentially random. The model is adequately fitted. Equation (14) is an example of the Hendry automatic time series modeling and forecasting to produce a "clean model" (Fig. 10.13).

We estimate a UER AR1 shown in Eq. (15) with impulse indicator saturation (IIS), differenced impulse indicator saturation variables (DIIS), and trend impulse indicator (TIS) saturation variables and a one-period lag in the LEI, G0M910, time series. We use the small (0.01) indicator level.

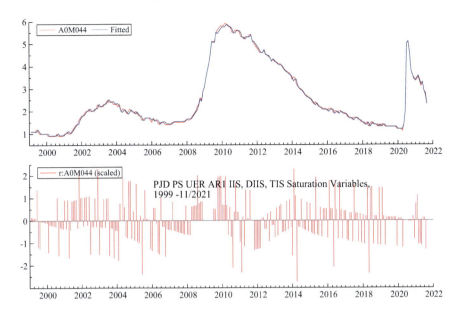

Fig. 10.13 Model PS UER AR1 IIS, DIIS, TIS saturation variables

The model estimation period is again the MZTT post-publication period, 1999–11/2021.

```
EQ(15) Modelling A0M044 by OLS

        The estimation sample is: 1999-02-01 - 2021-09-01

                  Coefficient  Std.Error  t-value  t-prob Part.R^2
A0M044_1            0.925972    0.01402     66.1   0.0000   0.9481
Constant            0.914897    0.1659      5.52   0.0000   0.1129
G0M910_1           -0.00883943  0.001211   -7.30   0.0000   0.1822
DI:2004-03-01       0.191341    0.04778     4.00   0.0001   0.0629
DI:2008-10-01       0.202501    0.04781     4.24   0.0000   0.0698
DI:2011-08-01       0.164663    0.05518     2.98   0.0031   0.0359
DI:2011-09-01       0.233208    0.05517     4.23   0.0000   0.0696
DI:2012-06-01       0.147175    0.04778     3.08   0.0023   0.0382
DI:2014-01-01      -0.143931    0.04778    -3.01   0.0029   0.0366
DI:2014-03-01       0.145131    0.04777     3.04   0.0026   0.0372
DI:2016-05-01      -0.143047    0.04778    -2.99   0.0030   0.0361
DI:2018-04-01       0.145242    0.04777     3.04   0.0026   0.0372
DI:2020-07-01       1.60112     0.06686    23.9    0.0000   0.7058
DI:2020-08-01       0.907491    0.06192    14.7    0.0000   0.4734
I:2002-12-01        0.184068    0.06837     2.69   0.0076   0.0294
I:2006-02-01        0.231814    0.06853     3.38   0.0008   0.0457
I:2008-12-01        0.207382    0.07019     2.95   0.0034   0.0352
I:2009-06-01        0.355330    0.07188     4.94   0.0000   0.0928
I:2009-09-01        0.327713    0.07084     4.63   0.0000   0.0822
I:2020-05-01       -0.305298    0.07551    -4.04   0.0001   0.0640
I:2020-06-01       -0.413191    0.08232    -5.02   0.0000   0.0954
I:2020-10-01       -0.871068    0.07900   -11.0    0.0000   0.3372
```

```
T1:2008-10-01      -0.0495361      0.01006     -4.92  0.0000   0.0921
T1:2009-04-01       0.159601       0.03509      4.55  0.0000   0.0797
T1:2009-06-01      -0.106706       0.02936     -3.63  0.0003   0.0524
T1:2016-07-01      -0.00409029    0.0008994    -4.55  0.0000   0.0796
T1:2020-03-01      -0.454312       0.02358    -19.3   0.0000   0.6083
T1:2020-06-01       0.821216       0.04216     19.5   0.0000   0.6135
T1:2020-10-01      -0.468046       0.04635    -10.1   0.0000   0.2991
T1:2021-01-01       0.202857       0.04960      4.09  0.0001   0.0654
T1:2021-04-01      -0.532531       0.1051      -5.07  0.0000   0.0970
T1:2021-05-01       0.960711       0.1514       6.35  0.0000   0.1442
T1:2021-06-01      -0.527587       0.07803     -6.76  0.0000   0.1606

sigma                0.0675497  RSS                    1.09054772
R^2                  0.998038   F(32,239) =       3798 [0.000]**
Adj.R^2              0.997775   log-likelihood         364.649
no. of observations       272  no. of parameters           33
mean(A0M044)         2.52941    se(A0M044)             1.43198

AR 1-7 test:       F(7,232)   =   0.47789 [0.8501]
ARCH 1-7 test:     F(7,258)   =   0.72116 [0.6542]
Normality test:    Chi^2(2)   =   1.2411  [0.5376]
Hetero test:       F(36,223)  =   0.89075 [0.6505]
RESET23 test:      F(2,237)   =   2.6010  [0.0763]
Model saved to C:\JBG\JGResearch\Palgrave Business Cycles\PJD TCB 112021\PJD PS
TCBData 11052021\Model PS UER AR1 IIS, DIIS, TIS Saturation and LEI L1 Variables.pdf
Model saved to C:\JBG\JGResearch\Palgrave Business Cycles\PJD TCB 112021\PJD PS
TCBData 11052021\Model PS UER AR1 IIS, DIIS, TIS Saturation and LEI L1
Variables.pdf.gwg
```

The estimated AR1 model, small IIS, DIIS, and TIS saturation, and one month of LEI variable in Eq. (15) produces a much lower Residual Sum of Squares (RSS) is 1.09, the AR1 benchmark, and its sigma, standard error, is 0.068, also far less than the AR1 model benchmark. The lagged LEI, G0M910, variables have the expected signs of the coefficient in the MZTT post-publication period. Increases in the LEI lead to reductions in the unemployment rate, out-of-sample! The model error terms are random. The model is adequately fitted. The model is adequately fitted. Equation (15) is an example of the Hendry automatic time series modellng and forecasting to produce a "clean model" (Fig. 10.14).

We estimate a UER AR1 shown in Eq. (16) with impulse indicator saturation (IIS), differenced impulse indicator saturation variables (DIIS), and trend impulse indicator (TIS) saturation variables and a one-period lag in the weekly unemployment claims time series, A0M005, time series. We use the small (0.01) indicator level.

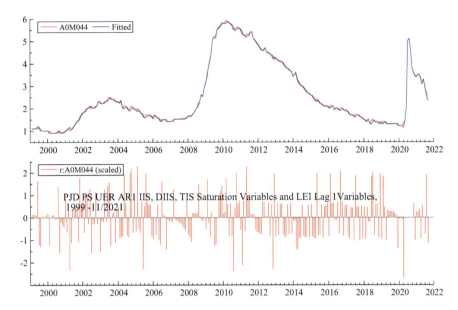

Fig. 10.14 Model PS UER AR1 IIS, DIIS, TIS saturation and LEI L1 variables

```
EQ(16) Modelling A0M044 by OLS
    The dataset is: C:\JBG\JGResearch\Palgrave Business Cycles\PJD PS OxMetrics
TCBData 11052021.csv
    The estimation sample is: 1999-02-01 - 2021-09-01

                Coefficient  Std.Error  t-value  t-prob  Part.R^2
A0M044_1           0.945824   0.004984     190.  0.0000    0.9933
Trend             -0.00208731 0.0001656   -12.6  0.0000    0.3964
A0M005_1           0.00125355 8.661e-05    14.5  0.0000    0.4640
DI:2002-12-01      0.160310   0.05104      3.14  0.0019    0.0392
DI:2008-11-01     -0.215527   0.05109     -4.22  0.0000    0.0685
DI:2009-07-01     -0.163403   0.05896     -2.77  0.0060    0.0308
DI:2009-08-01     -0.282529   0.05893     -4.79  0.0000    0.0867
DI:2012-06-01      0.150914   0.05103      2.96  0.0034    0.0349
DI:2020-02-01      1.36923    0.1061      12.9   0.0000    0.4078
DI:2020-03-01      4.08205    0.2667      15.3   0.0000    0.4918
DI:2020-04-01      3.06854    0.2112      14.5   0.0000    0.4660
DI:2020-06-01     -0.931934   0.08043    -11.6   0.0000    0.3568
DI:2020-07-01      1.00608    0.08658     11.6   0.0000    0.3582
DI:2020-08-01      0.523626   0.07119      7.36  0.0000    0.1827
DI:2020-10-01     -0.527308   0.06543     -8.06  0.0000    0.2116
DI:2020-11-01     -0.337407   0.07422     -4.55  0.0000    0.0787
DI:2020-12-01     -0.176198   0.06430     -2.74  0.0066    0.0301
DI:2021-06-01      0.273670   0.05106      5.36  0.0000    0.1061
I:2004-04-01      -0.250588   0.07300     -3.43  0.0007    0.0464
I:2009-06-01       0.368391   0.07423      4.96  0.0000    0.0924
I:2011-10-01      -0.250343   0.07299     -3.43  0.0007    0.0464
I:2014-04-01      -0.253471   0.07249     -3.50  0.0006    0.0481
```

```
T1:2005-12-01     -0.270217    0.07413    -3.65   0.0003   0.0521
T1:2006-01-01      0.499013    0.1464      3.41   0.0008   0.0458
T1:2006-02-01     -0.229657    0.07377    -3.11   0.0021   0.0385
T1:2019-12-01      1.34933     0.09124    14.8    0.0000   0.4747
T1:2020-02-01     -1.90046     0.1114    -17.1    0.0000   0.5462
T1:2020-06-01      0.667908    0.03730    17.9    0.0000   0.5699
T1:2020-10-01     -0.203354    0.02808    -7.24   0.0000   0.1781
T1:2021-05-01      0.0892660   0.009366    9.53   0.0000   0.2729

sigma                  0.0721666   RSS                  1.26033952
R^2                    0.997739    log-likelihood         344.970
no. of observations         272   no. of parameters           30
mean(A0M044)           2.52941     se(A0M044)             1.43198

AR 1-7 test:        F(7,235)   =    1.5012 [0.1676]
ARCH 1-7 test:      F(7,258)   =    0.48402 [0.8458]
Normality test:     Chi^2(2)   =    1.1253 [0.5697]
Hetero test:        F(37,229)  =    0.83054 [0.7461]
RESET23 test:       F(2,240)   =    2.8122 [0.0621]
Model saved to C:\JBG\JGResearch\Palgrave Business Cycles\PJD TCB 112021\PJD PS
TCBData 11052021\Model PS UER AR1 IIS DIIS TIS Saturation and WkUNCL L1 Variables.pdf
Model saved to C:\JBG\JGResearch\Palgrave Business Cycles\PJD TCB 112021\PJD PS
TCBData 11052021\Model PS UER AR1 IIS DIIS TIS Saturation and WkUNCL L1
Variables.pdf.gwg
```

The estimated AR1 model, small IIS, DIIS, and TIS saturation, and one month of lagged weekly unemployment claims variables in Eq. (16) produces a much lower Residual Sum of Squares (RSS) is 1.26, the AR1 benchmark, and its sigma, standard error, is 0.072, also far less than the AR1 model benchmark. The lagged weekly unemployment claims, A0M005, variable have the expected sign of the coefficients, positive. The model error terms are random. The model is adequately fitted. Equation (16) is a clean model.

```
EQ(17) Modelling A0M044 by OLS
        The dataset is: C:\JBG\JGResearch\Palgrave Business Cycles\PJD PS OxMetrics
TCBData 11052021.csv
        The estimation sample is: 2000-01-01 - 2021-09-01

                  Coefficient  Std.Error   t-value  t-prob Part.R^2
A0M044_1            0.872955    0.01474      59.2    0.0000   0.9375
G0M910_2           -0.00392038  0.0004177    -9.39   0.0000   0.2735
A0M005_1            0.000953651 8.780e-05    10.9    0.0000   0.3352
A0M005_2            0.000401876 4.148e-05     9.69   0.0000   0.2863
DI:2002-12-01       0.145301    0.05234       2.78   0.0060   0.0319
DI:2004-04-01      -0.184677    0.05238      -3.53   0.0005   0.0504
DI:2006-01-01      -0.152332    0.05234      -2.91   0.0040   0.0349
DI:2011-09-01       0.152812    0.05233       2.92   0.0038   0.0352
DI:2012-06-01       0.143533    0.05234       2.74   0.0066   0.0311
DI:2014-03-01       0.143481    0.05234       2.74   0.0066   0.0311
DI:2020-07-01       2.25312     0.06926      32.5    0.0000   0.8189
DI:2020-08-01       0.796524    0.06815      11.7    0.0000   0.3686
DI:2021-06-01       0.580953    0.09984       5.82   0.0000   0.1264
I:2008-11-01       -0.275384    0.07546      -3.65   0.0003   0.0538
```

```
I:2009-06-01           0.417377     0.07910     5.28   0.0000   0.1063
T1:2009-06-01         -0.0991239    0.02717    -3.65   0.0003   0.0538
T1:2009-08-01          0.102671     0.02775     3.70   0.0003   0.0553
T1:2018-04-01         -0.115665     0.03412    -3.39   0.0008   0.0468
T1:2018-05-01          0.116735     0.03590     3.25   0.0013   0.0432
T1:2020-02-01          2.28823      0.2119     10.8    0.0000   0.3326
T1:2020-04-01         -3.96374      0.3298    -12.0    0.0000   0.3817
T1:2020-07-01          2.51464      0.1280     19.6    0.0000   0.6226
T1:2020-09-01         -1.49125      0.1359    -11.0    0.0000   0.3399
T1:2020-10-01          0.627490     0.09741     6.44   0.0000   0.1506
T1:2021-05-01         -0.655519     0.1817     -3.61   0.0004   0.0527
T1:2021-06-01          1.17602      0.2947      3.99   0.0001   0.0637
T1:2021-07-01         -0.498866     0.1330     -3.75   0.0002   0.0567

sigma                  0.0740100   RSS                  1.28173107
R^2                    0.997450    log-likelihood        323.435
no. of observations         261   no. of parameters          27
mean(AOM044)           2.59119     se(AOM044)            1.42913

AR 1-7 test:        F(7,227)   =    2.0452 [0.0506]
ARCH 1-7 test:      F(7,247)   =    0.60055 [0.7552]
Normality test:     Chi^2(2)   =    0.16937 [0.9188]
Hetero test:        F(40,216)  =    1.0353 [0.4213]
RESET23 test:       F(2,232)   =    2.3947 [0.0935]
Model saved to C:\JBG\JGResearch\Palgrave Business Cycles\PJD TCB 112021\PJD PS
TCBData 11052021\Model PS UER AR1 IIS DIIS TIS Saturation WkUNCL LEI L12 Varianles.pdf
Model saved to C:\JBG\JGResearch\Palgrave Business Cycles\PJD TCB 112021\PJD PS
TCBData 11052021\Model PS UER AR1 IIS DIIS TIS Saturation WkUNCL LEI L12
Varianles.pdf.gwg
```

We estimate a UER AR1 shown in Eq. (17) with impulse indicator saturation (IIS), differenced impulse indicator saturation variables (DIIS), and trend impulse indicator (TIS) saturation variables and a twelve-period lag in the LEI, G0M910, and weekly unemployment claims time series, A0M005, time series. We use the small (0.01) indicator level.

The estimated AR1 model, small IIS, DIIS, and TIS saturation, and twelve months of lagged LEI variables in Eq. (17) produces a much lower Residual Sum of Squares (RSS) is 1.28, the AR1 benchmark, and its sigma, standard error, is 0.074, also far less than the AR1 model benchmark. The lagged LEI, G0M910, variables have the expected signs of the coefficient, negative, and the weekly unemployment claims coefficients have the expected coefficients, positive, in the estimated UER model. The model error terms are random. The model is adequately fitted (Fig. 10.15).

Finally, as we complete many of the seemingly infinite number of models one may estimate, must ask what do we know? The reader should realize that whether one works with the (raw) unemployment rate or the change in the unemployment rate, that both the LEI and Weekly Unemployment Claims data are statistically associated with unemployment. The reader should further recognize that a very large number of models on real-world data of the business cycle and its variables can be estimated, with very similar (low) RSS and standard errors and residuals that are not statistically different from being random (white noise). The data used in this chapter is as current as humanly possible, and the author thanks The Conference Board!

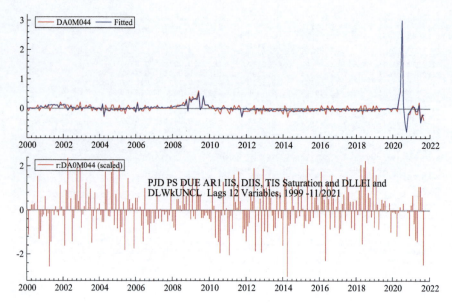

Fig. 10.15   Model PS DUE AR1 IIS DIIS TIS saturation and DLWkUNCL DLLEI L12 variables

10.8   Concluding Remarks and Extensions

In this chapter, we used the latest Conference Board database and built simple linear regression and multiple regressions in SAS to model the unemployment rate as a function if the Leading Economic Indicators, LEI, and one of its components, the weekly unemployment claims time series. We estimated many combinations of ordinary least square (OLS) and robust regression (ROB) models. We applied the Hendry and Doornik (2014) and Castle and Hendry (2019) automatic time series PCGive (OxMetrics) methodology to the unemployment rate. We report that the OxMetrics and AutoMetrics system substantially reduce regression sum of squares measures relative to a traditional variation on the random walk with drift model. The modeling process of including the Leading Economic Indicator in forecasting real GDP has been addressed before, but our results are more statistically significant, using the latest data for model verification. A similar conclusion is found for the impact of the LEI and weekly unemployment claims series leading the unemployment rate series. Breaks in time series must be estimated. Such results should excite practitioners!

References

Belsley, D. A., Kuh, E., & Welsch, R. E. (1980). *Regression diagnostics: Identifying influential data and sources of collinearity*. John Wiley & Sons. Chapter 2.

Castle, J. L., Clements, M. P., & Hendry, D. F. (2015). Robust approaches to forecasting. *International Journal of Forecasting, 31*, 99–112.

Castle, J. L., Doornik, J. A., & Hendry, D. F. (2013). Model selection in equations with many 'small' effects. *Oxford Bulletin of Economics and Statistics, 75*, 6–22.

Castle, J. L., & Hendry, D. F. (2019). *Modelling our changing world*. Palgrave Macmillan.

Castle, J. L., & Shepard, N. (2009). *The methodology and practice of econometrics*. Oxford University Press.

Clements, M. P., & Hendry, D. F. (1998). *Forecasting economic time series*. Cambridge University Press.

Dhrymes, P. J. (1978). *Introductory econometrics*. Springer.

Dhrymes, P. J. (2017). *Introductory econometrics* (Revised ed.). Springer.

Doornik, J. A. (2009). Autometrics. In J. L. Castle & N. Shepard (Eds.), *The methodology and practice of econometrics*. Oxford University Press.

Doornik, J. A., & Hendry, D. F. (2015). Statistical model selection with 'big data'. *Cogent Economics & Finance, 3*, 1–15.

Granger, C. W. J. (2001). *Essays in econometrics* (E. Ghysels, N. R. Swanson, & M. H. Watson, Eds.). Cambridge University Press.

Granger, C. W. J., & Newbold, P. (1977). *Forecasting economic time series*. Academic Press.

Guerard, J. B., Jr. (2001). A note on the effectiveness of the U.S. leading economic indicators. *Indian Economic Review, 36*, 251–268.

Guerard, J. B., Jr. (2004). The forecasting effectiveness of the U.S. leading economic indicators: Further evidence and initial G7 results. In P. Dua (Ed.), *Business cycles and economic growth: An analysis using leading indicators*. Oxford University Press.

Guerard, J. B., Jr., Thomakos, D., & Kyriazai, F. 2020. Automatic time series modelling and forecasting: A replication case study of forecasting real GDP, the unemployment rate, and the impact of leading economic indicators. *Cogent Economics & Finance, 8*. https://doi.org/10.1080/23322039.2020.1759483

Gunst, R. F., & Mason, R. L. (1980). *Regression analysis and its application*. Marcel Dekker Inc.

Hendry, D. F. (1980). Econometrics—Alchemy or science? *Economica, 47*, 387–406.

Hendry, D. F. (1986). Using PC-GIVE in econometrics teaching. *Oxford Bulletin of Economics and Statistics, 48*, 87–98.

Hendry, D. F. (2000). *Econometrics: Alchemy or science?* Oxford University Press.

Hendry, D. F., & Doornik, J. A. (2014). *Empirical model discovery and theory evaluation*. MIT Press.

Hendry, D. F., & Krolzig, H. M. (2005). The properties of automatic gets modelling. *The Economic Journal, 115*, c32–c61.

Hendry, D. F., & Nielsen, B. (2007). *Econometric modeling: A likelihood Approach*. Princeton University Press.

Krolzig, H. M., & Hendry, D. F. (2001). Computer automation of general-to-specific model selection procedures. *Journal of Economic Dynamics and Control, 25*, 831–866.

Kyriazi, F. S., Thomakos, D. D., & Guerard, J. B. (2019). Adaptive learning forecasting with applications in forecasting agricultural prices. *International Journal of Forecasting, 35*, 1356–1369.

Maronna, R. A., Martin, R. D., Yohai, V. J., & Salibian-Barrera, M. (2019). *Robust statistics: Theory and methods with R*. Springer.

Makridakis, S., & Hibon, M. (2000). The M3-competition: Results, conclusions and implications. *International Journal of Forecasting, 16*, 451–476.

Mincer, J., & Zarnowitz, V. (1969). The evaluation of economic forecasts. In J. Mincer (Ed.), *Economic forecasts and expectations*. Columbia University Press.

Montgomery, A. L., Zarnowitz, V., Tsay, R., & Tiao, G. C. (1998). Forecasting the U.S. unemployment rate. *Journal of the American Statistical Association, 93*, 478–493.

Thomakos, D., & Guerard, J. B., Jr. (2004). Naïve, ARIMA, transfer function, and VAR models: A comparison of forecasting performance. *The International Journal of Forecasting, 20*, 53–67.

Tsay, R. S. (1988). Outliers, level shifts, and variance changes in time series. *Journal of Forecasting, 7*, 1–20.

Tsay, R. S. (1989). Testing and modelling threshold autoregressive processes. *Journal of the American Statistical Association, 84*, 231–249.

Tsay, R. S. (2010). *Analysis of financial time series* (3rd ed.). Wiley.

Tsay, R. S., & Chen, R. (2019). *Nonlinear time series analysis*. Wiley.

Vinod, H. D. (2008). *Hands-on intermediate econometrics using R: Templates for extending dozens of practical examples*. World Scientific. ISBN 10-981-281-885-5.

Vinod, H. D., & Guerard, J. B., Jr. (2020). Causality studies of real GDP, unemployment, and leading indicators. In J. B. Guerard Jr. (Ed.), *Handbook of applied investment research*. World Scientific.

Zarnowitz, V. (1992). *Business cycles: Theory, history, indicators, and forecasting*. University of Chicago Press.

Zarnowitz, V. (2004). The autonomy of recent US growth and business cycle. In P. Dua (Ed.), *Business cycles and economic growth: An analysis using leading indicators* (pp. 44–82). Oxford University Press.

Zarnowitz, V., & Ozyildirim, A. (2001). On the measurement of business cycles and growth cycles. *Indian Economic Review, 36*, 34–54.

11

Conclusions and Summary

In Chapter 2, we introduced the reader to Mr. Mitchell, the first Director of Research at the National Bureau of Economic Research, NBER. We reviewed his *Business Cycles* (1913), and *Business Cycles: The Problems and its Settings* (1927) where Mr. Mitchell put forth the phases of the business cycle and laid the groundwork on how the NBER would conduct much of its business cycle research from its inception in 1920 until 1992. We reviewed the first NBER monograph, the Mitchell monograph, *Business Cycles and Unemployment* (1923), with its analysis of the Depression of 1921 and its recommendations for data collection, analysis, and recommendations to alleviate much of the suffering of unemployment in the U.S. economy in the early 1920s. Mr. Mitchell was trained in traditional (classical) economics. The Mitchell emphasis on empiricism and economic description and analysis of business conditions and cycles from 1862 to 1927 was reviewed.

In Chapter 3, we introduced the reader to the business cycles analyses of Mr. Warren Persons, who built models to develop a general business conditions index during the 1916–1932 time period. His models failed to forecast The Great Depression and failed to forecast its length and severity. His models were of marginal value to economists as only his stock price variables were statistically associated with real GDP growth during the 1875 to 1930 period. Mr. Joseph Schumpeter wrote a massive two-volume monograph, *Business Cycles*, in 1939. His book stressed non-business factors, exogenous factors, which can cluster innovations and drive economic growth, creating business fluctuations. Mr. Gottfried Haberler published his *Prosperity and Depression*

J. B. Guerard, *The Leading Economic Indicators and Business Cycles in the United States*, https://doi.org/10.1007/978-3-030-99418-1_11

in 1937, winning the David Wells Award at Harvard. Haberler integrated the Wesley Clair Mitchell and Irving Fisher-Hawtrey monetary theories of the business cycle. Mr. Otto Eckstein developed an econometric model to forecast the direction of real GDP growth and created a great commercial success, the Data Resources (DRI) Model. Is the model perfect? No. Was the model better than a naïve, no-change forecast; yes. The reader is introduced to several of the great (non-NBER) research monographs of business cycles in this chapter. There are some books that the reader must read to understand topics currently being debated.

Mr. Burns and Mr. Mitchell built upon the initial Mitchell volumes on business cycles to develop a framework to analyze 800 monthly series of economic data relative to their specific cycles, reference cycles, and amplitude and confirmatory movements within expansions and contractions. The Burns and Mitchell Measuring Business Cycles is a seminal treatment of economic variables with business cycles. Mr. Moore builds upon the Burns and Mitchell framework and pushes forward lists of the leading economic time series.

Mr. Zarnowitz continued the NBER analysis of business cycles in the tradition of Mr. Mitchell, Mr. Burns, and Mr. Moore, his frequent co-author. In Chapter 6, we reviewed the Mr. Zarnowitz econometric model testing, reporting that econometric models, while often beating naïve, no-change models, failed to identify turning points. Mr. Zarnowitz, in his NBER monograph, *Business Cycles: Theory, History, Indictors, and Forecasting*, parts III and IV, verified the statistical significance of the LEI in forecasting, particularly real GDP. Mr. Zarnowitz continued the analysis of Mr, Moore and reported that the NBER LEI continued to be less than satisfactory in predicting turning points in business cycles.

We applied the SAS and OxMetrics Hendry and Doornik automatic time series PCGive (OxMetrics) methodology to several well-studied macroeconomics series, real GDP, and the unemployment rate in Chapter 7. We discussed the analysis of Mr. Auerbach who statistically verified the predictive power of the Burns and Mitchell and Moore LEI during 1949–1977.

We reported that the OxMetrics and AutoMetrics system substantially reduced the residual sum of squares measures relative to a traditional variation on the random walk with drift model. The modeling process of including the Leading Economic Indicator in forecasting real GDP has been addressed before, but our results are more statistically significant. The LEI work of Professors Mitchell, Moore, and Zarnowitz has stood the test of time, 1959–2021.

In summary, let us review our most important results. First, a traditional AR(1) model of real GDP, 1959 – 11/2020 is not adequately fitted. The model residuals fail the Henry-Doornik econometric diagnostic tests.

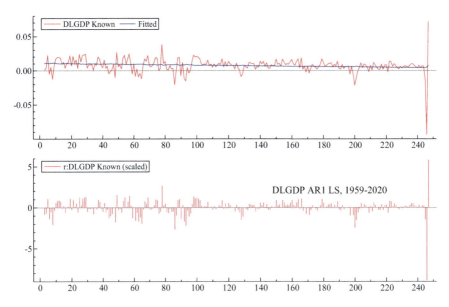

Fig. 11.1 The DLGDP AR1 LS, 1959–2020 is plagued by outliers, particularly in 2020

```
EQ 11-1     Modelling DLGDP Known by OLS
        The dataset is: C:\JBG\JGResearch\CFRM UW\TCB LEI US DLOG Data1959 2020 known.csv
        The estimation sample is: 3 - 247

                    Coefficient  Std.Error  t-value  t-prob Part.R^2
DLGDP Known_1       -0.0352231     0.06973   -0.505  0.6139   0.0011
Constant             0.0109301    0.001642    6.66  0.0000   0.1548
Trend             -2.79525e-05   1.031e-05   -2.71  0.0072   0.0295

sigma                0.0110927  RSS                0.0297774411
R^2                  0.0295605  F(2,242) =         3.686 [0.026]*
Adj.R^2              0.0215404  log-likelihood         756.730
no. of observations        245  no. of parameters          3
mean(Y)              0.0071898  se(Y)              0.0112141

AR 1-2 test:       F(2,240)   =    2.3193 [0.1005]
ARCH 1-1 test:     F(1,243)   =   44.468 [0.0000]**
Normality test:    Chi^2(2)   =   335.90 [0.0000]**
Hetero test:       F(4,240)   =   14.888 [0.0000]**
Hetero-X test:     F(5,239)   =   17.608 [0.0000]**
RESET23 test:      F(2,240)   =    1.2530 [0.2875]
```

The model residuals are plagued by huge outliers, particularly in 2020, see Fig. 11.1.

```
EQ 11-2    Modelling DLGDP Known by AutoMetrics
    The dataset is: C:\JBG\JGResearch\CFRM UW\TCB LEI US DLOG Data1959 2020 known.csv
    The estimation sample is: 3 - 247
```

	Coefficient	Std.Error	t-value	t-prob	Part.R^2
DLGDP Known_1	0.257205	0.04254	6.05	0.0000	0.1414
Trend	1.10023e-05	3.540e-06	3.11	0.0021	0.0417
DI:5	0.0165730	0.004197	3.95	0.0001	0.0656
DI:8	-0.0118439	0.004196	-2.82	0.0052	0.0347
DI:24	-0.0123005	0.004185	-2.94	0.0036	0.0374
DI:57	0.0130541	0.004842	2.70	0.0076	0.0317
DI:58	0.0120354	0.004845	2.48	0.0137	0.0270
DI:89	0.0135206	0.004177	3.24	0.0014	0.0451
DI:92	0.0199461	0.006014	3.32	0.0011	0.0472
DI:166	0.0102563	0.004189	2.45	0.0151	0.0263
DI:198	0.0134697	0.004826	2.79	0.0057	0.0339
DI:199	0.0135827	0.004825	2.81	0.0053	0.0345
DI:246	-0.0932582	0.004522	-20.6	0.0000	0.6570
I:49	0.0306761	0.006308	4.86	0.0000	0.0963
I:78	0.0295517	0.005971	4.95	0.0000	0.0994
I:86	-0.0289259	0.005963	-4.85	0.0000	0.0958
I:92	-0.0410945	0.008512	-4.83	0.0000	0.0950
T1:23	0.00109169	0.0002561	4.26	0.0000	0.0756
T1:49	-0.00838390	0.001982	-4.23	0.0000	0.0746
T1:51	0.00938465	0.002218	4.23	0.0000	0.0746
T1:63	-0.00584474	0.001393	-4.20	0.0000	0.0735
T1:66	0.00430023	0.001039	4.14	0.0000	0.0716
T1:244	-4.00406e-05	6.315e-06	-6.34	0.0000	0.1533

```
sigma                0.00590725  RSS              0.00774681531
R^2                  0.747535    F(22,222) =      29.88 [0.000]**
Adj.R^2              0.722516    log-likelihood       921.672
no. of observations       245   no. of parameters         23
mean(Y)              0.0071898   se(Y)            0.0112141

AR 1-2 test:      F(2,220)  =   2.4894 [0.0853]
ARCH 1-1 test:    F(1,243)  =   2.4270 [0.1206]
Normality test:   Chi^2(2)  =   4.8430 [0.0888]
Hetero test:      F(32,207) =   1.1952 [0.2291]
RESET23 test:     F(2,220)  =   3.9947 [0.0198]*
```

The application of the Castle and Hendry (2019) and Hendry and Doornik (2014) methodologies reduced the residual sum of squares, RSS, from 0.030 in EQ 11.1 to only 0.008 in EQ 11.2. The impulse- indicator-saturation (IIS, denoted I, in the program output) variables, the differenced impulse-indicator (DIIS, or DI in the program output), and trend saturation (TIS, or TI in the output) variables significantly reduce the residual sum of squares errors. The residual plots are now random, see Fig. 11.2.

More importantly, as we reported in the Appendix to Chapter 7, the models estimated in 2019 continued to work in 2020–2021 to substantially reduce the RSS. If EQ 11.2 was our final answer, many readers would be rightfully satisfied; however, the application of the Mitchell-Burns, Moore, and Zarnowitz LEI produces positive and statistically significant coefficients on the LEI one-period quarterly lag for the 1959–2020 period, a verification of the statistical significance of LEI lags reported Guerard (2001 and 2004), but only of one, not four as reported in the EViews work. See EQ 11.3. The reader notes the t-statistics on the LEI variable of 14.4.

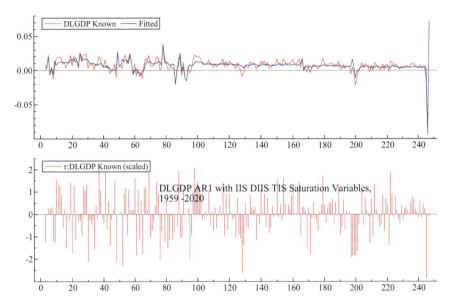

Fig. 11.2 DLGDP AR1 with IIS DIIS TIS Saturation Variables, 1959–2020

```
EQ 11-3     Modelling DLGDP Known by OLS
            The dataset is: C:\JBG\JGResearch\CFRM UW\TCB LEI US DLOG Data1959 2020 known.csv
            The estimation sample is: 6 - 247

                        Coefficient  Std.Error  t-value  t-prob Part.R^2
DLLEI_1                  0.295206     0.01835     16.1   0.0000   0.5305
DI:24                   -0.00941042   0.003583    -2.63  0.0092   0.0292
DI:29                    0.00993252   0.003583     2.77  0.0060   0.0325
DI:48                   -0.0157320    0.003588    -4.39  0.0000   0.0775
DI:76                   -0.0125296    0.004138    -3.03  0.0027   0.0385
DI:77                   -0.0193424    0.004148    -4.66  0.0000   0.0867
DI:89                    0.0161703    0.003587     4.51  0.0000   0.0815
DI:91                    0.0170264    0.004137     4.12  0.0001   0.0689
DI:92                    0.0119543    0.004138     2.89  0.0042   0.0352
DI:246                  -0.0495642    0.004135   -12.0   0.0000   0.3855
I:8                     -0.0219919    0.005117    -4.30  0.0000   0.0746
T1:189                   0.000100417  1.704e-05    5.89  0.0000   0.1317
T1:244                  -0.000107151  1.151e-05   -9.31  0.0000   0.2747

sigma                0.00506660  RSS              0.00587853827
R^2                  0.817413    log-likelihood        942.288
no. of observations       242   no. of parameters          13
mean(Y)              0.00717236  se(Y)                0.0112308

AR 1-2 test:      F(2,227)  =    1.3609 [0.2585]
ARCH 1-1 test:    F(1,240)  =    0.73059 [0.3935]
Normality test:   Chi^2(2)  =    1.1270 [0.5692]
Hetero test:      F(22,218) =    0.74088 [0.7940]
Hetero-X test:    F(24,216) =    0.71625 [0.8325]
RESET23 test:     F(2,227)  =    0.54158 [0.5826]
```

The RSS further falls to 0.006 and the model diagnostics indicate that the model is adequately fitted, and the residuals are "clean", see Fig. 11.3.

The adjusted R-squared rises from 0.022 in the AR(1) estimate, to 0.723 in the AutoMetrics univariate model (only real GDP) estimate, to 0.817 in the AutoMetrics bivariate model estimate. The reader sees the importance

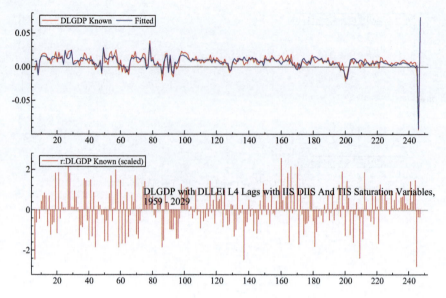

Fig. 11.3 DLGDP with DLLEI L4 Lags with IIS DIIS And TIS Saturation Variables, 1959–2029

of modeling outliers and structural breaks. Practitioners model real GDP; academicians, such as Professor Zarnowitz, model NBER and TCB coincidental indicators (CI). We will honor the Moore and Zarnowitz tradition and report in EQ 11.4.

EQ 11-4   Modelling the DL Coincidental Indicators (DLCI) in Terms
             of the Leading Economic Indicators: What do the LEI Lead?

```
The dataset is: C:\JBG\JGResearch\CFRM UW\TCB LEI US DLOG Data1959 2020 known.csv
The estimation sample is: 6 - 247

                Coefficient   Std.Error   t-value   t-prob  Part.R^2
Constant         0.00210545   0.0004113     5.12    0.0000   0.1105
DLLEI_1          0.218360     0.01515      14.4     0.0000   0.4962
DLLEI_3          0.0915720    0.01533       5.97    0.0000   0.1447
DI:8            -0.00914881   0.002464     -3.71    0.0003   0.0613
DI:23           -0.00951041   0.002450     -3.88    0.0001   0.0666
DI:43            0.00980474   0.002450      4.00    0.0001   0.0705
DI:48            0.00859624   0.002460      3.50    0.0006   0.0547
DI:62            0.00746649   0.002907      2.57    0.0109   0.0303
DI:63            0.0108214    0.002911      3.72    0.0003   0.0615
DI:76           -0.00975222   0.002835     -3.44    0.0007   0.0531
DI:77            0.00775393   0.002849      2.72    0.0070   0.0339
DI:84            0.00748619   0.002451      3.05    0.0025   0.0423
DI:93            0.00761856   0.002454      3.11    0.0022   0.0437
DI:245          -0.147567     0.003488    -42.3     0.0000   0.8946
I:47            -0.0151633    0.003552     -4.27    0.0000   0.0795
I:55             0.0129096    0.003574      3.61    0.0004   0.0582
I:87             0.0162533    0.003556      4.57    0.0000   0.0901
I:92            -0.0130057    0.003552     -3.66    0.0003   0.0597
I:127           -0.0105866    0.003490     -3.03    0.0027   0.0418
I:149            0.0108842    0.003531      3.08    0.0023   0.0431
I:200           -0.0152285    0.003639     -4.18    0.0000   0.0766
I:246           -0.0360271    0.005437     -6.63    0.0000   0.1723
T1:10            0.00292435   0.0005558     5.26    0.0000   0.1160
T1:59            0.00303827   0.0007104     4.28    0.0000   0.0798
T1:63           -0.00968005   0.001836     -5.27    0.0000   0.1164
T1:66            0.0108981    0.002061      5.29    0.0000   0.1170
T1:70           -0.0182005    0.003891     -4.68    0.0000   0.0940
T1:71            0.0145420    0.003147      4.62    0.0000   0.0919
T1:85           -0.000619773  0.0001452    -4.27    0.0000   0.0795
T1:158           0.000224478  6.075e-05     3.69    0.0003   0.0608
T1:176          -0.000189258  4.709e-05    -4.02    0.0001   0.0711

sigma               0.00346393   RSS               0.00253174342
R^2                 0.941140     F(30,211) =       112.5 [0.000]**
Adj.R^2             0.932772     log-likelihood          1044.22
no. of observations       242   no. of parameters            31
mean(DLGOM920)      0.00532372   se(DLGOM920)         0.0133596

AR 1-2 test:      F(2,209)  =  0.73914 [0.4788]
ARCH 1-1 test:    F(1,240)  =  0.27150 [0.6028]
Normality test:   Chi^2(2)  =  0.95662 [0.6198]
Hetero test:      F(39,193) =  0.46337 [0.9973]
RESET23 test:     F(2,209)  =  0.53878 [0.5843]
```

The lagged LEI variables lead the CI time series and are positive and statistically significant, with reported t-statistics of 14.40 and 5.97, respectively. The model is adequately fitted, as reported in the diagnostics. I believe Mr. Zarnowitz would be very pleased with both real GDP and CI analysis results, as he was with the author's work in 2001 and 2004.

Finally, we report the monthly MZTT analysis for the 1959–2020 period in EQ 11.5. Both the lags LEI and weekly unemployment claims time series are statistically significant, as reported in the monthly of Dhrymes (2017) and Guerard, Thomakos and Kyriazai (2020).

```
EQ 11-5      Modelling UER by OLS
      The dataset is: C:\JBG\JGResearch\CFRM UW\TCB LEI US DLOG Data1959 2020 known.csv
      The estimation sample is: 2 - 247

                    Coefficient  Std.Error  t-value  t-prob  Part.R^2
UER_1                 0.677305    0.02172     31.2   0.0000   0.8141
LEI_1                -0.0499301   0.005389    -9.27   0.0000   0.2789
WkUNCL_1              0.00191454  0.0004731    4.05   0.0001   0.0687
Constant             -1378.76    321.9       -4.28   0.0000   0.0763
Trend                 5.59285    1.300        4.30   0.0000   0.0770
DI:3                  0.549668    0.1314      4.18   0.0000   0.0731
I:64                  1.56167     0.1929      8.09   0.0000   0.2279
T1:9                  0.775927    0.1763      4.40   0.0000   0.0803
T1:10                -0.748960    0.1717     -4.36   0.0000   0.0789
T1:19                 0.256073    0.07675     3.34   0.0010   0.0477
T1:21                -0.224055    0.06259    -3.58   0.0004   0.0546
T1:65                 0.0450025   0.008035    5.60   0.0000   0.1238
T1:80                -0.128734    0.03781    -3.40   0.0008   0.0496
T1:85                 0.863507    0.1993      4.33   0.0000   0.0780
T1:86                -0.897672    0.1881     -4.77   0.0000   0.0931
T1:94                 0.400187    0.06155     6.50   0.0000   0.1600
T1:97                -0.262851    0.04282    -6.14   0.0000   0.1451
T1:168               -0.0157440   0.003352   -4.70   0.0000   0.0904
T1:199                0.0330277   0.009911    3.33   0.0010   0.0476
T1:215                0.352028    0.1172      3.00   0.0030   0.0390
T1:216               -0.372640    0.1130     -3.30   0.0011   0.0467
T1:243               -11.1722     0.1985     -56.3   0.0000   0.9345
T1:244                31.5632     1.775       17.8   0.0000   0.5876
T1:245               -25.9671     3.030      -8.57   0.0000   0.2486

sigma                 0.184864   RSS                 7.58678904
R^2                   0.989384   F(23,222) =     899.5 [0.000]**
Adj.R^2               0.988284   log-likelihood       78.8487
no. of observations    246       no. of parameters        24
mean(A0M043)          6.00935    se(A0M043)           1.7079


AR 1-2 test:      F(2,220)   =   2.5237 [0.0825]
ARCH 1-1 test:    F(1,244)   =   0.87694 [0.3500]
Normality test:   Chi^2(2)   =   0.99360 [0.6085]
Hetero test:      F(36,207)  =   0.72535 [0.8743]
RESET23 test:     F(2,220)   =   5.2896 [0.0057]**

Model saved to C:\JBG\JGResearch\Palgrave Business Cycles\Palgrave Monograph
01242022\Model UER Figure 11-2.pdf
Model saved to C:\JBG\JGResearch\Palgrave Business Cycles\Palgrave Monograph
01242022\Model UER Figure 11-2.pdf.gwg
```

We complemented the OxMetrics (and AutoMetrics) analysis with an application of the rolling window forecasting analysis which produced additional validation of the LEI and weekly unemployment claims series and the unemployment time series. We provided results for the best univariate and best bivariate models, in terms of their root mean-squared error rankings relative to the naïve benchmark, and the adaptive averaging autoregressive model ADA-AR and the adaptive learning forecast, ADL, produced the smallest root mean square errors and lowest mean absolute errors.

We applied the econometric causality testing methodologies of Clive Granger and his colleagues to corporate mergers and the unemployment rate, reporting statistically significant causality findings using the LEI and its components, stock prices, and weekly unemployment claims. Chapter 8 builds upon the regression and time series modeling in the previous chapter where we established the basis model for real GDP and the unemployment rate. We report Granger-Causality results of the unemployment rate, using both the SCA system, based on the modeling of Mr. Ruey Tsay and his colleagues, and the rolling window analysis of Kyriazi, Thomakos, and Guerard. We verified Granger-Causality and Root Mean Square Error (RMSE) forecasting errors substantially lower than the AR(1) and Sample Mean Forecasts that are often used as forecasting benchmarks of the unemployment rate.

In Chapter 9, we surveyed 70 years of portfolio selection through the works of Nobel Prize laureates James Tobin, Harry Markowitz, and William Sharpe. We reported the effectiveness of stock selection modeling in creating expected returns models for portfolio selection during the 1974–1990, 1998–2018, and 2001–2020 time periods. We reproduced how fundamental variables and earnings forecasting models continue to produce statistically significant asset selection in domestic and global stocks, 2003–11/2018. Regression models of fundamental factors and earnings forecasting factors continue to enhance portfolio returns. Momentum enhances portfolio returns primarily in non-U.S. equity markets. We report that the Markowitz mean-variance optimization is particularly efficient for producing efficient frontiers using a forecasted earnings acceleration model, CTEF, and a composite, robust-regression based ten-factor model, REG10. Have markets and stock selection models changed since Bloch, Guerard, Markowitz, Todd and Xu (1993) and Guerard and Mark (2003) published their studies? No. CTEF, REG9, and REG10 still dominate most other models. The risk models have changed evolved during the 1993–2018 period; the Axioma model has been introduced and Barra evolved and APT was sold to Sungard. The authors believe that financial anomalies exist and persist. Have the financial anomalies persisted through COVID? Yes, they have through December 2020. We report most of our results produced by the FactSet Research Systems, Inc., platform. Are markets efficient? No, not completely, but significant databases and computers are required to outperform.

Finally, in Chapter 10, we used the latest Conference Board database and built simple linear regression and multiple regressions in SAS to model the unemployment rate as a function of the Leading Economic Indicators, LEI, and one of its components, the weekly unemployment claims time series. We estimated many combinations of ordinary least square (OLS) and robust regression (ROB) models. We applied the Hendry and Doornik (2014) and Castle and Hendry (2019) automatic time series PCGive (OxMetrics) methodology to the unemployment rate. We report that the OxMetrics and AutoMetrics system substantially reduces regression sum of squares measures relative to a traditional variation on the random walk with drift model. The modeling process of including the Leading Economic Indicator in forecasting real GDP has been addressed before, but our results are more statistically significant, using the latest data for model verification. A similar conclusion is found for the impact of the LEI and weekly unemployment claims series leading the unemployment rate series. Such results should excite practitioners!

11.1   Where Do We Go from Here?

Where do we go from here? Mr. Guerard and Mr. Thomakos are completing our analysis of LEI and the money supply, M2, which will report statistically significant results that the LEI and M2 lead both real GDP and the unemployment rate during the 1959–2020 and 1995–2020 periods. In the next 2–5 years, the reader can expect to see additional results on the unemployment rate and the LEI when COVID is past. The reader can expect to see more econometric modelling of real GDP and combining econometric models with time series forecasts to reduce out-of-sample forecasting errors, in real-time. The reader can expect to see additional portfolio selection results for the 1976–2022 period, as the author celebrates the 100th birthday of Harry Markowitz in 2027. Finally, the reader should expect to see that earnings analysis, the I/B/E/S earnings forecast revisions of the Elton, Gruber, and Gultekin (1981) analysis, and the I/B/E/S work of Guerard, Markowitz, and Xu (2013, 2014, 2015, and 2021) continue to be statistically significant. The world is not perfect; models are not perfect; but we produce statistically significant results that enhance stockholder wealth in our portfolios. As Lord Keynes said, "in the long-run we are all dead"; let us celebrate being statistically significant while we are alive. The author can only hope that 100 years from now the Library of Congress will still contain the 11–13 volumes of Markowitz books and will contain a growing set of volumes celebrating portfolio theory and its applications, and its creators, Markowitz, Sharpe, Lintner, and Mossin.

C'est fini!

Appendix: The Theory and Estimation of Regression, Time Series Analysis, and Causality Modeling of the Unemployment Rate and the Leading Economic Indicators (LEI)

In February 2020, the U.S. unemployment rate was at a 50-year low. One of the great economic problems of the COVID pandemic is the dramatic increase in unemployment claims. In this appendix, we provide the background of linear regression, multiple regression, an introduction to time series modeling and forecasting, and causality testing. This Appendix will help the reader understand the statistics presented in Chapters 7, 8, and 10 analysis of the change in the unemployment rate as a function of the percentage changes in the Leading Economic Indicators, LEI, and one of the LEI components, the weekly unemployment claims time series. The Appendix will help the student understand the statistical modelling of portfolio selection in Chapter 9. We specifically address the unemployment rate in 2020 as the COVID virus closed down the U.S. economy in March 2020, with profound and highly significant impacts on U.S. output, as measured by Gross Domestic Product. Regression analysis is the primary technique discussed and estimated in this Appendix. More specifically, regression analysis seeks to find the "line of best fit" through the data points. The regression line is drawn to best approximate the relationship between the two variables. We extend the Appendix to include time series modeling and forecasting, automatic time series modeling, and Granger-Causality modelling.[1] Most

---

[1] English authors often spell modeling as modelling. We will use both spellings in the text and this Appendix.

J. B. Guerard, *The Leading Economic Indicators and Business Cycles in the United States*, https://doi.org/10.1007/978-3-030-99418-1

readers want to model and forecast economic time series, evaluate these fore-casts and the forecast errors, and build portfolios with regression modelling to outperform the stock market.

In simple regression analysis, one seeks to measure the statistical asso-ciation between two variables, X and Y. Regression analysis is generally used to measure how changes in the independent variable, X, influence changes in the dependent variable, Y. Regression analysis shows a statistical association or correlation among variables, rather than a causal relationship among variables. In this chapter, we address the relationship between the U.S. unemployment rate, the Leading Economic Indicator (LEI) and Weekly Unemployment Claims, a component of the LEI.

Estimating an Ordinary Least Square Regression Line

The case of simple, linear, least squares regression may be written in the form:

$$Y = \alpha + \beta X + \varepsilon \tag{A.1}$$

where Y, the dependent variable, is a linear function of X, the indepen-dent variable. The parameters α and β characterize the population regression line and ε is the randomly distributed error term. The regression estimates of α and β will be derived from the principle of least squares. In applying least squares, the sum of the squared regression errors will be minimized; our regression errors equal the actual dependent variable minus the estimated value from the regression line. If Y represents the actual value and $\hat{Y}$ the estimated value, their difference is the error term, e. Least square regression minimizes the sum of the squared error terms. The simple regression line will yield an estimated value of Y, $\hat{Y}$ by the use of the sample regression:

$$\hat{Y} = a + bX \tag{A.2}$$

In the estimation Eq. (A.2), a is the least squares estimate of α and b is the estimate of β. Thus, a and b are the regression constants that must be estimated. The least squares regression constants (or statistics) a and b are unbiased and efficient (smallest variance) estimators of α and β. The error term, $\hat{e}_i$, is the difference between the actual and estimated dependent variable value for any given independent variable values, X_i.

$$\hat{e}_i = Y_i - \hat{Y}_i \tag{A.3}$$

The regression error term, $\hat{e}_i$, is the least squares estimate of ε_i, the actual error term.[2]

To minimize the error terms, the least squares technique minimizes the sum of the squared error terms of the N observations,

$$\sum_{i=1}^{N} \hat{e}_i^2 \tag{A.4}$$

Thus, least squares regression minimizes:

$$\sum_{i=1}^{N} \hat{e}_i^2 = \sum_{i=1}^{N}\left[Y_i - \hat{Y}_i\right]^2 = \sum_{i=1}^{N}\left[Y_i - \left(\hat{a} + \hat{b}X_i\right)\right]^2 \tag{A.5}$$

To assure that a minimum is reached, the partial derivatives of the squared error terms function

$$\sum_{i=1}^{N} = \left[Y_i - \left(\hat{a} + \hat{b}X_i\right)\right]^2$$

will be taken with respect to a and b.

$$\frac{\partial \sum_{i=1}^{N} \hat{e}_i^2}{\partial \hat{a}} = 2\sum_{i=1}^{N}\left(Y_i - \hat{a} - \hat{b}X_i\right)(-1)$$

$$= -2\left(\sum_{i=1}^{N} Y_i - \sum_{i=1}^{N}\hat{a} - \hat{b}\sum_{i=1}^{N} X_i\right)$$

$$\frac{\partial \sum_{i=1}^{N} e_i^2}{\partial \hat{b}} = 2\sum_{i=1}^{N}\left(Y_i - \hat{a} - \hat{b}X_i\right)(-X_i)$$

$$= -2\left(\sum_{i=1}^{N} Y_i X_i - \hat{a}\sum_{i=1}^{N} X_i - \hat{b}\sum_{i=1}^{N} X_i^2\right)$$

---

[2] The reader is referred to an excellent statistical reference, such as Irwin Miller and J.E. Freund, *Probability and Statistics for Engineers*, (Englewood Cliffs, NJ: Prentice-Hall, 1965), S. Makridakis, S.C. Wheelwright, and R. J. Hyndman, *Forecasting: Methods and Applications* (New York: John Wiley & Sons, 1998, Third Edition), G.S. Maddala and K. Lahiri, *Introduction to Econometrics* (New York: John Wiley & Sons, 2009, Fourth edition), and P.J. Dhrymes, *Introductory Econometrics* (New York: Springer, 2017, Second Edition).

The partial derivatives will then be set equal to zero.

$$\frac{\partial \sum_{i=1}^{N} \hat{e}_i^2}{\partial \hat{a}} = -2\left(\sum_{i=1}^{N} Y_i - \sum_{i=1}^{N} \hat{a} - \hat{b}\sum_{i=1}^{N} X_i\right) = 0$$

$$\frac{\partial \sum_{i=1}^{N} \hat{e}_i^2}{\partial \hat{b}} = -2\left(\sum_{i=1}^{N} YX_i - \hat{a}\sum_{i=1}^{N} X_I \,\hat{}\,b\sum_{i=1}^{N} X_i^2\right) = 0$$

(A.6)

Rewriting these equations, one obtains the normal equations:

$$\sum_{i=1}^{N} Y_i = \sum_{i=1}^{N} \hat{a} + \hat{b}\sum_{i=1}^{N} X_i$$

$$\sum_{i=1}^{N} Y_i X_i = \hat{a}\sum_{i=1}^{N} X_i + \hat{b}\sum_{i=1}^{N} X_i^2$$

(A.7)

Solving the normal equations simultaneously for a and b yields the least squares regression estimates;

$$\hat{a} = \frac{\left(\sum_{i=1}^{N} X_i^2\right)\left(\sum_{i=1}^{N} Y_i\right) - \left(\sum_{i=1}^{N} X_i Y_i\right)}{N\left(\sum_{i=1}^{N} X_i^2\right) - \left(\sum_{i=1}^{N} X_i\right)^2}$$

$$\hat{b} = \frac{N\left(\sum_{i=1}^{N} X_i Y_i\right) - \left(\sum_{i=1}^{N} X_i\right)\left(\sum_{i=1}^{N} Y_i\right)}{N\left(\sum_{i=1}^{N} X_i^2\right) - \left(\sum_{i=1}^{N} X_i\right)^2}$$

(A.8)

An estimation of the regression line's coefficients and goodness of fit also can be found in terms of expressing the dependent and independent variables in terms of deviations from their means, i.e., their sample moments. The sample moments will be denoted by M.

$$M_{XX} = \sum_{i=1}^{N} x_i^2 = \sum_{i=1}^{N} (x_i - \bar{x})^2$$

$$= N\sum_{i=1}^{N} X_i - \left(\sum_{i=1}^{N} X_i\right)^2$$

$$M_{XY} = \sum_{i=1}^{N} x_i y_i = \sum_{i=1}^{N} (X_i - \overline{X})(Y_i - \overline{Y})$$

$$= N \sum_{i=1}^{N} X_i Y_i - \left(\sum_{i=1}^{N} X_i \right) \left(\sum_{i=1}^{N} Y_i \right)$$

$$M_{YY} = \sum_{i=1}^{N} y_i^2 = \sum_{i=1}^{N} (Y - \overline{Y})^2$$

$$= N \left(\sum_{i=1}^{N} Y_i^2 \right) - \sum_{i=1}^{N} (Y_i)^2$$

The slope of the regression line, b, can be found by:

$$\hat{b} = \frac{M_{XY}}{M_{XX}} \tag{A.9}$$

$$\hat{a} = \frac{\sum_{i=1}^{N} Y_i}{N} - \hat{b} \frac{\sum_{i=1}^{N} X_i}{N} = \overline{y} - \hat{b}\overline{X} \tag{A.10}$$

The standard error of the regression line can also be expressed in terms of the sample moments:

$$S_e^2 = \frac{M_{XX}(M_{YY}) - (M_{XY})^2}{N(N-2)M_{XX}}$$

$$S_e = \sqrt{S_e^2} \tag{A.11}$$

The major benefit in calculating the sample moments is that the correlation coefficient, r, and the coefficient of determination, R^2, can easily be found.

$$r = \frac{M_{XY}}{(M_{XX})(M_{YY})}$$

$$R^2 = (r)^2 \tag{A.12}$$

The coefficient of determination, R^2, is the percentage of the variance of the dependent variable explained by the independent variable. The coefficient of determination cannot exceed 1 nor be less than zero. In the case of

$R^2 = 0$, the regression line is $Y = \overline{Y}$ and no variation in the dependent variable is explained. If the dependent variable pattern continues as in the past, the model with time as the independent variable should be of good use in forecasting.

One can test whether the a and b coefficients are statistically different from zero, the generally accepted null hypothesis. A t-test is used to test the two null hypotheses:

$$H_{o_1} : a = 0$$

$$H_{A_1} : a \text{ ne } 0$$

$$H_{o_2} : \beta = 0$$

$$H_{A_2} : \beta \text{ ne } 0$$

where ne denotes not equal.

The H_0 represents the null hypothesis while H_A represents the alternative hypothesis. To reject the null hypothesis, the calculated t-value must exceed the critical t-value given in the t-tables in the appendix. The calculated t-values for a and b are found by:

$$
\begin{aligned}
t_a &= \frac{\hat{a} - \alpha}{S_e} \sqrt{\frac{N(M_{XX})}{M_{XX} + (N\overline{X})^2}} \\
t_b &= \frac{\hat{b} - \beta}{S_e} \sqrt{\frac{(M_{XX})}{N}}
\end{aligned}
\tag{A.13}
$$

The critical t-value, t_c, for the 0.05 level of significance with $N - 2$ degrees of freedom, can be found in a t-table in any statistical econometric text. One has a statistically significant regression model if one can reject the null hypothesis that the estimated slope coefficient is equal to zero.

We can create 95% confidence intervals for a and b, where the limits of a and b are:

$$\hat{a} + t_{a/2}S_e^+ \sqrt{\frac{(N\overline{X})^2 + M_{XX}}{N(M_{XX})}}$$

$$\hat{b} + t_{a/2}S_e \sqrt{\frac{N}{M_{XX}}} \tag{A.14}$$

To test whether the model is useful, an F-test is performed where:

$$H_o = \alpha = \beta = 0$$

$$H_A = \alpha \text{ ne } \beta \text{ ne } 0$$

$$F = \frac{\sum_{i=1}^{N} Y^2 \div 1 - \hat{b}^2 \sum_{i=1}^{N} X_i^2}{\sum_{i=1}^{N} \hat{e}^2 \div N - 2} \tag{A.15}$$

As the calculated F-value exceeds the critical F-value with $(1, N-2)$ degrees of freedom of 5.99 at the 0.05 level of significance, the null hypothesis must be rejected. The 95% confidence level limit of prediction can be found in terms of the dependent variable value:

$$\left(\hat{a} + \hat{b}X_0\right) + t_{a/2}S_e \sqrt{\frac{N(X_0 - \overline{X})^2}{1 + N + M_{XX}}} \tag{A.16}$$

Estimating Multiple Regression Lines

It may well be that several economic variables influence the variable that one is interested in forecasting. For example, the change in the unemployment rate as a function of changes in the Leading Economic Indicators or weekly unemployment claims. Multiple regression is an extremely easy statistical tool for researchers and management to employ due to the great proliferation of computer software. We use SAS and OxMetrics in this Appendix. The general form of the two-independent variable multiple regression is:

$$Y_t = \beta_1 + \beta_2 X_{2t} + \beta_3 X_{3t} + \varepsilon_t, \qquad t = 1, \ldots, N \tag{A.17}$$

In matrix notation multiple regression can be written:

$$Y = X\beta + \varepsilon \tag{A.18}$$

Multiple regression requires unbiasedness, the expected value of the error term is zero, and the X's are fixed and independent of the error term. The error term is an identically and independently distributed normal variable. Least squares estimation of the coefficients yields:

$$\hat{\beta} = \left(\hat{\beta}_1, \hat{\beta}_2, \hat{\beta}_3\right)$$
$$Y = X\hat{\beta} + \varepsilon \tag{A.19}$$

Multiple regression, using the least squared principle, minimizes the sum of the squared error terms:

$$\sum_{i=1}^{N} \hat{e}_1^2 = \hat{e}'\hat{e}$$
$$\left(Y - X\hat{\beta}\right)'\left(Y - X\hat{\beta}\right) \tag{A.20}$$

To minimize the sum of the squared error terms, one takes the partial derivative of the squared errors with respect to $\hat{\beta}$ and the partial derivative and set equal to zero.

$$\partial \frac{\left(\hat{e}'\hat{e}\right)}{\partial \beta} = -2X'Y + 2X'X\hat{\beta} = 0 \tag{A.21}$$

$$\hat{\beta} = \left(X'X\right)^{-1}X'Y$$

Alternatively, one could solve the normal equations for the two variables to determine the regression coefficients.

$$\Sigma Y = \hat{\beta}_1 N + \hat{\beta}_2 \Sigma X_2 + \hat{\beta}_3 \Sigma X_3$$
$$\Sigma X_2 Y = \hat{\beta}_1 \Sigma X_2 + \hat{\beta}_2 X_2^2 + \hat{\beta}_3 \Sigma X_3^2$$
$$\Sigma X_3 Y = \hat{\beta}_1 \Sigma X_3 + \hat{\beta}_2 \Sigma X_2 X_3 + \hat{\beta}_3 \Sigma X_3^2 \tag{A.22}$$

When we solved the normal equations, (A.7), to find the a and b that minimized the sum of our squared error terms in simple linear regression, and when we solved the two-variable normal equations, Eq. (A.31) to find the multiple regression estimated parameters, we made several assumptions. First, we assumed that the error term is independently and identically distributed; i.e., a random variable with an expected value, or mean of zero, and a finite, and constant, standard deviation. The error term should not be a function of time nor should the error term be a function of the size of the independent variable(s), a condition known as heteroscedasticity. One may plot the residuals as a function of the independent variable(s) to be certain that the residuals are independent of the independent variables. The error term should be a normally distributed variable. That is, the error terms should have an expected value of zero and 67.6% of the observed error terms should fall within the mean value plus or minus one standard deviation of the error terms (the so-called "Bell Curve" or normal distribution). Ninety-five percent of the observations should fall within the plus or minus two standard deviation levels, the so-called 95% confidence interval. The presence of extreme, or influential, observations may distort estimated regression lines and the corresponding estimated residuals. Another problem in regression analysis is the assumed independence of the independent variables in Eq. (A.22). Significant correlations may produce estimated regression coefficients that are "unstable" and have the "incorrect" signs. Let us spend some time discussing two problems discussed in this section, the problems of influential observations, commonly known as outliers, and the correlation among independent variables, known as multicollinearity.

There are several methods that one can use to identify influential observations or outliers. First, we can plot the residuals and 95% confidence intervals and examine how many observations have residuals falling outside these limits. One should expect no more than 5% of the observations to fall outside of these intervals. One may find that one or two observations may distort a regression estimate even if there are 100 observations in the database. The estimated residuals should be normally distributed, and the ratio of the residuals divided by their standard deviation, known as standardized residuals, should be a normal variable. We showed, in Eq. (A.29), that in multiple regression:

$$\hat{\beta} = (X'X)X'Y$$

The residuals of the multiple regression line is given by:

$$\hat{e} = Y' - \hat{\beta}X$$

Influential Observations and Possible Outliers and the Application of Robust Regression

The standardized residual concept can be modified such that the reader can calculate a variation on that term to identify influential observations. If we delete observation i in a regression, we can measure the impact of observation i on the change in estimated regression coefficients and residuals. Belsley, Kuh, and Welsch (1980) showed that the estimated regression coefficients change by an amount, DFBETA, where:

$$\text{DFBETA}_i = \frac{(X'X)^{-1}X'\hat{e}_i}{1 - h_i} \tag{A.23}$$

where

$$h_i = X_i(X'X)^{-1}X_i'$$

The h_i or "hat," term is calculated by deleting observation i. The corresponding residual is known as the studentized residual, sr, and is defined as:

$$sr_i = \frac{\hat{e}_i}{\hat{\sigma}\sqrt{1 - h_i}} \tag{A.24}$$

where $\hat{\sigma}$ is the estimated standard deviation of the residuals. A studentized residual that exceeds 2.0 indicates a potential influential observation [Belsley, et al., 1980]. Another distance measure has been suggested by Cook (1977), which modifies the studentized residual, to calculate a scaled residual known as the Cook distance measure, CookD. As the researcher or modeler deletes observations, one needs to compare the original matrix of the estimated residuals with the modified variance matrix. The COVRATIO calculation performs this calculation, where:

$$\text{COVRATIO} \substack{\rightarrow \\ \leftarrow} = \frac{1}{\left[\frac{n-p-1}{n-p} + \frac{\hat{e}_i*}{(n-p)}\right]^p (1 - h_i)} \tag{A.25}$$

where

n = number of observations,

p = number of independent variables, and
$\hat{e}_i*$ = deleted observations.

If the absolute value of the deleted observation is > 2, then the COVRATIO calculation approaches:

$$1 - \frac{3p}{n} \qquad\qquad (A.26)$$

A calculated COVRATIO that is larger than $\frac{3p}{n}$ indicates an influential observation. The DFBETA, studentized residual, CookD, and COVRATIO calculations may be performed within SAS. See Appendix A for the Belsley, Kuh, and Welsch (1980) influential observations and outlier analysis. The identification of influential data is an important component of regression analysis. One may create variables for use in multiple regression that make use of the influential data, or outliers, to which they are commonly referred.

The modeler can identify outliers, or influential data, and re-run the ordinary least squares regressions on the re-weighted data, a process referred to as robust (ROB) regression. In ordinary least squares, OLS, all data is equally weighted. The weights are 1.0. In robust regression one weights the data universally with its OLS residual; i.e., the larger the residual, the smaller the weight of the observation in the robust regression. In robust regression, several weights may be used. We will report the Huber (1973), Beaton-Tukey (1974), and Tukey MM-estimate with 99% efficiency, discussed in Maronna, Martin, Yohai, and Salibian-Barrera (2019) weighting schemes in Chapter 7. In the Huber (1973) robust regression procedure, one uses the following calculation to weigh the data:

$$w_i = \left(1 - \left(\frac{|\hat{e}_i|}{\sigma_i}\right)^2\right)^2 \qquad\qquad (A.27)$$

where

$\hat{e}_i$ = residual i,
σ_i = standard deviation of residual, and
w_i = weight of observation i.

The intuition is that the larger the estimated residual, the smaller the weight. A second robust re-weighting scheme is calculated from the Beaton-Tukey bisquare criteria where:

$$w_i = \left(1 - \left(\frac{\frac{|\hat{e}_i|}{\sigma_e}}{4.685}\right)^2\right)^2, \quad \text{if } \frac{|\hat{e}_i|}{\sigma_e} > 4.685;$$

$$1, \quad \text{if } \frac{|\hat{e}_i|}{\sigma_e} < 4.685. \tag{A.28}$$

The second major problem is one of multicollinearity, the condition of correlation among the independent variables. If the independent variables are perfectly correlated in multiple regression, then the $(X'X)$ matrix of Eq. (A.30), cannot be inverted and the multiple regression coefficients have multiple solutions. In reality, highly correlated independent variables can produce unstable regression coefficients due to an unstable $(X'X)^{-1}$ matrix. Belsley et al. advocate the calculation of a condition number, which is the ratio of the largest latent root of the correlation matrix relative to the smallest latent root of the correlation matrix. A condition number exceeding 30.0 indicates severe multicollinearity.

Efrom, Hastie, Johnstone, and Tibshirayi (2004) introduce LAR to the reader by discussing automatic model-building algorithms, including forward selection, all subsets, and back elimination. One can measure the goodness of fit in terms of predictive accuracy, but one uses a different manner, how well model subsets perform in terms of portfolio geometric means using out-of-sample variable weights. LAR is a variation of forward selection; that is the technique selects the variable with the largest absolute correlation, x_{j1}, with the response variable, y and performs simple linear regression of y on x_{j1}. The regression produces a residual vector orthogonal to x_{j1}, now considered to be the response or dependent variable. One projects the other predictor variables orthogonally to x_{j1}, and repeats the selection process. The application of K steps produces a set of predictor variables, $x_{j1}, x_{j2}, x_{j3}, \ldots, x_{jk}$ to construct a K-parameter linear model. Hastie et al. (2013) state that forward selection is an aggressive fitting technique that can be overly greedy, eliminating at a second step useful prediction correlated with x_{j1}.

Time Series Modeling and the Forecasting Effectiveness of Transfer Functions

In this section, we introduce the reader to time series modeling tools. Section "Estimating Multiple Regression Lines" of this chapter addresses time series modeling in practice. Section "Influential Observations and Possible Outliers and the Application of Robust Regression" presents the empirical evidence to support time series modeling of the U.S. real GDP time series. In section "Time Series Modeling and the Forecasting Effectiveness of Transfer Functions" we estimate a transfer function to test the forecasting effectiveness of the leading indicators in modeling real GDP. We use Autometrics, the automatic time series analysis and forecasting system developed by David Hendry and his colleagues to estimate structural breaks and outliers in U.S. Real GDP time series in section "Forecasting Effectiveness of Time Series Modelling Using AutoMetrics to Estimate Breaks with Saturation Variables" and changes in the U.S. unemployment rate in section "Granger–Causality Modeling and Testing". Outlier analysis and automatic time series modeling are highly statistically significant in the 1959–2018 time period and particularly relevant for root mean square error reductions in 2020.

Basic Statistical Properties of Economic Series

This chapter develops and forecasts models of economic time series in which we initially use only the history of the series. The chapter later explores explanatory variables in the forecast models. The time series modeling approach of Box and Jenkins involves the identification, estimation, and forecasting of stationary (or series transformed to stationarity) series through the analysis of the series autocorrelation and partial autocorrelation functions.[3] The autocorrelation function examines the correlations of the current value of the economic times series and its previous k-lags. That is, one can measure the correlation of a daily series of share prices, for example, by calculating:

$$p_{jt} = a + bp_{jt-1} \qquad \text{(A.29)}$$

where

p_{jt} = today's price of stock j;
p_{jt-1} = yesterday's price of stock j; and

---

[3] This section draws heavily from Box and Jenkins, *Time Series Analysis*, Chapters 2 and 3.

b is the correlation coefficient.

In a daily share price series, b is quite large, often approaching a value of 1.00. As the number of lags, or previous number of periods increase, the correlation tends to fall. The decrease is usually very gradual.

The partial autocorrelation function examines the correlation between p_{jt} and p_{jt-2}, holding constant the association between p_{jt} and p_{jt-1}. If a series follows a random walk, the correlation between p_{jt} and p_{jt-1} is one, and the correlation between p_j and p_{jt-2}, holding constant the correlation of p_{jt} and p_{jt-1}, is zero. Random walk series are characterized by decaying autocorrelation functions and a partial autocorrelation function by a "spike" at lag one, and zeros thereafter.

Let Z_t be a time series. In the general case, stationarity implies that the joint probability $[p(Z)]$ distribution $P(Z_{t1}, Z_{t2})$ is the same for all times t, t_1, and t_2 where the observations are separated by a constant time interval. The autocovariance of a time series at some lag or interval, k, is defined to be the covariance between Z_t and Z_{t+k}

$$\gamma_k = \mathrm{cov}\left[Z_t, Z_{t+k}\right] = E\left[(Z_t - \mu)(Z_{t+k} - \mu)\right]. \tag{A.30}$$

One must standardize the autocovariance, as one standardizes the covariance in traditional regression analysis before one can quantify the statistically significant association between Z_t and Z_{t+k}. The autocorrelation of a time series is the standardization of the autocovariance of a time series relative to the variance of the time series, and the autocorrelation at lag k, ρ_k, is bounded between $+1$ and -1.

$$\begin{aligned}
\rho_k &= \frac{E\left[(Z_t - \mu)(Z_{t+k} - \mu)\right]}{\sqrt{E\left[(Z_t - \mu)^2\right] E\left[(Z_{t+k} - \mu)^2\right]}} \\
&= \frac{E\left[(Z_t - \mu)(Z_{t+k} - \mu)\right]}{\sigma_Z^2} = \frac{r_k}{r_0}
\end{aligned} \tag{A.31}$$

The autocorrelation function of the process, $\{\rho k\}$, represents the plotting of r_k versus time, the lag of k. The autocorrelation function is symmetric and thus $\rho_k = \rho_{-k}$; thus, time series analysis normally examines only the positive segment of the autocorrelation function. One may also refer to the autocorrelation function as the correlogram. The statistical estimates of the autocorrelation function are calculated from a finite series of N observations, $Z_1, Z_2, Z_3, \ldots, Z_n$. The statistical estimate of the autocorrelation function at lag k, r_k, is found by:

$$r_k = \frac{C_k}{C_0}$$

where

$$C_k = \frac{1}{N} \sum_{t=1}^{N-k} (Z_t - \overline{Z})(Z_{t+k} - \overline{Z}), \qquad k = 0, 1, 2, ..., K.$$

C_k is, of course, the statistical estimate of the autocovariance function at lag k. In identifying and estimating parameters in a time series model, one seeks to identify orders (lags) of the time series that are statistically different from zero. The implication of testing whether an autocorrelation estimate is statistically different from zero leads one back to the t-tests used in regression analysis to examine the statistically significant association between variables. One must develop a standard error of the autocorrelation estimate such that a formal t-test can be performed to measure the statistical significance of the autocorrelation estimate. Such a standard error, S_e, estimate was found by Bartlett and, in large samples, is approximated by:

$$\text{Var } [r_k] \cong \frac{1}{N}, \text{ and}$$

$$S_e[r_k] \cong \frac{1}{\sqrt{N}}. \tag{A.32}$$

An autocorrelation estimate is considered statistically different from zero if it exceeds approximately twice its standard error.

A second statistical estimate useful in time series analysis is the partial auto-correlation estimate of coefficient j at lag k, ϕ_{kj}. The partial autocorrelations are found in the following manner:

$$\rho_j = \phi_{k1}\rho_{j-1} + \phi_{k2}\rho_{j-2} + \cdots + \phi_{k(k-1)}\rho_{jk-1} + \phi_{kk}\rho_{j-k} \qquad \text{or}$$

$$j = 1, 2, \ldots, k$$

$$
\begin{bmatrix}
1 & \rho_1 & \rho_2 & \cdots & \rho_{k-1} \\
\rho_1 & 1 & \rho_1 & \cdots & \rho_{k-2} \\
\vdots & \vdots & \vdots & \cdots & \vdots \\
\rho_{k-1} & \rho_{k-2} & \rho_{k-3} & \cdots & 1
\end{bmatrix}
\begin{bmatrix}
\phi_{k1} \\
\phi_{k2} \\
\vdots \\
\phi_{kk}
\end{bmatrix}
\begin{bmatrix}
\rho_1 \\
\rho_2 \\
\vdots \\
\rho_k
\end{bmatrix}
$$

The partial autocorrelation estimates may be found by solving the above equation systems for $k = 1, 2, 3, \ldots k$.

$$
\phi_{11} = \rho_1
$$

$$
\phi_{22} = \frac{\rho_2 - \rho_1^2}{1 - \rho_1^2} = \frac{\begin{vmatrix} 1 & \rho_1 \\ \rho_2 & \rho_2 \end{vmatrix}}{\begin{vmatrix} 1 & \rho_1 \\ \rho_1 & 1 \end{vmatrix}}
$$

$$
\phi_{33} = \frac{\begin{vmatrix} 1 & \rho_1 & \rho_1 \\ \rho_1 & 1 & \rho_2 \\ \rho_2 & \rho_1 & \rho_3 \end{vmatrix}}{\begin{vmatrix} 1 & \rho_1 & \rho_2 \\ \rho_1 & 1 & \rho_1 \\ \rho_2 & \rho_1 & 1 \end{vmatrix}}
$$

The partial autocorrelation function is estimated by expressing the current autocorrelation function estimates as a linear combination of previous orders of autocorrelation estimates:

$$
\hat{r}_1 = \hat{\phi}_{k1} r_{j-1} + \hat{\phi}_{k2} 2_{j-2} + \cdots + \hat{\phi}_{k(k-1)} r_{j+k-1} + \hat{\phi}_{kk} 2_{j-k} \qquad j = 1, 2, \ldots k.
$$

The standard error of the partial autocorrelation function is approximately:

$$
\operatorname{Var}\left[\hat{\phi}_{kk} \right] \cong \frac{1}{N}, \quad \text{and}
$$

$$
S_e[\phi_{kk}] \cong \frac{1}{\sqrt{N}}.
$$

The Autoregressive and Moving Average Processes

A stochastic process, or time series, can be repeated as the output resulting from a white noise input, α_t.[4]

$$\tilde{Z}_t = \alpha_t + \psi_1 \alpha_{t-1} + \psi_2 \alpha_{t-2} + \cdots$$

$$= \alpha_t + \sum_{j=1}^{\infty} \psi_j \alpha_{t-j}. \qquad (A.33)$$

The filter weight, ψ_j, transforms the input into the output series. One normally expresses the output, $\tilde{Z}_t$, as a deviation of the time series from its mean, μ, or origin

$$\tilde{Z}_t = Z_t - \mu.$$

The general linear process leads one to represent the output of a time series, $\tilde{Z}_t$, as a function of the current and previous value of the white noise process, α_t which may be represented as a series of shocks. The white noise process, α_t, is a series of random variables characterized by:

$$E[\alpha_t] \cong 0$$

$$\mathrm{Var}[\alpha_t] = \sigma_\alpha^2$$

$$\gamma_k = E[\alpha_t \alpha_{t+k}] = \sigma_\alpha^2 \ k \neq 0 \bigg|$$
$$0 \quad k = 0. \bigg|$$

The autocorrelation function of a linear process may be given by:

$$\gamma_k = \sigma_\alpha^2 + \sum_{j=0}^{\infty} \psi_j \psi_{j+k}.$$

---

[4] Please see Box and Jenkins, *Time Series Analysis*, Chapter 3, for the most complete discussion of the ARMA (p,q) models.

The backward shift operator, B, is defined as $BZ_t = Z_{t-1}$ and $B_j Z_t = Z_{t-j}$. The autocorrelation generating function may be written as:

$$\gamma(B) = \sum_{k=-\infty}^{\infty} \gamma_k B^k$$

For stationarity, the ψ weights of a linear process must satisfy that $\psi(B)$ converges on or lies within the unit circle.

In an autoregressive, AR, model, the current value of the time series may be expressed as a linear combination of the previous values of the series and a random shock, α_t.

$$\tilde{Z}_t = \phi_1 \tilde{Z}_{t-1} + \phi_2 \tilde{Z}_{t-2} + \cdots + \phi_p \tilde{Z}_{t-p} + \alpha_t$$

The autoregressive operator of order P is given by:

$$\phi(B) = 1 - \phi_1 B^1 - \phi_2 B^2 - \cdots - \phi_p B^p$$

or

$$\phi(B)\tilde{Z}_t = \alpha_t \qquad \text{(A.34)}$$

In an autoregressive model, the current value of the time series, $\tilde{Z}_t$, is a function of previous values of the time series, $\tilde{Z}_{t-1}$, $\tilde{Z}_{t-2}$, ... and is similar to a multiple regression model. An autoregressive model of order p implies that only the first p order weights are non-zero. In many economic time series, the relevant autoregressive order is one and the autoregressive process of order p, AR(p) is written as

$$\tilde{Z}_t = \phi_1 \tilde{Z}_{t-1} + \alpha_t$$

or

$$(1 - \phi_1 B)\tilde{Z}_t = \alpha_t$$

$$\tilde{Z}_t = \phi^{-1}(B)\alpha_t.$$

The relevant stationarity condition is $|B| < 1$ implying that $|\phi_1| < 1$. The autocorrelation function of a stationary autoregressive process,

$$\tilde{Z}_t = \phi_1 \tilde{Z}_{t-1} + \phi_2 \tilde{Z}_{t-2} + \cdots + \phi_p \tilde{Z}_{t-p} + \alpha_t$$

may be expressed by the difference equation:

$$P_k = \phi_1 \rho_{k-1} + \phi_2 \rho_{k-2} + \cdots + \phi_k \rho_{k-p} \quad k > 0$$

Or expressed in terms of the Yule-Walker equation as:

$$\rho_1 = \phi_1 + \phi_2 \rho_1 + \cdots + \phi_p \rho_{p-1}$$
$$\rho_2 = \phi_1 \rho_1 + \phi_2 + \cdots + \phi_p \rho_{p-2}$$
$$\hat{\rho}_p = \hat{\phi}_1 \rho_{p-1} + \hat{\phi}_2 \rho_{p-2} + \cdots + \hat{\phi}_p$$

For the first-order AR process, AR(1)

$$\rho_k = \phi_1 \rho_{k-1} = \hat{\phi}_p.$$

The autocorrelation function decays exponentially to zero when ϕ_1 is positive and oscillates in sign and decays exponentially to zero when ϕ_1 is negative.

$$\rho_1 = \phi_1$$

and

$$\sigma_2 = \frac{\sigma_\alpha^2}{1 - \phi_1^2} \tag{A.35}$$

The partial autocorrelation function cuts off after lag one in an AR(1) process.

In a q-order moving average (MA) model, the current value of the series can be expressed as a linear combination of the current and previous shock variables:

$$\tilde{Z}_t = \alpha_1 - \theta_1 \alpha_{t-1} - \cdots - \alpha_q \theta_{t-q}$$

$$= \left(1 - \theta_1 B_1 - \cdots - \theta_q B_q \right) \alpha_t$$

$$= \theta(B)\alpha_t$$

The autocovariance function of a q-order moving average model is:

$$\gamma_k = E\big[(\alpha_t - \theta_1\alpha_{t-1} - \cdots - \theta_q\alpha_{t-q})(\alpha_{t-k} - \theta_1\alpha_{t-k-1} - \cdots - \theta_q\alpha_{t-k-q})\big]$$

The autocorrelation function, ρ_k, is:

$$\rho_k = \begin{array}{ll} \frac{-\theta_k + \theta_1\theta_{k+1} + \cdots + \theta_{q-k}\theta_q}{1 + \theta_1^2 + \cdots + \theta_q^2} & k = 1, 2, \ldots, q \\ 0 & k > q \end{array}$$

The autocorrelation function of a MA(q) model cuts off, to zero, after lag q and its partial autocorrelation function tails off to zero after lag q. There are no restrictions on the moving average model parameters for stationarity; however, moving average parameters must be invertible. Invertibility implies that the π weights of the linear filter transforming the input into the output series, the π weights lie outside the unit circle.

$$\pi(B) = \psi^{-1}(B)$$

$$= \sum_{j=0}^{a} \phi^j B^j$$

In a first-order moving average model, MA(1)

$$\tilde{Z}_t = (1 - \phi_1 B)\alpha_t$$

and the invertibility condition is $|\theta_1| < 1$. The autocorrelation function of the MA(1) model is:

$$\rho_k = \begin{array}{ll} \frac{-\theta_1}{1 + \theta_1^2} & k = 1 \\ & k > 2. \end{array} \tag{A.36}$$

The partial autocorrelation function of an MA(1) process tails off after lag one and its autocorrelation function cuts off after lag one.

In many economic time series, it is necessary to employ a mixed autoregressive-moving average (ARMA) model of the form:

$$\tilde{Z}_t = \phi_1\tilde{Z}_{t-1} + \cdots + \phi_p\tilde{Z}_{t-p} + \alpha_t - \theta_1\alpha_{t-1} - \cdots - \theta_q\alpha_{t-q} \tag{A.37}$$

or

$$\left(1 - \phi_1 B - \phi_2 B^2 - \cdots - \theta_p B^p\right)\tilde{Z}_t = \left(1 - \theta_1 B - \theta_2 B^2 - \cdots - \theta_q B^q\right)\alpha_t$$

that may be more simply expressed as

$$\phi(B)\tilde{Z}_t = \theta(B)\alpha_t$$

The autocorrelation function of the ARMA model is

$$P_k = \phi_1 \rho_{k-1} + \phi_2 \rho_{k-2} + \cdots + \phi_p \rho_{k-p}$$

or

$$\phi(B)\rho_k = 0.$$

The first-order autoregressive–first-order moving average operator ARMA (1,1) process is written

$$\tilde{Z}_t - \phi_1 \tilde{Z}_{t-1} = \alpha_t - \theta_1 \alpha_{t-1}$$

or

$$(1 - \phi_1)\tilde{Z}_t = (1 - \theta_1 B)\alpha_t.$$

The stationary condition is $-1 < \phi_1 < 1$ and the invertibility condition is $-1 < \phi_1 < 1$. The first two autocorrelations of the ARMA (1,1) model is

$$\rho_1 = \frac{(1 - \phi_1\theta_1)(\phi_1 - \theta_1)}{1 + \theta_1^2 - 2\phi_1\theta_1}$$

and

$$\rho_2 = \phi_1 \rho_1.$$

The partial autocorrelation function consists only of $\phi_{11} = \rho_1$ and has a damped exponential.

An integrated stochastic progress generates a time series if the series is made stationary by differencing (applying a time-invariant filter) the data. In an integrated process, the general form of the time series model is

$$\phi(B)(1 - B)^d X_t = \theta(B)\varepsilon_t \tag{A.38}$$

where $\phi(B)$ and $\theta(B)$ are the autoregressive and moving average polynominals in B of orders p and q, ε_t is a white noise error term, and d is an integer representing the order of the data differencing. In economic time series, a first-difference of the data is normally performed.[5] The application of the differencing operator, d, produces a stationary ARMA(p,q) process. The autoregressive integrated moving average ARMA, model is characterized by orders p, d, and q [ARIMA(p,d,q)]. Many economics series follow a random walk with drift, an ARMA (1,1) may be written as:

$$\overline{V}^d X_t = X_t - X_{t-1} = \varepsilon_t + b\varepsilon_{t-1}. \tag{A.39}$$

An examination of the autocorrelation function estimates may lead one to investigate using a first-difference model when the autocorrelation function estimates decay slowly. In an integrated process, the corr(X_t, $X_{t-\tau}$) is approximately unity for small values of time, τ.

ARMA Model Identification in Practice

Time series specialists use many statistical tools to identify models; however, the sample autocorrelation and partial autocorrelation function estimates are particularly useful in modeling. Univariate time series modeling normally requires larger data sets than regression and exponential smoothing models. It has been suggested that at least 40–50 observations be used to obtain reliable estimates.[6] One normally calculates the sample autocorrelation and partial autocorrelation estimates for the raw time series and its first (and possibly second) differences. The failure of the autocorrelation function estimates of the raw data series to die out as large lags implies that a first difference is necessary. The autocorrelation function (ACF) estimates of an AR(p) process tails off after p. The autocorrelation function estimates of an MA(q) process

[5] Box and Jenkins, *Time Series Analysis*. Chapter 6; C.W.J. Granger and Paul Newbold, *Forecasting Economic Time Series* (New York: Academic Press, 1986, Second Edition), pp. 109–110, 115–117, 206.

[6] Granger and Newbold, *Forecasting Economic Time Series*. pp. 185–186.

should cut off after q.[7] To test whether the autocorrelation estimates are statistically different from zero, one uses a t-test where the standard error of $v\tau$ is[8]:

$$n^{-1/2}\left[1 + 2\left(\rho_1^2 + \rho_2^2 + \cdots + \rho_q^2\right)\right]^{1/2} \text{ for } \tau > q.$$

The partial autocorrelation function (PACF) estimates of an AR(p) process cut off after lag p and tails off after q for an MA(q) process. A t-test is used to statistically examine whether the partial autocorrelations are statistically different from zero. The standard error of the partial autocorrelation estimates is approximately:

$$\frac{1}{\sqrt{N}} \text{ for } K > p. \tag{A.40}$$

One can use the normality assumption of large samples in the t-tests of the autocorrelation and partial autocorrelation estimates. The identified parameters are generally considered statistically significant if the parameters exceed twice the standard errors.

The ARMA model parameters may be estimated using nonlinear least squares. Given the following ARMA framework generally pack-forecasts the initial parameter estimates and assumes that the shock terms are to be normally distributed.

$$\alpha_t = \tilde{W}_t - \phi_1 \tilde{W}_{t-1} - \phi_2 \tilde{W}_{t-2} - \cdots - \phi_p \tilde{W}_{t-p} + \theta_1 \alpha_{t-1} + \cdots + \theta_q \alpha_{t-q}$$

where

$$W_t = \overline{V}^d Z_t \text{ and } \tilde{W}_t = Wt - \mu.$$

The minimization of the sum of squared errors with respect to the autoregressive and moving average parameter estimates produces starting values for the p order AR estimates and q order MA estimates.

$$\left.\frac{\partial e_t}{-\partial \phi_j}\right|_{\beta_0} = \mu_{j,t} \text{ and } \left.\frac{\partial e_t}{-\partial \theta_i}\right|_{\beta_0} = X_{j,t}$$

---

[7] See Box and Jenkins, *Time Series Analysis*, p. 79.

[8] Box and Jenkins, *Time Series Analysis*. pp. 173–179. Nelson (1973) is one of the texts used in the 1970s for forecasting and is still a very useful guide to applied time series modeling.

It may be appropriate to transform a series of data such that the residuals of a fitted model have a constant variance or are normally distributed. The log transformation is such a data transformation that is often used in modeling economic time series. Box and Cox (1964) put forth a series of power transformations useful in modeling time series.[9] The data is transformed by choosing a value of λ that is suggested by the relationship between the series amplitude (which may be approximated by the range of subsets) and mean.[10]

$$X_t^\lambda = \frac{X_t^\lambda - 1}{X^{\lambda-1}} \tag{A.41}$$

where X is the geometric mean of the series. One immediately recognizes that if $\lambda = 0$, the series is a logarithmic transformation. The log transformation is appropriate when there is a positive relationship between the amplitude and mean of the series. A $\lambda = 1$ implies that the raw data should be analyzed and there is no relationship between the series range and mean subsets. One generally selects the λ that minimizes the smallest residual sum of squares, although an unusual value of λ may make the model difficult to interpret. Some authors may suggest that only values of λ of -0.5, 0, 0.5, and 1.0 be considered to ease in the model-building process.[11]

The Ljung-Box statistic is a variation on the Box-Pierce statistic and the Ljung-Box Q statistic tends to produce significant levels closer to the asymptotic levels than the Box-Pierce statistic for first-order moving average processes. The Ljung-Box statistic, the model adequacy check reported in the SAS system, can be written as

$$Q = n(n+2) \sum_{k=1}^{m} (n = k)^{-1} \hat{v}_k^2. \tag{A.42}$$

Residual plots are generally useful in examining model adequacy; such plots may identify outliers as we noted in the chapter. The normalized cumulative periodogram of residuals should be examined.

Granger and Newbold (1977) and McCracken (2002) use several criteria to evaluate the effectiveness of the forecasts with respect to the forecast errors.

---

[9] G.E. Box and D.R. Cox, "An Analysis of Transformations," *Journal of the Royal Statistical Society*, B 26 (1964), 211–243.

[10] G.M. Jenkins, "Practical Experience with Modeling and Forecasting Time Series," *Forecasting* (Amsterdam: North-Holland Publishing Company, 1979).

[11] Jenkins, op. cit., pp. 135–138.

In this chapter, we use the root mean square error (RMSE) criteria. One seeks to minimize the square root of the sum of the absolute value of the forecast errors squared. That is, we calculate the absolute value of the forecast error, square the error, sum the squared errors, divided by the number of forecast periods, and take the square root of the resulting calculation. Intuitively, one seeks to minimize forecast errors. The absolute value of the forecast errors is important because if one calculated only a mean error, a 5% positive error could "cancel out" a 5% negative error. Thus, we minimize the out-of-sample forecast errors. We need a benchmark for forecast error evaluation. An accepted benchmark [Mincer and Zarnowitz (1969)] for forecast evaluation is a no-change, NoCH. A forecasting model should produce a lower root mean square error (RMSE) than the no-change model. If several models are tested, the lowest RMSE model is preferred.

In the world of business and statistics, one often speaks of autoregressive, moving average, and random walk with drift models, or processes, as we have just introduced. It is well-known that the majority of economic series, including real Gross Domestic Product (GDP) in the U.S., follow a random walk with drift, RWD, and are represented with autoregressive integrated moving average (ARIMA) model with a first-order moving average operator applied to the first-difference of the data. The data is differenced to produce stationary, where a process has a (finite) mean and variance that do not change over time and the covariance between data points of two series depends upon the distance between the data points, not on the time itself. The RWD process, estimated with an ARIMA (0,1,1) model, is approximately equal to a first-order exponential smoothing model [Cogger (1974)]. The random walk with drift model has been supported by the work of Nelson and Plosser (1982). Let us return to The Conference Board data used in the previous chapter on regression and estimate an ARIMA RWD Model for U.S. GDP for the 1959Q2 to 2020Q3 time period.

Forecasting Effectiveness of Time Series Modelling Using AutoMetrics to Estimate Breaks with Saturation Variables

David Hendry and his colleagues at Oxford have developed statistical software breaks with saturation variables. These time series issues of outliers and breaks have been addressed before, but the Hendry software is easy to use and provides the reader and researcher with the ability to estimate statistically significant models using more recently developed time series modeling techniques. We employ the automatic time series modeling and forecasting of

Castle, Hendry, and Doornik (2012), Hendry and Doornik (2014), Doornik and Hendry (2015), Castle and Hendry (2019) with its emphasis on structural breaks in Chapter 5 for modeling the MZTT unemployment rate data. Montgomery, Zarnowitz, Tsay, and Tiao (MZTT, 1998) modeled the U.S. unemployment rate as a function of the weekly unemployment claims time series, 1948–1993. A similar conclusion is found for the impact of the LEI and weekly unemployment claims series leading the unemployment rate series. We report statistically significant breaks in these data, 1959–1993 and 1959–2020.

As an introductory example, let us consider the U.S. real GDP as can be represented by an autoregressive integrated moving average (ARIMA) model. The data is differenced to create a process that has a (finite) mean and variance that do not change over time and the covariance between data points of two series depends upon the distance between the data points, not on the time itself—a transformation to stationarity. In economic time series, a first-difference of the data is normally performed.[12] The application of the differencing operator, d, produces a stationary autoregressive moving average ARMA(p,q) model when all parameters are constant across time. Many economics series can be modeled with a simple subset of the class of ARIMA(p,d,q) models, particularly the random walk with drift and a moving average term. The random walk with drift economic time series behavior is not new and can be traced back to the works of Granger and Newbold (1977) and Nelson and Plossner (1982).

Automatic time series models have recently been discussed in Hendry (1986), Hendry and Krolzig (2001, 2005), Hendry and Nielsen (2007), Castle, Doornik, and Hendry (2013), Hendry and Doornik (2014), and Castle and Hendry (2019) and implemented in the Autometrics software.[13] Hendry sets the tone for automatic modelling by contrasting how statistically based his PC-Give and Autometrics work in contrast to the "data mining" and "garbage in, garbage out" routines, citing their forecasting efficiency and performance. If one starts with a large number of predictors, or candidate

---

[12] Box and Jenkins, *Time Series Analysis*. Chapter 6; C.W.J. Granger and Paul Newbold, *Forecasting Economic Time Series* (New York: Academic Press, 1986, Second Edition), pp. 109–110, 115–117, 206.

[13] Automatic time series modelling has advocated since the early days of Box and Jenkins (1970). Reilly (1980), with the Autobox System, pioneered early automatic time series model implementation. Tsay (1988) identified outliers, level shifts, and variance change models that were implemented in PC-SCA. SCA was used in modelling time series in MZTT (1998).

explanatory variables, say n, then the general model can be written:

$$y_t = \sum_{i=1}^{n} \gamma_i Z_{it} + u_t. \tag{A.43}$$

The (conditional) data generating processes is assumed to be given by:

$$y_t = \sum_{i=1}^{n} \beta_i Z_{(i),t} + \varepsilon_t, \tag{A.44}$$

where

$$\varepsilon_t \cong \text{IN}\left(0, \sigma_e^2\right) \text{ for any } n < N.$$

One must select the relevant regressors where $\beta_j \neq 0$ in (A.44). Hendry and his colleagues refer to equation (A.44) as the most general, statistical model that can be postulated, given the availability of data and previous empirical and theoretical research as the general unrestricted model (GUM). The Hendry general-to-specific modeling process is referred to as *Gets*. One seeks to identify all relevant variables, the relevant lag structure and cointegrating relations, forming near orthogonal variables, Z. The general unrestricted model, GUM, with s lags of all variables can then be written:

$$y_t = \sum_{i=1}^{n} \sum_{j=0}^{s} \beta_{i,j} x_{i,t-j} + \sum_{i=1}^{n} \sum_{j=0}^{s} k_{i,j} z_{i,t-j} + \sum_{j=1}^{s} \theta_j y_{t-j}$$

$$+ \sum_{i=1}^{T} \delta_i 1_{\{i=t\}} + e_t, \tag{A.45}$$

where

$$\varepsilon_t \sim \text{IN}\left(0, \sigma_e^2\right)$$

Furthermore, outliers and shifts for T observations can be modeled with saturation variables, see Doornik and Hendry (2015) and Hendry and Doornik (2014, Chapters 7 and 14).

Automatic modeling seeks to eliminate irrelevant variables; variables with insignificant estimated coefficients; lag-length reductions; and reducing saturation variables (for each observation); the nonlinearity of the principal components; and combinations of "small effects" represented by principal components.[14] One of the most significant enhancements of OxMetrics is its automatic time series modeling and forecasting in its saturation variables. As we noted in Chapter 7, the Autometrics algorithm of the OxMetrics package has been developed in Hendry (1986, 2000), Castle and Shepard (2009), Hendry and Nielsen (2007), Castle, Doornik, and Hendry (2013), Hendry and Doornik (2014), and Castle, Clements, and Hendry (2015), and Castle and Hendry (2019). When observations on a given phenomenon, population growth or unemployment, come from a process whose properties remain constant over time—for example, having the same mean and variance at all points in time—they are said to be stationary. That is, a time series is stationary when its first two moments, namely the mean and variance, are finite and constant over time and is said to be integrated of order zero, denoted I(0). Economies evolve and change over time in both real and nominal terms, sometimes dramatically as in major wars, the US Great Depression after 1929, the "Oil Crises" of the mid-1970s, or the more recent "Financial Crisis and Great Recession" over 2008–2012. There are two important sources of non-stationarity often visible in time series: evolution and sudden shifts. The former reflects slower changes, such as knowledge accumulation and its embodiment in capital equipment, whereas the latter occurs from (e.g.) wars and policy regime changes. Developing a viable analysis of non-stationarity in economics really commenced with the discovery of the problem of "nonsense correlations." These high correlations are found between variables that should be unrelated: for example, between the price level in the UK and cumulative annual rainfall shown in Hendry (1980). Granger and Newbold (1974) re-emphasized that an apparently "significant relation" between variables, but where there remained substantial serial correlation in the residuals from that relation, was a symptom associated with nonsense regressions. A structural break denotes a shift in the behavior of a variable over time, such as a jump in the money stock, or a change in a previous relationship between observable variables, such as between inflation and unemployment, or the balance of trade and the exchange rate. Many

---

[14] Doornik and Hendry (2013) remind the reader that the data generation process (DGP) is impossible to model, and the best solution that one can achieve is estimate the models to reflect the local DGP, through reduction, described above. The Auotmatic *Gets* algorithm reduces GUM to nest LGDP, the locally relevant variables. Congruency, in which the LGDP has the same shape and size as the GUM; or, models reflect the local DGP.

sudden changes, particularly when unanticipated, cause links between variables to shift. This is a problem that is especially prevalent in economics as many structural breaks are induced by events outside the purview of most economic analyses, but examples abound in the sciences and social sciences, e.g., volcanic eruptions, earthquakes, and the discovery of penicillin. The consequences of not taking breaks into account include poor models, large forecast errors after the break, mis-guided policy, and inappropriate tests of theories. Such breaks can take many forms. The simplest to visualize is a shift in the mean of a variable. This is a "location shift," from a mean of zero to 2. Forecasts based on the zero mean will be systematically terribly wrong. Knowing of or having detected breaks, a common approach is to "model" them by adding appropriate indicator variables, namely artificial variables that are zero for most of a sample period but unity over the time that needs to be indicated as having a shift. Indicators can be formulated to reflect any relevant aspect of a model, such as changing trends, or multiplied by variables to capture when parameters shift. It is possible to design model selection strategies that tackle structural breaks automatically as part of their algorithm, as advocated by Hendry and Doornik (2014). Even though such approaches, called indicator saturation methods (see Johansen and Nielsen 2009; Castle et al. 2015), lead to more candidate explanatory variables than there are available observations, it is possible for a model selection algorithm to include large blocks of indicators for any number of outliers and location shifts, and even parameter changes. An alternative approach models shifts, including recessions, as the outcome of stochastic shocks in nonlinear dynamic processes, the large literature on which was partly surveyed by Hamilton (2016). Such models assume there is a probability at any point in time, conditional on the current regime and possibly several recent past regimes, that an economy might switch to a different state. A range of models have been proposed that could characterize such processes, which Hamilton describes as "a rich set of tools and specifications on which to draw for interpreting data and building economic models for environments in which there may be changes in regime." However, an important concern is which specification and which tools apply in any given instance, and how to choose between them when a given model formulation is not guaranteed to be fully appropriate Information criteria have a long history as a method of choosing between alternative models. Various information criteria have been proposed, all of which aim to choose between competing models by selecting the model with the smallest information loss. The trade-off between information loss and model "complexity" is captured by the penalty, which differs between information criteria. For example, the AIC proposed by Akaike

(1973), sought to balance the costs when forecasting from a stationary infinite autoregression of estimation variance from retaining small effects against the squared bias of omitting them. Automated general-to-specific (Gets) approaches as in Hoover and Perez (1999), Hendry and Krolzig (2001), Doornik (2009), and Hendry and Doornik (2014). This approach will be the one mainly used in this book when we need to explicitly select a model from a larger set of candidates, especially when there are more such candidates than the number of observations. Perhaps the best-known example of an I(1) process is a random walk, where the current value is equal to the previous value plus a random error. Thus the change in a random walk is just a random error. Such a process can wander widely and was first proposed by Bachelier (1900) to describe the behavior of prices in speculative markets. To summarize, both the mean and the variance of I(1) processes change over time, and successive values are highly interdependent. When the data are I(2) there is a generalized form of cointegration leading to I(0) combinations. Equilibrium-correction mechanisms (EqCMs) can be written in a representation in which changes in variables are inter-related, but also include lagged values of the I(0) combinations. EqCMs have the key property that they converge back to the long-run equilibrium of the data being modeled. This is invaluable when that equilibrium is constant, but as we will see, can be problematic if there are shifts in equilibria. Location shifts are changes from the previous mean of an I(0) variable. Uncertainty abounds, both in the real world and in our knowledge thereof. However, some events are so uncertain that probabilities of their happening cannot be sensibly assigned. We call such irreducible uncertainty "extrinsic unpredictability," corresponding to unknown unknowns: see Hendry and Mizon (2014). A pernicious form of extrinsic unpredictability affecting inter-temporal analyses, empirical modeling, forecasting, and policy interventions is that of unanticipated location shifts, namely shifts that occur at unanticipated times, changing by unexpected magnitudes and directions. As I(1) time series can be transformed back to I(0) by differencing or cointegration, the Normal distribution often remains the basis for calculating probabilities for statistical inference, as in random sampling from a known distribution. Hendry and Mizon (2014) call this "intrinsic unpredictability," because the uncertainty in the outcome is intrinsic to the properties of the random variables. Large outliers provide examples of "instance unpredictability" since their timings, magnitudes, and signs are uncertain, even when they are expected to occur in general, as in speculative asset markets. At first sight, location shifts seem highly problematic for econometric modeling, but as with stochastic trends, there are several potential solutions. Differencing a time series will also inadvertently convert a location shift to an impulse (an impulse in the first difference is equivalent to a step-shift in the level). Secondly, time series can co-break, analogous to cointegration, in that location shifts can cancel between series. A possible solution is to find all the location shifts and outliers whatever their magnitudes and signs then include indicators for them in the model. To do so requires us to solve the apparently impossible problem of selecting from more candidate variables in a model than observations. Hendry added impulse indicators (which are "dummy variables" that are zero everywhere except for unity at one data point) for all observations pre-1952, which revealed three large outliers corresponding to a US Great Depression food program and postwar de-rationing. To check that his model was constant from 1953 onwards, he later added impulse indicators for that period, thereby including more variables plus indicators than observations, but only entered his model in two large blocks, each much smaller than the number of observations. This has led to a statistical theory for modeling multiple outliers and location shifts (see, e.g., Johansen and Nielsen 2009; Castle et al. 2015), available in our computational tool Autometrics (Doornik 2009) and in the package Gets (Pretis et al. 2018) in the statistical software environment R. This approach, called indicator saturation, considers a possible outlier, or shift at every point in time, but only retains significant indicators. Shifting distributions are indicative of structural change, but that can take many forms, from sudden location shifts, changes in trend rates of growth, or in estimated parameters reflecting changes over time in relationships between variables. Further, outliers that could be attributed to specific events, but are not modeled, can lead to seemingly fat-tailed distributions when in fact the underlying process generating the data is thin tailed. Incorrect or changing distributions pose severe problems for modeling any phenomena and need to be correctly dealt with for viable estimation and inference on parameters of interest. Empirical modeling that does not account for shifts in the distributions of the variables under analysis risks reaching potentially misleading conclusions by wrongly attributing explanations from such contamination to chance correlations with other included variables, as well as having non-constant parameters. While the dates of some major events like the Great Depression, oil and financial crises, and major wars are known ex post, those of many other events are not. Moreover, the durations and magnitudes of the impacts on economies of shifts are almost never known. Consequently, it behooves any investigator of economic (and indeed many other) time series to find and neutralize the impacts of all the in-sample outliers and shifts on the estimates of their parameters of interest. Shifts come at unanticipated times with many different shapes, durations, and magnitudes, so general methods to detect them are needed. "Ocular" approaches to spotting outliers in a model are insufficient: an apparent outlier may be captured by one of the explanatory variables, and the absence of any obvious outliers does not entail that a large residual will not appear after fitting. It may be thought that the considerable number of tests required to check for outliers and shifts everywhere in a sample might itself be distorting, and hence adversely affect statistical inference. In particular, will one find too many nonexistent perturbations by chance? That worry may be exacerbated by the notion of using an indicator saturation approach, where an indicator for a possible outlier or shift at every observation is included in the set of explanatory variables to be searched over. Even if there are just 100 observations, there will be a hundred indicators plus variables, so there are many trillions of combinations of models created by including or omitting each variable and every indicator, be they for outliers or for shifts starting and ending at different times. IIS creates a complete set of indicator variables. Each indicator takes the value 1 for a single observation and 0 for all other observations. As many indicators as there are observations are created, each with a different observation corresponding to the value 1. So, for a sample of T observations, T indicators are then included in the set of candidate variables. However, all those indicators are most certainly not included together in the regression, as otherwise a perfect fit would always result, and nothing would be learned. Although saturation creates T additional variables when there are T observations, Autometrics provides an expanding and contracting block search algorithm to undertake model selection when there are more variables than observations. To aid exposition, we shall outline the "split-half" approach analyzed in Hendry et al. (2008), which is just the simplest way to explain and analyze IIS, so bear in mind that such an approach can be generalized to a larger number of possibly unequal "splits," and that the software explores many paths. Including an impulse indicator for a particular observation in a static regression delivers the same estimate of the model's parameters as if that observation had been left out. Consequently, the coefficient of that indicator is equal to the residual of the associated observation when predicted from a model based on the other observations. Despite its apparently arcane formulation involving more variables plus indicators than available observations, the properties of which we discussed above, IIS is closely related to a number of other well-known statistical approaches. First, consider recursive estimation, where a model is fitted to a small initial subset of the data, say $K > N$ values when there are N variables, then observations are added one at a time to check for changes in parameter estimates. In IIS terms, this is equivalent to starting with impulse indicators for the last $T - K$ observations, then dropping those indicators one at a time as each next observation is included in the recursion. Second, rolling regressions, where a fixed sample length is used, so earlier observations are dropped as later ones are added, is a further special case, equivalent to sequentially adding impulse indicators to eliminate earlier observations and dropping those for later. IIS is designed to detect outliers rather than location shifts, but split-half can also be used to illustrate indicator saturation when there is a single location shift which lies entirely within one of the halves. For a single location shift, Hendry and Santos (2010) show that the detection power, or potency, of IIS is determined by the magnitude of the shift; the length of the break interval, which determines how many indicators need to be found; the error variance of the equation; and the significance level, α, as a Normal distribution critical value, $c\alpha$, is used by the IIS selection algorithm. Castle et al. (2012) establish the ability of IIS in Autometrics to detect multiple location shifts and outliers, including breaks close to the start and end of the sample, as well as correcting for non-Normality. A step-shift is just a block of contiguous impulses of the same signs and magnitudes. Although IIS is applicable to detecting these, then the retained indicators could be combined into one dummy variable taking the average value of the shift over the break period and 0 elsewhere, perhaps after conducting a joint F-test on the ex post equality of the retained IIS coefficients, there is a more efficient method for detecting step-shifts. We can instead generate a saturating set of $T - 1$-step-shift indicators which take the value 1 from the beginning of the sample up to a given observation, and 0 thereafter, with each step switching from 1 to 0 at a different observation. Step indicators are the cumulation of impulse indicators up to each next observation. The "T"th step would just be the intercept. The $T - 1$-steps are included in the set of candidate regressors. The split-half algorithm is conducted in exactly the same way, but there are some differences. First, while impulse indicators are mutually orthogonal, step indicators overlap increasingly as their second index increases. Second, for a location shift that is not at either end, say from T1 to T2, two indicators are required to characterize it. Third, for a split-half analysis, the ease of detection is affected by whether or not T1 and T2 lie in the same split, and whether location shifts occur in both halves with similar signs and magnitudes. Castle et al. (2015) derive the null retention frequency of SIS and demonstrate the improved potency relative to IIS for longer location shifts. Trend-Indicator Saturation. Thus, one way of capturing a trend break would be to saturate the model with a series of trend indicators, which generate a trend up to a given observation and 0 thereafter for every observation. However, trend breaks can be difficult to detect as small changes in trends can take time to accumulate, even if they eventually lead to very substantial differences. Let us assume that the theory correctly specifies the set of relevant variables. This could include lags of the variables to represent an equilibrium-correction mechanism. In the combined approach, the theory relation is retained while selecting over an additional set of potentially relevant candidate variables. These additional candidate variables could include disaggregates for household characteristics (in panel data), as well as the variables noted above. To ensure an encompassing explanation, the additional set of variables could also include additional lags and nonlinear functions of the theory variables, other explanatory variables used by different investigators, and indicator variables to capture outliers and shifts. The general unrestricted model (GUM) is formulated to nest both the theory model and the data-driven formulation. As the theory variables and additional variables are likely to be quite highly correlated, even if the theory model is exactly correct the model estimates are unlikely to be the same as those from estimating the theory model directly. However, the theory variables can be orthogonalized with respect to the additional variables, which means that they are uncorrelated with the other variables. Therefore, inclusion of additional regressors will not affect the estimates of the theory variables in the model, regardless of whether any, or all, of the additional variables are included. The theory variables are always included in the model, and any additional variables can be selected over to see if they are useful in explaining the phenomena of interest. Thus, data-based model selection can be applied to all the potentially relevant candidate explanatory variables while retaining the theory model without selection. In a stationary world, many famous theorems about how to forecast optimally can be rigorously proved (summarized in Clements and Hendry 1998): 1. causal models will outperform non-causal (i.e., models without any relevant variables); 2. the conditional expectation of the future value delivers the minimum mean-square forecast error (MSFE); 3. misspecified models have higher forecast-error variances than correctly specified ones; 4. long-run interval forecasts are bounded above by the unconditional variance of the process; 5. neither parameter estimation uncertainty nor high correlations between variables greatly increase forecast-error variances. Unfortunately, when the process to be forecast suffers from location shifts and stochastic trends, and the forecasting model is misspecified, then: 1. non-causal models can outperform correct in-sample causal relationships; 2. conditional expectations of future values can be badly biased if later outcomes are drawn from different distributions; 3. the correct in-sample model need not outperform in forecasting and can be worse than the average of several devices; 4. long-run interval forecasts are unbounded; 5. parameter estimation uncertainty can substantively increase interval forecasts; as can 6. changes in correlations between variables at or near the forecast origin. The problem for empirical econometrics is not a plethora of excellent forecasting models from which to choose, but to find any relationships that survive long enough to be useful: as we have emphasized, the stationarity assumption must be jettisoned for observable variables in economics. Location shifts and stochastic trend non-stationarities can have pernicious impacts on forecast accuracy and its measurement: Castle et al. (2019) provide a general introduction. Because I(1) processes cumulate shocks, even using the correct in-sample model leads to much higher forecast uncertainty than would be anticipated on I(0) data. Given the hazards of forecasting wide-sense non-stationary variables, what can be done? First, be wary of forecasting I(1) processes over long time horizons. Modelers and policymakers must establish when they are dealing with integrated series and acknowledge that forecasts then entail increasing uncertainty. The danger is that uncertainty can be masked by using misspecified models which can falsely reduce the reported uncertainty. An important case noted above is enforcing trend stationarity, as seen in Fig. 7.3, greatly reducing the measured uncertainty without reducing the actual, a recipe for poor policy and intermittent forecast failure. As Sir Alex Cairncross worried in the 1960s: "A trend is a trend is a trend, but the question is, will it bend? Will it alter its course through some unforeseen force, and come to a premature end?" Alternatively, as Mr. Hendry often says, it is said that the trend is your friend till it doth bend. Second, once forecast failure has been experienced, detection of location shifts can be used to correct forecasts even with only a few observations, or alternatively it is possible to switch to more robust forecasting devices that adjust quickly to location shifts, removing much of any systematic forecast biases, but at the cost of wider interval forecasts (see e.g., Clements and Hendry 1999). Nevertheless, we have also shown that one aspect of the explosion in interval forecasts from imposing an integrated model after a shift in an I(0) process (i.e., one that does not have a genuine unit root) is due to using just the forecast-origin value, and that can be reduced by using moving averages of recent values. In turbulent times, such devices are an example of a method with no necessary verisimilitude that can outperform the in-sample previously correct representation. Figure 7.9 illustrates the substantial improvement in the 1-step ahead forecasts of the log of UK GDP over 2008–2012 using a robust forecasting device compared to a "conventional" method. The robust device has a much smaller bias and MSFE, but as it is knowingly misspecified, clearly does not justify selecting it as an economic model—especially not for policy. Third, the huge class of equilibrium-correction models includes almost all regression models for time series, autoregressive equations, vector autoregressive systems, cointegrated systems, dynamic-stochastic general equilibrium (DSGE) models, and many of the popular forms of model for autoregressive heteroskedasticity (see Engle 1982). Unfortunately, all of these formulations suffer from systematic forecast failure after shifts in their long-run, or equilibrium, means. Indeed, because they have inbuilt constant equilibria, their forecasts tend to go up (down) when outcomes go down (up), as they try to converge back to previous equilibria. Consequently, while cointegration captures equilibrium correction, care is required when using such models for genuine out-of-sample forecasts after any forecast failure has been experienced. Fourth, Castle et al. (2018) have found that selecting a model for forecasting from a general specification that embeds the DGP does not usually entail notable costs compared to using the estimated DGP—an infeasible comparator with non-stationary observational data. Clements (2017) provide a careful analysis of forecast combination. A caveat emphasized by Hendry and Doornik (2014) is that some pre-selection is useful before averaging to eliminate very bad forecasting devices. For example, the GUM is rarely a good device as it usually contains a number of what transpire to be irrelevant variables, and location shifts in these will lead to poor forecasts. Granger and Jeon (2004) proposed "thick" modeling as a route to overcoming model uncertainty, where forecasts from all non-rejected specifications are combined. However, Castle (2017) showed that "thick" modeling by itself neither avoids the problems of model misspecification nor handles forecast-origin location shifts. Although "thick" modeling is not formulated as a general-to-simple selection problem, it could be implemented by pooling across all congruent models selected by an approach like Autometrics. One can consider the orthogonal regressor case in which one ranks the variables by their t-statistics, highest to lowest, and defines m to be the smallest, but statistically significant t-statistic, t_m^2, and discards all variables with t-statistics below the m largest t-values. We seek to select a model of the form:

$$y_t = \sum_{r=1}^{m} \delta_r Z_{\{r\},t} + n_t, \qquad (A.46)$$

where $Z_{\{r\},t}$ is a subset of the initial N variables, and that model may differ depending on which variables remain at the end of the selection process.[15] One progresses from the general unrestricted model to the "final" model in (A.46) by establishing that model residuals are approximately normal, homoscedastic, and independent. Model reduction proceeds by tree searches of insignificant variables. The last, non-rejected model is referred to as the

---

[15] In the selection process, one tests the null hypothesis that the parameter in front of a variable is zero. The relevant t-statistic from a two-sided test is used.

terminal equation. Selected model regressors have coefficients that are large relative to their estimated standard errors; since the estimators obtained by the initial model (A.5) are unbiased, the selected estimators are upward biased conditional on retaining $Z_{(j),t}$. The unselected variables will have downward biased estimators. By omitting irrelevant variables, the selection model does not "overfit" the model and the relevant (retained) variables have estimated standard errors close to those from the fitting equation (A.46).

The automatic time series modeling program (PCGets) or (Autometrics) is efficient, but Hendry and Nielsen (2007) state that the largest selection bias can arise from strongly correlated regressors. Autometrics deals with outliers and breaks in its automatic time series modeling. The Regression Sum of Squares, RSS, rises as the outlier criteria shrink. Autometrics apply can impulse-indicator saturation variables IIS, step-indicator saturation variables (SIS), differenced IIS (DIIS) , and trend saturation (TIS) to all marginal models. where there are significant indicators. The step-indicator saturation (SIS) variables are generalized IIS variables with higher statistical power to detect location shifts. One can include outlier detection indicators (impulse-indicator saturation, I, and step-indicator saturation, S) in the Autometrics analysis of the LEI component effectiveness estimates, which we report in Chapters 7 and 10.[16]

Granger-Causality Modeling and Testing

Koopmans (1950) was the first to propose that the right-hand side (RHS) variables in an econometric regression be "exogenous" in the sense of having independent or self-dependent data generating process (DGP) being "approximately causal" for the left-hand side (LHS) variable. Granger causality in Econometrics texts, Vinod (2008), refers to Granger (1969) who proposed tools for the detection of causal paths between two or more economic time series. Roughly speaking, we say that the Granger's causal path $X_i \overset{Gr}{\to} X_j$ holds if variable X_i helps to predict variable X_j. The idea can be formulated in terms of mean square error (MSE) of forecasting h steps ahead based on the information set $I_{nf,t}$, at time t. For example, we say that X_i Granger-causes

---

[16] The use of saturation variables avoids the issue of forcing a unit root to capture the shifts, leading to an upward biased estimate of the lagged dependent variable coefficient. The authors are indebted to Jenny Castle for her comments on the application of saturation variables, which she observes addresses this very well.

X_j if the MSEs satisfy the inequality:

$$\text{MSE}_h\left(I_{\text{nf},t},\ \text{with } x_i\right) < \text{MSE}_h\left(I_{\text{nf},t}, \text{without } x_i\right), \qquad (\text{A.47})$$

where we have spelled out the condition on the information set that forecasting MSE should be smaller when X_i is included compared to the MSE based on information without the benefit of related X_i variable.

Any statistical test based on lags and leads of effects is subject to the famous fallacy called "post hoc ergo propter hoc." The ancients were aware that a rooster crowing at sunrise before the sun rises was not the cause of the sunrise. Since Granger causality focuses on time precedence, it remains subject to the fallacy, although it obviously remains useful when used with care.

Assume we have $t = 1, 2, \ldots T$ observations. Consider a model having X_j on the left-hand side (LHS) and X_i plus a set of variables combined into generic X_k on the RHS:

$$X_{jt} = f(X_{it}, X_{kt}) + \epsilon_{j|ik}, \qquad (\text{A.48})$$

where we use a generic symbols f to denote a possibly nonlinear function and $\epsilon_{j|ik}$ to denote unobserved shocks or errors. We use nonlinear non-parametric kernel regressions to estimate the conditional expectation functions. The specification (A.2) implies the causal path (RHS $\rightarrow$ LHS) or $(X_i \rightarrow X_j)$.

We also consider a model for the opposite causal path, $(X_j \rightarrow X_i)$ obtained by flipping X_j with X_i:

$$X_{it} = f\left(X_{jt}, X_{kt}\right) + \epsilon_{i|jk}, \ . \qquad (\text{A.49})$$

By analogy with Granger causality, but avoiding the time-precedence requirement, the data support the causal path $(X_i \rightarrow X_j)$, provided the model (A.2) has a superior fit (smaller forecasting MSE) compared to the model (A.3). Theorem 1 in Vinod (2019) extends Granger's intuition to develop computational methods for assessing causal paths and their strength indices. There are at least three coequal empirical criteria, denoted by Cr1, Cr2, and Cr3, which quantify the empirical support for the causal path $(X_i \rightarrow X_j)$.

The criterion Cr1 evaluates finite sample implications of consistency of conditional expectation functions of flipped kernel regressions. The true unknown errors $\epsilon_{j|ik}$ should be orthogonal to the regressors with probability limit satisfying:

$$plim_{T \to \infty}(\in_{j|ik} X_{it})/T = 0 \qquad (A.50)$$

Koopmans (1950) formulated the consistency requirement of Eq. (A.50) as exogeneity of X_i, and went on to require that each RHS variables should "approximately cause" the LHS variable. We plug observable residuals into the (consistency) exogeneity condition (A.50), yielding two sets of T multiplications $\in_{j|ik} X_{it}$ and $\in_{i|jk} X_{jt}$, where we replace the true unknown errors $\in_{.|..}$ by corresponding residuals $e_{.|..}$.

Our Cr1 assumes that closeness to zero of these observable expressions reveals relative speeds of convergence. The criterion Cr2 checks which flip has "lower" absolute values of residuals. We use asymmetric generalized partial correlation coefficients from Vinod (2014) as our third criterion Cr3.

Since it is not possible to prove why one criterion should dominate others, we use the "preponderance of evidence" standard by constructing a unanimity index $ui \in [-100, 000]$. We simply use a weighted sum of the three criteria denoted by ui. Given a 5% threshold, say, (or $\tau = 5$), the index allows us to propose the following decision rules:

Rule 1: If $(ui < -\tau)$, the causal path is: $X_i \to X_j$.
Rule 2: If $(ui > +\tau)$, the causal path is: $X_j \to X_i$.
Rule 3: If $(|ui| \leq -\tau)$, we obtain bi-directional causality: $X_i \leftrightarrow X_j$, that is, the variables are jointly dependent.

Complete computational details for using these decision rules on any given data set are a part of an open-source and free software package called "generalCorr," Vinod (2017), in a computer language called R. It is readily available in an open forum for further checking and development. The R package comes with three vignettes that provide theoretical details about the algorithms used, as well as examples.

The unemployment rate time series of the U.S. can be modeled with an AR(1) process, a one-period lag in weekly unemployment claims time series, with the expected positive coefficient, and a one-period lag in the LEI time series, with the expected negative coefficient. We report in Chapter 6 the validation of the MZTT analysis. There is a substantial RSS reduction and normal and homoscedastic error terms. Causality testing with the SCA system, using the Box and Jenkins (1970 and Tsay (1988 and 2020) methodologies produced statistical evidence that the DLLEI time series causes changes in the differenced U.S. unemployment rate time series.

Influential Observations and Outlier Detection

Influential observations are identified as observations, that when omitted, significantly influence estimated model coefficients and errors.

$$\hat{y} = x\hat{\beta} \qquad \hat{y}(i) = x\widehat{\beta_{\varepsilon}}$$

$$z_i = (x_i, y_i) \; when \; z_i \; is \; omitted$$

$$r_i = r_i(\beta)$$

Belsley, Kuh, and Welsch (1980) reported a set of criteria to identify influential observations. SAS reports the Cook Distance, Rstudent, COVRATIO, DFBETA, and DFFITS criteria.

The Cook distance of z_i is

$$D_i = \frac{1}{p^* s^2} ||\hat{y}(i) - \hat{y}||^2$$

$$p^* = \text{rank}\,(X),\, s^2 = \frac{1}{n - p^*} \sum_{i-1}^{n} r_i^2$$

H, the Hat Matrix, has a diagonal element, $h_1, \ldots h_n$ are the leverages of $x_1, \ldots x_n$

$$H = X(X'X)^{-1}x_i$$

$$h_i = X_i^i(X'X)^{-1}x_i$$

When observation i is omitted

$$D_i = \frac{r_i^2}{s^2} \frac{h_i}{p^*(1 - h_i)^2}$$

Student's version of $r_{(i)} =$

$$s_{(i)}^2 = s(i) = \frac{n - p - 1}{n - p} s^2 - \frac{e_i^2}{(n - p - 1)(1 - h_i)}$$

$$\text{COVRATIO} = \left[\left(\frac{n - p - 1}{n - p} \right) + \frac{e_i^{*2}}{n - p} \right)^P (1 - h_i) \right]$$

DFBETA $=$ change in regression coefficients iluminating observation i

Compare to variance of b_j

$$\sigma^2 (X^1 X)^{-1} x_i$$

$$= b_j - b_{j(i)} = \frac{c_{ji} - e_i}{1 - h_i}$$

$$\text{var}(b_j) = \sigma^2 \sum_{k-1}^{n} c_j k^2$$

$$\text{DFFITS} = \left[\frac{h_i}{1 - h_i} \right]^{1/2} \frac{e_i}{s_i \left(\sqrt{1 - h_i} \right)}$$

RSTUDENT

$$e_i^* = \frac{e_i}{s(i) \sqrt{1 - h_i}}$$

$$\text{COVRATIO} = \frac{1}{\left[\frac{n-p-1}{n-p} + \frac{e_i^{*2}}{n-p} \right]^P (1 - h_i)}$$

Points with COVRATIO $- 1$ investigated for $3p/n$

$$\sqrt{1 - h_i} \frac{r(i)}{s(i)} = \frac{1}{\sqrt{1 - h_i}} \frac{v_i}{s(i)}$$

The U.S. Leading Economic Indicators

Let us follow The Conference Board Components and their definitions, as of November 29, 2019:

BCI-01 Average weekly hours, manufacturing

The average hours worked per week by production workers in manufacturing industries tend to lead the business cycle because employers usually adjust work hours before increasing or decreasing their workforce.

BCI-05 Average weekly initial claims for unemployment insurance

The number of new claims filed for unemployment insurance are typically more sensitive than either total employment or unemployment to overall business conditions, and this series tends to lead the business cycle. It is inverted when included in the leading index; the signs of the month-to-month changes are reversed, because initial claims increase when employment conditions worsen (i.e., layoffs rise and new hirings fall).

BCI-08 Manufacturers' new orders, consumer goods, and materials (in 1982 $)

These goods are primarily used by consumers. The inflation-adjusted value of new orders leads to actual production because new orders directly affect the level of both unfilled orders and inventories that firms monitor when making production decisions. The Conference Board deflates the current dollar orders data using price indexes constructed from various sources at the industry level and a chain-weighted aggregate price index formula.

BCI-130 ISM new order index

This index reflects the levels of new orders from customers. As a diffusion index, its value reflects the number of participants reporting increased orders during the previous month compared to the number reporting decreased orders, and this series tends to lead the business cycle. When the index has a reading of greater than 50 it is an indication that orders have increased during the past month. This index, therefore, tends to lead the business cycle. ISM new orders are based on a monthly survey conducted by Institution for Supply Management (formerly known as National Association of Purchasing Management). The Conference Board takes normalized value of this index as a measure of its contribution to LEI.

BCI-33 Manufacturers' new orders, non-defense capital goods excl. aircraft (in 1982 $)

This index, combing with orders from aircraft (in inflation-adjusted dollars) are the producers' counterpart to BCI-08.

BCI-29 Building permits, new private housing units

The number of residential building permits issued is an indicator of construction activity, which typically leads to most other types of economic production.

BCI-19 Stock prices, 500 common stocks

The Standard & Poor's 500 stock index reflects the price movements of a broad selection of common stocks traded on the New York Stock Exchange.

Increases (decreases) in the stock index can reflect both the general sentiments of investors and the movements of interest rates, which is usually another good indicator for future economic activity.

BCI-107 Leading Credit Index™

This index consists of six financial indicators: 2-years Swap Spread (real time), LIBOR 3 month less 3-month Treasury-Bill yield spread (real time), Debit balances at margin account at broker dealer (monthly), AAII Investors Sentiment Bullish (%) less Bearish (%) (weekly), Senior Loan Officers C&I loan survey—Bank tightening Credit to Large and Medium Firms (quarterly), and Security Repurchases (quarterly) from the Total Finance-Liabilities section of Federal Reserve's flow of fund report. Because of these financial indicators' forward-looking content, LCI leads to economic activities.

BCI-129 Interest rate spread, 10-year Treasury bonds less federal funds

The spread or difference between long and short rates is often called the yield curve. This series is constructed using the 10-year Treasury bond rate and the federal funds rate, an overnight interbank borrowing rate. It is felt to be an indicator of the stance of monetary policy and general financial conditions because it rises (falls) when short rates are relatively low (high). When it becomes negative (i.e., short rates are higher than long rates and the yield curve inverts) its record as an indicator of recessions is particularly strong.

BCI-125 Avg. Consumer Expectations for Business and Economic Conditions

This index reflects changes in consumer attitudes concerning future economic conditions and, therefore, is the only indicator in the leading index that is completely expectations-based. It is an equally weighted average of consumer expectations of business and economic conditions using two questions, Consumer Expectations for Economic Conditions 12-months ahead from Surveys of Consumers conducted by Reuters/University of Michigan, and Consumer Expectations for Business Conditions 6-months ahead from Consumer Confidence Survey by The Conference Board. Responses to the questions concerning various business and economic conditions are classified as positive, negative, or unchanged.

Identifying Influential Observations in a Regression

In the following regression estimate, is the differenced-log (DLOG) Leading Economic Indicator, LEI, lagged one period, L1LEI, and the differenced-log (DLOG) Weekly Unemployment Claims, lagged one period, L1WKUCL, a statistically significant determinant of the differenced unemployment rate (DUE)? Why?

The REG Procedure

Model: MODEL1
Dependent Variable: DUE
Analysis of Variance

Source	DF	Sum of Squares	Mean Square	F Value	Pr > F
Model	2	1.30406	0.65203	496.48	<.0001
Error	737	0.96790	0.00131		
Corrected Total	739	2.27196			

Root MSE	0.03624	R-Square	0.5740
Dependent Mean	0.00021158	Adj R-Sq	0.5728
Coeff Var	17128		

Parameter Estimates

Variable	DF	Parameter Estimate	Standard Error	t Value	Pr > |t|
Intercept	1	-0.00035475	0.00139	-0.26	0.7985
L1LEI	1	0.01676	0.21061	0.08	0.9366
L1WKUCL	1	0.37861	0.01530	24.74	<.0001

Note in the OLS-estimated regression only the one-period lagged Weekly Unemployment Claims variable is statistically significant.

Let us identify potentially influential observations on the basis of Studentized Residuals, the hat diagonal elements, DFFITS, and DFBETAS.

Model: MODEL1
Dependent Variable: DUE

Output Statistics

Obs	Residual	RStudent	Hat Diag H	Cov Ratio	DFFITS	DFBETAS Intercept	L1LEI	L1WKUCL
1	.	.	.	.	.	.	.	.
2	.	.	.	.	.	.	.	.
3	-0.0418	-1.1557	0.0055	1.0041	-0.0858	-0.0201	-0.0737	-0.0372
4	-0.0372	-1.0287	0.0044	1.0041	-0.0681	-0.0239	-0.0455	-0.0019
5	0.001244	0.0343	0.0017	1.0058	0.0014	0.0013	-0.0002	-0.0006
6	-0.0225	-0.6227	0.0039	1.0064	-0.0390	-0.0130	-0.0316	-0.0206

7	0.003085	0.0852	0.0020	1.0060	0.0038	0.0025	0.0018	0.0021
8	0.0109	0.3013	0.0016	1.0053	0.0122	0.0093	0.0045	0.0045

			Hat Diag	Cov		-----------DFBETAS-----------		
Obs	Residual	RStudent	H	Ratio	DFFITS	Intercept	L1LEI	L1WKUCL
9	0.0185	0.5120	0.0024	1.0055	0.0253	0.0185	-0.0021	0.0118
10	0.0635	1.7568	0.0028	0.9944	0.0937	0.0774	-0.0525	-0.0663
11	-0.0341	-0.9421	0.0034	1.0039	-0.0550	-0.0313	-0.0051	-0.0364
12	-0.1357	-3.7855	0.0033	0.9508	-0.2170	-0.1517	0.0701	-0.0747
13	0.0731	2.0322	0.0098	0.9971	0.2019	0.0491	0.0880	-0.0750
14	-0.0870	-2.4100	0.0014	0.9821	-0.0909	-0.0888	0.0140	-0.0025
15	0.1318	3.6705	0.0019	0.9527	0.1609	0.1512	-0.0746	-0.0820
16	-0.0802	-2.2226	0.0027	0.9868	-0.1161	-0.0778	0.0013	-0.0637
17	-0.007407	-0.2044	0.0015	1.0054	-0.0078	-0.0072	-0.0001	0.0017
18	0.0303	0.8354	0.0020	1.0032	0.0370	0.0273	0.0067	0.0195
19	0.0119	0.3291	0.0016	1.0052	0.0130	0.0104	0.0044	0.0041
20	0.002460	0.0679	0.0015	1.0056	0.0027	0.0024	0.0000	0.0007
21	-0.0483	-1.3352	0.0029	0.9997	-0.0723	-0.0355	-0.0397	-0.0522
22	0.1168	3.2478	0.0019	0.9639	0.1411	0.1333	-0.0644	-0.0700
23	-0.0224	-0.6197	0.0023	1.0048	-0.0298	-0.0175	-0.0150	-0.0188
24	0.0674	1.8644	0.0019	0.9919	0.0820	0.0772	-0.0410	-0.0110
25	0.003986	0.1100	0.0015	1.0056	0.0043	0.0043	-0.0015	-0.0012
26	0.0329	0.9095	0.0045	1.0052	0.0609	0.0179	0.0501	0.0381
27	-0.0332	-0.9166	0.0032	1.0038	-0.0517	-0.0239	-0.0289	-0.0386
28	0.0621	1.7199	0.0041	0.9962	0.1109	0.0461	0.0550	-0.0227
29	0.0121	0.3343	0.0036	1.0072	0.0200	0.0074	0.0157	0.0102
30	-0.004667	-0.1289	0.0026	1.0066	-0.0066	-0.0035	-0.0037	-0.0001
31	0.0410	1.1325	0.0039	1.0027	0.0705	0.0261	0.0501	0.0102
32	-0.0748	-2.0715	0.0029	0.9896	-0.1114	-0.0512	-0.0761	-0.0696
33	0.0524	1.4511	0.0053	1.0008	0.1056	0.0300	0.0773	0.0104
34	-0.0460	-1.2718	0.0015	0.9990	-0.0499	-0.0446	-0.0004	-0.0138
35	-0.0332	-0.9180	0.0036	1.0043	-0.0552	-0.0225	-0.0360	-0.0030
36	-0.0169	-0.4684	0.0073	1.0105	-0.0401	-0.0063	-0.0361	-0.0224
37	-0.0233	-0.6422	0.0017	1.0041	-0.0266	-0.0197	-0.0106	-0.0018
38	-0.0583	-1.6129	0.0015	0.9950	-0.0620	-0.0522	-0.0165	-0.0158
39	0.0251	0.6942	0.0042	1.0063	0.0449	0.0142	0.0367	0.0192
40	0.0108	0.2970	0.0014	1.0052	0.0113	0.0106	-0.0003	-0.0024
41	-0.0124	-0.3411	0.0017	1.0054	-0.0143	-0.0102	-0.0066	-0.0027
42	-0.0223	-0.6161	0.0017	1.0043	-0.0258	-0.0207	-0.0030	-0.0112
...								
75	-0.0894	-2.4768	0.0019	0.9812	-0.1076	-0.0717	-0.0549	-0.0467
76	0.0381	1.0538	0.0026	1.0022	0.0539	0.0278	0.0338	0.0084
77	-0.0426	-1.1768	0.0016	1.0001	-0.0474	-0.0360	-0.0194	-0.0119
78	0.0231	0.6380	0.0018	1.0042	0.0269	0.0226	0.0002	-0.0101
79	-0.0455	-1.2575	0.0016	0.9993	-0.0509	-0.0383	-0.0213	-0.0139
80	-0.0103	-0.2842	0.0020	1.0057	-0.0126	-0.0081	-0.0066	-0.0061
81	-0.0499	-1.3798	0.0031	0.9994	-0.0768	-0.0348	-0.0478	-0.0549
82	0.0248	0.6859	0.0032	1.0054	0.0387	0.0255	-0.0031	-0.0248
83	-0.007031	-0.1942	0.0034	1.0074	-0.0114	-0.0045	-0.0084	-0.0029
84	-0.0311	-0.8593	0.0035	1.0045	-0.0506	-0.0192	-0.0393	-0.0280
85	0.0110	0.3030	0.0025	1.0063	0.0153	0.0079	0.0100	0.0039
86	-0.0781	-2.1625	0.0030	0.9882	-0.1187	-0.0552	-0.0724	-0.0843

Obs	Residual	RStudent	Hat Diag H	Cov Ratio	DFFITS	DFBETAS Intercept	L1LEI	L1WKUCL
87	0.005916	0.1633	0.0015	1.0055	0.0063	0.0053	0.0017	0.0004
88	0.0696	1.9304	0.0051	0.9941	0.1384	0.0674	0.0079	-0.0879
89	0.0331	0.9151	0.0015	1.0021	0.0353	0.0299	0.0086	0.0007
90	-0.0521	-1.4414	0.0028	0.9984	-0.0760	-0.0628	0.0433	0.0012
91	-0.004675	-0.1290	0.0018	1.0058	-0.0054	-0.0053	0.0026	0.0012
92	-0.008599	-0.2373	0.0017	1.0056	-0.0098	-0.0095	0.0041	0.0012
93	-0.0181	-0.4987	0.0023	1.0053	-0.0237	-0.0218	0.0146	0.0120
94	-0.005170	-0.1427	0.0018.	1.0058	-0.0060	-0.0058	0.0028	0.0013
95	-0.0366	-1.0106	0.0017	1.0016	-0.0417	-0.0404	0.0171	0.0044
96	0.0440	1.2151	0.0014	0.9995	0.0461	0.0440	-0.0044	0.0055
97	0.006667	0.1840	0.0017	1.0057	0.0077	0.0070	-0.0018	0.0013
98	-0.004221	-0.1165	0.0019	1.0059	-0.0050	-0.0037	-0.0014	0.0009
99	-0.0710	-1.9670	0.0054	0.9937	-0.1444	-0.0606	-0.0261	-0.1119
100	0.006951	0.1918	0.0015	1.0054	0.0074	0.0062	0.0019	0.0002
101	-0.0234	-0.6458	0.0021	1.0045	-0.0296	-0.0193	-0.0118	-0.0176
102	0.0702	1.9423	0.0029	0.9917	0.1056	0.0645	0.0175	-0.0484
103	-0.004190	-0.1157	0.0023	1.0063	-0.0056	-0.0033	-0.0028	0.0000
104	-0.0171	-0.4714	0.0022	1.0054	-0.0223	-0.0131	-0.0123	-0.0130
105	0.0352	0.9724	0.0030	1.0032	0.0535	0.0274	0.0257	-0.0077
106	0.0450	1.2437	0.0017	0.9995	0.0514	0.0374	0.0225	0.0191
107	-0.0273	-0.7530	0.0014	1.0031	-0.0278	-0.0259	-0.0022	-0.0023
108	0.005600	0.1546	0.0021	1.0061	0.0072	0.0053	0.0006	-0.0030
109	-0.0545	-1.5096	0.0066	1.0015	-0.1234	-0.0235	-0.1040	-0.0931
110	0.0256	0.7061	0.0014	1.0034	0.0260	0.0245	0.0015	0.0013
111	0.007985	0.2205	0.0024	1.0063	0.0108	0.0085	-0.0024	-0.0068
112	-0.0539	-1.4896	0.0014	0.9964	-0.0549	-0.0525	-0.0001	0.0018
113	-0.004857	-0.1340	0.0014	1.0054	-0.0050	-0.0045	-0.0006	-0.0008
114	0.0614	1.6976	0.0018	0.9942	0.0722	0.0501	0.0352	0.0147
115	0.008295	0.2289	0.0015	1.0053	0.0087	0.0076	0.0016	-0.0003
116	-0.0631	-1.7438	0.0014	0.9932	-0.0660	-0.0583	-0.0109	-0.0155
117	-0.0313	-0.8642	0.0018	1.0028	-0.0365	-0.0355	0.0179	0.0098
118	0.0141	0.3886	0.0029	1.0064	0.0211	0.0096	0.0147	0.0053
119	0.0117	0.3243	0.0022	1.0059	0.0153	0.0090	0.0089	0.0028
120	0.001589	0.0438	0.0015	1.0056	0.0017	0.0017	-0.0005	-0.0004
121	-0.0305	-0.8421	0.0022	1.0034	-0.0392	-0.0269	-0.0089	-0.0230
122	0.0103	0.2841	0.0015	1.0052	0.0109	0.0096	0.0015	-0.0011
123	-0.000652	-0.0180	0.0014	1.0054	-0.0007	-0.0006	-0.0000	-0.0000
124	0.0190	0.5251	0.0016	1.0046	0.0213	0.0188	-0.0005	-0.0073
125	0.006469	0.1785	0.0014	1.0054	0.0068	0.0059	0.0014	0.0000
126	0.0309	0.8539	0.0035	1.0046	0.0504	0.0413	-0.0394	-0.0256
127	-0.0189	-0.5214	0.0020	1.0050	-0.0235	-0.0213	0.0106	-0.0001
128	-0.0173	-0.4791	0.0027	1.0058	-0.0248	-0.0213	0.0158	0.0042
...								
570	-0.0304	-0.8388	0.0026	1.0038	-0.0428	-0.0349	0.0197	-0.0052
571	0.0513	1.4201	0.0034	0.9993	0.0830	0.0655	-0.0526	-0.0619
572	-0.0139	-0.3846	0.0024	1.0059	-0.0187	-0.0167	0.0113	0.0034
573	-0.0359	-0.9920	0.0025	1.0026	-0.0495	-0.0444	0.0328	0.0256
574	-0.0256	-0.7064	0.0016	1.0036	-0.0279	-0.0277	0.0100	0.0048
575	0.0239	0.6604	0.0017	1.0040	0.0269	0.0266	-0.0115	-0.0078

...

Obs	Residual	RStudent	Hat Diag H	Cov Ratio	DFFITS	DFBETAS Intercept	L1LEI	L1WKUCL
576	-0.0368	-1.0157	0.0018	1.0017	-0.0434	-0.0408	0.0182	0.0014
577	0.0504	1.3937	0.0014	0.9976	0.0531	0.0460	0.0114	0.0011
578	-0.0150	-0.4130	0.0025	1.0059	-0.0205	-0.0184	0.0135	0.0104
579	-0.0309	-0.8542	0.0015	1.0026	-0.0333	-0.0326	0.0090	0.0007
580	0.0447	1.2344	0.0017	0.9996	0.0516	0.0429	0.0033	-0.0170
581	-0.0385	-1.0628	0.0020	1.0015	-0.0481	-0.0441	0.0239	0.0032
582	0.0603	1.6688	0.0018	0.9946	0.0709	0.0667	-0.0265	-0.0349
583	0.0121	0.3331	0.0019	1.0055	0.0144	0.0137	-0.0071	-0.0023
584	-0.0182	-0.5032	0.0020	1.0050	-0.0223	-0.0213	0.0123	0.0088
585	0.0139	0.3852	0.0030	1.0065	0.0211	0.0179	-0.0154	-0.0076
586	0.008349	0.2307	0.0040	1.0079	0.0147	0.0115	-0.0118	-0.0087
587	-0.0175	-0.4828	0.0027	1.0059	-0.0252	-0.0215	0.0162	0.0043
588	0.0489	1.3534	0.0045	1.0011	0.0906	0.0686	-0.0741	-0.0340
589	-0.009354	-0.2586	0.0055	1.0093	-0.0192	-0.0138	0.0165	0.0086
590	-0.008997	-0.2492	0.0086	1.0125	-0.0232	-0.0148	0.0212	0.0151
591	0.0342	0.9474	0.0059	1.0064	0.0731	0.0516	-0.0641	-0.0360
592	-0.0432	-1.1972	0.0083	1.0066	-0.1093	-0.0695	0.0969	0.0409
593	0.0822	2.2789	0.0040	0.9871	0.1450	0.1140	-0.1178	-0.0814
594	0.0341	0.9431	0.0056	1.0061	0.0711	0.0509	-0.0619	-0.0370
595	0.0182	0.5035	0.0022	1.0052	0.0234	0.0211	-0.0122	-0.0018
596	0.0191	0.5318	0.0190	1.0223	0.0740	0.0385	-0.0698	-0.0317
597	-0.0105	-0.2914	0.0071	1.0109	-0.0246	-0.0165	0.0220	0.0115
598	0.0351	0.9752	0.0157	1.0161	0.1231	0.0669	-0.1151	-0.0522
'''								
722	-0.0621	-1.7183	0.0014	0.9935	-0.0654	-0.0619	0.0053	-0.0093
723	0.001005	0.0277	0.0014	1.0054	0.0010	0.0010	-0.0000	-0.0000
724	-0.0443	-1.2228	0.0015	0.9995	-0.0470	-0.0457	0.0085	0.0137
725	0.002790	0.0770	0.0014	1.0055	0.0029	0.0029	-0.0006	-0.0005
726	0.0253	0.6985	0.0014	1.0035	0.0265	0.0264	-0.0064	-0.0031
727	-0.007587	-0.2094	0.0014	1.0053	-0.0079	-0.0077	0.0011	-0.0004
728	0.0142	0.3923	0.0015	1.0050	0.0153	0.0139	0.0001	-0.0038
729	-0.0606	-1.6768	0.0017	0.9943	-0.0687	-0.0674	0.0293	0.0126
730	0.0347	0.9590	0.0020	1.0024	0.0433	0.0409	-0.0245	-0.0196
731	-0.0308	-0.8503	0.0017	1.0029	-0.0353	-0.0346	0.0163	0.0087
732	-0.001433	-0.0395	0.0014	1.0054	-0.0015	-0.0014	-0.0000	-0.0001
733	0.0114	0.3150	0.0017	1.0053	0.0128	0.0119	-0.0030	0.0017
734	-0.000093	-0.002567	0.0020	1.0061	-0.0001	-0.0001	-0.0000	0.0000
735	0.2219	6.2864	0.0016	0.8597	0.2554	0.2501	-0.1017	-0.0339
736	0.2528	15.7616	0.7384	1.6038	26.4777	-0.9960	6.2446	24.0222
737	-0.2689	-8.1582	0.0994	0.8599	-2.7108	-0.9589	2.3713	0.4742
738	0.0472	1.3314	0.0413	1.0398	0.2764	0.0503	0.0033	-0.2109
739	0.0754	2.1109	0.0242	1.0105	0.3324	0.0451	0.1196	-0.1608
740	-0.1514	-4.2429	0.0087	0.9421	-0.3975	-0.0594	-0.3278	-0.0772
741	0.0521	1.4478	0.0113	1.0069	0.1547	0.0515	0.0057	-0.1101
742	-0.0714	-1.9775	0.0046	0.9929	-0.1351	-0.0778	0.0230	0.1016

Sum of Residuals	0
Sum of Squared Residuals	0.96790
Predicted Residual SS (PRESS)	1.86050

The BOLD (RStudent) Studentized Residuals exceed 2.00 or are less than −2.00, indicating influential observations.

The BOLD DFFITS exceed 0.109 indicating influential observations.

The BOLD DFBETAS are large and are paired with DFFITS exceed 0.109 indicating influential observations.

The bold RStudent, DFFITS, and DFBETAS statistics indicate that the 2020 time period is dominated by influential observations.

Selected References

Ashley, R. (1998). A new technique for postsample model selection and validation. *Journal of Economic Dynamics and Control, 22*, 647–665.

Ashley, R., Granger, C. W. J., & Schmalensee, R. (1980). Advertising and aggregate consumption: An analysis of causality. *Econometrica, 48*, 149–1167.

Ashley, R. A. (2003). Statistically significant forecasting improvements: How much out-of-sample data is likely necessary? *International Journal of Forecasting, 19*, 229–240.

Beaton, A. E., & Tukey, J. W. (1974). The fitting of power series, meaning polynomials, illustrated on bank-spectroscopic data. *Technometrics, 16*, 147–185.

Belsley, D. A., Kuh, E., & Welsch, R. E. (1980). *Regression diagnostics: Identifying influential data and sources of collinearity* (Chapter 2). Wiley.

Box, G. E. P., & Jenkins, G. M. (1970). *Time series analysis: Forecasting and control*. Holden-Day.

Castle, J., & Shepard, N. (2009). *The methodology and practice of econometrics*. Oxford University Press.

Castle, J., Clements, M. P., & Hendry, D. F. (2015). Robust approaches to forecasting. *International Journal of Forecasting, 31*, 99–112.

Castle, J. L., & Hendry, D. F. (2019). *Modelling our changing world*. Palgrave Macmillan.

Chen, C., & Lee, C. J. (1990). A VARMA test on the Gibson Paradox. *Review of Economics and Statistics, 72*, 96–107.

Chen, C., & Liu, L.-M. (1993a). Joint estimation of model parameters and outliers in time series'. *Journal of the American Statistical Association, 88*, 284–297.

Chen, C., & Liu, L.-M. (1993b). Forecasting time series with outliers. *Journal of Forecasting, 12*, 13–35.

Clements, M. P., & Hendry, D. F. (1998). *Forecasting economic time series.* Cambridge University Press.

Cochrane, D., & Orcutt, G. H. (1949). Application of least squares regression to relationships containing autocorrelated error terms. *Journal of the American Statistical Association., 44*, 32–61.

Dhrymes, P. (2017). *Introductory econometrics* (Rev. ed.). Springer.

Efron, B., Hastie, T., Johnstone, J., & Tibshirani, R. (2004). Least angle regression. *The Annals of Statistics, 32*, 407–499.

Granger, C. W. J., & Newbold, P. (1977). *Forecasting economic time series.* Academic Press.

Granger, C. W. J. (1969). Investigating casual relations by economic models and cross-spectral methods. *Econometrica, 37*, 424–438.

Granger, C. W. J. (1980). Testing for causality: A personal viewpoint. *Journal of Economic Dynamics and Control, 2*, 329–352.

Granger, C. W. J. (2001). *Essays in econometrics* (2 vols., E. Ghysels, N. R. Swanson, & M. W. Watson, Eds.). Cambridge University Press.

Guerard, J. B. (1985). Mergers, stock prices, and industrial production: An empirical test of the Nelson hypothesis. In *Time series analysis: Theory and practice* (7th ed.). O.D. Anderson. Amsterdam North-Holland Publishing Company.

Guerard, J. B., Jr, Xu, G., & Wang, Z. (2019). *Portfolio and investment analysis with SAS: Financial modeling techniques for optimization.* SAS Press.

Gunst, R. F., & Mason, R. L. (1980). *Regression analysis and its application.* Marcel Dekker Inc.

Hastie, T., Tibshirani, R., & Friedman, J. (2016). *The elements of statistical learning: Data mining, inference, and prediction* (2nd ed., 11th printing). Springer.

Hamilton, J. R. (1994). *Time series analysis.* Princeton University Press.

Hendry, D. F. (1980). Econometrics-alchemy or science? *Economica, 47*(1980), 387–406.

Hendry, D. F. (1986). Using PC-give in econometrics teaching. *Oxford Bulletin of Economics and Statistics, 48*, 87–98.

Hendry, D. F. (2000). *Econometrics: Alchemy or science?* Oxford University Press.

Hendry, D. F., & Krolzig, H. M. (2005). The properties of automatic gets modelling. *The Economic Journal, 115*, c32–c61.

Hendry, D. F., & Doornik, J. A. (2014). *Empirical model discovery and theory evaluation.* MIT Press.

Huber, P. J. (1973). Robust regression: Asymptotics, conjectures, and Monte Carlo". *Annals of Statistics, 1*, 799–821.

Klein, L. (1950). *Economic fluctuations in the United States, 1941.* Wiley.

Krolzig, H.-M., & Hendry, D. F. (2001). Computer automation of general-to-specific model selection procedures. *Journal of Economic Dynamics & Control*, 831–866.

Makridakis, S., Wheelwright, S. C., & Hyndman, R. J. (1998). *Forecasting: Methods and applications* (3rd ed., Chapters 5, 6). Wiley.

Mansfield, E. (1994). *Statistics for business and economics* (5th ed.). W. W. Norton.

Maronna, R. A., Martin, R. D., & Yohai, V. J. (2006). *Robust statistics; Theory and methods with R*. Wiley.

Maronna, R. A., Martin, R. D., Yohai, V. J., & Salibian-Barrera, M. (2019). *Robust statistics; Theory and methods with R* (2nd ed.). Wiley.

Miller, I., & Freund, J. E. (1965). *Probability and statistics for engineers*. Prentice-Hall.

Mincer, J., & Zarnowitz, V. (1969). The evaluation of economic forecasts. In J. Mincer (Ed.), *Economic forecasts and expectations*. Columbia University Press.

Montgomery, A. L., Zarnowitz, V., Tsay, R., & Tiao, G. C. (1998). Forecasting the U.S. unemployment rate. *Journal of the American Statistical Association, 93*, 478–493.

Nelson, C. R., & Plossner, C. I. (1982). Trends and random walks in macroeconomic time series: Some evidence and implications. *Journal of Monetary Economics, 10*, 139–162.

Moore, G. H. (1961). *Business cycle indicators* (2 vols.). Princeton University Press.

Murphy, J. L. (1973). *Introductory econometrics*. Richard D. Irwin Inc.

Nelson, C. R., & Plosser, C. I. (1982). Trends and random walks in macroeconomic time series. *Journal of Monetary Economics, 10*, 139–162.

Thomakos, D., & Guerard, J. (2004). Naïve, ARIMA, transfer function, and VAR models: A comparison of forecasting performance. *The International Journal of Forecasting, 20*, 53–67.

Tsay, R. S. (1989). Testing and modelling threshold autoregressive processes. *Journal of the American Statistical Association, 84*, 231–249.

Tsay, R. S. (1988). Outliers, level shifts, and variance changes in time series. *Journal of Forecasting, 7*(1988), 1–20.

Tsay, R. S. (2010). *Analysis of financial time series* (3rd ed.). Wiley.

Tsay, R. S., & Chen, R. (2019). *Nonlinear time series analysis*. Wiley.

Vinod, H. D. (2008). *Hands-on intermediate econometrics using R: Templates for extending dozens of practical examples*. World Scientific. ISBN 10-981-281-885-5.

Zarnowitz, V. (1992). *Business cycles: Theory, history, indicators, and forecasting*. University of Chicago Press.

Index

A

Adaptive learning model 311, 313, 315, 322

American Telephone and Telegraph 46

Amplitude 46, 47, 82, 85–87, 90, 93, 95, 96, 99, 103–107, 142, 147, 148, 151, 582, 614

Analysts' forecasts 128, 164, 346, 363, 388

AO 302

AR(1) process 114–116, 246, 247, 251, 252, 264, 311, 313–315, 322, 324, 582, 585, 589, 609, 629

Ashley Granger Schmalensee (AGS) 300, 309

AutoMetrics 114, 163, 242, 244, 264, 265, 268, 322, 578, 582, 585, 588, 589, 603, 615, 616, 627

Autoregressive 133–135, 163, 242, 267, 544, 549, 551, 554, 555, 558, 559, 562, 571, 588, 607–609, 611–613, 615

Autoregressive integrated moving average (ARIMA) 74, 114, 165, 241, 615, 616

Autoregressive-moving average (ARMA) 242, 607, 610–613, 616

Axioma 337, 368, 377, 383, 385, 406, 589

B

Bank clearings 6, 7, 9, 46, 50–55, 84, 86, 87, 104, 105, 108

Barra 337, 368, 369, 406, 589

Beta 343–346, 349–352, 365, 368, 371, 372

Bisquare 185, 187, 190, 230, 234, 366, 367, 484, 490, 494, 496, 529, 532, 535, 536, 538, 540, 543, 602

Bivariate vector autoregressive model 267

Blin, John 337

Book-to-price 349, 350

Book value-to-price 355, 357

Bradstreet index of commodity
   prices 53
Burns, Arthur 19, 20, 23, 24, 30,
   32, 36, 38, 46, 48, 79–99,
   101–110, 113, 125, 126, 138,
   139, 142, 151, 156, 174, 245,
   582
Business barometer 44, 49, 52, 57
Business conditions 8, 25, 32, 36,
   37, 39, 41, 44, 45, 48–50,
   52–55, 57, 58, 77, 101, 150,
   581, 632
Business cycles 191, 331, 581, 582
Business failures 8, 31, 40, 52, 53,
   84, 93–95, 104, 105, 108,
   110, 119, 143
Business fluctuations 19, 21, 24, 41,
   47, 50, 58, 72, 78, 80, 97, 98,
   106, 139, 581
Business forecasting 20, 102

C

Capital asset pricing model (CAPM)
   343, 344, 352
Capital market line 344
Cash flow-to-price 355, 357
Castle, Jennifer 616, 627
Casual Paths 298
Coincidental indicators 63, 108,
   122, 586
Constraints 10, 346, 348, 372
Contractionary period 84, 86, 96,
   103, 109, 145
COVID 1, 4, 73, 79, 138, 191,
   250, 268, 314, 324, 386, 399,
   406, 436, 456, 476, 589–591
Cowles Foundation 58, 88, 90, 91,
   95
Crashes 31, 56, 123
Crisis 13, 14, 19, 24, 28–32, 34, 35,
   39–43, 47, 48, 59, 65, 69, 70,
   79, 156, 191, 247, 298, 299,
   332, 367

CTEF 346, 364, 367, 376, 377,
   382–385, 388, 399, 406, 589

D

Depression 1, 4, 5, 7, 9, 10, 12–15,
   19, 24–26, 29, 32–45, 47, 50,
   52, 56–59, 61–65, 67, 69, 79,
   80, 83, 93, 94, 104, 105, 108,
   111, 117, 126, 140–142, 152,
   156, 581
DFBETAS 183, 195, 436, 456, 476,
   525
DFFITS 183, 195, 204, 422, 436,
   456, 476, 525, 630
Dhrymes, Phoebus 593
Differenced 25, 47, 55, 67, 68, 71,
   72, 93, 94, 147, 151, 155,
   241, 244, 254, 255, 260, 266,
   547, 615, 616, 629
Differenced-Impulse-Indicator-
   Saturation Variable (DIIS)
   244, 247, 248, 252, 254, 255,
   257, 260, 262, 269, 274, 275,
   415, 547, 549, 551, 554, 556,
   558, 559, 562, 565, 566, 569,
   571, 572, 574, 576, 577, 584,
   627
Dodd, David 356
Donut strategy 384
Doornik, Jurgen 114, 164, 165,
   242, 243, 268, 543, 544, 569,
   578, 582, 584, 589, 616–618
Dow Jones Industrial Average 105,
   107, 110, 143, 344
Downturns 4, 6–9, 16–18, 61, 69,
   113, 122, 140, 152, 154, 155
DRI model 71–77, 90, 125, 144,
   145

E

Earnings-to-price 350, 351, 355,
   357

Eckstein, Otto 20, 49, 71–78, 90,
    116, 144, 145, 582
Econometrics 125, 291, 596, 627
Efficient Frontier 337–339, 357,
    368, 383, 385, 406, 589
Empiricism 15, 48, 91, 581
Estimated beta 344, 345, 349, 350
Expansionary period 85, 103, 118,
    142, 145

F

Factor returns 337, 399
Falling prices 4, 11, 13–15, 63, 70
Federal Reserve Bank 1, 6, 110
Financial anomalies 331, 355, 367,
    377, 406, 589
Fisher, Irving 10–15, 42, 43, 45, 55,
    65, 78, 113, 139, 582
Fisk, Jay 6
Forecasting 18, 20, 46, 48, 50, 52,
    54, 55, 57, 58, 65, 73, 74,
    106, 110, 114, 120, 121,
    124–128, 130, 132, 133,
    136–140, 143, 145, 156, 160,
    163–165, 168, 169, 191, 242,
    250, 265–268, 291, 292, 298,
    309, 311, 315, 324, 331, 346,
    363, 366, 406, 415, 543, 544,
    569, 574, 578, 582, 588–591,
    596, 597, 603, 613, 615, 616,
    627, 628
Forecast revisions 137, 164, 346,
    363, 590
Friedman, Milton 7, 9, 10, 23, 35,
    36, 55, 56, 58, 93, 113, 114,
    138, 139, 153, 154
Freight Loadings 50
F-statistic 203, 238
Fundamental analysis 52

G

General Electric 36

Geometric mean (GM) 341, 358,
    374, 382, 602, 614
Gets 243, 617
GLER 366, 367
Gordon, Robert A. 15–18, 58, 74,
    88, 89, 117, 144
Gordon, Robert J. 76, 77, 117
Graham, Benjamin 356
Granger-causality 298, 299, 311,
    314, 324, 588, 591, 627
Granger, C.W.J 7, 20, 134–136,
    164, 242, 291, 292, 324, 365,
    588, 612, 614, 616, 627, 628
Greenbacks 7, 23, 57, 58
Gross Domestic Product (GDP) 1,
    4, 64, 74, 75, 109, 123, 127,
    141, 146, 147, 151, 165, 175,
    183, 185, 187, 190, 241, 245,
    247, 249, 250, 268, 322, 324,
    578, 581, 582, 586, 587, 590,
    615
Gross National Product (GNP) 5,
    8–10, 15, 57, 64, 73, 75, 76,
    108–111, 118, 126, 127, 141,
    143–146, 151, 153, 343
Growth 5, 6, 8, 9, 15, 16, 20, 21,
    40, 48, 58, 59, 61, 62, 64, 72,
    75, 76, 78, 109, 110,
    117–119, 121–123, 126, 127,
    134, 137, 139–142, 146–154,
    156, 299, 345, 350, 351, 356,
    365, 581
Gruber, Martin 128, 331, 342, 343,
    355, 357, 358, 363, 590

H

Haberler, Gottfried 20, 49, 60–71,
    77, 78, 581
Harvard Economic Service (HES)
    44, 49, 50, 55, 56, 58
Hat Diag 191, 424

Hendry, David 114, 136, 164, 165,
   242–244, 268, 543, 544, 569,
   603, 615–618, 627
HETERO 250
Hoover, Herbert 19, 36, 97

I

Impulse-indicator-saturation (IIS)
   variable 243, 244, 247–249,
   415, 545, 547, 551, 556, 559,
   562, 566, 572, 574, 577
Index of General Business
   Conditions 45, 49, 51, 55–57,
   59, 62, 65, 139
Industrial production 7, 45, 90, 105,
   108–110, 113, 122, 147–149,
   151, 294
Influential observations 170–172,
   177, 178, 183, 193, 194, 204,
   419, 422, 439, 519, 599–601,
   630, 633
Information ratio (IR) 369, 374
Innovation 41, 58–62, 72, 78, 117,
   123, 581
Institutional Broker Estimation
   Services (I/B/E/S) 355, 363,
   364, 367, 369, 376, 388, 590
Interest rates 191
Investability 398

J

Jennifer Castle 230
Juglar 10, 40, 44, 117

K

Keynes, John 191
Kitchin 63, 88, 117
Kondratieff 9, 10, 44, 62, 63, 88,
   117
Koopmans, Tjalling 88–91, 291,
   293, 627, 629

L

Lags 13, 44–46, 51, 53, 54, 82–84,
   86, 93, 96, 98, 105, 116, 134,
   151, 152, 187, 190, 192, 243,
   250, 259, 264, 265, 292, 294,
   300, 301, 309, 311, 313, 315,
   322, 558, 562, 566, 577, 584,
   587, 604, 605, 612, 617, 628
Leading Economic Indicators (LEI)
   20, 48, 63, 64, 90, 108, 110,
   113, 114, 119, 120, 125, 127,
   138, 163–165, 169, 175, 183,
   185, 187, 190–192, 203, 212,
   230, 245, 248–250, 255, 258,
   264, 268, 293, 294, 298–300,
   309, 316, 322, 324, 415, 416,
   490, 506, 549, 551, 566, 572,
   574, 577, 578, 582, 584, 589,
   591, 592, 597, 616, 627, 629,
   631
Leads 13–18, 20, 26–28, 35, 37, 41,
   44–46, 51, 53, 65–70, 83, 84,
   86, 87, 93, 94, 98, 102,
   105–108, 110, 112, 113, 116,
   119, 127, 144, 145, 151, 152,
   155, 175, 183, 185, 187, 190,
   250, 504, 506, 510, 605, 607,
   628, 632, 633
Leverage 28, 177, 193, 194, 349,
   351, 365, 371, 630
Liabilities 25, 31, 37, 38, 93, 94,
   104, 105, 108, 110, 143, 351
Liquidation 14, 18, 24, 28, 29,
   34–36, 61, 63, 94

M

M2 119, 143, 152, 153, 322, 590
Mahalanobis distance 294
Mark, Andrew 337, 364, 366, 406,
   589
Markowitz, Harry 20, 21, 138, 139,
   331, 332, 336, 337, 340–343,
   355, 357, 358, 363, 365–368,

374, 376, 382–384, 398, 399, 406, 569, 589, 590

Maronna, R.A. 172, 294, 367, 377, 601

Marschak, Jacob 95–99

Martin, R.D. 172, 294, 367, 601

Mathematical assignment program (MAP) 346, 347, 349, 371

Mean absolute errors (MAE) 145

Mean-Variance Portfolio Construction 342, 369

Mean-variance tracking error at risk 377

Measurement without Theory 88, 89, 92

Mitchell, Wesley 1, 15, 19, 20, 23–40, 42–48, 55, 65, 66, 68, 70, 72, 78–99, 101–104, 106–109, 113, 125, 126, 138, 140, 142, 144, 151, 154, 156, 582

Money supply 5, 7–13, 32, 58, 69, 70, 92, 110, 113, 114, 116, 118, 119, 139, 143, 152, 153, 322, 590

Moore, Geoffrey 19, 20, 90–92, 94, 99, 101–114, 116–121, 124–126, 138, 139, 142–144, 150, 156, 174, 175, 245, 415, 582, 584, 586

Moving average 158, 159, 242, 607, 609–616

Multi-factor risk model 349

N

National Bureau of Economic Research (NBER) 1, 6, 9, 19, 20, 23, 24, 36, 39, 47, 48, 64, 79, 80, 83, 86, 88–90, 92, 93, 98, 101, 102, 105, 106, 108–111, 113, 114, 116, 118, 120–122, 124–126, 138–143,

147, 150, 155, 156, 332, 581, 582, 586

National income 15, 71, 97

New incorporations 108

New orders 17, 18, 31, 34, 35, 108, 110, 118, 143, 144, 151, 245, 632

Nobel Prize 20, 88, 144, 145

Normality 116, 246, 252, 254, 544, 551, 555, 559, 570, 571, 613

O

Optimism 25, 41, 66, 68

Optimization 332, 337, 340, 348, 374, 376, 385, 399, 406, 589

Ordinary least squares (OLS) 132, 172, 183, 184, 203, 293, 344, 358, 366, 367, 416, 419, 438, 442, 459, 461, 578, 589, 601

Outlier 172, 177, 184, 194, 294, 358, 382, 599–601, 603, 614–617, 627

OxMetrics 163, 165, 169, 242, 245–252, 254, 255, 258, 260, 262, 264, 265, 268, 269, 274, 275, 280, 286, 322, 543, 544, 569, 578, 582, 588, 589, 597

P

Panic of 1873 6, 7

Panic of 1893 9, 10

Paper production 105, 107

PCGive 242, 268, 578, 582

Peaks 1, 6, 8, 9, 44, 53, 62, 71, 74, 81, 82, 84–86, 92, 94–96, 103–106, 109, 110, 112–114, 119–121, 139–141, 147, 150–152, 155

Pig-iron production 9, 39, 46, 54, 105

Portfolio selection 21, 138, 331, 342, 349, 358, 591

Price momentum 365, 367
Profit margin 5, 17, 18, 24, 25, 34,
    65, 105
Profits 21, 28, 39
Prosperity 4, 7, 10, 17–19, 24,
    26–29, 31, 33–35, 37, 38,
    40–42, 44, 45, 47, 50, 52,
    61–63, 65, 69, 79, 80, 94, 95,
    105, 140, 150

Q
Quantity Theory of Money 12, 23,
    33, 43, 66, 139
Quarterly mergers 298

R
Randomly distributed error 166,
    344, 366, 592
Real GDP 7, 20, 48, 78, 122, 124,
    126, 127, 156, 163, 165, 175,
    183, 185, 187, 190, 247, 249,
    250, 268, 322, 324, 582, 585,
    588, 590, 603, 616
Recession 4, 8, 16, 18–20, 36, 44,
    45, 47, 55, 56, 62–65, 71–74,
    76, 77, 80, 83, 86, 87, 94,
    103, 106–111, 117, 120–123,
    126, 127, 141, 142, 144,
    146–151, 154, 156, 331, 332
Recovery 8, 9, 16, 24–26, 35, 50,
    56, 57, 66, 103, 104, 109,
    113, 121–123, 141, 142
Reference cycle 81, 84, 86, 90, 98,
    99, 108, 582
REG8 357, 363, 364, 376, 377,
    382, 383
REG9 364, 376, 382–385, 388,
    399, 406, 589
REG10 366, 369, 376, 377, 382,
    383, 388, 399, 406, 589
Regression analysis 164, 165, 170,
    172, 366, 367, 415, 418, 419,
    438, 518, 525, 527, 529, 532,
    535, 536, 538, 540, 543, 591,
    592, 599, 601, 604, 605
Regression coefficient 170, 171, 173,
    294, 358, 374, 598–600, 602
Regression modeling/Regression
    modelling 165, 592
Rendings Fels 5
RESET 246, 252
Residual Sum of Squares (RSS) 116,
    247, 249, 255, 258, 259, 264,
    274, 280, 286, 544, 547, 549,
    551, 554, 555, 558, 559, 562,
    565, 569–572, 574, 577, 584,
    585, 627, 629
Revival 8, 9, 16, 17, 24–27, 34, 35,
    42, 44, 45, 62, 63, 65, 67, 69,
    70, 80, 86, 87, 94, 102,
    105–108, 142
Risk-return tradeoff 339, 368, 378,
    399
Robust regression 163, 172, 185,
    187, 190, 201, 211, 230, 234,
    294, 315, 322, 358, 366, 367,
    382, 415, 419, 436, 442, 480,
    481, 484, 487, 490, 494, 496,
    499, 502, 510, 518, 525, 529,
    535, 538, 578, 589, 600, 601
Rolling windows 266, 322
Root-Mean-Square-Error (RMSE)
    92, 267, 268, 299, 311,
    313–315, 322, 324, 589, 615
Rosenberg, Barr 349, 350, 353, 364
R-squared 203, 300, 585
RStudent 183, 195, 204, 419, 422,
    436, 442, 456, 476, 525
Rutledge Vining 88, 90

S
Sales-to-price 355, 357
Salibian-Barrera, M. 172, 294, 367,
    377, 382, 601

Saturation variables 114, 116, 244, 247, 249, 252, 254, 255, 262, 543, 547, 551, 556, 559, 562, 566, 572, 574, 577, 615, 617, 618, 627

Schumpeter, Joseph 10, 20, 23, 24, 30, 38, 41, 49, 58–63, 66, 77, 78, 88, 97, 154, 581

Scientific computing associates (SCA) 291, 299

Security Market Line (SML) 344

Sharpe ratio 358, 372, 382, 399

Sharpe, William 138, 331, 355, 406, 589

Sinai, Allen 76, 77, 116

Skewness 341, 372

Sound money 12, 23

Specific cycle 81, 82, 84–87, 107, 148

Specific Returns 367, 377, 382, 383

Speculation 5, 17, 26, 46, 54, 55, 63, 141, 356

Standard & Poor's 110, 143, 632

Standard deviation 44, 46, 54, 84, 118, 135, 136, 141, 142, 170, 171, 333, 334, 336, 342, 349–351, 368, 374, 599–601

Standard error 244, 544, 547, 549, 551, 554, 555, 558, 559, 562, 565, 569–572, 574, 576, 577, 595, 605, 606, 613, 627

Standardized residuals 171, 177, 193, 194, 599, 600

Statistically significant 7, 48, 57, 114, 116, 125, 126, 137, 138, 163, 175, 185, 187, 190, 192, 203, 230, 243, 265, 294, 299, 300, 322, 324, 350, 351, 355, 358, 364, 366, 367, 369, 372, 376, 377, 382, 383, 388, 415, 416, 418, 419, 438, 439, 459, 487, 490, 494, 496, 499, 502, 506, 514, 518, 527, 532, 536, 540, 543, 582, 587, 589, 590

Stekler, Herman 120, 121, 138

Step-indicator-saturation variable 244, 249

Stock prices 6, 8, 16–19, 21, 26, 28–31, 36, 46, 53–55, 57, 78, 84, 87, 93, 94, 103–105, 107, 108, 110, 113, 114, 116, 119, 143, 174, 293, 294, 298, 324, 588

T

The Conference Board (TCB) 20, 114, 122, 127, 174, 191, 245, 316, 322, 415, 577, 615, 631–633

The Great Depression 4, 15, 58, 64, 78, 111, 142, 581

The Purchasing Power of Money 11, 13

Theta Forecasts 317

Theta model 267

Thomakos, Dimitrios 7, 164, 175, 190, 265, 266, 298, 299, 311, 322, 324, 589, 590

Time series 19, 44–46, 48, 50–54, 57, 60, 61, 80–87, 89, 92, 95–97, 99, 102–110, 114, 115, 119, 123, 127, 135, 142–144, 157, 163–165, 191, 242, 244, 246, 250, 251, 260, 264, 265, 268, 291, 298–300, 322, 324, 415, 543, 544, 549, 556, 559, 569, 574, 577, 578, 582, 588, 589, 591, 592, 603–605, 607, 608, 610, 612–616, 627, 629

Tobin, James 332, 406, 589

Total returns 382

Transitionary periods 13

Treynor, Jack 369

Troughs 47, 81, 82, 84, 86, 87, 92, 94, 96, 103, 104, 106, 108,

112, 119–121, 123, 124, 139, 147, 151, 152, 155

T-statistics 243, 294, 369, 584, 587, 626

Turning points 7, 9, 18, 64, 70, 72, 82, 83, 87, 92, 94, 96, 102, 105, 106, 112, 120, 121, 124, 125, 127, 128, 137, 144, 145, 150, 156, 582

Turnover 92, 94, 104, 350, 358, 376, 398

U

Unemployment 5, 7, 16, 17, 20, 36–39, 56, 64, 65, 72–74, 76, 79, 90, 97, 108–110, 113, 118, 124, 127, 141, 147, 149, 150, 156, 163–165, 169, 175, 191, 192, 212, 230, 250, 257, 265–267, 274, 281, 286, 298–301, 309, 313, 315, 324, 415, 416, 438, 510, 518, 544, 577, 588, 590–592, 597, 603, 616, 629, 632

Unemployment rate (UER) 192, 195, 201, 203, 212, 230, 234, 269, 274, 416, 544, 547, 554, 556, 558, 559, 566, 569, 577

USER 258, 366, 367, 369, 370

V

Value 4, 5, 11, 13–15, 18, 25, 28, 29, 35, 37, 43, 53, 57, 58, 60, 66, 75, 77, 78, 81–83, 85, 93, 94, 97, 98, 116, 128, 132–134, 136, 137, 153, 157–159, 164, 166, 170, 267, 346, 348, 351, 365, 371, 382, 544, 592, 596–599, 601, 603, 604, 607–609, 612–615, 626, 629, 632

Variance 130, 132, 134, 135, 168, 172, 241, 341, 350, 352, 353, 384, 595, 600, 604, 614–616, 631

Vector autoregressive (VAR) 145, 153, 299

Velocity 11, 12, 14, 43, 153, 154

W

Warren Persons 44, 49, 55, 58, 77, 581

Waves 61, 62, 85

Weekly unemployment claims (WkUNCL) 163, 164, 166, 169, 175, 191, 192, 250, 260, 262, 264, 265, 267, 268, 274, 281, 298–301, 309, 324, 438, 459, 510, 544, 554–556, 558, 559, 562, 565, 569, 574, 576–578, 587–590, 592

Weighted latent Root Regression (WLRR) 358

Wholesale prices 5–7, 9, 17, 25, 31–33, 35, 37, 39, 44, 45, 47, 50–52, 54, 55, 72, 84, 93, 105, 107, 108

World War I 58, 93, 356

World War II 1, 16, 102, 117, 120, 121, 146, 147

X

Xu, Ganlin 138, 366, 590

Y

Yohai, V.J. 172, 377, 601

Z

Zarnowitz, Victor 141–156, 163, 173–175, 190, 191, 245, 415, 582, 586

Printed by Printforce, the Netherlands